Lynn Hill

ARTFORMS

ARTFORMS

AN INTRODUCTION TO THE VISUAL ARTS

FIFTH EDITION

DUANE AND SARAH PREBLE

HarperCollinsCollegePublishers

About the Cover
HAND from the Hopewell Mound, Ohio. c. 150.
Ohio Historical Society.
Cover photograph by Dirk Bakker.

Throughout history the human hand has been both a source of art and a symbol of creativity. The Hopewell Indian mica Hand is an ancient work of art with universal, timeless quality.

Editor-in-Chief: Laurie E. Likoff
Developmental Editors: Judith Leet, Mark Getlein, Joan Rose
Cover and Text Designer: Malia Preble of DeFrancis Studio
Page Layouts: Melissa Rogers of Barbara Pope Book Design
Photo and Permissions Editor: Elsa Peterson
Production Assistant: Jeffrey Taub
Line Art: George Retseck
Maps: Jane Eckelman, Manoa Mapworks
Color Separations: Quality Graphic Services
Printer and Binder: Arcata Graphics/Kingsport
Cover Printer: Coral Graphic Services, Inc.

For permission to use copyrighted material, grateful acknowledgment is made to the copyright holders on pp. 517-518, which are hereby made part of the copyright page.

Library of Congress Cataloging-in-Publication Data

Preble, Duane.
Artforms: an introduction to the visual arts / Duane and Sarah Preble. — 5th ed.
p. cm.
Includes bibliographical references and index.
ISBN 0-06-500834-0
1. Composition (Art) 2. Visual perception. 3. Art—History. I. Preble, Sarah. II. Title.
N7430.P69 1994
700—dc20 93-4725
CIP

97 98 9 8 7 6 5

To all who come to know the artist within

Contents

Preface

From the first edition, in 1972, we have sought to make ARTFORMS as visually exciting as the individual works of art reproduced in it. In this edition we have built on the strengths of earlier versions: clear organizational structure, straightforward writing, and high quality illustrations.

ARTFORMS grew out of a desire to introduce art through an engaging visual experience. It is written and designed to help readers build an informed foundation for individual understanding and enjoyment of art. By introducing art theory, practice, and history in a single volume, we aim to draw students into a new or expanded awareness of the visual arts. Our goal is to engage readers in the process of realizing their own innate creativity.

The fifth edition is refined and updated throughout and contains new chapters as well as new features: brief biographies and essays. The biographies explore the lives of artists in relation to their work, and the essays look into some of today's most thought-provoking art issues. The table of contents is longer than in previous editions because we have more clearly identified topics and sub-topics and improved on total organization.

Part 1 introduces the nature of art, aesthetics, creativity, and purposes of art. Part 2 presents the communicative language of vision: form and content, visual elements, and principles of design. It also includes a new chapter on style (Chapter 6). Experience with the language of visual form introduced in Chapters 3 through 6 provides a foundation for developing critical thinking and for considering issues of evaluation and art criticism, which are discussed in Chapter 7. The visual and verbal vocabulary covered in Part 2 prepares the reader to sample the broad range of art disciplines, media, and processes presented in Parts 3, 4, and 5. Parts 6 and 7 introduce historic world styles and related cultural values. Although the development of Western art is emphasized, these chapters are written to encourage readers to become aware of the rich heritage of art throughout the world. Part 7 explores the many ways the art of today has evolved out of the art of the past. The final chapter discusses art of the recent decade and the roles of artists today.

The domain of the visual arts ranges from drawing and painting to architecture and urban design, from making furniture to making films and videos. To limit the length rather than the scope of ARTFORMS, we have had to be both highly selective and broad in outlook. Beyond fostering appreciation of major works of art, our primary concern is to open eyes and minds to the richness of the visual arts as unique forms of human communication and to convey the idea that the arts enrich life best when we experience, understand, and enjoy them as integral parts of the process of living.

The title of this book has a dual meaning. It evolved from the original title, which was a condensation of the concluding sentences of the draft for the first edition: "Man creates art. Art creates man." *Man Creates Art Creates Man* was further condensed into ARTFORMS, which contains the idea in one word: as we create forms, we are in turn shaped by that which we have created.

Research for five editions of ARTFORMS has taken us around the world and into the studios of many artists. We found it highly rewarding to meet and talk with artists as well as collectors, gallery and museum staff members, photographers, and scholars, who generously shared their work and expertise with us. We were sustained by the help and enthusiasm of the many people who have been directly involved in this group effort. Some are identified in captions or credits; we regret that space does not permit us to name them all.

A few people deserve special mention for their major contributions. We are particularly grateful to the staff at HarperCollins for enabling us to be actively involved in the design and production of this edition. Editor-in-Chief Laurie Likoff was remarkably patient and cooperative in working with authors who expected a fine art book on a textbook budget. Developmental editors Mark Getlein, Judith Leet, and Joan Rose and Photo and Permissions editor Elsa Peterson all went far beyond the call of duty in their dedication to the project. Designers Malia Preble and the staff of DeFrancis Studio as well as Melissa Rogers and the staff of Barbara Pope Book Design handled the limitations and ever-changing demands of the project with creative skill. The staffs at Quality Graphics and Arcata Graphics/ Kingsport went way beyond business-as-usual as they helped us meet deadlines and maintain the high-quality reproductions for which ARTFORMS is known.

Thanks also to our many colleagues at the University of Hawaii, the Honolulu Academy of Arts, The Contemporary Museum, and the Hawaii State Library who generously shared their knowledge and resources. Peter Chamberlain merits special mention for his help with the section on computer imaging. Silvia Salgado's assistance with the early stages of the project is greatly appreciated. Stephanie Chun's editorial expertise was enormously helpful in the final stages. We are grateful to Tom Dorsaneo for shepherding the crucial final weeks of production.

Most important to this book are the artists, past and present, known and unknown, whose art is presented here and those people who have had the foresight to preserve meaningful products of human creativity.

We would like to express our appreciation to the following reviewers who contributed many helpful suggestions:

Jack Breckinridge, Arizona State University, Tempe
Val Christensen, Missouri Southern State College
William Cordiner, University of Northern Colorado
Pat Craig, California State University, Fullerton
Christina Dinkelacker, Memphis State University
Paula Drewek, Macomb Community College
Joan Esch, University of New Hampshire
Paul Grootkerk, Mississippi State University
Felix Heap, Boise State University
Jed Jackson, Southern Illinois University
Douglas Johnson, University of Wisconsin, River Falls
Susan Josepher, Metropolitan State College of Denver
Klaus H. Kallenberger, Middle Tennessee State University
Richard Karberg, Cuyahoga Community College—East
John Parker, Fullerton College
Robbie Reid, Foothills College
Cheryl Souza, Kapiolani Community College
Michael Stone, Cuyahoga Community College—West
Jean E. Swanson, North Hennepin Community College
George Vail, Gloucester County College
Kurt Wild, University of Wisconsin, River Falls

Once again, it has been an awe-inspiring experience to be part of a cooperative venture as large and complex as the publication of ARTFORMS.

Duane and Sarah Preble

PART 1

WHAT IS ART FOR?

Consider...

Have you ever tried to explain something to someone—then picked up a pencil to show exactly what you meant?

Are any paintings, posters, or photographs displayed where you live or work? If so, how do you feel about them? Do they enhance your life?

Do you think artists are born with special gifts, or do you think they acquire skills through practice and effort?

Most of us were active artists as children, and then we stopped making art. Do you still draw or paint or take photographs? If not, why not?

CHAPTER 1

The Nature of Art

In Pierre Bonnard's painting DINING ROOM IN THE COUNTRY the sunlight of a French countryside makes colors glow. The pale blue door reflects the green outside. The door and blue-violet tablecloth set off the rich red-orange wall. Bits of reflected color on the cup and plates echo the colors of the flowers outside. A hazy, late afternoon stillness fills the air. Cats, flowers, fruit, and a woman leaning on the window sill add to this expression of unhurried life in the country.

The painting is Bonnard's interpretation of his own home—an invitation to enter his world and view life through his eyes. Bonnard was deeply moved by the scenes he depicted, and he took delight in sharing his vision. He found it more effective to do this with paint than with words.

Art is not something apart from us. It grows from common—as well as uncommon—human insights, feelings, and experiences. When we are so deeply moved by an experience that we want to share it with others, we are where art begins.

Art does not need to be "understood" to be enjoyed. Like life itself, it can simply be experienced. Yet the more we understand what art can offer, the richer our experience of it will be.

WHAT IS ART?

Art—like beauty, truth, and life itself—is larger than any single definition. One widely used dictionary defines it this way:

> ***art*** *(art), n. 1. the quality, production, or expression of what is beautiful, appealing, or of more than ordinary significance.*[1]

A *work of art* is the aesthetic expression of an idea or experience formed with skill through the use of a medium. A *medium* is a particular material, along with its accompanying technique. (The plural is *media.*) Artists select media that best suit the ideas and feelings they wish to present. When a medium is used in such a way that the object or performance contributes to our understanding or enjoyment of life, we experience the final product as art.

Media that have long been favorites include clay, fiber, stone, wood, and oil paint. By mid-twentieth century, modern technology had added new media, including video and computers, to the nineteenth-century contributions of photography and motion pictures. Art made with a combination of different materials is referred to as *mixed media.*

When people speak of *the arts,* they are usually referring to music, dance, theater, literature, and the visual arts. Each art form is perceived by our senses in different ways, yet each grows from a common need to give substance to feelings, ideas, insights, and experiences. The focus of this book is the visual arts, including drawing, painting, sculpture, film, and architecture.

Much of our communication is verbal, yet any single medium of expression has its limitations.

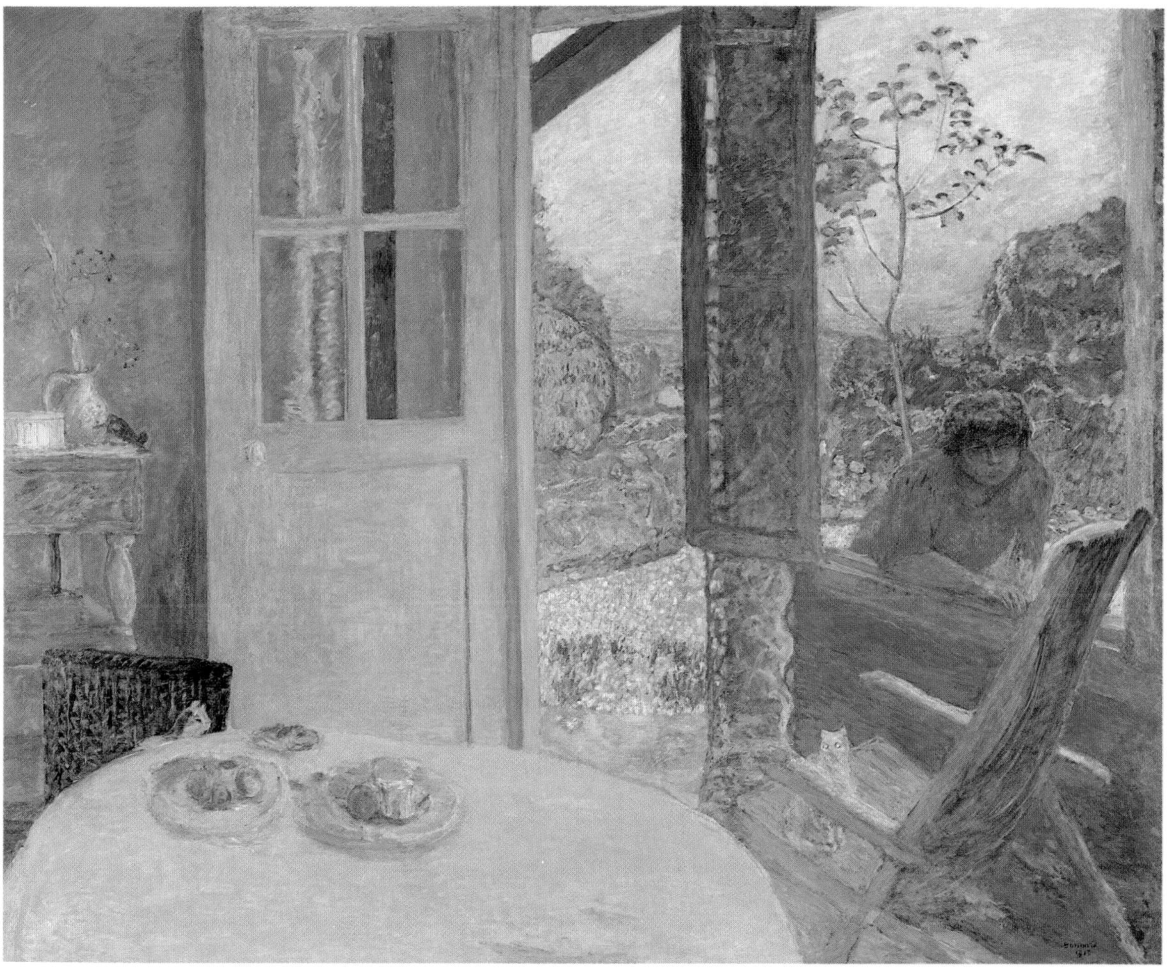

1 Pierre Bonnard. DINING ROOM IN THE COUNTRY. 1913.
Oil on canvas. 64¾" × 81".
The Minneapolis Institute of Arts. The John R. Derlip Fund.

Certain ideas and feelings can be communicated only through visual forms, while other insights can be expressed only through music. American painter Georgia O'Keeffe said: "I found that I could say things with colors and shapes that I couldn't say in any other way—things I had no words for."[2] The arts provide ways to communicate meanings that go far beyond ordinary verbal exchange. The entire range of thought and feeling is the subject of art.

IS ART A NECESSITY?

Is it necessary for us to give physical form to things we feel, think, and imagine? Must we gesture, dance, draw, speak, sing, write, and build? To be fully human, it seems we must. In fact, the ability to create is one of the special characteristics of being human. The urge to make and enjoy what we call art has been a driving force throughout human history.

All societies have produced objects and rituals that extend communication and meet physical and spiritual needs. Some objects—from simple tools to vast temple complexes—have been designed to meet both physical and spiritual needs simultaneously.

Traditional societies do not separate art from the rest of life. That is, they seldom distinguish between the practical function of an object and its spiritual and aesthetic significance. Healing, beauty, and spiritual meaning are inseparable within the context of the Navajo SANDPAINTING CEREMONY.

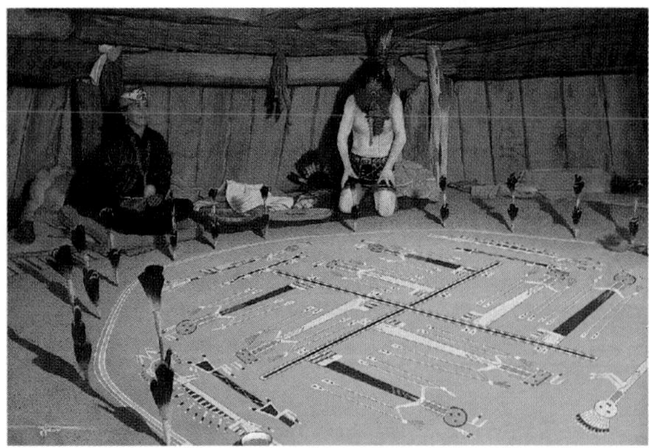

2 David Yazzie.
SANDPAINTING CEREMONY. c. 1985.
Oil on canvas. 24" × 36".
Courtesy of Indian Trader West, Santa Fe.

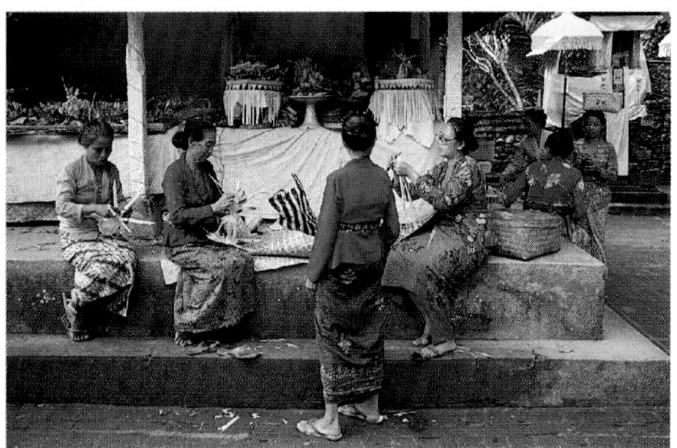

3 PREPARING FOR A FESTIVAL, Bali. 1992.
Photograph: Carl Hefner, Honolulu.

Some traditional societies do not even have a word for art. The highly artistic Balinese—shown here PREPARING FOR A FESTIVAL—claim that they have no art, that they do everything as well as they can. In such societies, the arts express important traditional values and give form to the spiritual life of both the individual and the community. Because the arts embody creative energy, they often act as ritual, magic, and practical technology all at once. Arts such as singing, dancing, carving, and image-making bring participants into unity with nature's forces and thereby give access to the creative energy of the universe. The artistic expressions of spiritual life are not treasured as performances or decorative objects, but as harmonizing vehicles of power, as offerings of praise and gratitude. It is the creative process and the power of the object rather than the object itself that is of value.

Our high-tech, multicultural society has few shared traditions, so we have few traditional art forms. We tend to think of "art" as something produced only by "artists"—uniquely gifted people. Because "art" is often separated from community life in contemporary society, many people believe they have no artistic "talent." This belief makes them hesitate to create their own art or even to explore the art of others. In modern societies, works we call art are displayed in galleries and museums—far removed from the everyday life experiences of the people who created them.

This is unfortunate; people living in highly technological societies need art as much as the members of culturally rich, traditional societies need it. Science and the arts serve humanity in complementary ways. Both involve creative thinking and problem solving. Science seeks answers to questions about the outer, physical world; these answers form the basis of our technology. The arts foster the development of our inner world—the intuitive, emotional, spiritual, and creative aspects of being human. Reality is explained through the sciences and revealed through the arts. People need both science and art if they are to balance function with meaning.

History provides the best evidence of our need for the arts. When a dictator or conquering group seeks domination over a people, and perhaps has already won a military victory, the next step is to find ways to destroy the culture—to eliminate the language, traditions, and the arts of the oppressed. Artists of all kinds are among the first to be controlled or silenced. Hitler's and Stalin's control of the arts, and the suppression of the languages and ritual arts of Native Americans come to mind.

As groups and individuals, we can survive incredible physical hardships far more easily than the loss of our personal creativity and cultural foundations. Our languages, our arts, our traditions and beliefs are at the core of who we are.

PURPOSES AND FUNCTIONS OF ART

Art can inspire, beautify, inform, persuade, entertain, and transform. It can also deceive, humiliate, and anger. Art can arouse our emotions, spark our imaginations, delight our senses, lead us to think in new ways, and help each of us develop a personal sense of truth. A given work of art may serve several functions all at once.

When we look at art of the past—or even current art—we cannot always know exactly what its creators had in mind. To understand their purposes and functions, we find it is useful to place art and artifacts in contexts and categories.

The terms "fine art" and "applied art" are used to distinguish the two basic types of artistic intention. *Fine art* refers to art created for purely aesthetic expression, communication, or contemplation. Painting and sculpture are the best known of the fine arts. *Applied art* is art in which aesthetic values are used in the design or decoration of utilitarian objects. In applied art, the "art" function can be as important as the object's other functions—but in many cases the art aspect is secondary to the object's practical utility. Vincent van Gogh's painting VINCENT'S CHAIR is called fine art, whereas the SIDE CHAIR designed by Charles and Ray Eames is called applied art.

Because people in earlier societies were inclined to share common religious beliefs and views of the world, artists and craftspeople were trained to produce traditional objects and images for agreed-upon purposes. In contrast, people in modern urban societies have no widely accepted attitudes about the meaning and function of art. We frequently have difficulty responding to and evaluating the art of our own time—or even understanding the purposes it serves.

We can increase our understanding by exploring past and present reasons for making art, and by examining how art has functioned over time. By interpreting the art and artifacts of our ancestors—from stone carvings and paintings to dwellings and sacred sites—we are able to learn about the attitudes, feelings, and ways of life of earlier peoples. In a recent excavation of a 70,000-year-old grave,

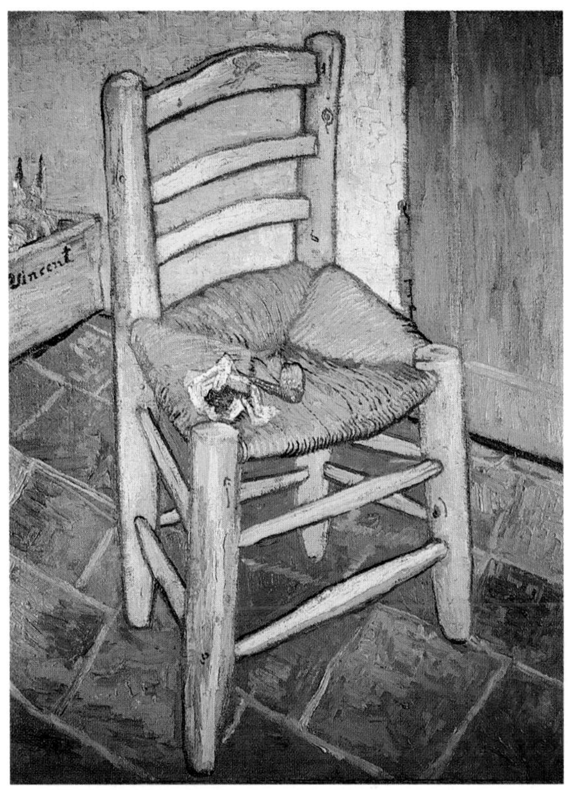

4 Vincent van Gogh.
VINCENT'S CHAIR. 1888-1889.
Oil on canvas. 36½" × 29".
Reproduced courtesy of the Trustees, The National Gallery, London.

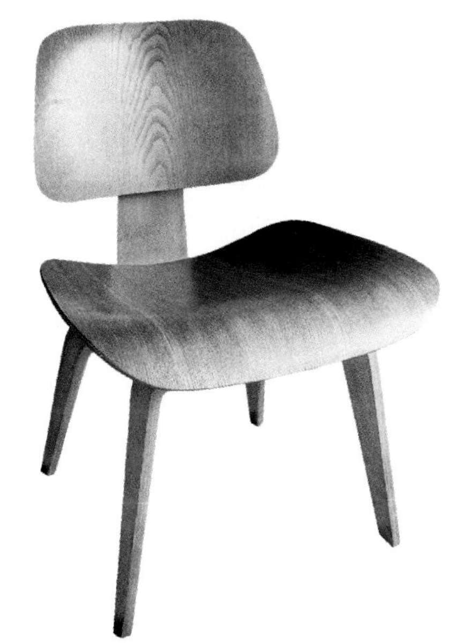

5 Charles and Ray Eames.
SIDE CHAIR. c. 1942.
Molded plywood.

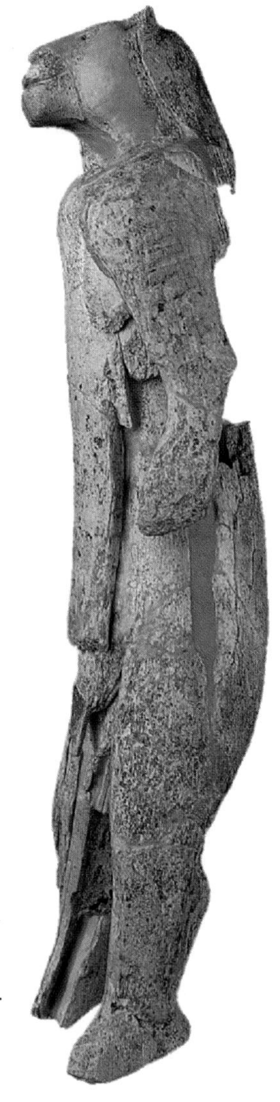

6 PALEOLITHIC HUMAN FIGURE WITH LION'S HEAD. C. 32,000 B.C.
Ivory. Height 28 cm.
Museum der Stadt Ulm, Germany.

the remains of flowers were found and interpreted as the earliest known sign of honoring the deceased.

Art for Communicating Information

Because art can make a strong statement, one clearly understood by a broad spectrum of people, it is often used to impart information in both literate and nonliterate societies. During the Middle Ages in Europe, stained-glass windows and church sculpture taught Bible stories to an illiterate population. Art continues to inform the nonliterate as well as literate people around the world. Photography, film, and television have proven to be particularly useful for recording and communicating. Through artistic presentation, information often becomes more accessible and memorable than it would be through words alone.

According to ancient tradition in India, the purposes of the arts are to educate the illiterate, to enlighten the literate, and to entertain the enlightened. In today's high-tech societies, the commercialization of art often short-circuits these age-old functions—and the arts become mere entertainment for the illiterate.

Art for Day-to-Day Living

Objects of all kinds, from ancient, carefully crafted flint knives to sleek sports cars, have been conceived to delight the eye as well as to serve more obviously useful functions. Well-designed utilitarian objects and spaces—from chairs to communities—bring pleasure and efficiency into our daily lives. To the degree that the visual arts improve the quality of our surroundings, they are environmental arts.

In a general sense, the visual arts include all human creations in which visual form has been a major consideration during design and production. Nearly all the objects and spaces we use in our private and public lives were designed by art and design professionals. We live in buildings, towns, and cities designed with the quality of their visual form—as well as their other functions—in mind. We are involved with art/design whenever we make decisions about how to style our hair, what clothes to wear, or how to furnish and arrange our living spaces. As we make such choices, we are engaged in universal art-related processes—making visual statements about who we are and the kind of world we like to see around us.

Art For Spiritual Sustenance

In many societies, all the arts have a spiritual component. Spiritual or magical purposes apparently inspired the making of the world's earliest figure carvings and cave paintings. It appears that early human beings developed what we now call art and religion simultaneously. Long before the developments of farming and writing, the arts helped sustain bands of hunter-gatherers. Prehistoric peoples

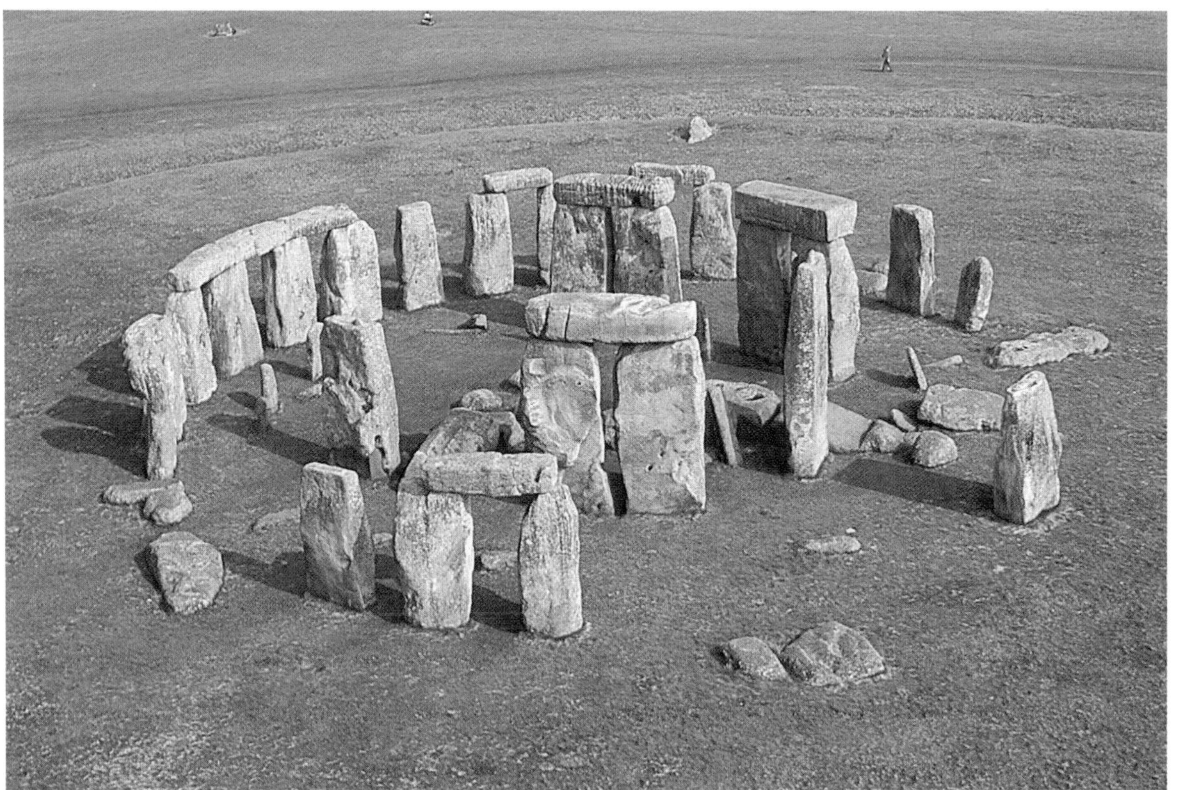

7 STONEHENGE. Wiltshire, England.
Photograph: English Heritage.

were motivated by such concerns as physical survival, the need to record events, and a desire to magically control the animals they hunted for food. See the GREAT HALL OF BULLS found in the caves of Lascaux on page 280.

The strong feelings of identity that early human beings felt toward animals is made apparent in a 34,000-year-old ivory carving of a human body with a lion's head. The small sculpture may have been made to bring the lion's superior hunting power into the body of the figure's owner. It may portray a sacred animal deity, or it may represent a person wearing the head and neck fur of a lion as a disguise for hunting or for a ritual or ceremony.

Clearly, early re-creations of the physical forms of animals dealt with the most pressing issues of day-to-day existence. Works such as this carving and the ANTELOPE FIGURES on page 310 helped people deal with their need for food as well as with their spiritual concerns, and these works often provided an important focus for ritual practices.

Among the best known ritual structures built by stone-age human beings is the complex of huge boulders at Stonehenge, England. It was constructed at a time when religion and science were one unified quest for understanding. Four series of giant stones, surrounding an altar stone, stand within a circular trench 300 feet in diameter. Most archaeologists agree that STONEHENGE was built in several phases, around 2000 B.C., to serve some sort of religious or scientific function. Few scholars agree on the specific purpose of the stone monument, but some have concluded that STONEHENGE was used to calculate solar and lunar movements, including eclipses.

Many works of ancient and tribal religious art continue to elicit strong responses, even when we know very little about the intentions of their makers. The CANOE PROW FIGURE from the Solomon Islands (page 306) employs symbolism meaningful

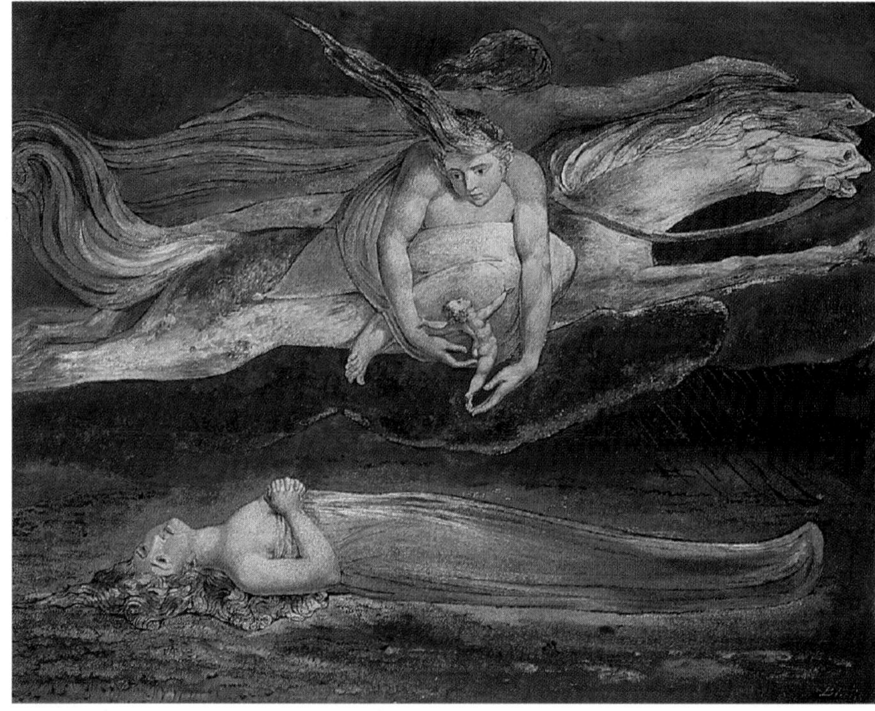

8 William Blake.
PITY. c. 1795.
Color print finished in pen and watercolor.
16¾" × 21¼".
Tate Gallery, London.

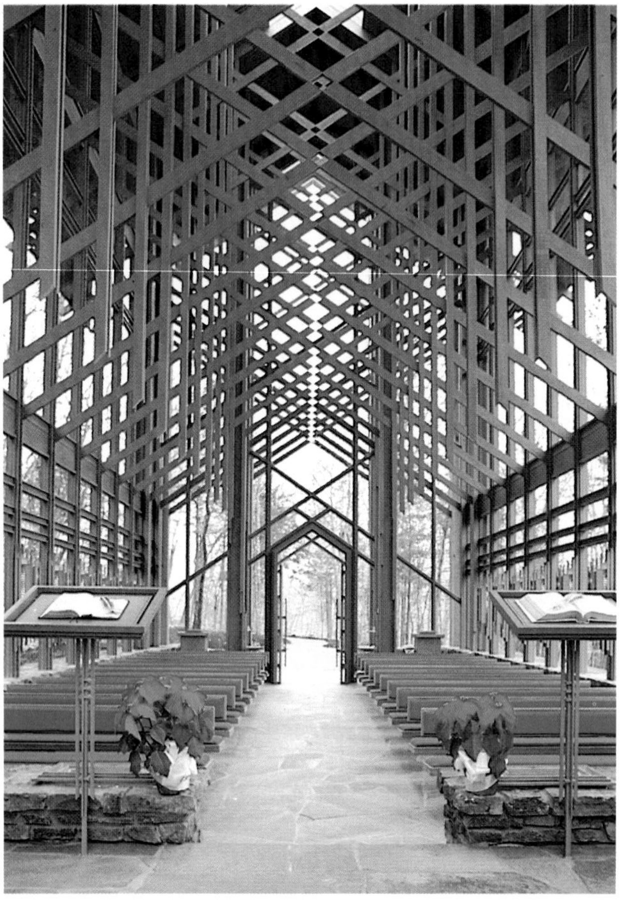

9 E. Fay Jones & Associates.
THORNCROWN CHAPEL.
Eureka Springs, Arkansas.
1981.
Photograph: Thomas England.

to that culture. The figure was carved and attached to the prow of a canoe to ensure the safety of the boat's passengers. Its present function—whether displayed in a museum or reproduced in a book—is to convey cross-cultural information, while pleasing us with its form and imagery.

In many indigenous societies, artists are spiritual leaders identified as shamans or medicine men. Such artist-counselor-healers create their community-centered art within strong traditional limits and provide cultural and spiritual continuity from generation to generation.

All of the world's major religions have used art to inspire and instruct the faithful, even though several of the great spiritual leaders—Gautama Buddha, Jesus Christ, and Mohammed—cautioned their followers against worshiping idols. Art continues to fulfill personal, spiritual needs for many people. The most obvious application of this function is seen in places of worship—where sculpture, paintings, stained-glass windows, and the architecture itself may create an atmosphere for inspiration and devotion.

Nondenominational Christian THORNCROWN

CHAPEL was built in a secluded spot along a wooded trail high in the Ozark mountains. Knowing that heavy construction equipment would damage the wooded setting, architect E. Fay Jones designed the entire structure out of materials that two people could carry along a narrow hillside path. The innovative design provides inspiration on several levels—from the aesthetic and the spiritual to the ecological.

William Blake, eighteenth-century English visionary poet and artist, was a mystic who found reality inseparable from imagination. He considered it natural to converse with angels and biblical prophets, and he referred to his paintings as "Visions of Eternity" that gave visual form to ultimate truth. In Blake's view, the human was an expression of the spiritual, and the visions of the inner eye were more important than the sights of the visible world. His paintings and engravings are filled with the radiance of his imagination—particularly his illustrations of the Bible, his own writings, and works by Milton and Dante. PITY, from Blake's *The First Book of Urizen,* depicts the departing soul of a woman as it is gathered up by angels sweeping past on ghostly white horses.

Art does not have to exist in a religious context to move us spiritually. A wide variety of art forms can have magical, uplifting qualities that evoke a sense of awe, wonder, and appreciation akin to what has been described as a mystical experience. See Weston's PEPPER on page 19.

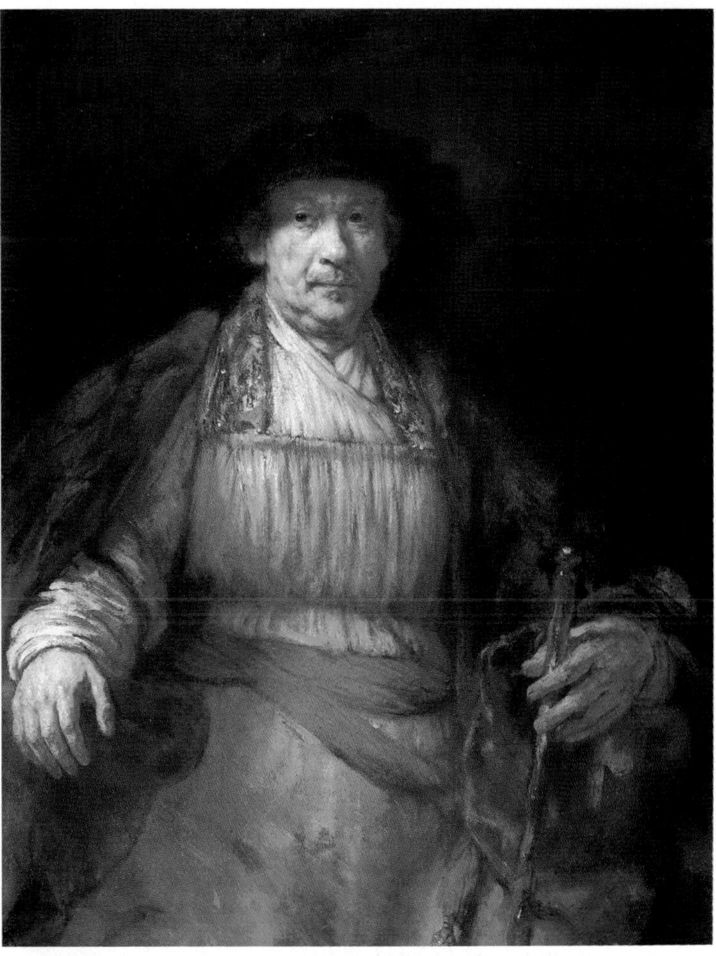

10 Rembrandt van Rijn.
SELF-PORTRAIT. 1658.
Oil on canvas. 33¼" × 26".

Art for Personal Expression

Certain artists reveal themselves so clearly that we feel we know them. Seventeenth-century Dutch artist Rembrandt van Rijn expressed his attitude toward life through more than two thousand paintings, drawings, and prints.

From the age of twenty until his death at sixty-three, Rembrandt drew and painted more than ninety self-portraits. He was fascinated by the expressive possibilities of the human body and found himself to be the most readily available model. Like a good actor, he used his own face as a resource for studying life. By portraying himself at intervals throughout his adult life (see also pages 101 and 364), Rembrandt left a visual autobiography of timeless interest. In most of his self-portraits he viewed himself with objectivity and with the same interest that he brought to his other human subjects (see page 163).

Rembrandt's SELF-PORTRAIT of 1658 is brought to life by the eyes, which suggest a man of penetrating insight. By studying himself carefully, Rembrandt went beyond himself; he created a visual statement about how it feels to be alive, to be human.

Twentieth-century American artist Romare Bearden was fascinated by the pageant of daily life he witnessed in the rural south and in Harlem,

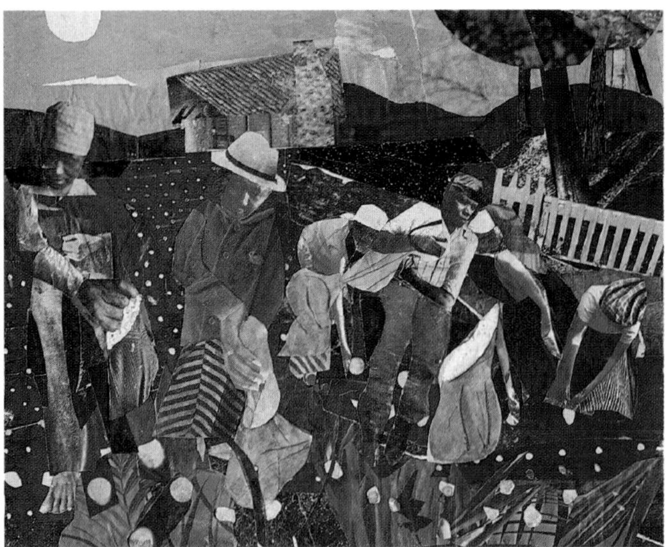

11 Romare Bearden.
WATCHING THE GOOD TRAIN GO BY: COTTON. 1964.
Photo-collage, watercolor, gouache, and pencil on paperboard.
11⅛" × 14".
Hirshhorn Museum and Sculpture Garden, Smithsonian Institution.
Gift of Joseph H. Hirshhorn, 1966.

New York. Bearden created memorable images of humanity by observing, distilling, then reconstructing the life he saw around him. In WATCHING THE GOOD TRAIN GO BY, Bearden communicated his insights with dynamic shapes using a richly varied paint and collage technique.

Qualities of dream and ritual lend an air of mystery to INTERIOR WITH PROFILES. In ROCKET TO THE MOON, collage fragments build a scene of quiet despair and stoic perseverance. A barely visible rocket heads for the moon, while urban life remains punctuated by two red stoplights. The artist makes an ironic visual statement: Bearden placed America's accomplishments in space next to our inner cities' stalled social and economic progress.

Both Bearden and Rembrandt were concerned with the effectiveness of their communication to others, but equally important was meeting their own inner needs for expression. Their situations were quite different from that of a graphic designer such as Saul Bass (see page 235), who was meeting the government's need for a stamp as well as expressing his own artistic sensibilities. Stamp design lies somewhere on the continuum between highly self-expressive art (such as Bearden's and Rembrandt's) and self-effacing product design (see page 238).

Within the broad range of the visual arts, there is a considerable difference in the amount and type of personal expression. The designs of a coin or a chair offer much less information about the personal concerns of the artist than do the designs of a painting or a piece of sculpture.

An element of self-expression exists in all art, even when the art is produced cooperatively by many individuals, as in filmmaking and architecture. In each case, the intended purpose of the work affects the nature of the personal expression.

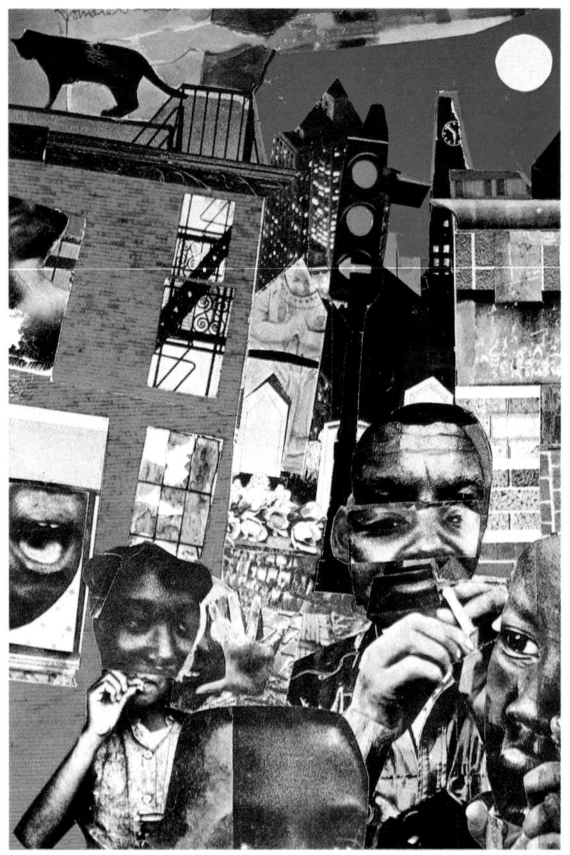

12 Romare Bearden.
ROCKET TO THE MOON. 1967.
Collage. 12½" × 9".
Collection of Nanette Rohan Bearden, New York.

ROMARE BEARDEN (1914–1988)

Romare Bearden paid tribute to the richness of his African-American experience through his art. He sought :

"to paint the life of my people as I know it—passionately and dispassionately as Bruegel painted the life of the Flemish people of his day . . . because much of that life is gone and it had beauty. Also, I want to show that the myth and ritual of Negro life provide the same formal elements that appear in other art, such as a Dutch painting by Pieter de Hooch." [3]

(See paintings by Bruegel on page 356 and de Hooch on page 90.)

The child of educated, middle-class parents, Bearden spent his early childhood in rural North Carolina, then moved north with his family to Harlem, in New York City. He attended New York University, where he earned a degree in mathematics and drew cartoons for the *NYU Medley*. He went on to draw humorous and political cartoons for magazines and a newspaper. During the Depression, he attended the Art Students League in New York, where he was encouraged to say more in his drawings than he said in his cartoons. He held his first exhibition in 1940—about the same time that he became a social worker in New York, a job he held on and off until 1966.

After serving in the army during World War II, Bearden used his G.I. Bill education grant to study at the Sorbonne in Paris. There he came to know a number of intellectuals and writers of African descent, including James Baldwin. Bearden was inspired to make the philosophical perspective of his ethnic heritage a cornerstone of his art.

Bearden was critical of programs that supported African-American artists by encouraging them to work in European academic traditions rather than out of their own lives. He believed that, just as African-Americans had created their own musical forms such as jazz and blues, they should invent their own visual art. He urged fellow African-American artists to create art out of their own life experiences, as had jazz greats Ellington, Basie, Waller, and Hines, who were among Bearden's friends. Bearden himself was a musician and songwriter who said he painted out of the tradition of the blues.

His study of art history led Bearden to admire Cubist and Surrealist paintings (see pages 421 and 432) and African sculpture (pages 310–312), as well as work by European masters. These works of art were among the many important influences on his creative development. Bearden worked in a variety of styles prior to the 1960s, when he arrived at the combined collage and painting style for which he is best known.

Although he learned from direct association with the previous generation of international artists, Bearden's focus remained the African-American experience. He kept a list of key events from his life on the wall of his studio. Often, Bearden drew upon memories of his childhood in rural North Carolina. The idea of homecoming fascinated him. "You can come back to where you started from with added experience and you hope more understanding. You leave and then return to the homeland of your imagination," he said.[4]

Despite his emphasis on his own experiences, Bearden cannot simply be labeled an African-American artist. As with the work of any true artist, his art is beyond classification. "What stands up is structure," he said.

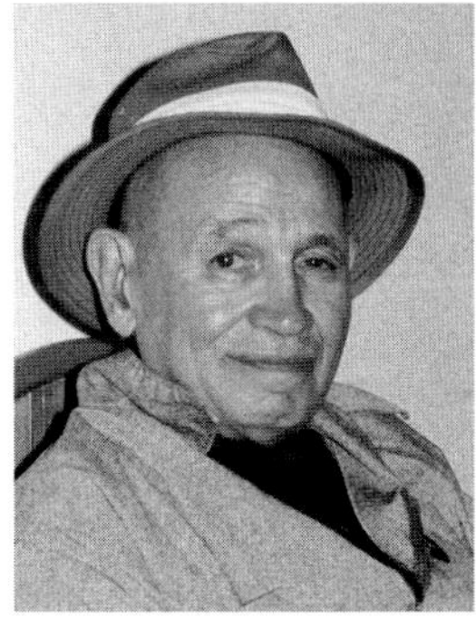

13 Romare Bearden.
Photograph: Bernard Brown.

"What I try to do with art is amplify." If he had just painted a North Carolina farm woman, " . . . it would have meaning to her and people there. But art amplifies itself to something universal."[5]

An exhibition of Bearden's works held at the Studio Museum in Harlem in 1991 was appropriately titled "Memory and Metaphor." His vivid photocollage/paintings are alive with references to his own heritage and life experiences, yet they eloquently portray universal concerns.

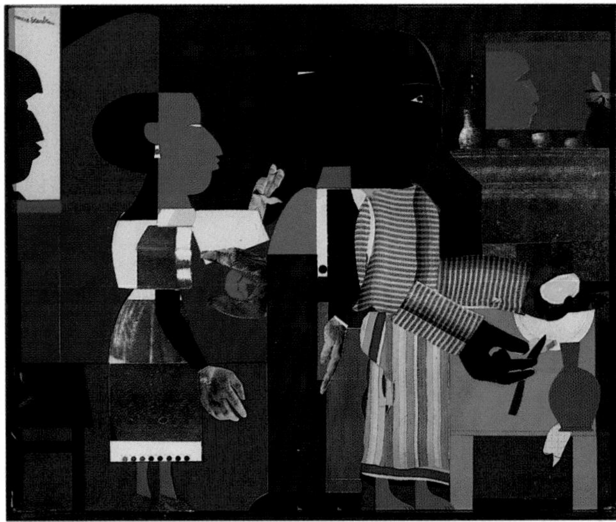

14 Romare Bearden. INTERIOR WITH PROFILES. 1969.
Collage. 39¾" × 49⅞".
First National Bank of Chicago.

THE POPULAR-ART/FINE-ART DIALOG

If art existed only in museums, it would soon lose all relevance to our lives. One of the ways art gets renewed is through its on-going dialog with the everyday world of popular culture.

During the twentieth century, artists have aggressively questioned and expanded art's traditional limits. They have borrowed and adapted art forms from many styles and sources including tribal societies, folk artists, and children, as well as from popular mass media. For example, Joan Miró and Paul Klee (see page 430,) brought the playfulness found in children's pictures into their own art.

The resulting transformations in art have affected contemporary design from clothing to automobiles, from advertising to music videos. And just as applied artists often draw upon the work of fine artists, so fine artists sometimes look to the popular applied arts for inspiration. The outpourings of the mass media dominate modern society. Images ranging from commercial products to rock videos flash quickly around the world via newspapers, magazines, and television. These images have provided subjects and styles for many fine artists who incorporate mundane objects and symbols in their work as part of their response to their surroundings. Such responses are not new. Since prehistoric times artists have helped their communities deal with day-to-day reality by portraying what they see around them.

In his painting I SAW THE FIGURE 5 IN GOLD, Charles Demuth drew upon the signs common to twentieth-century cities. The style echoes a graphic-design style of the twenties. Flags, maps, stenciled

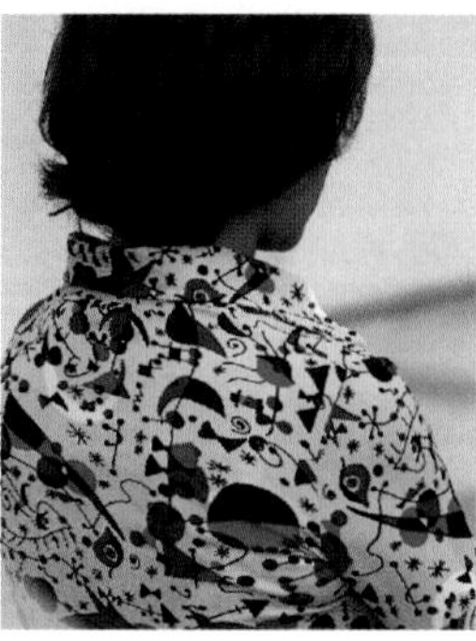

16 TEXTILE DESIGN INFLUENCED BY JOAN MIRÓ. 1976.

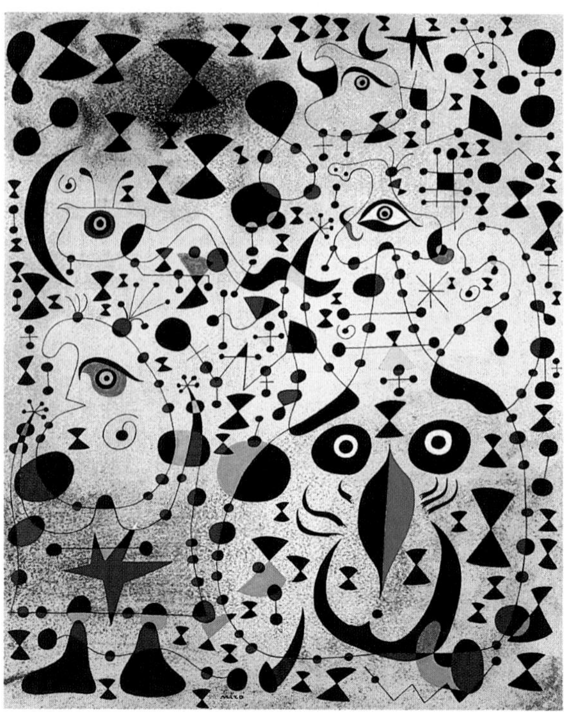

17 Joan Miró.
BEAUTIFUL BIRD REVEALING THE UNKNOWN TO A PAIR OF LOVERS. 1941.
Gouache and oil wash on paper. 18" × 15".
The Museum of Modern Art, New York.
Acquired through the Lillie P. Bliss Bequest.

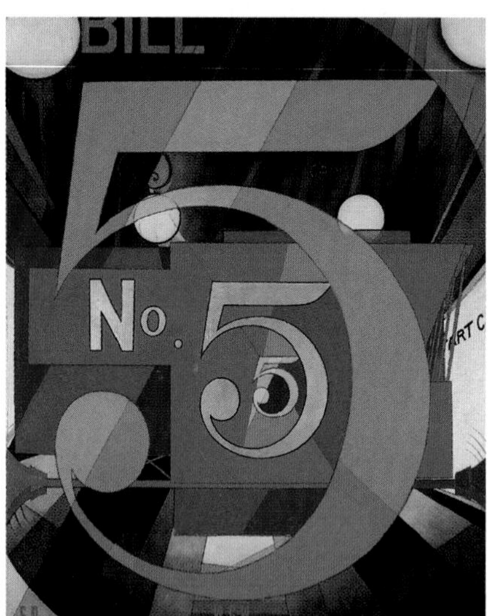

15 Charles Demuth.
I SAW THE FIGURE 5 IN GOLD. 1928.
Oil on composition board. 36" × 30".
The Metropolitan Museum of Art, New York.
Alfred Stieglitz Collection, 1949 (49.59.1).

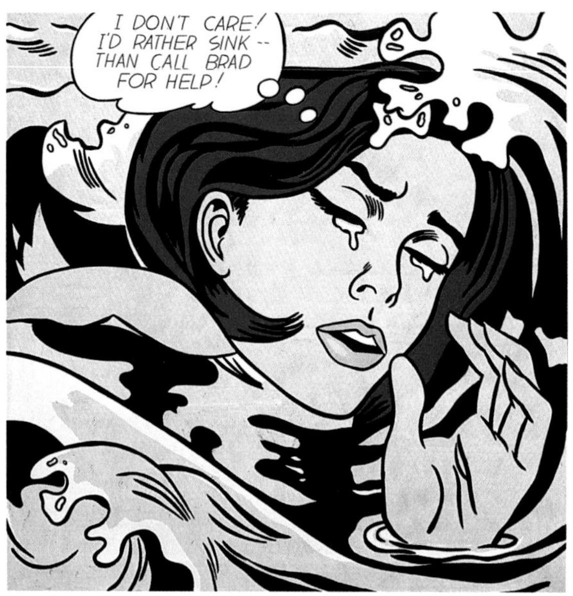

18 Roy Lichtenstein.
DROWNING GIRL. 1963.
Oil and synthetic polymer paint on canvas. 67⅝" × 66¾".
The Museum of Modern Art, New York. Philip Johnson Fund and gift of Mrs. Bagley Wright.

THE POPULAR-ART/FINE-ART DIALOG

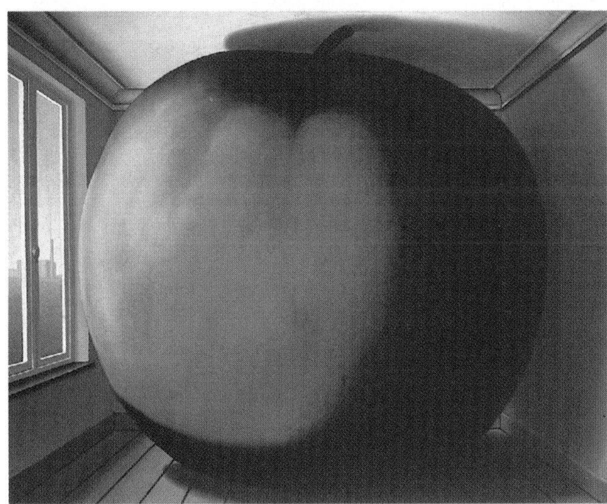

19 René Magritte.
THE LISTENING ROOM I. 1953.
Oil on canvas. 38 cm × 45.8 cm.

Art director and designer Tom Wolsey collaborated with photographer Henry Wolf to create a highly intriguing series of ads for Karastan Rug Mills. The inspiration came from paintings such as THE LISTENING ROOM I by one of Wolsey's heroes, the Surrealist painter René Magritte.

Historically, artists have been influenced by one another and have borrowed from their contemporaries as well as their predecessors. What is new is the greatly expanded quantity of visual material available to people worldwide. Just a few generations ago, people knew only the art they saw as original works; it is only within the last century that print, film, and television have made reproductions of the art of the world available to people everywhere. Throughout the twentieth century we have seen artists and designers incorporate influences from diverse sources as they freed themselves from the constraints of narrow historical views.

20 Henry Wolf.
KARASTAN RUG MILLS ADVERTISEMENT.
"NESTING INSTINCT." 1986.
Composite photograph.
40.5 cm × 54.5 cm.
Tom Wolsey, Art Director.

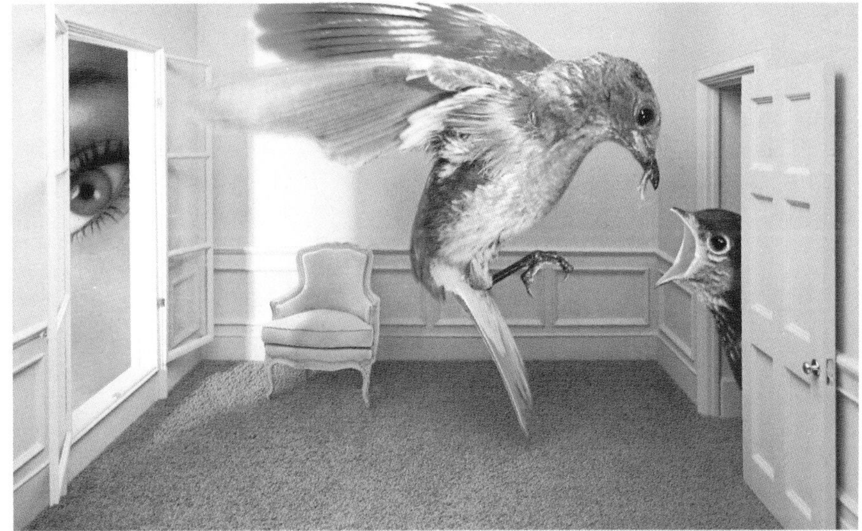

numbers, and targets are seen in many of Jasper John's paintings and prints. (See his TARGET WITH FOUR FACES on page 458. See also Andy Warhol's CAMPBELL SOUP CANS on page 461.) James Rosenquist made visual statements influenced by styles found in billboard advertising (see page 461), and Roy Lichtenstein adopted a comic book style and subject matter as seen in his painting DROWNING GIRL.

Going the other way, graphic designers and others working in applied arts have borrowed heavily from painters. We see how a textile designer was influenced by the abstract style of the painter Joan Miró.

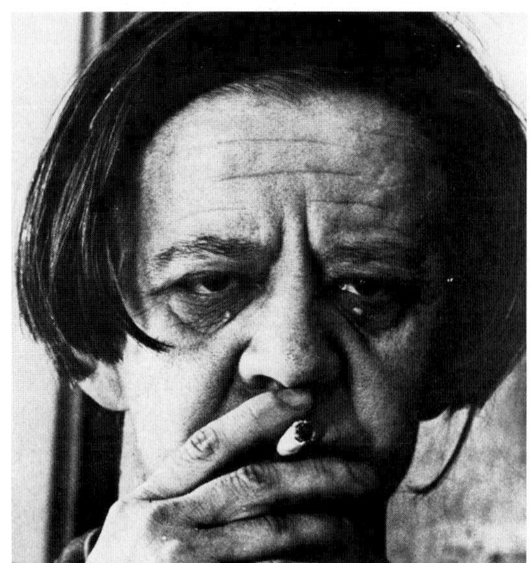

21 AMERICAN CANCER SOCIETY POSTER. c. 1969.

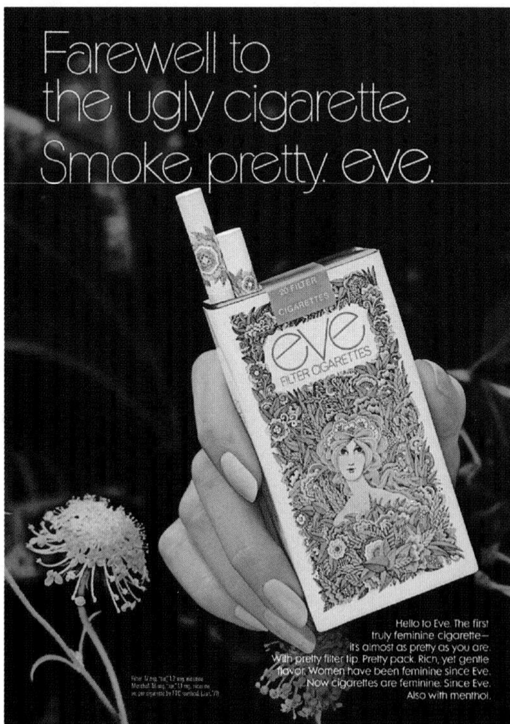

22 Herb Lubalin.
EVE CIGARETTE ADVERTISEMENT. 1970.

Art for Social and Political Purposes

Art has served, criticized, described, shaped, and been shaped by human societies. From ancient times to the present, religious and political leaders throughout the world have directed and at times even placed rigid controls on the style and content of art.

Architecture, painting, and sculpture—and more recently film and television—have been used to project and glorify images of deities, political leaders, even corporations. In seventeenth-century France, King Louis XIV built an enormous palace with a formal garden at Versailles. It was built to symbolize the strength of the monarchy—to impress and intimidate the nobility with the Sun King's power (see page 367). Today we have buildings such as Trump Tower in New York City, businessman Donald Trump's high-rise monument to himself.

We are surrounded by persuasive "art" in the form of commercial advertisements. Posters, billboards, and television commercials seek to sell us everything from toothpaste to presidential candidates. Some years ago nonsmokers enjoyed the AMERICAN CANCER SOCIETY poster. Many women smokers, on the other hand, were influenced by the EVE CIGARETTE ADVERTISEMENT designed to counteract the Cancer Society's poster.

Advertising designers often use the persuasive powers of art to slant the truth. We see their messages every day on television and in the print media. Not all persuasive art is commercial, however. Art can be an effective instrument for educating, directing popular values, molding public opinion, and gaining and holding political power. Art, like science, is not inherently good or evil. It is the way art is used that makes the difference.

Political and religious leaders wielded the power of art to help control the minds of the masses long before the advent of modern communications media. In the twentieth century, art's capacity to influence behavior has been greatly increased by photography, film, and television. Adolf Hitler's ability to inspire people to follow his mad dreams was greatly intensified and extended by the master-

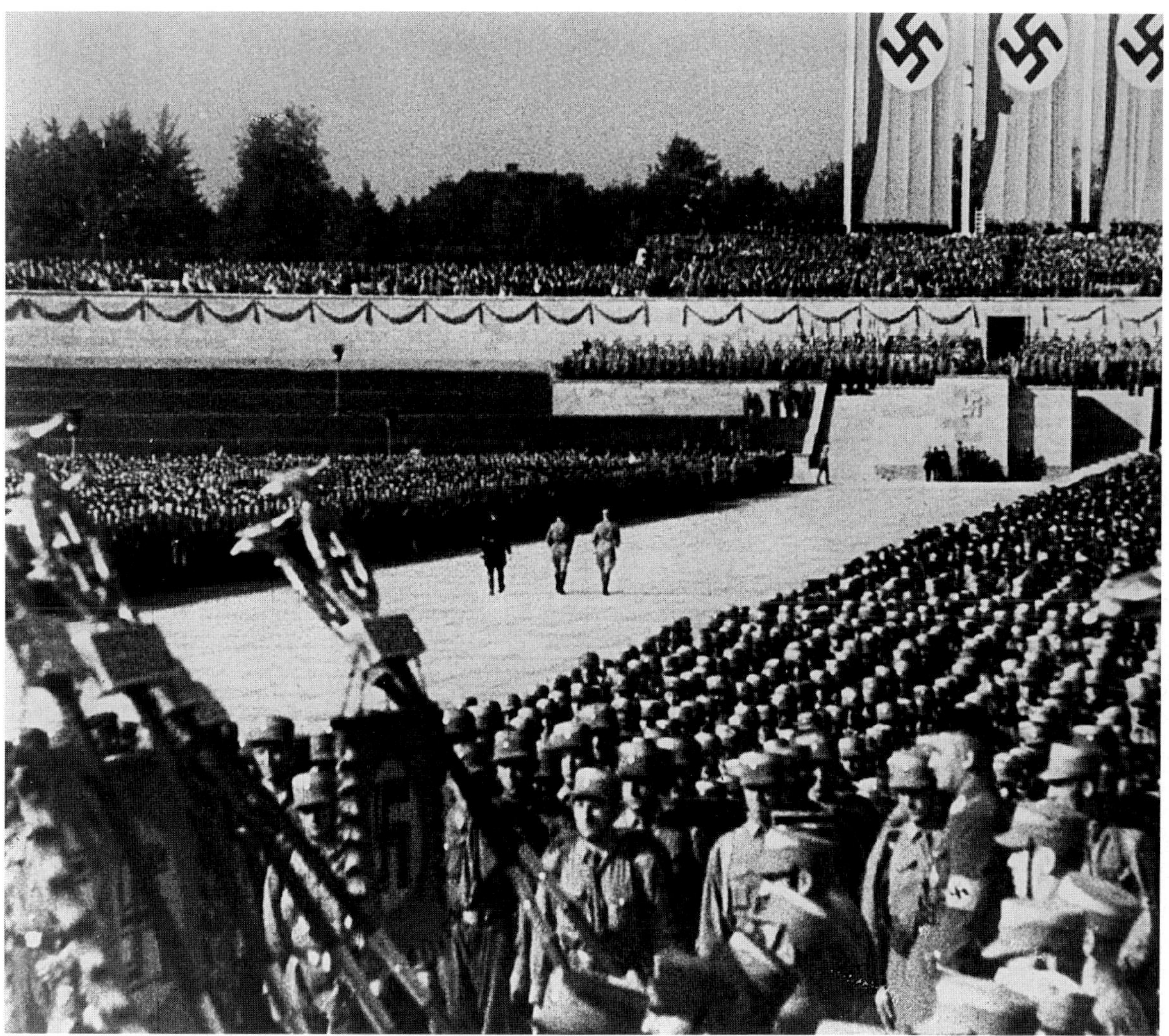

23 Leni Riefenstahl.
TRIUMPH OF THE WILL. 1934.
Film.
The Museum of Modern Art Film Stills Archive, New York.

ful filmmaking of Leni Riefenstahl. In her 1934 film TRIUMPH OF THE WILL, Riefenstahl created what Hitler ordered: a highly effective instrument for political propaganda. Writing about her experiences, she said her aim was to bring the word of the Führer to the German people and to the world.

The major question raised by Riefenstahl's work for Hitler goes far beyond the Nazi films she produced. What is an artist's moral responsibility? What is the impact of such powerful artistic achievement on the whole human race? In this case, an artist of great talent applied her artistic ability to influence the hearts and minds of millions of people—with disastrous results.

Many artists, including political cartoonists and photographers, have used their art to protest injustice and to promote peace, environmental protection, and human rights. Margaret Bourke-White's photograph LOUISVILLE FLOOD VICTIMS on page 178 is a protest against racial inequality; Picasso's GUERNICA on page 443 is a strong antiwar statement.

Robert Arneson, best known for his whimsical self-portraits (see page 217), has also created works

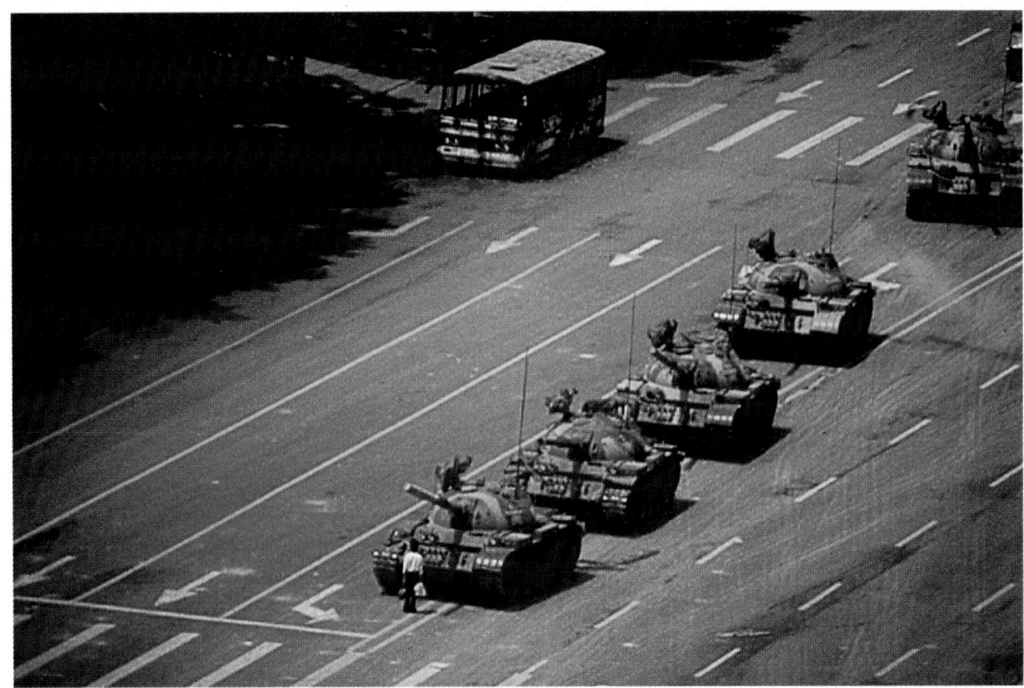

24 Stuart Franklin.
CONFRONTATION NEAR TIANANMEN SQUARE. 1989.
Photograph.

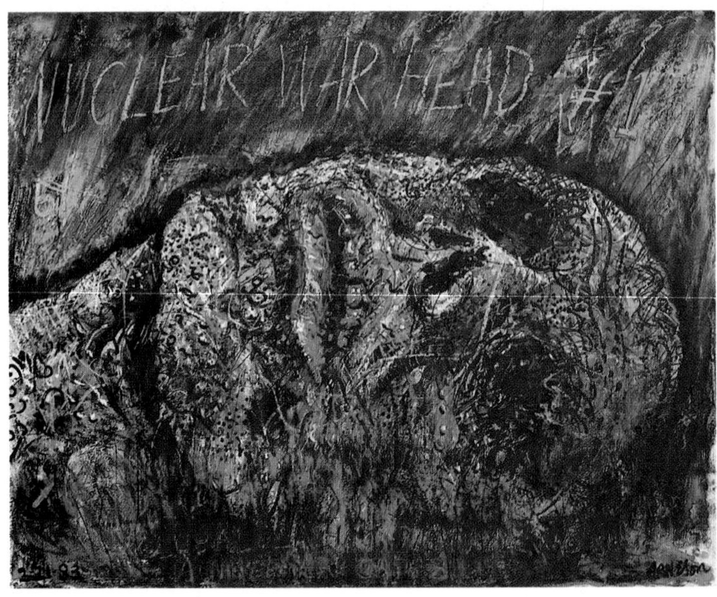

25 Robert Arneson.
NUCLEAR WAR HEAD. 1983.
Acrylic oil sticks, alkyd on paper. 43" × 53".
Courtesy of the artist.

in clay and on paper that deal with the threat of nuclear holocaust. Works such as NUCLEAR WAR HEAD come from a sense of social concern.

Few can forget the photographs and televised images of a lone civilian blocking the path of oncoming tanks during the CONFRONTATION NEAR TIANANMEN SQUARE following the massacre of 1989. While Riefenstahl glorified blind patriotism, Stuart Franklin captured one man's courageous act of defiance against tyranny. (See also Goya's similar protest, on page 375.)

The art of our culture reflects who we are and our relationships to our surroundings and to one another. Art can provide beauty and inspiration, but it may also uncover disturbing truths. In the powerful distortions in some works of art we may recognize destructive aspects of ourselves and of society. This very recognition can inspire inner development and an increased social and political awareness. Today, when cross-cultural understanding, open-mindedness, and creative problem solving are urgently needed, art can elevate our consciousness and deepen our humanity.

CHAPTER 2

Art and Experience

Art encourages us to experience our lives more vividly by causing us to reexamine our thoughts and renew our feelings. The essence of art is the spark of insight and the thrill of discovery—first experienced by the maker, then built into the work of art, and finally experienced by the viewer. Russian novelist and philosopher Leo Tolstoy described the process:

To evoke in oneself a feeling one has experienced, and having evoked it..., then by means of movement, line, color, sounds or forms expressed in words, so transmit that same feeling—this is the activity of art.[1]

Life is a succession of experiences. As we live our lives, experiences flow past in a stream of what may seem like disconnected events and impressions. Art helps us to become aware of the significance of the moment and the interrelationships of events—and thereby to experience life fully.

While animals are keenly aware of their world through their senses, human beings have lost some of the ability to experience life intensely in the present moment. Caught up in thoughts and emotions, and often separated from direct experiences with nature, many human beings adopt dulled, programmed responses to their environments.

The best art can cut through our tendency to experience life with complacency and prejudgment. Such art sharpens our perceptions of life by re-creating human experience in fresh forms, bringing a renewed sense of the significance and connectedness of life.

An art maker learns to be fully aware during the act of artistic creation. An artist has to be continuously open to change, open to new possibilities and interpretations. Art created in a spirit of openness has vitality and honesty built into its very structure. When the art maker has an insight that she or he succeeds in building into the work of art, then the work will express that insight—that level of awareness.

PERCEPTION AND AWARENESS

Of all our planet's resources, the most precious is human awareness.

Don Fabun[2]

Perception and awareness are closely related. To *be aware* means to be conscious, to know something. To *perceive* is to become aware through the senses, particularly through sight or hearing, and to understand through that awareness.

In the visual arts, we seek awareness through our sense of sight and through the development of visual thinking. Surprising as it may seem, much of our sensory awareness is learned. The eyes are blind to what the mind cannot see. The following story provides an unusually dramatic example.

Joey, a New York City boy with blind parents,

was born with cerebral palsy. Because of his disabilities, as well as those of his parents, Joey was largely confined to his family's apartment. As he grew older, he learned to get around the apartment in a walker. His mother believed him to be of normal intelligence, yet clinical tests showed him to be blind and mentally retarded. At age five, Joey was admitted to a school for children with a variety of disabilities, and for the first time he had daily contact with people who could see. Although he bumped into things in his walker and felt for almost everything, as a blind person does, it soon became apparent that Joey was not really blind. *He simply had never learned to use his eyes.* The combined disabilities of Joey and his parents had prevented him from developing normal visual awareness. After working with specialists and playing with sighted children for a year, his visual responses were normal. Those who worked with him concluded that Joey was a bright and alert child.

To varying degrees, we are all guided—or limited, as Joey was—in the growth of our awareness by parents, teachers, and others who influence us.

Even common words and concepts can sometimes limit our sensory impressions. When we look at an object only in terms of a label or a stereotype, we miss the thing itself; we tend to see a vague something called "tree" or "chair" rather than *this* tree, this *particular* chair, or this *unique* object or person. As artist Robert Irwin pointed out, "seeing is forgetting the name of the thing one sees."[3]

As we become more conscious of our own sensory experiences, we open up new levels of awareness. Ordinary things become extraordinary when seen without prejudgment. Is Edward Weston's photograph of a pepper meaningful to us because we like peppers so much? Probably not. To help us see anew, Weston created a memorable image on a flat surface with the help of a common pepper. A time exposure of over two hours gave PEPPER #30 a quality of glowing light—a living presence that resembles an embrace. Through his sensitivity to form, Weston revealed how this pepper appeared to him. Notes from his *Daybook* describe his insights about this photograph:

August 8, 1930

I could wait no longer to print them—my new peppers, so I put aside several orders, and yesterday afternoon had an exciting time with seven new negatives.

First I printed my favorite, the one made last Saturday, August 2, just as the light was failing—quickly made, but with a week's previous effort back of my immediate, unhesitating decision. A week?—Yes, on this certain pepper,—but twenty-eight years of effort, starting with a youth on a farm in Michigan, armed with a No. 2 Bull's Eye [Kodak] 3½ × 3½, have gone into the making of this pepper, which I consider a peak of achievement.

It is a classic, completely satisfying—a pepper—but more than a pepper: abstract, in that it is completely outside subject matter... this new pepper takes one beyond the world we know in the conscious mind.[4]

April 24, 1930

Clouds, torsos, shells, peppers, trees, rocks, smokestacks are but interdependent, interrelated parts of a whole, which is life.—Life rhythms felt in no matter what, become symbols of the whole.[5]

LOOKING AND SEEING

Degrees of visual awareness can be distinguished by the verbs "look" and "see." Looking implies taking in what is before us in a purely mechanical way; seeing is a more active extension of looking. If we care only about function, we simply need to look quickly at a doorknob in order to grasp and turn it. But when we get excited about the shape and finish of a doorknob or the bright clear quality of a winter day, we go beyond simple functional looking to a higher level of perception called "seeing."

Sixteenth-century German artist Albrecht Dürer developed his powers of seeing to such a high degree that he was able to reveal to others the wonder of an ordinary patch of wild plants. His

26 Edward Weston.
PEPPER #30. 1930.
Photograph.

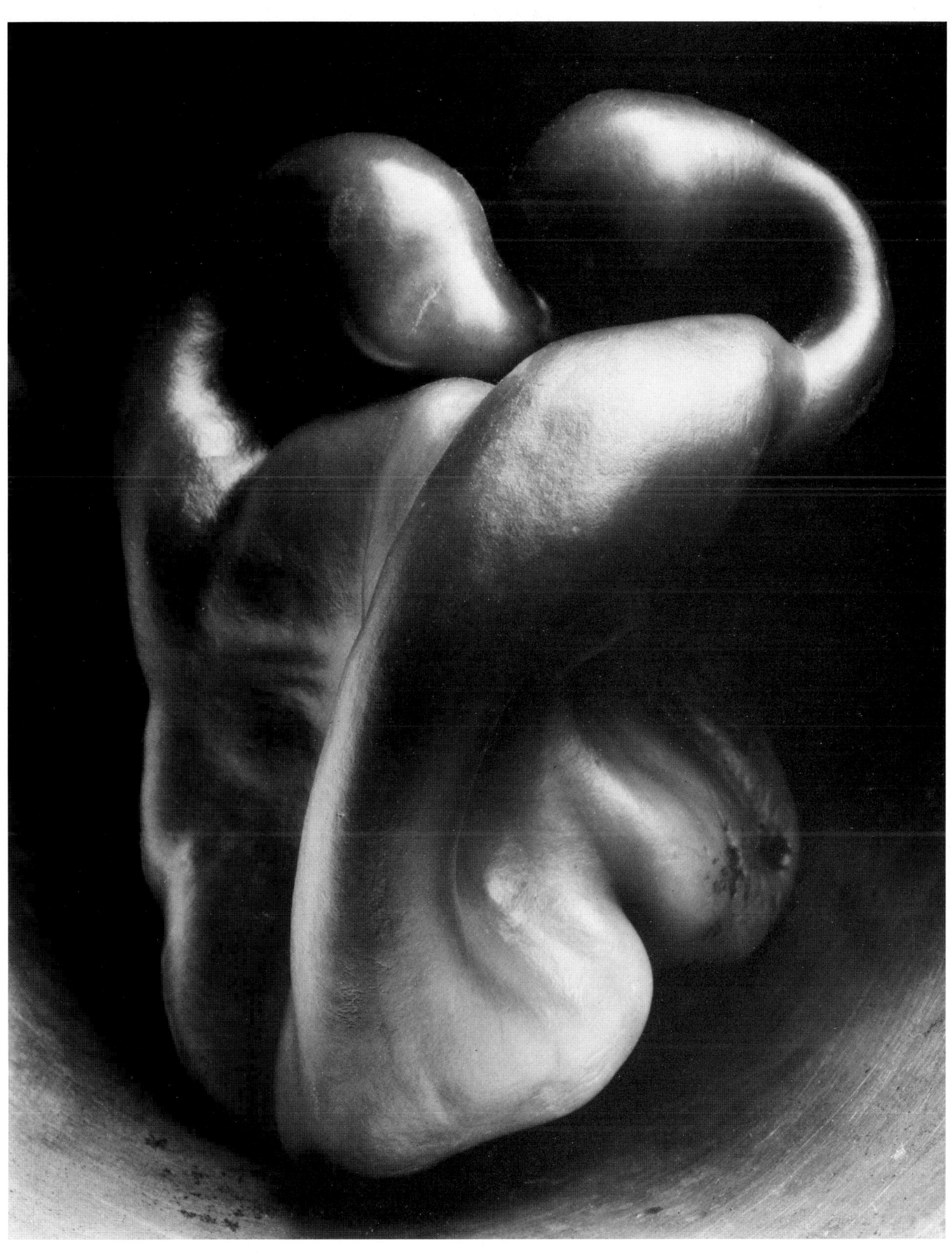

watercolor painting, appropriately titled THE GREAT PIECE OF TURF, shows a commonplace subject seen as though for the first time. Such careful observations of nature helped initiate the development of modern science.

Have we lost the ability to see with the precision of Dürer? Could you get down on your hands and knees and observe a patch of grass with as much careful attention? A botanist could list the plant types, but would she or he always go beyond scientific identification to see the unique forms of each plant and the interrelationships among them?

Our technological, media-oriented society bombards us with stereotyped or "canned" images that may deaden our awareness. Such visual noise or visual pollution may overload us and dull our senses. Even before the development of television, twentieth-century French artist Henri Matisse wrote about the effort it takes to move beyond stereotypes—to see fully:

To see is itself a creative operation, requiring an effort. Everything that we see in our daily life is more or less distorted by acquired habits, and this is perhaps more evident in an age like ours when cinema, posters, and magazines present us every day with a flood of ready-made images which are to the eye what prejudices are to the mind. The effort needed to see things without distortion takes something very like courage.[6]

VISUAL THINKING

A great deal of our thinking is visual thinking. To visualize is to use imagination and visual memory consciously to preview events or plans before they occur. The process of visualization provides a means by which ideas, images, and goals can be materialized. As a horticulturalist says, "Before you can have beautiful roses on your lawn or in your greenhouse, you have to have beautiful roses in your mind."[7] This is equally true for a meal, a shirt, a vacation, a painting, or a building. Visualization is used by all artists. Some plan their works by mentally picturing them as completed images; others visualize their pieces as they develop them, letting one idea lead to another.

An individual's life experiences determine the nature of both inner visualization and outer seeing. For example, twelve people painting the same subject—even working from the same vantage point—will make twelve different images based on their personal experiences, values, interests, and eyesight. A conservationist, a farmer, and a developer will see the same landscape differently, as will a painter and a photographer.

Even the same individual can have a variety of responses to a given subject. When we look at a photograph of a house, for example, we see an enclosed, three-dimensional volume. On an intellectual level we may assume it contains rooms, while our emotions may lead us to make associations with "home." Creative visual thinking draws from these varied levels of meaning and integrates the complementary modes of rational and intuitive human intelligence associated with the right and left sides of the brain.

ART AND BEAUTY

In the West, contradictory views exist regarding "art" and "beauty." Beginning with the ancient Greeks, Westerners have been preoccupied with beauty. Criteria for beauty, as well as art, often are based on culturally accepted standards rather than individual responses or personal intuition.

Today we often use the word "beautiful" to refer to things that are simply pretty. "Pretty" means pleasant or attractive to the eye, whereas "beautiful" means having qualities of a high order, qualities that delight the eye, engage the intellectual or moral sense, or do all these things simultaneously. In the words of architect Louis Kahn, "Beautiful doesn't necessarily mean good-looking."[8]

It is important to consider possibilities beyond the conventional or established standards of beauty and ugliness. If art's only function were to please the senses, ugliness would have no place in art. But

27 Albrecht Dürer. THE GREAT PIECE OF TURF. 1503. Watercolor. 16¼" × 12⅜".
Albertina Collection, Vienna

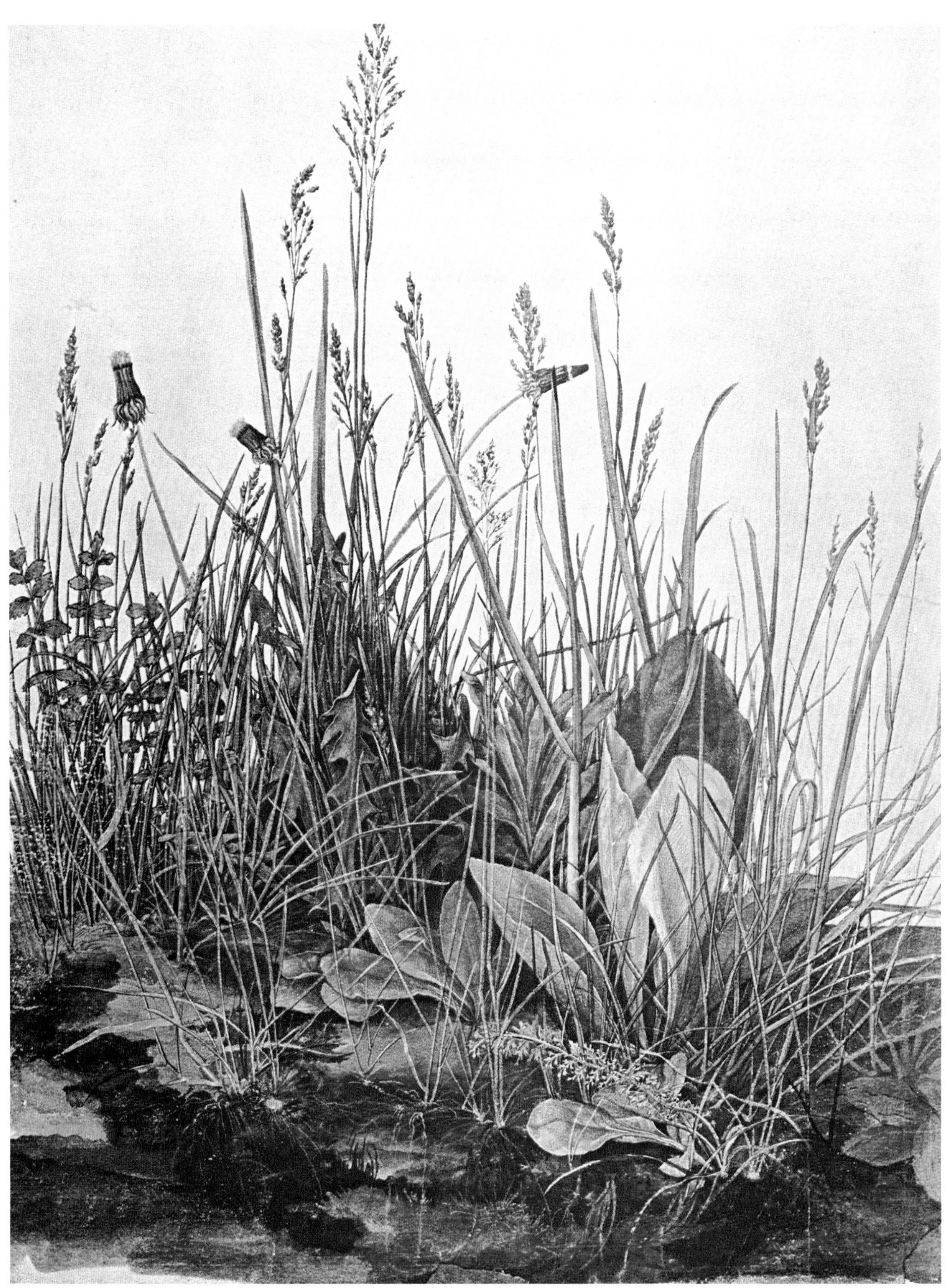

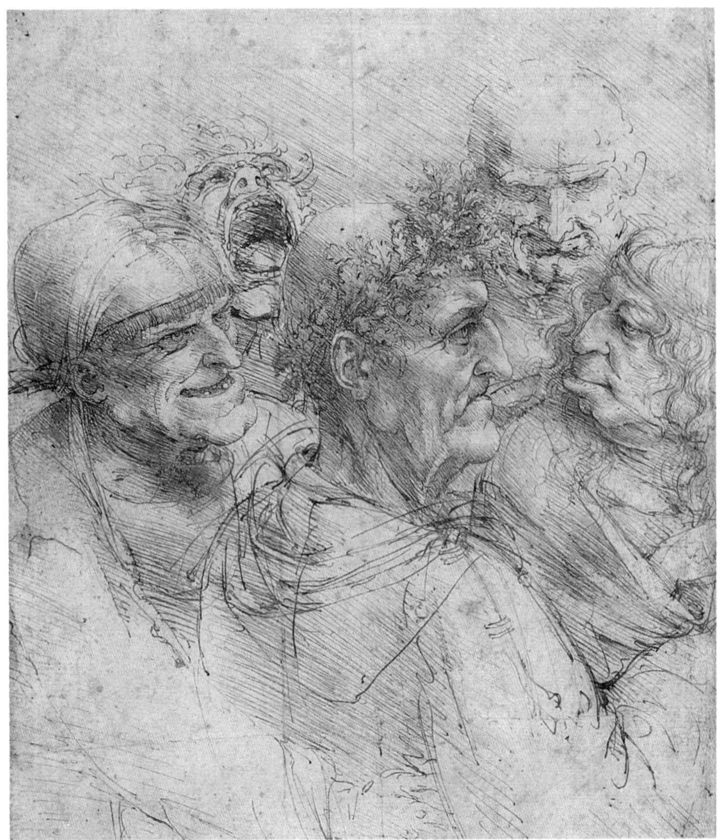

28 Leonardo da Vinci.
FIVE GROTESQUE HEADS. c. 1490.
Pen and brown ink. 10¼" × 8½".
Windsor Castle, Royal Library. © 1993 Her Majesty Queen Elizabeth II.

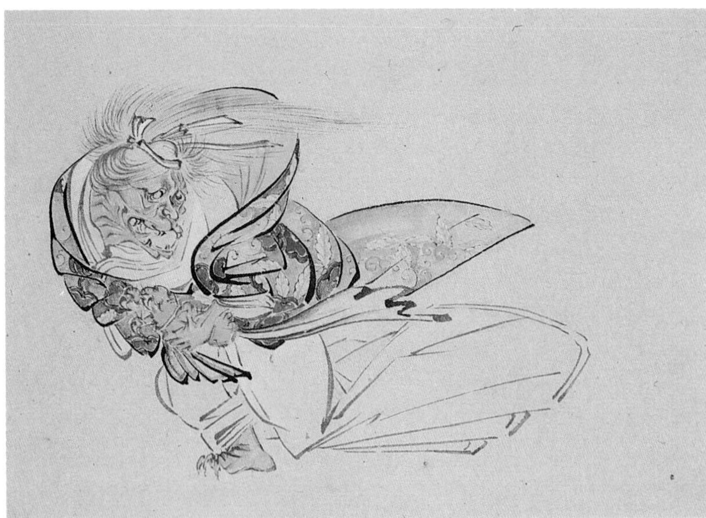

29 Shibata Zeshin.
DETAIL OF DANCING RASHOMON. 19TH CENTURY.
Ink and color on paper. Hanging scroll, 14⅝" × 20½".
Honolulu Academy of Arts. Gift of James E. O'Brien.

since we don't expect all works of drama or literature to be pretty or pleasant, why should we have different expectations of the visual arts? Leonardo da Vinci, Shibata Zeshin, Pablo Picasso, and Otto Dix were artists from different times and places who actively explored dimensions of "ugliness."

Street life fascinated Italian Renaissance artist Leonardo da Vinci. He was particularly interested in studying people of striking appearance, people either very beautiful or very ugly. Leonardo found ugliness to be as worthy of attention as beauty. In fact, he considered ugliness a variation of beauty, and this feeling can be seen in his FIVE GROTESQUE HEADS. In his *Treatise on Painting*, he advised others always to carry a pocket notebook in which to make quick drawings of whatever they observed. He also drew from memory, as described by sixteenth-century artist and biographer Giorgio Vasari:

Leonardo used to follow people whose extraordinary appearance took his fancy, sometimes throughout a whole day, until he could draw them as well by memory as though they stood before him.[9]

Elegant lines, charged with energy, depict the garments and frame the ghastly head in a detail from nineteenth-century Japanese artist Shibata Zeshin's DANCING RASHOMON. Zeshin created the terrifying figure from his imagination in order to dramatize a key moment in a story.

HEAD, the study by twentieth-century Spanish artist Pablo Picasso for his famous painting GUERNICA (see page 443), was part of his personal response to the pre-World War II bombing of Guernica, a small Spanish town. For him, the event symbolized the cruelty and brutal ugliness of war. This painting continues to stand as a political statement against the forces that cause such horrors.

Otto Dix, who served in the German army for four years during World War I, depicted the terrible anguish of war in his etching WOUNDED SOLDIER. In the economically and politically troubled postwar period, he criticized his society for its decadence. With unrelenting honesty, Dix documented the brutalities of gas and trench warfare.

In contrast to Leonardo's and Zeshin's drawings, in which ugliness is gracefully drawn, every line in Dix's etching carries the grotesque quality of the larger subject—the horror of war. As Picasso's drawing and Dix's etching illustrate, even horrible events can provide the basis for constructive communication through art. Artists can help us to learn without our having to live through such horrors.

AESTHETICS

Aesthetics is the branch of philosophy that studies fundamental issues in the arts. When we seek basic guidelines for creating, interpreting, or evaluating works of art, or when we wonder why one work is more beautiful, memorable, or provocative than another, we engage in aesthetic thinking. When we are so moved by something that we lose ourselves in the experience, our response may be called an aesthetic experience. *Aesthetic* refers to an awareness of beauty or to that quality in a work of art or other manmade or natural form which evokes a sense of elevated awareness in the viewer. The opposite of aesthetic is anesthetic.

In eighteenth-century Europe, when aesthetics became a separate branch of philosophy, the concept of beauty was its main concern. Today, many other aspects of art are considered. Aesthetics investigates how the arts affect feelings and how those feelings influence learning and other aspects of culture. Aesthetics helps us to compare different types of art and guides our evaluation of the whole range of art. Questions raised by aesthetics include: How does art differ from other human enterprises? When is something art? How does art affect our perceptions, moods, values, and beliefs? Is art good for society and for individuals? When is art beneficial? When is it dangerous? Do artists and their art ever threaten the social order?

Scholars in many civilizations study the ways in which works of art affect their people. Asian aesthetic views have remained traditional and stable over the centuries. In India, philosophers say the aesthetic experience takes place in a transaction between a prepared viewer and a true work of art. Further, the aesthetic experience resides neither in

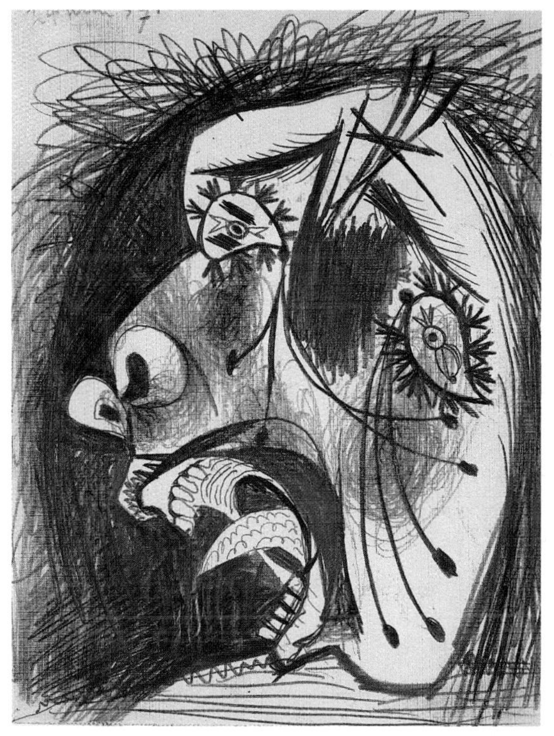

30 Pablo Picasso.
HEAD (STUDY FOR GUERNICA). May 24, 1937.
Pencil and gouache. 11⅜" × 9¼".
Museo del Prado, Madrid. (See page 443.)

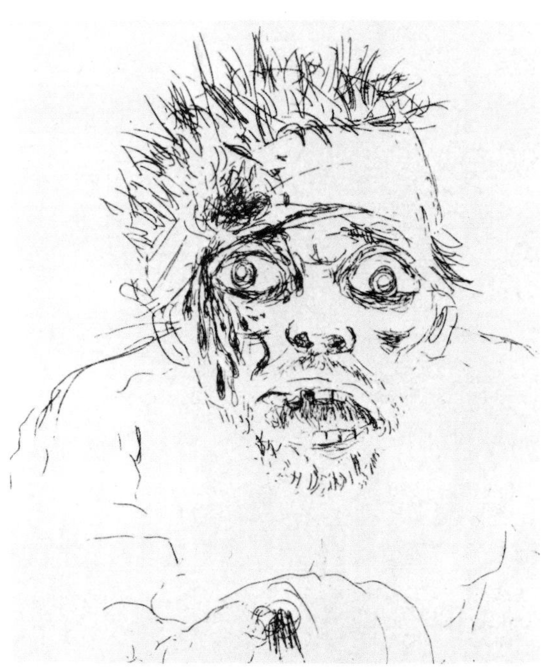

31 Otto Dix.
WOUNDED SOLDIER. 1924.
Etching. 7¾" × 5½".
Galerie der Stadt. Stuttgart.

the beholder nor in the object, but in the interaction of the two. In Japan, a work of art is said to provoke inexpressible awe. In China, the work of art is expected to express the vitality of the artist—which is consistent with the energy of the universe—so that viewers may be vitalized through their experiences of the art.

In the West, theories of aesthetics can be broadly categorized as subjective, objective, or a balance of the two. The *subjective* approach holds that judgment is personal, changeable, and unchallengeable, and that all individual responses are equally valid. Here the artwork's aesthetic value rests in the response of the viewer rather than in the work itself. On the other hand, *objective* theories presume unchanging standards upon which absolute judgments can be made about all art, regardless of time and place. Nearly any such fixed set of standards results in rejecting the art of many cultures and periods.

Between the extremes of objectivism and subjectivism are *relativist* theories whose proponents claim that aesthetic value derives from the interaction between the subjective response of the viewer and the intrinsic qualities of the art object. With this relativist approach, each culture and each period forms its own standards.

Cultures without a theory or even a word for art have nevertheless recognized some works as having higher quality and thus greater power than others. While art experts and museum curators in our culture generally agree on which examples of world art from the past deserve viewers' time and attention, their opinions can be very different from those of their predecessors and may seem outdated fifty years from now. There is, however, far less consensus among experts regarding the art produced today.

Some people equate the word "aesthetic" with taste. Many artists and art critics oppose this view, maintaining that art has nothing to do with taste; they think that so-called good taste can actually limit an honest response.

"Good taste" almost always refers to an already established way of seeing. Innovative artists, seeking new ways of seeing, often challenge the established conventions of taste. During the last two hundred years, developments in most Western art can be seen as successive overturnings of previous generations' standards or taste. This search for new levels of awareness explains why many traditional aesthetic theories seem inadequate when applied to much contemporary art.

Chapter 7, pages 125–130, offers a practical, step-by-step approach to the appreciation and evaluation of works of art, from ancient to current forms.

CREATIVITY

The source of all art, science, and technology—in fact, all of human civilizations—is creative imagination, or creative thinking. As scientist Albert Einstein declared, "Imagination is more important than knowledge."[10]

What do we mean by this ability we call creativity? Psychologist Erich Fromm wrote:

> *In talking about creativity, let us first consider its two possible meanings: creativity in the sense of creating something new, something which can be seen or heard by others, such as a painting, a sculpture, a symphony, a poem, a novel, etc., or creativity as an attitude, which is the condition of any creation in the former sense but which can exist even though nothing new is created in the world of things. . . .*
>
> *What is creativity? The best general answer I can give is that creativity is the ability to see (or to be aware) and to respond.*[11]

Creativity is as fundamental to experiencing and appreciating a work of art as it is to making one. Insightful seeing is itself a creative act; it requires open receptivity—putting aside habitual modes of thought.

Studies of creativity have described traits of people who have maintained or rediscovered the creative attitude. These include the abilities to:

- wonder and be curious
- be open to new experience
- see the familiar from an unfamiliar point of view

- take advantage of accidental events
- make one thing out of another by shifting its function
- generalize from particulars in order to see broad applications
- synthesize, integrate, and find order in disorder
- be in touch with unconscious sources, yet be intensely conscious
- be able to analyze and evaluate
- know oneself, have the courage to be oneself in the face of opposition
- be willing to take risks
- be persistent: to work for long periods—perhaps years—in pursuit of a goal

As Fromm said, creativity is an *attitude.* We all have the potential to be creative, yet most of us were not encouraged to develop our creativity. We can do so by becoming willing to explore new relationships and insights.

The creative process often begins when one is inspired by an idea or faced with a problem. It can start with something as simple as "fooling around." There are as many ways to create as there are creative people, but creative processes generally have certain sequential characteristics in common:

preparation Framing or formulating the question(s) may be the most important step; information is gathered and open-minded exploration takes place.

incubation All the preparatory work is set aside and you take time off to relax and to let intuitive insights come forward.

illumination Sometimes referred to as the *aha!* experience, it occurs when a sudden hunch or insight leads to a valuable final result.

verification or revision You test your solution, and others respond by confirming or denying your success; revision may lead you to begin the steps again. Artists as well as scientists often find that their results lead them to start over with a related project.

Imaginative visualization is a major part of the creative process. When we form images in the mind's eye, we cultivate imaginative experiences outside actual events. The arts make this creative, intangible life of the mind tangible—visible in the visual arts, audible in music, verbal in literature.

Creativity developed through art experiences enhances creative problem solving and communicating in other areas of life. Opportunities for creative expression are extremely important: they develop our abilities to integrate experiences of the outside world with those of our inner selves.

CHILDREN'S ART

Our basic attitudes about art and our own creativity are shaped during childhood. Because artistic efforts are among our most personal endeavors, children tend to be particularly vulnerable to disinterest, demeaning comparisons, and disparaging remarks about such efforts. To ignore or belittle creative expression is like saying, your expression is not worthwhile; therefore, *you* are not worthwhile. When natural creative drives are blocked, they can become the sources of antisocial, even destructive, behavior.

Art-making processes provide the means to give constructive form to our personal insights and experiences. Expressing their innermost concerns, attitudes, beliefs, feelings, and thoughts is natural for people of all ages. To deny children the development of these aspects of their natures is to deny them answers to the basic questions of life, to diminish their humanity, and to jeopardize their futures.

For all of us—and especially for the very young—mental and emotional growth depends upon a sense of self-worth. Because artistic endeavors have many equally "correct" solutions, each person—child or adult—has the opportunity to succeed. At certain ages and stages of development, children need plenty of encouragement to be able to express themselves without fear of being "wrong." In the arts, each child gets a chance to have his or her own right answer, to have his or her own voice heard.

By realizing the importance of the arts in human development, we can encourage the efforts of children, we can come to understand what happened to our own creative growth, and perhaps we can even reactivate our own creativity.

Most abilities of creative people are also characteristic of children during the first few years of life. Nearly all children have rich, creative imaginations. What becomes of this extraordinary capacity? According to John Holt, author of *How Children Fail,*

> *we destroy this capacity above all by making them afraid—afraid of not doing what other people want, of not pleasing, or of making mistakes, of failing, of being wrong. Thus we make them afraid to gamble, afraid to experiment, afraid to try the difficult and unknown.*[12]

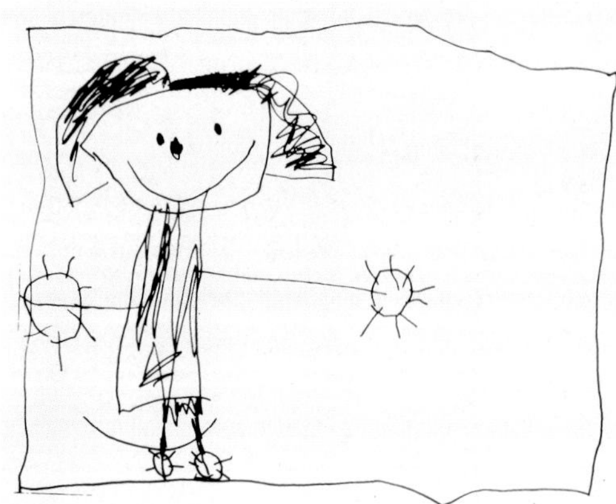

32 Malia, age 4.
SELF-PORTRAIT.

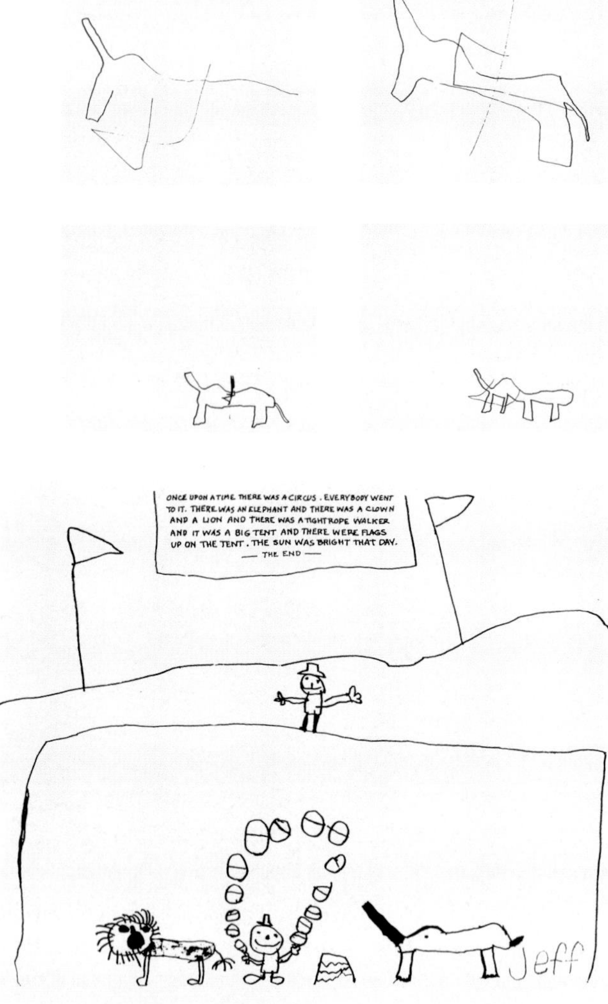

33 Jeff, age 4.
CIRCUS.

Young children use a universal visual language. All over the world, drawings by children ages two to six show the same stages of growth, from individualized mark-making or scribbling to developing shapes to making recognizable subjects. Until they are about six or seven years old, children depict the world in symbolic rather than realistic ways. Most of their images are mental constructions rather than records of visual observations.

In the United States, children's dissatisfaction with their own art usually begins around age nine or ten, when they want their pictures to look like photographs or images produced by trained adult artists. Children become frustrated because they cannot draw the way they have learned to see. Too often this frustration results in a lifetime of blocked creativity, of feeling "untalented."

Self-assurance shows clearly in the smiling SELF-PORTRAIT by four-year-old Malia. The line drawn around the edge of her paper shows an awareness of the whole space. One hand with radiating fingers reaches out, giving strong asymmetrical balance to the composition. Malia accomplished this drawing spontaneously without any adult guidance or conscious knowledge of design.

Young children often demonstrate a fine, intuitive sense of composition, as seen in the pictures by Malia, Jeff, and Kathryn. Unfortunately, we lose much of this intuitive sense of balanced composition as we begin to look at the world from a conceptual, self-conscious point of view. At age four or five, children begin to draw things they have seen. Jeff's series of drawings shows a four-year-old's struggle to draw an elephant soon after going to see a circus for the first time. Jeff began with the most characteristic part of the elephant—the trunk. He tried several times, impatiently crossing out all but one of his first drawings. (Trial and error is an important part of the creative process.) He not only wanted to draw an elephant, he wanted the elephant to be the right size and in the right place, so that his entire vision of the circus could be complete. When he was satisfied with his elephant, he turned the paper over and drew the full circus, including an elephant, a lion, a juggler, and a tightrope walker in action. The scene was so real for him that he asked his father to write down the story while he told about his picture.

Jeff's drawing is a record of his wonderful experience at the circus and evidence of his growing ability to communicate visually—actually to draw what he had in his mind. His own drawing was far more meaningful to him and everyone who saw it than any circus coloring book could have been.

Most children who have been given coloring books, workbooks, and predrawn printed single sheets become overly dependent on such impersonal, stereotyped props. In this way, children often lose the urge to invent unique images based on their own experiences. The two drawings of BIRDS show this process: the child first interprets the bird in a personal, fresh way, but later adopts the trite forms of a conventional workbook or coloring book. Without opportunities for personal expression, children lose self-confidence and the urge to be creative.

The richly colored painting by a group of third-graders in New York City's Public School 69 was made as part of the Studio in a School Association (SIAS) program. To achieve their imaginative

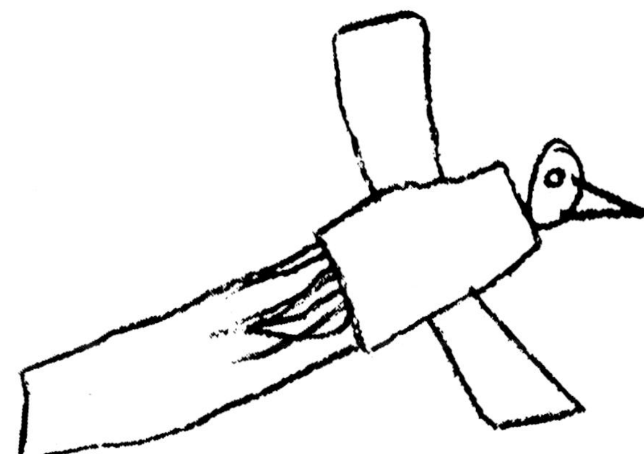

34 Anonymous Child.
BIRDS.
a This picture shows one child's drawing of a bird before exposure to coloring books.

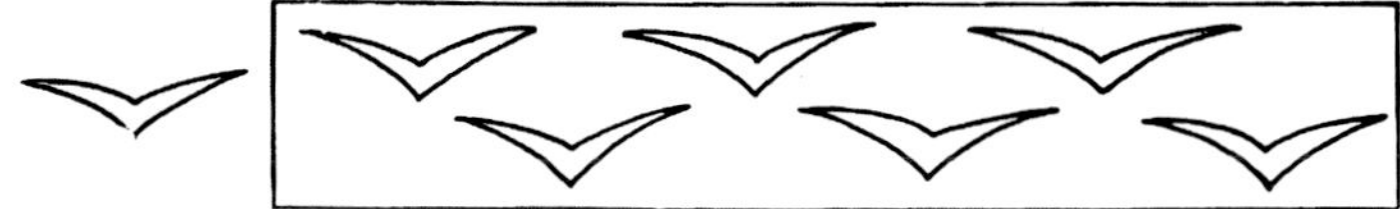

b Then the child colored a workbook illustration.

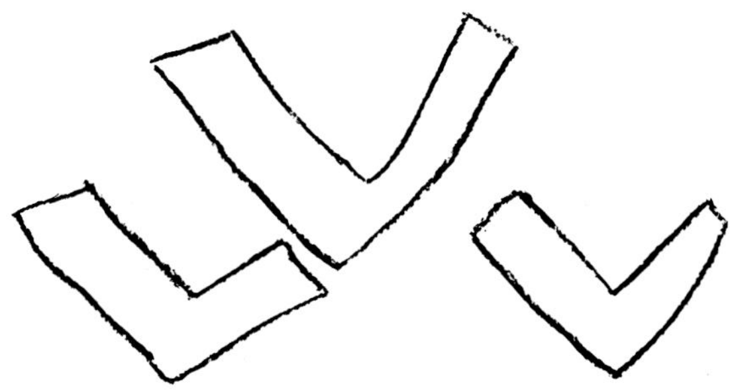

c After coloring the workbook birds, the child lost creative sensitivity and self-reliance.

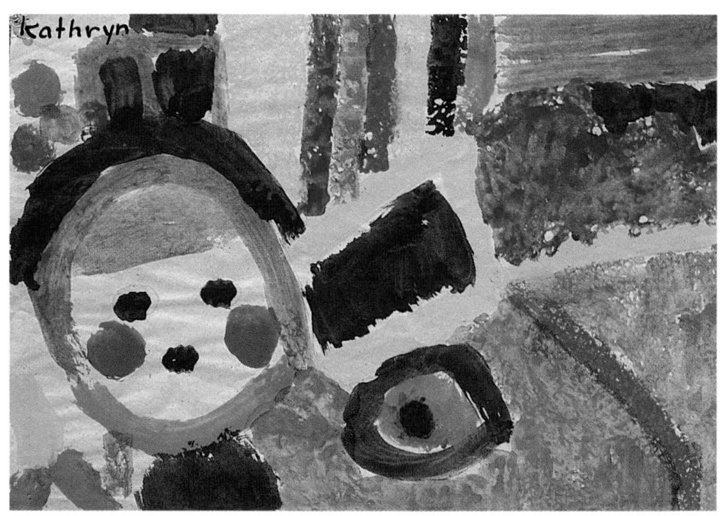

35 Kathryn, age 5.

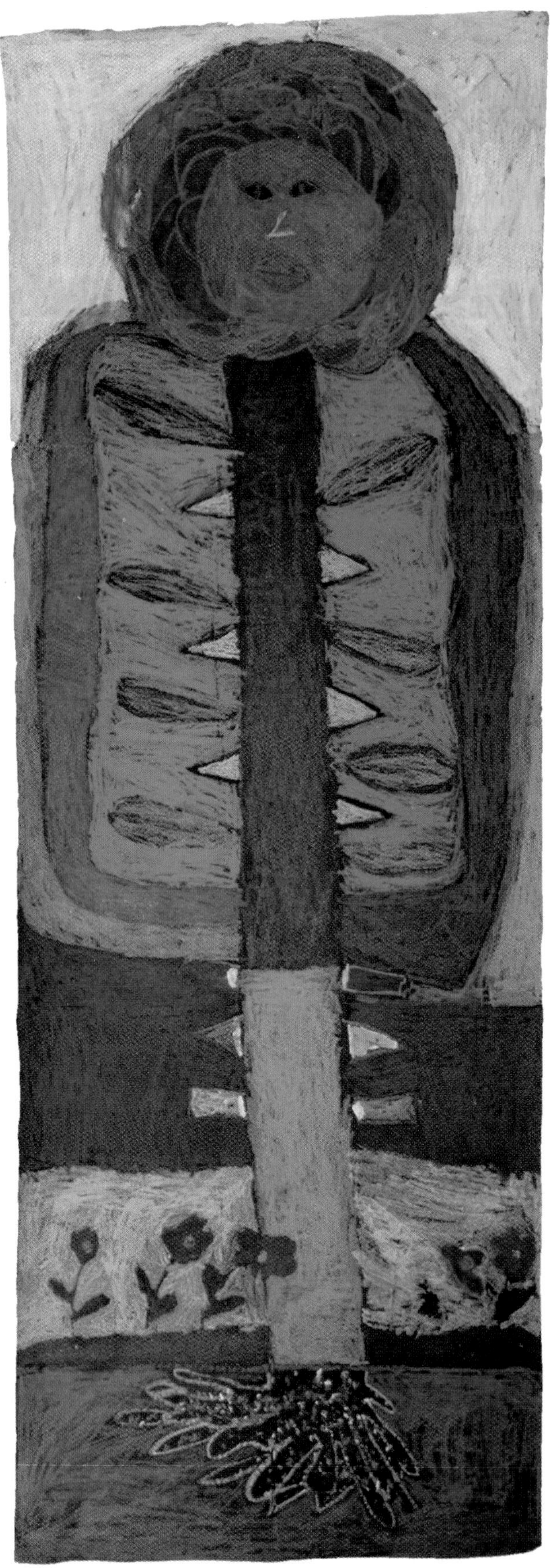

painting FLOWER WITH A FACE, seven- and eight-year-old children pooled the individual artistic skills they had developed since preschool days.

If presented well, the arts can greatly facilitate all other aspects of education. When the arts are poorly taught, treated as a frill, or eliminated from a school curriculum, only the children strong in verbal and mathematical skills may be considered intelligent and successful. Those whose learning strengths are visual, spatial, musical, or interpersonal may be branded failures at an early age.

What happens when we are unable to communicate our most significant ideas and experiences? What happens when no one has time to listen to our stories or look at our drawings? When our creativity is not encouraged, we may lose confidence in our special insights and perceptions. We may lose the sense of wonder. Certainly we lose some of our ability to shape our own lives creatively. Yet in spite of attacks on their original creativity, adults can rediscover and strengthen their all-but-forgotten creative intelligences.

FOLK ART AND NAIVE ART

The urge to create is universal; it has little to do with art training. The terms *folk art* and *naive art* refer to art made by people with no formal art training. *Folk art* applies to artists who are part of established regional traditions of style, theme, and craftsmanship. In earlier times, particularly in rural areas, communication and influences from the outside world were limited, and thus many folk art traditions remained relatively unchanged for long periods.

Handsome quilted bedcovers are treasured works of American folk art. The vibrant colors in Amish quilts stand in surprising contrast to the

36 Morgan Diamond, G-Young Kang, Cristine Muscatello, Melissa Parker, Allison Stakossky, Matthew Utnick. Grade 3, Studio in a School at PS 69, Staten Island, New York.
FLOWER WITH A FACE.
Oil pastel on paper.
The Studio in a School Association.

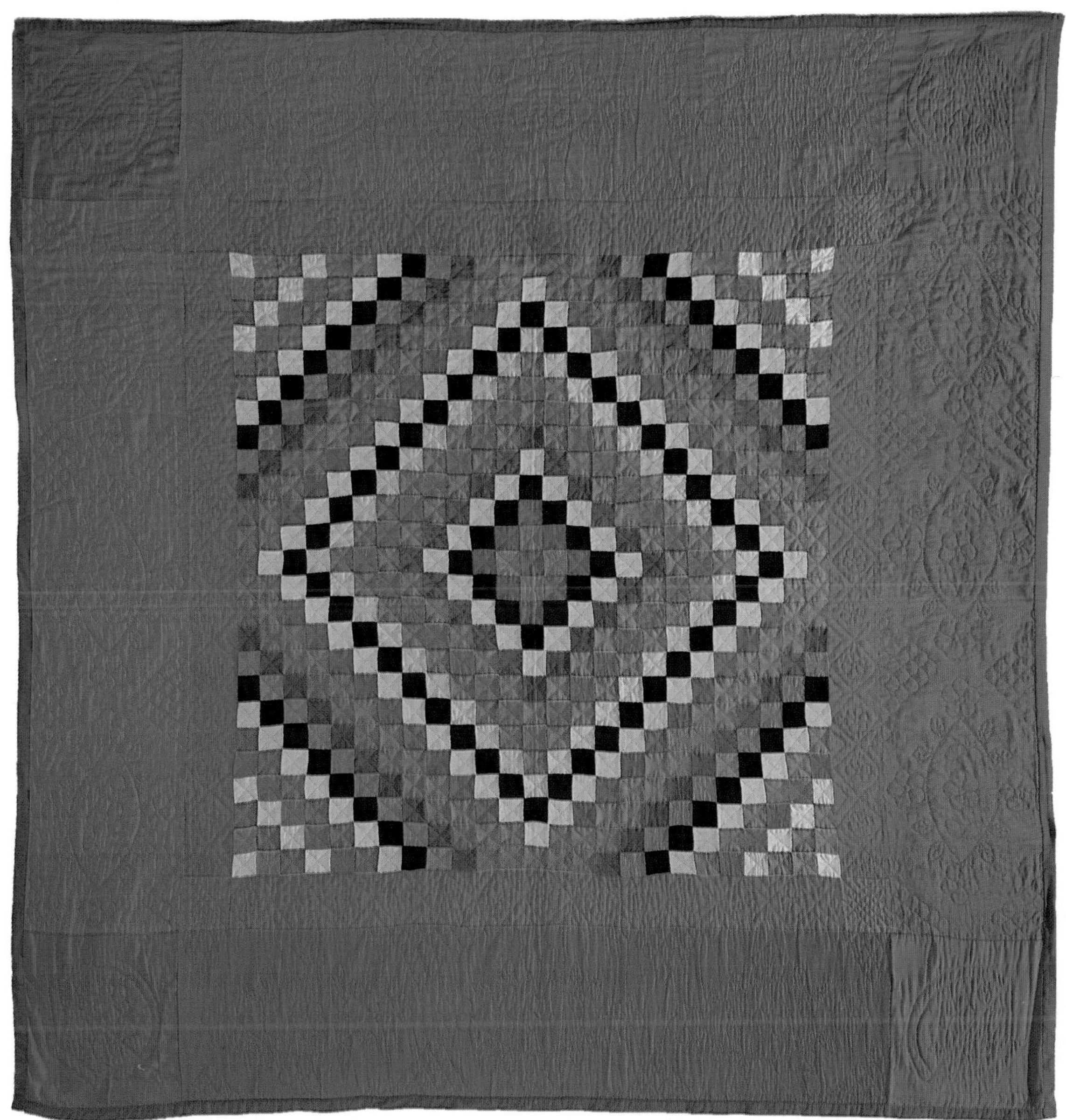

37 AMISH QUILT. "AROUND THE WORLD."
Lancaster County, Pennsylvania. c. 1900.
Cotton and wool, 84" × 84".
Honolulu Academy of Arts. Gift in memory of Alice Kamokila Campbell.

plain and simple lives of the women who make them. The Amish, with their traditional preference for black or subdued hues in clothing, have recently moved toward a greater use of color, yet this doesn't compare with the free use of color the Amish enjoy in their quilts. Mainstream culture now undoubtedly influences the choice of colorful fabrics for quilts, but some scholars maintain that the use of rich, often bright colors in their quilts is an expressive outlet for people who lead what outsiders see as somber lives. The use of geometric shapes and contrasting colors in this AMISH QUILT resembles the shapes and colors in prints and paintings by some leading contemporary artists (see page 83). Geometric quilts are part of Amish culture, and quilt makers know that they belong to a long tradition. (For contrast, see the more recent folk quilt on page 223.)

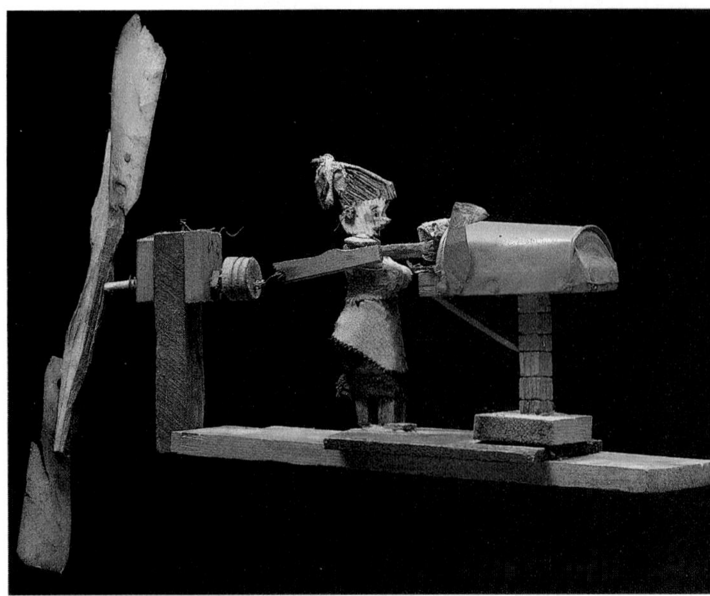

38 Steve Ashby.
RECEIVING A PACKAGE. c. 1970.
Carved and painted wood. 18" × 20" × 7".
Collection of Chuck and Jan Rosenak.
Photograph: © Joel Breger.

Folk artist Steve Ashby was a farmhand, waiter, and gardener who enjoyed carving in his spare time. He made small figures from found objects, wood scraps, and saw-cut plywood and then painted them with model-airplane paint. RECEIVING A PACKAGE is a whirligig. The wind turns the propeller, which moves a series of parts and causes the woman's arm to move in and out of the mailbox. The figure's charm is enhanced by the addition of motion.

Naive art, often considered a type of folk art, is made by people largely unaware of art history or the art trends and fashions of their time. Unlike folk art, naive art is personal expression created apart from any tradition. In some cases "naive" is a misleading word; in terms of their own vision and the often high quality of their work, naive artists can be both wise and sophisticated.

We tend to think of folk art and naive art as being pretechnological; yet these forms of expression continue to be practiced throughout the world. Imaginative, original art by those who consider themselves "just plain folk" has some of the fresh, unselfconscious quality we see in children's art.

Many naive artists seem to develop their art spontaneously, without regard to art of the past or present. Sanford Darling was sixty-three, retired, and recently widowed when he began to paint. Using a three-inch brush and green semigloss enamel, he painted his first picture—on a wall of his house in Santa Barbara, California. With additional colors and other brushes, he soon filled the entire wall. Over a period of years, he covered the rest of his house, inside and out, with landscapes and other scenes from his memory. Among Darling's images were things he had seen during a six-month tour of the South Pacific and the Orient as well as scenes from his youth on a Wisconsin farm. He continued to paint pictures on his furniture and on the backs of small rugs. The photo SANFORD DARLING IN HIS KITCHEN shows a room domi-

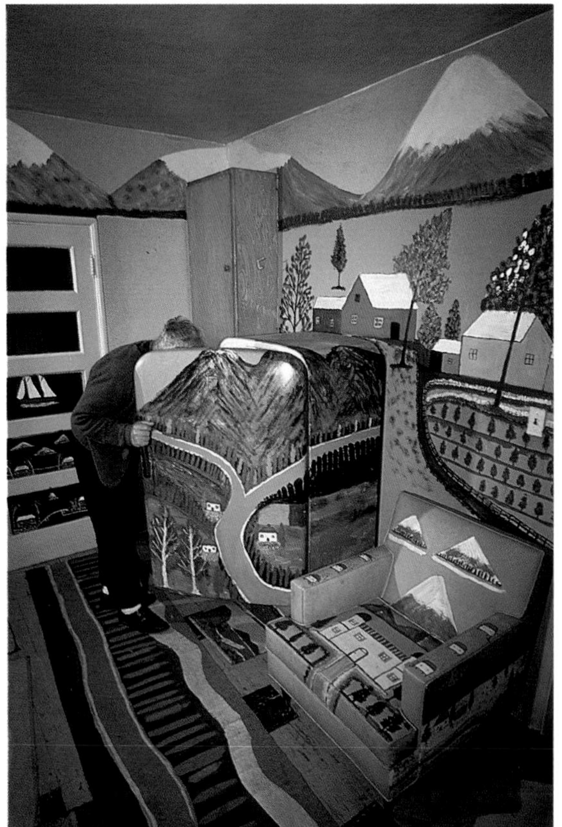

39 SANFORD DARLING IN HIS KITCHEN.
Photograph: Ralph Crane.
Life Magazine. © 1971 Time Warner, Inc.

nated by landscapes, including a river that flows across the refrigerator.

The sculptural spires in Watts, California, known commonly as "Watts Towers," were titled NUESTRO PUEBLO (Our City) by naive artist Sabatino Rodia, the Italian tile setter who built them. Rodia exemplifies the artist who visualizes new possibilities for ordinary materials. He worked on his cathedrallike towers for thirty-three years, making the fantastic structures from cast-off materials, such as metal pipes and bed frames, held together with steel reinforcing rods, mesh, and mortar. Incredibly, he built the towers without power tools, rivets, welds, or bolts.

As they grew up from his tiny triangular backyard, he lovingly and methodically covered their surfaces with bits and pieces of broken dishes, tile, melted bottle glass, shells, and other colorful "junk" from the vacant lots of his neighborhood. Rodia's towers and the thoughts they represent are testimony to the creative process.

The works of some naive artists become well known and are recognized by collectors and other art lovers, but many are known only within their own communities. Haitian artist Pauléus Vital painted the life and work of his people with such

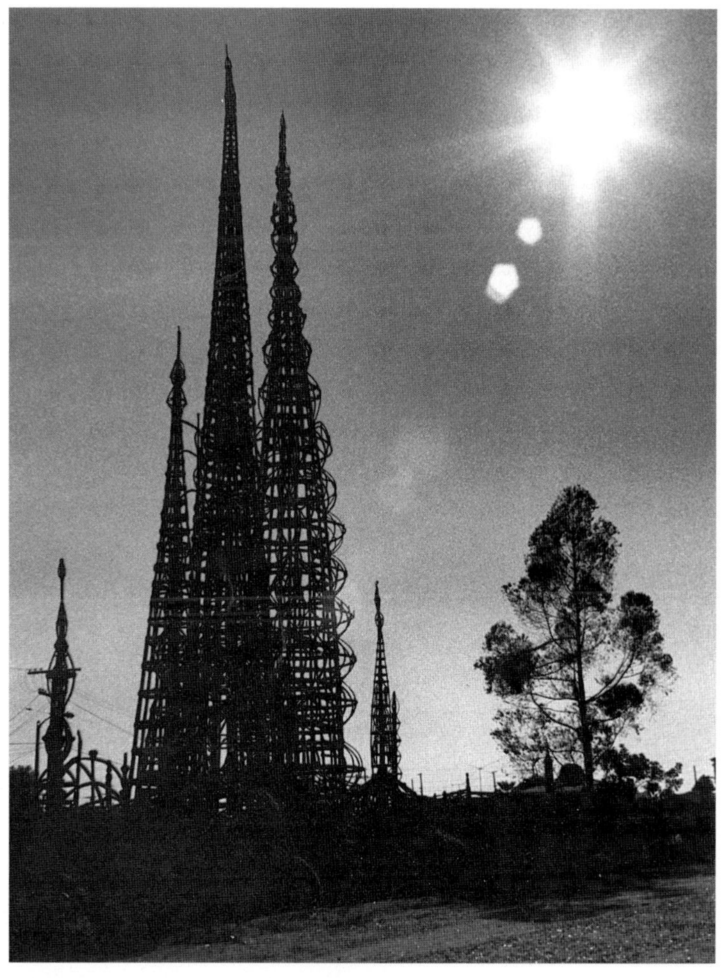

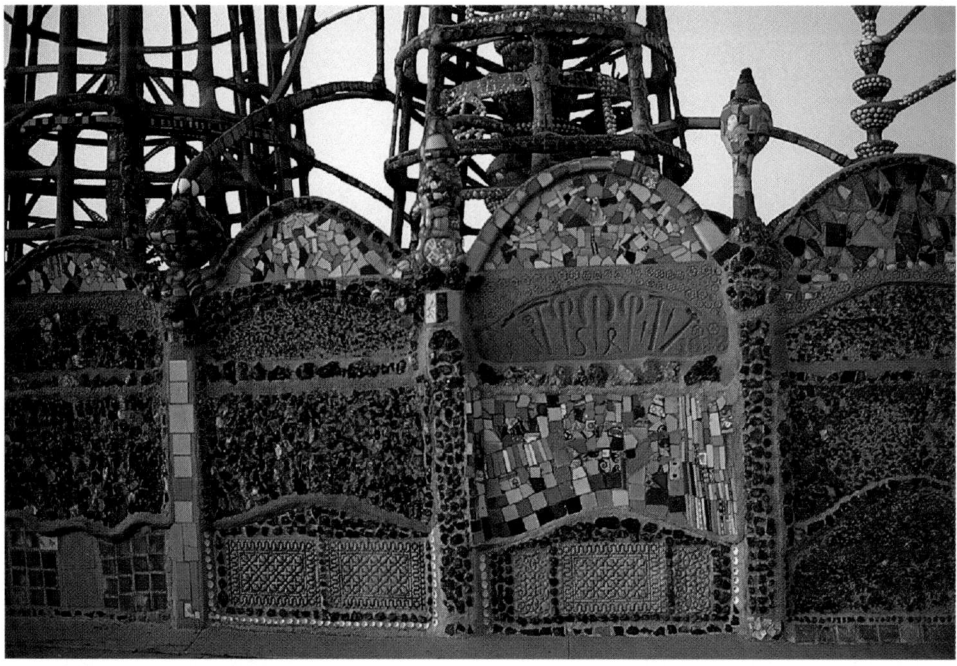

40 Sabatino "Simon" Rodia.
a NUESTRO PUEBLO. Watts, California. 1921–1954.
Mixed media. Height 100'.

b Detail of NUESTRO PUEBLO.
Enclosing wall
with construction-tool impressions.

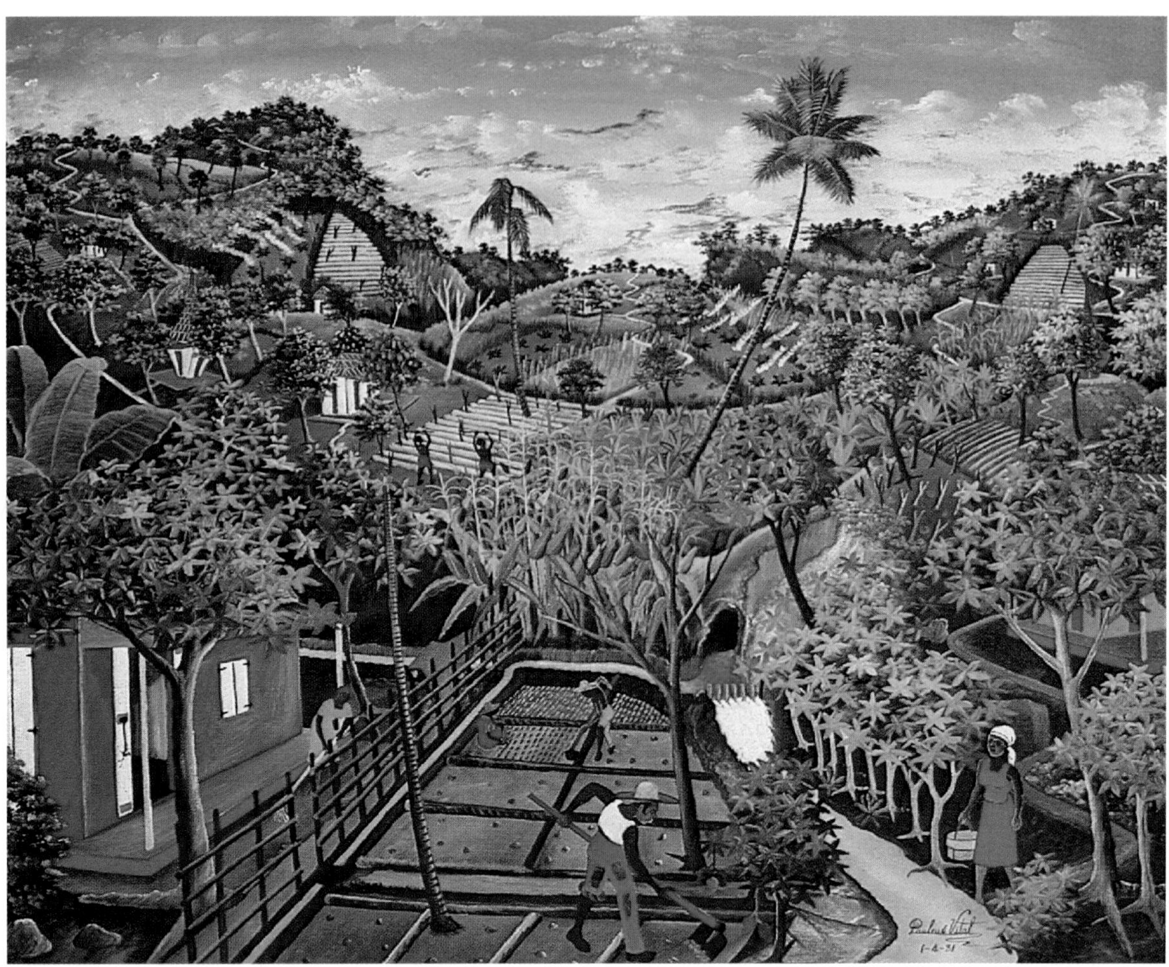

41 Pauléus Vital.
LANDSCAPE AT SABLES CABARET. 1981.
Acrylic on canvas. 24" × 29½".
Collection Selden Rodman, Oakland, N.J.

honest enthusiasm and skill that his images continue to speak clearly, even to the hearts and minds of those who live far beyond his island. Vital's LANDSCAPE AT SABLES CABARET captures in rich detail the Haitian intimacy with nature—the people working to bring forth the bounty of the land.

TRAINED ARTISTS

In the past, the world's trained artists learned by working as apprentices to accomplished masters. Through practical experience, they gained necessary skills and developed knowledge of their society's art traditions. Today most art-educated American artists are "trained" in art schools or in college or university art departments. Learning in such settings develops sophisticated knowledge of a vast array of alternative points of view, both contemporary and historical.

In contrast to naive artists, who demonstrate unmannered originality, trained artists often show a self-conscious awareness of their relationship to art history. This can be either an asset or a burden. Knowledge of art history provides a wealth of material to draw from, but it can lead to an egocentric struggle to be profound and original.

Whether naive or trained, artists must be independent thinkers—must have the courage to go beyond group mentality. In this way artists offer not what others have seen, but fresh insights that extend the experiences of those who see their art.

PART 2

THE LANGUAGE OF VISUAL EXPERIENCE

Consider . . .

Close your eyes and picture a house. It is your house? Is it the house with a chimney you always drew as a child? Is the house "real" or "abstract"?

We all have visual memory. Recall your own most vivid visual memory and begin to describe it in detail.

Why is handwriting sometimes accepted as legal evidence in court? What does that tell you about individual drawing styles?

How do cartoonists show the passage of time? How do they show movement? What other visual media can express time and/or movement?

Does color affect your emotions? What color would you choose to express sadness? Joy? Boredom? Anger? Do you avoid using certain colors in your clothing or in your art?

CHAPTER 3

Visual Communication

The language of vision determines, perhaps even more subtly and thoroughly than verbal language, the structure of our consciousness.

S. I. Hayakawa[1]

The most direct avenue to the mind is through the eyes. As S. I. Hayakawa pointed out, our visual experience of the world is so profoundly influential that it constitutes a nonverbal language all its own. This is the language that art uses to communicate.

In art, the visual experience is essential. Words used to describe that experience are simply a means of discussing the nature of our perceptions. Words can help us analyze—and therefore better understand—the infinite ways in which artists construct visual forms.

Since words and visual images are two different "languages," talking about visual arts with words is always an act of translation—and is one step removed from actually experiencing art. Ultimately, our eyes have their own connections to our minds and emotions. Only by cultivating these connections are we able to take full advantage of what art has to offer.

ART AND APPEARANCES

"That painting of the woman looks exactly like her." Viewers often equate art with making replicas of people, objects, and places. They reason that the more "real" the art looks, the better it must be. Actually, art is concerned with interpretation rather than replication. A real horse, a painting of a horse, and a sculpture of a horse each has its own reality—and each of these realities is substantially different from the others.

The visual language of art has its origins in the "real" world of things as we ordinarily see, think, and feel about them. Artists may depict much of what they see in the physical world, they may alter appearances, or they may invent forms not seen in either the natural or human-made worlds. Regardless of their approaches, most artists invite viewers to see beyond mere appearances. To describe an artwork's relationship to the physical world, we use the terms *representational, abstract,* and *nonrepresentational* (or *nonobjective*).

Representational Art

Representational art (sometimes called *objective* or *figurative art*) depicts the appearance of things. It re-presents—presents again—objects we recognize from the everyday world. Objects that representational art depicts are called the *subject* or *subject matter.* The subjects of Bonnard's DINING ROOM IN THE COUNTRY (page 3) and Kollwitz's SELF-PORTRAIT (page 121) are as straightforward as the titles.

Many people respond to representational art because it can be easily identified and therefore seems understandable. But as you look at art more seriously, you begin to notice not how much a rep-

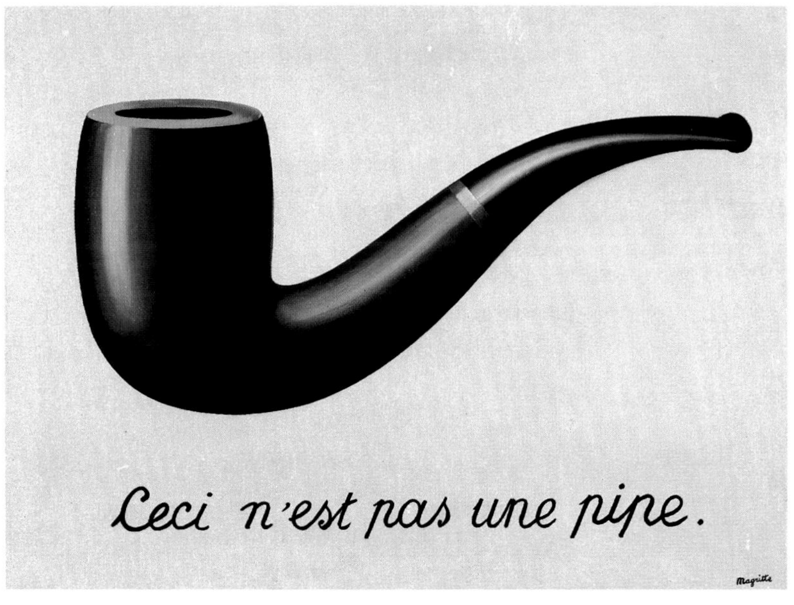

42 René Magritte.
LA TRAHISON DES IMAGES
(THE TREASON OF IMAGES). c. 1928-1929.
Oil on canvas. 23⅝" × 37".
Los Angeles County Museum of Art. Purchased with funds provided by the Mr. and Mrs. William Preston Harrison Collection.

43 William Harnett.
A SMOKE BACKSTAGE. 1877.
Oil on canvas. 7" × 8⅛".
Honolulu Academy of Arts. Gift of John Gregg Allerton.

resentational painting or sculpture resembles its subject matter, but how little. If you compare the colors in a photograph of your own dining room with the bright reds and greens of Bonnard's painting of his dining room, you will see a vast difference in "realness." Yet the Bonnard painting is considered to be representational art because it clearly depicts recognizable fruit, cats, furniture, woman, and landscape.

Representational art includes a wide range of styles, from the fool-the-eye realism of William Harnett to personally expressive images such as those by Matisse (see pages 116–119), to heroic distortions such as those in Michelangelo's PIETA (page 102).

The most "real" looking paintings are in a style called *trompe l'oeil* (pronounced "tromp loy")—French for "fool the eye." Paintings in this illusionistic style impress us because they look so "real." In Harnett's painting A SMOKE BACKSTAGE, the assembled objects are close to life-size, which contributes to the illusion. We feel that we could almost reach out and touch an actual pipe.

Belgian painter René Magritte presents the viewer with a different pictorial and written statement about the nature of representational art. The

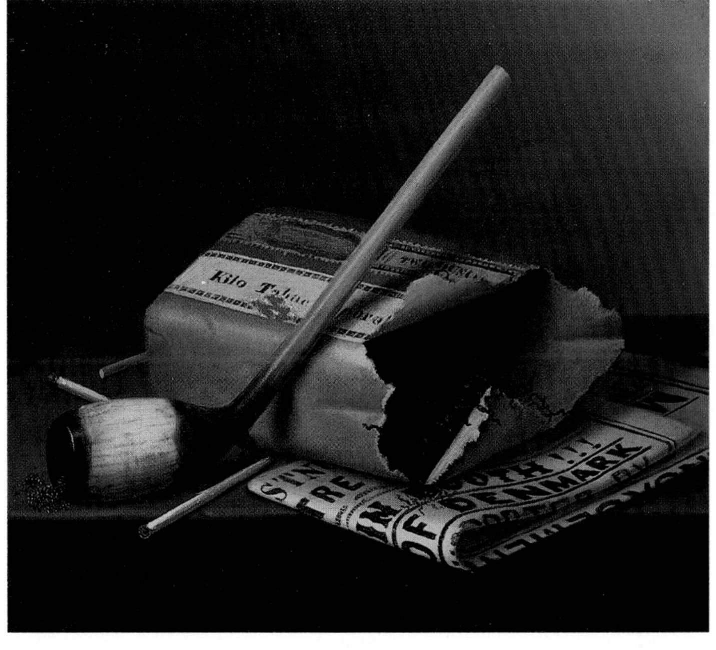

subject of the painting appears to be a pipe, but written in French on the painting are the words, *"Ceci n'est pas une pipe."* ("This is not a pipe.") The viewer wonders, "If this is not a pipe, what is it?" The answer, of course, is that it is a painting! Magritte's title, THE TREASON OF IMAGES, suggests what the artist had in mind.

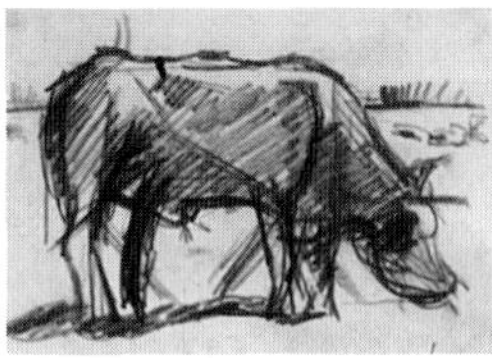

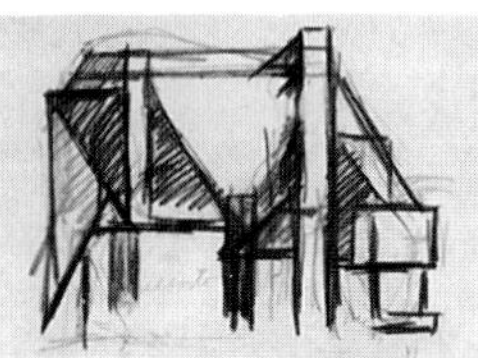

44 Theo van Doesburg.
ABSTRACTION OF A COW, four stages.

Studies for COMPOSITION (THE COW). c. 1917.
Pencil, each 4⅝" × 6¼".
The Museum of Modern Art, New York. Purchase.

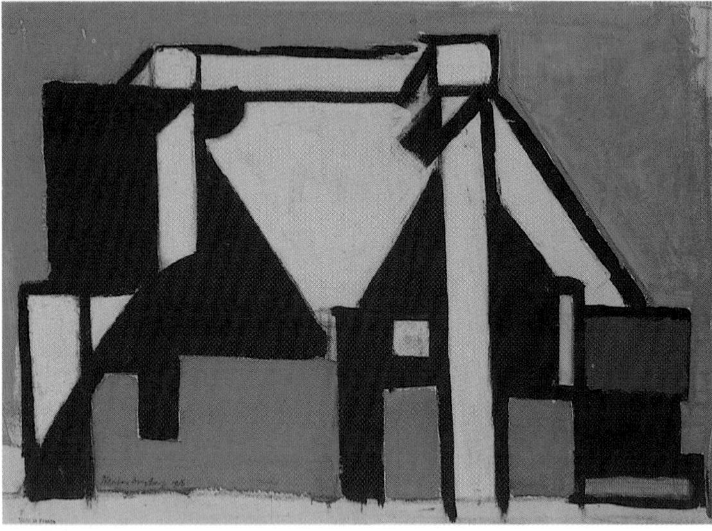

COMPOSITION (THE COW). 1916.
Gouache. 15⅝" × 22¾".
The Museum of Modern Art, New York. Purchase.

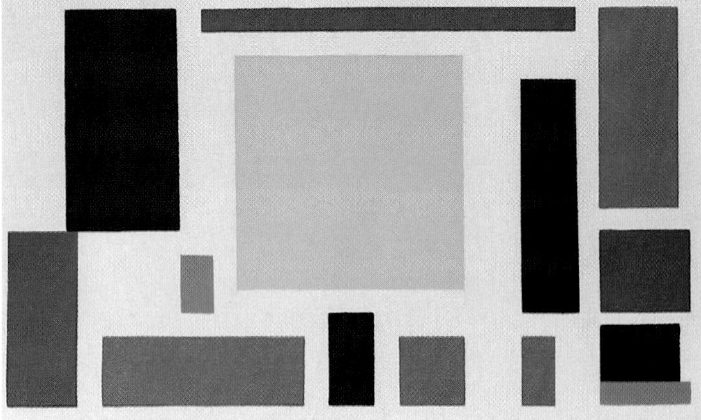

COMPOSITION (THE COW). 1916-1917.
Oil on canvas. 14¾" × 25".
The Museum of Modern Art, New York. Purchase.

Matisse told of an incident that illustrated his views on the difference between art and nature. A woman visiting his studio pointed to one of his paintings and said, "But surely, the arm of this woman is much too long." Matisse replied, "Madame, you are mistaken. This is not a woman, this is a picture."[2]

Abstract Art

"To abstract" means to extract the essence of an object or idea. In art, the word *abstract* can mean either (1) works of art that have no reference at all to natural objects, or (2) works that depict natural objects in altered, simplified, distorted, or exaggerated ways. In this book, we use abstract in the second sense.

In abstract art, the artist changes the object's natural appearance in order to emphasize or reveal certain qualities. Just as there are many approaches to representational art, there are many approaches to abstraction. We may be able to recognize the subject matter of an abstract work quite easily, or we may need the help of a clue (such as a title). The interaction between how an actual subject typically looks and how a particular artist presents it is part of the pleasure and challenge of abstract art. In a basic sense, all art is abstraction, because it is not possible for an artist to reproduce exactly what is seen.

Varying degrees of abstraction are evident in Theo van Doesburg's series of drawings and paintings, ABSTRACTION OF A COW. Although Van Doesburg's works are titled "Cow," he based the series on the form of a bull. He apparently wanted to see how far he could abstract the bull through simplification and still have his image symbolize the essence of the animal. Van Doesburg used the subject as a point of departure for a composition made up of colored rectangles. If we saw only the final painting of a bull, and none of the earlier ones, we would see it as a nonrepresentational painting. (See also the steps to abstraction in paintings by Piet Mondrian on pages 438–439.)

Nonrepresentational Art

Nonrepresentational art (sometimes called *nonobjective* or *nonfigurative art*) presents visual forms with no specific references to anything outside themselves. Just as we can respond to the pure sound forms of music, so we can respond to the pure visual forms of nonrepresentational art. Although Louise Nevelson's works (see also pages 122–124) have titles that indicate themes, the pieces do not (and are not meant to) represent specific, nameable things, and thus they are nonrepresentational.

While nonrepresentational art may at first seem more difficult to grasp than representational or abstract art, it can offer fresh ways of seeing. Absence of subject matter actually clarifies the way all visual form affects us. Once we learn how to "read" the language of visual form, we can respond to art and the world with greater understanding and enjoyment.

How differently we respond to two American works, Frank Stella's THRUXTON 3X and Louise Nevelson's BLACK CHORD. Stella's scrambled, cheerfully vulgar colors may remind us of amusement parks or joyfully spray-painted graffiti. (The modern city laughs.) The soft black of Nevelson's sculpture may recall a muted place of mystery, such as a church or an attic full of memories. (The modern city meditates.)

Notice that the shapes in Stella's work break free of a confining frame like pieces of a jigsaw puzzle tumbling out onto the floor, giving the work a feeling of immense energy. In Nevelson's sculpture, on the other hand, all pieces are carefully contained, like precious objects filed according to a system we may never fathom. In some boxes, lids block our view of the contents, increasing the sense of mystery. The title BLACK CHORD reminds us that music, too, is an art that needs no subject matter to be expressive.

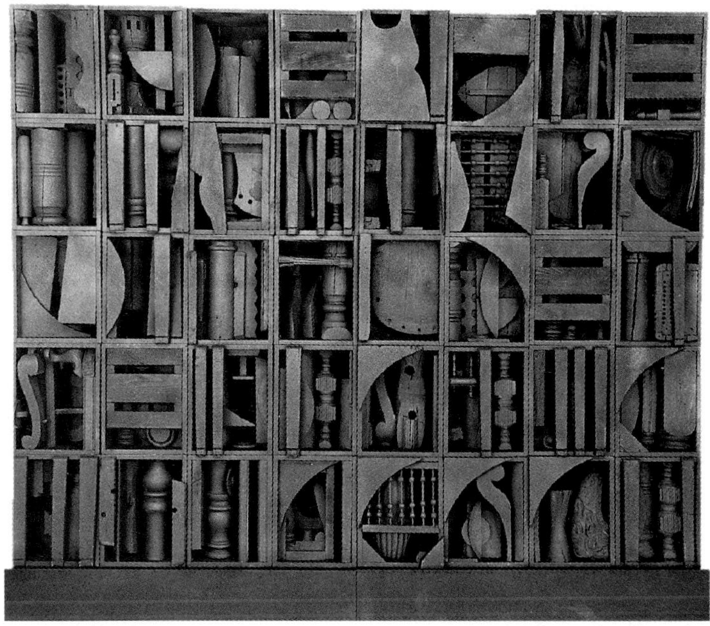

45 Louise Nevelson.
BLACK CHORD. 1964.
Painted wood. 96" × 120" × 11½".
Collection Joel Ehrenkranz.

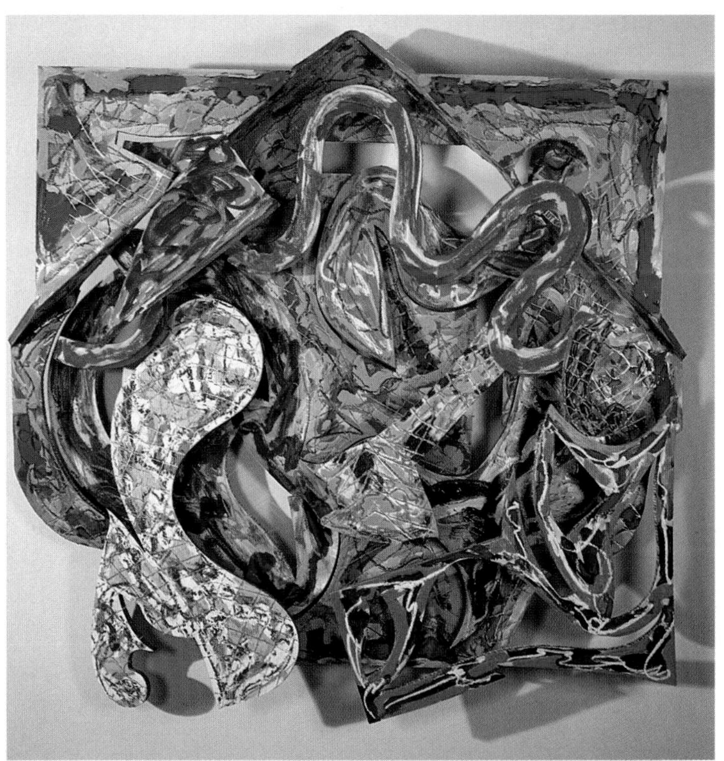

46 Frank Stella.
THRUXTON 3X. 1982.
Mixed media on etched aluminum. 75" × 85" × 15".
The Shidler Collection, Honolulu, Hawaii.

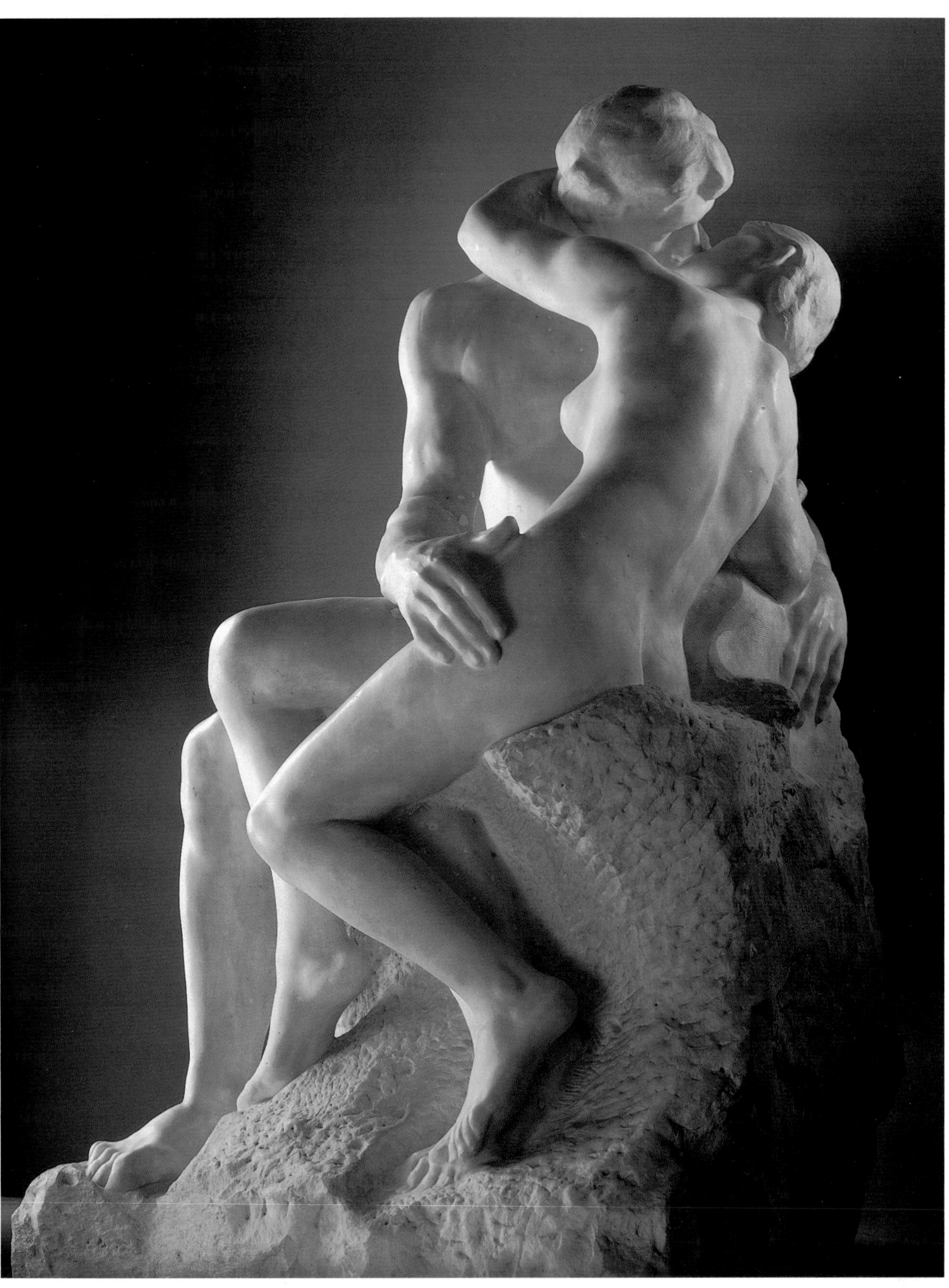

FORM AND CONTENT

Form is what we see; content is what we interpret as the meaning of what we see. In this book, *form* refers to the total effect of the combined visual qualities within a work, including such components as materials, color, shape, line, and design. *Content* refers to the message or meaning of the work of art—what the artist expresses or communicates to the viewer. Content determines form and is expressed through it; thus the two are inseparable. As form changes, content changes—and vice versa.

For example, the valentine ❤ heart—which is used to represent the human heart—is a symbol of love. If someone were to give you a huge, beautifully made red velvet valentine, so large it had to be pulled on a cart, you would probably be overwhelmed by the gesture. The content would be Love! But if you were to receive a faint photocopied outline of a heart on a cheap piece of paper, you might read the content as: *love*—sort of—a very impersonal kind. And if you were to receive a shriveled, greenish brown, slightly moldy image of a heart, you might read the content as *Ugh!*

One way to understand how art communicates experience is to examine works that have the same subject but vary greatly in form and content. THE KISS by Auguste Rodin and THE KISS by Constantin Brancusi show how two sculptors interpret an embrace. In Rodin's work, the life-size human figures represent ideals of the masculine and feminine: Rodin captured the sensual delight of that highly charged moment when lovers embrace. Our emotions are engaged as we overlook the hardness of the marble out of which the illusion was carved. The implied natural softness of flesh is accentuated by the rough texture of the unfinished marble supporting the figures.

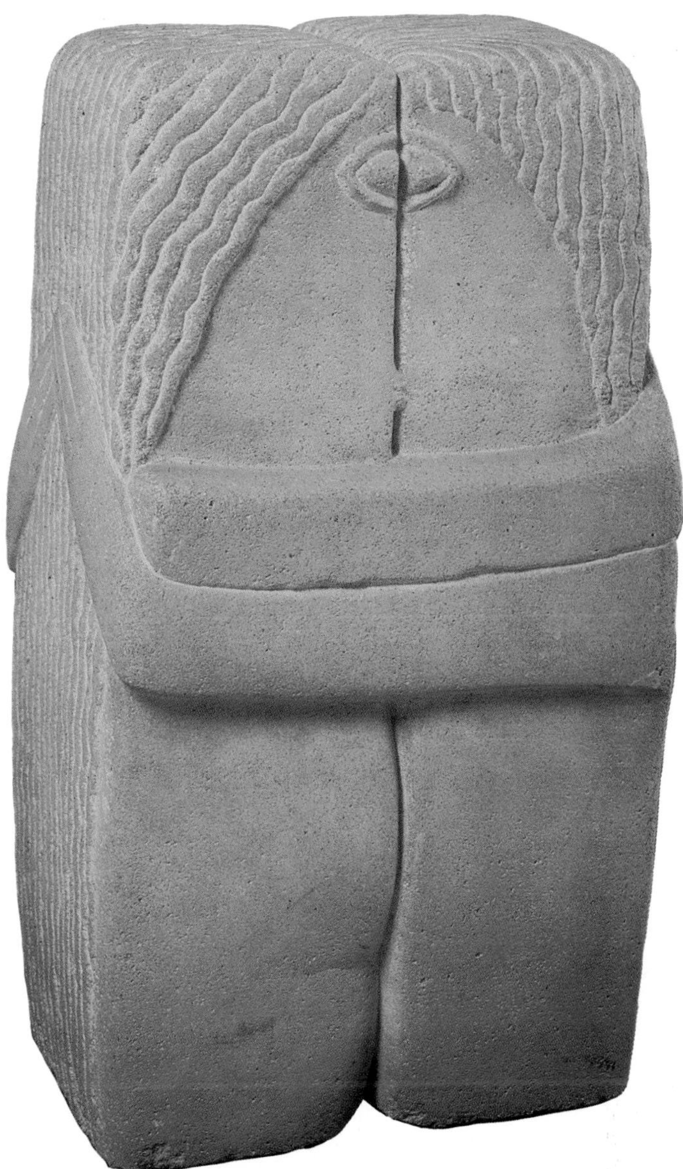

48 Constantin Brancusi.
THE KISS. c. 1912.
Limestone. 23" × 13" × 10".
Philadelphia Museum of Art, The Louise and Walter Arensberg Collection.

In contrast to Rodin's sensuous approach, Brancusi used the solid quality of a block of stone to express lasting love. Through minimal cutting of the block, Brancusi symbolized—rather than illustrated—the concept of two becoming one. He chose geometric abstraction rather than representational naturalism to express love. Rodin's work expresses the *feelings* of love while Brancusi's expresses the *idea* of love.

47 François Auguste René Rodin.
THE KISS. 1886.
Marble. Height 5'11¼".
Musée Rodin, Paris (S1002).
Photograph: Bruno Jarret.

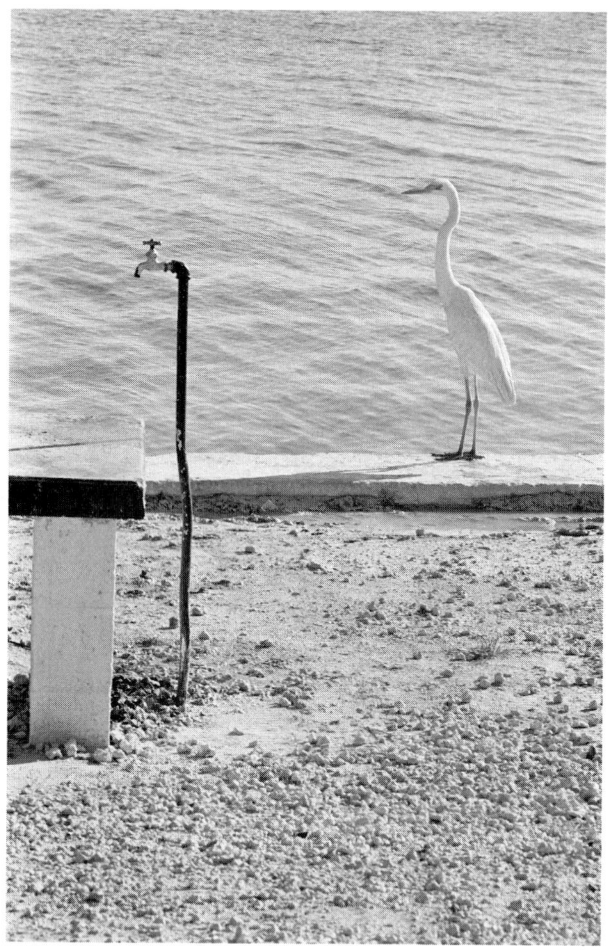

49 Elliott Erwitt. FLORIDA. 1968. Photograph.

50 VISUAL METAPHOR. Student Project.

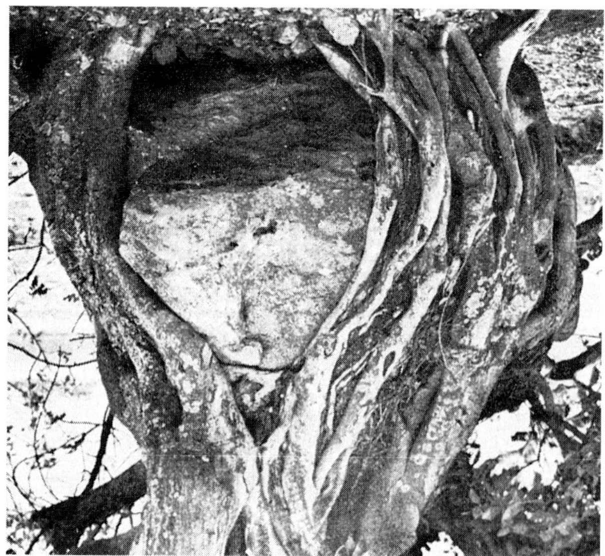

SEEING AND RESPONDING TO FORM

The creative act is not performed by the artist alone; the spectator brings the work in contact with the external world by deciphering and interpreting its inner qualifications and thus adds his contribution to the creative act.

Marcel Duchamp[3]

Obviously, effort is required to produce a work of art. Less obvious is the fact that responding to a work of art also requires effort. The artist is the source or sender; the work is the medium carrying the message. We, as viewers, must receive and experience the work if the communication is to be complete. The words of American composer John Cage bring this to our attention:

Most people mistakenly think that when they hear a piece of music, that they're not doing *anything, but something is being done* to *them. Now this is not true, and we must arrange our music, we must arrange our Art, we must arrange everything, I believe, so that people realize that they themselves are doing it, and not that something is being done to them.*[4]

Whether we realize it or not, learning to respond to form is part of learning to live in the world. We guide our actions by "reading" the forms of people, things, and events that make up our environment. Even as infants, human beings have an amazing ability to remember visual forms such as faces, and we interpret content based on our previous experiences with these forms. Each form is capable of

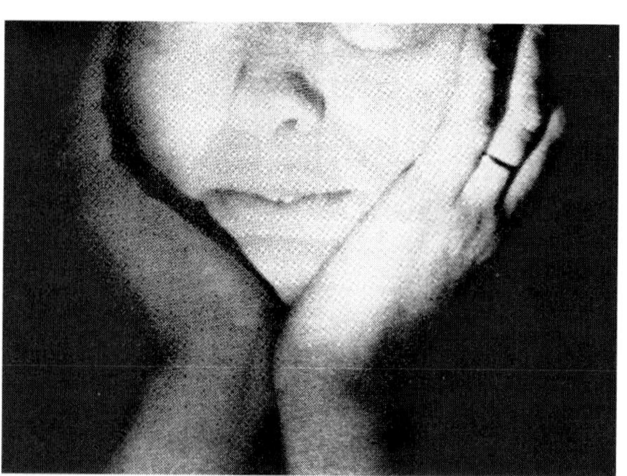

evoking some kind of response from each of us.

Subject matter can interfere with our perception of form. One way to learn to see form without subject is by looking at pictures upside down. Inversion of recognizable images frees the mind from the process of identifying and naming things. Familiar objects become unfamiliar, enabling the artist to concentrate on the design. Art teachers have found that having students copy a picture placed upside down can dramatically improve seeing, and thereby improve representational drawing skills, by encouraging concentration on spatial relationships rather than on preconceptions.

Another exercise in learning to see form is to search for images that are similar in form but dissimilar as nameable objects. For example, when we notice that the form of fingers supporting a head is similar to roots grasping a rock (in an inverted photograph), we are seeing beyond names to pure form. Such similarities can become visual metaphors, as in Elliott Erwitt's photograph, FLORIDA.

Georgia O'Keeffe responded to nature's forms in her own way. In paintings such as ORIENTAL POPPIES and JACK-IN-THE-PULPIT NO. V, she shared her awareness. She said of these paintings:

Everyone has many associations with a flower—the idea of flowers. Still—in a way—nobody sees a flower—really—it is so small—we haven't the time—and to see takes time, like to have a friend takes time. If I could paint the flower exactly as I see it no one would see what I see because I would paint it small like the flower is small.

So I said to myself—I'll paint what I see—what the flower is to me but I'll paint it big and they will be surprised into taking time to look at it.[5]

Those who have seen O'Keeffe's paintings of flowers and the American Southwest (see also page 447) often go on to see actual flowers and desert landscapes in new ways.

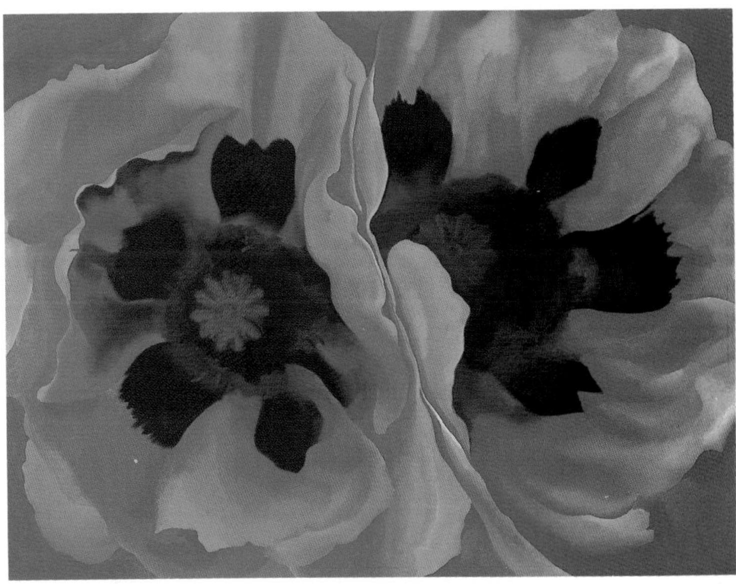

51 Georgia O'Keeffe.
ORIENTAL POPPIES. 1928.
Oil on canvas. 30" × 40⅛".
University Art Museum, University of Minnesota, Minneapolis. Purchase (37.1).

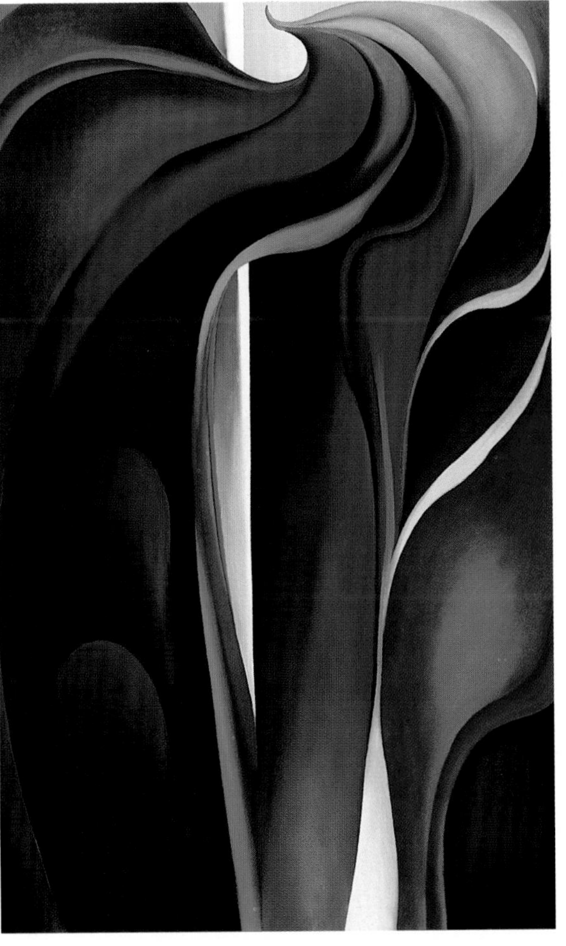

52 Georgia O'Keeffe.
JACK-IN-THE-PULPIT NO. V. 1930.
Oil on canvas. 48" × 30".
Estate of Georgia O'Keeffe.

GEORGIA O'KEEFFE (1887–1986)

During her long, productive life, Georgia O'Keeffe became nearly as well known as her distinctive paintings. She represented, to many people, the popular concept of the isolated, eccentric "artist." She lived a spare, often solitary life, and approached both her life and her art in her own unique way.

O'Keeffe was born in Sun Prairie, Wisconsin, and spent her childhood on her family's farm. While in high school, she had a memorable experience that gave her a new perspective on the art-making process. As she passed the door to the art room, O'Keeffe stopped to watch as a teacher held up a jack-in-the-pulpit plant so that the students could appreciate the unusual shapes and subtle colors. Although O'Keeffe had enjoyed flowers in the marshes and meadows of Wisconsin, all of her drawing and painting had been done from plaster casts or copied from photographs or reproductions. This was the first time she realized that one could draw and paint from real life. Twenty-five years later she produced a powerful series of paintings based on flowers.

O'Keeffe studied at the Art Institute of Chicago, the Art Students League in New York, and Columbia University Teachers College. From Arthur Wesley Dow of Columbia, she learned to appreciate Japanese design, to fill space in a beautiful way, and to balance light and dark. As a student, she was also influenced by the first wave of European abstract paintings reaching the United States from Europe.

From 1912 to 1918, she spent four winters teaching school in the Texas Panhandle. The Southwest landscape left a strong impression on her and influenced her later decision to move to New Mexico—where the desert became her favorite subject.

O'Keeffe's first important artworks, produced in 1915, consisted of abstract charcoal drawings suggesting natural forms and vivid watercolor landscapes. A friend of O'Keeffe's showed those drawings to influential photographer and gallery owner Alfred Stieglitz, who exhibited them in his avant-garde Gallery 291 in New York. Thus began one of the best-known artistic and romantic liaisons of the twentieth century. O'Keeffe and Stieglitz were married in 1924, and O'Keeffe's work was exhibited annually in various galleries owned by Stieglitz until his death in 1946. They were strong supporters of one another's work.

Although associated with American modernist artists, O'Keeffe developed her own style, which is both sensuous and austere. Her paintings of the 1920s include the series of greatly enlarged flowers, landscapes, and geometrically structured views of New York City. In her mature style, O'Keeffe rejected realism in favor of simplified flat patterns and color harmonies inspired by Japanese art.

From 1929 to 1949 O'Keeffe spent summers in Taos, New Mexico, surrounded by the desert she loved. After Stieglitz died, she settled permanently on an isolated ranch near the village of Abiquiu, where she remained until her death in 1986 at age ninety-eight. In people's minds she lives on as a model of creative individuality and strength.

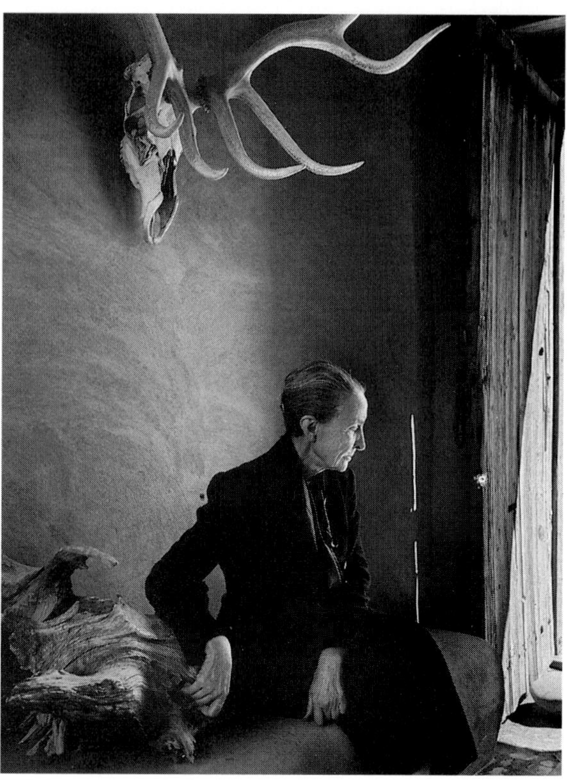

53 Yousuf Karsh. GEORGIA O'KEEFFE. 1956. Photograph.
© Karsh of Ottawa.

ICONOGRAPHY

As we have noted, form conveys content even when no nameable subject matter is represented. But when subject matter is present, meaning is often based on traditional interpretations.

Iconography is the symbolic meaning of signs and subjects. Not all works of art contain iconography. In those that do, it is often the symbolism (rather than the obvious subject matter) that carries the deepest levels of meaning. The identification and specific meanings of significant subjects, motifs, forms, colors, and positions are the central concern of iconographic interpretation.

Examples of iconography from different times and places reveal a wealth of cultural meanings. Today, the term iconography is usually associated with a religious or cultural area of iconographic study, such as Egyptian or Christian iconography.

The primary subject in Albrecht Dürer's THE KNIGHT, DEATH AND THE DEVIL is a man in armor on horseback; behind him are a corpselike figure and a horned monster. Meanings of the objects in the detailed scene would have been well known to Christians of Dürer's time because they were familiar with Christian iconography. The knight in armor, for instance, symbolized the good Christian who follows the right path despite the persistence of Death and the Devil.

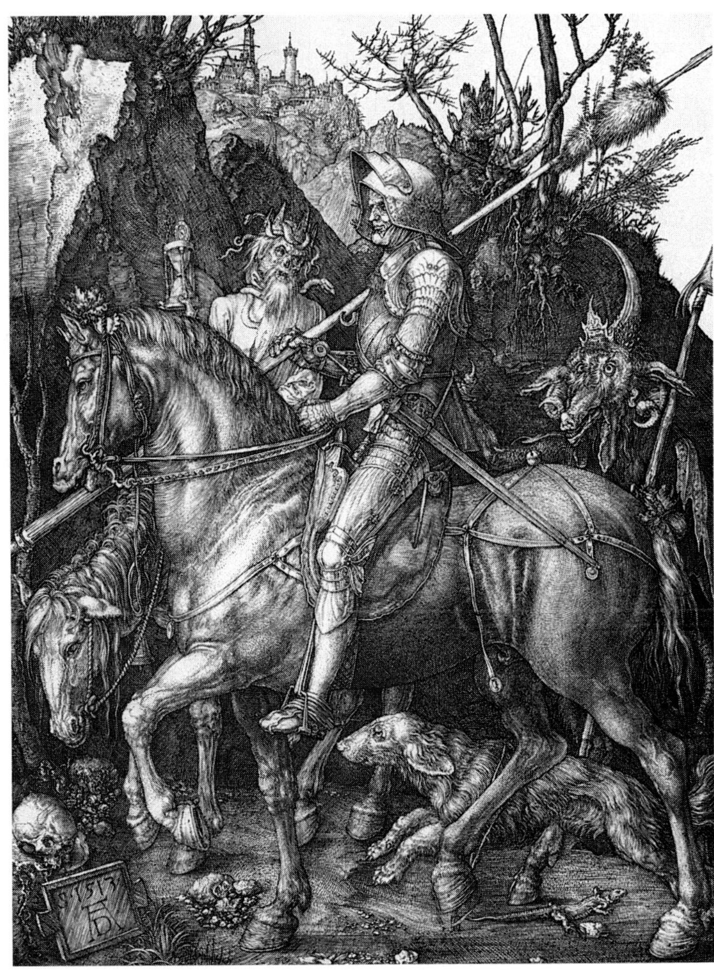

54 Albrecht Dürer.
THE KNIGHT, DEATH AND THE DEVIL. 1513.
Engraving. 9¾" × 7⅜".
The Brooklyn Museum, Gift of Mrs. Horace O. Havemeyer.

The knight must ride through the darkness of the "valley of the shadow of death" to reach the City of God, seen in the background. An hourglass in the hand of Death symbolizes human mortality or the brevity of life. Serpents in Death's hair are ancient symbols of death and also Christian symbols of the Devil. The dog, a symbol of faithfulness in both religion and marriage, symbolizes the faith the knight must have if he is to reach his goal. A dragonlike lizard is an emblem of evil and is seen here going in an opposing direction. Dürer organized all these separate references in a way that leaves no doubt that the Christian knight will reach his goal. The idealized form and dominant central position of the knight and his powerful horse convey a sense of assurance.

One of the world's finest examples of relief sculpture, known as DESCENT OF THE GANGES (see next page), was carved in a huge granite outcropping in the town of Māmallapuram, in southern India. Included in the large composition are over a hundred figures of humans, deities, flying pairs of angels without wings, life-size elephants, and a variety of other animals, all converging at the Ganges River in an elaborate depiction of intertwining Hindu legends. As in Dürer's engraving, the composition is filled with symbolic subject matter.

The center of the carving represents the descent of the sacred Ganges from heaven to earth, making the land fertile. The cobra-like figures of the King

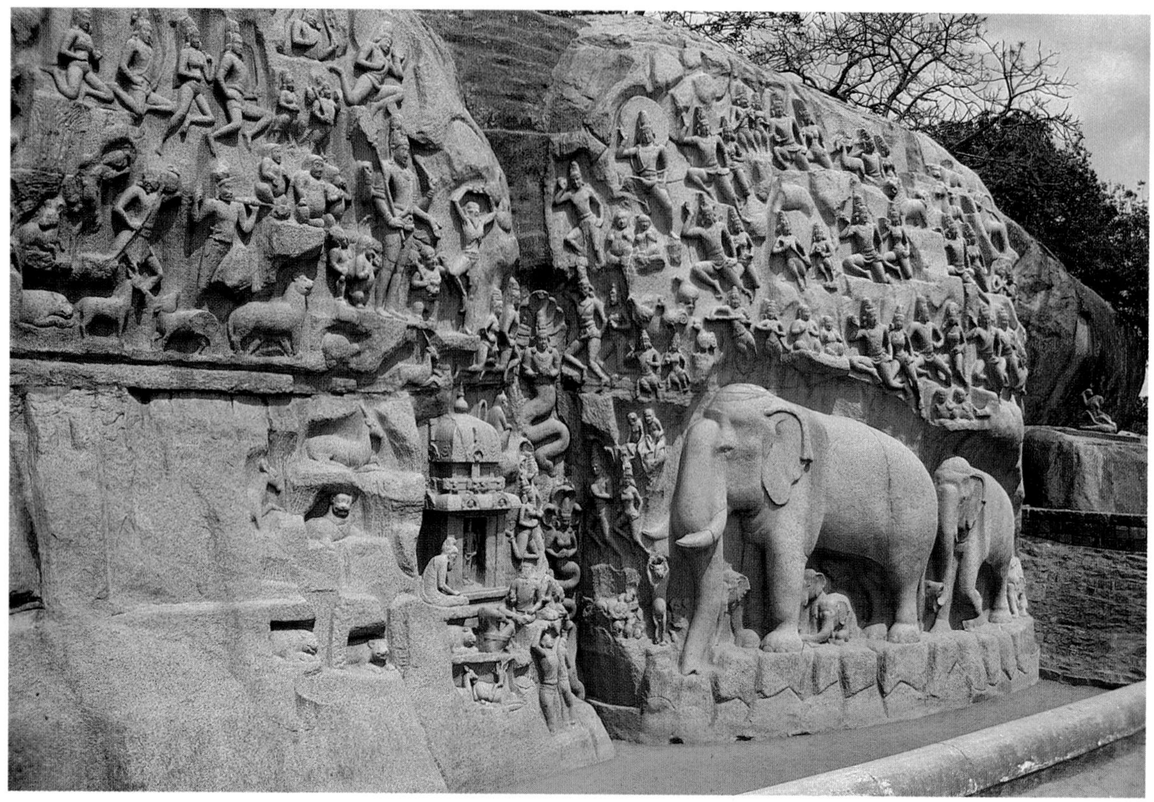

and Queen of the Nagas are serpent deities that portray the great river. While these figures dominate the center of the relief, other legends are incorporated into the composition.

In front of the largest elephant is a wonderful depiction of a cat and mice. According to an old folk tale, beside the Ganges, a cat pretending to be an ascetic stood with upraised paws and gazed at the sun. The cat convinced the mice that she was holy and thus worthy of worship. As the mice closed their eyes in reverence, the cat snatched them for dinner.

The whole sculpture relates to the annual miracle of the return of the life-giving waters of the river. Appropriately, the many figures appear to be emerging from the stone as if from a flow of water.

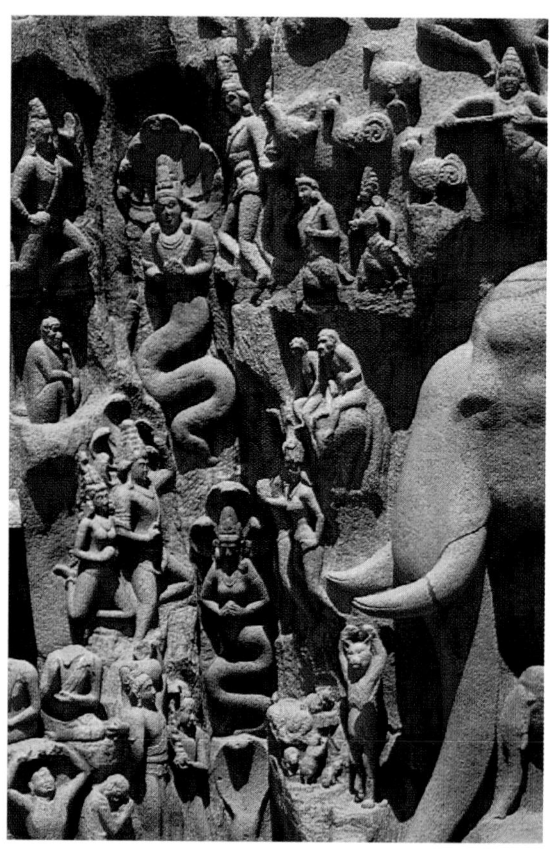

55 DESCENT OF THE GANGES.
Māmallapuram, India. 7th century.
Granite. Height approximately 30'.
a Overview.
Photograph: Jerome Feldman, Hawaii Loa College.
b Detail.
Photograph: Duane Preble.

Symbols, both personal and universal, continue to inspire today's artists. For example, some painters and photographers combine the images of ordinary objects in ways that express qualities far beyond what the objects would mean by themselves. Such images symbolize shared human concerns: time, chance, death, fate, and desire.

When an artist depicts objects loaded with symbolic implications, all of the associations carried by the symbols interact as in a well-told story.

Seventeenth-century French painter Georges de La Tour is best known for his candle-lit paintings. In MAGDALEN WITH SMOKING FLAME the candlelight illuminates timeless, symbolically loaded subjects: candle, skull, and mirror—objects frequently depicted in work inspired by Ecclesiastes 1.2: "Vanity of vanities, all is vanity." The significance of the objects is magnified by the touch of Magdalen's hand on the skull and by her expression. She seems to be reflecting on her own mortality.

Audrey Flack's WHEEL OF FORTUNE presents some of the same objects associated with vanity: skull, hourglass, mirror, candle, and jewels. The large, elaborately detailed painting is loaded with personal significance. It deals with the tragedy of her autistic daughter, pictured in the upper left. Death looms large, symbolized by the skull and it's reflection, yet, as Flack points out, "the hand mirror momentarily exposes a rainbow, signifying the beyond, the afterlife."[6]

Flack sees this painting as a strong protest against simply accepting fate. The image, incorporating current as well as universal symbolic references, deals with the need to work with one's fate in a constructive, life-affirming way.

Most of us have created at least one personal symbolic collage or assemblage in the form of a scrapbook, a bulletin board, an illustrated journal, or a collection of keepsakes.

In LEGACY, student David Kaneko juxtaposed national symbols and historic figures to convey his concern for the values of the country his generation will inherit.

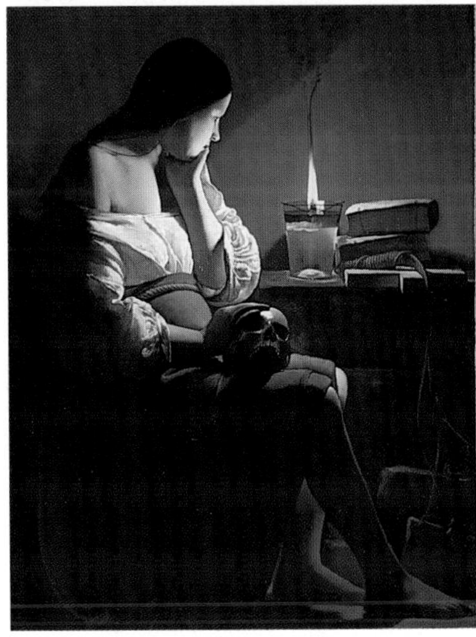

58 Georges de La Tour.
MAGDALEN WITH SMOKING FLAME. c. 1640.
Oil on canvas. 46½" × 35½".
Los Angeles County Museum of Art.

56 David Kaneko.
LEGACY. 1991.
Collage. 20" × 15".
Courtesy of the artist.

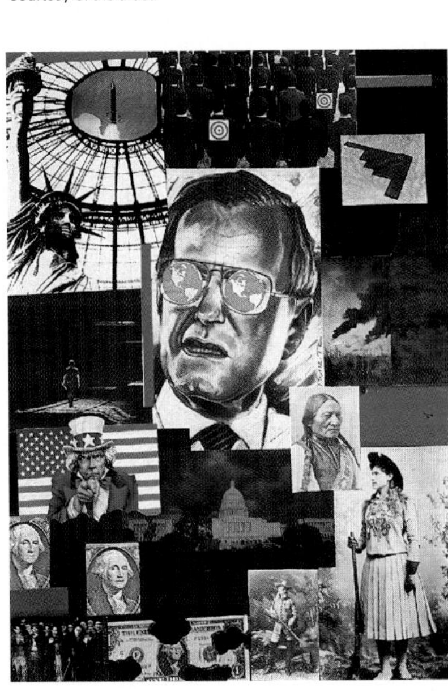

57 Audrey Flack.
WHEEL OF FORTUNE. 1977-1978.
Oil over acrylic on canvas. 8' × 8'.
Collection of Louis, Susan, and Ari Meisel.
Photograph courtesy of Louis K. Meisel Gallery, New York.

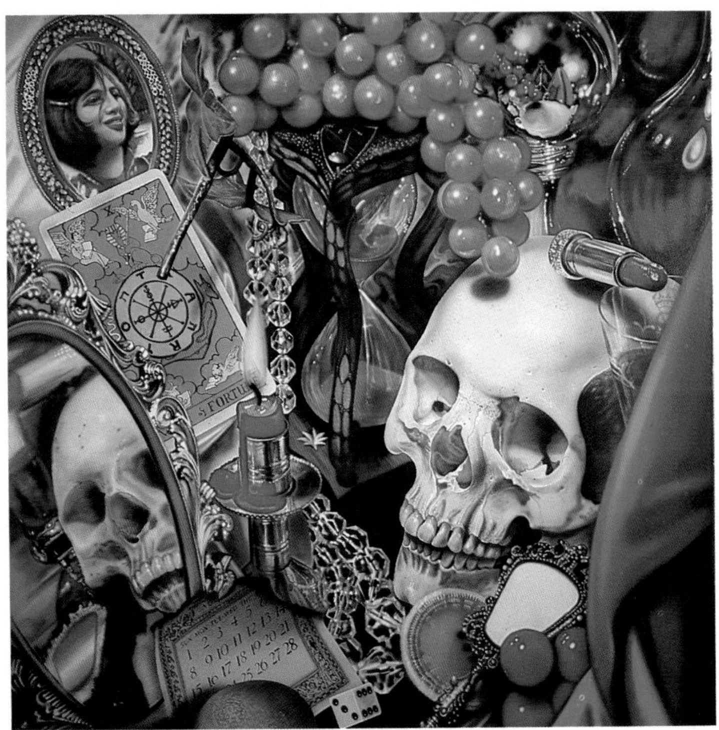

CHAPTER 4

Visual Elements

Remember that a picture—before being a war horse, a nude woman, or some anecdote—is essentially a plane surface covered with colours assembled in a certain order.

Maurice Denis[1]

Painter Maurice Denis could have gone on to say that the *plane,* the two-dimensional picture surface, may also be covered with lines, shapes, textures, and other aspects of visual form (visual elements). Sculpture consists of these same elements organized and presented in three-dimensional space. Because of their overlapping qualities, it is impossible to draw rigid boundaries between the elements of visual form.

For example, a glance at Swiss artist Paul Klee's LANDSCAPE WITH YELLOW BIRDS reveals his playful interpretation of the subject. Fluid, curving *lines* define abstract *shapes.* Klee simplified and flattened the solid *masses* of natural plant and bird forms so that they read as flat shapes against a dark background *space.* Such abstraction emphasizes the fantastic, dreamlike quality of the subject. The whimsical positioning of the upside-down bird suggests a moment in *time* without *motion. Light* illuminates and enhances the yellow *color* of the birds and the unusual colors of the leaves. Surface *textures* provide further interest to each area of the painting.

This chapter introduces the visual elements identified in LANDSCAPE WITH YELLOW BIRDS: line, shape, mass, space, time, motion, light, color, and texture. Not all these elements are important, or even present, in every work of art; many works emphasize only a few elements. In order to understand their expressive possibilities, it is useful to analyze—one at a time—the expressive qualities of each of the aspects of visual form.

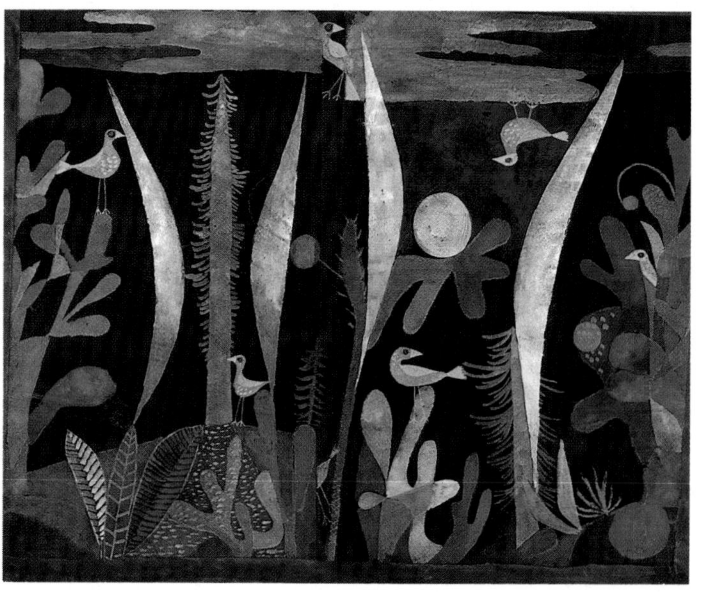

59 Paul Klee.
LANDSCAPE WITH YELLOW BIRDS. 1932.
Watercolor, newspaper, black base. 14" × 17⅜".
Private Collection. © 1993 by Cosmopress, Geneva.

LINE

We write, draw, plan, and play with lines. Our individualities and feelings are expressed as we write our one-of-a-kind signatures or make other unmechanical lines. Line is our basic means for recording and symbolizing ideas, observations, and feelings; it is a primary means of visual communication.

Our habit of making all kinds of lines obscures the fact that pure geometric line—line with only one dimension, length—is a mental concept. "Line" does not exist in the three-dimensional physical world. "Lines" are actually linear forms in which length dominates over width. Wires and branches are long cylinders, while cracks and grooves are long, narrow depressions. Wherever we see an edge, we can perceive the edge as a line—the place where one object or plane appears to end and another object or space begins. In a sense, we often "draw" with our eyes, converting edges to lines.

In art and in nature, *lines* can be seen as paths of action—records of the energy left by moving points. Many intersecting and contrasting linear paths form the composition in Ansel Adams's photograph RAILS AND JET TRAILS.

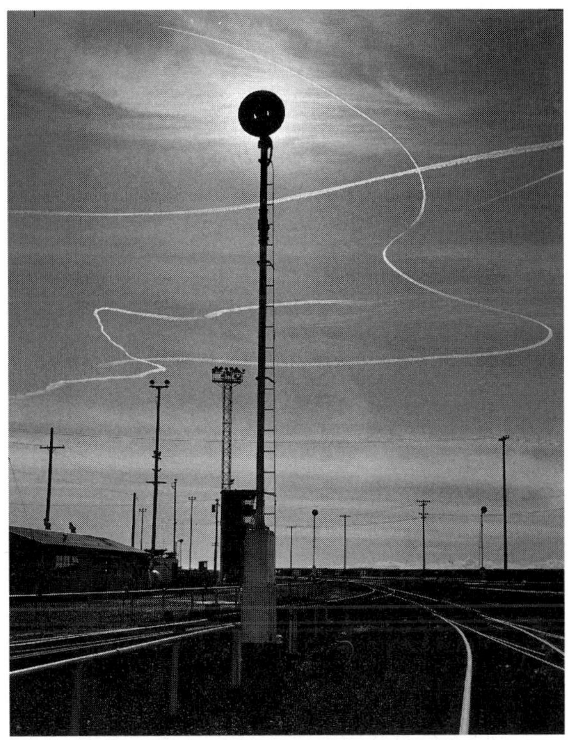

60 Ansel Adams.
RAILS AND JET TRAILS, ROSEVILLE, CALIFORNIA. 1953.
Photograph.

Characteristics of Line

Lines can be active or static, aggressive or passive, sensual or mechanical. Lines can indicate directions, define boundaries of shapes and spaces, imply volumes or solid masses, and suggest motion or emotion. Lines can also be grouped to depict qualities of light and shadow and to form patterns and textures. Note the line qualities in the LINE VARIATIONS.

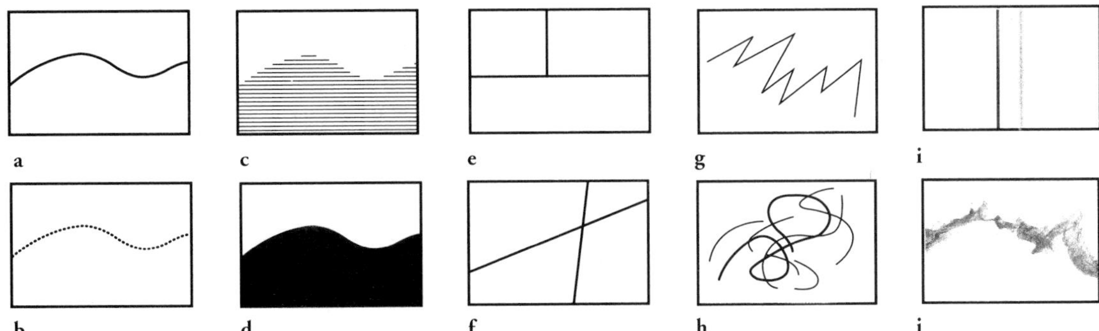

61 LINE VARIATIONS
a Actual line.
b Implied line.
c Actual straight lines and implied curved line.
d Line created by an edge.
e Vertical line (attitude of alert attention).
Horizontal line (attitude of rest).
f Diagonal lines (slow action, fast action).
g Sharp, jagged line.
h Dance of curving lines.
i Hard line, soft line.
j Ragged, irregular line.

Consider the range of qualities expressed in the playful visual statement by Saul Steinberg, in the spontaneous dance of gestural line in Jackson Pollock's DRAWING, and in the vibrant energy of painted lines in Bridget Riley's CURRENT. TWO ACROBATS is one of many whimsical pieces of wire sculpture in which Alexander Calder took advantage of the descriptive and expressive potential of lines.

Recording the contours of three-dimensional objects as outlines (edges) of shapes on a two-dimensional surface is a fundamental process of drawing—and one of the most important functions of line in art. In the descriptive drawing BLUE GINGER, contour lines depict the edges of leaves. Notice the contrasting ways contour lines are used to express lyric sensuality and brusque aggressiveness in the Japanese woodcut prints by Kiyonobu (WOMAN DANCER WITH FAN AND WAND) and Kiyotada (ACTOR IN A DANCE MOVEMENT).

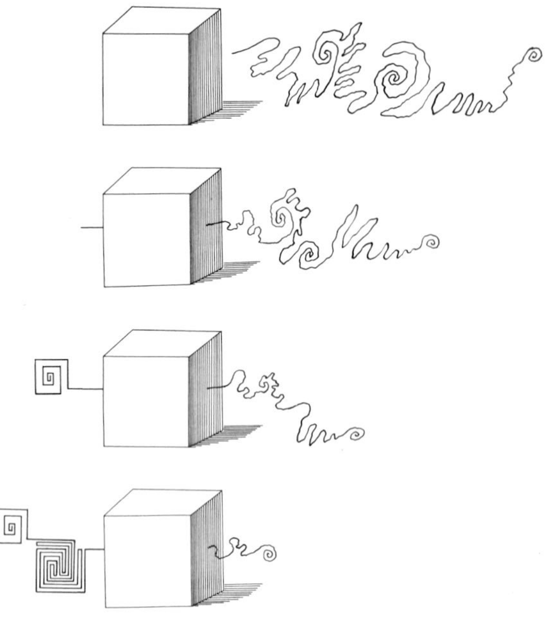

62 Saul Steinberg.

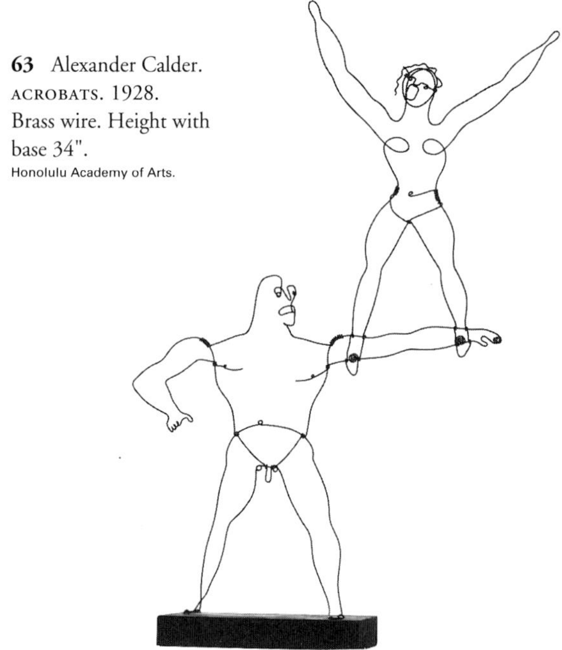

63 Alexander Calder.
ACROBATS. 1928.
Brass wire. Height with base 34".
Honolulu Academy of Arts.

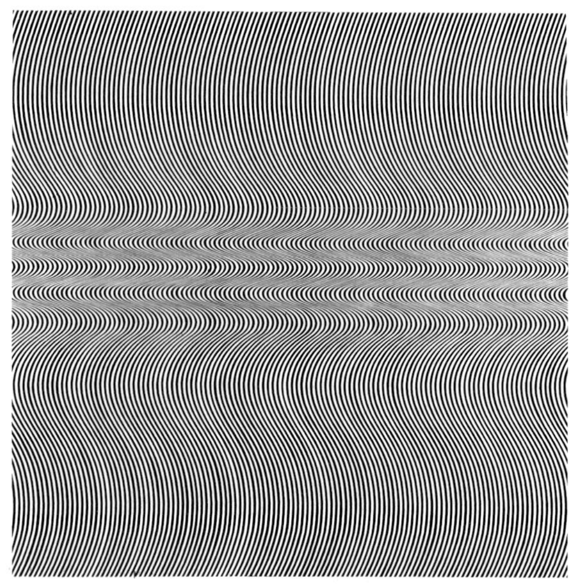

64 Bridget Riley.
CURRENT. 1964.
Synthetic polymer paint on composition board. 58⅜" × 58⅞".
The Museum of Modern Art, New York. Philip Johnson Fund.

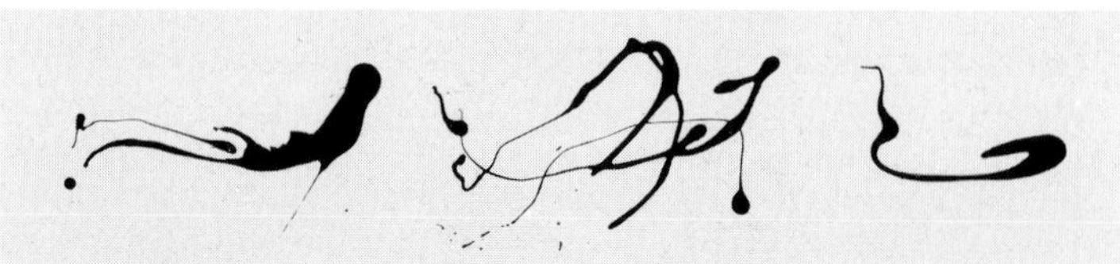

65 Jackson Pollock.
DRAWING. 1950.
Duco on paper. 1'10¼" × 4'11¾".
Staatsgalerie, Stuttgart.

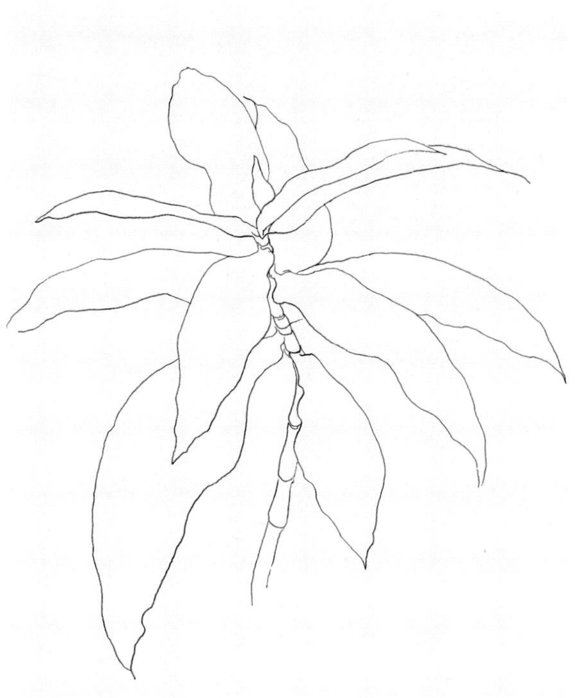

66 Duane Preble.
BLUE GINGER. 1993.
Pencil. 13¾" × 11".

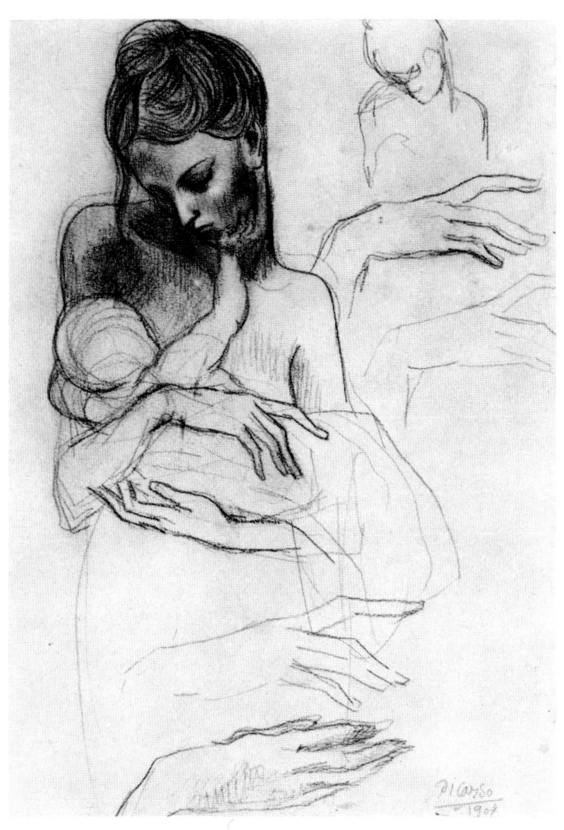

69 Pablo Picasso.
MOTHER AND CHILD AND FOUR STUDIES OF HER RIGHT HAND. 1904.
Black crayon on tan wove paper. 338 mm × 267 mm.
Courtesy of the Fogg Art Museum, Harvard University Art Museums.
Bequest of Meta and Paul J. Sachs.

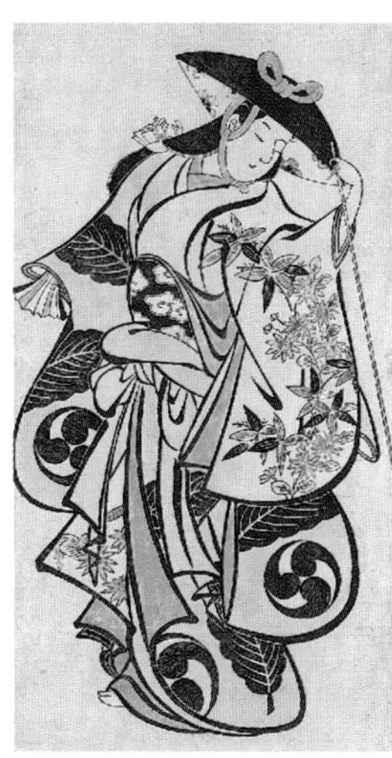

67 Attributed to Torii Kiyonobu I
WOMAN DANCER WITH FAN AND WAND. c. 1708.
Hand-colored woodcut.
21¾" × 11½".
Metropolitan Museum of Art, New York.
Harris Brisbane Dick Fund, 1949.

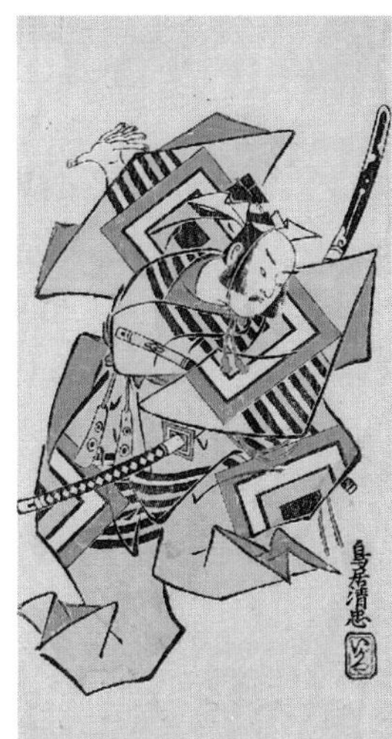

68 Torii Kiyotada.
ACTOR IN A DANCE MOVEMENT. c. 1715.
Hand-colored woodcut.
11¼" × 6".
Metropolitan Museum of Art, New York.
Harris Brisbane Dick Fund, 1949.

Because the drawing MOTHER AND CHILD is a study for a painting, we can follow Picasso's visual thinking as he drew. He concentrated on the angles of the woman's head and hands, and he was particularly concerned with the positions of the fingers of her right hand. Contour lines are used to describe the basic shape and structure of her hands. A variety of lines are used to portray the details of the woman's features, the texture of her skin, the pattern of her hair, and the light falling on her head and shoulders. After describing the contours of the figures, Picasso made groups of parallel straight lines drawn across each other in several directions (called *cross-hatching*) to develop the darks of the shadow areas. (See further discussion of lines under Drawing beginning on page 140.)

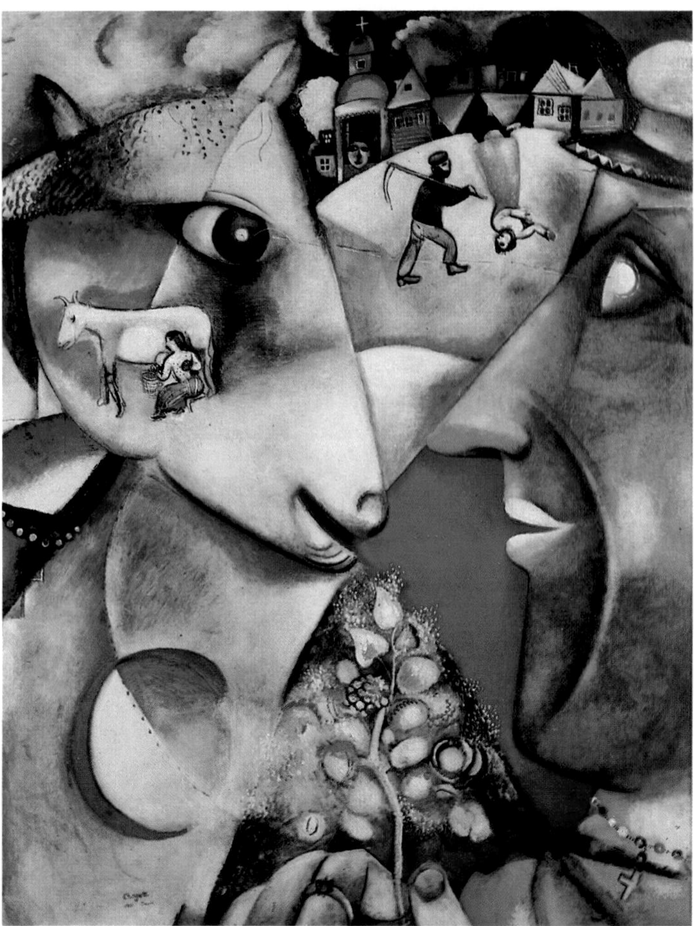

70 Marc Chagall.
I AND THE VILLAGE. 1911.
Oil on canvas. 75⅝" × 59⅝".
The Museum of Modern Art, New York. Mrs. Simon Guggenheim Fund.

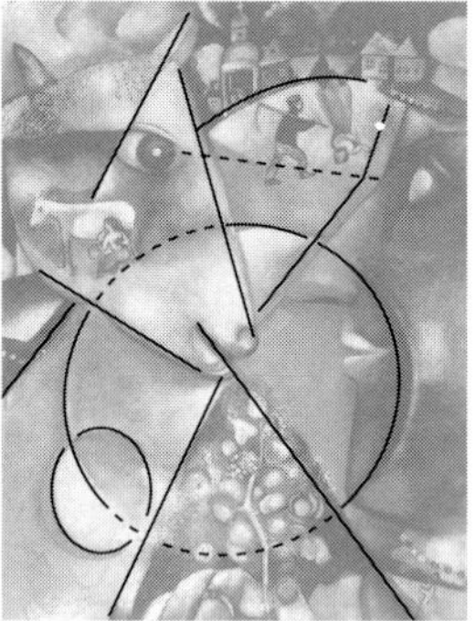

Implied Line

Implied lines suggest visual connections. An implied line in Picasso's drawing A MOTHER AND CHILD (page 49) is indicated by the downward gaze of the mother as she looks at her baby. Implied lines that form geometric shapes can serve as an underlying organizational structure. In I AND THE VILLAGE, Marc Chagall used implied lines to create a circle that brings together scenes of Russian Jewish village life. Notice that he also playfully drew in the implied sightline between man and animal.

SHAPE

The words shape, mass, and form are sometimes used interchangeably. Here we use *shape* to refer to the expanse within the outline of a two-dimensional area or within the outer boundaries of a three-dimensional object. When we see an animal in daylight, we may respond to its mass. If it is silhouetted against a sunset, we may see it only as a flat shape. A shape becomes visible when a line or lines enclose an area or when an apparent change in value (lightness or darkness), color, or texture sets an area apart from its surroundings. In BLUE GINGER (page 49), lines define variations in similar leaf shapes.

We can approach the infinite variety of shapes through two general categories: organic and geometric. *Geometric shapes*—such as circles, triangles, and squares—tend to be precise and regular. *Organic shapes* are irregular, often curving or rounded, and tend to seem relaxed and more informal than geometric shapes. The most common shapes in the human-made world are geometric. While some geometric shapes exist in nature—in such forms as crystals, honeycombs, and snowflakes—most shapes in nature are organic.

In I AND THE VILLAGE, Chagall used a geometric structure of circles and triangles to organize the organic shapes of people, animals, and plants. He softened the severity of geometric shapes to achieve a natural flow between the various parts of the painting. Natural subjects were abstracted toward geometric simplicity in order to strengthen visual impact and symbolic content.

When a shape appears on a *picture plane* (the flat picture surface), it simultaneously creates a second shape out of the background area. We refer to the subject or dominant shapes as *positive* or *figure shapes;* background areas are *negative* or *ground shapes.* The figure-ground relationship is a fundamental aspect of perception; it allows us to sort out and interpret what we see. Because we are conditioned to see only objects, and not the spaces between and around them, it takes a shift in awareness to see the negative shapes as seen in A SHAPE OF SPACE. An artist, however, must consider both positive and negative shapes simultaneously, and treat them as equally important to the total effectiveness of an image.

Interactions between figure shapes and ground shapes are heightened in some images. NIGHT LIFE can be seen as white shapes against black or as black shapes against white, or the figure-ground relationship can shift back and forth. In both this and M. C. Escher's woodcut SKY AND WATER, the shifting of figure and ground contributes to a similar content: the interconnectedness of all things.

At the top of Escher's print, we see dark geese on a white ground. At the bottom, we see light fish on a black ground. In the middle, however, fish and geese interlock so perfectly that we are not sure what is figure and what is ground. As our awareness shifts, fish shapes and bird shapes trade places, a phenomenon called *figure-ground reversal.*

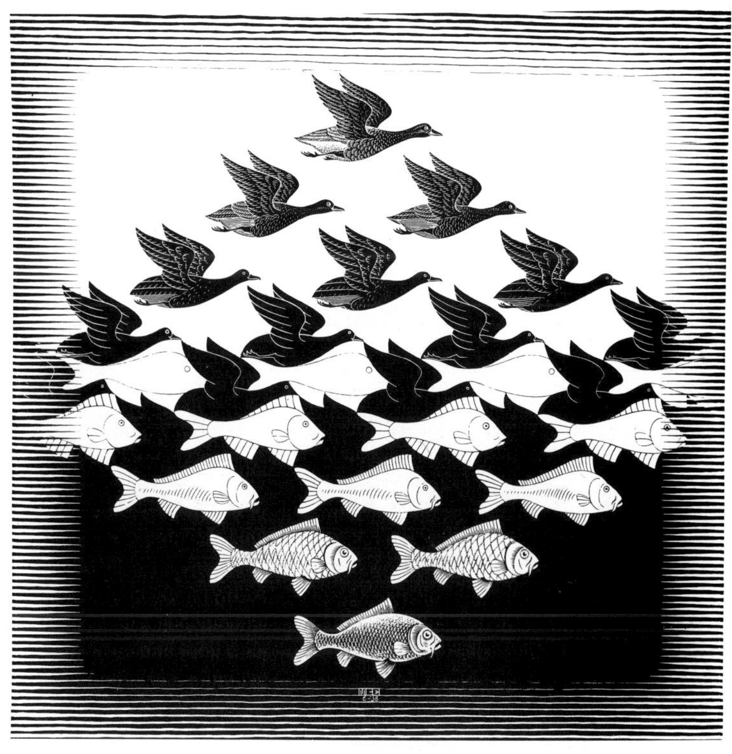

72 M. C. Escher.
SKY AND WATER I. 1938.
Woodcut. 17⅛" × 17¼".

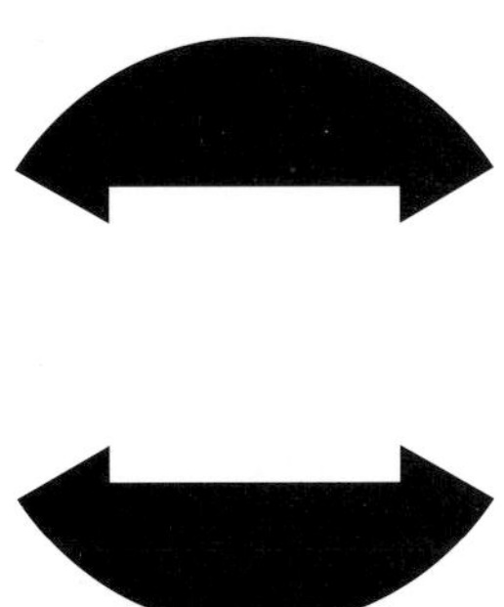

71 A SHAPE OF SPACE (IMPLIED SHAPE).

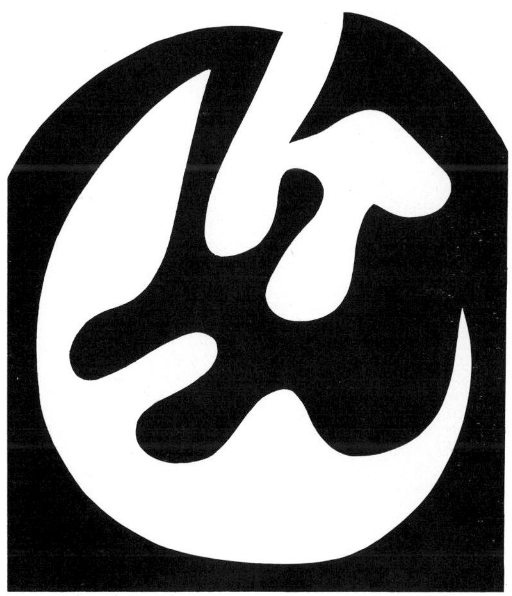

73 NIGHT LIFE (FIGURE-GROUND REVERSAL).

MASS

While a two-dimensional area is referred to as a shape, a three-dimensional area is called a *mass*—the physical bulk of a solid body of material. When mass encloses space, the space is called *volume.* The word mass is occasionally used interchangeably with the words form and volume.

Mass in Three Dimensions

Mass is often a major element in sculpture and architecture. Massiveness was one of the dominant characteristics of ancient Egyptian architecture and sculpture. Egyptians sought this quality and perfected it because it expressed their desire to make art for eternity.

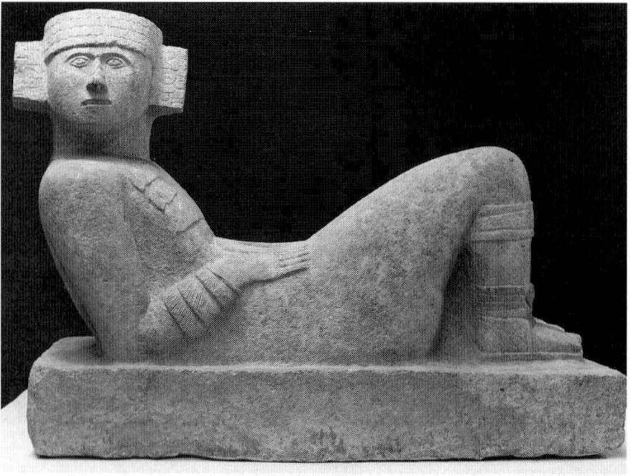

74 CHACMOOL (GOD OF BENEFICIAL RAINS). 10th-12th century. Toltec. Stone. Length 42".
National Anthropology Museum, Mexico City.

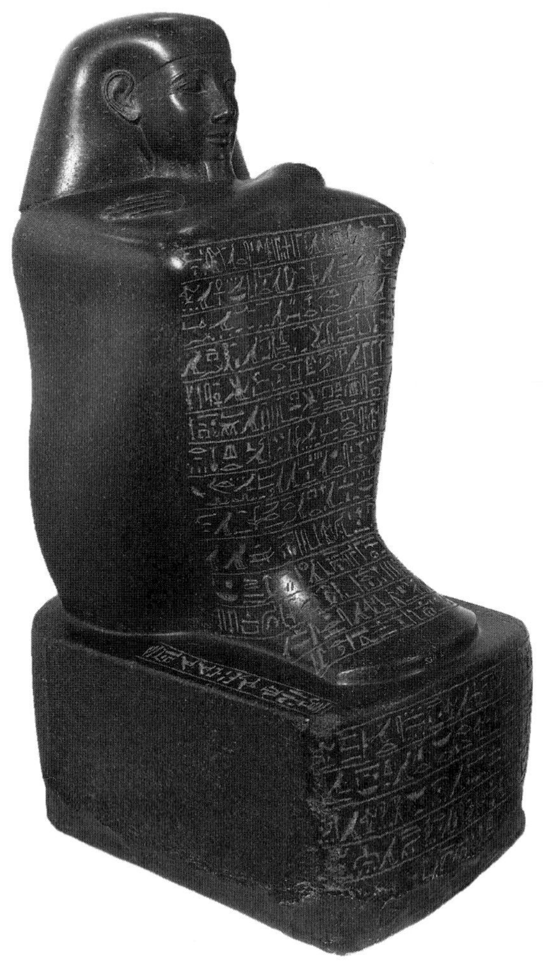

QENNEFER, STEWARD OF THE PALACE was carved from hard black granite and retains the cubic, blocklike appearance of the quarried stone. None of the limbs projects outward into the surrounding space. The figure sits with his knees drawn up and arms folded, his neck obscured by a ceremonial headdress. The body is abstracted and implied with minimal suggestion. This piece is a prime example of *closed form*—form that does not openly interact with the space around it. Here, compact mass symbolizes permanence. Egyptian portrait sculpture acted as a symbolic container for the soul of an important person in order to insure eternal life.

In contrast to the massive Egyptian portrait, contemporary sculptor Alberto Giacometti's MAN POINTING conveys a sense of fleeting presence rather than permanence. The tall, thin figure appears eroded by time and barely existing. Giacometti used little solid material to construct the figure, so we are more aware of a linear form in space than of mass. The figure reaches out; its *open form* interacts with the surrounding space, which seems to overwhelm it, suggesting the fragile, impermanent nature of human existence.

75 QENNEFER, STEWARD OF THE PALACE. c. 1450 B.C. Black granite. Height 2'9".
Copyright British Museum, London.

Giacometti's art reveals an obsession with mortality that began when he was twenty, following the death of an older companion. Later, the fleeting essence of human life became a major concern visible in his work. For Giacometti, both life and the making of art were continuous evolutions. He never felt that he succeeded in capturing the changing nature of what he saw, and therefore he considered all of his works unfinished.

British artist Henry Moore used mass in a way that is different from either Giacometti or the Egyptian sculptor. RECLINING FIGURE was the first major work in Moore's long series of female figures begun soon after he saw a CHACMOOL figure from Pre-Columbian Mexico, similar to the one shown here. Moore was inspired by the way monumentality and strength of the human form are emphasized over detail in this and other Toltec works.

In RECUMBENT FIGURE, Moore related the rounded forms of a woman's body to the wind-worn stone and bone forms he had admired since childhood. Moore made his abstract figure relatively compact in mass, but he put a large hole through the figure, allowing space to flow through as well as around the form. In this way, he created a dynamic, interactive relationship between mass and space. Notice that in talking about mass, we have also had to talk about space. An object is always seen in relation to the space it occupies, and the character of that interaction carries some of the work's meaning.

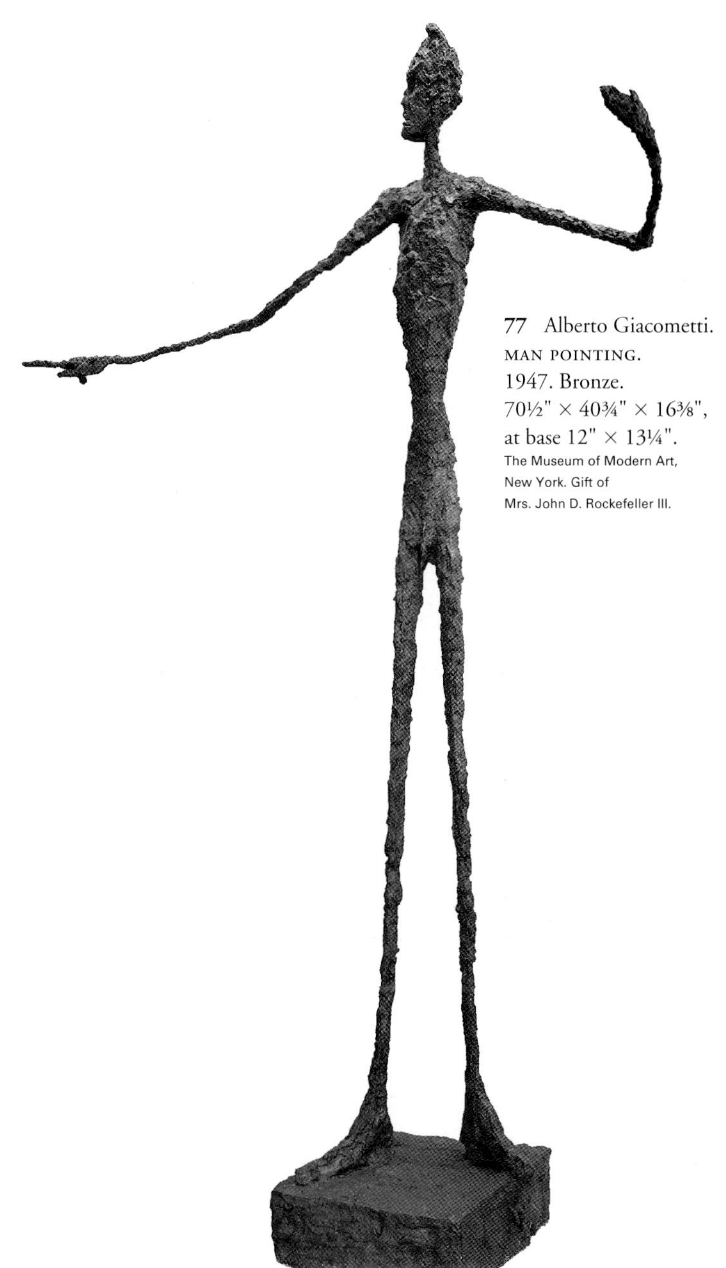

77 Alberto Giacometti.
MAN POINTING.
1947. Bronze.
70½" × 40¾" × 16⅜",
at base 12" × 13¼".
The Museum of Modern Art, New York. Gift of Mrs. John D. Rockefeller III.

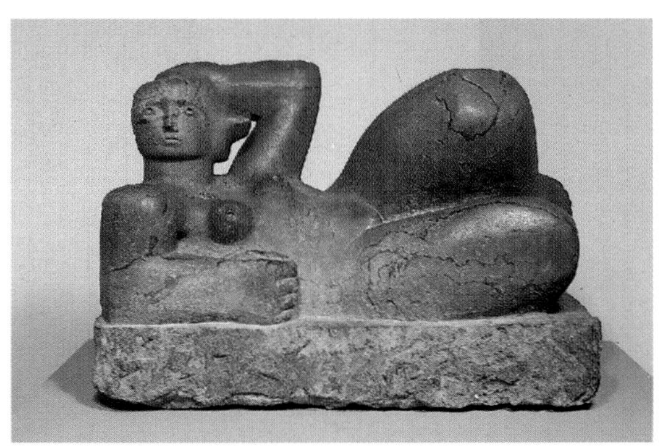

76 Henry Moore.
RECLINING FIGURE. 1929.
Brown hornton stone. Length 33".
Leeds City Art Gallery, England.

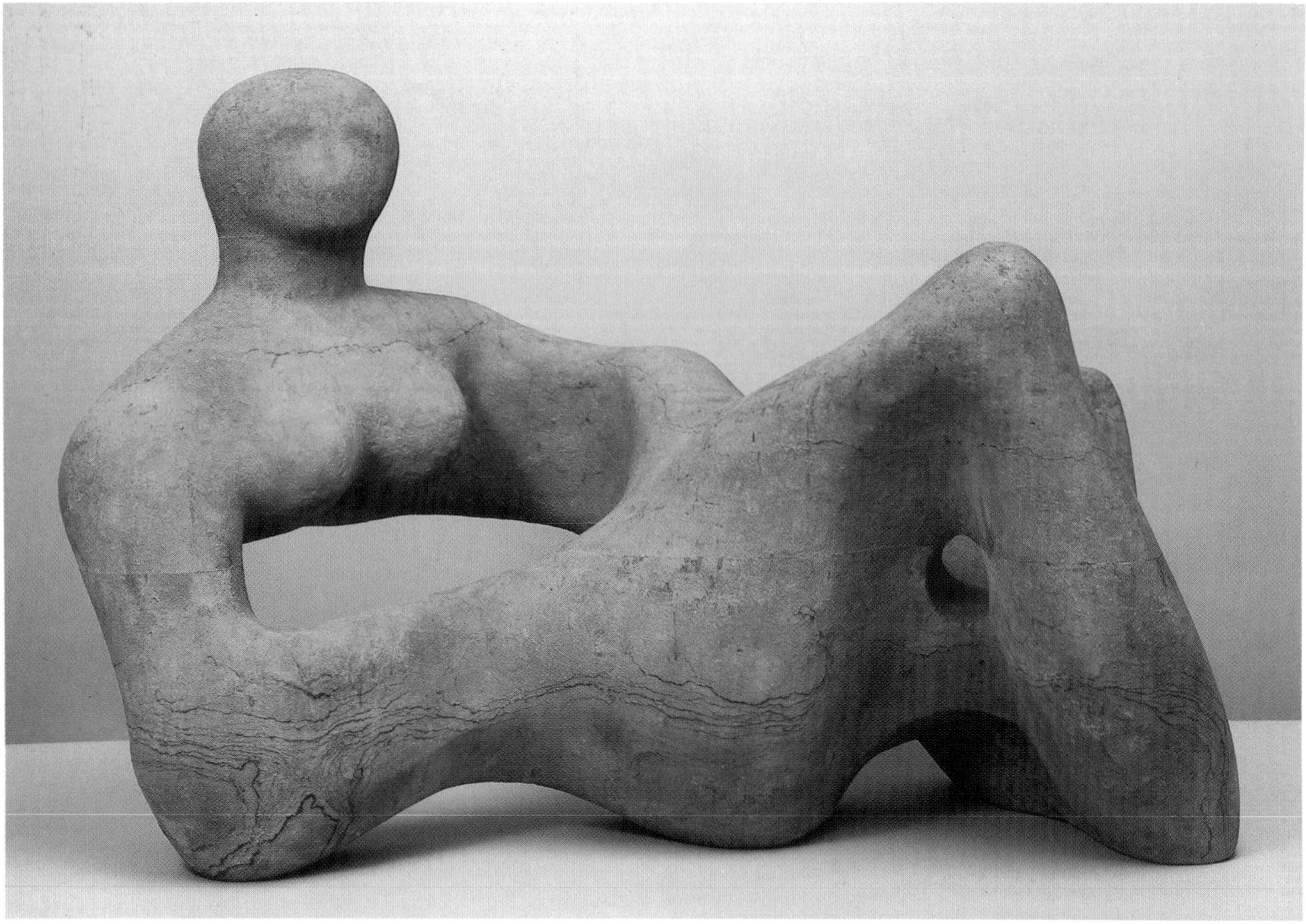

78 Henry Moore.
RECUMBENT FIGURE. 1938.
Green horton stone. Length 54".
Tate Gallery, London.

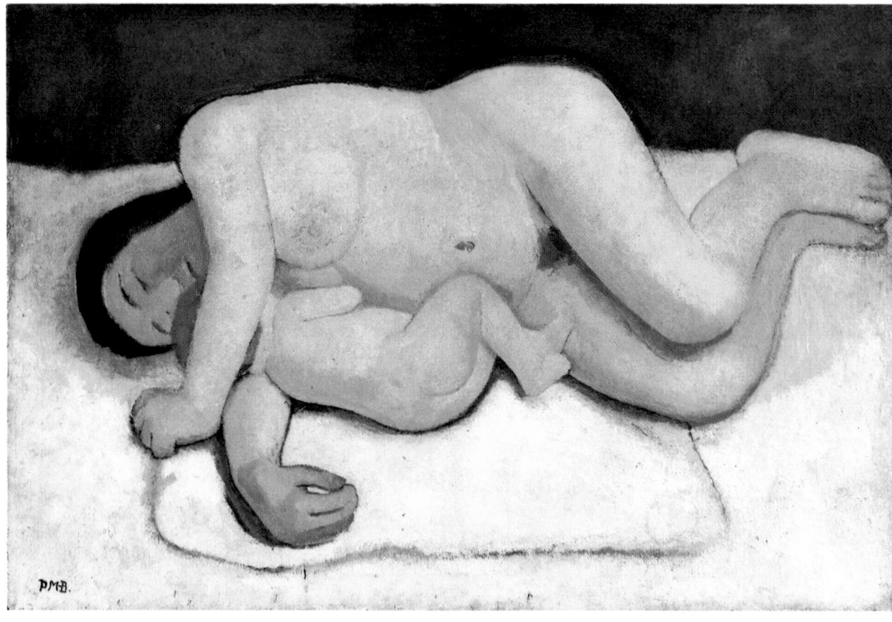

79 Paula Modersohn-Becker.
MOTHER AND CHILD. 1907.
Oil on canvas. 18 cm × 24 cm.
Private collection, Bremen, Germany.

Mass in Two Dimensions

In two-dimensional media such as painting and drawing, mass must be implied. Compare the sculptural quality implied in the painting MOTHER AND CHILD by German artist Paula Modersohn-Becker with the actual three-dimensional form of Henry Moore's RECUMBENT FIGURE. Modersohn-Becker's figures look solid because she applied paint in gradations from light to dark, giving the appearance that light is shining on the curving surfaces from above. The texture of the thick paint further emphasizes the solid quality of the figures.

In HEAD OF A YOUNG MAN, Picasso drew lines that seem to wrap around and define a head in space, implying a solid mass. The drawing gives the appearance of mass because the lines both follow the curvature of the head and build up dark areas to suggest mass revealed by light. Picasso's use of lines convinces us that we are seeing a fully rounded head. At the same time, the vigor of Picasso's lines calls our attention to the flat surface, reminding us that the image is a two-dimensional drawing.

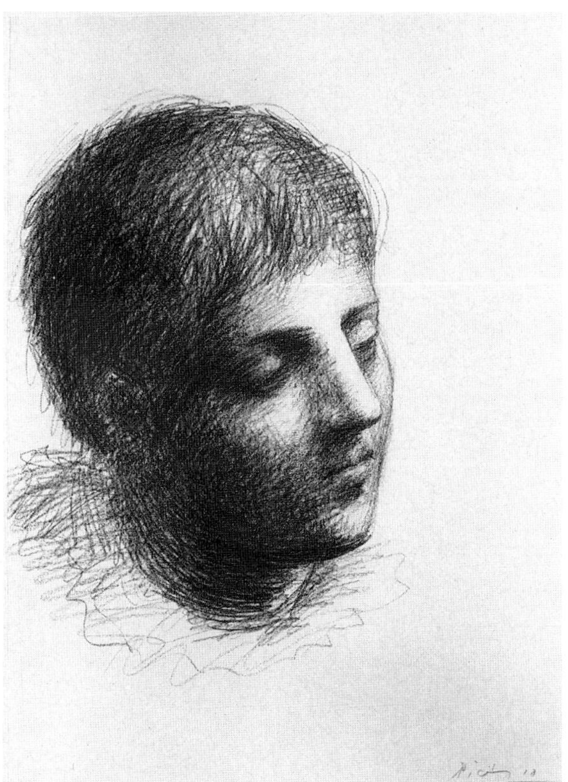

80 Pablo Picasso.
HEAD OF A YOUNG MAN. 1923.
Conté crayon. 24½" × 18⅝".
The Brooklyn Museum, New York. Carrll H. DeSilver Fund.

HENRY MOORE (1898–1986)

When Henry Moore was eleven years old, he learned one day in Sunday school about a man named Michelangelo. Deeply impressed by stories of the artist's greatness, he decided to become a sculptor himself—a *great* sculptor. This was an unusual dream for someone of Moore's background, for he lived in a small town in the bleak north country of England, the ninth of ten children of a coal miner. But he never gave up on his dream and neither did his parents nor his teachers. After serving as a soldier in World War I, Moore was accepted at the Leeds School of Art, and from there he won a scholarship to the Royal College of Art in London.

Moore's training was conservative and academic. He insisted later that all art students should have a thorough grounding in drawing and anatomy to anchor their work. In his art, however, he rejected classical ideals of beauty in favor of something he felt was ultimately more powerful and primal—a language of expressive form such as he found in ancient Cycladic (page 410) and Mexican Pre-Columbian sculpture, in ancient stone monuments like Stonehenge (page 7), and in the sea-worn boulders and cliff formations of the English coast ("nature sculptures," he called them).

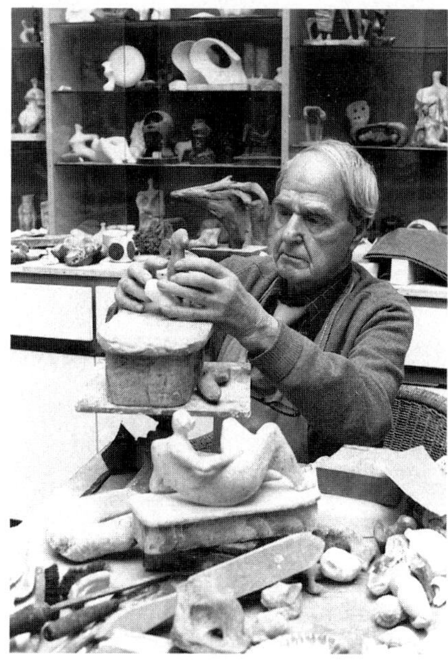

81 HENRY MOORE.
Photograph: © Gemma Levine.

In one important respect, though, Moore was deeply nourished by the Western tradition, for he believed that the human body was the basic subject of sculpture and through it one could say everything that needed to be said. He abstracted and opened the figure to bring human form into resonance with the natural forms he loved. "I am trying to add to people's understanding of life and nature," he said simply, "to help them open their eyes and to be sensitive."[2]

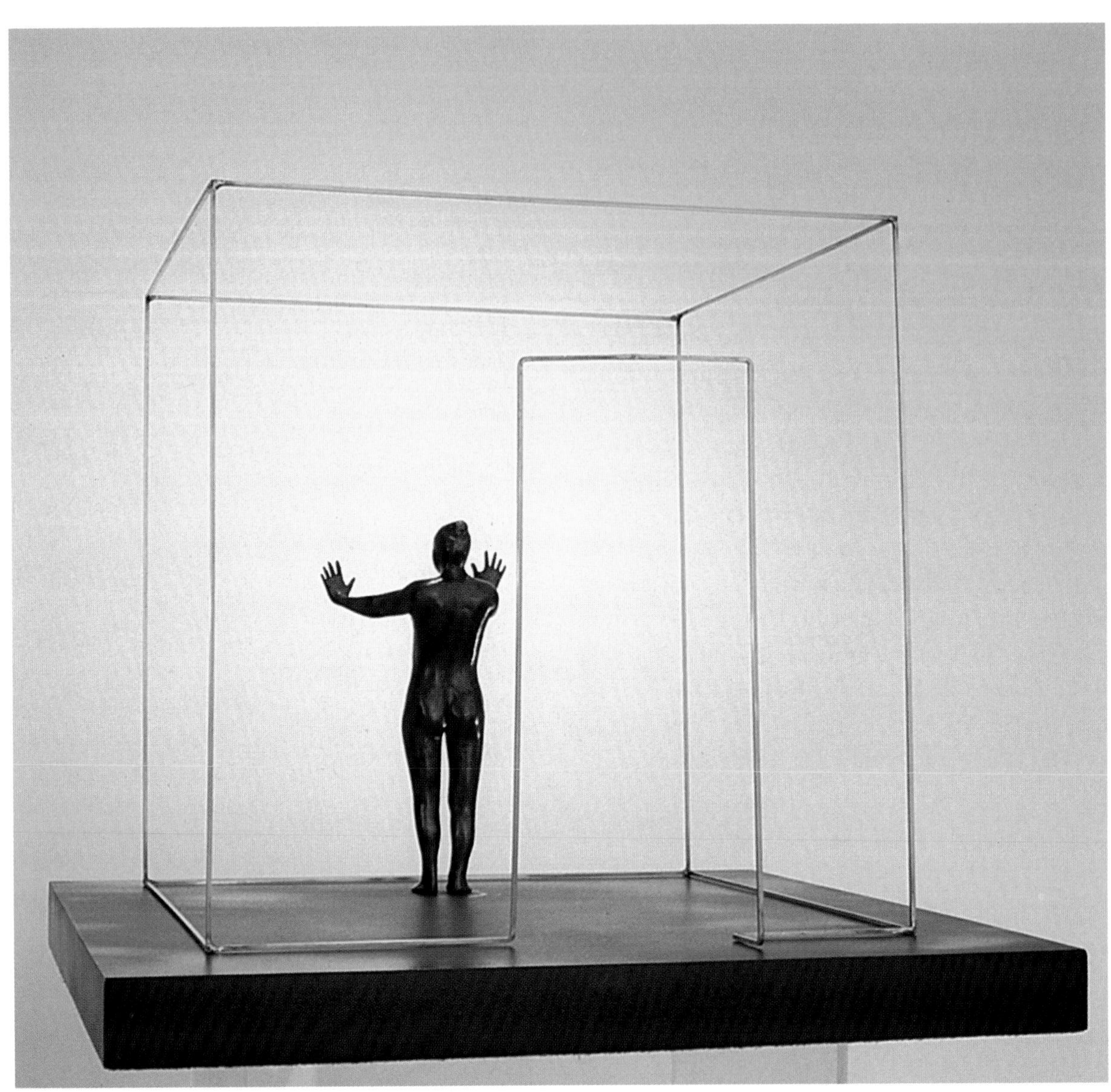

82 Beatriz Kohn.
WHAT IS ALL ABOUT? 1986.
Bronze and micarta. 20" x 24" x 24".
Courtesy of the artist.

SPACE

Space is the indefinable, general receptacle of all things—the void. It is continuous, infinite, and ever present. The visual arts are sometimes referred to as *spatial* arts because most of these art forms are organized in space. In contrast, music is a *temporal* art because musical elements are organized primarily in time. In film, video, and dance, form is organized in both time and space.

Space in Three Dimensions

Of all the visual elements, space is the most difficult to convey in a book. To experience three-dimensional space, we must be in it—as Beatriz Kohn's figure is in it. The artist used the rectilinear frame, the gesture of the figure, and the title WHAT IS ALL ABOUT? to convey a sense of our existence in space.

Architects are especially concerned with the qualities of space. Imagine how you would feel in a small room with a very low ceiling. What if you raised the ceiling to fifteen feet? What if you added skylights? What if you replaced the walls with glass? In each case, you would have changed the character of the space, and by doing so, radically changed your experience.

We experience space beginning with our own positions in relation to other people, objects, surfaces, and voids at various distances from ourselves. Each of us has a sense of personal space—the area surrounding our bodies—that we like to protect, and the extent of this invisible boundary varies from person to person and from culture to culture.

While we experience the outside of a building as mass, we experience the inside as volume and as a sequence of enclosed spaces. The best architecture provides a variety of spatial experiences. When a long, dim corridor opens into a large, light-filled room, the thrill we experience was planned for us by the architect.

Eero Saarinen designed the TWA TERMINAL at Kennedy Airport to express the wonder of air travel. The basic structure, consisting of four huge curving shells of reinforced concrete, is like a huge abstract sculpture. Two of the shells stretch out like the wings of a bird and evoke the feeling of flight. The

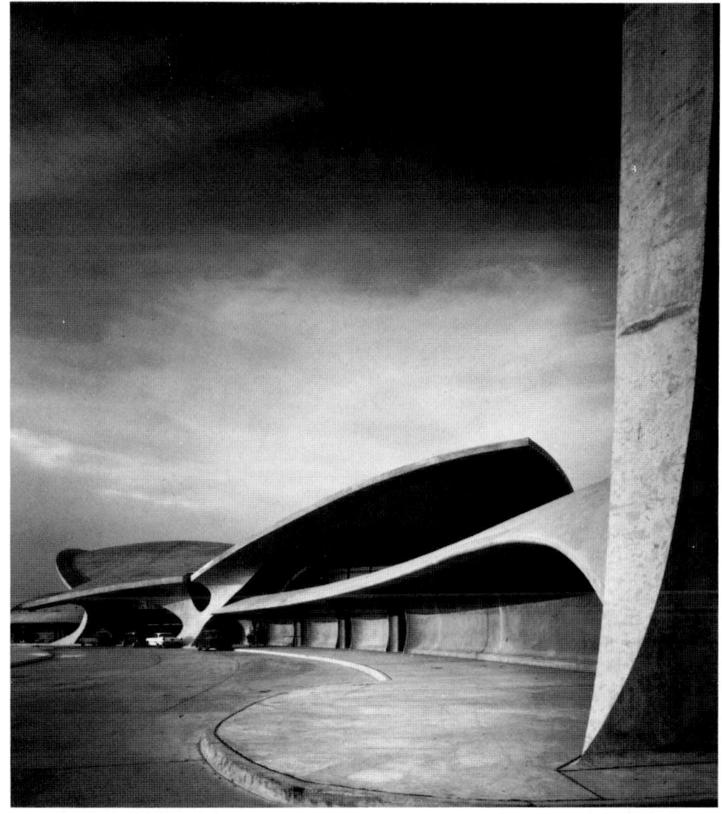

83 Eero Saarinen.
TWA TERMINAL. Kennedy Airport, New York. 1956-1962.
a Exterior.
Photograph: Ezra Stoller/© ESTO.

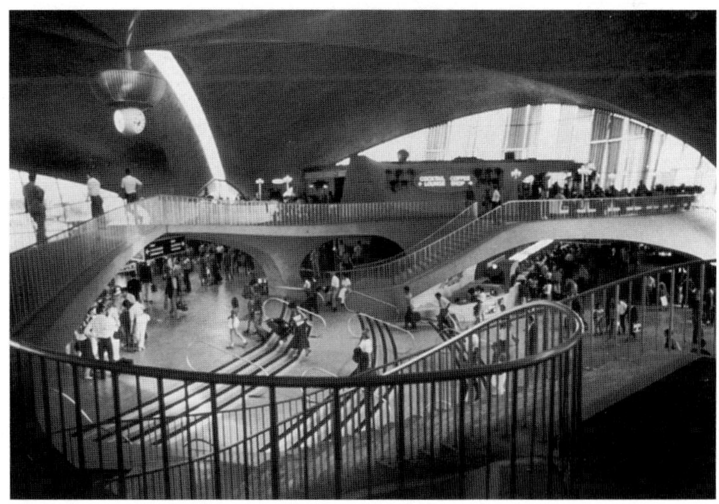

b Interior.
Photograph: Duane Preble.

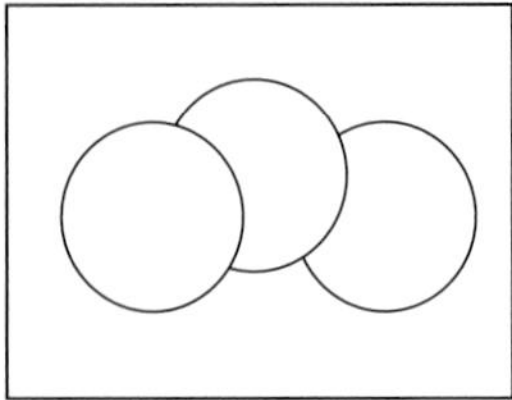

a Overlap.

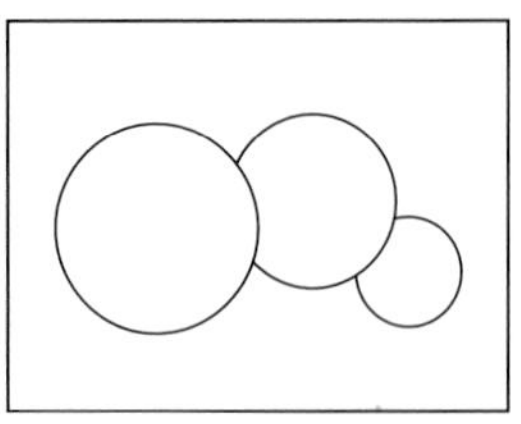

b Overlap and diminshing size.

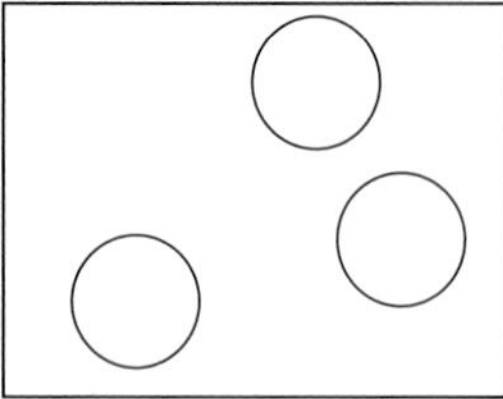

c Vertical placement.

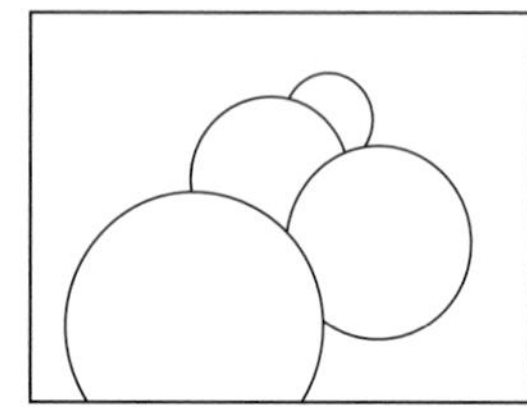

d Overlap, vertical placement, and diminishing size.

84 CLUES TO SPATIAL DEPTH.

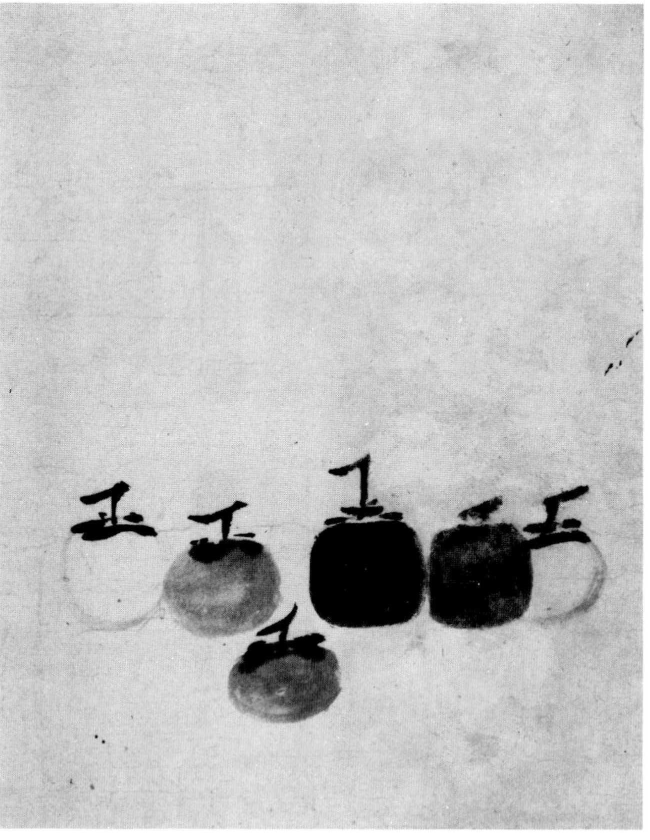

85 Mu Qi (Mu Ch'i)
SIX PERSIMMONS. c. 1269.
Ink on paper. 17⅝16" × 14¼".
Ryoko-in, Daitoku-ji, Kyoto, Japan.

exterior announces the character of the interior. Inside, Saarinen continued the streamlined feeling: instead of a series of rooms and corridors, he created an open, flowing space that seems to shift constantly as we walk around in it. Saarinen intended this building to lift people's spirits.

Space in Two Dimensions

With three-dimensional objects and spaces, such as sculpture and architecture, we must move around to get the full experience. With two-dimensional works, such as drawing and painting, we see the space of the surface all at once. In drawings, prints, photographs, and paintings, the actual space of each picture's surface *(picture plane)* is defined by its edges—usually the two dimensions of height and width. Yet within these limited boundaries, an infinite number of spatial qualities can be implied.

The Illusion of Depth Almost any mark on a picture plane begins to give the illusion of a third dimension: depth. Clues to seeing spatial depth are learned in early childhood. A few of the major ways of indicating space on a picture plane are shown in the diagrams of CLUES TO SPATIAL DEPTH.

When shapes overlap, we immediately assume from experience that one is in front of the other (diagram a). Overlapping is the most basic way to achieve the effect of depth on a flat surface. The effect of overlap is strengthened by *diminishing size,* which gives a sense of increasing distance between each of the shapes (diagram b). Our perception of distance depends on the observation that distant objects appear smaller than near objects. A third method of achieving the illusion of depth is with *vertical placement:* objects placed low on the picture plane (diagram c) appear to be closer to the viewer than objects placed high on the plane. This is how we see most things in actual space. Creating illusions of depth on a flat surface usually involves one or more such devices (diagram d).

In medieval Europe, pictorial space was used to portray symbols and tell stories, and it was not intended to be illusionistic. In Angelo Puccinelli's

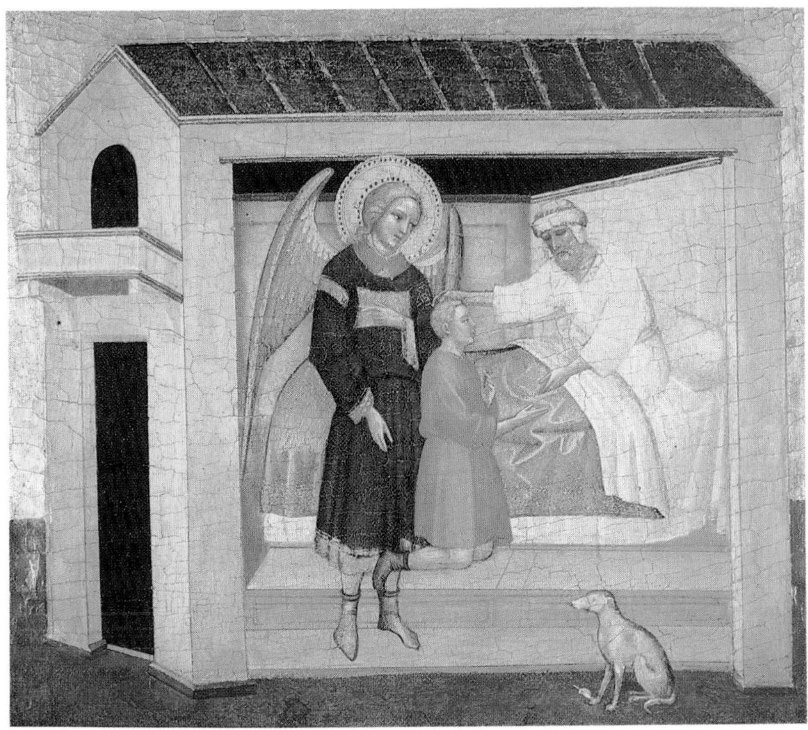

86 Angelo Puccinelli.
TOBIT BLESSING HIS SON.
c. 1350-1399.
Tempera on wood. 14⅞" x 17⅛".
The Philbrook Museum of Art, Tulsa, Oklahoma.
Samuel H. Kress Collection.

painting TOBIT BLESSING HIS SON, is it possible to tell whether the angel is behind or in front of the son? It does not matter, of course, since angels do not usually appear in logical, earthly space. More to the point is that the house appears far too small for the figures. It's a symbol of a house, with a wall removed so that we can see what's going on inside.

We can be conscious of the flat surface or of the illusion of depth when we examine a picture. Artists can emphasize either the reality or the illusion—or strike a balance between these extremes. For centuries, Asian painters have paid careful attention to the relationship between the reality of the flat picture plane and the implied depth they wish to create. Mu Qi's ink painting SIX PERSIMMONS has only a subtle suggestion of depth in the overlap of two of the persimmons. By placing the smallest persimmon lowest on the picture plane, Mu Qi further minimized the illusion of depth; since we interpret the lower part of the picture as being closer to us, we might expect the persimmon there to be larger.

The persimmons appear against a pale background that works as both flat surface and as infinite space. The shapes of the fruit punctuate the open space of the ground. Imagine what would happen to this painting if some of the space at the top were cut off. Space is far more than just what is left over after the important forms have been placed; it is an integral part of the total visual design.

The Persian miniature painting INCIDENT IN A MOSQUE (see next page) by Shaykh Zadeh is an intricate organization of flat planes fitted together in shallow, implied space. Islamic painters of Persia (now called Iran) have typically shown human activity going on both inside and outside architectural spaces to clarify important aspects of a story. Here we see people looking through a high window, others looking over a wall, and people inside a mosque. Figures and architectural forms are stacked up across the surface as if seen from a high vantage point. The floor, with its tile pattern and richly decorated carpets, is also seen as if from above. There is no diminishing size in the figures or in the steps to the raised seat to indicate distance from the viewer. On the contrary, two of the smallest figures are in front. Depth is shown by overlap and vertical placement, with those figures farthest from us placed

87 Shaykh Zadeh.
INCIDENT IN A MOSQUE.
Persia. c. 1536-1537.
Opaque watercolor on paper.
28.9 cm × 17.8 cm.
Photograph courtesy of the Arthur M. Sackler Museum, Harvard University Art Museums. Private collection.

highest in the composition. The painting has its own spatial logic consistent with the Persian style, which emphasizes narrative clarity and richness of surface design.

Perspective In general usage, the word perspective refers to point of view. In the visual arts, *perspective* refers to any system of representing three-dimensional objects in space on a two-dimensional surface.

In the West, we have become accustomed to *linear perspective* (also called simply *perspective*), a system designed to depict the way objects in space appear to the eye. This system was developed by Italian architects and painters in the fifteenth century, at the beginning of the Renaissance.

Linear perspective is based on the way we see. We have already noted that objects appear smaller when seen at a distance than when viewed close up. Because the spaces between objects also appear smaller when seen at a distance, parallel lines appear to converge as they recede into the distance, as shown in the first of the LINEAR PERSPECTIVE diagrams. Intellectually, you know that the edge lines of the road must be parallel, yet they seem to converge, meeting at last at what we call a *vanishing point* on the horizon—the place where land and sky appear to meet. On a picture surface, the horizon (or *horizon line*) also represents your eye level as you look at a scene.

Eye level is an imaginary plane, the height of the artist's eyes, parallel with the ground plane and extending to the horizon, where the eye level and ground plane appear to converge. In a finished picture, the artist's eye level becomes the eye level of anyone looking at the picture. The eye level of the artist determines the height of the horizon line in relation to other objects in the picture. Although the horizon is frequently blocked from view, it is necessary for an artist to establish the combined eye-level/horizon line to construct images using linear perspective.

With the LINEAR PERSPECTIVE system, an entire picture can be constructed from a single, fixed position called a *vantage point,* or *viewpoint.* The first diagram (a) shows one-point (one vanishing point) perspective with the parallel sides of a road appearing to converge and a row of trees appearing smaller as their distances from the vantage point increase.

Diagram (b) shows cubes drawn in one-point linear perspective. The cubes at the left are at eye level; we can see neither their top nor their bottom surfaces. You might imagine them as buildings.

The cubes in the center are below eye level: we can look down on their tops. These cubes are drawn from a high vantage point, a viewing position above the subject. The horizon line is above these cubes and their perspective lines go up to it. Imagine these as boxes on the floor seen from above.

The cubes at the right are above our eye level; we can look up at their bottom sides. We would say that these cubes are drawn from a low vantage point. The horizon line is below these cubes and their perspective lines go down to it. You might imagine these as boxes sitting on a glass shelf high above your head.

88 LINEAR PERSPECTIVE.
a One-point linear perspective.
b One-point linear perspective. Cubes above eye level, at eye level, and below eye level.
c Two-point linear perspective.

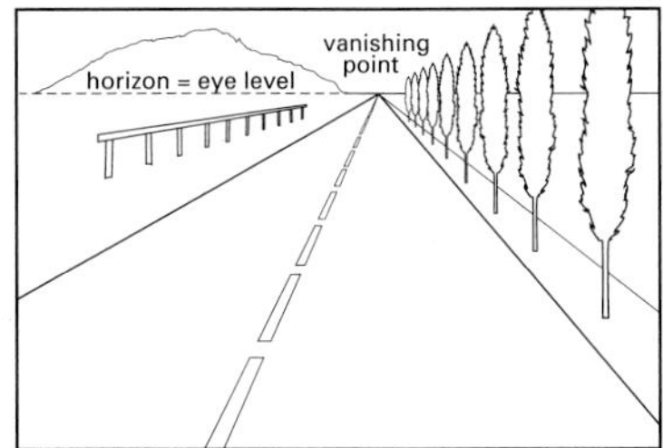

a

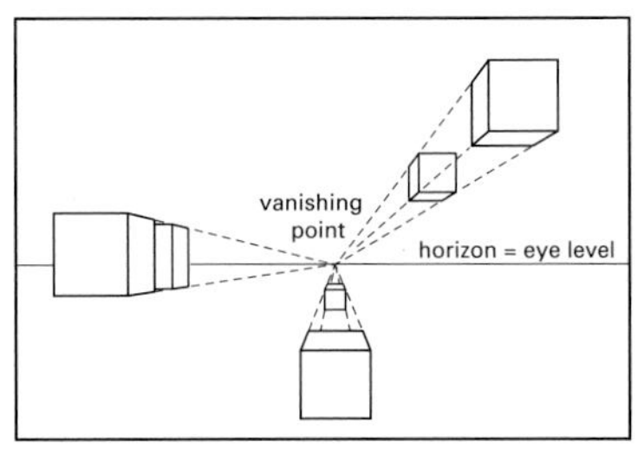

b

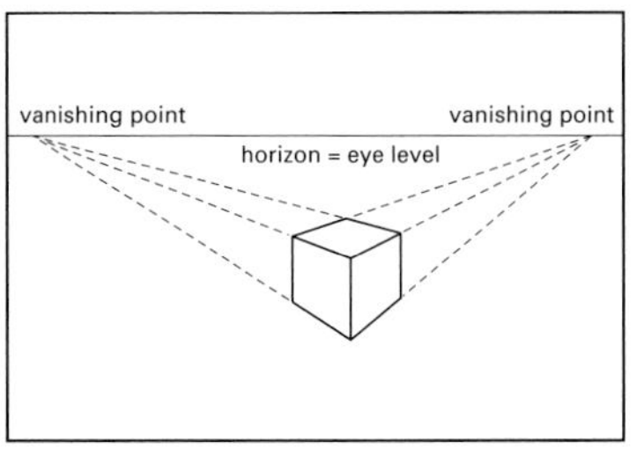

c

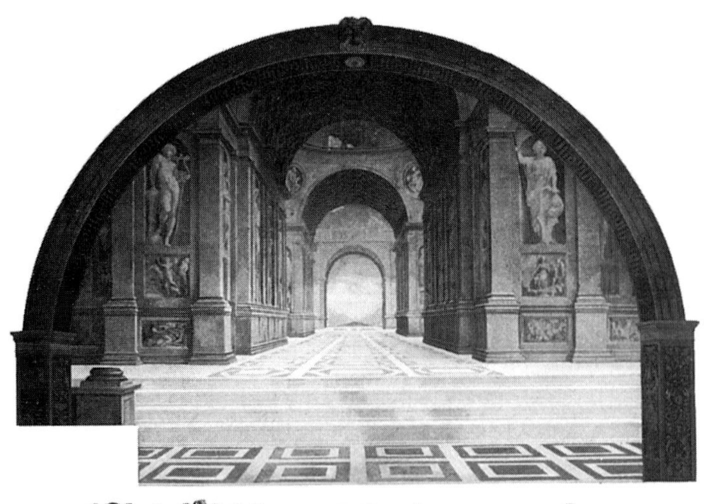
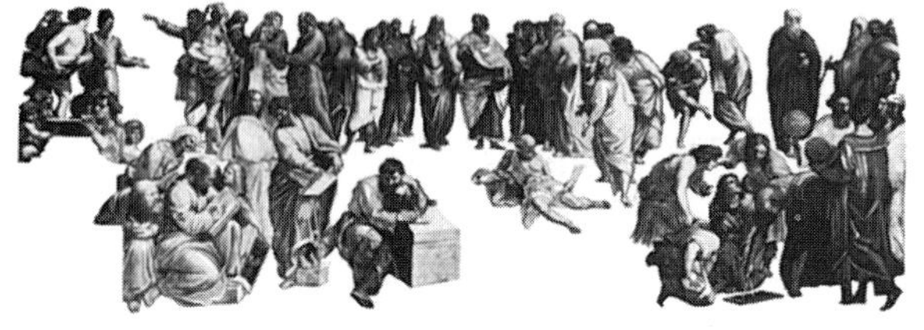

89 Harry Clow.
Study of Raphael's THE SCHOOL OF ATHENS.

In *one-point perspective,* all the major receding "lines" of the subject are actually parallel, yet visually they appear to converge at a single vanishing point on the horizon line. In *two-point perspective,* two sets of parallel lines appear to converge at two points on the horizon line, as in diagram (c).

When a cube or any other rectilinear object is positioned so that a corner, instead of a side, is closest to us, we need two vanishing points to draw it. The parallel lines of the right side converge to the right; the parallel lines of the left side converge to the left. There can be as many vanishing points as there are sets and directions of parallel lines.

Horizontal parallel lines moving away from the viewer above eye level appear to go down to the horizon line; those below eye level appear to go up to the horizon line. It is easy to find the eye level in diagram a because the horizon line is visible; it is not so easy in the painting THE SCHOOL OF ATHENS.

In THE SCHOOL OF ATHENS, Raphael Sanzio (called simply Raphael) invented a grand architectural setting in the Renaissance style to provide an appropriate space for his depiction of the Greek philosopher-teachers Plato and Aristotle and their students. The size of each figure is drawn to scale according to its distance from the viewer; thus the entire group seems natural. Lines superimposed over the painting reveal the basic one-point perspective system used by Raphael. The cube in the foreground, however, is not parallel to the picture plane or to the painted architecture and is in two-point perspective.

An artist can use perspective for symbolic emphasis. We infer that Plato and Aristotle are the most important figures in this painting because they are placed at the center of the series of receding archways and are framed by the one farthest away. Even more important, they are placed on both sides of the vanishing point in the zone of greatest implied depth.

Raphael achieved a balance between the forward push of the figures and the tremendous pull into deep space created by the linear perspective. At the point where the viewer is pulled farthest back in space, the two figures step forward, creating dynamic

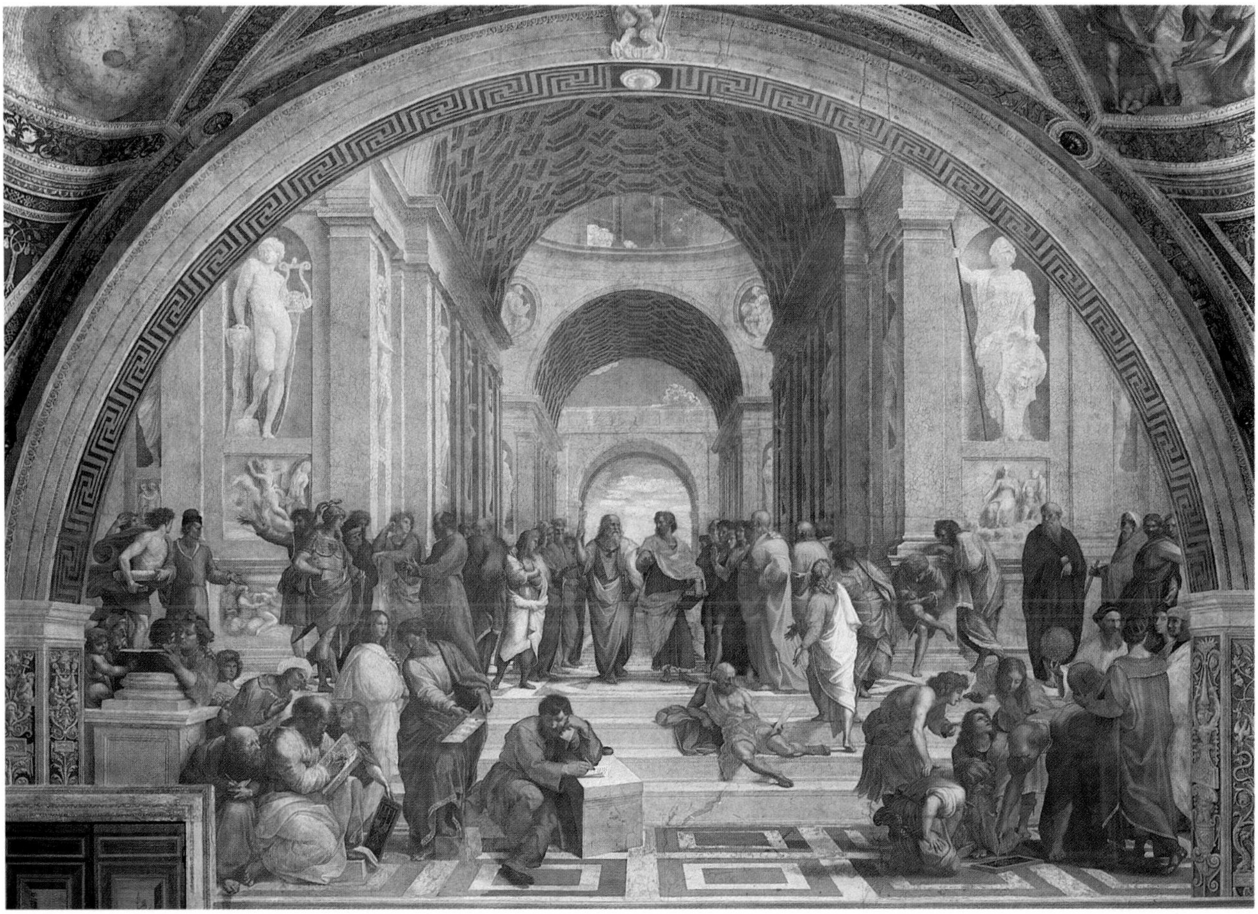

90 Raphael Sanzio.
THE SCHOOL OF ATHENS. 1509.
Fresco. Approx. 18' × 26'.
Stanza della Segnatura, Vatican, Rome.

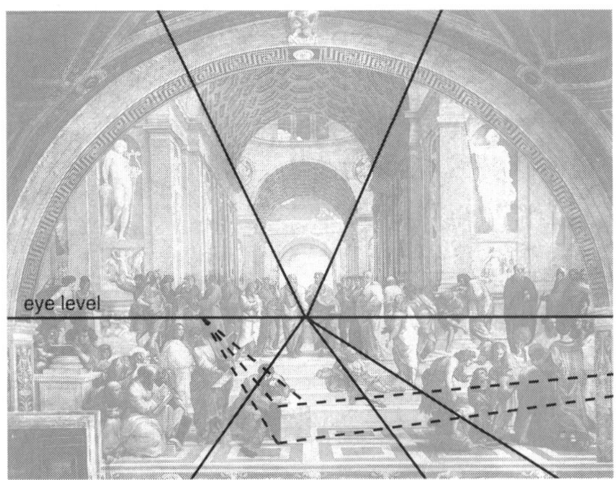

Perspective lines showing eye level, main vanishing point, and left vanishing point for the stone block in the foreground.

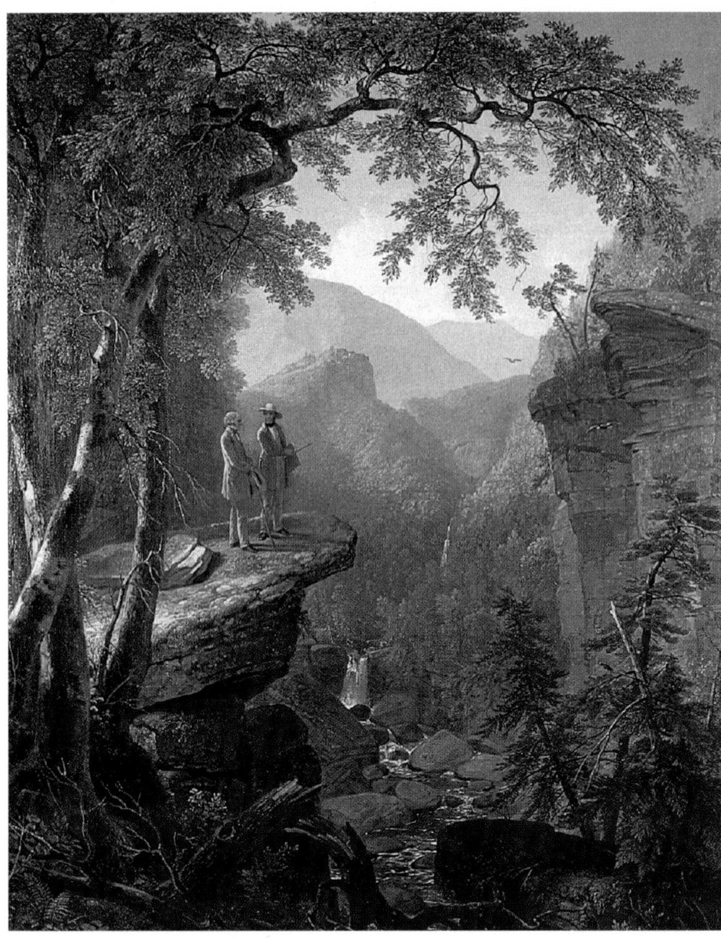

91 Asher Brown Durand. KINDRED SPIRITS. 1849. Oil on canvas. 44" × 36". Collection of the New York Public Library. Astor, Lenox and Tilden Foundations.

tension. If the figures—particularly the two main figures—were removed, as shown in the diagram on page 62, the resulting "hole" would be so distracting that it would be difficult to see anything else in the painting. Our attention would be pulled right through the painted surface into implied infinite space. When we look at the figures without the architecture, we see that the upper row of figures, including Plato and Aristotle, were made smaller than the foreground figures because of their distance from the viewer. It is also clear that without the perspective structure of the painting, we cannot identify the two most important figures.

Atmospheric or *aerial perspective* is a nonlinear means for giving an illusion of depth. The illusion of depth is created by changing color, value, and detail. In visual experience of the real world, as the distance increases between the viewer and faraway objects such as mountains, the increased quantity of air, moisture, and dust causes the distant objects to appear increasingly bluer and less distinct. Color intensity is diminished, and contrast between light and dark is reduced.

Asher Brown Durand used atmospheric perspective in his painting KINDRED SPIRITS to provide a sense of the vast distances in the North American wilderness. The illusion of infinite space is balanced by dramatically illuminated foreground details, by the figures of the men, and by Durand's lively portrayal of trees, rocks, and waterfalls. We identify with the figures of painter Thomas Cole and poet William Cullen Bryant as they enjoy the spectacular landscape. As in THE SCHOOL OF ATHENS, the implied deep space appears as an extension of the space we occupy.

Artists of China have differed from their European counterparts in their use of atmospheric perspective. In Shen Chou's painting POET ON A MOUNTAIN TOP, near and distant mountains are suggested by washes of ink and color on white paper. The light gray of the farthest mountain implies space and atmosphere. Traditional Chinese landscape paintings present poetic symbols of landforms rather than realistic representations. (See page 295 for a discussion of the philosophical con-

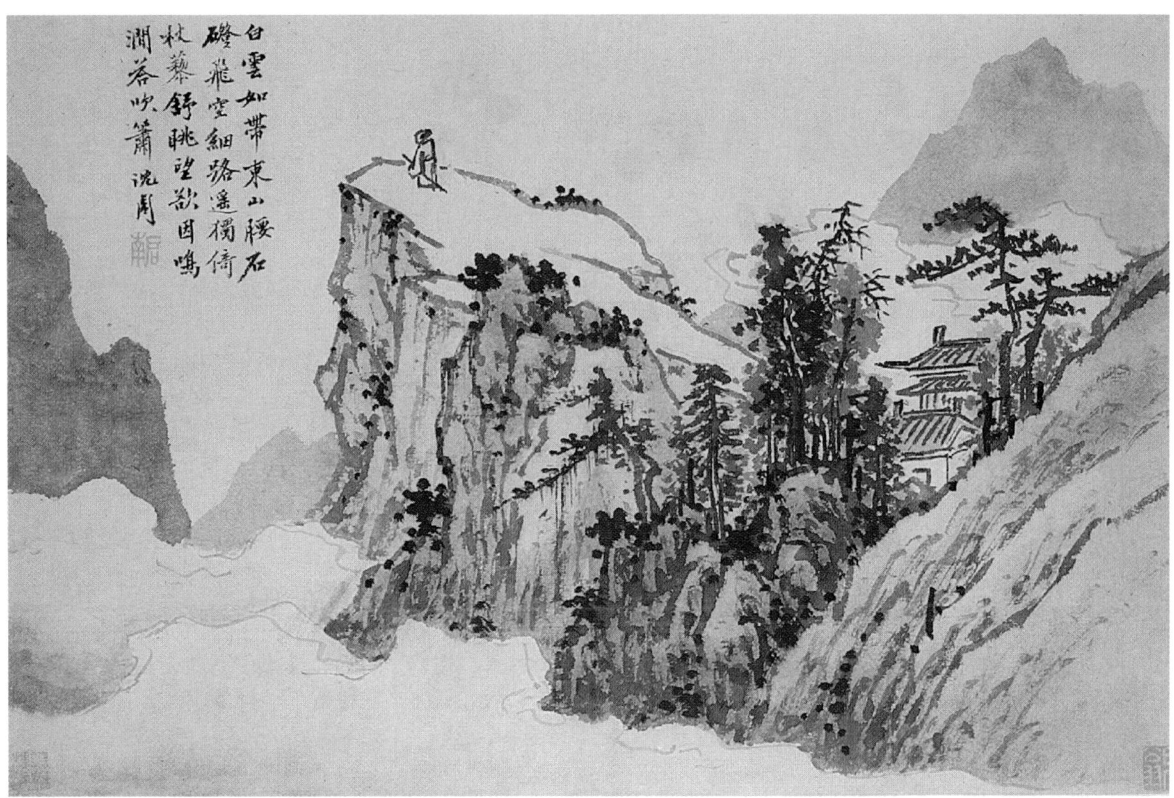

cepts behind "space" in Chinese painting.) While KINDRED SPIRITS draws the viewer's eye into and through the suggested deep space, POET ON A MOUNTAIN TOP leads the eye across (rather than into) space.

A third system for suggesting depth is isometric perspective, which is employed by engineers and is often used by traditional Eastern artists. In *isometric perspective,* parallel lines remain parallel; they do not converge as they recede. Instead, rectangular planes that turn away from the viewer are drawn as parallelograms. The illustration ISOMETRIC PERSPECTIVE (page 66) shows a cube drawn in isometric perspective. Industrial designers and architects also find isometric perspective useful because it enables them to maintain accurate measurements in working drawings. The detail from the Chinese hanging scroll EIGHTEEN SCHOLARS shows furniture and another hanging scroll in isometric perspective. Notice that INCIDENT IN A MOSQUE (page 60) shows isometric perspective in the top surfaces of the steps that lead up to the raised seat.

92 Shen Chou.
POET ON A MOUNTAIN TOP, (Chang-li yuan-t'iao).
Album leaf mounted as a handscroll.
Ink and light color on paper. 15¾" × 23¾".
The Nelson-Atkins Museum of Art, Kansas City, Missouri. Nelson Fund (46-51/2).

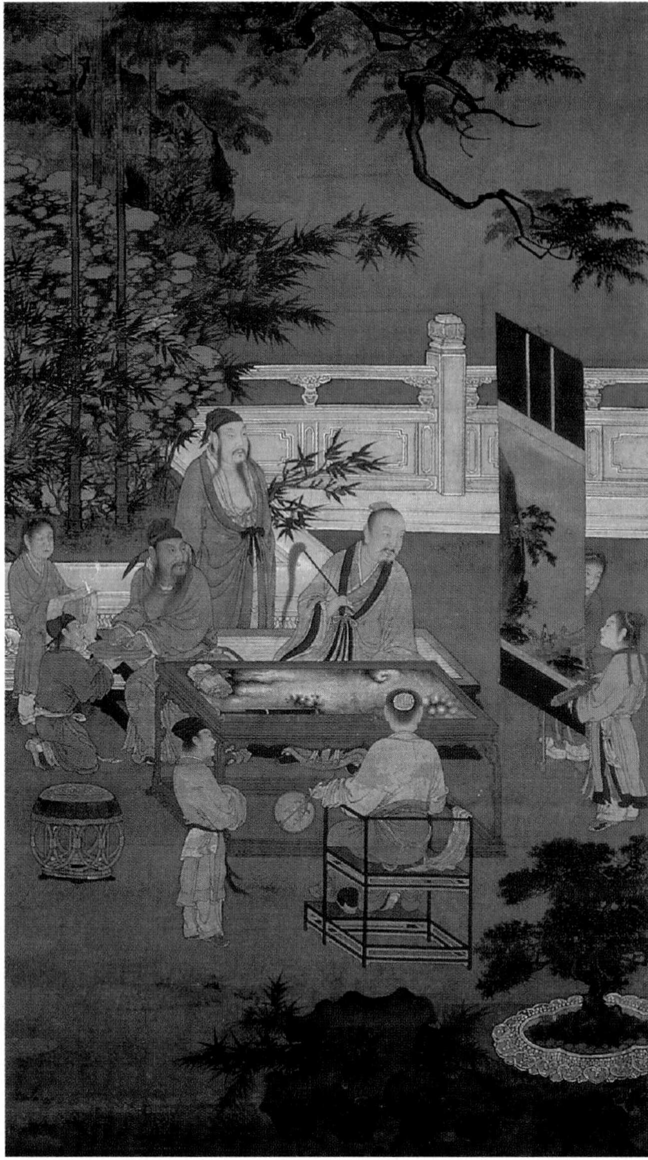

93 Anonymous.
Detail of EIGHTEEN SCHOLARS. Song Dynasty (960-1279).
Hanging scroll. Ink and color on silk. 174.1 cm × 103.1 cm.
National Palace Museum, Taipei, Taiwan.

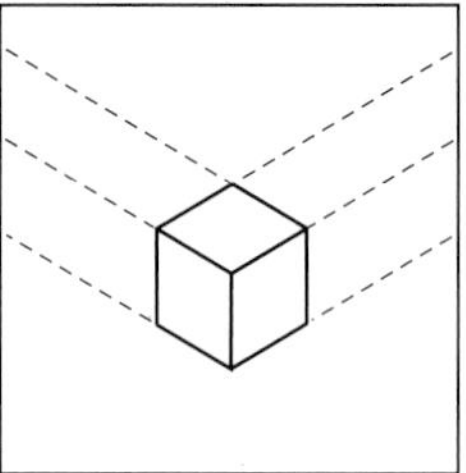

94 ISOMETRIC PERSPECTIVE.

Beyond Perspective For over four hundred years linear perspective has been used to suggest space in Western painting. The Renaissance concept of a painting as a window onto realistic space was not seriously challenged until the early twentieth century. The concept was reinforced first by the development of optical sighting devices and more recently by cameras and photographs. Today, our perception of linear perspective in photographs is so ingrained that it has become part of the way we see, sometimes making it difficult for us to appreciate the accomplishments of cultures that use other methods for depicting space.

At the end of the nineteenth century, European painters began to feel limited by the single vantage point that linear perspective enforces and found inspiration in the Asian approach to pictorial space. Of these artists, French painter Paul Cézanne was the most influential. In THE TURN IN THE ROAD, he constructed a kind of pictorial space that was unfamiliar to the Europeans of his time. Because the vantage point is high above the ground plane—as it usually is in Chinese paintings—we are not led into this painting as we were in Durand's landscape. Cézanne intentionally tipped up the road plane, making it a major shape in the composition, and he used more than one vantage point. We look *out* at the houses, but we look *down* at the road. Departing from the idea of a window view from one position, he adjusted the planes of houses, walls, and the road to strengthen the overall visual dynamics of his composition. The space implied in the painting is relatively shallow. Cézanne's goal was to reconcile in his own way the three dimensions of nature with the two dimensions of the picture plane. After four hundred years of the painting-as-a-window tradition, Cézanne's approach led Western artists to rethink pictorial space.

Thanks to the pioneering efforts of Cézanne and others, as well as our access to art from other cultures, linear perspective is today simply one of several spatial devices an artist may or may not choose to use. Many leading artists of the twentieth century have chosen to avoid illusions of depth in

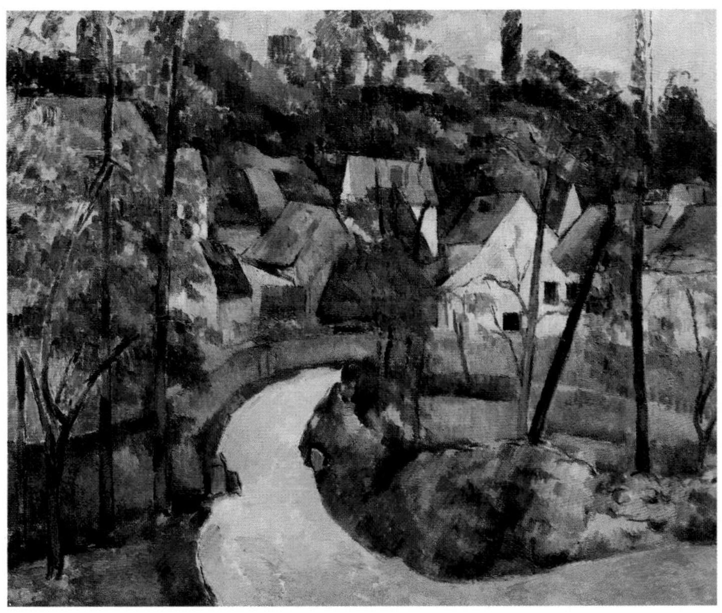

95 Paul Cézanne.
THE TURN IN THE ROAD. 1879-1882.
Oil on canvas. 23⅞" × 28⅞".
Bequest of John T. Spaulding. Courtesy, Museum of Fine Arts, Boston.

their work. It is a difference in intention rather than skill that results in various methods for depicting space in pictures.

In FIRE AT EVENING, Paul Klee avoided the use of linear perspective to create an illusion of three-dimensional space. The painting is one of a series he made after a trip to Egypt, where his imagination was stimulated by patterns of agriculture and by the glow of fires that were used for cooking, warmth, and light. Although no perspective system was used, this composition, inspired by landscape, has a subtle feeling of depth. The interaction of push and pull in space is suggested by the contrast between warm and cool, light and dark colors. Rhythmic bands of muted colors capture the magic of twilight and set off the advancing red-orange "fire." A glowing pink above an intense blue suggests the last fading light of day along the horizon. Klee achieved a feeling of landscape while maintaining the visual flatness of the picture plane.

Artists such as Paul Klee have reaffirmed the two-dimensional reality of the picture surface. They have used it to create spatial configurations, multiple views, and even a sense of time and motion relevant to the changing insights and concerns of our age (see pages 416–422).

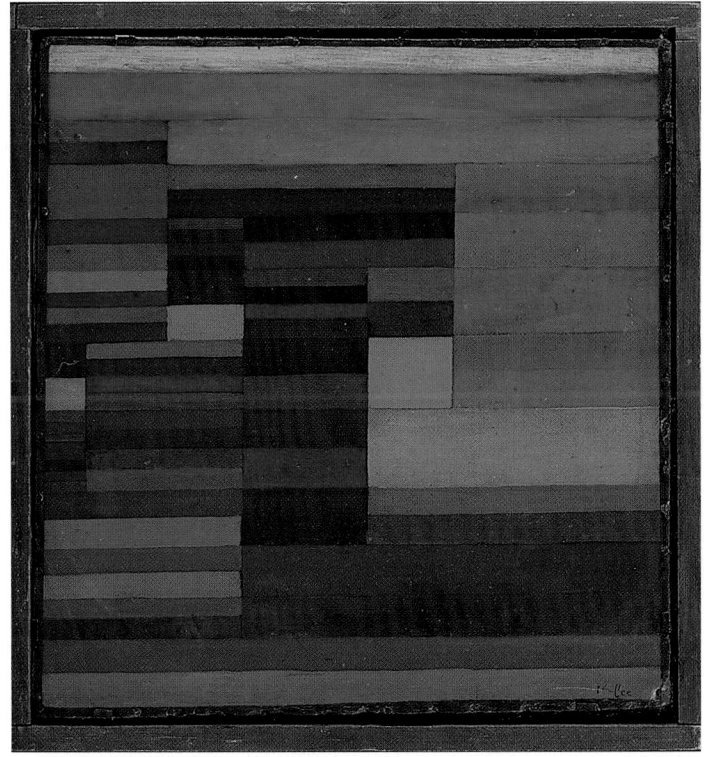

96 Paul Klee.
FIRE AT EVENING (FEUER ABENDS). 1929.
Oil on cardboard. 13⅜" × 13¼".
The Museum of Modern Art, New York. Mr. and Mrs. Joachim Jean Aberbach Fund.

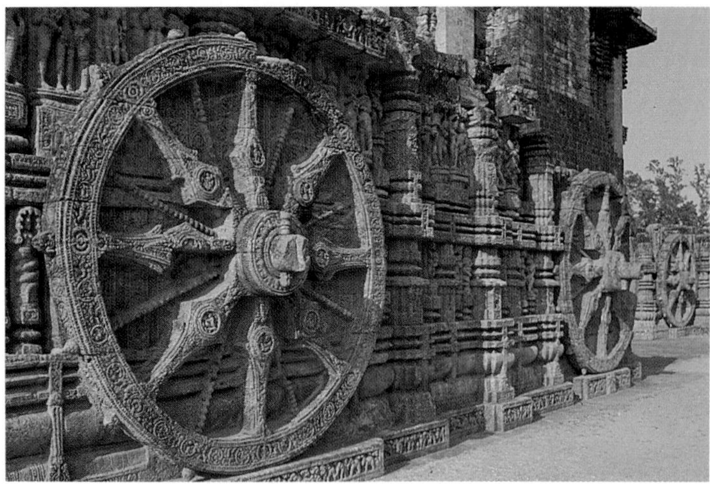

97 WHEELS OF THE SUN CHARIOT.
Surya Deul Temple, Konarak, India. c. 1240.
Photograph: Prithwish Neogy.

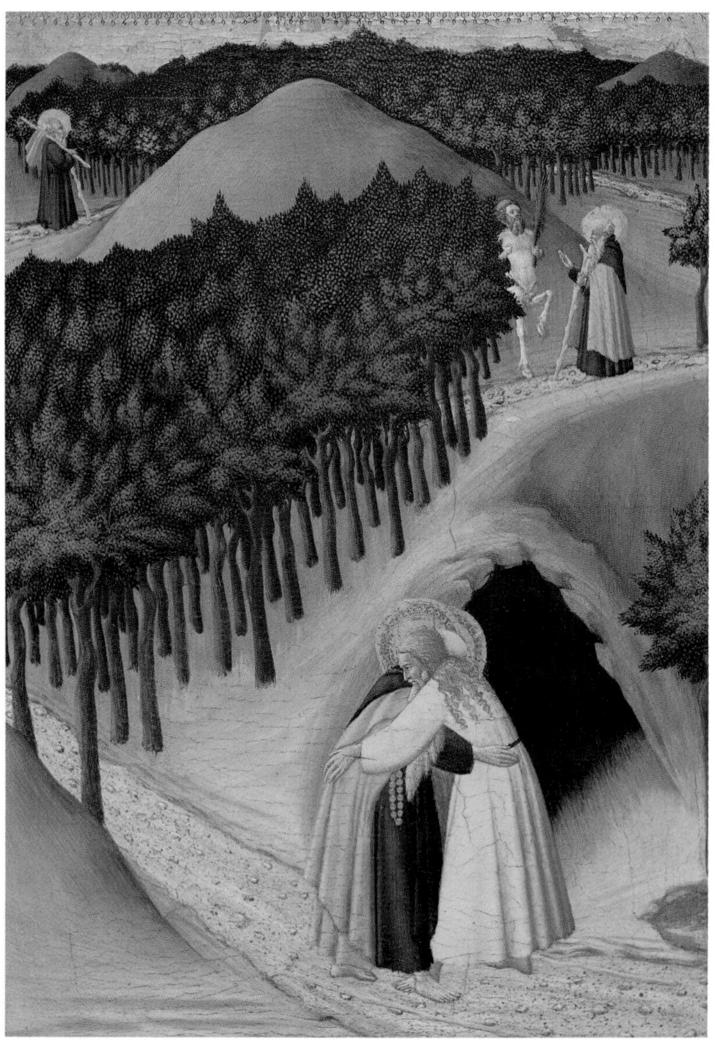

TIME AND MOTION

Time is a nonspatial continuum—the fourth dimension—in which events occur in succession. Because we live in a combined environment of space and time, our experience of time often depends on our movement in space and vice versa. Although time itself is invisible, it can be made perceptible in art. Time and motion become major elements in visual media such as film, video, and kinetic (moving) sculpture.

Many traditional Asian philosophies and religions teach that, ultimately, time is cyclic. The Wheel of the Law in Buddhism, which originated in ancient Hindu symbolism, stands for time seen in the cycle of the seasons; in the cycle of birth, death, and rebirth; and in longer cycles of celestial creation, preservation, dissolution, and re-creation. This view of time is one of the symbolic references expressed in WHEELS OF THE SUN CHARIOT of Surya Deul Temple at Konarak, India.

The Judeo-Christian tradition of Western culture teaches that time is linear—continually moving forward. Sassetta implied the passage of linear time in his painted narration of THE MEETING OF SAINT ANTHONY AND SAINT PAUL. The painting depicts key moments during Saint Anthony's progression through time and space, including the start of his journey in the city, which is barely visible behind the trees. He first comes into view as he approaches the wilderness; we next see him encountering the centaur; finally, he emerges into the clearing in the foreground, where he meets Saint Paul. The road upon which he travels implies continuous forward movement in time.

The comic strip is a contemporary narrative art form that also relies on implied sequential time. Consistency in the identifying features of the figures makes the illusion of passing time understandable. In comics, stories are read from left to right, with each panel framing a segment of the

98 Sassetta and Workshop of Sassetta.
THE MEETING OF SAINT ANTHONY AND SAINT PAUL. c. 1440.
Tempera on wood. 18¾" × 13⅝".

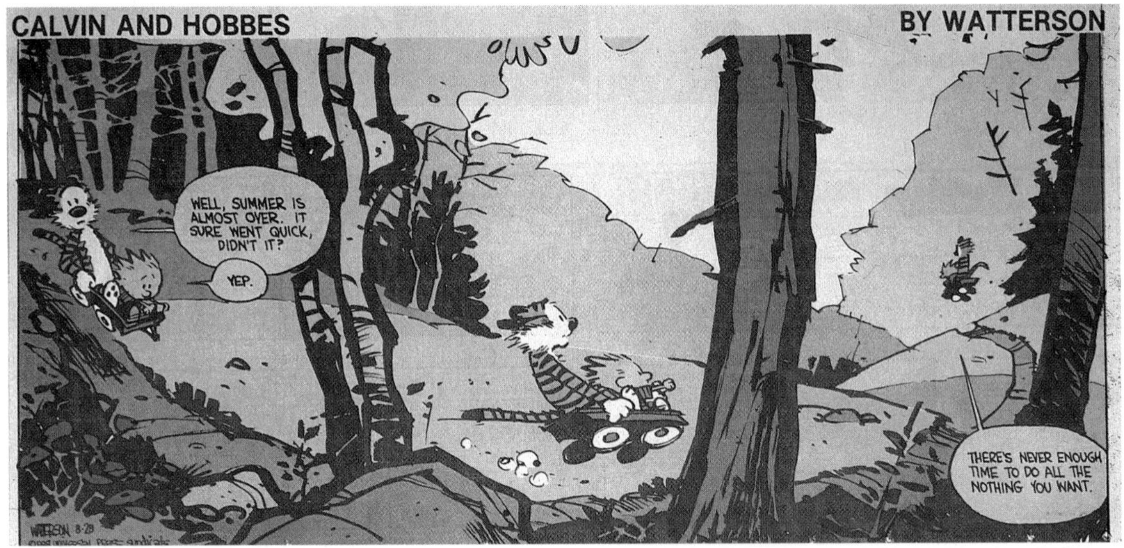

99 Bill Watterson. CALVIN AND HOBBES. 1989. Distributed by Universal Press Syndicate. Reprinted with permission.

action and indicating the passage of time. Bill Watterson often uses frames in his CALVIN AND HOBBES comic strips, but here he departed from this practice. Like Sassetta, he employed strategically placed trees to divide time into segments. Watterson drew Calvin and Hobbes moving rapidly, seen at three separate moments in time.

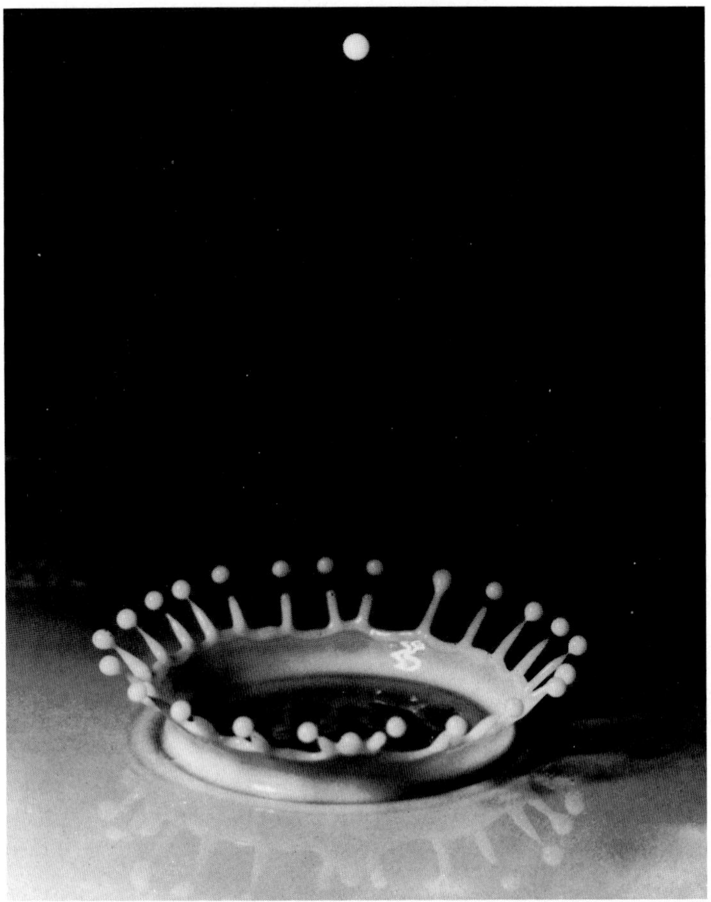

100 Harold Edgerton. MILK SPLASH RESULTING FROM DROPPING A BALL. 1936. Photograph.

Stopping Time

The desire to record events in time goes back to before written history. More recently this urge helped to inspire the development of photography. Initially, only static, inanimate objects could be photographed, but improvements in the process made it possible to photograph people standing or sitting very still; and by the end of the nineteenth century even a galloping horse could be photographed.

In the early twentieth century, electronics engineer Harold Edgerton explored the unseen world of things in high-speed motion. He invented the strobe light and pioneered its use in photography. In stroboscopic photography, light pulses flash on a moving subject at regular intervals in order to "stop" the action and record it (without blurring) on film. Such means have greatly increased our understanding of the changes in objects as they move. Edgerton's high-speed photograph of a MILK SPLASH (taken at one-millionth of a second) reveals

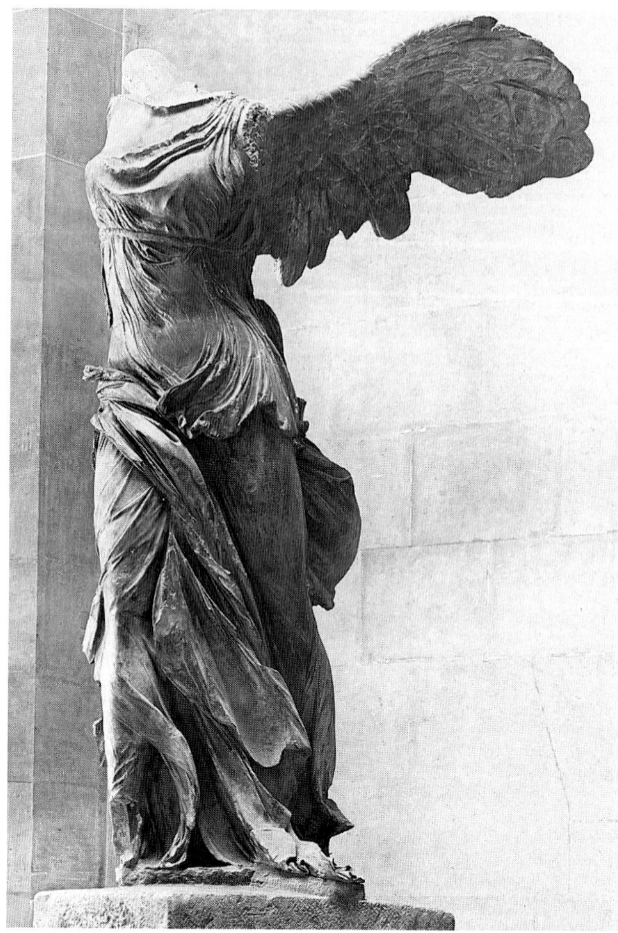

101 NIKE OF SAMOTHRACE. c. 200 B.C.
Musée du Louvre, Paris.

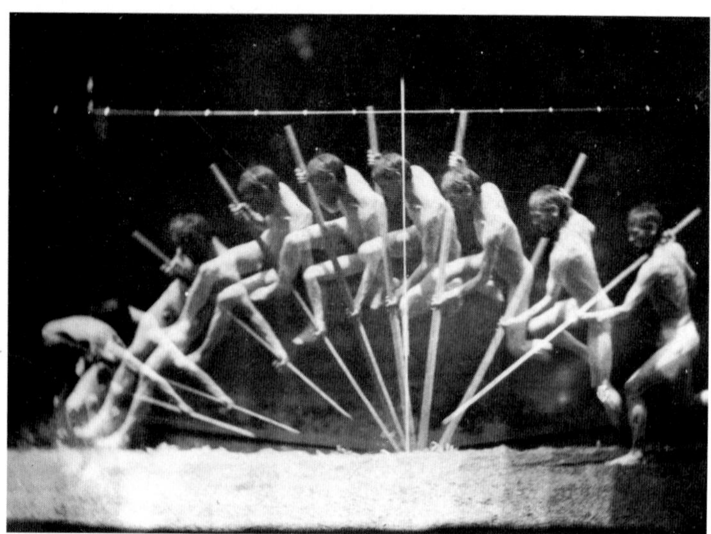

102 Thomas Eakins.
MAN POLE VAULTING. 1884.
Multiple-exposure photograph. 9.5 cm. × 12.3 cm.
The Metropolitan Museum of Art, New York. Gift of George Bregler, 1941 (41.142.11).

the beauty of the "crown" of a milk drop, which is not visible to the unaided human eye.

Manipulating Time

The word *movies* underscores the central feature of the filmmaker's art: the appearance of motion. In films, still pictures are shown at the rate of twenty-four images per second, creating the illusion of actual motion. Past, present, and future time can be implied and intermixed, and events that occur too quickly or too slowly to be perceived can be made visible by slowing them down or speeding them up. In both film and television, the impression of time can be compressed, expanded, run backwards, and rerun.

Implying Motion

To give a lifelike feeling, artists often search for ways to create a sense of movement. One of the world's most inspired depictions of movement is the (damaged) Greek marble carving known as NIKE OF SAMOTHRACE, in which the invisible force of wind seems to bring a dynamic quality of life and movement to the elegant and powerful form of Nike, Greek goddess of victory. More than two thousand years later, a twentieth-century sculptor took an abstract approach to depicting figures in motion (see page 425).

A sense of motion may be created by actual or implied changes in position. In 1884, American painter and pioneer photographer Thomas Eakins used a single camera and a movable photographic plate to capture sequential images that show the movements of a MAN POLE VAULTING. Eakins also designed a camera with revolving discs to produce stop-action stills, anticipating the principle of the motion picture camera.

Early multiple-exposure photographs of figures in motion influenced French artist Marcel Duchamp (see page 426) and Italian Futurist painter Giacomo Balla. In DYNAMISM OF A DOG ON A LEASH, Balla suggests movement through rhythmic repetition. (This method for showing motion is now often used by cartoonists.) His painting depicts the concept presented in the *Futurist Painting Technical Manifesto* of 1910:

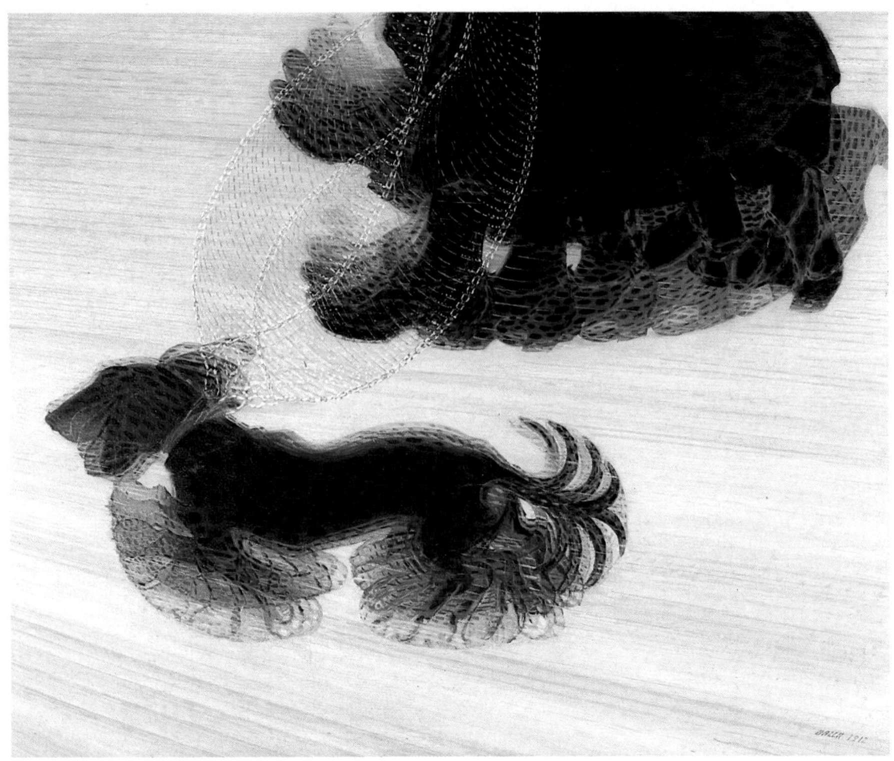

103 Giacomo Balla.
DYNAMISM OF A DOG ON A LEASH. 1912.
Oil on canvas. 35⅜" × 43¼".
Albright Knox Art Gallery, Buffalo, New York. Bequest of A. Conger Goodyear and gift of George F.Goodyear (1964).

In fact, all things move and run, all things change rapidly. The profile before our eyes is never static but constantly appears and disappears. Given the persistence of the image in the retina, moving objects are multiplied, changing their shapes as they pursue one another like lively vibrations across space.[3]

Actual Motion

Before the advent of electric motors, artists created moving sculpture by harnessing the forces of wind and water. Fountains as well as kites, banners, and flags have been popular since ancient times.

Alexander Calder's mobiles, such as BIG RED, rely on air movement to perform their subtle dances. Calder, a leading inventor of kinetic sculpture, was one of the first twentieth-century artists who made movement a major feature of their art.

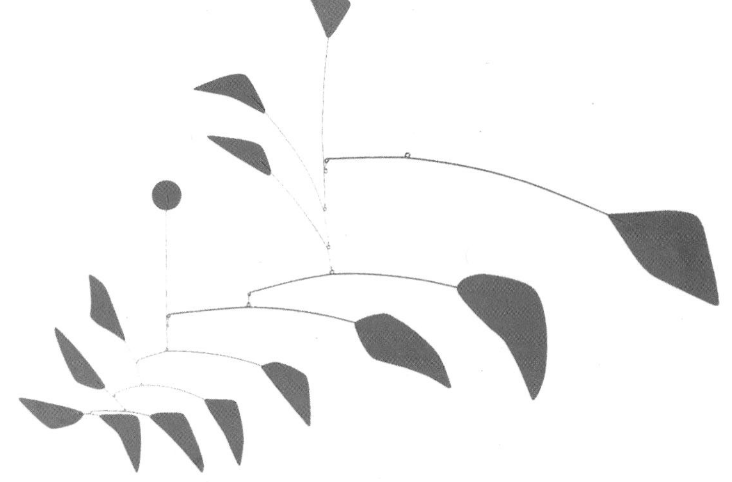

104 Alexander Calder.
BIG RED. 1959.
Painted sheet metal and steel wire.
74" × 114".
Collection of Whitney Museum of American Art, New York. Purchase, with funds from the Friends of the Whitney Museum of American Art (61.46).

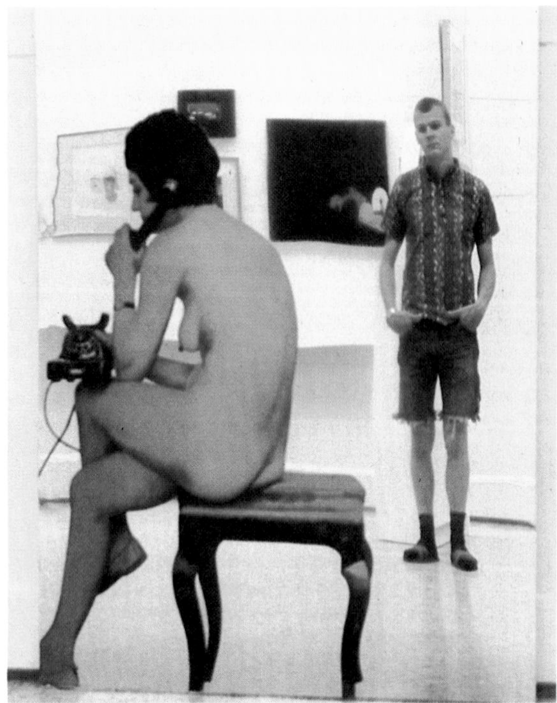

105 Michelangelo Pistoletto.
NUDE WOMAN TELEPHONING. 1965.
Paint on highly polished steel. Life-size figure.
Private collection.
Photographs: Basil Langton/Photo Researchers, Inc.
a With male viewer.

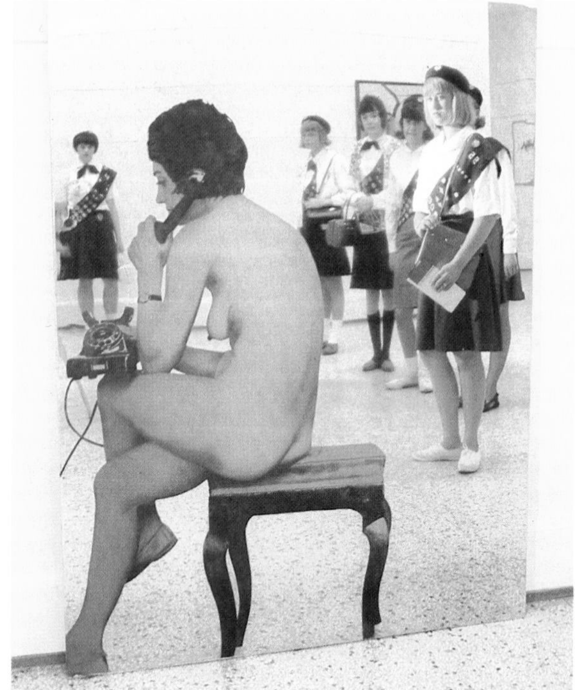

b With Girl Scouts.

Movement of the viewer is important in Michelangelo Pistoletto's NUDE WOMAN TELEPHONING. Pistoletto painted the figure on paper, then glued the painting to a reflective, stainless steel surface that acts as a mirror. The only way to suggest time and motion in a reproduction is to show Pistoletto's painting as seen at two different times. The nude woman continues telephoning, whether she is watched by a young man or by Girl Scouts. If we were there, we would see a variety of groupings and we would see actual motion—perhaps our own.

LIGHT

Our eyes are light-sensing instruments. Everything we see is made visible by the radiant energy we call light. Sunlight, or natural light, although perceived as white, actually contains all the colors of light that make up the visible part of the electromagnetic spectrum. Light can be directed, reflected, refracted (bent), diffracted, or diffused. The various types of artificial light include incandescent, fluorescent, neon, and laser. The source, color, intensity, and direction of light greatly affect the way things appear; as light changes, surfaces illuminated by it also appear to change.

Seeing Light

A simple shift in the direction of light dramatically changes the way we perceive the sculpture of ABRAHAM LINCOLN by Daniel Chester French. When the monumental figure was first installed in the Lincoln Memorial in Washington, D.C., the sculptor was disturbed by the lighting: the character of the Lincoln figure was radically altered by sunlight reflected from the floor of the entrance to the building. Light alone had changed the content of French's portrait from wise leader to frightened novice. The problem was corrected by placing spotlights in the ceiling above the statue. Because the spotlights are stronger than the natural light reflected from the white marble floor, they illuminate the figure with the kind of overhead light we are accustomed to seeing.

Light coming from a source directly in front of or behind objects seems to flatten three-dimensional form and emphasize shape. Light from above or from the side, and slightly in front, most clearly reveals the form of objects in space.

Implied Light

The mystical energy of light appears to radiate toward the viewer in Arnold Schmidt's UNTITLED painting. Here lines alone were used to imply light emanating from within the image.

In art terminology, *value* (sometimes called *tone*) refers to the relative lightness and darkness of surfaces. Value ranges from white through various grays to black. Value may be seen as a property of color or independent of color. Subtle relationships between light and dark areas determine how things look. To suggest the way light reveals form, artists use changes in value. A gradual shift from lighter to darker tones can give the illusion of a curving surface, while an abrupt value change usually indicates an abrupt change in surface direction.

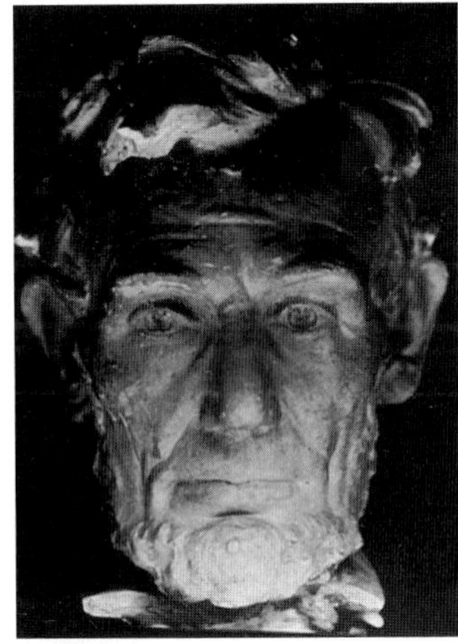

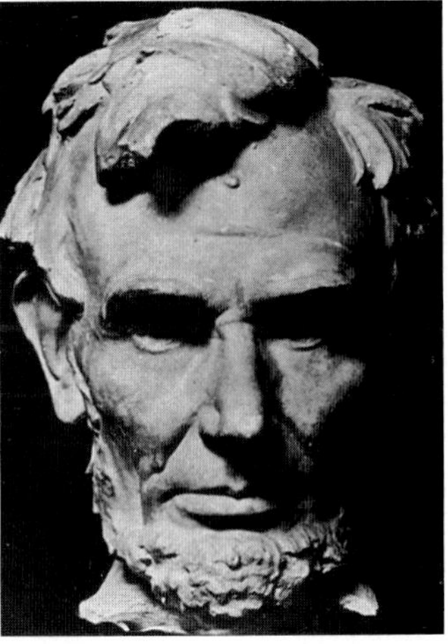

106 Daniel Chester French. Head of ABRAHAM LINCOLN demonstrating lighting problem. 1922.
a Original daylight.

b With the addition of artificial light.

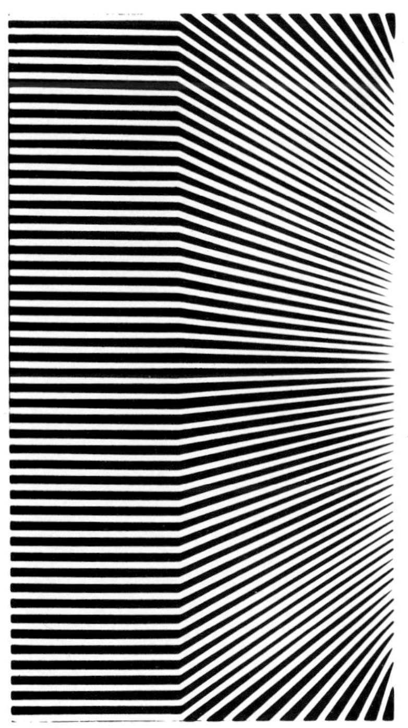

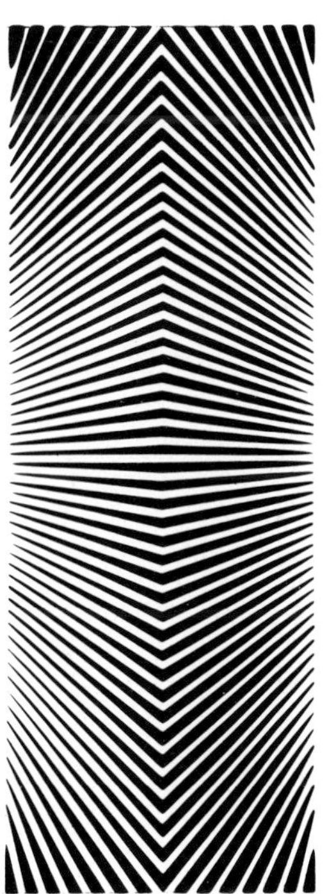

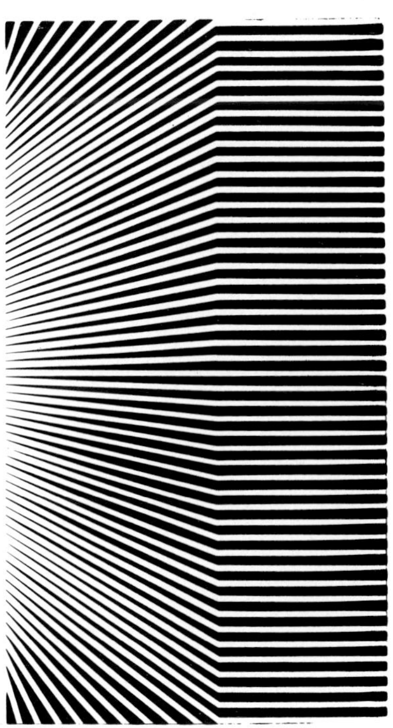

107 Arnold Schmidt
UNTITLED. 1965.
Synthetic polymer paint on canvas. 48⅛" × 8'⅛".
The Museum of Modern Art, New York. Gift of Mr. and Mrs. Herbert Bernard.

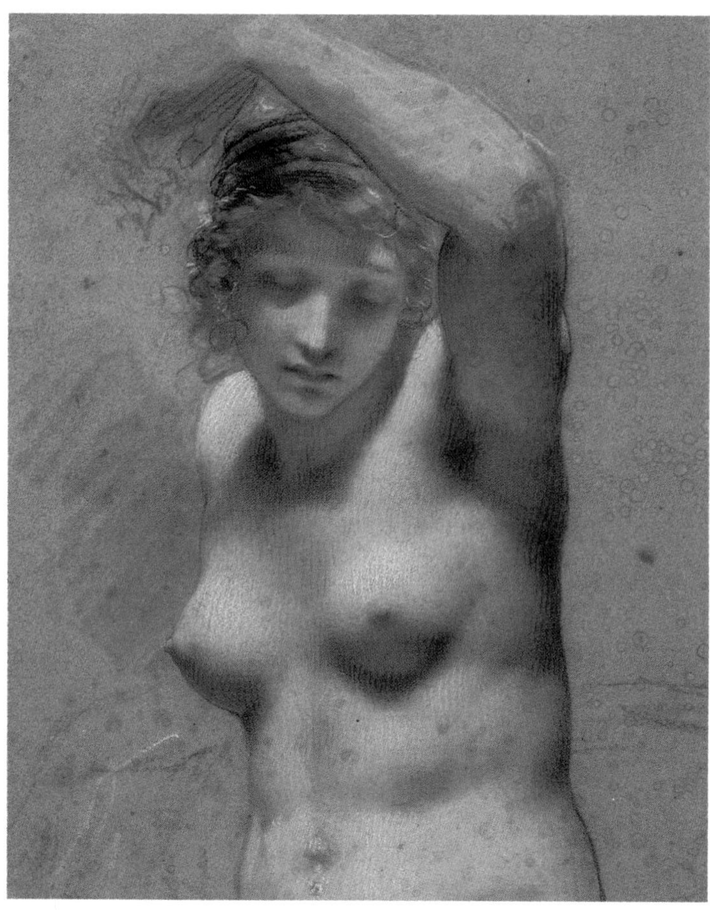

108 Pierre-Paul Prud'hon.
STUDY OF A FEMALE FIGURE. c. 1814.
Charcoal and black-and-white chalks on blue paper. 11" × 8¾".
Philadelphia Museum of Art. The Henry P. McIlhenny Collection in memory of Frances P. McIlhenny.

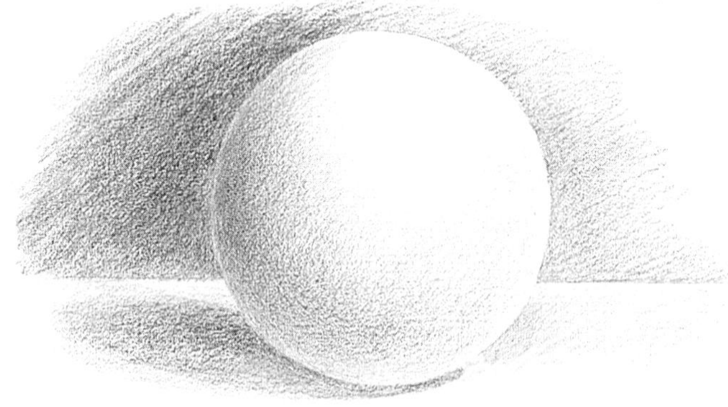

The diagram DARK/LIGHT RELATIONSHIPS shows that we perceive relationships rather than isolated forms: the gray bar has the same gray value over its entire length, yet it appears to change from one end to the other as the value of the background changes.

The DRAWING OF LIGHT ON A SPHERE illustrates *chiaroscuro*—the use of gradations of light and shade, in which forms are revealed by the subtle shifting from light to dark areas, without sharp outlines. This technique, developed in the Renaissance, makes it possible to create the illusion that figures and objects depicted on a flat surface appear as they do in natural light conditions. Chiaroscuro, originally an Italian word, is now used in English to describe the interaction of light and shade in two-dimensional art. The word's origins suggest its meaning: *chiaro* means light or clear, and *oscuro* means dark or obscure.

With black and white chalk on a middle-value blue-gray paper, Pierre-Paul Prud'hon used chiaroscuro to create the illusion of roundness in STUDY OF A FEMALE NUDE. Because the blue paper has a value between white and black, it acts as a connective value between the highlights and shadows. If you follow the form of the figure, you will see how it appears first as a light area against a dark background (note the right shoulder), then as a dark area against a lighter background (as in the underpart of the breast on the same side). The background remains the same, appearing first dark, then light.

Sometimes, as in the area between the shoulder and the breast on this figure, the edge of an object

109 DRAWING OF LIGHT ON A SPHERE.
Value gradations suggest light on a curving surface.

110 DARK/LIGHT RELATIONSHIPS.
Value scale compared to uniform middle gray.

will almost disappear when its value at that point becomes the same as the value behind it and the figure and ground appear to merge. Yet because we expect to see the form as continuous, our minds fill in the invisible line of the continuous edge.

The preoccupation with mass or solid form as revealed by light is a Western tradition—another bequest of Renaissance realism. Traditional Chinese and Japanese paintings, in contrast, make no use of pictorial modeling in light and shade (see page 300). When the Japanese first saw Western portraits, they wanted to know why one side of the face was dirty!

When gradations of value are minimized, images can take on a more forceful appearance. Without middle values, dark and light areas adjoin one another directly. The resulting strong contrast between light and dark gives a work dramatic impact that may be essential to its content. *Strong value contrast* emphasizes the tragic subject of Francisco de Zurbarán's SAINT SERAPION. In compositional terms, its major shape is a light rectangle against a dark background.

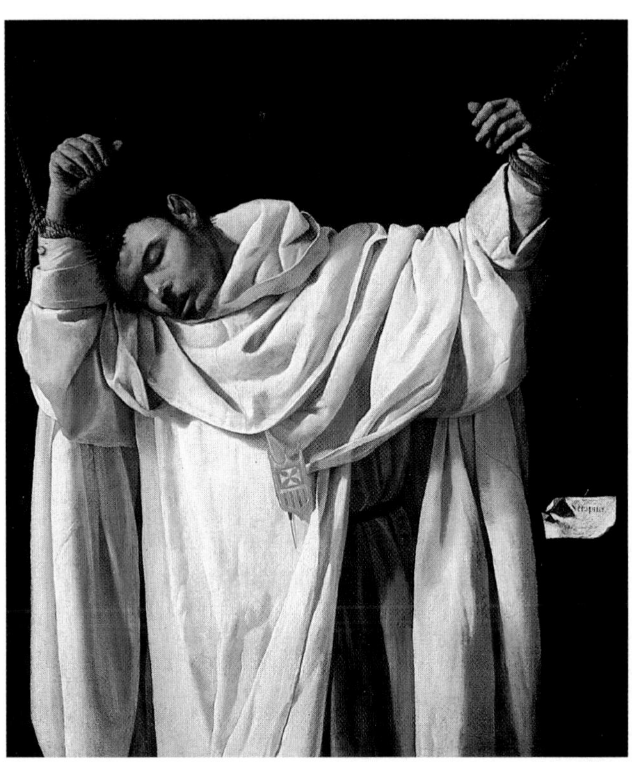

111 Francisco de Zurbarán.
SAINT SERAPION. 1628.
Oil on canvas. 47¼" × 41".
Wadsworth Atheneum, Hartford, Connecticut. The Ella Gallup Sumner and Mary Catlin Sumner Collection.

Minimal value contrast is a major aspect of Kasimir Malevich's WHITE ON WHITE. The simplicity of this unique painting is enhanced by the closely keyed value relationship of one white square placed on another. The simplicity of Malevich's painting calls attention to the visual quality of minimal value contrast. A subtle color shift between the cool square figure and its warm background plays a key role in the work. A very different example of minimal value contrast is INJURED BY GREEN by Richard Anuszkiewicz (see page 83). Both paintings have low value contrast; yet Malevich minimized color contrast, while Anuszkiewicz maximized it.

An image or space with minimal value contrast that uses light or high values exclusively is said to be *high key*; if it employs only dark or low values, the work is *low key.* The painting WHITE ON WHITE is high key. The terms high key and low key are also

112 Kasimir Malevich.
SUPREMATIST COMPOSITION: WHITE ON WHITE. 1918 (?).
Oil on canvas. 31¼" × 31¼".
The Museum of Modern Art, New York.

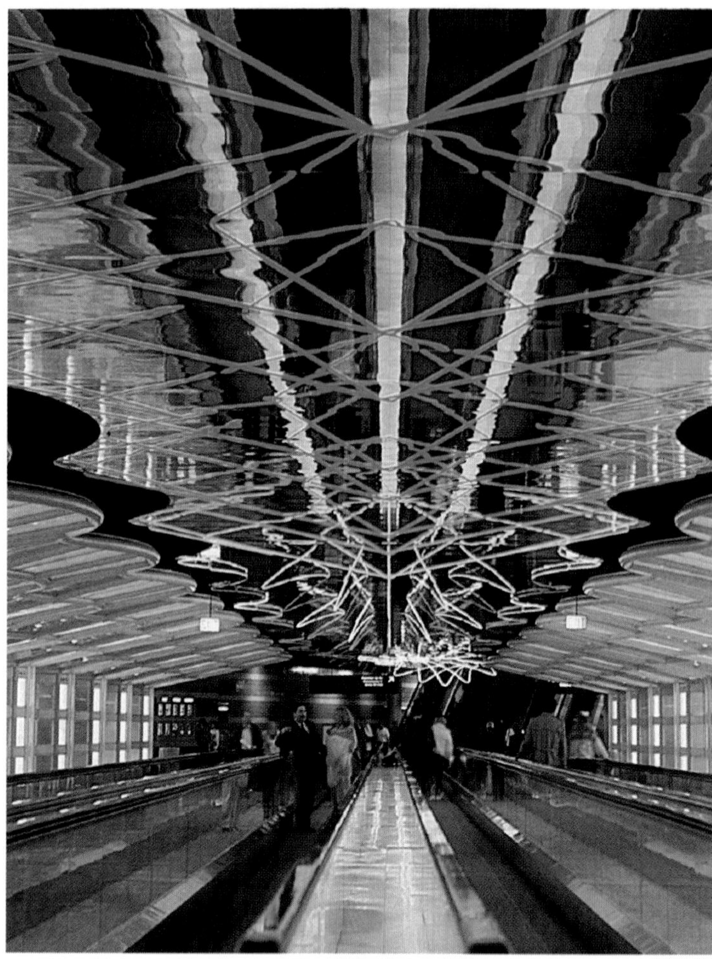

113 Michael Hayden.
SKY'S THE LIMIT. 1987.
United Airlines Terminals, O'Hare International Airport, Chicago. Neon tubes, mirrors, controlled by computers with synchronized music. Length 744'.
Photograph: Courtesy United Airlines.

used in interior design to refer to the combined effect achieved by limiting the values of wall and floor covering, furniture, and room illumination. Hospitals tend to be high key; bars tend to be low key.

Color, direction, quantity, and intensity of light strongly affect our moods, mental abilities, and general well-being. California architect Vincent Palmer has experimented with the color and intensity of interior light, and he has found that he can modify the behavior of his guests by changing the color of the light around them. Light quality affects people's emotions and physical comfort, thereby changing the volume and intensity of their conversations and even the lengths of their visits.

As light technology has developed, and people's awareness of the important functions of light have increased, lighting designers have become more important. Qualities of light must be carefully considered in most of the visual arts, but especially in photography, cinematography, television, stage design, architecture, and interior design.

Light as a Medium

Some contemporary artists use artificial light as their medium. Michael Hayden employs neon light with spectacular effect in his installation SKY'S THE LIMIT. The sculpture runs the entire length of the ceiling of an underground pedestrian walkway in the United Airlines Terminal at Chicago's O'Hare Airport. The work modifies space in a cycle of changing, moving light patterns, as neon tubes of colored light turn on and off in computer-timed sequences with musical accompaniment.

Light used in combination with visual media and sound has become of increasing interest to contemporary artists. Lighting has also become important in performances of all kinds, including rock concerts and videos.

COLOR

Color, a component of light, affects us directly by modifying our thoughts, moods, actions, and even our health. Psychologists, as well as designers of schools, offices, hospitals, and prisons, have acknowledged that colors can affect work habits and mental conditions. People surrounded by expanses of solid orange or red for long periods often experience nervousness and increased blood pressure. In contrast, some blues have a calming effect, causing blood pressure, pulse, and activity rates to drop to below normal levels.

Dressing in terms of our color preferences is one way we express ourselves. Leading designers of everything from clothing and cars to housewares and interiors recognize the importance of individual color preferences, and they spend considerable time and expense determining the colors of their products.

Most cultures use color symbolically, according to established customs. Leonardo da Vinci was influenced by earlier traditions when he wrote, "We shall set down for white the representative of light, without which no color can be seen; yellow for earth; green for water; blue for air; red for fire; and black for total darkness."[4]

In China and Japan, traditional painters have often limited themselves to black ink on white. Prior to the mid-nineteenth century, color was used in limited, traditional ways in Western art. In the 1860s and 1870s, influenced by the new science of color, the French Impressionist painters revolutionized the way we see and use color (see pages 114–115 and 387–390).

The Physics of Color

What we call "color" is the effect on our eyes of light waves of differing wavelengths or frequencies. When combined, these light waves make white light—the visible part of the electromagnetic spectrum. Individual colors are components of white light.

The phenomenon of color is a paradox: color exists only in light, but light itself seems colorless to the human eye. All objects that appear to have color are merely reflectors or transmitters of the colors that must be present in the light that illuminates them. In 1666, British scientist Sir Isaac Newton discovered that white light is composed of all the colors of the spectrum. He found that when the white light of the sun passes through a glass prism, it is separated into the bands of color that make up the *visible spectrum.*

Because each color has a different wavelength it travels through the glass of the prism at a different speed. Red, which has the longest wavelength, travels more rapidly through the glass than blue, which has a shorter wavelength. A rainbow results when sunlight is refracted and dispersed by the spherical forms of raindrops, producing a combined effect like that of the glass prism. In both cases, the sequence of spectral colors is: red, orange, yellow, green, blue, indigo, and violet.

Pigments and Light

Our common experience with color is provided by light reflected from pigmented surfaces. Therefore the emphasis in the following discussion is on pigment color rather than on color coming from light alone.

When light illuminates an object, some of the light is absorbed by the surface of the object and some is reflected. The color that appears to our eyes as that of the object (called *local color* or *object color*) is determined by the wavelengths of light being reflected. Thus a red surface illuminated by white light (full-spectrum light) appears red, because it reflects mostly red light and absorbs the rest of the spectrum. A green surface absorbs most of the spectrum except green, which it reflects; and so on with all the hues.

When all the wavelengths of light are absorbed by a surface, the object appears black; when all the wavelengths are reflected, the surface appears white. Black and white are not true colors: white, black, and their combination, gray are *achromatic* (without the property of hue) and are often referred to as *neutrals.*

Each of the millions of colors human beings can distinguish is identifiable in terms of just three

114 COLOR INTENSITY AND VALUE.
From the book *The Elements of Color* by Johannes Itten.
New York: Van Nostrand Reinhold, New York.

variables: hue, value, and intensity.

- *Hue* refers to a particular wavelength of spectral color to which we give a name. Colors of the spectrum—such as yellow and green—are called hues.
- *Value* refers to relative lightness or darkness from white through grays to black. Pure hues vary in value. On the COLOR INTENSITY AND VALUE chart, pure hues are aligned with their equivalent gray on the value scale (left column). Hues in their purest forms are also at their usual values. Pure yellow is the lightest of hues; violet is the darkest. Red and green are middle-value hues. Black and white pigments can be important ingredients in changing color values. Black added to a hue produces a *shade* of that hue. For example, when black is added to orange, the result is a brown; when black is mixed with red, the result is maroon. White added to a hue produces a *tint.* Lavender is a tint of violet; pink is a tint of red.
- *Intensity,* also called *saturation* or *chroma,* refers to the purity of a hue or color. A pure hue is the most intense form of a given color; it is the hue at its highest saturation, in its brightest form. With pigment, if white, black, gray, or another hue is added to a pure hue, its intensity diminishes and the color is thereby dulled.

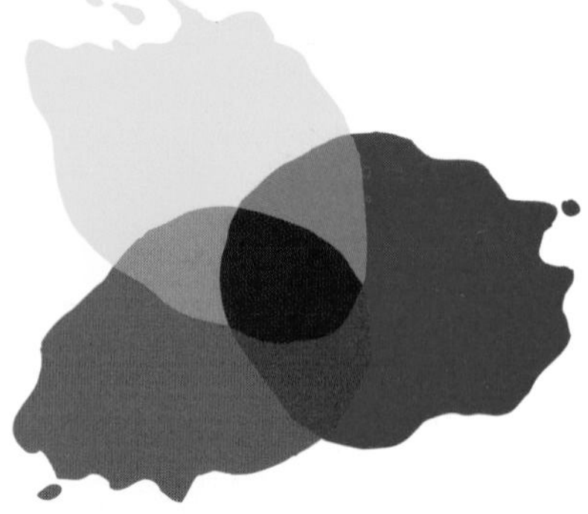

115 PIGMENT PRIMARIES: SUBTRACTIVE COLOR MIXTURE.

When the pigments of different hues are mixed together, the mixture appears duller and darker because pigments absorb more and more light as their absorptive qualities combine. For this reason, pigment mixture is called *subtractive color mixture.* Mixing red, blue, and yellow will produce a dark gray, almost black, depending on the proportions and the type of pigment used.

Most people are familiar with the three PIGMENT PRIMARIES: red, yellow, and blue. Printers use *magenta* (red), *yellow,* and *cyan* (blue) because magenta and cyan provide the specific purplish red and greenish blue that work best for four-color printing.

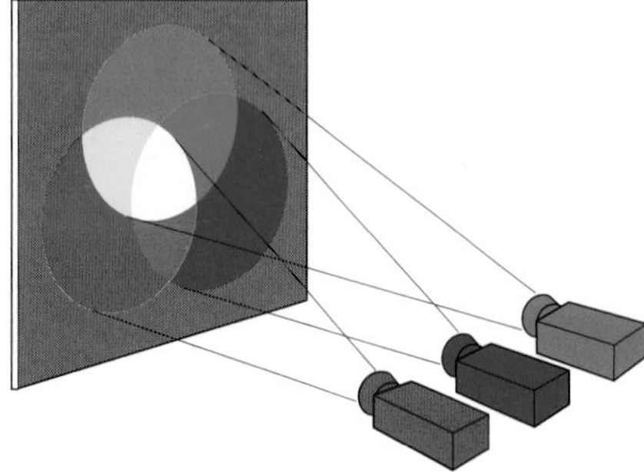

116 LIGHT PRIMARIES: ADDITIVE COLOR MIXTURE.

A lesser-known triad is the three LIGHT PRIMARIES: red, green, and blue or blue-violet—actual electric light colors that produce white light when combined. Such a mixture is called *additive color mixture.* Combinations of the light primaries produce lighter colors: red and green light, when mixed, make yellow light. Color television employs additive color mixture.

The Color Wheel

Several major pigment color systems are in use today, each with its own basic hues. The *color wheel* is a twentieth-century version of the circle concept first developed in the seventeenth century by Sir Isaac Newton. After Newton discovered the spectrum, he found that both ends could be combined into the hue red-violet, making the color wheel concept possible. Numerous color systems have followed since that time. The color system we show is based on twelve pure hues and can be divided into the following groups:

- *Primaries:* red, yellow, and blue. These are the pigment hues that cannot be produced by an intermixing of other hues. They are also referred to as primary colors.
- *Secondaries:* orange, green, and violet. The mixture of two primaries produces a secondary hue. Secondaries are placed on the color wheel between the two primaries of which they are composed. When we mix secondaries ourselves, they do not have the brilliance of oranges, greens, and violets manufactured from pigments specifically chosen to produce those pure hues.
- *Intermediates:* red-orange, yellow-orange, yellow-green, blue-green, blue-violet, and red-violet. Each intermediate is located between the primary and the secondary of which it is composed.

The blue-green side of the wheel is *cool* in psychological temperature, and the red-orange side is *warm.* Yellow-green and red-violet are the poles dividing the color wheel into warm and cool hues. The difference between warm and cool colors may come chiefly from psychological association. We can see relative warm and cool differences in any combination of hues. Color affects our feelings about size and distance as well as temperature. Cool colors appear to contract and recede; warm colors appear to expand and advance, as in the WARM/COOL COLORS diagram. See also Klee's painting FIRE AT EVENING on page 67.

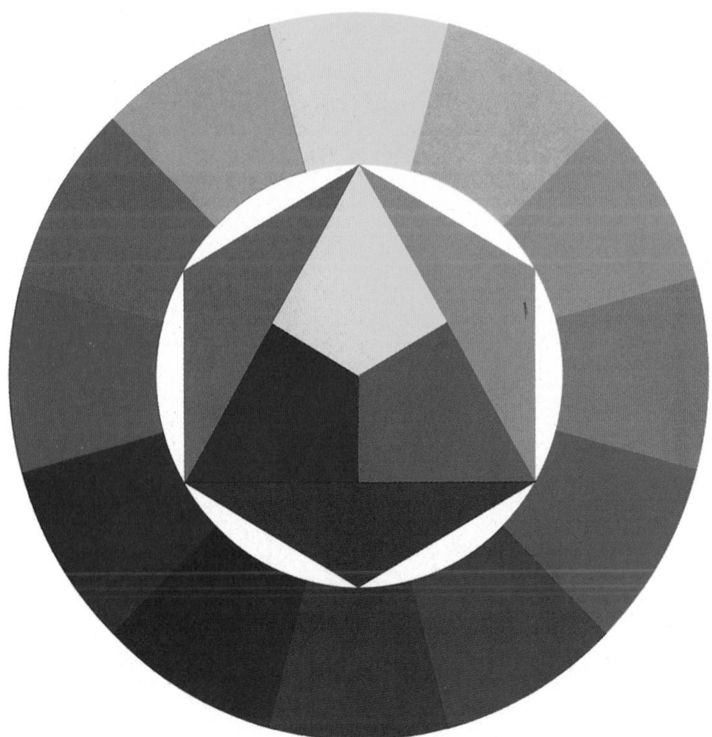

117 COLOR WHEEL.
From the book *The Elements of Color* by Johannes Itten.
New York: Van Nostrand Reinhold, New York.

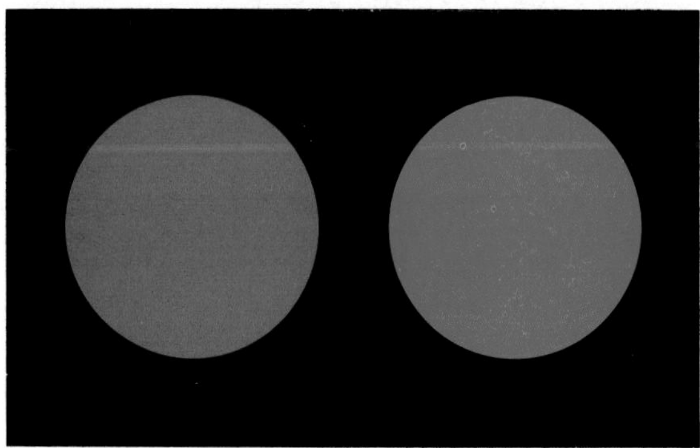

118 WARM/COOL COLORS.

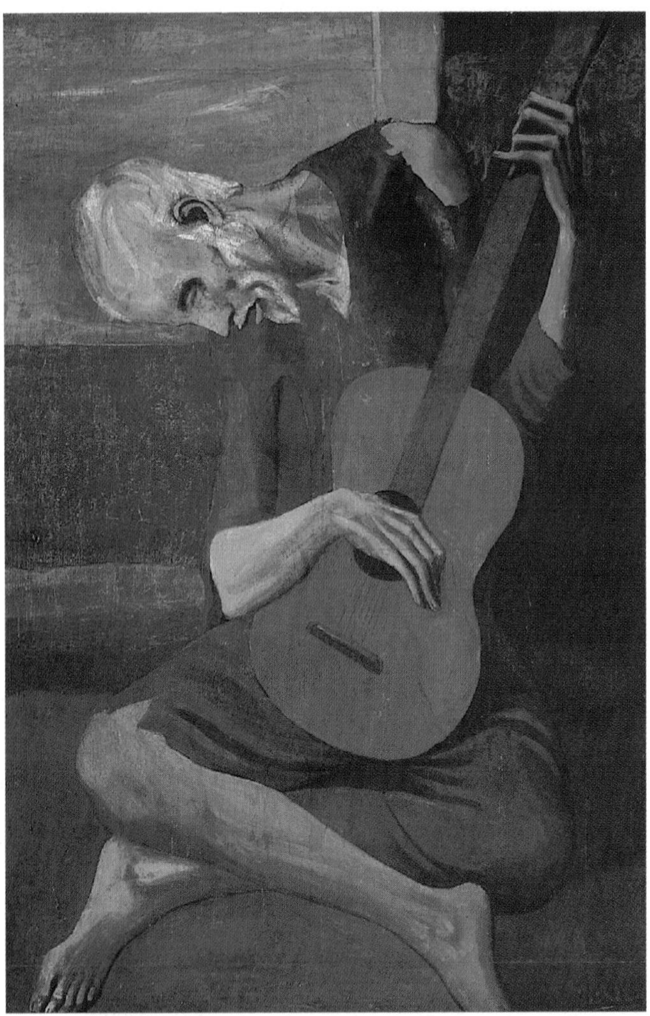

119 Pablo Picasso.
THE OLD GUITARIST. 1903.
Oil on panel. 122.9 cm × 82.6 cm.
Helen Birch Bartlett Memorial Collection, (1926.253).

Color sensations more vibrant than those achieved with actual pigment mixture can be obtained when dots of pure color are placed together so that they blend in the eye and mind, creating the appearance of other hues. This is called *optical color mixture.* For example, we see rich greens when many tiny dots or strokes of yellow-green and blue-green are placed close together.

Painter Georges Seurat developed this concept in the 1880s as a result of his studies of Impressionist paintings and recent scientific discoveries of light and color. He wanted his paintings to capture the brilliance and purity of natural light. Seurat called his method divisionism; it is now usually called *pointillism.* The result is similar to modern four-color printing, in which tiny dots of ink in the printer's three primary colors—magenta (a bluish red), yellow, and cyan (a greenish blue)—are printed together in various amounts with black ink on white paper to achieve the effect of full color. Seurat, however, used no black. Compare the detail of Seurat's A SUNDAY ON LA GRANDE JATTE with the color separations and the enlarged detail of the reproduction of Botticelli's BIRTH OF VENUS. (The complete paintings appear on pages 395 and 346.) The eye perceives subtle blends as it optically mixes tiny dots of intense color in both Seurat's painting and four-color printing.

Color groupings that provide distinct color harmonies are called *color schemes.* The most common color schemes are monochromatic, analogous, and complementary.

Monochromatic: Monochromatic color schemes are based on variations in the value and intensity of a single hue. In a monochromatic scheme, a pure hue is used alone with black and/or white, or mixed with black and/or white. Picasso's THE OLD GUITARIST is a monochromatic painting that employs tints and shades of blue that are set off by the neutral grayish brown of the guitar. This is one of a series of predominantly blue paintings Picasso made in his early twenties. During his own period of poverty and struggle, Picasso identified with and depicted the poverty and suffering of the poor in

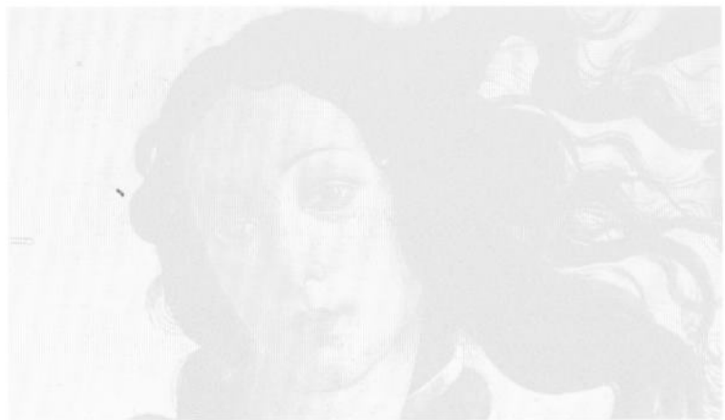

a Yellow.

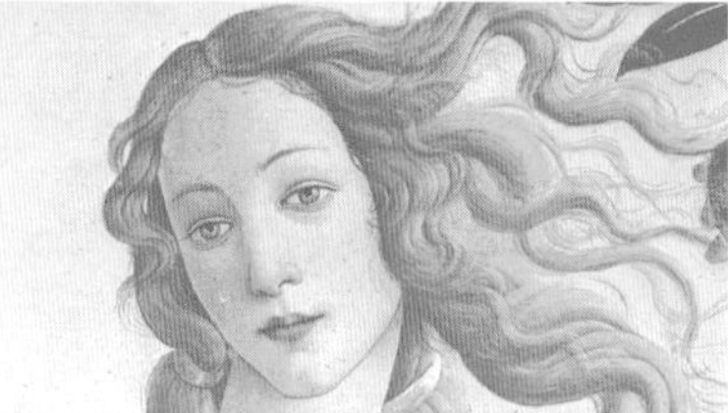

b Magenta.

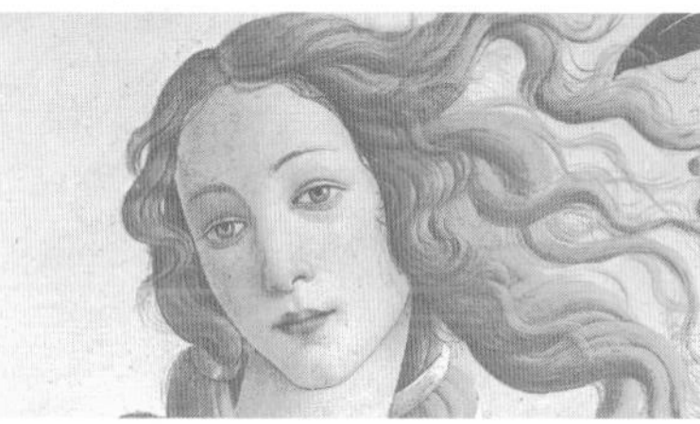

c Yellow and magenta.

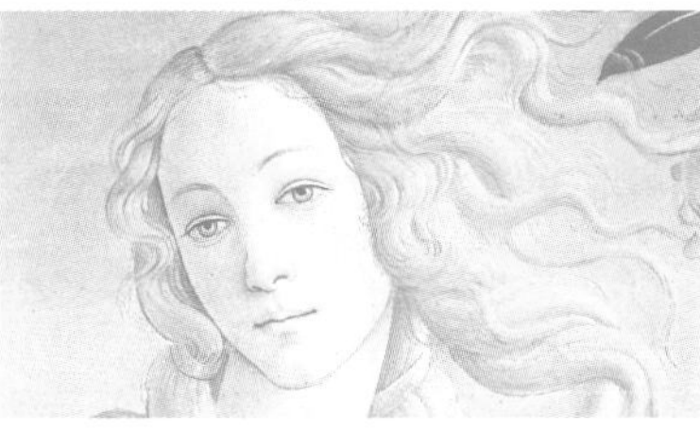

d Cyan.

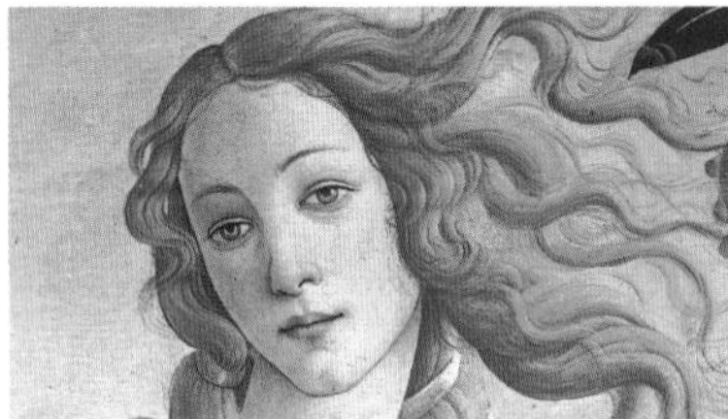

e Yellow, magenta, and cyan.

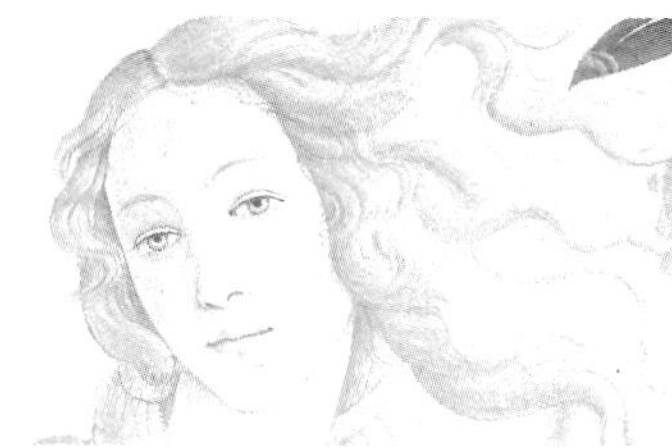

f Black.

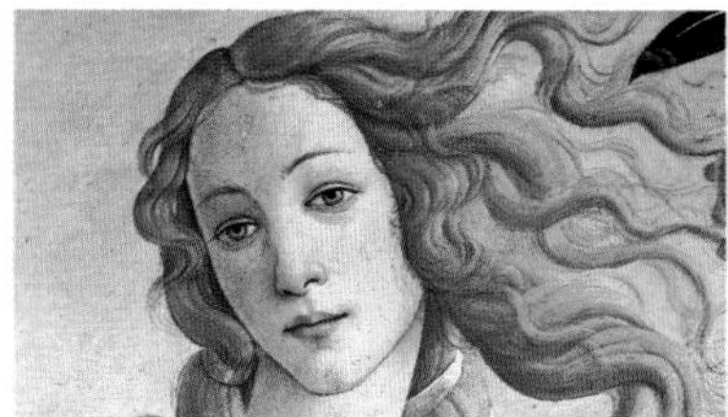

g Yellow, magenta, cyan, and black.

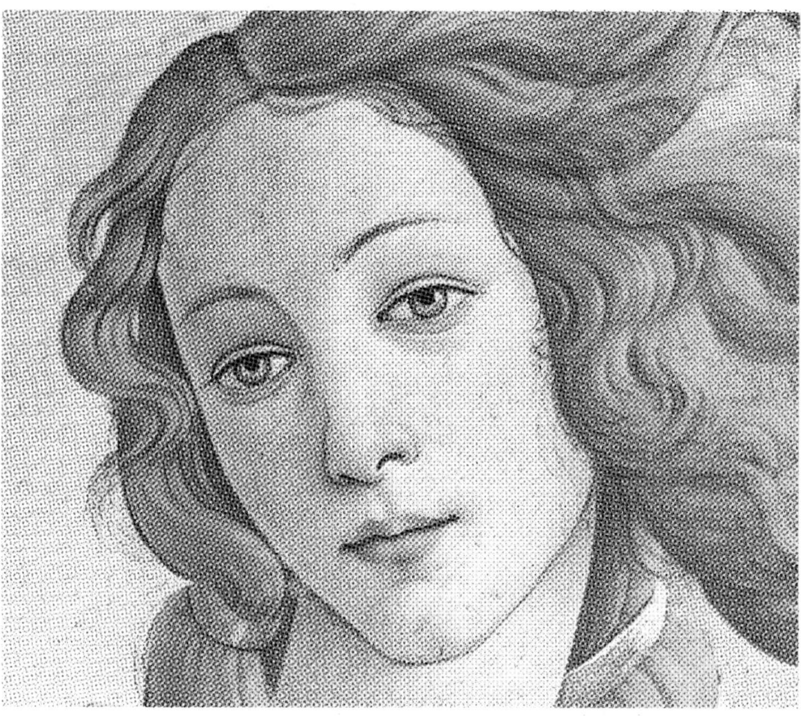

120 COLOR PRINTING
h Color printing detail of Botticelli's BIRTH OF VENUS showing mechanical dot pattern of offset photolithography. (See complete painting on page 346)

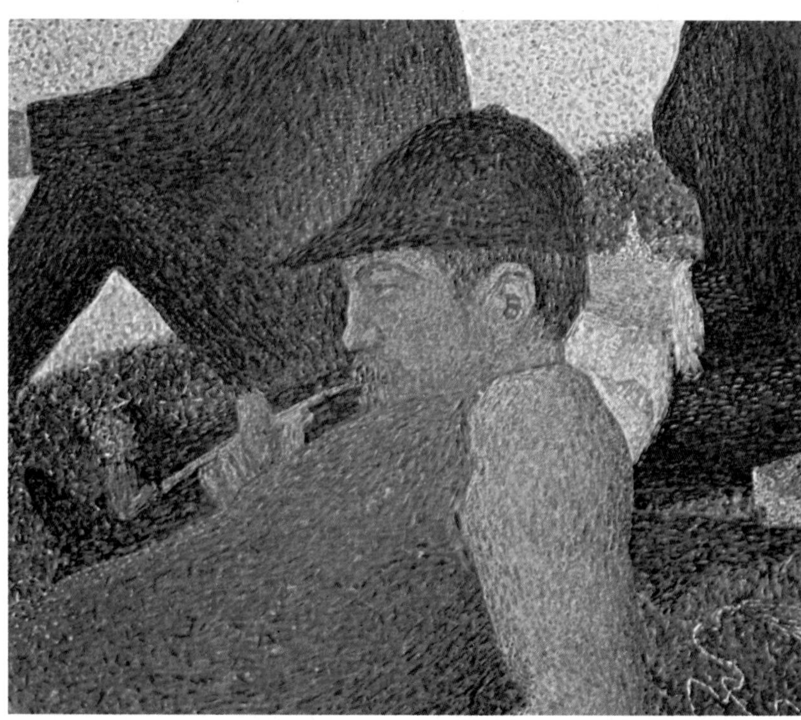

121 OPTICAL COLOR MIXTURE.
Detail of Seurat's A SUNDAY ON LA GRANDE JATTE showing divisionist technique. (See complete painting on page 395.)

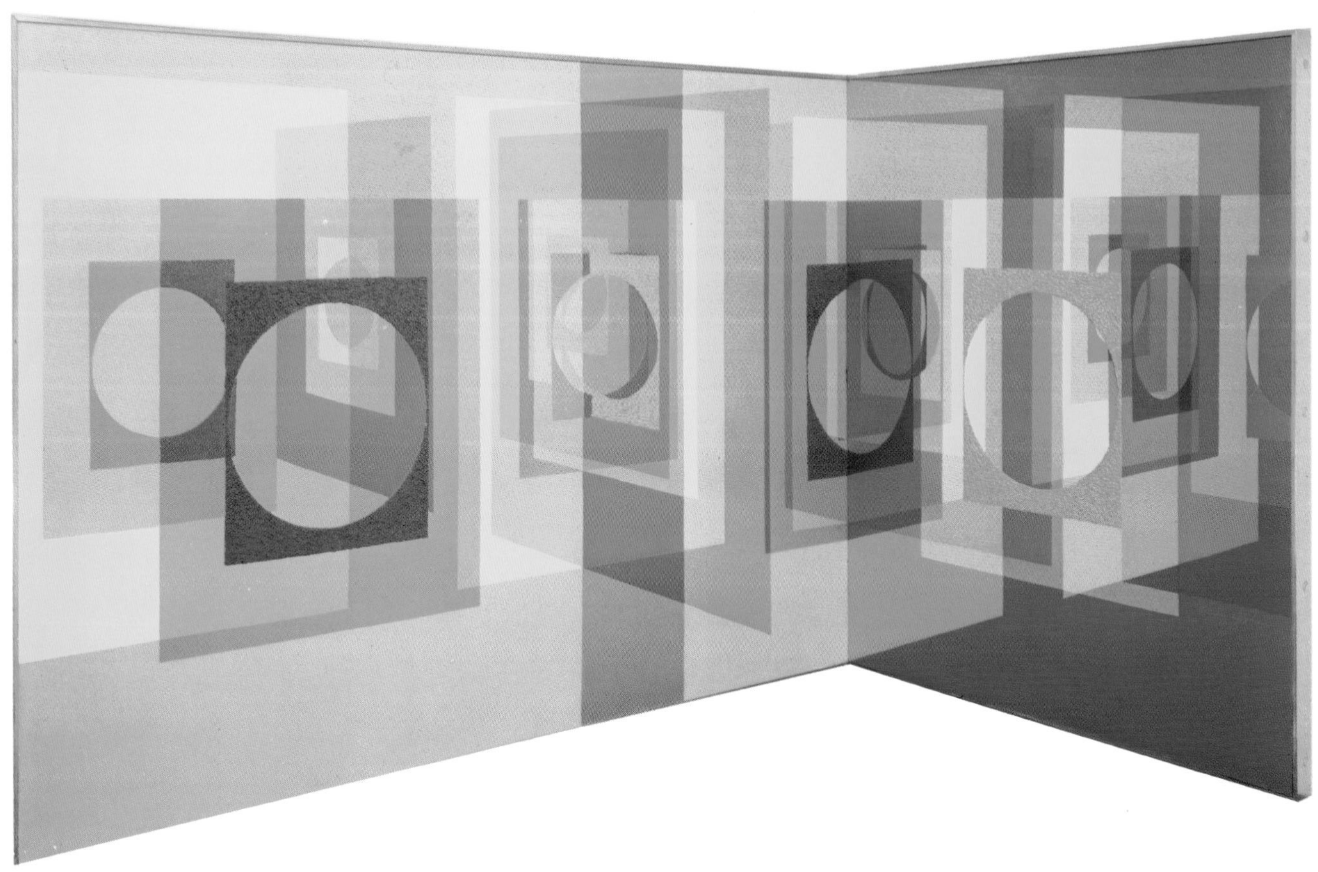

122 Ben Cunningham.
CORNER PAINTING. 1948-1950.
Oil on canvas. 25½" × 36½"; 25½" × 21½".
Collection of Mrs. Ben Cunningham.

his neighborhood. The pervasive blue color heightens the melancholy mood conveyed by the posture and distortions of the figure.

Analogous: Analogous color schemes are based on colors adjacent to one another on the color wheel, each containing the same pure hue, such as a color scheme of yellow-green, green, and blue-green. Ben Cunningham's CORNER PAINTING contains the analogous colors yellow, yellow-orange, orange, and red-orange and neutral or achromatic browns. Tints and shades of each analogous hue may be used to add variations to this color scheme. Cunningham transcended the usual rectangular format in CORNER PAINTING, where his manipulation of color relationships and his precise perspective give an illusion of depth. In this one painting, Cunningham mastered the spatial effects of color as transparent film, as hollow volume, and as impenetrable surface. One can look at, through, and into Cunningham's painting.

Complementary: Complementary color schemes emphasize two hues directly opposite each other on the color wheel, such as red and green. When mixed together in almost equal amounts, complementary hues form neutral grays; but when placed side by side as pure hues, they contrast strongly and intensify each other. Because they can be identical in value, the complementary hues red-orange and blue-green tend to "vibrate" more when placed next to each other than do other complements. The complements yellow and violet provide the strongest value contrast possible with pure hues.

The complement of a primary is the opposite secondary, which can be obtained by mixing the other two primaries. For example, the complement of yellow is violet. The interaction of the complementary hues red and green is the dominant feature of the painting INJURED BY GREEN by Richard Anuszkiewicz.

It should be noted that these examples provide only a basic foundation in color theory. Most artists work intuitively with color harmonies more complex than the schemes described above.

The Optical Effect of Color

A color can appear to change as colors around it are changed. In INJURED BY GREEN, Richard Anuszkiewicz painted a uniform pattern of dots in two sizes. Behind them, the red-orange background appears to change, but it is the same color throughout.

Intensity builds from the outer edges of the painting toward the center, where we are "injured"—temporarily color-blinded—by a diamond-shaped area containing yellow-green dots of the same value as the red background. The diamond is surrounded by a square of blue-green dots. These two hues are on either side of green on the color wheel—and green is the complement of red. The yellow-green and blue-green form the split complements of red. Thus Anuszkiewicz used split complements of matching value to give this central area its pulsing energy.

The eye sees an *afterimage* when prolonged exposure to a visual form causes excitation and subsequent fatigue of the retina. Color afterimages are caused by partial color blindness temporarily induced in the normal eye when some of its color receptors (cones) become fatigued and are therefore desensitized. For example, staring at a red spot for thirty seconds under a bright white light will tire the red receptors in that segment of the retina on which the red spot is focused, rendering the viewer less sensitive to red light, or partially red-blind. When the red spot is removed, the eye sees a blue-green spot on the white surface because the tired red receptors react weakly to the red light reflected by that area of the surface. The blue and green

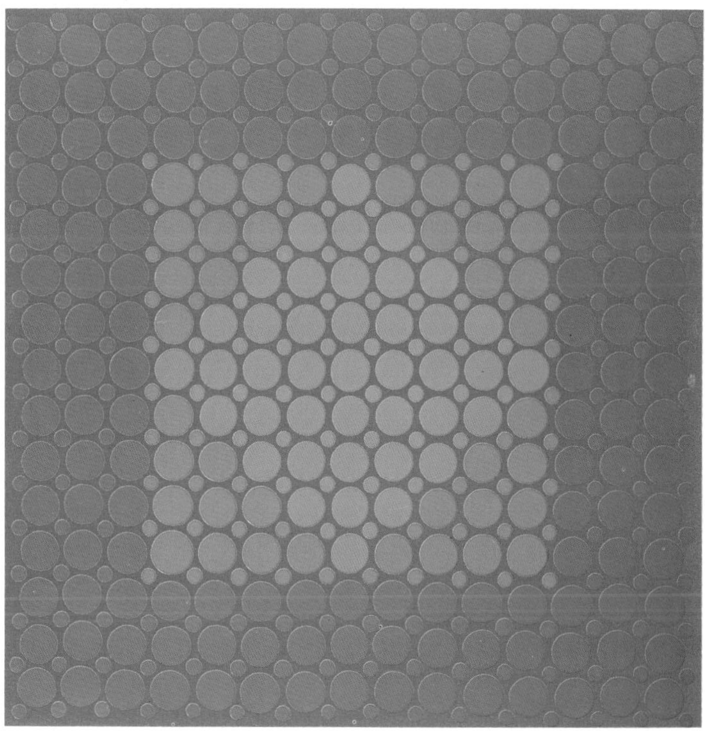

123 Richard Anuszkiewicz.
INJURED BY GREEN. 1963.
Acrylic on board. 36" × 36".
Collection of Janet S. Fleisher, Philadelphia.

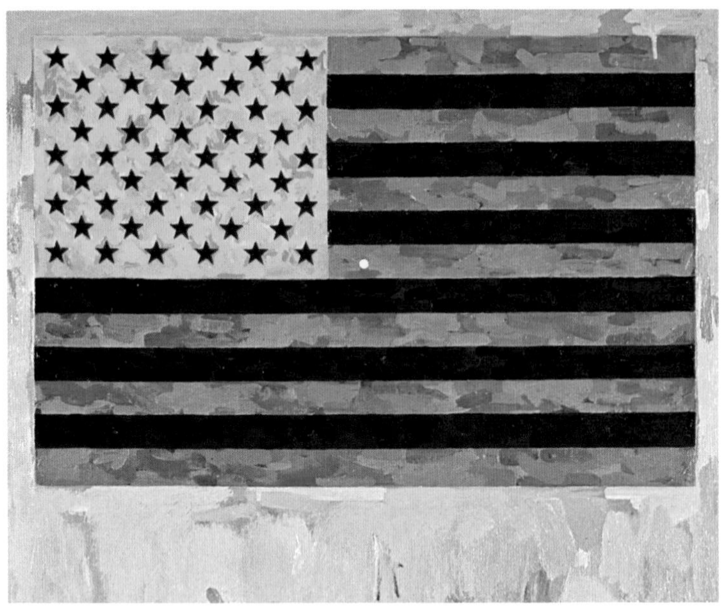

124 Jasper Johns.
Detail of FLAGS. 1965.
Oil on canvas with raised canvas.
Full painting 72" × 48".
Private collection. © 1994 Jasper Johns/VAGA New York.

receptors, meanwhile, respond strongly to the reflected blue and green light in the white light, producing an apparent blue-green dot that is not actually present on the surface. On a neutral surface, therefore, the hue of an afterimage will always be the complement of the hue of the original image or stimulus.

Try this more complex example of the afterimage phenomenon: stare for about thirty seconds at the white dot in the center of the flag in the detail of Jasper Johns's painting FLAGS, and then look at a white area of paper beneath it. (View the reproduction of FLAGS in or near sunlight to experience the full effect.)

In art, as in the everyday world, the appearance of an object's or a shape's color is relative to adjacent colors and the color and intensity of the light. As light decreases, individual colors appear less distinct. In bright light, colors reflect one another, causing changes in the appearance of local color. In his painting DINING ROOM IN THE COUNTRY (page 3), Pierre Bonnard emphasized these shifts in local color and added poetic color harmonies of his own invention. Color is central to Bonnard's art. He began with an ordinary scene and heightened its effect on us by concentrating on the magical qualities of light and color.

TEXTURE AND PATTERN

In the visual arts, *texture* refers to the tactile qualities of surfaces or to the visual representation of those qualities. Children explore their surroundings by touching everything within reach, and they learn to equate the feel with the look of surfaces. As adults we know how most things feel, yet we still enjoy the pleasures that touching gives; we delight in running our hands over the fur of a pet or the smooth surface of polished wood.

All surfaces have textures that may be experienced by touching or through visual suggestion. We categorize textures as either actual or simulated. *Actual* textures are those we can feel by touching, such as polished marble, wood, sand, or swirls of thick paint. *Simulated* (or implied) textures are those created to look like something other than

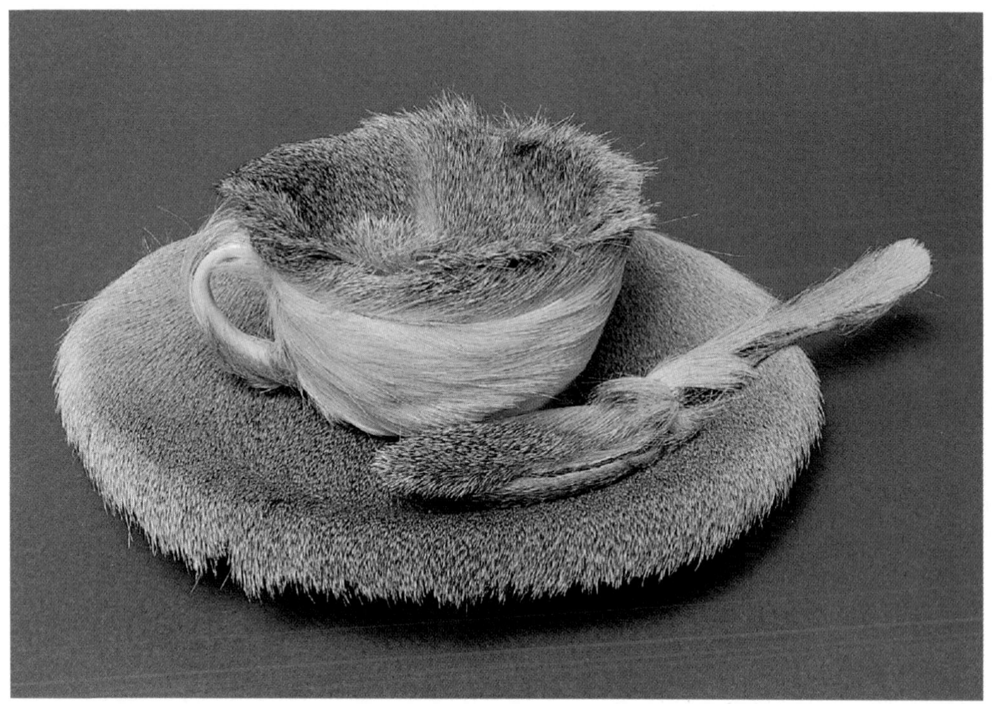

125 Meret Oppenheim. OBJECT (LE DEJEUNER EN FOURRURE). 1936. Fur covered cup 4¾" diameter; saucer 9⅜" diameter; spoon 8" long; overall height 2⅞". The Museum of Modern Art, New York. Purchase.

paint on a flat surface. A painter can simulate textures that look like real fur or wood but to the touch would feel like smooth paint. Artists can also invent actual or simulated textures. The invented, delicately granulated gold texture behind the figures in Gustav Klimt's THE KISS (page 87) is simulated and would have little or no textural feeling if we could touch it. We can appreciate most textures even when we are not permitted to touch them, because we know, from experience, how they would feel.

Meret Oppenheim's fur-covered teacup, titled OBJECT, is a rude tactile experience. She presented an intentionally contradictory object designed to evoke strong responses ranging from revulsion to amusement. The actual texture of fur is pleasant, as is the smooth texture of a teacup, but the combination makes the tongue "crawl." The abundant social and psychological implications are intended.

Sculptors and architects make use of the actual textures of their materials and the relationships between them. They can also create new textures in the finishing of surfaces. Compare the eroding surfaces of Alberto Giacometti's figure on page 53 with the youthful, skinlike textures of the figures in

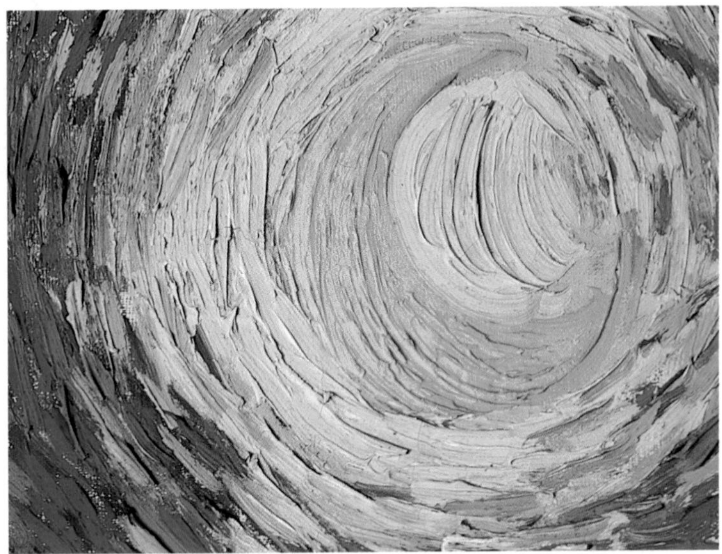

126 Vincent van Gogh.
Detail of STARRY NIGHT. 1889.
(See page 399.)

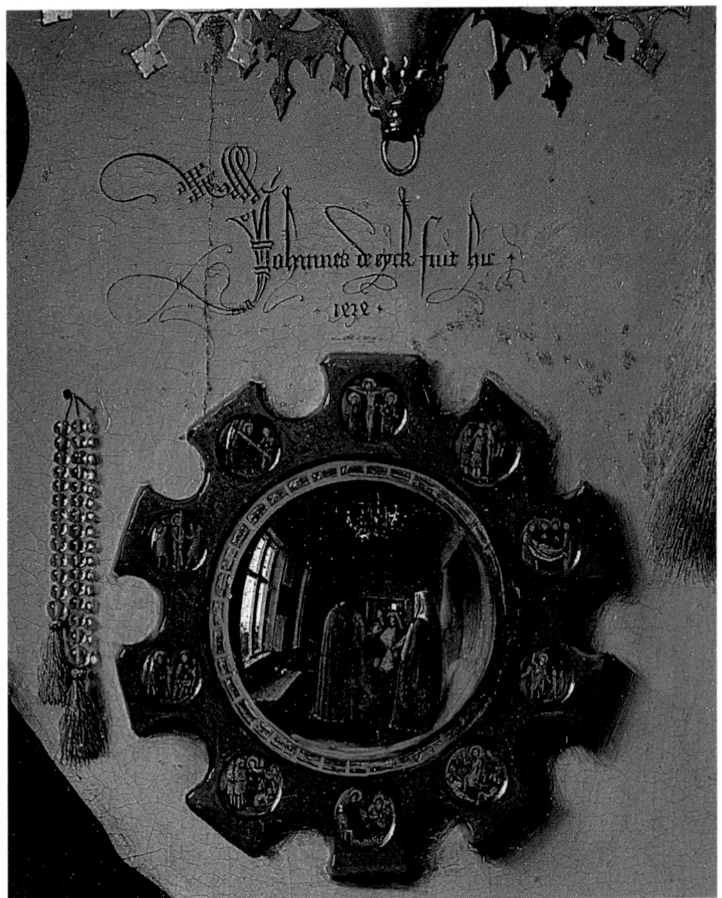

127 Jan van Eyck.
Detail of GIOVANNI ARNOLFINI AND HIS BRIDE. 1434.
(See page 355.)

Rodin's THE KISS on page 38, which in itself has strong textural contrast. Each artist used texture to heighten emotional impact.

A painter may develop a rich tactile surface as well as implied or simulated texture. Actual texture on a two-dimensional surface is seen in the detail of Van Gogh's STARRY NIGHT (the entire painting appears on page 399). With brush strokes of thick paint, called *impasto,* Van Gogh invented textural rhythms that convey his emotional intensity.

Five centuries earlier, Netherlandish painter Jan van Eyck used tiny brush strokes to show, in minute detail, the incredible richness of various materials. In GIOVANNI ARNOLFINI AND HIS BRIDE, Van Eyck simulated a variety of textures; in this section of the painting, we see the textures of the glass mirror, amber beads, and a corner of a whisk broom. Other textures including fur, hair, and wood are seen in the entire painting, reproduced on page 355.

Pattern is an art term that generally refers to repetitive, ordered surface designs such as those found in textiles, tiles, and wallpaper. A pattern may also be seen as a textural quality, depending on its scale. When precisely structured textures are enlarged, they can appear as patterns, and some small patterns can be seen as textures. In Klimt's painting THE KISS, the simulated textures of skin and hair are enhanced by the elegant, invented texture of the gold background, by the various decorative patterns of the garments, and by the floral patterns beneath the figures.

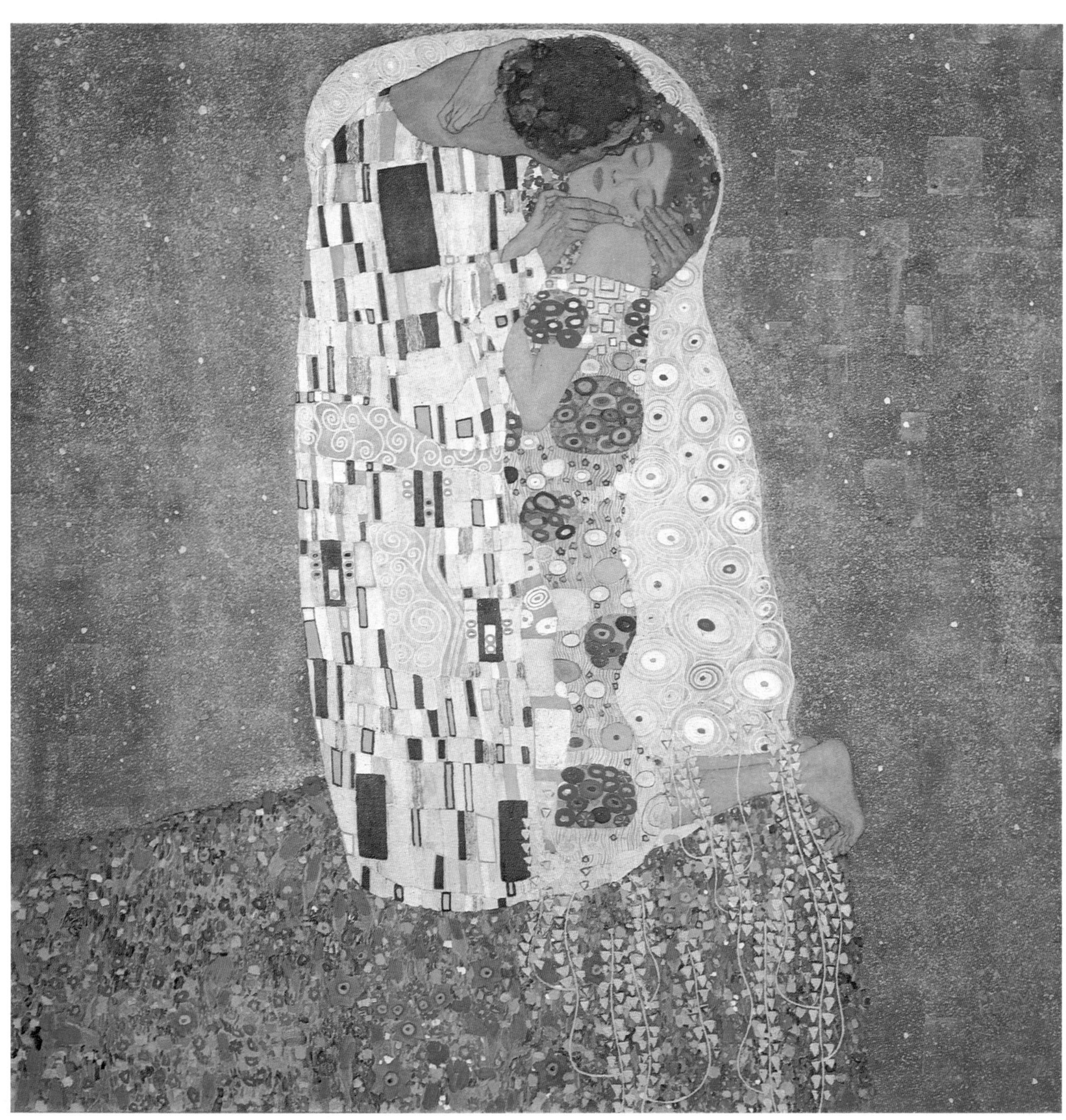

128 Gustav Klimt.
THE KISS. 1908.
Oil on canvas. 71" × 71".
Osterreichische Galerie, Vienna.

CHAPTER 5

Principles of Design

Organized perception is what art is all about.

Roy Lichtenstein[1]

Artists and designers organize visual elements in order to create significant form. In two-dimensional arts, such as painting and photography, this organization is usually called *composition.* But a broader term that applies to the entire range of visual arts is *design.*

Design grows from our basic need for meaningful order. The word *design* is used to indicate both the process of organizing visual elements and the product of that process.

There are no absolute rules for good design. There are only principles or general guidelines for effective visual communication. We study them for the same reason artists do: to develop our innate design sense, to give ourselves a vocabulary for talking to one other about what we see, and to become more sensitive to the expressive and relational qualities of form. In this chapter we look at seven key terms (or sets of terms) used to identify major principles of design:

unity and variety
balance
emphasis and subordination
directional forces
contrast
repetition and rhythm
scale and proportion

Together they provide an understanding not only of how artists work but how design affects us. We are continually affecting and being affected by design—our own designs and the designs of others. Whenever we make plans, select clothing, place items on a plate, or arrange furniture, we are designing. The selection and ordering of the objects and events in our daily lives are related to the design process in art. In both, the process is at its best when it is a lively, open dialogue between the intention and intuition of the designer and the innate character of the materials employed.

Gestalt psychology provides a way to understand our most basic response to design phenomena. *Gestalt* (German for "form") refers to our perception of configurations so integrated that they have qualities beyond a mere sum of their parts. Our perception of such designs in art or nature relies on the desire and ability to perceive order. Our need to unify our experiences of forms causes us to seek closure. If there is too little information, our minds seek to fill in what is missing; if there is too much information our minds leave out what is unnecessary.

UNITY AND VARIETY

Unity and variety are complementary concerns. *Unity* is the appearance or condition of oneness; *variety* provides diversity. In design, we use unity to describe the feeling that all the elements in a work

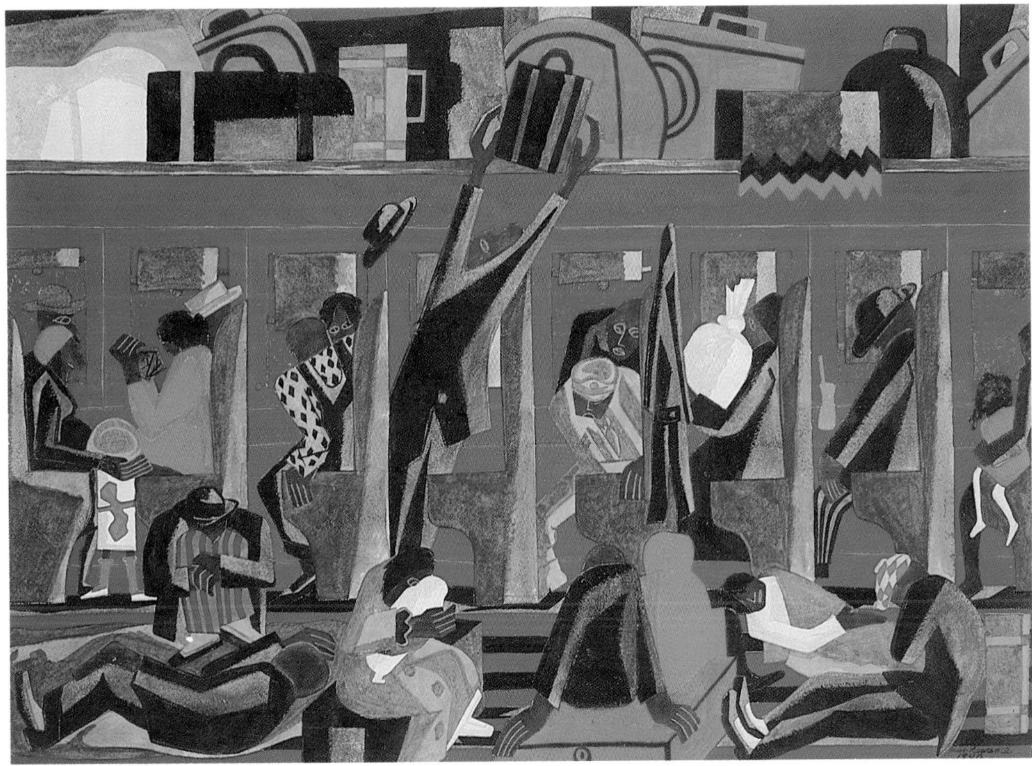

129 Jacob Lawrence. GOING HOME. 1946. Gouache. 21½" × 29½". Collection, IBM Corporation, Armonk, New York.

belong together and make up a coherent and harmonious whole. When a work of art has unity, the artist and the viewer feel as if nothing could be changed without damaging overall quality and strength.

Variety acts as a counterbalance to extreme unity. The balance between the boredom of too much sameness and the chaos of uncontrolled variety creates continuity, vitality, and interest in both art and life.

Artists select certain aspects of the visual form in order to clarify and intensify the expressive character of their subjects or themes. In his painting GOING HOME, Jacob Lawrence abstracted the elements of his subject, people traveling on a train. He established visual themes with the lines, shapes, and colors of the train seats, figures, and luggage, and then he repeated and varied those themes. Notice the varied repetition in the green chair seats and window shades. As a unifying element, the same red is used in a variety of shapes. The many figures and objects in the complex composition form a unified design through the artist's skillful use of abstraction, theme, and variation.

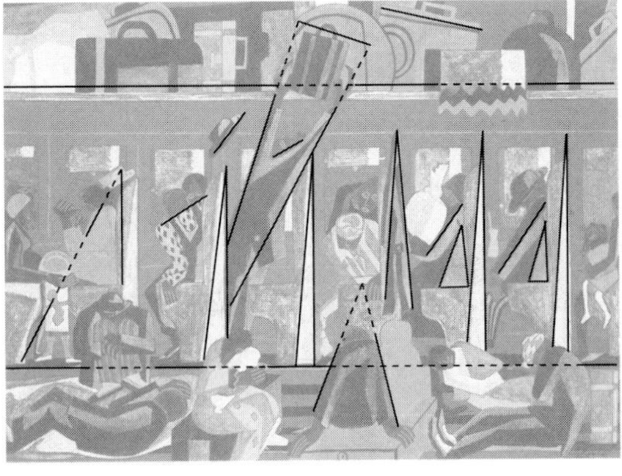

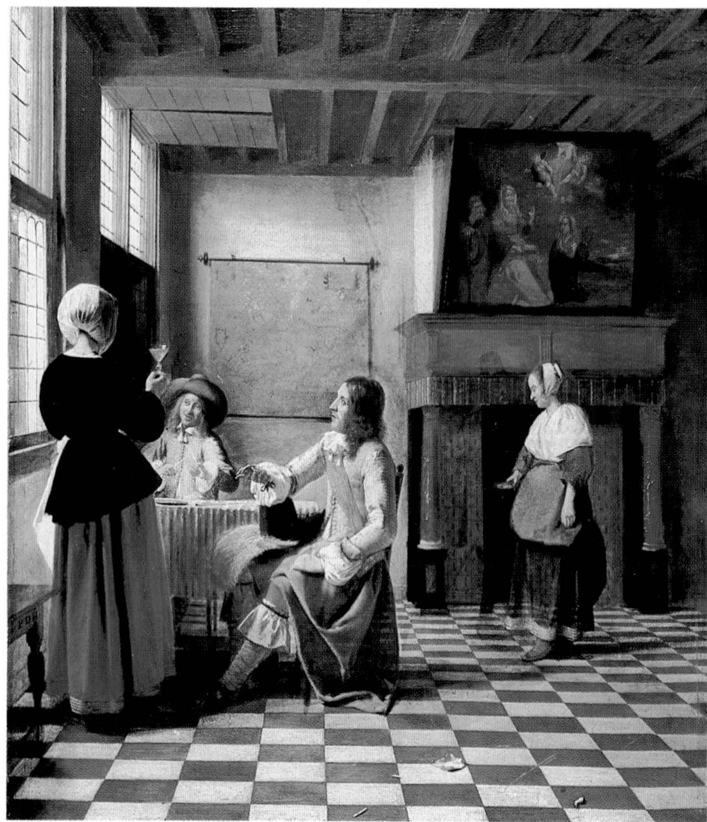

130 Pieter de Hooch.
INTERIOR OF A DUTCH HOUSE. 1658.
Oil on canvas. 29" × 35".

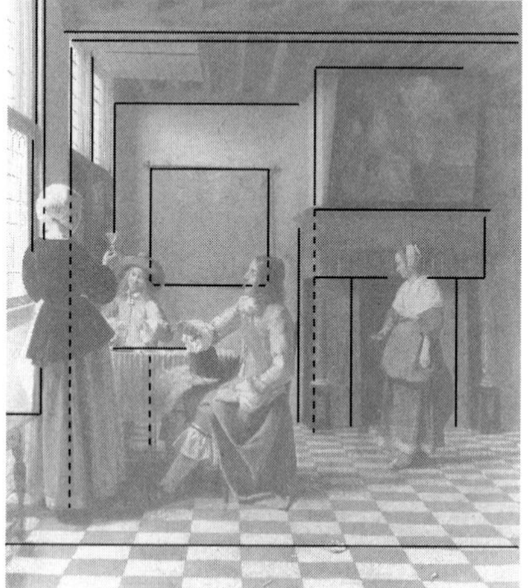

Lawrence is known for the lively harmony of his distinctive compositions. Although he has made a conscious decision to work in an unsophisticated, almost childlike manner, he is keenly aware of the importance of design. Lawrence studies other artists' work, and he has been influenced by a number of nineteenth- and twentieth-century painters whose works he finds particularly forceful. "I like to study the design to see how the artist solves his problems and brings his subjects to the public."[2]

The flat quality of GOING HOME contrasts with the illusion of depth in Pieter de Hooch's INTERIOR OF A DUTCH HOUSE. Each artist depicted a scene from daily life in a style relevant to the century in which he painted. In each case, the painter's use of space helped unify the composition. Painters De Hooch, Raphael (see page 63), and David (see page 373) all "borrowed" the unity that architecture imposes on actual space in order to unify pictorial space and provide a cohesive setting for the interaction of figures.

In De Hooch's painting, the pattern of floor tiles and windows plays off against the larger rectangles of map, painting, fireplace, and ceiling. The overall unifying theme is one of rectangular shapes. De Hooch repeated the horizontal and vertical proportions that begin with the format (nearly square) of the picture plane. He then created a whole family of varied rectangles, as indicated in the accompanying diagram. The shapes and colors in the figures around the table relate to the shapes and colors of the figures in the painting above the fireplace—another use of theme and variation.

Alberto Giacometti's sculpture CHARIOT brings together diverse subjects—a standing female figure and two wheels. Unity is achieved through the use of a thin linear quality and rough texture in the figure, wheels, and axle, as well as through the use of bronze for the entire piece. The unity provided by the consistent handling of these elements leads us to see all aspects of the sculpture as a single mysterious entity. Our interest is held by the varied components and by the tension of the figure poised precariously atop a two-legged table on wheels. And this brings us to the principle called balance.

BALANCE

For sculptors such as Giacometti, balance is both a visual issue and a structural necessity. The dynamic interplay between opposing forces is one of the basic conditions of life. Equally basic is the dynamic process of seeking balance.

Balance is the achievement of equilibrium, the condition in which acting influences are held in check by opposing forces. We crave balance in life and in art, and we are disturbed when we feel its absence. In art, our instinct for physical balance finds its parallel in a desire for visual balance. A painting can depict an act of violence or imbalance—a frenzied battle or a fall from a tightrope—but unless the painting itself is balanced, it will lack the expressive power necessary to convince us that the battle was terrible, the fall disastrous. Instead it will merely convince us that it is not a very good painting. For examples of well-balanced paintings of chaotic events, see Delacroix's DEATH OF SARDANAPALUS on page 378 and Picasso's GUERNICA on page 443.

The two general types of balance are symmetrical (formal) and asymmetrical (informal).

Symmetrical Balance

By *symmetrical balance* we mean what biologists call bilateral symmetry: the left and right sides are exact or near mirror images of each other.

Architects often employ symmetrical balance to give unity and formal grandeur to a building's facade or front side. For example, in 1792 James Hoban won a competition for his DESIGN FOR THE PRESIDENT'S HOUSE with a drawing of a symmetrical, Georgian-style mansion (see next page). Today, two centuries and several additions later, we know it as The White House.

In architecture, as elsewhere, symmetrical design is useful because it is easier to comprehend than asymmetry. Symmetry is also useful because it creates a powerful unity—even in large, complex buildings—setting them apart from nearby structures. Finally, symmetry tends to be visually inactive. We certainly want our symbolically important government buildings to be motionless and stable.

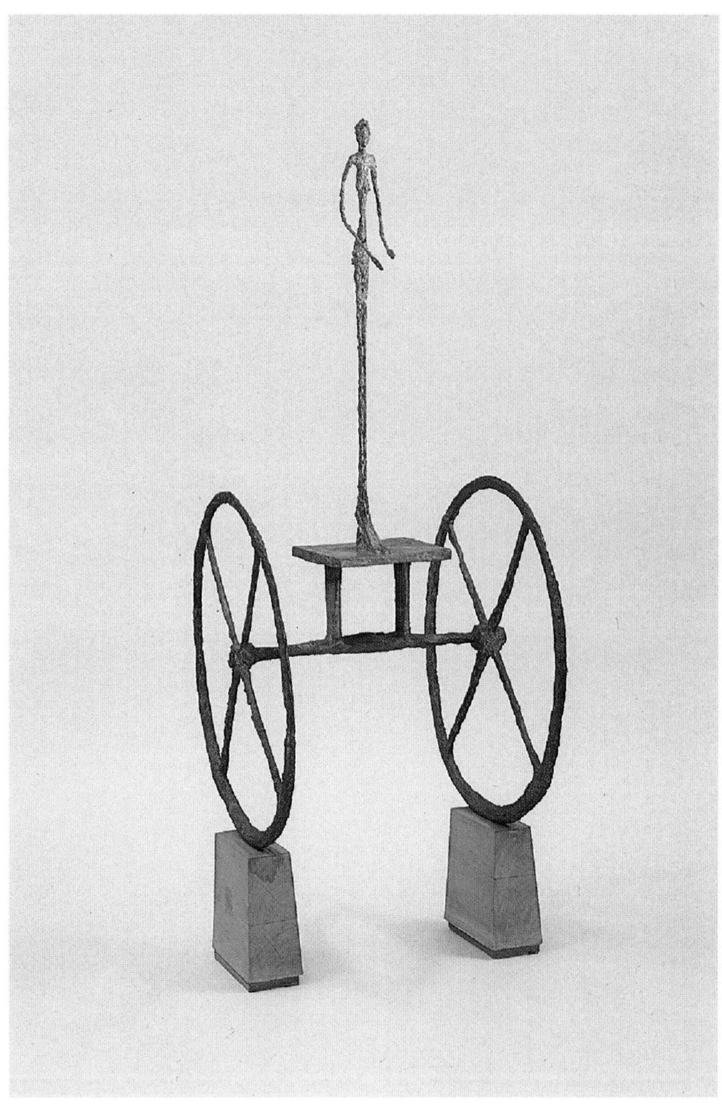

131 Alberto Giacometti.
CHARIOT. 1950.
Bronze. 57" × 26" × 26⅛".
The Museum of Modern Art, New York. Purchase.

132 James Hoban.
DESIGN FOR THE PRESIDENT'S HOUSE.
Elevation. 1792.
Maryland Historical Society, Baltimore.

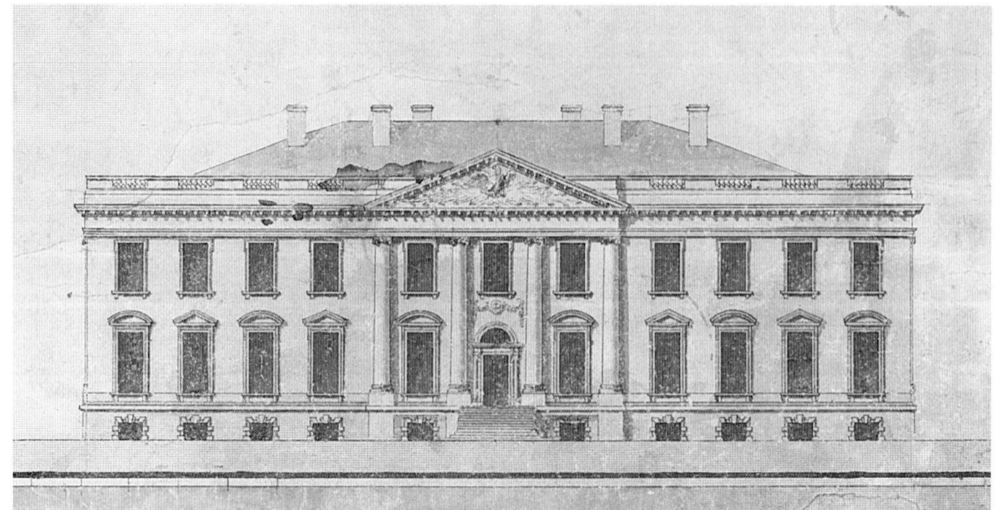

133 Hans Holbein.
ANNE OF CLEVES. 1539.
Oil on wood panel. 25⅝" × 18⅞".
Musée du Louvre, Paris.

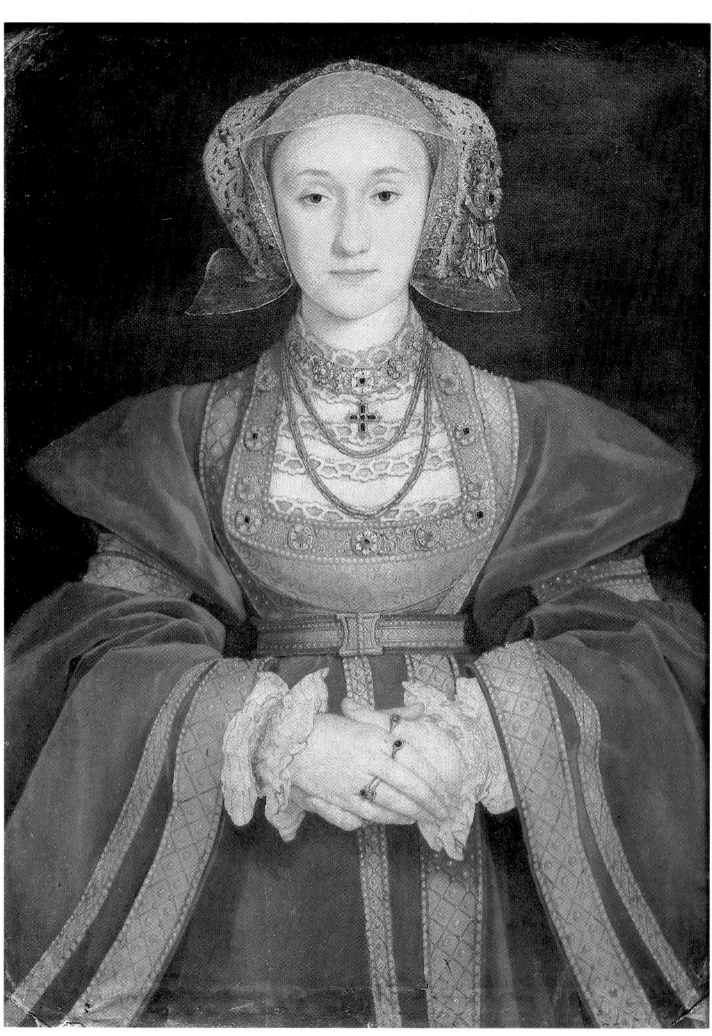

However, symmetry is not always so formal and static. For contrast, see the use of sweeping curves to suggest motion in the symmetrical TWA TERMINAL shown on pages 57 and 261.

All the qualities that make symmetry desirable in architecture make it generally less desirable in sculpture and two-dimensional art. We usually do not want these arts to be static, nor do we want them to be too easy to comprehend visually. Thus, while artists admire symmetry for its formal qualities, they rarely employ it rigidly.

Hans Holbein used symmetrical balance to give his portrait of ANNE OF CLEVES formal dignity. But the composition is not as completely symmetrical as it first appears. If you align a ruler vertically on the pendant cross and belt buckle, which fall exactly on the vertical *axis* (an imaginary line down the middle of a form or picture), you will see that the head sits slightly to the left of center. A subtle light coming from the right enhances this leftward motion. In the lower half of the composition, the bold asymmetrical bands of the skirt exert a delicate counterthrust to the right. But the sleeve ruffle on the left also attracts our attention. Because we see the ruffle's complete shape, and because it contrasts with the dark velvet, it provides a ballast. By means of these and other subtle shifts of balance around the vertical axis, Holbein relieved the static quality of symmetry while retaining its formal power.

Asymmetrical Balance

With *asymmetrical balance,* the two sides are not the same. Instead, various visual phenomena are balanced—according to their visual and referential weights—around a felt or implied center of gravity. By *referential weights* we mean the psychological impact (weight) of recognizable subjects—as seen in the diagram VISUAL WEIGHT, where our attention is drawn more to the child's face than to the blurred image. Asymmetrical balance is far more difficult to achieve than symmetrical balance, but it is more flexible, subtle, and dynamic.

What exactly are the visual properties or weights of colors and forms, and how does an artist go about balancing them? As with design itself, there are no rules, only principles. Here are a few about visual balance:

- A large form is heavier, more attractive or more attention-getting than a small form. So two or more small forms can balance one large form.
- A form gathers visual weight as it nears the edge of a picture. So a small form near an edge can balance a larger form near the center.
- A complex form is heavier than a simple form. So a small complex form can balance a large simple form.

Color complicates things. For example, here are three color principles that allow you to overturn the three principles of form just given:

- Warm colors are heavier than cool colors. So a single small yellow form can balance a large dark blue form.
- Intense colors are heavier than weak or pale colors (tints and shades). So a single small bright blue form near the center can balance a large pale blue form near an edge.
- The intensity, and therefore the weight, of any color increases as the background color approaches its complementary hue. So on a green background, a small simple red form can balance a large complex blue form.

While guidelines such as these are interesting to study and can be valuable to an artist if she or he gets "stuck," they are really "laboratory" examples. The truth is that most artists rely on a highly

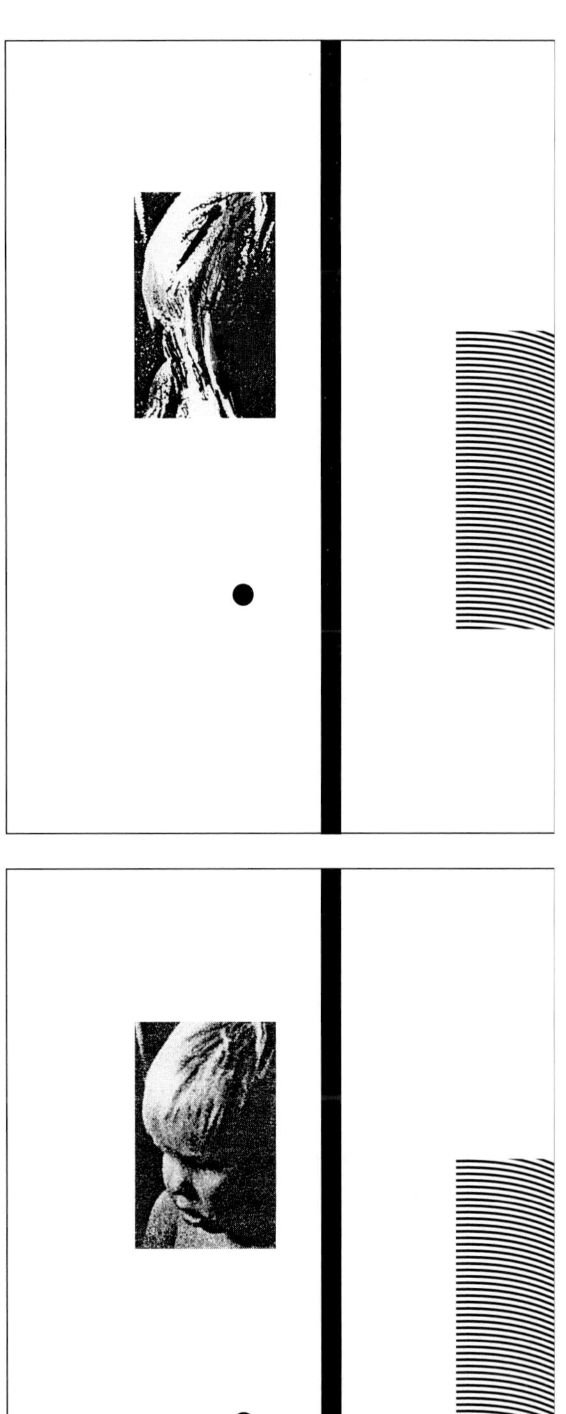

134 VISUAL WEIGHT.

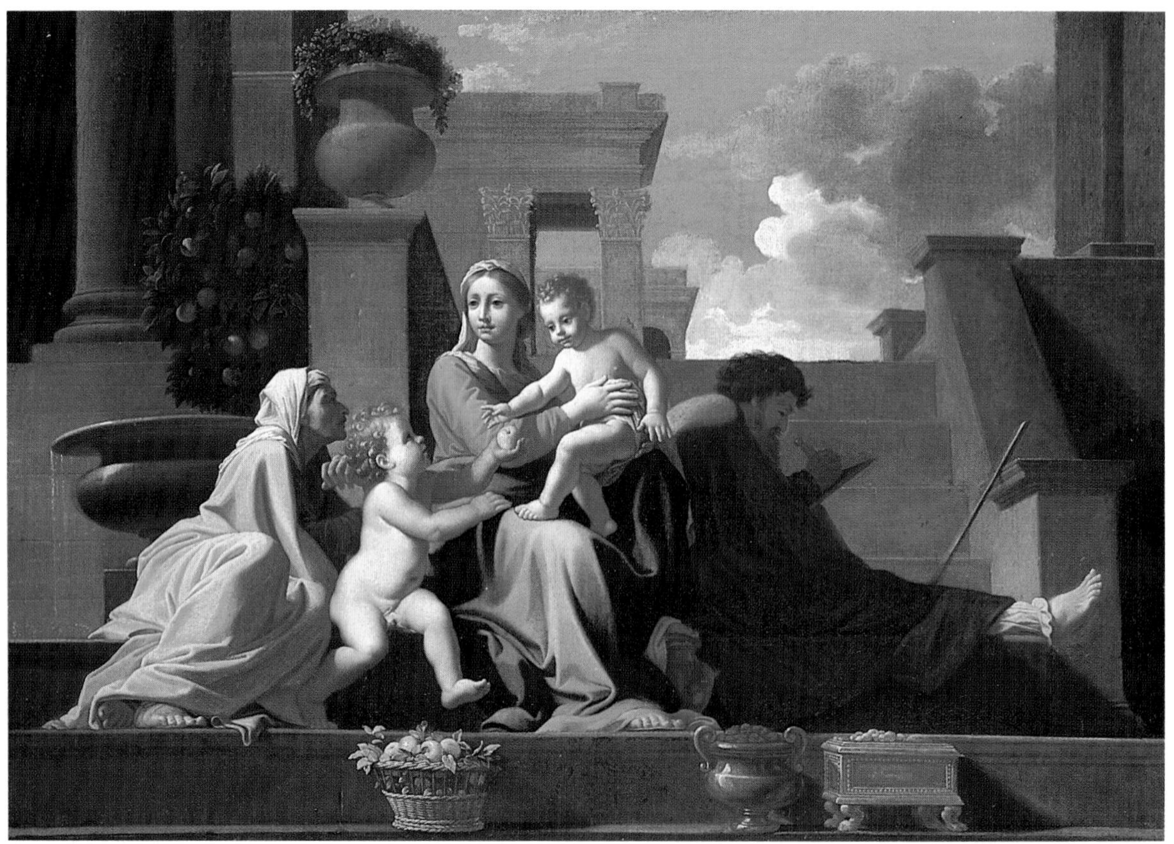

135 Nicholas Poussin.
HOLY FAMILY ON THE STEPS. 1648.
Oil on canvas. 27" × 38½".

developed sensitivity to what "looks right" in order to arrive at an acceptable balance. Simply put, a picture is balanced when it feels balanced.

A classic example of balance is Nicolas Poussin's HOLY FAMILY ON THE STEPS. Poussin combined both asymmetrical and symmetrical elements in this complex composition. He grouped the figures in a stable, symmetrical pyramidal shape. The most important figure, the infant Jesus, is at the center of the picture, the strongest position. In case we don't see that right away, Poussin guided our attention by making the traditional red and blue of Mary's robes both light and bright, and by placing Jesus's head within a halolike architectural space.

But then Poussin offset the potential boredom of this symmetry with an ingenious asymmetrical color balance. He placed Joseph, the figure at the right, in deep shadow, undermining the clarity of the stable pyramid. He created a major center of interest at the far left of the picture by giving St. Elizabeth a bright yellow robe. The interest created by the blue sky and clouds at the upper right counterbalances the figures of St. Elizabeth and the infant John the Baptist. But the final master stroke that brings complete balance is Joseph's foot, which Poussin bathed in light. The brightness of this small, isolated shape with the diagonal staff above it is enough to catch our eye and balance the color weights of the left half of the painting.

While the overall composition of HOLY FAMILY ON THE STEPS is balanced asymmetrically, the painting's center of gravity is still the central vertical axis. In JOCKEYS BEFORE THE RACE, on the other hand, Edgar Degas located the center of gravity on the right. To reinforce it, he drew it in for us as a pole. (Degas was known for innovative compositions; see also pages 143 and 392.) At first glance, all our attention is drawn to our extreme right, to the nearest and largest horse. But the solitary circle of the sun in the upper left exerts a strong fascination. The red cap, the pale pink jacket of the distant jockey, the subtle warm/cool color intersection at the horizon, and the recession of the horses all help to move our eyes over to the left portion of the picture, where a barely discernible but very important vertical line directs our attention upward.

In JOCKEYS BEFORE THE RACE, a trail of visual cues moves our attention from right to left. If we are sensitive to them, we will perform the act of balancing the painting. If we are not, the painting will seem forever unbalanced. Degas relied on the fact that seeing is an active, creative process and not a passive one.

Notice that both Poussin and Degas used strong diagonals in their designs. In the Poussin, Elizabeth's robe at the lower left begins an implied diagonal line that continues up through the cloud at the upper right. In the Degas, the large horse in the lower right, our first center of attention, is counterbalanced by the sun in the upper left. Diagonal opposition is common in asymmetrical compositions, and looking for it can often help you find the key to the balance.

A good way to explore a picture's balance is to imagine it painted differently. Block out Joseph's light-bathed foot in the Poussin, then see how the lack of balance affects you. Cover the jockey's red cap in the Degas and you'll see the spark of life go out of the painting.

Asymmetrical balance in architecture is difficult to show in photographs. In Frank Lloyd Wright's KAUFMANN HOUSE (see page 262), you can sense that the asymmetrically placed horizontal forms are firmly held, visually, by the implied gravity of the vertical tower. But what you cannot see is how the play of forms shifts constantly for the observer who walks around the house, how the forms maintain a balance that can be seen from every angle.

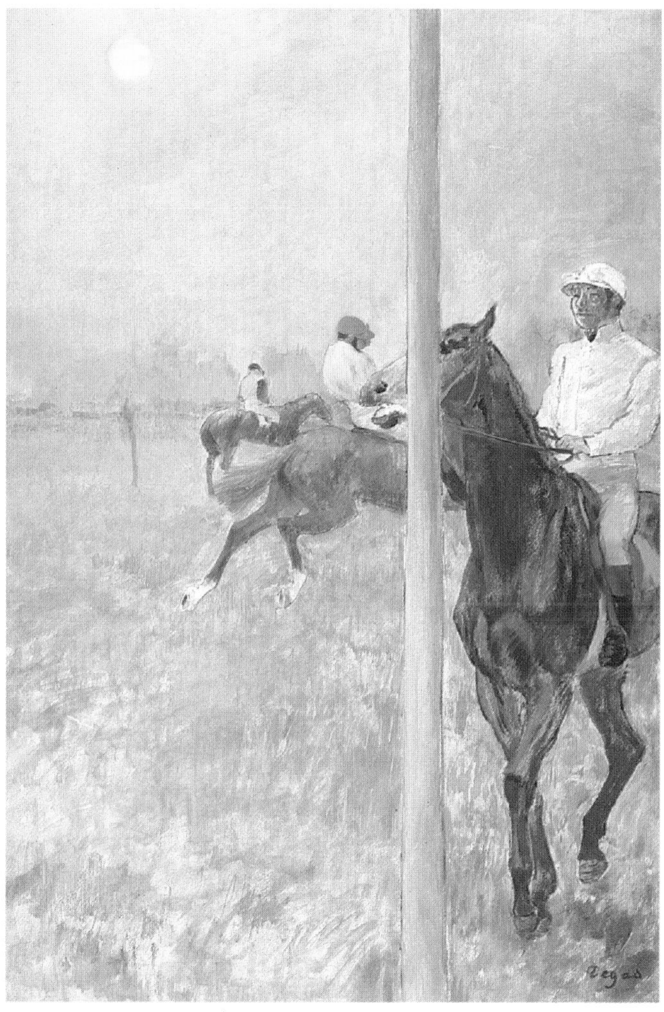

136 Edgar Degas.
JOCKEYS BEFORE THE RACE. 1878-1879.
Oil with touches of pastel on paper stretched on pasteboard.
42½" × 29".
The Barber Institute of Fine Arts, The University of Birmingham.

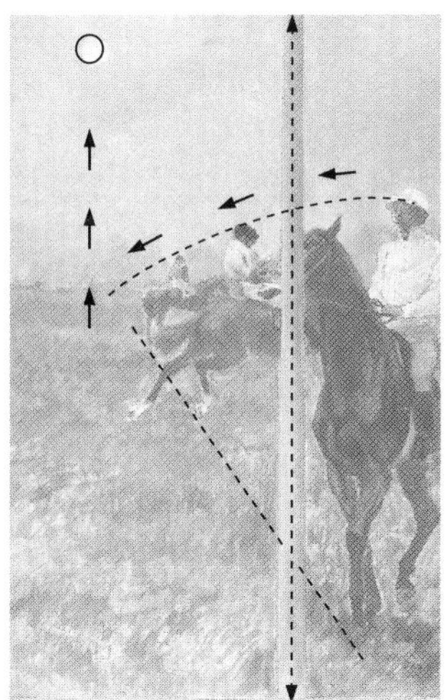

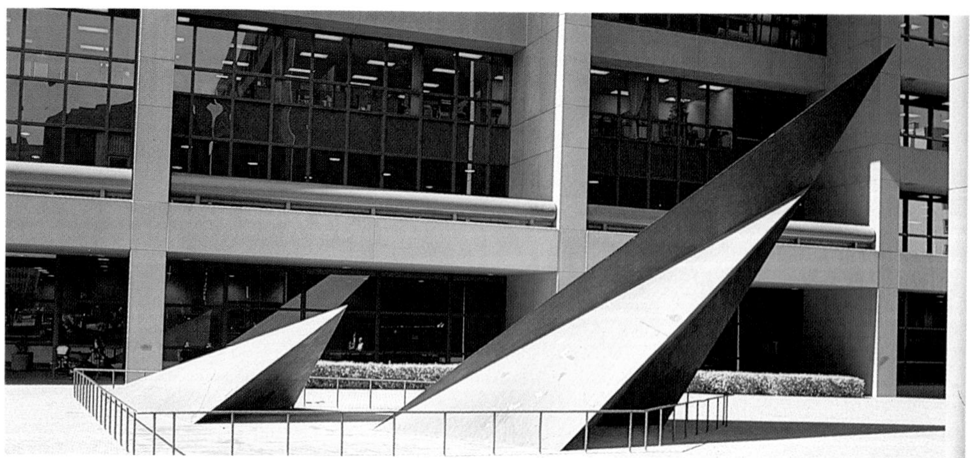

137 Beverly Pepper. EXCALIBUR. San Diego Federal Building. 1976. Painted steel. 35' × 45' × 45'. Photograph: Philipp Scholz Ritterman.

Besides the visual balance we seek in all art, works of sculpture and architecture need structural balance or they will not stand up. Feelings about visual balance are intimately connected to our experience with actual physical balance. It appears that Beverly Pepper designed her large sculpture EXCALIBUR to look somewhat unbalanced as a way of giving an intriguing tension to her soaring diagonal structures. We know the triangular forms are securely attached to the ground, yet they look precarious. When the work is viewed from this and other angles, the smaller piece seems to provide an anchor—a visual pull that acts as a counterweight to the larger form.

EMPHASIS AND SUBORDINATION

Emphasis is used to draw our attention to an area or areas. If that area is a specific spot or figure, we call it a *focal point.* Position, contrast, color intensity, and size can all be used to create emphasis.

Through *subordination,* an artist creates neutral areas of lesser interest that keep us from being distracted from the areas of emphasis.

Emphasis, subordination, and directional forces are ways in which an artist balances and controls the sequence of our seeing and the amount of attention we pay to the various parts of any work of art. We have seen them at work in two paintings just examined.

In HOLY FAMILY ON THE STEPS (page 94), Poussin placed the most important figure in the center, the strongest location in any visual field. In JOCKEYS BEFORE THE RACE (page 95), Degas took a different approach, using size, shape, placement, and color to create areas of emphasis *away* from the center. The sun is a separate focal point created through contrast (it is lighter than the surrounding sky area and the only circle in the painting) and through placement (it is the only shape in that part of the painting). Sky and grass areas, however, were painted in muted color with almost no detail so that they would be subordinate to, and thus support, the areas of emphasis.

DIRECTIONAL FORCES

Directional forces are "paths" for the eye to follow provided by actual or implied lines. Implied directional lines may be suggested by a form's axis, by the imagined connection between similar or adjacent forms, or by the implied continuation of actual lines. Studying directional lines and forces often reveals a work of art's underlying energy and basic visual structure.

Looking at JOCKEYS BEFORE THE RACE, we find that our attention is pulled to a series of focal points: the horse and jockey at the extreme right, the vertical pole, the red cap, the pink jacket, and the blue-green at the horizon. The dominant directional forces in JOCKEYS are diagonal. The focal points mentioned above create an implied directional line. The face of the first jockey is included in this line.

The implied diagonal line created by the bodies of the three receding horses acts as a related directional force. As our eyes follow the recession, encouraged by the attraction of the focal points, we perform the act of balancing the composition by correcting our original attraction to the extreme right.

Just as our physical and visual feelings for balance correspond, so do our physical and visual feelings about directional lines and forces. As we noted in Chapter 4, the direction of lines produces sensations similar to standing still (|), being at rest (—), or being in motion (/). Therefore, a combination of vertical and horizontal lines provides stability. For example, columns and walls and horizontal steps provide a stable structure for HOLY FAMILY ON THE STEPS. The vertical pole and horizon provide stability in Degas's JOCKEYS.

Francisco Goya's etching BULLFIGHT provides a fascinating example of effective design based on a dramatic use of directional forces. To emphasize the drama of man and bull, Goya isolated them in the foreground as large, dark shapes against a light background. He created suspense by crowding the spectators into the upper left corner.

Goya evoked a sense of motion by placing the bullfighter exactly on the diagonal axis that runs from lower left to upper right (diagram a). He reinforced the feeling by placing the bull's hind legs along the same line.

Goya further emphasized two main features of the drama by placing the man's hands at the intersection of the image's most important horizontal and vertical lines. He also directed powerful diagonals from the bull's head and front legs to the pole's balancing point on the ground (a). The resulting sense of motion to the right is so powerful that everything in the rest of the etching is needed to balance it.

By placing the light source to the left, Goya extended the bull's shadow to the right, forming a relatively stable horizontal line. The man looks down at the shadow, creating a directional force that causes us to look also. When we do, we realize that the implied lines reveal the underlying structure to be a stable triangle (diagram b). Formally, the triangle serves as a balancing force; psychologically, its missing side serves to heighten the tension of the situation.

The dynamism of the man's diagonal axis is so strong that the composition needed additional balancing elements, so Goya used light to create two more diagonals in the opposite direction (diagram c). The area of shadow in the background completes the balance by adding visual weight and stability to the left.

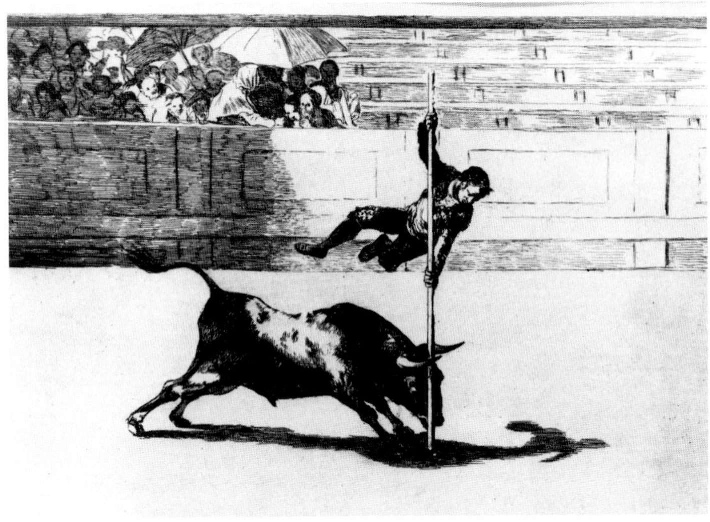

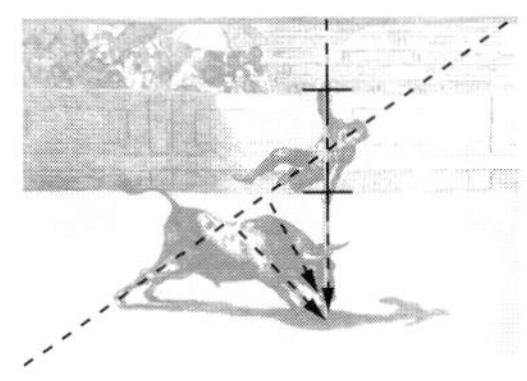

a

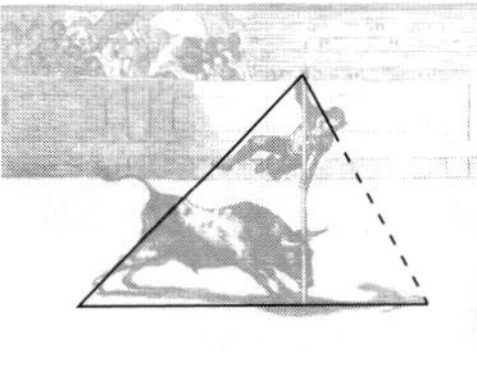

b

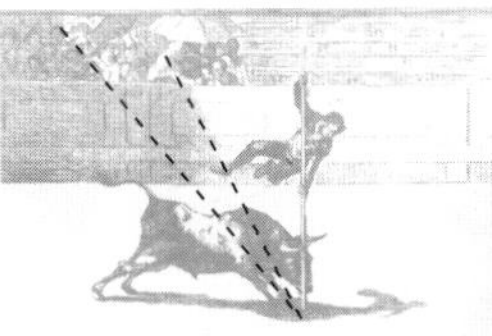

c

138 Francisco Goya. BULLFIGHT. 1810-1815. Etching. 12¼" × 8⅛". Fine Arts Gallery of San Diego.

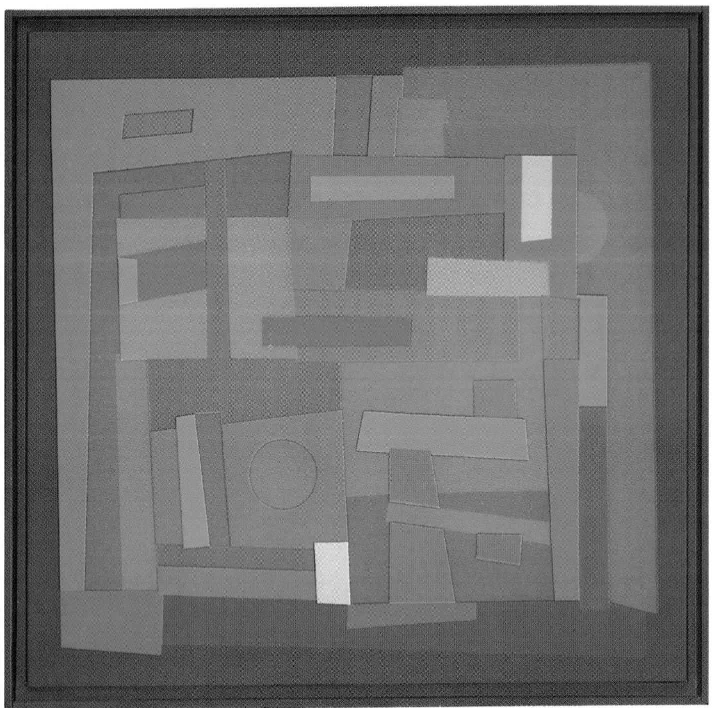

139 Ad Reinhardt.
NUMBER 30. 1938.
Oil on canvas. 40½" × 42½".
Private collection, on extended loan to the Whitney Museum of American Art (P31.77).

It has taken many words and several diagrams to describe the visual dynamics that make the design of Goya's etching so effective. However, our eyes take it in instantly. Good design is efficient; it communicates its power immediately.

CONTRAST

Contrast is the juxtaposition of strongly dissimilar elements. Dramatic effects may be produced when dark is set against light, large against small, bright colors against dull. Without contrast, visual experience would be monotonous.

Contrast may be seen in the thick and thin areas of a single brush stroke. It may also be seen in the juxtaposition of regular geometric and irregular organic shapes, or in hard (sharp) and soft (blurred) edges. Contrast can provide visual interest, emphasize a point, and express content.

In Ad Reinhardt's NUMBER 30, color contrasts occur between warm and cool colors. Reinhardt limited his design to geometric shapes as a way of focusing attention on both shape and color interactions. The point of greatest emphasis is the lone red circle that relates to the other geometric shapes but strongly contrasts with them.

REPETITION AND RHYTHM

The repetition of visual elements give a composition unity, continuity, flow, and emphasis. As we saw earlier, De Hooch's INTERIOR OF A DUTCH HOUSE (page 90) is organized around the repetition of rectangular shapes.

In Raphael's MADONNA OF THE CHAIR, curved shapes echo the circular format of the painting. The curve of the edge of the painting is repeated in the curve of Mary's head, neck, and arm, and in the interlocking curve of the infant Jesus. The repeated curves provide flow and continuity, while the vertical axis of the chair post stabilizes the curving directional forces that dominate the composition.

When repeated forms are organized in a series, rhythms are created. *Rhythm* refers to any kind of movement or structure with a regular repetition of dominant and subordinate elements in sequence. We generally associate rhythm with temporal arts such as music, dance, and poetry. Visual artists also use rhythm, as an organizational and expressive device. In the visual arts, rhythm is created through the regular recurrence with related variations of elements.

Repetition and rhythm are effectively employed in one of history's most carefully observed and elegantly painted depictions of flying birds: THE HUNDRED GEESE. (Only a small section of the handscroll is shown here.) There is some controversy over who painted it and when, but no one can question the painter's incredible awareness of birds in flight and at rest and the skillful use of ink gradations. It is likely that the flying birds shown here are actually the same bird depicted in various stages of flight, emerging from the distance and coming into sharper focus. The artist succeeded in creating the illusion of space and continous motion long before the invention of film and television.

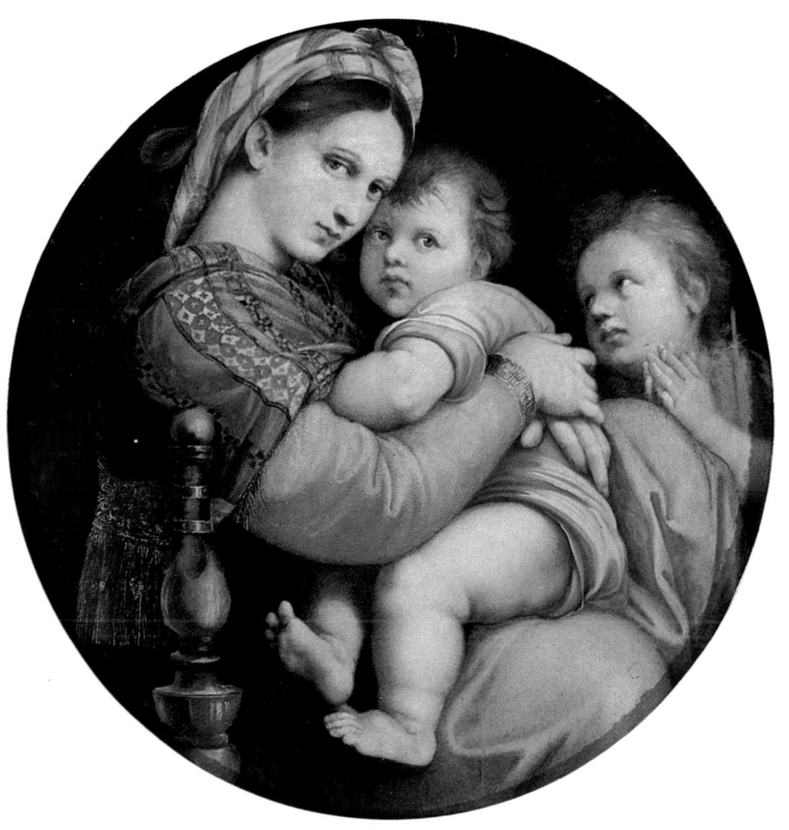

140 Raphael Sanzio.
MADONNA OF THE CHAIR. c. 1514.
Oil on wood. Diameter 2'4".
Pitti Gallery, Florence.

141 Attributed to Ma Fen.
Detail of THE HUNDRED GEESE.
12th century. Ink on paper, mounted as a handscroll.
Entire scroll 13¾" × 15'10⅞".
Honolulu Academy of Arts.

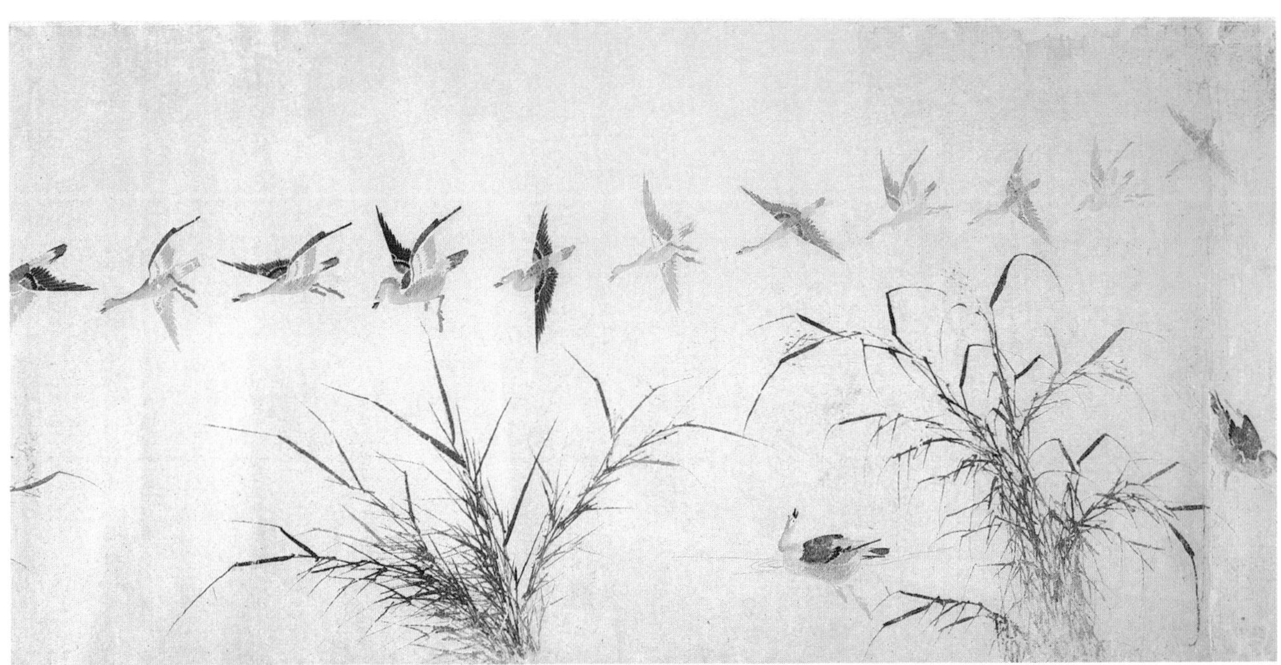

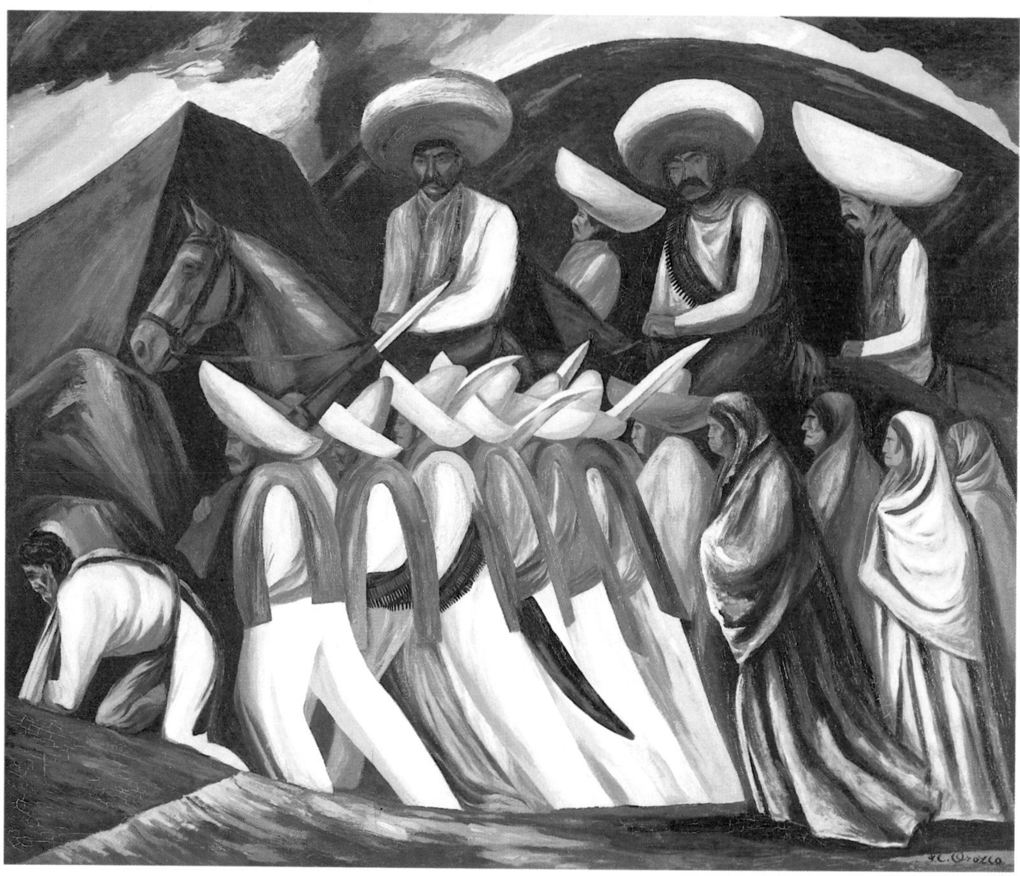

142 José Clemente Orozco.
ZAPATISTAS. 1931.
Oil on canvas. 45" × 55".
The Museum of Modern Art, New York. Anonymous gift.

A strong rhythm dominates José Clemente Orozco's ZAPATISTAS. The line of similar, diagonally placed figures grouped in a rhythmic sequence expresses the determination of oppressed people in revolt. The rhythmic diagonals of their hat brims and bayonets all contribute to a feeling of action. In fact, diagonal lines dominate the entire composition.

The design of Duchamp's NUDE DESCENDING A STAIRCASE (page 426) also presents a rhythmic progression, indicating movement and change through a dynamic sequence of interacting lines and shapes.

SCALE AND PROPORTION

Scale refers to the size of an object in relation to an ideal or normal size, other objects, its environment, or its format. *Proportion* is the size relationship of parts to a whole or to each other.

Claes Oldenburg's humorous CLOTHESPIN is much larger in scale than one expects a clothespin to be. The presence of people in the photograph clarifies the scale. Oldenburg also used proportion to transform an ordinary object into something monumental. He redesigned the form of a clothespin by elongating the handle ends, giving the work an anthropomorphic quality that mere enlargement would not have produced. Is it a monumental icon for a society dominated by mass-produced objects? Or does it simply make us realize that there is visual dignity even in small, ordinary things? Or both?

Scale is one of the first decisions an artist makes when planning a work of art. How big will it be? We experience scale in relation to our own size, and this experience constitutes an important part of our response to works of art.

We see many relationships in terms of scale. You have probably noticed that when a short person stands next to a tall person, the short one seems shorter and the tall one taller. Their relationship exaggerates their relative height difference. In the diagram SCALE RELATIONSHIPS, the inner circles at the center in both groups are the same size, but they appear to be quite different.

When the size of any work is modified for reproduction in a book, its character changes. The sizes of almost all the art objects in this book have been changed to fit them on the pages. One of the few exceptions is Rembrandt's SELF-PORTRAIT IN A CAP. This tiny etching, which the artist did when he was twenty-four years old, is reproduced here the actual size of the original print. It captures a fleeting expression of intense surprise. At this scale,

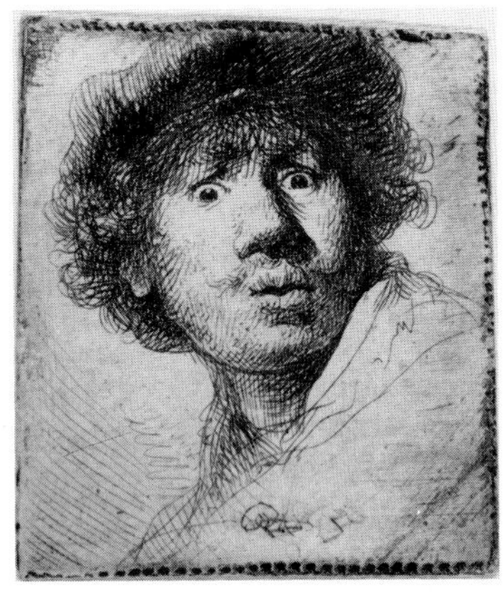

145 Rembrandt van Rijn.
SELF-PORTRAIT IN A CAP, OPEN MOUTHED AND STARING. 1630.
Etching. 2" × 1⅞".
British Museum, London.

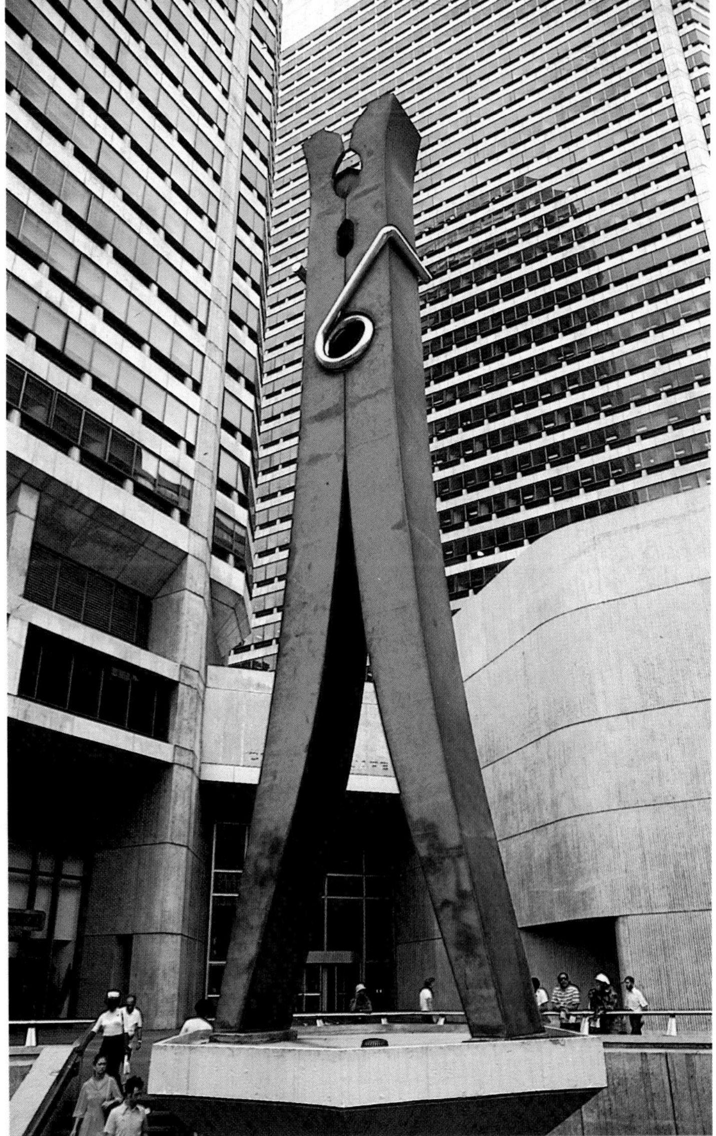

143 Claes Oldenburg.
CLOTHESPIN. Centre Square, Philadelphia. 1976.
Cor-ten steel. Height 45'.

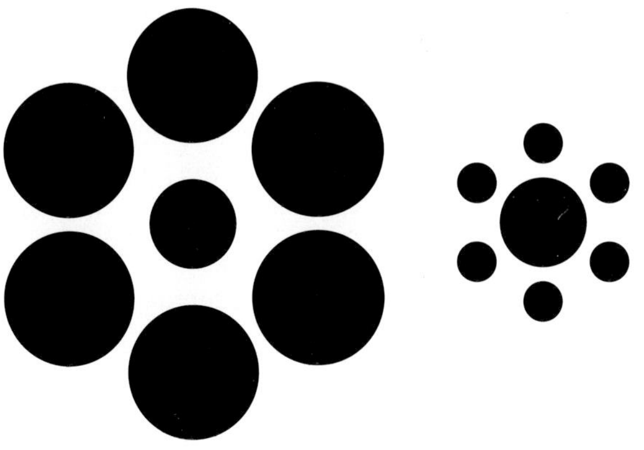

144 SCALE RELATIONSHIPS.

it reads as an intimate notation of human emotion. On the other hand, Michelangelo Buonarroti's sculpture of DAVID (page 352) and Picasso's GUERNICA (page 443) have been reduced in this book to tiny fractions of their actual sizes, thereby greatly changing the impact of each. Because works of art are distorted in a variety of ways when they are reproduced, it is important to experience original art whenever possible.

The term *format* refers to the size and shape—and thus to the scale and proportion—of a two-dimensional picture plane, such as a piece of paper, a canvas, a book page, or a video screen. For example, the format of this book is a vertical 8½-by-11-inch rectangle, the same format used for typing paper and most notebooks. Three common formats favored by traditional painters in China and Japan have been the long horizontal handscroll, the tall, vertical hanging scroll, and the fan. The circular or "tondo" format was used during the Renaissance by Raphael (see page 99) and others. Some recent artists have used huge formats (see page 462).

The format an artist chooses affects the total composition (design) of a particular work. Matisse makes this clear in his *Notes of a Painter:*

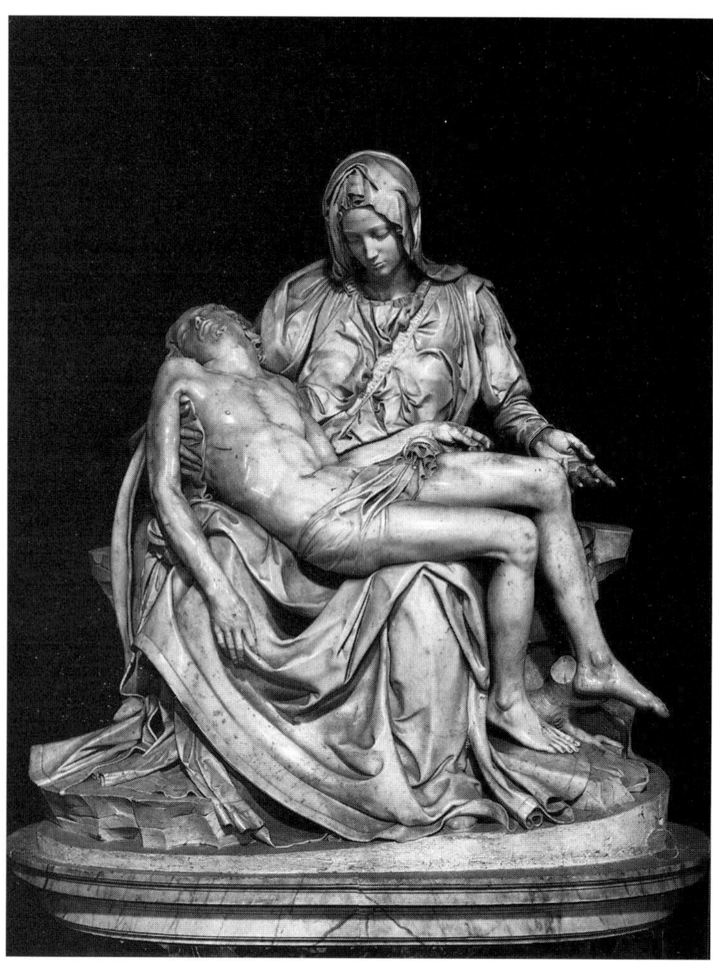

146 Michelangelo Buonarroti.
PIETÀ. 1501.
Marble. Height 6' 8½".
St. Peter's Basilica, Rome.

Composition, the aim of which should be expression, is modified according to the surface to be covered. If I take a sheet of paper of a given size, my drawing will have a necessary relationship to its format. I would not repeat this drawing on another sheet of different proportions, for example, rectangular instead of square.[3]

Proportions within a work of art are often designed to express symbolic meaning. The use of unnatural proportions to show the relative importance of figures is called *hierarchic proportion* by art historians. In the Egyptian wall painting on page 321, the nobleman is presented as the most important person, and the women scaled in proportion to their ranks.

Change in proportion can make a major difference in how we experience a given subject. This becomes apparent in comparing two *pietàs* (*pietà,*

Italian for "pity," refers to a depiction of Mary holding and mourning over the body of Jesus).

Creating a composition with an infant on its mother's lap is much easier than showing a fully grown man in such a position. In his most famous PIETÀ, the young Michelangelo solved the problem by dramatically altering the human proportions of Mary's figure. Michelangelo made the heads of the two figures the same size but greatly enlarged Mary's body in relation to that of Christ, disguising her immensity with folds of drapery. Her seated figure spreads out to accommodate the almost horizontal curve of Christ's limp body. Imagine how the figure of Mary would appear if she were standing. Michelangelo made Mary's body into that of a giant; if she were a living human being rather than a work of art, she would stand at least seven feet tall!

Because the proportions of the figure of Christ are anatomically correct and there are abundant naturalistic details, we overlook the proportions of Mary's figure; yet the distortion is essential to the way we experience the content of the work.

Compare Michelangelo's work with another PIETÀ created almost a century earlier by an unknown sculptor. In the earlier work, the proportions are true to life, yet at first they seem unnatural. Christ's body appears to stick out awkwardly, without support. The sense of discomfort caused by the more normal proportions emphasizes the grief and tension appropriate to the subject. Such emphasis on suffering contrasts with the emphasis on serenity in Michelangelo's design.

The simple observation that some proportions are more pleasing to us than others has led to attempts throughout history to discover a rule that would generate "perfect" proportions. The ancient Greeks, whose philosophers held that numerical relationships reflected and formed the key to the structure of the universe, developed the most influential and enduring of these proportions, a relationship known as the GOLDEN SECTION, the Golden Ratio, or Divine Proportion. Many have believed it to be an essential component of harmony and possibly an integral part of life itself. This mathematical proportion appears often in the patterns of

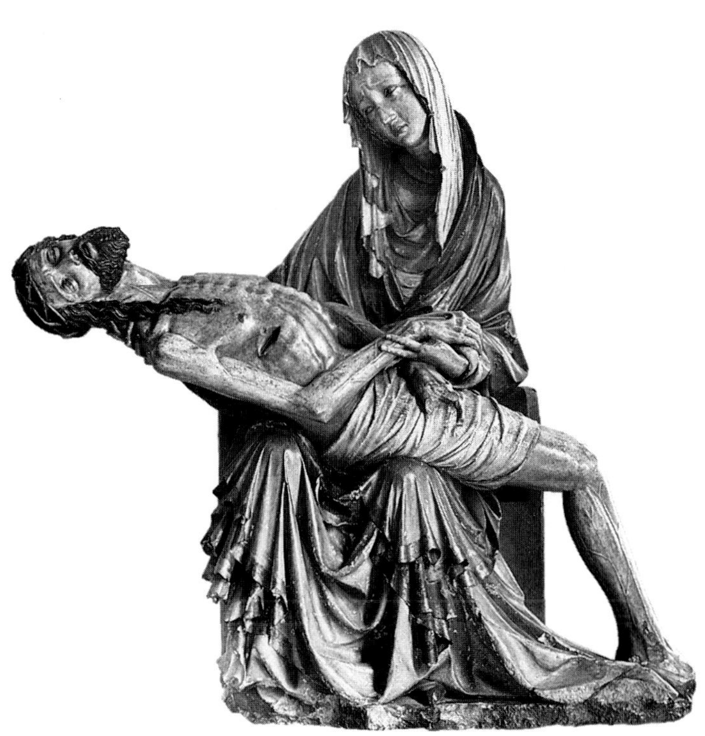

147 Master of the Beautiful Madonna.
PIETÀ. c. 1415.
Polychromed stone.
St. Mary's Church, Gdansk, Poland.

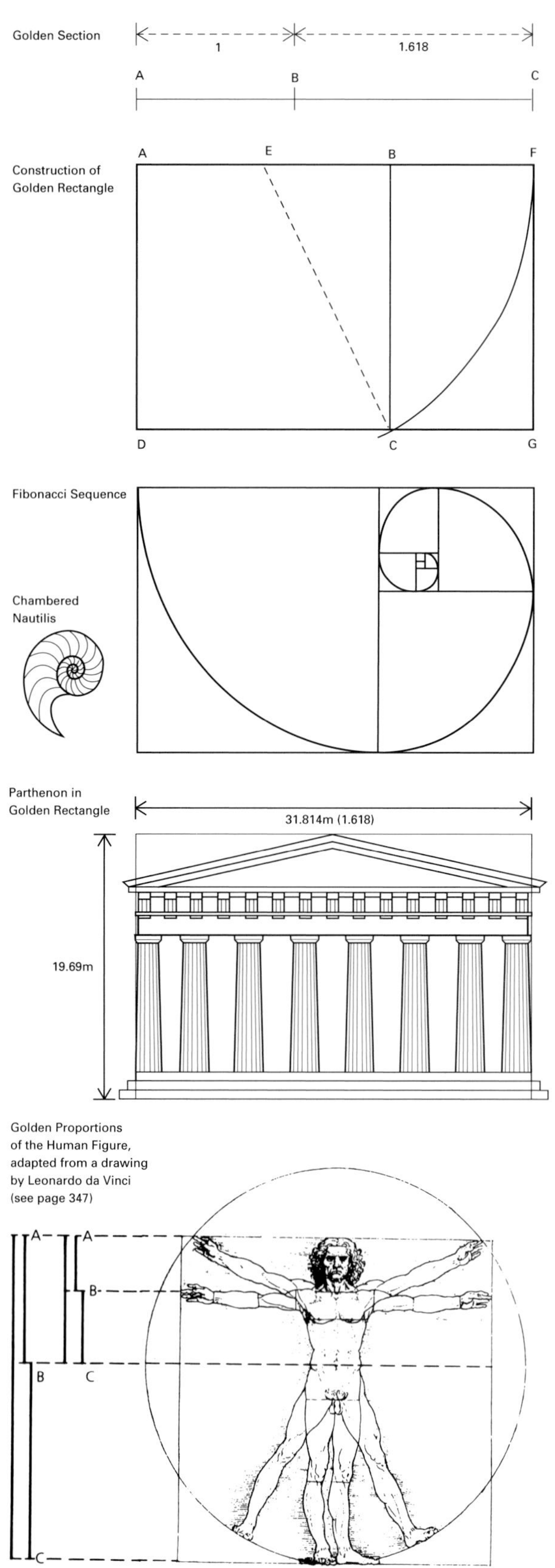

nature, and it has fascinated artists and mathematicians for thousands of years. Greek philosopher Plato considered it the key organizing principle of the cosmos.

To achieve the Golden Ratio, a line is divided into two unequal segments: the small segment has the same ratio to the larger as the larger segment has to the whole. In the thirteenth century, mathematician Leonardo Fibonacci discovered the numerical sequence generated by the Golden Ratio. The Fibonacci sequence (1, 1, 2, 3, 5, 8, 13, 21, 34, 55, etc.) is interesting because each number in the series is the sum of the two preceding numbers. The ratio of each number to its predecessor gets closer and closer to the Golden Ratio as the numbers get larger. The Fibonacci sequence, extended to include angles and spirals, can be found in the natural world in the chambered nautilus and spiral nebulae.

In the GOLDEN SECTION diagram, this "divine proportion" can be seen most clearly in line (AC), divided at a particular point that will yield unequal sections in which the shorter section (AB) is to the longer (BC) as the longer is to the entire length (AC). The Golden Proportion is thus expressed AB/BC = BC/AC. A rectangle with sides proportioned in accordance with the Golden Section is known as a Golden Rectangle.

Those who discovered and developed the concept of the Golden Section thought of it not as a mechanical formula, but as an ideal basis for art and architecture. The early Greeks designed temples with this harmonic proportion as a guide. Expressed in numbers, the Golden Proportion is .618034 to 1.

148 GOLDEN PROPORTIONS.

DESIGN SUMMARY

A finished artwork affects us because its design seems inevitable. And yet design is not inevitable at all. Faced with a blank piece of paper, an empty canvas, a lump of clay, or a block of marble, an artist begins a process involving many decisions, false starts, and changes in order to arrive at an integrated whole. In this chapter, we have presented some of the principles of design that guide the art-making process.

By photographing the progress of his LARGE RECLINING NUDE, Henri Matisse left us a rare record of the process of designing. Twenty-four photographs were taken over a period of four months; we reproduce four of them.

Matisse was sixty-six years old when he painted this picture. He had been painting for over forty-five years, yet he still searched for fresh solutions in every painting he started. The elegance of the final version of LARGE RECLINING NUDE looks effortless. The proportions are serene and confident. It all looks so easy. But it wasn't; the photographs tell of a patient process of search and discovery leading to a strong final design.

In some cases, before he began repainting, Matisse attached pieces of colored paper to the surfaces of his paintings to determine how the possible changes would look. At each stage, he selected and strengthened those aspects of the image that contributed most to the overall design. Finally, when he felt that everything worked together, he stopped.

In the earliest versions, Matisse struggled with awkward spacing and disjointed proportions. He gradually resolved these problems and added the rhythmic background grid pattern, which contrasts with the sweeping shapes of the figure. In the final painting, the bold distortions of the figure add up

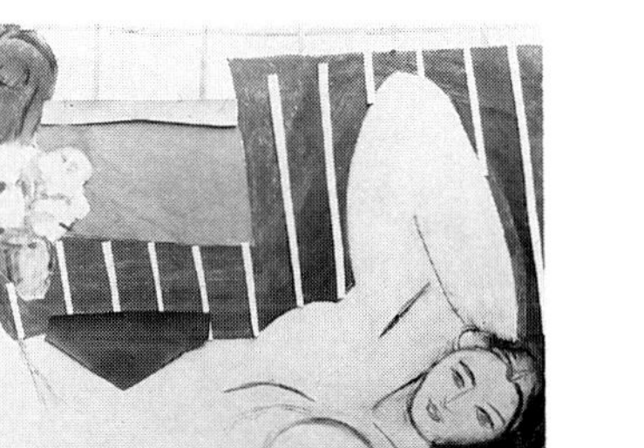

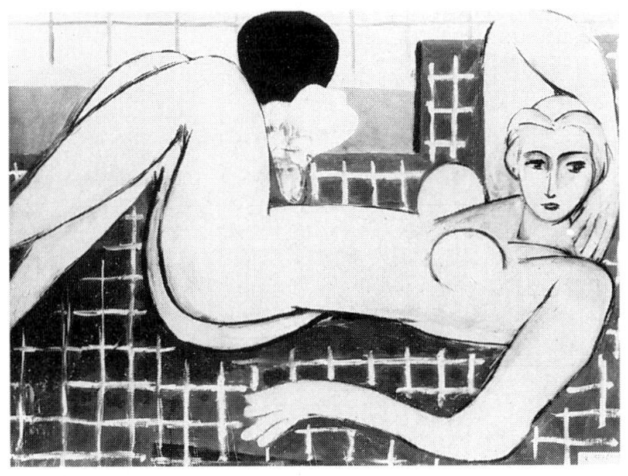

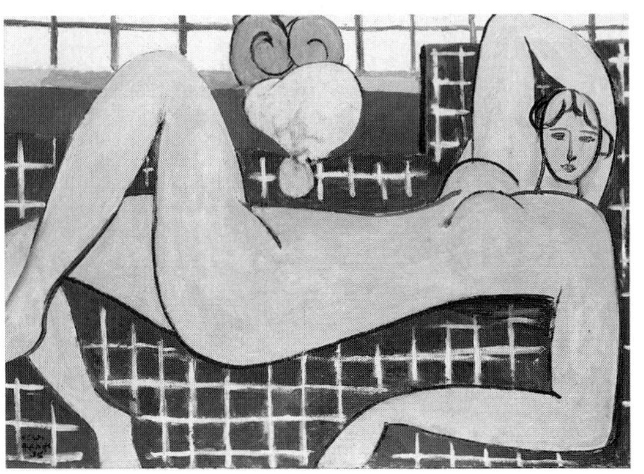

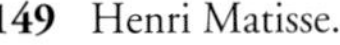

149 Henri Matisse.
Photographs of four states of LARGE RECLINING NUDE.
The Baltimore Museum of Art. The Cone Collection.
a State 1, May 3, 1935.
b State 9, May 29, 1935.
c State 13, September 4, 1935.
d Final painting, September 15, 1935.

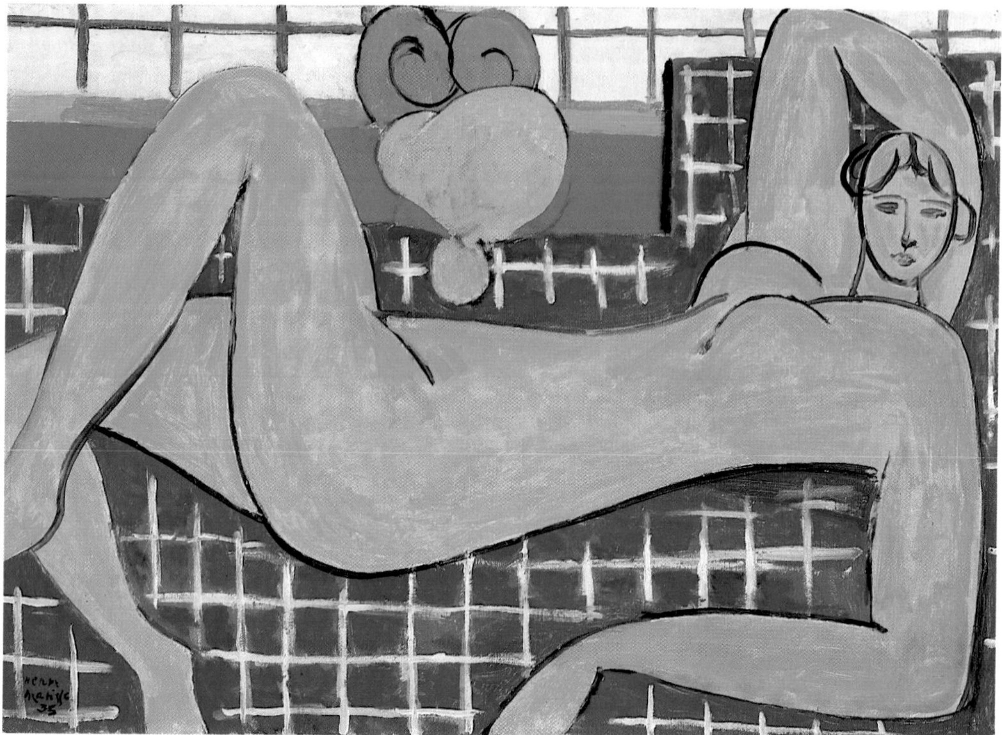

150 Henri Matisse. LARGE RECLINING NUDE. (formerly called "The Pink Nude"). September 15, 1935. Oil on canvas. 26" × 36½". The Baltimore Museum of Art: The Cone Collection, formed by Dr. Claribel and Miss Etta Cone of Baltimore, Maryland. (BMA 1950.258)

to a memorable abstraction of the subject. The sensuous curves of the nude echo the curves of the abstracted flowers and spiraling chairback. The rectangles and grids of the background provide a contrast that is simple but never dull.

For Matisse, expression in a composition was not limited to the passion mirrored in a face or to the gesture of a figure.

The entire arrangement of my picture is expressive: the place occupied by the figures, the empty spaces around them, the proportions, everything has its share.[4]

Three works with the same subject, done by Edvard Munch, demonstrate how variations in design and media can effectively change the aesthetic impact of a given subject. These three works, each showing a couple embracing, were completed over a period of six years.

In the painting KISS BY THE WINDOW, a couple is placed on the far right side of the canvas, their figures joined. They appear to be hiding behind the curtain. Munch's way of showing a couple's feeling of oneness is already present in the greatly simplified, if somewhat awkward, composite shape of the embracing figures. On the far left, a tree and light from windows balance the couple and produce an interesting asymmetrical tension. The nearly monochromatic blue-green tends to cool an otherwise hot subject. Simple curves play off against straight edges, contrasting the curved figures and the curtain with the straight lines of the window.

The second work, THE KISS, is a drypoint in which a nude couple is nearly centered in front of a window. (Drypoint is discussed on page 162.) Munch boldly emphasized the outlines of the figures and again made them into one relatively simple shape. By removing the line that would normally divide the faces, he emphasized their unity. Drawn lines create a texture on the figures that enhances the rhythmic movement and energy of their outlines. The shapes of the dark curtains frame the embracing couple and add dramatic emphasis by providing strong value contrast with the light of the

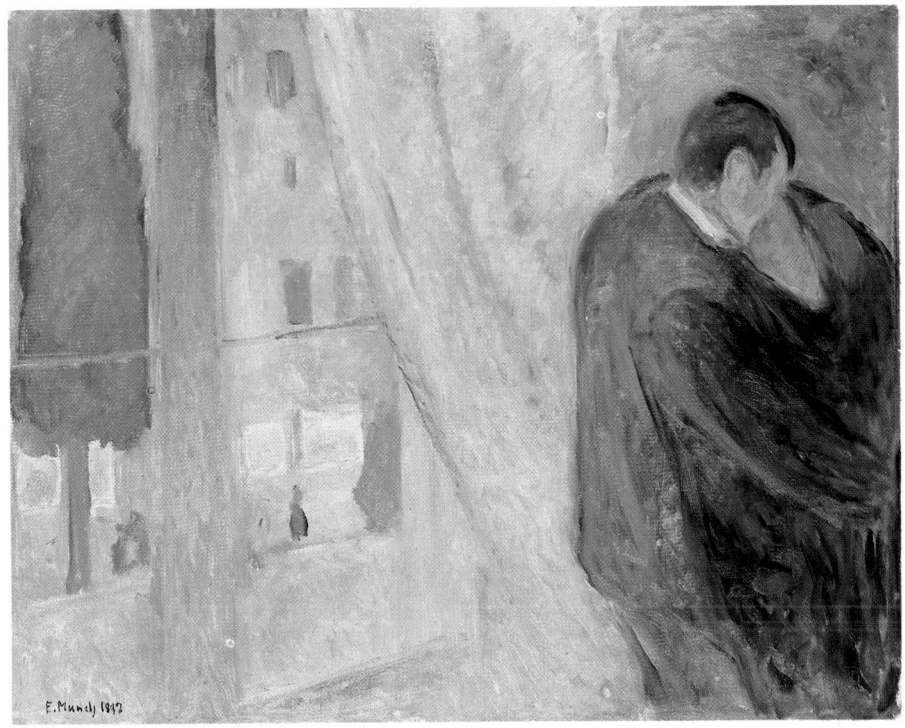

151 Edvard Munch.
KISS BY THE WINDOW. 1892.
Oil on canvas. 72.3 cm x 90.7 cm.
National Gallery, Oslo.

window. This contrast brings a feeling of passion not present in the other two images.

For the painting, Munch chose a horizontal format that offsets the many vertical directional lines and active diagonal curves within the frame. The drypoint's format is vertical, which gives the image a more active quality in spite of its almost symmetrical composition. In the third work, a woodcut also called THE KISS (see next page), the nearly square format produces a relatively quiet balance of directional forces. Here, shapes have been flattened and even more simplified than the shapes in the painting.

The entire image is highly abstract. Wood texture printed as background—from an uncut second block—provides a vertical rhythmic pattern, offering a counterpoint to the gently curving lines and single shape of the embracing couple. By removing indications of light and shadow and eliminating suggestions of spatial depth, location, and all unnecessary details of anatomy, Munch created maximum effect with a minimum of means. He

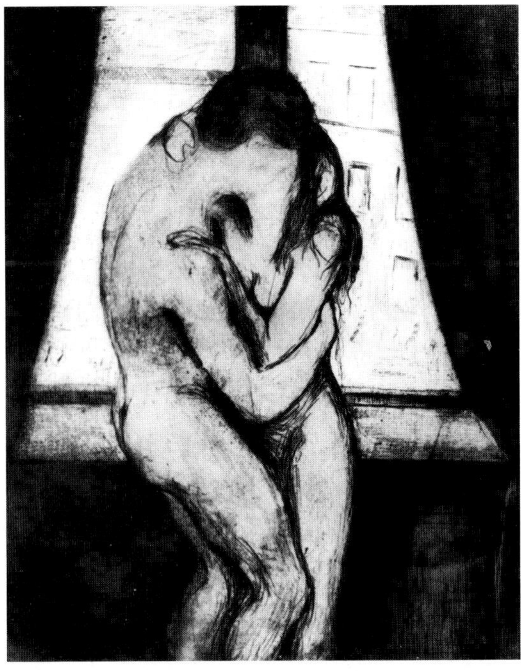

152 Edvard Munch.
THE KISS. 1895.
Drypoint and aquatint.
343 mm × 278 mm.
Albertina Collection, Vienna.

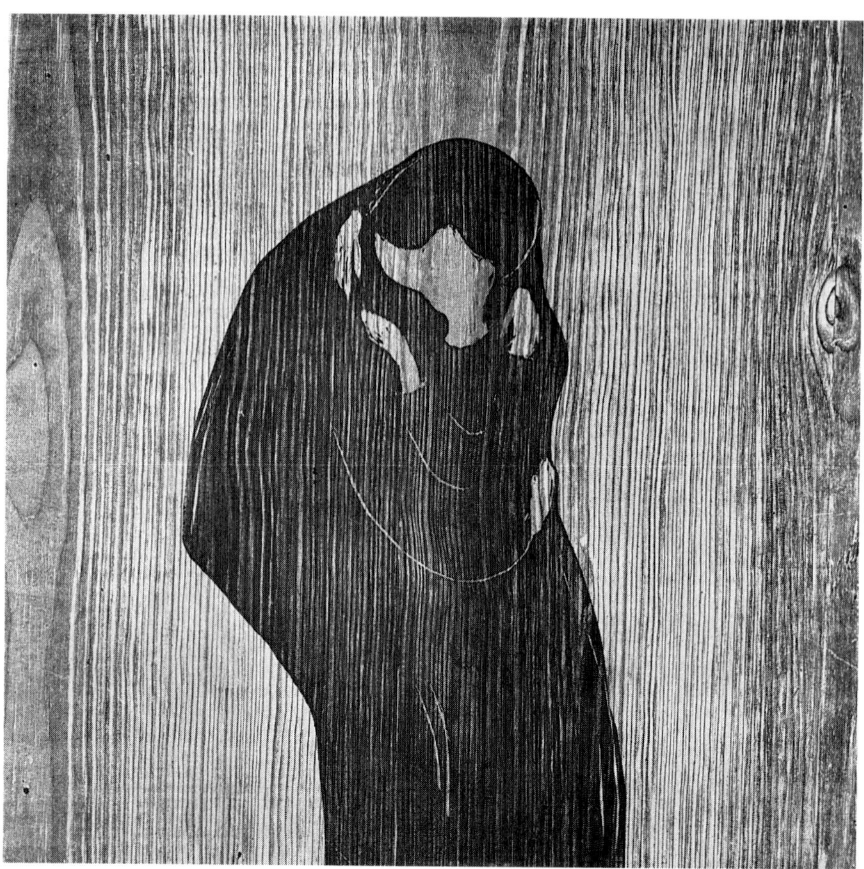

153 Edvard Munch. THE KISS. 1897-1898. Woodcut. 465 mm × 467 mm. Albertina Collection, Vienna.

distilled the subject to its essence. But he did not achieve this result all at once; it evolved from one work to the next in a series that included several versions not shown here. In each of the three images reproduced here, Munch demonstrated his sensitivity to the format he chose and the unique character of each medium. Of Munch's many versions of THE KISS, the woodcut is the best known, perhaps because its design so effectively symbolizes feelings of oneness associated with a kiss.

To be successful, the design process must involve sensitive, effective decisions concerning all aspects of the form being created. The artist must evaluate each decision as it is implemented and make further changes as needed, as Matisse did in LARGE RECLINING NUDE. The goal is to refine all the interrelationships within the evolving form—to respond to both planned and unplanned events as they occur.

Whether the visual art is drawing or computer graphics, sculpture or architecture, basic elements and principles of design remain the same. The results, however, are determined by the artist's interaction with the unique form-making possibilities and the limitations of each material and technique.

The design of the objects and spaces we live with makes a big difference in how we think and feel, whether we are aware of design or not. An awareness of visual form and its effect on us helps us discriminate between what contributes to our lives and what does not.

EDVARD MUNCH (1863–1944)

In the late nineteenth century, while Austrian physician Sigmund Freud was originating psychoanalysis, Norwegian artist Edvard Munch was making states of mind visible in his paintings and prints.

Soon after his birth (the second of five children), Munch's family moved to Christiana (now Oslo). Family relationships were close throughout Munch's life, but his childhood was clouded by illness and death.

When he was five his mother died of tuberculosis, and when he was fourteen his elder sister died of the same illness. His strict and pious father, a military medical doctor, was periodically obsessed—almost to the point of insanity—by grief and religious anxiety. Edvard himself was frail, and ill health caused long absences from school. He wrote:

Disease and insanity were the black angels on guard at my cradle.... In my childhood I felt always that I was treated in an unjust way, without a mother, sick, and with threatened punishment in Hell hanging over my head.[5]

Munch's artistic career began at age seventeen. Poor health had once again interrupted his formal schooling and put an end to his father's hope that he would become an engineer. With his family's approval, he entered art school.

His early works were conventional in terms of subject matter and style. Some can be considered illustrations. But by 1884 Munch had joined the world of bohemian artists and writers in Oslo, and his art had begun to change. He made several visits to Paris, where he was influenced by the Impressionists and Symbolists, particularly by Gauguin's shapes and symbolic color (see pages 400–401). Munch's work shows the tipped-up ground plane and flat-shape emphasis inspired by Gauguin, and the emotional intensity and linear energy of Van Gogh. But Munch carried these qualities further. His symbolic compositions and sense of impending disaster are unique (see THE SHRIEK on page 403).

From 1892 to 1908 Munch lived mainly in Germany, with frequent stays in Norway and visits to France and Italy. In the 1890s, Munch developed a new, intensely emotional way of expressing feelings in his art. By eliminating unnecessary details, and by using line, shape, value, and color freely in symbolic ways, he communicated heightened emotions.

His art draws on those experiences and emotions central to his life: love, sexual desire, jealousy, loneliness, fear, sickness, death, and despair. He explained his choice of psychologically charged subject matter:

There should be no more paintings ... of people reading and women knitting. In the future they should be of people who breathe, who feel emotions, who suffer and love.[6]

The early loss of his mother and sister—the two women closest to him—undoubtedly contributed to his obsession with male-female love. Munch's view of love is often seen as a basic struggle between the sexes. One cannot help but wonder if the works reproduced here sprang in part from Munch's need to express his love and his unfulfilled desire for a lasting love relationship with a woman.

He often repeated a subject two, three, or more times, usually starting with a painting and moving on to prints, as seen on previous pages. In the process, he strengthened and clarified his composition and intensified the message of his imagery. Through art, Munch used his personal psychological journey to create universally significant archetypal symbols.

The anxieties so evident in much of his work were confessions of his own tortured soul. A fear of insanity, which had weighed on him for many years, became a reality. In 1908 he suffered a complete mental collapse, the result of heavy drinking, overwork, and the end of a long and troubled love affair. He returned to Denmark and entered a clinic, where he remained for several months. Although he realized that his mental instability spurred his artistic genius, he made a conscious effort to recover. As part of this effort, he abandoned his emotionally intense imagery. His style remained vigorous, but the internal anguish of much of his earlier work was replaced by less personally charged visions.

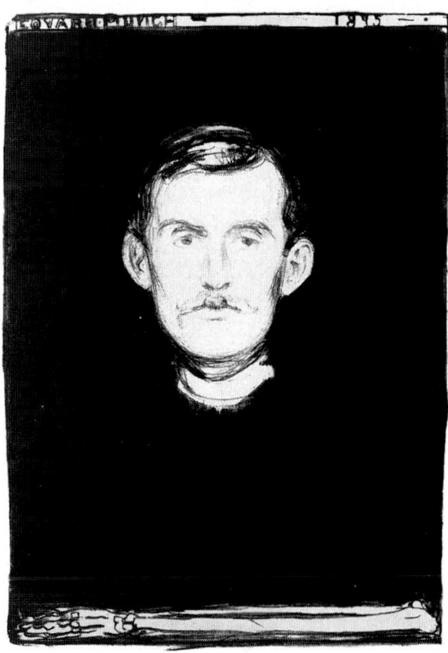

154 Edvard Munch.
SELF-PORTRAIT. 1895.
Lithograph, printed in black.
Composition 18⅛" × 12¾".
The Museum of Modern Art, New York.
Gift of James L. Goodwin in memory of Philip L. Goodwin.

Munch's powerful imagery places him among the most influential artists of his time. He and Van Gogh are considered the two main sources of Expressionist art in the twentieth century.

CHAPTER 6

Style

The word "style" is common in everyday speech. Designers try to influence our purchases with frequent changes of clothing and car styles. We wear our hair in a particular style. We recognize the distinctive styles of our favorite musicians. We even speak of the style of an era, such as 1950's-style music. Style is a consistent, recognizable, and noteworthy manner of expression or way of behaving.

In art, *style* refers to a consistent and characteristic handling of media, elements of form, and principles of design that make a work of art identifiable as the product of a particular person, group, historic period, or place. Some art styles are more distinct and easily identifiable than others. Individual and shared values, experiences, and techniques are among the major sources of artistic styles. During the course of a lifetime, an artist may change his or her style.

Besides personal, group, period, and geographic styles, a number of other terms describe general stylistic approaches. This chapter provides an overview of the ways in which styles reveal artists' attitudes and intentions. It uses style as a way to help us compare and better understand the art of different artists, periods, and cultures.

Terms such as classical and classicism, romantic and romanticism, formal and formalist describe styles. While the terms classicism and romanticism are not opposites, they are frequently used to describe opposing tendencies, as are the terms formalism and expressionism.

Classicism refers to art based on qualities of logical order, clarity, and harmony found in the art of ancient Greece and Rome. When applied to Greek art, the term *Classical* refers to works created during the fifth and fourth centuries B.C., when Greek art reached its peak of excellence (see pages 323–325). After the decline of the Greeks and Romans, their general style was looked back upon and admired by later sculptors, architects, and their patrons.

Neoclassicism (new classicism) is the term used for the eighteenth- and nineteenth-century revival of Classical Greek and Roman forms. Throughout the world, aspects of the Classical Greek style have been imitated widely; we can see examples of Classical columns on banks and government buildings in nearly every large town and city.

The marble sculpture created by ancient Greek artists retains its strength and power for today's viewers. But "classical" is also used more broadly to describe art based on regular structure or symmetry, emphasizing horizontal and vertical directional forces and static or stable balance. In an even wider sense, the word classic is used to indicate lasting excellence, such as a classic film or piece of music.

Romanticism refers to either a specific, late eighteenth- and nineteenth-century style or a general tendency in art and literature that emphasizes strong feelings, the power of the imagination, and the value of intuition. Romanticism arose to challenge Neoclassicism in Europe in the late eighteenth century and lasted until the mid-nineteenth century. Romantic artists espoused the idea that intuition and emotion are just as compelling as reason and order. While classicism and romanticism are used to identify specific historic styles, the terms are also applied to basic approaches to art.

In simple terms, the classic resolves tension in favor of stability and calm; the romantic fosters tension, instability, and passion. The painting by Delacroix on page 378 embodies the essence of Romanticism, while David's painting on page 373 is a leading example of Neoclassicism.

FORMAL AND EXPRESSIVE STYLES

The more recent terms *formal* and *formalist* refer to an emphasis on order, formality, and studied proportions, and they are therefore related to a classical approach. In formal compositions, the emphasis is on rational structure rather than intuitive expression. Formalist art reveals the artist's deliberate control of the elements of visual form, such as line, mass, and color, with little or no indication of personal feelings. It looks carefully constructed, based on the principles of design. (See Mondrian's formalist paintings on page 439.)

In contrast, *expressionist* art emphasizes immediate feelings and heightened passions. It is likely to be bold, to make use of distortion or abstraction, and it may include inventive or symbolic use of color. Expressionist art sometimes appears to have been done quickly, in an unplanned or spontaneous manner, even when it was not. (See Kandinsky's expressionist painting on page 415.)

Stylized refers to art that follows established artistic conventions rather than direct observations of the surrounding world. Ancient and tribal societies with long-standing traditions develop their own stylized conventions for subject matter. Byzantine painting (see page 334) and Egyptian painting and sculpture (see pages 320–321) have easily recognizable styles, with much use of stylized forms. In the Byzantine stylization of the face, eyes are surrounded with dark shadows, noses are long and thin, and mouths narrow; Egyptian stylization depicts eyes front-view, noses and mouths side-view.

PERIOD AND CULTURAL STYLES

Just as a society develops its own language and customs, so it develops its own beliefs (religion) and style of material forms (clothing, buildings, art of all kinds). Taken together, these social and physical forms comprise "culture." Each society finds ways to represent what it values or feels is important.

Style is an important part of every culture's identity. It is both culturally conditioned and culturally expressive. Just as an artist is the product of a culture, so too is he or she the product of the experience of a particular era. Within any culture, styles undergo changes over time while still expressing the broad cultural viewpoint. We cannot disassociate the way a style looks from our feelings about a particular culture and its time in history.

The elegant EYE symbol is well known and distinctive; a glance may be enough to recognize the period and culture that created it. This symbol is used in two different ways in the wall painting shown on page 321.

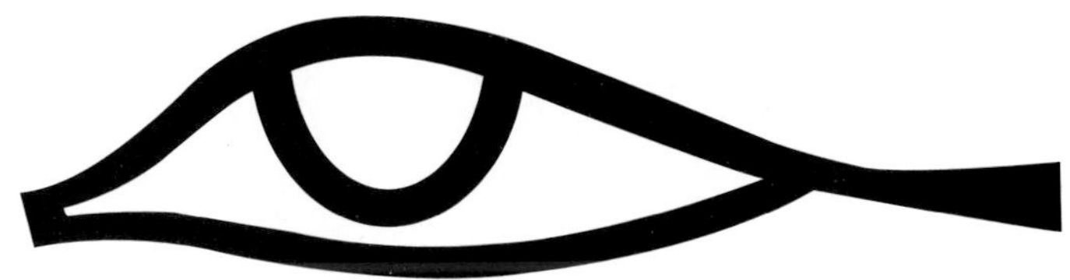

155 EYE.

Another popular period style, *Art Nouveau* (French for "new art"), was an international decorative style of the late nineteenth and early twentieth centuries. The style is characterized by sinuous lines or contours, sometimes called "whiplash" lines, to describe their serpentine curves and how they reverse themselves in unexpected ways. Art Nouveau appeared in nearly all art forms, from furniture and housewares to posters, typography, jewelry, glass, painting, sculpture, and architecture. Its sources include an antimechanical, return-to-crafts movement in England, the flat, curving

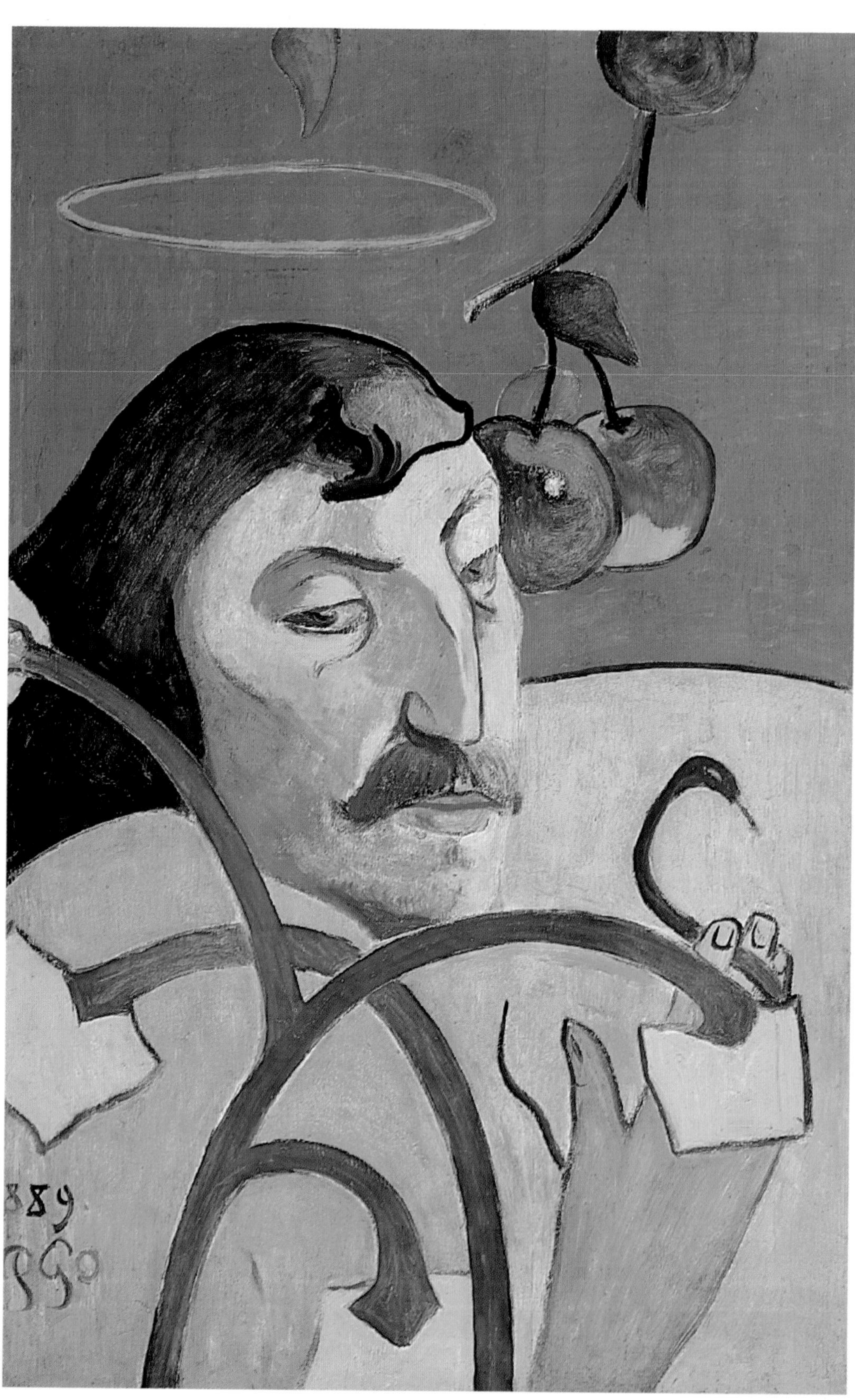

156 Paul Gauguin.
SYMBOLIST SELF-PORTRAIT WITH HALO. 1889.
Oil on wood. 31¼" × 20¼".

shapes and patterns of Japanese woodcut prints (see page 300), decorative linear plant forms, and the art of Symbolist painters such as Paul Gauguin. Notice the line quality of the vinelike snake in Gauguin's SYMBOLIST SELF-PORTRAIT WITH HALO.

Although they drew from many sources, the artists who worked in the Art Nouveau style were antihistorical. They tried to free themselves from what they saw as superficial realism and the revivals of earlier historical styles. Art Nouveau reached its peak around 1900 and dominated the arts of Europe and the United States until World War I. The style was revived in the 1960s and continues to have broad appeal today. The elegant linear embellishment of the stairway in Victor Horta's TASSEL HOUSE, Henry van de Velde's twisting, turning, plantlike CANDELABRUM, and the flamboyant curves in Alphonse Mucha's poster advertising the bicycle company CYCLES PERFECTA are typical of Art Nouveau.

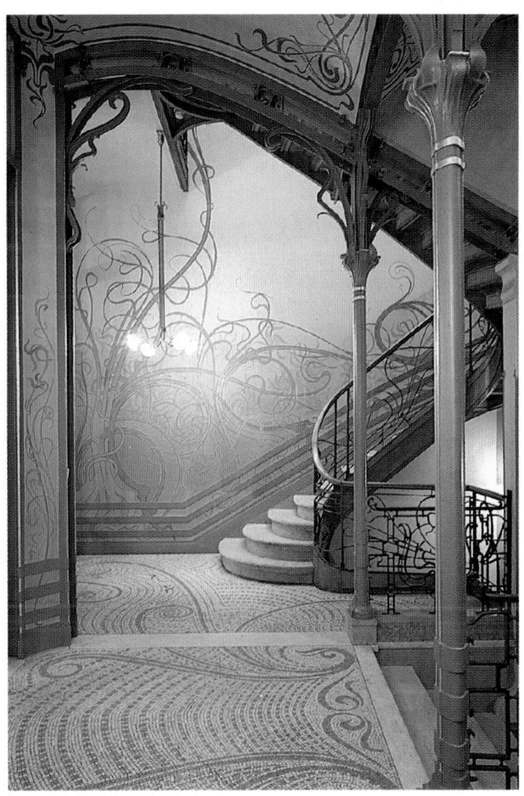

157 Victor Horta.
STAIRCASE, TASSEL HOUSE, Brussels. 1892-1893.

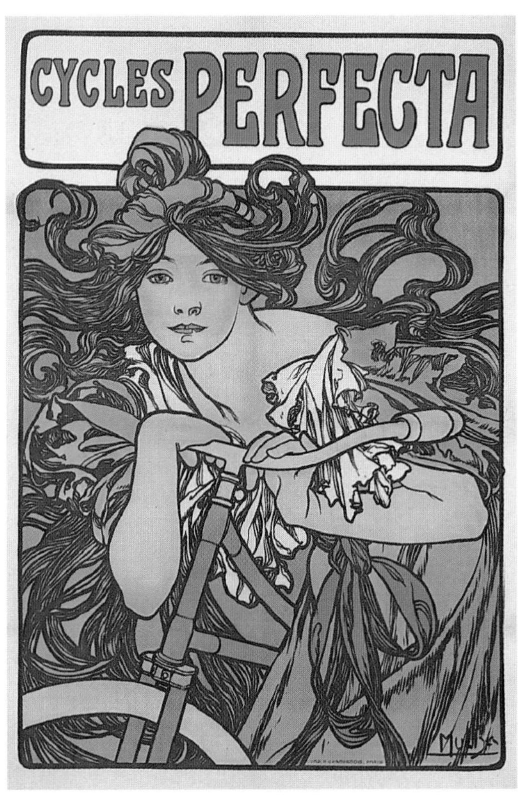

158 Alphonse Mucha.
CYCLES PERFECTA.
Poster.

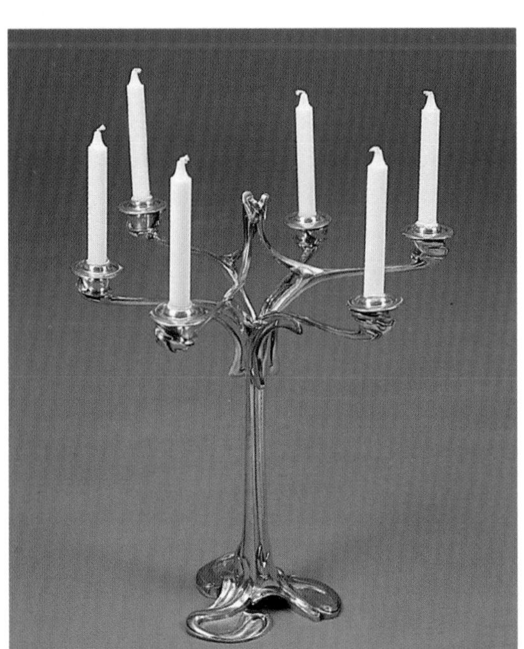

159 Henry van de Velde.
CANDELABRUM. c. 1902.
Silver-plated bronze.
Industrial Arts Museum, Trondheim, Norway.

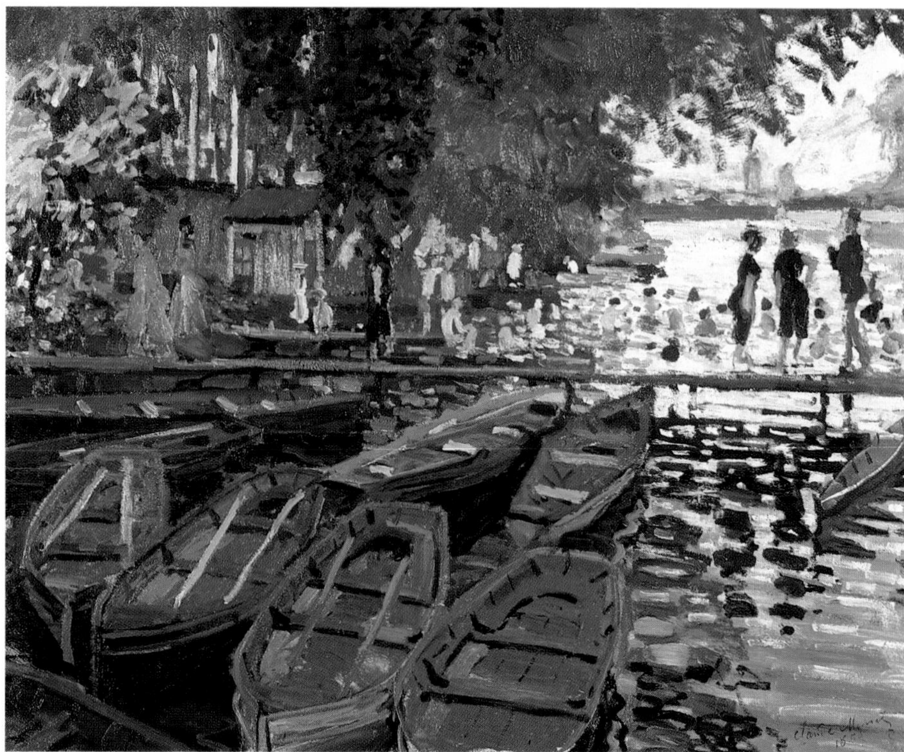

160 Claude Monet. BATHING AT LA GRENOUILLÈRE. 1869. Oil on canvas. 73 cm × 92 cm.

GROUP STYLE

Impressionism is a late nineteenth-century French style of painting. Impressionists depicted scenes of contemporary life and landscape in a freely painted, light, colorful manner that was quite unlike the tightly polished, dark-toned canvases of the popular art of the time. Claude Monet and Pierre-Auguste Renoir, early advocates of this new approach, were part of a loosely knit group that included Edgar Degas, Edouard Manet, and Mary Cassatt, an American (see pages 386 and 392–393).

Rather than depict myths or scenes from ancient Rome, members of the group painted their fleeting impressions of the leisure activities, urban scenes, and rural landscapes of their day. The Impressionists were among the first artists to paint outdoors, directly from their subjects. Until then, the standard practice was to sketch the subject, then complete the painting in the studio.

Another revolutionary feature of the style was the unfinished quality of the completed paintings. In contrast to other painters of the time, Impressionists did not hide their brush strokes. Monet and Renoir developed the rapid painting techniques the Impressionists used for representing transitory effects of light. Monet's BATHING AT GRENOUILLÈRE and Renoir's BALL AT THE MOULIN DE LA GALETTE reveal the artists' interest in the ways light activates color to create the mood of a particular moment and place.

The Impressionists' subject matter included indoor as well as outdoor subjects and was largely urban and middle-class in outlook. Even when an Impressionist artist looked at a landscape, it was often from a city dweller's point of view.

Although Impressionism is now the best-known and best-appreciated group style in Western art, it was not always so. The approach was highly controversial from its inception in the late 1860s until the early twentieth century—when even more radical departures from tradition were introduced. The Impressionists' way of seeing and painting laid the groundwork for many of the revolutionary movements and styles of the twentieth century. (See also the discussion of Impressionism in the history section, pages 387–394.)

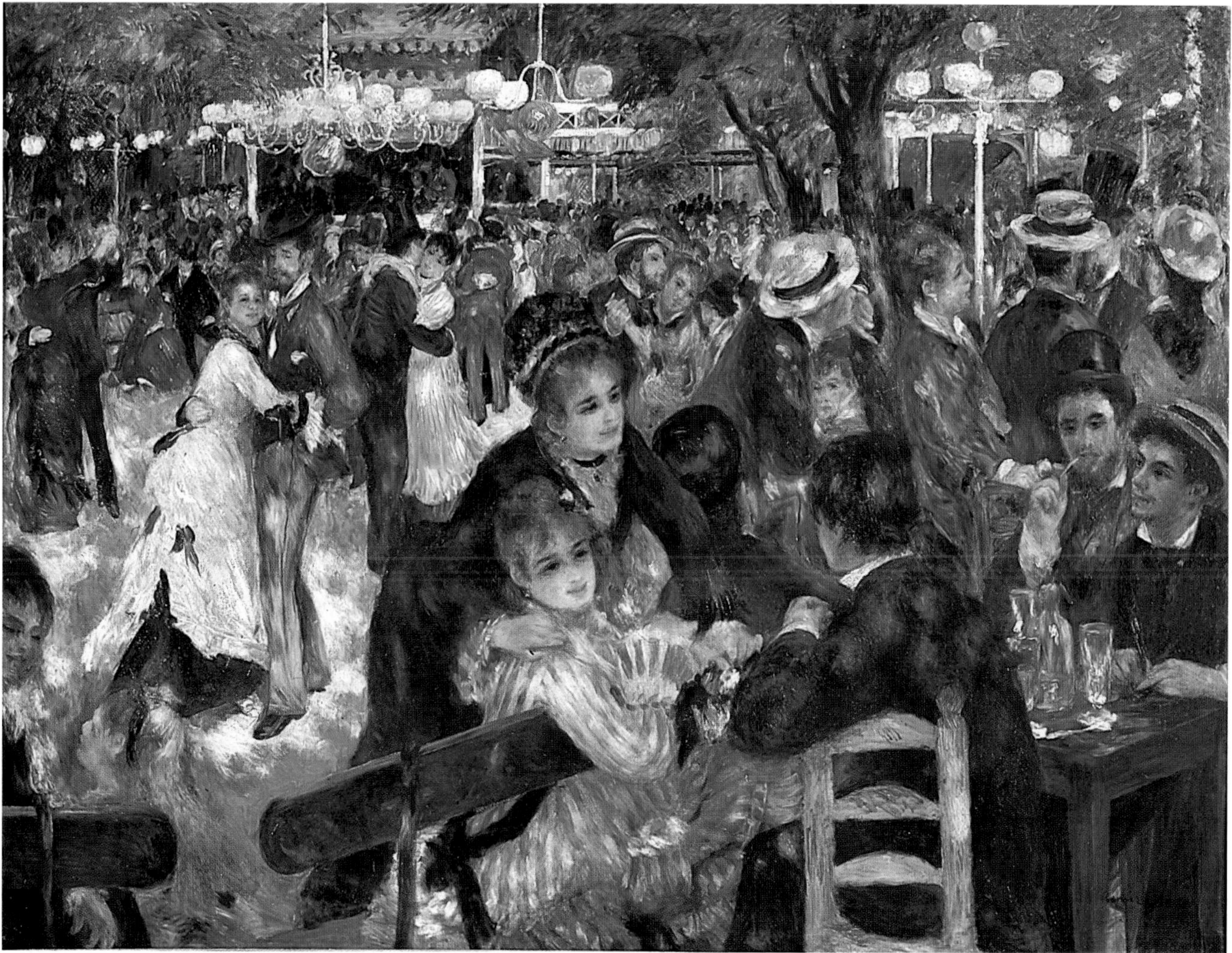

161 Pierre-Auguste Renoir.
BALL AT THE MOULIN DE LA GALETTE. 1876.
Oil on canvas. 51½" × 69".
Musée d'Orsay, Paris.

PERSONAL STYLE

Just as each of us has a recognizable style of writing that is part of our expressive identity, individual artists have characteristic modes of personal expression. Personal styles evolve naturally as artists assimilate influences and mature. Many artists' early works are linked with the art of their periods, peers, and teachers. As an artist's ideas evolve, wide variations in style may occur. Even when an artist's basic attitude remains the same, experiences, influences, and affiliations with other artists and art movements may generate major changes in style.

The works of the three artists we consider next demonstrate individual, consistent points of view

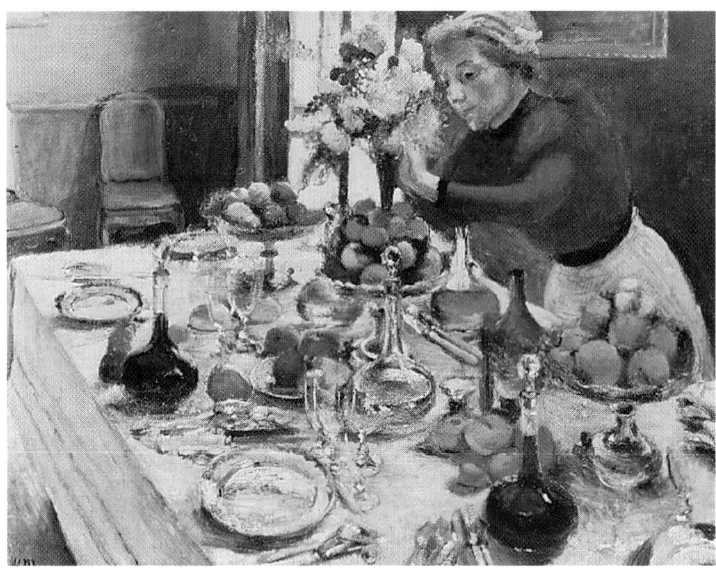

162 Henri Matisse.
LA DESSERTE. 1897.
Oil on canvas. 39½" × 51½".
Private collection. © Succession H. Matisse.

and therefore show fairly consistent personal styles, with some important variations over time. Each of these artists shows a unity of vision or purpose that differs markedly from the others. Although their lives overlapped in time, they came from different countries and held very different attitudes. Henri Matisse and Käthe Kollwitz were primarily interested in depicting people; Louise Nevelson preferred to work with nonrepresentational forms.

During the 1890s, Matisse was at work developing the skills of a painter. Although the Symbolist reaction against Impressionism was in full swing, Matisse was still studying the lessons of Impressionism. LA DESSERTE sums up what he had learned. Its freely painted surface and rich luminosity were adapted from Impressionist depictions of light. Its composition makes something solid out of Impressionism's fleeting moment. But Matisse didn't remain in the Impressionist mode for long. With its tilted tabletop and slightly compressed sense of depth, LA DESSERTE gives a glimpse of major changes to come.

Matisse was good at balancing tradition and innovation. When an artistic idea fired his imagination, he made it completely his own. Between 1908 and 1917, Matisse made several trips to Algeria, Morocco, and Germany, searching for ways to enliven his painting with more rhythmic lines and brighter colors. HARMONY IN RED shows the results of his search. The subject matter is almost identical to that of LA DESSERTE, yet the overall effect could hardly be more different. The abstract, decorative qualities of Art Nouveau and the rich fabric designs Matisse found in North Africa influenced a colorful linear pattern of point and counterpoint.

First painted as *Harmony in Blue*, the painting was sold by Matisse; later he asked to have it back so he could repaint the canvas with an overall red to achieve a better balance of color. The dominant warm red, animated by a bold pattern of blues and greens, brings the tablecloth and wall together. Although the subjects—table, room, and window-framed landscape—immediately suggest the illusion of depth, Matisse translated the third dimension of the real world into a lively flat surface. The tabletop, with no forward edge, has become a spatially ambiguous plane of color upon which bright shapes rest weightlessly.

Matisse made substantial changes in style as he encountered new experiences and influences, yet he felt a continuity between his earlier and later work:

I foresee the danger of appearing to contradict myself. I feel very strongly the tie between my earlier and my recent works, but I do not think exactly the way I thought yesterday. Or rather, my basic idea has not changed, but my thought has evolved, and my modes of expression have followed my thoughts.[1]

Matisse became more and more independent. Throughout most of his life he was not associated with any group style. In 1908, he wrote:

The purpose of a painter must not be conceived as separate from his pictorial means, and these pictorial means must be the more complete (I do not mean complicated) the deeper is his thought. I am unable to distinguish between the feeling I have for life and my way of expressing it.[2]

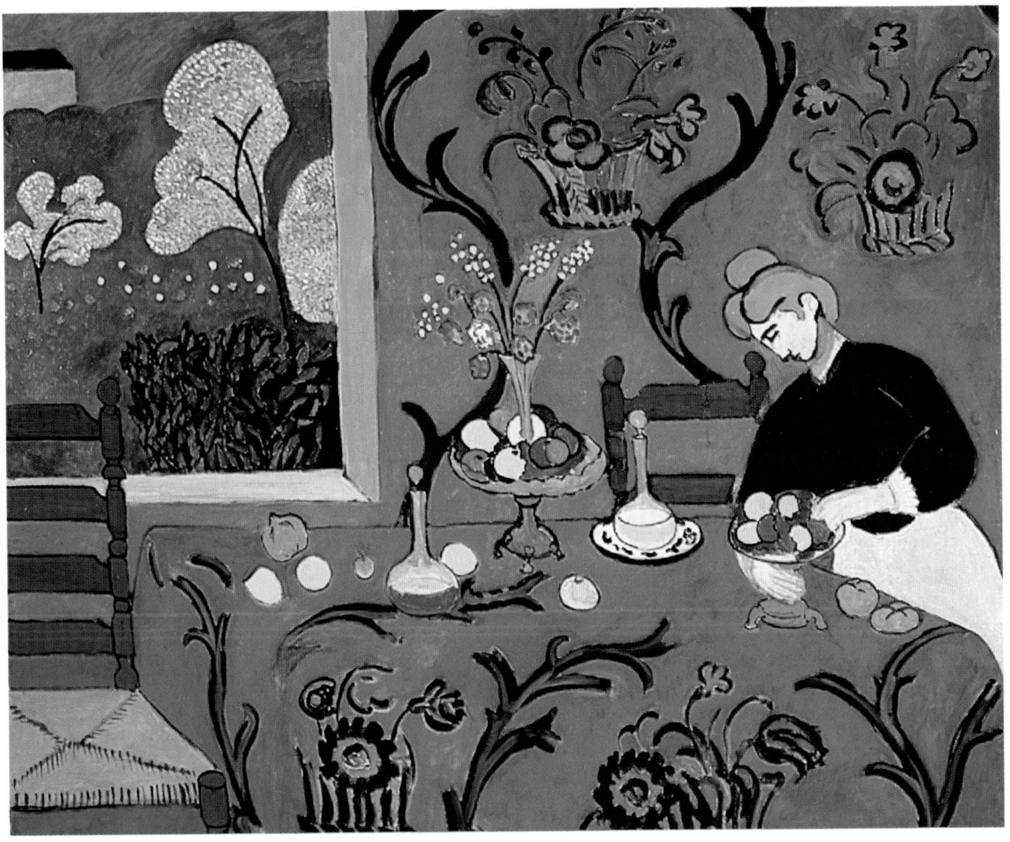

163 Henri Matisse.
HARMONY IN RED. 1908-1909.
Oil on canvas. 72" × 97".
State Hermitage Museum, St. Petersburg, Russia.

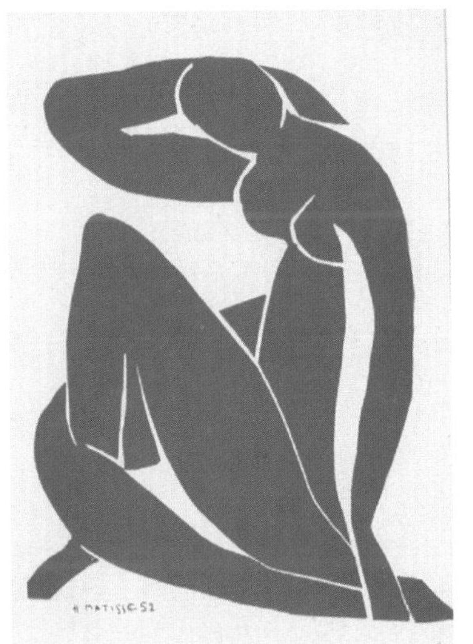

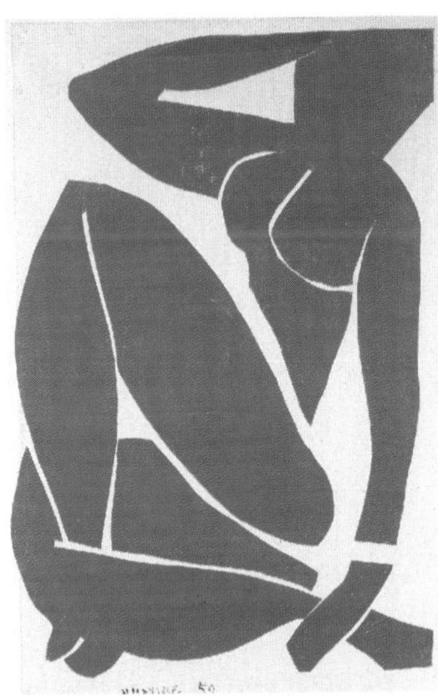

164 Henri Matisse.
BLUE NUDE IV AND BLUE NUDE III. 1952.
Gouache cutouts. 105 cm × 85 cm, 109 cm × 74 cm.
Private collection.

Matisse wrote the above a few years before he created NASTURTIUMS AND THE DANCE (see page 119), a painting that illustrates his point. It shows a corner of his studio, including a chair and a sculpture stand topped with a vase of flowers. A section of his large painting *The Dance* rests against the wall. In NASTURTIUMS AND THE DANCE, Matisse expressed what the French call *joie de vivre,* or "joy of life." It is reflected in every line, shape, and color. We find evidence of Matisse's sense of delight throughout most of his work—even his self-portrait (see next page) has an expressive, playful quality.

The collages (or cutouts) titled BLUE NUDE III and BLUE NUDE IV were made when Matisse was bedridden, less than two years before his death. Despite his failing health, his enthusiasm for life is evident. In fact, his late works are some of his most powerful and joyful.

HENRI MATISSE (1869–1954)

When French artist Henri Matisse was eighteen years old, his father sent him to Paris to study law. A year later, he passed his examinations and took a dull job as a clerk in a lawyer's office. Then an attack of appendicitis changed the direction of his life. During the long convalescence at his parents' home, his mother tried to amuse him with a gift of a box of paints, brushes, and a do-it-yourself book on painting. The result was extraordinary. By the age of twenty-one, Matisse knew he wanted to be a painter. He returned to Paris and became a full-time art student. In the methodical manner of a lawyer, he began his artistic career by becoming thoroughly proficient in the traditional techniques of French art. Throughout his life he worked at adding to both his knowledge and his skills, while being careful to preserve his original naiveté.

For Matisse, a painting was a combination of lines, shapes, and colors before it was a depiction of nameable objects. His personal style was based on intuition; yet he acknowledged the importance of his years of study. He masterfully assimilated influences from the arts of the Near East and Africa and from other painters. Paul Gauguin, who invented color combinations and flat, outlined shapes new to Western art, was a particularly significant influence (see pages 400–401).

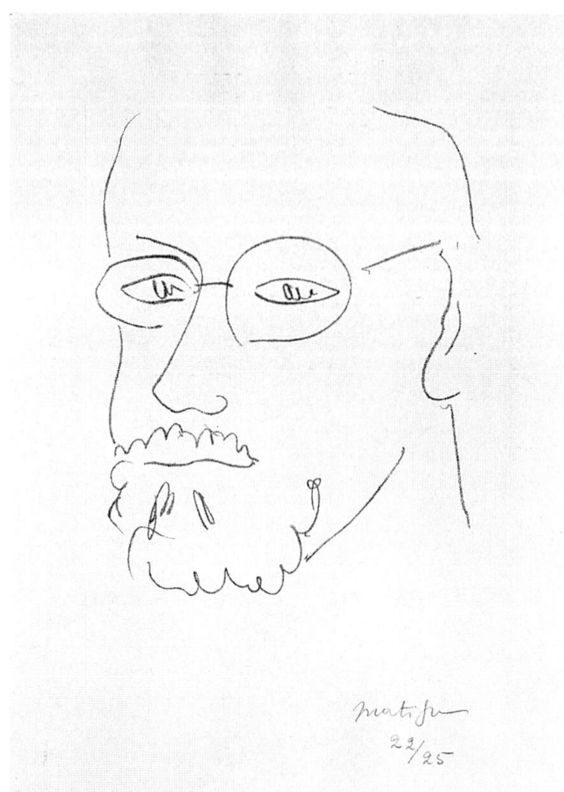

165 Henri Matisse. SELF-PORTRAIT, THREE-QUARTER VIEW. 1948. Lithograph printed in black, composition. 9" × 7¼". The Museum of Modern Art, New York. The Curt Valentin Bequest.

Matisse's primary interest was in expressing his passionate feeling for life through the free use of visual form, with the human figure his main subject.

What interests me most is neither still life nor landscape but the human figure. It is through it that I best succeed in expressing the nearly religious feeling that I have towards life.[3]

Matisse sought to hide his own artistic struggles so that his work would appear effortless and light. He was concerned, however, that young people would think his paintings were done casually—even carelessly—and would mistakenly conclude that years of disciplined work and study were unnecessary.

The dominant qualities in Matisse's art are lyric color and vitality. Behind the playful appearance lie radiant bigheartedness, grace, and wisdom. Although he lived through both world wars and was aware of acute suffering, Matisse chose to express joy and tranquility in his art.

What I dream of is an art of balance, of purity and serenity, devoid of troubling or depressing subject matter, an art which might be for every mental worker, be he businessman or writer, like an appeasing influence, like a mental soother, something like a good armchair in which to rest from physical fatigue.[4]

166 Henri Matisse. NASTURTIUMS AND THE DANCE. 1912. Oil on canvas. 75¾" × 45". Pushkin Museum of Fine Arts, Moscow.

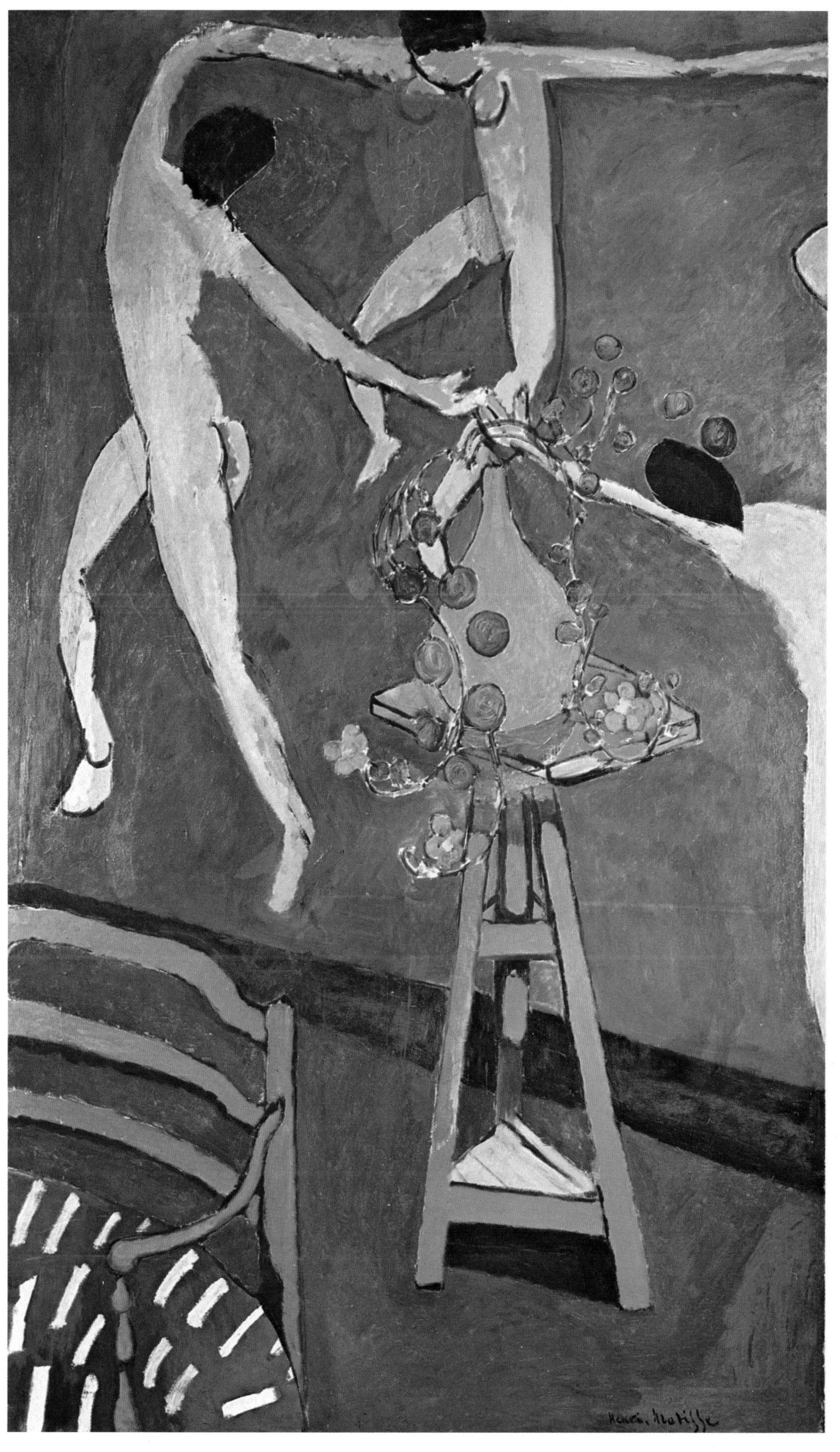

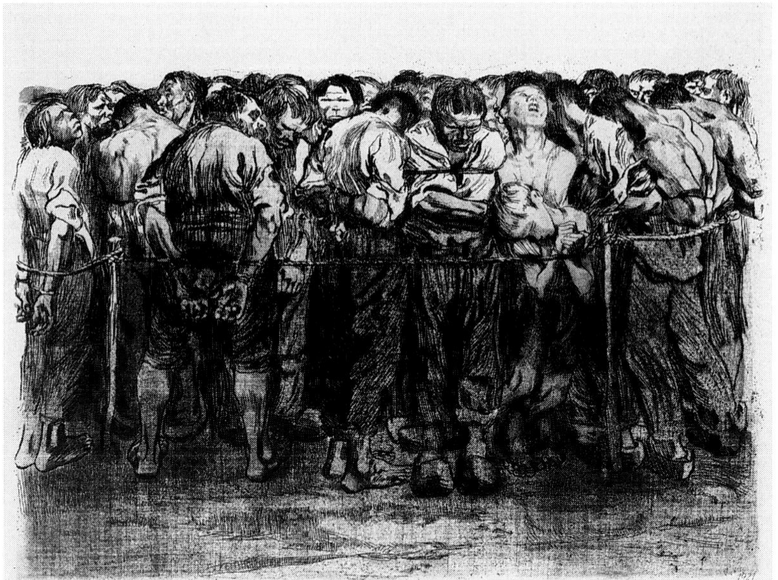

167 Käthe Kollwitz.
THE PRISONERS. 1908.
Etching and soft-ground.
12⅞" × 16⅝".
Library of Congress, Washington, D.C.

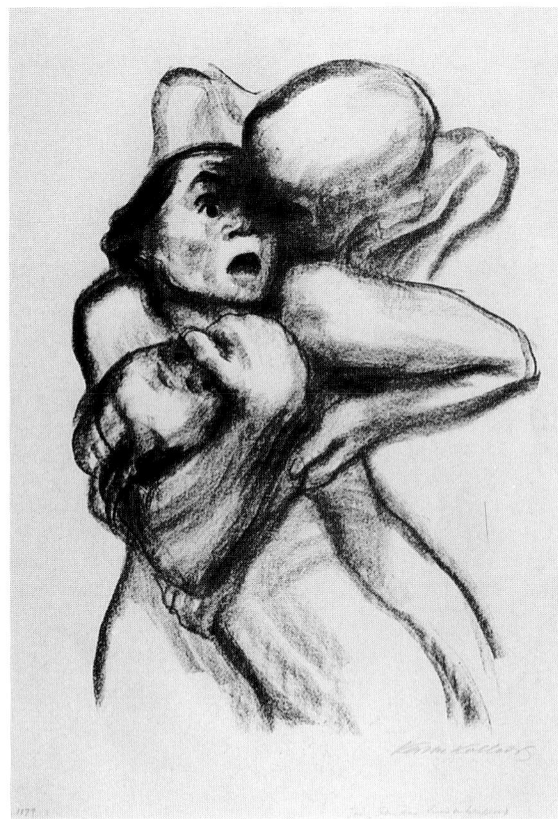

168 Käthe Kollwitz.
DEATH SEIZING A WOMAN. 1934.
Plate IV from the series DEATH (1934-1936).
Lithograph, printed in black. 20" × 14 7/16".
The Museum of Modern Art, New York. Purchase.

Käthe Kollwitz, a contemporary of Matisse, expressed a very different attitude in her art. (As Matisse said, an artist's expression "must derive inevitably from his temperament."[5]) Kollwitz's experience and temperament were totally unlike Matisse's. The three prints reproduced here were made over a period of twenty-six years, yet they are remarkably consistent in mood and graphic quality. THE PRISONERS, done in 1908, was one of a series of prints inspired by Kollwitz's interest in a peasant revolution that occurred in Germany in 1525.

DEATH SEIZING A WOMAN was one of eight prints in Kollwitz's last major print series. She reduced the idea to its essentials to increase the print's dramatic impact. The mother clutches her child in a protective grasp and stares ahead in terror, as a symbolic figure of death presses down on her. Bold, converging lines focus attention on the mother's expression of fear. The strong sculptural quality in Kollwitz's drawings and prints developed from her study of Rembrandt, as well as from her own experience making sculpture.

Her SELF-PORTRAIT depicts a person of kindness and great strength. Kollwitz's powerful graphic images are pleas for compassion. In the face of war, death, and human cruelty, they encourage empathy, charity, and conscience.

KÄTHE KOLLWITZ (1867–1945)

It is not surprising that Käthe Kollwitz became an artist of fiercely independent views. She was born in Königsberg, East Prussia, to parents who had strong moral and social convictions. The values of her social-democrat father and her maternal grandfather (a rebel Lutheran pastor) were early influences on the direction of her life and art.

By the time Kollwitz was five, she was drawing extensively; by the time she was twelve, her father, who had already recognized her artistic potential, made sure she received the best art training available. At sixteen, Kollwitz made her first narrative drawings of workers. Although few academies or colleges accepted women, she continued her advanced studies with the help of a few mature artists and was finally able to attend the Women's Art School in Munich.

When she was nineteen she realized that her ideas would be most powerfully expressed if she limited herself to black and white. From then on, her work took the form of drawings, prints, and sculpture. In her diary she wrote:

In my own work I find that I must keep everything to a more and more abbreviated form.... so that all the essentials are strongly stressed and the inessentials almost omitted.[6]

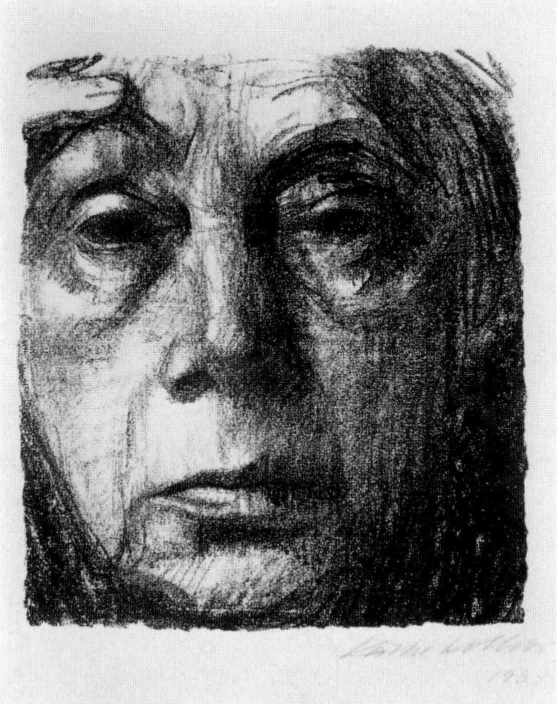

169 Käthe Kollwitz. SELF-PORTRAIT. 1934. Lithograph. 8¹⁄₁₆" × 7³⁄₁₆". Philadelphia Museum of Art. Given by Dr. and Mrs. William Wolgin.

At twenty-three she married Karl Kollwitz, a doctor who had decided to practice medicine in one of Berlin's poorest districts. The couple acted as social workers, often welcoming troubled people into their home.

Kollwitz worked as a graphic artist and sculptor through her years of motherhood and right up to her death at seventy-seven. Her haunting images express strength, compassion, and self-discipline. A strong identification with the suffering of others is seen in her prints and drawings, many of which appear to be self-portraits. Although she lost a son in World War I and a grandson in World War II, her personal grief was secondary to her abiding concern for humanity. Kollwitz dreamed of a united world—one that would elevate human life above the misery she expressed in much of her art.

The tragic situation in post–World War I Germany led her to use art as a tool for social change. Believing that art should be for everyone, she chose not to make expensive paintings. Instead, she made inexpensive prints (posters, lithographs, and woodcuts) that ordinary people could afford (see the discussion of prints, beginning on page 158). The seriousness of her art is balanced by her technical mastery and her ability to construct formal beauty.

In 1919, Kollwitz was elected the first woman member of the Prussian Academy of Arts in Berlin, a position that included full professor status. But her anti-Nazi sympathies caused her expulsion from that teaching position in 1933. The Nazis considered her degenerate and forbade exhibition of her work.

She died in 1945, just days before World War II ended, outlawed in her own country but recognized internationally as one of the world's outstanding artists. Kollwitz was one of the few women artists whose greatness was publicly recognized prior to the middle of the twentieth century.

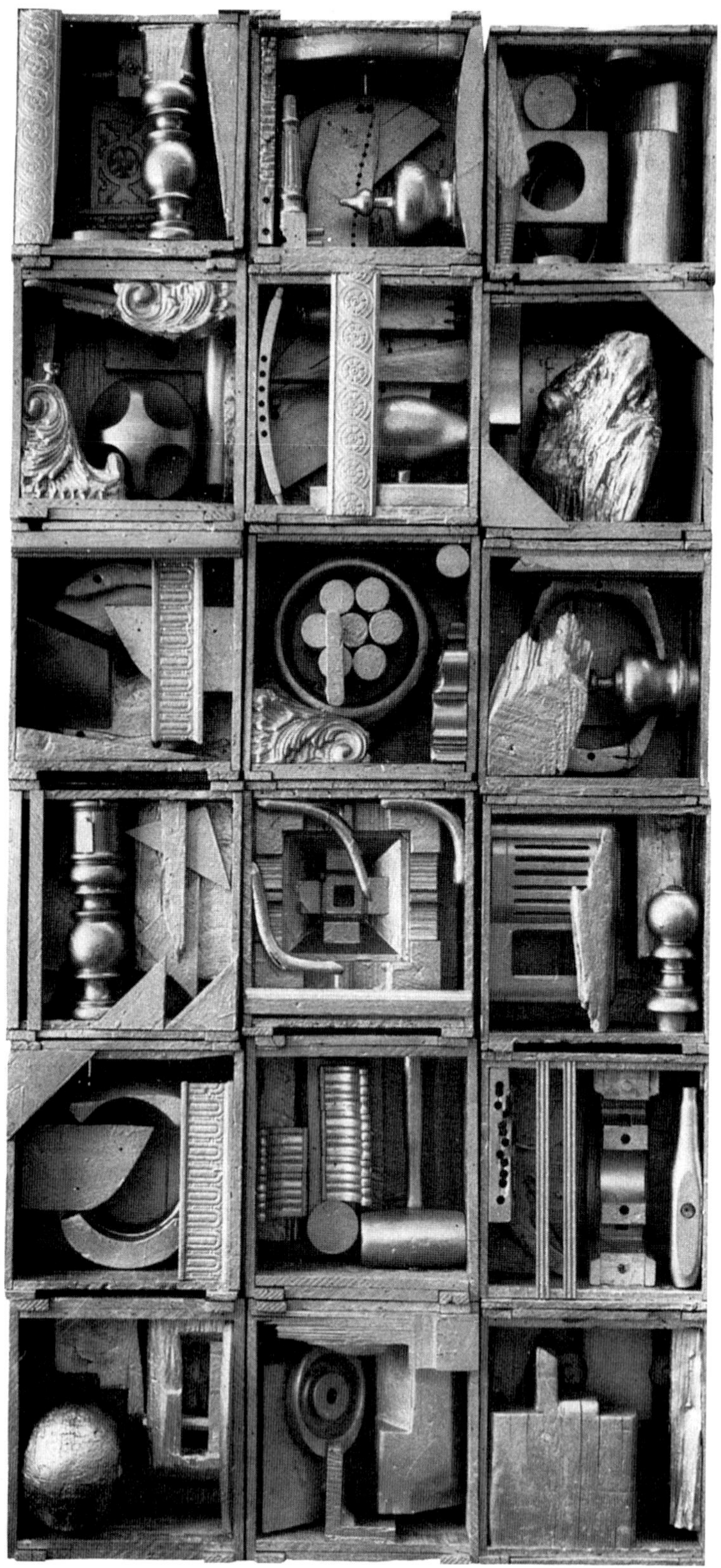

Louise Nevelson was born much later than Matisse and Kollwitz, yet all three were alive during the first forty-five years of this century. While the other two artists were interested in figurative art, Nevelson's work is nonrepresentational.

Nevelson began making sculpture out of scrap wood in the 1950s. She was an early exponent and leading practitioner of sculpture as environment. Her relief walls have, on occasion, been made to extend around entire rooms. In ROYAL TIDE #1, the carefully combined pieces of wood include bits of old furniture and architectural trim. Each compartment is both a composition in itself and part of a complex total form. Nevelson painted such stacked-box constructions a single unifying color, usually black, white, or gold—colors she considered aristocratic.

In the late 1960s and 1970s, Nevelson turned from wood to plastic and aluminum, then to steel—a material suitable for large outdoor works. SHADOWS AND FLAGS, a group of seven pieces, stands in what is now Louise Nevelson Plaza in New York City.

Toward the end of her life, she returned to wood, making pictorial collages such as VOLCANIC MAGIC X.

Calling herself an "architect of shadows," Nevelson was concerned with space and shadow in all her assemblages. She described her sculpture in various media as variations on a theme, revealing a unity of approach to form. She stated:

Different people have different memories. Some have memories for words, some for action—mine happens to be for form.[7]

170 Louise Nevelson.
ROYAL TIDE #1. 1961.
Gilded wood. 8' × 3'.
Collection of Jean and Howard Lipman.

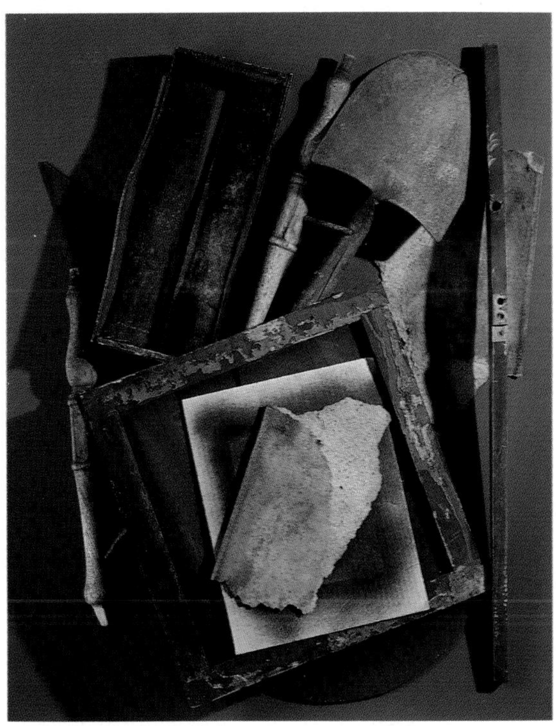

171 Louise Nevelson.
VOLCANIC MAGIC X. 1985.
Wood, paper, and metal. 40" × 32" × 6".
Courtesy of the Pace Gallery, New York.

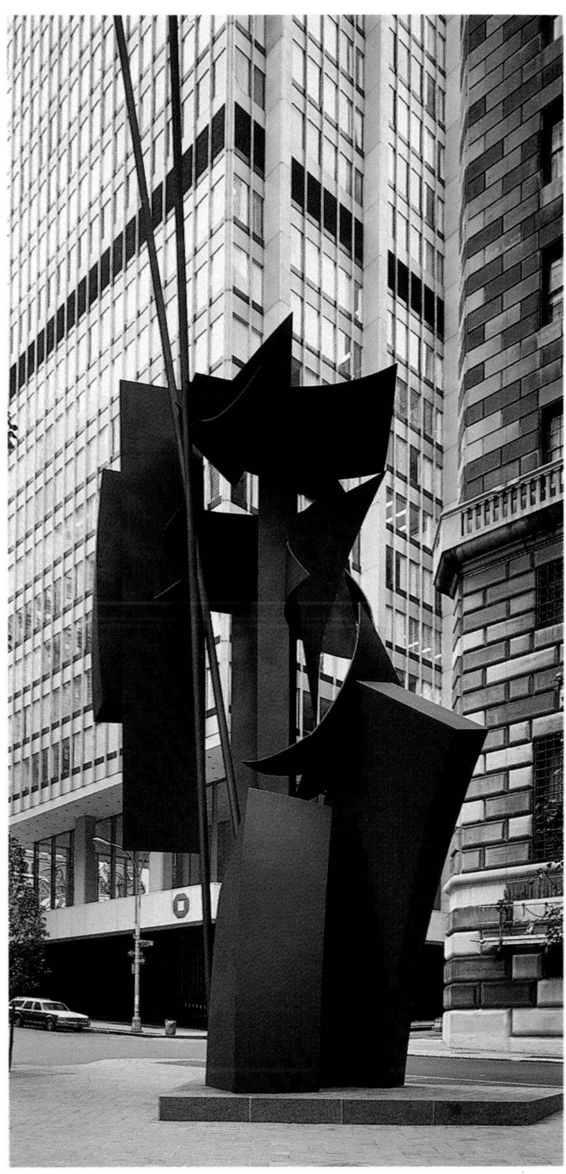

172 Louise Nevelson.
Detail of SHADOWS AND FLAGS.
Louise Nevelson Plaza, New York. 1977-1978.
Painted cor-ten steel. Height 72'.
One of seven sculptures.
Photograph: © Tom Crane, 1978.

While we have viewed the art of Matisse, Kollwitz, and Nevelson in terms of personal style, we can also see each style as an expression of its time and in relation to twentieth century art movements. Parts 6 and 7 include an overview of major historic styles and examine the ways in which styles in art both reveal and help shape the cultural, political, and social history of their times.

Now that the purposes and the language of art have been discussed, the groundwork has been laid to consider how individual works of art are evaluated.

LOUISE NEVELSON (1900–1988)

It wasn't until she was in her fifties that Louise Nevelson was seen as a leading American sculptor.

Born Louise Berliawsky in Russia, she was brought to the United States by her parents when she was five. Her family settled in Rockland, Maine, where they lived near a few other Jewish families, isolated from the life of the town.

In school, problems with the new language caused her to discover that she could express herself through art. Her success in drawing gave her the sense of self-worth she needed and led her to dream of becoming an artist. Of the visual arts, she later said: "It's the quickest way of communicating, and I think it's the most joyous."[8]

After graduating from high school she married businessman Charles Nevelson, partly as a way to escape the limits of her small town. The couple moved to New York City when she was twenty. There—following the birth of her son—she pursued her interest in the arts by studying music, drama, poetry, and dance as well as the visual arts.

Wishing to go deeper, Nevelson—now thirty—began to study art seriously at the Art Students League. Then, in 1931, in a gesture of independence, she sailed alone to Europe to study with Hans Hofmann, the foremost teacher of the new abstract art.

In her search for self-fulfillment, she divorced her husband and for more than twenty years struggled to survive as an artist. Despite many years of rejection and neglect, Nevelson managed to develop a highly original body of work.

Early in her career, Nevelson worked in a variety of styles and media, making drawings, prints, and paintings, as well as sculpture in stone, bronze, clay, and wood. It was not until the 1950s that she developed her mature style based on solid geometric forms. Nevelson's best-known works are large assemblages made up of numerous boxes filled with "found" wood fragments she picked up on the streets of New York City and in vacant lots and lumber yards.

She had this to say about the origin and evolution of her constructive style:

I never wanted to make sculpture. I didn't want to make anything like that. I felt my great search was for myself, the inner being of myself, and that was the best way I knew to project how I was feeling about everything in the world. Consequently, it wasn't that I made anything for anybody. Now, we call it "work" and I don't like to call it work at all. It really is a projection of an awareness. People don't understand that when you project from yourself you are really at the height of your awareness, and that means you are at your best.[9]

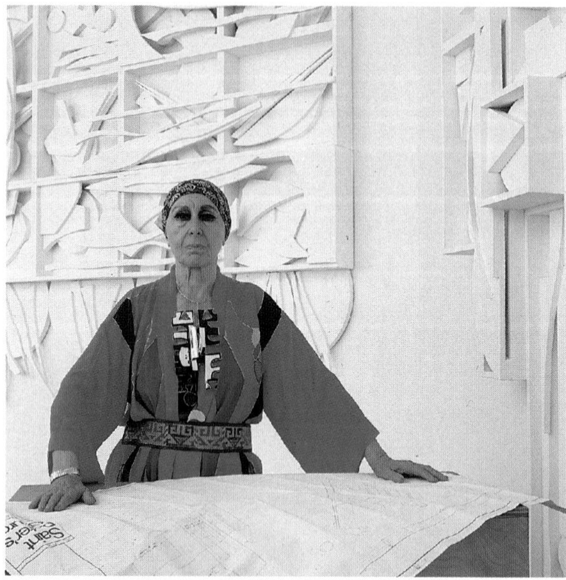

173 LOUISE NEVELSON.
Photograph: © 1984 Hans Namuth.

Nevelson's sculpture demonstrates her belief that, in art as well as in life, it is not what you start with that counts; it is what you make of it. From scrap, she created regal structures with an air of timelessness. They are at once old and new. They have lived, and they are alive. Nevelson captured the essence of the art process:

The joy, if you want to call it that, of creation, is that it opens life to you.... It opens and you become more aware and more aware and that is the wonder of it.[10]

CHAPTER 7

Evaluation and Criticism

Before exploring further the many ways of making art, it is important to consider two interrelated issues: evaluation (is the art worthwhile?) and art criticism (who decides whether it is worthwhile?).

EVALUATION

Have you ever heard someone say, I don't know anything about art, but I know what I like? Each of us decides what she or he likes or doesn't like many times a day. When we select one thing over another, or appreciate the special value of something, we are evaluating.

Creative experience is a process of selecting and evaluating. For the artist, the creative process involves selecting and evaluating each component before deciding to include it in the final form. After the work is completed, the viewer's enjoyment comes from sensing the quality that has been achieved. How do artists and viewers evaluate art to determine whether it has quality?

Quality is relative. How a work of art is evaluated varies from person to person, from country to country, and from age to age. Few famous artists or styles have had unchanging reputations. The Impressionist painters of the late nineteenth century (see pages 114–115 and 387–394) were ridiculed by critics, museums, and the public. Their style differed too radically from those of their predecessors for easy acceptance in their own time. Today, Impressionist paintings have an honored place in museums and are eagerly sought by the public.

Value judgments in art necessarily involve subjectivity. It is not possible to measure artistic quality objectively in the same way we measure the wingspan of an airplane or the capacity of a computer. Quality in art has little to do with the complexity or the difficulty of technique.

Those who seek a yardstick for measuring artistic quality often apply some of the principles the ancient Greeks believed art must contain: truth, beauty, order, harmony, and moral goodness. In the late twentieth century, however, there is much less agreement on the meaning of these concepts than there was in ancient Greece.

Prior to the nineteenth and twentieth centuries, cultural changes occurred slowly. People within each society had generally agreed-upon values and standards in nearly all areas, including the arts. During our century of rapid change, many artists have intentionally sought to go beyond or to deny long-established traditions. Related shifts in thinking have occurred in science and philosophy.

Strangely, it is easier for many people to accept the work of pioneering scientists than that of pioneering artists. If we close our eyes and minds to new work that is hard to understand, we will miss the opportunity to learn from fresh insights. Our concept of what is "good art" changes as we mature and develop our aesthetic awareness and critical thinking skills.

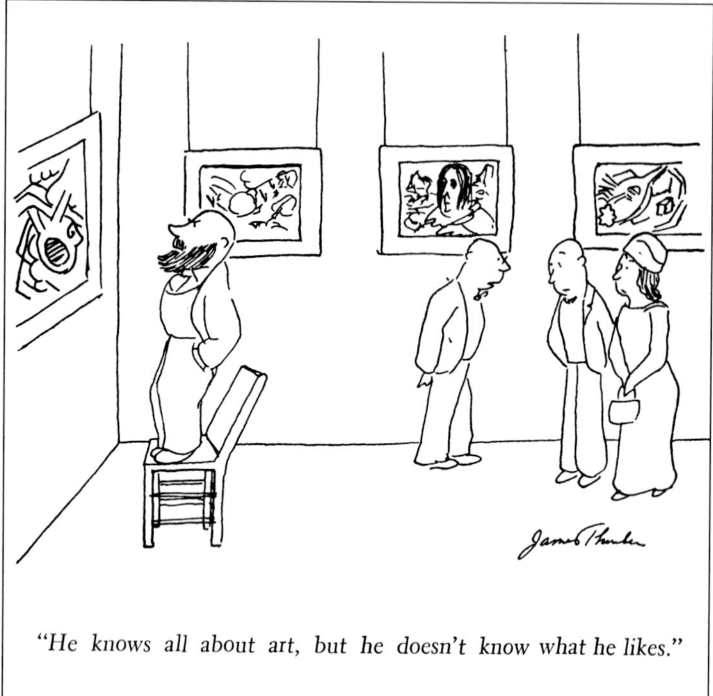

174 James Thurber.

When we look at a work of art and find that we are pleased (or displeased), it is useful to discover why. We tend to like what is familiar and easy to comprehend. In order to increase our enjoyment of art, it is necessary to increase our visual awareness and knowledge. Teachers, authors, and art critics can offer their insights and add new dimensions to our understanding. With effort, we can learn to recognize aesthetic quality even in works we would not want to live with.

Whether we are approaching art for our own enjoyment or for a class assignment, it is most rewarding to begin with an open, receptive mind—to go beyond prejudgments. Give yourself time to get acquainted and to respond.

In addition to making drawings or composition studies of significant works, one of the best ways to experience a work of art is through writing. When the writing is about a visual form, the process of interpretive translation from nonverbal to verbal can greatly heighten one's personal experience of not only the particular work being written about, but all subsequent encounters with art and art-making. Levels of awareness in other areas may be enhanced.

Writing even a paragraph or brief essay causes you to take the time to really engage in seeing and responding to a work of art, to become conscious of the reasons for your initial gut-level reaction. Senses, emotions, and memories come together with knowledge as we think about how to communicate through words what we see and feel.

You might start by considering what you see. Describe its physical qualities. What is it made of? How big is it? Go into detail about what you see. If you are writing, describe the work as if you were helping a blind person "see" it. What colors and shapes are used? What subjects (if any) are represented?

What you have just done is the beginning of formal analysis—a discussion of the way various visual elements and design principles are used to affect viewers' thoughts and feelings. Terms introduced in Chapters 3 through 5 will be helpful; use them to describe the use of elements such as line, shape, color, and space. How was the work designed? Is it balanced? What is emphasized? Rhythm? Proportion? Contrast? Is there unity as well as variety?

Follow the analysis of form with a subjective interpretation of the meaning or symbolism of the work. How does the work make you feel? How or why does it evoke these feelings? Think again about your first description. At this point, go well beyond "I like it" or "I don't like it."

Can you tell what the artist had in mind? If so, was that intention realized? Was it worth the effort? Is it valuable from your point of view?

The process just described is a simplified version of that used by an art critic.

ART CRITICISM

The term *art criticism* refers to making discriminating judgments, both favorable and unfavorable. Art criticism may include the above process (description, formal analysis, interpretation, and value judgment) plus biographical and historical information.

Biographical or historical information often provides clues to a work's context and therefore to its intended meaning. Criteria upon which many art professionals agree include degree of originality, sensitivity to the appropriate use of materials, and consistency of concept, design, and execution.

Art critics evaluate art exhibitions and events and publish their views in newspapers, magazines, exhibition catalogues, and books. While critics or teachers may pass personal judgment on a work, one of their primary functions is to help others look closely at a work and make their own evaluations. By opening the dialog for others to discuss the issues, critics help viewers clarify their own positions regarding meaning and quality.

As long as there have been art patrons and critics, the relationship between them and artists has been problematic. We are looking over the artist's shoulder in Pieter Bruegel's drawing THE PAINTER AND THE CONNOISSEUR—or are we? Maybe we do not wish to be identified with the "connoisseur," who clutches his money pouch as he looks through his spectacles at Bruegel's work-in-progress. Of course, Bruegel, being an artist, gave us the story from the artist's point of view; if we identify with anyone, it is with Bruegel.

Ideally, each person who views a work of art will make his or her own evaluation of its quality, but preconceptions often cloud the process. Many of us read the artists' names and titles of works in museums before we allow ourselves to respond. For example, we have heard that Leonardo da Vinci's MONA LISA (page 348) is a great work of art. If this is foremost in our minds when we see MONA LISA, our direct experience of the painting is affected by our preconception—by the idea that it is great art hanging in the famous Louvre Museum in Paris. This preconception is increased by the fact that we find the painting in a special bulletproof glass case, and largely obscured by the crowds of people who flock to see it (page 369). The painting's fame not only prevents many people from making their own judgments, it causes it to be so protected that we can barely see it at all.

The art market "boom" of the 1970s and 1980s has further clouded the problem of evaluating art. The artistic fashions of the moment may be the result of market "hype" rather than the presence of new art of high quality or the rediscovery of earlier art of long-lasting value. When a work sells at an auction for thousands, even millions, of dollars, does that make it an exceptionally good work of art?

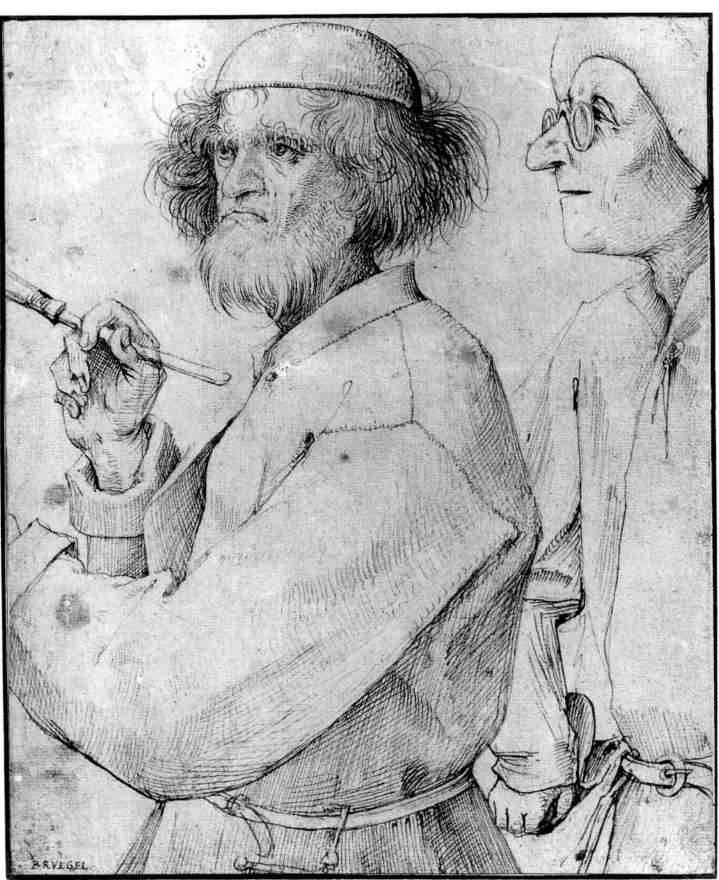

175 Pieter Bruegel.
THE PAINTER AND THE CONNOISSEUR. c. 1568.
Pen and bistre. 10" × 8⅜".
Albertina Collection, Vienna.

Even museums make mistakes in evaluating art. Decades ago, several American museums sold off large parts of their collections of nineteenth-century American paintings. Now that such paintings are popular once again, the same institutions wish they had them back.

The current gap between the public's taste and the preferences of art museum curators, many practicing artists, patrons, and critics is the result of revolutionary innovations in the arts. Today's art is as complex, varied, and contradictory as the world it reflects and extends. Accordingly, art criticism—

the way art is explained and evaluated—has also changed.

One of the most important art critics of the twentieth century, Clement Greenberg, wielded enormous power during the 1950s and early 1960s. His 1961 *Art and Culture* was the most influential book about art in twenty-five years. He was the first American critic to look at art as a succession of movements or styles. He was convinced that there is a mainstream of art, and that all art that matters—that is immortal—is within this mainstream. He traced this stream from the sixteenth century through Cubism of the early twentieth century. He decided that, after Cubism (see pages 416–422), a purely abstract art was the logical extension of the mainstream.

At the height of his influence, Greenberg's critical style was authoritarian. He set absolute standards for modern painting, which he felt should be purely visual—all meaningful content was to be avoided. According to his view, paintings should be abstract, impersonal, and have totally flat pictorial space.

Greenberg looked for an artist who would express these aesthetic "virtues" and found such an artist in Jackson Pollock (see page 451). Since Greenberg's view of Pollock's greatness is still widely accepted today, it is easy to forget that it took extraordinary courage for a beginning critic to praise such a radical and almost unknown painter as Pollock was at the time.

At the opposite end of the critical spectrum from Greenberg is Lucy Lippard, a well-respected art critic whose approach is one of open-mindedness. She is well known for her passionate advocacy of works outside the mainstream of art—works often created by women and minority artists. She prefers art with content and criticism that isn't bound up in technical jargon. "I wish criticism could be loosened up to the point where it would really follow the art...," Lippard says. "Not in a sense of no criteria ... but for the most part riding with the art."[1]

As art criticism departs from the Greenbergian notion that art history flows in a single, well-defined stream, the role of the critic as centralized authority begins to crumble. Previously—even before the twentieth century—the critic's job was to see that the "rules" of art were followed. However, as the rest of this book makes clear, these rules are increasingly being broadened, changed, and broken. Accordingly, some say that the critic's role is no longer to offer a definitive explanation and evaluation of art—that is, the critic is no longer the sole judge of meaning and value, and the viewer a mere consumer of art.

Whatever his or her point of view, the critic's task is to make well-supported arguments, not pronouncements of personal taste. He or she must establish criteria broad enough to encompass a wide range of aesthetic styles and intentions.

In the last analysis, although we can describe, analyze, interpret, and appraise art, there is no final, absolutely correct way to evaluate art. The process of evaluation is rewarding in itself because it draws the evaluator/viewer into the creative process.

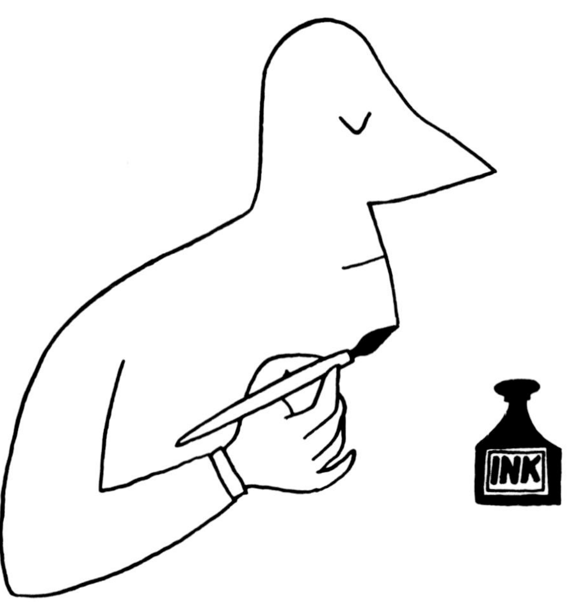

176 Saul Steinberg.

ROBERT HUGHES (BORN 1938)

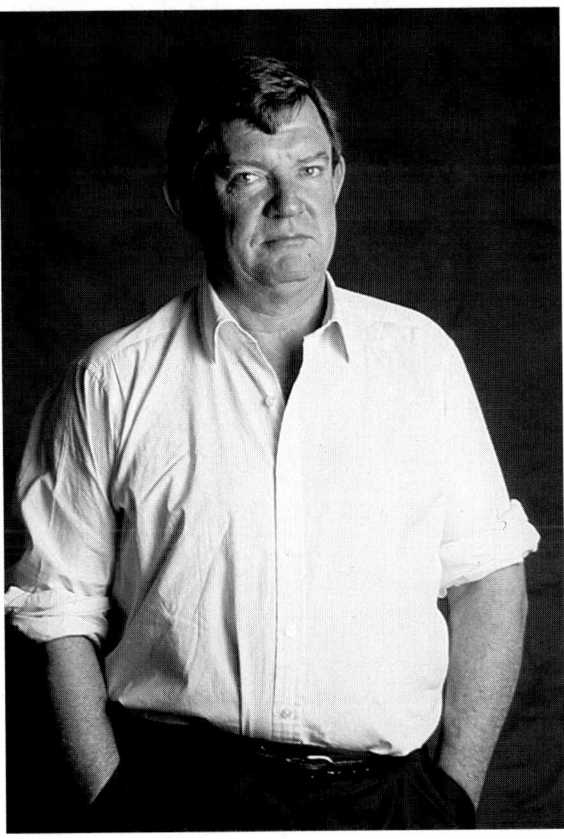

177 ROBERT HUGHES.
Photograph: Joyce Ravid/Onyx.

As his 1991 book title suggests, Robert Hughes is *Nothing If Not Critical.* The outspoken art critic is known to millions for his art reviews in *Time* magazine and for his 1980 television series on modern art and the accompanying book, both titled *The Shock of the New.*

Born in Australia, Hughes dropped out of the Sydney University School of Architecture in his senior year to write his first book, *The Art of Australia.* He was working as a cartoonist for a small magazine in Sydney in 1958 when the art critic was fired. Hughes remembers the editor rushing into his office shouting, "I've just fired the art critic ... *you* must know something about art. *You* are now the art critic."[2]

Hughes emigrated to England in 1964 and "lucked into" freelance critic jobs with London newspapers in 1966, but he says he didn't really get in gear until he got to America in 1970. He has been the art critic for *Time* since 1970, sending in twenty-four art reviews a year from his home on Shelter Island, a ferry ride away from Manhattan.

Whether he is writing about a contemporary artist or one who lived hundreds of years ago, Hughes's personal convictions are passionately stated. He is at his most witty and provocative when he writes about contemporary art, and he can be as eloquent when he contemptuously dismisses works as when he raves about particular pieces and artists.

"Drawing... is not what [this artist] does," he once wrote. "He never learned to do it, and probably never will.... The line has all the verve of chewed string. It starts here and finishes there, but that's all you can say for it: nothing happens along the way."[3]

Hughes prefers to write about art he likes—and there is a great deal that he does. He wrote a rave review of an exhibit of the works of nineteenth-century painter Georges Seurat:

One of the miracles of his art is his ability to analyze light, not through the simple juxtaposition of dabs of color but by a layering of tiny brush marks built up from the underpainted ground, so that the eventual surface becomes a fine-grained pelt, seamless and yet infinitely nuanced, from which captured light slowly radiates.[4]

While his writings are widely read, Hughes is not among the handful of twentieth-century critics (including Greenberg) who have had a strong influence on the directions and fortunes of art. Often at odds with art galleries and museums, Hughes is a critic not only of art and artists but of the cultural context in which art is created, exhibited, and sold. He is recognized as a "quixotic upholder of a cultural and intellectual standard he alternately mourns, celebrates, and nurtures."[5]

Hughes's critical approach is a valuable one. He believes that the work of a critic is to open up the discussion, to challenge us to make up our own minds after we have read his opinion. "Criticism isn't about saying 'I think this, therefore you should think this.' It's about getting people to look and to think, and to do it on their own," Hughes states firmly.[6]

ON VISITING AN ART MUSEUM

...or, How to Enjoy Looking at Art Without Being Overwhelmed by Museum Fatigue

Art museums can be mind-expanding or sleep-inducing, depending on how you approach them. It is a mistake to enter a museum with the belief that you should like everything you see—or even that you should see everything that is there. Without selective viewing, the visitor to a large museum is likely to come down with a severe case of museum exhaustion.

The English word *museum* comes from the Greek *mouseion,* "place of the muses." "Muse" indicates the spirit or power believed to be capable of inspiring and watching over poets, musicians, and other artists—or any source of inspiration. A museum is for musing, a place devoted to collecting, caring for, studying, and displaying objects of lasting value and interest.

Unfortunately, museum visitors are often overwhelmed by the many rooms full of art and background information. Some may feel that they should have an extensive knowledge of art history before they even enter a museum. Even the entrance to a museum can be a bit intimidating ("Step this way. Serious art. No smiling.") or it can be inviting and welcoming ("Come on in. Relax. Make yourself comfortable.").

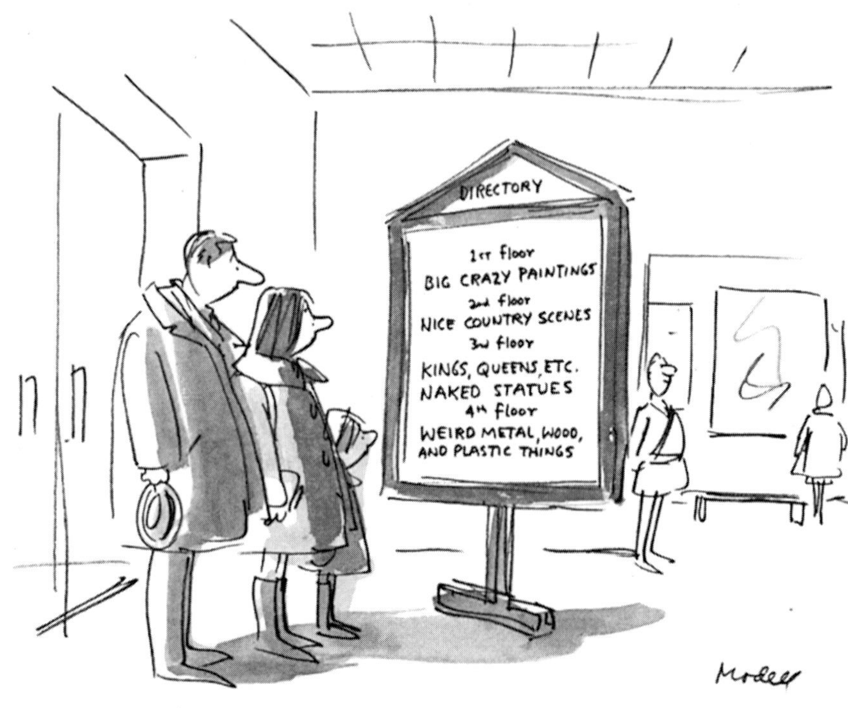

178 Frank Modell.

There is a way to enjoy an art museum without experiencing overload. If you were to go to a fine restaurant and try to sample everything on the menu, you would probably get sick. In both restaurants and museums, selection is the key to a positive experience.

It makes sense to approach an art museum the way a seasoned traveler approaches a city for a first visit: find out what there is to see. In the museum, inquire about the schedule of special shows, then see those exhibitions and outstanding works that interest you. Museums are in the process of rethinking their buildings and collections in order to meet the needs of changing populations and changing values. It is not unusual to find video exhibits, performances of all kinds, and film showings as part of regular museum programming.

If you are visiting without a specific exhibition in mind, follow your interests and instincts. Browsing can be highly rewarding. Zero in on what you feel are the highlights, savoring favorite works and unexpected discoveries.

For those traveling abroad, *Mona Winks* is a useful guide to many of Europe's top museums. This lighthearted book includes a collection of self-guided tours covering the highlights of some twenty European museums and cultural centers.[7]

Don't stay too long in a museum. Take breaks. Perhaps there is a garden or cafe in which you can pause for a rest. The quality of your experience is not measured by the amount of time you spend in the galleries or how many works you see. The most rewarding experiences can come from finding something that "speaks" to you, then sitting and enjoying it in leisurely contemplation.

PART 3

TWO-DIMENSIONAL MEDIA

Consider...

Have you ever said, I can't draw? Does that mean you can't write your name or draw a map? What do people really mean when they say they can't draw?

Imagine an art gallery containing two framed artworks. One is a large, colorful painting and the other is a small black-and-white print. Would you approach each of them in the same way? How might your experience of them be different?

Which invention has had a bigger impact on the course of world history, the printing press or the automobile?

A primary function of the camera is that it "stops" time. We use photography to keep exact records of visual events. Does the camera ever lie?

What effect does the rapid transmission of visual images (via newspapers, magazines, television) have on the world?

CHAPTER 8

Drawing

The desire to draw is as natural as the desire to talk. As children, we draw long before we learn to read and write. In fact, making letter forms is a kind of drawing—especially when we first learn to "write." Some of us continue to enjoy drawing; others return to drawing as adults. Those who no longer draw probably came to believe they did not draw well enough to suit themselves or others. Yet drawing is a learned process. It is a way of seeing and communicating, a way of paying attention.

In the most basic sense, to draw means to pull, push, or drag a marking tool across a surface to leave a line or mark. Most people working in the visual arts utilize drawing as a major tool for visual thinking—for recording and developing ideas.

Because drawing is less abstract than writing, developing drawing skills may be easier than learning to write. Drawing is the most immediate and accessible way to communicate through imagery. Through drawing we can share ideas, feelings, experiences, and imaginings. Sometimes a drawing does several of these things simultaneously.

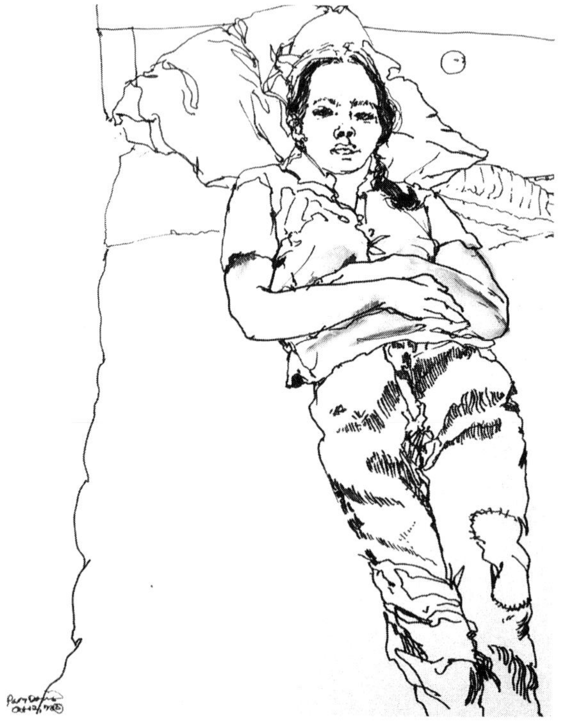

179 Pamela Davis.
CAROL. 1973.
Felt-tip pen. 19⅕" × 17".
Courtesy of the artist.

The lines in Pamela Davis's drawing of CAROL are lively and inventive, describing the way the subject looked to Davis as she drew. Shading in the central area was made by smearing the felt-tip pen lines with wet fingers.

Many people find it valuable to keep a sketchbook handy to serve as a visual diary, a place to develop and maintain drawing skills and to note whatever catches the eye or imagination. From sketchbook drawings, some ideas may develop and reach maturity as finished drawings or complete works in other media. Leonardo da Vinci kept many of his exploratory drawings and writings in notebooks. He drew this study of THREE SEATED

FIGURES next to idea sketches for some mechanical devices. Another study, DESIGNS FOR INVENTIONS, is the work of Iris, age eight. These two sets of drawings made to aid visual thinking—one by a world-renowned artist, scientist, and engineer and one by an untrained child—underscore the nature of the thinking and drawing process.

Drawing from direct observation is neither more nor less important than drawing from imagination or memory. However, the process of drawing from observation helps people learn to see more attentively and develops the ability to draw from either memory or imagination. In *The Zen of Seeing* (from which the PENCIL DRAWING is taken), medical doctor Frederick Franck describes drawing as a means to heighten visual awareness:

I have learned that what I have not drawn, I have never really seen, and that when I start drawing an ordinary thing I realize how extraordinary it is, sheer miracle: the branching of a tree, the structure of a dandelion's seed puff.[1]

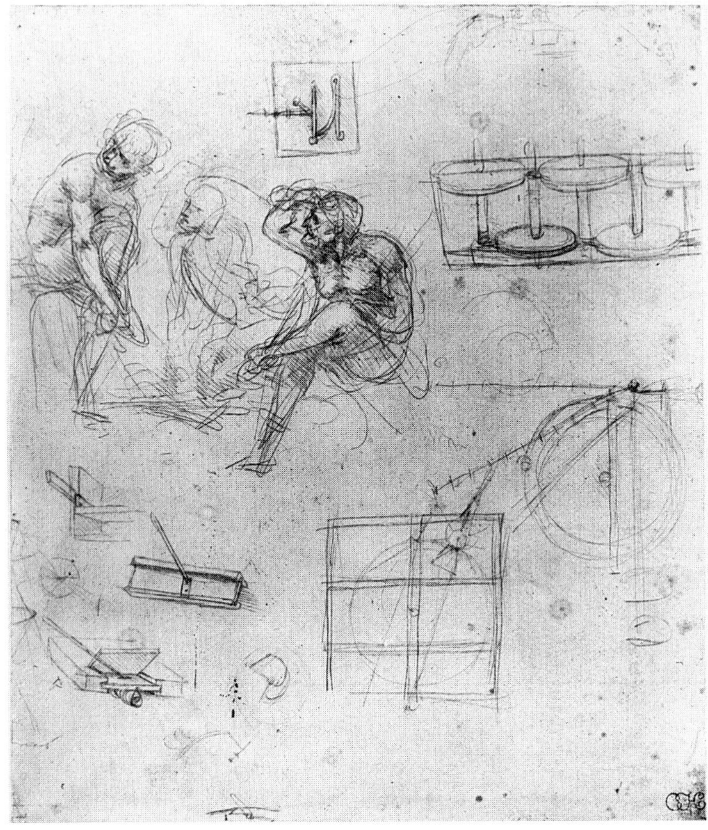

181 Leonardo da Vinci.
THREE SEATED FIGURES AND STUDIES OF MACHINERY. c. 1490.
Silver-point on very pale pink, prepared surface.
Ashmolean Museum, Oxford.

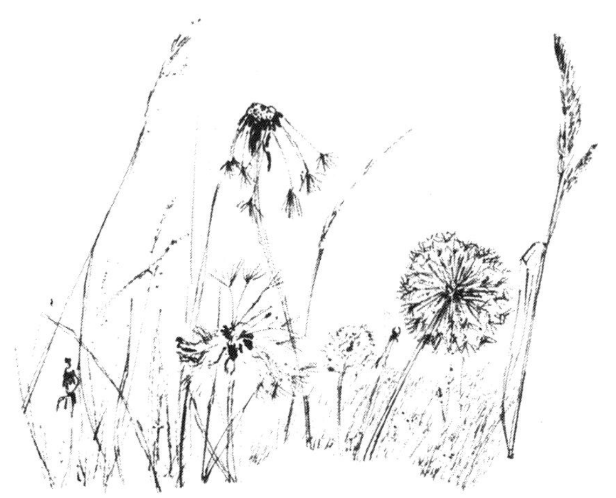

180 Frederick Franck.
PENCIL DRAWING from his book *The Zen of Seeing.*

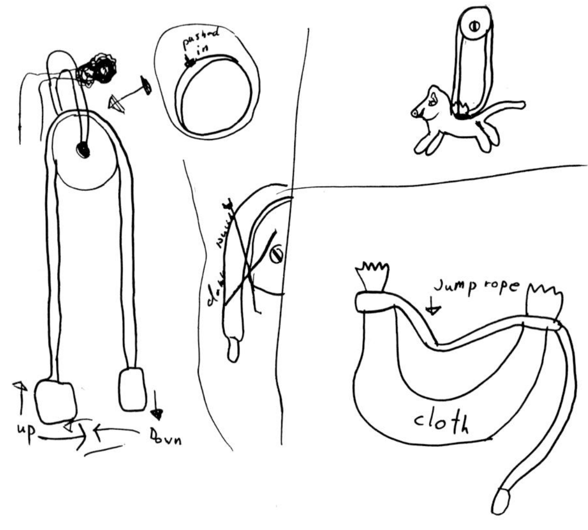

182 Iris Chamberlain, age 8.
DESIGNS FOR INVENTIONS. 1992.
Felt-tip pen. 8½" × 11".

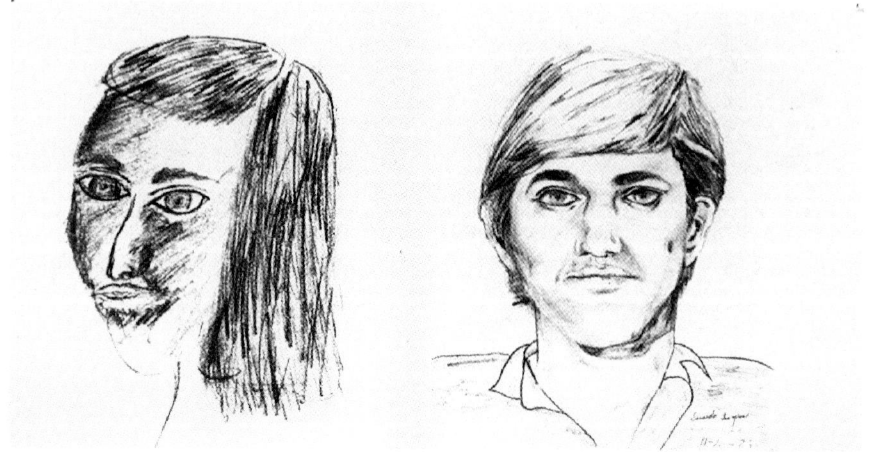

183 Gerardo Campos, September 2, 1973.(left) Gerardo Campos, November 10, 1973.(right) From Betty Edwards, *Drawing on the Right Side of the Brain.*

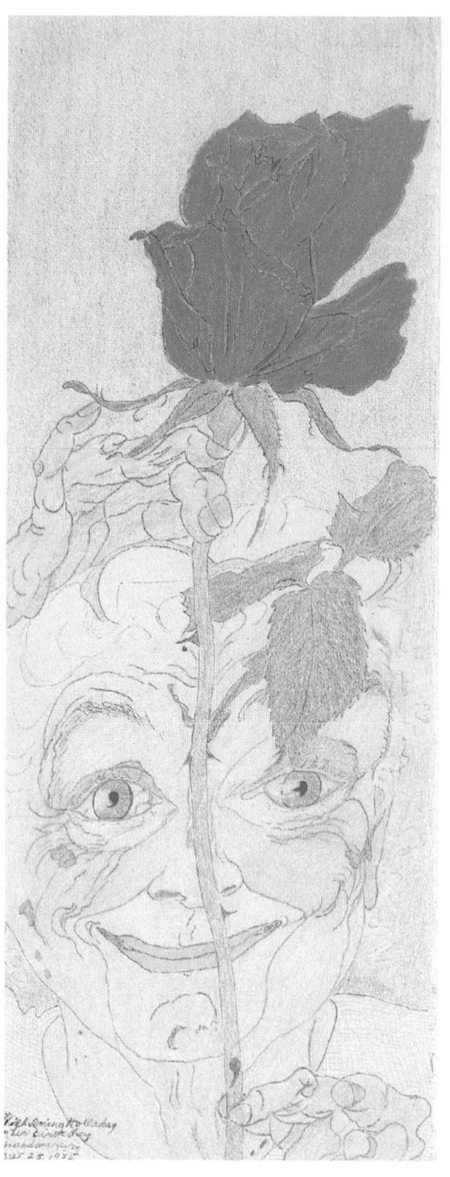

Through her classes and her book *Drawing on the Right Side of the Brain*, Betty Edwards has created effective sequences of mind-releasing exercises that enable people to draw what they see.[2] When her students make a shift from verbally dominated preconceptions to pure visual awareness, they really begin to see what they are looking at. Before-and-after student drawings, such as those shown above, show the typical change in the ability to see—and thus to draw—achieved in just a few weeks.

Learning to draw to your own satisfaction can transform your outlook on life. Elizabeth Layton was in her sixties and had been suffering from depression for many years when she took a drawing course that "turned her around." She learned to create representational images with blind (or pure) contour drawing. With this drawing method, one focuses attention on the edge lines of a subject rather than on the subject itself. Ever since she learned contour drawing, Layton has been drawing with enthusiasm and gaining wide recognition for the quality of her drawings.

Layton's pencil and pastel drawing SELF-PORTRAIT HOLDING ROSE WITH THORNS speaks of a newfound love of life and an understanding of its beauty—with all its thorns.

184 Elizabeth Layton.
SELF-PORTRAIT HOLDING ROSE WITH THORNS. 1985.
Pastel with pencil on paper. 18" × 7".
The National Museum of Women in the Arts. Gift of Wallace and Wilhelmina Holladay.

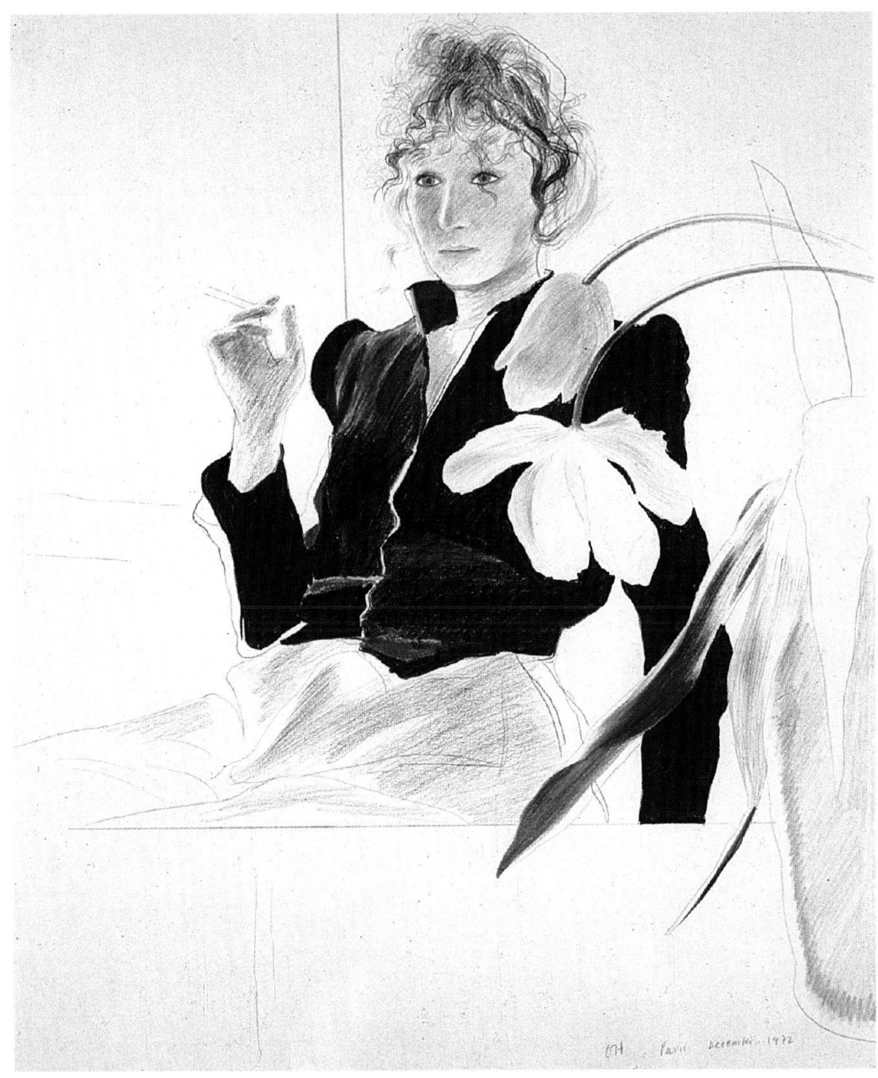

185 David Hockney.
CELIA IN A BLACK DRESS WITH WHITE FLOWERS.
1972.
Crayon. 17" × 14".

In drawing, as in every human activity, it seems some people have more natural aptitude than others. David Hockney feels his great interest in drawing spurred him to draw frequently, and this constant practice developed whatever ability he has. And it seemed he was drawing all the time—twelve hours a day when in art school. Hockney's intriguing crayon drawing CELIA IN A BLACK DRESS WITH WHITE FLOWERS exemplifies the level of expertise he developed. Hockney wrote:

Obviously I had some facility, more than other people, but sometimes facility comes because one is more interested in looking at things, examining them, and making a representation of them, more interested in the visual world, than other people are.[3]

Some artists, like Picasso, demonstrated exceptional drawing ability as young children. Others, such as Paul Cézanne and Vincent van Gogh, did not show obvious drawing ability when they committed themselves to art. Their skills developed through diligent effort. In spite of early difficulties, they succeeded in teaching themselves to draw. Seeing and drawing are learned processes, not just inborn gifts.

Van Gogh learned a great deal about both seeing and painting through his practice of drawing. He was just beginning his short career as an artist when he made the drawing of a CARPENTER shown below. Although stiff, and clumsy in proportion, the drawing reveals Van Gogh's careful observation and attention to detail. OLD MAN WITH HIS HEAD IN HIS HANDS, made two years after his CARPENTER, shows that Van Gogh had learned a great deal about seeing and drawing in those two years. By this time, Van Gogh was able to portray the old man's grief as well as the solidity of the figure and to give a suggestion of his surroundings. The groups of parallel lines appear to have been drawn quickly, with sensitivity and self-assurance.

Good drawing may appear deceptively simple, yet it can take years of patient work to be able to draw easily and effectively. According to one account, a person viewing a portrait drawn by Matisse with only a few lines asked the artist with some disgust, "How long did it take you to do this?" "Forty years," replied Matisse (see his SELF-PORTRAIT on page 118).

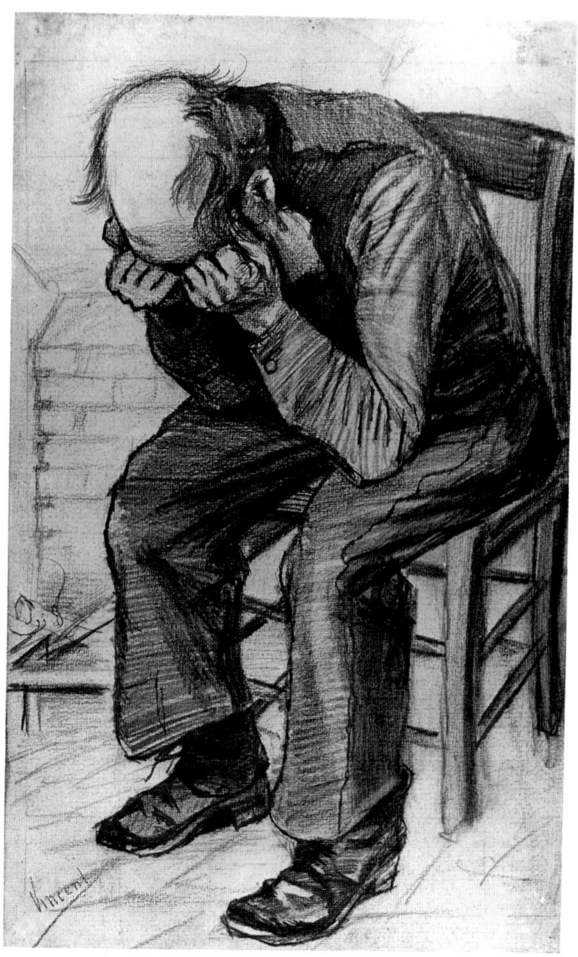

186 Vincent van Gogh.
OLD MAN WITH HIS HEAD IN HIS HANDS. 1882.
Pencil on paper. 19$^{11}/_{16}$" × 12$^{3}/_{16}$".
Vincent van Gogh Foundation/Van Gogh Museum, Amsterdam.

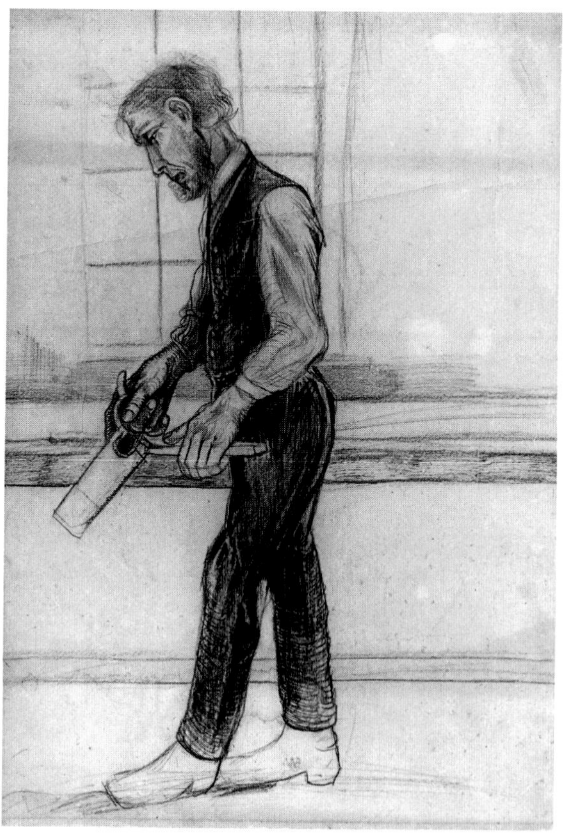

187 Vincent van Gogh.
CARPENTER. c. 1880.
Black crayon. 22" × 15".
Rijksmuseum Kröller-Müller, Otterlo, Netherlands.

VINCENT VAN GOGH (1853–1890)

Today the art of Vincent van Gogh is internationally known and admired. So it is hard to believe that Van Gogh worked as an artist for only ten years and that during his lifetime his art was known only to a few. In fact, he sold only one painting.

Van Gogh was born in Holland. His father was a minister, his grandfather a famous preacher; three uncles, and later his brother, were art dealers—a background that paved the way for Vincent's lifelong concern with both art and religion.

From age sixteen, he worked for a firm of art dealers, first in The Hague and later in London and Paris. During this period he began what was to become his famous correspondence with his brother Theo. It is primarily through these extraordinary letters (published in a book, *Dear Theo*) that we have come to know Van Gogh's short, intense, yet highly creative life.

After six years working for art dealers, he returned to Holland to study theology. In 1878, at age twenty-five, he became a lay preacher among impoverished miners in Belgium. While not successful at preaching, Van Gogh was effective at nursing victims of mining disasters and disease. When his compassion spurred him to give most of his own clothes and other possessions to the poor, the missionary society that had hired him dismissed him for his literal interpretation of Christ's teachings. Van Gogh remained in Belgium, living in acute poverty and spiritual turmoil until he decided to apply himself to becoming an artist. He made his commitment to art not because he possessed any obvious talent, but because he saw art as the means through which he could communicate with others. Although determined to be a painter, Van Gogh believed that he had to master drawing before he allowed himself to use color. Miners and farm laborers were his first models. As he worked on developing his skill, Vincent—the name he used to sign his finished works—was supported by his brother Theo, who regularly sent money and provided encouragement through his letters.

Van Gogh studied briefly at the art academy in Antwerp, but he was largely self-taught. In 1886 he joined his brother in Paris, where he met the leading French Impressionist and Post-Impressionist painters. Under their influence, Van Gogh's paintings, which had been limited to the somber tones of traditional Dutch painting, became much lighter and brighter in color (see his SELF-PORTRAIT WITH GRAY HAT).

In 1888 he moved to southern France, where—in less than two years—he produced most of the paintings for which he is known. There, armed with the Impressionists' bright, free color, and inspired by the intense semi-tropical light, Van Gogh took color even further. He developed a revolutionary approach to color based on the way colors and color combinations symbolize ideas and emotional content. His new understanding of expressive color led him to say that "the painter of the future will be a colorist such as has never existed."

Van Gogh's use of pure colors and his bold strokes of thick paint created images of emotional intensity that had a great impact on artists—especially expressionist painters—of the twentieth century. Before Van Gogh, most Western painters used color to describe the appearance of their subjects. After Van Gogh, painters began to realize that color could make feelings and states of mind visible.

From his teenage years, Van Gogh's intense personality caused him to be rejected by the women with whom he fell in love, and later it drove away potential friends such as Paul Gauguin (see page 402). Such rejection in turn contributed to several emotional breakdowns. Spells of fervent painting were interrupted by periods of illness and depression. Increasing illness led him voluntarily to enter a mental hospital, where he was able to paint during his periods of improved health and mental clarity. After leaving the hospital he returned to Paris, then settled in a nearby town under the watchful eye of a doctor known to be a friend of artists. There, in a frenzy of creative productivity, he completed about seventy paintings in sixty-five days—the last two months of his life. Van Gogh's loneliness and despair drove him to suicide at age thirty-seven.

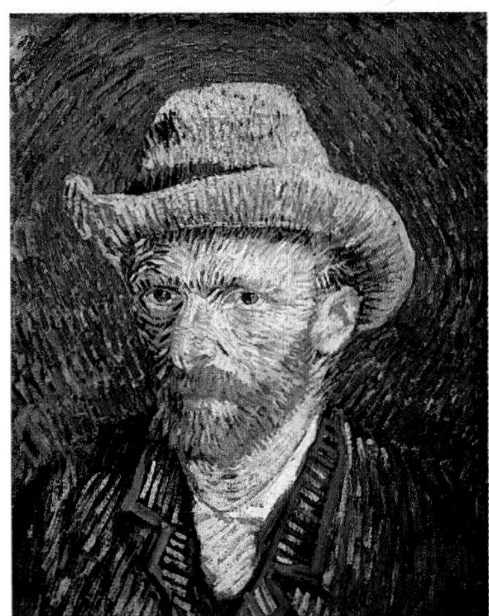

188 Vincent van Gogh.
SELF PORTRAIT WITH GRAY HAT. 1887.
Oil on canvas. 17¼" × 14¾".
Vincent van Gogh Foundation/Van Gogh Museum, Amsterdam.

An emphasis on the tragic aspects of Van Gogh's now legendary life has produced a popular view of the man that tends to obscure his great contribution to art. In spite of his difficulties, Van Gogh produced almost two thousand works of art within a mere ten years. Although most of his contemporaries could not see the value of his art, his paintings and drawings are displayed today in major museums world-wide, and exhibitions of his works attract record crowds.

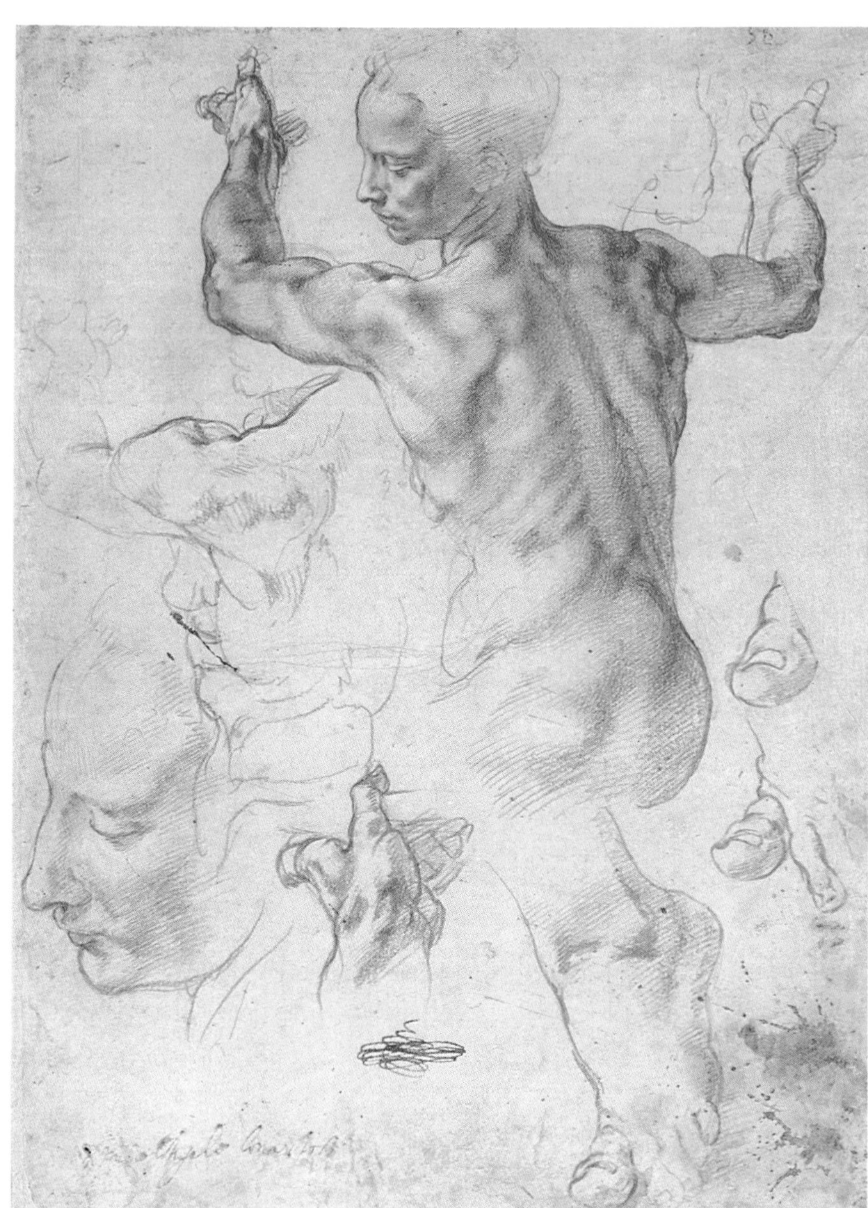

189 Michelangelo Buonarotti. Studies for the LIBYAN SIBYL on the Sistine Chapel ceiling. c.1508.
Red chalk. 11⅜"× 8⅜".
The Metropolitan Museum of Art, New York, Purchase (1924), Joseph Pulitzer Bequest.

PURPOSES OF DRAWING

A drawing can function in one or more of three ways:

- as a personal notation, sketch, or record of something seen, remembered, or imagined
- as a study for another, usually larger and more complex work such as a sculpture, a building, a film, a painting—or another drawing
- as an end in itself, a complete work of art

When Michelangelo made his detailed studies for the LIBYAN SIBYL, he had no idea that reproductions of his sheet of working drawings would be admired at least as much as his finished painting of the figure on the ceiling of the Sistine Chapel.

This magnificent drawing of a mythical female figure was drawn from a male model. The studies are a record of search and discovery as Michelangelo carefully drew what he observed. His understanding of anatomy helped him to define each muscle. The flow between the head, shoulders, and arms of the figure is based on Michelangelo's feeling for visual continuity as well as his attention to detail.

The parts of the figure that he felt needed further study were drawn repeatedly. To achieve the dark reds, Michelangelo evidently licked the point of the chalk.

A simple, tiny sketch, quickly done, can be the starting point for a far larger and more complex work. Picasso did many studies in preparation for a major painting, GUERNICA—a huge work measuring more than 11 feet high by 25 feet long (a larger reproduction appears on page 443). Forty-five of Picasso's studies are preserved, nearly all dated. In such drawings, an artist can work out problems of overall design or concentrate on small details.

The first drawing for GUERNICA shows what can be identified in later stages as a woman with a lamp, apparently an important symbol to Picasso. The woman leans out of a house in the upper right. On the left, a bull appears with a bird on its back. Both the bull and the woman with the lamp are major elements in the final painting. The first drawing was probably completed in a few seconds, yet its quick gestural lines contain the essence of the large, complex painting.

Although artists do not generally consider their preliminary sketches as finished pieces, studies by leading artists are often treasured both for their intrinsic beauty and for what they reveal about the creative process. Picasso recognized the importance of documenting the creative process from initial idea to finished painting:

It would be very interesting to preserve photographically, not the stages, but the metamorphoses of a picture. Possibly one might then discover the path followed by the brain in materializing a dream. But there is one very odd thing to notice, that basically a picture doesn't change, that the first "vision" remains almost intact, in spite of appearances.[4]

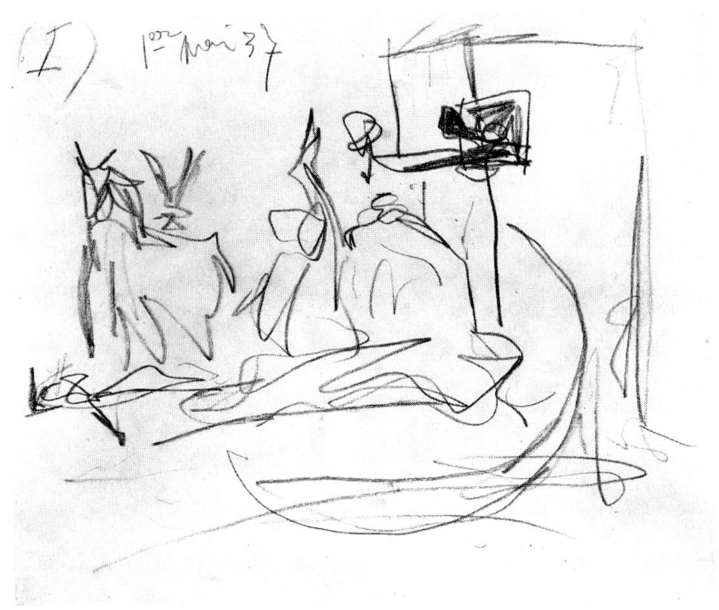

190 Pablo Picasso.
First composition study for GUERNICA. May 1, 1937.
Pencil on blue paper. 8¼" × 10⅝".
Museo del Prado, Madrid.

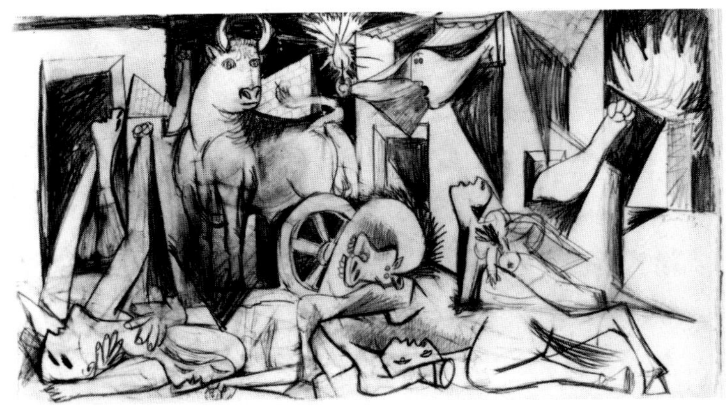

191 Pablo Picasso.
Composition study for GUERNICA. May 9, 1937.
Pencil on white paper. 9½" × 17⅞".
Museo del Prado, Madrid.

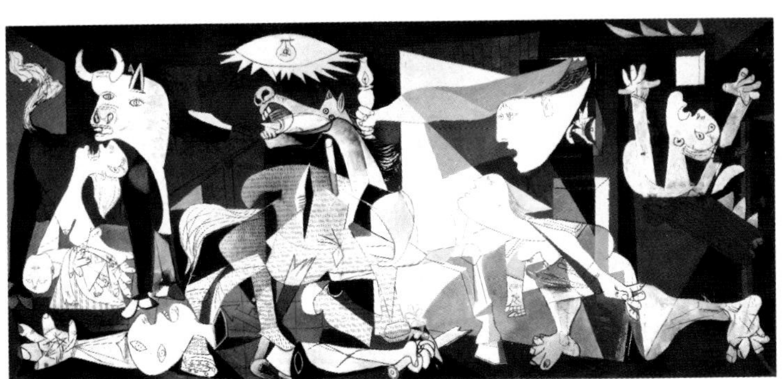

192 Pablo Picasso.
GUERNICA. 1937.
Oil on canvas. 11'5½" × 25'5¼".
Museo del Prado, Madrid. (See larger reproduction on page 443.)

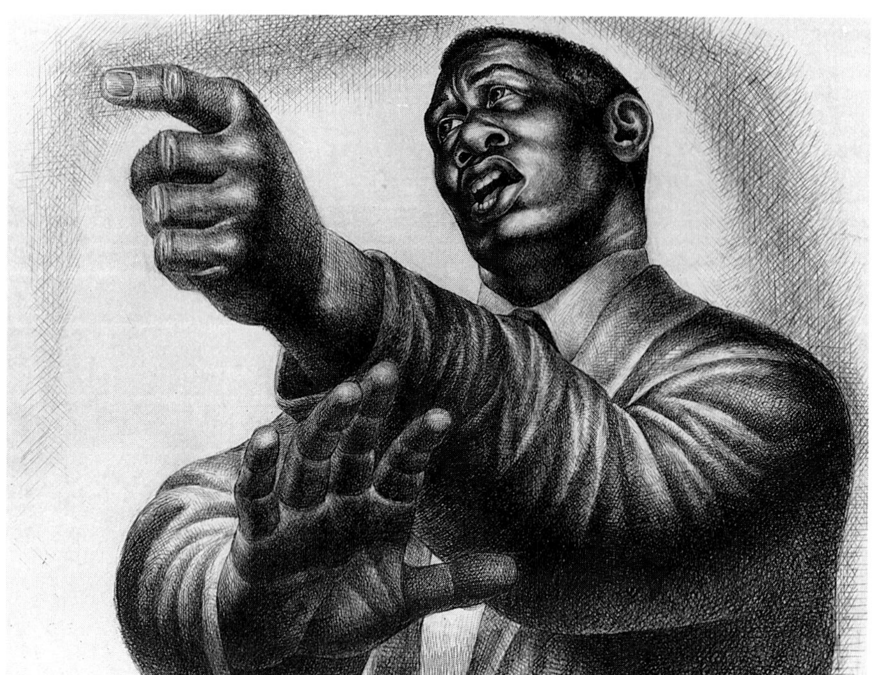

193 Charles White.
PREACHER. 1952.
Ink on cardboard. 21⅜" × 29⅜".
Collection of Whitney Museum of American Art, New York. Purchase (52.25).

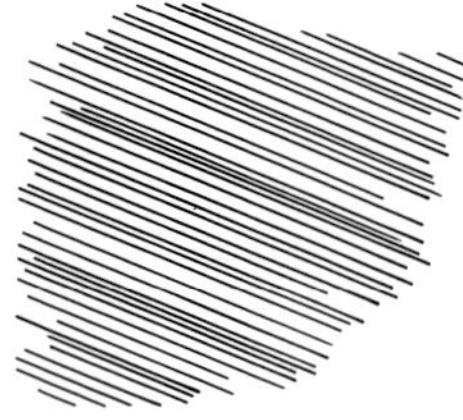

194 Types of Hatching.
a Hatching.

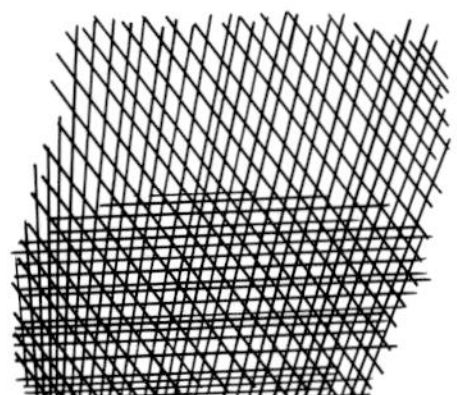

b Cross-hatching.

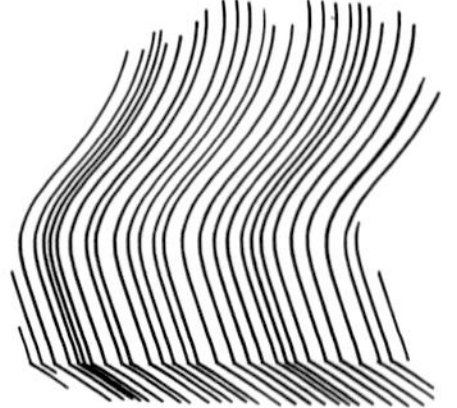

c Contour hatching.

Another type of preparatory drawing is the cartoon. The original meaning of cartoon, still used by art professionals, is a full-sized drawing made as a guide for a large work in another medium, particularly a fresco painting, mosaic, or tapestry.

In today's common usage, the word *cartoon* refers to a narrative drawing emphasizing humorous or satirical content. Cartoons and comics are among the most widely enjoyed drawings. Young people fond of drawing cartoons often go on to develop their drawing skills in other ways.

Each drawing tool and each type of paper has its own characteristics. The interaction between these materials and the technique of the artist determines the nature of the resulting drawing. The illustration DRAWING TOOLS shows the different qualities of marks made by various common drawing tools.

Another illustration shows how values can be built up with parallel lines, called *hatching,* or with *cross-hatching* of various types. Charles White used cross-hatched ink lines in PREACHER to build up the figure's mass and gesture in a forceful manner. Through the use of contour hatching, White gave the figure a feeling of sculptural mass. The strongly foreshortened right hand and forearm add to the drawing's dramatic impact.

DRY MEDIA

Dry drawing media include pencil, charcoal, conté crayon, and pastel. Drawing pencils include those made of graphite varying from soft (dark) to hard (light) and high-quality colored pencils in a wide range of colors.

Darkness and line quality are determined both by the degree of hardness of the pencil and by the texture of the surface to which it is applied. Paper with some *tooth* or surface grain will receive pencil marks more readily than paper that is smooth. Pencil lines can vary in width or length, can be made by using the side of the pencil point in broad strokes, and can be repeated as hatching. A considerable range of values can be produced by varying the pressure on a medium-soft drawing pencil.

A rich variety of values and inventive shapes made with light (hard) and dark (soft) grades of drawing pencils fills Judith Murray's drawing OBSIDIAN. Light and dark shapes, patterns, and textures play off against each other in a lively improvisation. The central black curving shape rises, helped by the energy of the shapes below and around it. Diagonally positioned, crystal-like triangular structures soar and return in dynamic interplay.

The sticks of charcoal used today are similar to those used by prehistoric people to draw on cave walls. With charcoal, dark passages can be drawn quickly. The various hard-to-soft grades of charcoal now available for drawing provide a flexible medium for both beginning and advanced artists.

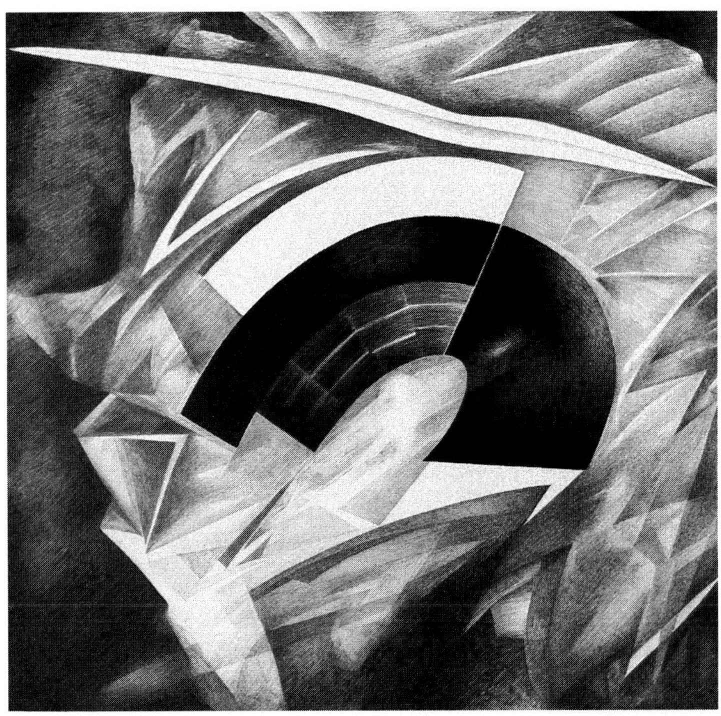

195 Judith Murray.
OBSIDIAN. 1988.
Pencil on arches paper. 22½" × 30".
Courtesy of the artist. Collection of Howard and Terry S. Walters, New Jersey.

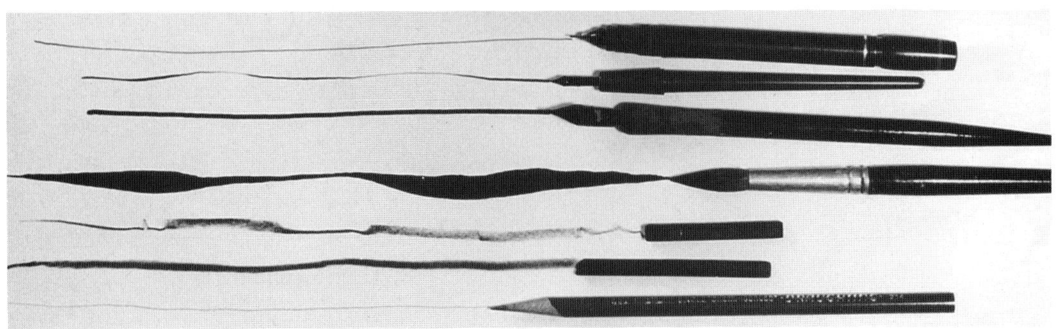

196 Drawing tools and their characteristic lines.

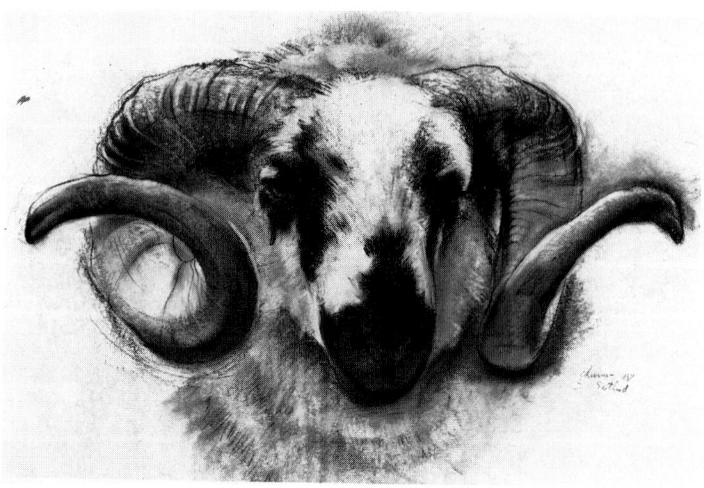

197 William Abbott Cheever.
RAM'S HEAD.
Charcoal on paper. 19" × 23".
Addison Gallery of American Art, Phillips Academy, Andover, Massachusetts.

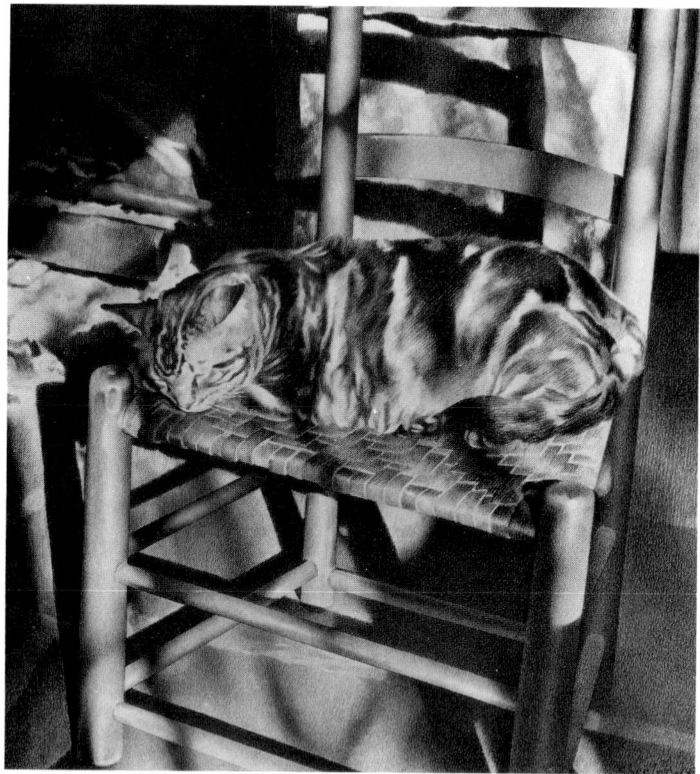

198 Charles Sheeler.
FELINE FELICITY. 1934.
Conté crayon on white paper. 14⅛" x 13¼".
Courtesy of Fogg Art Museum, Harvard University Art Museums, Louise E. Bettens Fund.

Because the charcoal particles do not bind to the surface of the paper, charcoal is easy to smudge, blur, or erase. This quality is both an advantage and a drawback: it enables one to make changes readily, but finished works can easily smear. A completed charcoal drawing may be set or "fixed" with a thin varnish called *fixative,* which is sprayed over it to help bind the charcoal to the paper.

William Cheever's RAM'S HEAD shows the wide range of values and strokes possible with charcoal. Sharp outlines define the horns, making them look hard. Soft, feathery strokes create the illusion of fur. Charcoal is an ideal medium for creating the velvety blacks seen in the nose and shadow areas. In this vigorous drawing, the illusion of a ram's head is played off against the reality of charcoal on paper.

Conté crayon is a semi-hard chalk with enough oil in the binder to cause it to adhere to smooth paper. It can produce varied lines or broad strokes that are relatively resistant to smudging. Wax-based crayons, such as those given to children, are avoided by serious artists; they lack flexibility, and most fade over time. Because the strokes do not blend easily, it is difficult to obtain bright color mixtures with wax crayons. Many professional artists now use oil crayons.

In Charles Sheeler's conté crayon drawing FELINE FELICITY, crisp edges work together with light and shade to form an intricate pattern. Sheeler was a leading photographer of the early twentieth century as well as a painter and draftsman. In all media, his work has a strong sense of structured design.

Georges Seurat used conté crayon to build up the illusion of three-dimensional form through value gradations (chiaroscuro) in his drawing THE ARTIST'S MOTHER. Seurat actually drew a multitude of lines; yet in the final drawing the individual lines are obscured by the total effect of finely textured light and dark areas. He selected conté crayon on rough paper as a means of concentrating on basic forms and on the interplay of light and shadow.

Natural chalks of red, white, and black have been used for drawing since ancient times. Pastels, produced since the nineteenth century, have characteristics similar to natural chalk. They have a freshness and purity of color because they are comprised mostly of pigment, with very little binding material. Because no drying is needed, there is no change in color, as occurs in some paints when they dry. Soft pastels do not allow for much detail, so they force the user to work boldly. Blending of strokes with fingers or a paper stump made for the purpose produces a soft blur that lightly mixes the colors. Pastels yield the most exciting results when not overworked.

French artist Edgar Degas shifted from oil painting to pastels in his later years, and occasionally he combined the two. He took advantage of the vibrant strokes of color and subtle blends possible with pastel. Although carefully constructed, his compositions look like casual, fleeting glimpses of everyday life. In BREAKFAST AFTER THE BATH, bold contours give a sense of movement to the whole design.

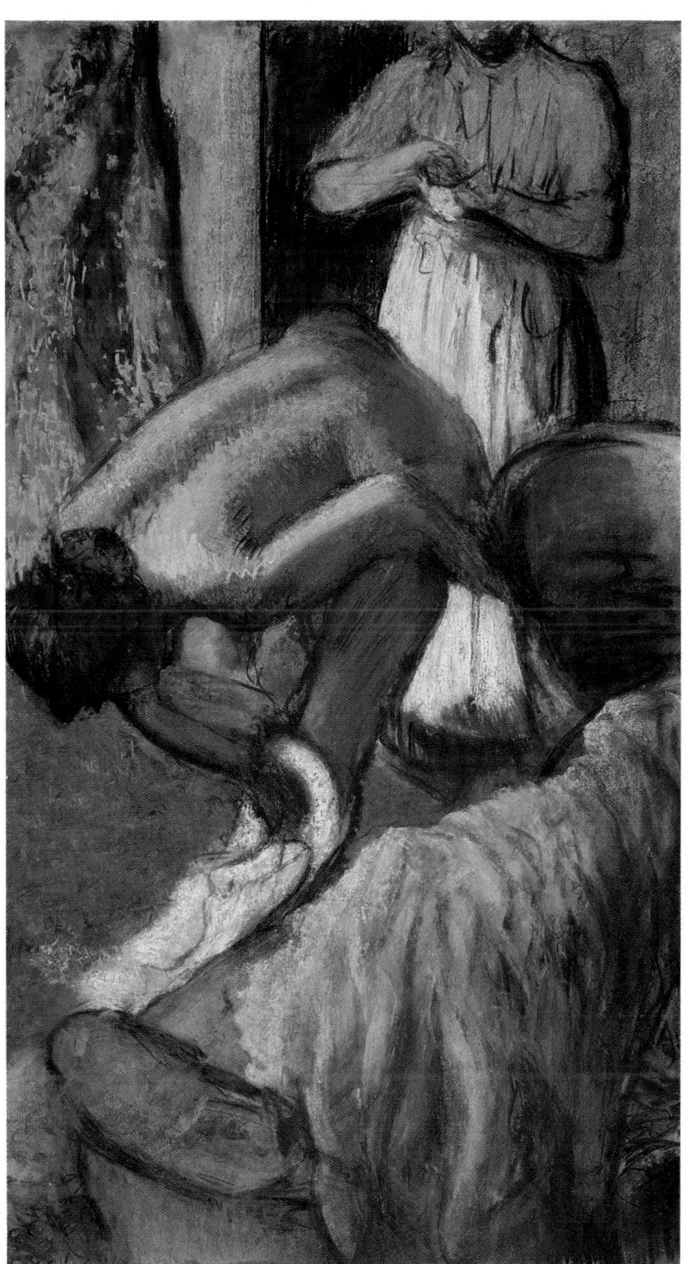

199 Edgar Degas.
BREAKFAST AFTER THE BATH
(YOUNG WOMAN DRYING HERSELF). c. 1894.
Pastel on paper. 98.7 cm × 58.7 cm.
Presented by the Gilman Foundation, New York to the Tel Aviv Museum and the Tel Aviv University.

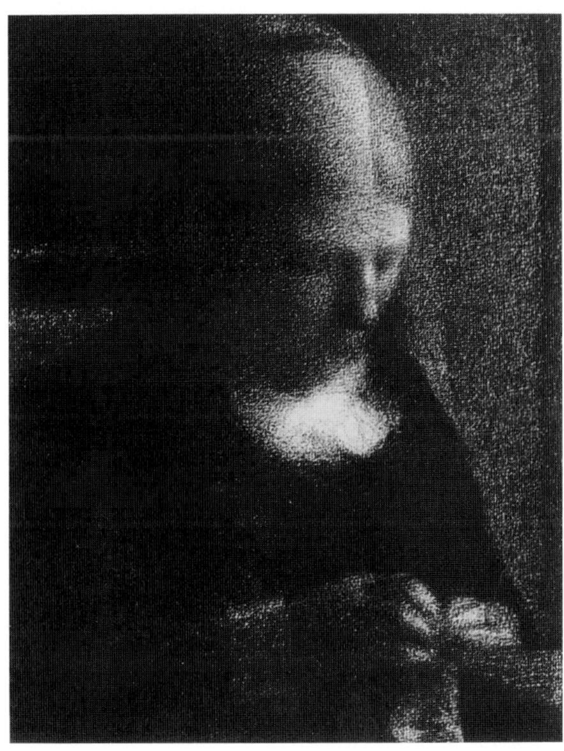

200 Georges Seurat.
THE ARTIST'S MOTHER (WOMAN SEWING). c. 1883.
Conté crayon on paper. 12¼" × 9½".
The Metropolitan Museum of Art, New York. Purchase. Joseph Pulitzer Bequest, 1955 (55.21.1).

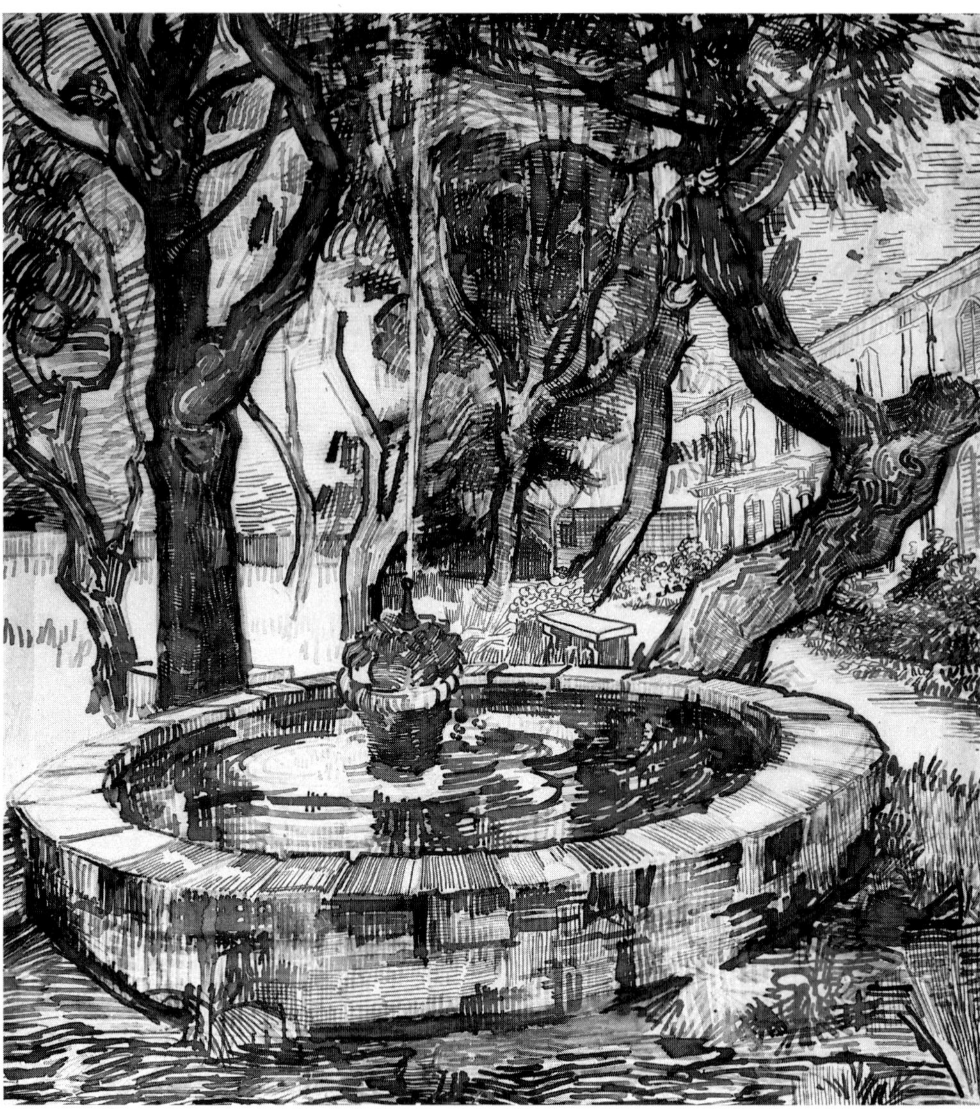

201 Vincent van Gogh. THE FOUNTAIN IN THE HOSPITAL GARDEN. 1889. Pen and ink. 18⅞" × 17¾". Vincent van Gogh Foundation/Van Gogh Museum, Amsterdam.

LIQUID MEDIA

Black or colored inks are the most common drawing liquids. Some brush drawings are made with *washes* of ink thinned with water. Such ink drawings are similar to watercolor paintings. Felt- and fiber-tipped pens are widely used recent additions to the traditional pen-and-ink media (see Pamela Davis's drawing on page 132).

In THE FOUNTAIN IN THE HOSPITAL GARDEN, Van Gogh used a Japanese bamboo pen and ink for his vigorous lines, varying the darkness of lines by using both full strength and diluted ink. Rhythmic line groups suggest the play of light and shadow on the various surfaces.

Nineteenth-century Japanese artist Hokusai, a skilled and prolific draftsman, is said to have created about 13,000 prints and drawings during his lifetime. He experienced the feelings of self-doubt known to many, yet he prevailed with courage and humor. His statement about the development of his artistic ability should encourage any young person to persevere:

I have been in love with painting ever since I became conscious of it at the age of six. I drew some pictures which I thought fairly good when I was fifty, but really nothing I did before the age of seventy was of any value at all. At seventy-three I have at last caught every aspect of nature—birds, fish, animals, insects, trees, grasses, all. When I am eighty I shall have developed still further and will really master the secrets of art at ninety. When I reach one hundred my art will be truly sublime, and my final goal will be attained around the age of one hundred and ten, when every line and dot I draw will be imbued with life.

(signed) Hokusai

The art-crazy old man[5]

In TUNING THE SAMISEN, the expressive elegance of Hokusai's lines was made possible by his control of the responsive brush. In the Orient, writing and drawing are done with the same or similar brushes, often using the same strokes. Oriental brushes are ideal for making calligraphic lines because they hold a substantial amount of ink and readily produce both thick and thin lines. Hokusai played the uniformly thin lines of head, hands, and instrument against the bold spontaneous strokes indicating the folds of the kimono. As the woman tuned the strings of her samisen, he captured a moment of concentration with humor and insight.

Rembrandt also used brush, ink, and ink wash for the drawing of his wife, SASKIA ASLEEP. The result is at once bold and subtle, representational and abstract, finished and unfinished. Rembrandt's spontaneous line technique bears comparison to the Oriental brush-painting tradition seen in the works of Hokusai. While Rembrandt used shading to give the illusion of three-dimensional form, Hokusai suggested the bulk of the figure with line alone.

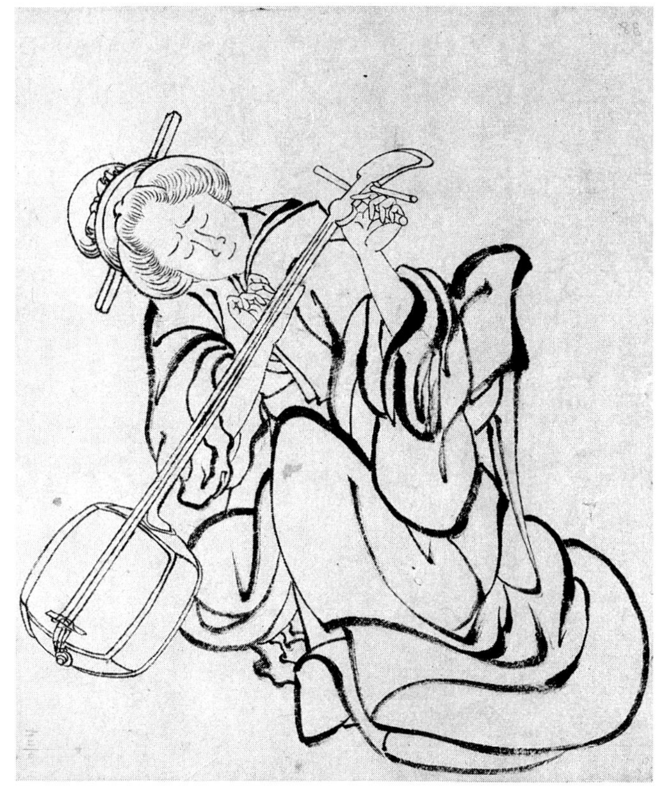

202 Hokusai.
TUNING THE SAMISEN.
c. 1820-1825.
Brush drawing. 9¾" × 8¼".
Courtesy of Freer Gallery of Art, Smithsonian Institution, Washington, D.C. (04.241).

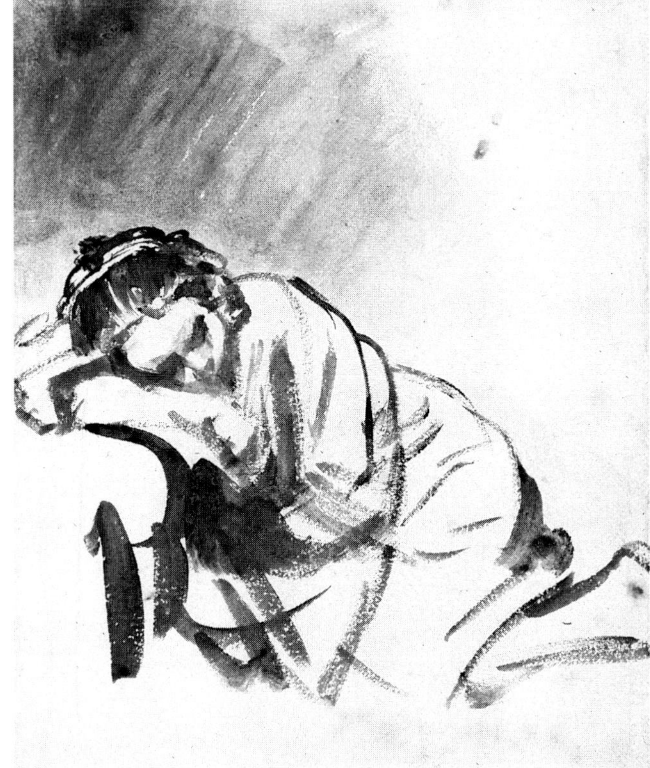

203 Rembrandt van Rijn.
SASKIA ASLEEP. c. 1642.
Brush and wash. 9½" × 8".
British Museum, London.

CHAPTER 9

Painting

To many people, the word art means painting. The long, rich history of painting, the strong appeal of color, and the endless image-making possibilities—both representational and abstract—explain painting's prominence and popularity.

Drawing and painting are closely related, somewhat overlapping processes. In fact, many paintings, such as Winslow Homer's SLOOP, NASSAU, are essentially brush drawings over light pencil sketches with color as a major element. Paintings tend to be larger, more formal, more colorful, and they are often completed more slowly than drawings—but there are many exceptions. There is no distinct separation between painting and drawing.

The people who made the earliest cave paintings used natural pigments obtained from plants and nearby deposits of minerals and clays. Pigments used in cave paintings at Lascaux, France—including blacks from charred woods, reds and yellows from ochres (impure iron ore), and white from chalk deposits—have lasted more than 17,000 years (see page 280). Today many types of ready-made paints are available, in synthetic as well as natural colors. Each type of paint has its own unique advantages and disadvantages.

Paints consist of three components: pigment, binder (or medium), and vehicle. The *pigment* provides color; the *binder* mixes with the pigment to hold the pigment particles together without dissolving them and to attach the pigment to the *ground* (the prepared surface to which the paint is applied); and the *vehicle* spreads the pigment. With oil paints, turpentine is the vehicle and linseed oil is the binder. With traditional tempera, water is the vehicle and egg yolk is the binder.

Pigments are powdered coloring agents that have long been derived from plant, animal, and mineral sources. In the nineteenth and twentieth centuries, major advances in the chemical industry have made it possible to produce synthetic pigments that extend the available range of colors. The durability of both natural and synthetic pigments has also been improved. Most of the same pigments are used both in manufacturing the various paint media and in the dry drawing media such as colored pencils and pastels. The slight color of each binder affects the hue and intensity of common pigments in different ways; thus the same pigments look slightly different in each of the various paint types.

Because art terminology is notoriously ambiguous, it is helpful to note the overlapping meanings of the term *medium.* In the broad context of the whole field of visual arts, medium means a material and its accompanying technique. In the context of painting, medium can also refer to the binder, or mixture of binder and vehicle, added to paint to facilitate its application without diluting color intensity.

Paints are usually applied to a flat *support,* such as stretched canvas for oils or paper for watercolors. To achieve a ground, the surface of the support

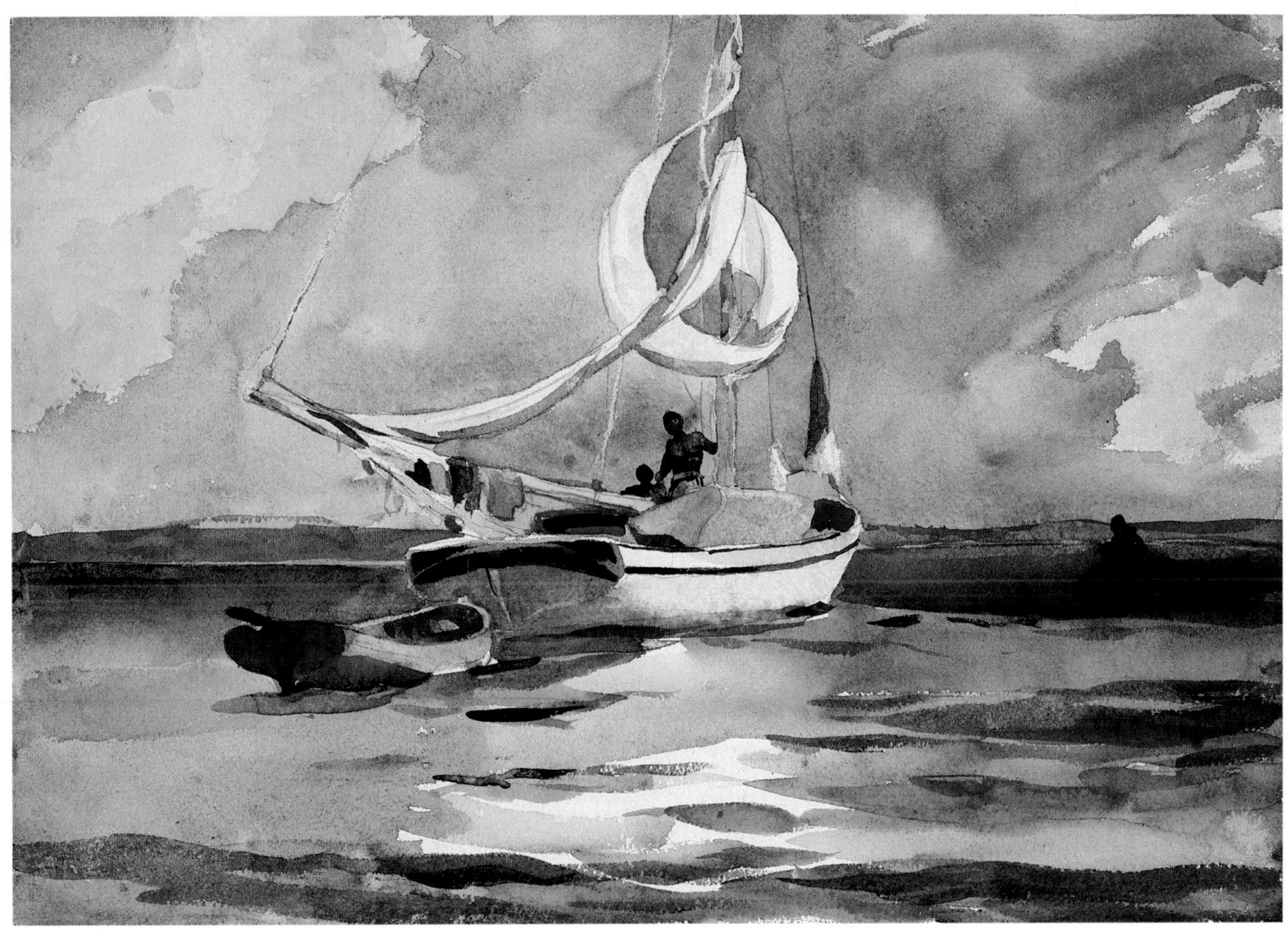

204 Winslow Homer.
SLOOP, NASSAU. 1899.
Watercolor on paper. 15" × 21½".
The Metropolitan Museum of Art. Amelia B. Lazarus Fund, 1910 (10.228.3).

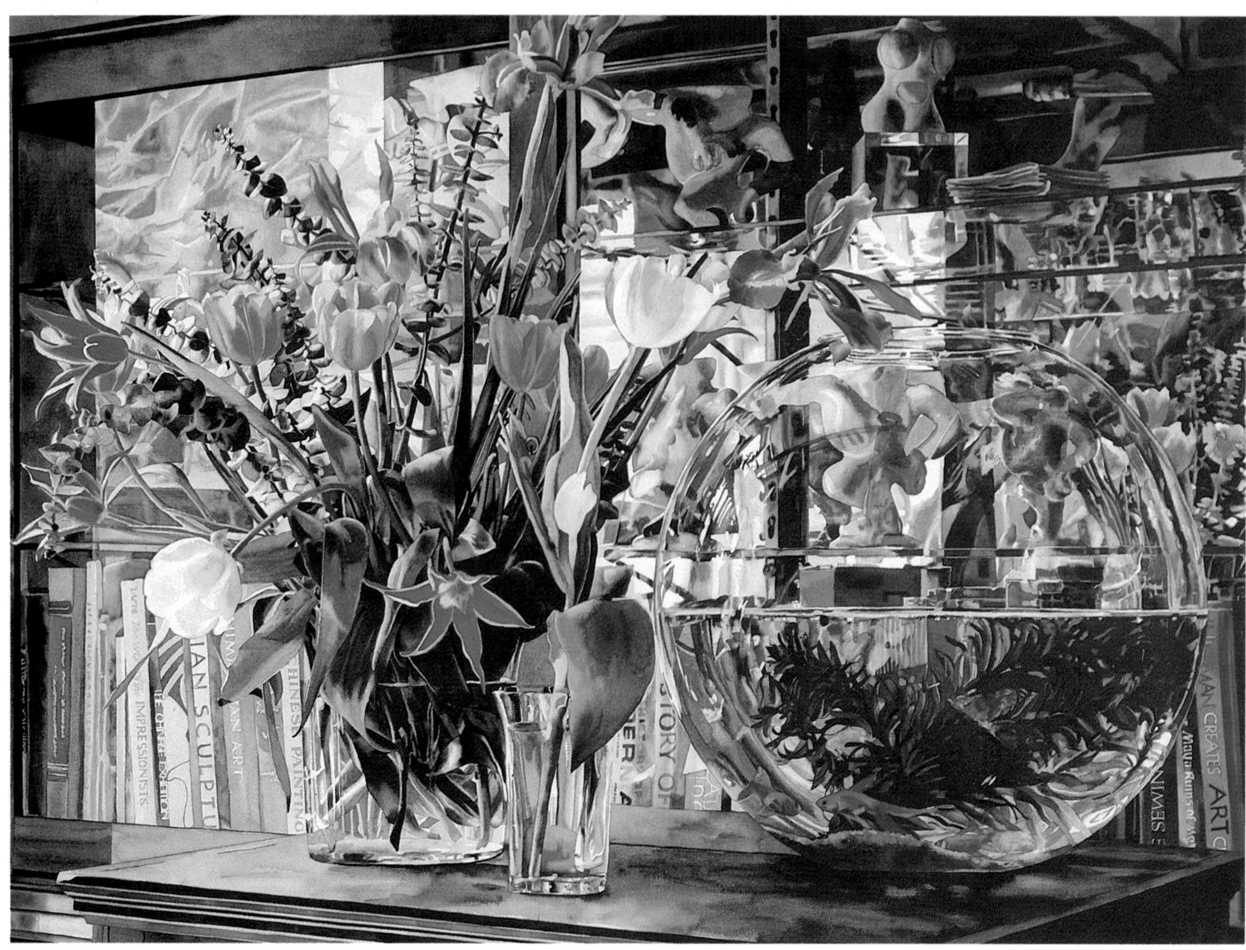

205 Carolyn Brady.
WHITE TULIP. 1980.
Watercolor on paper. 31½" × 44".
Private collection. Photograph courtesy of Nancy Hoffman Gallery, New York.

(usually canvas) is prepared by sizing or priming, or both. Because supports are often too absorbent to permit controlled application of paint, a *size,* or sealer, is usually applied to lessen absorbency and fill in the pores of the material. For oil painting in particular, size is needed on canvas and paper to protect them from disintegrating from the drying action of linseed oil in oil paint. To complete the surface preparation for painting, an opaque *prime* coat, or *ground,* usually white, is often applied after or instead of sizing. For watercolors, sizing and priming are unnecessary; a paper surface provides both the support and the ground.

In Rembrandt's time, the seventeenth century, painters or their assistants laboriously mixed finely ground pigments with oil by hand until the paint reached a desirable fineness and consistency. Today, high-quality paints are packaged in convenient tubes or jars, ready for immediate use.

A student or beginning artist will want to experiment with the various types of paint available, learning firsthand the possibilities of each paint medium. Watercolor, tempera, oils, and synthetic or acrylic paints are among the choices, but for the last five hundred years, oil paint has been the favorite medium of most painters. In recent years, artists have begun to use synthetic (usually acrylic) paints for spraying, pouring, dripping, and other innovative methods of application.

WATERCOLOR

Watercolor paintings are made by applying pigments suspended in a solution of water and gum arabic (a resin from the acacia tree) to white paper. Rag paper is the preferred support because of its superior absorbency and unchanging whiteness. Blocks of paint available in metal or plastic boxes are modern versions of the dried blocks of watercolor used for thousands of years. Professional artists use high-quality pigments sold in tubes.

Watercolor is basically a staining technique. The paint is applied in thin, translucent washes that allow light to pass through the layers of color and to reflect back from the white paper. Highlights are obtained by leaving areas of white paper unpainted. Opaque (nontranslucent) watercolor is sometimes added for detail. Watercolors are well suited to spontaneous as well as carefully planned applications. Despite the simple materials involved, watercolor is a demanding medium because it does not permit easy changes or corrections. Overwork a watercolor, and you lose its characteristic freshness.

Watercolor's fluid spontaneity makes it a favorite medium for painters who want to catch quick impressions outdoors. The translucent quality of watercolor washes particularly suits depictions of water, atmosphere, light, and weather.

American artist and illustrator Winslow Homer is best known for his watercolors. In SLOOP, NASSAU, Homer used the bright whiteness of the bare paper to form the highlights of ocean waves, boat, and sails. From light pencil lines to finished painting, his whole process is visible. Homer captured the mood of weather—in this case, the particular qualities of light and color in the calm just before a storm. A keen observer of nature, he learned that, for him, a quick impression made with watercolor was visually stronger than a painting filled with carefully rendered details.

Homer's watercolors are distinguished by their strong design. In SLOOP, NASSAU, he created rhythms with the loops of the sails, the repeated lines of the boats, the softly undulating waves, and the storm clouds. With a couple of short, deft strokes he painted a third figure to the right—an essential element in the balance of the composition.

In another vein, Carolyn Brady's elaborately developed photorealist watercolors stress the interplay of patterns found in familiar surroundings. WHITE TULIP is so filled with visual information that our eyes do not remain long on any one part of the composition. Exuberant color and lively surface reflections are held together in an unusual, carefully composed design. Brady must have planned and worked on the painting for many hours; yet her mastery of the medium enabled her to retain a fresh, spontaneous quality. (It was not until after we had selected this example of contemporary realism in watercolor that we noticed the book *Man Creates Art Creates Man,* the first edition of

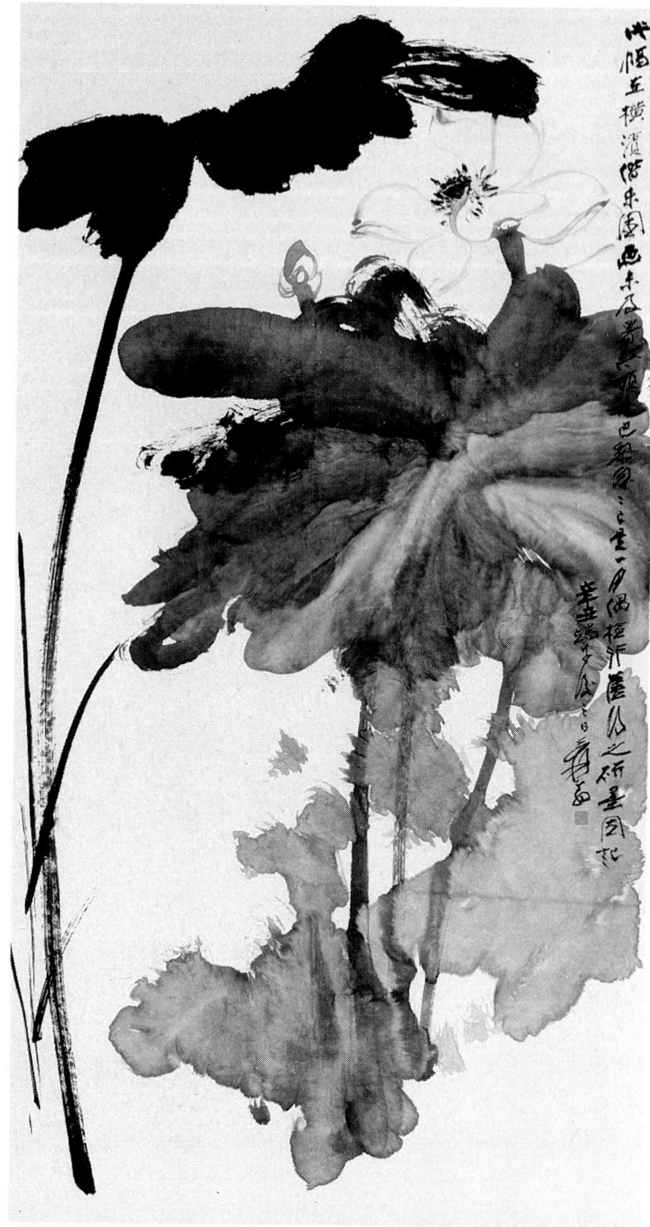

206 Chang Dai-Chien.
LOTUS. 1961.
Brush and ink on paper. 70¾" × 38¼", mounted on silk scroll, 106½" × 44⅞".
The Museum of Modern Art, New York. Gift of Dr. Kuo Yu-Shou.

Artforms, on the bookshelf in the painting.)

In traditional Chinese watercolor technique, the artist employs black ink as well as color and often uses the water-based ink without color. For the Chinese, a skillfully made black ink painting is a fully developed artwork, accorded at least as much honor as a painting with color. A modern example of this ancient attitude and technique is Chang Dai-Chien's ink painting LOTUS. In some areas Chang applied the ink full strength; in others he diluted it with water to achieve value gradations from light gray to black. A dry brush line appears in the soft middle part of the stroke that represents the stem supporting the highest leaf. In the lower right, diluted ink was allowed to blur the previously painted stem lines.

In China, both the artist and the viewer are expected to know the basic precepts of Chinese painting and the attitudes that animate them (see pages 294 and 295).

Watercolor mixed with opaque (nontranslucent) white pigment is called *gouache* (or designer's gouache or designer's colors). With gouache one can work from dark to light by adding white to colors, whereas with true watercolor, one works from the white of the paper to progressively darker layers of translucent color. Gouache can be used to create effects similar to those obtainable with oil paint with less trouble and expense. However, gouache is neither as permanent nor as flexible as oil, and its colors are much lighter in value when dry than they are when first applied.

TEMPERA

Tempera was used by the ancient Egyptians, Greeks, and Romans. It was highly developed during the Middle Ages, when it was used for small paintings made on wood panels, such as the BYZANTINE MADONNA on page 334. Since ancient times, the principal tempera medium has been egg tempera, in which egg yolk, or occasionally egg white, is the binder. (The binding qualities of egg yolk are well known to anyone who has washed breakfast dishes.) Today the word *tempera* is sometimes used to include water-soluble paints with binders of glue, casein, egg, or egg and oil emulsion. All tempera paints are water-thinned.

Egg tempera has a luminous, slightly *matte* (not shiny) surface when dry. Its clear, brilliant quality results from painting on a ground of very white gesso. *Gesso* is a preparation of chalk or plaster of Paris and glue applied to a support as a ground for tempera and oil paintings.

Egg tempera is good for achieving sharp lines and precise details, and it does not darken with age. However, its colors change during drying, and blending and reworking are difficult because of the rapid drying. Traditional tempera painting requires complete preliminary drawing and pale underpainting because of its translucency and the difficulty in making changes. Overpainting consists of applying layers of translucent paint in small, careful strokes. Because tempera lacks flexibility, movement of the support may cause the gesso and pigment to crack. A rigid support, such as a wood panel, is preferred.

Fra Filippo Lippi was one of the finest colorists of his day. In MADONNA AND CHILD, he methodically built up thin layers of color, creating a smooth, almost luminous surface. Tempera is well suited for depicting translucencies such as those created by Lippi in the halo and neck scarf. His naturalistic yet poetic portayal brought a worldly dimension to religious subject matter.

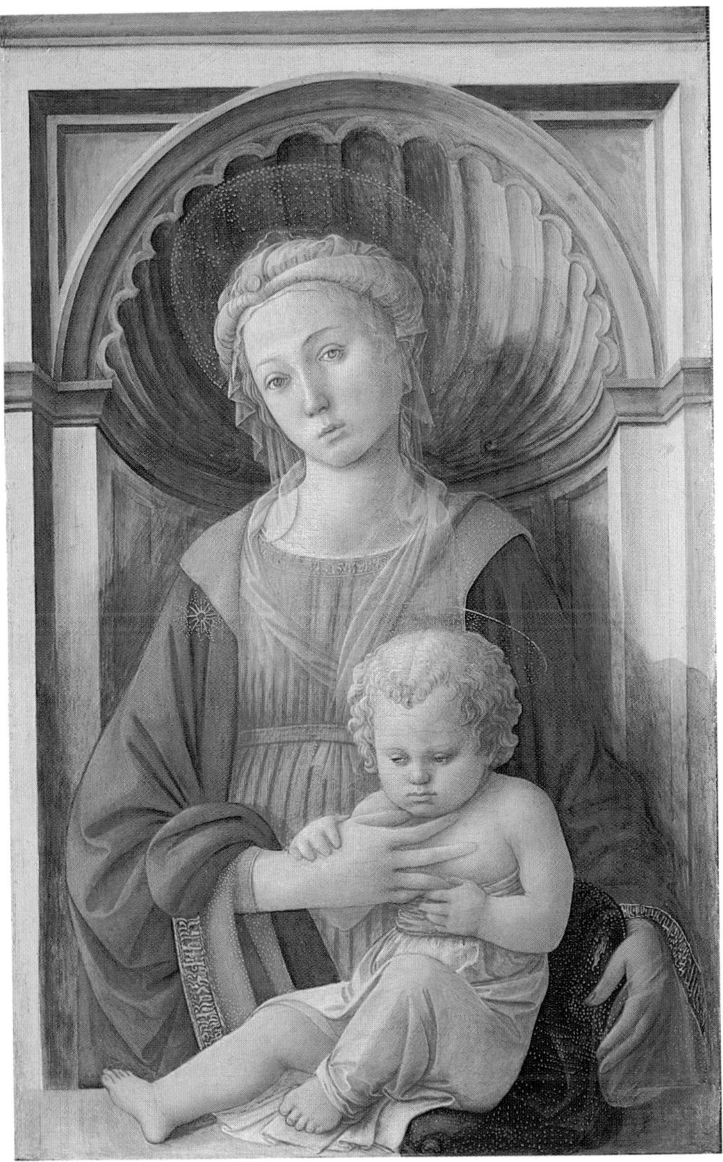

207 Fra Filippo Lippi.
MADONNA AND CHILD. c. 1440-1445.
Tempera on wood. 31⅜" × 20⅛".

OIL

In the Western world, oil paint has been a favorite medium for five centuries. Pigments mixed with various vegetable oils, such as linseed, walnut, and poppyseed, were used in the Middle Ages for decorative purposes, but not until the fifteenth century did Flemish painters fully develop the use of paint made with linseed oil pressed from the seeds of the flax plant. In this early period, artists applied oil paint to wood panels covered with smooth layers of gesso, as in the older tradition of tempera painting.

The Van Eyck brothers, Hubert and Jan, are credited with developing oil painting techniques and bringing them to their first perfection. They achieved glowing, jewel-like surfaces that remain

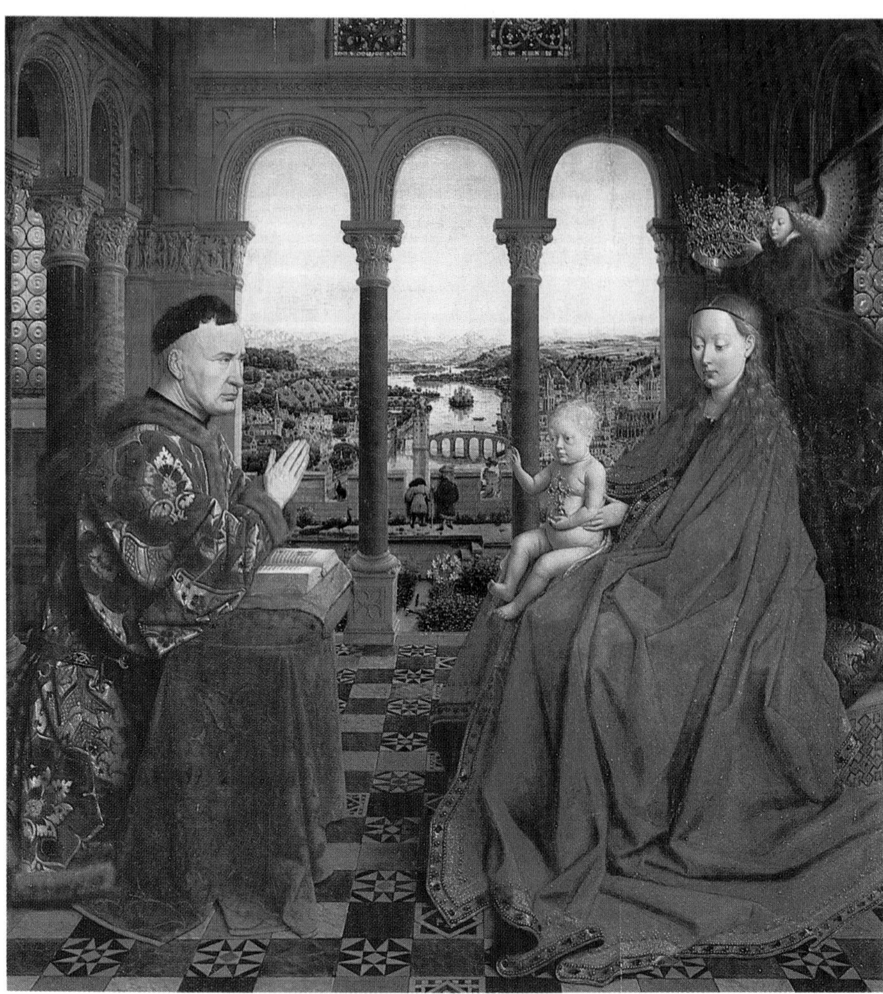

208 Jan van Eyck.
MADONNA AND CHILD WITH THE CHANCELLOR ROLIN.
c. 1433-1434.
Oil and tempera on panel.
26" × 24⅜".
Musée du Louvre, Paris.

delightfully fresh to the present day. Jan van Eyck's MADONNA AND CHILD WITH THE CHANCELLOR ROLIN is an example of his early mastery of the oil technique (see also Van Eyck's GIOVANNI ARNOLFINI AND HIS BRIDE on page 355).

MADONNA AND CHILD WITH THE CHANCELLOR ROLIN was painted on a small gesso-covered wood panel. After beginning with a brush drawing in tempera, Van Eyck proceeded with thin layers of oil paint, moving from light to dark and from opaque to translucent colors. The luminous quality of the surface is the result of successive oil glazes. A *glaze* is a very thin, transparent film of color applied over a previously painted surface. To produce glazes, oil colors selected for their transparency are diluted with glazing medium—usually a mixture of oil, thinner, and varnish. Glazes give glowing depth to painted surfaces by allowing light to pass through and reflect from lower paint layers.

Here the sparkling jewels, the textiles, and the furs are each given their own refined textures. Within the context of the religious subject, Van Eyck demonstrated his enthusiasm for the delights of the visible world. Veils of glazes in the sky area provide atmospheric perspective and thus contribute to the illusion of deep space in the enticing view beyond the open window. The evolution in the new oil painting technique made such realism possible.

Oil has many advantages not found in other traditional media. Compared to tempera, oil paint can provide both increased opacity—which yields better covering power—and, when thinned, greater transparency. Its slow drying time, first considered a drawback, soon proved to be a distinct advantage, permitting strokes of color to be blended and repeated changes made during the painting process. Unlike pigment in tempera, gouache, and acrylics, pigment colors in oil change little when drying; however, oil medium (primarily linseed oil) has a tendency to darken and yellow slightly with age. Because of the flexibility of dried oil film, sixteenth-century Venetian painters who wished to paint large, could replace heavy wood panels with canvas stretched on wood frames. A painted canvas is not only light, but it can be unstretched and rolled (if the paint layer is not too thick) for transporting. Canvas continues to be the preferred support for oil paintings.

Oil can be applied thickly or thinly, wet into wet or wet onto dry. When applied thickly, it is called *impasto.* When a painting is painted wet into wet and completed at one sitting, the process is called the *direct painting* method.

This method was used in Rembrandt's SELF-PORTRAIT. Our detail shows how the impasto of light and dark paint both defines a solid-looking head and presents the incredible richness of Rembrandt's painterly brushwork.

In Rembrandt's SELF-PORTRAIT and in Frank Auerbach's HEAD OF MICHAEL PODRO, the artists' responsiveness to both the reality of their subjects and the physical nature of paint and painting is highly visible. Because the thick, paste-like quality of oil paint is celebrated rather than hidden, viewers participate in the process of conjuring up images when viewing Rembrandt's rough strokes and Auerbach's smears and globs of paint. Both artists created paintings that project strong images when seen at a distance and present amazingly rich tactile surfaces when viewed close up.

The wide range of approaches possible with oil paint becomes apparent when we compare Van Eyck's subtly glazed colors with the impasto surfaces of Rembrandt, Auerbach, and Hans Hofmann.

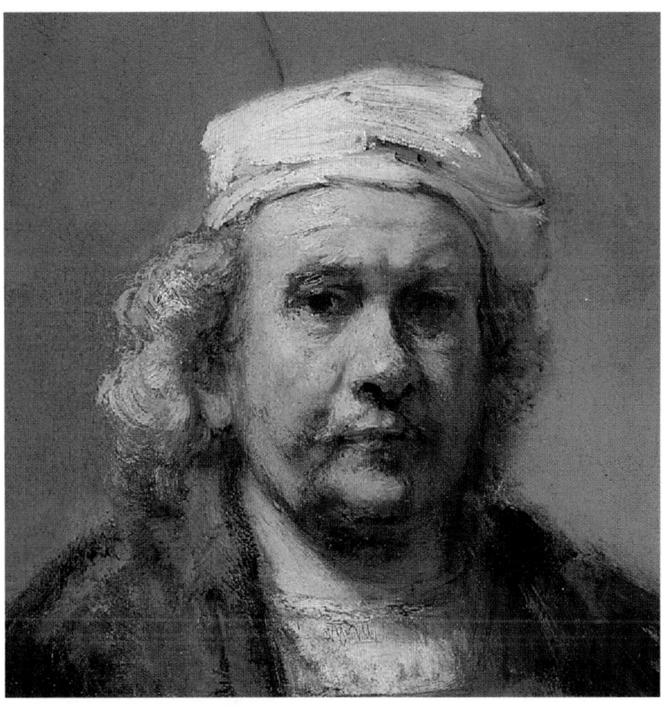

209 Rembrandt van Rijn.
Detail of SELF-PORTRAIT. 1663.
Oil on canvas. Full painting 45" × 38".
Iveagh Bequest, Kenwood House (English Heritage), London.

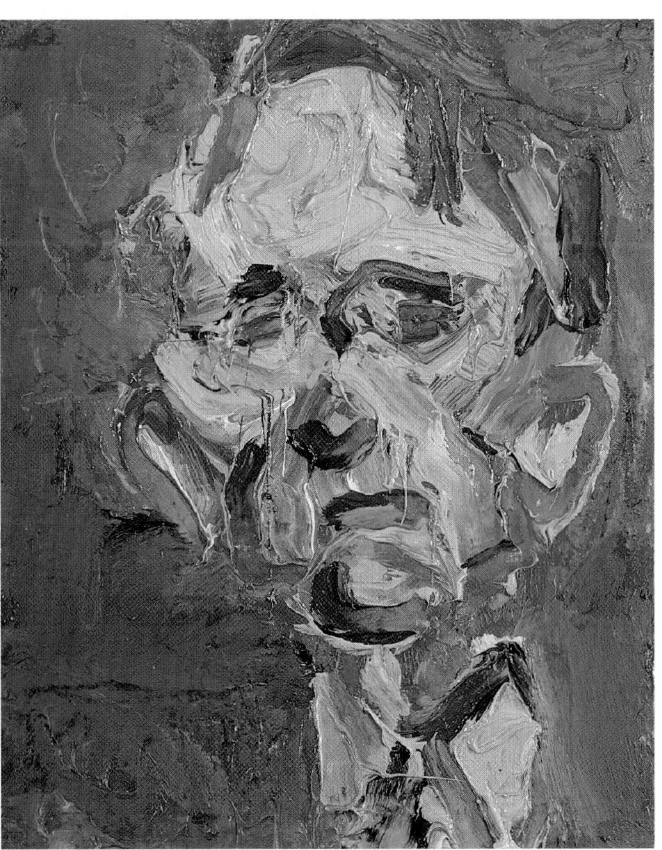

210 Frank Auerbach.
HEAD OF MICHAEL PODRO. 1981.
Oil on board. 13" × 11".
Private collection. Photograph: Marlborough Fine Art, London.

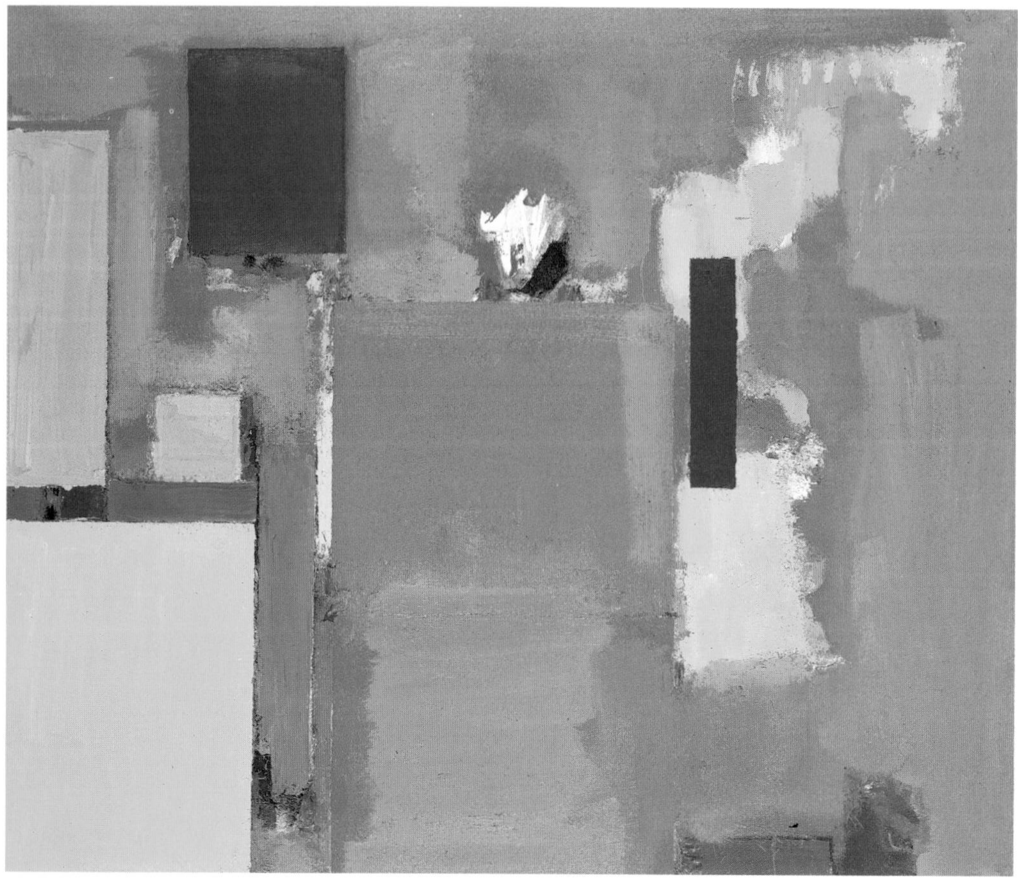

211 Hans Hofmann.
THE GOLDEN WALL. 1961.
Oil on canvas. 60" × 72¼".
Mr. and Mrs. Frank G. Logan Prize Fund (1962.775). © 1993
The Art Institute of Chicago. All rights reserved.

In both his art and his teaching, Hofmann emphasized the translation of personal states of being into nonrepresentational form. In THE GOLDEN WALL, he worked with the dynamics of advancing and receding color, movement, and countermovement. Static, hard-edge rectangles assert their presence in a field of vigorous, irregular shapes. The painting creates its own self-contained environment.

ACRYLIC

Foremost among the synthetic painting media currently in wide use are *acrylics.* Pigments are suspended in acrylic polymer medium, which provides a fast-drying, flexible film. These relatively permanent paints can be applied to a wider variety of surfaces than traditional painting media. Most acrylics are water-thinned and water-resistant when dry. Because acrylic resin medium is highly transparent, colors can maintain a high degree of intensity; but unlike oils, acrylics rarely darken or yellow with age. Their rapid drying time restricts blending and reworking possibilities, but it greatly reduces the time involved in layering processes such as glazing.

Acrylics work well when paint is applied quickly with little blending—witness the splash in David Hockney's A BIGGER SPLASH—or when brushed on in flat areas as in the rest of the painting. The strong contrast between the dramatic freedom of the paint application of the splash and the thinly painted, geometric shapes of house, chair, pool rim, and diving board gives lively energy to the suburban scene. The acrylic contributes clean, sharp colors painted with many hard edges, suggesting psychological isolation even amid the good life in sunny southern California.

Acrylic paint is inert when dry and, unlike oil paint, will not damage cloth fibers over a long period of time. Thus acrylics can be applied directly to unprimed canvas or paper. This quality has resulted in a variety of staining techniques in which the paint, thinned with water, acts more as a dye than as a coating on the surface of the canvas. Morris Louis used this technique in BLUE VEIL.

In recent years, many painters have used airbrushes to apply their paint. An *airbrush* is a small-scale paint sprayer, capable of projecting a fine, controlled mist of paint. It provides an even paint application without the personal touch seen in individual brush strokes, and it is therefore well suited to the impersonal imagery and subtle gradations of color values found in many paintings of the 1960s and 1970s, such as Audrey Flack's WHEEL OF FORTUNE on page 45.

Acrylics lend themselves well to the spontaneous approaches taken by many of today's artists. They are appreciated for their fast-drying property and for their ability to provide a strong, stable base, ground, or glue for mixed media techniques.

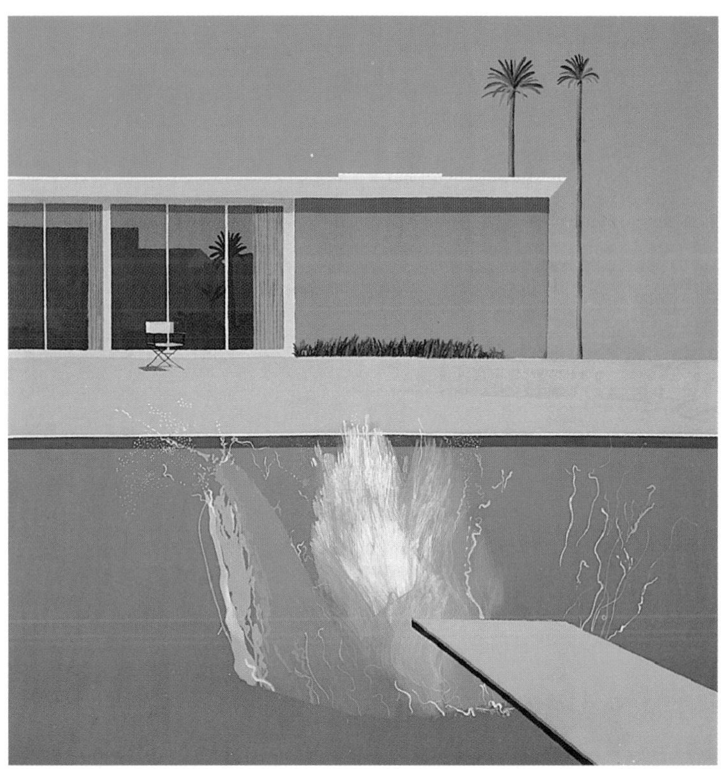

212 David Hockney.
A BIGGER SPLASH. 1967.
Acrylic on canvas. 96" × 96".
The Tate Gallery, London.

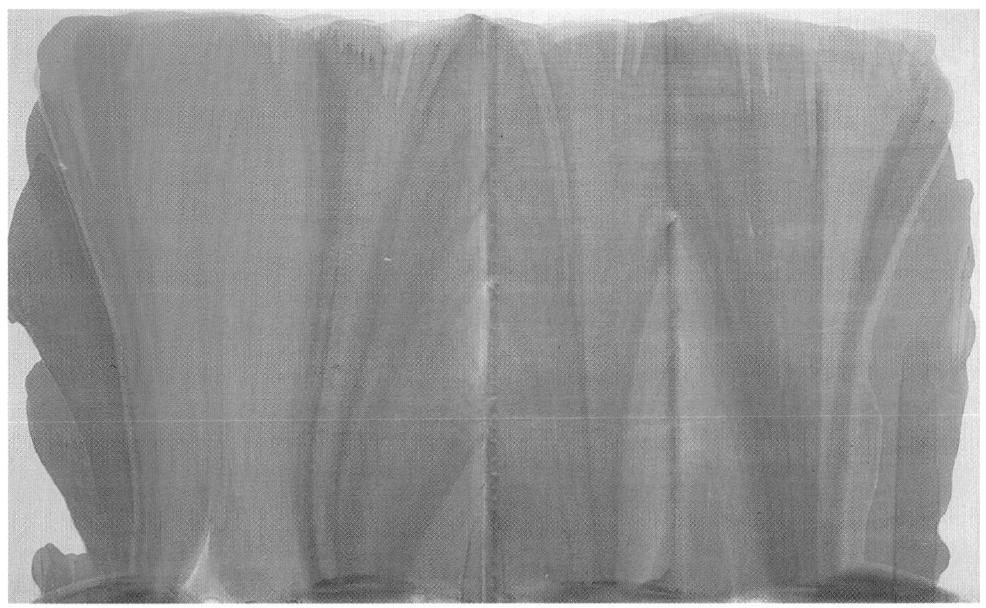

213 Morris Louis.
BLUE VEIL. 1958-1959.
Acrylic resin paint on canvas.
233 cm × 396.2 cm.
Courtesy of Fogg Art Museum, Harvard University Art Museums. Gift of Lois Orswell and Gifts for Special Uses Fund.

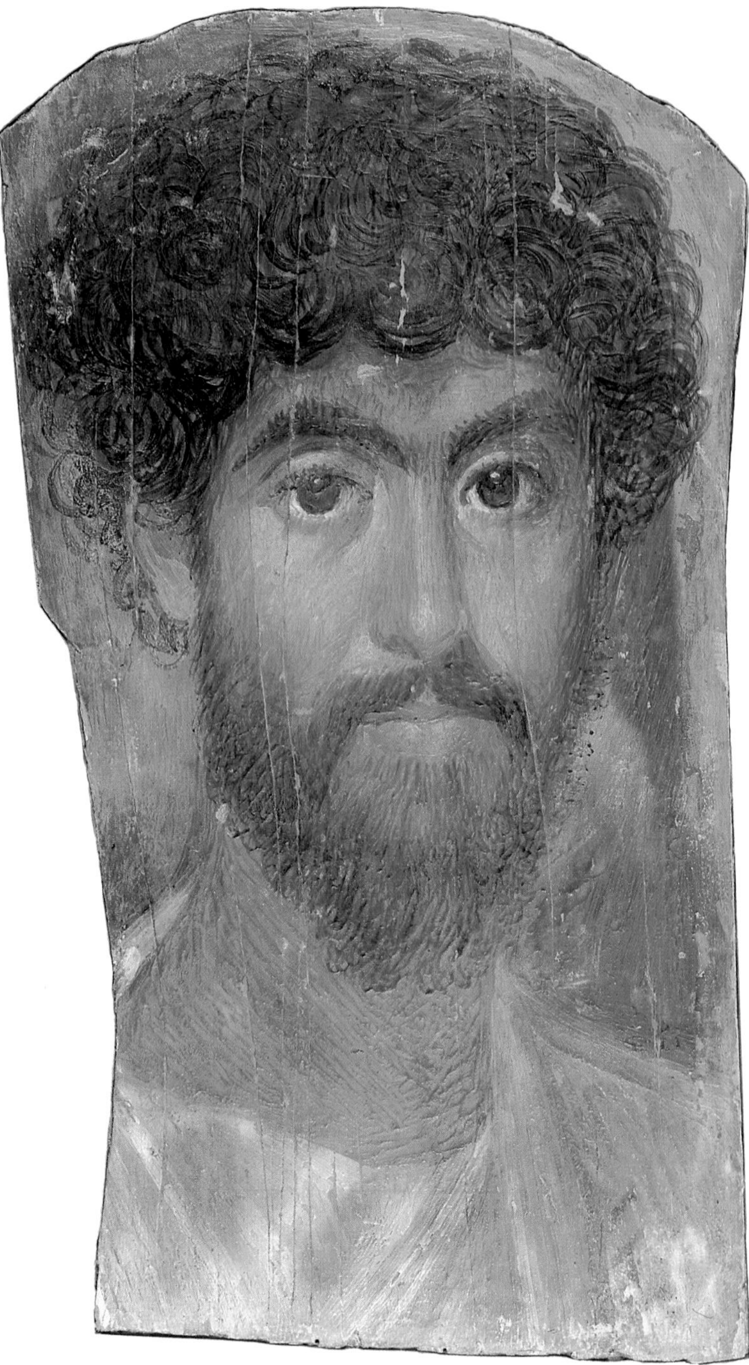

214 MUMMY PORTRAIT OF A MAN. A.D. 160-170.
From Fayum, Egypt.
Encaustic on wood. 14" × 8".
Albright-Knox Art Gallery, Buffalo, New York. Charles Clifton Fund (1938).

ENCAUSTIC

In the ancient medium of *encaustic,* pigments are suspended in hot beeswax, resulting in lustrous surfaces that bring out the full richness of colors. Early Christian Egyptians, known as Copts, developed encaustic painting to a high art in the second century. Coptic sarcophagus portraits, such as MUMMY PORTRAIT OF A MAN, were painted on wood. In these portraits, lifelike vigor and the sense of individuality remain strong and colors have retained their intensity after almost two thousand years.

Early practitioners found it difficult to keep the wax binder of encaustic at the right temperature for proper handling; with modern electrical heating devices, it is easier to maintain workable temperatures. Nevertheless, encaustic is used by only a few painters today. One of the best-known proponents of encaustic painting is Jasper Johns (see his TARGET WITH FOUR FACES on page 458).

FRESCO

True fresco, or *buon fresco,* is an ancient wall-painting technique in which very finely ground pigments suspended in water are applied to a damp lime-plaster surface. Generally, a full-size drawing called a *cartoon* is completed first, then transferred to the freshly laid plaster wall before painting. Because the plaster dries quickly, only the portion of the wall that can be painted in one day is prepared; joints are usually arranged along the edges of major shapes in the composition.

The painter works quickly in a rapid staining process similar to watercolor. Lime, in contact with air, forms transparent calcium crystals that chemically bind the pigment to the moist lime-plaster wall. The lime in the plaster thus becomes the binder, creating a smooth, extremely durable surface. Once the surface has dried, the painting is part of the wall. Completion of the chemical reaction occurs slowly, deepening and enriching the colors as the fresco ages. Colors reach their greatest intensity fifty to one hundred years after a fresco is painted, yet the hues always have a muted quality.

The artist must have the design completely worked out before painting, because no changes

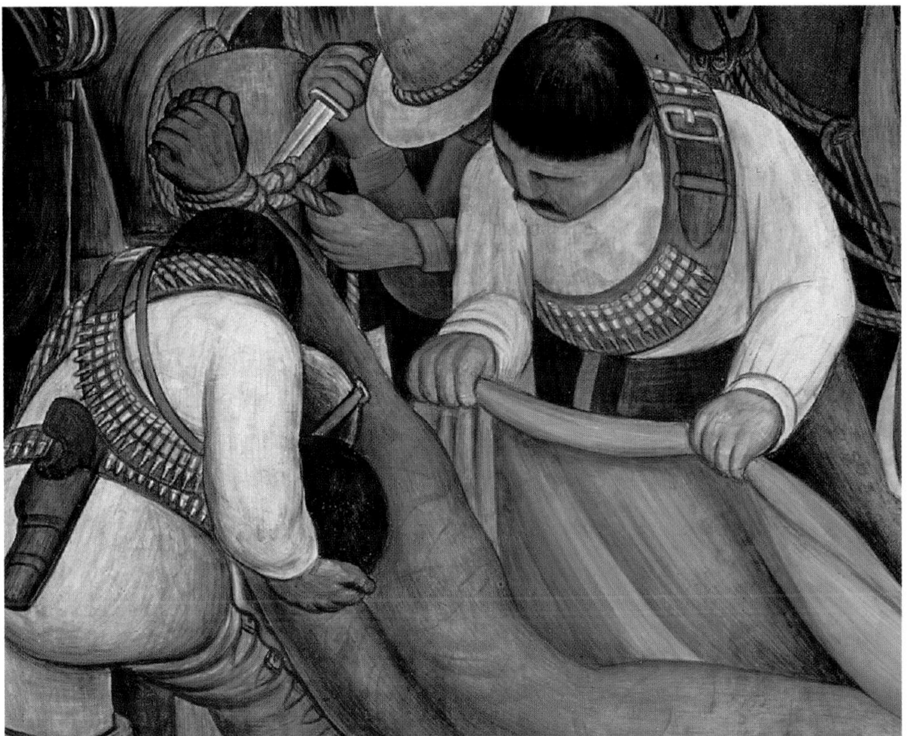

215 Diego Rivera.
Detail of THE LIBERATION OF THE PEON. 1931.
Fresco. Full painting 74" × 95". (See page 445.)
Philadelphia Museum of Art. Given by Mr. and Mrs. Herbert C. Morris.

can be made after the paint is applied to the fresh plaster. It may take twelve to fourteen straight hours of work just to complete two square yards of a fresco painting. Fresco technique does not permit the delicate manipulation of transitional tones; but the luminous color, fine surface, and permanent color make it an ideal medium for large murals.

Secco fresco, another ancient wall-painting method, is done on finished, dried lime-plaster walls. With this technique, tempera paint is applied to a clean, dry surface or over an already dried *buon fresco* to achieve greater color intensity than is possible with *buon fresco* alone.

Fresco has been used in Asian and Western cultures for at least four thousand years. In Renaissance Italy, it was the favored medium for decorating church walls. Giotto's LAMENTATION in the Padua Chapel (see page 343), painted in both *buon fresco* and *secco fresco,* is characteristic of frescoes from this period. Probably the best known fresco paintings are those by Michelangelo on the Sistine Chapel ceiling in the Vatican in Rome, Italy (see page 353). After the Renaissance and Baroque periods, fresco became less popular, eclipsed by the more flexible oil medium. However, a revival of the fresco technique began in Mexico in the 1920s, encouraged by the new revolutionary government's support for public murals.

By leading the revival in fresco mural painting for public buildings, Diego Rivera was able to break away from the limited studio and gallery audience and make art a part of the life of the people. His style blends European and native art traditions with contemporary subject matter. THE LIBERATION OF THE PEON is one of eight portable frescoes that Rivera made for his 1931–1932 exhibition at the Museum of Modern Art in New York (the complete painting appears on page 445). Notice the texture of the plaster; even at the reduced size shown here, Rivera's typical fresco brushwork is visible.

CHAPTER 10

Printmaking

The term *printmaking* describes a variety of media developed to create multiple images. So much in our society is printed—newspapers, books, posters, magazines, greeting cards, billboards—that it is hard to imagine a time in which all human-made images were produced by hand, one at a time. Before 1415, every book and manuscript in Europe was hand-lettered and hand-illustrated. In contrast, multiple copies of *Artforms* are printed quickly by a mechanical printing method called *offset lithography.*

The ability to reproduce pictures with a printing press was as important to human development as the invention of movable type. The technologies for both printing and papermaking came to Europe from China. By the ninth century, the Chinese were printing pictures; by the eleventh century, they had invented (but seldom used) movable type. Printmaking as we know it today was developed in Europe by the fifteenth century—first to meet the demand for inexpensive religious icons and playing cards, then to illustrate books printed with the new European movable type. Since the fifteenth century, the art of printmaking has been closely associated with the illustration of books.

Prior to the twentieth century, most printing was for the purpose of commercial reproduction rather than making original art. As recently as the late nineteenth century, printmakers were still needed to copy drawings, paintings, and even early photographs by making plates to be used, along with movable type, for illustrating newspapers and books.

As photomechanical methods of reproduction were developed, handwork by craftsmen played an increasingly minor part in the printing process. Artists, however, have continued to use the old handcrafted printmaking processes to take advantage of their uniquely expressive properties. By designing and printing multiple originals, today's printmakers can sell their works for much less than one-of-a-kind paintings. Such works, conceived as *original prints,* are not to be confused with reproductions (see the discussion on page 170).

Nearly all original prints are numbered to indicate the total number of prints pulled or printed in the edition, and to give the number of each print in the sequence. The figure 6/50 on a print, for example, would indicate that the edition totaled fifty prints and that this was the sixth print pulled.

As part of the printmaking process, artists make prints called *progressive proofs* at various stages to see how the image on the block, plate, stone, or screen is developing. When a satisfactory stage is reached, the artist makes a few prints for his or her record and personal use. These are marked AP, meaning *artist's proof.*

Printmaking methods range from simple to complex. Traditionally, we divide these methods into four basic categories: relief, intaglio, lithography, and screenprinting.

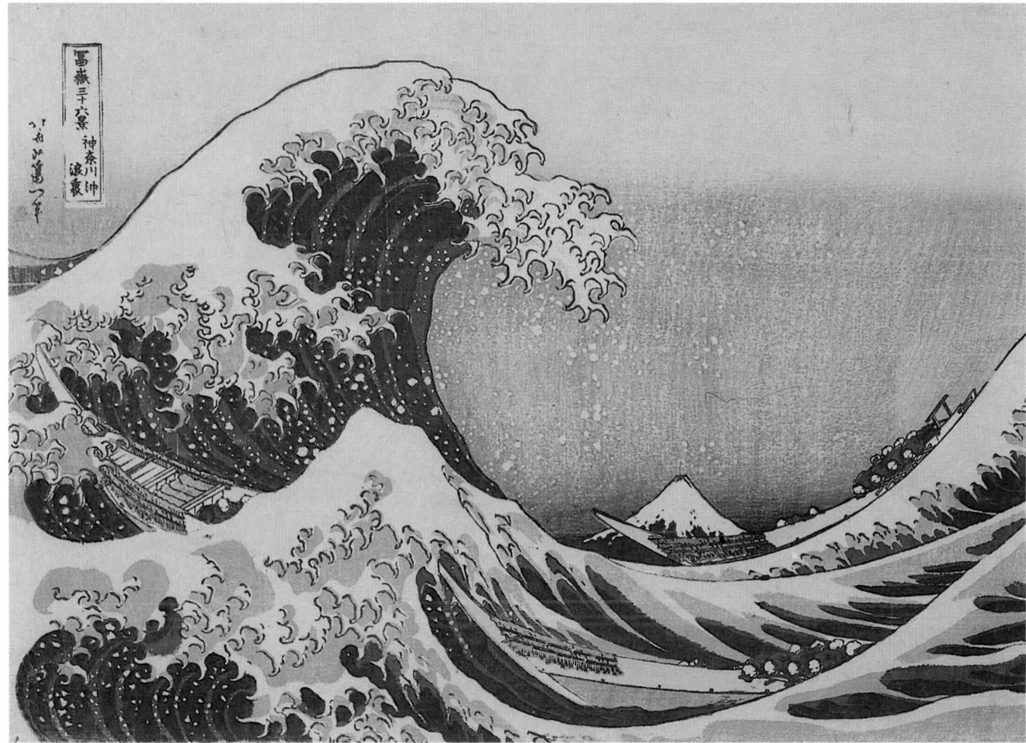

216 Hokusai.
WAVE AT KANAGAWA from the series THIRTY-SIX VIEWS OF MOUNT FUJI. c. 1830.
Color woodblock print.
10¼" × 15⅛".
Honolulu Academy of Arts.
The James A. Michener Collection.

RELIEF

In a *relief* process, the printmaker cuts away all parts of the printing surface not meant to carry the ink, leaving the design to be printed "in relief " at the level of the original surface. The surface is then inked, and the ink is transferred to paper with pressure. Relief processes include *woodcuts, wood engravings,* and *linoleum* (or *lino*) *cuts.* Images made by rubber stamps and wet tires are examples of relief-printed marks in the everyday world.

The traditional woodcut process lends itself to designs with bold black-and-white contrast. The image-bearing block of wood, usually a soft wood, is a plank cut along the grain. Color can be printed with single or multiple blocks. As with most printmaking techniques, when more than one color is used, individually inked blocks—one for each color—are carefully *registered* (lined up) to insure that colors will be exactly placed in the final print.

Block printing from woodcuts originated in China and became a highly developed art in Japan in the seventeenth through the nineteenth centuries. Japanese woodblock prints were made through a complex process that used multiple blocks to achieve subtle and highly integrated color effects. Through this art form, Westerners came to know Japanese art in the late nineteenth century.

During the century since his death, Japanese artist Hokusai's color woodcut prints have become well known around the world. Hokusai worked in close collaboration with highly skilled craftsmen to realize the final prints. For each of his woodcuts, specialists transferred Hokusai's watercolor brush painting to as many as twenty blocks, then cut the blocks. In Hokusai's famous print WAVE AT KANAGAWA, a clawing mountain of water dwarfs tiny fishermen in their boats, climaxing the rhythmic curves of the churning ocean. The only stable element is the distant peak of Mt. Fuji. A more realistic rendering would not have been as effective in capturing the awesome power of the sea. This print is one of Hokusai's thirty-six famous views of Mount Fuji seen from various locations.

The stylized detail in Hokusai's print is quite different from the intentional primitiveness of the woodcut PROPHET by German artist Emil Nolde.

Each cut in the block contributes to the expressive image of an old man's face and reveals the character of the wood and the wood-cutting process. The light-and-dark pattern created through simplification of the features gives emotional intensity to the image. Nolde's direct approach is a recent development in the long tradition of German printmaking that included the work of Albrecht Dürer.

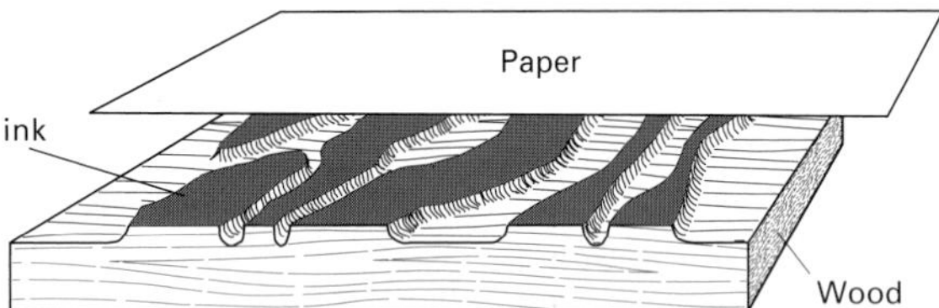

217 RELIEF

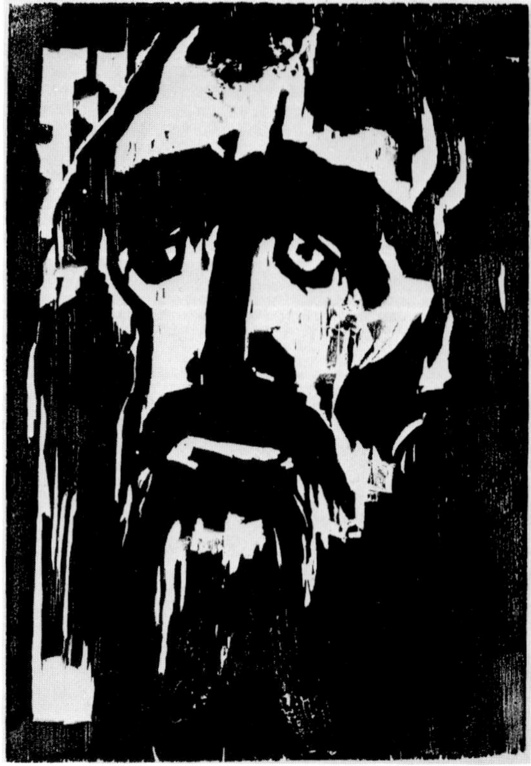

219 Emil Nolde.
PROPHET. 1912.
Woodcut. 12½" × 8⅞"; sheet: 15¾" × 13 15/16".

INTAGLIO

Intaglio printing is the opposite of relief: areas below the surface hold the ink. *Intaglio* comes from the Italian *itagliare,* "to cut into." The image to be printed is either cut or scratched into a metal surface by steel or diamond-tip tools, or it is etched into the surface by acid. To make a print, the printmaker first daubs the plate with viscous printer's ink, then wipes the surface clean, leaving ink only in the etched or grooved portions. Damp paper is then placed on the inked plate, and a print is made when the dampened paper picks up the ink in the grooves as it passes beneath the press roller. The pressure of the roller creates a characteristic plate mark around the edges of the print. Intaglio printing was traditionally done from polished copper plates, but now zinc, steel, aluminum, and even plastic are often used. Engraving, drypoint, and etching are intaglio processes.

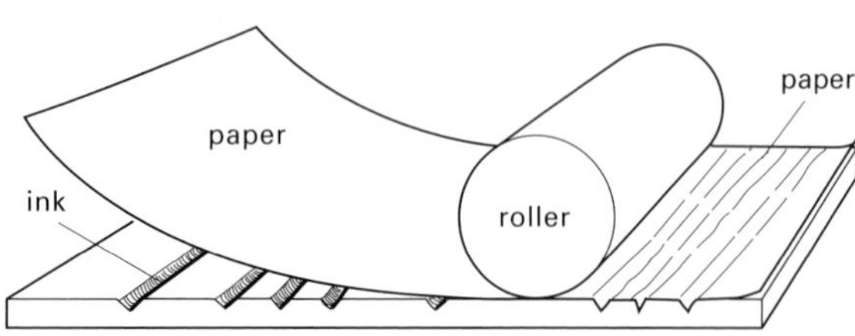

218 INTAGLIO

Engraving

In *engravings,* lines are cut into the polished surface of the plate with a *burin,* or engraving tool. This exacting process takes strength and control. Lines are made by pushing the burin through the metal to carve a groove, removing a narrow strip of metal in the process. A clean line is desired, so any rough edges of the groove must be smoothed down with a scraper. Engraved lines cannot appear as freely drawn as etched lines because of the pressure needed to cut the grooves. The precise, smooth curves and parallel lines typical of engravings can be seen in the engraved portraits that appear on the paper currency we use.

The complex richness of engraved lines may also be seen in Albrecht Dürer's magnificent engraving THE KNIGHT, DEATH AND THE DEVIL, reproduced here close to its actual size. Thousands of fine lines define the shapes, masses, spaces, values,

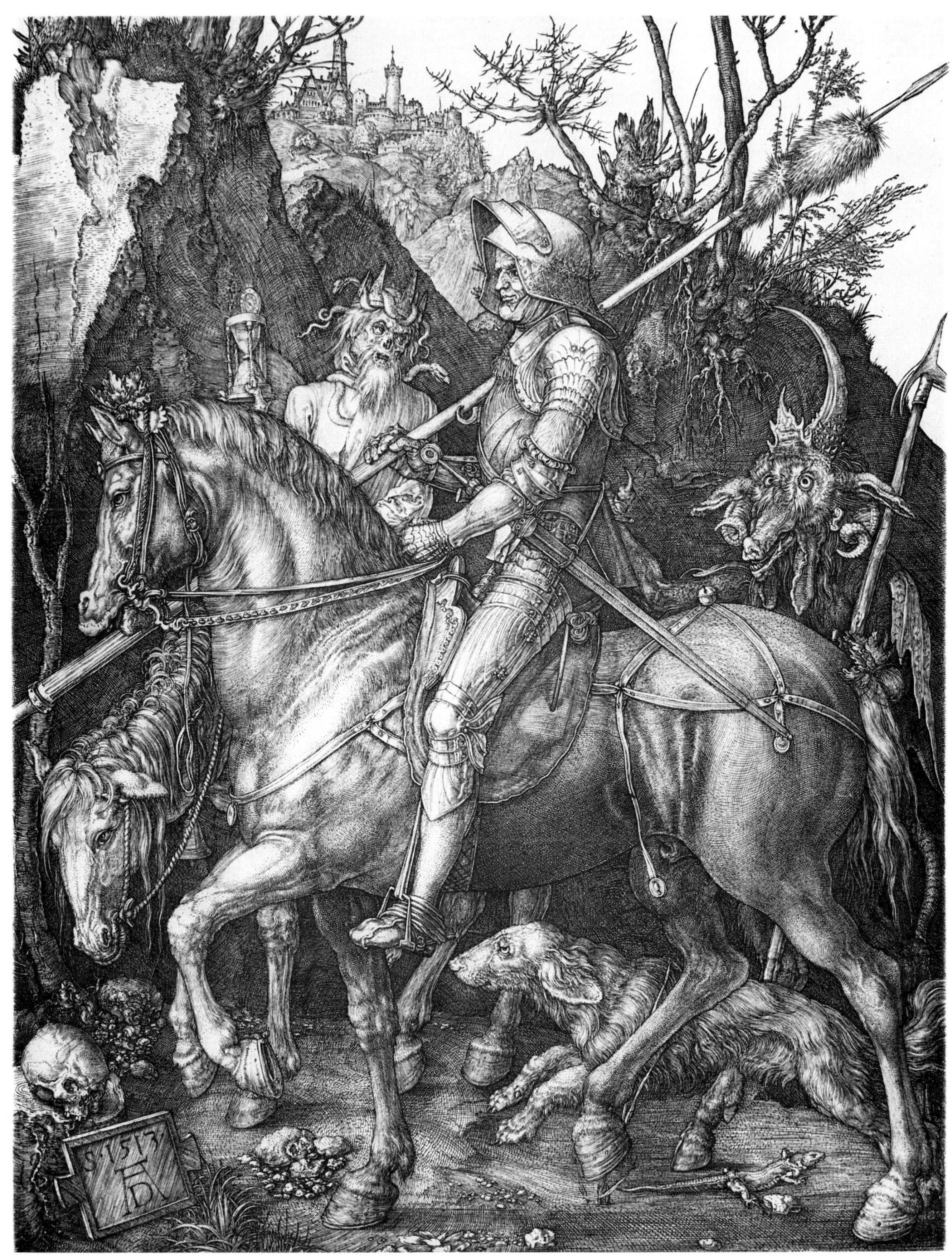

220 Albrecht Dürer.
THE KNIGHT, DEATH AND THE DEVIL. 1513.
Engraving. 9¾" × 7⅜".
The Brooklyn Museum. Gift of Mrs. Horace O. Havemeyer.

and textures of the objects depicted. The precision of Dürer's lines seems appropriate to the subject—an image of the noble Christian knight moving with resolute commitment, unswayed by the forces of chaos, evil, and death that surround him (a discussion of the print's iconography appears on page 43).

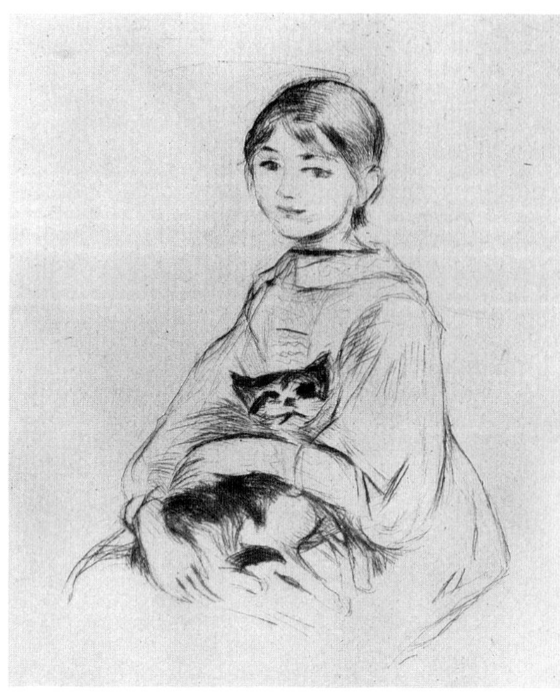

221 Berthe Morisot.
LITTLE GIRL WITH CAT. 1889.
Drypoint. 6" × 5".

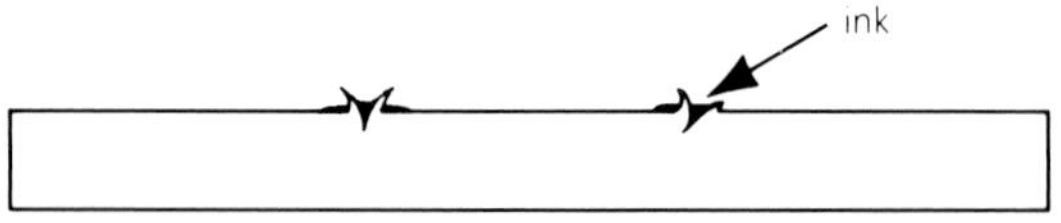

222 DRYPOINT PLATE

Drypoint

Drypoint is similar to line engraving. Using a thin, pencil-like, pointed tool with a steel or diamond tip, the artist digs lines into a soft copper or zinc plate. The displaced metal leaves a *burr,* or rough edge, similar to the row of earth left by a plow. The burr catches the ink and, when printed, leaves a slightly blurred line. Because the burr is fragile and deteriorates rapidly from the pressure of the printing press rollers as prints are made, drypoint editions are by necessity small. Skillful draftsmanship is required, for drypoint lines are difficult to execute and almost impossible to correct. The soft, somewhat sketchy line quality in Berthe Morisot's gentle depiction of LITTLE GIRL WITH CAT is characteristic of drypoint prints.

Etching

The process of making an *etching* begins with preparing a metal plate with a *ground*—a protective coating of acid-resistant material that covers the copper or zinc. The printmaker then draws easily through the ground with a pointed tool, exposing the metal. Then the plate is immersed in acid. Where the drawing has exposed the metal, acid "bites" into the plate, making a groove that varies in depth according to the strength of the acid and the length of time the plate is in the acid bath.

Because they are more easily produced, etched lines are generally more relaxed or irregular than engraved lines. Note the difference in line quality between an etching and an engraving—the freedom versus the precision—by comparing the lines in Rembrandt's etching CHRIST PREACHING with the lines in Dürer's engraving THE KNIGHT, DEATH AND THE DEVIL.

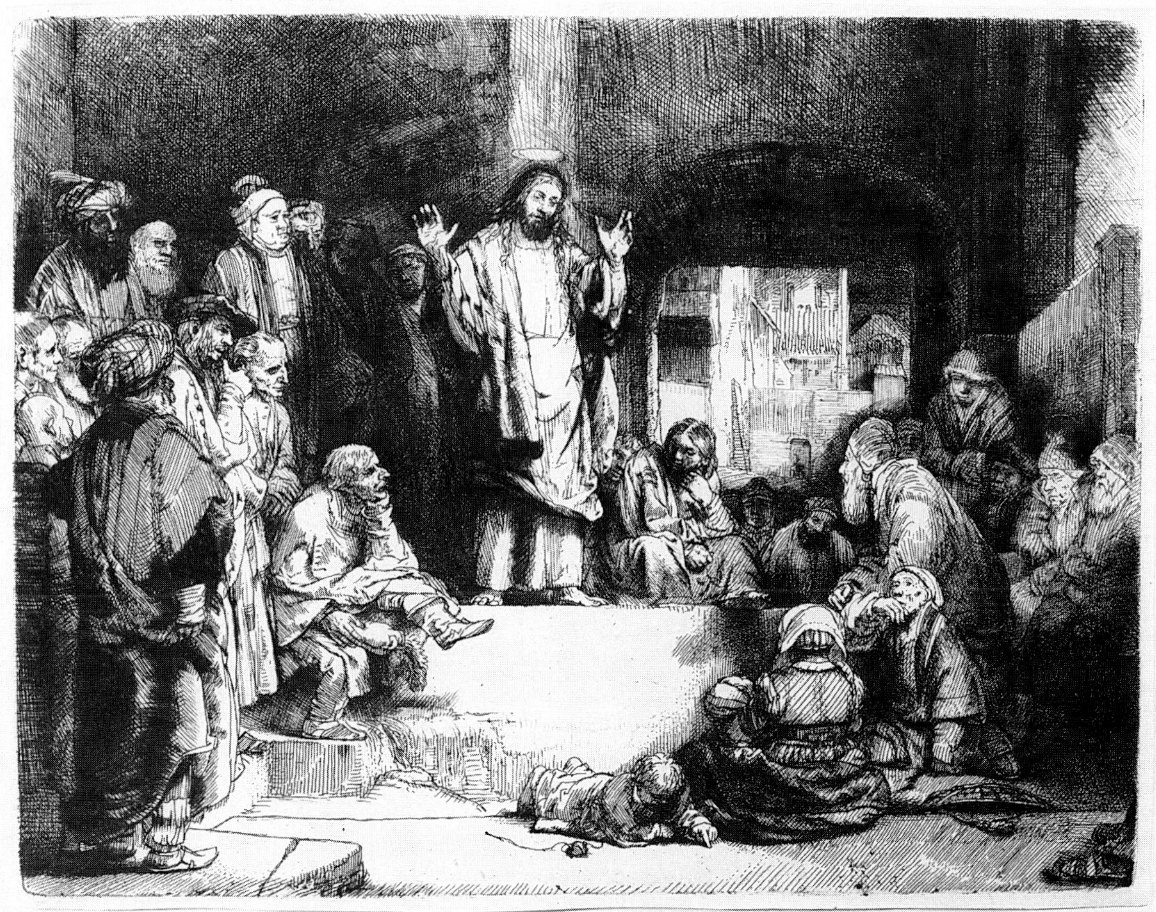

223 Rembrandt van Rijn.
CHRIST PREACHING. c. 1652.
Etching. 6" × 8⅛".
The Metropolitan Museum of Art, New York.
The H.O. Havemeyer Collection, 1929. (29.107.18).

In CHRIST PREACHING, Rembrandt's personal understanding of Christ's gentle compassion is in harmony with the decisive yet relaxed quality of the artist's etched lines. This etching shows Rembrandt's typical use of a wide range of values, achieved with drypoint as well as etching. Skillful use of light and shadow draws attention to the figure of Christ and gives clarity and interest to the whole image. In a composition in which each figure is similar in size, Rembrandt identifies Jesus as the key figure by setting him off with a light area below, a light vertical band above, and implied lines of attention leading to him from the faces of his listeners.

Aquatint is an etching process used to obtain uniform values in black-and-white or color prints. Contemporary aquatints are prepared with acid-resistant spray paints. When the plate is placed in

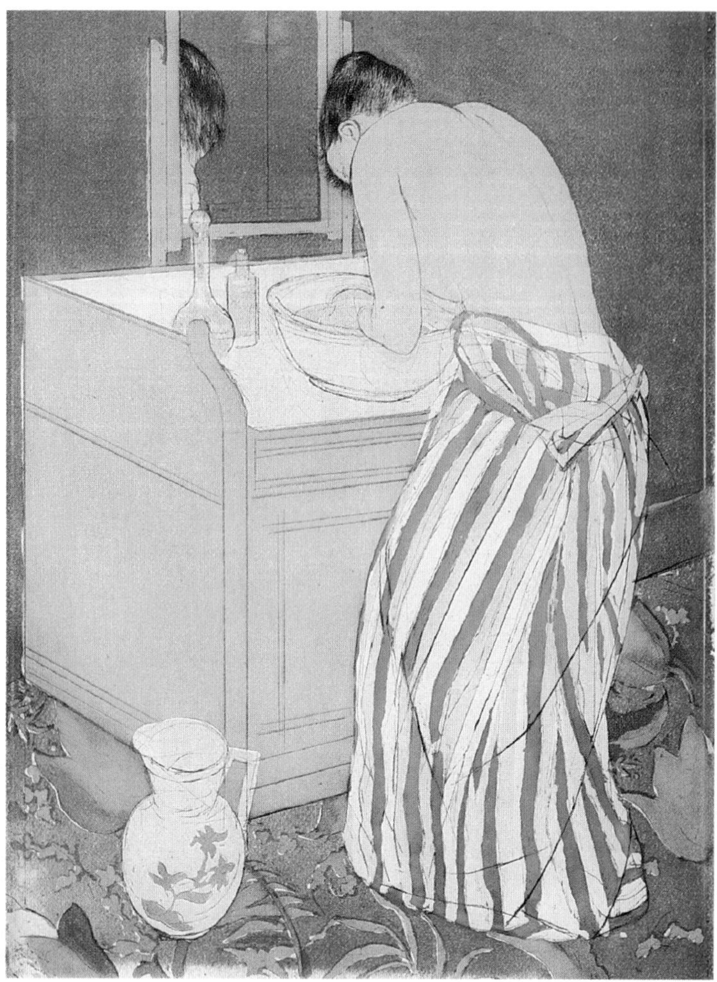

224 Mary Cassatt.
WOMAN BATHING. 1891.
Drypoint, soft ground etching, and aquatint. 14⅛" × 10⅛".
Courtesy Museum of Fine Arts, Boston. Hayden Fund.

acid, the exposed areas between the paint particles are eaten away to produce a rough surface capable of holding ink. Values thus produced can vary from light to dark, depending on how long the plate is in the acid. Because aquatint is not suited to making thin lines, it is usually combined with a linear print process such as engraving, drypoint, or line etching.

American artist Mary Cassatt's prints and paintings show the influence of the strong flat shapes and elegant lines of Japanese woodblock prints (see page 300). In her print WOMAN BATHING, Cassatt's use of aquatint provides light and dark areas of subtle color, while her drypoint lines give definition and linear movement to the composition.

LITHOGRAPHY

Etching and engraving date to the fifteenth and sixteenth centuries respectively, but lithography was not developed until early in the nineteenth century.

Lithography is a surface printing process based on the mutual antipathy of oil and water. It lends itself well to a direct manner of working because the artist draws an image on the surface of the stone or plate, without any cutting. Its directness makes lithography faster and somewhat more flexible than other methods. A lithograph is often difficult to distinguish from a drawing.

Using litho crayons, litho pencils, or a greasy liquid called *tusche,* the artist draws the image on flat, fine-grained Bavarian limestone (or on a metal surface that duplicates the character of such stone). After the image is complete, it is chemically treated

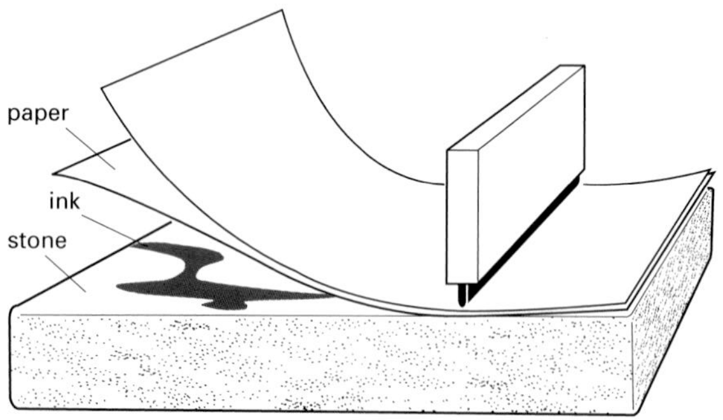

225 LITHOGRAPHY

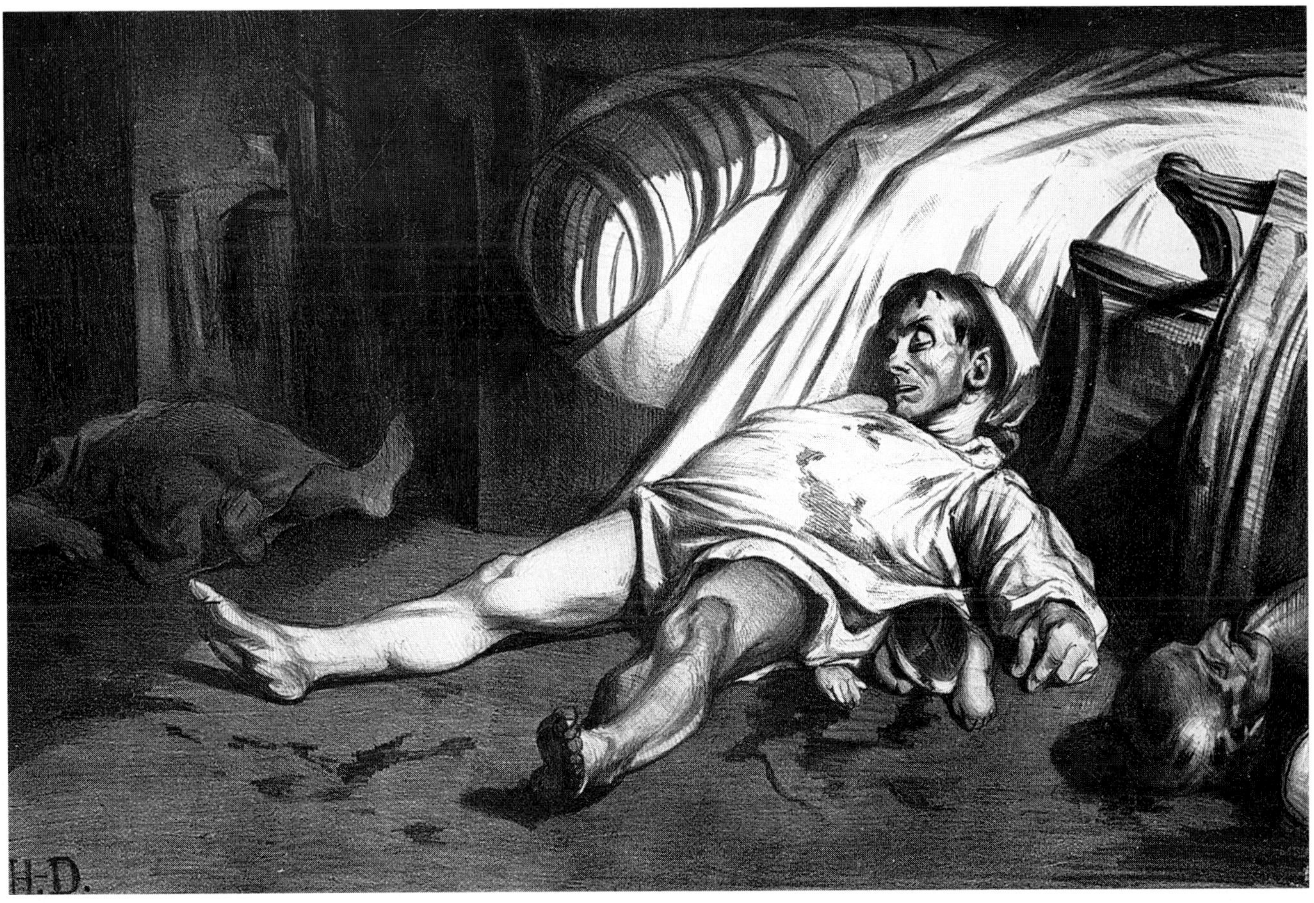

226 Honoré Daumier.
RUE TRANSNONAIN. 1834.
Lithograph. 11¼" × 17⅜".
The Cleveland Museum of Art. Gift of Ralph King. (CMA 24.809).

with gum arabic and a small amount of acid to "fix" it on the upper layer of the stone. The surface is then dampened with water and is inked. The oil-based ink is repelled by the water in the blank areas, but it adheres to the greasy area of the image. As in other print processes, when the surface is covered with paper and run through a press, the image is transferred to the paper.

Although lithography was a relatively new medium in the early 1800s, it had a major impact on society because prints could be produced quickly and easily. Before the development of modern printing presses, it provided the illustrations for newspapers, posters, and handbills. Honoré Daumier, one of the first great lithographic artists, made his living drawing satirical and documentary lithographs for French newspapers. His personal style was well suited to the direct quality of the lithographic process.

In RUE TRANSNONAIN, Daumier carefully reconstructed an event that occurred during a period of civil unrest in Paris in 1834. The militia claimed that a shot was fired from a building on Transnonain Street. Soldiers responded by entering the apartment and killing all the occupants. Daumier's lithograph of the event was published the following day. The lithograph clearly reflects the artist's feelings, but it also conveys information in the way news photographs and television do today. Rembrandt's influence is evident in the composition of strong light and dark areas that increase the dramatic impact of Daumier's image.

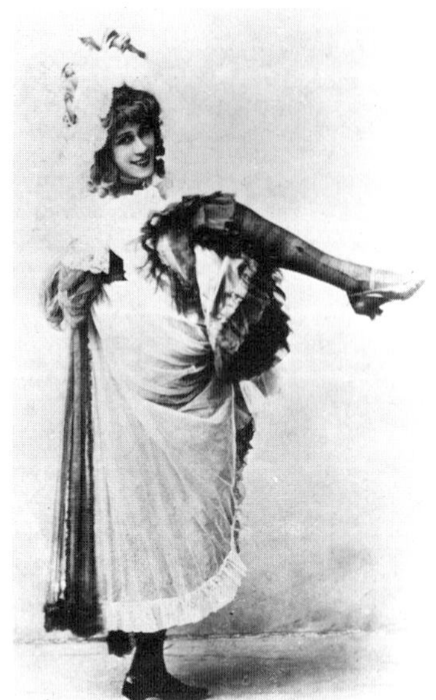

227 Henri de Toulouse-Lautrec.
JANE AVRIL. c. 1893.
Photograph.

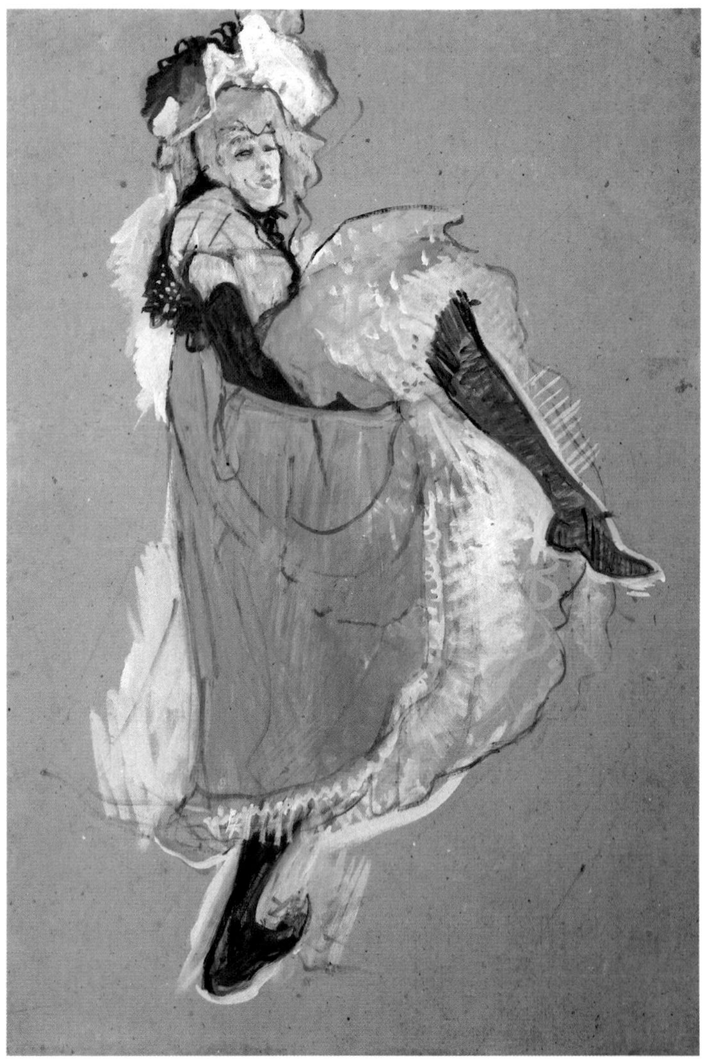

228 Henri de Toulouse-Lautrec.
JANE AVRIL. c. 1893.
Oil study on cardboard.
38" × 27".
Private collection.

The freedom and directness of lithography made the technique ideal for the spontaneous, witty approach of Henri de Toulouse-Lautrec. In the space of about ten years, this prolific artist created over three hundred lithographs. Many of them were designed as posters advertising everything from popular nightclub entertainers to bicycles. His posters of cabaret singer and dancer Jane Avril made her a star and simultaneously gave Parisians of the 1890s a firsthand look at "modern art" by a leading artist. Toulouse-Lautrec's innovations in lithography, including spatter techniques, large format, and use of vivid color, greatly influenced both lithographic art and graphic design in the twentieth century.

The popular lithographic poster JANE AVRIL appears to have begun with an awkward photograph and come to life in a dynamic oil sketch. The sketch was then incorporated as the key element in a strong lithograph, drawn with brush and liquid tusche on the litho stone. Compare the angles of the feet and legs in the photograph with those in the sketch. Toulouse-Lautrec used diagonal lines and curves to introduce a sense of motion missing in the photograph. In the print, he placed Jane Avril in a nightclub setting and balanced her figure with the silhouetted shape of a bass player. A dark line emerging from the bass frames the dancer. Toulouse-Lautrec's strong use of shapes and fluid brush lines retains much of the vigor of the sketch and reflect his admiration for Japanese prints.

229 Henri de Toulouse-Lautrec.
JANE AVRIL. JARDIN DE PARIS. c. 1893.
Lithograph printed in color. 48⅝" × 35⅛".
The Museum of Modern Art, New York. Gift of A. Conger Goodyear.

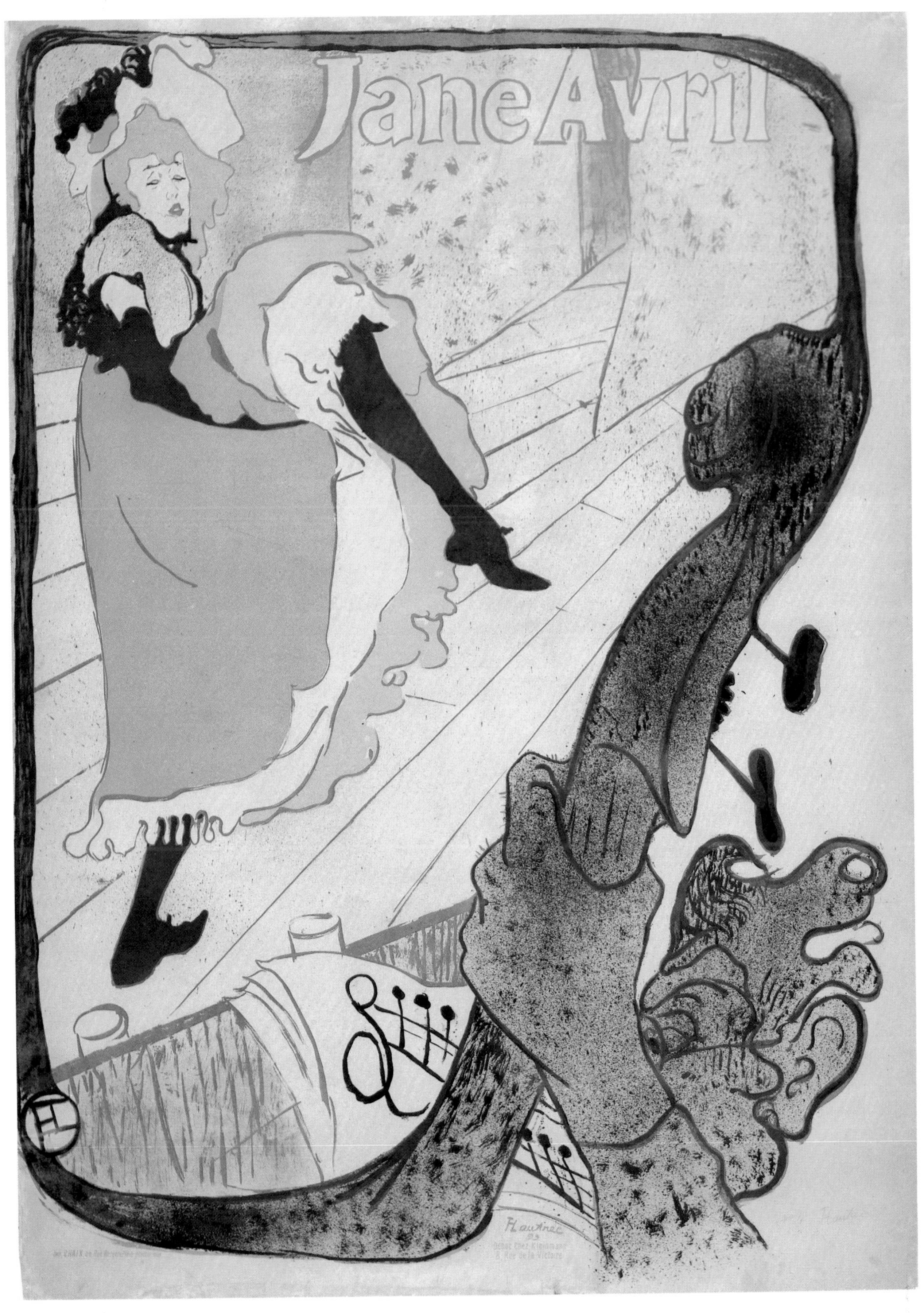
Jane Avril

SCREENPRINTING

Modern *screenprinting* is a refinement of the ancient and relatively simple technique of stencil printing. Early in this century, stencil technique was improved by adhering the stencil to a screen made of silk fabric stretched across a frame (synthetic fabric is used today). With a rubber-edged tool (called a *squeegee*), ink is then pushed through the fabric in the open areas of the stencil to make an image of the stencil on the material being printed. Because silk was the traditional material used for the screen, the process is also known as *silkscreen* or *serigraphy* (*seri* is Latin for silk).

Screenprinting is well suited to the production of images with areas of uniform color. Each separate color requires a different screen, but registering and printing are relatively simple. There is no reversal of the image in screenprinting—in contrast to relief, intaglio, and lithographic processes in which the image on the plate is "flopped" in the printing process.

The latest development in screenprinting is the photographic stencil, or *photo screen,* achieved by attaching light-sensitive gelatin to the screen fabric.

Capitalizing on the impersonal, mass-media look provided by this technique, Andy Warhol popularized photo-screenprinting. MARILYN is one of a series of works based on media stars. Warhol's choice of garish colors relates to the media hype surrounding Marilyn Monroe.

In contrast to Warhol's opaque, flat areas of color, Allyn Bromley's prints are comprised of overlapping translucent layers of color. She has brought a painterly quality to the previously flat, posterlike look of screenprinting. In PROTEA, Bromley combined photographic as well as hand-drawn, photoscreen images.

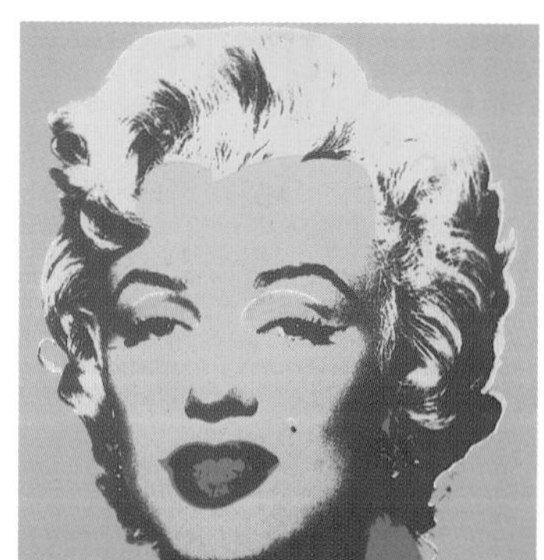

230 Andy Warhol.
MARILYN. 1967.
Serigraph on paper. 36" × 36".
The Tate Gallery, London.

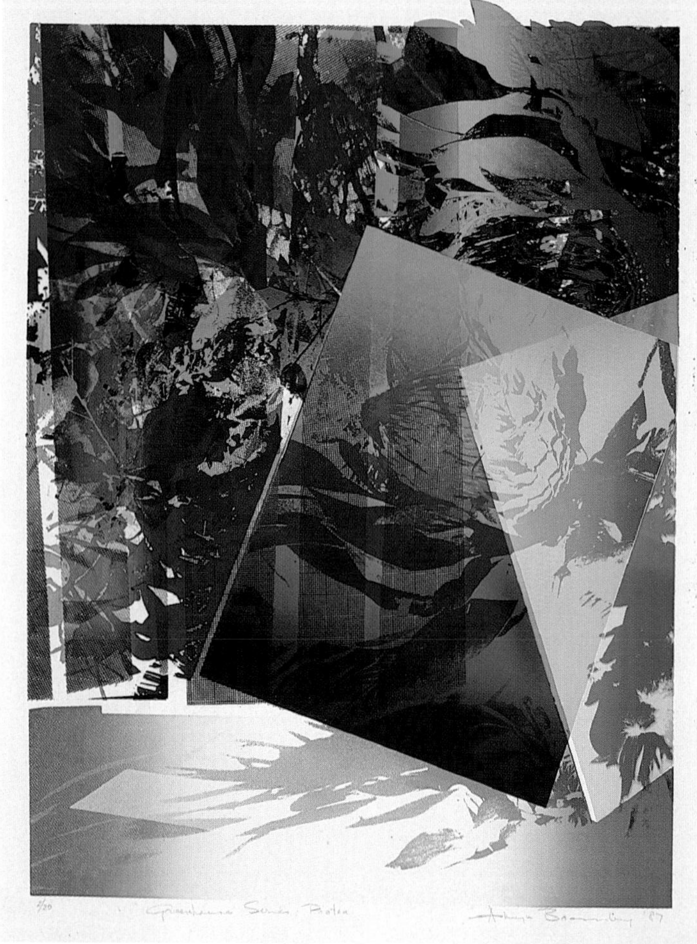

231 Allyn Bromley.
PROTEA. 1987.
Screenprint. 30" × 22".
Courtesy of the artist.

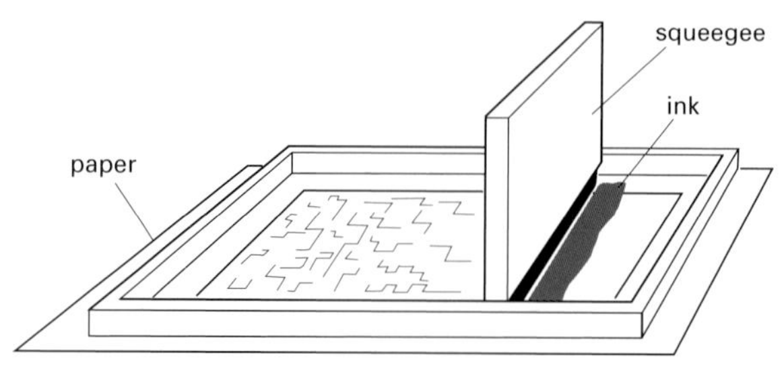

232 SCREENPRINTING

CURRENT DIRECTIONS

Since the sixties, the evolution of American printmaking has been dramatic in its use of new techniques and formats. Artists and master printers have developed equipment and techniques for making very large prints and combining several print techniques in a single work. Much of the innovation takes place in workshops, where master printers work with artists.

Monotypes

As the printmaking revival peaked in the 1970s, it was supplemented by a nontraditional, process-oriented practice called monotype. The word itself is a contradiction: *mono* means one and *type* carries connotations of multiple impressions of the same image. A *monotype* is both a printing method and a one-of-a-kind print taken from a flat surface, such as metal, glass, or plastic, on which an image has been freshly drawn or painted. Paper is pressed down on the still-wet plate to produce a single print. The process of printing largely removes the image from the plate.

Wayne Thiebaud's FREEWAY CURVE is one of a series of monotypes related to his cityscape paintings. Thiebaud's delight in pushing around thick paint is here translated into the monotype process. The high-speed frenzy of California freeways is captured with freshness and enthusiasm.

Combined Print Techniques

Because form and content are more important than technique, many artists combine media or techniques to achieve the results they desire.

An example is Joan Hall's huge wall piece DEBRIS, for which she took both a mixed-printmaking and an even broader mixed-media approach. Her use of materials and techniques exemplifies some of today's attitudes toward pushing the limits of a discipline such as printmaking.

Hall's imagery comes from her responses to "water crossings" and explorations. In DEBRIS, she deals with her concern for protecting the oceans from pollution.

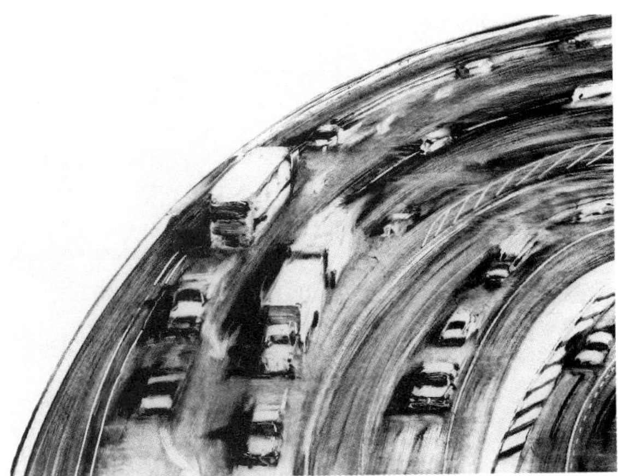

233 Wayne Thiebaud.
FREEWAY CURVE. 1977.
Monotype. 22⅜" × 29⅞".
Collection of Harry W. and Mary Margaret Anderson.

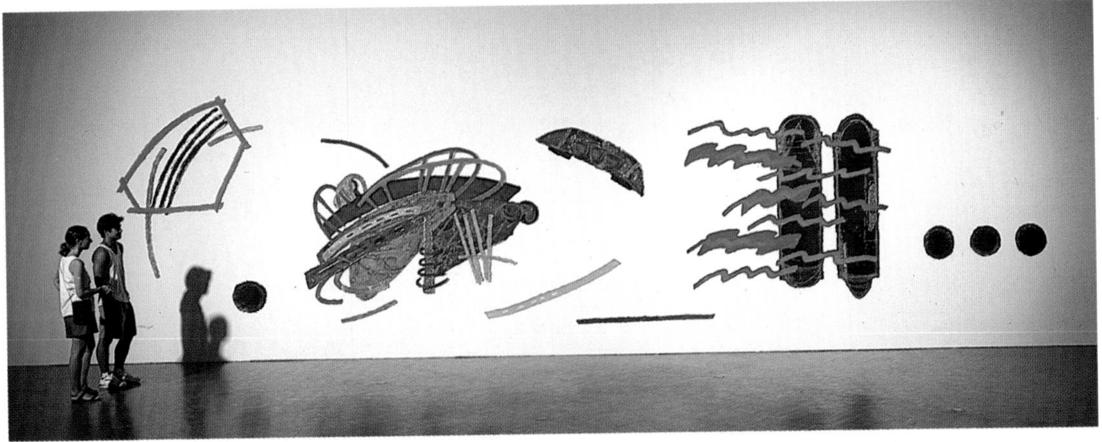

234 Joan Hall. DEBRIS. 1992.
Intaglio, relief, collagraph, and lithography on handmade paper.
10'8" × 30'.
Courtesy of the artist.

HANDMADE ORIGINALS IN AN AGE OF MECHANICAL REPRODUCTION

The concept of original "fine" prints may seem out of place at a time when good reproductions are readily available. Although reproductions are merely mechanically made copies, without the exact color or texture of the original, they do make the art of the world available to us as never before.

Original prints, regardless of type, are those printed by the artist or under the artist's supervision from plates, blocks, stones, or stencils made by, or in collaboration with, the artist. The term *reproduction* signifies a photomechanical copy of an original work of art. Any print that is made from a preexisting work of art, whether through photographic techniques or by skilled copyists, is a reproductive print or reproduction. Any work that is made by photographic reproduction or by a purely mechanical process is not an original print.

The terms original print and fine print signify the artist's intent: to create multiple originals rather than copies of a single, preexisting original such as a painting. The printmaker works directly by hand to create the printing surface (or matrix) on stone, wood, metal, plastic, or any material that may be used to transfer images (or make impressions).

Buying original prints by artists, especially young or emerging artists, is an excellent way to acquire and enjoy original works of art at modest expense. However, the buyer should beware. The recent practice of selling photomechanical reproductions at high prices, under the guise of "limited edition prints," has confused many people who are unaware of the difference between reproductions and original prints. The advertising of art as a commodity for investment has led unscrupulous dealers to intentionally obscure the distinction between original prints and reproductions. It is important for buyers to recognize the difference between inexpensively produced reproductions, which should sell for a few dollars, and original prints that should be priced as works of art.

Some artists use photomechanical means to reproduce their own pieces; these reproductions are then sold as "signed prints" or posters, sometimes called "art prints." The marketing of signed reproductions is based on the artist's feeling that it is most important to get one's work seen and be able to make a living from selling it. This practice raises ethical and practical questions about the value and quality of an original, the value of a signature on a reproduction, and the extent to which art should be shaped and motivated by profit.

How can you tell a reproduction from an original print? If close scrutiny with a magnifying glass reveals a rigid pattern of small dots of the type shown on page 81, then the work is a reproduction, not a handmade original print. But there are exceptions; some highly sophisticated printing systems, including laser scanners, produce reproductions that do not have dot patterns. Original serigraphs (screenprints) have layers of ink that look like paint on top of, rather than absorbed by, the paper. Original etchings and engravings are produced with a printing press, which causes the edge of the plate to leave an indentation in the paper called a *plate mark.*

Most original prints are signed and numbered by the artist in the lower margin to indicate personal involvement and approval. Original prints are usually produced in quantities called limited editions. All the prints in an edition are nearly identical, and each is called an original work. The artist generally destroys the plate, block, or screen after the edition has been printed in order to ensure the integrity of his or her work. In many states, laws now require artists to provide cancellation proofs when they sell limited editions of their prints. A cancellation proof shows that the original printing surface has indeed been permanently altered (frequently with a big X across the image), and that no further prints of the original image can be made. Such regulation by law is designed to protect both artists and buyers against abuses of the traditional printmaking edition system.

The hands-on involvement of the originating artist is the crucial factor determining the value of a fine print: Original prints are always printed by the artist or by a printer working directly under the artist's supervision. Any work produced through photomechanical processes or without the artist's personal involvement from start to finish is a reproduction.

Before purchasing an original print, buyers should request complete disclosure information, including the name of the artist who created the matrix (block, plate, stone, screen) used to make the print; the method used for printing; the type of paper used; the name of the printer, if different from the artist; the number of impressions in existence; the manner in which the prints in the edition are numbered and identified; the number of artist's proofs; and the current status of the original matrix. By protecting the integrity of original prints, we make it possible for people to purchase high-quality art at affordable prices.

CHAPTER 11

Camera Arts and Computer Imaging

Much of our present understanding of life comes from images made with still, motion picture, and television cameras. When we get caught up in the compelling realism of photography, film, or television, we may easily forget that the camera arts are recent extensions of a long pictorial tradition rooted in the desire to make lifelike images of our significant experiences. Each new technique in the history of art relies heavily on its predecessors.

Photography has been influenced by Western painting, and in turn it has influenced painting. Cinematography grew from and continues to rely on the basic principles of still photography. And television is influenced by painting, photography, and cinematography. When we are struck by a particular shot in a film or video, we often say it looks like a painting. And, in turn, television and other photographic imagery influence the more traditional visual and performing arts. Apart from all these mutual influences, cameras provide a means through which both past and present art can be reproduced and enjoyed by people in all parts of the world.

PHOTOGRAPHY

Photography literally means "light-writing" or "light-drawing." Basically, it is a method for capturing optical images on light-sensitive or photosensitive surfaces, and, as such, it is well suited to the process of making meaningful visual statements. Like drawing, photography can be either an art medium or a widely used practical tool. Among those who rely on photography as a tool are artists working in a variety of other media, social and physical scientists, and, most of all, news and advertising photographers and other people working in communications.

As an art form, photography reveals the photographer's personal ways of seeing and responding. Ten photographers working with the same subject will make ten different photographs, with each photographer conveying those aspects of the subject he or she feels are most significant. Individual styles would not be evident in photographs if photography were not a means of personal expression and communication.

Although ads for some cameras would have us believe a particular brand will almost automatically produce "great pictures," it is the photographer, not the equipment, that makes the difference between an ordinary snapshot and a work of art. Before releasing the shutter, a skilled photographer makes many choices regarding subject, light, angle, focus, distance, and composition, as well as type of camera, lens, and film. The best photographers have learned to visualize their photographs before releasing the shutter. American photographer Ansel Adams spoke of the need to give considerable time and effort to the making of a photograph for the result to be worthwhile:

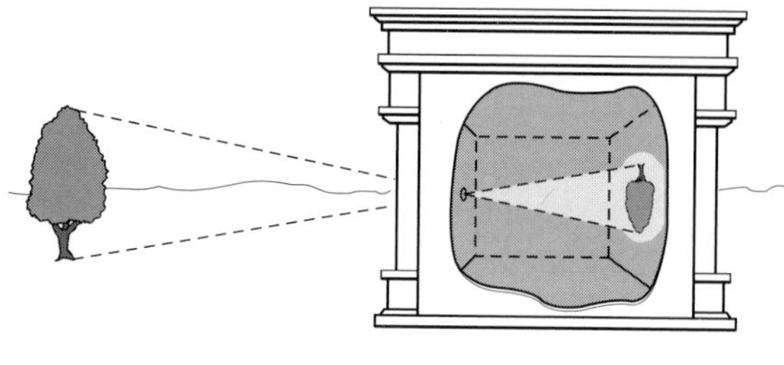

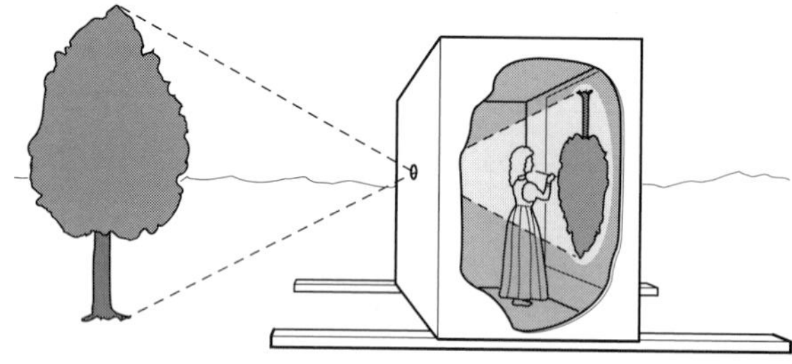

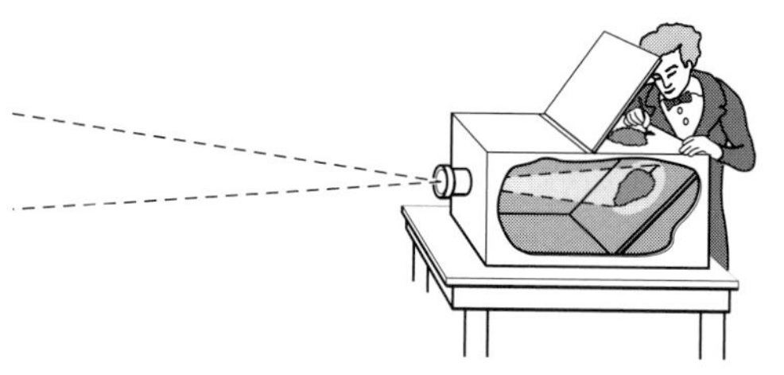

235 EVOLUTION OF THE CAMERA OBSCURA, PREDECESSOR OF THE MODERN CAMERA.
a 16th-century camera obscura.
b 17th-century portable camera obscura.
c 17th–19th-century table model camera obscura.

I have often thought that if photography were difficult in the true sense of the term—meaning that the creation of a simple photograph would entail as much time and effort as the production of a good watercolor or etching—there would be a vast improvement in total output. The sheer ease with which we can produce a superficial image often leads to creative disaster. We must remember that a photograph can hold just as much as we put into it, and no one has ever approached the full possibilities of the medium.[1]

Edwin Land, who developed the Polaroid camera, also emphasized the process of taking a photograph when he described how even automatic, "instant" cameras can help us learn to see:

At its best, photography can be an extra sense, or a reservoir for the senses. Even when you don't press the trigger, the exercise of focusing through a camera can make you better remember thereafter a person or a moment. When we had flowers in this office recently to use as test objects, it was a great experience to take pictures of them. I learned to know each rose. I now know more about roses and leaves, and that enriched my life. Photography can teach people to look, to feel, to remember in a way that they didn't know they could.[2]

The Development of Photography

The basic concept of the camera preceded actual photography by more than three hundred years. The desire of Renaissance artists to make accurate depictions of nature was the impetus behind the eventual invention of photography as we know it. See page 343.

The forerunner of the modern camera was the *camera obscura,* literally "dark room." The concept of photography grew out of the observation that reflected sunlight passing through a small hole in the wall of a darkened room projects onto the opposite wall an inverted image of whatever lies outside. In the fifteenth century, Leonardo described the device as an aid to observation and picture making.

As a fixed room, or even as a portable room, the camera obscura was too large and cumbersome to be widely used. In the seventeenth century, when it was realized that the person tracing the image did not have to be inside, the CAMERA OBSCURA evolved into a portable dark box. During the course of this pre-camera evolution, a lens was placed in the small hole to improve image clarity. Later an angled mirror was added to right the inverted image, enabling anyone, skilled or unskilled, to trace the projected pictures with pen or pencil (see the table model CAMERA OBSCURA).

It was not until about 1826 that the first vague photographic image was made by Joseph Nicéphore Niépce. He recorded and fixed on a sheet of pewter an image made by exposing the sensitized metal plate to light for eight hours. During the next decade, the painter Louis Jacques Mandé

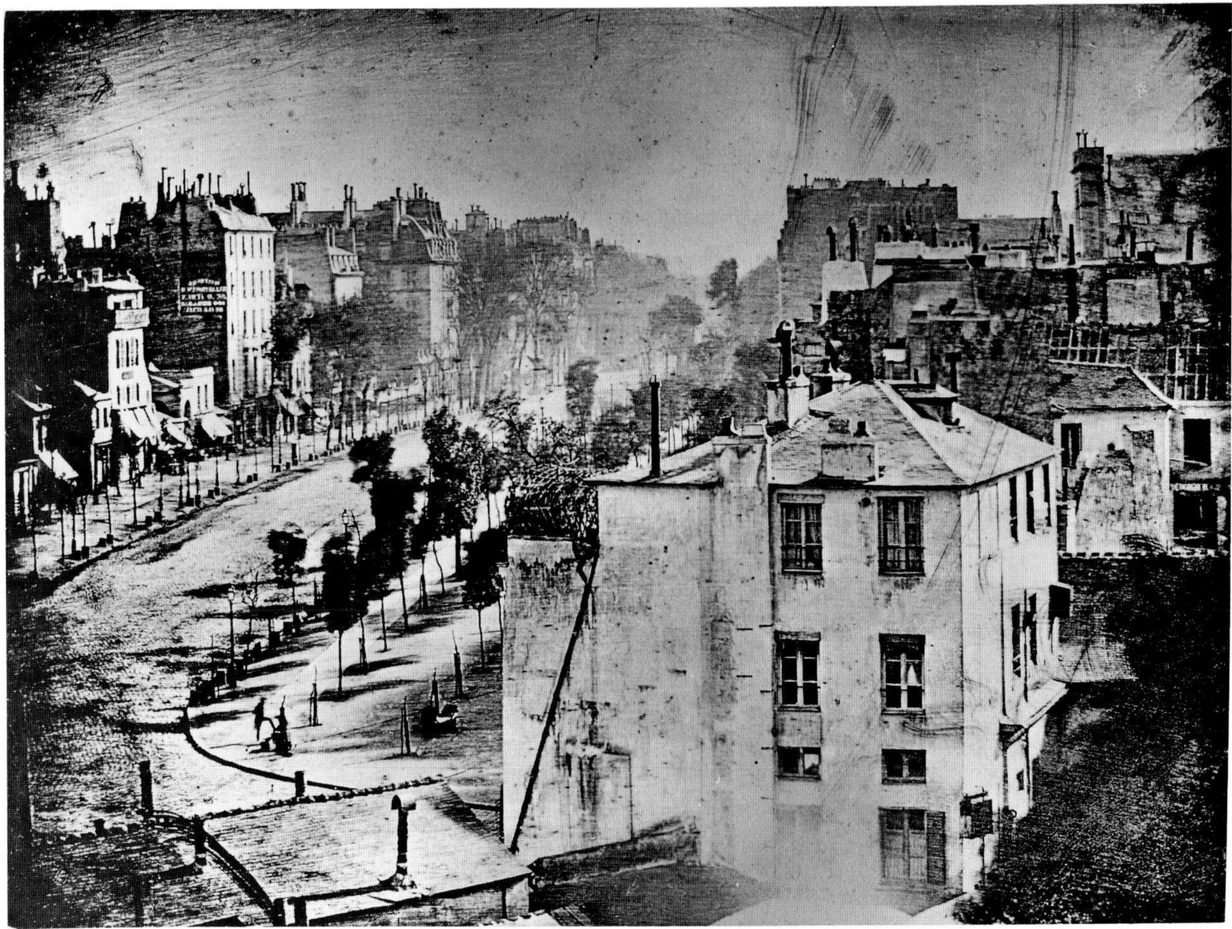

236 Louis Jacques Mandé Daguerre
LE BOULEVARD DU TEMPLE. 1839.
Daguerreotype.
Bayerisches National Museum, Munich. (R6312).

Daguerre further perfected Niépce's process and produced some of the first satisfactory photographs, known as *daguerreotypes.*

At first, because the necessary exposure times were so long, photography could record only stationary objects. In Daguerre's photograph of LE BOULEVARD DU TEMPLE taken in Paris in 1839 (the year his process was made public), the streets appear deserted because moving figures made no lasting light impressions on the plate. However, one man, having his shoes shined, stayed still long enough to become part of the image. He is visible on the corner in the lower left, the first person to appear in a photograph. It was a significant moment in history: now images of people and things could be made without the trained hand of a traditional artist. Although some painters at the time felt the new medium constituted unfair competition and spelled the end of art, the invention of photography actually marked the beginning of a period when art would be more accessible to all through photographic reproductions; it also marked not the end but the beginning of a great outpouring of art—particularly painting.

Before the development of the camera, it was usually only royalty and the wealthy who could afford to have their portraits painted. By the mid-nineteenth century, people of average means were going in great numbers to photography studios to sit unblinking for several minutes in bright sunlight to have their pictures taken.

From the beginning, portrait photography was

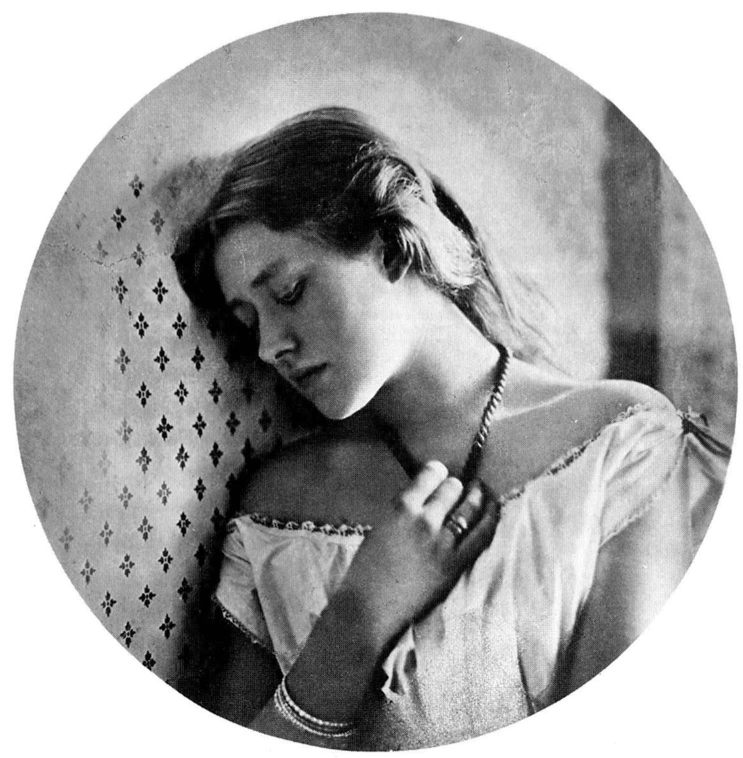

237 Julia Margaret Cameron.
ELLEN TERRY AT AGE SIXTEEN. 1863.
Carbon print. Diameter of circle 240 mm.
The Metropolitan Museum of Art,
The Alfred Stieglitz Collection, 1949 (49.55.323).

heavily influenced by the traditions of portrait painting. The art of portrait photography was raised to a high level by English artist Julia Margaret Cameron. In 1864, she became an avid photographer and began to create some of the most expressive portraits ever made with a camera. Cameron pioneered the use of close-ups and carefully controlled lighting to enhance the images of her subjects, who were often family members and famous friends. In the portrait of British actress ELLEN TERRY AT AGE SIXTEEN, the dominant light comes from behind the subject, leaving the face in shadow and emphasizing the subject's introspective mood.

Many nineteenth-century photographers looked for ways to duplicate what painters had already done—and thereby failed to find their medium's unique strengths. Painters, meanwhile—partially freed by photography from their ancient role as recorders of events, places, and people—looked for other avenues to explore. Yet some leading painters were greatly influenced by photography (see pages 381 and 384).

The Technology of Photography

Although the technology of modern cameras is highly sophisticated and complex, the basic unit is still simply a lightproof box with an opening, or *aperture,* set behind a *lens* designed to focus, or order, the light rays passing through it. It also has a *shutter* to control the length of time the light is allowed to strike the light-sensitive film or plate held within the body of the camera.

The diagram HUMAN EYE AND CAMERA shows how the camera can be compared to a simplified mechanical replica of the human eye. The major differences are that the eye receives a continuous flow of changing images that are interpreted by the brain, whereas the still camera depends on light-sensitive film to record an image and can only pick up a single image at a time. Also, a pair of eyes sees in stereoscopic vision, while a camera's vision is monoscopic. Monoscopic vision tends to flatten the visual field, whereas with stereoscopic vision we see slightly more of an object from two different angles, thereby heightening our perception of three-dimensional space, or depth.

The adjustable aperture in the lens of a sophisticated camera is similar to the changing pupil of the human eye, as shown in the diagram. By changing the aperture, a photographer adjusts the amount of light entering the camera and simultaneously determines the depth of the area in sharp focus—called the *depth of field*—in the photograph. A large aperture gives a relatively shallow depth of field. By closing down the size of the opening, the photographer increases the area in focus, as shown in the diagram. The smaller the aperture, the greater the depth of field. To understand how this works, hold up your thumb about a foot in front of your face and focus your eyes on it. Notice how objects behind it are out of focus. Now curl the fingers of your other hand to make a very small tunnel and hold it up to your eye. The light reflected off your thumb will pass through the tunnel to your eye. As you look at your thumb through the small opening or aperture, you will notice that both your thumb and what is just behind it come into sharper focus.

The various types of *film* are essentially transparent plastic strips or single sheets, coated with light-sensitive emulsion. Exposed and developed print film is called a *negative* because the light and dark areas of the original subjects are reversed. Color positive film, such as slide film, produces a positive image that can be projected or printed. Photojournalists are now able to use high-resolution digital camera systems that can store many more images than even the longest rolls of film. Digital images can be quickly transferred, without loss of quality, through a computer modem (via telephone) to magazine or newspaper publishers.

Working in a darkroom, the photographer (or a technician) prints a negative by placing it in an *enlarger,* which projects and enlarges the negative image onto light-sensitive paper. Placed in a chemical bath, the paper darkens in those areas where it has been exposed to light, thus producing a positive image. After the chemical action of the developer is stopped in an acid solution called the *stop bath,* the image is chemically *fixed* to prevent further change.

In cameras of all types, the quality of the lens is most important. Lenses are designed to gather and

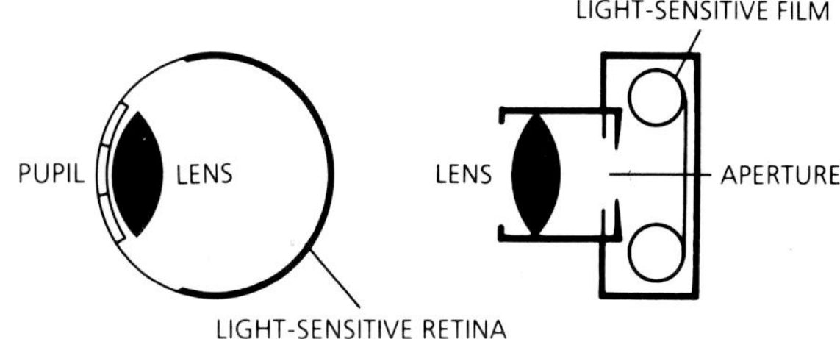

238 HUMAN EYE AND CAMERA.

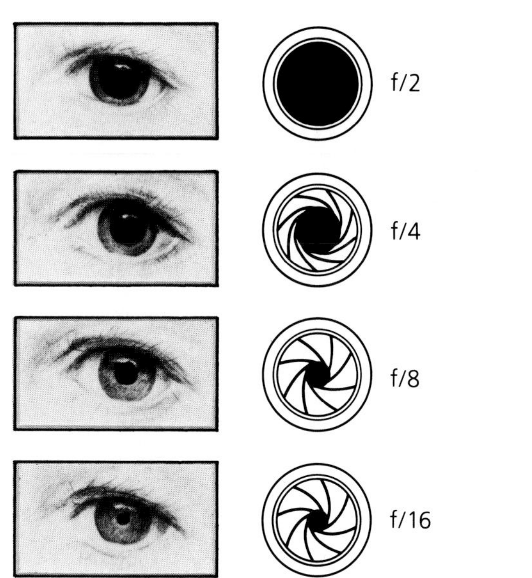

239 PUPIL OF HUMAN EYE AND APERTURE OF CAMERA.

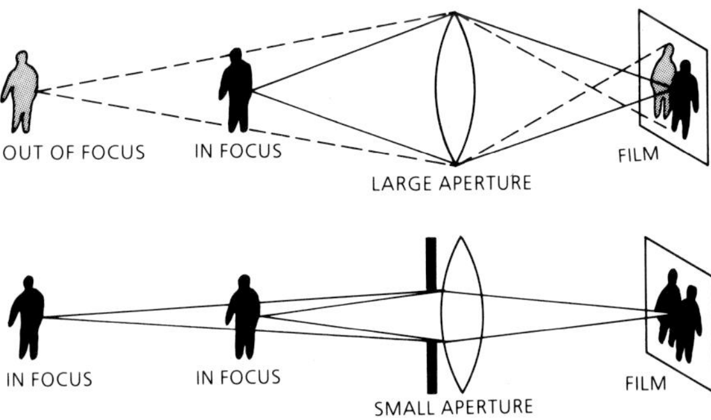

240 CHANGES IN DEPTH OF FIELD WITH APERTURE ADJUSTMENTS.

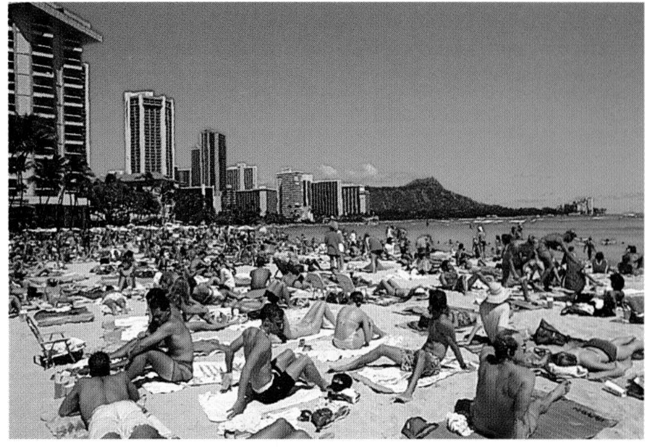

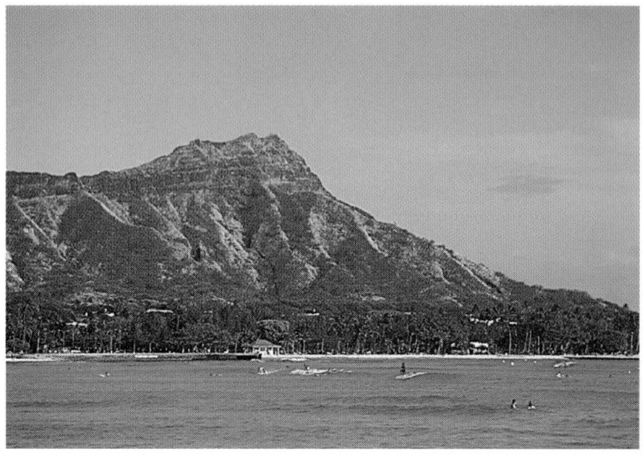

241 PHOTOGRAPHS OF WAIKIKI AND DIAMOND HEAD.
a With a wide-angle (24 mm) lens.
b With a telephoto (135 mm) lens.

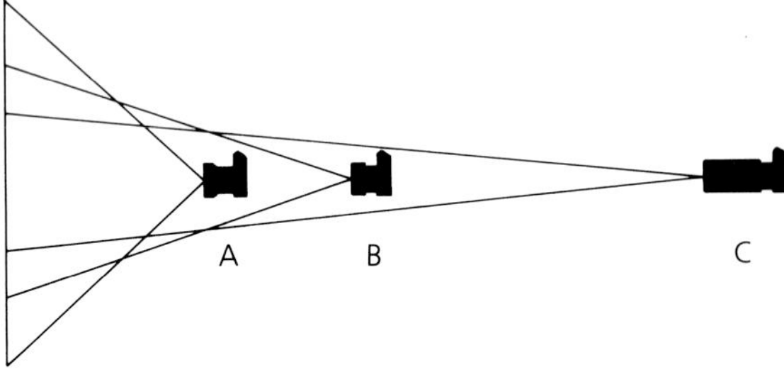

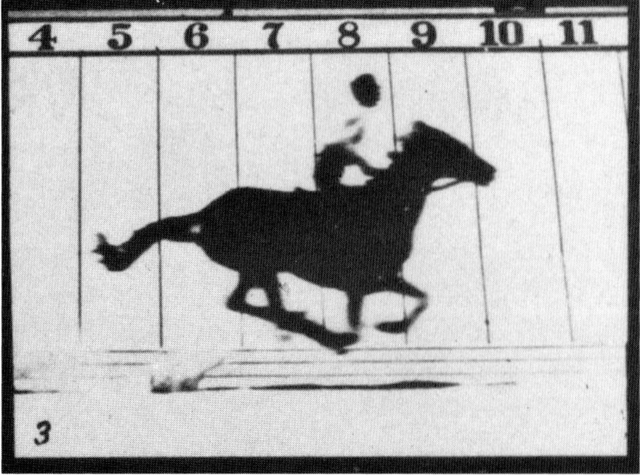

concentrate a maximum amount of available light in order to transmit a sharply focused image quickly. The most versatile cameras allow for interchangeable lenses capable of various angles of view. The ANGLE OF VIEW diagram shows approximate angles of view with normal, telephoto, and wide-angle lenses. A zoom lens permits the focal length of the lens to be adjusted to various distances from close to far.

The WAIKIKI photographs were taken from the same position, on the same beach, using different lenses. The shot taken with a wide-angle lens takes in the crowded beach and massive high-rise hotels of the new Waikiki, while the telephoto shot edits out the congested resort area to show only a few surfers enjoying the waves—to imply an unspoiled island paradise. As this simple example shows, photography is not always as objective an observer as many would believe. It can stretch the truth, and it can mislead.

Stopping Time

Since prehistoric times, artists have tried to portray the appearance of people and animals in action. One of photography's special strengths is its ability to capture a moment in time. Eadweard Muybridge pioneered stop-action photography, making the world's first serious studies of people and animals in motion and providing the groundwork for the development of motion pictures. GALLOPING HORSE was one of those studies; see also page 185.

Today it is common for cameras to have shutter speeds of up to 1/1000 of a second and faster. High shutter speeds used with corresponding film and film processing are crucial for sports photographers and others who seek to stop action in their photographs. Dennis Oda's REBOUND arrests the

242 ANGLE OF VIEW.
a Wide-angle lens.
b Normal lens.
c Telephoto lens.

243 Eadweard Muybridge.
GALLOPING HORSE. 1879.
Photograph.
International Museum of Photography at George Eastman House, Rochester, New York.

ball in midair and, with the help of a telephoto lens, brings the viewer into the action at a moment of great intensity. The overhead vantage point gives an unusual view of the action. Because the players are seen from above, their arms and legs form diagonals that emphasize the action of the moment. The circular shapes of the heads, hoop, and ball create a sub-theme in the composition.

Henri Cartier-Bresson created another type of stop-action photograph in BEHIND THE GARE ST. LAZARE, PARIS. Although the actual image was caught in an instant, Cartier-Bresson made many important choices that led him to release the shutter at just the right time. A fraction of a second later, the man's foot would have hit the pavement and the visual tension between his heel and his shadow would have been missed. Most amazing is the way the shape of the running man is echoed by the dancer on the poster in the background as well as by his own reflection. According to Cartier-Bresson, capturing the "decisive moment" is the result of such split-second "composing":

To me, photography is the simultaneous recognition, in a fraction of a second, of the significance of an event as well as of a precise organization of forms which give that event its proper expression.[3]

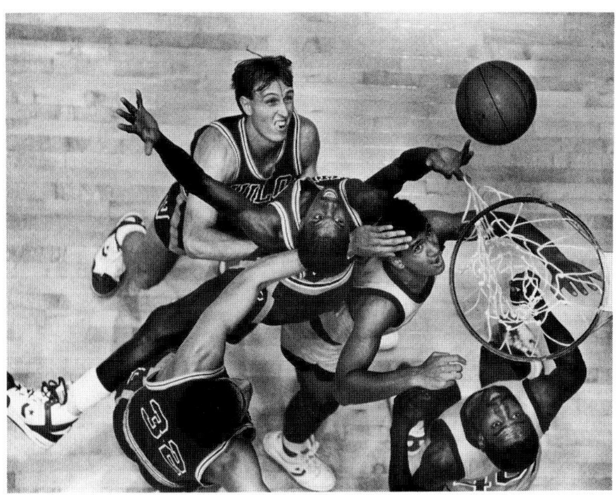

244 Dennis Oda.
REBOUND. 1987.
Photograph.
Courtesy of the artist, Honolulu.

Photography and Social Change

With the ever growing circulation of mass media, each generation now produces its own set of memorable photographs. The photographs we remember best are moving not only because of the way their subjects are presented, but because we know the photographer was there. We join the photographer as witnesses. The significance of such images lies not simply in their ability to inform us, but in their power to stir our emotions.

Only a few decades after the invention of the medium, photographers began to bring public attention to human suffering caused by war, poverty,

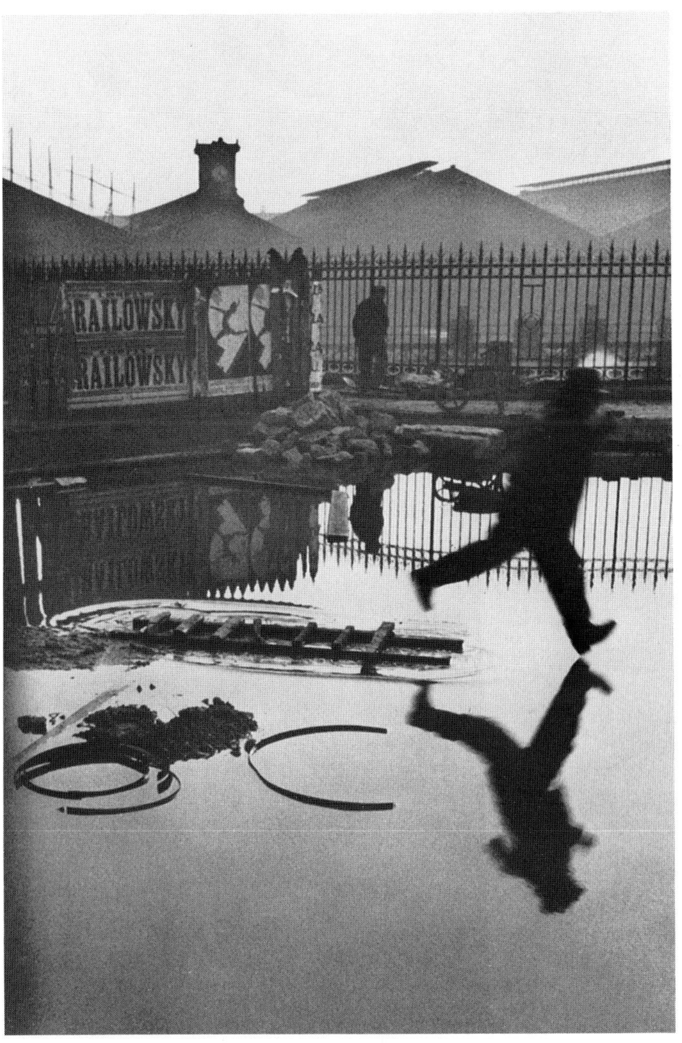

245 Henri Cartier-Bresson.
BEHIND THE GARE ST. LAZARE, PARIS. 1932.
Photograph.
© Henri Cartier-Bresson/Magnum Photos.

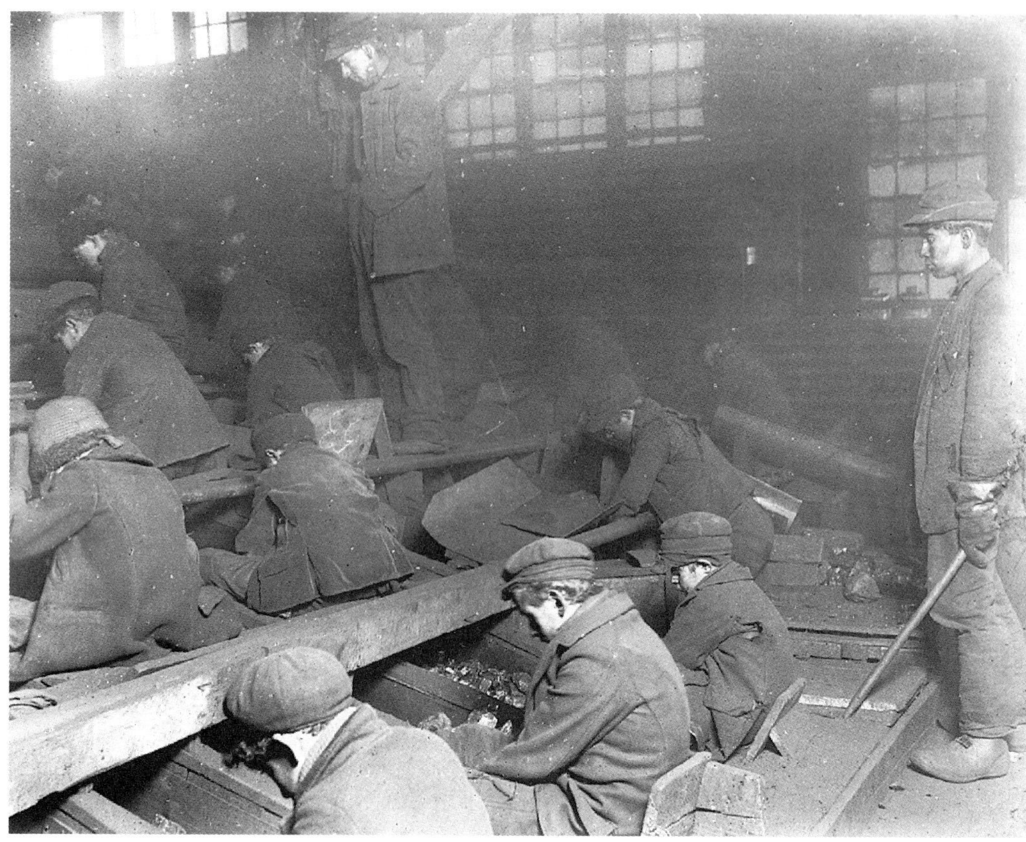

246 Lewis Hine.
COAL BREAKERS, PENNSYLVANIA. 1910.
Photograph.
International Museum of Photography at George Eastman House, Rochester, New York.

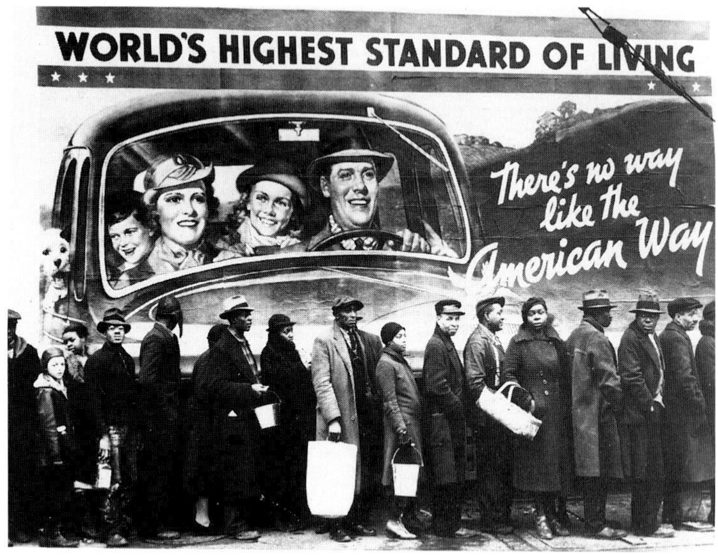

247 Margaret Bourke-White.
LOUISVILLE FLOOD VICTIMS. 1937.
Photograph.
Life Magazine, © Time Warner, Inc.

hunger, and neglect. The new tool made believable visual statements in ways that no other media could. Of all the arts, photography is uniquely suited not only to documenting historic events and social problems but to bringing about the kind of empathetic awareness that leads to social reform.

Early in this century, long before television, American sociologist Lewis Hine used his skill as a photographer to communicate his concern for the plight of working children. COAL BREAKERS, PENNSYLVANIA is one of a series of photographs that show young children working long hours in coal yards, cotton mills, and food-processing factories. These photographs brought such abuses to the attention of the public and played a significant role in the creation of child labor laws.

During the Great Depression of the 1930s, a number of photographers led the public toward concern for those less fortunate than themselves. Margaret Bourke-White's LOUISVILLE FLOOD VICTIMS confronts us with the brutal difference between the glamorous life promised in advertising and the reality that many face every day. If it were not for the dated styles of the car and clothing, this photograph could be about today's homeless.

In the same decade, Bourke-White introduced the concept of the photographic essay—an approach that was soon adopted by other photographers. A *photo essay* is a collection of photographs on a single subject, arranged to tell a story or convey a mood in a way not possible with a single photograph. Photo essays are now an important part of international journalism.

Another American master, Dorothea Lange, photographed people on the streets of San Francisco during the thirties (see A DEPRESSION BREADLINE, page 446). Her famous portrait MIGRANT MOTHER was part of a report on the living conditions of migrant farm workers commissioned by the state of California. Lange's photographs emphasize human dignity and strength in the face of adversity; John Steinbeck reportedly found inspiration for his novel *Grapes of Wrath* in her work.

More recently, Nick Ut's telephoto shot of TERRIFIED VIETNAMESE CHILDREN had great political impact when it appeared in American newspapers and magazines during the Vietnam War. This widely reproduced photograph was credited with bringing about increased public opposition to American involvement in the Vietnam War.

Americans saw few comparable images of the many civilian casualties of the Gulf War in 1991. Because government officials had realized the impact of such photographs on the American public, photographers were permitted very limited access to the Gulf War.

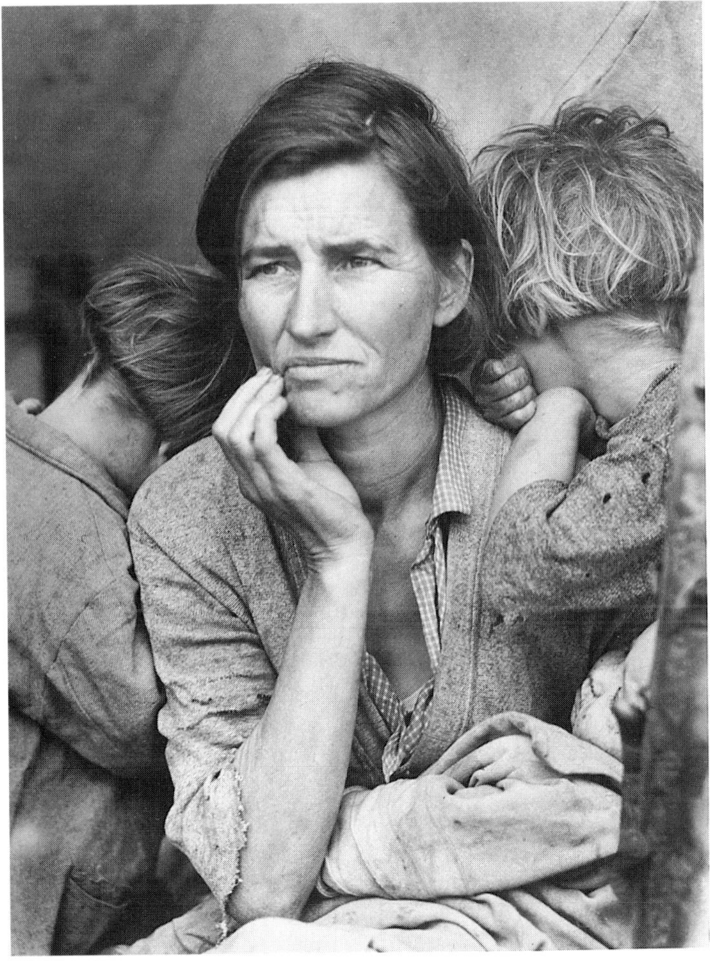

248 Dorothea Lange.
MIGRANT MOTHER, NIPOMO, CALIFORNIA.
1936.
Photograph.
Library of Congress.

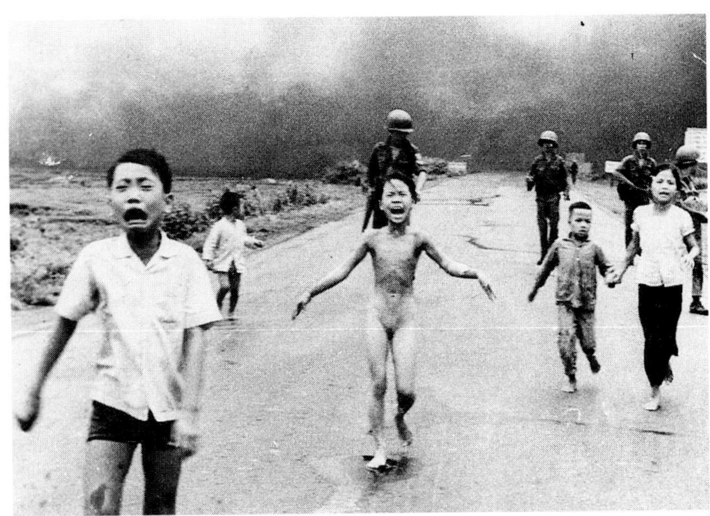

249 Huynh Cong "Nick" Ut.
TERRIFIED VIETNAMESE CHILDREN FLEE AFTER NAPALM STRIKE. 1972.
Photograph.
AP/Wide World Photos.

ANSEL ADAMS (1902–1984)

As a youth, Adams aspired to become a pianist, but his experiences with photography and his love of the natural environment led him in another direction.

When he was fourteen, Adams took a Kodak box Brownie to Yosemite Valley. What he saw and photographed fired his imagination. From ages eighteen to twenty-two, while continuing his music studies, Adams spent summers working as caretaker of the Sierra Club's conservation headquarters in Yosemite National Park. There he connected with the values, friends, and resources that formed the focus for the rest of his life.

He became a lifelong advocate of environmental preservation. In his many published essays on the concept of national parks, Adams stressed this uniquely American contribution to democracy. He spent much of his adult life championing the national park idea.

At twenty-eight, Adams decided to become a photographer rather than a pianist. The work habits he had developed through long hours of piano practice paid off in the perseverance and technical precision he brought to the making of photographs. One of his best-known statements reveals his attitude toward both the craft and the art of photography: "The negative is the [musical] score. The print is the performance."[4]

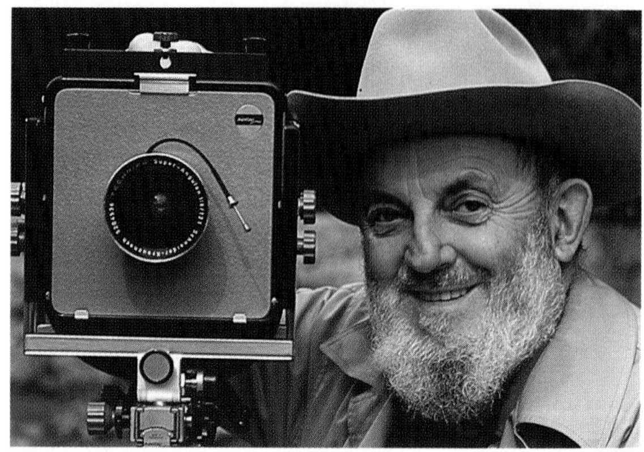

250 ANSEL ADAMS.
Photograph: T. Sennett/Magnum.

In 1932, Adams was a co-founder of the leading photographic group f64. The following year, a trip around the United States culminated in his meeting Alfred Stieglitz (see page 423) who gave Adams an exhibition at his famous, avant-garde New York gallery.

His 1935 book *Making a Photograph* marked the beginning of Adams's immense influence on American photography, especially the technique and aesthetic of the unretouched "straight" print.

Adams wrote some of the most useful photography manuals of his time, now seen as classics. His zone system is widely used for controlling light and dark—from preliminary visualization of the composition, to the exposure of the negative, to the precise control of values in the final print. For Adams, the camera was an artist's tool rather than a recording device, and this can be seen in the personal feeling and interpretation he brought to his prints. "People look at my pictures and then accept them, in a sense, as reality."[5]

A master of his art and a fun-loving, down-to-earth person, Adams was also a devoted teacher. His photographs of nature, people, and other subjects (see page 47) reveal the breadth of his awareness and concerns.

Master photographer Minor White wrote of Adams's art:

Nature never seems so grand, romantic, sensuous, and magical elsewhere, nor the buildings so architectural, nor the artifacts of man and details close to the ground so full of presence. . . .[6]

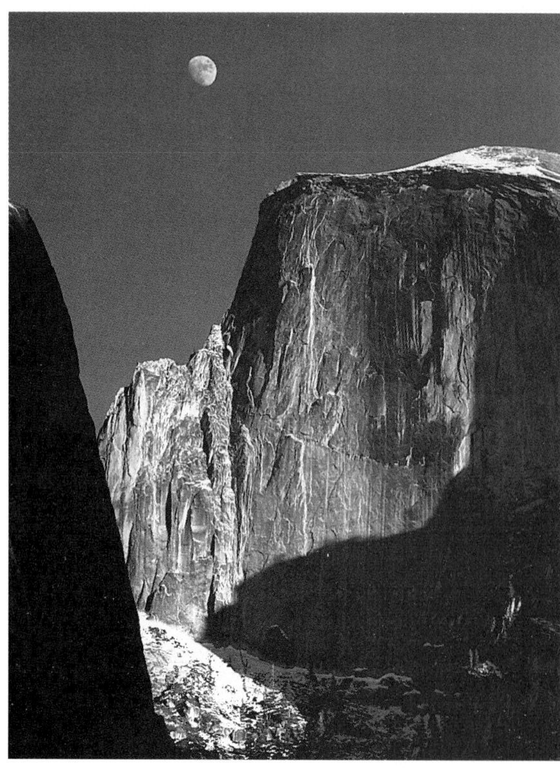

251 Ansel Adams.
MOON AND HALF DOME, YOSEMITE NATIONAL PARK, CALIFORNIA. c. 1960.
Photograph.

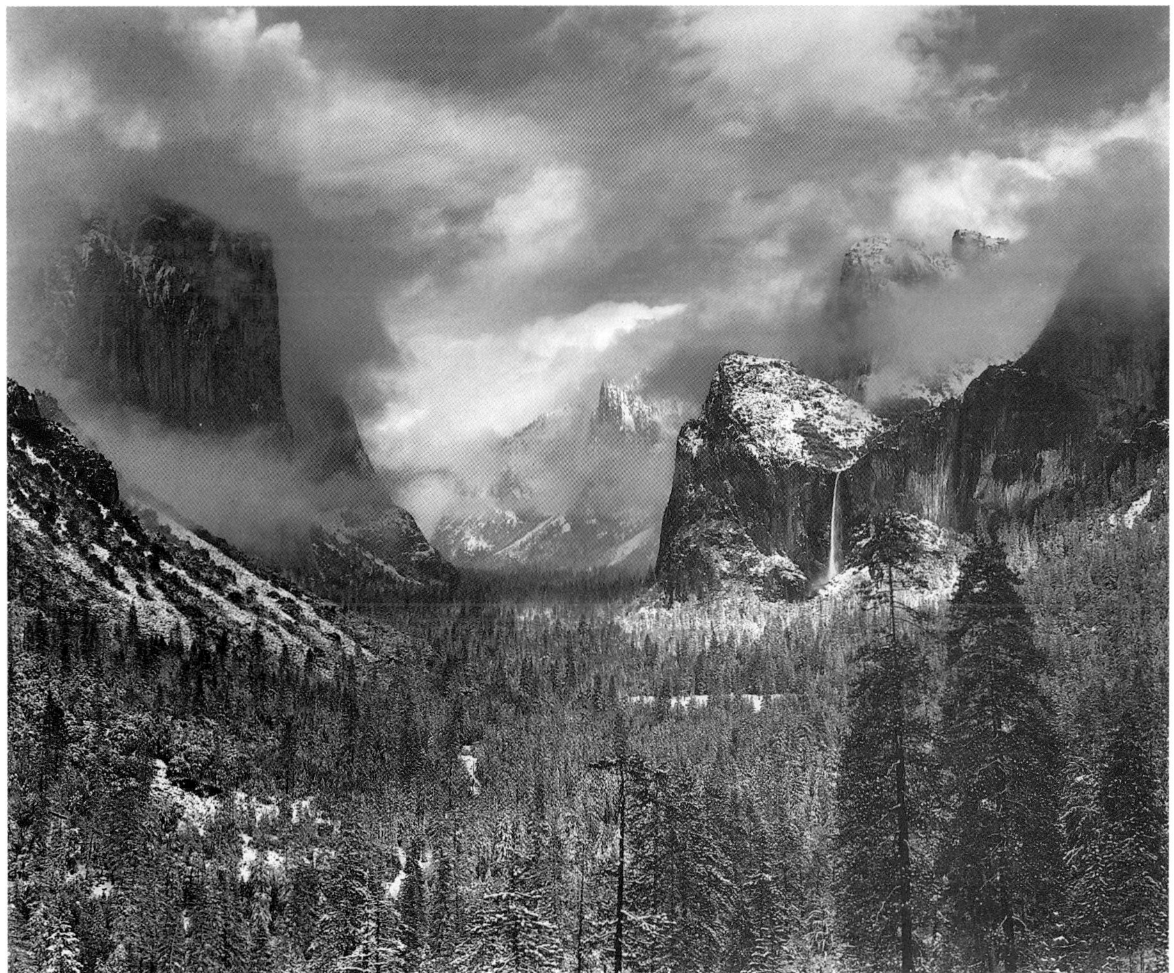

252 Ansel Adams.
CLEARING WINTER STORM, YOSEMITE NATIONAL PARK, CALIFORNIA. 1944.
Photograph.

In addition to focusing on social problems, photography has aided environmentalists. Ansel Adams used the power of his photographs and his reputation as an artist to increase public awareness of the beauty of nature and to draw attention to the great need for environmental protection. The symphonic grandeur of WINTER STORM, YOSEMITE NATIONAL PARK reflects his vision of the eloquence of nature's design. His dramatic orchestration of a range of white to black values creates a brilliant image of the cathedral-like grandeur of Yosemite. The stark beauty of the massive rock peaks contrasts with the soft intermingling of clouds.

Adams viewed aspects of nature as the symbols of spiritual life, capable of transcending the often conflicting prescriptions of society. Nature becomes a timeless metaphor for spiritual harmony in his majestic black-and-white photographs, which reflect a lifelong passion for art and nature.

In Yosemite and the High Sierra, where Adams spent a lifetime working, he recognized the perfect symbiosis between art and environment. It was here that he discovered the almost magical blending of the emotional experiences of nature and the aesthetic experiences of art.

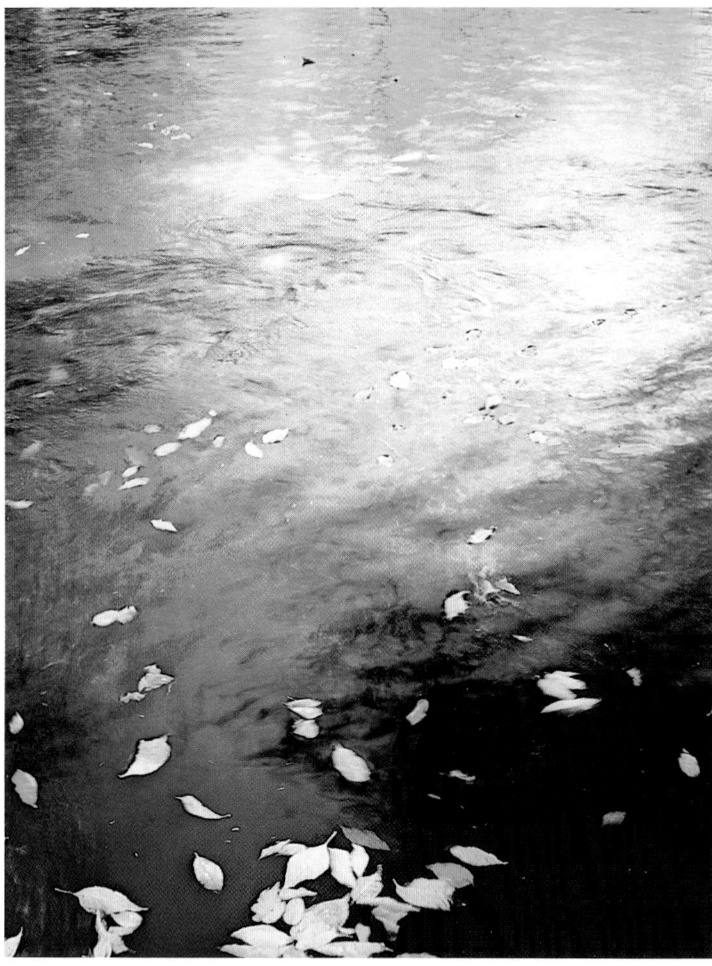

253 Eliot Porter.
POOL IN A BROOK, NEW HAMPSHIRE, OCTOBER 4, 1953.
Photograph.

Color Photography

Photography began as a black-and-white (sometimes brown-and-white) process, and for the first one hundred fifty years, black and white was preferred by most serious photographers. Through much of the twentieth century, technical problems with color persisted: film and printing papers were expensive, and, over time, the prints frequently faded. Even when fairly accurate color became available, many photographers felt that color tended to dilute the abstract power of the black-and-white image.

The development of color photography took a step forward in 1907 with the invention of positive color transparencies. In 1932, the Eastman Kodak Company began making color film based on the divisionist color theories of painter Georges Seurat (see page 395). Then, in 1936, the invention of Kodachrome provided an even simpler technique that substantially improved the versatility and accuracy of color film. Further progress in the relative permanence of color prints has led to several decades of creative activity in color photography.

For those who accept its potential and its complexity, color expands expressive possibilities because it is the most evocative element in visual language.

By the time Eliot Porter took up color photography he was already well known as a black-and-white photographer with an eye for subtle detail. He was meticulous in the printing of his negatives. Rather than travel the world looking for sensational vistas, Porter took the time to notice the beauty in nature close at hand. A tireless, patient photographer, he was known to wait for hours or days for the right light and weather conditions to take photographs such as POOL IN A BROOK.

Pushing the Limits

Artists have explored a variety of techniques to go beyond photography's assumed limits. The term *photomontage* describes the technique in which parts of photographs are cut out and reassembled to form new, often thought-provoking combinations. In Hannah Höch's photomontage THE MULTI-

MILLIONAIRE (see page 429), the expected relationships between familiar subjects are transformed.

The manipulated images of Jerry Uelsmann have added new dimensions to the art of photography and encouraged younger photographers to go beyond straightforward photography. Uelsmann was inspired by O. J. Rejlander's mid-nineteenth-century multiple-negative photographs (see page 380). In the darkroom—which he calls "a visual research lab"—Uelsmann combines parts of images from several negatives to make one print. By manipulating the print, he achieves a mystical quality influenced by the dreamworld explorations of surrealist painters (see page 432). In the UNTITLED print seen here, trees float above the reflected image of a giant seed pod, invoking a mood of timeless generative forces. Uelsmann explains his intentions:

I am involved with a kind of reality that transcends surface reality. More than physical reality, it is emotional, irrational, intellectual, and psychological. It is because of the fact that these other forms of reality don't exist as specific, tangible objects that I can honestly say that subject matter is only a minor consideration which proceeds after the fact and not before.[7]

The set-up photographs of Sandy Skoglund and John Pfahl (see page 471) challenge viewers in different ways. Skoglund draws and constructs dreamlike interior settings in which she then poses live models. Pfahl manipulates our perception of space by reinforcing the flatness of the photographic surface.

Sonia Landy Sheridan has pioneered the use of photocopy machines and computers as artists' tools. These tools support her research in the creative use of imaging technology, which she calls "generative systems." In FLOWERS, the translucent colors that fill the background were produced by shining fluorescent and tungsten lights into the copy machine. Trained as a traditional artist, Sheridan began to

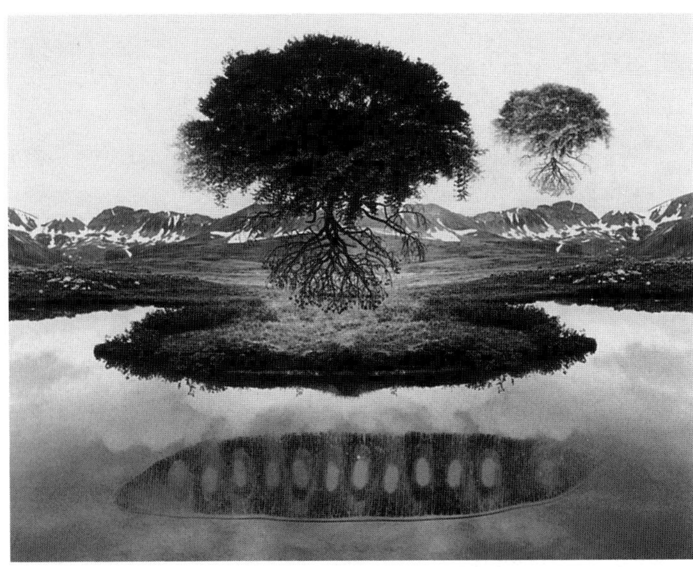

254 Jerry Uelsmann.
UNTITLED. 1969. Photograph.
Courtesy of the artist.

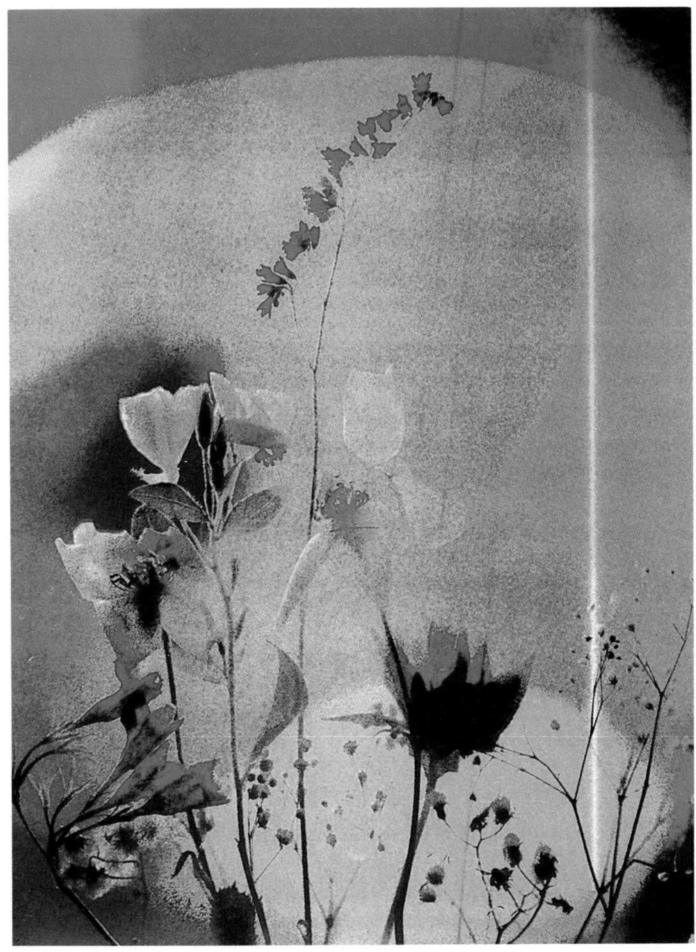

255 Sonia Landy Sheridan.
FLOWERS. 1976.
3M color-in-color print. 8½" × 11".
Courtesy of the artist.

shift in the late 1960s to creative uses of technological processes. Rather than wait for technology to catch up to her ideas, she worked with the 3M Company to develop tools to generate some of the images she envisioned.

The invention of photography and the increasing availability of photographs and cameras have changed art more than any other invention to date, freeing it from its former narrative and documentary roles. Artists were now at liberty to explore the possibilities of abstraction and nonrepresentation.

FILM: THE MOVING IMAGE

For thousands of years, artists have tried, with varying success, to depict motion and the passage of time. Prehistoric painters portrayed time sequences on cave walls; the Assyrians, the Egyptians, and the Romans presented time progressions in low-relief sculpture; French artists of the Middle Ages painted frescoes in strips to show stages in biblical stories; and traditional Chinese and Japanese artists painted scrolls that told stories visually as the paintings were unrolled a section at a time (see page 298). But it was only recently, with the development of movies, that motion and time found full, lifelike expression in the visual arts. Films are often so convincing in their illusion that we do not think about the craft that brings them into being.

The Development of Film

The development of the film medium began with the application of photography to existing, rather simple, multi-image devices designed to give the illusion of motion by spinning or flipping sequential drawings of figures in various stages of movement. These were the precursors of today's animated films. As soon as camera lenses and film were sufficiently light sensitive (fast enough) to record action, photographs became the primary means for depicting motion.

Eadweard Muybridge began making still photographs of stages of continuous movement in the 1870s when he was hired by Leland Stanford to determine whether a running horse has all four hooves off the ground at once. Muybridge lined up a series of still cameras beside a racetrack. Each camera was fixed with a string to be tripped by the horse's front legs, causing the GALLOPING HORSE to be photographed every few seconds as it ran past. Later, Muybridge discovered that when he projected the resulting photographs in rapid succession, the horse appeared to move. The persistence of the horse images on the observer's eye gave the illusion of continuous motion and became the basis of filmmaking. These photographs not only sparked the development of cinematography, but have had a major influence on the way artists represent animals in motion and have forever changed the way we see movement.

Soon others began experimenting with sequences of projected photographs. Their investigations led to the invention of the motion picture camera in 1889 by Thomas Edison and his assistant, William Dickson. Edison and Dickson had developed a camera that used rolls of coated celluloid film, with a peep-show device for viewing. Anything that moved—from FRED OTT'S SNEEZE to traffic on a city street—was used to demonstrate the exciting new technology.

In film, the illusion of motion is made possible by phenomena of the human eye and mind. When photographs of a sequence of consecutive movements, shot at the rate of twenty-four per second, are projected at the same speed, we see what appears to be continuous motion at normal speed. There are two reasons for this: the brief retention of an image by the retina after the stimulus is removed, called persistence of vision, and the process of perception by which the mind attempts to order and make sense of incomplete information. Although we are convinced we are seeing continuous motion on the screen of a movie theater, we are actually sitting in the dark, staring at a blank screen for about one hour out of every two hours of movie!

Film and Visual Expression

Film's rhythmic, time-based structure makes motion picture photography a very different sort of visual art from painting or even from still photography. A painter or photographer designs a single moment, but a filmmaker must design sequences that work together in time as well as space.

Each piece of film photographed in a continuous running of the camera is called a *shot.* Film makes possible a dynamic relationship among three kinds of movement: the moving objects within a shot, the movement of the camera toward and away from the action, and the movement created by the sequence of shots.

Much of the power of film comes from its ability to reconstruct time in the context of believable space; yet film is not inhibited by the constraints of clock time. It can convincingly present the past, the present, and the future, or it can mix all three in any manner. Film time can affect us more deeply than clock time, because film sequences can be constructed to approximate the way we feel about time. In addition to editing, filmmakers can manipulate time by slowing or accelerating motion. The filmmaker's control over time, sequence, light, camera angle, and distance can create a feeling of total, enveloping experience so believable that it becomes a new kind of reality.

The making of a film is a collaborative effort, coordinated and given a coherent form by the director. Leading directors have created their own styles and are known for certain kinds of content.

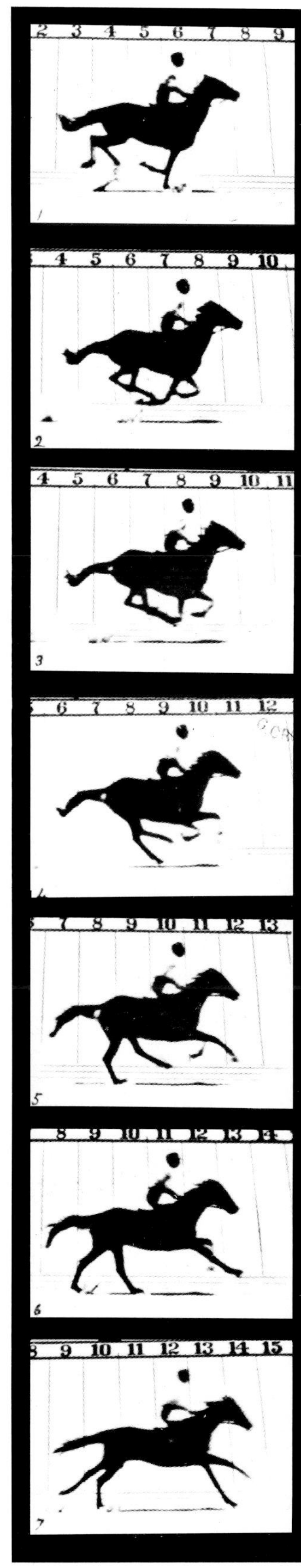

256 Eadweard Muybridge. GALLOPING HORSE. 1878. Photographs.
International Museum of Photography at George Eastman House, Rochester, New York.

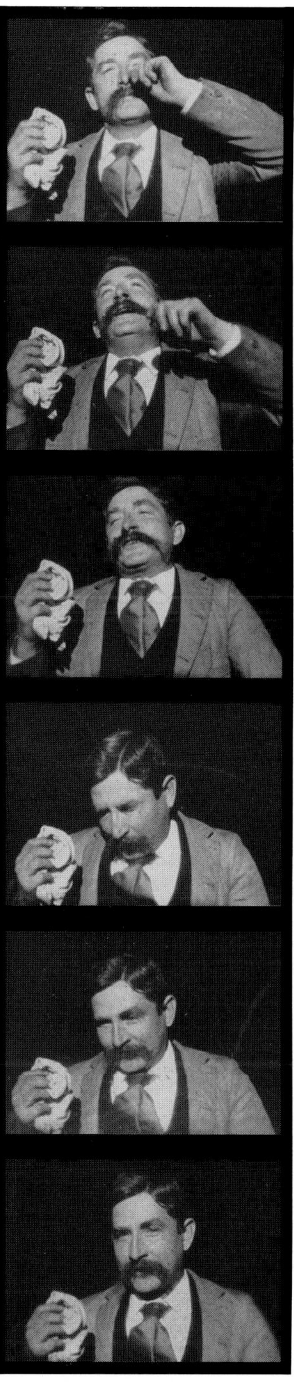

257 Thomas Edison and W. K. Dickson. FRED OTT'S SNEEZE. 1889. Film.

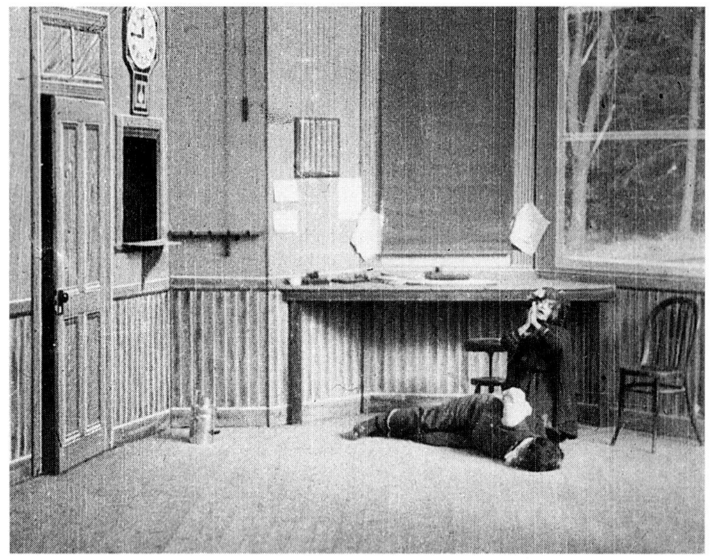

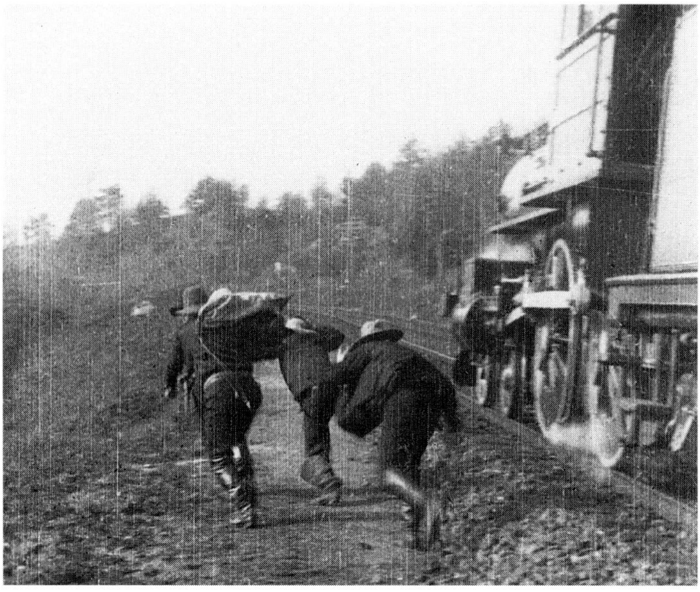

258 Edwin S. Porter.
THE GREAT TRAIN ROBBERY. 1903.
Film.
The Museum of Modern Art Film Stills Archive, New York.

Technical Developments: Creating a New Language of Vision

The development of film as a significant art form came slowly. At first, film was nothing more than a sideshow novelty. In order to gain public acceptance, early filmmakers tried to make their movies look like filmed theatrical performances. Actors made entrances and exits in front of a fixed camera as though it were a member of the audience at a stage play. Early films were not only limited to a fixed view, they were silent because the technology for recording sound did not come until more than thirty years after the invention of motion picture photography. The total reliance on the visual image forced pioneer filmmakers to develop the visual language of film that continues to be basic to the art.

Between 1907 and 1916, American director D. W. Griffith helped bring the motion picture from its infancy as a nickelodeon amusement to full stature as a means of artistic expression. Griffith introduced the idea of the moving camera by releasing it from its fixed, stagebound position in order to better express narrative content. The camera was placed at a distance from the action, where it would best reveal the dramatic meaning of a scene. Each scene thus came to be composed of several shots taken from different angles, thereby greatly increasing the viewer's feeling of involvement.

Assembling a scene from several shots involves *film editing,* a process in which the editor selects the best shots from raw footage, then reassembles them into meaningful sequences and finally into a total, unified progression.

Narrative editing was introduced by Edwin S. Porter in his 1903 film THE GREAT TRAIN ROBBERY. Porter set up his camera in several locations to shoot the various parts of the story, then he glued all the shots together and projected them in a logical sequence designed to tell a story. The nearly twelve-minute film was taken in fourteen scenes, each one a single shot. Later, Griffith used *parallel editing* to compare events occurring at the same time in different places (person in danger and approach of would-be rescuer) or in different times, as in his film INTOLERANCE, in which he cut back and forth between four stories set in four periods of history.

To underscore the importance of editing, we have only to consider the cutting ratio. The cutting ratio tells how much film footage was finally used, compared to what was discarded. In the traditional Hollywood movie, the ratio is at least ten to one, or ten feet thrown away for every foot used. To fine-tune a motion picture, the editor will sometimes add or remove just a few inches of film—equal to less than one second of viewing time.

One of film's most characteristic techniques was discovered when Griffith's camera operator accidentally let the shutter of his camera close slowly, causing the light to gradually darken. Griffith decided that this might be a good way to begin and end love scenes. *Fading in* or *out* remains a common transition between scenes.

Griffith was the first to use the close-up and the longshot while most movies were still stage-bound. A *close-up* shows only the actor's face. Today the close-up is one of the most widely used shots; but when Griffith first wanted to try a close shot, his cameraman balked at the idea of a head without a body! In a *longshot* the camera photographs the subject from a distance to emphasize large groups of people or a panoramic setting.

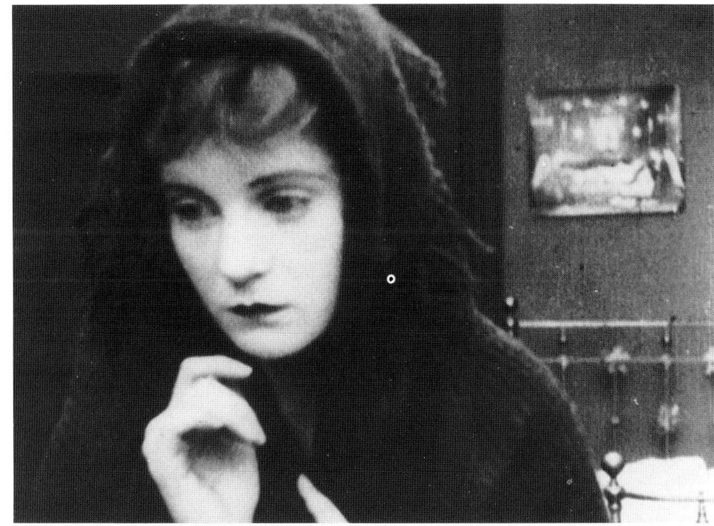

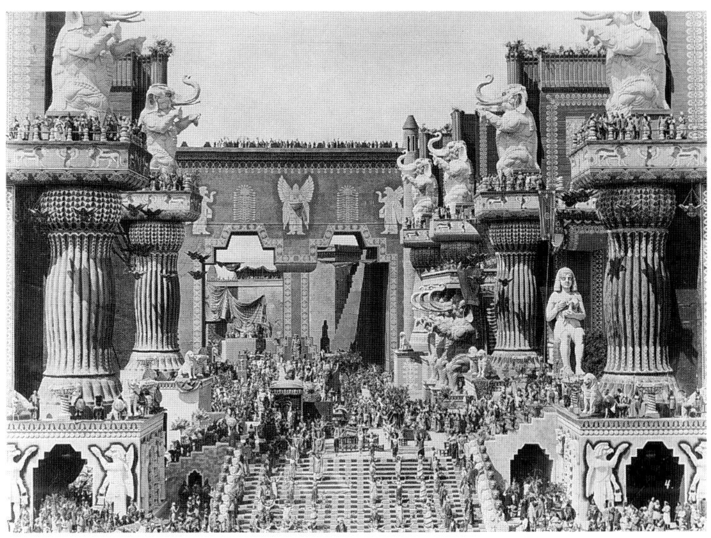

259 D. W. Griffith.
INTOLERANCE. 1916.
Film.
a Close-up ("Little Dear One").
b Longshot (Belshazzar's Feast).
The Museum of Modern Art Film Stills Archive, New York.

An International Language

When films were silent, movies could be produced in many countries for an international audience, without concern for language barriers. Following the Russian Revolution in 1917, Sergei Eisenstein emerged as a major film artist, honored as much in the West as in the Soviet Union. Eisenstein greatly admired Griffith's film techniques and, after careful study, developed them further, becoming one of the first filmmakers to produce epic films of high quality.

One of Eisenstein's major contributions was his skilled use of montage to heighten dramatic intensity. *Montage,* introduced by Griffith in 1916, is the editing technique of combining a number of very brief shots, representing distinct but related subject matter, in order to create new relationships,

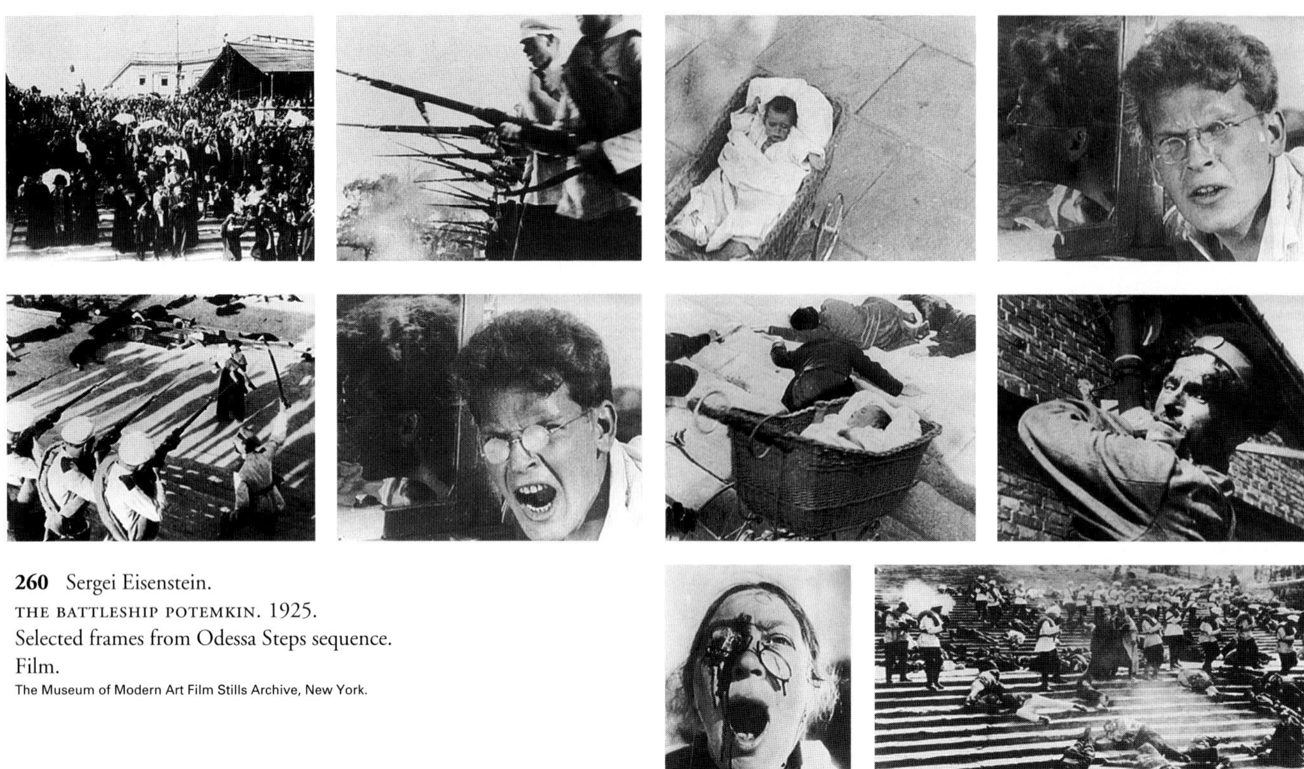

260 Sergei Eisenstein.
THE BATTLESHIP POTEMKIN. 1925.
Selected frames from Odessa Steps sequence.
Film.
The Museum of Modern Art Film Stills Archive, New York.

build strong emotion, or indicate the passage of time. With the use of montage, a great deal seems to happen simultaneously, in a short time.

In his film THE BATTLESHIP POTEMKIN, Eisenstein created one of the most powerful sequences in film history: the terrible climax of a failed revolt. The montage of brief shots, edited into a sequence of no more than a few minutes, effectively portrays the tragedy of the historic event. Rather than shoot the entire scene with a wide-angle lens from a spectator's perspective, Eisenstein took many close-ups to give viewers the sensation of being caught in the middle of the violence as a participant. He intermixed hundreds of shots to create relationships among elements such as a crowd on the steps, a rolling baby carriage, a horror-stricken student, and a Cossack about to strike. Eisenstein personalized the story by alternating close-up shots of individuals with sweeping scenes of chaos. The juxtaposition of movement and motionlessness, close-ups and longshots gives audiences a powerful sense of the fear and tragedy involved, second only to actually being in a situation of similar intensity.

Charlie Chaplin came to prominence about 1915, when pressure from audiences and industry competition caused "stars" to be created and publicized. He began his career as a member of a pantomime troupe, and he went on to become not only the leading comedian of his time, but a director, producer, writer, and even a composer of the background music for some of his films. He built a team consisting of cameraman, leading lady, and comic actors, who worked with him for many years. A perfectionist, he reshot particular scenes dozens, even hundreds of times. In 1931, four years after the introduction of sound in film, Chaplin chose to stay with the silent tradition in CITY LIGHTS (except for music and sound effects) even though "talkies" were then being made by all other Hollywood filmmakers.

The arrival of sound in 1927 added a new

dimension to film, but it did not change the medium's fundamental grammar. Color was introduced in the 1930s; the wide screen and three-dimensional images in the 1950s; 360-degree projection was first seen by the public in the 1960s. Most of these techniques, however, had been conceived of and researched by 1910.

After World War I, Hollywood became the film capital of the world, a position it held until the 1960s. In the thirties, most Hollywood films simply repeated plot formulas already proven successful at the box office. Then, in 1941, at age twenty-five, Orson Welles made his film debut with CITIZEN KANE, an international landmark in filmmaking. Welles coauthored the script, directed, and played the leading role in the thinly disguised account of the life of newspaper tycoon William Randolph Hearst. Because of its outstanding aesthetic quality and meaningful social message, CITIZEN KANE immediately set new standards for filmmaking. Welles and his cinematographer, Gregg Toland, pioneered the use of extreme camera angles, such as the low vantage point, which allows Kane (Welles) to be seen as a towering presence, and the tilt, shown here, which emphasizes Kane's crooked politics.

Recent decades have seen the growing significance of regional film production and national styles. Since 1950, many strong directors working in Europe, China, Japan, and, India, as well as in the United States, have greatly extended the expressive range of film.

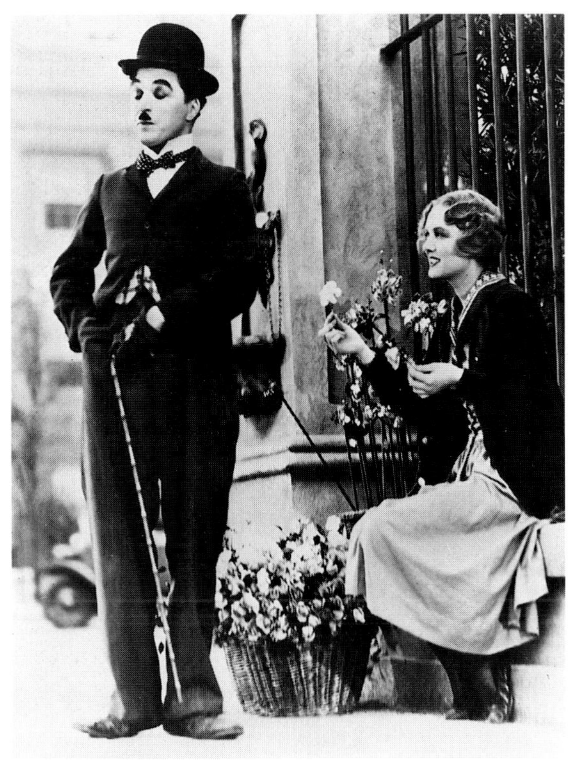

261 Charlie Chaplin.
CITY LIGHTS. 1931.
Film.
The Museum of Modern Art Film Stills Archive, New York.

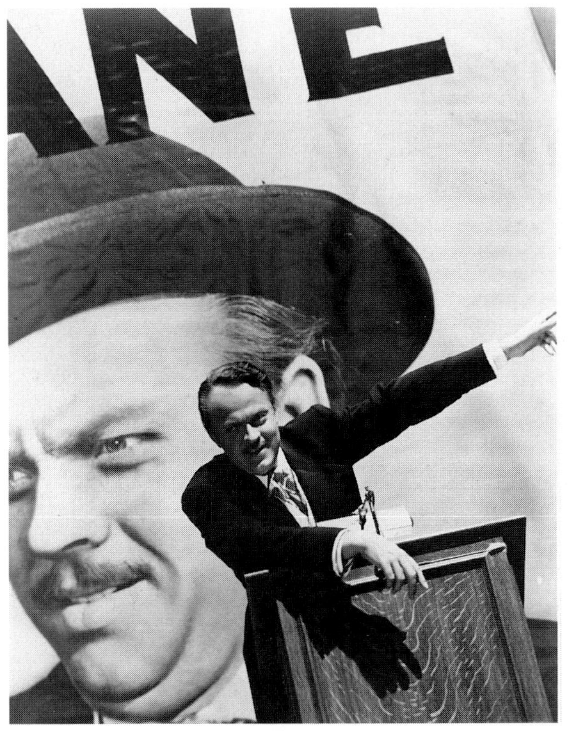

262 Orson Welles.
CITIZEN KANE. 1941.
Film.
Museum of Modern Art Film Stills Archive, New York.

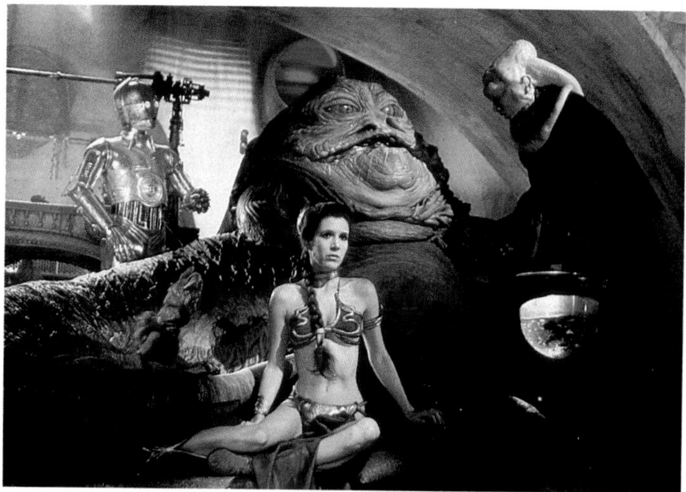

263 George Lucas.
The lair of Jabba the Hutt from RETURN OF THE JEDI. 1983.
Film.
Courtesy of Lucasfilm Ltd.

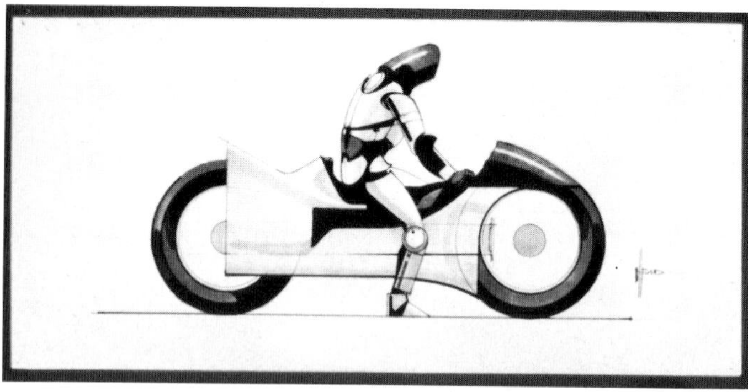

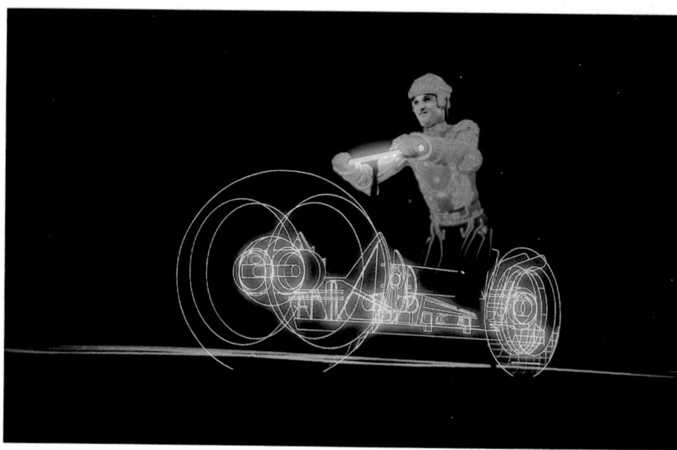

264 TRON. 1982.
a Syd Mead.
Study for the light cycles in TRON.
b Bruce Boxleitner on a light cycle from the film TRON.
© 1982 Walt Disney Productions.

Special Effects and New Technology

In recent years, some of the biggest box office successes have exploited special effects made possible by a merging of old techniques and new technology. Teams of artists and technicians work with producer-directors such as George Lucas, creator of the *Star Wars* trilogy, to provide working sketches, models, animation, and sets that are fantastic yet believable.

Industrial Light and Magic (ILM), the special effects division of George Lucas's company, Lucasfilm Ltd., was the leading special effects studio of the late 1970s and 1980s. The ILM team takes ideas from script to storyboard to models to film. A *storyboard* is a series of drawings or paintings arranged in a sequence like a comic strip and used to visualize the major shots in a film. ILM spends at least a week on a sequence that will last less than two seconds in the finished film. Only with computers can the complex alignment of all the elements of camera, light, model, and background be achieved.

Lucas is also responsible for the increased use of computers to edit film. With Edit Droid, a device developed by Lucas, a film editor can rearrange film footage almost as easily as a text editor can move words or sections of copy on a word processor.

Lucas is one of a handful of talented producer-directors who have dominated the Hollywood scene since 1975 by putting their creativity into technique rather than content. Their movies are capable of providing enough suspense, amazement, and terror to attract and hold the attention of millions of viewers. Some critics, however, question the lasting value of films that deal with assaults from alien galaxies, deathrays, and great white sharks.

In a similar tradition, Walt Disney Productions' epic science fiction film TRON, in spite of a fairly weak story line, was praised for its wonderfully inventive visual form, achieved through computer animation. Designer and visual futurist Syd Mead is widely known for his masterful illustrations of futuristic architecture, transportation systems, and computerized environments. Mead created conceptual drawings for the fantastic light cycles and high-tech settings in TRON. The film features a trip through an imagined video-game universe of light, color, and energy—all inside a computer. Appropriately, TRON was the first movie to employ animated computer graphics successfully, revealing the computer as a versatile tool in the hands of inventive filmmakers.

Today, film is an international, intercultural language—the most persuasive of the arts. When the believable realism of photography was combined with the equally convincing appearance of motion, film became the supreme illusion of reality. When visual motion was synchronized with sound, two major facets of total sensory experience were joined. Film can make us feel we are actually participating in events as they occur. No other medium is capable of engaging us so completely.

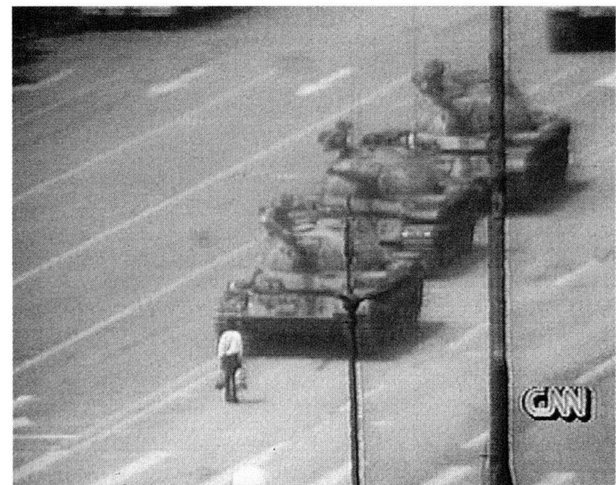

265 UNARMED PROTESTOR CONFRONTS TANKS NEAR TIANANMEN SQUARE. Beijing, China. 1989.

TELEVISION

Television, literally "vision from afar," is the electronic transmission of still or moving images and sound by means of cable or wireless broadcast. In countries where commercial television dominates, it is primarily a distribution system for advertising, news, and entertainment.

Broadcast Television

Television became all-pervasive in a very short time: in January 1949, only 2.3 percent of American homes had TV; by 1954, more than half had a set; and in 1991, 98 percent had one or more sets. It is now the most powerful, almost inescapable, means of mass communication.

Early TV broadcasts, except for televised movies, were always live. With the introduction in the 1960s of magnetic videotape, which records audio and visual material simultaneously, it became possible for light and sound waves collected and converted by television cameras to be stored for later transmission. The capacity to combine live and canned segments instantaneously gives television even greater flexibility and immediacy than film.

In July 1969, an estimated 400 million people around the world watched as the first moon landing became a milestone in human history. In 1989, through television, the free world joined Germany in celebrating the dismantling of the Berlin Wall and delighted in the incredible bravery of one citizen who defied a line of tanks during Tiananmen Square demonstrations in Beijing. In the TIANANMEN SQUARE shot, the camera's angle of view, the angle of the line of tanks, and the scale of the lone figure against the bulk of the tanks all contribute to the power of this image.

The ways in which TV is used shape attitudes and behavior around the world. The influence of television violence—the new pornography—on real life violence has been well documented. On the positive side, selective TV viewing can be highly educational as well as entertaining.

Video Art

The terms *video* and *video art* came into use in the late 1960s and were used to identify television activity by individuals or groups that were not (and did not want to be) part of the broadcast "establishment." In spite of attempts by makers of video to distance themselves from commercial broadcast television, many techniques developed during video experimentation have since been applied to commercial television.

Video equipment became affordable and accessible to artists in 1965, when Sony Corporation introduced its portable half-inch videotape system known as the Porta-Pak. Using the new equipment,

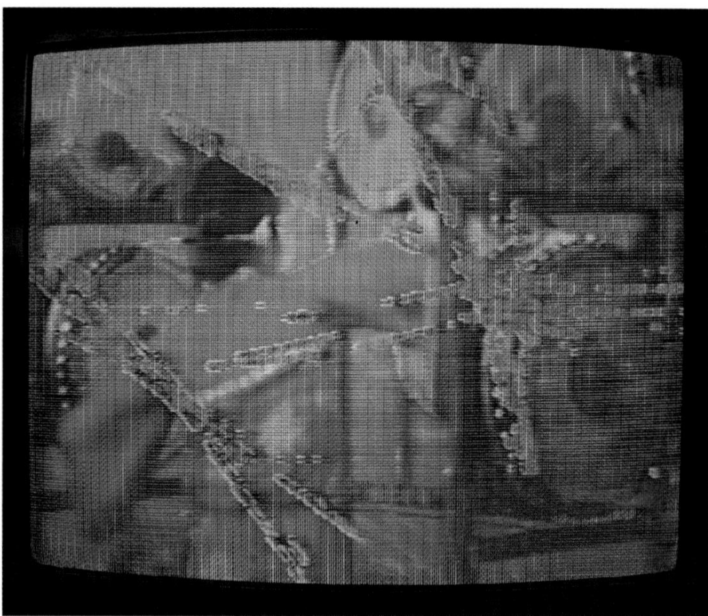

266 Nam June Paik and John Godfrey.
GLOBAL GROOVE. 1973.
Video. Produced by the Television Laboratory at WNET/13.
Photograph: Michael Danowski. Courtesy of Electronic Arts Intermix.

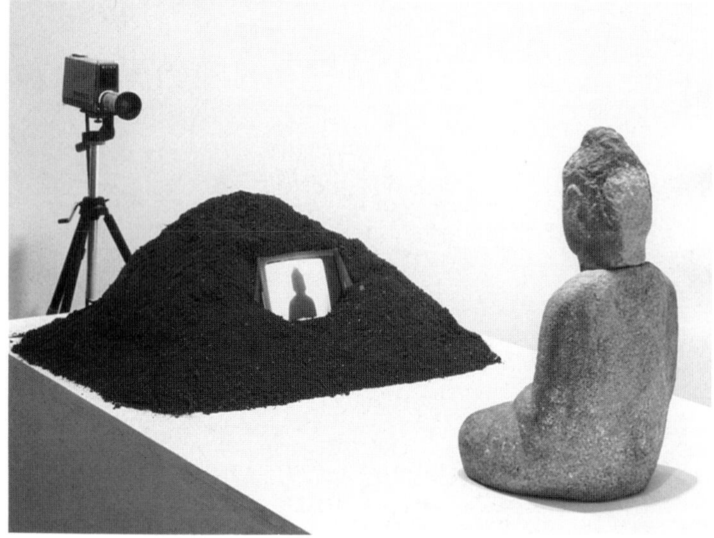

267 Nam June Paik.
TV BUDDHA. 1982.
Video.
Photograph: ©1982 by Peter Moore.

video pioneers went beyond the commercially-driven conformity of network television offered by the major networks. One dominant trend in their work is an emphasis on the need for contact with everyday reality. Today's lightweight video cameras now make it possible to go into the streets and the countryside to record ordinary people in real-life situations.

Korean-born musician, scientist, artist, and engineer Nam June Paik is the foremost pioneer of video art and the first to explore the multiple possibilities of manipulated television imagery as seen in GLOBAL GROOVE. In the 1960s, Paik became widely known for developing the video synthesizer, an optical color generator capable of transforming inputs from black-and-white cameras into colorful abstractions. Paik's musical background gives his manipulated forms a richness and depth not found in the work of some of his followers. TV BUDDHA, one of Paik's thought-provoking installations, is a humorous statement on the mysterious interplay between self and image. It challenges assumptions about what television is, and it gives a new perspective on the place of television in our lives.

Avant-garde and mass media merge in music videos, which have provided a free-form creative outlet for video artists working apart from standard commercial television. The highly imaginative imagery seen in the best music videos complements the music it is designed to support. Dada and Surrealism (see pages 427–434) have strongly influenced music video, which in turn has influenced television commercials and feature films. Television has gone from serving largely as a transmission vehicle for film to becoming a medium of conscious creativity.

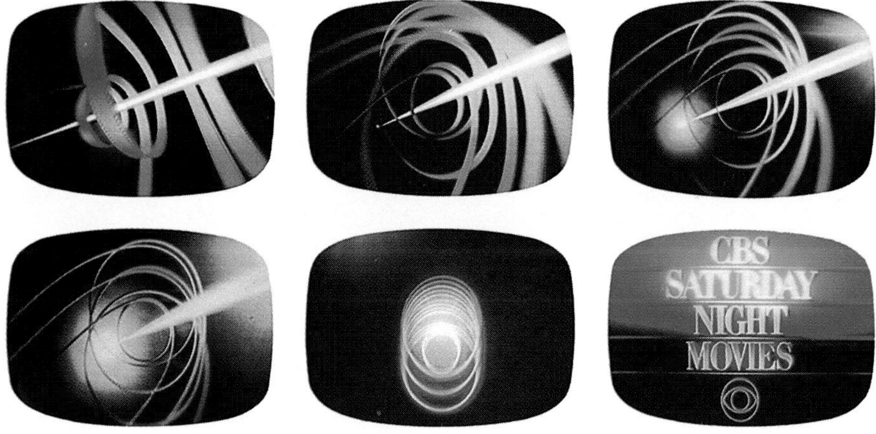

268 John LePrevost, art director; Jay Tietzell, producer.
CBS MOVIE OPENER. 1983. Computer-generated animation.

COMPUTER-GENERATED IMAGERY

Self-expressive and commercial applications of computer-generated imagery have emerged from the melding of science, technology, and art. Within the visual arts alone the work of many disciplines has changed, contributed to, and benefited from the advent of this amazing multifunctional technology. Artists with dramatically divergent points of view and levels of aesthetic sophistication are using computers either to create previously impossible forms or to speed up or make more manageable forms that would have been too complex and too time-consuming. In the fields of broadcast television, video, and filmmaking alone, the computer is replacing or supplementing earlier special effects tools such as miniature models and trick photography.

As we mentioned earlier, each time a new medium is introduced, the first artists to adopt it tend to work with it as if it were a familiar, traditional medium. Some of the first artists to use computers drew, painted, or designed in habitual ways before exploring aspects of image-making that took advantage of the computer's special capabilities.

Computer screens are cathode ray tubes (CRTs) just like TV screens. The artmaking capacity of computer-linked equipment ranges from producing finished art, such as color prints, film, and videos, to generating ideas for works that are ultimately made in another medium. Computers are also used to solve design problems by facilitating the visualization of alternative solutions. The computer's capacity to store images-in-progress enables the user to save unfinished images while exploring ways of solving problems in the original. Thus sculptors, photographers, filmmakers, designers, and architects can take advantage of the tools created by programmers of computer software.

The multipurpose characteristics of the computer have accelerated the breakdown of boundaries between media specializations. A traditional painter working with a computer can be easily seduced into employing photo imaging or even adding movement and sound to a work. A photographer can retouch, montage, change values, "paint over," or color black-and-white images. Computers facilitate the writing, design, and printing of, and the color separations for, books such as *Artforms.*

For many years now, computers have been used to design exciting television feature titles, such as the CBS MOVIE OPENER. The spatial gymnastics of rotating letters or logos is made possible by computer-aided animation and image manipulation.

Ed Emshwiller was an early pioneer of inventive computer-generated videos. He worked as a painter before switching to filmmaking in the 1960s and then to video in 1972. Although he had achieved recognition as an avant-garde filmmaker, Emshwiller saw new possibilities in the use of computer technology to generate video images. Video provided some of the immediacy of painting, along

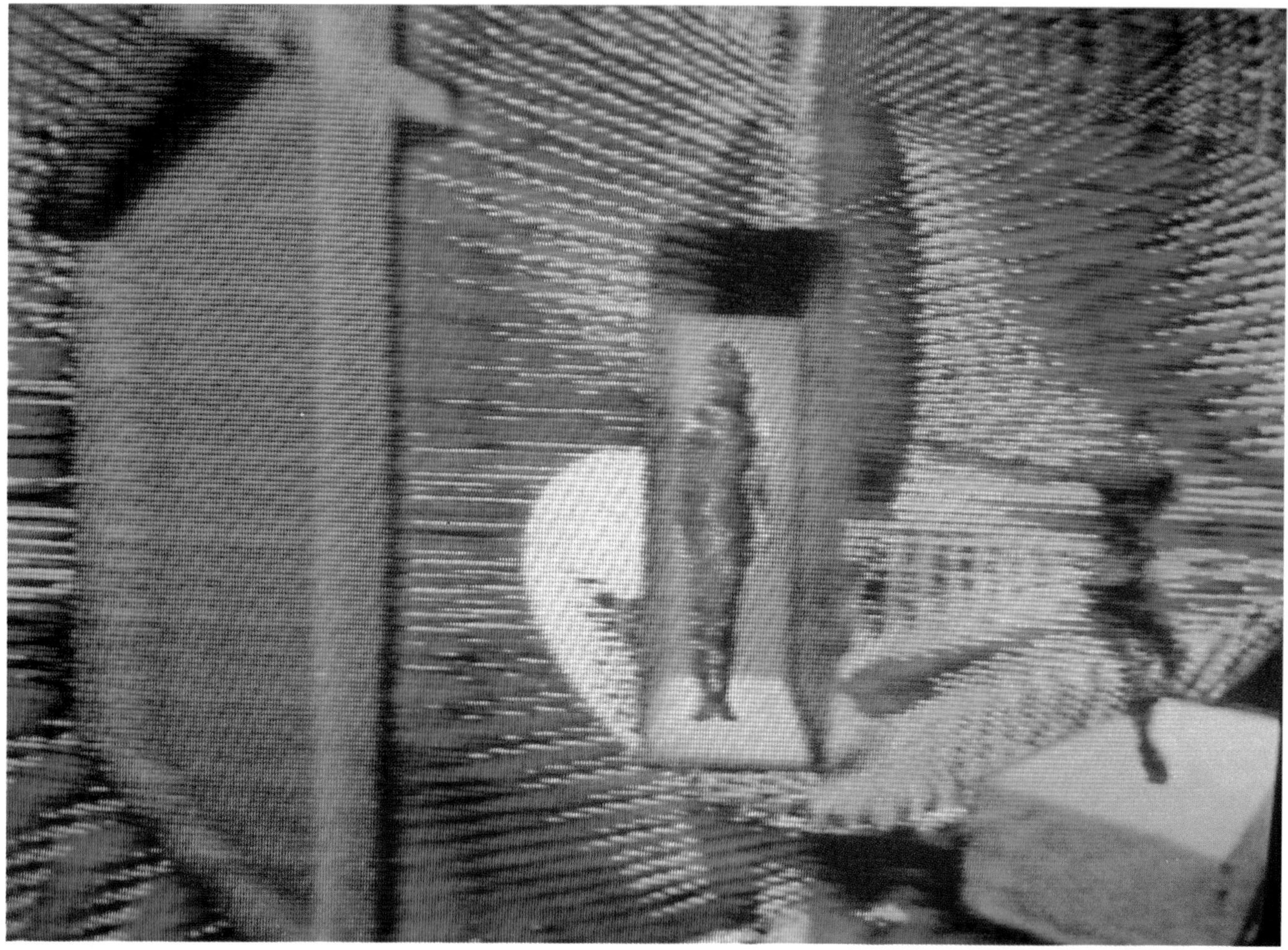

269 Ed Emshwiller.
SCAPE-MATES. 1973.
Computer-generated video. 30 minutes.
The Television Laboratory, WNET, New York.

with greater image-making flexibility than film. With SCAPEMATES, Emshwiller created a thirty minute kaleidoscopic fantasy that blends two dancers within an ever-changing computer-generated world. He orchestrated his visions with the help of skilled video and computer engineers.

Emshwiller's choreography began with black and white artwork, from which he designed basic shapes and movements with a computer. The live dancers, videotaped separately against a black background, were then merged with and color-keyed into the environment. Final background and color were added with a synthesizer.

Computer marking tools include a variety of electronic "drawing" and "painting" instruments; the effect is similar to having a collection of pens and brushes of different widths capable of producing various line qualities. Paint programs offer vast color choices, brush options, and even the ability to blend and smear colors as though they were wet paint.

Some artists transcend the "user" status through committed involvement and collaboration with technical wizards who share an interest in the artistic vision. Both Sonia Sheridan (see page 183) and Lillian Schwartz, formerly working with 3M and AT&T Bell Laboratories respectively, have collaborated with engineers and physicists in the development of new technology.

For over twenty years Lillian Schwartz has pioneered the use of the computer as an artistic tool. After studying traditional art forms, she became interested in merging art and technology. She began drawing with a light pen in 1968 and has since used computers to make graphics, film, and video, as well as images that resemble watercolors and oil paintings. As a consultant to Bell Laboratories, Schwartz collaborated with engineers and physicists in the development of computer-generated color images and effective techniques for the use of computers in film and animation. In 1984, she created the first computer-generated graphics commissioned by the Museum of Modern Art—to announce the reopening of the expanded museum. Pictured is one frame from her award-winning thirty-second TELEVISION ANNOUNCEMENT advertising the museum.

Elizabeth Zinn's image-making on a computer followed years of painting with watercolor and acrylics. The translucency and layering of color she enjoyed in watercolor led her to related explorations with a software program developed specifically as a tool for artists. Her seascape SPECTRA was made entirely on a computer by selecting, cutting, and overlaying portions of previously made computer images. Irregular shapes of clouds, sky, and ocean are suggested with flowing, shimmering surfaces and sunset colors seen as if through subtly fractured layers of space.

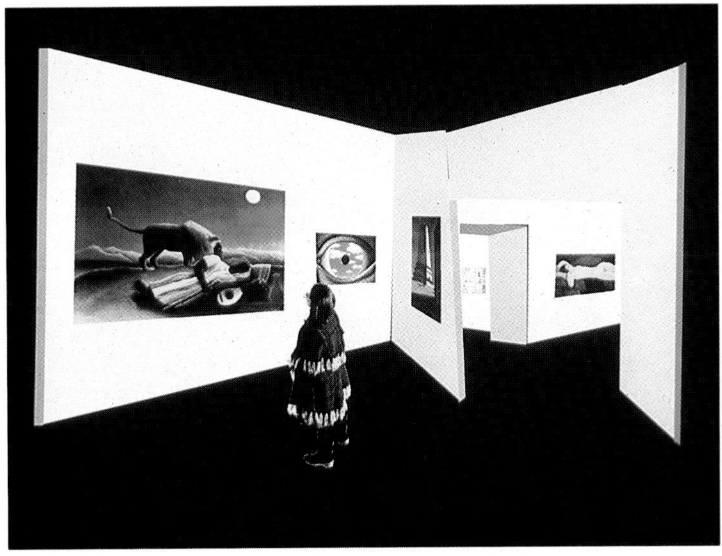

270 Lillian Schwartz.
From the TELEVISION ANNOUNCEMENT FOR THE REOPENING OF THE MUSEUM OF MODERN ART. 1984.
Computer-generated video.

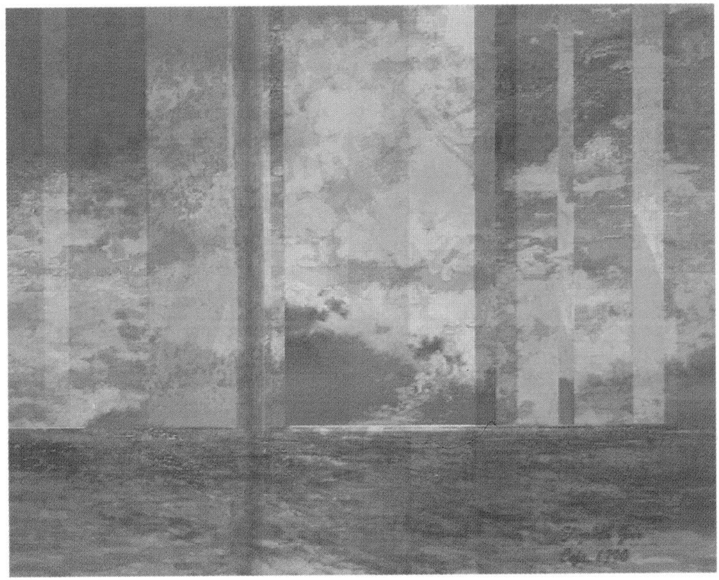

271 Elizabeth Zinn.
SPECTRA. 1990.
Computer painting.
Courtesy of the artist.

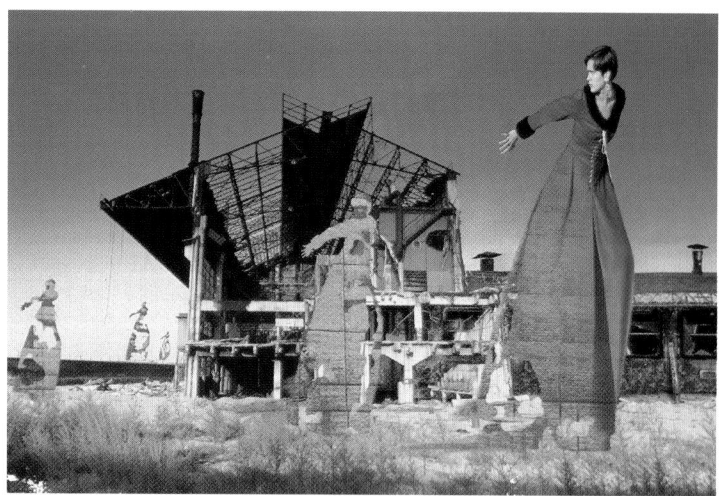

272 Corinne Rodriguez.
L' ECHAPPÉE. 1991.
Computer manipulated photographic images.
Paris Cité 1991 International Competition for Creative Technologies.

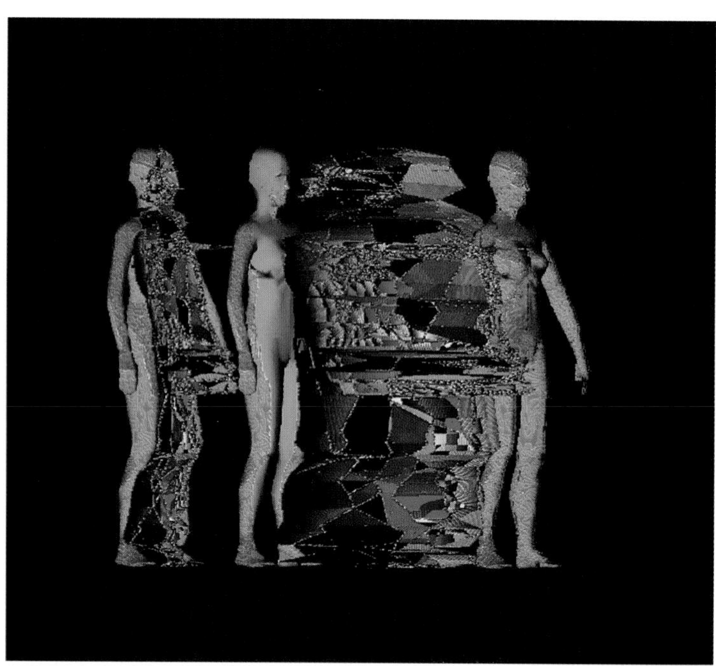

273 Duane Palyka.
PICASSO TWO. 1985.
Computer painting.
Computer Graphics Laboratory, New York Institute of Technology.

Zinn stores her completed images on computer discs from which photographic and color laser prints can be made. The images can also be transferred from discs to a film recorder that produces slides. Slides may be laser-printed onto paper or canvas, or made into color-photo prints.

The crisp resolution available with some software programs enabled Corinne Rodriguez to use photographic imagery to invent the highly convincing picture she calls L'ECHAPPÉE. By compositing (montaging) and using geometric distortion and elaborate photo-retouching on computer, Rodriguez has created a surrealist, dreamworld event out of diverse subject elements.

Since the late sixties computer scientist Duane Palyka has worked to integrate the contributions of science, technology, and art. With degrees in both math and art, Palyka understands the distinctly different mental processes involved in computer programming and art making. He believes the emerging computer art field can be advanced by individuals who both develop programs (tool makers) and work as artists (tool users). In addition to creating and exhibiting images such as PICASSO TWO, Palyka teaches programming skills to college students and artists.

The creation of intricate sculptural pieces is facilitated by using computers as controlling centers for output and input signals rather than as tools for information storage and retrieval (information processing). A special advantage of computers is their unique interactive, interdisciplinary capacity when it comes to programming virtual or actual environmental installations. With computer control, kinetic light and sound sculptures, such as Michael Hayden's THE SKY'S THE LIMIT, shown on page 76, or timed water sculpture, can attain new levels of complexity and sophistication.

All artists and designers working with three-dimensional forms appreciate programs that enable them to experiment using the rotational motion of implied three-dimensional images. In this way forms and spaces can be viewed from all angles. Bruce Beasley designed his cast-bronze sculpture BREAKOUT with a computer graphics program used by engineers. It allowed him to try variations, rotate, change proportions, and modify details in more complete ways than visual thinking and drawing ever could. When thousands of parts and angles are involved, the computer facilitates every stage from initial visualization to final building plans. Two shots from the monitor show Beasley's sculpture in profile and as separate parts ready for cutting from steel plates.

Architects and urban designers also use computer graphics programs to construct hypothetical three-dimensional structures and spaces. With computers they can see how inside and outside spaces will look without building models. To see how a planned new building will look in the context of an existing neighborhood, designers and their clients need only to feed the necessary old and new information into the computer, then move through the simulated community space.

Computer-aided architectural design has already proven to be extraordinarily useful, as seen in Mark Crosley's KITCHEN PLANS. With the aid of computers, architects can create floor plans, elevations, perspectives, and a range of working drawings. After perspective views are presented to the client, recommended changes can be made on the computer in minutes. Computer sequences make it easier for architects and clients to study and adjust spaces before plans are finalized. Now clients can feel as if they are moving in and around a proposed building while there is still time to make changes.

Just as the synthesizer continues to open up new possibilities in music and change the way we think about sound, so the computer has changed the way some artists and many illustrators and designers accomplish the visual thinking necessary for artistic production. Modern tools, however, are simply facilitators. No matter how complex and sophisticated they are, tools by themselves do not make art or turn their users into artists.

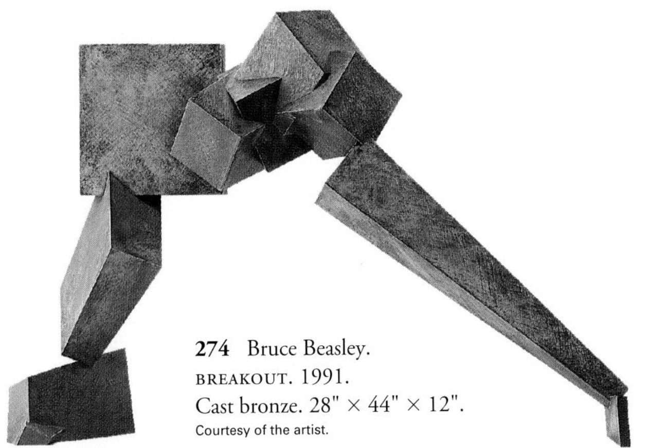

274 Bruce Beasley.
BREAKOUT. 1991.
Cast bronze. 28" × 44" × 12".
Courtesy of the artist.

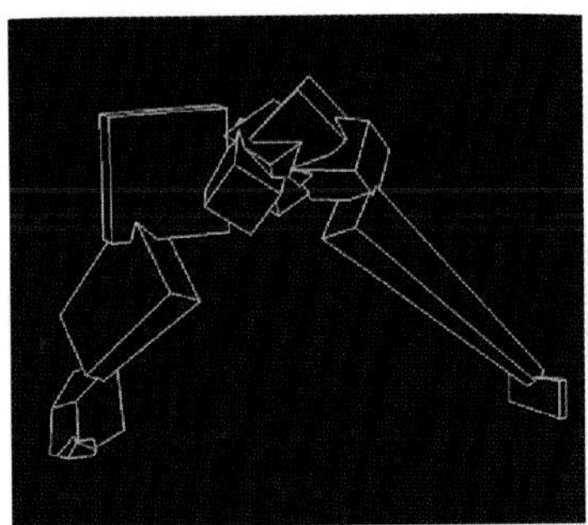

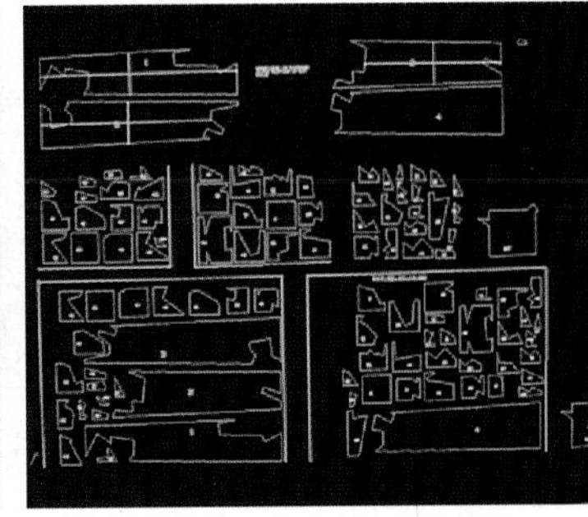

275 Bruce Beasley.
Computer studies for BREAKOUT.
a Model drawn with three-dimensional imaging software.
b Two-dimensional pattern used to create the sculpture.
Courtesy of the artist.

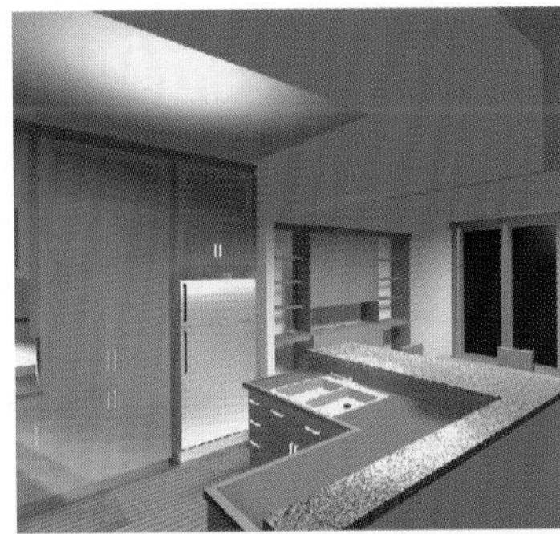

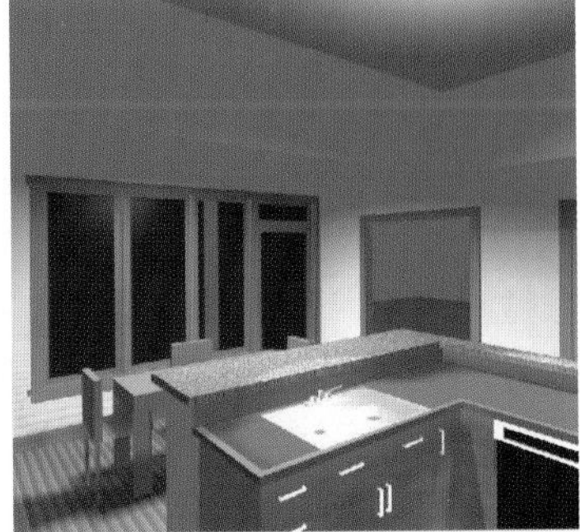

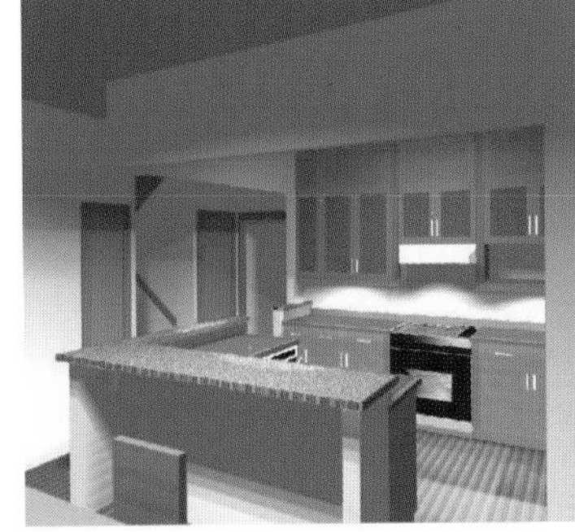

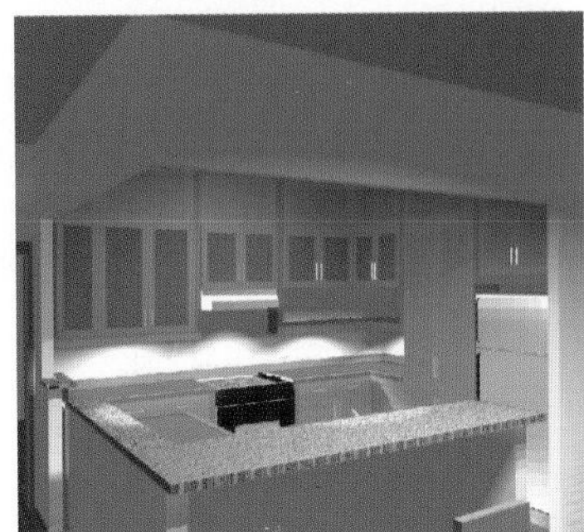

276 Design and rendering by Mark Lauden Crosley.
Computer-generated KITCHEN PLANS using AutoCAD and 3D Studio software from Autodesk, Inc. 1993.
Courtesy of the artist.

ART AND LIFE IN CYBERVILLE

Cybernetics is the relatively new science that studies the extraordinary interactions between nature's automatic control and communication systems (such as the human nervous system) and human-made electromechanical systems (computers). The prefix *cyber* refers to human-computer interrelationships.

Computers are hidden within the everyday tools of modern life. And most adults are happy simply to be the oblivious users of the technology that enables them to do things faster, better, more easily. But for the younger generation the situation is often different: The children of Cyberville know the resolution and operating system updates of their computers and Nintendo programs; their parents, meanwhile, can't set the clocks on their VCRs; eleven-year-old Sally must show her art teacher how to use the school's new paint program.

We cannot deny that the rapid increase in accessibility of computer-based technology has had a powerful influence on all aspects of life, including the arts. Artists respond in the same variety of ways as everyone else: some reject it and try to avoid it, some take it for granted, some embrace it, some try to find new ways to use it, and some become obsessed with it. Those creative thinkers who respond to its potential seek both to understand and to take advantage of it—to direct it toward realizing their visions. Such innovators can be identified as cyber artists: those who use their understanding of the rapidly evolving technology as a means of extending its application and development.

Computer-based technology has been in the mainstream since the 1970s. Terms like multimedia, hypermedia, and interactive media are coming into common usage. In computer terms, *multimedia* simply implies a computer system set up to control, process, and integrate text, static and moving images, and sound—in any combination and through a variety of input and output devices. *Hypermedia* refers to interactive capabilities that allow the user to affect and interact instantaneously with an ongoing sequence. Many artists interested in real-time or participatory processes have moved logically through performance or video into hypermedia activity.

Hypermedia mimics the ways we naturally experience and interact with the world. We construct our sense of something bit-by-bit while looking at various parts sequentially. The more we look, the deeper we explore, the more we discover, the more we learn. Content can be presented with combinations of text, image, and sound, each determined by the artist's personal or collaborative skills and sensibilities. Through personal choice, the user determines the areas and depth of involvement. Since hypermedia is multidirectional, concepts, facts, images, and sounds can be cross-referenced as well as constructed or deconstructed.

At the next level, interactive multimedia allows us to place ourselves in artificially constructed settings. This is called *virtual reality,* the term for interactive multimedia systems that allow users to have the sensation of being immersed in spaces that respond to their moves and manipulations. The user dons a helmet designed to block out the sights and sounds of the outer world in order to hear and see simulated sounds and images. The experience differs from sitting close to the TV, and wearing headphones, in that the sounds and images respond to your movement: when you turn your head to the left, the whole environment is seen as if you were moving within it and the sounds you hear change accordingly. As fully as possible, a total experience is simulated. Even aspects of touch and smell are being explored. These systems are still big-budget items, limited to places like Disney World and major research facilities.

As this technology becomes more accessible, commercial, industrial, and artistic uses of virtual reality will become commonplace. We will be able to explore and interact with entirely imagined worlds. It should not be hard to imagine the incredible possibilities this will open up. What will we do with such technology?

Virtual realities can extend the natural human ability to visualize, but the form and quality of these artificial environments will be restricted to their designers' capacity for meaningful visual thinking. So far, many such "realities" have the limited ambiance of a cartoon video game.

Human consciousness doesn't seem to be changing as fast as technology. Television programming will continue to offer experiences ranging from the educational and entertaining, to the mind-numbing and x-rated. Given the probably irreversible competitive edge that TV, video, and computer games already have on the classroom, virtual reality could have a positive effect on education because it demands interactive involvement, decision making, and experiential learning—activity types proven to stimulate the growth of creative intelligence.

We have already assimilated technology into our lives as users, and we have entrusted its development and control to commercial interests. The affordability of personal computers that can serve as production-quality multimedia tools has finally put media power into the hands of the general population and the independent artist. It is clear that we need to expend the extra effort necessary to understand and participate in decisions that will determine our techno future. Much of this responsibility will fall on the creative communicator, the artist.

PART

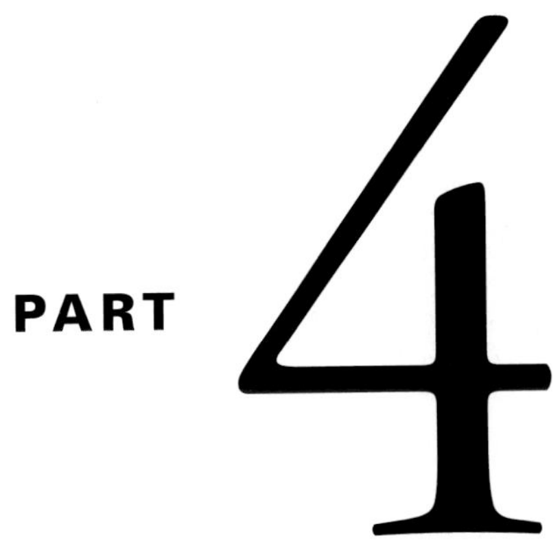

THREE-DIMENSIONAL MEDIA

Consider...

In what ways does a sculpture of a human being differ from a painting of one?

Do you think one medium seems more "real" than the other? More expressive of individuality or feeling?

You can see all of a painting at one time, but you usually have to move around a sculpture, seeing parts of it from each angle. How does this make your experience of a sculpture different from that of a painting?

If something is functional, can it still be art?

Is there a difference between "art" and "craft"?

CHAPTER 12

Sculpture

Sculpture exists in space, as we do. The total experience of a sculpture is the sum of its surfaces and profiles. Even when touching is not permitted, the tactile quality of sculpture is an important dimension. In most cases, sculpture is experienced through the movement of the viewer.

FREESTANDING AND RELIEF

Sculpture meant to be seen from all sides is called *in-the-round* or *freestanding.* When we view freestanding sculpture, we receive impressions from each side as we move around the piece. No one had to suggest moving around Calder's OBUS to the little girl in our photograph. A single photograph shows only one view of a sculpture under one lighting arrangement; so unless we can see many photographs or, better yet, a video, or best of all, view the piece firsthand, we receive only a limited impression of the sculpture.

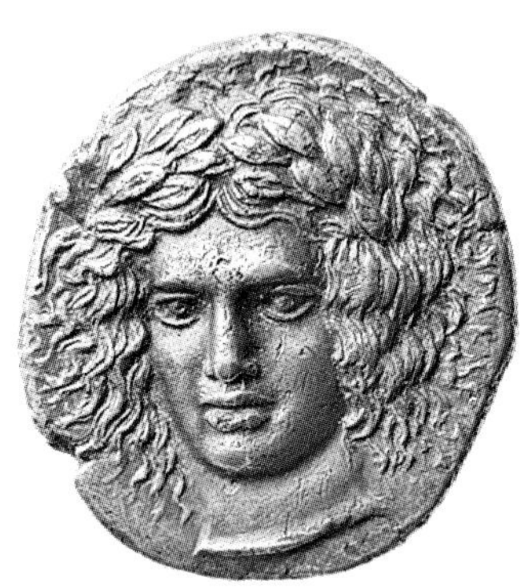

277 APOLLO. c. 415 B.C.
Greek silver coin. Diameter 1⅛".

A sculpture that is not freestanding but projects from a background surface is in relief. In *low-relief* (or *bas-relief*) sculpture, the projection from the surrounding surface is slight and no part of the modeled form is undercut. As a result, shadows are minimal. Most coins, for example, are works of low-relief sculpture. A high point in the art of coin design was reached on the island of Sicily during the classical period of ancient Greece. The APOLLO coin, shown here slightly larger than actual size, has a strong presence in spite of being in low relief and very small.

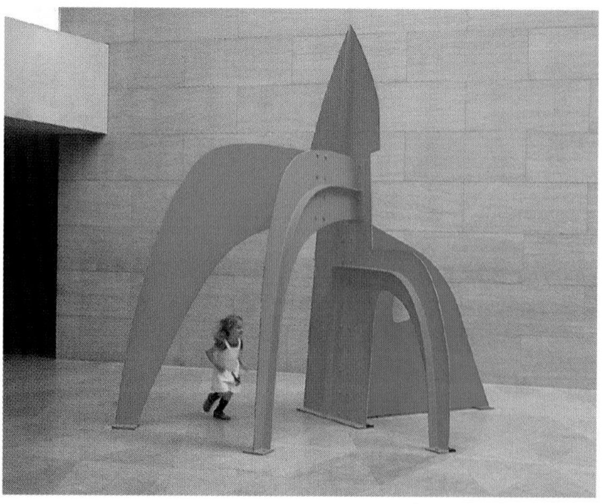

278 Alexander Calder.
OBUS. 1972.
Painted steel. 142½" × 152" × 89⅝".
The National Gallery of Art, Washington, D.C. Mr. & Mrs. Paul Mellon Collection.

In *high-relief* sculpture, more than half of the natural circumference of the modeled form projects from the surrounding surface, and figures are often substantially undercut.

Italian Renaissance sculptor Lorenzo Ghiberti was trained as a goldsmith, then worked briefly as a painter before establishing himself as a leading sculptor. He is best known for his bronze relief doors, particularly the east doors made for the Baptistry of Florence Cathedral. The tall doors are divided into ten rectangular panels. One of the finest depicts the biblical story of ISAAC, JACOB, AND ESAU. Ghiberti drew on his experience as a painter to create the illusion of depth through both pictorial and sculptural means. Figures in the foreground are in such high relief that they almost appear to be detached from the surface. By making the figures on the left and right edges overlap the frame, Ghiberti put them even farther into our space. Figures in the middle ground and background are in progressively lower relief. He used a thin layer of gold to provide an elegant finish to the cast-bronze surface. When Michelangelo saw these doors he said, "They are so beautiful that they might be the gates of paradise."[1] The remark became famous, and since then the doors have been known as the Gates of Paradise.

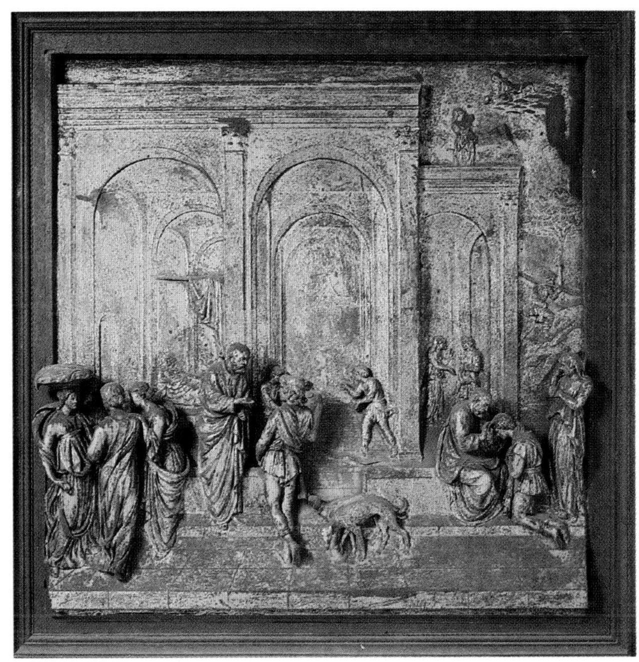

279 Lorenzo Ghiberti.
ISAAC, JACOB, AND ESAU, detail of the east doors "GATES OF PARADISE." Baptistry, Florence Cathedral. 1435.
Gilt bronze. 31¼" × 31¼".

METHODS AND MATERIALS

Traditionally, sculpture has been made by modeling, casting, carving, assembling, or a combination of these processes.

Modeling

Modeling is a *manipulative* and often *additive* process: pliable material such as clay, wax, or plaster is built up (added to), removed, and pushed into a final form. Giacomo Manzù used clay to model the HEAD OF MICHAEL PARK, which was later cast in bronze. Manzù intentionally left tool and finger marks as evidence of his spontaneous modeling technique.

In their working consistencies, materials such as wax, clay, and plaster are soft. To prevent sagging, sculptors usually start all but very small pieces with a rigid inner support called an *armature.*

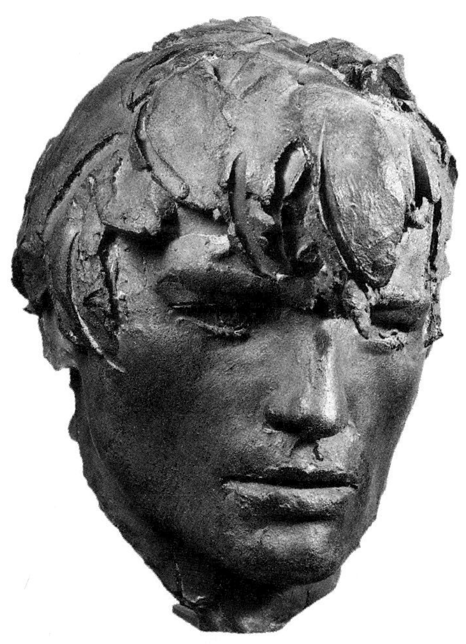

280 Giacomo Manzù.
HEAD OF MICHAEL PARK. 1964.
Bronze. Height 11".
Photograph courtesy of the artist.

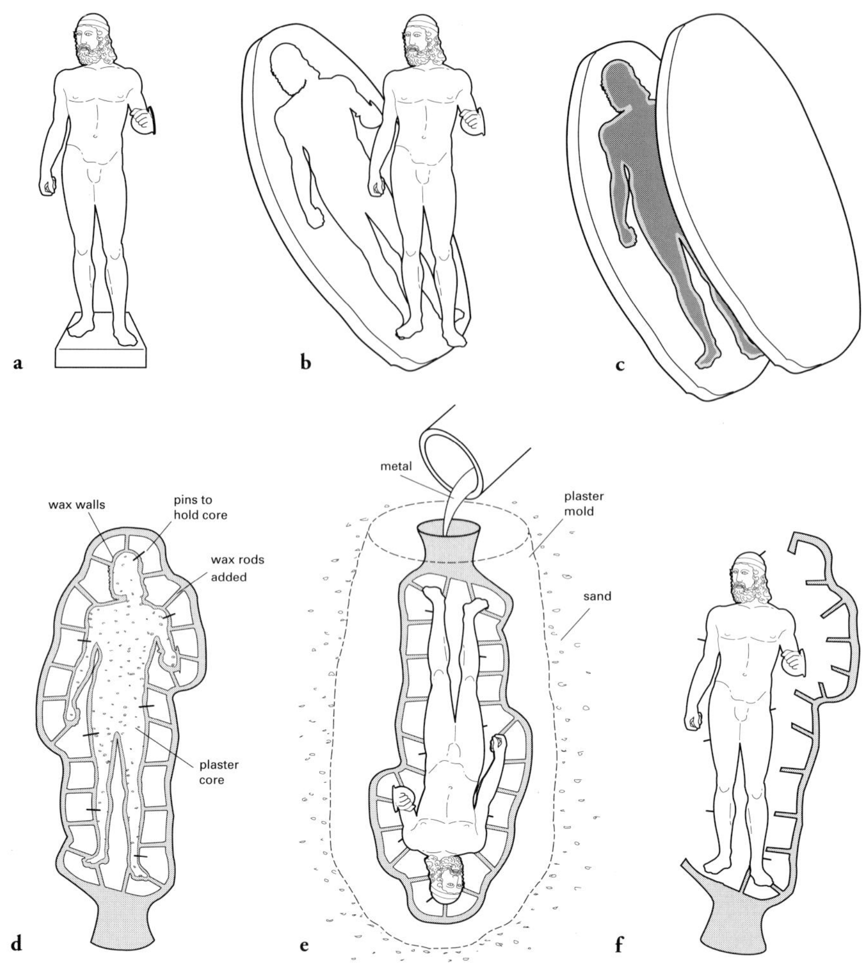

281 LOST WAX CASTING PROCESS.
a Clay or plaster full-size model of intended sculpture.
b Synthetic rubber negative mold. This is an accurate impression of the contours.
c Negative mold is coated with a layer of wax. The wax is applied to the thickness desired for the final sculpture—which will be hollow.
d The space inside the wax is filled with a mixture of wet plaster, called *investment.* After it dries, the plaster core is held in place with a series of metal pins. The synthetic rubber mold is removed. A network of hollow metal rods is added to the outside of the wax model.
e The wax model, with its rods and plaster core, is coated with another layer of plaster, creating an outer plaster mold. The mold is placed in a kiln and the wax is then melted away (hence the term *lost wax*), leaving an empty space between the plaster core and outer mold that is the exact shape and thickness of the desired sculpture. When molten metal is poured into the space vacated by the wax the rods serve as channels, allowing the metal to flow into every crevice and air to escape.
f After the metal has cooled, the outer mold, inner core, and metal rods are removed. Rough spots are filed away and the piece is polished.
Drawings a through f and accompanying text adapted from *Living with Art,* Third Edition, by Rita Gilbert, Published by McGraw-Hill, Inc.

Casting

Casting processes make it possible to execute a work in an easily handled medium (such as clay) and then to preserve the results in a more permanent material (such as bronze). Because most *casting* involves the substitution of one material for another, casting is also called the *substitution* or *replacement* process. The process of bronze casting was highly developed in ancient China, Greece, Rome, and parts of Africa. It has been used extensively in the West from the Renaissance to modern times.

Casting involves three broad steps. First, a *mold* is taken from the original work (also called the *pattern*). The process of making the mold varies, depending on the material of the original and the material used in the casting. Materials that can be poured and will harden can be used to cast: clay diluted with water, molten metal, concrete, or liquid plastic. Second, the original sculpture is removed from the mold and the casting liquid is poured into the resulting hollow cavity. Finally, when the casting liquid has hardened, the mold is removed.

Some casting processes employ molds or flexible materials that allow many casts to be made from the same mold; with other processes, such as the *lost wax process* shown in the drawings, the mold is destroyed to remove the hardened cast, thus permitting only a single cast to be made.

Castings can be solid or hollow, depending on the casting method. The cost and the weight of the material often help determine which casting method will be used for a specific work.

The process of casting a large object like Giacometti's MAN POINTING (page 53) is extremely complicated. Except for small pieces that can be cast solid, most artists turn their originals over to foundry experts, who make the molds and do the casting. To create her poignant SLEEPWALKER, Marianna Pineda initially built up the figure using clay over a wire armature. In this case, the transposition from clay to bronze involved two molds and two castings. The artist took a mold from the clay figure, then made a plaster cast of the figure. She took the plaster figure to a foundry where a mold was made from the plaster, and the final cast was poured in bronze.

In recent years, many sculptors have turned to modern synthetic media such as plastics, which can be cast and painted to look like a variety of other materials—even human flesh. Sculpture made with materials such as polyvinyl or epoxy resin are often formed in separate pieces in plaster molds, then assembled and unified with the addition of more layers of plastic. Although molds are used, the initial pouring process differs from conventional casting because forms are built up in layers inside mold sections rather than made out of material poured into a single mold all at once.

Sculpture has the special power to come much closer to duplicating models than even the most naturalistic painting. A sculptural counterpart to the photorealism of painting can be seen in John

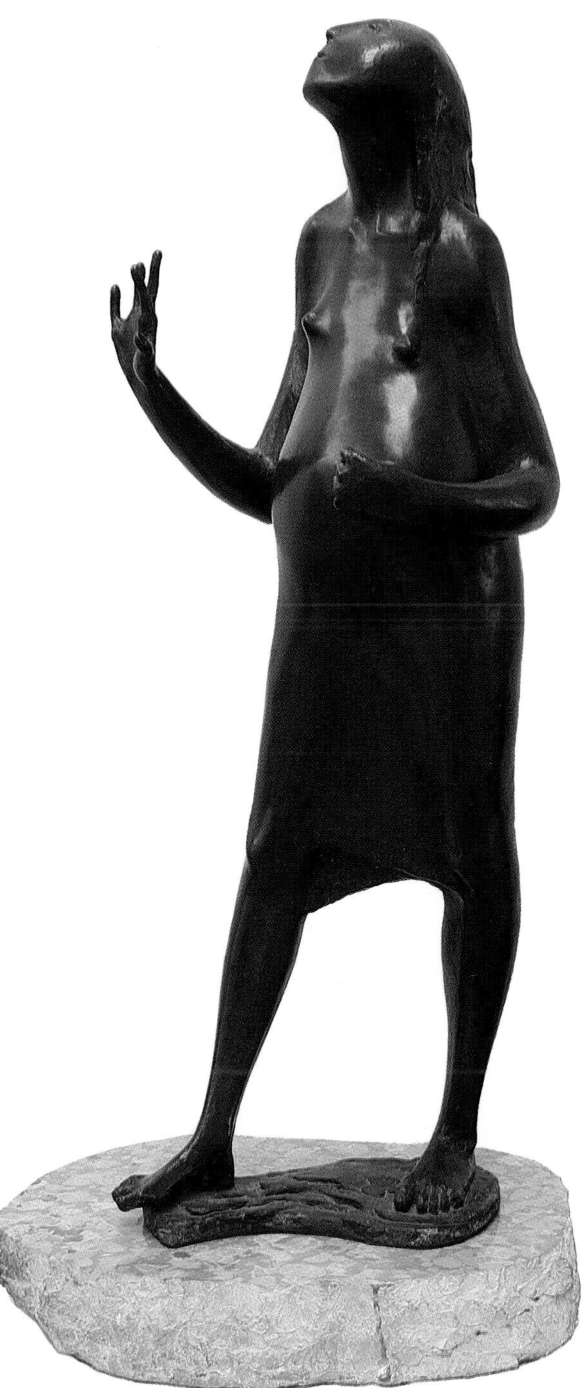

282 Marianna Pineda.
SLEEPWALKER. 1950.
Bronze, unique cast. Height 38".
Collection of the artist. Photograph: Nina Tovish, Cambridge, Massachusetts.

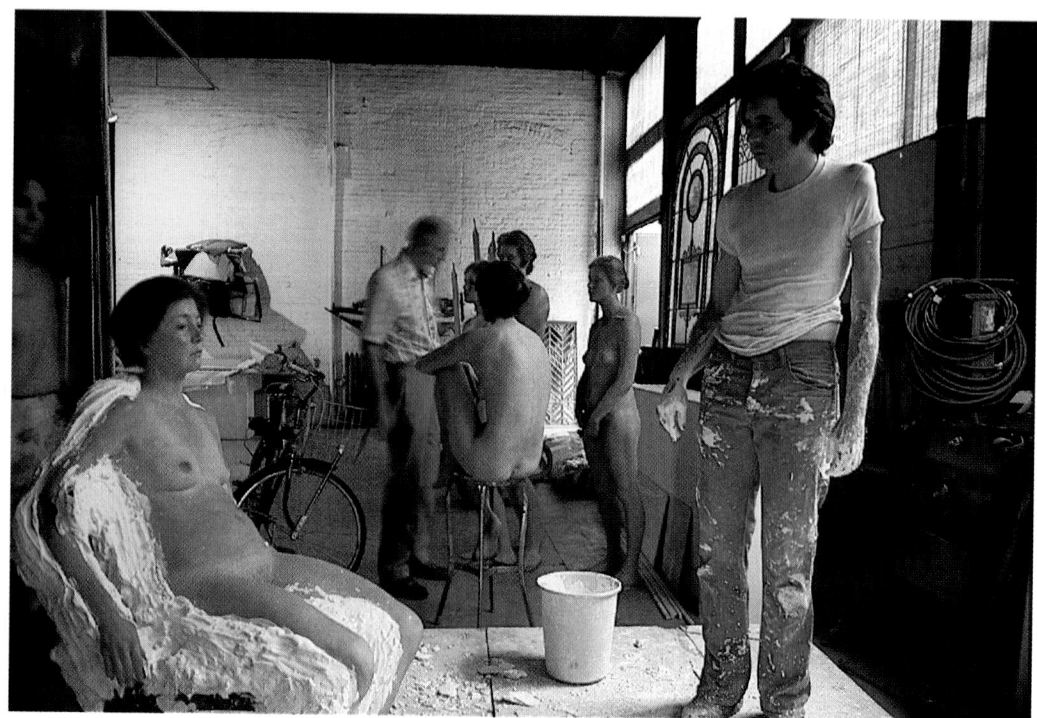

283 John DeAndrea. Several works, including CLOTHED ARTIST WITH MODEL, and live viewer. Photographed in 1976 in the storeroom of OK Harris Gallery, New York.

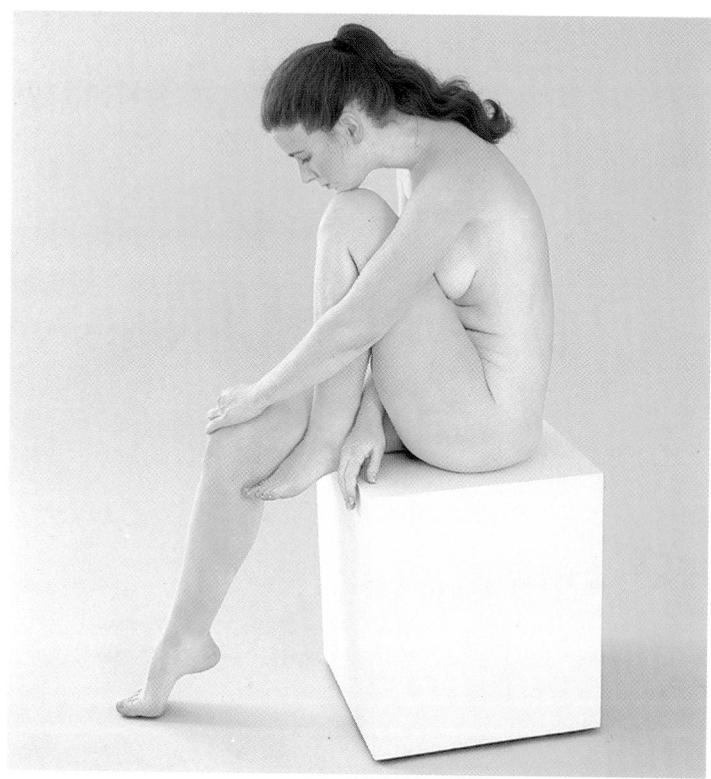

DeAndrea's MARLA and CLOTHED ARTIST WITH MODEL. DeAndrea casts his life-size *superrealist* figures, then paints them in minute detail.

Viewing these sculptures face to face can be unsettling. During a tour of the OK Harris gallery in New York City, a group of students was taken into a storeroom. Behind the huge racks of paintings they saw several unclothed models. The models appeared to be waiting to be cast by a sculptor, who seemed to be in the process of making a cast of a young woman. It took many seconds for the students to realize that all of the figures, including the sculptor in the plaster-covered blue jeans and his model, were actually sculptures rather than live people. By challenging perceptual assumptions, DeAndrea's work heightens awareness.

284 John DeAndrea. MARLA. 1986. Oil on polyvinyl. 44" × 16" × 32". Collection of Laila and Thurston Twigg-Smith, Honolulu. Photograph courtesy of Carlo Lamagna Gallery, New York.

Carving

Carving away unwanted material to form a sculpture is a *subtractive* process. Michelangelo preferred this method. Close observation of his chisel marks on the surfaces of the unfinished awakening slave reveals the steps he took toward increasingly refined cutting—even before he had roughed out the proportions of the figure from all sides. Because Michelangelo left this piece in an unfinished state, it seems as though we are looking over his shoulder midway through the carving process. For him, the act of making sculpture was a process of releasing the form he had seen in his mind's eye from within the block of stone. This is one of four unfinished figures of slaves that Michelangelo abandoned in various stages.

Carving is the most difficult of the three basic sculptural methods because it is a one-way technique that provides little or no opportunity to correct errors. Before beginning to cut, the sculptor must visualize all angles of the finished form within the original block of material. Examples of Michelangelo's finished carvings are his DAVID on page 352 and his early PIETÀ on page 102.

In Ernst Barlach's MAN DRAWING HIS SWORD, the strength of the figure is enhanced by the emphasis on the expressive mass of the material. Barlach retained the massive quality of the heavy blocks of wood that were first joined and then carved to produce MAN DRAWING HIS SWORD. Chisel marks left on the surface add textural interest and draw the viewer into the carving process. Despite its modest size, the piece has a monumental presence.

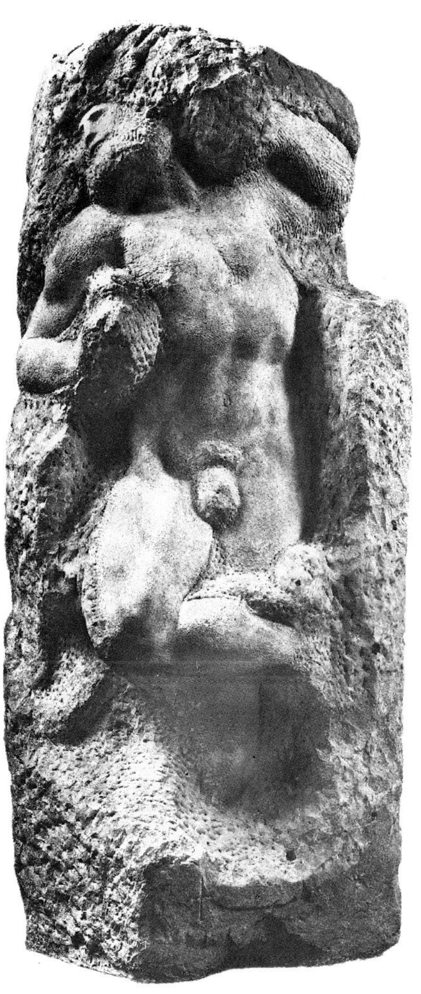

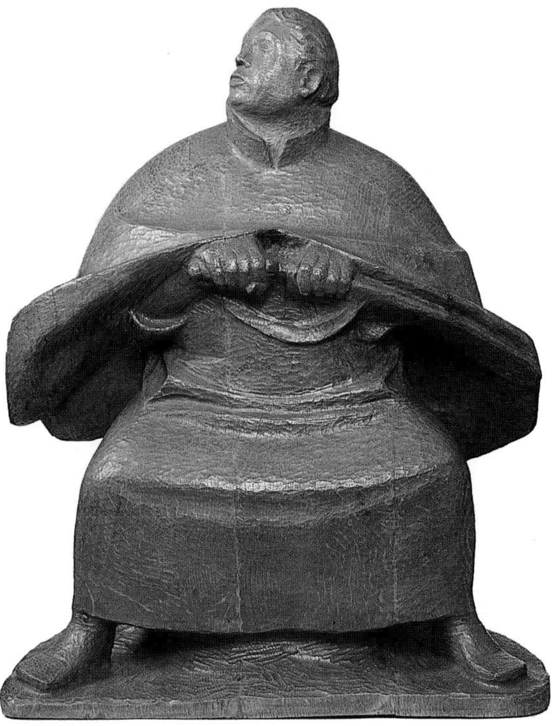

285 Michelangelo Buonarroti.
THE AWAKENING SLAVE.
1530-1534.
Marble. Height 9'.
Academy Gallery, Florence.

286 Ernst Barlach.
MAN DRAWING HIS SWORD.
1911.
Wood. Height 31".
Ernst Barlach Haus, Hamburg, West Germany.

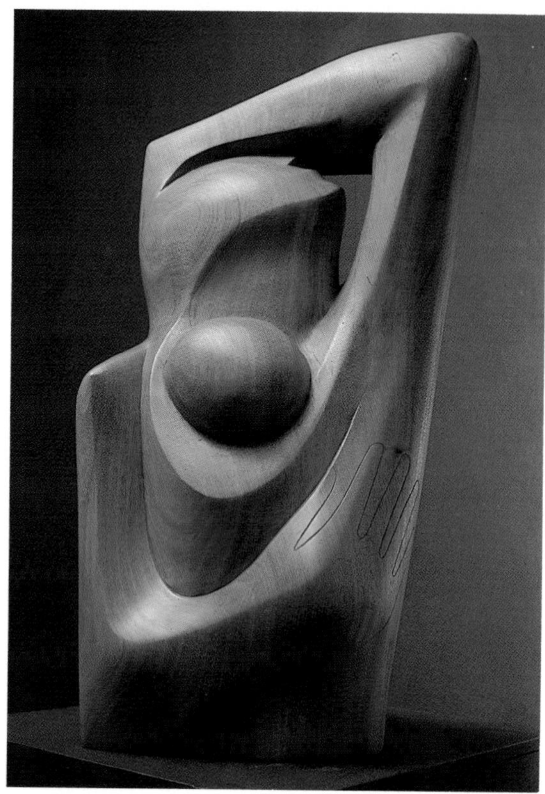

287 Elizabeth Catlett.
MOTHER AND CHILD #2. 1971.
Walnut. Height 38".
Collection of Alan Swift. Photograph courtesy of Samella Lewis.

Contemporary artist Elizabeth Catlett's carved MOTHER AND CHILD is an expression of an artist who is also a mother. The gesture of the mother suggests anguish, perhaps over the struggles all mothers know each child will face. Both figures have been abstracted to their essence in a composition of bold sweeping curves and simplified shapes. Solidity of the mass is relieved by the open space between the uplifted chin and raised elbow and by the convex and concave surfaces. A subtle carved line indicating the mother's right hand accents the surface of the abstract form. The matte-finished smooth wood invites the viewer to touch.

Constructing and Assembling

Before the present century, the major sculpturing techniques were modeling, carving, and casting. After Picasso constructed his Cubist GUITAR in 1912 (see page 421), *assembling* methods became popular. Such works are called *constructions.*

In the late 1920s, Spaniard Julio Gonzalez pioneered the use of the welding torch for cutting and welding metal sculpture. The invention of oxyacetylene welding in 1895 had provided the necessary tool for welded metal sculpture, but it took three decades for artists to realize the new tool's potential. Gonzalez had learned welding while working briefly in the Renault automobile factory. After several decades—and limited success—as a painter, Gonzalez began assisting Picasso with the construction of metal sculpture. Subsequently Gonzalez committed himself to sculpture and began to create his strongest, most original work. In 1932 he wrote:

> *The Age of Iron began many centuries ago by producing very beautiful objects, unfortunately mostly weapons. Today it makes possible bridges and railroads as well. It is time that this material cease to be a murderer and the simple instrument of an overly mechanical science. The door is wide open, at last! for this material to be forged and hammered by the peaceful hands of artists.*[2]

Gonzalez welded iron rods to construct his linear abstraction MATERNITY. It is airy and playful. In

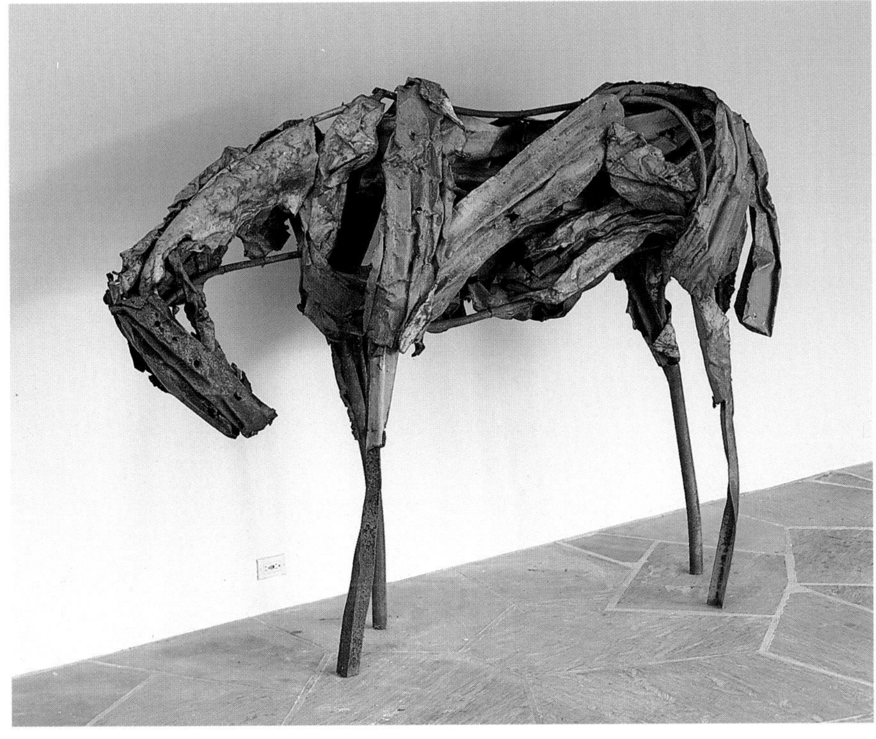

288 Deborah Butterfield.
NAHELE. 1986.
Scrap metal. 72" × 102" × 39".
Courtesy The Contemporary Museum, Honolulu.
Photograph: Brad Goda.

289 Julio Gonzalez.
MATERNITY. 1934.
Welded iron. Height 49⅞".
Tate Gallery, London.

290 Julio Gonzalez.
THE MONTSERRAT. 1936-1937.
Sheet iron. Height 5'5".
Stedelijk Museum, Amsterdam.

contrast, THE MONTSERRAT, created a few years later, is a much more representational figure. The title, after Catalonia's holy mountain, suggests that the figure is a symbol of Spanish will and resistance to Nazi aggression.

The direct metalworking technique was quickly adapted by other leading sculptors, including Alexander Calder and David Smith (see pages 210 and 456). Smith, an early practitioner of metal construction, used such industrial materials as I-beams, pipes, and rolled metal plates as raw materials, and he adopted industrial methods of fabrication.

Since the 1970s, Deborah Butterfield has created figures of horses from found materials such as sticks and scrap metal. Much of Butterfield's time is spent on a ranch in Montana where she trains and rides horses and makes sculpture. Painted, crumpled, rusted pieces of metal certainly seem an unlikely choice for expressing a light-footed animal, yet Butterfield's NAHELE and other abstract horses have a surprisingly lifelike presence. The artist intends her sculpture to *feel* like horses rather than simply look like them. The old car bodies used for

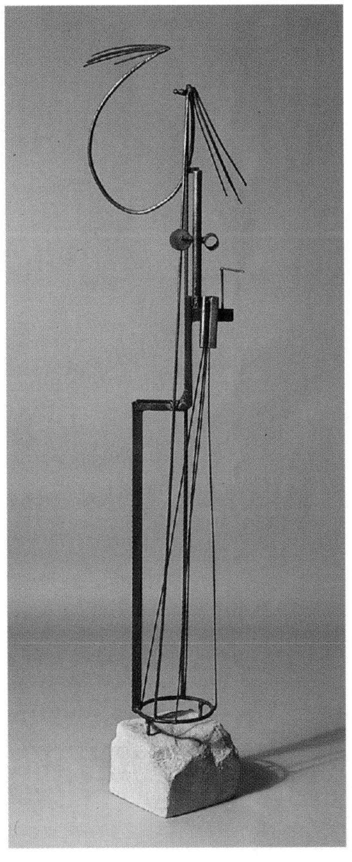

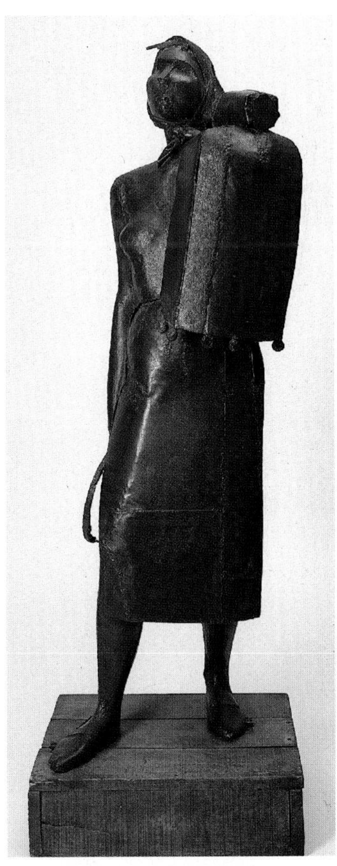

many of her welded and wired metal horses add a note of irony: the horseless carriage becomes a horse.

For some works, sculptors assemble preexisting objects so that their original identities are still apparent, yet radically changed by the new context. This subcategory of constructed sculpture is called *assemblage.* In Picasso's BULL'S HEAD, the creative process has been distilled to a single leap of imagination.

One day I found in a pile of jumble an old bicycle saddle next to some rusted handle bars.... In a flash they were associated in my mind.... The idea of this Bull's Head came without my thinking of it ... I had only to solder them together....[3]

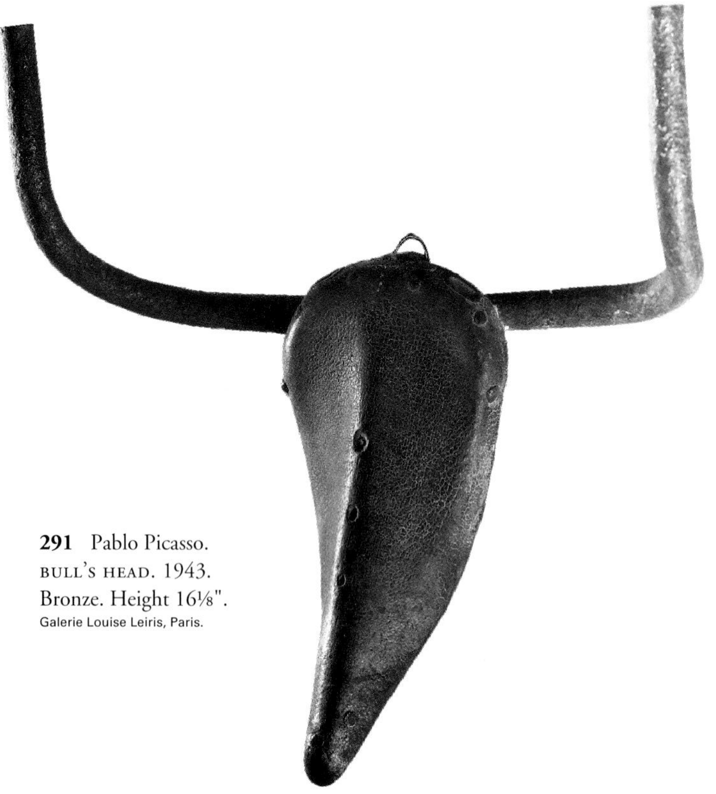

291 Pablo Picasso.
BULL'S HEAD. 1943.
Bronze. Height 16⅛".
Galerie Louise Leiris, Paris.

Almost anyone could have done the work of putting them together, yet the idea for the piece came from Picasso's active imagination. This metamorphosis of ordinary manufactured objects into animal form and spirit is magical. The final piece was cast in bronze to give it unity and durability.

What is wonderful about bronze is that it can give the most incongruous objects such a unity that it's sometimes difficult to identify the elements that make them up. But it's also a danger: if you only see the bull's head and not the saddle and handlebars from which it is made, the sculpture loses its interest.[4]

Today's artists frequently use a variety of media within a single work. Rather than present a long, awkward list of materials, artists often identify such combinations as "mixed media." The media involved may be all two-dimensional, all three-dimensional, or a mixture of the two.

Marisol is a sculptor who incorporates drawing and painting in her pieces. The mother and children in THE FAMILY are seen as if sitting for a family photograph. With humble materials, Marisol presents the dignity of ordinary folks. The combination of actual commonplace objects, such as

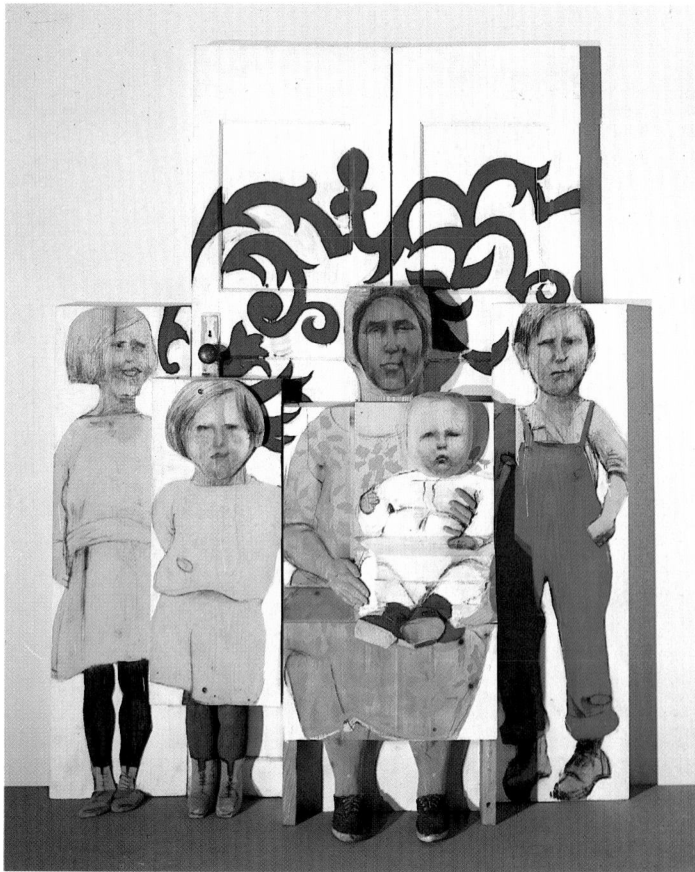

292 Marisol. THE FAMILY. 1962.
Painted wood and other materials in three sections.
6'10⅝" × 65½".
The Museum of Modern Art, New York. Advisory Committee Fund.

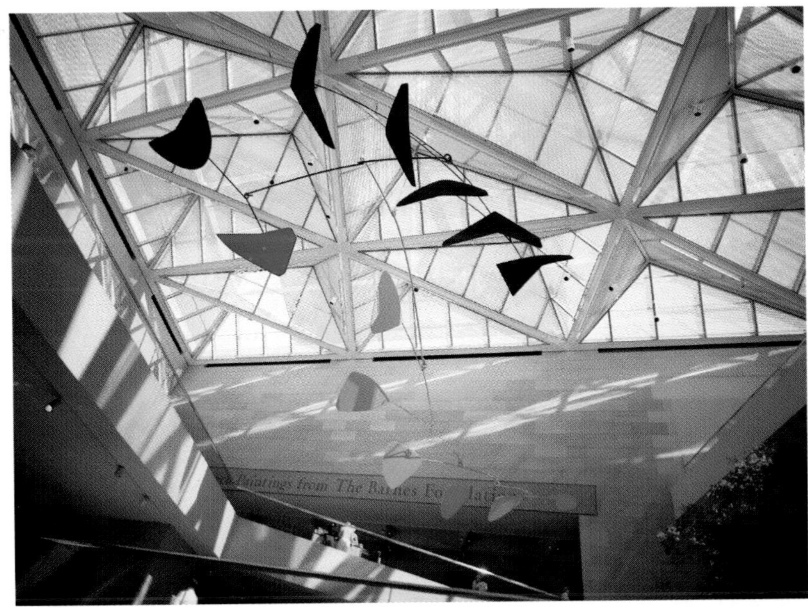

293 Alexander Calder.
UNTITLED. 1976.
Painted aluminum and tempered steel.
29'10½" × 76'.

shoes and doors, with careful carpentry, carving, casting, drawing, and painting, is typical of Marisol's work.

KINETIC SCULPTURE

Alexander Calder was among the first to explore the possibilities of *kinetic sculpture*, or sculpture that moves. Marcel Duchamp christened Calder's kinetic sculptures *mobiles*—a word Duchamp had coined for his own work in 1914 (see page 458). Sculptors' traditional emphasis on mass is replaced in Calder's work by a focus on shape, space, and movement (see page 200). By 1932, he was designing inventive wire and sheet-metal constructions. Calder's huge UNTITLED mobile is the centerpiece of the contemporary wing of the National Gallery of Art in Washington; its slow, graceful movement is caused by natural air currents within the building.

The humorous, motorized work of Jim Jenkins contrasts with Calder's air-activated mobiles. In COORDINATED PROGRAMMING, the hands simultaneously pat the "head" and rub the "stomach." Because the piece is hung from the ceiling with cables, the motion of the hands causes the whole "figure" to twist and turn. The piece evokes thoughts about our "dance" with technology. Do we control technology, or does it control us?

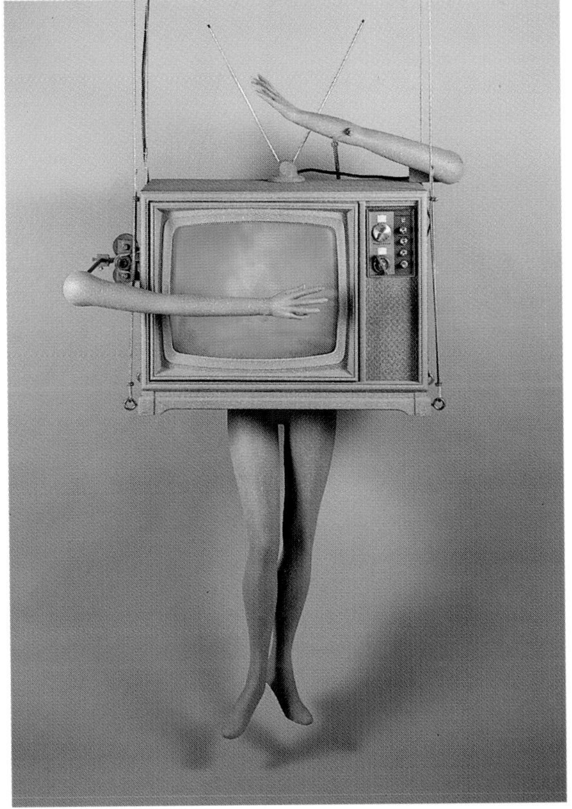

294 Jim Jenkins.
COORDINATED PROGRAMMING. 1987.
Television, mannequin limbs, and motor. 6' × 4' × 3'.
Photograph: Jeff Atherton. Courtesy of the artist.

ALEXANDER CALDER (1898–1976)

As a child, Alexander Calder made toys for his little sister and friends out of bits of wire, wood, and other odds and ends. This playful inventiveness never left him, and it leads viewers to see his mature sculptures as visual toys for adults. No other description quite explains the sense of well-being his sculptures can produce.

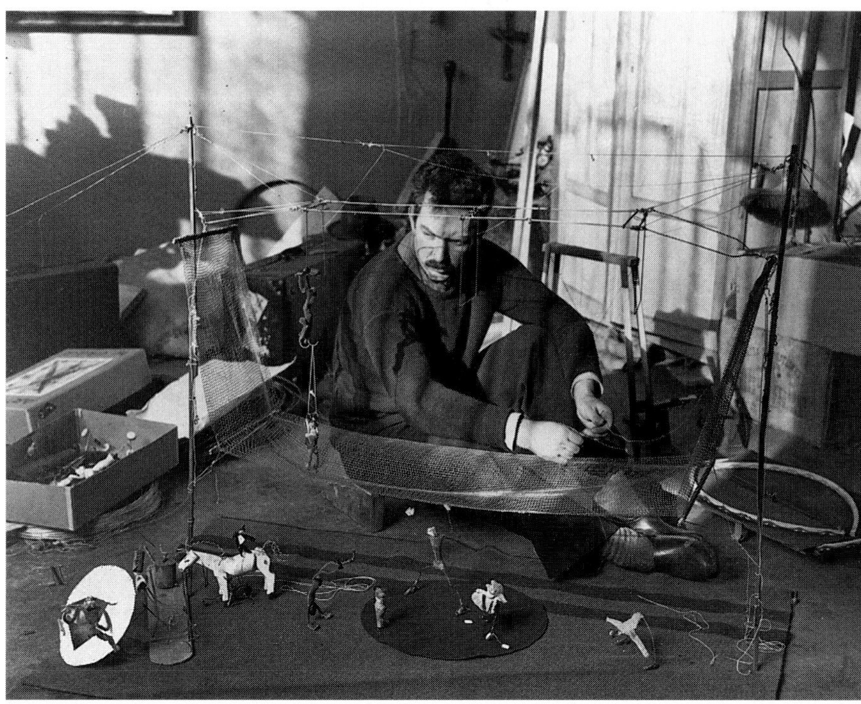

295 ALEXANDER CALDER. 1929.
Photograph: Andre Kertész.

Alexander (Sandy) Calder was born in Lawton, Pennsylvania. His father and grandfather were both sculptors—you can see their work outdoors in many American cities. His mother was a painter. As artists, they encouraged creativity in their children, and young Sandy had his own workshop at home.

Despite his upbringing among artists, Calder decided on a career as an engineer, earning a degree from Stevens Institute of Technology in New Jersey. But after he had been out of school for a few years, he felt the urge to start drawing again. He studied at the Art Students League in New York, then in 1925 he went to Paris, the center of energy for new art at the time.

Calder first enchanted others with his delightful wire sculptures, whimsical three-dimensional drawings of animals and entertainers (see page 48). Perhaps his best-loved wire work is a grand troupe of circus performers and animals. Today CIRCUS is in a museum, in a glass case where it can't be touched. But the artist used to treat his friends to gala performances, complete with music and lights, announcing each act like a ringmaster and putting his wire performers through their paces. Life, play, and art all ran together in Calder's world.

A 1930 visit to Piet Mondrian (see page 438) opened Calder's eyes to the possibilities of abstraction. "I liked his paintings well enough," the sculptor later recalled. "But those little black or colored rectangles—I should have liked to see them move."[5] From this insight he developed his famous *mobiles*—delicately balanced constellations of metal discs on wires that move in the breeze or at a touch.

Calder became one of the most popular artists of his day. He married happily and had two daughters, one of whom carries on the family artistic tradition as a children's book illustrator. His time was divided between a farmhouse in France and one in Connecticut, and from his huge barnlike studios there emerged a long and joyous series of mobiles, stabiles (stationary constructions), paintings, jewelry, stage sets, and designs for tapestries and rugs.

Today Calder's large sculptures can be seen in many city squares and modern buildings. They have become a part of our daily lives, just as he wanted. "A sculpture must be as useful as signaling poles placed in sea-lanes and waterways, with their red discs, yellow squares, and black triangles," he said. "It must be designed as a real urban signal [as] well as a sculpture."[6] Calder's sculptures beam a strong signal of freedom and delight into modern life.

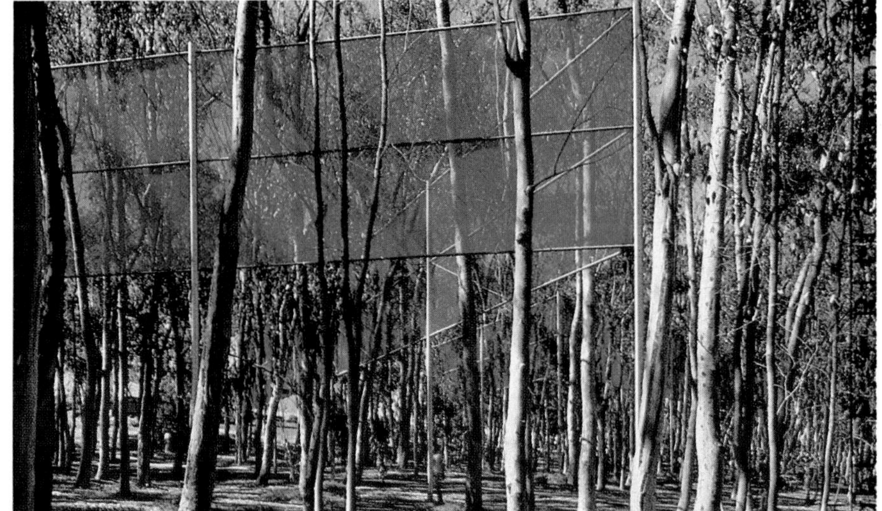

296 Robert Irwin.
TWO RUNNING VIOLET V FORMS.
University of California, San Diego. 1983.
Steel chain-link fencing with blue-violet plastic coating mounted on 5" diameter stainless steel poles.
Height 25'.
Stuart Foundation Sculpture Collection.
Photograph courtesy of the artist.

SITE-SPECIFIC SCULPTURE

Sculpture designed for a particular place—called *site-specific*—has become a major type of contemporary art. Many artists have sought to move beyond the limitations of sculpture as portable, collectible commodities and sculpture on pedestals, such as statues of historic figures. In addition, commissions for art in public places usually involve designing permanent works for specific locations. The best of site-specific sculpture interacts with its location in such a complete and complementary way that the surroundings become part of the piece and the sculpture helps define the character of the place.

Robert Irwin moves beyond the physical presence of an isolated form, often assumed to be the chief characteristic of sculpture. In his TWO RUNNING VIOLET V FORMS installation in a eucalyptus grove on the campus of the University of California at San Diego, the form itself is not the center of attention but the vehicle for noticing the ever-changing light and color moods of the site.

Herbert Bayer and Robert Smithson (see page 466) have worked with the environment on a large scale. Each of their earth sculptures *(earthworks)* uses materials from its surrounding area and is conceived in terms of the character of the site.

Herbert Bayer's MILL CREEK CANYON EARTHWORKS, commissioned by King County, Washington, is one of a number of sculpted landscapes designed, in part, to restore areas damaged by environmental abuse. Beginning with a stream, a marshy area, and the intriguing spaces of a natural canyon, Bayer designed a park space that solves a drainage problem. Sculpted grass mounds, a circular pond, interconnecting paths and bridges, and the existing stream invite playful activities and provide a refreshing retreat for people of all ages.

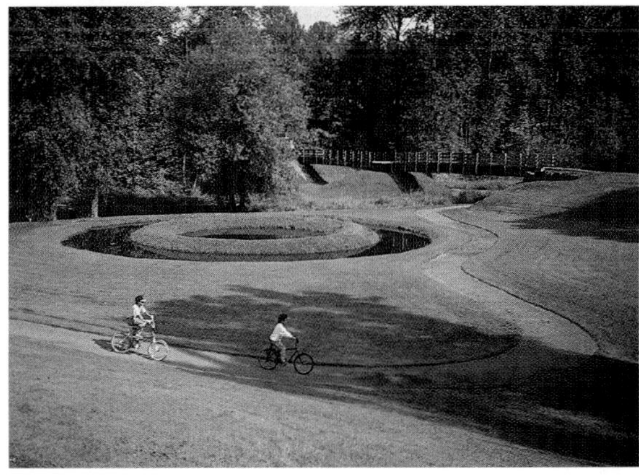

297 Herbert Bayer.
Detail of MILL CREEK CANYON EARTHWORKS.
Kent, Washington. 1979-1982.

Although of great interest to today's artists, the idea of site-specific sculptural forms is not entirely new. One of the world's most impressive site-specific installations is the prehistoric monument at STONEHENGE (see page 7). Another site-specific work is the VIETNAM WAR MEMORIAL shown on page 493.

CHAPTER 13

Crafts: Traditional and Contemporary

Crafts were an integral part of daily life from prehistoric times until the Industrial Revolution in the mid-eighteenth century. Today it is hard to imagine a time when all utensils, furnishings, and tools necessary for the sustenance of daily life were handmade by those who would use them or by skilled craftsworkers (artisans).

In traditional societies, such as that of the N'DEBELE VILLAGE in South Africa, and others in Africa and Indonesia, crafts are still an integral part of daily life, and the close relationship between user, maker, and individual object continues. In industrialized societies such as ours, however, this relationship has been lost. Machines have taken over the essential tasks of weaving cloth, making dishes, and fashioning metal utensils—with the vast majority of our everyday objects now produced by mechanical methods. Nevertheless, we can still derive satisfaction from using our own hands to make utilitarian objects, and we feel a related pleasure when we use something handmade.

Over the past several decades, a dramatic resurgence in the study and practice of traditional crafts has occurred, a trend often referred to as the Crafts Movement. In addition to revitalizing ceramics, weaving, and woodworking—historically the most widely practiced crafts—the movement has resurrected a variety of other crafts, particularly in metal, glass, and mixed media.

CRAFT AND ART

The line separating craft and art is difficult to trace. All art begins with craft, for if a work is not well made, there is little chance that we will experience it as art. Historically, few societies have seen crafts as separate or "minor arts" as we in the West have come to define them. In ancient Greece, for example, a painting on a vase was as highly esteemed as a wall painting (see page 322).

In order to grasp the art/craft relationship, imagine a long line—with *art* at one end and *craft* at the other. We can categorize as *art* those works in which concern for form and content are primary; we can identify as *craft* those works in which concern for process and materials are dominant. On this art/craft line, the distinction between a painting by Rembrandt and a coffee mug from a craft fair is clear. However, the distinctions grow blurred toward the center, where art and craft become intermingled. For example, innovative craft-based artists have succeeded in challenging the distinctions between sculpture made of stone and that made of clay or fiber (see page 224). Many contemporary artists and craftsworkers prefer to see the imaginary art/craft line as an open continuum, one in which the artist's intention is more important than his or her choice of technique and materials.

There are at least three general groups of craftspeople: (1) people without formal training, includ-

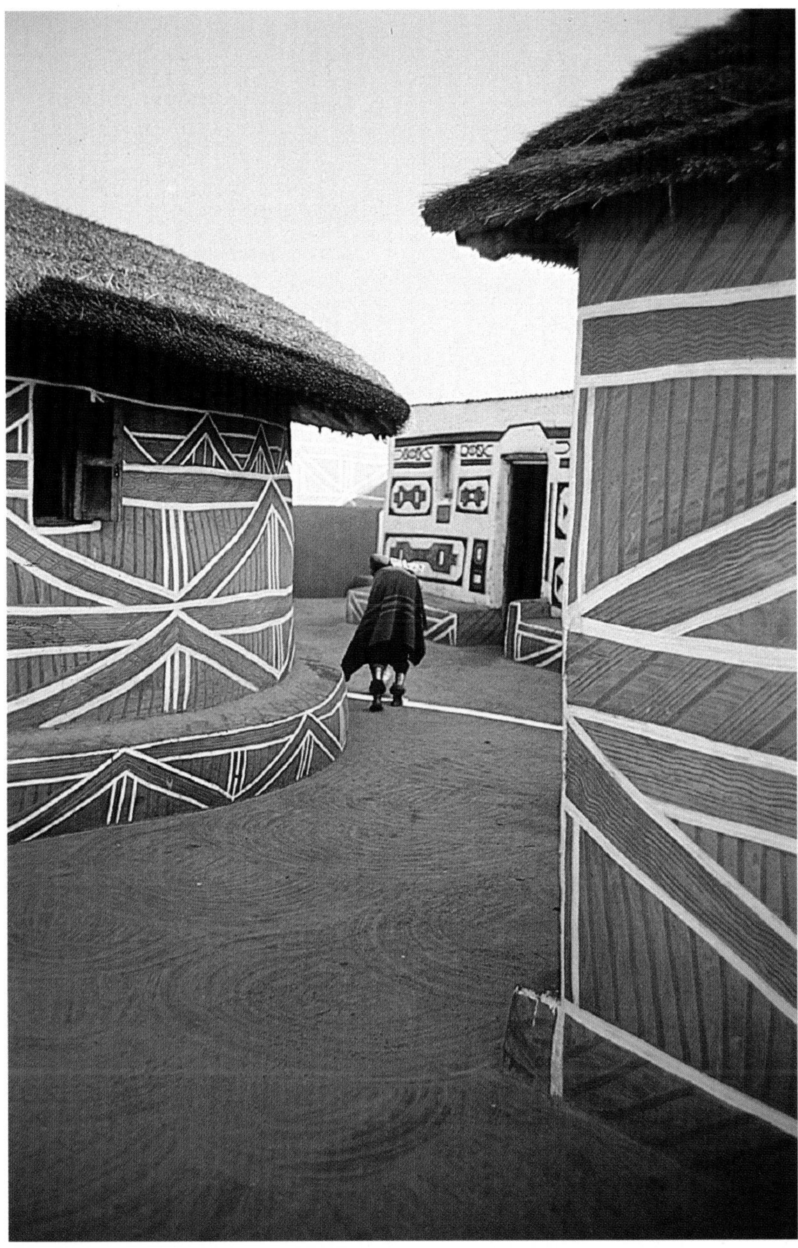

298 N'DEBELE VILLAGE, SOUTH AFRICA. 1960.
Photograph: Pete Turner.

ing folk artists (see pages 28-30) and amateurs, most of whom make things for pleasure rather than for income; (2) craftsworkers who make a living producing a marketable and recognizable "line" of items, such as handmade jewelry, clothing, or tableware; (3) craft artists, who use craft media to make one-of-a-kind objects of artistic merit, regardless of sales potential. Craft artists tend to lead the way in inventive design and innovative use of materials. Partly because of their success, there has been an increased mixing of media and techniques in nearly all areas of artistic expression during the last several decades.

As noted, industrialization has severed the direct contact between consumer and maker. Interestingly, it has also given new freedom to craft artists, allowing them to create objects without concern for quantity, economy, and practicality. In fact, industrialization has made it possible for craft artists to produce purely expressive rather than

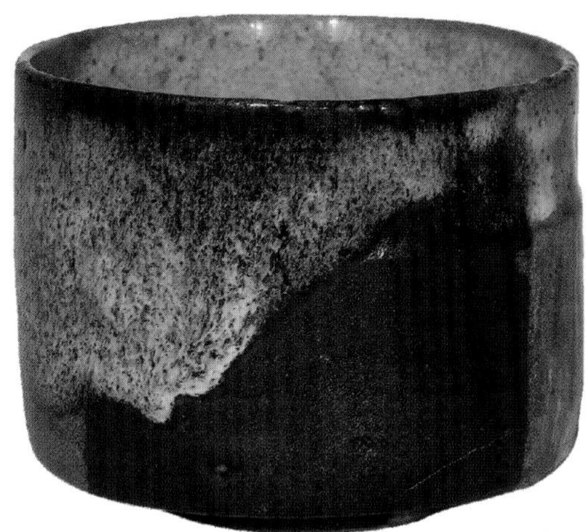

299 TEA BOWL. Satsuma ware. 17th century.
Diameter of mouth 10.7 cm.
Courtesy of the Freer Gallery of Art, Smithsonian Institution, Washington D.C.

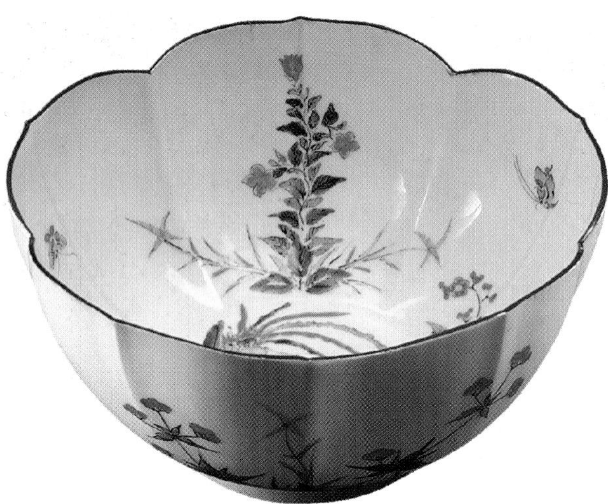

300 Kakiemon V.
BELL-FLOWER-SHAPED BOWL. 17th century.
Porcelain with overglaze enamels. Height 7.6 cm.
Stanford University Museum of Art (61.20). Gift of Mrs. Philip N. Lilienthal, Jr.

functional works. Today, much work in the traditional craft media has no function other than to evoke pleasure or to provoke thought—aims we usually associate only with the fine arts.

While we have no name for this new craft-as-art phenomenon, it is a continuing pleasure to see works in which form and content, medium and function become one—in which craft is undeniably art. Rather than worrying about labels, we should look for the work of those craft artists whose pieces radiate the kind of inner vitality found in the best handmade articles of pre-industrial times.

CLAY

Bits of broken clay pots found at archaeological sites provide valuable clues to thousands of years of human civilization. Clay has long been a valuable raw material. It offers flexibility of form and also provides relative permanence because of its capacity to harden when exposed to heat.

The art and science of making objects from clay is called *ceramics,* and a person who works with clay is called either a *potter* or a *ceramist.* A wide range of objects can be made of fired clay, including tableware, vases, bricks, sculpture, and many kinds of tiles. Most of the basic ceramic materials were discovered, and processes developed, thousands of years ago.

The ceramic process is relatively simple. Potters create functional pots or purely sculptural forms from soft, damp clay using hand-building methods such as slab, coil, or pinching, or by *throwing*—that is, by shaping clay on a rapidly revolving wheel. Invented in Mesopotamia about six thousand years ago, the potter's wheel allows potters to produce circular forms with great speed and uniformity. In the hands of a skilled worker, the process looks effortless, almost magical, but it takes time and practice to perfect one's technique.

After being shaped, a piece is allowed to dry thoroughly. Next it is *fired* in a *kiln*—a kind of oven where heat transforms the clay chemically into a hard, stonelike substance.

To decorate ceramics, glazes are often used. A *glaze* is a specially formulated liquid "clay paint"

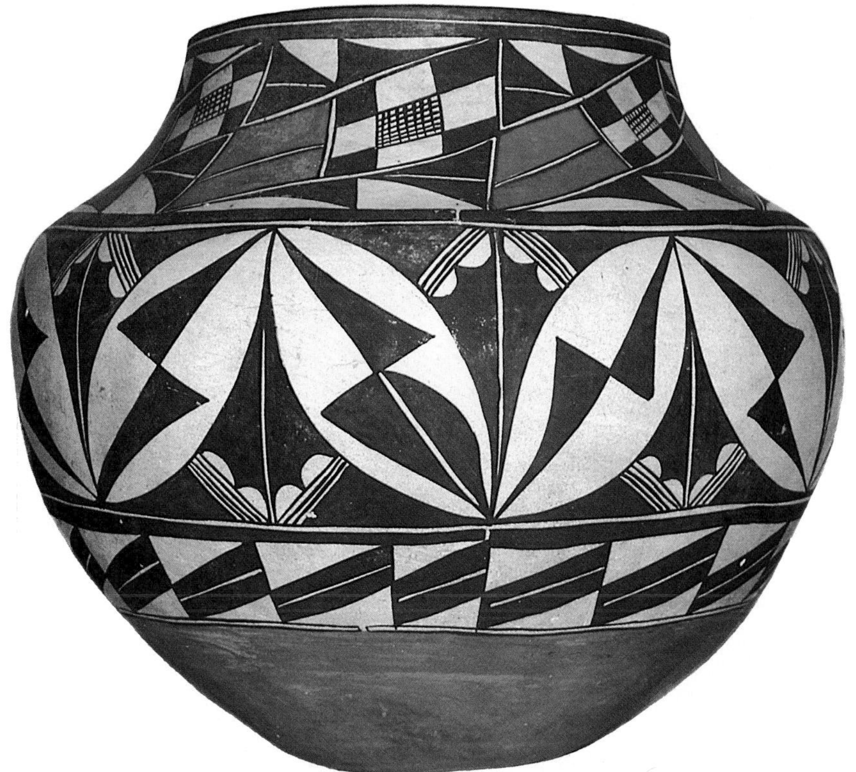

301 Maria Chino.
CEREMONIAL WATER JAR. 1927.
White clay, decoration in black and red.
11¼" × 13½".
Honolulu Academy of Arts.
Gift of Mrs. Charles M. Cooke, Sr.

with a silica base. During firing, the glaze vitrifies (turns to a glasslike substance) and fuses with the clay body, creating a nonporous surface. Glazes can be colored or clear, translucent or opaque, glossy or dull, depending on their chemical composition.

Two seventeenth-century Japanese bowls, a TEA BOWL and a BELL-FLOWER-SHAPED BOWL, illustrate the extreme contrast in style that can occur when widely differing values, techniques, and materials are applied to the making of objects with similar functions. The TEA BOWL, inspired by the Japanese tea ceremony, is of stoneware. Stoneware clays contain impurities (including some that impart color) that cause them to be used for making unrefined wares. Earthy spontaneity, including graceful, unanticipated glaze drips, is highly valued by tea masters. In contrast, the porcelain BELL-FLOWER-SHAPED BOWL is delicate and fragile-looking and appears to have taken a long time to make. Porcelain is made with a pure, fine-grained, translucent clay body. Both pieces are fine traditional examples, yet they express greatly contrasting approaches and appeal to very different tastes.

Some present-day potters use ancient methods, firing their pots in open fires that reach only low and generally varied temperatures. Maria Chino of Acoma Pueblo in New Mexico made this CEREMONIAL WATER JAR using the methods of her ancestors. Traditionally, the making of such an Acoma vessel takes four or five days, during which the artist eats and sleeps very little. During this process, the soul of the artist is said to be united with the spirit of the pot. Chino hand-built this pot using thick coils, smoothing each one as she added it. She applied the unglazed design using red and black oxides, leaving some areas of white clay exposed. The motifs are her own. Breaks in the bands that separate the upper and lower portions of the design provide openings for the spirit after the work was completed.

In the mid-1950s, Peter Voulkos brought craft tradition together with art expression and thus extended the horizons of both art and craft. He and a group of his students led the California sculpture movement that broke through preconceptions about limits of clay as a medium for sculpture. With his rebellious spirit, Voulkos revitalized ceramic art and helped touch off new directions in other craft media. His monumental GALLAS ROCK brings the emotional energy of Abstract Expressionist painting (see pages 452–454) to three-dimensional form.

Both Peter Voulkos and Toshiko Takaezu were influenced by the earthiness and spontaneity of some traditional Japanese ceramics, such as the TEA BOWL, as well as by expressionist painting, yet they have taken very different directions. Voulkos's pieces are rough and aggressively dynamic, while Takaezu's CERAMIC FORMS offer subtle, restrained strength. Takaezu's sculptural forms become the foundation for rich paintings of glaze and oxide. She reflects on her love of the clay medium:

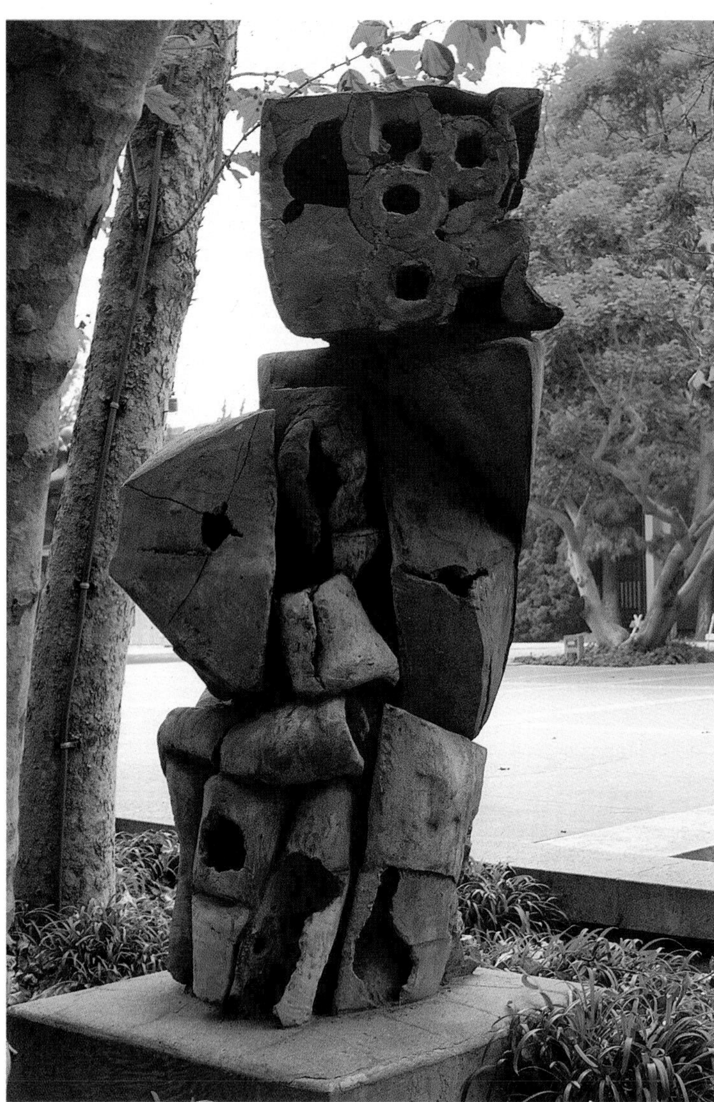

302 Peter Voulkos.
GALLAS ROCK. 1960.
Glazed ceramic. Height 6'.
University of California at Los Angeles.

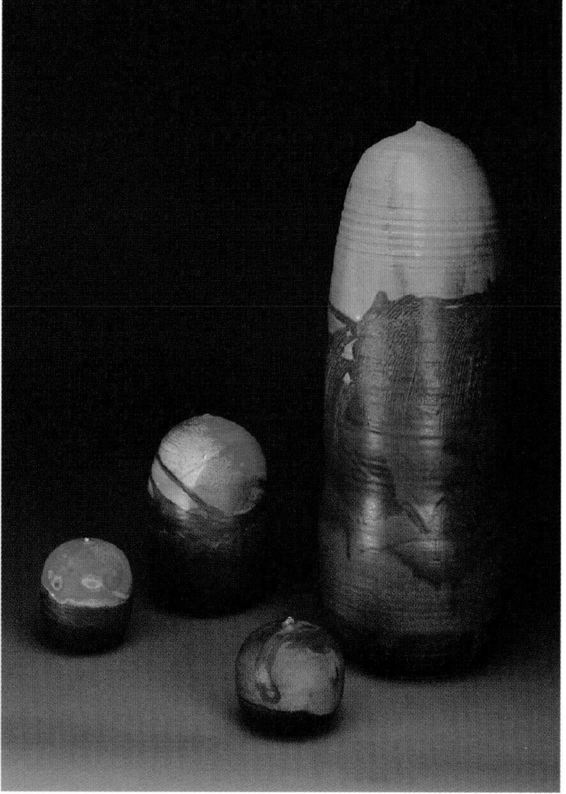

303 Toshiko Takaezu.
CERAMIC FORMS. 1986.
Stoneware.
Photograph: Macario, Kaneohe, Hawaii.

When working with clay I take pleasure from the process as well as from the finished piece. Every once in a while I am in tune with the clay, and I hear music, and it's like poetry. Those are the moments that make pottery truly beautiful for me.[1]

Robert Arneson considered all art self-portraiture, and he underscored his assertion by creating many whimsical images of himself. He made CALIFORNIA ARTIST in response to an attack on his work by a New York critic who said that, because of California's spiritual and cultural impoverishment, Arneson's work could have no serious depth or meaning. Arneson's life-size ceramic self-portrait has holes in place of eyes, revealing an empty head. The artist depicted himself as a combination biker and aging hippie—complete with the appropriate cliches on and around the base. Those who think that clay is only for making bricks and dinnerware were acknowledged by Arneson, who put his name on the bricks, as any other brickmaker would. Arneson stated his point of view:

I like art that has humor, with irony and playfulness. I want to make "high" art that is outrageous, while revealing the human condition which is not always high.[2]

Until the twentieth century, ceramic processes evolved very slowly. In recent years, new formulations and even synthetic clays have become available. Other changes have included more accurate methods of firing and improved techniques and equipment. The most significant change has come in the use of clay as a conceptual and sculptural art medium. Broadening attitudes regarding the possibilities of clay have helped open up thinking about the expressive potential of other traditional materials.

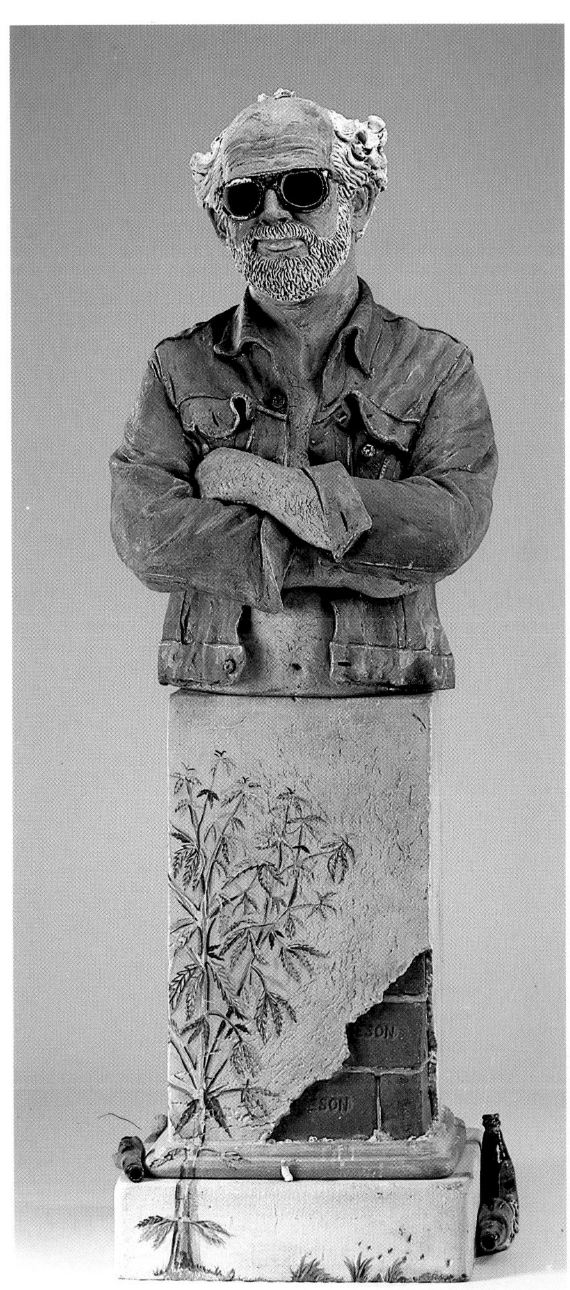

304 Robert Arneson.
CALIFORNIA ARTIST. 1982.
Glazed ceramic. 78" × 28" × 21".
San Francisco Museum of Modern Art.

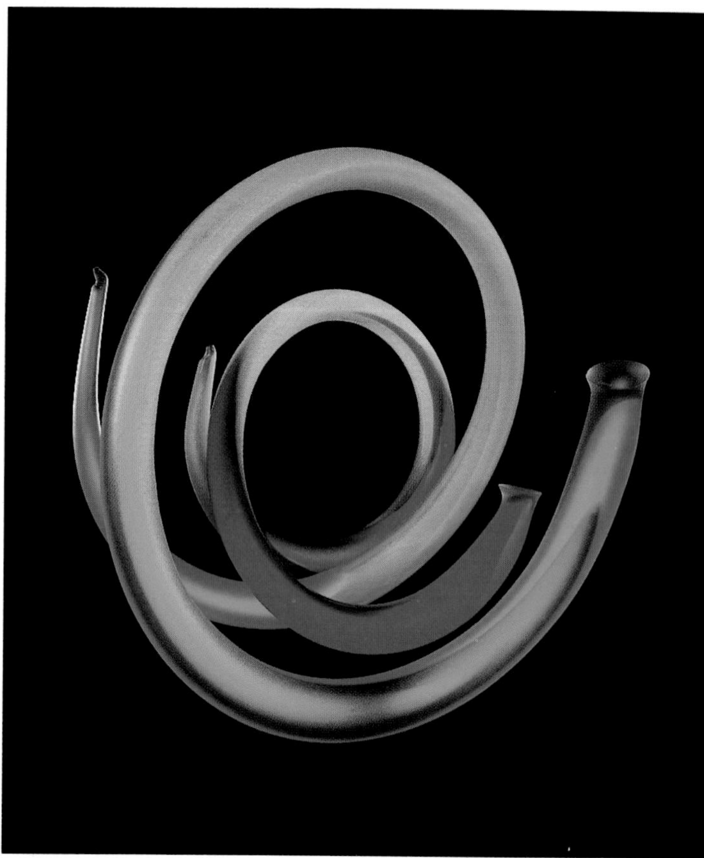

305 Paul Seide.
FROSTED RADIO LIGHT from the SPIRAL SERIES. 1986.
Blown and manipulated glass, charged with neon and mercury vapor from a transmitted radio field.
48.4 cm × 53.5 cm.
The Corning Museum of Glass. Part gift of Mike Belkin.

GLASS

Glass is an exotic and enticing art medium. Chemically, glass is closely related to ceramic glaze. As a medium, however, it offers a wide range of possibilities that are unique to glass. Hot or molten glass is a sensitive, amorphous material that is shaped by blowing, casting, or pressing into molds. As it cools, glass solidifies from its molten state without crystalizing. After it is blown or cast, glass may be cut, etched, fused, laminated, layered, leaded, painted, polished, sandblasted, or slumped (softened for a controlled sag). The fluid nature of glass produces qualities of mass flowing into line as well as translucent volumes of airy thinness.

Glass has been used for at least four thousand years as a material for practical containers of all shapes and sizes. During the Middle Ages, stained glass was used extensively in Gothic churches and cathedrals (see page 341). Glass is also a fine medium for decorative inlays in a variety of objects including jewelry. Elaborate blown-glass pieces have been made in Venice since the Renaissance.

Because our primary contact with glass is with utilitarian objects such as food and beverage containers, mirrors, and windows, we often overlook the fact that glass is an excellent sculptural material. Although it is said that the character of any material determines the character of the expression, this is particularly true of glass. Molten glass requires considerable speed and skill in handling. The glassblower combines the centering skills of a potter, the agility and stamina of an athlete, and the grace of a dancer to bring qualities of breath and movement into crystalline form.

Dynamic line, light, and vibrant color unite to tease the senses in Paul Seide's FROSTED RADIO LIGHT. Between years of study at the University of Wisconsin, Seide learned the technology of vacuum bombardment and pumped ionized rare gases at Egan Neon Glassblowing School in New York. While in the city, he gained an appreciation for the art of our era, particularly Fauve color and the linear energy of Pollock's paintings (see pages 412 and 451). Seide creates his light sculptures by blowing glass tube forms and filling them with rare gases, each originating its own color frequency when electrically activated.

The fluid and translucent qualities of glass are used to the fullest in Dale Chihuly's SEAFORM SERIES. Chihuly produces such pieces with a team of glass artists working under his direction. In this series, he arranges groups of pieces and carefully directs the lighting to suggest delicate undersea environments. Chihuly—artist, teacher, and entrepreneur—founded the Pilchuck Glass School, the primary force in making the Seattle area one of the world's largest centers for glass art.

Although it can take years to master the techniques of glass, the search is for significant expressive form. As with other media, technique is something nearly anyone can learn, but the art is in how the technique is used. Glass is so seductive and intriguing that some lesser artists never get beyond the beauty of the material itself.

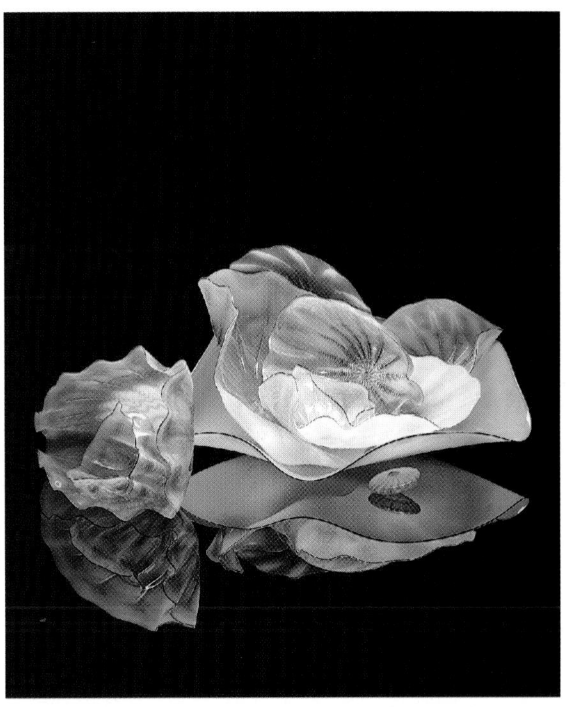

306 Dale Chihuly.
MAUVE SEAFORM SET WITH BLACK LIP WRAPS from the SEAFORM SERIES. 1985.
Blown glass.
Courtesy of Chihuly Studio.
Photograph: Dick Busher.

METAL

Metal's primary characteristics are strength and formability. The types of metal most often used for sculpture can be hammered, cut, drawn out, welded, joined with rivets, or cast. Early metalsmiths created tools, vessels, armor, and weapons.

Perhaps the largest number of craft artists using metal today are those who make jewelry. Contemporary jewelry often combines unusual materials with more traditional metals and precious stones. The best examples can be appreciated as miniature sculpture.

Mark Pierce is among the many craft artists who have recently explored new materials and techniques. Pierce invents jewelry forms by merging his experience as a painter with his work as a jewelry designer. Through research, Pierce developed the polymer-aluminum process he uses for creating EARRINGS and other jewelry.

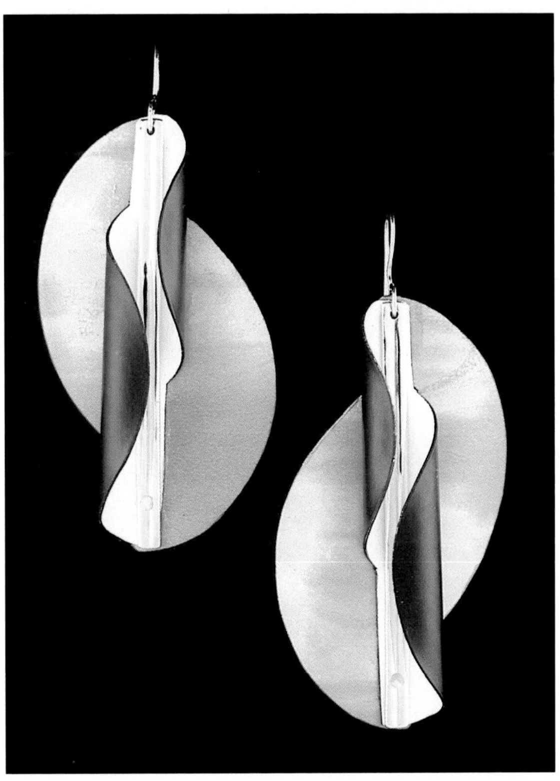

307 Mark Pierce.
EARRINGS. 1982.
Polished brass and luminar.
2¼" × 1⅜" × ½".
Courtesy of the artist.

The shapes, patterns, and contrasting size relationships make the PRE-COLUMBIAN PENDANT memorable for both the intensity of its highly unified design and its rich details. The boldness of the piece gives it a monumentality that belies its small size. In contrast, linear complexity and lyric, organic curves and spaces cause Albert Paley's large hand-wrought and forged GATE to appear delicate when seen in a small reproduction.

Paley began his metalworking career making jewelry and gradually shifted to larger pieces such as the GATE, commissioned for the entrance of the Renwick Gallery museum shop. Few artists today possess the technical skill required to forge red-hot iron. Paley enjoys handling a material that physically resists him. Whether he is working on small pieces or large ones, Paley employs a variety of metals, woven together in harmonious interplay. A lively relationship between lines and spaces creates the high energy of his ornamental gates. The curves—revealing Art Nouveau influence (see page 113)—have the sensual fluidity of hot pliable metal, while the center verticals recall the rigid strength of iron and steel. Bundles of straight lines unify and solidify the composition. The twelve-hundred-pound Renwick GATE took Paley and his assistant seven months to complete.

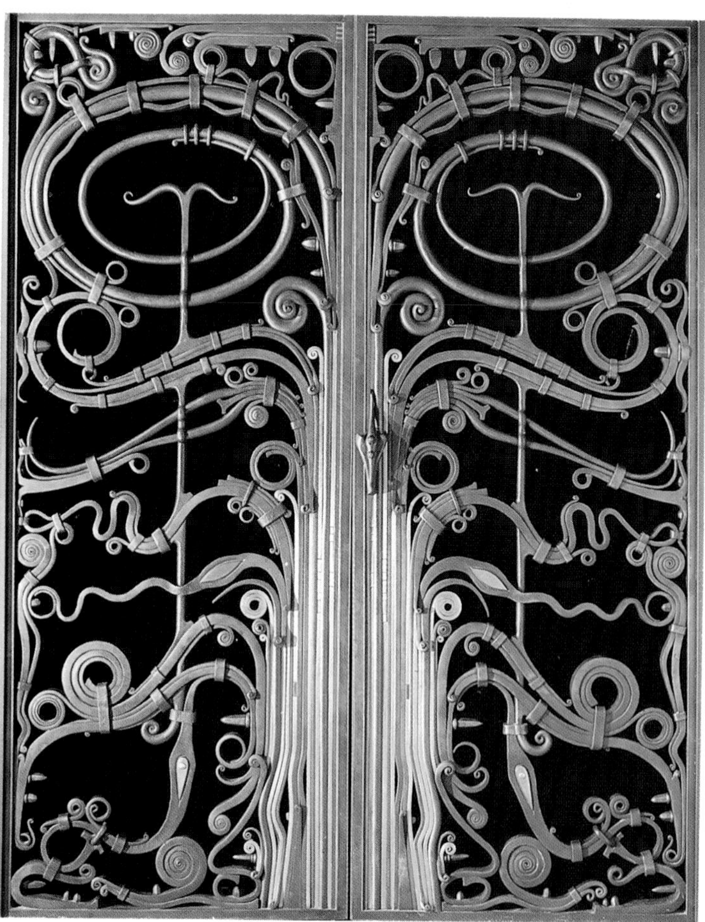

308 Albert Paley.
GATE. 1974.
Steel, brass, copper, hand-wrought and forged.
90¾" × 72".
National Museum of American Art, Smithsonian Institution, Washington, D.C. Commissioned for the Renwick Gallery (1975.117.1).

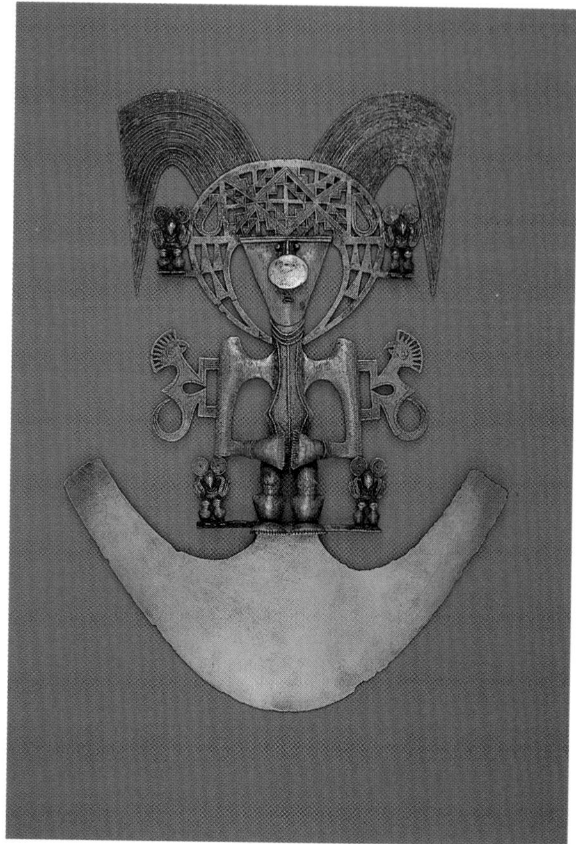

309 PRE-COLUMBIAN PENDANT.
Cast in a gold-copper alloy, gilded.
Copyright British Museum, London.

WOOD

The living spirit of wood is given a second life in craft forms. Growth characteristics of individual trees remain visible in the grain of wood long after the trees are cut, giving wood a vitality not found in other materials. Its abundance, versatility, and warm tactile qualities have made wood a favored material for human use.

In his bowl forms, Bob Stocksdale celebrates the natural colors, textural patterns, and grains of various woods. As he shapes the TURNED WOOD BOWLS, contour and wall thickness are determined by his sensitivity to the particular character of each type and piece of wood. Stocksdale brings out the color variations and the grain that make each piece of wood unique.

Most furniture purchased today is produced by industrial mass-production methods. However, people with the skill to make their own—or enough money to buy custom-made pieces—can enjoy the rich experience of living with handcrafted furniture.

Sam Maloof makes unique pieces of furniture and repeats some designs he finds particularly satisfying. The ROCKING CHAIR and other designs Maloof creates express his love and understanding of wood and of the hand processes he uses to shape wood into furniture. Flowing curves in his ROCKING CHAIR reveal his sensitive melding of form and function. Although he employs assistants who help him to duplicate his best designs, he limits quantity. Because he enjoys knowing that each piece is cut, assembled, and finished according to his own standards, Maloof has rejected offers from manufacturers who want to mass-produce his designs. He prefers to retain quality control and the special characteristics that are inevitably lost when designs are factory-produced rather than handmade. Many pieces of furniture are pleasing to look at, and many are comfortable to use, but relatively few fulfill both functions so successfully.

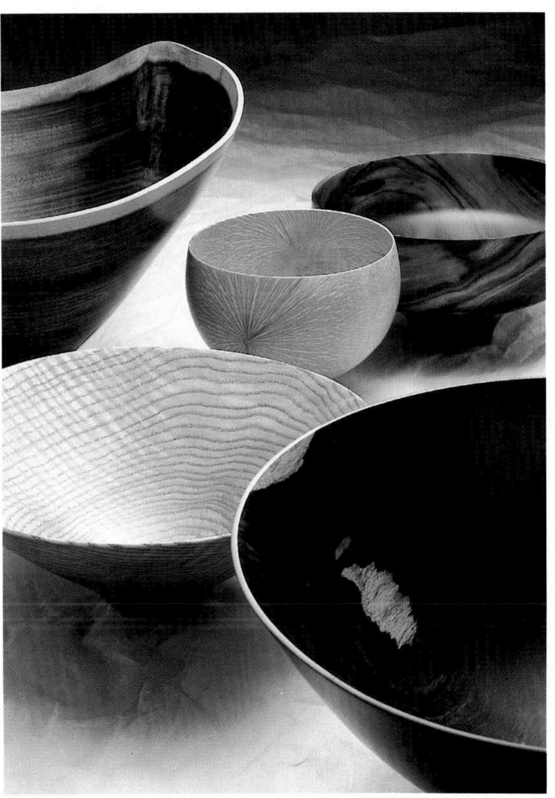

310 Bob Stocksdale.
TURNED WOOD BOWLS. 1982.
Clockwise from top right: ebony, 10¾" diameter; ash, 8½" diameter; blackwood, 11¼" diameter; macadamia, 4½" diameter; ironwood, 6½" diameter.
Photograph: Nora Scarlett.

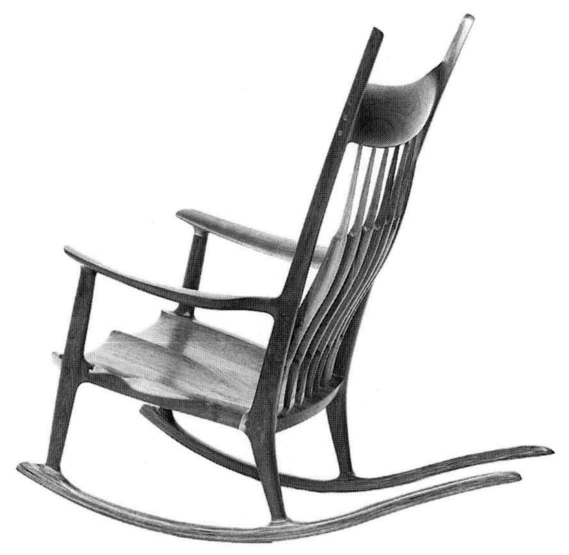

311 Sam Maloof.
ROCKING CHAIR. 1986.
Fiddleback maple.
Photograph courtesy of the artist.

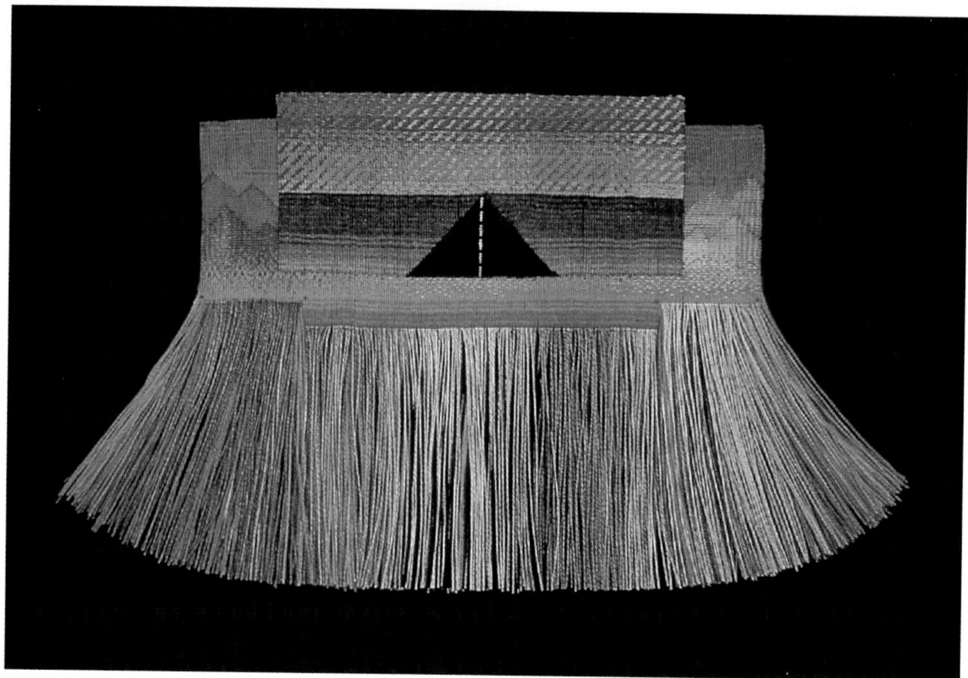

312 Diane Itter.
PATTERN SCAPE. 1985.
Linen, knotted. 10" × 11".
Photo courtesy of the American Craft Museum, New York.

FIBER

Fiber art includes such processes as weaving (both loom and nonloom techniques), stitching, basket making, surface design (dyed and printed textiles), wearable art, and handmade papermaking. These fiber processes use natural and synthetic fibers in both traditional and innovative ways. Artists working with fiber (as with artists working in any medium) draw on the heritage of traditional practices and also explore new avenues of expression.

All weaving is based on the interlacing of lengthwise fibers, *warp,* and the cross fibers, *weft* (also called *woof*). Weavers create patterns by changing the numbers and placements of interwoven threads, and they can choose from a variety of looms and techniques. Simple hand looms can produce very sophisticated, complex weaves. A large tapestry loom, capable of weaving hundreds of colors into intricate forms, may require several days of preparation before work begins.

Prolific, highly influential artist Diane Itter created a major body of work consisting of off-loom, small-scale knotted structures made of linen threads. PATTERN SCAPE is one of Itter's many pieces made with a technique she developed. Working from the center out, through patterned repetition, she constructed complex color-rich forms thread by thread. Of her work she said:

I have come to realize what it is about the textile arts that fascinates me. Among other things... it is the capacity to be both painter and sculptor at the same time. That is, the visual image is created by the integration of color and structure—one cannot exist without the other. In addition, the textile arts allow me a way of working which is both personal and intimate yet potentially monumental in concept and universal in nature. By limiting both my technique (knotting) and my materials (linen) I am able to concentrate all my energies on full exploration of the visual image. After many years of working, I am still fascinated by the infinite variety of images I can create within the set limits.[3]

Many modern African-American quilt designs were inspired by traditional African textiles, while others are related to European-American traditions.

STRING, a collaborative work, was pieced by Rosie Lee Tompkins and restructured and quilted by Willia Ette Graham. Its contrasting strips of light and dark, hot and cool colors flow in an inventive rhythmic pattern. Most of the pieces are velvet, which gives the quilt an exceptionally rich surface that cannot be seen as well in a photograph as in the quilt itself. This quilt exhibits a strong African-American aesthetic of improvisation that contrasts with the regularity and frequent symmetry of European-American quilts such as the Amish quilt on page 29. In its spontaneous energy and impact, STRING is related to the vital spirit of jazz.

Faith Ringgold's paintings, quilts, and soft sculptures speak eloquently of her life and ideas. Happy memories of her childhood in Harlem in the 1930s provide much of her subject matter. MRS. JONES AND FAMILY represents Ringgold's own family. Commitment to women, the family, and cross-cultural consciousness are at the heart of Ringgold's work. With playful exuberance and whimsy, she draws on history, recent events, and her own experiences for her depictions and narratives of class, power, race, and gender. Her highly sophisticated use of naiveté gives her work the appeal of the best folk art.

After attending college and graduate school in New York, she taught high school for many years before she began teaching at the University of California, San Diego. Ringgold has been a strong advocate for greater representation of African Americans in art museums and galleries.

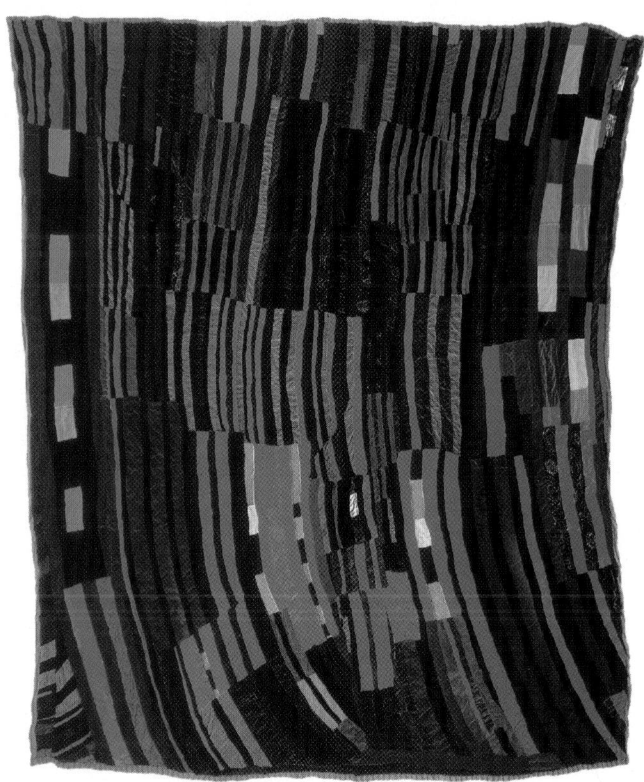

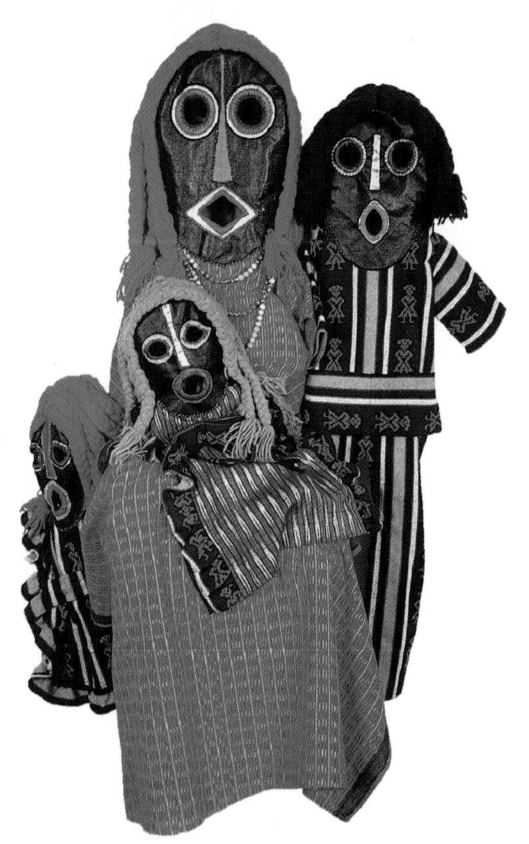

313 Pieced by Rosie Lee Tompkins; restructured and quilted by Willia Ette Graham.
STRING. 1985.
Mixed fabrics. 100" × 85½".
Private collection. Photograph courtesy of the San Francisco Craft and Folk Art Museum.

314 Faith Ringgold.
MRS. JONES AND FAMILY. 1973.
Sewn fabric and embroidery. 60" × 12" × 16".
Courtesy Bernice Steinbaum Gallery.

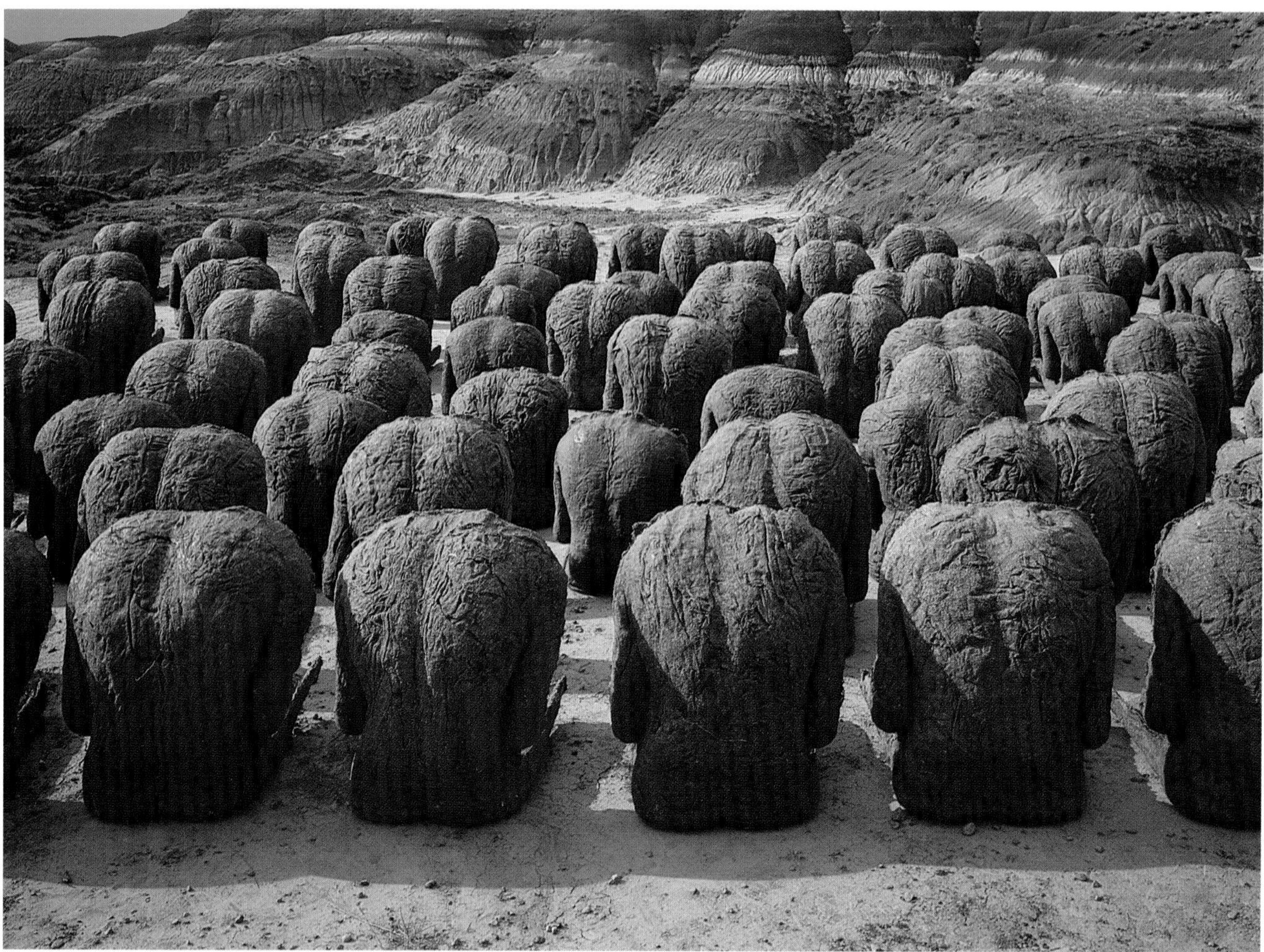

315 Magdalena Abakanowicz.
BACKS. 1976-1982.
80 pieces, burlap and glue: 24" × 19⅝" × 21⅝"; 27¼" × 22" × 26"; 28¼" × 23¼" × 27¼".
Photograph: © 1981 Dirk Bakker, Detroit, Michigan.

Innovations in off-loom fiber work have taken the fiber arts into the realm of sculpture in a variety of ways. Magdalena Abakanowicz has been at the leading edge of nontraditional uses of fiber since the 1960s. Her powerful series called BACKS has an unforgettable quality, at once personal and universal; the earthy color and textures of the formed burlap suggest the capacity to endure dire hardships and to survive with strength. Her forms have what she feels all art must have: mysterious, bewitching power. The artist speaks of her motives:

I want the viewer to penetrate the inside of my forms. For I want him to have the most intimate contact with them, the same contact one can have with clothes, animal skins, or grass.[4]

It was her fellow fiber artists who first recognized and gave appreciative support to Abakanowicz's work. Abakanowicz has earned a place in the mainstream of art history both for the quality of her art and for her breakthrough uses of fiber for major works of sculpture. As Peter Voulkos had done with ceramics, Abakanowicz changed the way we think of fiber as a medium.

For Abakanowicz, materials and techniques are

MAGDALENA ABAKANOWICZ (BORN 1930)

Art and life have both been challenges for Magdalena Abakanowicz. Born to a wealthy family with vast land-holdings in rural Poland, Abakanowicz grew up without companions her own age. She was raised largely by servants and, as a child, saw little of her distant mother (who had wanted her to be a boy) or her aloof, aristocratic father. Her pretty, conforming elder sister received the parental attention Magda craved.

First one teacher, then another was hired, but Magda resisted memorizing formulas and facts. Education, as it was presented to her, was alien and distasteful. She escaped outdoors at every opportunity.

Left to her own resources, she developed a rich imagination and a sense of oneness with the natural and supernatural dimensions of the world. She spent long hours alone, exploring the wonders and mysteries of nature. The surviving animistic beliefs of her peasant neighbors colored her reveries. Of her early childhood, she wrote:

Bark and twigs were full of mysteries; and later so was clay. I molded objects whose meaning was known only to me. They fulfilled functions in performances and rituals which I created for myself alone.... Imagination collected all that was impenetrable and uncertain, hoarding secrets that expanded into worlds.[5]

She was nine years old when World War II uprooted her family from their country estate. She recalls watching her mother answer a rude knock at the door, only to be greeted by a group of drunken soldiers who began to shoot. Her mother's right arm was severed at the shoulder and her left hand was injured. "The capable wise hand suddenly became a piece of meat, separate."[6]

Magda did not know how to hate and could not understand such hate and violence. Her wartime memories include seeing and hearing a great deal of shooting, fire, and destruction, as well as helping look after people who had been horribly maimed and seeing many of them die.

After losing everything in the war, her family supported itself by running a newspaper kiosk. In school, Magdalena was an outsider, unable to relate to other children.

Abakanowicz found that circumstances required her to be flexible in her creativity. She became an artist who did weaving because that medium best suited her circumstances at the time. Cloth could be folded and stored under her bed.

When she applied to the Academy of Fine Arts in Warsaw she had to hide her family's background because children of the prewar aristocracy were not admitted to institutions of higher education. While she disliked the academically restrictive school, she knew she needed the diploma in order to join the artists union.

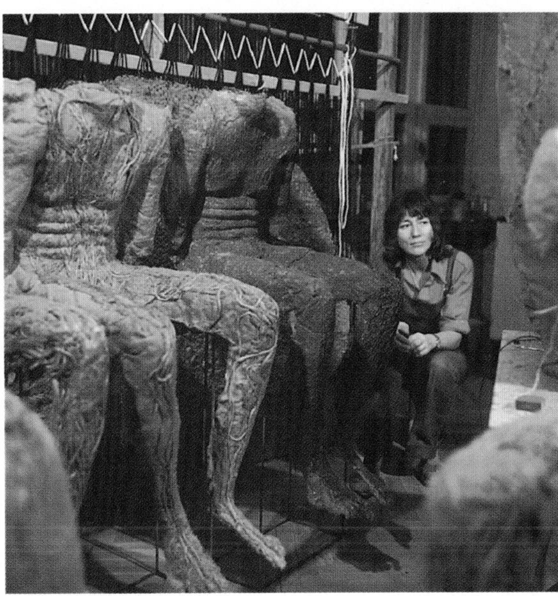

316 MAGDALENA ABAKANOWICZ IN HER STUDIO.
Photograph: Andrzej Michlewski, Warsaw.

As a young adult, Abakanowicz faced the need to support herself in a poor country; battled an educational system in which new approaches were not allowed; was forced to work in small spaces; and struggled against the prevailing traditional ideas about acceptable and unacceptable uses of fiber.

In the sixties, she became known for her large woven wall reliefs and a series of ceiling-hung structures that she saw as abstract figures. In the mid-seventies, she began a series made of stiffened burlap that represented human figures in a more direct way. In the late eighties, she began working in bronze with human and animal figures while continuing her work in burlap. In each medium, the power of her distinctive forms is unique and unmistakable. Throughout, her art presents a feeling of both tragedy and wisdom. As participant and witness, Abakanowicz is fully aware of the cruelty and deep suffering, as well as the profound mysteries, of life.

Her headless, anonymous bodies and disembodied heads suggest loss of self, externally imposed uniformity, traumatic memories of World War II, and Cold War survival mentality. Abakanowicz sees her art as expressions of her personal experience; others see both broad and specific political implications.

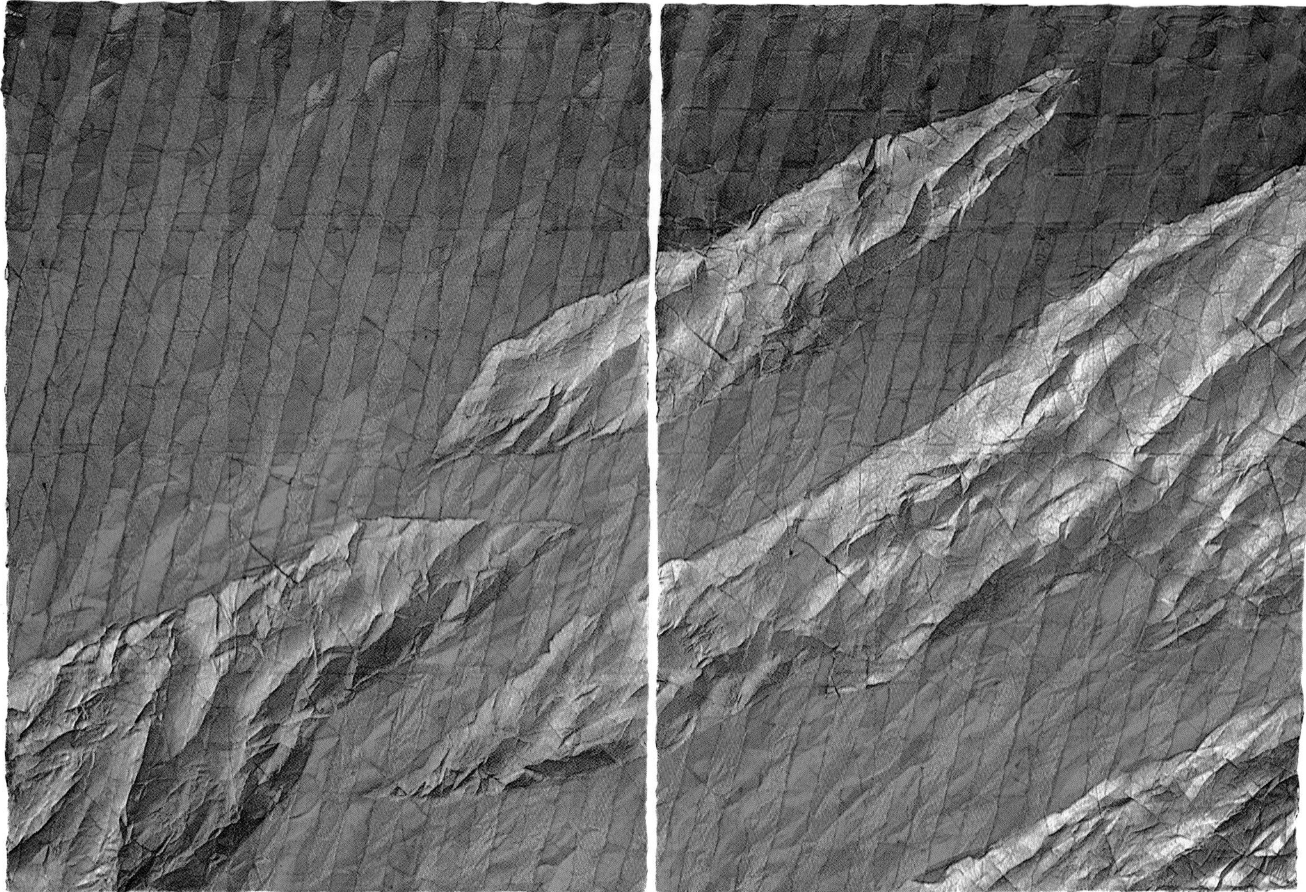

317 Nance O'Banion.
MIRAGE SERIES: TOO. 1984.
Handmade abaca paper, paint on bamboo. 4' × 6'.
Photograph: Elaine Keenan. Courtesy of the Allrich Gallery, San Francisco.

instruments of communication, not ends in themselves. After proving that humble fibers could be shaped into fine art, she has changed her materials many times, exploring wood, stone, and bronze.

One of the most common materials manufactured from fiber is paper. In recent years, there has been a revival of the ancient craft of making paper by hand. Inventive craft artists have greatly expanded our understanding of paper's potential as an expressive medium.

Nance O'Banion worked in printed textiles prior to her involvement in papermaking, and she often combines her handmade paper with other types of fiber. In the two-part composition MIRAGE SERIES: TOO, O'Banion created an intriguing interplay of textures, patterns, shapes, and colors. Cloudlike forms appear in relief, accentuated by subtly painted shadows. Their light, majestic shapes are set off by the contrasting warm and cool colors of the rhythmically striped background.

The fibers we are closest to in everyday life are our clothes. Artists who make and sell wearable art offer us intimate contact with their creations. Art to wear, along with other avenues of investigation and innovation in craft media, demonstrates the craft-based artist's important role in bringing art to life.

Craft media are used today in both traditional and new ways, and they increasingly overlap and are combined with the practices and intentions of other visual arts.

PART 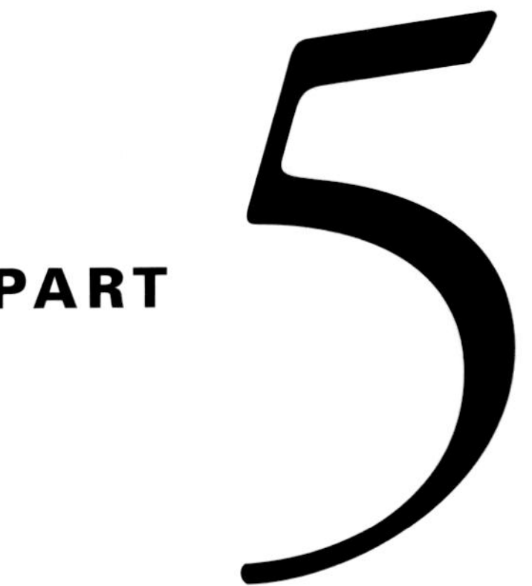

DESIGN DISCIPLINES

Consider...

Are there car emblems, TV graphics, postage stamps, or posters you particularly admire? What do you like about them?

In choosing a car, do you place more emphasis on its prospective gas mileage or on how the car looks? What percentage of the price of a new car goes for appearance?

What approaches to architecture are most appropriate to your climate? Is there a house style that is particularly popular in your area? Is it an appropriate design for the location (site) and climate?

Why are urban planning and design particularly crucial for cities and suburbs?

Who should decide the balance among streets, buildings, and open spaces—developers, politicians, city planners, or voters?

CHAPTER 14

Design and Illustration

Designing is a process basic to all the visual arts. Here and in the following chapters we use the word *design* to refer to the process of applying aesthetic sensitivity and creative problem-solving skills to meeting specific needs. These needs may be presented to designers by clients, or they may be initiated by designers themselves.

Even when a project is initiated by the designer, the emphasis is on meeting the needs of others rather than on being self-expressive. The aesthetic issues addressed by an illustrator, a clothing designer, or an architect are not entirely different from those considered by a painter or a sculptor. The differences between a graphic designer and a painter lie in their priorities.

A painter begins with a need to express a personal idea or to fulfill the requirements of a commission in *a personally expressive mode.* Conversely, a graphic designer begins by addressing a client's need for an advertisement, a book cover, or a logo, yet the solution will always contain some degree of that designer's personal expression. "Artists" and "designers" work along a continuum—from pure self-expression at one end to problem solving at the other. Some designers see themselves as artists, while others consciously reject that label, preferring to think of themselves as creative problem solvers.

Every manufactured object, printed image, and constructed space has been designed by someone. A professional designer's role is to enhance living by applying a developed sense of aesthetics and utility to the design of the human-made world. From alarm clocks to airplanes, from living rooms to public spaces, design is a basic necessity, not a cosmetic afterthought. Design helps to shape as well as to transmit culture.

As consumers, we are aware that some things are well designed and some are not. When the form and function of an object do not complement each other, the object is poorly designed. Good design solves problems; bad design creates problems.

In the West, twentieth-century design has been strongly influenced by the Bauhaus, a school founded by Walter Gropius in Weimar, Germany, in 1919. The Bauhaus brought together many leading artists, architects, and designers. Working as an inspired team, the faculty combined the study of fine arts (such as drawing and painting) with crafts (such as weaving and furniture making) and developed an aesthetic based on visual structure and sound craftsmanship. Faculty and students worked together on design projects. The school's mission was to improve society through design, bringing humanistic and artistic sensitivity to industrial society.

The Bauhaus stressed a clean functionalism and effective design in everyday objects. The school's basic philosophy—that form follows function—related to Bauhaus director Mies van der Rohe's idea that "less is more" (see page 258). Together these concepts had an enormous, and at times negative, impact on the design and architecture that followed.

During the 1920s, the school and its outstanding faculty attracted students from all over the world. In 1933, however, the Nazis began increasing intimidation of Bauhaus students and faculty. Hitler felt that all art should support his political agenda and glorify the German people. He considered Bauhaus art and ideas degenerate. In that same year, Mies van der Rohe closed the school, refusing to submit to further suppression of artistic freedom.

After the Bauhaus closed, some of the faculty moved to the United States. Laszlo Moholy-Nagy opened the Institute of Design in Chicago to carry on the Bauhaus goals. The teaching of design in the United States continues to reflect the influence of the Bauhaus philosophy, with its emphasis on formal visual structure and functional simplicity. The impact of the all-embracing design concepts of the Bauhaus remains very much with us today, evident in disciplines as diverse as architecture, industrial design, textile design, typography, and painting. The Bauhaus was not only a design movement, it was a social movement as well. Central to its vision was the belief that people must command technology and use it for creative purposes in order to guide human destiny.

In this chapter, we touch on just a few of the many design disciplines, moving from designing images and small objects to designing interiors. We focus on graphic design (including typography), illustration, industrial design, textile design, and interior design. In Chapter 15, we present architecture and environmental design. Other disciplines that influence our lives include the design of clothing and packages, which we will leave to magazines and other books.

GRAPHIC DESIGN

The term *graphic design* refers to the process of working with printed words and images to create solutions to problems of visual communication. It ranges in scale and complexity from postage stamps and trademarks to billboards and television commercials. Much of graphic design involves designing materials to be printed, including books, magazines, brochures, packages, and posters, such as April Greiman's THE MODERN POSTER.

Graphic designers work with typography, photography, and illustration. The design of *Artforms,* for example, is the art of graphic designers at DeFrancis Studio and Barbara Pope Book Design, who carefully considered and integrated the illustrations, text, and publishing requirements presented to them by the authors and editors.

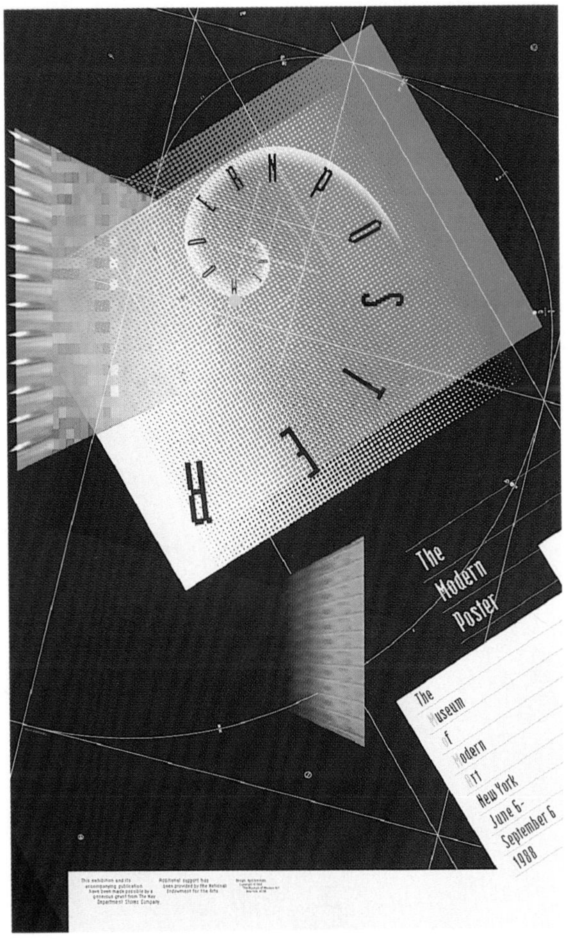

318 April Greiman.
THE MODERN POSTER. 1988.
Offset lithograph. 39" × 24½".
The Museum of Modern Art, New York. Exhibition Fund.

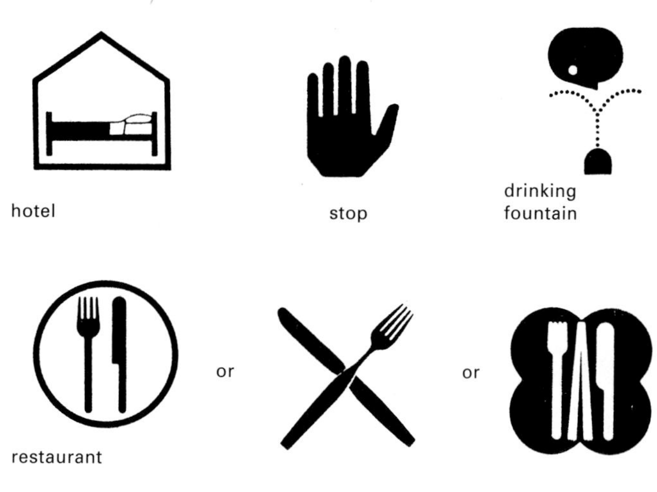

319 Henry Dreyfuss.
SYMBOLS. 1972.

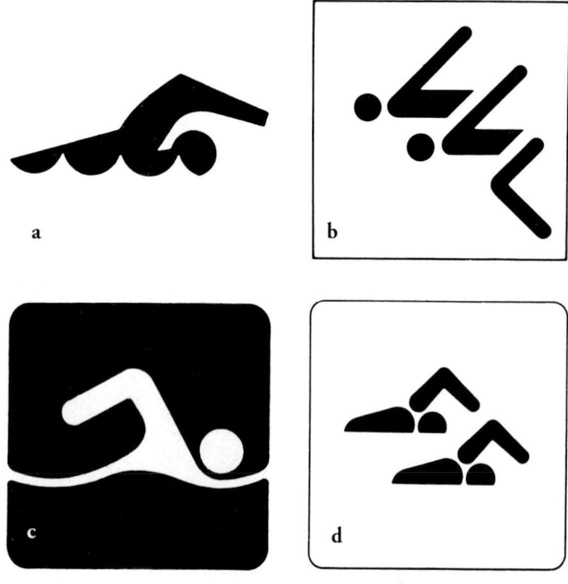

320 OLYMPIC SYMBOLS FOR SWIMMING. 1964-1984.
a 1964 Masaru Katsumie, assisted by Yoshiro Yamashita.
b 1972 & 1976 Otl Aicher.
c 1980 Variation on Aicher's design.
d 1984 Keith Bright, assisted by Ken Parhurst.

Signs and Symbols

Often the name, product, or purpose of a company or organization is given a distinctive and memorable appearance by a graphic designer. An identifying mark, or trademark, based on letter forms is known as a *logo* (short for *logotype*). An identifying mark based on pictorial (rather than typographic) sources is called a *symbol.*

Symbols that instantly communicate important information without words have met the needs of travelers in foreign countries. When such symbols are not easily understood, they cause more problems than they solve. Designer Henry Dreyfuss saw the need for an international symbol system, then pioneered the development of universally recognized SYMBOLS. His 1972 *Symbol Sourcebook* combined his own ideas with the work of other designers.

OLYMPIC SYMBOLS have become widely reproduced and admired. Prior to 1964, they were more literal than symbolic—more representational than abstract. For the 1964 Tokyo Olympics, Masaru Katsumie designed the first true symbols, and they remain among the finest. Perhaps the best-known OLYMPIC SYMBOLS are those Otl Aicher designed for the 1972 Munich games. In Montreal in 1976 they were used again, with slight modification.

For the NEW CANAAN LIBRARY SYMBOL, the challenge was to create an identifying mark for the library that would integrate the idea of books with the idea of leaves—a major feature of the surrounding Connecticut landscape. The eye-teasing symbol consists of lines and shapes in a design that employs figure/ground reversal.

321 Don Ervin.
NEW CANAAN LIBRARY SYMBOL. 1975.
Pen and ink. ⅞" × ⅞".

A memorable logo or symbol is the key element in a consistent design program, allowing a business or other organization to benefit from public recognition and an understanding of what the organization is selling or promoting. A highly effective corporate identity program was designed for Apple Computer, Inc. Apple's design program, based on a new "white look," was expanded from print media to include corporate signing. The company retained its APPLE COMPUTER, INC. SYMBOL, designed earlier by Robert Janoff, and placed it in a large white field. In the world marketplace, the striking rainbow-striped apple transcends language barriers as a distinctive symbol for the company's products.

In the fifties, William Golden designed a striking logo/symbol combination for the Columbia Broadcasting System. His CBS EYE captures the essence of Columbia Broadcasting System's television programming by placing the company's initials at the center of an abstract eye.

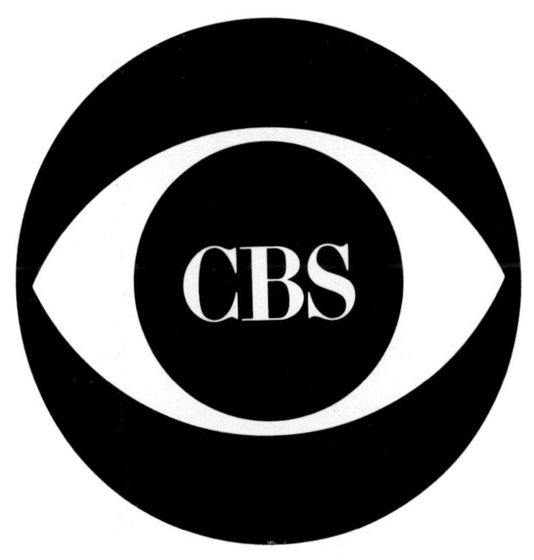

322 William Golden.
CBS EYE. c. 1951.

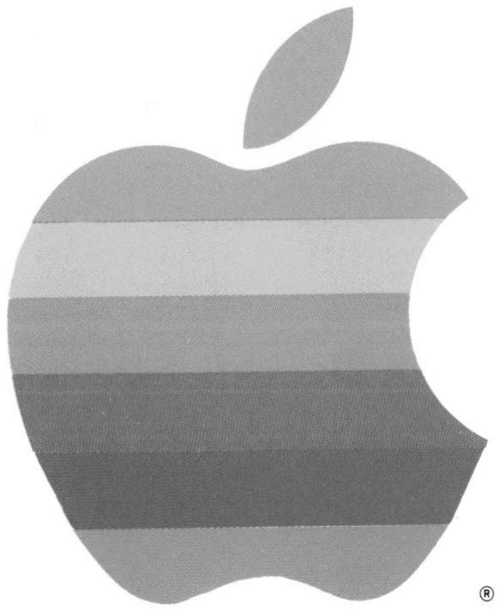

323 Ronn Harsh, designer; Rob Gemmell, art director; Tom Suiter, creative director.
APPLE COMPUTER, INC. SYMBOL.
a Symbol with color bars.

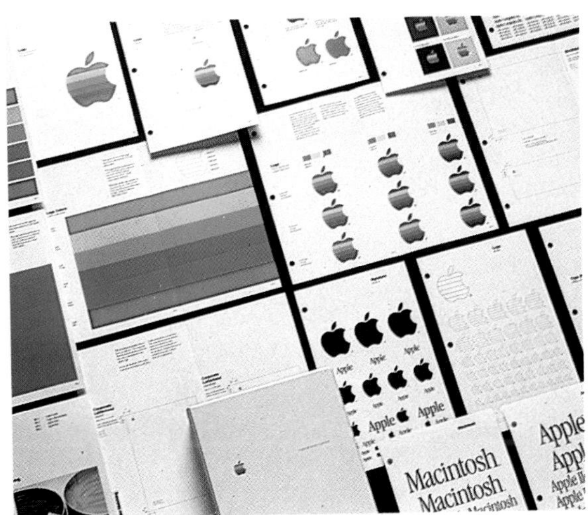

b Corporate identity manual.

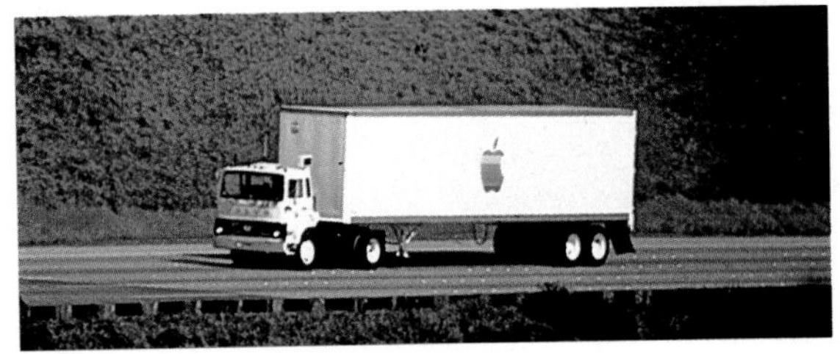

c Truck with symbol.

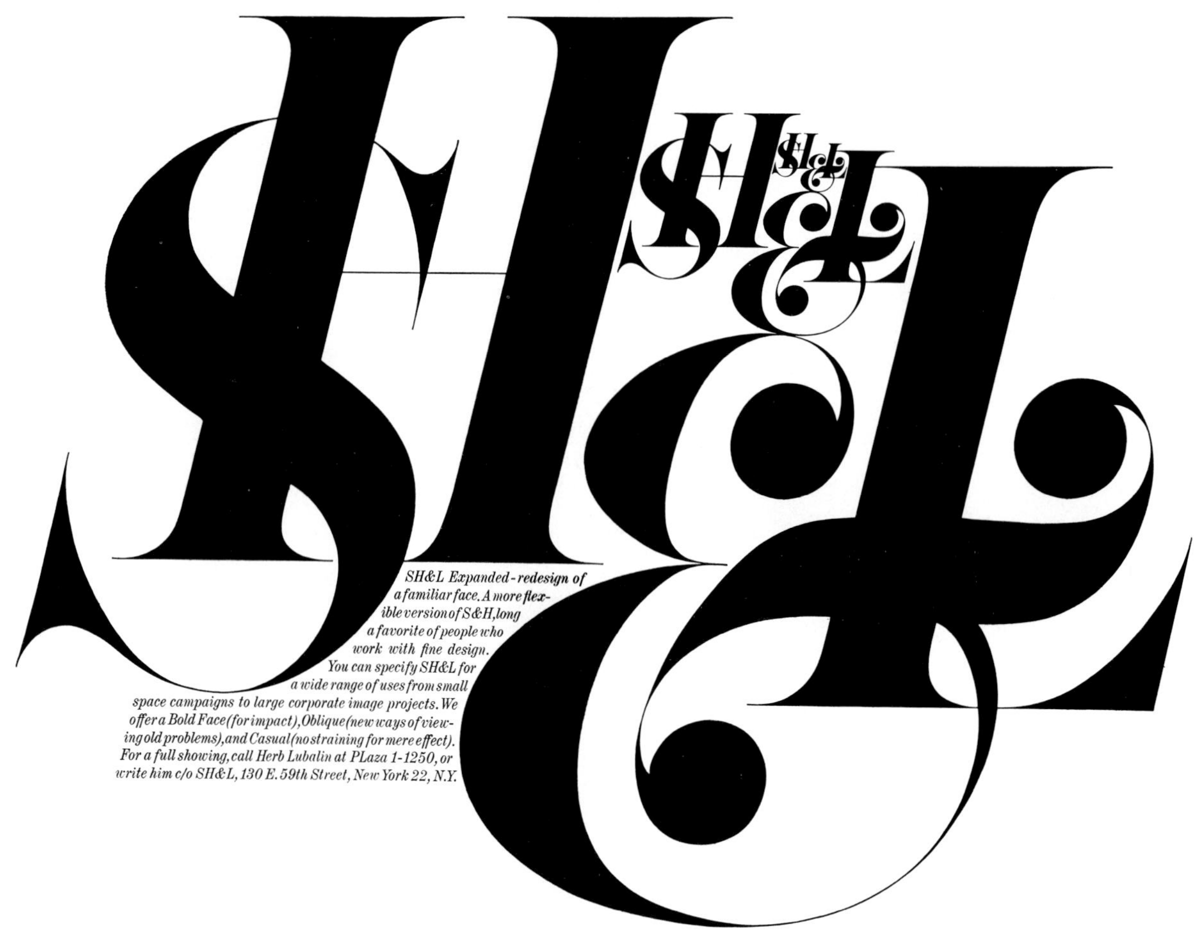

324 Herb Lubalin.
SH&L LOGO. c. 1962.
Courtesy Sudler & Hennessey, Inc., New York.

Typography

Letter forms are art forms. *Typography* is the art and technique of composing printed material from letter forms *(typefaces)*. Designers, hired to meet clients' communication needs, frequently create designs that relate nonverbal images and printed words in complementary ways.

Just a few decades ago, when people committed words to paper, their efforts were handwritten or typewritten—and nearly all typewriters had the same typeface, the name of which was unknown to most users. Now anyone who uses a computer can select typefaces, or fonts. With the advent of the personal computer, a great many people who had no training or background in design could suddenly create documents that looked typeset and produce desktop publications such as newsletters and brochures. But computer programs, like pen-

325 Herb Lubalin, assisted by Alan Peckolick and Tom Carnase.
MOTHER & CHILD, logo for a magazine (never produced). 1965.
By permission of Herb Lubalin, Lubalin Peckolick Associates.

cils, paintbrushes, and cameras, are simply tools that *may* facilitate artistic aims.

Since German printer Johann Gutenberg's invention of the printing press in the fifteenth century, thousands of typefaces have been created—helped recently by computer technology. For the text of Artforms, Adobe Garamond was selected for its grace and readability.

Many typefaces are based on the capital letters carved in stone by early Romans. **Roman** letters are made with thick and thin strokes, ending in *serifs*—short lines with pointed ends, at an angle to the main strokes. In typesetting, the term 'roman' is used to mean not *italic*. San serif (without serifs) typefaces have a modern look due to their association with the Bauhaus movement's modernist designs. They are actually ancient in origin. **Black letter** typefaces are based on Northern medieval manuscripts and are rarely used today.

Graphic designer Herb Lubalin first gained an international reputation for elegant typographic designs such as his SH&L LOGO for the firm Sudler, Hennessey and Lubalin. In his most innovative work, form and content are inseparably united, as in his logo design intended for a magazine devoted to parenting, MOTHER AND CHILD. The magazine was never produced, but the logo—an apt symbol of the mother-and-child-relationship—is now well-known to designers and students of design.

Through the modification of letter forms, words become pictorial expressions of content in the book cover for a children's book on OIL and in the trade-

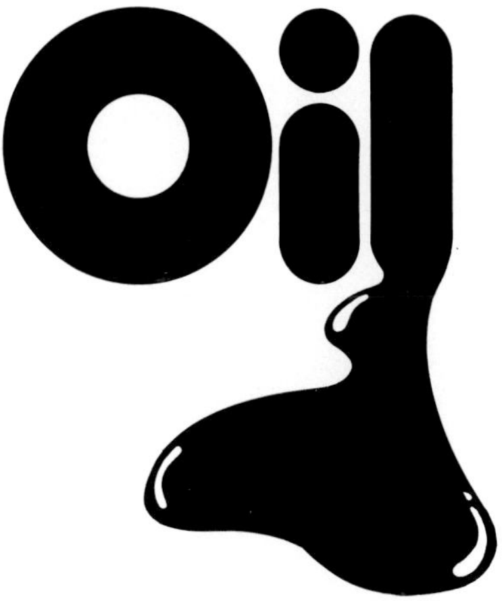

326 Nancy Tafuri and Thomas Tafuri, artists; Judy Mills, art director.
OIL, design for jacket for children's book by Barbara Lowery.
© 1976 by Franklin Watts, Inc. Used with permission of the publisher.

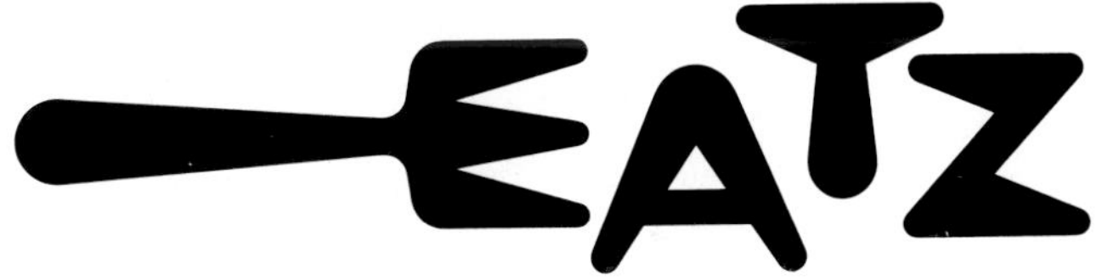

327 Marty Neumeier.
EATZ RESTAURANTS LOGO.
Courtesy of Neumeier Design Team.

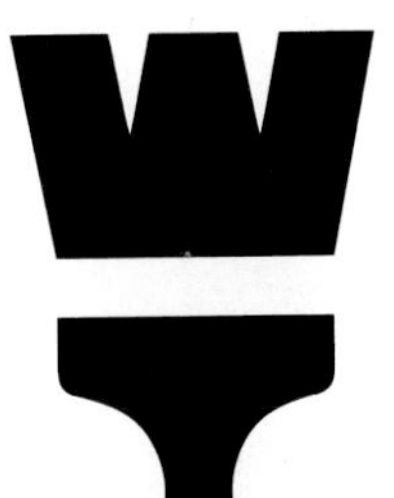

328 D. C. Stipp.
WILLIS PAINTING CONTRACTORS LOGO.
Courtesy of D. C. Stipp, designer, R.B.M.M.

mark for EATZ, a chain of fast-food restaurants. The single initial W transforms the bristles of a paint-brush in a logo for WILLIS PAINTING CONTRACTORS.

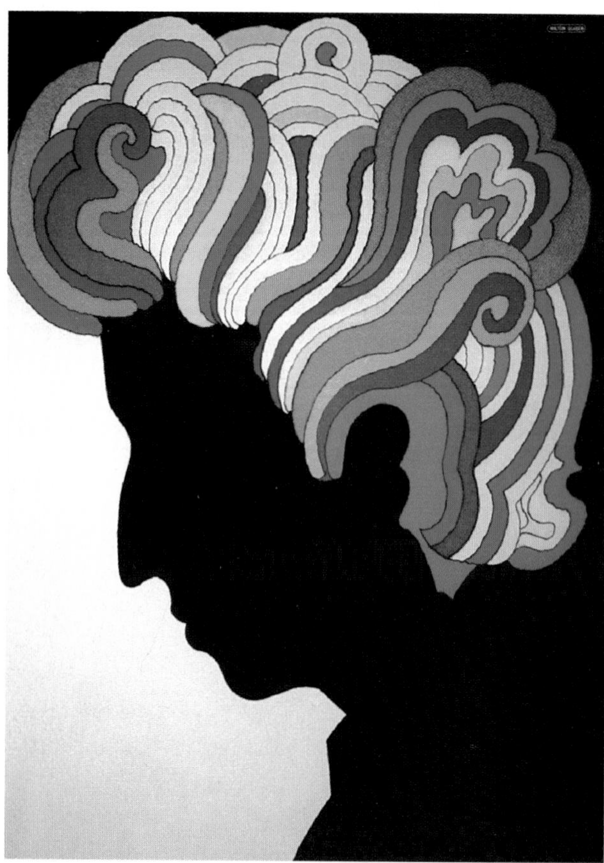

329 Milton Glaser.
BOB DYLAN POSTER. 1967.

Posters, Advertisements, and Other Graphics

A poster is a concise visual announcement that provides information through the integrated design of typographic and pictorial imagery. An effective poster attracts attention and conveys its message in a flash. The creativity of a poster designer is directed toward a specific purpose, which may be to advertise or persuade.

The concept of the modern poster is more than a hundred years old (see page 167), but it wasn't until the 1920s and 1930s that printing methods made possible high-quality mass production. Since the 1950s, other means of advertising have overshadowed posters. While they now play a lesser role than they once did, well-designed posters still provide powerful means of instant communication. Posters of all sorts have become so popular as inexpensive images to be framed and hung on walls that printing and selling posters has become big business. Poster design has influenced and been influenced by contemporary fine art. (See the work of Barbara Krueger on page 482.)

Milton Glaser's 1967 poster for BOB DYLAN, the singer and songwriter, has become a graphic icon for the sixties generation. Here, bright colors are set off by black and white. The colored hair patterns were inspired by Islamic design (see page 315) and the psychedelic movement.

In Steff Geissbuhler's ALVIN AILEY poster, the action and exuberance of the Ailey company's dancing is given dramatic and primary importance; typography plays a diminished but supporting role.

Brand Advertising Agency used a photograph of live model Denise Tegtman by Dick Greene and Arnold Paley in an advertisement for Safety-Kleen, a company that recycles industrial wastes. This surreal reinterpretation of our symbol of freedom

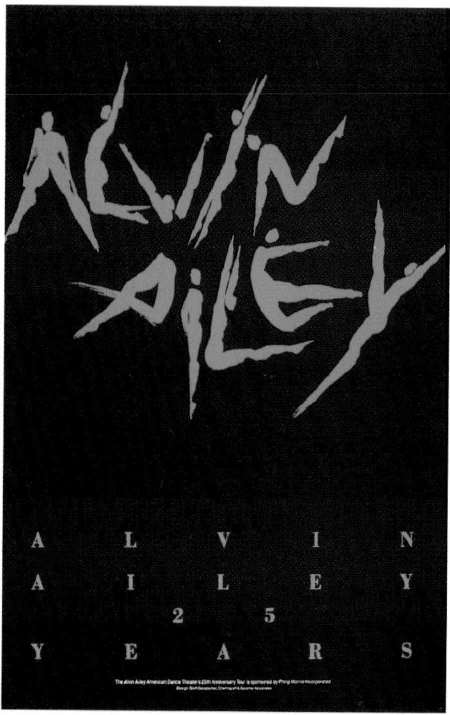

330 Steff Geissbuhler.
POSTER FOR THE ALVIN AILEY AMERICAN DANCE THEATER. 1983.

sinking into a sea of pollution uses humor and shock value to address a serious problem. Although CLEAN UP YOUR ACT, AMERICA started as a print ad, it was so well received that it was also printed as a poster.

In today's world of bold, ever-present commercial messages, it has become increasingly challenging for designers to create eye-catching visual images. Some graphic designers are turning to more subtle approaches to convey information. April Greiman is an advocate of Post-Modern design, which emerged in the 1970s in opposition to the clear, rational design of the previous decades (see the discussion of Post-Modernism on pages 475 and 476). Her design publicizing an exhibition called THE MODERN POSTER at the Museum of Modern Art (see page 229) shows the influence of computers and high-tech space imagery. Color bars and rectangles, lines and textured areas run in all directions and seem to float and reach beyond the boundaries of the composition.

Saul Bass, a major contributor to American graphic design, created a bright spot among the generally dull United States postage stamps with a design celebrating the benefits from the cooperation of SCIENCE AND INDUSTRY. Appropriately, Bass used a computer to design the perspective grid and industrial forms which rise in an imaginary landscape.

In advertising, the arts frequently work together. Television advertising is a kind of operatic art form that calls upon writers, musicians, and actors as well as directors, camera operators, and graphic designers. In printed advertising, a writer, a designer, and often an illustrator or photographer work as a team.

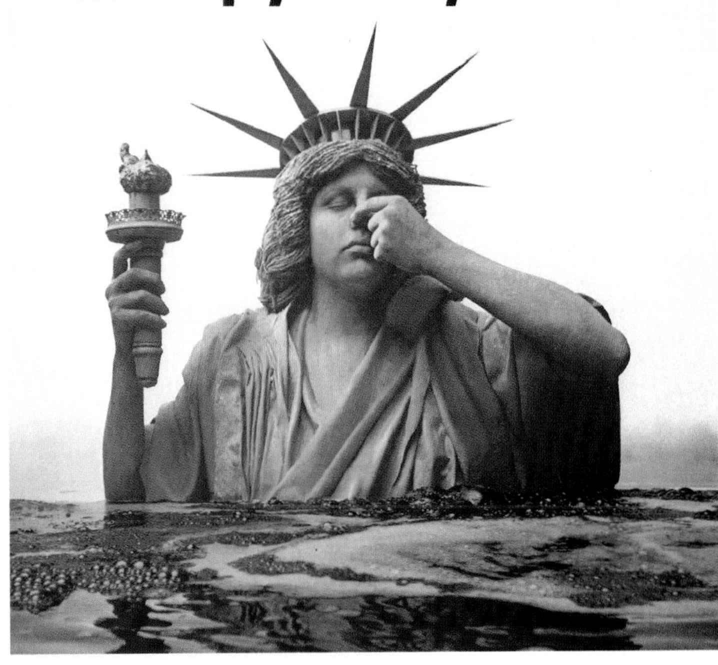

331 CLEAN UP YOUR ACT, AMERICA.
Advertisement for Safety-Kleen.
Dick Greene and Arnold Paley, photographers for Brand Advertising.

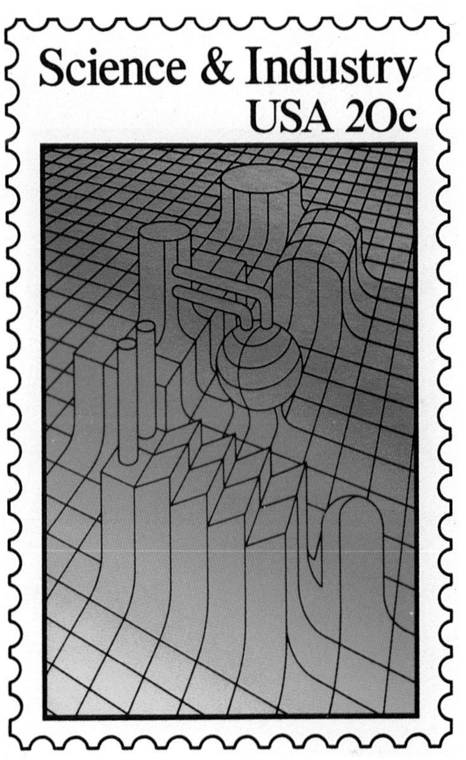

332 Saul Bass.
SCIENCE AND INDUSTRY STAMP. 1983.
Computer-aided design. 1½" × 1".

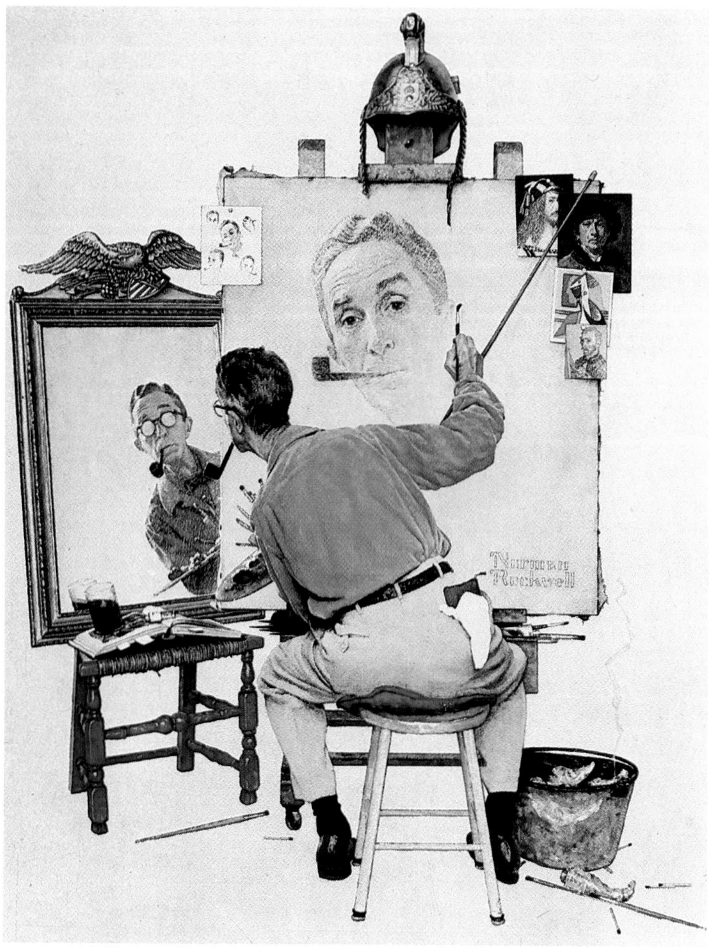

333 Norman Rockwell.
TRIPLE SELF-PORTRAIT. Cover for *Saturday Evening Post.* February 13, 1960.
Oil on canvas.

ILLUSTRATION

An *illustration* is a picture or decoration created to enhance the appearance of written material or to clarify its meaning. Illustrators create images for books, magazines, reports, album covers and CD cases, greeting cards, and advertisements.

Modern illustration has evolved in conjunction with the development of printing processes. Nineteenth-century French artist Honoré Daumier was among the first to use lithography for illustration (see page 165). Recent photomechanical reproduction processes have enabled illustrators to employ drawing, painting, and photographic techniques. Computer programs further extend the capabilities of illustrators. Although most illustration is now done with photography, some areas—notably children's books, fashion illustration, and greeting cards—continue to rely on drawn or painted images.

The distinction between illustrations and art displayed in galleries and museums has to do with the purpose the work is intended to serve, rather than the medium in which the work is made, since both illustrations and art can be drawings, paintings, or photographs.

American illustrator Norman Rockwell was best known for the many *Saturday Evening Post* magazine covers he created between 1916 and 1963. He specialized in warm, humorous, often sentimental scenes of everyday small-town life, drawn with a wealth of meaningful detail. His TRIPLE SELF-PORTRAIT is intriguing on several levels. The face looking back at us from the mirror looks anxious and somewhat comical, with a drooping pipe and blank reflections for eyes. The Rockwell on the easel appears younger, more handsome and jaunty, without glasses, and with pipe firmly clenched. Perhaps the real Norman Rockwell is the third figure—with his back to us. Self-portraits by Dürer, Rembrandt, Picasso, and Van Gogh are tacked to the upper right corner of his easel. He may be suggesting that "painters" can show themselves as they look, feel, or imagine they are, while "illustrators" rarely depict themselves—and, when they do, aren't sure where they fit in the art world. (Compare Vermeer's self-portrait on page 366.)

Until the mid-1950s, there was a fairly clear distinction between the fine arts of drawing and painting and the commercial art of illustration. Since then, the two areas have moved closer together. Starting in the 1960s, some magazine editors encouraged personal expression, and this led a number of illustrators to move in the direction of more abstract, symbolic, or poetic depictions, which brought their work closer to that of gallery artists.

Brad Holland belongs to this new breed of illustrator. His images are specific but not literal, and he is most concerned with meeting his own criteria. Holland began his art career by working for a year as a book illustrator at Hallmark in Kansas. He proceeded to New York, where his struggle to make a living was hampered by his insistence that he be allowed to work in his own way. His originality and the quality of his imagery eventually led to commercial success as a magazine illustrator. His distinctive style has influenced other illustrators. Many of Holland's illustrations have an eerie, demonic quality, which may have made him a logical choice to do the KHOMEINI cover for *Time*'s "Man of the Year" issue in 1980.

Most editors seek illustrators after they have selected stories or articles. To Holland's surprise and delight, a few editors have reversed this practice, giving writers story assignments intended to accompany his existing drawings.

Maurice Sendak's name has become synonymous with children's book illustration. Though he has illustrated many books by other authors, he is best known for those he wrote himself. His style varies from quite simple line drawings, with little or no indication of background, to elaborate cross-hatched and textured drawings in which every inch of the composition is filled.

Sendak's make-believe creatures delight adults as well as children. His READING IS FUN poster uses animals from his book *Where the Wild Things Are.* Sendak rejects the notion that illustrations for

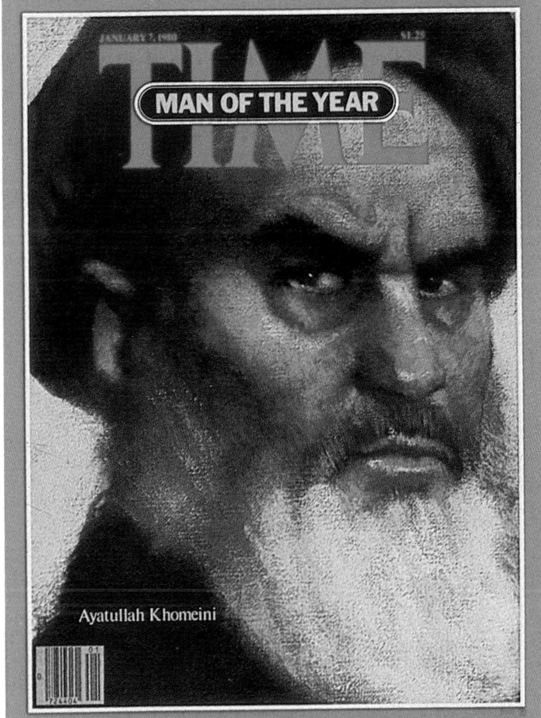

334 Brad Holland.
AYATULLAH KHOMEINI. January 7, 1980. *Time.*

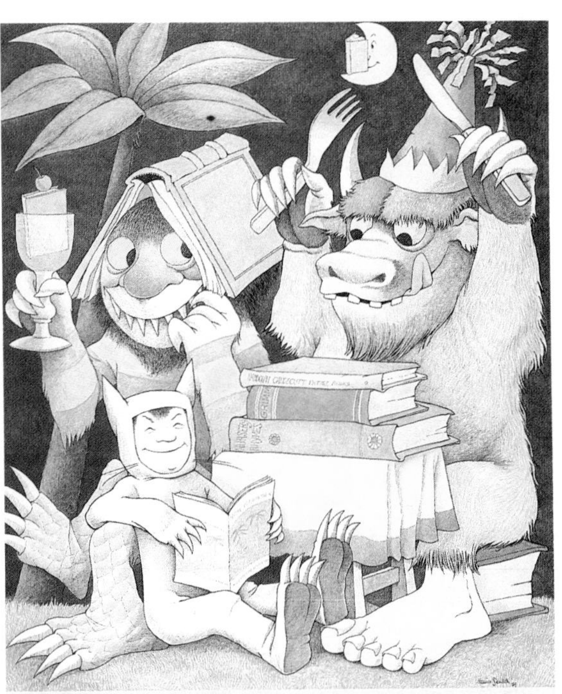

335 Maurice Sendak.
READING IS FUN. Poster.

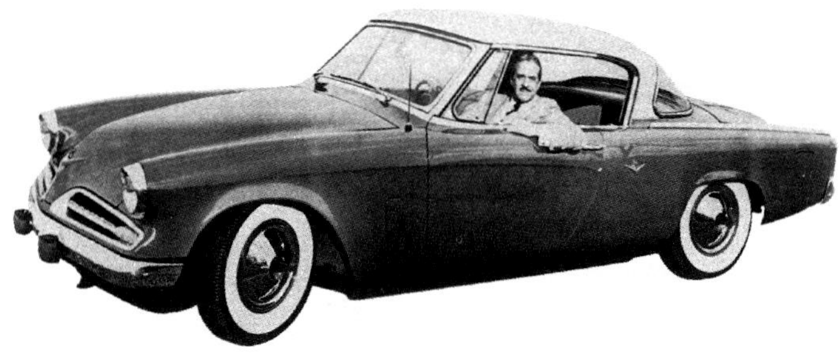

336 Raymond Loewy.
STUDEBAKER STARLINER.
1953.

337 Raymond Loewy.
MXRL AUTOMOBILE. 1974.

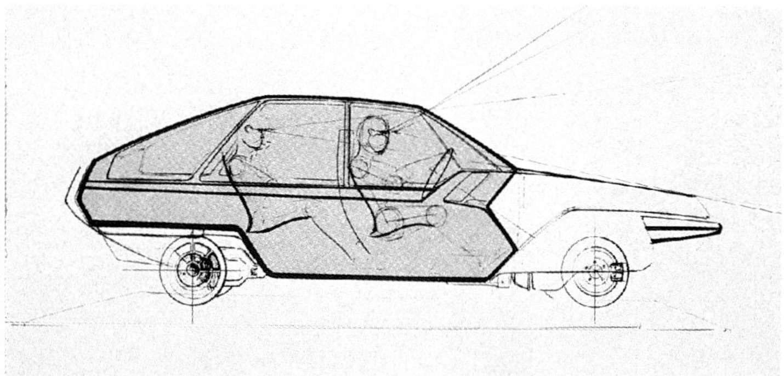

a Sketch by Raymond Loewy.

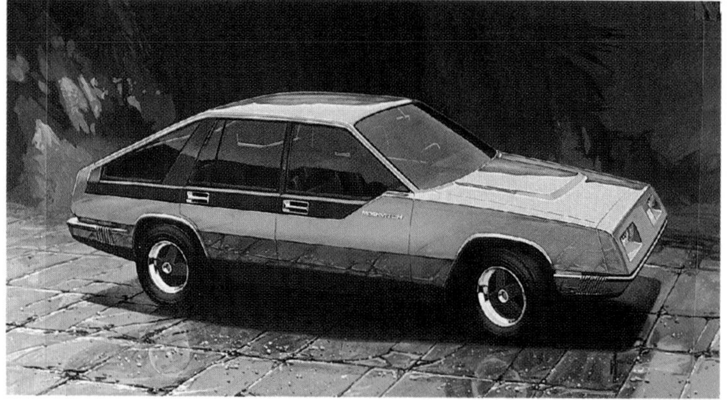

b Presentation drawing by Syd Mead.

children's books must be devoid of anything frightening; his playfully menacing creatures provide children with a healthy way to confront some of their fears of the unknown. Sendak's work has had a strong influence on other illustrators.

INDUSTRIAL DESIGN

What we work on is going to be ridden in, sat upon, looked at, talked into, activated, operated, or in some way used by people.... If the point of contact between the product and the people becomes a point of friction, then the industrial designer has failed. If people are made safer, more comfortable, more eager to purchase, more efficient—or just plain happier—the designer has succeeded.

Henry Dreyfuss[1]

Industrial design is aesthetics working within industry. Its purposes are to design objects for machine production, to relate technology to human sensibilities, and to enhance objects designed primarily for functional use. An industrial designer can work on items as simple as a bottle cap or as complex as a computer. Always, the designer needs to be able to learn anew. He or she must become familiar with how the object being designed will be fabricated, how the object must work, and how it can make a meaningful, economical contribution to the process of living.

In the mid-nineteenth century, products of the relatively new Industrial Revolution were often dressed up with Egyptian or Rococo (see page 367) ornamentation. The need for industrial design did not become clear until the twentieth century, when objects designed by Raymond Loewy, Henry Dreyfuss, and others caused industrial design to be seen as a respected and needed profession.

Raymond Loewy's guiding philosophy was to unite function, beauty, comfort, and safety in the design of affordable and profitable products for everyday use. His automobile designs were among his most outstanding achievements; the 1953 STUDEBAKER STARLINER was so far ahead of its time that people blinked in disbelief when they saw it. Later, the car had an influence on other designers.

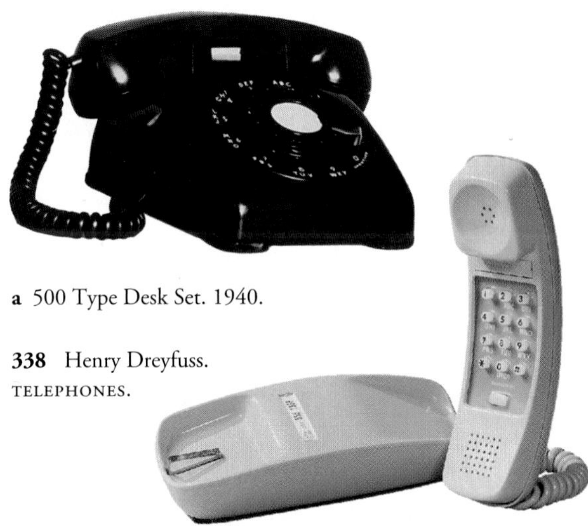

a 500 Type Desk Set. 1940.

b Touch Tone Trimline. 1968. Photographs reproduced with permission of AT&T Archives.

338 Henry Dreyfuss. TELEPHONES.

Loewy's international reputation led him to work on projects in the Soviet Union—an almost unthinkable venture at the height of the Cold War. In 1974, Loewy completed drawings and a rendering for the MXRL, a reliable, economical car without costly stylistic elaborations. But the communist regime canceled the project before production could begin.

The work done by industrial designers is so much a part of our everyday life that we scarcely notice it. Yet if all the designs influenced by such designers as Raymond Loewy and Henry Dreyfuss were suddenly removed, the impact would be staggering. Dreyfuss helped set design standards for technology through his designs for such products as the Honeywell thermostat, the interiors of the DC-10 jet, the Hoover vacuum cleaner, and the Singer sewing machine. The research Dreyfuss and his industrial design teams conducted on telephone use led to the design of AT&T's black-cradle 500 desk phone and, later, to the Trimline, Princess, and original Touch Tone TELEPHONES. Although many Dreyfuss-designed classics have been replaced by newer models, his design creed—that attractive form comes from within and is determined by purpose rather than applied as external decoration—continues to guide today's designers.

RAYMOND LOEWY (1893–1986)

French-born American industrial designer Raymond Loewy grew up dreaming of building cars and trains; today his name is practically synonymous with industrial design. He, along with Henry Dreyfuss and a few others, established the industrial design profession in the 1920s.

As a child, Loewy spent so much time filling his notebooks with sketches of airplanes, locomotives, and cars that his parents decided that he should be educated as an engineer. At age twenty-one, however, his engineering studies were interrupted by World War I. After four years, Loewy was discharged as a captain. He came to the United States, where he worked as a fashion illustrator for *Vogue, Harper's Bazaar,* and other magazines, and as a freelance window designer for department stores.

After redesigning an old-fashioned Gestetner duplicating machine in 1927, he decided to become an industrial designer. In 1934, he was hired to improve the appearance of a refrigerator and ended up redesigning the whole unit, inside and out. Its success was the start of a long and influential career.

Loewy's reputation was enhanced by his international network of design offices. His sense of image and style—in combination with a keen business sense, a good imagination, and strong design ability—drew attention not only to Raymond Loewy but to the new profession of industrial design.

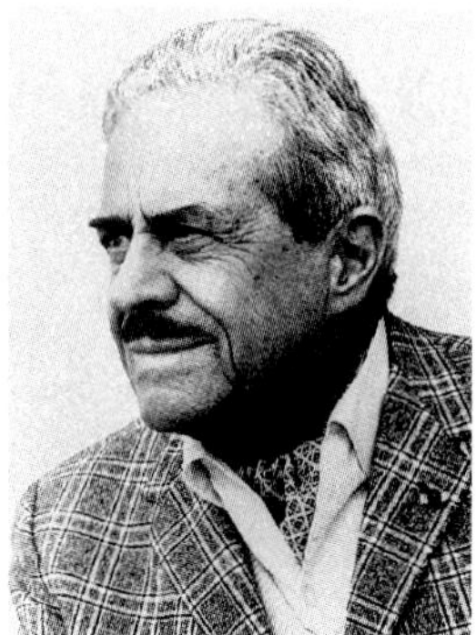

339 RAYMOND LOEWY.

His international reputation was built on a diversity of products and on the complete design service his company provided clients. Although he thought of himself as an industrial designer, he and others in his international firm also worked as graphic and packaging designers.

From 1925 to 1985, the United States led the world in the development of industrial mass production. During this period, Loewy played a larger role than any other designer in shaping everyday life. His designs included objects and images as diverse as soda bottles, cigarette packages, trains, and airplanes. Loewy designed the symbols and logos of Shell, Exxon, and Canada Dry; the Greyhound bus; the first streamlined car; and the sleeping berths on the NASA space shuttle. His motto, "Never leave well enough alone," became the title of his autobiography.

There is a considerable difference between redesigning to improve an object's total function and restyling an exterior to increase sales. When it comes to basic transportation, for example, one brand of automobile may function as well as another. The consumer's decision to buy a particular model is often based largely on appearance; a high percentage of the purchase price of the average American car is for visual design alone. Retooling the machinery that makes cars—or any complex manufactured product—is the most expensive aspect of design. It is change in design, rather than design itself, that is costly.

Each type of object to be designed presents a special set of challenges to the industrial designer. In 1929, Bauhaus-trained architect Ludwig Mies van der Rohe designed a chair that has long been seen as a classic: his LOUNGE CHAIR is a graceful and comfortable place for one or two people to sit. Verner Panton's molded plastic STACKING CHAIR is uniquely balanced to provide flowing, sculptural support for the body. Panton was the first to achieve single-piece cantilevered chair construction. He began by using rigid polyurethane and later (when his chairs were mass-produced) molded fiberglass and polyester.

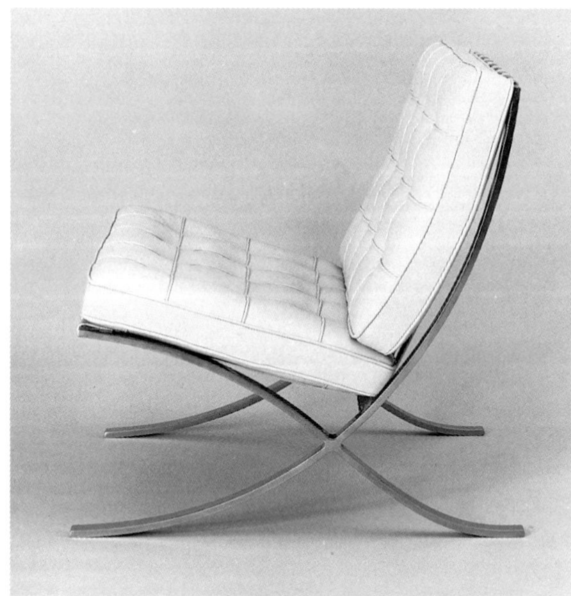

340 Ludwig Mies van der Rohe.
LOUNGE CHAIR (BARCELONA CHAIR). 1929.
Chrome-plated steel bars, leather. Height 29½".
The Museum of Modern Art, New York.
Gift of the manufacturer, Knoll Associates, Inc.

TEXTILE DESIGN

Textile design generally refers to designs created to be mass-produced by either weaving or printing on fabric.

Jack Lenor Larsen has become one of America's best known weavers and textile designers. An enthusiastic traveler, he finds inspiration in the fabrics he studies and collects throughout the world. Larsen says he weaves his experiences into his fabrics, as in LABYRINTH. He uses techniques, color, and materials from many cultures, yet he synthesizes them into designs and collections uniquely his own. He is a major innovator as well as a fine traditional craftsman.

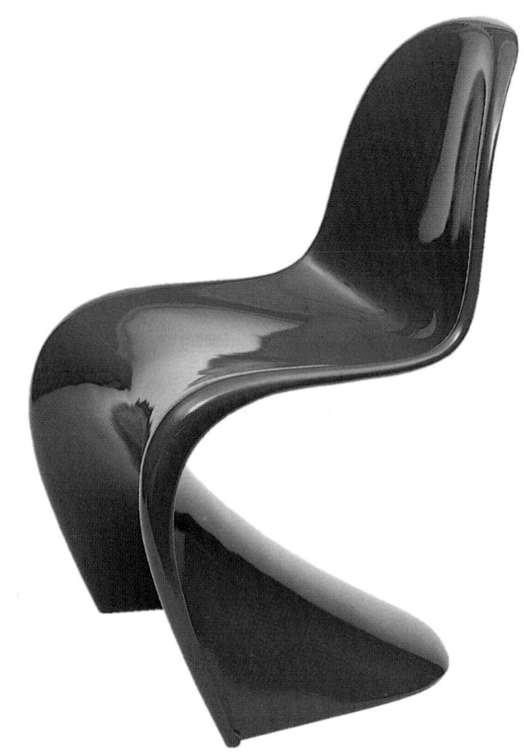

341 Verner Panton.
STACKING SIDE CHAIR. 1959-1960 (manufactured 1967).
PU-foam Baydur. 32⅝" × 19¼" × 23½".
The Museum of Modern Art, New York. Gift of Herman Miller AG.

Although the majority of Larsen's designs are now woven on power looms, he continues to weave most of his first samples by hand. Some of his large commissions are woven in India and Africa, where the traditional techniques that Larsen employs originated. This practice has helped to revitalize ancient crafts and benefited local economies.

In the early 1950s, Armi Ratia started the Marimekko company in Finland. Designer Maija Isola joined her, and together they caused a revolution in the textile-printing industry. Marimekko broke away from conventional floral motifs and monotonous ornamentation. The firm became known for its bold designs using large areas of color, designs so appealing that people often stretched MARIMEKKO FABRIC DESIGNS on frames and hung them as though they were paintings.

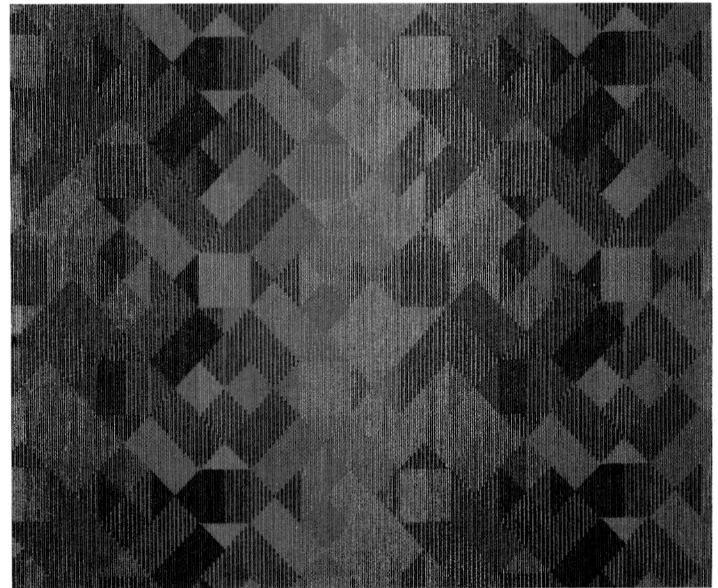

342 Jack Lenor Larsen.
LABYRINTH. 1981.
Upholstery fabric, Jacquard "repp," worsted wool and cotton, worsted wool face.
Project director: Mark Pollock, Larsen Design Studio.

INTERIOR DESIGN

Interior living spaces are often designed, whether consciously or unconsciously, by those who inhabit them. Professional and amateur designers have an awareness of the expressive character of architectural spaces. In addition, they have the ability to visualize how surfaces and furnishings can be combined to achieve a desired effect.

Enjoyable interiors are determined by the values and lifestyles of the occupants. For this reason, some of the best interior design is done by individuals for themselves. Important aspects of the design process include developing ideas about the intended purpose of the space and the desired mood; relating interior and exterior when applicable; organizing rooms to suit specific needs; selecting and arranging furniture for comfort and ease of circulation; and coordinating materials, colors, and textures.

Interior designers Robert Bray and Michael Schaible are concerned primarily with spatial qualities. Bray's studio apartment was designed as a starting point to which other elements could be added at a later date. After he began living in the apartment, however, Bray decided that he did not want to add anything, that he preferred the beauty of the bare walls to the beauty of paintings. The uncluttered simplicity gives a spacious feeling to the small

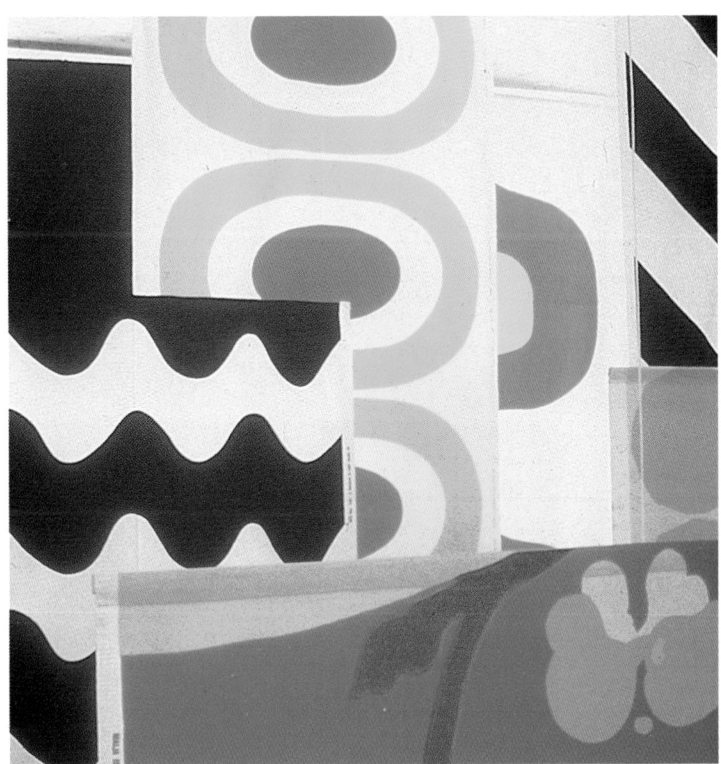

343 MARIMEKKO FABRIC DESIGNS. 1963.
Cotton.

room and makes the BRAY RESIDENCE a tranquil refuge from the intensity of Manhattan. A variety of floor levels divides the room, providing visual interest without making the space appear smaller. The highest level is flush with the window sills, creating a flow between interior and exterior space.

Interior design may include reshaping the architecture of the interior. When they work with clients, Bray and Schaible feel that getting spaces down to basic, functional essentials is the first and most important step, even when clients already own beautiful furnishings and art objects. Such an approach enables those with limited funds to add furniture and art objects slowly.

Bray's sleek apartment contrasts with the more earthy MALOOF RESIDENCE. Sam and Alfreda Maloof created a home filled with art and enhanced by warm wood tones. Their residence and workshop express their lifestyle. Sam designed and built the house, from the supporting structure to the elegant details. Even the door latches and hinges are beautifully handcrafted. The house is filled with Sam's furniture (see his rocking chair on page 221) and with ancient and contemporary art. Persian rugs and an outstanding collection of Native American rugs, pots, and baskets complement the natural wood of the house. In the large kitchen-dining area, walls of concrete block painted orange and magenta contrast with the walls of rough-hewn redwood. The house is an ongoing work of love that has engaged the Maloofs for over thirty years.

Designers apply aesthetic principles to meet everyday needs. Their art contributes to our efficiency and well-being.

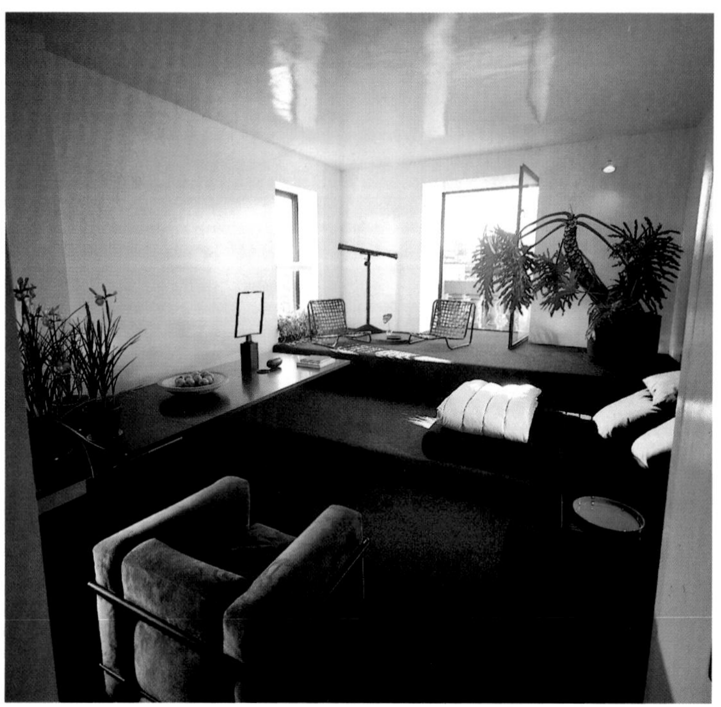

344 Bray-Schaible Design, Inc.
BRAY RESIDENCE.
Photograph: Jaime Ardiles-Arce.

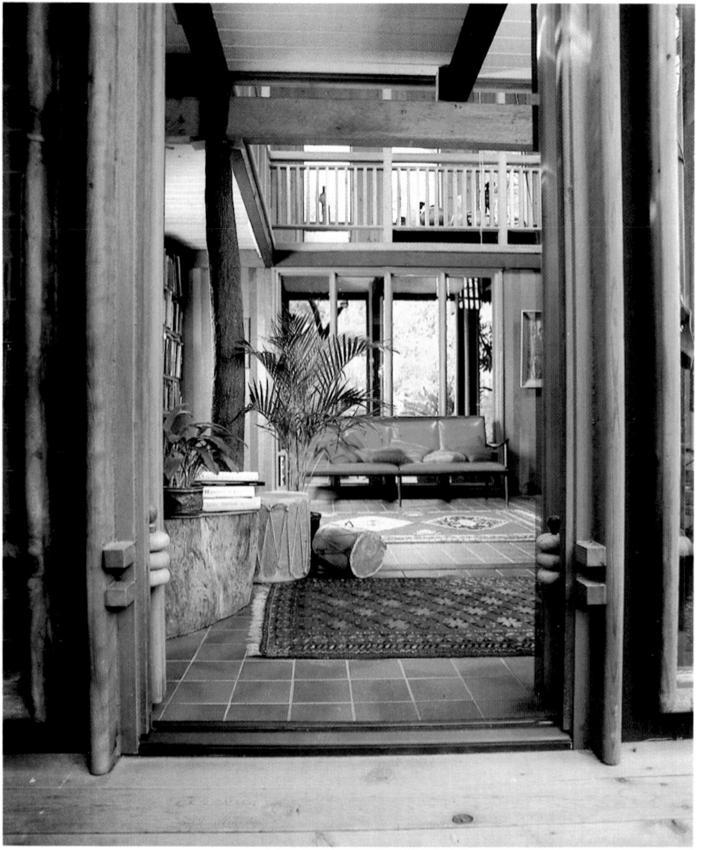

345 Sam and Alfreda Maloof.
MALOOF RESIDENCE.
Photograph: © Jonathan Pollack, 1984.

CHAPTER 15

Architecture and Environmental Design

ARCHITECTURE

Architecture is often overlooked and misunderstood as an art form—first, because of its constant presence; second, because it is generally seen as a necessity rather than an expressive statement. Of course it is both. As the art form that surrounds us in our daily lives, architecture has long made human survival both possible and enjoyable.

Architecture is the art and science of designing and constructing buildings for practical, aesthetic, and symbolic purposes. Since it grows out of basic human needs and aspirations, architecture offers one of the clearest records of a society's values. For at least five thousand years, people around the world have developed impressive techniques for building structures that go far beyond providing mere shelter.

Throughout most of human history people built their own homes, gathered or grew their own food, and made their own clothes. The essential skills for these tasks were passed on from generation to generation, from parents to children, from master to apprentice. Yet even before industrialization and the rapid growth of cities, knowledge of the building crafts was lost to all but a few. In order to provide livable housing for the world's growing population, educated people need knowledge of architectural possibilities.

Architects must address and integrate three key issues: function (how a building is used); form (how it looks); and structure (how it stands up).

We come to understand a building through a succession of experiences in time and space. Unlike a painting, a building cannot be seen or experienced all at once; to enjoy the pleasures architecture offers, one must explore buildings inside and out.

Walk around your house or apartment. How do you respond to the entrance? The height of the ceilings? Wall and floor colors, textures, materials? Window sizes and placements? The stairs, if any? Have you ever noticed how your response changes as you move from a dark, low-ceilinged entranceway to a bright, high-ceilinged room?

An Art and a Science

As an art, architecture is concerned with the design of the space-defining expressive form achieved throughout a total structure.

As a science, architecture is a physics problem: How does a structure hold up its own weight and the loads placed upon it? Architecture must be designed to withstand the forces of compression, or pushing (→←), tension, or pulling (←→), bending, or curving (↳ ↲), and any combination of these physical forces.

Today's architecture has three essential components, which can be compared to elements of the human body: a supporting skeleton or frame; an

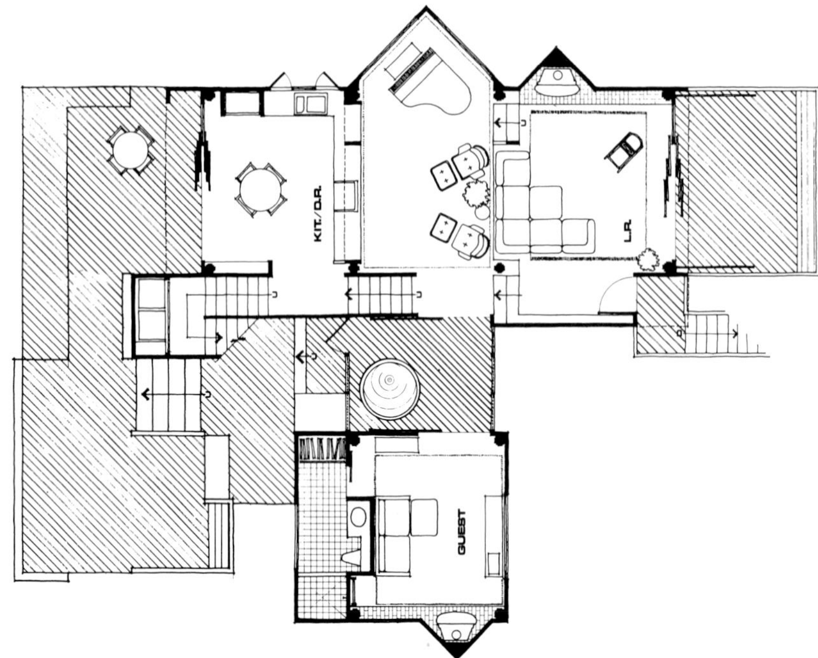

346 Beverly Hoversland.
ARCHITECTURAL DRAWINGS.

a Plan.

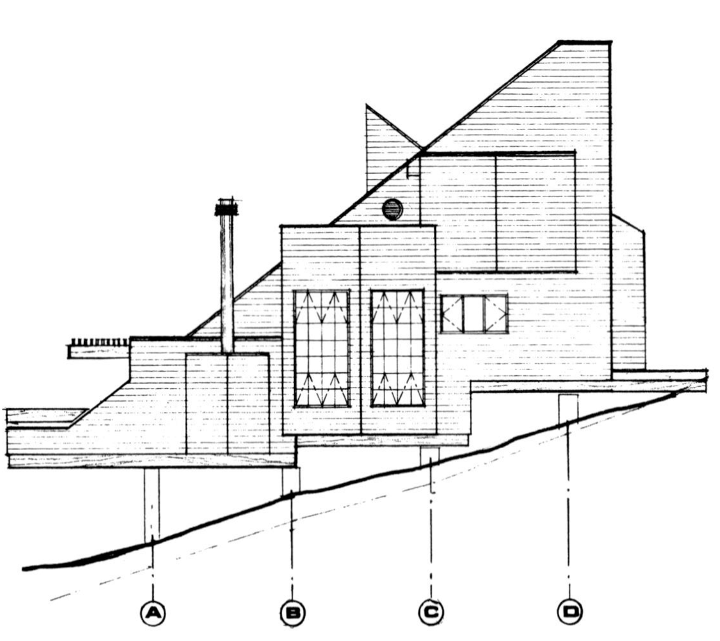

b Elevation.

outer skin; and operating equipment, similar to the body's vital organs and systems. The equipment includes plumbing; electrical wiring; appliances; and systems for cooling, heating, and circulating air as needed. In earlier centuries, structures of wood, brick, or stone had no such equipment, and the skeleton and skin were one.

To develop and present their ideas, architects make drawings and scale models. ARCHITECTURAL DRAWINGS include (a) *plans,* in which the structure is laid out in terms of the relationships among spaces as seen from above (without the roof); (b) *elevations,* in which individual exterior walls are drawn to scale as if seen straight on, thus indicating the exact proportions of such elements as wall heights and window placements; (c) *sections,* in which slices or cross sections are drawn showing details along an imaginary vertical plane passing through the proposed structure; and (d) *perspective renderings,* which give pictorial rather than schematic views of finished buildings as they will appear on their sites. Perspective renderings help the architect and the client visualize the building in relation to land contours, landscaping, and adjacent streets and buildings.

Style, Materials, and Methods

The evolution of architectural techniques and styles has been determined by the materials available and by the changing needs and values of society. In prehistoric times, when nomadic hunter-gatherers became farmers and village dwellers, housing evolved from caves and tents to substantial structures. During the Age of Faith (the High Middle Ages), the tallest buildings were stone churches; during our own age of commerce, the tallest buildings are steel and glass office towers.

By the nineteenth century, historic styles had been carefully catalogued so that architects in Europe, the United States, and other parts of the world could borrow and adapt freely, depending on the tastes of the architects and their clients. This practice of borrowing and combining from diverse styles, called *eclecticism,* had dominated architecture from the late eighteenth century to the mid-

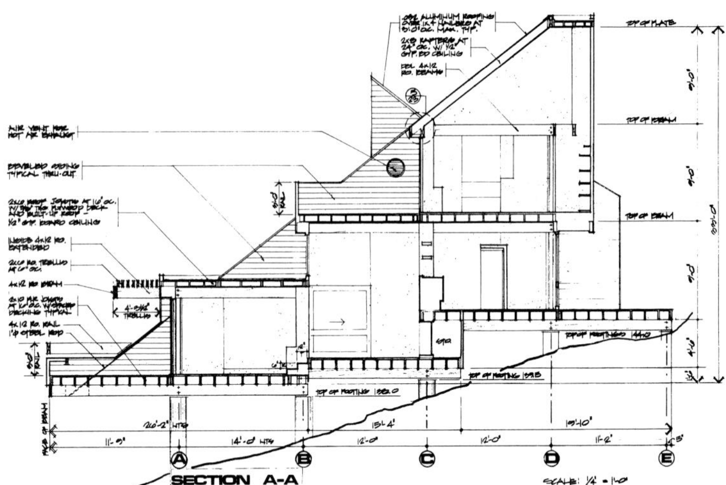

c Section.

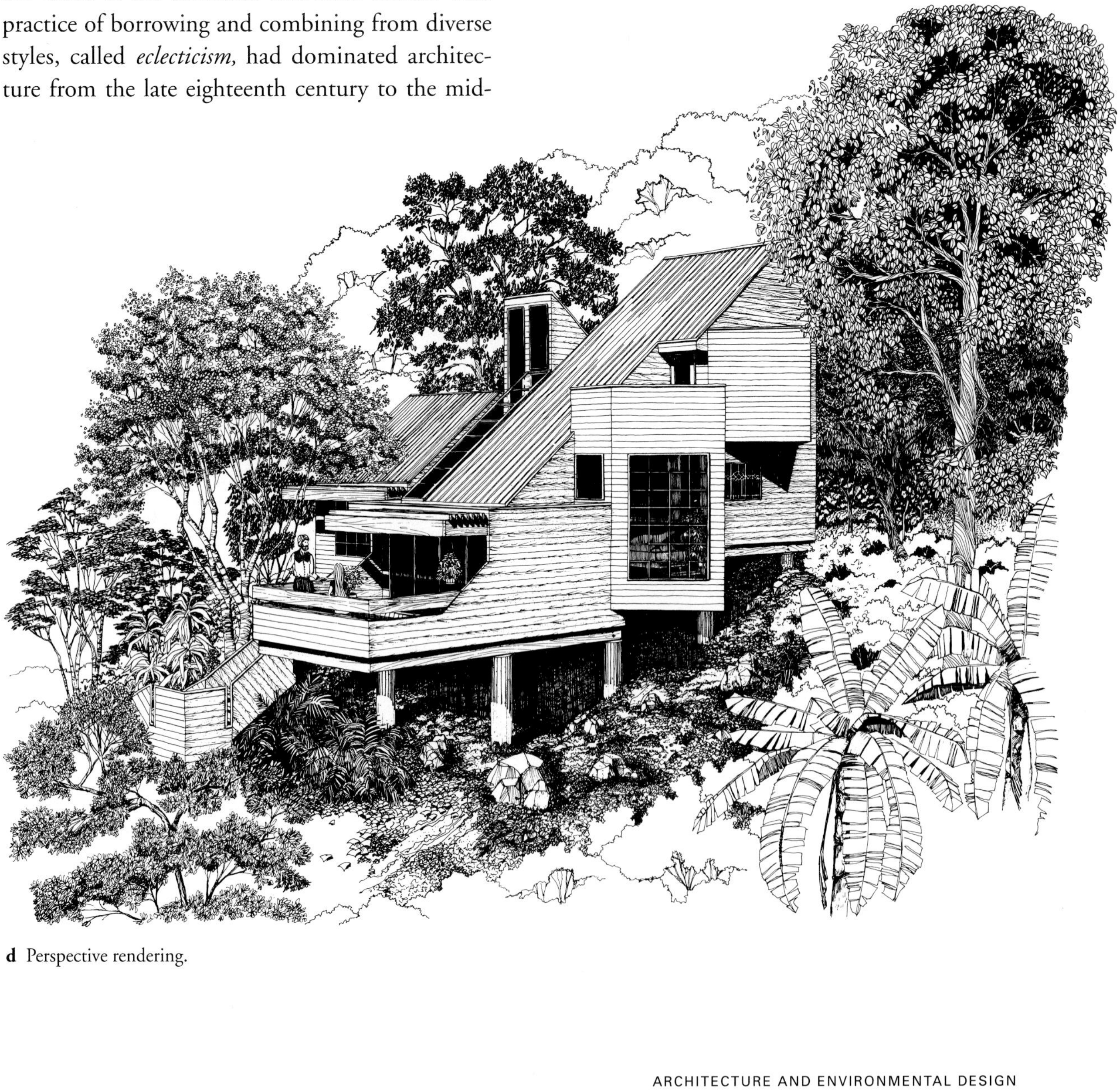

d Perspective rendering.

twentieth century. The term *revival* is used to describe architecture that is closely dependent on one particular historic style. In church design, the Byzantine, Romanesque, Baroque, and Gothic styles dominated. For public and commercial buildings, Renaissance, Greek, and Roman designs were preferred and often mixed. These preferences lasted well into the twentieth century, as numerous banks, churches, schools, and government buildings in American cities attest.

Until this century, builders learned from trial and error. Because early building designers (as well as those in nonindustrialized countries today) could design structures only out of materials at hand, regional styles developed that blended well with their sites and climates. In recent times, modern transportation and the spread of advanced technologies have made it possible to build almost anything anywhere. The consequence is a loss of a sense of place. Urban architecture in many parts of the world now looks very much alike: similiar steel-and-glass high-rise buildings dominate the skylines of most cities.

The so-called modern architecture, which originated in the early twentieth century and gained strength until the sixties, was in part a revolt against eclecticism. Modernism promoted the stripped-to-essentials, form-follows-function approach (see page 257 and pages 440–441). Since the sixties, a new wave of eclectic practices called Post-Modern has become a major trend (see pages 475–476).

Wood, Stone, and Brick

Since the beginning of history, most structures have been made of wood, stone, or brick. Each of these natural materials has its own strengths and weaknesses. For example, wood, which is light, can be used for roof beams, whereas stone, which is heavy and generally good in compression, can be used for load-bearing walls but isn't effective as a beam. Much of the world's major architecture has been constructed of stone because of its permanence, availability, and beauty. In the past, entire cities grew from the time-consuming task of cutting and fitting stone upon stone.

Post and Beam Prior to the twentieth century, two dominant structural types were in common use: post-and-beam (also called post-and-lintel) and arch systems, including vaulting. (The term *lintel,* preferred by art historians, is usually associated with stone; *beam,* preferred by today's architects and builders, is usually associated with wood, steel, and steel-reinforced concrete.) Most of the world's architecture, including modern steel structures, has been built with POST-AND-BEAM CONSTRUCTION: Vertical posts or columns support horizontal beams and carry the weight of the entire structure to the ground.

The form of post-and-beam buildings is determined by the strengths and weaknesses of the materials used. Stone beam lengths must be short and columns (posts) relatively thick to accommodate stone's brittleness. Wood beams may be longer, and posts thinner, because wood is lighter and more flexible. The strength-to-weight ratio of modern steel makes it possible to build with far longer beams and thus create much larger interior spaces.

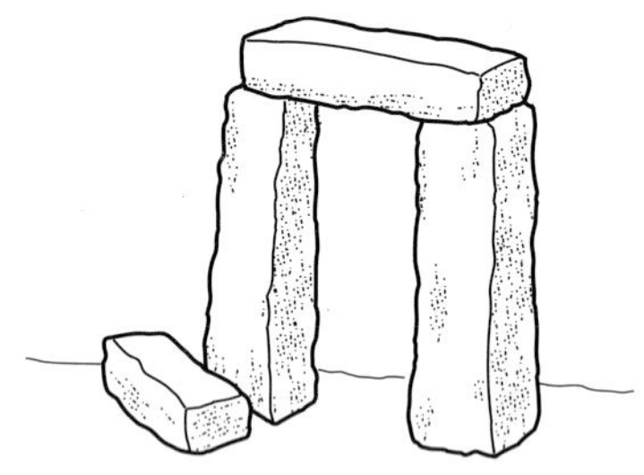

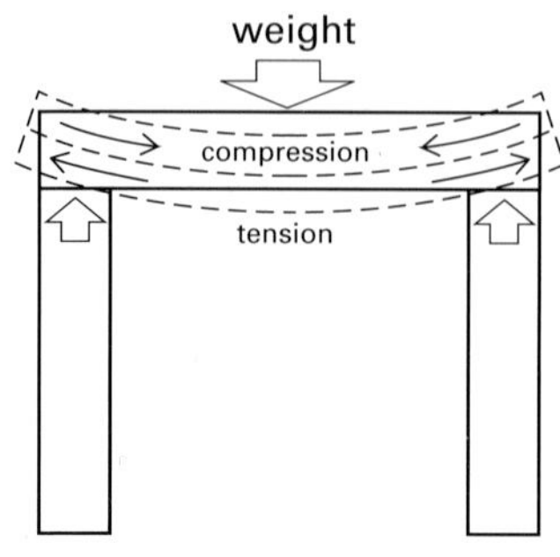

347 POST-AND-BEAM CONSTRUCTION.

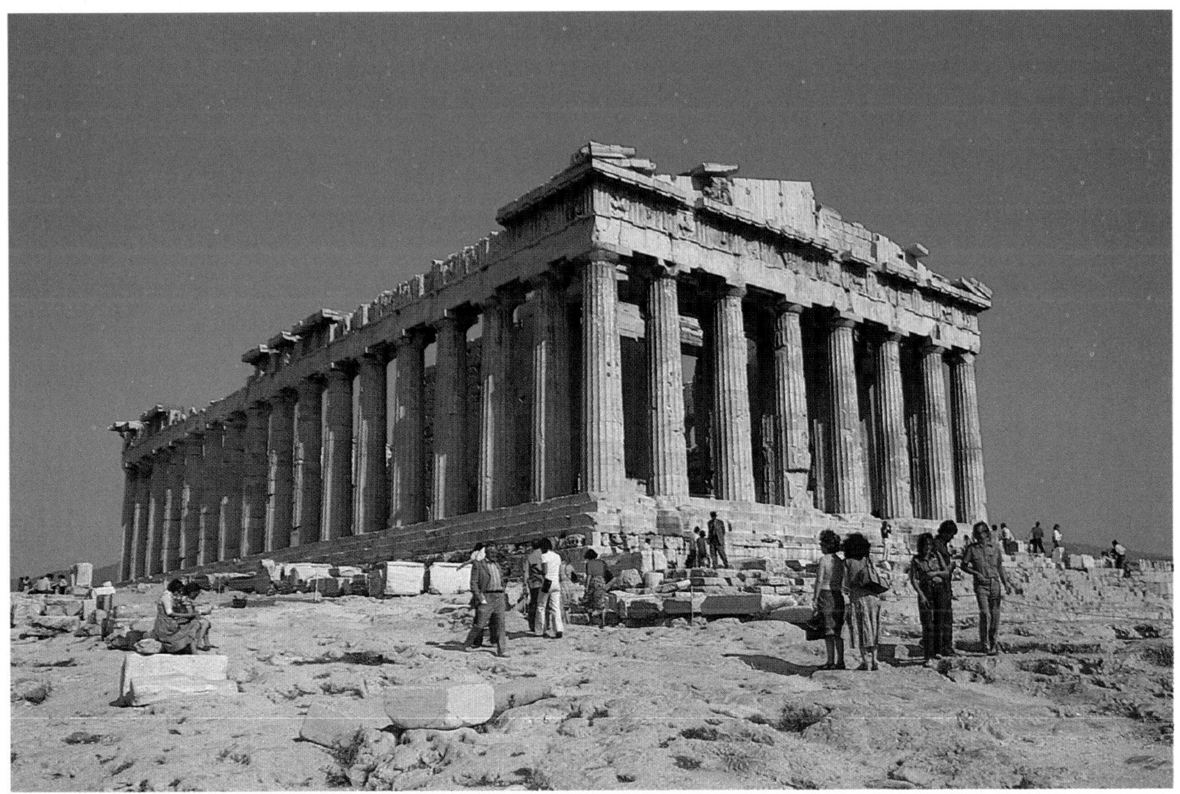

348 Ictinus and Callicrates.
PARTHENON. Athens, Greece. 447-432 B.C.
View from the northwest.

The monumental stone post-and-lintel structures of the Egyptian temples at Luxor appear to have been derived from earlier constructions in which supporting posts (columns) were made of bundles of reeds. A row of columns spanned or connected by beams is called a *colonnade,* as seen in the COLONNADE AND COURT OF AMENHOTEP III.

Following the lead of the Egyptians, the Greeks further refined stone post-and-beam construction. For more than two thousand years, the magnificence of the PARTHENON and other classical Greek architecture has influenced world architecture. Roman, Renaissance, Greek Revival, and modern architects have studied and found inspiration in classical architecture. Even today we find Greek-style government buildings with classical columns in most of the world's cities. See discussion and illustration of the Greek orders on page 325.

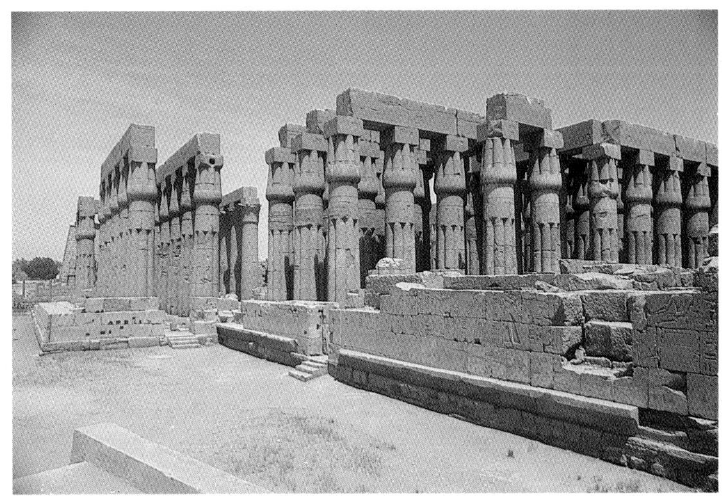

349 COLONNADE AND COURT OF AMENHOTEP III.
Temple of Amun-Mut-Khonsu. Luxor, Egypt.
c. 1390 B.C.

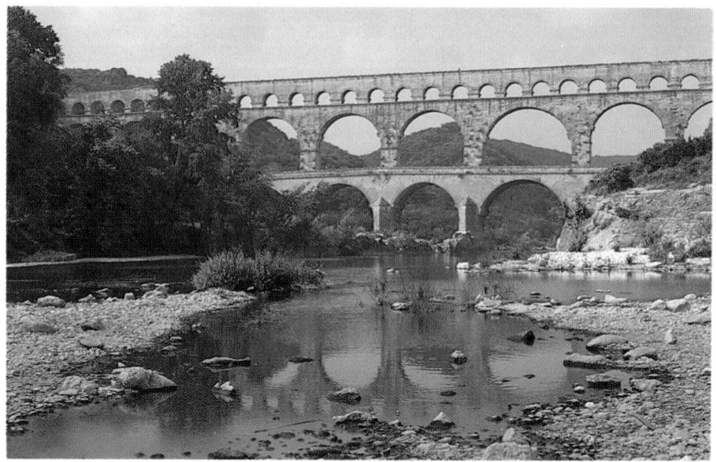

350 PONT DU GARD.
Nimes, France. A.D. 15.
Limestone. Height 161', length 902'.

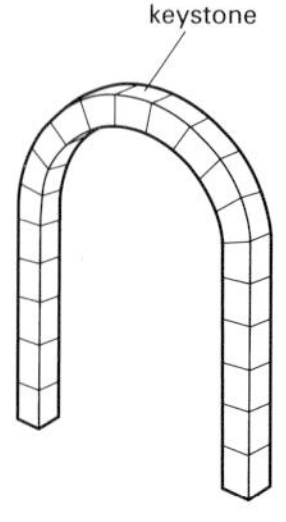

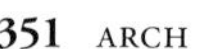

351 ARCH

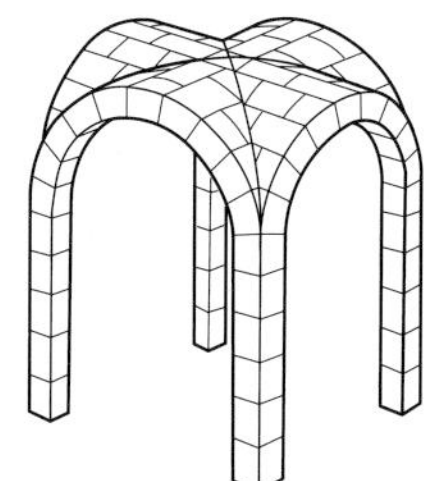

352 GROIN VAULT

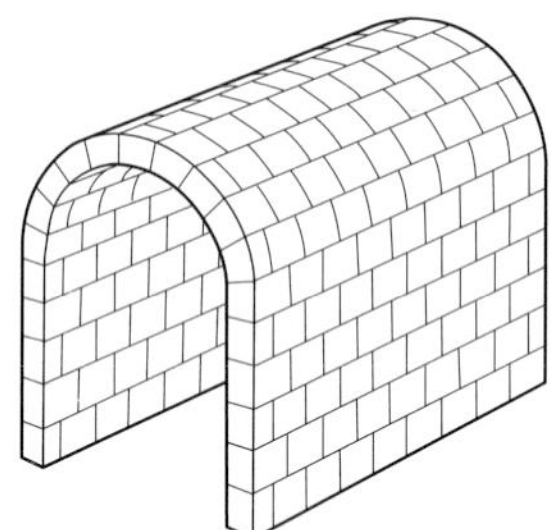

353 BARREL VAULT

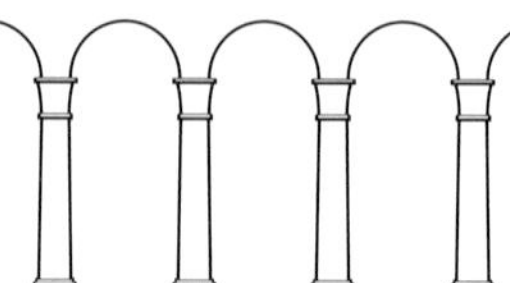

354 ARCADE

Round Arch, Vault, and Dome Both Egyptian and Greek builders had to place their columns close together because stone is weak in the tension required of a beam. A structural invention had to be made before this physical limitation of short spans could be overcome and new architectural forms created. That invention was the semicircular ARCH, which when extended in depth creates a tunnel-like structure called a BARREL VAULT. Roman builders perfected the round arch and developed the GROIN VAULT, formed by the intersection of two barrel vaults.

A *vault* is a curving ceiling or roof structure, traditionally made of bricks or blocks of stone tightly fitted to form a unified shell. In recent times, vaults have been constructed of materials such as cast reinforced concrete.

Early civilizations of western Asia and the Mediterranean area built arches and vaults of brick, chiefly for underground drains and tomb chambers. But it was the Romans who first used the arch extensively in above-ground structures. They inherited the stone arch and vault from the Etruscans, who occupied central Italy between 750 and 200 B.C.

A stone arch can span a longer distance and support a heavier load than a stone beam because much lower levels of stress develop—and no tension. The Roman arch is a semicircle made from wedge-shaped stones fitted together with joints at right angles to the curve. During construction, temporary wooden supports carry the weight of the stones. The final stone that is set in place at the top of the arch is called the *keystone.* When the keystone is placed, a continuous arch with loadbearing capacity is created, and the wooden supports can be removed. A series of such arches supported by columns forms an ARCADE.

As master builders, the Romans created cities, roads, and aqueducts throughout their vast empire in most of Europe, the Near East, and North Africa. The aqueduct called PONT DU GARD, near Nimes, France, is one of the finest remaining examples of the functional beauty of Roman engineering. The combined height of the three levels of arches is 161 feet. Uncemented stone blocks, weighing up to two tons each, make up the large arches of the two lower tiers. Water was once carried in a conduit at the top, with the first level serving as a bridge for traffic. That the aqueduct is still standing after two thousand years attests to the excellence of its design and construction.

Roman architects borrowed Greek column design and combined it with the arch, enabling them to greatly increase the variety and size of their architectural spaces. The Romans also introduced concrete as a material for architecture. Cheap, stone-like, versatile, and strong, concrete allowed the Romans to cut costs, speed construction, and build on a grand scale.

By the beginning of the fourth century, as Roman rulers shifted from outlawing Christianity to officially adopting the religion, meeting places were needed for rapidly growing congregations. Church leaders sought to have buildings designed and built specifically for Christian use. Christian architects used Roman assembly halls, called basilicas, as their models, rather than Greek or Roman temples. Yet Christian churches then and now continue to use some elements, such as columns, adapted from Greek and Roman temples.

The Roman civic basilica sheltered an oblong space with a high wooden roof supported by outer walls and by two or more inner rows of piers. Adapted for Christian churches, the center area became the nave and the narrower outer areas became the side aisles. Above the roofs of the side aisles, the upper exterior wall (called the *clerestory*) contained windows that illuminated the interior of the nave. With its three-aisled basilica plan, the church of S. APOLLINARE IN CLASSE exemplifies this type of early Christian architecture.

At one or both ends of the basilica, the Romans built a semicircular space called an *apse* in which they placed a statue of their emperor. In Christian churches, such as S. APOLLINARE, the apse is where the altar is placed. Two small wings on either side, at the apse end of the building, were first used for storing accessories. Eventually, these additions were enlarged, providing later church buildings with the characteristic Latin cross floor plan.

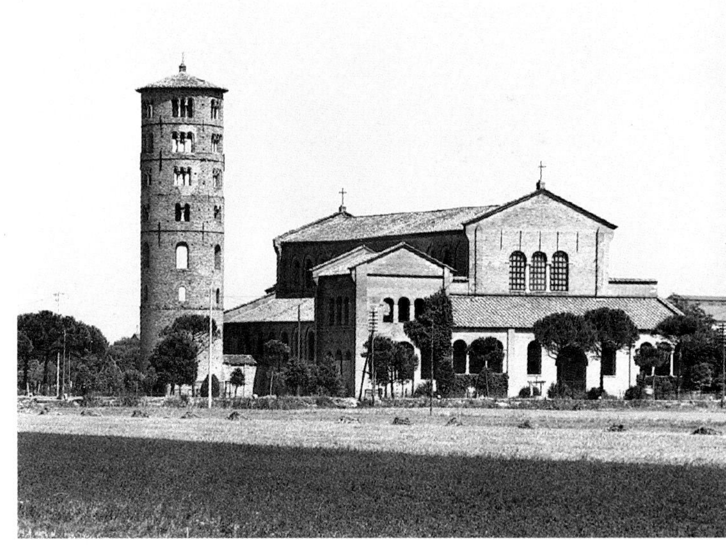

355 S. APOLLINARE IN CLASSE.
Ravenna, Italy. 533-549.
a Exterior.

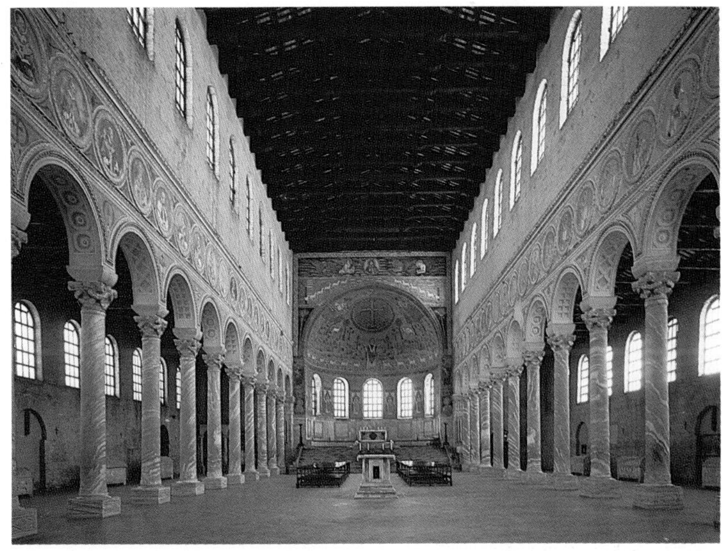

b Interior.

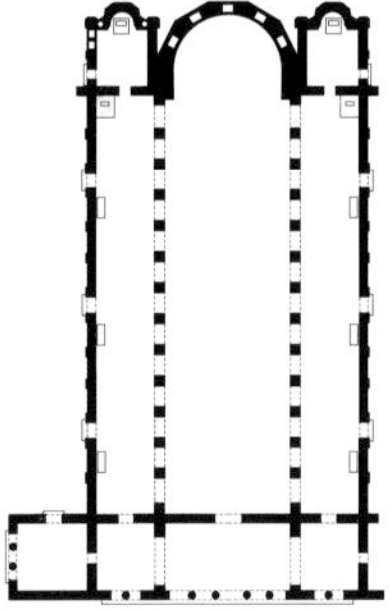

c Plan.

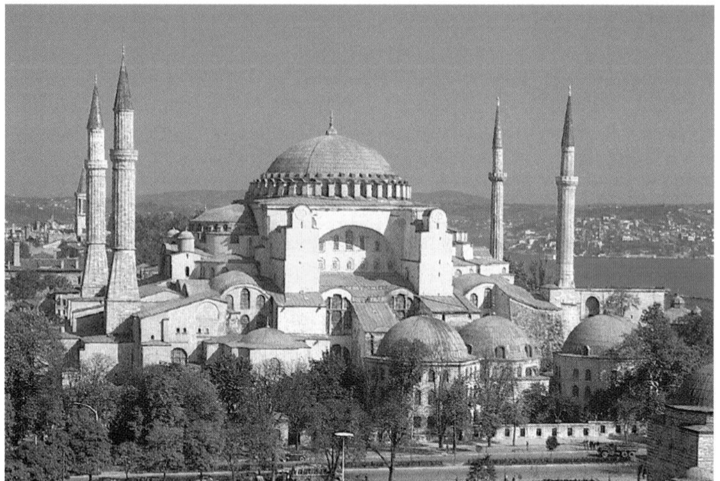

356 HAGIA SOPHIA. 532-535.
a Exterior.
Photograph: © Erich Lessing/Magnum.

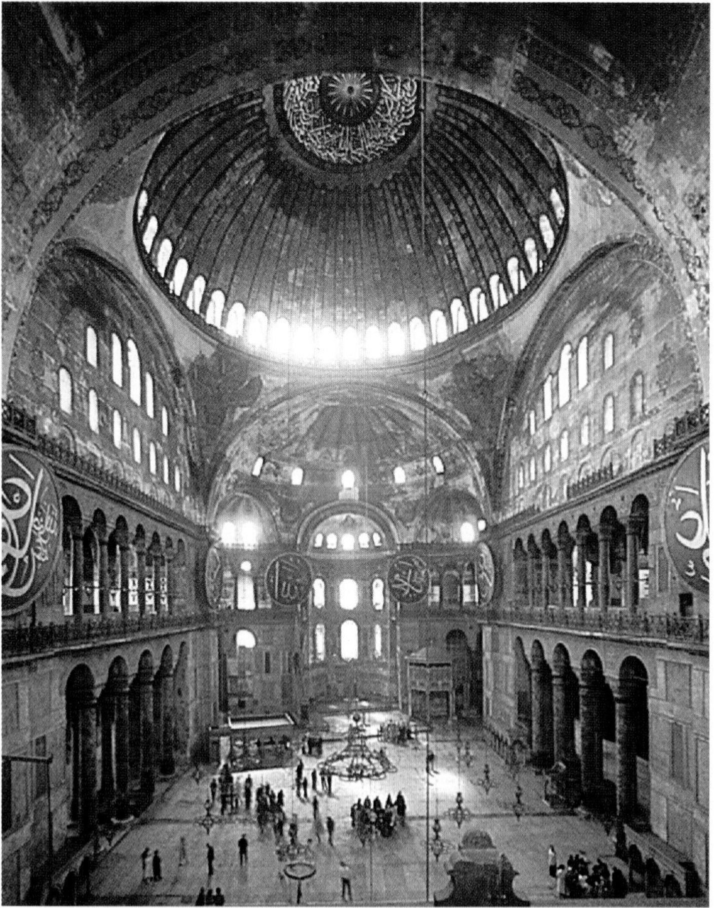

b Interior.
Photograph: Marvin Trachtenberg.

An arch rotated 360 degrees on its vertical axis creates a DOME. Domes may be hemispherical, semihemispherical, or pointed. In general usage the word *dome* refers to a hemispherical vault built up from a circular or polygonal base. Like an arch, the weight of a dome pushes downward and outward all around its circumference. Therefore, the simplest support is a cylinder with walls thick enough to resist the downward and outward thrust. The Roman PANTHEON (page 328) is a dome on a cylinder. Great domes such as those on the PANTHEON and the SULTAN AHMET MOSQUE (page 316) allow large, open interior areas.

One of the most magnificent domes in the world was designed for the Christian Byzantine cathedral of HAGIA SOPHIA in Istanbul, Turkey. It was built in the sixth century as the central sanctuary of the Eastern Orthodox Church. After the Islamic conquest of 1453, minarets were added and it was used as a mosque. It is now a museum. In contrast to the PANTHEON's dome on a cylinder, the domes of HAGIA SOPHIA and the SULTAN AHMET MOSQUE rest on square bases. (See pages 330–334 for more on the Byzantine era.)

HAGIA SOPHIA's distinctive dome appears to float on a halo of light—an effect produced by the row of windows encircling its base. The huge dome is supported on what appears to be a larger dome with its top and sides removed. Curving triangular sections called *pendentives* carry the enormous weight from the circular base of the upper dome downward to a square formed by supporting walls.

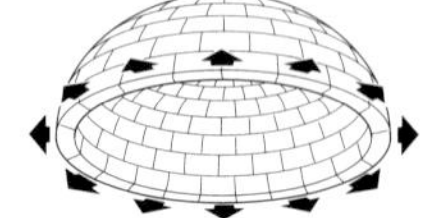

357 DOME
a Dome (arch rotated 360°).

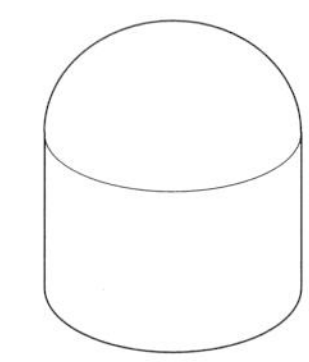

b Dome on a cylinder.

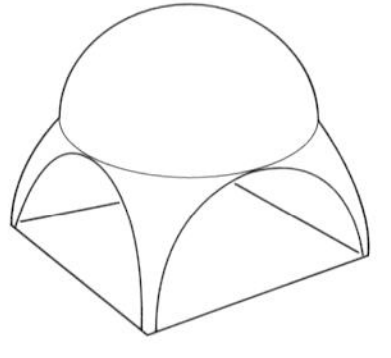

c Dome on pendentives.

(For a twentieth-century dome, see Buckminster Fuller's U.S. PAVILION on page 261.)

During the Dark Ages (after the fall of the Roman Empire), the Roman art of vaulting all but died out as the technical knowledge for engineering such structures was gradually lost. Builders used arches only for bridges and for arcades along the side walls of church interiors and courtyards. By the eleventh and twelfth centuries, however, the master builders of Europe, seeking to replace the fire-prone wooden roofs of churches with something less flammable, returned to employing barrel vaults based on the Roman concept. The resulting distinct style of the Early Middle Ages is called Romanesque. Although it was influenced by many different styles (Byzantine, Celtic, Viking, and others), its Roman heritage is apparent in its basilica plan (used by Early Christians), columns, arches, and barrel vault. While there are numerous regional variations, Romanesque churches, cathedrals, and monasteries are characterized by massive walls and Roman elements such as round arches and vaults.

Romanesque vaults, made of separate stone blocks pressing one on another, exert both downward and outward pressure. To carry the great weight of the stone ceilings (vaults), inner columns and outer walls had to be thick, with relatively small window openings. The cross section of ST. SERNIN shows how main vaults of the nave rest on arcades, with the sideways thrust carried to the outer walls by vaults over the side aisles. Dark interiors were the shortcoming of Romanesque churches such as ST. SERNIN. (The light fixtures and altar decorations are later additions.) What was needed was the development of a masonry vaulting system that would admit more natural light.

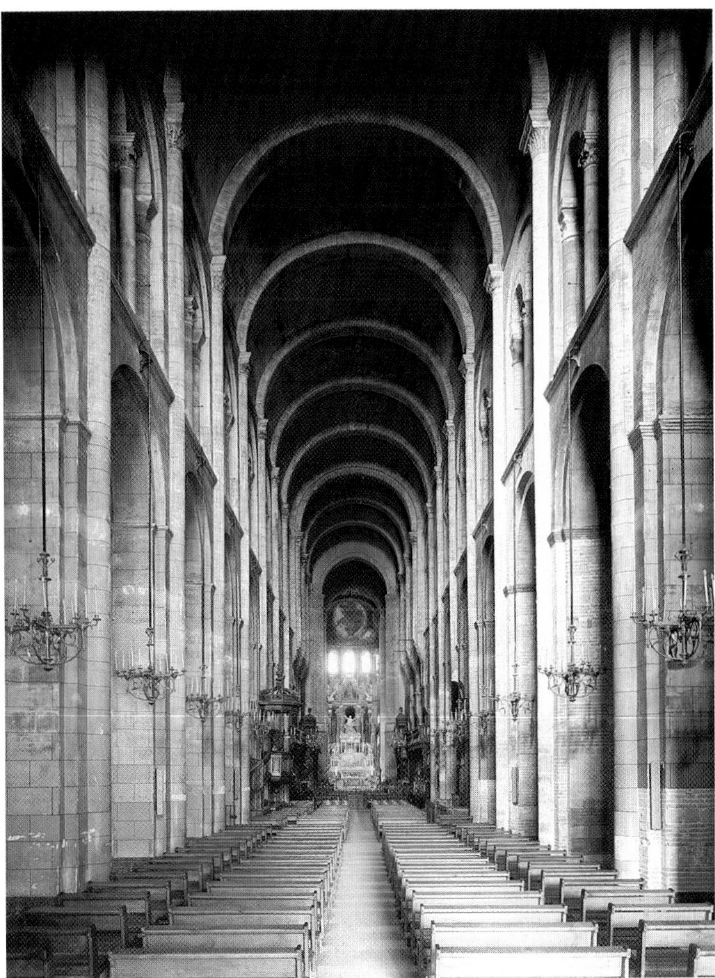

358 ST. SERNIN. Toulouse, France. c. 1080-1120.
a Nave and choir.

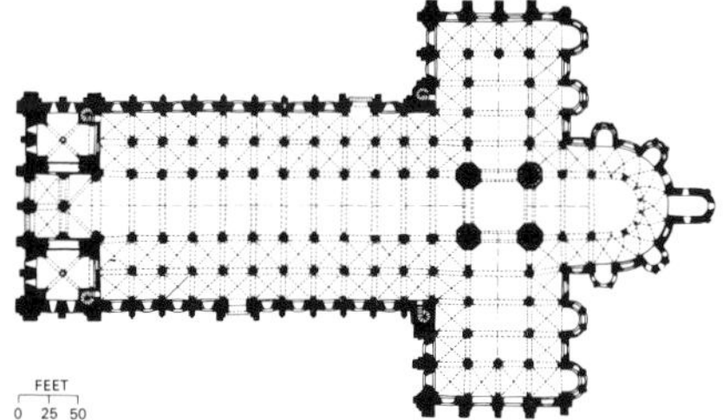

b Plan.

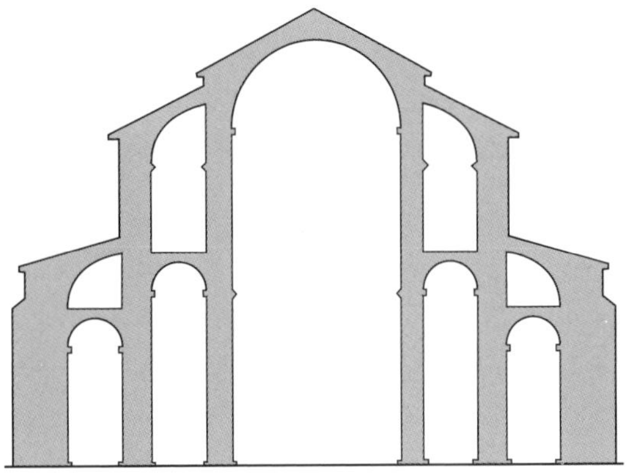

c Cross section.

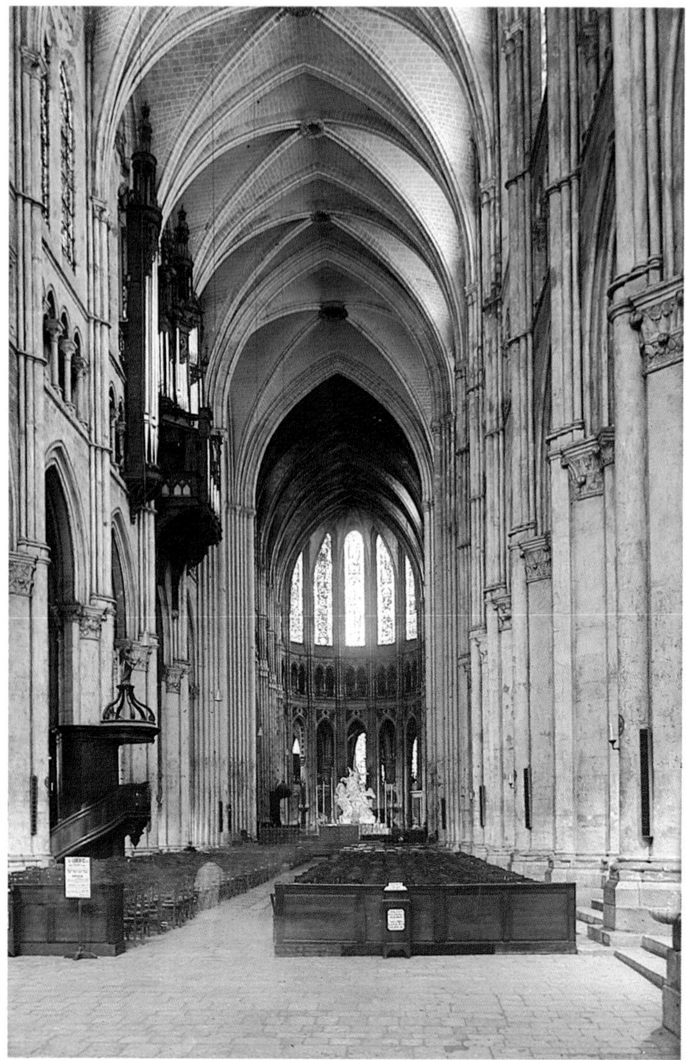

359 NOTRE DAME DE CHARTRES. Chartres, France. 1145-1513. Interior, nave. Height 122', width 53', length 130'.

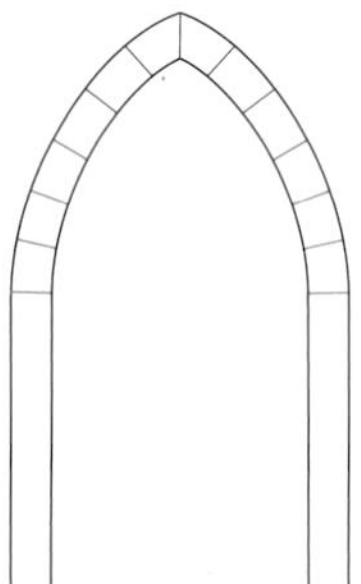

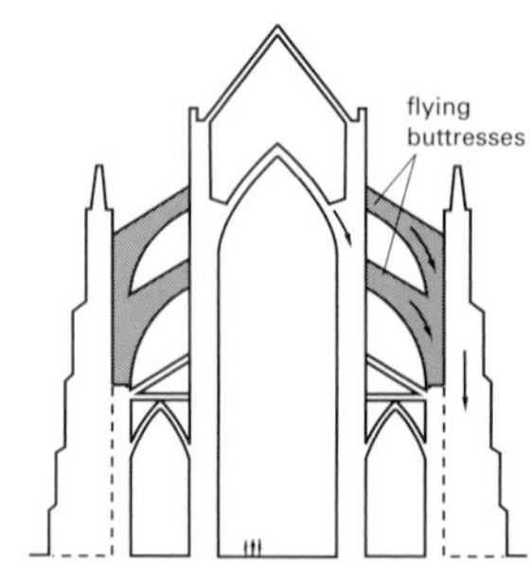

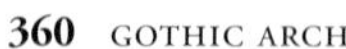

360 GOTHIC ARCH. **361** FLYING BUTTRESS.

The period was one of great experimentation with vaulting and supporting structures. Imaginative sculpture (see page 338) and colorful patterns enliven walls, entrances, and altars. The first Romanesque churches, built in a time of feudal warfare, provided powerful symbols of security in a hostile world.

Pointed Arch and Vault The pointed GOTHIC ARCH was the next great structural advance after the rounded or semicircular arch and its offspring, the dome. This new shape seems a small change, but its effect on the building of cathedrals was spectacular. Vaults based on the pointed arch made it possible to build wider naves. It was not merely the geometry of the pointed arch, but also the exterior buttresses and the trusses supporting the roof that allowed builders to go higher and to make thinner walls with larger window areas.

Although a pointed arch is steeper and therefore sends its weight more directly downward, a substantial sideways thrust must still be countered. Gothic builders accomplished this by constructing elaborate supports called *buttresses* at right angles to the outer walls. In the most developed High Gothic cathedrals, the outward force of the arched vault is carried to large buttresses by stone half-arches called *flying buttresses.*

By placing part of the structural skeleton on the outside, Gothic builders were able to make their cathedrals higher and lighter in appearance (see page 339). Since the added external support of the buttresses relieved the cathedral walls of much of their structural function, large parts of the wall could be replaced by enormous stained-glass windows, allowing more light (a symbol of God's grace and love) to enter the sanctuary. From the floor of the sanctuary to the highest part of the interior above the main altar, the windows increase in size, causing the upper part of the interior to appear dissolved in light. Stones carved and assembled to form thin ribs and pillars make up the elongated columns along the nave walls, which emphasize verticality and give the cathedral its active sense of upward thrust. (We discuss the stylistic features of Gothic architecture in more detail in Chapter 18.)

Gothic cathedrals, built in Europe from the twelfth to the sixteenth centuries, are among the most inventive and awe-inspiring architectural achievements of all time. Their enthusiastic spirit of ascendance symbolizes an era of renewed religious faith and economic prosperity. In contrast to the heavy, relatively dark interiors of their Romanesque predecessors, the interiors of Gothic cathedrals such as NOTRE DAME DE CHARTRES are more open to light and seem almost weightless as they soar upward (see also pages 339 and 341). Light enriched by the colors of stained glass and soaring interior space expressed the devotion and spiritual aspirations of the people who built these monuments. During this period, Christian belief helped to unify much of European society.

New Materials, New Techniques

No basic structural technique was added to the Western architectural vocabulary after the Gothic pointed arch and vault until the nineteenth century. Instead, architects designed a variety of structures—at times highly innovative—in which combinations of borrowed elements played important new roles. Forms and ornamentation from the Greek and Roman periods were revived again and again and given new life in different contexts.

In the nineteenth century, eclectic and revival architecture consisted primarily of elements applied to exteriors, while interior spaces were designed in more contemporary ways, often taking advantage of new technical resources. Cast iron became technically useful during the Industrial Revolution, and it led to new types of structures in which heavy, load-bearing walls were no longer needed. Iron has much greater strength than most stone and can span much larger distances. The engineering of structures with iron was a prelude to the development of steel toward the end of the nineteenth century and steel-reinforced concrete in the twentieth.

Truss and Balloon Frame Construction It is possible to build strong structures with relatively thin wooden boards. One method is to use TRUSSES, such as those used for structural support in Gothic cathedral roofs. A *truss* is a triangular framework used to span, reinforce, or support. Another method is balloon framing, in which heavy timbers are replaced with thin studs held together only with nails. In the nineteenth century, the availability of cheap wood in the United States led to the BALLOON FRAME innovation in wood construction for houses and other small structures. Oldtimers, who were unwilling to use the new method, called it balloon framing because they thought it was as fragile as a balloon. The method—widely used since its 1833 introduction—made possible the rapid settlement of the Western frontier.

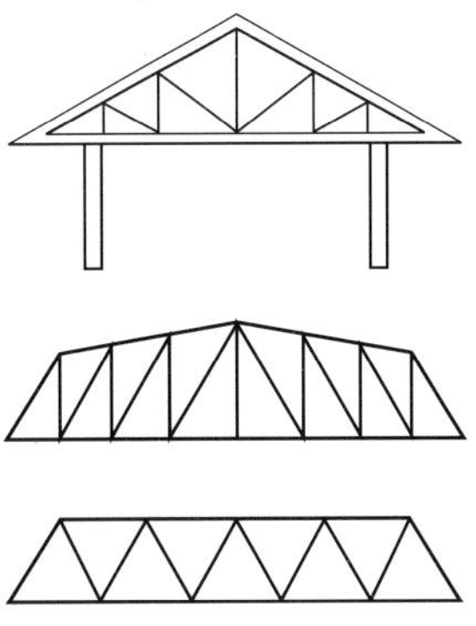

362 TRUSSES.

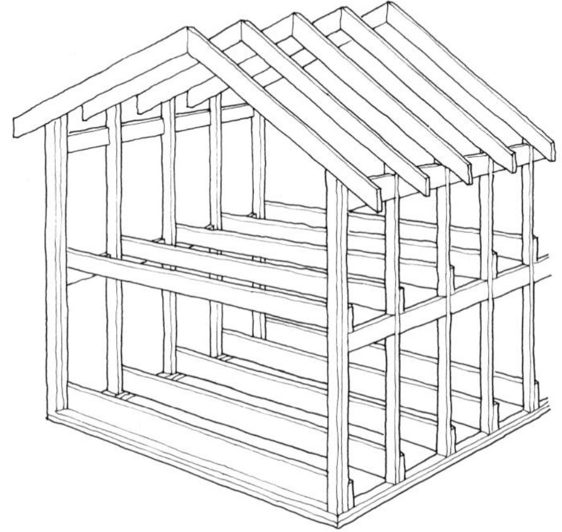

363 BALLOON FRAME.

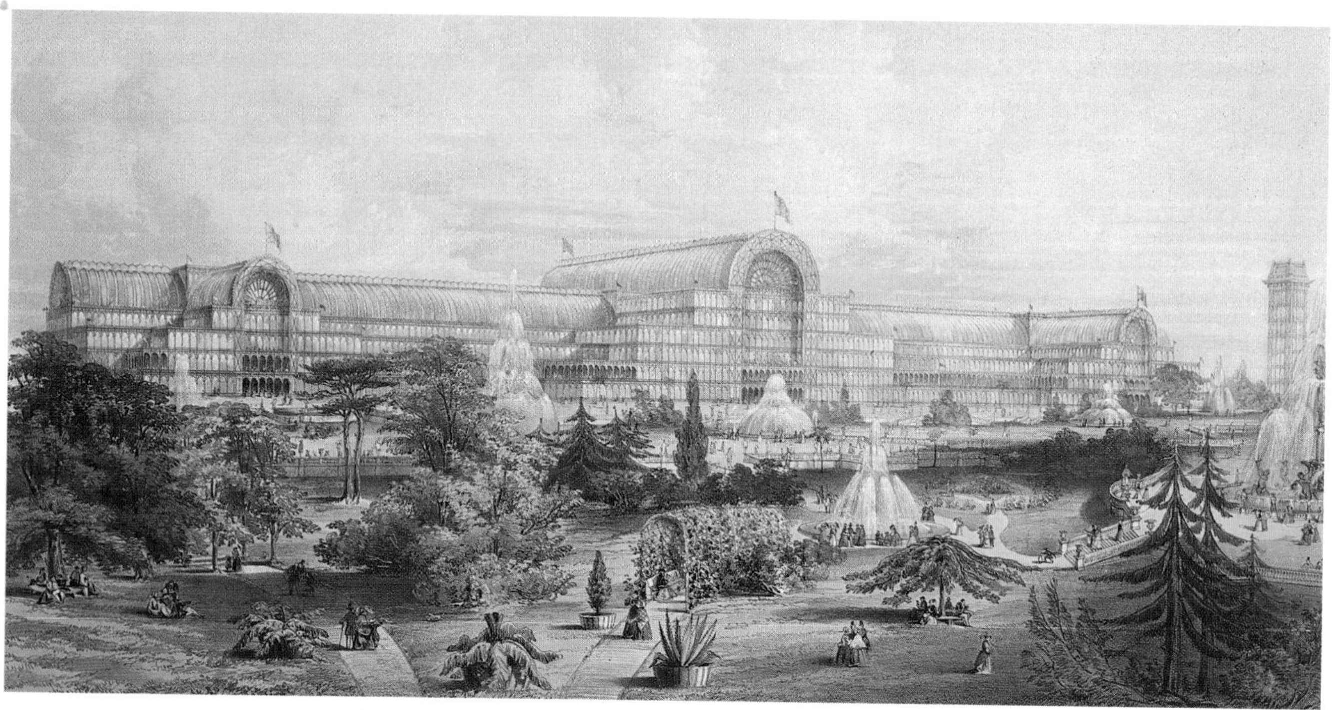

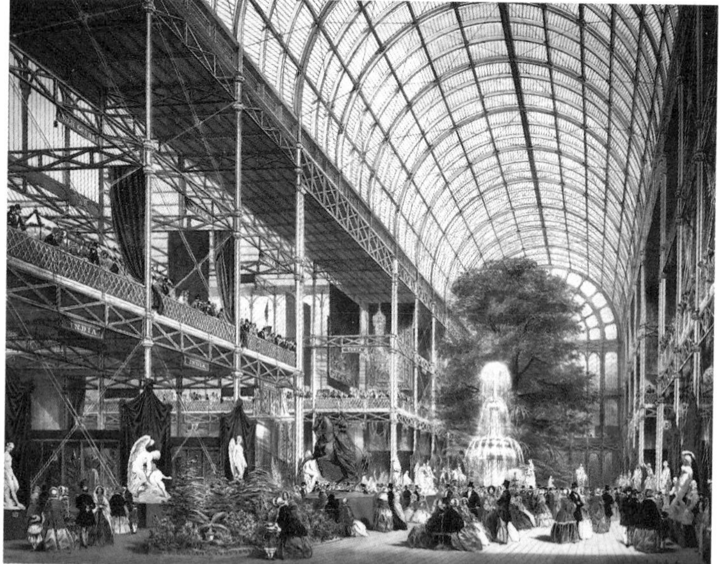

364 Joseph Paxton.
CRYSTAL PALACE.
London. 1850-1851 (destroyed by fire in 1936).
Cast iron and glass. Width 408', length 1851'.
a Exterior. (Lithograph by Vincent Brooks. Victoria and Albert Museum, London. Crown Copyright.)
b Interior. (Etching by Lothar Buchar. Victoria and Albert Museum, London. Crown Copyright.)

Cast Iron By the mid-nineteenth century, the world was being transformed by science and industry. New inventions of the industrial age led to a revolution in architecture. First cast iron, then steel, then steel-reinforced concrete, electricity, and the invention of the high-speed elevator gave architects a set of materials and technologies that changed the design of city buildings.

After the iron industry was established, cast and wrought iron became important building materials. Stronger and more fire-resistant than wood, iron led to lighter exterior walls and more flexible uses of interior space. Factories, bridges, and railway stations were among the new types of buildings for which cast iron was used.

The CRYSTAL PALACE, designed by Joseph Paxton, was a spectacular demonstration of what cast iron could do. It was designed and built for the Great Exhibition of the Works of Industry of All Nations, the first international exposition, held in London in 1851. The building was designed to show off the latest mechanical inventions, and it was perfectly suited to the task. This was the first time new industrial methods and materials were eloquently presented in architecture. In its day, the CRYSTAL PALACE was recognized as a highly original expression of the spirit of the new age.

In this building there was no borrowing of earlier styles. Paxton used relatively lightweight, factory-made modules (standard-size structural units) of cast iron and glass. By freeing himself from past styles and masonry construction, Paxton created a whole new architectural vocabulary. The light, decorative quality of the glass and cast-iron units was created not by applied ornamentation, but by the structure itself. The modular units provided enough flexibility for the entire structure to be assembled on the site, right over existing trees, and later disassembled and moved across town. Unfortunately, a fire destroyed the building in 1936.

Paxton's successful innovation was a new application of the concept "form follows function," expressed earlier by Renaissance architect Leon Battista Alberti and later made famous by American architect Louis Sullivan.

The 984-foot EIFFEL TOWER in Paris, designed and built by civil and aeronautic engineer Gustave Eiffel in 1889, epitomizes the inventive spirit of the new cast-iron structures of the mid- to late nineteenth century. At the time of its design and construction, the tower was highly controversial because of its disruption of the low skyline of Paris. (All cities were low-rise then.) When it was built, it was the world's tallest freestanding structure. Even now, as the city's most visible symbol, it dominates the Paris skyline.

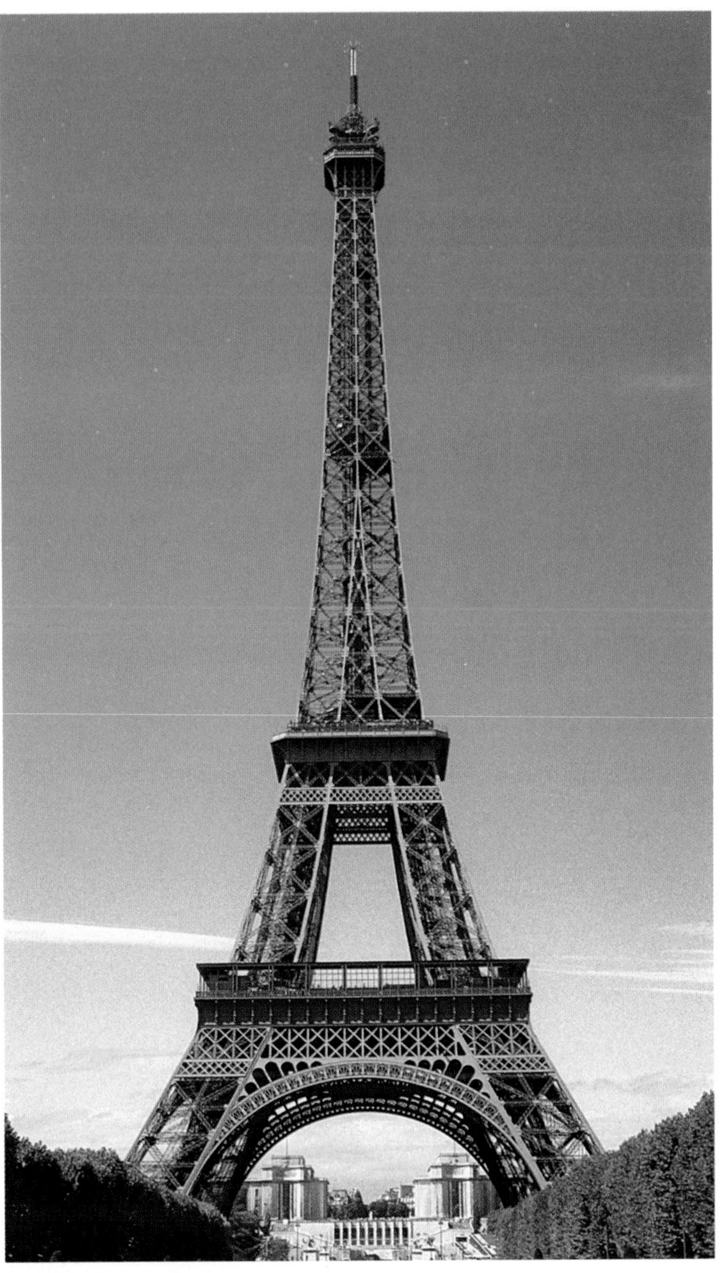

365 Alexandre Gustave Eiffel.
EIFFEL TOWER. 1889.
Iron frame. Height: 984'.
Photograph: Harry G. Kasanow, Honolulu.

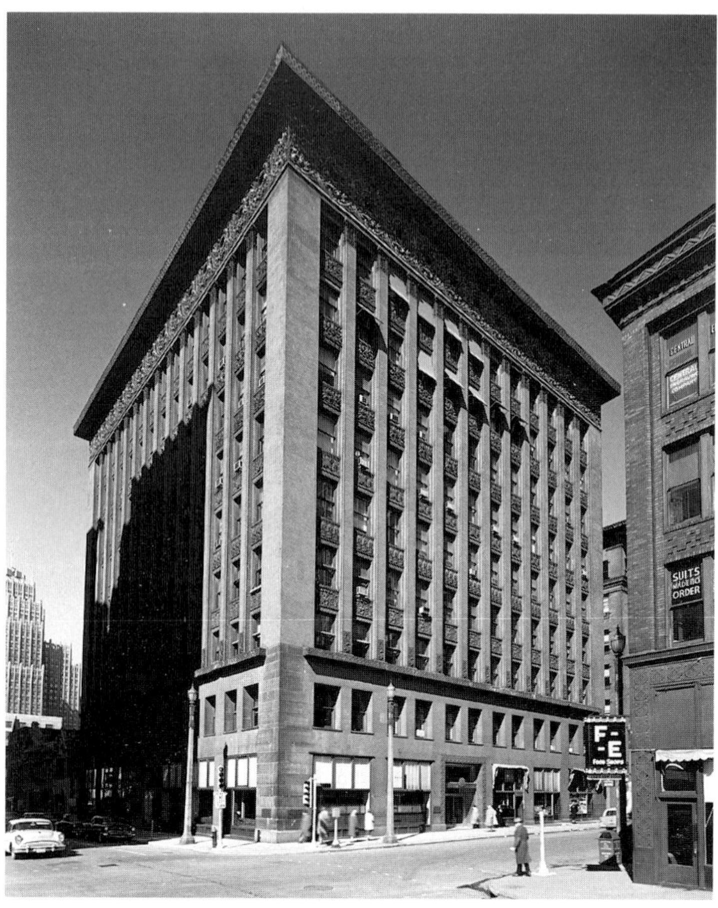

366 Louis Sullivan.
WAINWRIGHT BUILDING. St. Louis. 1890-1891.

Steel and Reinforced Concrete The next breakthrough in construction methods for large structures came between 1890 and 1910 with the development of high-strength structural steel, used by itself and as the reinforcing material in reinforced concrete. The extensive use of cast-iron skeletons in the mid-nineteenth century had prepared the way for multistory steel-frame construction in the 1890s.

New building techniques and materials, as well as new functional needs, demanded a fresh approach to structure and form. The movement began to take shape in commercial architecture, became symbolized by early skyscrapers, and found one of its first opportunities in Chicago, where the big fire of 1871 had cleared the way for a building boom.

Leading the Chicago school was Louis Sullivan, regarded as the first great modern architect. He rejected eclectic practices and sought to meet the needs of his time by using building methods and materials made available by the new technology. Sullivan had a major influence on the early development of what became America's and the twentieth century's most original contribution to architecture: the skyscraper.

Sullivan's first high-rise building, the WAINWRIGHT BUILDING in St. Louis, Missouri, was made possible by the invention of the elevator and by the development of steel used for the structural skeleton. The building breaks with nineteenth-century tradition in a bold way. Its exterior design reflects the internal steel frame and emphasizes the height of the structure by underplaying horizontal elements in the central window area. Sullivan demonstrated his sensitivity and adherence to the harmony of traditional architecture by dividing the building's facade into three distinct zones, reminiscent of the base, shaft, and capital of Greek columns (see page 325). These areas also reveal the various functions of the building, with shops at the base and offices in the central section. The heavily ornamented band at the top (cornice) acts as a capital, stopping the vertical thrust of the piers located between the office windows. All of Sullivan's buildings bear his distinctive terra-cotta ornamentation.

The interdependence of form and function is

found in nature and in well-designed human forms. Sullivan's observation that "form ever follows function" eventually helped architects to break with their reliance on past styles and to rethink architecture from the inside out.[1]

In this spirit, a new architecture arose in Europe between 1910 and 1930. It rejected decorative ornamentation and eclecticism, as well as traditional stone and wood construction, and it broke away from the earlier idea of a building as a mass. The resulting International Style (also called International Modern) expressed the function of each building, its underlying structure, and a logical (often asymmetrical) plan. (You can read more about the International Style and the more recent Post-Modern reaction to it on pages 440–441 and 475–476.)

With a simple drawing of the DOMINO CONSTRUCTION SYSTEM, Le Corbusier—French architect, painter, and city planner—demonstrated the basic components of steel-column and reinforced-concrete-slab construction. This concept was used extensively later in the century as architects adopted the look, and sometimes the principles, of the International Style. Le Corbusier's idea of supporting floors and roof on interior load-bearing columns instead of load-bearing walls made it possible to vary the placement of interior walls and the nature of exterior coverings. His sense of style was inspired by the efficiency of machines and an awareness of the importance of natural light.

Walter Gropius carried out the principles of the International Style in his new building for the BAUHAUS when the school moved to Dessau, Germany (see also page 228). The workshop wing, built between 1925 and 1926, follows the basic concept illustrated in Le Corbusier's drawing. Because the reinforced-concrete floors and roof were supported by steel columns set back from the outer edge of the building, exterior walls did not have to carry any weight: they could be *curtain walls* made of glass. Even interior walls were non-load-bearing and could be placed anywhere they were needed.

In the United States, the development of the high-rise building reached a climax in New York.

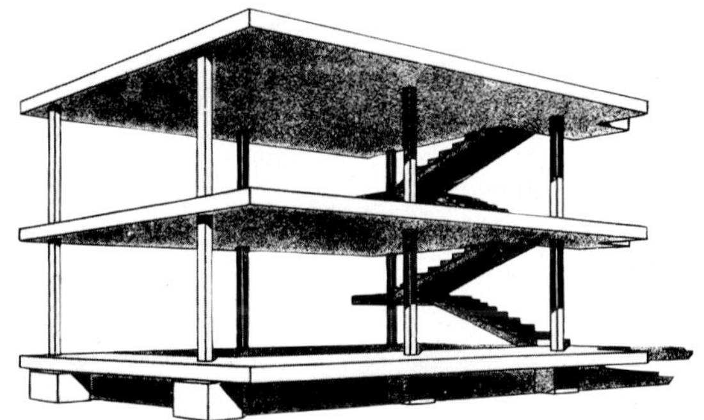

367 Le Corbusier.
DOMINO CONSTRUCTION SYSTEM. 1914-1915.

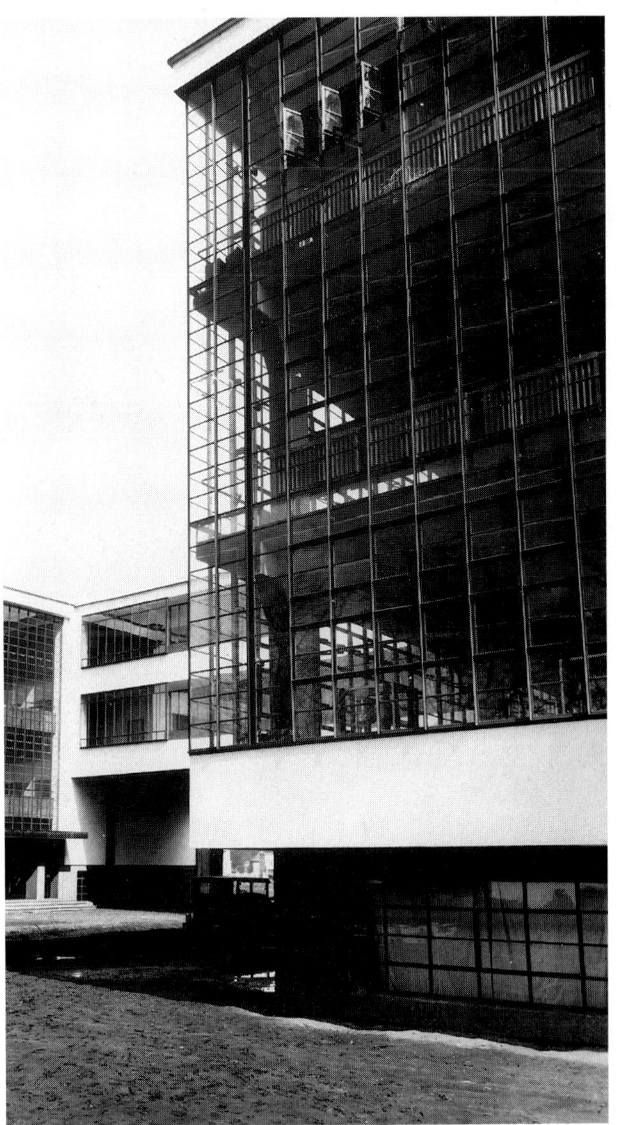

368 Walter Gropius.
BAUHAUS. Dessau, Germany. 1925-1926.

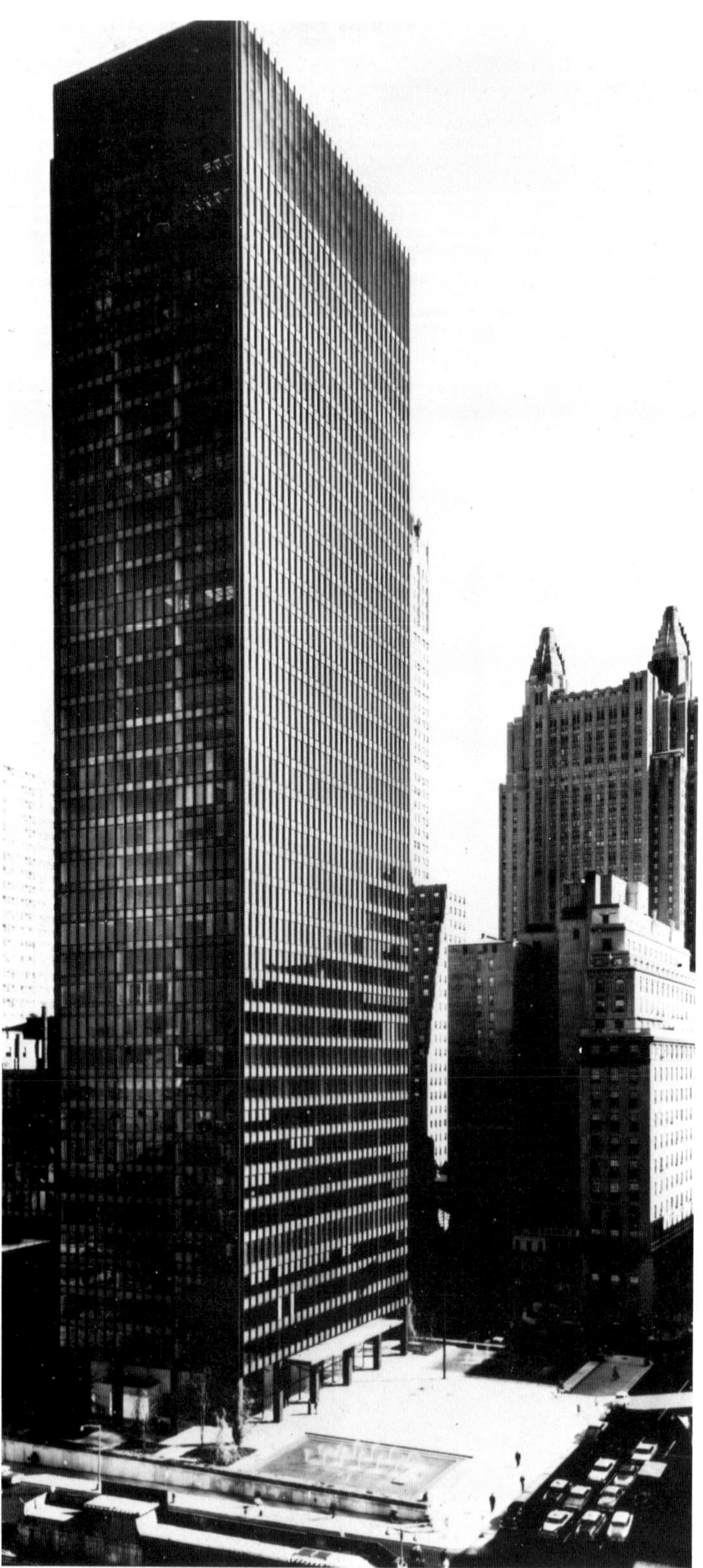

369 Ludwig Mies van der Rohe and Philip Johnson. SEAGRAM BUILDING. New York. 1956-1958.
Photograph: Ezra Stoller © Esto.

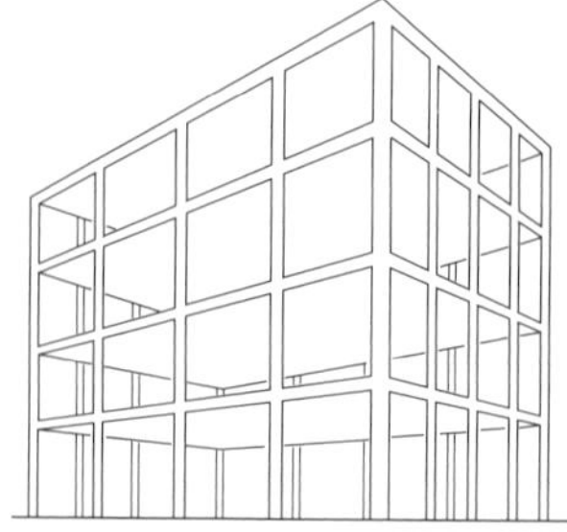

370 STEEL-FRAME CONSTRUCTION.

On the city's small, heavily populated Manhattan Island, tall buildings provided a way to supply more residential and commercial space. By 1915, New York was suffering from poor air circulation and reduction of sunlight because so many skyscrapers were built straight up from the sidewalk. By the 1920s, a new *set-back* law required architects to terrace their structures back from the street to allow sunlight to enter what were becoming dark canyons (see page 273).

Le Corbusier's idea for alleviating urban crowding by using tall, narrow buildings fronted by open space, and Sullivan's concept for high-rise buildings that express the grid of their supporting STEEL-FRAME CONSTRUCTION came together in the SEAGRAM BUILDING, designed by Mies van der Rohe and Philip Johnson. Non-load-bearing glass walls had been a major feature of Mies's plans for skyscrapers conceived as early as 1919, but it wasn't until the 1950s that he had the chance to build such structures. In the SEAGRAM BUILDING, interior floor space gained by the height of the building allowed the architects to leave a large, open public area at the base. The vertical lines emphasize the height and provide a strong pattern that is capped by a top section designed to give a sense of completion. The austere design embodies Mies van der Rohe's famous statement "less is more."

Mies van der Rohe was a leading proponent of the International Style, which had an enormous, if sometimes negative, influence on world architecture. It has often replaced unique, place-defining regional styles. By mid-century, modern (now called modernist) architecture had become synonymous with the International Style. The uniformity of glass-covered rectilinear grid structures was considered the appropriate formal dressing for the bland anonymity of the modern corporation.

During the building boom of the 1950s and 1960s, buildings using huge expanses of glass were popular with architects and were not seriously questioned by clients until the energy crisis of the early 1970s. The thin glass skins of such buildings cause them to require costly heating, cooling, and ventilating systems that consume large amounts of electricity. Concerned architects have since created more energy-efficient designs.

Energy efficiency was a major consideration in the design of CITICORP CENTER, completed in 1977. The square floor plan of the tower requires less energy to heat or cool than any plan except a circle. The building's exterior has twice the usual amount of insulation, including double layers of reflective glass, and much less glass surface area than older International Style office buildings. Other energy-saving features include a heat reclamation system and a sloping roof designed to utilize solar energy.

The architects, Stubbins Associates and Emery Roth and Sons, expanded on the idea of maximizing the amount and quality of ground-level public space. The height and placement of the four columns that support the square tower increase the feeling of spaciousness at street level.

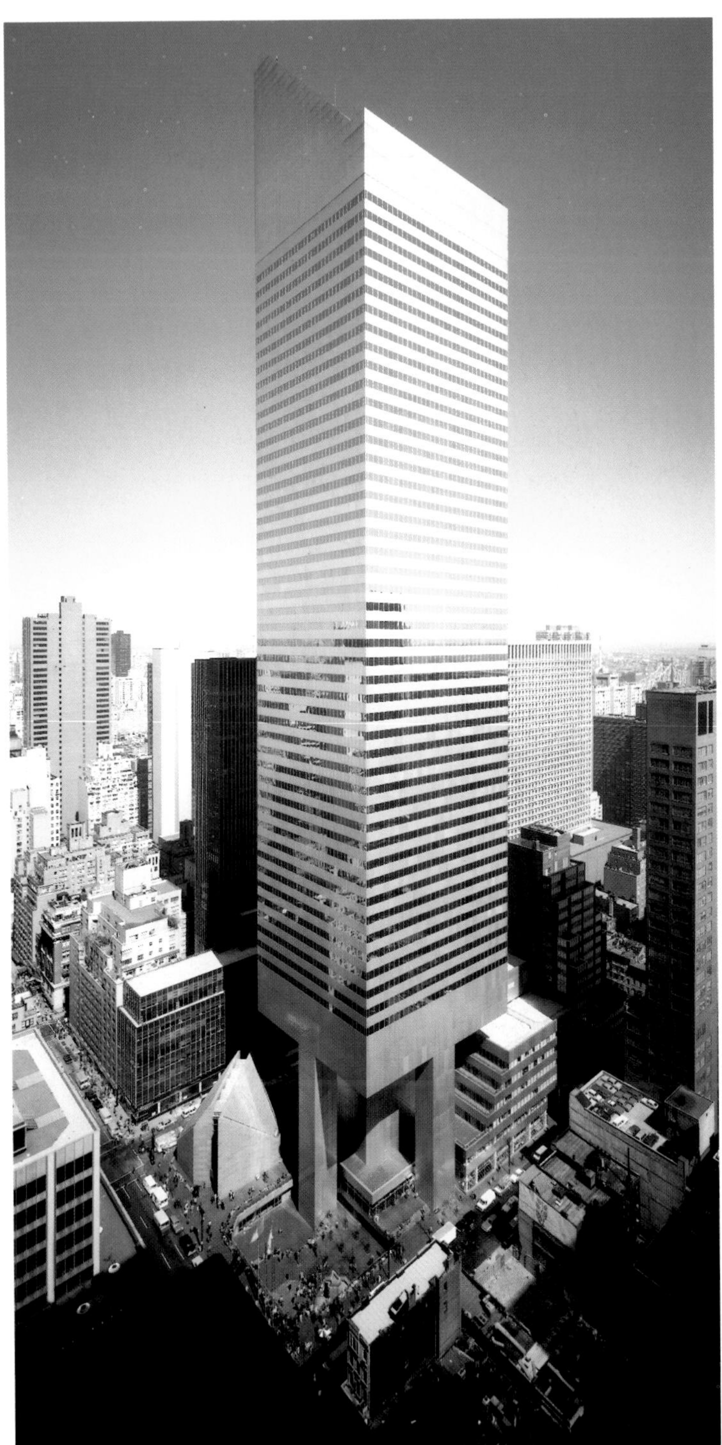

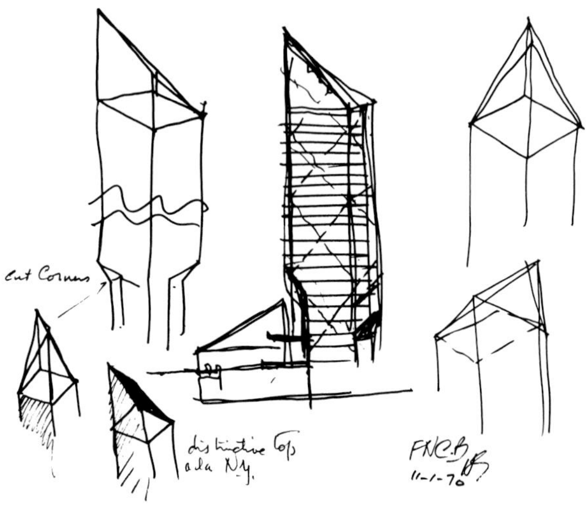

371 The Stubbins Associates, Inc., and Emery Roth and Sons.
a CITICORP CENTER. New York. Completed in 1977.
Photograph: © Edward Jacoby/APG.
b Idea sketches for CITICORP CENTER.

Recent Innovations

Reinforced concrete and steel have provided the raw materials for a variety of new structural forms. The giant roofs of Kenzo Tange's indoor stadiums, built in Tokyo for the 1964 Olympics, are supported by a SUSPENSION STRUCTURE of the type employed previously for bridge construction. Tange's tentlike OLYMPIC STADIUMS integrate spatial, structural, and functional requirements.

In the main building, which houses the swimming pools, Tange and structural engineer Yoshikatsu Tsuboi designed an interior space with seating for fifteen thousand. The vast open area under the roof was made possible by suspending the roof from steel cables strung from huge concrete abutments at either end of the building (rather than supporting the roof with interior columns). In spite of the structure's large size, the entire building complements rather than dwarfs human scale. Diving platforms, seats, and air-conditioning vent pipes on the end wall are part of the unified sculptural design.

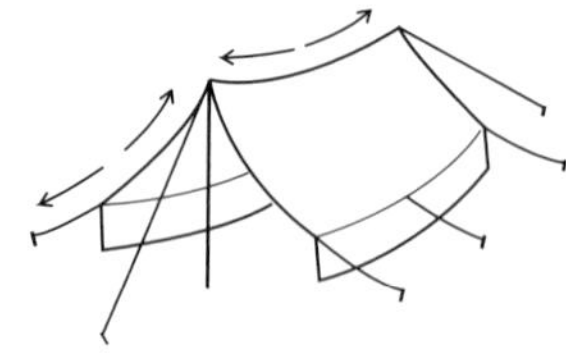

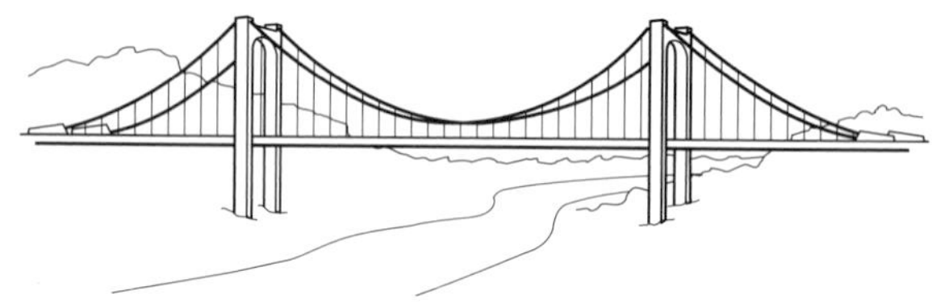

372 SUSPENSION STRUCTURES.

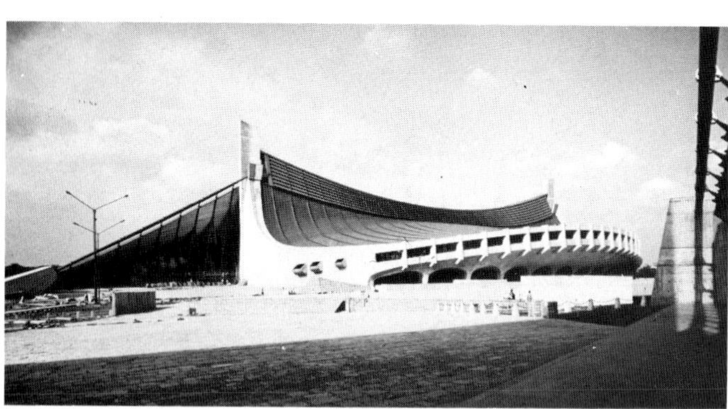

a Exterior, natatorium.

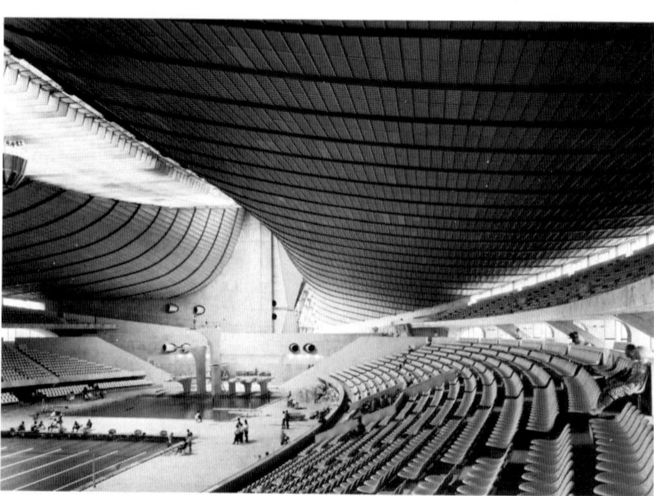

b Interior, natatorium.

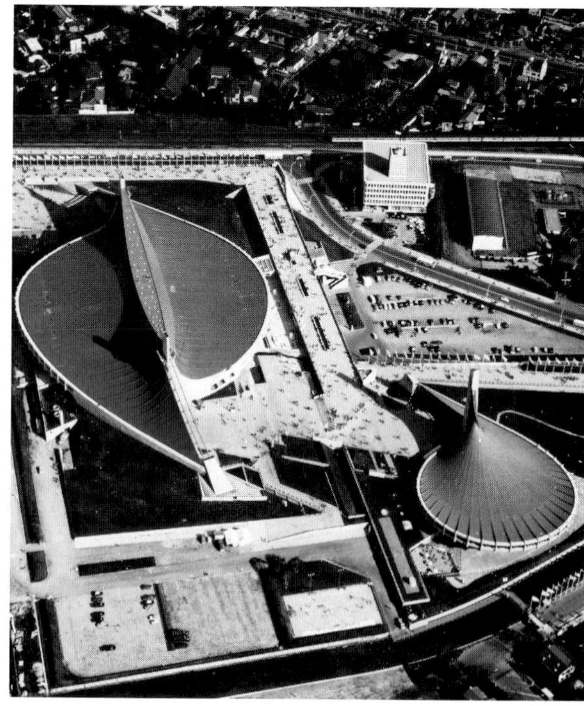

c Aerial view.

373 Kenzo Tange.
OLYMPIC STADIUMS (YOYOGI SPORTS CENTER).
Tokyo, Japan. 1964.

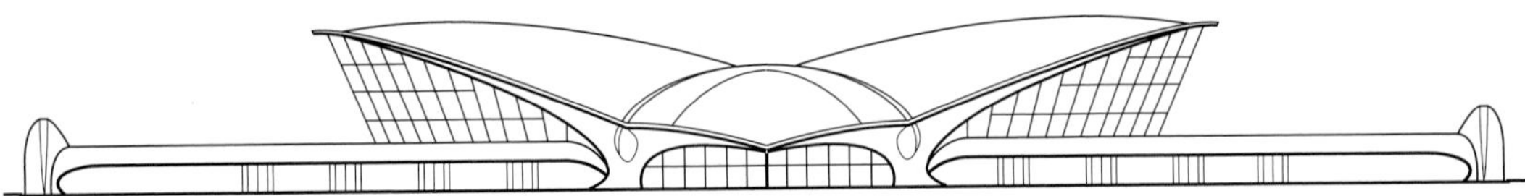

374 SHELL STRUCTURE (TWA TERMINAL). (See page 57.)

An aerial view shows how the sweeping curves of the buildings unite the two structures and energize the spaces between and around them. The proportions of the many curves, both inside and out, give the complex a sense of graceful motion and balance.

By the late twentieth century, improved construction techniques and materials, new theories regarding structural physics, and computer analyses of the strengths and weaknesses in complex structures led to the further development of fresh architectural forms including hanging roofs (as mentioned above) and such innovations as the SHELL STRUCTURE, the FOLDED PLATE ROOF, and the PNEUMATIC or air-inflated structure.

Inventor, architect, and structural engineer R. Buckminster Fuller pointed out that carefully guided technology can provide maximum benefit with minimum cost. Fuller put this concept to work when he developed the principle of the GEODESIC DOME, related to polyhedrons found in nature and inspired by the revolutionary 1922 dome designed by Walter Bauersfeld in Germany. Fuller's goal was not to imitate nature but to recognize and employ her principles. The strength of the GEODESIC DOME makes it possible to enclose more space with less material than any other structural system.

A geodesic dome can be erected from lightweight, inexpensive standardized parts in a very short time. Usually a skeleton is constructed of modular, linear elements joined together to form single planes; as these are combined they form the surface of a dome, such as the U.S. PAVILION, EXPO-67. The resulting structure can be covered with a variety of materials to make the enclosed space weatherproof.

Geodesic domes embody Fuller's goal of doing more with less. They are now used to construct a variety of buildings, including houses, research facilities, and greenhouses.

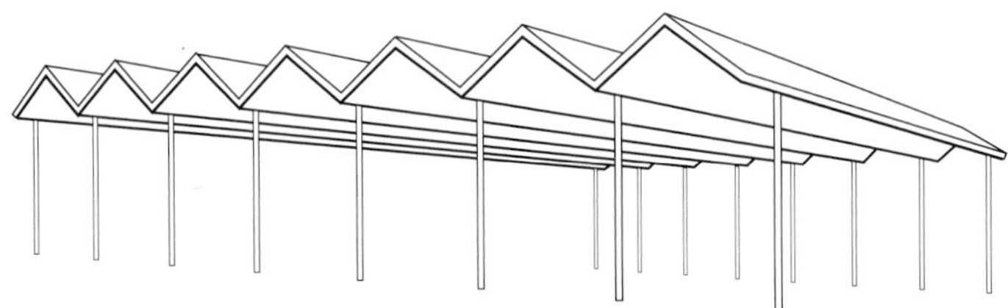

375 FOLDED PLATE ROOF.

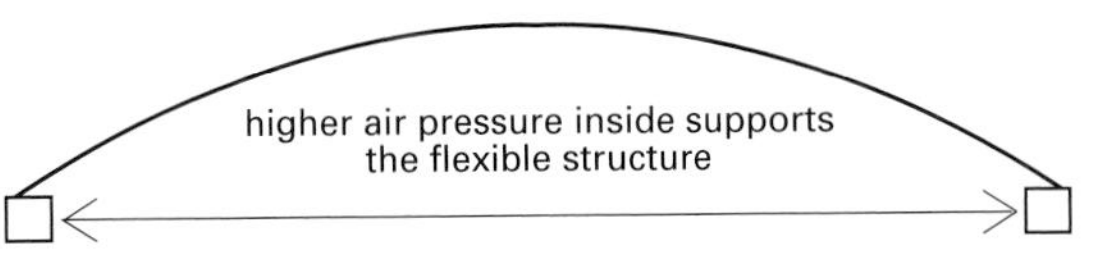

376 PNEUMATIC STRUCTURE.

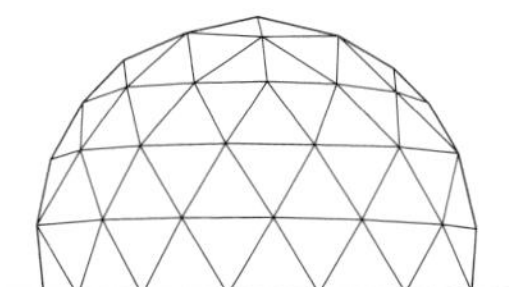

377 GEODESIC DOME.

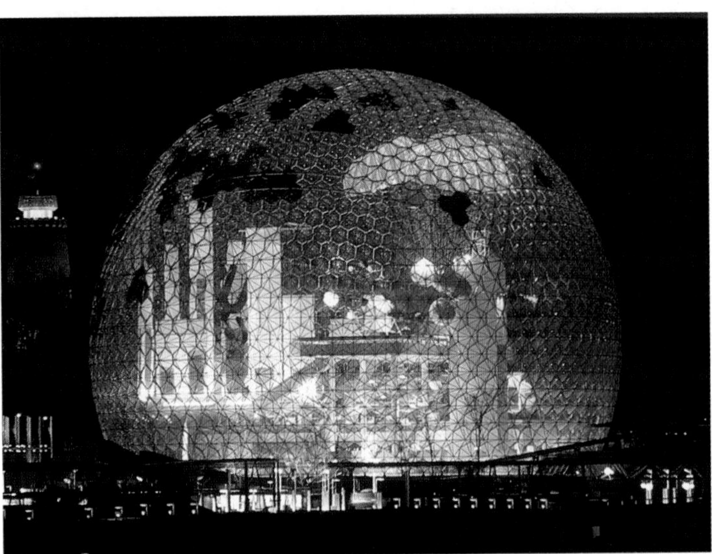

378 R. Buckminster Fuller.
U.S. PAVILION, EXPO-67. Montreal. 1967.
Photograph: © Russe Kinne/Comstock.

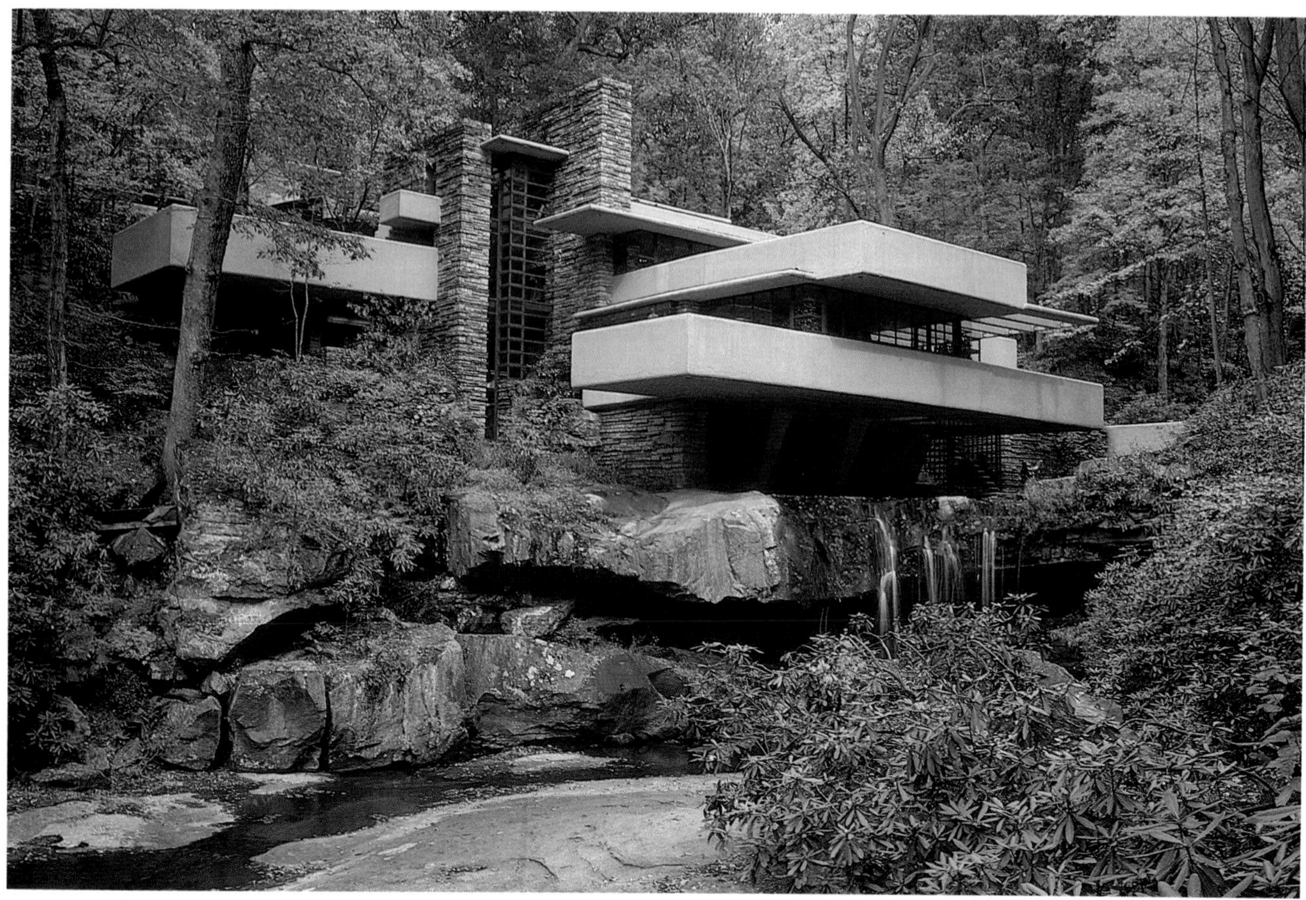

379 Frank Lloyd Wright.
FALLING WATER (EDGAR KAUFMANN RESIDENCE).
Bear Run, Pennsylvania. 1936.
a Exterior.
Photograph: Thomas A. Heinz.

(opposite page)
b Living room.
Photograph: Christopher Little.

Where We Live

Large public structures such as temples, churches, office buildings, and stadiums have historically been at the forefront of architectural innovation, for into them an entire society puts its energy and resources. But one fundamental purpose of architecture is to provide us with a place to live, and our most intimate contact with architectural design is in our own homes. In this section we look at houses designed by architects as well as those designed and built by indigenous peoples.

In Harmony with Nature Major influences on today's domestic architecture came from Japan through Frank Lloyd Wright. Wright was among the first to use open planning in houses. In a break with the tradition of closed, boxlike houses, Wright eliminated walls between rooms, enlarged windows, and discovered that one of the best ways to open a closed-in room was to place windows in cor-

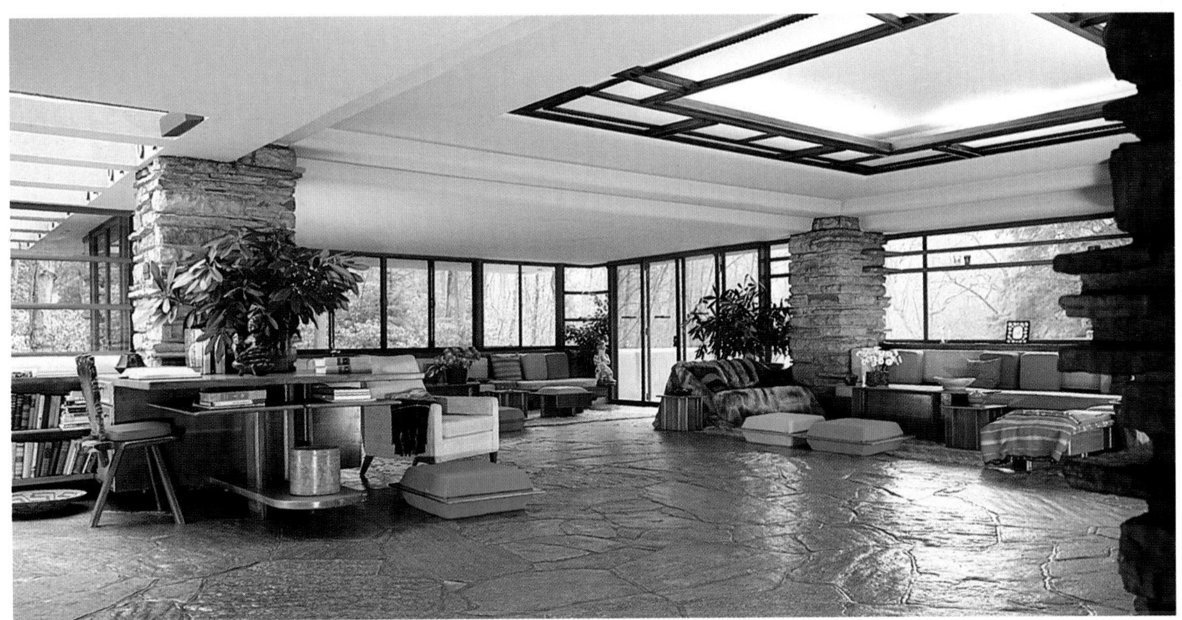

ners. With these devices, he created flowing spaces that opened to the outdoors, welcomed natural light, and related houses to their sites and climates.

Wright also made extensive use of the cantilever. When a beam or slab is extended a substantial distance beyond a supporting column or wall, the overhanging portion is called a CANTILEVER. Before the use of steel and reinforced concrete, cantilevers were not used to a significant degree because the available materials could not extend far enough to make the concept viable. Early demonstrations of the possibilities of this structural idea include the extensive overhanging roof of Wright's ROBIE HOUSE, page 424, and the extended floor and roof slabs in Le Corbusier's drawing of 1914–1915, page 257.

One of the boldest and most elegant uses of the principle occurs in Wright's KAUFMANN RESIDENCE (also known as FALLING WATER) at Bear Run, Pennsylvania. Horizontal masses cantilevered from supporting piers echo the rock ledges on the site and seem almost to float above the waterfall. Vertical accents were influenced by surrounding tall, straight trees. The intrusion of a building on such a beautiful location seems justified by the harmony Wright achieved between the natural site and his equally inspiring architecture.

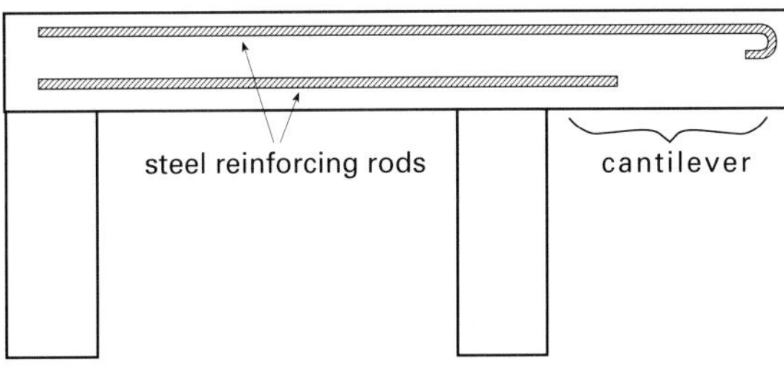

380 CANTILEVER.

FRANK LLOYD WRIGHT (1869–1959)

Frank Lloyd Wright, the most influential twentieth-century American architect, was born in Wisconsin, the son of a Baptist minister.

At sixteen, Wright took a job with a local builder while studying civil engineering part-time at the University of Wisconsin. A year later, in 1887, he went to Chicago, where he worked as an apprentice in the newly formed architectural firm of Adler & Sullivan. When Louis Sullivan was designing the Wainwright Building (page 256), Wright was his chief draftsman. Eager to do his own work, Wright began designing houses on his own at night. Sullivan took offense at this practice, and Wright left the firm. Wright, however, was strongly influenced by Sullivan and continued throughout his life to refer to him as *Lieber Meister* (beloved master).

By 1893, Wright had opened his own office in the rapidly growing community of Oak Park, Illinois, where he designed a series of houses with low horizontal lines that echoed the flat prairie landscape. This distinctive approach became known as his prairie style.

That same year, at the Columbian Exposition in Chicago, Wright saw a Japanese tea house. The encounter had a great effect upon him and led to a deep interest in Japanese architecture and long stays in Japan. He found the asymmetrical balance, large extended eaves, and flexible open plan (with sliding doors and walls) of traditional Japanese houses (see page 301) more sensitive to nature and to human life than the often static symmetry of traditional American homes.

Wright sought to bring his own poetic sense of nature into harmony with the new materials and the engineering technology of the machine age. In terms of both structure and aesthetics, Wright was a radical innovator. He used poured reinforced concrete and steel cantilevers in houses at a time when such construction was usually confined to commercial structures. His KAUFMANN RESIDENCE is dramatically cantilevered over a waterfall, and two of his major buildings were designed with flowing interior spaces and spiral ramps. Among his many notable buildings was the structurally innovative Imperial Hotel in Tokyo, built between 1916 and 1922. His use of the cantilever in this hotel was criticized as a violation of sound construction—until after the devastating quake of 1923, when it remained one of the few undamaged buildings in the city.

In his later years, Wright continued his large practice and devoted considerable time to writing and to teaching apprentices in his workshop-homes. Throughout his career Wright was guided by his awareness that buildings have a profound, life-shaping influence on the people who inhabit them.

Among Wright's many unrealized projects was a plan for a mile-high skyscraper. His last major work was the controversial Solomon R. Guggenheim Museum, built in the late fifties. Its immense spiraling ramp enables viewers to see exhibitions in a clearly defined continuous path, but the sloping, eye-filling space tends to overpower the presentation of other works of art.

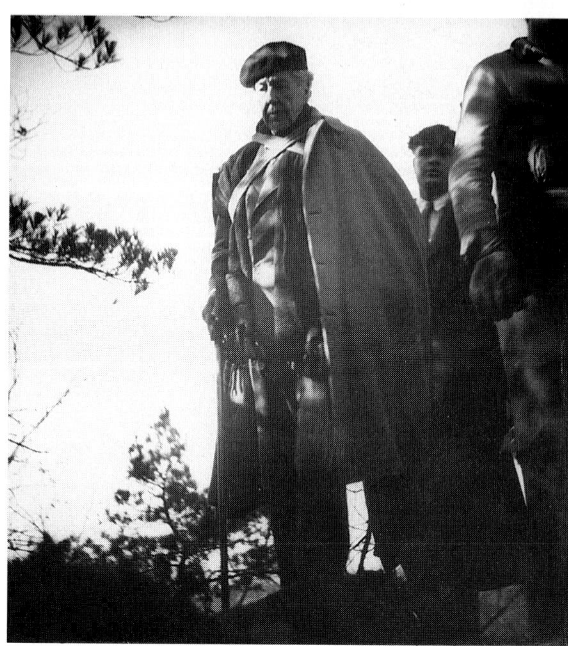

381 FRANK LLOYD WRIGHT. 1936.
Photograph: Edmund Teske, Los Angeles.

Wright's guiding philosophy is most apparent in his houses, where his concern for simplicity and his sensitivity to the character of space and materials express what he defined as an organic ideal for architecture. According to Wright, the word *organic* goes beyond its strictly biological meaning to refer to the integration of all aspects of a form, the part to the whole and the whole to the part. In architecture, this meant determining the form of a building by designing in terms of the unique qualities of the site, proceeding from the ground up, and honoring the character of the natural conditions, as well as the materials and purposes of the structure. Wright spoke of organic architecture as having a meaning beyond any preconceived style:

> *exalting the simple laws of common sense—or of super-sense if you prefer—determining form by way of the nature of materials, the nature of purpose so well understood that a bank will not look like a Greek Temple, a university will not look like a cathedral, nor a fire-engine house resemble a French château.... Form follows function? Yes, but more important now [with organic architecture] form and function are one.*[2]

Conserving Energy In recent years the sharp increase in energy costs has motivated many architects to reexamine their design concepts. Daylight is a key factor in architecture. Now, more than ever, there is a need to maximize natural light and minimize energy-consuming artificial light.

For decades we saw the development of costly, energy gobbling technology designed to shield us from climatic changes. Late in the twentieth century, architects and builders again began to realize that energy-saving architecture can be designed to offer comfortable year-round temperatures by taking advantage of renewable energy sources. They began designing with nature rather than striving to conquer her. The need to find ways to conserve energy has led to a rediscovery of the logic of earlier INDIGENOUS ARCHITECTURE designed to complement, rather then compete with, regional climates.

For preindustrial societies, the sun was a reliable source of heat. It was a matter of comfort and even survival to understand how to build in relationship to the sun, and to work with natural warming and cooling cycles. The traditional adobe brick of the Southwest insulates against the extreme temperature changes of the desert. Thick adobe walls work well for both pueblos and contemporary solar structures designed for the Southwest.

Modern houses based on the concept of using solar radiation from walls were first built in the late 1930s, but they collected too much heat by day and lost too much heat at night. This heat-storage problem is solved in David Wright's houses, in which the masses of the buildings store solar heat and retain it for long periods with the help of full external insulation.

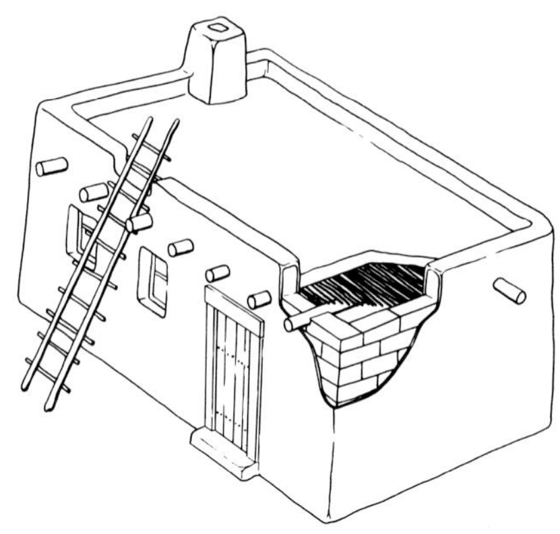

382 INDIGENOUS ARCHITECTURE, designed for various climates
a Hot, arid climate. The southwest Pueblo Indian adobe house insulates against high daytime temperatures and low nighttime temperatures.

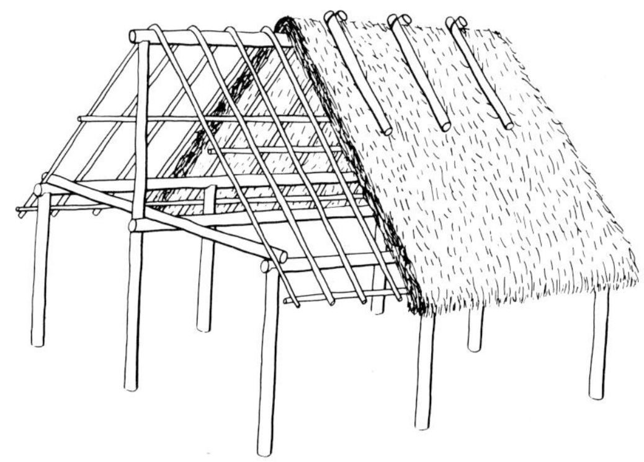

b Hot, humid climate. The Seminole Indian house in Florida permits air circulation and reduces the effects of high humidity.

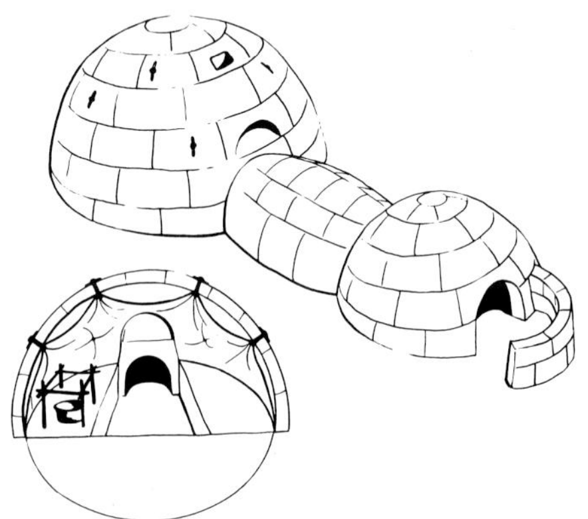

c Cool climate. The Eskimo igloo's heat-saving entrance and snow-block walls rely on the insulating principle of trapped air.

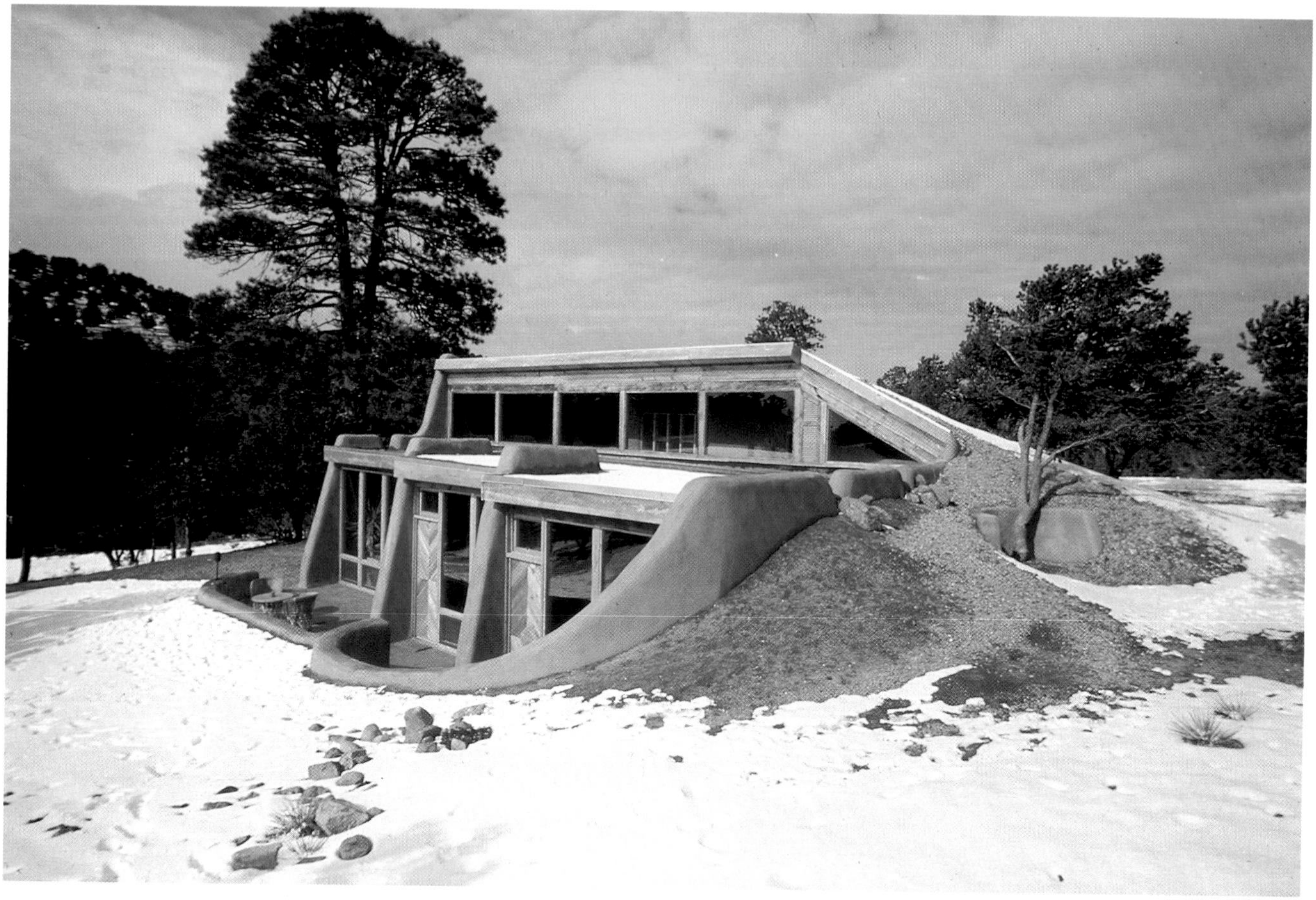

383 David Wright. SUN CAVE. Santa Fe, New Mexico. 1979.

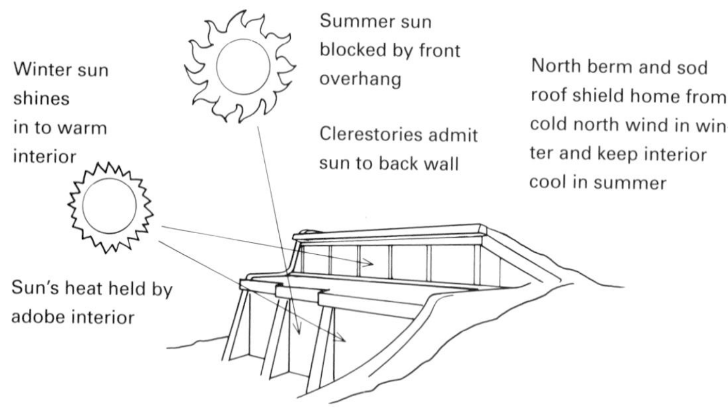

In 1979, David Wright designed a home called SUN CAVE, constructed near Santa Fe, New Mexico, by builder Karen Terry. It is an earth-sheltered house, inspired by Southwest pueblo-style architecture and based on the concept of a direct-gain passive (nonmechanical) solar heating system.

The entire house is a solar collector and heat-storage system. On sunny days, heat from the sun passes through south-facing double-glass windows and is absorbed by red-brick flooring and 12-inch-thick adobe walls. The floor is the primary heat-storage area. After absorbing heat during the day, both floor and walls radiate the collected heat during the night and during overcast periods of daytime. Air circulates naturally to counterbalance day and night and seasonal warming and cooling cycles. The building enclosure is capable of storing enough heat to keep the home comfortable for several sunless days. Cooling is provided by good cross-ventilation. SUN CAVE comfortably handles temperature changes from below 0° F to 85° F with changes of as much as fifty degrees in a twenty-four-hour period. The success of this house is due largely to the simplicity of its design.

In the mid-nineteenth century, as people harnessed waterpower to run sawmills, the production of precut, standardized lumber caused a revolution in home building. Lumber, plywood, wallboard, and window frames are now manufactured in standard sizes, and architects design with such sizes in mind. Cabinets, once handcrafted on the site, are now usually factory-produced. Even an architect-designed, custom-built house such as SUN CAVE may contain many standardized components. Cost-cutting standardization is a major aspect in the transition of architecture from handcrafted to industrial production. Prefabrication offers the best hope for meeting the urgent international need for low-cost, quality housing.

For Everyone a Home and a Garden Architect Moshe Safdie has designed new forms of stacked modular living units as an alternative to urban sprawl and megalithic high-rise apartments. He is motivated by the idea that relatively low-cost housing can be designed to minimize land consumption yet provide privacy and a sense of individual living units. This concept is not new. It has worked well for generations in communities such as NORTH PUEBLO in Taos, New Mexico, a traditional, energy-efficient, climate-related, high-density community surrounded by open space.

HABITAT '67, built for the World Exposition in Montreal in 1967, was Safdie's first demonstration of this stacked-unit concept. He minimized costs by prefabricating apartment units in a factory and stacking them on the site. Although the components were standardized, they could be placed in a variety of configurations, thus keeping the total structure from becoming monotonous. The roof of one unit becomes the garden for another. Walkways and covered parking areas are included. The design allows for a dense concentration of people, yet it provides many of the advantages of single,

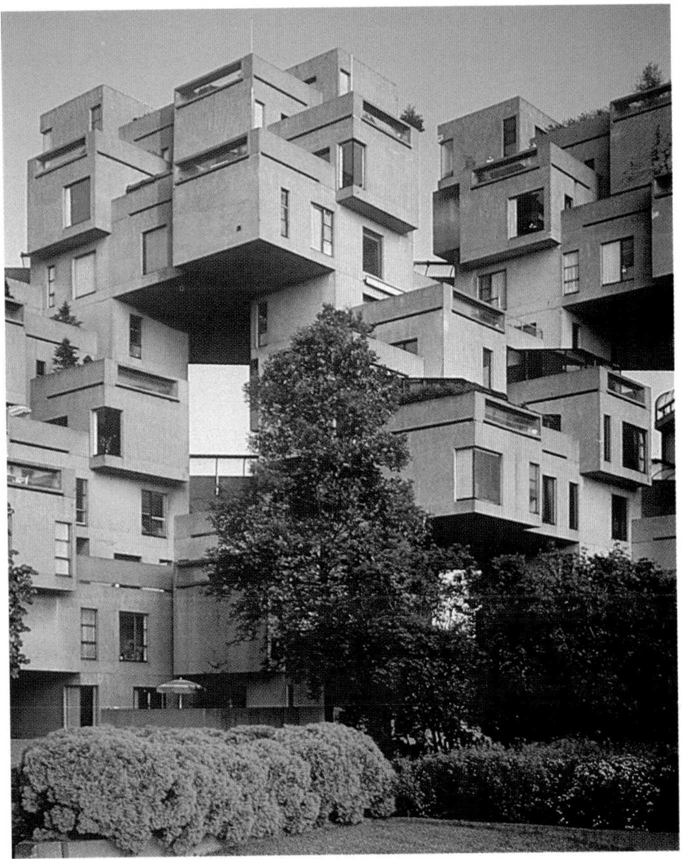

384 Moshe Safdie and David Barott. Boulva Associated Architects. HABITAT '67. Montreal. 1967.
Photograph: Timothy Hursley, The Arkansas Office.

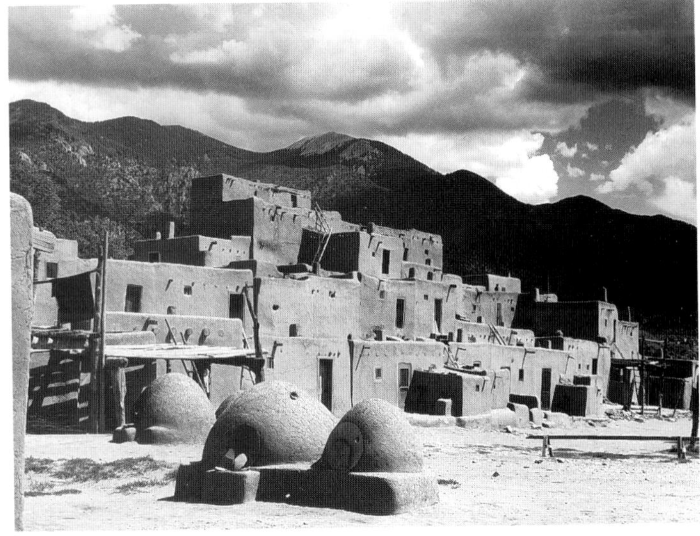

385 NORTH PUEBLO. Taos, New Mexico.
Photograph: Laura Gilpin.

unattached dwellings. Much of Safdie's design philosophy is summarized in his phrase, "For everyone a garden."

Architects, builders, community leaders, and volunteers in communities around the world are focusing their creative efforts on solving the housing crisis. As population pressures continue to grow and material and labor costs spiral, a few dedicated architects and builders offer solutions. The more we are able to understand the architecture of past and present, the better we are able to visualize possibilities for the future.

ENVIRONMENTAL DESIGN

The design of the human-made environment is about as far as art can get from art objects in museums, yet architecture and environmental design are among the most important of the arts in terms of long-range human well-being. Environmental design refers to design processes aimed at guiding changes in outdoor spaces; the term applies to everything from landscape architecture to the planning of cities and regions.

Nature, left to its own evolutions and cycles, is one thing. The natural environment, modified by human beings to meet the changing demands of a fast-growing population, is quite another. Landscape architect and planner Ian McHarg has pointed out that site-planning techniques are too often aimed at subduing, rather than complementing, nature. Since any site or area in its natural state consists of a balance of complex natural forces, changes (such as cutting down trees, bulldozing hillsides, or channeling streams) may invite disaster. Human rearrangement of nature can lead to soil erosion and flooding as well as the destruction of the ecological balance that sustains the lives of a variety of species.

Designers of human-made environments must take nature's designs into consideration. In his influential 1971 book *Design with Nature,* McHarg recommends that area developments of all kinds begin with an analysis of each part of an ecosystem—and that only those projects that can be completed without major side effects be undertaken.

The philosophical basis for the environmental movement was provided in the eighteenth century by Thomas Jefferson, and in the nineteenth century by writers Ralph Waldo Emerson and Henry David Thoreau, by painters including Asher Durand (page 64), Thomas Cole and Robert Duncanson (page 377), and by early landscape photographers. Because these farsighted leaders could see the damage caused by exploitive attitudes and practices, they called attention to the importance of setting aside areas of great natural beauty for future generations.

By the mid-twentieth century, the public had begun to realize that the conservation of natural areas was only a part of what was needed to defend a threatened planet. In the sixties, a new level of ecological awareness led the environmental movement to seek to protect the quality and continuity of life through land use controls and the prevention of pollution, as well as the conservation and restoration of natural areas.

People began to understand that environmental problems are best addressed from the perspectives of many disciplines, including science and art. From the beginning, the visual arts offered avenues to heightened awareness and helped to develop visual thinking. The principles of effective visual design—such as proportion, balance, unity, and variety, introduced in Chapter 5—apply as much to environmental design as to the other visual arts.

Now, with a new level of environmental awareness, participatory planning (citizen participation in the planning processes) helps provide a basis for sound decision making. Environmental designers need the ideas and support of informed citizens who are aware of the benefits of environmental planning and design.

The city of Davis, California, has become a model for the twenty-first century—a demonstration of how participatory planning can create exciting, life-enhancing communities. One of the citizens' shared visions resulted in a pollution-free transportation system. LINEAR PARKS wind through the community, passing under streets to provide

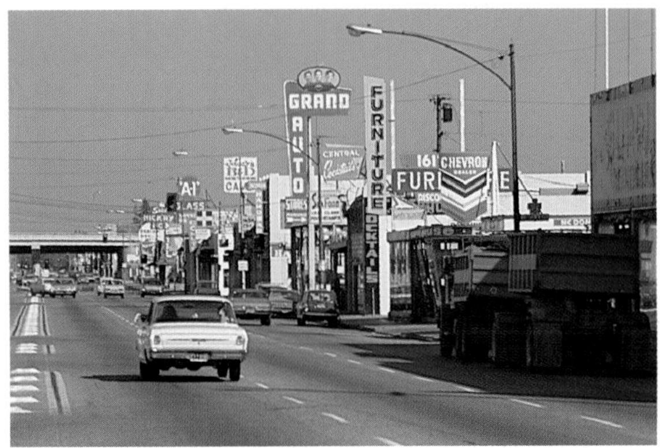

386 a STREET WITH VISUAL POLLUTION.

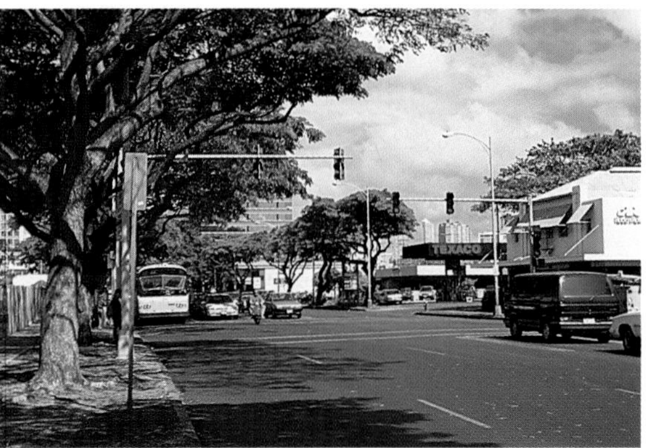

b STREET WITHOUT VISUAL POLLUTION.

people with safe access to shopping, recreational areas, and schools along pleasant, graceful pathways.

When outside our homes and places of work, our usual view of our communities is the one we have traveling along streets. Photographs of two similar city streets show the difference in quality between a street with many kinds of visual pollution and one that shows an effort to minimize visual pollution.

What follows is a sampling of the many ways an awareness of environmental design options can lead to true progress in the effort to improve the quality of life.

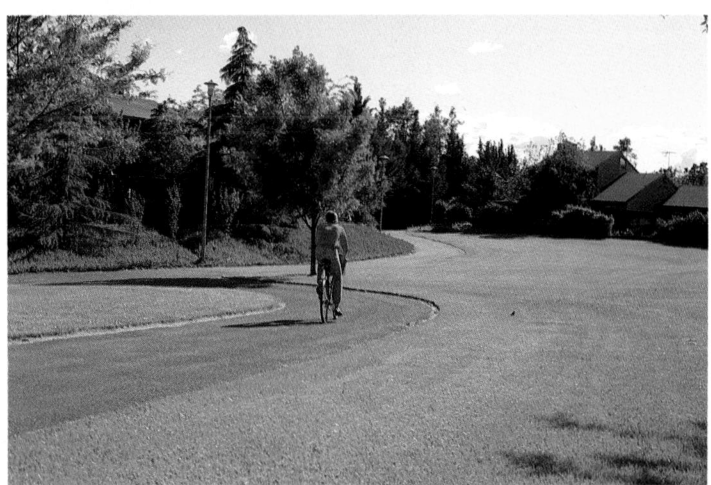

387 LINEAR PARK WITH BIKEWAY.
Davis, California. 1977.
Photograph: Alison Portello.

Landscape Architecture

Landscape architecture deals with the interrelationships among land forms and the plants and constructed elements upon them. It is the art of working with both natural and human-made elements to provide visual enjoyment and refreshing places for relaxation and recreation.

Approaches range from formal, geometrically organized designs to informal, natural-looking compositions (see pages 367 and 301). Landscape architects frequently work with planners and architects to enhance the surroundings of buildings and to help buildings relate visually to their sites and to one another.

Landscape architects design spaces as diverse as indoor gardens, parks, golf courses, and campus courtyards. Their works range in size from vast

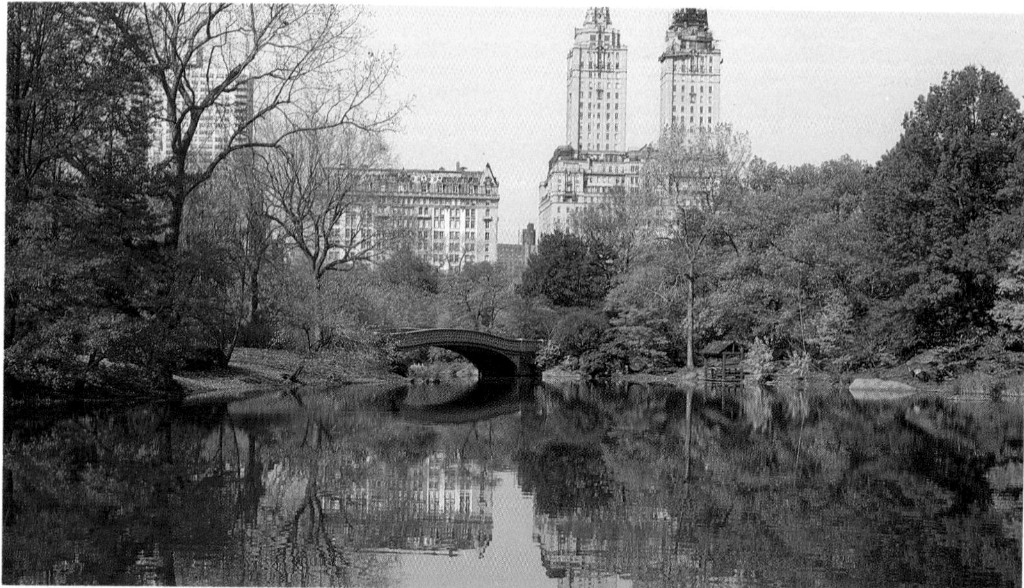

388 Frederick Law Olmsted and Calvert Vaux. CENTRAL PARK. New York. 1857-1887.
Photograph: David Bradford, Envision, New York.

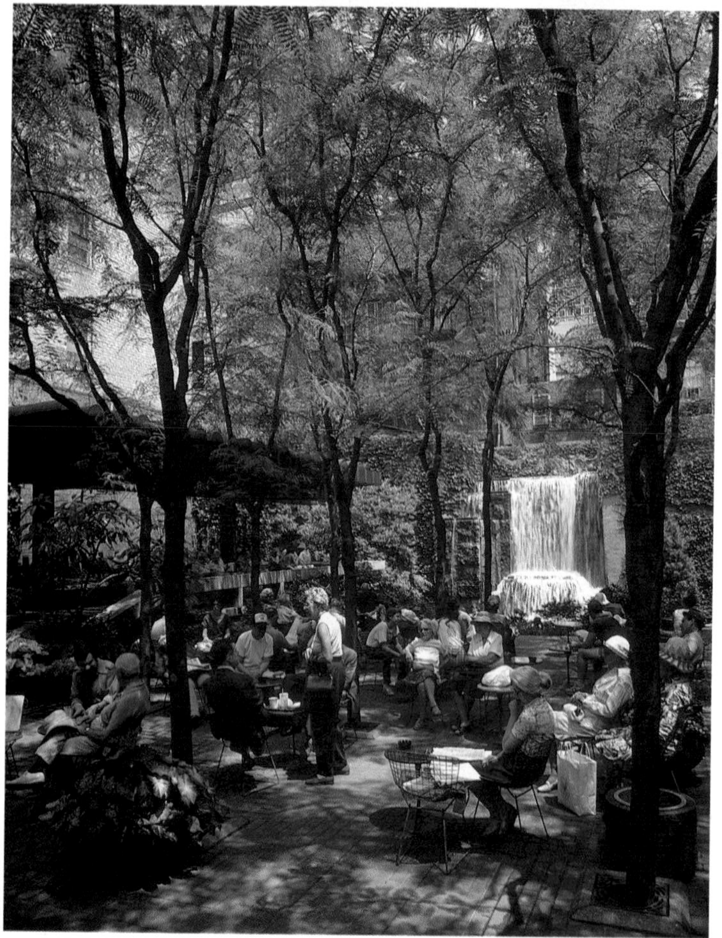

389 Hideo Sasaki. GREENACRE PARK. New York. 1979.
Owned and maintained by the Greenacre Foundation.

projects, such as CENTRAL PARK in New York City or Golden Gate Park in San Francisco, to small parks and home gardens. Gardens and large landscaped areas provide a refreshing balance to the often jarring intensity of cities.

Frederick Law Olmsted was a noted writer before he gained fame as a landscape architect. He and Calvert Vaux designed the plan for CENTRAL PARK. After the City of New York acquired the land in 1856, Olmsted was hired to supervise the execution of the design. The well-planned 840-acre park was one of the first attempts in the United States to work with nature to create a natural-appearing public park. It followed the informal landscaping style of eighteenth-century English country estates, augmenting the natural rolling terrain with lakes and ponds, paths, and small roads. CENTRAL PARK also includes a zoo, a skating rink, bridle paths, an outdoor theater, and a formal garden.

Olmsted's success with this unique project brought him invitations to design many major parks in American cities, including the Capitol grounds in Washington, D.C., South Park in Chicago, and a system of parks and parkways for the city of Boston. His influence on the profession of landscape architecture remains strong. Millions of people who never heard of landscape architecture enjoy the beauty of his parks.

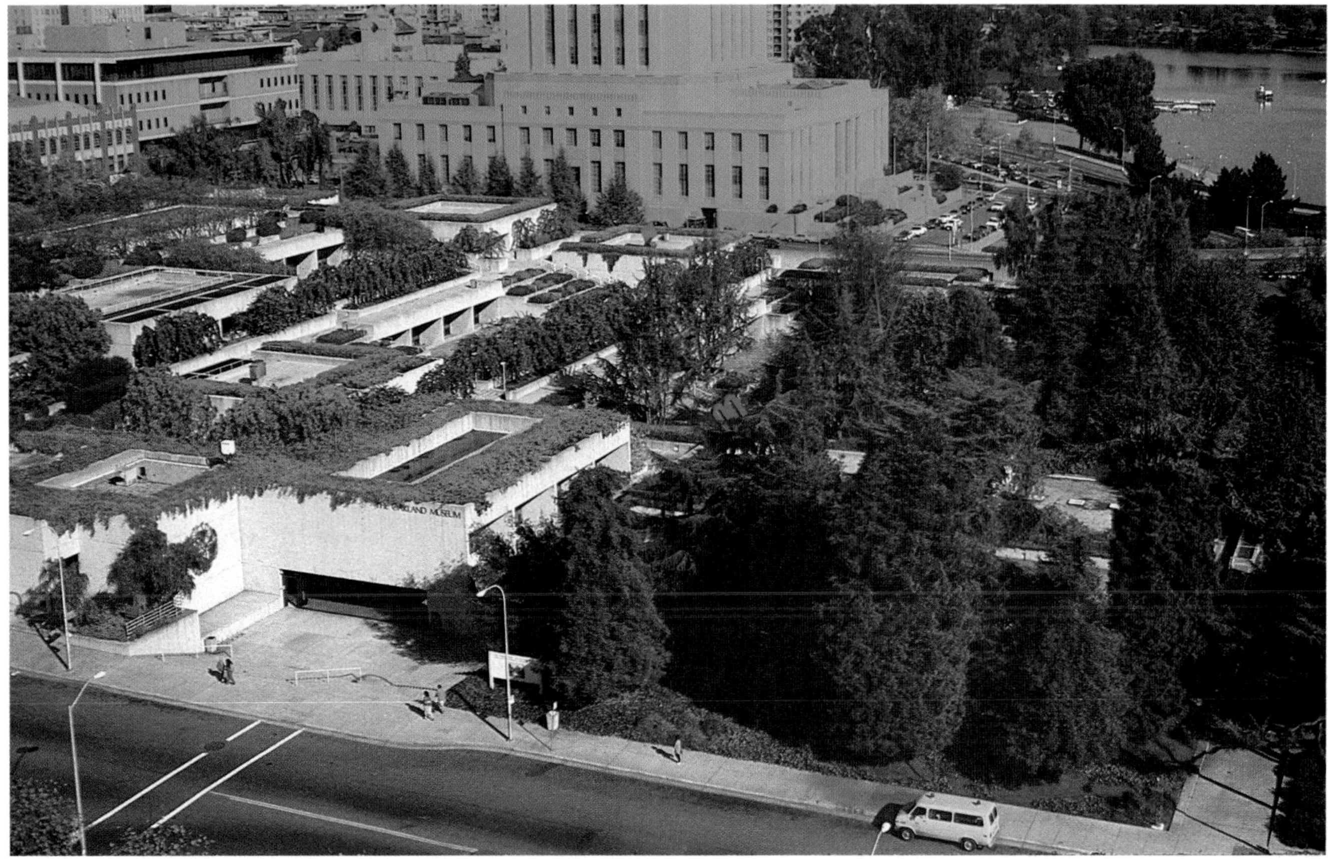

390 Kevin Roche and Associates.
OAKLAND MUSEUM. Oakland, California. 1969.

Generations ago, a town was often built around an open area known as the village square or common. Today, as cities grow in population density, we have the need for parks for every neighborhood; yet the land in cities becomes ever more expensive. The concept of small or vest-pocket parks has evolved to meet present circumstances: when an old building is torn down, a tiny park can be built on a single lot that is too small to allow for substantial new construction.

GREENACRE PARK provides a place for the public to relax in the middle of New York City. Trees and the sound of water help minimize traffic noise and offer refreshing relief from the harshness of the city. During the lunch hour, the park is so heavily used that people sit on the steps and railings rather than go elsewhere, demonstrating the need for well-designed outdoor urban spaces. In residential areas, parks provide recreational and play areas accessible to nearby residents.

When major growth takes place in densely populated cities, there is often a conflict between those who want more open green space and those who support more construction. Architect Kevin Roche came up with a solution to such conflicting demands when he designed the OAKLAND MUSEUM in Oakland, California. The building, partially underground, is roofed with a series of garden terraces designed by landscape architect Daniel Kiley. On the terraces, plantings and pleasant places to sit are integrated with outdoor sculpture.

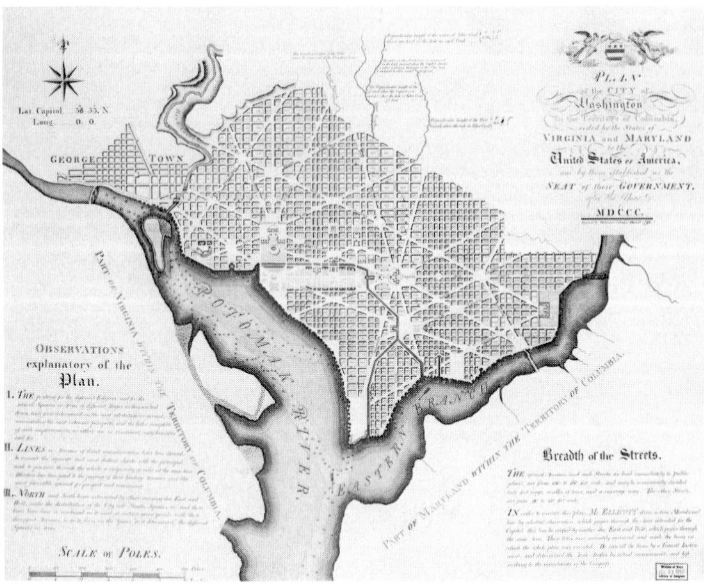

391 Pierre Charles L'Enfant.
PLAN FOR WASHINGTON, D.C. 1792.
Library of Congress, Washington, D.C.

Urban and Regional Design

Urban design involves designing developments, subdivisions, new communities, or sections of existing towns and cities so they will be efficient, healthy, and pleasing environments. As the name implies, *regional design* deals with outlying areas. The term *environmental design* is sometimes used interchangeably with both of these terms—or is used to refer to them collectively. Environmental designers work with planners, who draw up guidelines and master plans based on studies of present and projected social, economic, and physical needs.

The professions of urban and regional design overlap the disciplines of architecture, landscape architecture, and transportation design. Environmental designers help establish and work within zoning laws that determine land use and population density through open-space requirements. Such restrictions set height limits on buildings and establish setback laws which regulate the distance a building must be from property lines. Visual contact with natural and manufactured landmarks is preserved or created through view corridors and view planes that prevent new construction from blocking such features.

A band of continuous parks, farmland, or natural areas called a *greenbelt* can be preserved or developed at the edge of a city as a boundary to preserve the identity of communities and to prevent haphazard urban growth from spreading into rural areas and nearby communities.

The concept of city planning and design is very old. Many ancient cities, including Babylon and Nineveh, were built from plans. Long before anyone was identified as a designer or planner, people built infrastructures of paths, roads, bridges, and water systems, as well as community settlement patterns, public plazas, and parks. Ancient Chinese, Greek, and Roman cities were built with grids of intersecting streets with carefully placed public squares. The Romans had highly developed systems for water supplies and drainage, and they employed zoning concepts.

Too often towns and cities have grown spontaneously, without long-range plans. Urban development presented relatively few problems until the last few generations, because populations grew slowly and building technology was limited. As the Earth's population rapidly increases, environmental planning and design, or their absence, make an enormous difference in the quality of life around the world.

In the United States, the best-known city plan is the original PLAN FOR WASHINGTON, D.C., conceived by French-born engineer Pierre Charles L'Enfant in 1792, when the area was mostly "wilderness." Working under the direction of George Washington and Thomas Jefferson, L'Enfant designed a radial pattern, with the Capitol at the center, overlaid on the usual rectangular grid. The plan sets off and serves government buildings. With its broad avenues, grand vistas, and open public areas, the L'Enfant plan gave great dignity to the capital city, even though the design was often ignored in succeeding years and parts of the plan were not implemented until 1901.

The scheme for Washington, D.C., was devised at a time when horse-drawn carriages were the primary means of transportation. Grand diagonal avenues crossing the grid and intersections punctuated by monuments provided interest for people in slow-moving carriages, but they can be confusing obstacles for today's hurried automobile drivers.

On a small scale, the accidental city has intriguing variety and complexity; but in a large and rapidly expanding metropolitan area, haphazard growth can be dehumanizing and dangerous.

Master planner James Rouse points out that far too often

> *our cities grow by sheer chance, by accident, by the whim of the private developer and public agencies. A farm is sold and the land begins to sprout houses instead of potatoes. Forests are cut. Valleys are filled. Streams are turned into storm sewers. An expressway is hacked through the landscape. Then a cloverleaf, then a regional shopping center, then office buildings, then highrise apartments. In this way, the bits and pieces of a city are splattered across the landscape. By this irrational process, non-communities are born, formless places without order, beauty or reason, with no visible respect for either people or the land.*[3]

Two mechanical inventions—the elevator and the automobile—have had an enormous influence on the design of our cities and suburbs. The elevator made the skyscraper and the high-rise city possible, while the automobile enabled people to escape to the suburbs and beyond.

Early in the twentieth century, the height and density of construction in lower Manhattan transformed streets such as EXCHANGE PLACE into dark corridors. In 1916, zoning laws were enacted that required new construction to be stepped back as buildings increased in height. Those who sought to use every allowable square inch of commercial space complied with these laws by designing buildings that were stair-stepped like wedding cakes.

392 Berenice Abbott. EXCHANGE PLACE. 1933. Photograph.

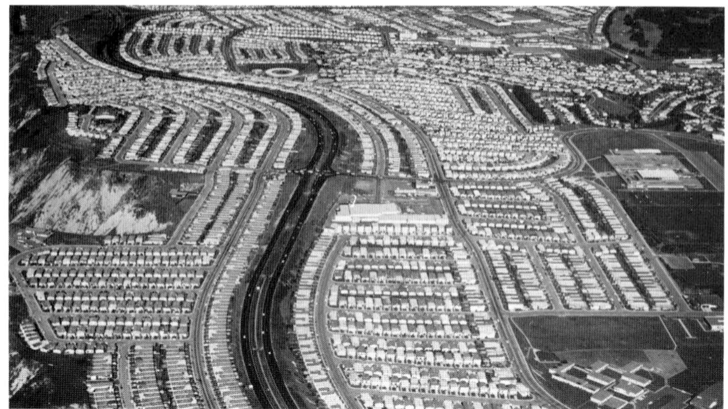

393 DALY CITY, CALIFORNIA. c. 1960.
Photograph: Donald W. Aitken.

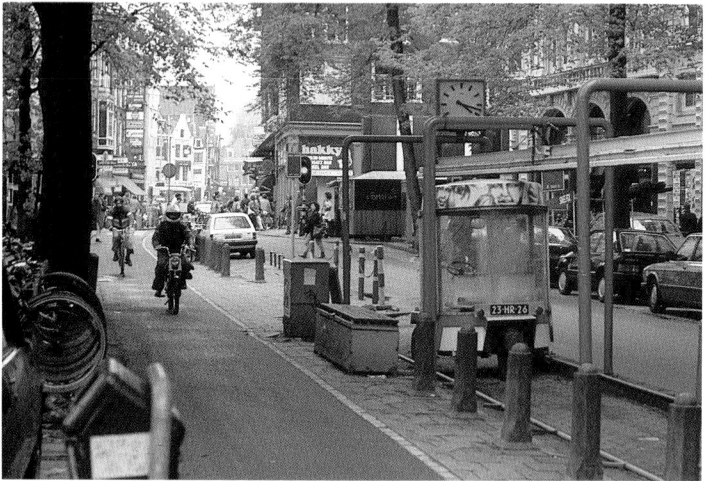

394 BIKEWAY IN AMSTERDAM.

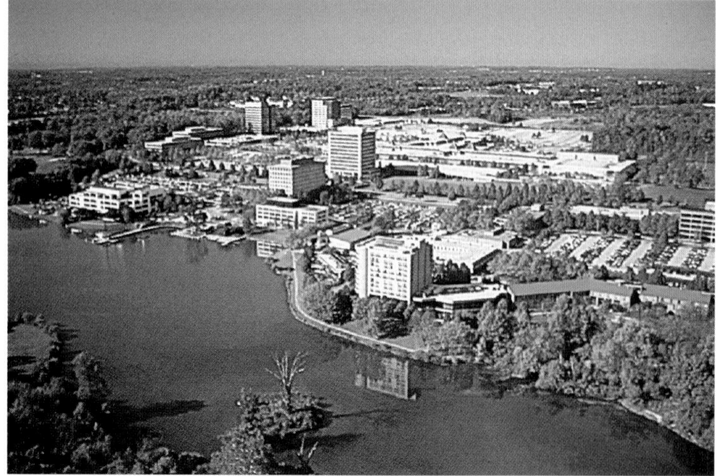

395 Downtown COLUMBIA, MARYLAND.
Photograph courtesy of the Rouse Company.

As the automobiles made it possible to work in a city and live in a town, sprawling suburbs such as DALY CITY began filling in the spaces between cities. Cars beget highways, and highways discourage alternate means of transportation in a vicious cycle. Henry Ford did not envision the impact his product would have when he wrote:

I will build a motor car for the great multitude.... But it will be so low in price that no man making a good salary will be unable to own one—and enjoy with his family the blessings of hours of pleasure in God's great open spaces.[4]

Because individual transportation choices shape communities, transportation design is a major environmental design issue. Transportation planners and designers work on ways to handle increasing automobile traffic as well as to plan mass-transit systems attractive and efficient enough to entice people away from automobiles. The key to economically viable transportation is to provide a variety of options. In Amsterdam and a few other cities, lanes of roads are designated BIKEWAYS, exclusively for bicyclists.

Although freeways solve problems related to the movement of vehicular traffic, in some places they have become barriers between parts of cities, creating new kinds of ghettos. It is important that we design transportation options that enhance rather than disrupt community life.

The planned community concept is one approach to minimizing the consumption of land and retaining open green space. The idea involves concentrating people in specific communities capable of meeting all their basic daily needs, including stores, schools, services, and job opportunities. The best of the planned communities usually include apartments, townhouses, and cluster houses, with shared open space and extensive recreational facilities.

COLUMBIA, MARYLAND, is one of many planned cities built since 1960 that initially were unable to provide enough jobs. A percentage of Columbia residents commute to jobs in Baltimore or Washington, D.C., but the planned city is gradually attracting corporations interested in moving away from high land costs in older cities and relocating in or near the new communities, where land is cheaper and a labor force is nearby.

Changing the overall design of existing cities is economically impossible and in most cases undesirable. Yet changes within cities are being made all the time, with some sensitive blending of old and new. Often there has been no blend, and occasionally incredible confrontations occur between the old and the new, as when the size of a new building causes it to dwarf older, smaller structures.

JOHN HANCOCK TOWER, facing Copley Square in Boston, has been criticized by people who object to its dominating size and see its sleek form as incompatible with the styles of nearby older buildings. Others have admired its monumental scale and enjoyed the dramatic contrast of its sheer crystalline form with Henry Richardson's nineteenth-century TRINITY CHURCH.

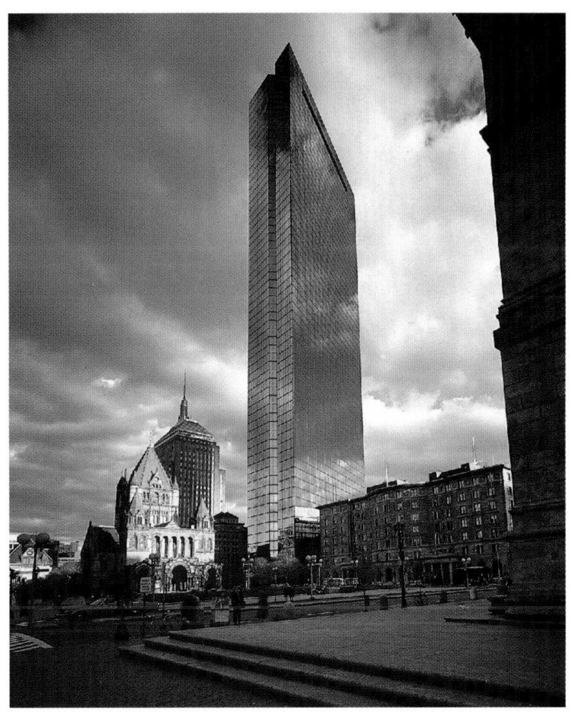

396 Henry Hobson Richardson. TRINITY CHURCH. 1877. I. M. Pei and Partners. JOHN HANCOCK TOWER. 1974. Copley Square, Boston.
Photograph: © Steve Rosenthal.

BATTERY PARK CITY is a large complex built on a landfill just west of the World Trade Center in New York City. The development was first conceived in 1966, but a series of changing plans and financing problems held up the project for over ten years. In 1979, the New York State Urban Development Corporation took over the project. Under its subsidiary, Battery Park City Authority, a combination of city management and private investment was formed. As a first step, a master plan and urban design guidelines for the area were prepared.

The plan, based on studies and comparative analysis, defined street patterns, building masses, public and private space, waterfront treatment, and connections and relationships to the adjoining section of lower Manhattan. Both the planner and the architect made conscious efforts to relate the new complex to the older, nearby buildings, rather than to the tall box skyscrapers built in the 1950s, 1960s, and 1970s. The planners' guidelines speci-

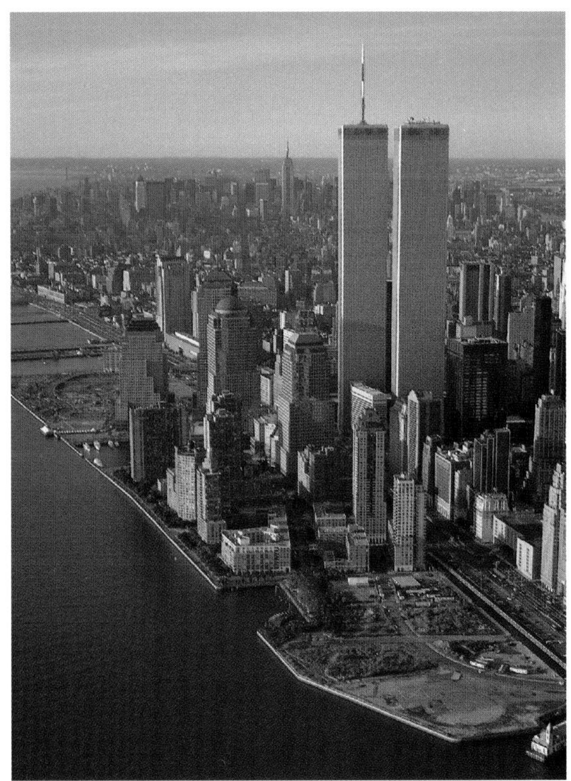

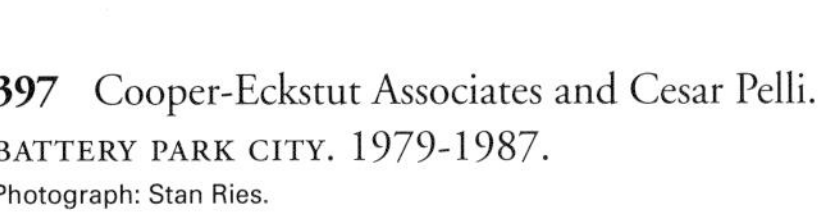

397 Cooper-Eckstut Associates and Cesar Pelli. BATTERY PARK CITY. 1979-1987.
Photograph: Stan Ries.

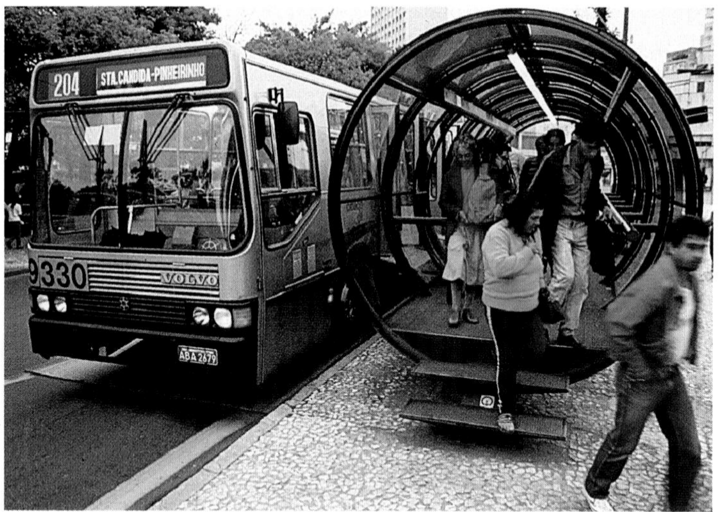

398 BUS STATION, CURITIBA, BRAZIL.

fied that the buildings be stepped back to relate them both physically and symbolically to Manhattan's old, lower building heights and profiles.

The BATTERY PARK CITY commercial complex is built on fourteen of the ninety-two acres of the city within a city. It includes four tall office buildings and two lower, domed, octagonal buildings, joined by a three-acre tree-shaded plaza with a terrace that steps down to the Hudson River. The varied buildings forms are unified by identical granite and glass facades. The spectacular complex, with its mile-long waterfront walkway, is a landmark addition to New York City. It is also an unusual achievement of state and city management combined with private investment in a mutually beneficial partnership.

While many of the world's cities provide declining qualities of life, a few exceptional places have turned the tide and achieved greatly improved livability. The city of CURITIBA, BRAZIL, has become an inspirational model of progress; some call it "the third-world city that works."

Three-term mayor Jaime Lerner provided the vision as well as the planning and management skills that have led to Curitiba's success. His professional experience as an architect and urban planner led him to bring public transit, parks, bike paths, recycling, and jobs to the city that now calls itself "the ecological capital of the world." Lerner chooses to use simple, modestly priced solutions to seemingly impossible problems. Other cities (including many in developing countries) have gone heavily into debt to build underground subways and buildings that are little more than monuments to national vanity. However, Lerner rejects grandiose projects, preferring to think small.

Over a span of twenty years, Curitiba, a city of 1.6 million, went from being a typical, inefficient city choked with cars and smog to a city with an efficient, well-used bus system (including express buses that use express lanes) and a downtown area in which streets have been converted into pleasant, landscaped pedestrian walkways.

A ninety-mile bicycle path, which goes through the downtown area and several city parks, is an important part of Curitiba's urban transportation. It is used for both recreation and commuting. The bus system was streamlined with the addition of "tube stations," which provide shelter and shade and enable passengers to pay their fare before entering the bus, and result in faster boarding.

We tend to think of towns and cities as things that just happen, not as human constructions that can be designed imaginatively and aesthetically in tune with nature.

While standing under a row of flowering trees, Lerner said, "There is little in the architecture of a city that is more beautifully designed than a tree."[5]

The same creative process used by artists in other disciplines applies to solving environmental design problems. Whether we begin with the desire to create something new or the need to change or preserve something that already exists, we are faced with the challenge of paying attention to the character of the materials, the existing situation, and the ideas we started with. Nowhere is this creative process more urgently needed than in the design of our environments.

PART 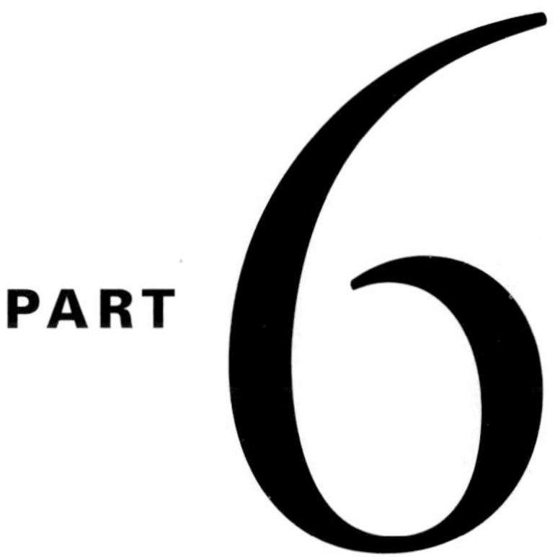

ART AS CULTURAL HERITAGE

Consider . . .

Picasso once said, "If a work of art cannot live always in the present it must not be considered at all." What do you think he meant?

Glance through Chapter 17 (pages 284–316) without reading the text. How much can you learn about each civilization by looking at its art and architecture? For example, compare the Indian temple with the Japanese palace. What differences are apparent in each culture's view of beauty?

What is the difference between studying history without the arts and studying history through or in relation to the arts?

Notice the change in the subject matter as you glance through Chapter 20. How would you characterize the artistic interests of the eighteenth and nineteenth centuries, when compared with those of the Renaissance (Chapter 19)?

CHAPTER 16

Prehistoric to Early Civilization

Art history makes history visible and accessible. It is a record of how the people of the past—our ancestors—lived, felt, and acted in widely separated parts of the world at different periods of time.

Art history differs from other kinds of history because works of art from the past are with us in the present. One-to-one communication occurs even when artist and viewer are separated by thousands or even tens of thousands of years. This communicative power of art makes it possible for us to glimpse some of the experiences of those whose lives preceded ours, to better understand societies other than our own, and to see beyond our own cultural limitations. Although interesting, old science is no longer of practical use, but old art can be as life-enriching as new art.

Our knowledge of art history is constantly growing. Excavations and restorations continue to bring ancient works to light. In rare cases such as the excavation of Pompeii in Italy, an entire city is being revealed.

Modern techniques of photoreproduction and printing have helped to make the art of the whole world available to us. Through reproductions, we can now see more fine works of ancient Egyptian and Chinese art, for example, than the people of those cultures were themselves able to see.

If numbers of years get in your way as you study history, consider time in terms of generations. Since the beginning of human life on Earth, the average time interval between the birth of parents and the birth of their offspring has varied from about eighteen to thirty-three years. When we figure that roughly twenty-five years is the average generation, we can come closer to the people of the past by realizing that most of us have three generations within our own families, and many have four. The United States became a country only nine generations ago; the Italian Renaissance occurred just twenty generations ago; Jesus Christ lived eighty generations ago; Gautama (Siddhartha) Buddha lived about one hundred generations ago. The end of the prehistoric period is less than three hundred generations back.

Finally, we urge you to consider that there is no "better" or "best" when comparing the art of different societies, or even the art of different times within the same society. Rather, differences in art reflect differences in points of view. Pablo Picasso put the subject of art history in perspective this way:

To me there is no past or future in art. If a work of art cannot live always in the present it must not be considered at all. The art of the Greeks, the Egyptians, the great painters who lived in other times, is not an art of the past; perhaps it is more alive today than it ever was. Art does not evolve by itself, the ideas of people evolve and with them their mode of expression.[1]

THE PALEOLITHIC PERIOD

Roughly two million years ago, in east central Africa, early hominids first made crude stonecutting tools. The making of these tools enabled our predecessors to extend their powers and thereby gain a measure of control over their surroundings. From this beginning, human beings developed the ability to reason and visualize: to remember the past, to relate it to the present, and to imagine possible futures. As we became form-creating creatures, our ability to form mental images—and the development of hands capable of making those images—set us apart from other animals. As Jacob Bronowski stated in *The Ascent of Man,* "Every animal leaves traces of what it was; man alone leaves traces of what he created."[2] Imagination is our special advantage.

About one million years ago in Africa, and more recently in Asia and Europe, people made more refined tools by chipping flakes from opposite sides of stones to create sharp cutting edges. It took another 250,000 years or so for human beings to develop choppers and hand axes that were symmetrical and refined in shape. An awareness of the relationship of form to function, and of form as enjoyable in itself, was the first step in the history of art.

Examples of what we call prehistoric art were discovered during the last hundred years in what is now Europe. Current scientific dating places the earliest of these findings at about forty thousand years ago, toward the end of the last Ice Age. As the southern edge of the European ice sheet slowly retreated northward, hunter-gatherers followed the animals on which they depended for food. They carved and painted images of these animals on cave walls deep in the earth. The level of expertise demonstrated in these works suggests that they were preceded by generations of slow artistic development. Interestingly, researchers have not yet found any evidence that a long evolution led to the fully developed art forms known to us from this period.

A variety of hand-size carvings have been found at prehistoric sites in Europe. The small, somewhat abstract female PALEOLITHIC FIGURE (shown here actual size) was carved from the tusk of a mammoth, a prehistoric elephant. The exaggerated emphasis on hips and breasts suggests that the figure was symbolic and designed to help ensure fertility. Therefore, we might assume that prehistoric people gave primary credit to women for the most evident creative act: the birth of a new person. Current research suggests that these figures may be the earliest known works of religious art, depicting the Paleolithic image of the Creator—the Great Mother Goddess. Similar objects, including a few highly abstract male and composite male-female forms, have been found at other Paleolithic sites in Europe and as far east as Siberia. Such carvings probably had a very important function in the lives of Ice Age hunters, but we can only guess at what they meant to the people who made them.

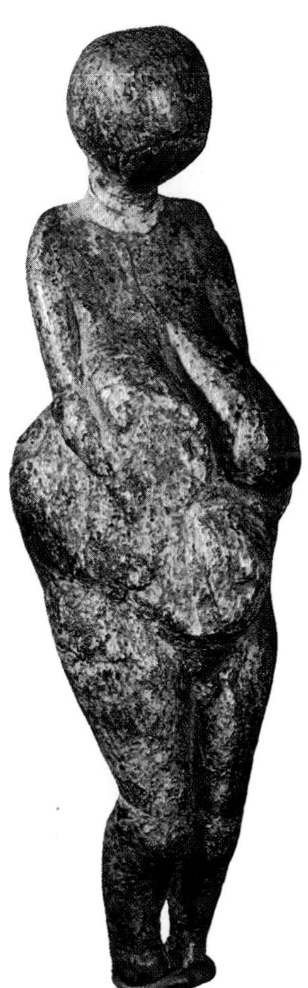

399 PALEOLITHIC FIGURE. c. 25,000 B.C.
Mammoth ivory. Height 4¾".
Museum of Anthropology and Ethnography of the Academy of Science, St. Petersburg.

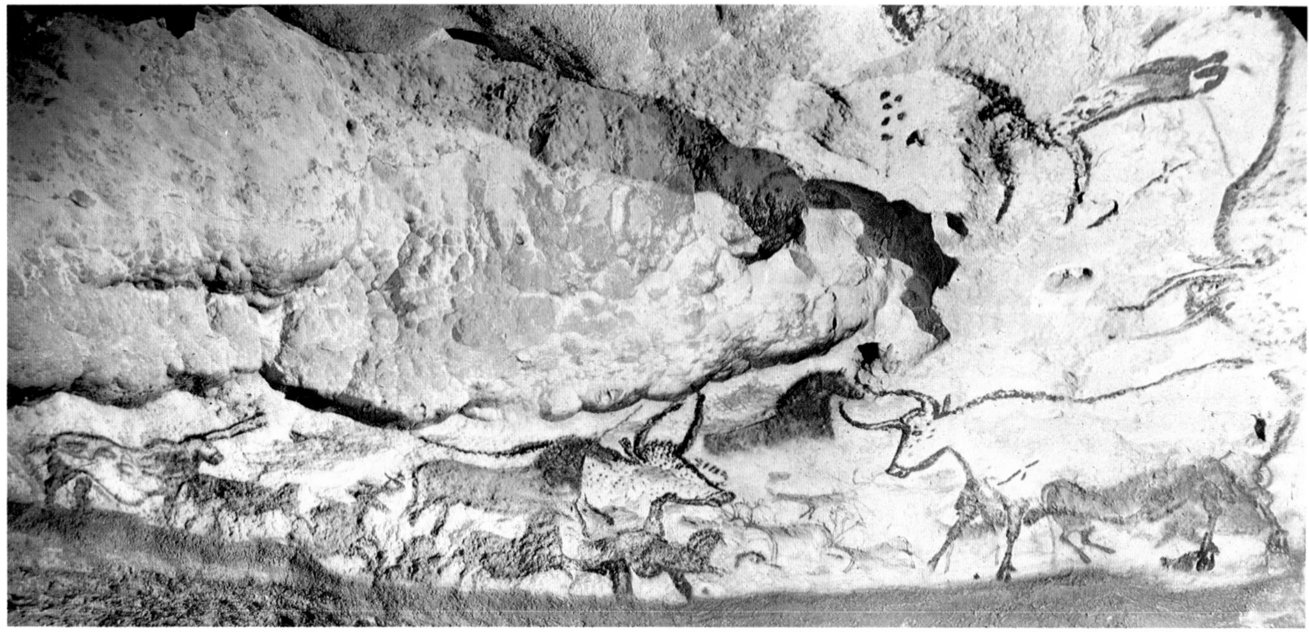

400 LASCAUX CAVES. LEFT-HAND WALL, GREAT HALL OF BULLS.
Dordogne, France. c. 15,000-10,000 B.C.
Polychrome rock painting.

Human figures rarely appear in Paleolithic paintings; those that do tend to be more simplified and abstract than the images of animals. Animals portrayed in sculpture and paintings of this period have an expressive naturalism. The maker of HEAD OF A NEIGHING HORSE combined careful observation with skill; the small carving not only accurately portrays the horse, it shows the artist's empathy with the frightened, possibly dying animal.

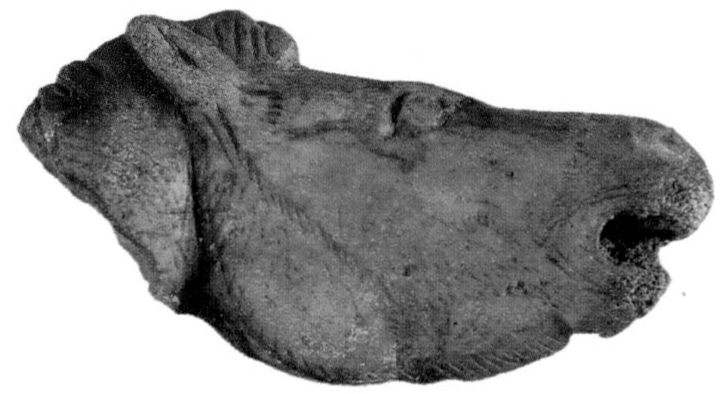

401 HEAD OF A NEIGHING HORSE. Le Mas d'Azil, Ariège, France. c. 30,000-10,000 B.C.
Reindeer antler. Length 2".
Museum of National Antiquities, St.-Germaine-en-Laye, France.

The LASCAUX CAVES in southern France contain examples of the magnificent art of the late Paleolithic period. These are some of the earliest paintings known. On walls of the inner chambers, large and small animals were painted in as many as thirteen different styles, from small and delicate to very large and bold. The largest bull at Lascaux (at lower right of the GREAT HALL OF BULLS) is eighteen feet in length. Successive images were painted over earlier ones. Each of the vigorous, naturalistic styles was made in a different time period. Depictions are obviously based on careful observation gained through considerable direct contact with the animals that roamed the land at that time. The paintings were made by the light of oil-bearing stone lamps. At Lascaux, and at many other Paleolithic sites, geometric signs or symbols often appear along with the animal and occasional human figures.

Scholars long believed that the purpose of naturalistic Paleolithic art was to bring the spirits of animals into rituals related to the hunt. Many authors stress this theory. However, careful study of footprints and other archaeological remains has recently led some experts to theorize that Lascaux and similar sites were used as sanctuaries where youth were initiated in ceremonies based on symbolic and metaphysical associations with the animals portrayed.

THE NEOLITHIC PERIOD

The transition from Old Stone Age, or Paleolithic, to New Stone Age, or Neolithic, cultures marked a turning point in human history. It seems to have occurred first in the Middle East, between 9000 and 6000 B.C., when people made the gradual transition from the precarious existence of nomadic hunters and food gatherers to the relatively stable life of village farmers and herders. The agricultural revolution—this major shift from nomadic groups to small agricultural communities—stabilized human life and produced early architecture and other technological developments. Out of necessity, people learned new techniques for working with seasonal rhythms. Food and seeds had to be stored, so it is not surprising that clay storage pots are among the most significant artifacts of the period.

Neolithic art reflects this great shift in living patterns. The vigorous, naturalistic art of Paleolithic hunters was largely replaced by the geometrically abstract art of Neolithic farmers. From about 10,000 to 3000 B.C., emphasis was placed on abstract designs for articles of daily use. The motifs, or dominant themes, used on clay pots were often derived from plant and animal forms.

The painted EARTHENWARE BEAKER is from Susa, the first developed city on the Iranian plateau. Solid bands define areas of compact decoration. The upper zone consists of a row of highly abstract long-necked birds, followed by what appears to be a band of dogs running in the opposite direction. The dominant image is an ibex or goat abstracted into triangular and circular shapes. The significant difference between the naturalism of Paleolithic animal art and the abstraction of Neolithic art becomes clear when we compare this goat with the naturalistic bulls of Lascaux.

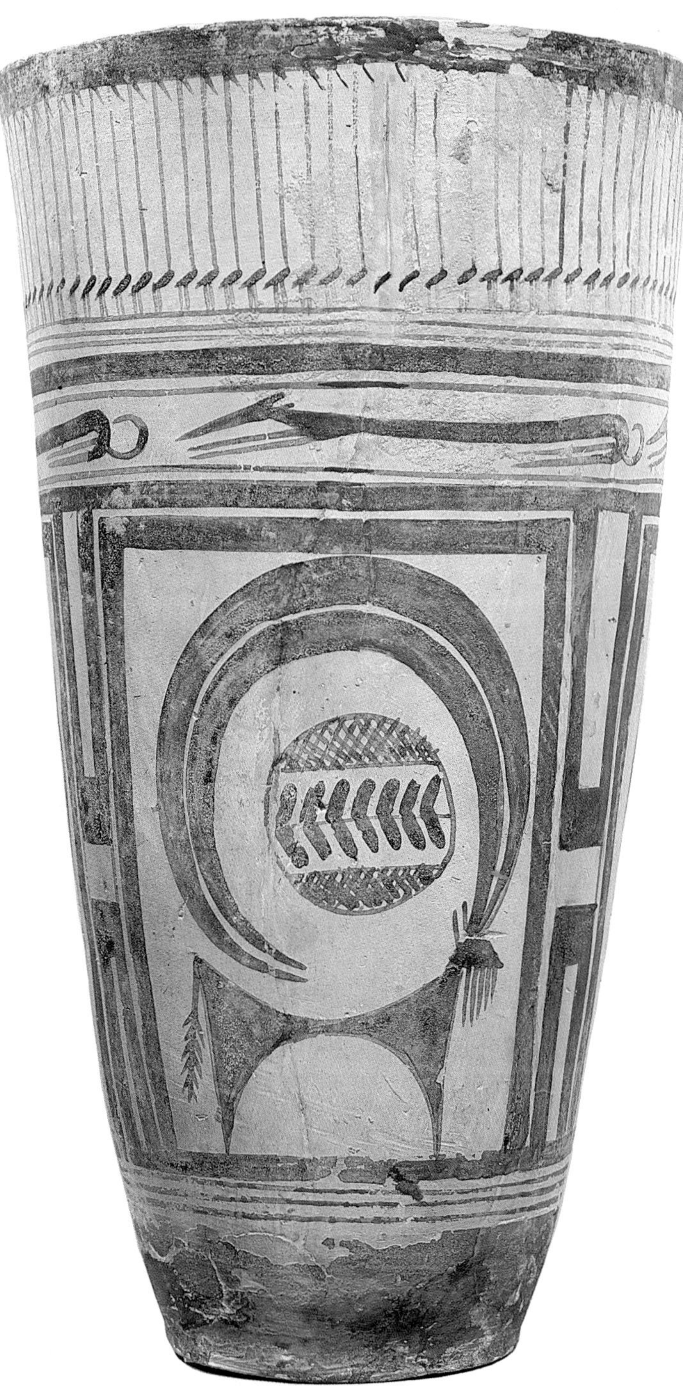

402 EARTHENWARE BEAKER. Susa.
c. 5000-4000 B.C.
Painted terra-cotta. Height 11¼".
Musée du Louvre, Paris.

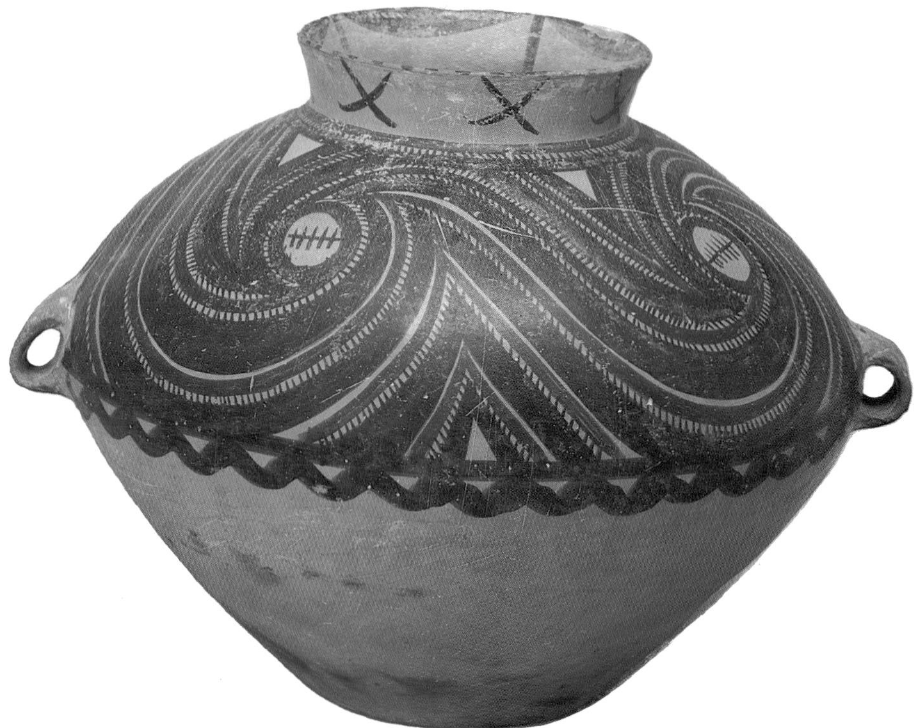

403 BURIAL URN.
Kansu type. China.
c. 2000 B.C.
Earthenware.
Height 14⅛".
Seattle Art Museum. Eugene Fuller Memorial Collection (51/194).

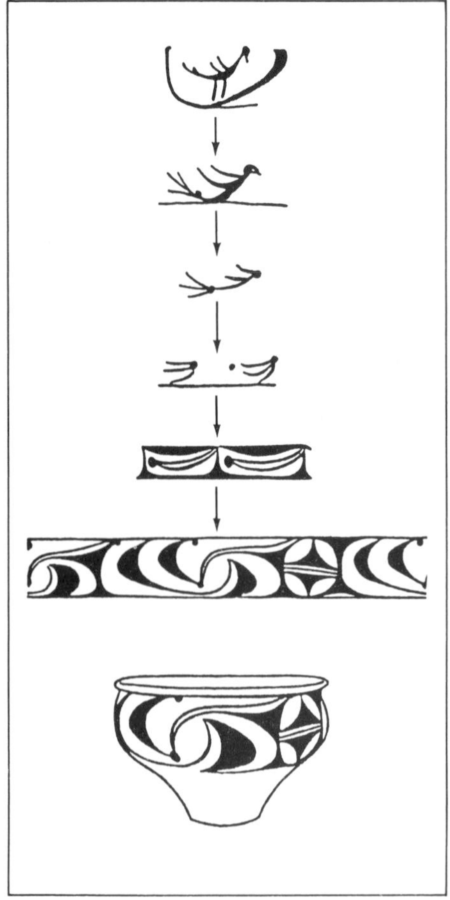

404 AN EVOLUTION OF ABSTRACTION.
From Neolithic pottery, Shensi Province, China.
Courtesy of Charles Weber.

We can see how Neolithic abstract designs were derived from representational images in AN EVOLUTION OF ABSTRACTION, the series of drawings copied from pieces of pottery found in Shensi Province in China. As the decorative designs evolved over generations, the clearly recognizable bird image became more and more abstract, and eventually it formed the basis for the totally nonrepresentational band around the pot shown in the drawing. Such playing with figure-ground reversal is also found in modern painting and design (see page 241).

Some of the finest Neolithic pottery was made in China. The well-preserved BURIAL URN from Kansu Province is decorated with a bold interlocking design, which may have been abstracted from spirals observed in nature. The design in the center of the spirals is probably derived from the bottoms of cowrie shells.

It is quite possible that nonrepresentational signs often found in Paleolithic caves along with naturalistic images of animals were meant to communicate specific information. All of the world's greatest writing systems grew out of a search for visual equivalents for speech and were preceded by various types of pictography, or "picture writing." The pictographic origin of some characters in modern Chinese writing is well known. Less well known is that some letters of the Roman alphabet used in English came from pictographs that stood for objects or ideas.

THE BEGINNINGS OF CIVILIZATION

Artifacts indicate that early civilizations emerged independently, at different times, in many parts of the world. We use the term *civilization* to distinguish cultures, or composites of cultures, that have fairly complex social orders and relatively high degrees of technical development. Key elements are food production through agriculture and animal husbandry, metallurgy, occupational specialization, and writing. All of these developments were made possible by the move to cooperative living in urban as well as agricultural communities.

Among the earliest major civilizations were those in four fertile river valleys: the Tigris and Euphrates rivers in Iraq, the Nile River in Egypt, the Indus River in west Pakistan and India, and the Yellow River in northern China. It is in these valleys that we find evidence of the beginnings of civilization as we know it.

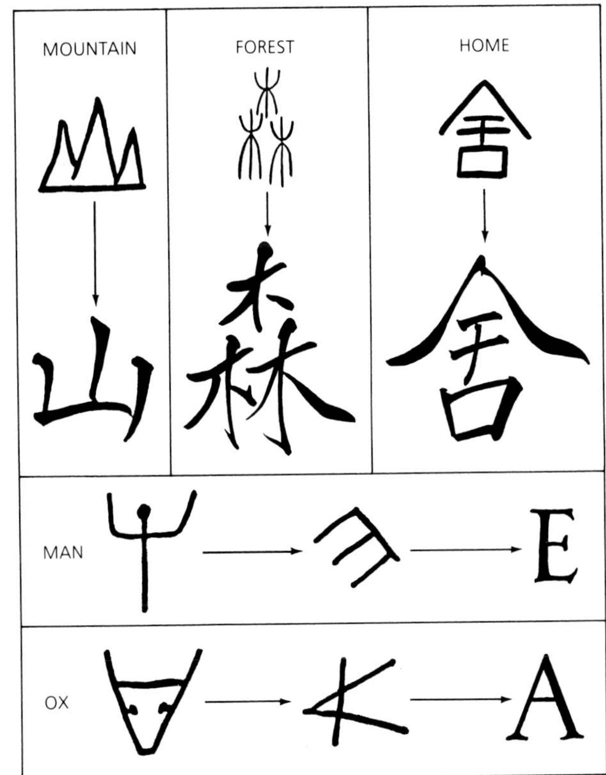

405 PICTOGRAPHS TO WRITING, EAST AND WEST.

406 EARLIEST CENTERS OF CIVILIZATION, 3500–1500 B.C.

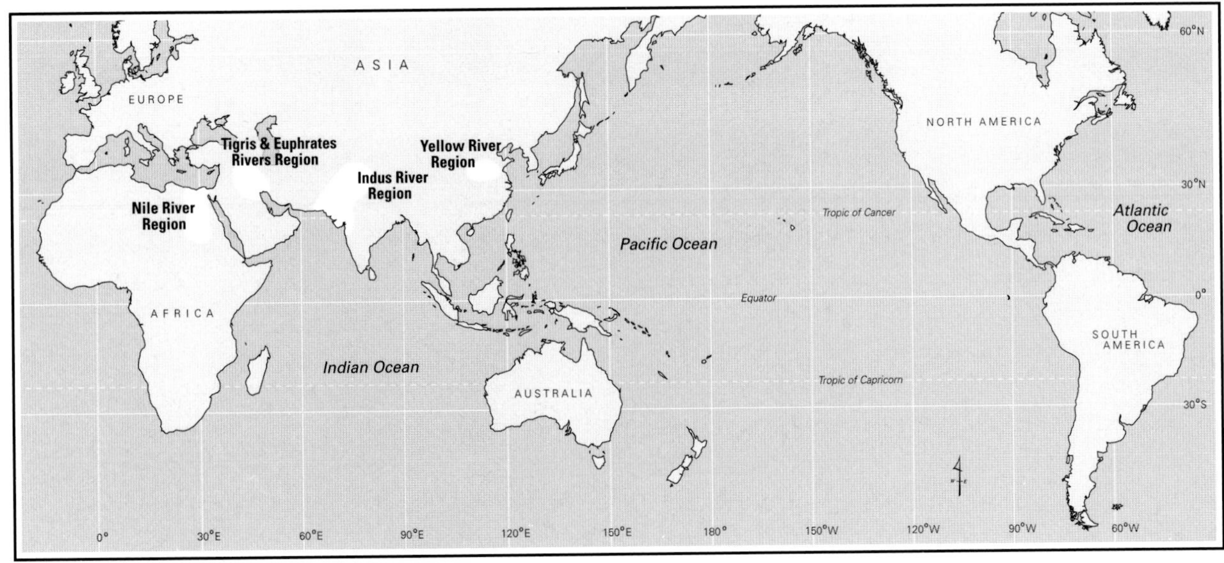

CHAPTER 17

Beyond the Western World

Most of the readers of this book live in a Western culture; therefore, the emphasis in the following chapters is on the evolution of art in the West. Yet the majority of the world's cultures are not Western. In this chapter, we take a brief look at a sampling of traditional arts of non-European-based cultures.

Learning about other cultures not only helps us put our own civilization in perspective, it helps us understand the art of our own time. In the twentieth century, non-Western art has become increasingly studied and appreciated in the West, and it has influenced many European and American artists. Through travel, photography, books, and museums, artists around the world are increasingly aware of and influenced by art from cultures beyond their own. In the global village of the late twentieth century, art (along with science, technology, economics, and language) often transcends national and cultural boundaries.

INDIA

In the 1930s, excavations at the sites of the ancient cities of Mohenjo-daro and Harappā revealed the remains of a well-organized society with advanced city planning and a high level of artistic production. The two cities served as focal points for a civilization that extended for one thousand miles along the fertile Indus Valley between 3000 and 5000 years ago. (Most of this valley, where Indian culture began, became part of Pakistan under the Indian Independence Act of 1947.)

Ancient Indus Valley sculpture already shows the particularly sensual naturalism that characterizes much of later Indian art. This quality enlivens the small, masterfully carved MALE TORSO from Harappā. The lifelike surface gives the torso an energized quality as if it were animated by breath. The figure's protruding abdomen may reveal an early understanding of the importance of *prana,* or life-giving breath, a concept perpetuated by the ancient tradition of hatha yoga.

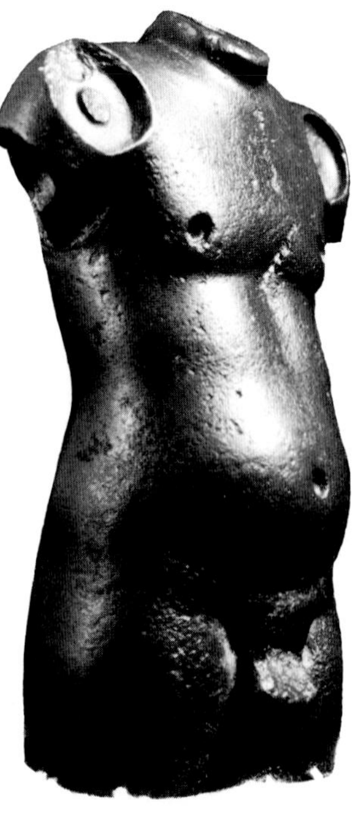

407 MALE TORSO.
Harappā, Indus Valley.
c. 2400-2000 B.C.
Limestone. Height 3½".
National Museum of India, New Delhi. Photograph: Prithwish Neogy.

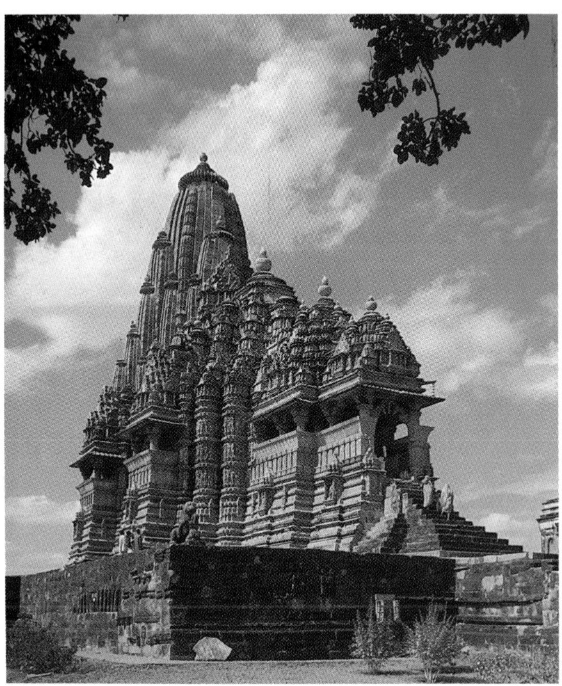

408 a KANDARYA MAHADEVA TEMPLE. Khajurāho, India. 10th-11th centuries.
Photograph: Prithwish Neogy.

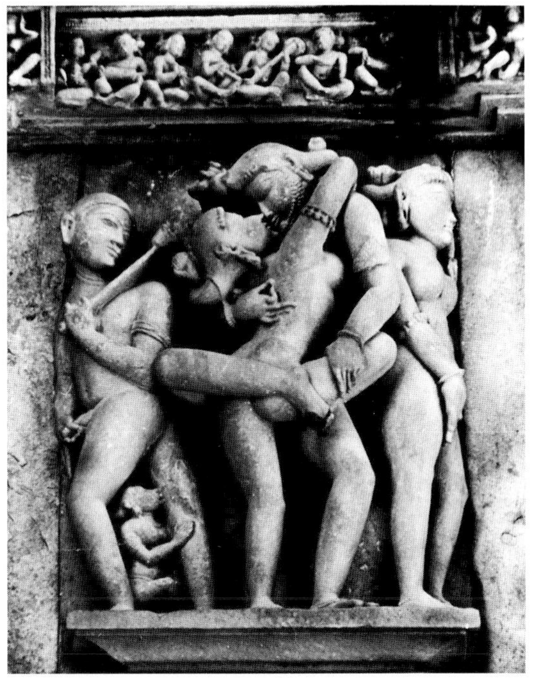

b Scene from KANDARYA MAHADEVA TEMPLE.
Photograph: Holle Bildarchiv.

Relatively few works of art have survived from the period between 1800 B.C., when the Indus Valley civilization declined, and 300 B.C., when the first Buddhist art appeared. Nevertheless, the years in that interval were important ones for the development of Indian thought and culture.

Starting around 1500 B.C., the Indian subcontinent was invaded and gradually conquered by nomadic Aryan tribes from the northwest. The Aryans' beliefs, gods, and social structure formed the foundation of Hinduism—a set of religious, philosophical, and cultural practices that would underlie all subsequent development of Indian civilization. Interestingly, the Aryans, being nomads, were neither painters nor architects. What came into being as Indian art is a synthesis of indigenous Indian art forms and the religious ideas of the nomadic, non-image-making Aryans.

Many individual religions developed from the core beliefs of Hinduism. In the sixth century B.C., two highly influential spiritual leaders preached more meditative and socially tolerant versions of Hinduism. They were Gautama Buddha, founder of Buddhism, and Mahavira, founder of Jainism. Buddhism especially was to have a profound influence not only in India, but in China, Japan, Korea, and Southeast Asia.

Hindu Art

The Hindu KANDARYA MAHADEVA TEMPLE at Khajurāho in north central India was built a century earlier than its Gothic European counterpart, CHARTRES CATHEDRAL (see page 339). Both have a vertical emphasis in their designs. Both are complex stone structures that appear to rise effortlessly from the horizontal countryside as if they were organic and continuing to grow. On the Indian temple, a series of small towers builds to a climax in a single large tower. The rounded projecting forms, symbolizing both male and female sexuality, seem to celebrate the procreative energy found in nature and felt within ourselves.

Unlike CHARTRES, KANDARYA contains not a large space for congregational worship, but a small

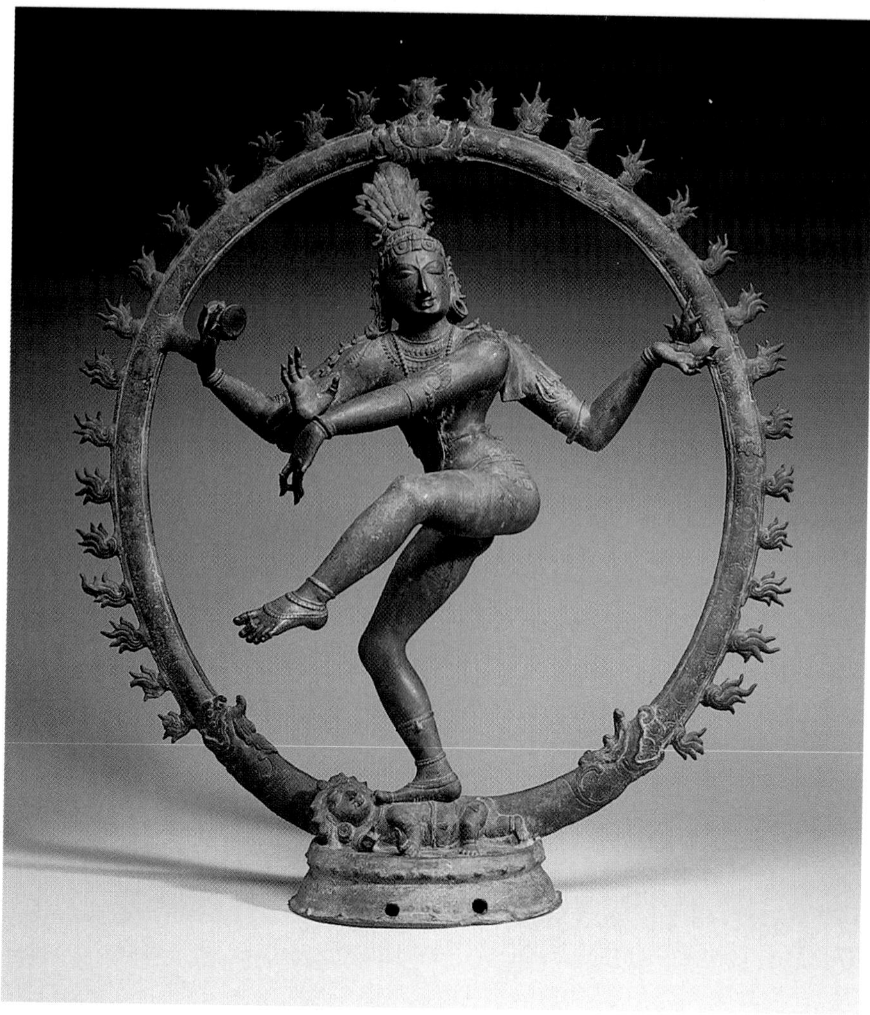

409 SHIVA NĀTARĀJA, LORD OF THE DANCE. 11th century.
Copper. 43⅞" × 40".

sanctum for individual worship of the sacred image within. In its solidity, it recalls THE GREAT STUPA at Sāñchī (see page 289).

Shown on page 285 is one of six erotic scenes from the abundant sculpture on the outside of KANDARYA TEMPLE. To the Hindu worshiper, union with God is filled with a joy analogous to the sensual pleasure of erotic love. The natural beauty and fullness of the human figures emphasize maleness and femaleness. Fullness seems to come from within the rounded forms, as seen in the earlier MALE TORSO from Harappā. The intertwining figures symbolize divine love in human form—an allegory of ultimate spiritual unity. In India, and elsewhere in the non-Western world, no separation is made between what we call the sacred and secular spheres of life.

The complex pantheon of Hindu gods and goddesses depicted in Indian art represents all aspects of human aspirations and experience. In later Hindu belief, Shiva—one of the greatest gods—encompasses in cyclic time the creation, preservation, dissolution, and re-creation of the universe. To show these roles, Shiva is given various forms in Hindu sculpture. In this eleventh-century image,

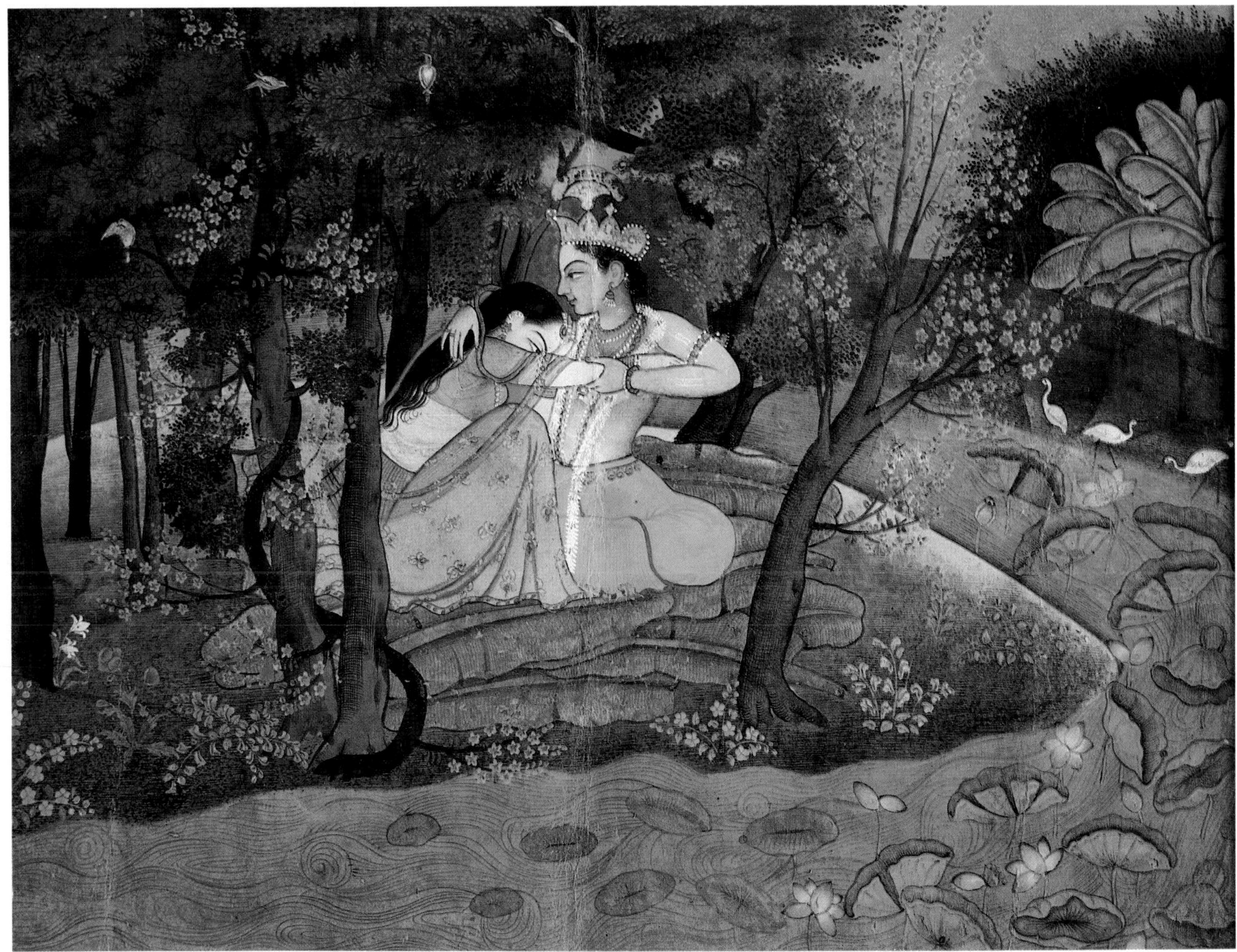

410 HINDU DEITIES KRISHNA AND RADHA IN A GROVE. c. 1780.
Gouache on paper. 123 mm × 172 mm.

SHIVA NĀTARĀJA, Lord of the Dance, performs the cosmic dance within the orb of the sun. As he moves, the universe is reflected as light from his limbs. The sculpture implies movement so thoroughly that motion seems contained in every aspect of the piece. Each part is alive with the rhythms of an ancient ritual dance. Multiple arms increase the sense of movement and hold symbolic objects.

In the seventeenth and eighteenth centuries, northern Indian artists, influenced by the miniature painting traditions of Persia (see page 60), developed their own related, yet unique styles of painting. Figures in serene landscapes and religious legends were popular subjects. HINDU DEITIES KRISHNA AND RADHA IN A GROVE is characteristic of the romantic content and gracefully flowing linear style of painters of the hill state of Kangra. This painting echoes some of the sumptuousness and sensuality of early Indian sculpture. The legends of Krishna contain a wealth of erotic references. As in Hindu temple sculpture (see page 285), erotic themes in the painted legends of Krishna lead to deeper symbolic meanings. Amorous summons are transformed into the appeal of the divinity.

Buddhist Art

Early Buddhism did not include the worship of images. As with Christianity, however, religious practice needed visual icons as support for contemplation; thus images of the Buddha began to appear. The many styles of Buddhist art and architecture vary according to the cultures that produced them. As Buddhism spread from India to Southeast Asia and across central Asia to China, Korea, and Japan, it influenced (and was influenced by) native religious and aesthetic traditions.

The Indian Gupta dynasty (c. 320–540) is notable for major developments in politics, law, mathematics, and the arts. Although slightly damaged, the carved stone STANDING BUDDHA is a fine

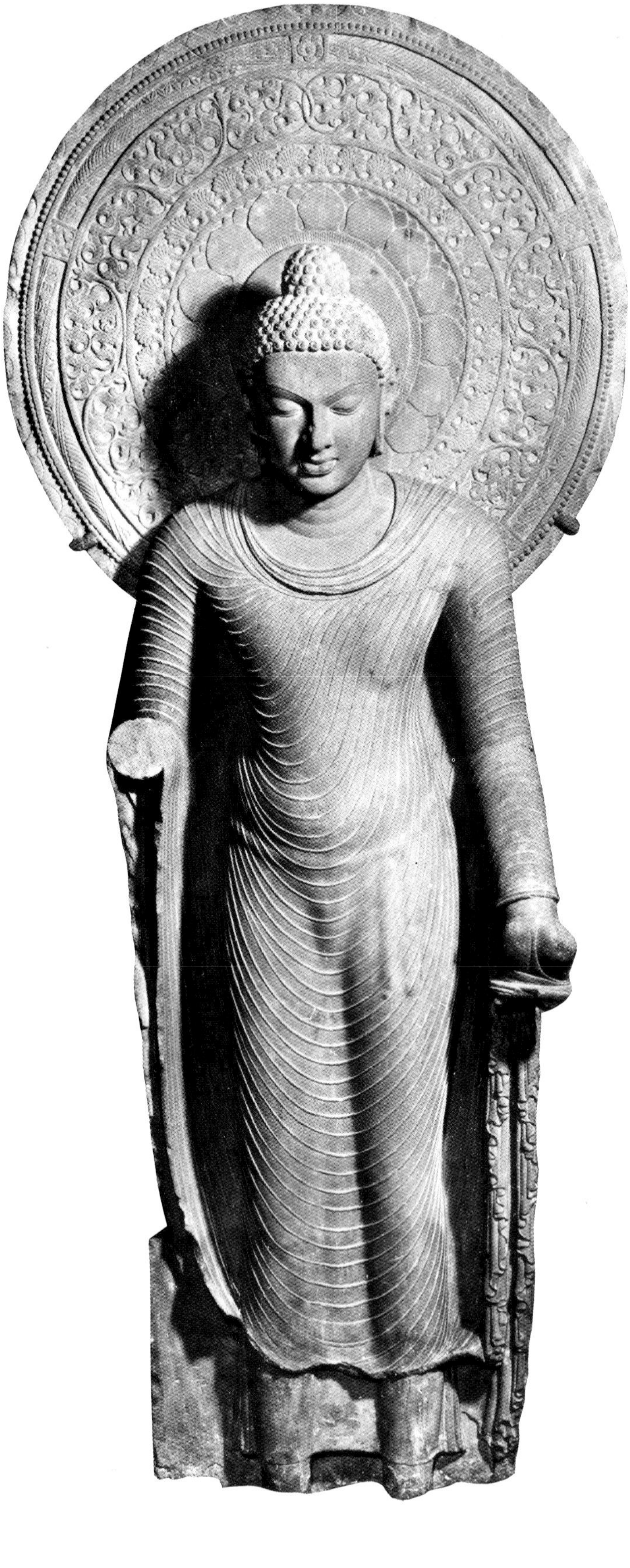

411 STANDING BUDDHA. 5th century.
Red sandstone. Height 5'3".
Indian Museum, Calcutta.

412 "BEAUTIFUL BODHISATTVA" PADMAPANI.
Detail of a fresco from Cave 1, Ajanta, India. c. 600-650.

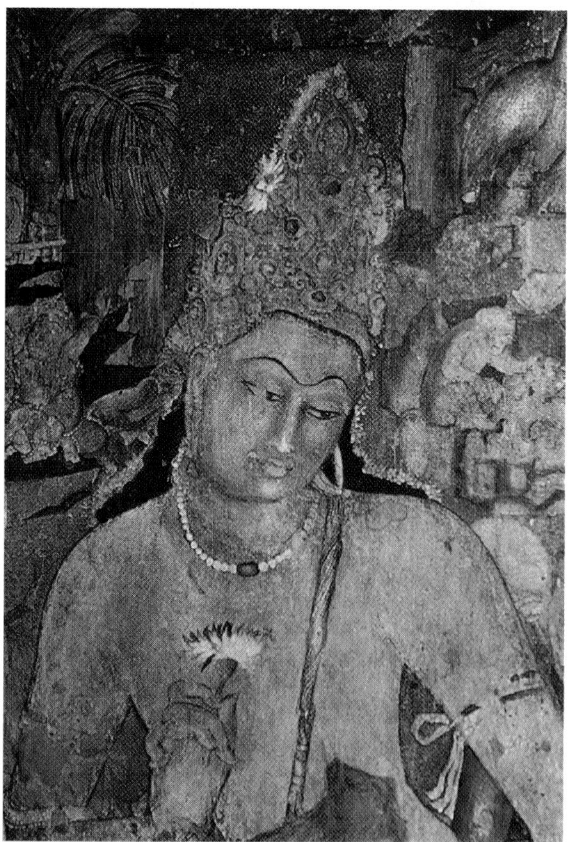

example of Gupta sculpture. In its cool, idealized perfection, the refined Gupta style marks a period of high achievement in Indian art. Once again, the simplified mass of the figure seems to push out from within as though the body were inflated with breath. The rounded form is enhanced by curves repeated rhythmically down the figure. The drapery seems wet as it clings to and accentuates the softness of the body.

Similar Gupta elegance and linear refinement are found in the noble figure known as the "BEAUTIFUL BODHISATTVA" PADMAPANI, part of a series of elaborate paintings in the Ajanta Caves. According to Buddhist teaching, a Bodhisattva is one who is qualified for Buddhahood but, out of compassion, forgoes *nirvana* (the state in which the soul is released from desires and attachments) in order to help others reach enlightenment. Fine linear definition of the figure accents full, rounded shapes, exemplifying the Gupta ideal of relaxed opulence.

The beginnings of Buddhist architecture are seen in solid, domelike structures called *stupas,* which evolved from earlier Indian burial mounds. At THE GREAT STUPA at Sāñchī, four gates symbolize north, south, east, and west. The devout walk around the stupa in a ritual path, symbolically taking the Path of Life around the World Mountain.

We can trace the EVOLUTION OF BUDDHIST ARCHITECTURE from its origin in India to its later manifestations in other parts of Asia. Buddhist pagodas developed from a merging of the Indian stupa with the traditional Chinese watchtower. The resulting broad-eaved tower structure was in turn adopted and changed by the Japanese.

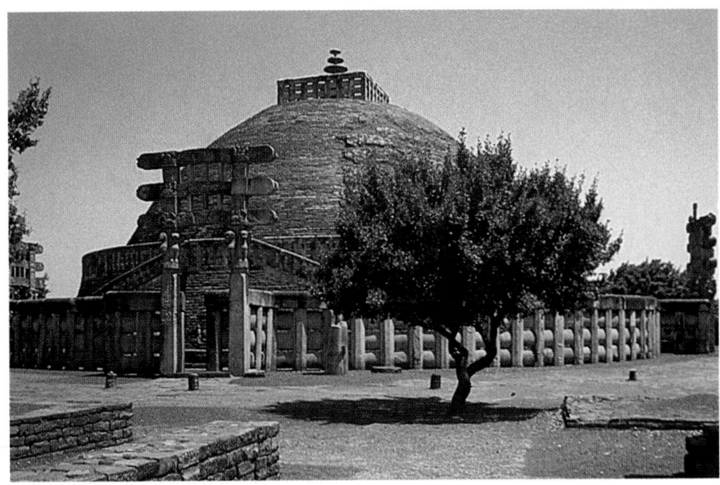

413 a THE GREAT STUPA. Sāñchī, India. 10 B.C.-A.D. 15.
Photograph: Prithwish Neogy.
b Eastern gate of THE GREAT STUPA.
Photograph: Hans Hinz.

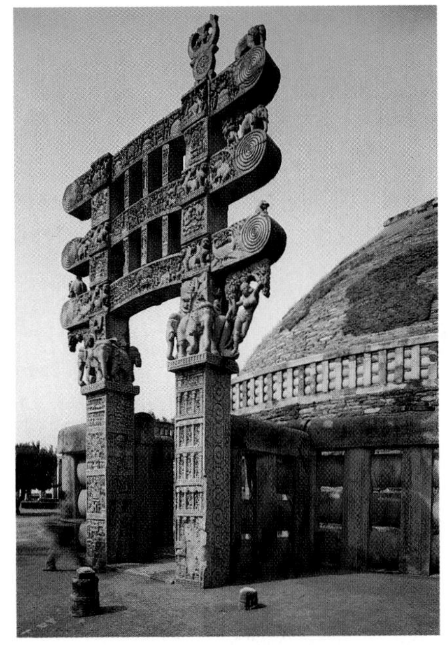

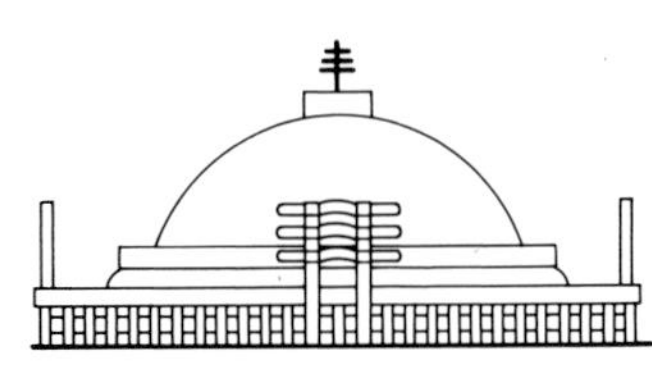

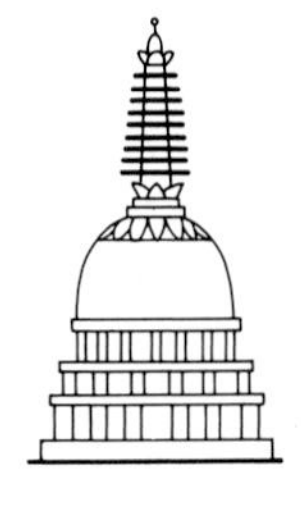

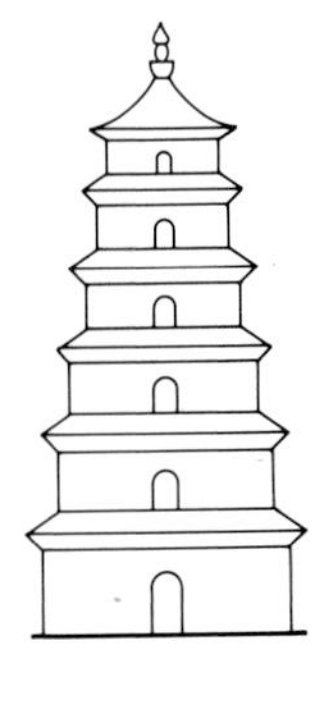

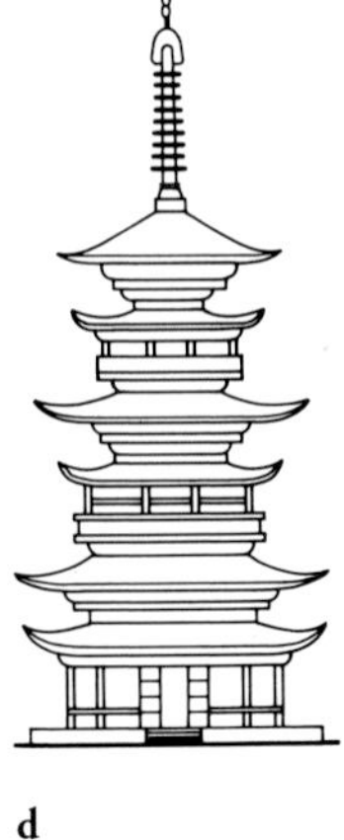

a b c d

414 EVOLUTION OF BUDDHIST ARCHITECTURE.
a Early Indian stupa. 3rd century to early 1st century B.C.
b Later Indian Stupa. 2nd century A.D.
c Chinese pagoda. 5th to 7th centuries.
d Japanese pagoda. 7th century.

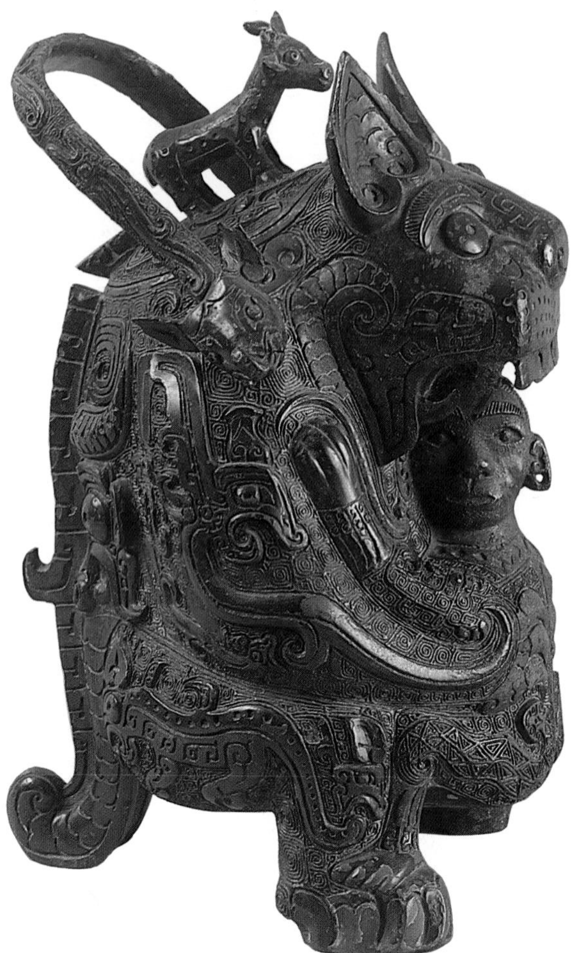

415 RITUAL VESSEL. China. c. 1100-1000 B.C.
Cast bronze. Height 14".
Musée Cernushi, Paris.

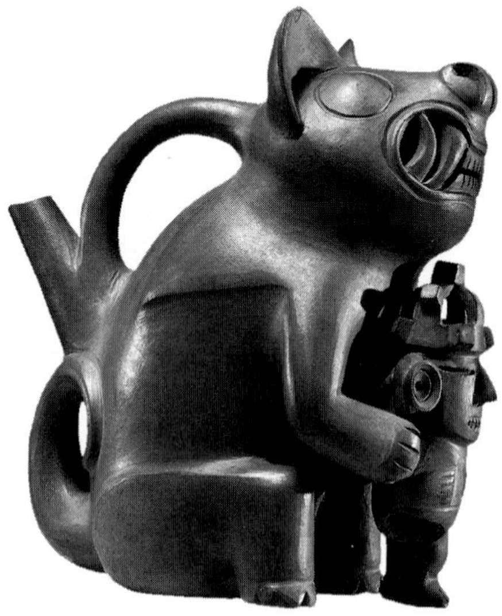

416 VESSEL IN THE SHAPE OF A FELINE HOLDING A MAN.
Virú, Peru. c. 1200 B.C.
Pink clay. Height 8½".

CHINA

Few Westerners are familiar with the complexity of Chinese history or with its greatly varied art styles.

Some of the world's finest cast-bronze objects were produced in China during the Shang dynasty (sixteenth to eleventh centuries B.C.). In the RITUAL VESSEL, there is an overall compactness. As on other Shang containers, surfaces are covered with an intricate composite of animal forms: sometimes fragments of animals are combined, sometimes complete animals are depicted. In this piece, a deer acts as a handle for the lid; just in back of the deer, an elephant's trunk comes out of a tiger's mouth, providing a third support. The man seems about to be devoured—his head is shown within the ferocious jaw of the tiger spirit—but at the same time his hands are relaxed as he reaches to the animal for protection. An intriguing aspect of this vessel is the gentle expression on the man's face in relation to the aggressive, protective power of the animal.

The VESSEL IN THE SHAPE OF A FELINE from Peru is remarkably similar to the Chinese RITUAL VESSEL. Both objects are compact, abstract depictions of catlike animal guardians, differing primarily in their surface treatments. Such similarities in subject matter and form may be evidence that storm winds and ocean currents helped move ships from Asia to the Americas long before the voyages of Magellan.

Recent excavations of tombs from the Han dynasty (206 B.C.–A.D. 221) uncovered the magnificent second-century FLYING HORSE found at Wu-Wei in Kansu. The sculptor gave a feeling of weightlessness to the horse by delicately balancing it on one hoof atop a flying swallow. The curvaceous form and powerful energy of this elegant horse is typically Chinese.

Throughout most of Chinese history, animals have been the preferred subject for sculptors. Aside from tomb figures, there are few early Chinese representations of the human body in art. The most important tradition of sculpture based on the human figure began as Buddhism reached China from India some time during the first century A.D. Chinese artists then adopted the idealized, sacred

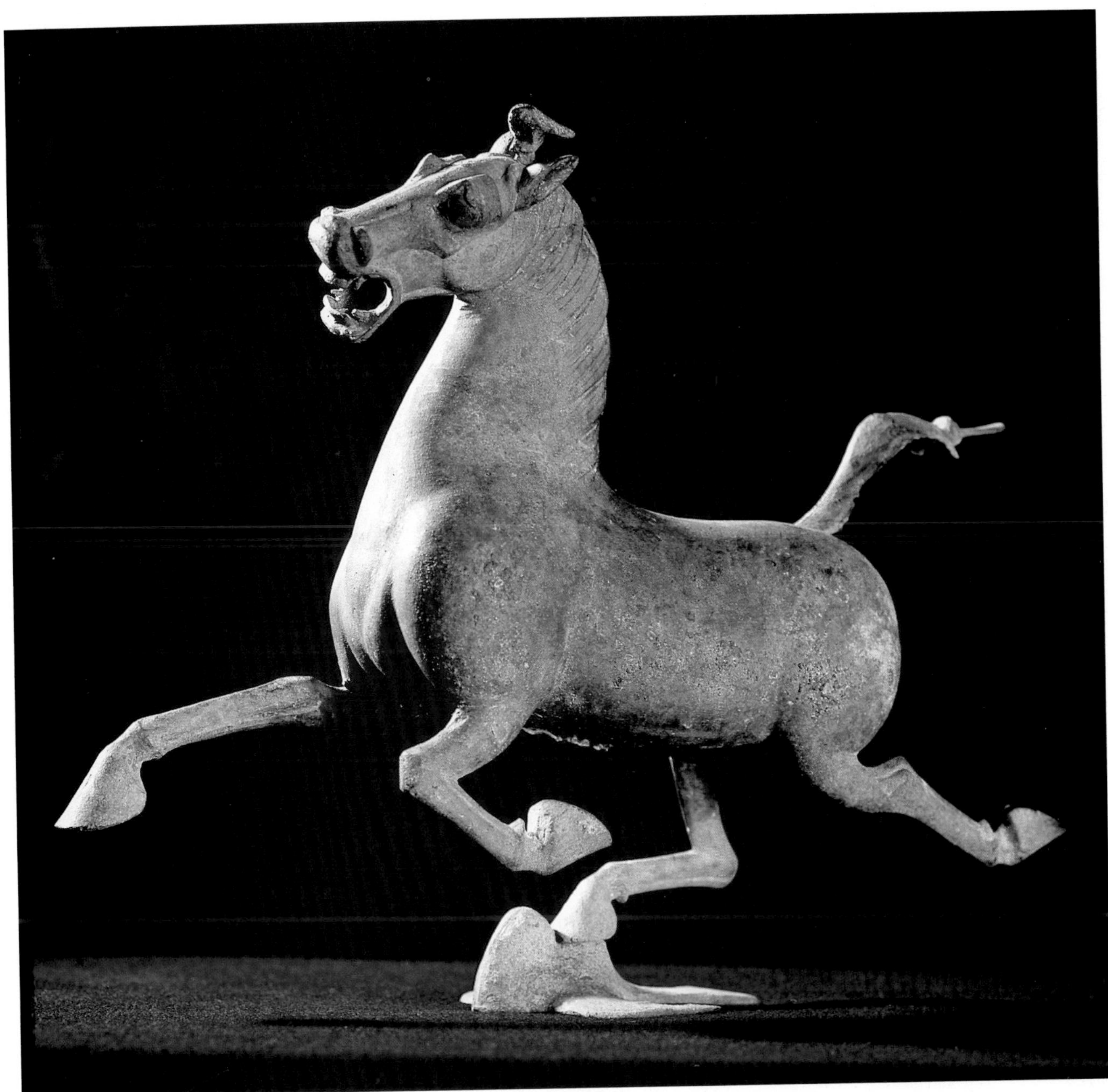

417 FLYING HORSE. Wu-Wei. Han dynasty, 2nd century. Bronze. 13½" × 17¾".

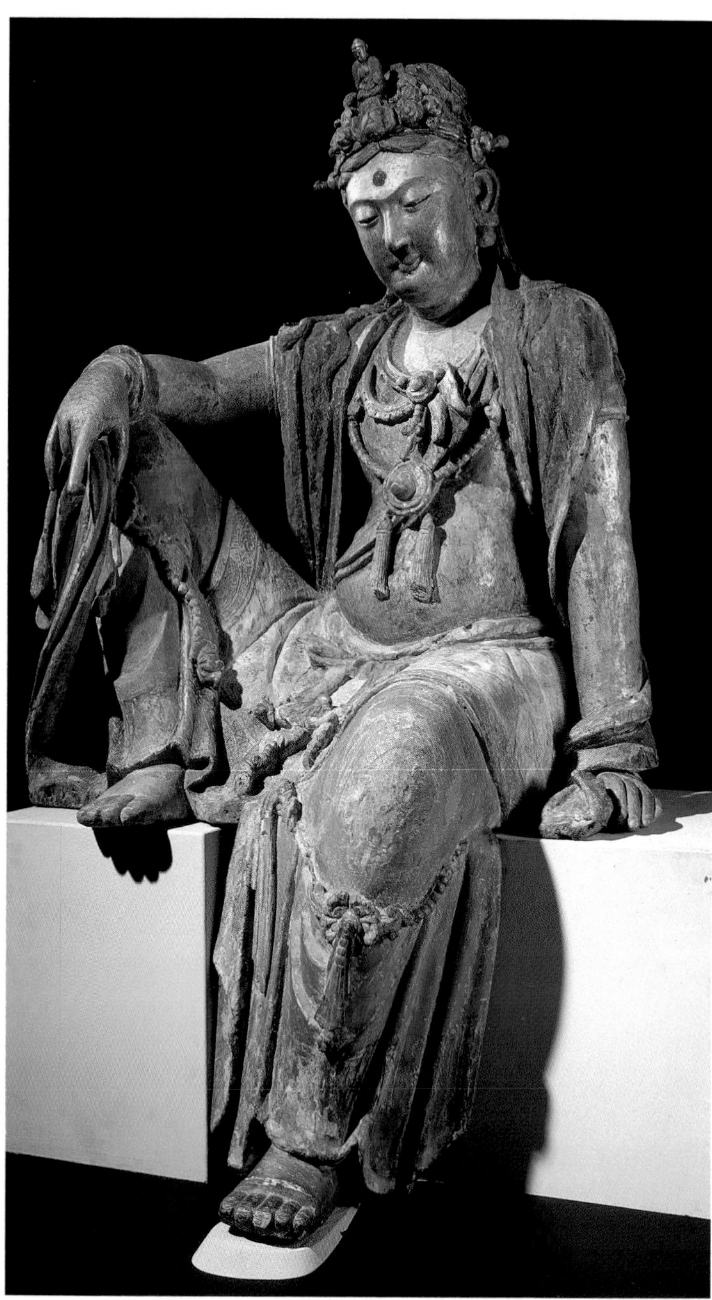

418 BODHISATTVA GUAN YIN (KUAN YIN).
Song (Sung) dynasty, c. 12th century.
Carved wood decorated in gold, lacquer, and polychrome.
Height 55½".
Harvey Edward Wetzel Fund. Courtesy, Museum of Fine Arts, Boston.

images of Indian sculptors, with only minor changes. Some of the finest figures—those that express Buddhist compassion—are known as Avalokitesvara in India, Guan Yin (Kuan Yin) in China, and Kwannon in Japan. The gentle smile and relaxed posture of the GUAN YIN symbolize kindness, patience, and wisdom.

In painting, even more clearly than in sculpture, we see the Chinese reverence for nature. Traditionally, Chinese painters sought to manifest the spirit residing in every form. The painter was taught to meditate before wielding a brush in order to achieve a balance between the impression received through the eyes and the perception of the heart and mind. After prolonged contemplation of nature, the artist painted from memory, working with ink and light color on silk or paper. Through painting, individuals nourished spiritual harmony within themselves and revealed divine energy to others. This approach is based on Daoism, the principal religious philosophy of China. Daoism focuses on the relative nature of all things: there can be no death without life, no good without evil, and so forth. Behind the duality and illusion of the so-called real world is a unifying principle called the Dao. In Chinese, *Dao* means path or way. It is the way the universe functions, as seen in the effortless flow of interacting forces of nature.

In order to assimilate fully their rich tradition, Chinese painters copy (with personal variations) the works of earlier artists. Even fully mature painters will often produce a work in the style of an older master they particularly admire.

The Northern Song dynasty (960–1126) was a particularly important period for painting in China. During the eleventh century, a group of artist-intellectuals developed a new spirit in artistic expression known as *literati painting*. Many of the early literati painters, who were both political leaders and accomplished calligraphers, held that the artist's true character and emotions could be expressed through the abstract forms of calligraphic characters—and even through individual brush strokes. They were critical of those who painted for commercial rather than aesthetic reasons.

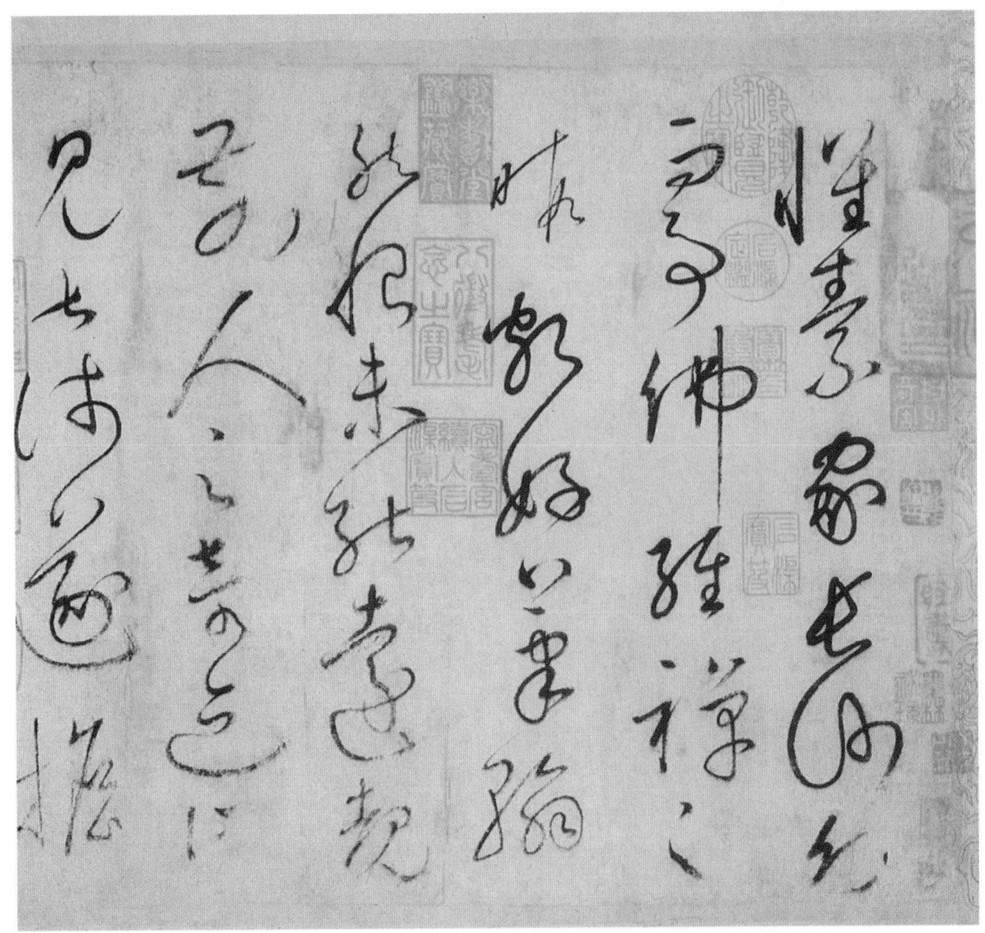

419 Huai-su.
Detail of AUTOBIOGRAPHY.
Tang dynasty,
7th-10th centuries.
Ink on paper.
National Palace Museum, Taipei, Taiwan.

Long valued in China, calligraphy is still considered a higher art than painting. Since ancient times, Chinese leaders of all kinds have been expected to express the strength of their character through elegant writing. By introducing calligraphic brush techniques for expressive purposes, literati painters sought to elevate painting to the levels that calligraphy and poetry had already attained. Huai-su, in AUTOBIOGRAPHY, and later masters drew inspiration from fourth-century Daoist poet, statesman, and master calligrapher Wang Hsi-chih. His style of writing, an improvement on earlier styles, has served as an inspirational model for generations of calligraphers to the present day. Wang Hsi-chih's stature in China is comparable to Shakespeare's and Rembrandt's in the West and indicates the Chinese people's long-standing admiration for great calligraphy. What is remarkable is how few original examples of his writing survive.

The flowering of calligraphy as an art form was due partly to the popularity of the new literati style of writing that freed scholars from the angular formality of characters used in official script. The fluid script enabled artists and poets to express themselves in a personal and energetic manner. With the spontaneous, gestural design of each brush stroke, the artist conveys the emotional as well as the intellectual content of the word or character being written. Poetry lies in the execution of the stroke as well as the phrase.

In China, painting and writing are closely related, and Chinese artists often include poems within their paintings. The same brushes and ink are used for both, and in both each brush stroke is important in the total design. Artists "paint" their poems as much as they "write" their paintings.

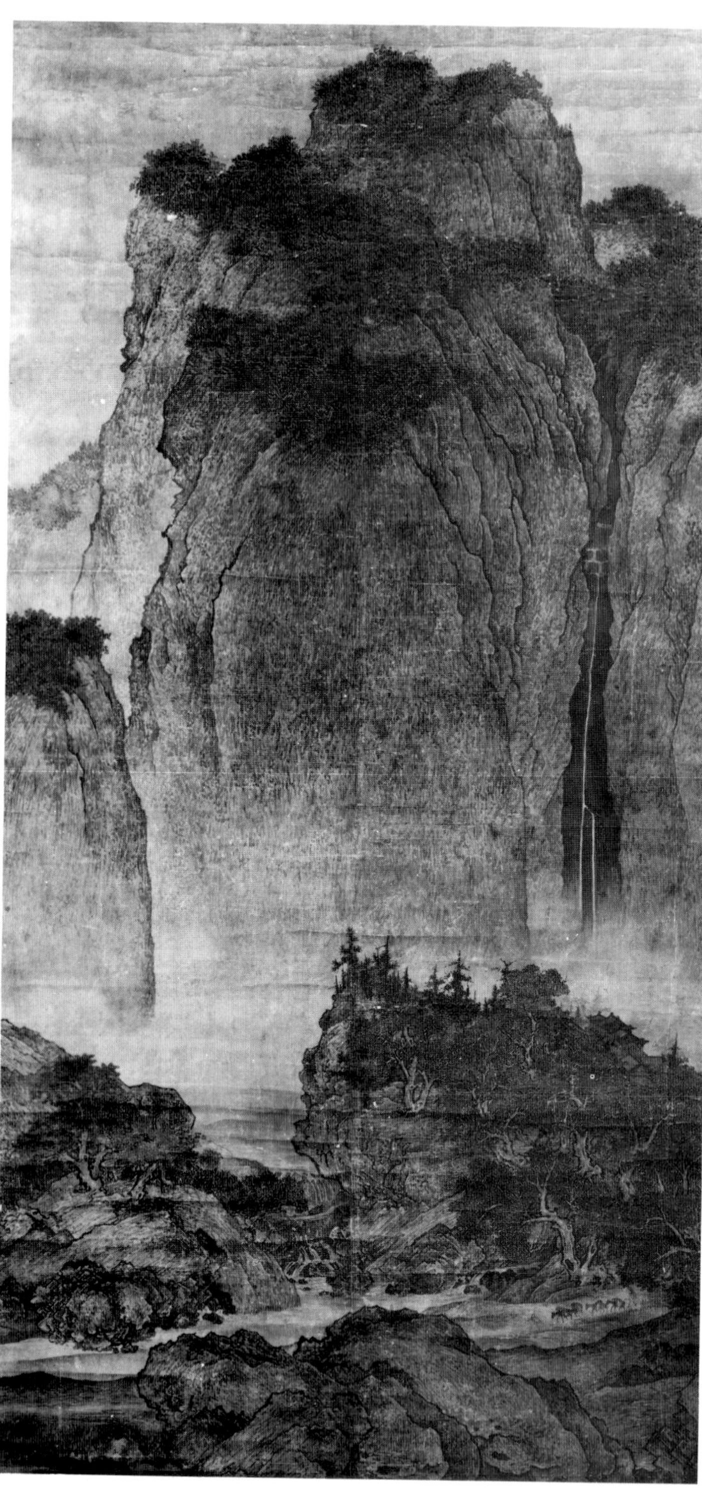

420 Fan Kuan (Fan K'uan).
TRAVELERS AMONG MOUNTAINS AND STREAMS. Early 11th century.
Hanging scroll, ink on silk. Height 81¼".
National Palace Museum, Taipei, Taiwan.

His contemporaries regarded court painter Fan Kuan as the greatest landscape painter of the Song dynasty. In his large hanging scroll TRAVELERS AMONG MOUNTAINS AND STREAMS, intricate brushwork captures the spirit of trees and rocks. Artists used many kinds of brush strokes, each identified by descriptive names such as "raveled rope," "raindrops," "ax cuts," "nailhead," and "wrinkles on a devil's face." Here "raindrop" and other types of brush strokes suggest the textures of the vertical face of the cliff. Men and donkeys, shown in minute scale, travel a horizontal path dwarfed by high cliffs rising sharply behind them. To highlight the stylized waterfall as the major accent in the design, Fan Kuan painted the crevice behind the waterfall in a dark wash and left the off-white silk unpainted to suggest the falling water. The vertical emphasis of the composition is offset by the almost horizontal shape of the light area behind the rocks in the lower foreground.

When a vertical line intersects a horizontal line, the opposing forces generate a strong center of interest. Fan Kuan took advantage of this phenomenon by extending the implied vertical line of the falls to direct the viewer's attention to the travelers. Figures give human significance to the painting and, by their small scale, indicate the vastness of nature. Effectiveness of the monumental landscape is achieved in part by grouping the fine details into a balanced design of light and dark areas.

The painting embodies ideas of Daoism and Neo-Confucianism, China's two major philosophical and spiritual traditions, which see nature as both emptiness and substance, interacting passive and active forces (*yin* and *yang*) that regulate the universe. Harmony on Earth is achieved through a balance of these forces—female and male, void and solid, dark and light.

In both central and southern China, steep, mist-shrouded peaks such as HUANGSHAN MOUNTAIN have inspired Chinese painters for centuries. In the seventeenth century, Li Li-Weng wrote, "First we see the hills in the painting, then we see the painting in the hills." His words remind us that, although art depends on our perception of na-

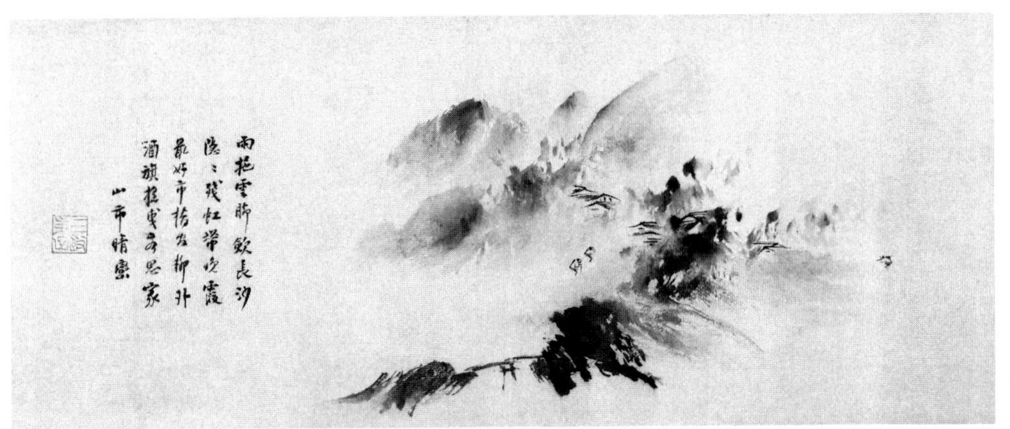

421 Yu-Jian (Yu-Chien). MOUNTAIN VILLAGE IN A MIST. 13th century. Ink on paper. Height 13". Idemitsu Museum of Arts, Tokyo.

ture, art also helps us to see nature with fresh eyes.

Northern Song literati painters helped prepare the way for another school of painting that flourished in Buddhist monasteries. Chan (as Zen Buddhism is called in China) painters in the thirteenth century developed a bold style that used abbreviated, abstract references. Compared to the detailed representation in Fan Kuan's TRAVELERS AMONG MOUNTAINS AND STREAMS, priest Yu-Jian's painting of MOUNTAIN VILLAGE IN A MIST shows a simplified, gestural impression of a landscape. In this painting, the relationship of human beings to nature is again expressed by the figures and the barely suggested roof lines in an atmosphere of mist-obscured mountains. The white, unpainted surface is as visually strong as the brushwork. Where Fan Kuan's painting is detailed and formal, Yu-Jian's is suggestive and informal.

Many Chinese painters intentionally leave their paintings incomplete to free the imagination and to avoid the implication that completeness is possible.

Before the twentieth century, no European or American artist would have left such large areas unpainted. Traditional Chinese painters, however, see space as a ground of possibilities, as positive rather than negative. Forms are suspended in Yu-Jian's painting, emerging and vanishing in ambiguous ways. Here the paper refers to sky, clouds, or mist, implying that what cannot be seen at this moment will appear at another moment and then disappear again. Chinese philosophy emphasizes the changing, interactive nature of thing-ness and no-thing-ness.

An unpainted surface standing for sky or clouds can also be a surface to write upon. Brush marks that indicate the landscape are expected to evoke a remembered experience rather than present what the eyes see. Here, the accompanying writing is a poem that also stimulates the memory image. The poem and the painting are parallel expressions. The practice of adding inscriptions to paintings reached maturity with the literati painters of the thirteenth and fourteenth centuries, and it has continued to the present in Chinese painting.

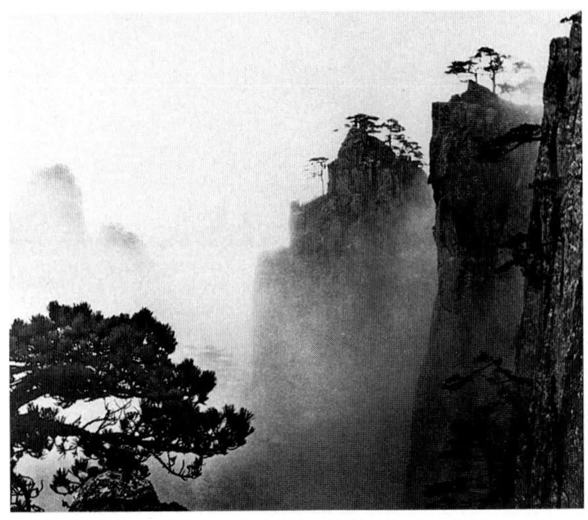

422 HUANGSHAN MOUNTAIN AFTER A RAIN. c. 1980. Photograph.

JAPAN

The indigenous (native) religion of Japan is an ancient form of nature and ancestor worship called Shinto. In this religion, forests and huge stones are considered holy places where gods dwell. The Shinto shrines at Ise are on a sacred site within a forest. The present MAIN SHRINE at Ise has been completely and exactly rebuilt every twenty years since the seventh century. Builders take wood for the shrine from the forest with gratitude and ceremonial care. As a tree is cut into boards, the boards are numbered so that the wood that was joined in the tree is reunited in the shrine. No nails are used; the wood is fitted and pegged. In keeping with the Shinto concept of purity, surfaces are left unpainted. The shrines at Ise combine simplicity with subtlety. Refined craftsmanship, sculptural proportions, and spatial harmonies express the ancient religious and aesthetic values of Shinto.

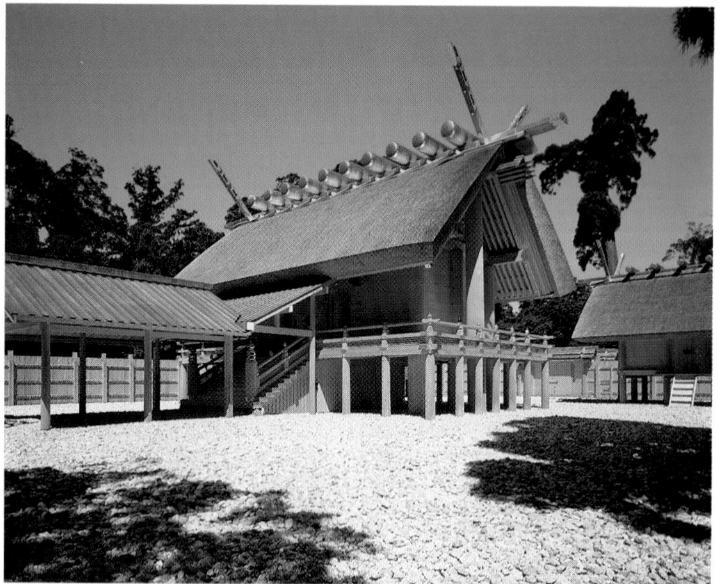

423 MAIN SHRINE. Ise, Japan. c. 685, rebuilt every twenty years.

In a wave of cultural borrowing that occurred more than a thousand years ago, the Japanese imported Buddhism, the Chinese writing system, and the art and architecture of Tang dynasty (seventh to tenth centuries) China—all strong influences in Japanese society today.

Buddhism came to Japan by way of Korea in the sixth century. The subsequent conversion to Buddhism stimulated an outpouring of art. Unkei, one of the greatest Buddhist sculptors of Japan, carved and painted a portraitlike sculpture of MUCHAKU, a legendary Indian priest. The sculpture is one of the few naturalistic figures known in Asia in which the force of individual personality is used to portray spiritual values. MUCHAKU's face expresses the sublime tranquility sought in Buddhism.

Zen Buddhism, which spread to Japan from China in the thirteenth century, provided a philosophical basis within which aesthetic activities were given meaning beyond their physical form. Zen

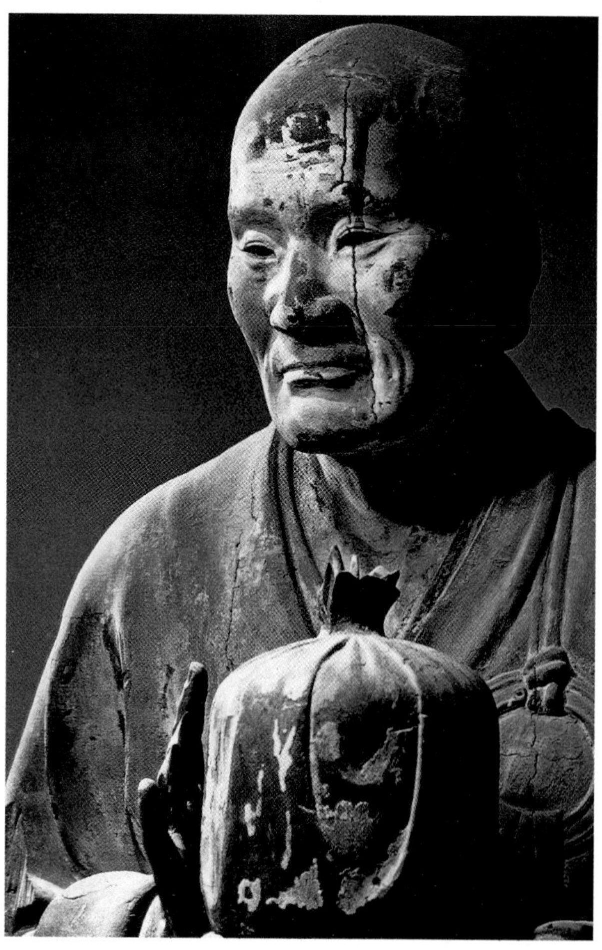

424 Unkei.
Detail of MUCHAKU. c. 1208.
Wood. Height 75".
Kofuku-ji Temple, Nara, Japan.

teaches that enlightenment can be attained through meditation and contemplation. The influence of Zen on Japanese aesthetics can be seen in spontaneous and intuitive approaches to poetry, calligraphy, painting, gardens, and flower arrangements.

Zen Buddhist priest Sesshū is considered the foremost Japanese master of ink painting. In 1467, he traveled to China where he studied the works of Southern Song masters and saw the countryside that inspired them. Chinese Chan (Zen) paintings, such as Mu Qi's SIX PERSIMMIONS (page 58) and Yu-Jian's MOUNTAIN VILLAGE IN A MIST, were greatly admired by the Japanese, and many were brought to monasteries in Japan.

Sesshū adapted the Chinese style and set the standard in ink painting for later Japanese artists. He painted in two styles. The first was formal and complex, while the second was a simplified, somewhat explosive style, later called *haboku,* meaning "flung ink." HABOKU LANDSCAPE is abstract in its simplification of forms and freedom of brushwork. Sesshū suggested mountains and trees with single, soft brush strokes. The sharp lines in the center foreground indicating a fisherman, and the vertical line above the rooftops representing the staff of a wine shop, are in contrast to the thin washes and darker accents of the suggested landscape.

Many Japanese artists used the format of the horizontal handscroll (thought to have originated in China) as a way of leading viewers on a journey through landscape. Some handscrolls measure as long as 50 feet, and all were meant to be seen, a small section at a time, by only two or three people. Japanese painters found the handscroll particularly

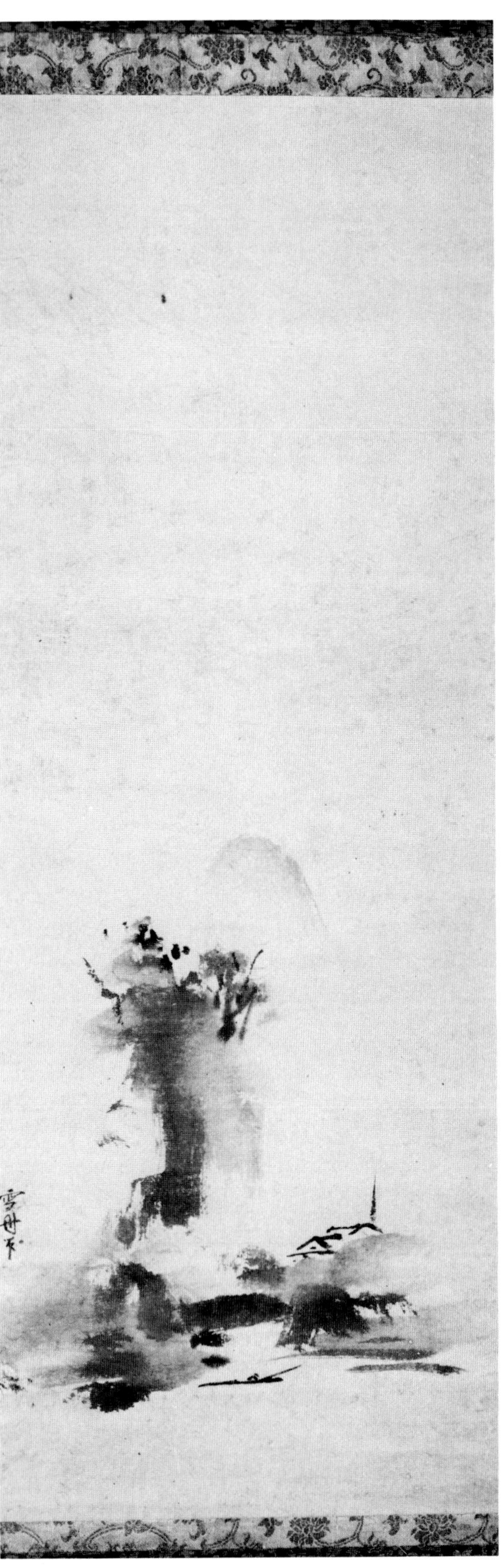

425 Sesshū.
HABOKU LANDSCAPE. 15th century.
Hanging scroll, ink on paper. 28¼" × 10½".
The Cleveland Museum of Art. The Norweb Collection (CMA 55.43).

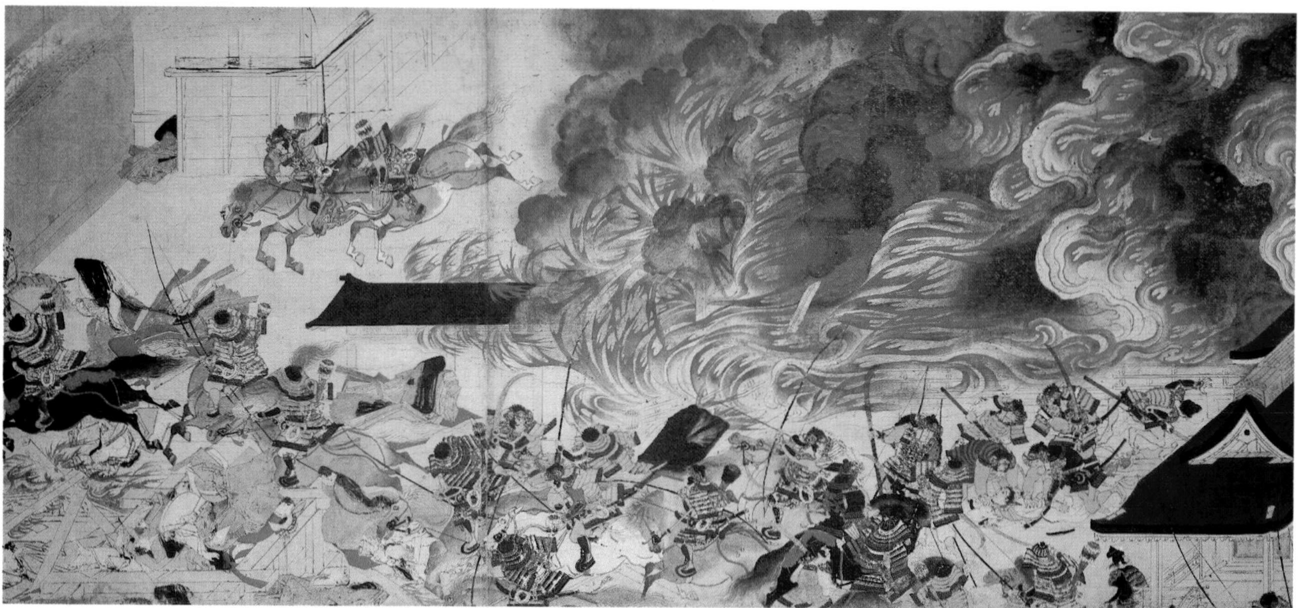

426 BURNING OF THE SANJO PALACE, from the HEIJI MONOGATARI. 13th century.
Section of the handscroll, ink and color on paper. Height 41.3 cm.
Fenollosa-Weld Collection. Courtesy, Museum of Fine Arts, Boston.

effective for long narrative compositions that depict the passage of time. BURNING OF THE SANJO PALACE is from the HEIJI MONOGATARI, a scroll that describes the Heiji insurrection of 1159. As the scroll is unrolled from right to left, the viewer follows a succession of events expertly designed to tell the story. Through effective visual transitions, the horror and excitement of the action are connected. The story builds from simple to complex events, reaching a dramatic climax in the scene of the burning palace, a highly effective depiction of fire. The color of the flames emphasizes the excitement of the historic struggle. Parallel diagonal lines and shapes, used to indicate the palace walls, add to the sense of motion and provide a clear geometric structure in the otherwise frantic activity of this portion of the scroll. Today such historic dramas are presented through film or television.

In traditional Japan, folding screens provided privacy by separating areas within rooms. Artists have used the unique spatial properties of the screen format in highly original ways. In contrast to the European easel painting that functions like a window in the wall, a painted screen within the living space of a home becomes a major element in the interior. The usefulness of a folding screen is part of the subject of the screen known as TAGASODE.

Tawaraya Sōtatsu's large screen WAVES AT MATSUSHIMA consists of a pair of six-panel folding screens (only one is shown here). The screens are designed so that together, or separately, they form complete compositions.

In keeping with well-established Japanese artistic practices, Sōtatsu created a composition charged with the churning action of waves, yet as solid and permanent in its design as the rocky crags around which the waters leap and churn. He translated his loving awareness of natural phenomena into a decorative, abstract design. Spatial ambiguity in the sky and water areas suggests an interaction that the viewer is to feel rather than read as a literal transcription of nature. In addition to rhythmic patterns that fill much of the surface, boldly simplified shapes and lines are contrasted with highly refined details and eye-catching surprises. A flat, horizontal gold shape in the upper left, accentuated with a black line, signifies a cloud and reaffirms the picture plane. The strongly asymmetrical

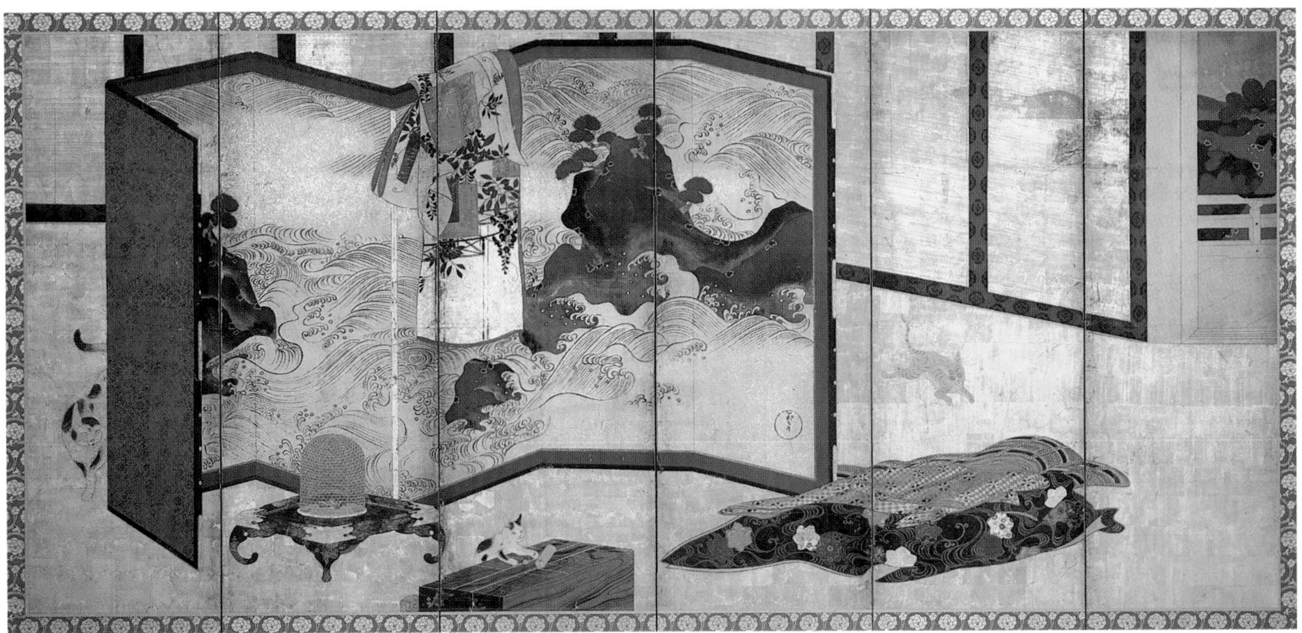

427 Anonymous. TAGASODE.
Painted screen.
Courtesy of the Freer Gallery of Art, Smithsonian Institution, Washington, D.C. (07.127).

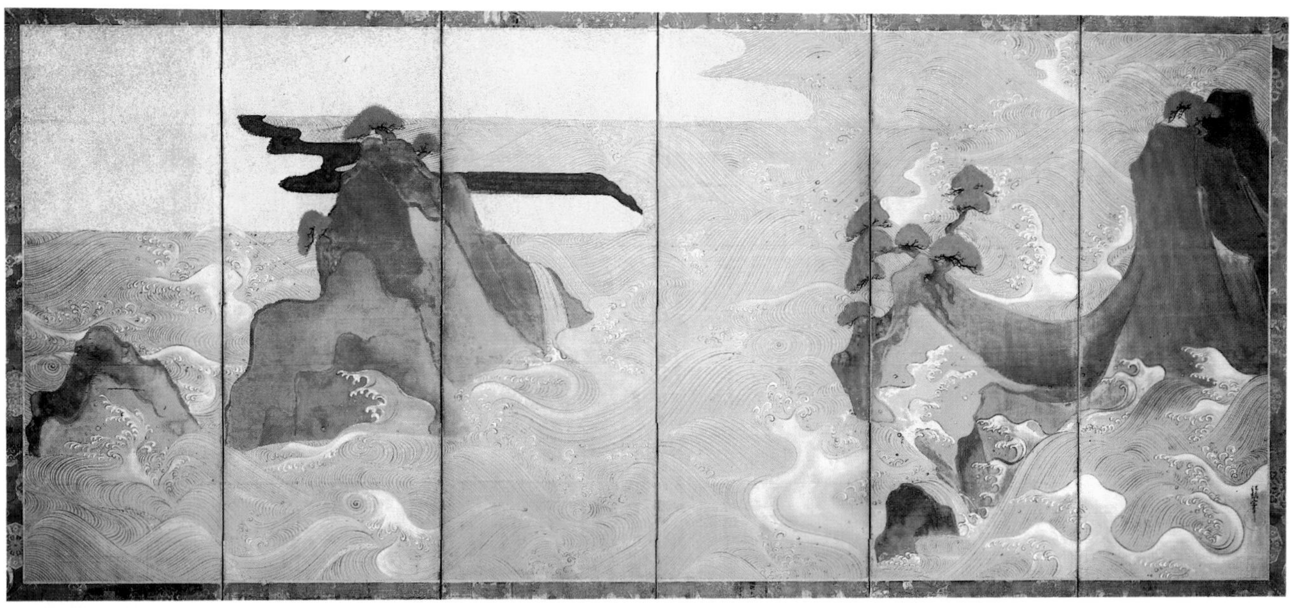

428 Tawaraya Sōtatsu.
WAVES AT MATSUSHIMA.
Early 17th century.
Painted screen, paper.
Each panel 59⅞" × 141¼".
Courtesy of the Freer Gallery of Art, Smithsonian Institution, Washington, D.C. (06.231).

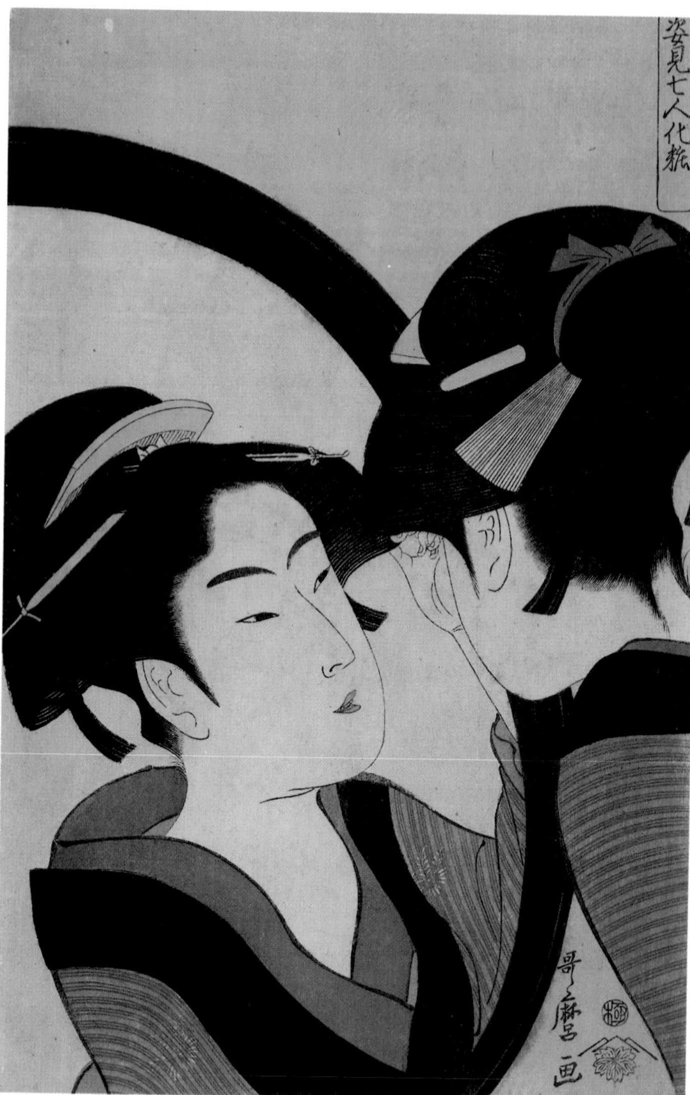

429 Kitagawa Utamaro.
REFLECTED BEAUTY, from the series SEVEN WOMEN SEEN IN A MIRROR. c. 1790.
Color woodblock print. 14¼" × 9½".
Honolulu Academy of Arts. The James A. Michener Collection.

design, emphasis on repeated patterns, and relatively flat spatial quality are all typical of much Japanese painting from the sixteenth to the nineteenth centuries.

By the mid-seventeenth century, the art of woodcut printing had developed to meet the demand for pictures by the newly prosperous merchant class. Japanese artists took the Chinese woodcut technique and turned it into a popular art form. For the next two hundred years, hundreds of thousands of these prints were produced. The prints are called *ukiyo-e,* meaning "pictures of the floating world," because they depict scenes of daily life, particularly the life of the entertainment centers of the time.

Kitagawa Utamaro's woodcut REFLECTED BEAUTY transforms the then ordinary subject into a memorable image consisting of bold, curving outlines and clear, unmodeled shapes. As with most Japanese paintings and prints, flat shapes are emphasized by avoiding shading. The center of interest is the reflected face of the woman, set off by the strong curve representing the mirror's edge. In contrast to Western compositions with centered balance and subjects well within the frame, here the figure is thrust in from the right and cut off abruptly by the edge of the picture plane, rather than presented completely within the frame. This type of radically cropped composition was one of the elements of Japanese art that most intrigued European artists in the nineteenth century. The influence can be seen in Gauguin's THE VISION AFTER THE SERMON on page 400.

Japanese architects have also demonstrated the sensitive orchestration of clearly defined forms. KATSURA PALACE, a seventeenth-century Japanese imperial villa, was built in Kyoto beside the Katsura River, the waters of which were diverted into the garden to form ponds. All elements—land, water, rocks, and plants—were integrated in a garden design that blends humanmade and natural elements. Because palace walls are sliding screens, they can provide flexible interconnections between interior and exterior spaces.

Compared to VERSAILLES (see page 367), another seventeenth-century imperial villa, KATSURA is very humble. Unlike VERSAILLES, the KATSURA PALACE complex was planned with no grand entrance either to the grounds or to the buildings. Instead, one approaches the palace along garden paths, and as one proceeds along these paths, unexpected views open up. Earth contours, stones, and waterways are combined to symbolize—on a small scale—mountains, rivers, fields, inlets, and beaches. The tea house, which imitates the tradi-

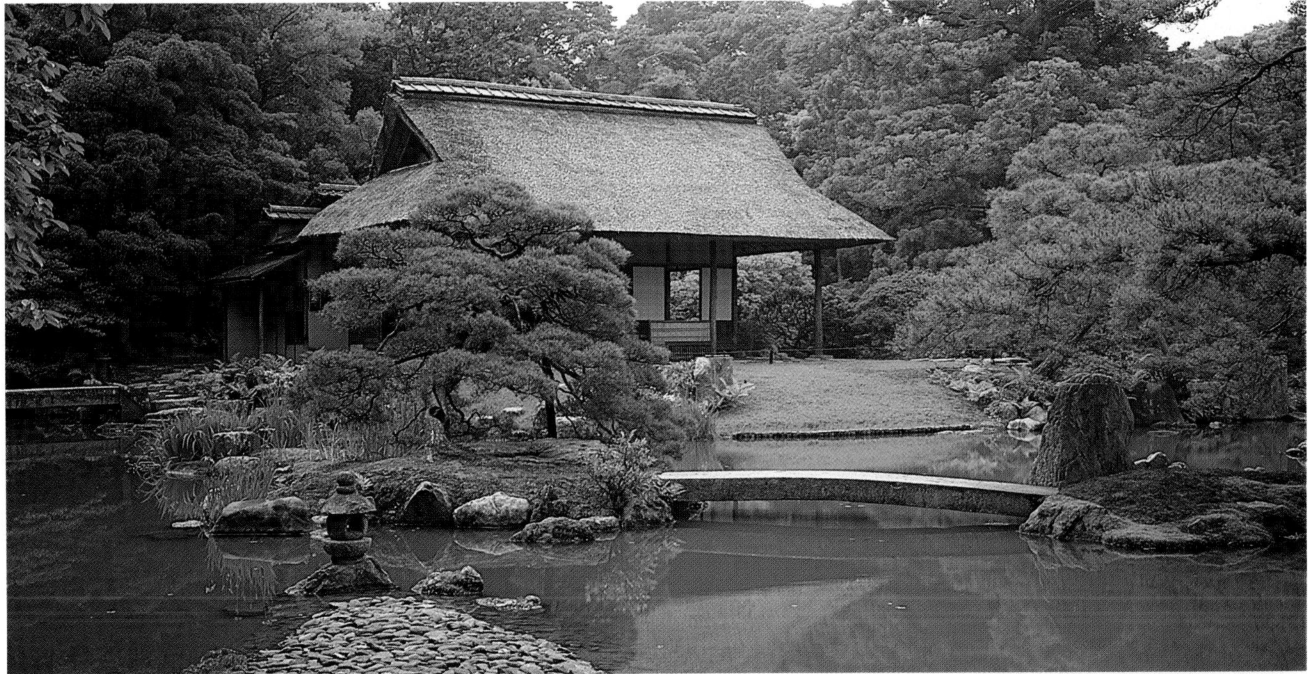

430 KATSURA DETACHED PALACE. Kyoto, Japan. 17th century.
a Gardens and tea house.
Photograph courtesy of Kenzo Yamamoto.

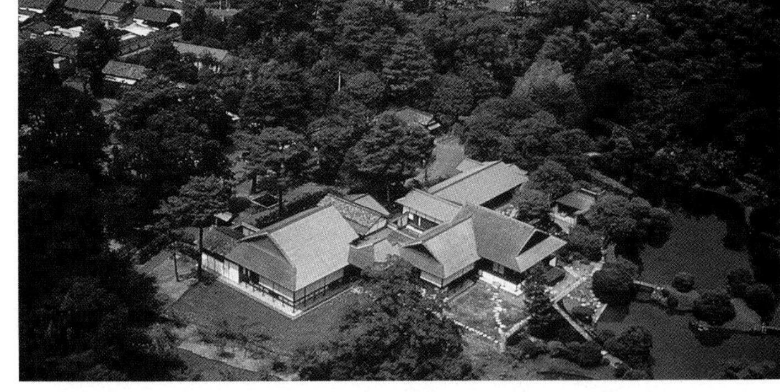

b Aerial view of imperial gardens and villa.
Photograph courtesy of Obayashi-Gumi, Construction Company.
c Interior of imperial villa.
Photograph: Ezra Stoller © Esto.

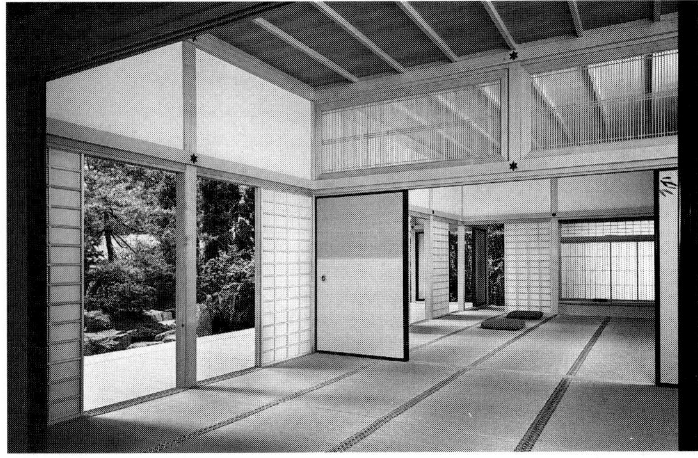

tional Japanese farmhouse, is constructed of common, natural materials. It provides the appropriate setting for the tea ceremony, which embodies the attitudes of simplicity, naturalness, and humility that permeate the entire palace grounds.

Domestic architecture has long been an important part of Japanese art. Modest houses, as well as palaces and Buddhist temples, have traditionally employed many of the structural and aesthetic principles of Shinto shrines. In the past, Japanese homes were related to the land and were often set in or built around a garden. Today small gardens provide intimacy with natural beauty, even in crowded city environments.

Traditional Japanese houses, such as those at KATSURA, are built of wood using post-and-beam construction. The result is essentially a roof on posts, allowing walls to be sliding screens rather than supports. The Japanese use of unpainted wood and the concept of spatial flow between indoors and outdoors have been major influences on twentieth-century architects in the West. (See Frank Lloyd Wright on page 263.)

PRE-COLUMBIAN CENTRAL AND SOUTH AMERICA

At the end of the last ice age, when the civilizations of India and China were emerging from the Neolithic stage, parallel developments were taking place in Central and South America. The major societies of this region were the Maya, the Aztec, and the Inca.

The Maya, who lived in what are now parts of Mexico, Guatemala, and Honduras, developed a written language, an elaborate calendar, advanced mathematics, and large temple complexes of stone. Maya also created fine ceramic vessels and sculpture. Figures such as MAYA MAN AND WOMAN stress volume, natural gestures, and costume detail.

431 MAYA MAN AND WOMAN. Mexico. c. 700. Buff clay with traces of color. 10½" × 5¾" × 3⅜". Honolulu Academy of Arts. Purchase.

The hundreds of stone temples at Tikal suggest that Mayan priests had great power. TEMPLE I, built during the classical Maya period, A.D. 300–900, rises over a great plaza in a Guatemalan rain forest. The 200-foot-high pyramid has a temple at the top consisting of three rooms. Another Maya temple pyramid contained a burial chamber deep inside, similar to those found in Egyptian pyramids. Walls and roofs of Maya stone temples were richly carved and painted.

Little is known about the Toltec civilization that developed in central Mexico between the ninth and thirteenth centuries, following the decline of the Maya and preceding the rise of the Aztecs. During a time of conflict and change, the Toltecs initiated a major new era in the highlands of central Mexico, distinguished by architectural innova-

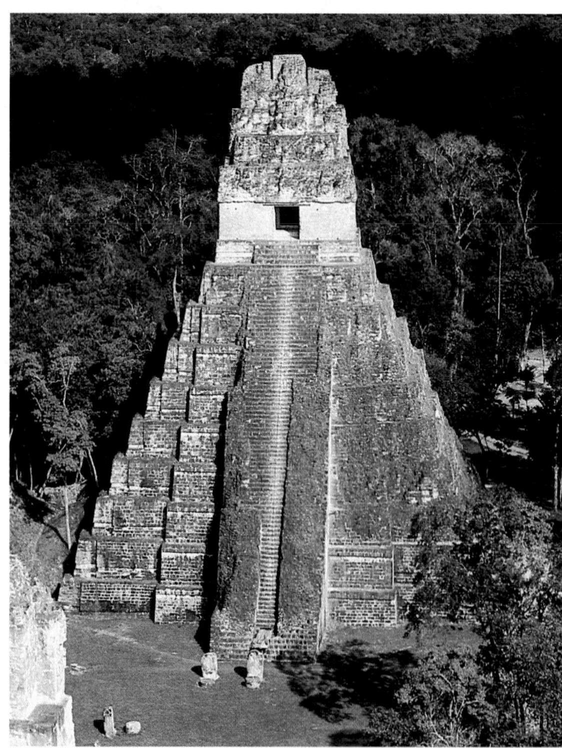

432 TEMPLE I. Maya. Tikal, Guatemala. c. 300-900. Photograph: Hans Namuth.

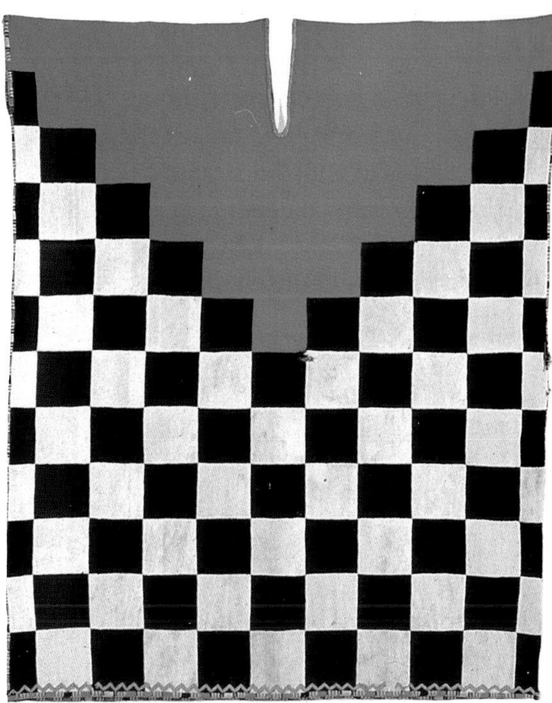

433 INCA SHIRT. Peru. c. 1438-1532.
Tapestry weave in alpaca wool. 34" × 31".

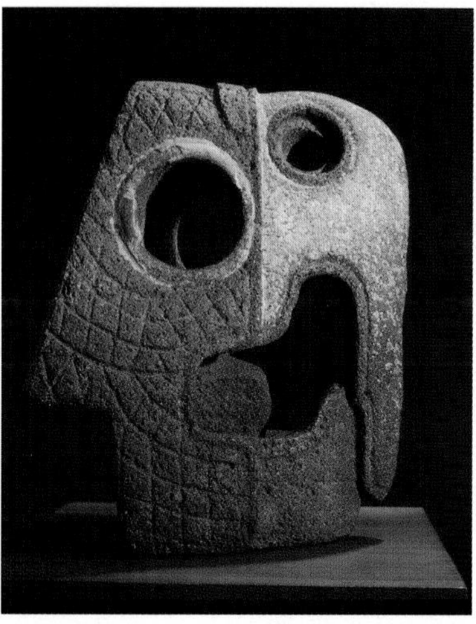

434 HEAD OF A MACAW.
Toltec. Teotihuacan,
Mexico. c. 1200.
Stone. Height 22½".
National Museum of Anthropology, Mexico City.

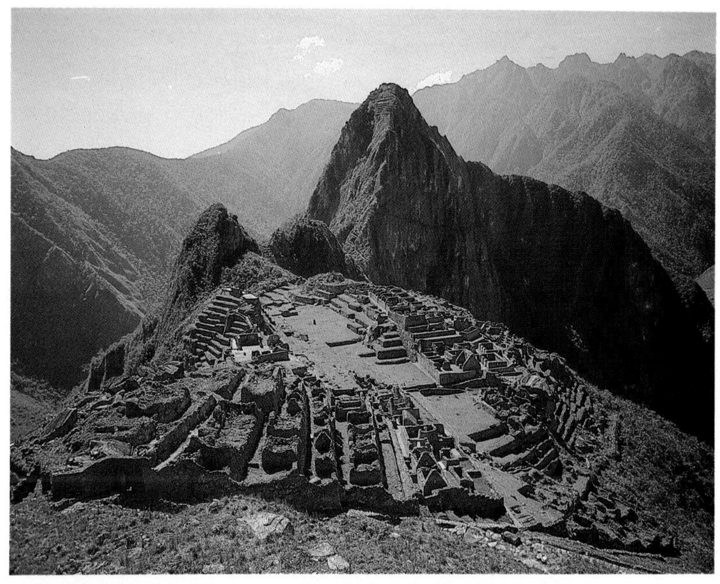

435 MACHU PICCHU. Inca. Peru. Early 16th century.
Photograph: Ewing Krainen.

tions and massive carved figures. One of the recurrent Toltec forms is the recumbent idol from Chichen Itza known by the Mayan name CHACMOOL (see page 52). It is believed that the bowl held at the figure's waist—possibly for sacrificial offerings—relates to ensuring a steady supply of water. Also of Toltec origin is the highly abstract HEAD OF A MACAW. The holes indicating an eye, nostril, and mouth create a dynamic interplay between negative spaces and positive shapes.

In the Andes of South America, Inca culture flourished for several centuries prior to the Spanish conquest in 1532. We have Spanish reports from the time telling of the magnificence of Incan art, but most of the culture's exquisite gold objects were melted down soon after the conquest, and all but a few of the refined fabrics have perished with age and neglect. Inca weaving is typified by the rich color and geometric patterns found in this very old but contemporary-looking sleeveless INCA SHIRT.

The Incas are perhaps best known for their supremely skillful shaping and fitting of stones. Their masonry is characterized by mortarless joints and the "soft" rounded faces of granite blocks. MACHU PICCHU, "the lost city of the Incas," was built on a ridge in the eastern Andes, in what is now Peru, at an elevation of 8,000 feet. The city, which escaped Spanish detection, was planned and constructed in such a way that it seems to be part of the mountain.

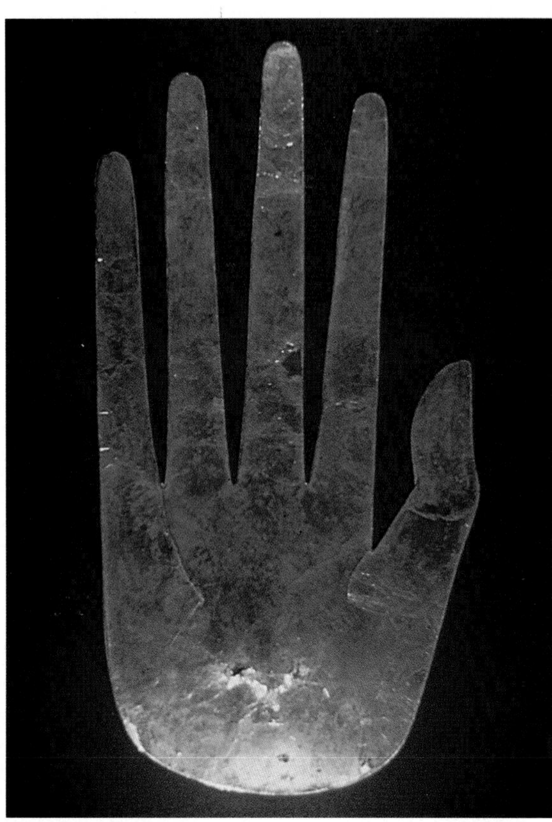

436 HAND. Hopewell Mound, Ohio. c. 150.
Mica. 11⅕" × 6".
Ohio Historical Society, Columbus.

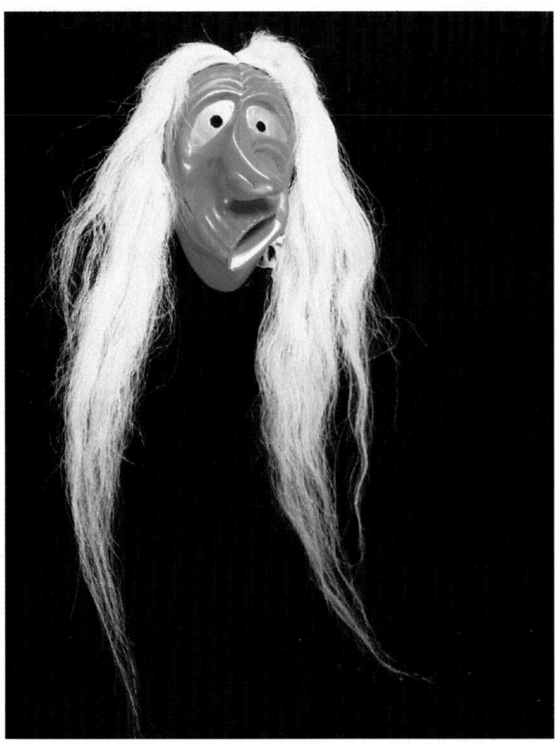

NATIVE NORTH AMERICA

The native art of North America has received less attention than that of the urban cultures of Central and South America. At one time there were great numbers of North American tribes, each with its own unique culture and style of art, yet only a handful of these societies survive today.

The Hopewell culture flourished from the second century B.C. to the sixth century A.D. Large Hopewell burial mounds, most of which were built in what is now Ohio, contained rich offerings placed in elaborate log tombs. Hopewell artists included wood and stone carvers, potters, coppersmiths, and specialists who worked in shell and mica. The HAND, found in a burial mound, has a striking, abstract quality; elongated fingers and a glowing surface strengthen its mysterious presence. Cut from a glistening, translucent sheet of mica, it seems to celebrate the coordination of eye and hand, mind and spirit, that is the source of all art.

Among the finest works of the Iroquois are the masks of the False Face Secret Society. The masks are worn for curing sickness caused by False Faces—grotesque, bodyless beings that stalk the dark forest, waiting to bewitch people into illness. To bring life energy into a mask, the mask is roughed out in the living tree, then cut off, finished, painted, and decorated. "CROOKED NOSE," a type of Onondaga mask, depicts a mythical personage who dared to challenge the creator and consequently was tricked into smashing his own face. He then became a protector against disease. (The Onondaga are part of the Iroquois confederacy of the Native American tribes of the Eastern woodlands.)

Masks worn in healing ceremonies, dances and dramas affect the performers as well as the audience. The spirit, represented by the mask, evokes a trance state and is said to take possession of the performer.

437 "CROOKED NOSE," FALSE FACE SOCIETY CURING MASK.
Onondaga, Iroquois.
Painted wood, copper, and horse hair.
Cranbrook Institute of Science Museum, Bloomfield Hills, Michigan.

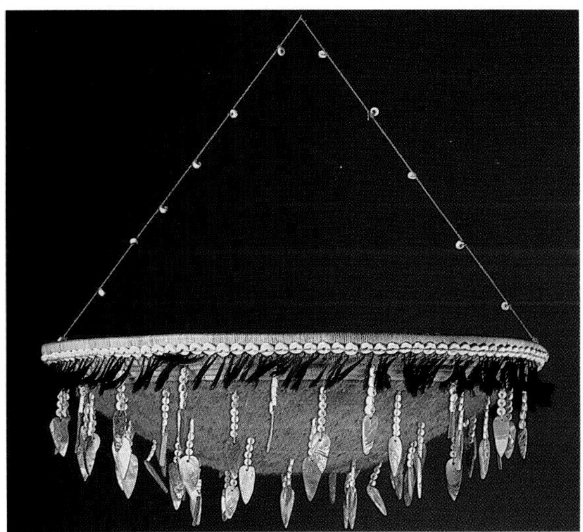

438 POMO FEATHER BASKET.
California. c. 1945.
3¼" × 13½".
Courtesy of the Southwest Museum, Los Angeles.

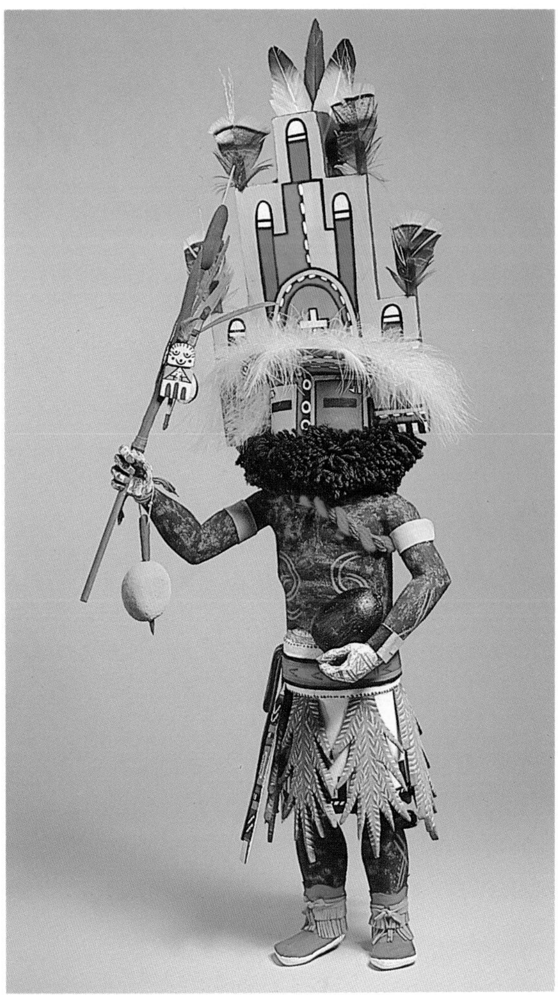

439 Marshall Lomakema.
HOPI KACHINA. 1971. Painted wood.
Courtesy of National Museum of the American Indian/Smithsonian Institution.

Pueblo tribes of the Southwest are among the few Native American groups to succeed in keeping their cultures alive. Most Pueblo peoples recognize the spirits of invisible life forces. These spirits, known as *kachinas,* are impersonated by masked and costumed male members of the tribes, who visit the villages in a variety of forms including birds, animals, clowns, and demons. During ceremonies they dance, present kachina figures to delighted children, provide humor, and occasionally give public scoldings. The carved and painted KACHINAS are made by Hopi and Zuni fathers and uncles as a means of teaching children their sacred traditions.

Much of the surviving Native American art is in the form of clay vessels (see the modern Acoma pottery on page 215). Before their cultures and most of their people were destroyed, Native Americans of the Pacific Coast region produced some of the world's finest baskets. In northern California, Pomo artists made baskets of such incredible tightness that they could hold water. There was great variety in size, shape, and decoration—from large containers up to four feet in diameter to tiny gift baskets less than a quarter of an inch across. Pomos wove strong geometric designs into many of their baskets and used ornaments such as feathers and shells to embellish others. Women were responsible for the highest artistic achievements in Pomo culture, the brightly colored FEATHER BASKETS. Treasured pieces were made as gifts designed solely to delight the eye.

Northwest Coast tribes developed highly imaginative arts to depict their mythology. Tlingit and other Northwest Coast tribes are known for elegant abstractions of animal subjects. The compact designs of their painted relief carvings are reminis-

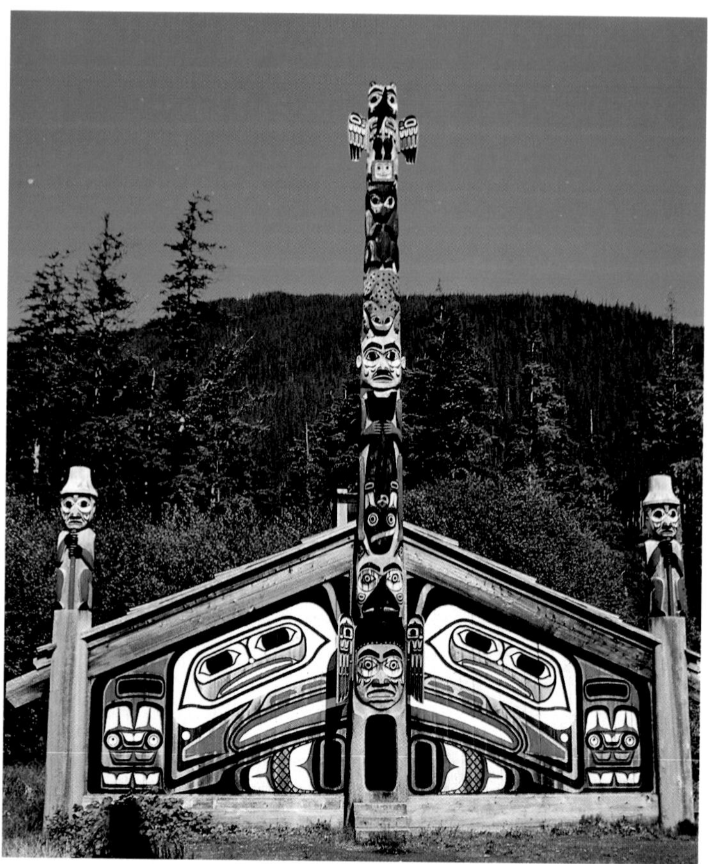

440 TLINGIT COMMUNITY HOUSE.
Ketchikan, Alaska.
Photograph: Steve McCutcheon.

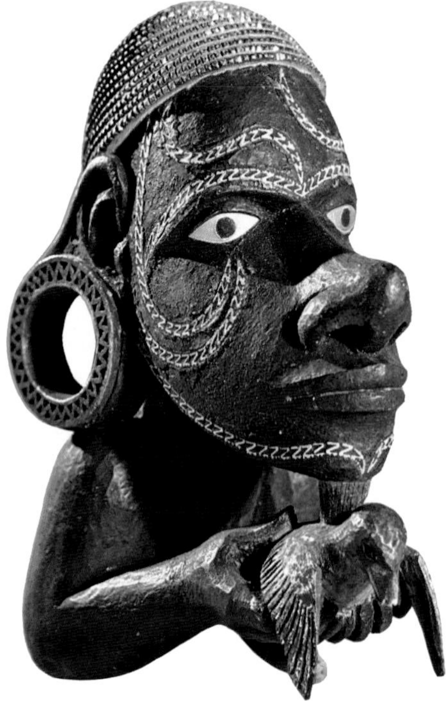

441 CANOE PROW FIGURE.
Maravo Lagoon, New Georgia, Solomon Islands.
Collected 1929.
Wood with mother-of-pearl.
Height 6½".
Museum of Ethnology, Basel, Switzerland.

cent of the abstract animal forms found on ancient Chinese bronzes (see page 290). On house walls, boxes, and blankets, major features of a totemic animal form are laid out in two-dimensional schematic patterns. (A *totem* is an object such as an animal or plant that serves as an emblem of a family or clan and often symbolizes original, prehuman ancestors.) The rounded shapes of totemic animals are presented in integrated symmetrical designs.

With its wide, gently sloping roof, elaborately painted facade, and totem poles, the TLINGIT COMMUNITY HOUSE is characteristic of the art and architecture of the region. Tlingit totem poles, shorter and thinner than those of other Northwest tribes, combine original design elements with features borrowed from neighboring tribes.

OCEANIA AND AUSTRALIA

Oceania is the collective name for the thousands of Pacific islands that comprise Melanesia, Micronesia, and Polynesia. It is difficult to generalize about Oceanic art, since the cultures, physical environments, and raw materials vary greatly over an enormous area.

Oceanic peoples were among the first of the world's great navigators. They developed very little pottery because of a shortage of clay, and they were not acquainted with metal until traders introduced it in the eighteenth century. For tools, they used stone, bone, or shell; for houses, canoes, mats, and cloth, they used wood, bark, and small plants. Feathers, bone, and shells were employed not only for utensils and sculpture, but for personal adornment.

In the Solomon Islands and New Ireland, part of Melanesia, wood carvings and masks are designed to serve ritual purposes. In the art of many societies, birds appear with human figures to act as guides or messengers between the physical world of the living and the spiritual world of deceased ancestors. The bird held by the CANOE PROW FIGURE from the Solomon Islands guides voyagers by acting as a protective spirit, watching out for shoals and reefs. The carving is only the size of a hand, but it looks much larger because of the boldness of its form. The exaggerated nose and jaw help give the head its forward thrust. Against the blackened wood, inlaid mother-of-pearl provides strongly contrasting white eyes and rhythmically curving linear ZZZ bands. Like the Chinese and Peruvian vessels on page 290, it exemplifies the symbolic power of art.

In New Ireland, masks are made for funerary rites that commemorate tribal ancestors, both real and mythical. In this MASK, the elaborately carved, openwork panels are painted in strong patterns that accentuate—and at times oppose—the dynamic forms of the carving. Snail-shell eyes give the mask an intense expression. As in the Solomon Islands' CANOE PROW FIGURE, a bird plays a prominent role.

In contrast to the art of Melanesia, the works made in Micronesia and in much of Polynesia are streamlined and highly finished. The Kapingamarangi COCONUT GRATER shows a fine integration of form and function. One sits on the "saddle" of the animal-like form and grates coconuts using the serrated blade at its head. The STANDING FIGURE from Nukuoro Atoll has a similar distinctive spare

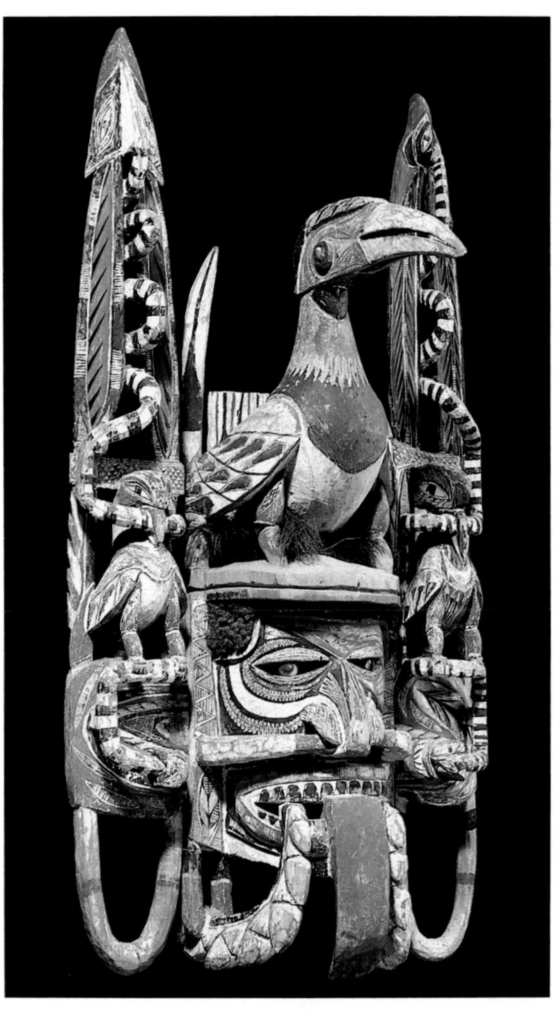

443 MASK. New Ireland. c. 1920.
Painted wood, vegetable fiber, shell. 94 cm × 53 cm.
Fowler Museum of Cultural History, UCLA.

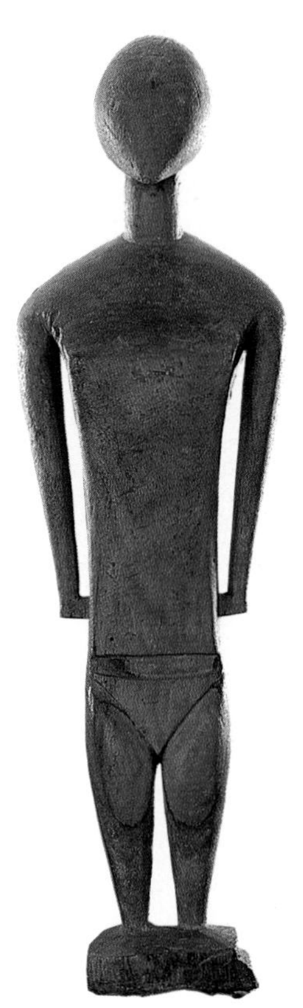

442 STANDING FIGURE.
Nukuoro Atoll, Caroline Islands. Probably 19th century.
Wood. Height 15 9/16".
Honolulu Academy of Arts. Exchange.

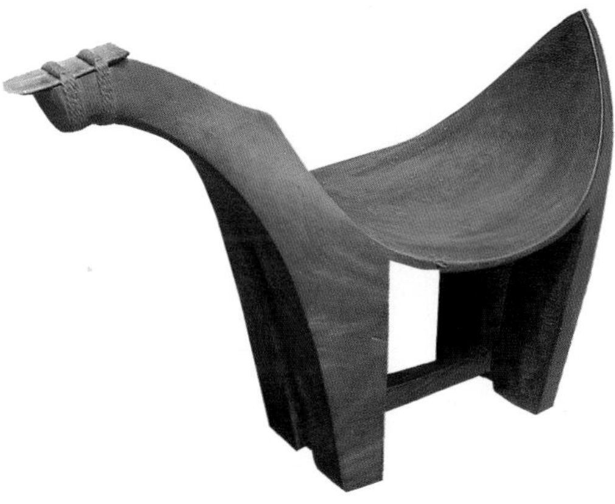

444 COCONUT GRATER.
Kapingamarangi, Caroline Islands. 1954.
Wood, shell blade attached with sennet. Height 17".
Private collection.

quality. Although both Kapingamarangi and Nukuoro are in the southern part of Micronesia, they are culturally Polynesian.

Polynesia covers a large, triangular section of the Pacific, from New Zealand to Hawaii to Easter Island. It is not surprising that the widely separated Polynesian islands and island groups developed greatly varied arts that include both delicate and boldly patterned bark cloth, featherwork, shellwork, woodcarvings, and huge rockcarvings.

The rich color and stunning designs of Hawaiian feather helmets and cloaks are among the world's most magnificent royal attire. Captain James Cook (the first European to "discover" the Hawaiian Islands) compared Hawaiian featherworks to "the thickest and richest velvet which they resemble both as to the feel and the glossy appearance."[1] In this FEATHER CAPE, the geometric figure and ground shapes are in pleasing relationship to one another as well as to the overall shape of the cape.

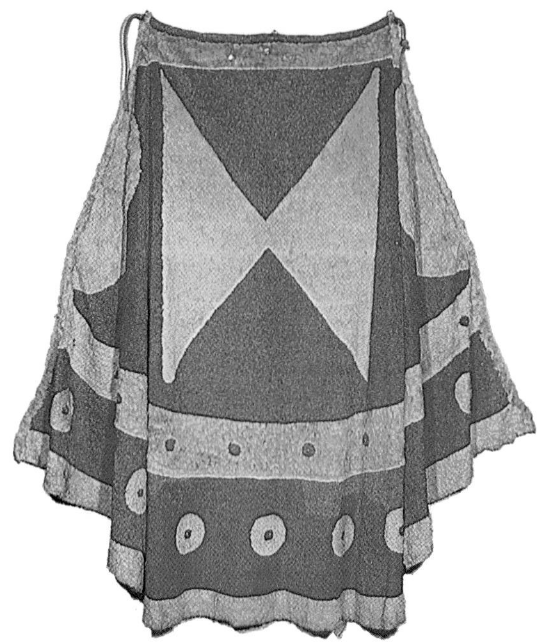

445 FEATHER CAPE. Hawaii. 18th century. Network with feathers knotted into the mesh. Height 4'1".
Copyright British Museum, London.

An outstanding example of semi-abstract Hawaiian sculpture is this forceful ʻAUMAKUA (ancestral deity) found in the lava-tube burial cave of a chief or high priest. By eliminating extraneous details and carefully articulating the parts of the body, the sculptor increased the impact of the female figure's bold stance. Its intensity is enhanced by the attached reddish human hair, shell eyes, and open mouth with bone teeth. The arms-out, knees-bent, feet-apart position, brings the figure to life with an inner power. Full upper arms taper to small forearms and even smaller hands. There is consistent use of full, rounded, almost inflated mass throughout. The well-polished dark wood and inset material show a high degree of craftsmanship.

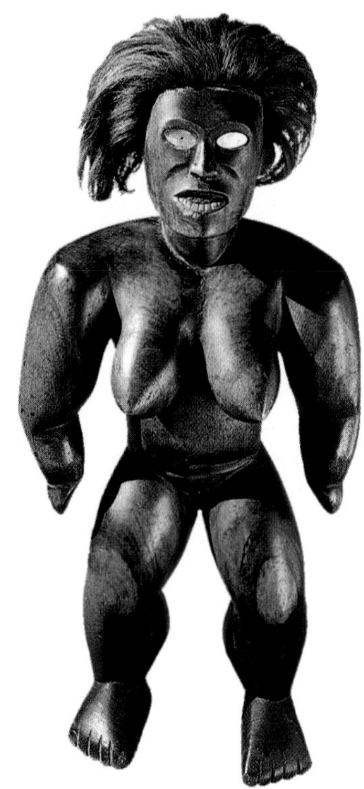

446 ʻAUMAKUA.
Koa(?) wood. 74 cm × 34.5 cm × 18.5 cm.
Bishop Museum, Honolulu.

For some 20,000 years—or for about 15,000 years before the invention of writing and what we call "history"—the aborigines of Australia have maintained an intimate bond with nature, as demonstrated by their art. While most other human groups gradually changed from wandering food foragers to settled farmers, manufacturers, and merchants, the aborigines continued to live as seminomadic hunter-gatherers without clothing or

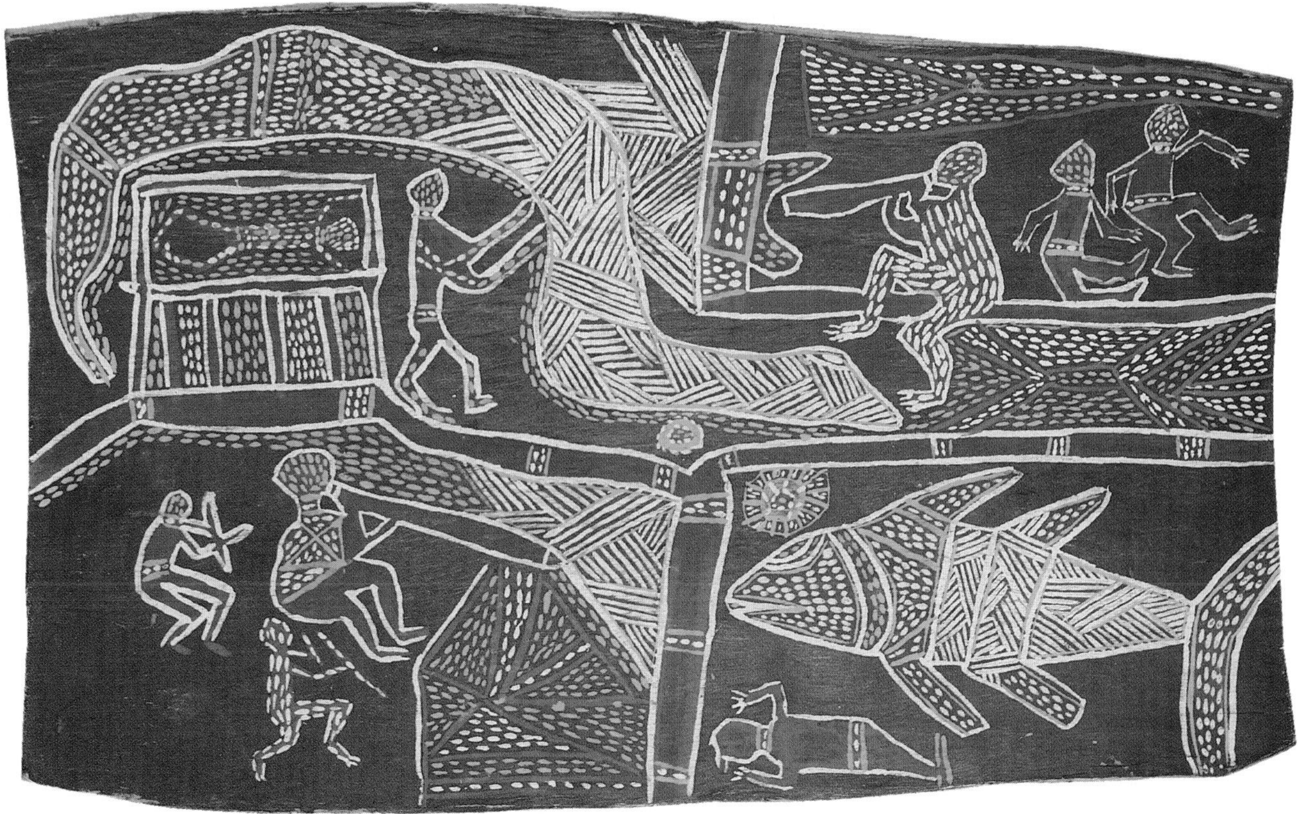

447 Bunia.
FUNERARY RITES AND SPIRIT'S PATHWAY AFTER DEATH.
Australian Aboriginal bark painting.
Groote Eylantdt, Arnhem Land.

permanent shelters and with only a few simple, highly effective tools.

The recognition of their dependence on nature is evident in nearly all art done by aborigines and other primal peoples. Australian aborigines see the bond between themselves and nature as a totemic relationship established by creative beings in the mythical or Eternal Dreamtime. The many disciplines and practices related to spiritual life vary from tribe to tribe, but Dreamtime spirits are prominent in nearly all groups.

In the bark painting entitled FUNERARY RITES, animal and human symbols tell a story, with time segments shown in four sections. In the top left section, a dying man lies on a funeral platform; in the lower left, a didjeridu player and two dancers perform for him until he dies. In the upper right, the spirit of the dying man and his two wives also dance until he dies. After his death, the man's spirit leaves the platform and begins the journey to the spirit world; along the way he crosses over the great snake. In the lower right, he uses a stone to kill a large fish for food for the journey.

In recent years, paintings (particularly those on bark) by Australian aborigines have attracted considerable attention from art collectors and galleries. Aboriginal myths have long been communicated through painting, singing, chanting, and dancing, but there are few places left in Australia where the myths enshrined in the visual and performing arts are still faith-sustaining.

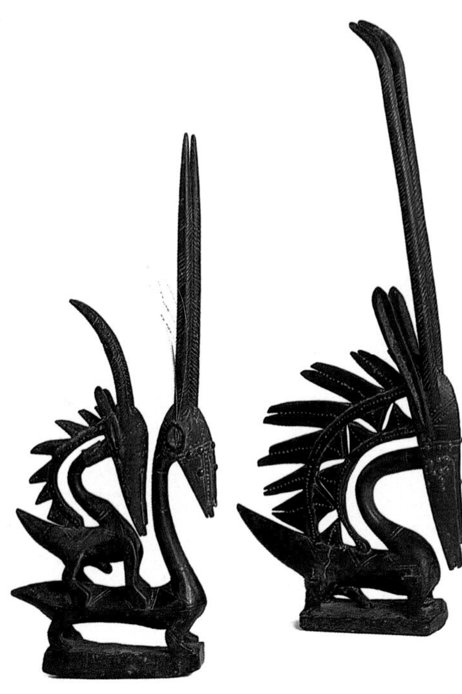

448 MALE AND FEMALE ANTELOPE FIGURES (TYI WARA DANCE HEADDRESSES).
Bamana peoples. Mali, Africa. Late 19th or early 20th century.
Wood, brass tacks, string, cowrie shells, iron, quills.
Height of female 79.8 cm, height of male 97.8 cm.
Ada Turnbull Hertle Fund (1965.6-7)

449 PAIR OF TYI WARA DANCERS.
Photograph: Pascal James Imperato.

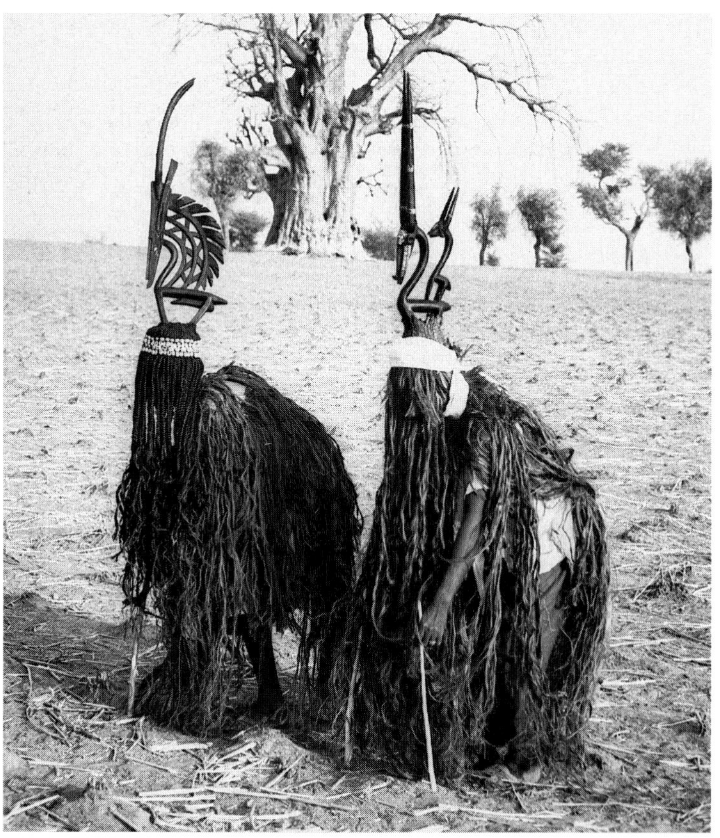

AFRICA

The arts of sub-Saharan Africa are extremely varied, and the diversity of styles reflects the diversity of cultures in the vast continent. Most styles from the past are highly abstract, but some groups have produced naturalistic works. Among African artforms highly valued in the West are masks and figures of terra-cotta, bronze, stone, and wood, particularly those made for ceremonial use. However, some traditional African art has been made of perishable material such as mud or chalk.

In Africa, as in most of the world before the modern era, sculpture may not merely symbolize a spirit; it may be believed actually to embody or contain it. Where such traditions prevail, the sculptor of sacred objects must follow established rituals while carving.

The Bamana people of Mali are renowned for their carved wooden ANTELOPE FIGURE headdresses, which young men attach to basketry caps and wear on top of their heads during agricultural ceremonies. When a new field is cleared, the most diligent male workers are selected to perform a dance of leaps in imitation of the mythical *tyi wara,* who taught human beings how to cultivate crops. The dance always includes both male and female TYI WARA FIGURES: the female is identified by a baby on her back, the male by a stylized mane. Organically abstracted antelope bodies become energized, almost linear forms. Rhythmic curves are accented by a few straight lines in designs that emphasize an interplay of solid mass and penetrating space.

As the Gothic era began in twelfth-century Europe (see page 339), a highly sophisticated art was being produced for the royal court of Ife, a sacred Yoruba city in southwestern Nigeria. In Ife, a naturalistic style of courtly portraiture developed that was stylistically and technically unlike anything to be found in Europe at the time and was unique among the inventive abstract forms created by most African cultures. The MALE PORTRAIT HEAD, a representational portrait of an individual, demonstrates its maker's great skill in the difficult craft of lost-wax bronze casting. Such thin-walled,

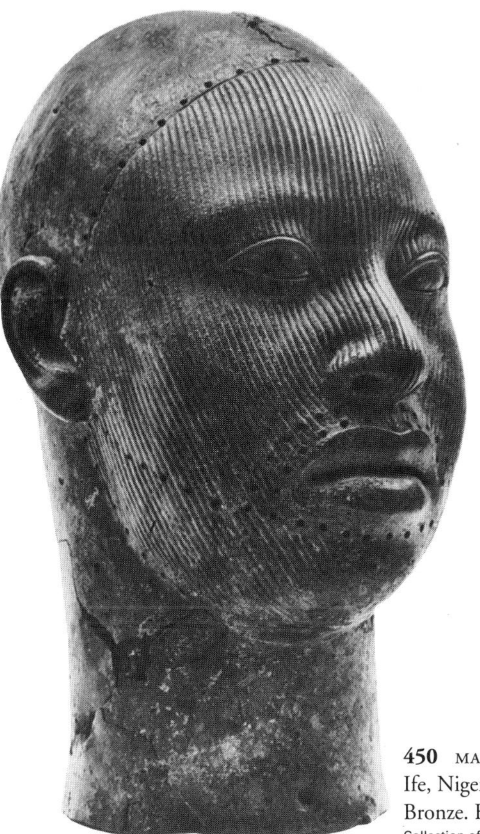

450 MALE PORTRAIT HEAD.
Ife, Nigeria. 12th century.
Bronze. Height 13½".
Collection of the Oni of Ife.

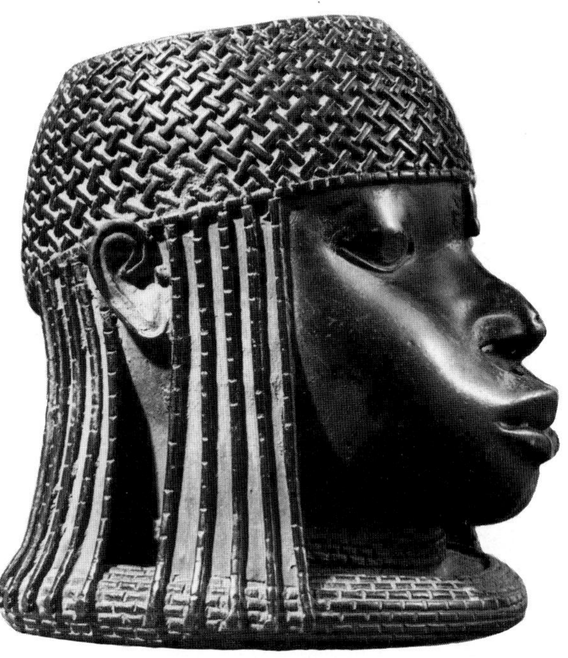

451 BENIN HEAD. Nigeria. 16th century.
Bronze. Height 9¼".
The Metropolitan Museum of Art, New York. The Michael C. Rockefeller Memorial Collection. Bequest of Nelson A. Rockefeller, 1979 (79.206.86).

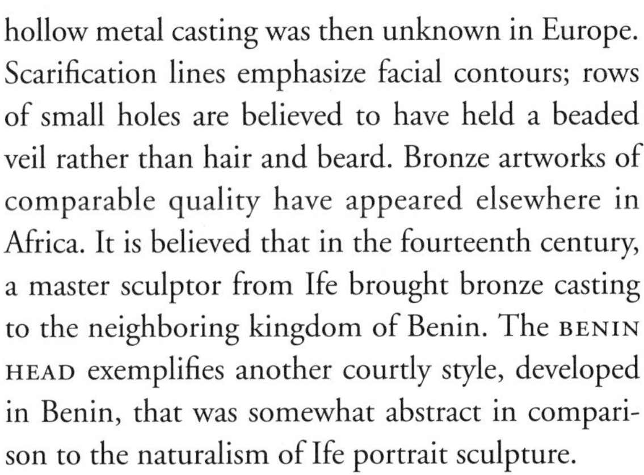

hollow metal casting was then unknown in Europe. Scarification lines emphasize facial contours; rows of small holes are believed to have held a beaded veil rather than hair and beard. Bronze artworks of comparable quality have appeared elsewhere in Africa. It is believed that in the fourteenth century, a master sculptor from Ife brought bronze casting to the neighboring kingdom of Benin. The BENIN HEAD exemplifies another courtly style, developed in Benin, that was somewhat abstract in comparison to the naturalism of Ife portrait sculpture.

When sixteenth-century Europeans first arrived in the kingdom of Benin, they were amazed to see cast bronze sculptures, palaces, and a tightly organized city that compared favorably to their own capital cities. The ivory PORTRAIT OF A QUEEN MOTHER from Benin was carved in the sixteenth century, and modern versions are still worn on the oba's (king's) chest, or at his waist during important ceremonies. The crown consists of a row of alternating human heads and catfish. The heads were

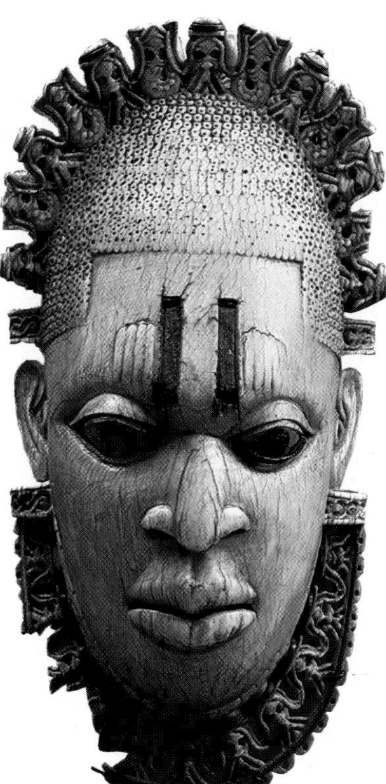

452 PORTRAIT OF A QUEEN MOTHER.
Benin district, Nigeria.
16th century.
Ivory, iron inlays. Height 9⅜".
The Metropolitan Museum of Art, New York. The Michael C. Rockefeller Memorial Collection. Gift of Nelson A. Rockefeller, 1972.

inspired by the "strange" dress, long, straight hair, and beard styles of Portuguese visitors.

The bold, uninhibited style of art of the grasslands region of Cameroon looks far removed from the aristocratic styles of Ife and Benin, even though it also was developed for royal courts. The separate areas of the LARGE DANCE HEADDRESS are clearly defined by different patterns and textures. This heavy sculpture, worn by court officials, does not copy the human head but reinterprets it.

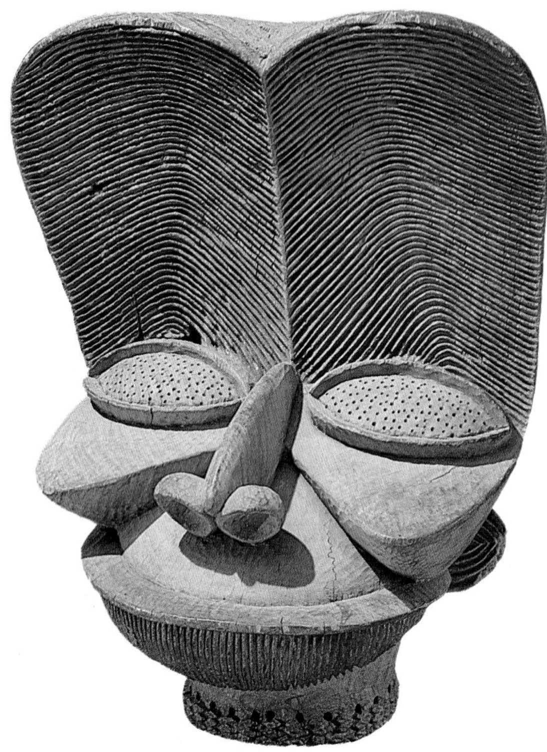

453 LARGE DANCE HEADDRESS.
Bamenda area, Cameroon, Africa. 19th century.
Wood. Height 26½".
Rietberg Museum, Zurich. Von der Heydt Collection.

The art of pattern design is highly developed in many parts of Africa. In northern Nigeria, people embellish GOURDS with inventive incised patterns. The smooth surfaces lend themselves to carving and painting. Gourds are grown in Africa for numerous purposes, including for storage and serving containers, musical instruments, and ritual objects.

In many African textile traditions, long, narrow strips of cloth are woven and then sewn together to make a piece of fabric large enough for a garment or blanket. For the BLANKET from Sierra Leone, strips with varied design motifs were woven so that the rhythmic patterns of the lengthwise pieces would line up to form crosswise stripes. Natural dye colors, rhythmic motifs, and subtle patterns are combined in elegant harmonies.

Today, traditional African fabrics are used for both traditional and Western style clothing. The tie-dye process involves tying portions of the fabric with fine twine or string so that they will not absorb the dye. In the NIGERIAN FABRIC, the dye is derived from the indigo plant. The geometric design has an inventive energy similar to that of the gourd designs.

The art of Africa south of the Sahara first became known in Europe in the fifteenth century. It attracted little attention, however, until it was rediscovered around the turn of this century by a few European artists who were impressed by its power and who brought it to the attention of their colleagues. Expressive and highly sophisticated abstract sculpture from Africa and Oceania became major

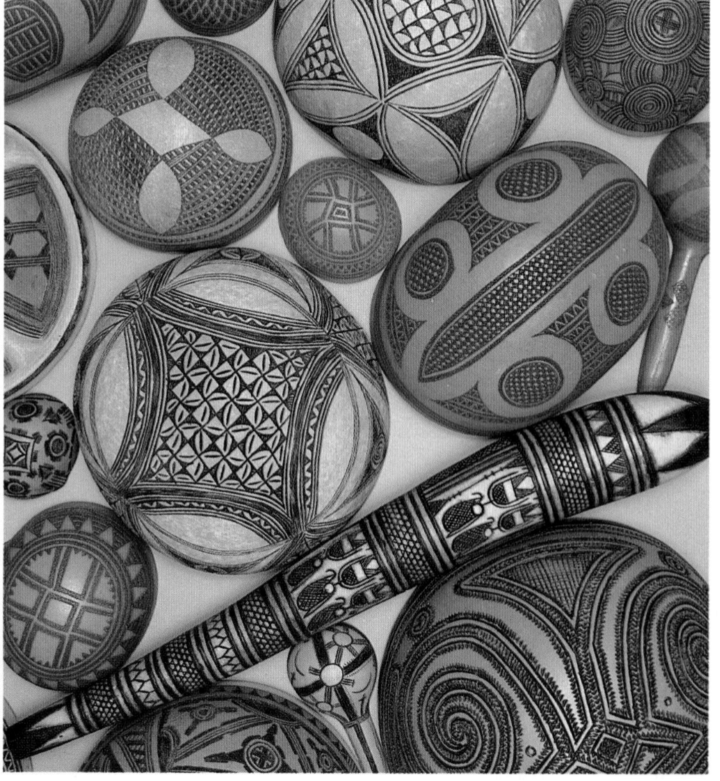

454 GOURDS. Northern Nigeria. 20th century.
Fowler Museum of Cultural History, UCLA.
Photograph: Richard Todd.

influences on twentieth-century Western art (see page 416).

Looking only at the traditional arts of non-Western peoples is misleading. Within the indigenous societies of Africa, the pre-Columbian Americas, Oceania, and Australia, many traditional arts are no longer practiced and many of those that survive have lost their central roles in maintaining meaningful community life. Modern commerce, mass-produced material goods, and commercial mass media have transformed life around the world. Some societies with long-standing cultural traditions have been radically changed by these "modern" influences.

The impact of the amazing cross-cultural currents in today's global village is apparent in the work of Ghanaian artist Kane Kwei. His LAMBORGHINI COFFIN takes us beyond traditional African prototypes. In Ghana, as in many societies, the coffin is more than a container for the body: it is a vehicle to the next world. Traditionally, Ghanaian coffins reflect the profession, interests, or stature of the deceased. In 1970 Kwei, who had worked primarily as a carpenter, was asked to make a coffin in the shape of a boat. It was greatly admired at the funeral and brought Kwei so many commissions that he started his own business: a fish for a fisherman, a cocoa pod for a planter, a Mercedes Benz for the owner of a taxi fleet. Kwei's coffins came to the attention of American gallery owner Ernie Wolfe, who encouraged him to make a variety of cars, which were exhibited in museums and galleries in the United States. From 1970 until his death in 1992, Kwei added a new dimension to his Ashanti tradition.

Past art and traditional values are invigorating a variety of contemporary art forms. Many so-called Third-World artists have traveled, studied, or at least seen both traditional and modern art from Western as well as non-Western societies. An awareness of international art has strengthened some artists' desire to create forms that emerge from, and express, their personal and cultural perspectives.

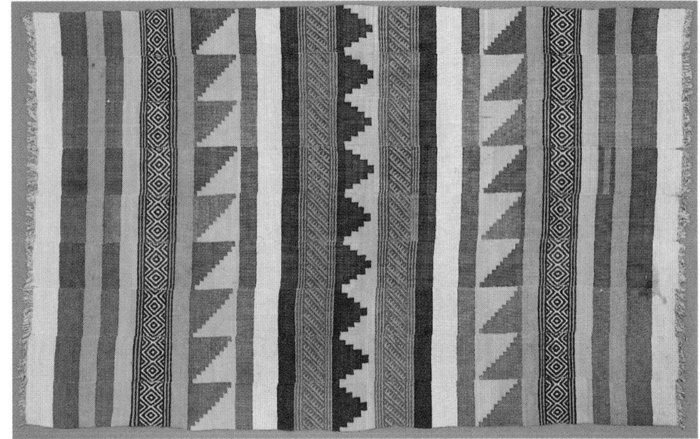

455 BLANKET.
Mende peoples, Sierra Leone.
Cotton, 80⅛" × 49⅝".
National Museum of African Art, Smithsonian Institution, Washington, D.C.

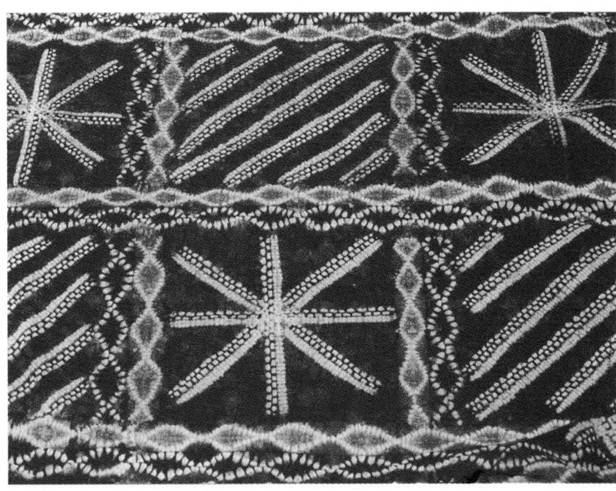

456 NIGERIAN FABRIC. 1992.
Cotton, tie-dyed with idigo. 16½" × 24".

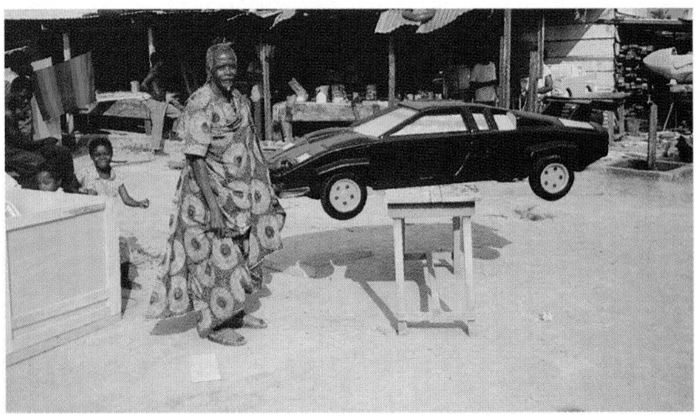

457 Kane Kwei with his LAMBORGHINI COFFIN. 1991.
Photograph: Ernie Wolfe III. Courtesy Turkana Primitive/Ernie Wolfe Gallery, Los Angeles.

ISLAM

Islam is the third major world religion to build on the teachings of the biblical prophets of the Middle East. Although based on the revelations of prophet Mohammed, Islam shares fundamental beliefs and religious history with its predecessors Judaism and Christianity. An adherent of Islam is called a Muslim—Arabic for "one who submits to God." Muslims do not separate reality into sacred and secular; all Islamic art is evidence of heavenly reality within the earthly sphere.

Islamic history began in 622 with Mohammed's flight, known as the Hegira, to what is now Medina on the Arabian peninsula. The new religion spread quickly into much of what was once the Eastern Roman and Byzantine empires, then fanned out to include North Africa, Spain, India, and areas of Southeast Asia. Islam is now the principal religion in the Middle East, North Africa, and much of Asia.

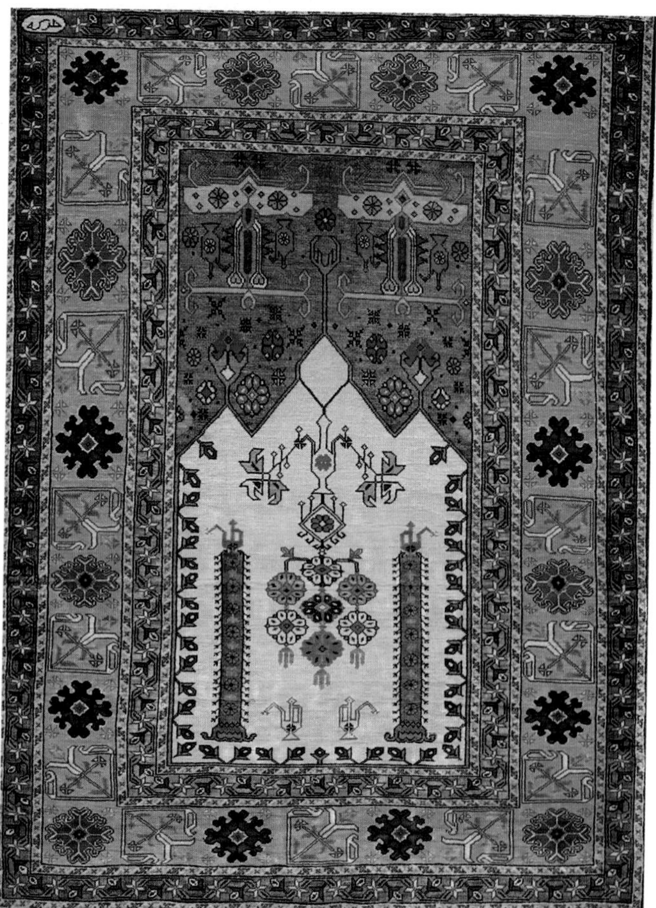

By allowing the peoples of conquered lands to retain their own religions and cultures, Islamic invaders facilitated their conquests. This strategy enabled the Muslim invaders, who had little art of their own, to borrow from earlier artistic traditions. At its height, from the ninth through the fourteenth centuries, Islamic culture developed into a synthesis of the religions, artistic and literary traditions, and scientific knowledge of the entire ancient world. Muslims adopted and built on the achievements of their predecessors, in contrast to the medieval Christians who rejected "pagan" pre-Christian civilization and scholarship. Muslim scholars translated the legacy of Greek, Syrian, and Hindu knowledge into Arabic, and Arabic became the language of scholarship from the ninth through the thirteenth centuries for Syrians, Jews, Persians, and Moors as well as Arabs. As Islam flourished, medieval Europe languished from intolerance, isolationism, and feudalism. Islamic civilization produced outstanding achievements in the arts, sciences, administration, and commerce that were not attained in Europe until the height of the Renaissance, in the late fifteenth century.

The fully developed Islamic style was derived primarily from the Byzantine art of Eastern Christianity (see pages 330–334), the earlier art of Persia (now Iran), and the nomadic art of Central Asia (see pages 335–336).

Orthodox Islam prohibits the representation of human figures because of the association with idol worship. The art that evolved within this restriction was highly inventive, based on geometric patterns and floral motifs. The most characteristic Islamic design form is the *arabesque,* a type of flowing linear decoration based on plant forms. Decoration of surfaces is the dominant feature of all Islamic design; intricate patterns (often including writing) cover entire surfaces of walls, rugs, manuscript pages, and even small utensils.

So-called Oriental rugs, long popular in the

458 PRAYER RUG. Hereke, Turkey. 20th century. Silk. 30" × 21".
Courtesy the Indich Collection, Honolulu. Photograph: Brad Goda.

West, are the most familiar of the Islamic arts in the non-Arab world. Skillfully woven small rugs, made for worshipers to kneel on as they pray, are among the finest Islamic textiles. PRAYER RUG designs are usually based on either the MIHRAB (prayer niche) or on the concept of the garden of paradise.

Calligraphy is the most honored Islamic art because it is used to enhance the beauty of the word of God. The most respected practice for a calligrapher is the art of writing the words of the Koran, the sacred text of Islam, which Muslims believe was revealed by Allah (God) to Mohammed in Arabic. In the Islamic world, the written text of THE KORAN is the divine word in visible form. According to Islamic tradition, God's first creation was the *qualam,* the slant-cut reed pen.

The decorative qualities of Arabic scripts combine well with both geometric and floral design motifs. While calligraphy is considered the major art in the Islamic world, architecture is also significant and is directly related to many artistic activities. Walls are adorned with stucco reliefs, tiles, and tile mosaics—many of which feature calligraphy.

As the Muslim conquest spread, Islamic architects borrowed building techniques as well as surface designs from the styles of those they conquered. In Islamic communities, even homes and government and commercial buildings have religious elements. Various arch forms were adopted and developed by Islamic builders, who found that horseshoe and pointed arches created larger and more open spaces than semicircular arches. Other characteristic features of Islamic architecture include onion domes, *minarets* (towers from which worshipers are called to prayer), and open courtyards for preparing for worship.

Mosques are communal houses of prayer. As Islam spread, many new mosques were built; in addition, many existing buildings, including Christian churches and various kinds of temples, were appropriated as mosques. Within the mosque, the wall closest to Mecca has in its center a highly decorated niche called a MIHRAB, which provides orientation, directing the faithful to pray in the direction of Mecca.

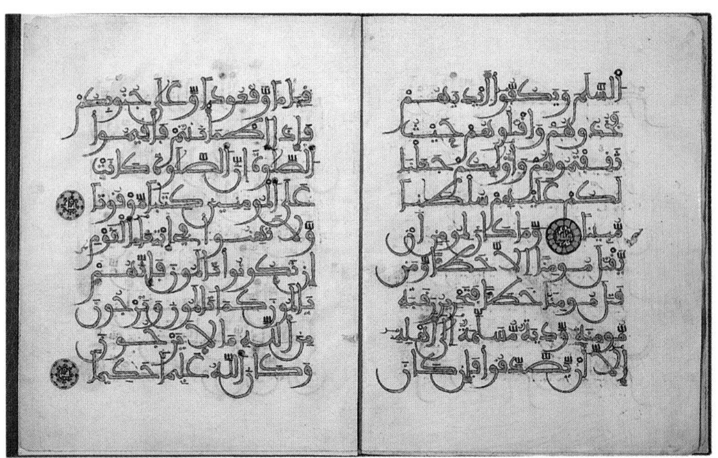

459 TEXT OF THE KORAN.
North Africa or Spain. 11th century.
Colors on paper.
MS no. 1544. Reproduced by kind permission of the Trustees of the Chester Beatty Library, Dublin.

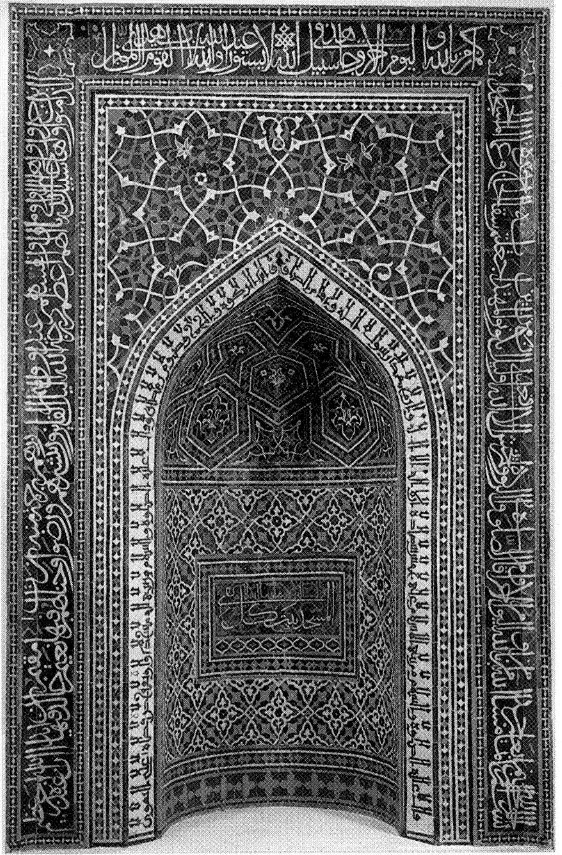

460 MIHRAB. Iran. c. 1354.
Glazed ceramic, cut and assembled in mosaic. 11'3" × 7'6".
The Metropolitan Museum of Art. Harris Brisbane Dick Fund, 1939. (39.20).

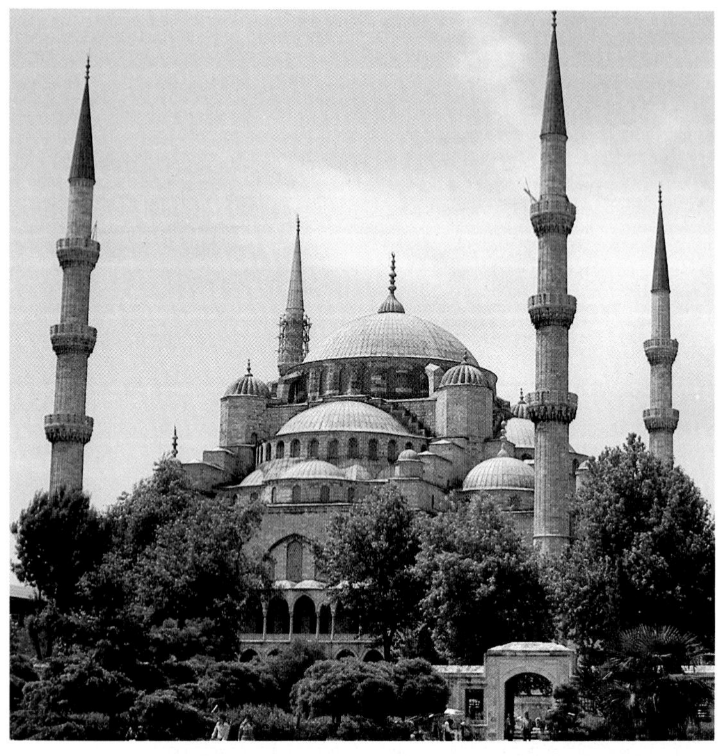

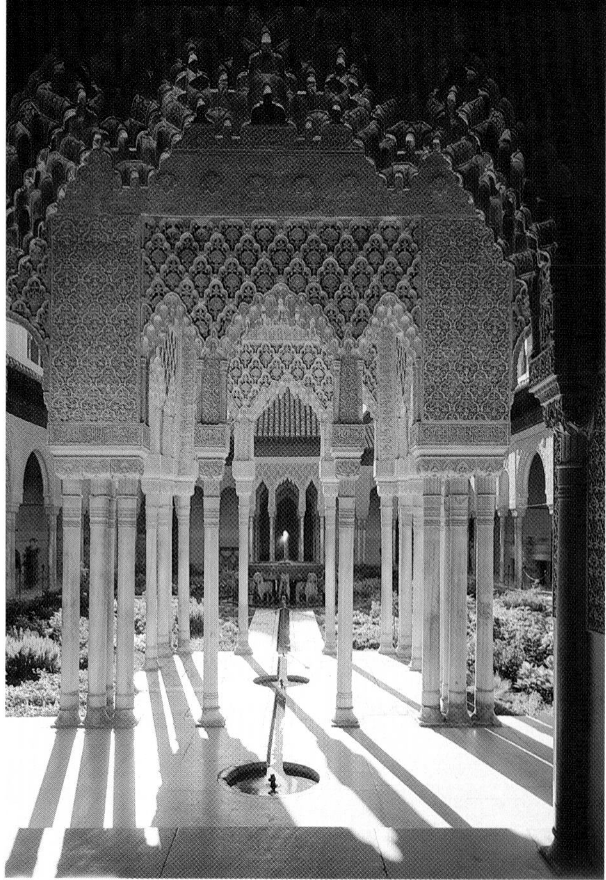

SULTAN AHMET MOSQUE, in Istanbul, is distinguished by many minarets and by its central dome illuminated by windows. Wall surfaces are covered with blue and green tiles.

The culture of Islamic Spain reached a peak of achievement in Moorish art and architecture exemplified by the ALHAMBRA, a great citadel of the Moorish kings of Spain. Halls and chambers surround a series of open courts, including the COURT OF THE LIONS, which contains arches resting on 124 white marble columns. Many of the walls seem to consist entirely of translucent webs of intricate decoration in marble, alabaster, glazed tile, and carved plaster. Light coming through the small openings in the decoration gives many of the rooms and courtyards a luminous splendor.

Secular Islamic painting was greatly influenced by the Mongol invasion of the Middle East in the thirteenth century. A decorative style of painting emerged in which figures, landscape, and ornamental patterns combine in intricate, colorful compositions (see page 60).

The geographic center of present-day Islamic culture coincides with the section of Iraq known in ancient times as Mesopotamia. In the next chapter, we begin our discussion of the art of the ancient world with the early civilization that developed in this fertile plain where the art of the Western world was born.

461 SULTAN AHMET MOSQUE. Istanbul, Turkey. 1609-1616.
Photograph: Tom Klobe.

462 COURT OF THE LIONS, ALHAMBRA.
Grenada, Spain. 1309-1354.

CHAPTER 18

Ancient through Medieval

The ancient civilizations of Mesopotamia and Egypt ran almost parallel in time, arising in the fourth millennium B.C. and lasting some three thousand years. Yet they were quite different from each other. Urban civilization developed earlier in Mesopotamia than it did in Egypt. The Nile Valley of Egypt was protected by formidable deserts, and the Egyptians enjoyed thousands of years of relatively unbroken self-rule. The Tigris-Euphrates Valley of Mesopotamia, however, was vulnerable to repeated invasion, and the area was ruled by a succession of different peoples. Each civilization therefore developed its own distinctive art forms.

MESOPOTAMIA

It was the Greeks who named the broad plain between the Tigris and Euphrates rivers Mesopotamia, "the land between the rivers." Today, this plain is part of Iraq. The first Mesopotamian civilization arose in the southernmost part of the plain in an area called Sumer. The Sumerian people developed the world's first writing.

In the city-states of Sumer, religion and government were one; authority rested with priests who claimed divine sanction. The Sumerians worshiped a hierarchy of nature gods in temples set on huge platforms called *ziggurats,* which stood at the center of each city-state. Ruins of many early Mesopotamian cities are still dominated by eroding ziggurats such as the ZIGGURAT OF UR-NAMMU. The biblical Tower of Babel was actually a ziggurat.

463 ZIGGURAT OF UR-NAMMU. Iraq. c. 2100 B.C.
a Reconstruction drawing.
The University Museum, University of Pennsylvania, Philadelphia.
b Incomplete restoration.
Photograph: Superstock.

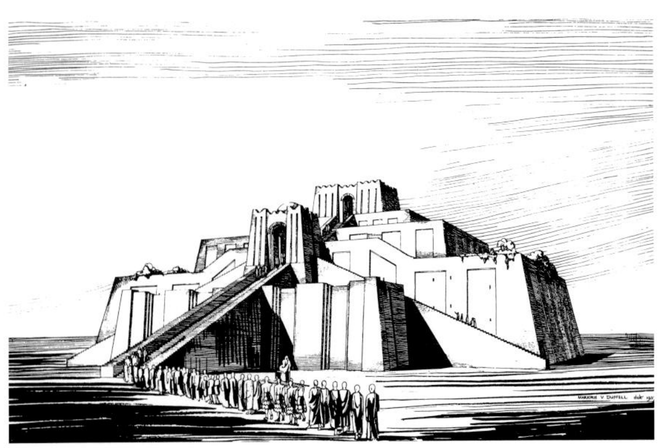

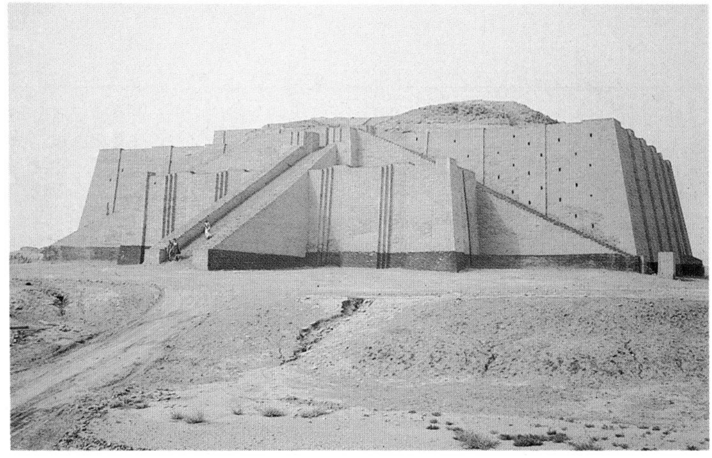

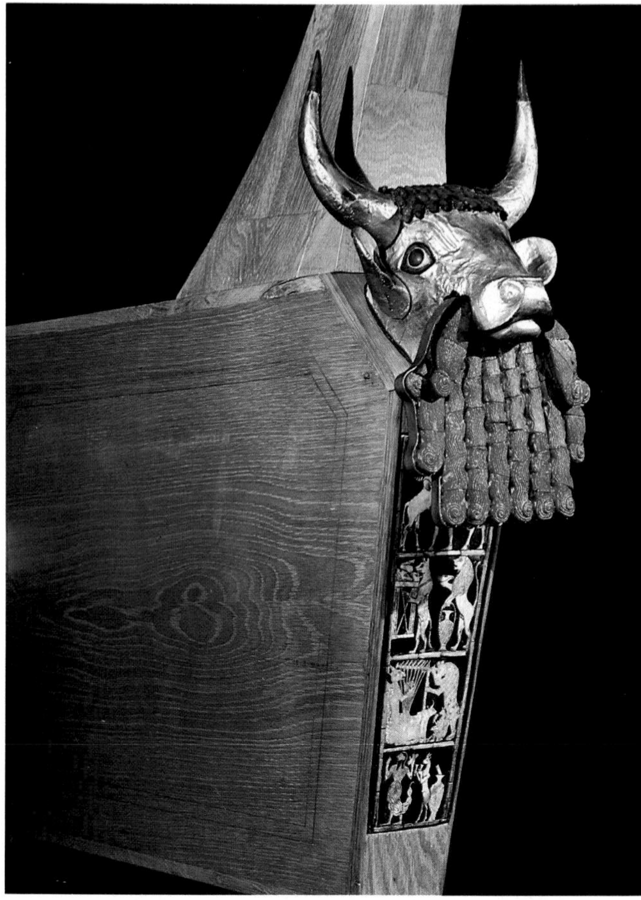

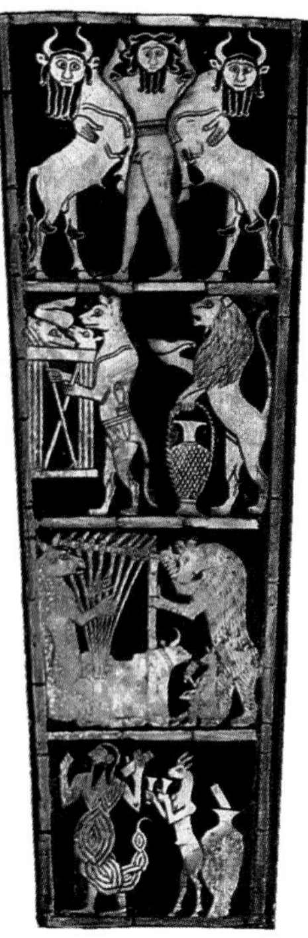

b Front plaque.

464 Reconstructed LYRE. From "The King's Grave" tomb RT 789, Ur. c. 2650-2550 B.C.
Wood with gold, lapis lazuli, shell, and silver.
The University Museum, University of Pennsylvania, Philadelphia (T4-29).
a Soundbox.

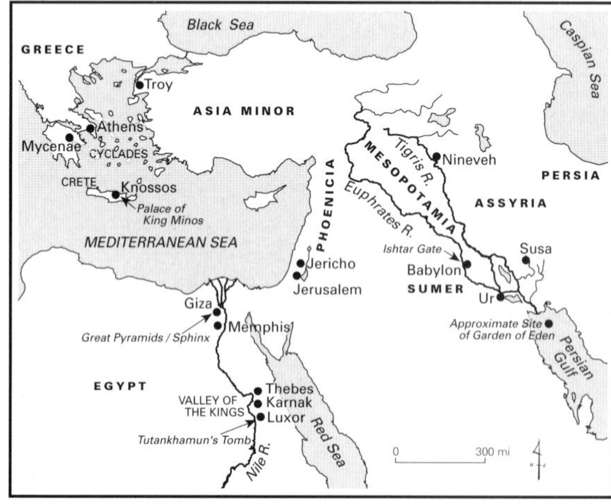

465 THE ANCIENT NEAR EAST.
Map adapted from *Living with Art*, Third Edition, by Rita Gilbert, published by McGraw-Hill, Inc. Copyright ©1992 by Rita Gilbert. All rights reserved. Adapted with permission of McGraw-Hill, Inc.

Ziggurats symbolized the concept of the "sacred mountain" that links heaven and earth. They were filled with sun-baked bricks and faced with fired bricks often glazed in different colors. Two or more successively smaller platforms stood on the solid base, with a shrine on the uppermost platform. On these heights, close to heaven, the city's god might dwell, and there the ruling priests had their sanctuaries. A lack of stone led to the use of brick and wood for building, and consequently very little Mesopotamian architecture remains.

We can imagine the splendor of Sumerian court life by studying the reconstruction of the elegant royal LYRE found in the king's tomb in the ancient city of Ur. The narrative panel on the front and the bull's head are original. The bearded bull's head is a symbol of royalty often seen in Mesopotamian art. In contrast, the bulls and other imaginative animals inlaid on the harp's soundbox are depicted in a simplified narrative style that seems somewhat comical to us. They take on human roles, as do the animals in the later Greek fables of Aesop. The upper panel, which shows a man embracing two bearded bulls, is a type of heraldic design developed by the Su-

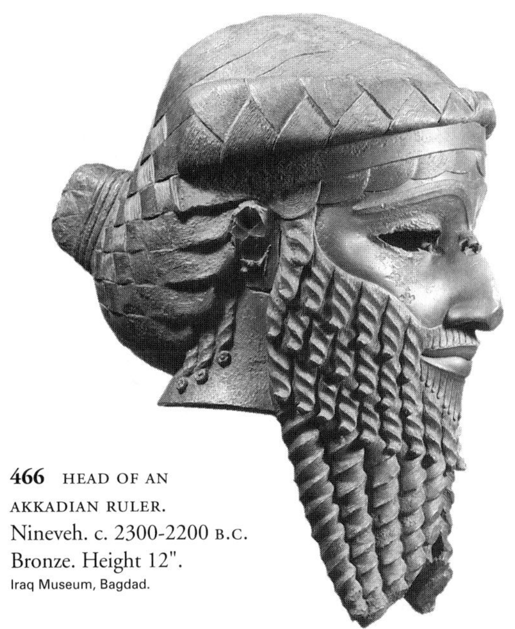

466 HEAD OF AN AKKADIAN RULER.
Nineveh. c. 2300-2200 B.C.
Bronze. Height 12".
Iraq Museum, Bagdad.

merians that was to influence the art of many later cultures. Both the upper panel and the panel at the bottom—a goat attending a scorpion-man—are believed to be scenes from the great classic of Sumerian literature, the *Epic of Gilgamesh.*

The region of Mesopotamia north of Sumer was called Akkadia. By about 2300 B.C., the scattered city-states of Sumer had come under the authority of a single Akkadian king. The magnificent HEAD OF AN AKKADIAN RULER portrays such an absolute monarch. Clearly, this fully mature work evolved from a long tradition. The elaborate hairstyle and rhythmic patterning show the influence of Sumerian stylization. The handsome face expresses calm inner strength. Such superb blending of formal design with carefully observed naturalism is a characteristic of both later Mesopotamian and Egyptian art.

Politically, Mesopotamia was an area of continual local rivalries, foreign invasions, and the rise and fall of military powers. Against such a background, the development and continuity of cultural traditions seem particularly remarkable.

EGYPT

Deserts on both sides of the Nile diminished outside influences and enabled Egypt to develop distinctive styles of architecture, painting, and sculpture that remained relatively unchanged for 2,500 years—longer than the time from the birth of Christ to today. In our age of rapid cultural and technological change, it is difficult to imagine such a stable society.

We are most familiar with the Egyptian art that was made for the tombs of pharaohs, the rulers who were considered god-kings. Egyptian religious belief was distinguished by its emphasis on life after death; preservation of the body and care for the dead were considered essential for extending life beyond the grave. Upon death, the bodies of royalty and nobility were embalmed and, together with accompanying artifacts, tools, and furniture, buried in GREAT PYRAMIDS or in hidden underground tombs.

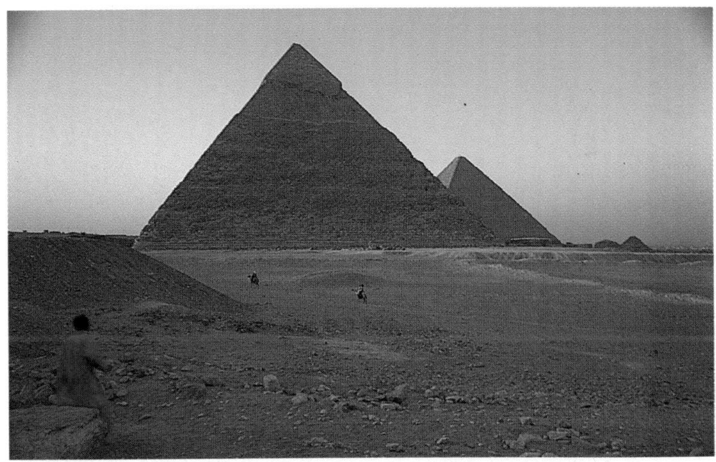

467 GREAT PYRAMIDS OF GIZA. Egypt.
Khafre, c. 2600 B.C.; Khufu, 2650 B.C.

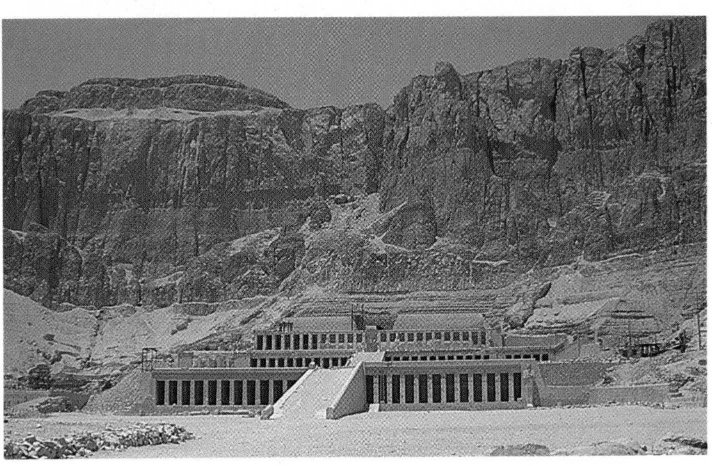

468 FUNERARY TEMPLE OF QUEEN HATSHEPSUT.
Deir el-Bahari. c. 1480 B.C.
Photograph: Jerome Feldman, Hawaii Loa College.

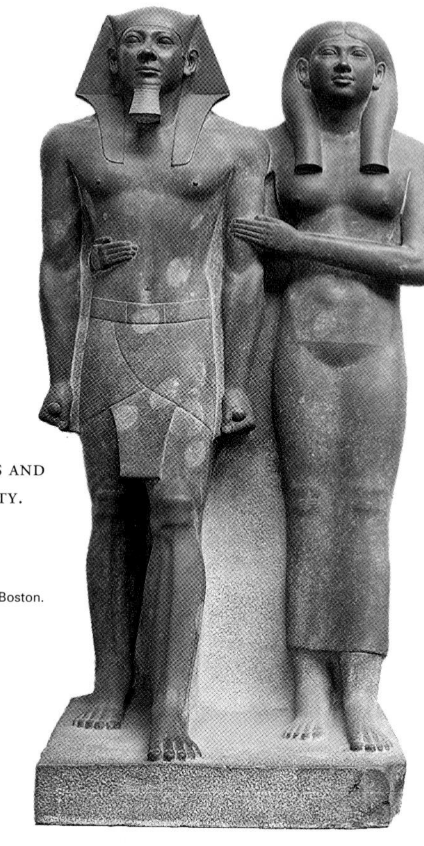

469 KING MYCERINUS AND QUEEN KHAMERERNEBTY. 2599-2571 B.C. Schist. Height 54½". Harvard-MFA Expedition. Courtesy, Museum of Fine Arts, Boston.

Architecture was the most impressive of the ancient arts, and the names of many early Egyptian architects have been preserved. Among the finest and best preserved examples of Egyptian architecture is the FUNERARY TEMPLE OF QUEEN HATSHEPSUT, designed by Senmut, the queen's chancellor and architect. The design and placement of ramps and colonnades echo and complement the rock cliffs behind the temple (see previous page).

Egyptian sculpture is characterized by a preference for compact, solidly structured figures that embody some of the qualities of strength and geometric clarity found in Egyptian architecture. The final form of a piece of sculpture was determined by an underlying geometric plan that was first sketched on the surface of the block. The sculptor of KING MYCERINUS AND QUEEN KHAMERERNEBTY paid considerable attention to human anatomy yet stayed within the traditionally prescribed geometric scheme. The strength, clarity, and lasting stability expressed by the figures result from this union of naturalism and abstraction. With formal austerity, the couple stands in the frontal pose (straight forward, not turning) that had been established for royal portraits. Even so, the figures express warmth and vitality; the queen touches Mycerinus in a sympathetic, loving way. Typical of monumental sculpture of this era are the formal pose with left foot forward, the false ceremonial beard, and figures that remain attached to the block of stone from which they were carved.

Tutankhamen ("King Tut"), who died at age eighteen, is the best known Egyptian pharaoh because his was the only Egyptian tomb discovered in modern times with most of its contents intact. The volume and value of the objects in the small tomb make it clear why grave robbers have been active in Egypt since the days of the first pharaohs. Tutankhamen's inlaid gold MASK FROM MUMMY CASE is but one of hundreds of extraordinary artifacts from the tomb. Its formal blend of naturalism and abstract idealism is distinctly Egyptian.

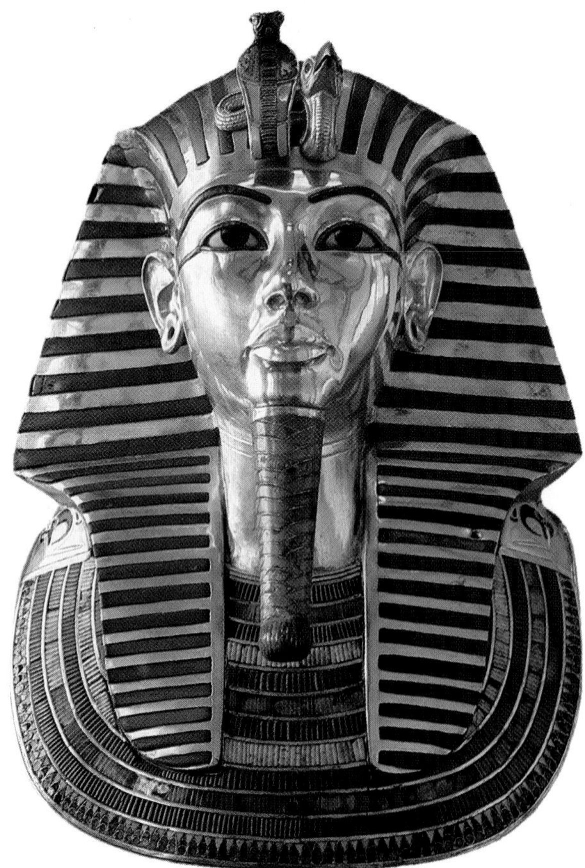

470 TUTANKHAMEN, MASK FROM MUMMY CASE. c. 1340 B.C. Gold inlaid with enamel and semiprecious stones. Height 21¼". Egyptian Museum, Cairo.

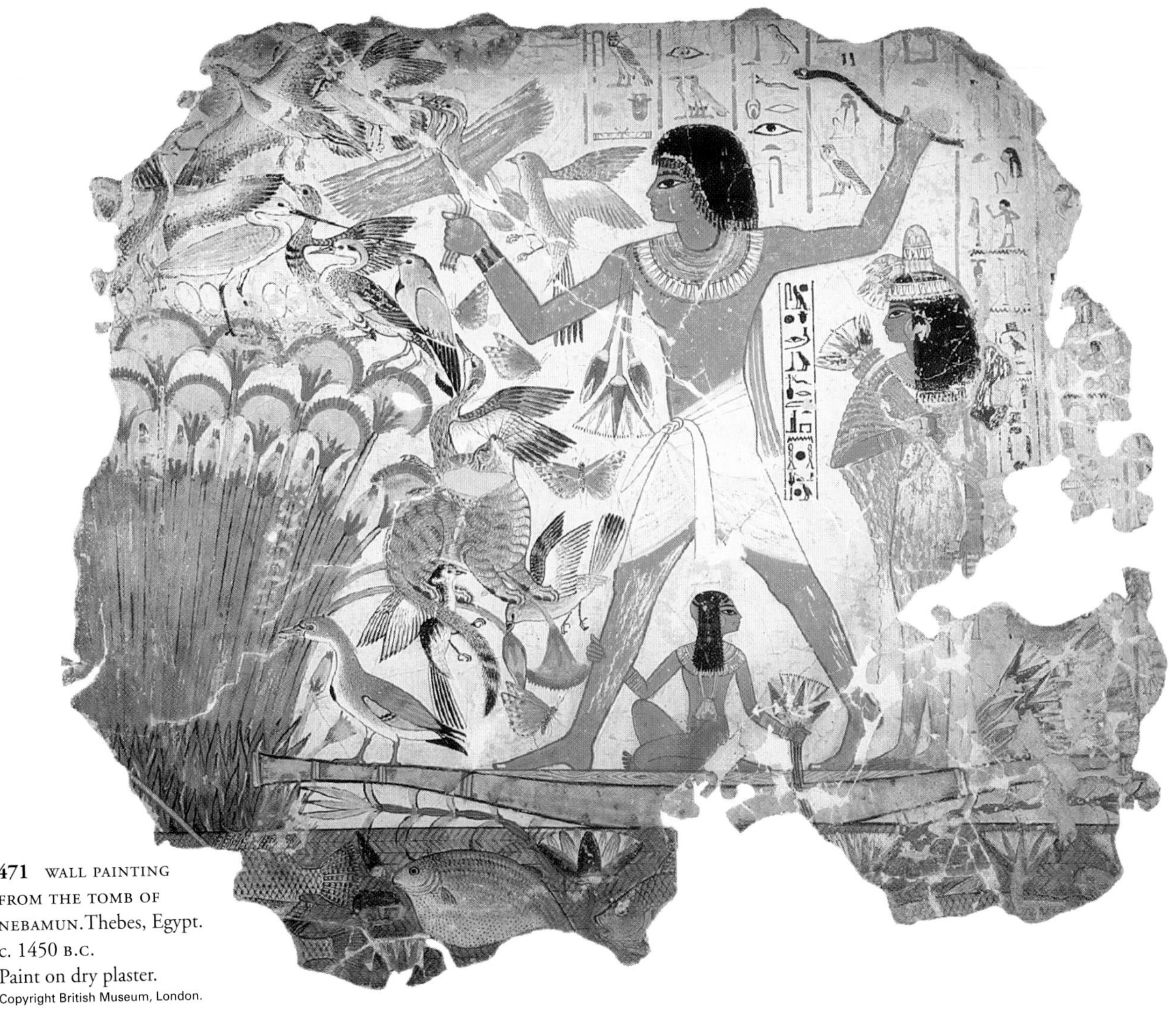

471 WALL PAINTING FROM THE TOMB OF NEBAMUN. Thebes, Egypt. c. 1450 B.C. Paint on dry plaster.

A distinctive feature of Egyptian painting, relief carving, and even sculpture in the round is the presentation of the human figure either in a completely frontal position or in profile. Egyptian artists portrayed each object and each part of the human body from what they identified as its most characteristic angle, thus avoiding the ambiguity caused by random or chance angles of view.

In the WALL PAINTING FROM THE TOMB OF NEBAMUN, the painter of the hunting scene presents a wealth of specific information without making the painting confusing. Flat shapes portray basic elements of each subject in the clearest, most identifiable way. The head, hips, legs, and feet of the nobleman who dominates this painting are shown from the side, while his eye and shoulders are shown from the front. Sizes of human figures are determined by social rank, a system known as *hierarchic proportion;* the nobleman is the largest figure, his wife is smaller, his daughter smaller still.

The family stands on a boat made of papyrus reeds; plants grow on the left at the shore. The entire painting is teeming with life, and the artist has even taken great care to show life below the water's surface. Egyptian attention to accurate detail lets us identify species of insects, birds, and fish. The difference between the naturalism used to depict animals and the abstraction of human beings is reminiscent of a similar tendency in Paleolithic art.

As in many Chinese paintings, two parallel ways of conveying information have been used—one pictorial, the other verbal. The hieroglyphics (Egyptian writing) can be read today by experts.

GREECE

To the extent that Mesopotamians were caught up in warfare and Egyptians concentrated on the afterlife, the ancient Greeks focused on life here and now. The Greeks distinguished themselves from other peoples of Europe and Asia by their attitude toward being human. They came to regard humankind as the highest creation of nature—the closest thing to perfection in physical form, coupled with the power to reason. Greek gods had human weaknesses, and Greek mortals had godlike strengths.

With this attitude came a new concept of the importance of the individual. The Greek focus on human potential and achievement led to the development of democracy and to the perfection of naturalistic images of the human figure in art. Philosopher Plato taught that behind the imperfections of transitory reality was the permanent, ideal form. Thus, to create the ideal individual (the supreme work of nature) became the goal of Greek artists.

Greek civilization passed through three broad stages: the Archaic period, the Classical period, and the Hellenistic period. In the art of the Archaic period (from the late seventh to the early fifth centuries B.C.), we see the Greeks assimilating influences from Egypt and the Near East. Greek writers of the time tell us that Greek painters were often better known than Greek sculptors. Yet what we now see of Greek painting appears only on pottery because there are no known surviving wall or panel paintings. The elegant GREEK VASE shown here suggests the level of achievement of Greek potters as well as painters. It is in the Archaic, "black-figured" style and shows Achilles and Ajax, two heroes from Homer's writing, playing draughts. Although their eyes are still shown from the front in the Egyptian manner, the new liveliness in the bodies is based on observation rather than convention or preconception.

Numerous life-size nude male and clothed female figures were carved in stone or cast in bronze during this era. The Archaic-style KOUROS, carved at about the same time the vase was painted, has a rigid frontal position that is an adaptation from Egyptian sculpture. (*Kouros* is Greek for male youth;

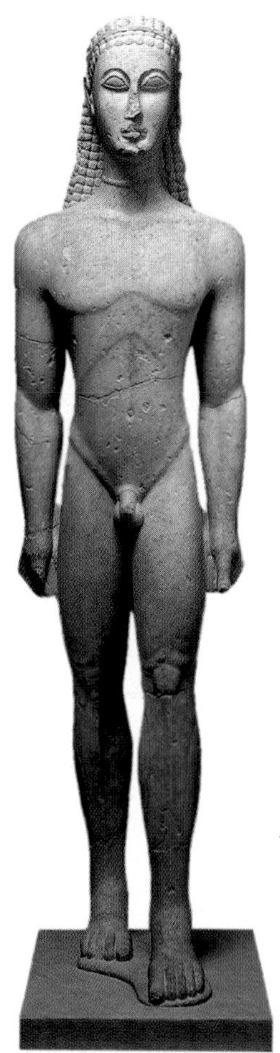

472 STATUE OF A YOUTH (KOUROS). c. 610-600 B.C. Marble. Height 76". The Metropolitan Museum of Art, New York. Fletcher Fund, 1932. (32.11.1)

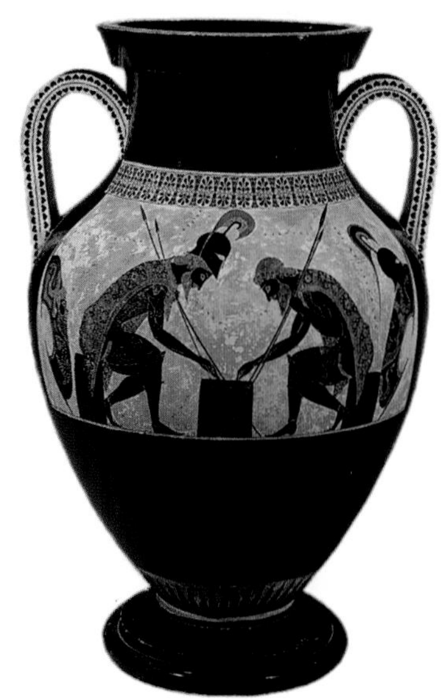

473 Exekias. GREEK VASE, ACHILLES AND AJAX PLAYING DRAUGHTS. c. 540 B.C. Black-figured style. Height 24". Vatican Museum.

kore is the word for female youth.) The Egyptian figure of MYCERINUS (page 320) and the KOUROS both stand with arms held straight at the sides, fingers drawn up, and left leg forward with the weight evenly distributed on both feet.

In spite of the similarity of stance, however, the character of Greek sculpture is already quite different from Egyptian. The KOUROS is freestanding, not attached to the back slab of the original block, and has an overall sense of energy not found in Egyptian sculpture.

Within one hundred years after the making of the KOUROS figure, Greek civilization had entered its Classical phase (480–323 B.C.). The rigid poses of Egyptian and early Greek figures gave way to a greater interest in anatomy and more relaxed poses. Sculpture became increasingly naturalistic as well as idealized, and it began to show the body as alive and capable of movement.

The WARRIOR, one of two bronze sculptures found in 1972 in the Mediterranean off the coast of Italy, is a fine example of Greek Classicism. The figure stands with its weight resting on one foot. As a result, the hip and shoulder lines are no longer in a frontal, parallel position, but they counterbalance one another. This form of balance is known as *contrapposto,* meaning counterposed. The Greeks and then the Romans used it to give a lifelike quality to figures at rest. Centuries later, their sculpture would inspire Renaissance artists to use the same technique (see Michelangelo's DAVID, page 352).

Classical Greek sculpture was much more than the accurate representation of live models. Greek sculptors infused life into bronze or marble, guided by the ideal proportions they established for the depiction of human figures. The WARRIOR shows a balance between the ideal male figure and a convincing image of a man in the prime of life. Details include eyes of bone and glass-paste, bronze eyelashes, nipples of copper, and silver-plated teeth.

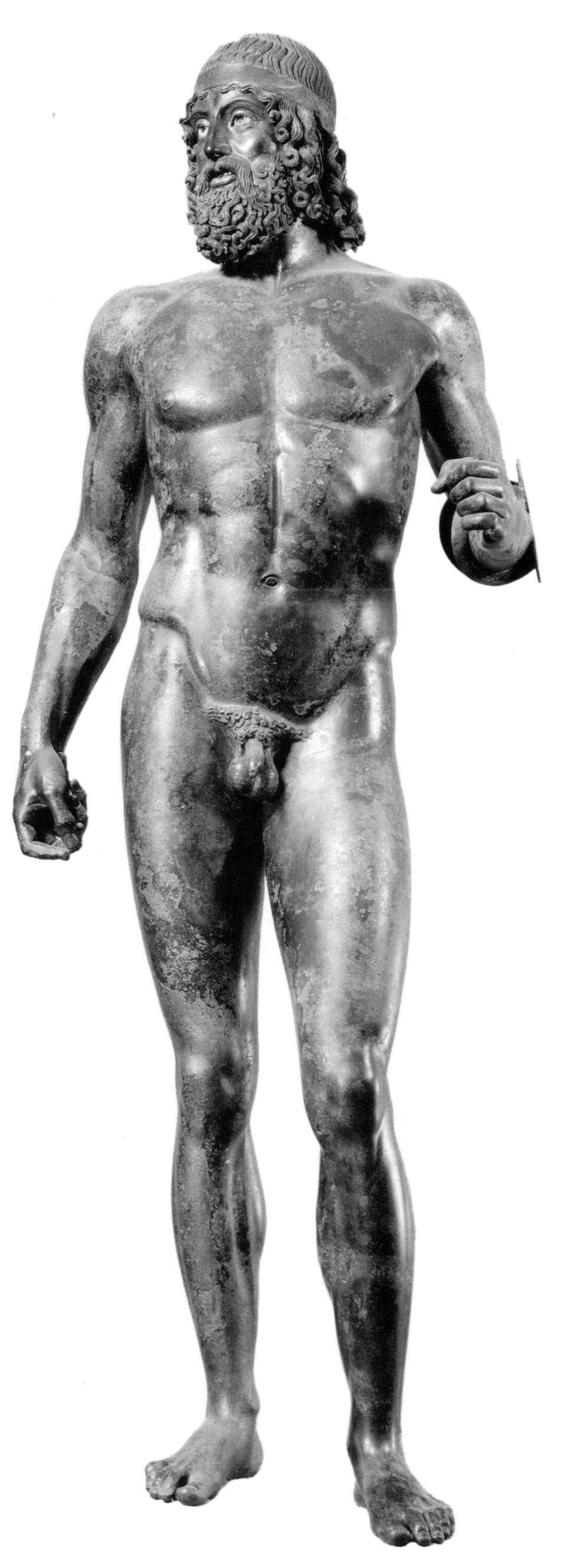

474 WARRIOR. 5th century B.C.
Bronze with inlaid bone, glass-paste, silver, and copper.
Height 78⁴/₅".
National Museum, Reggio Calabria, Italy.

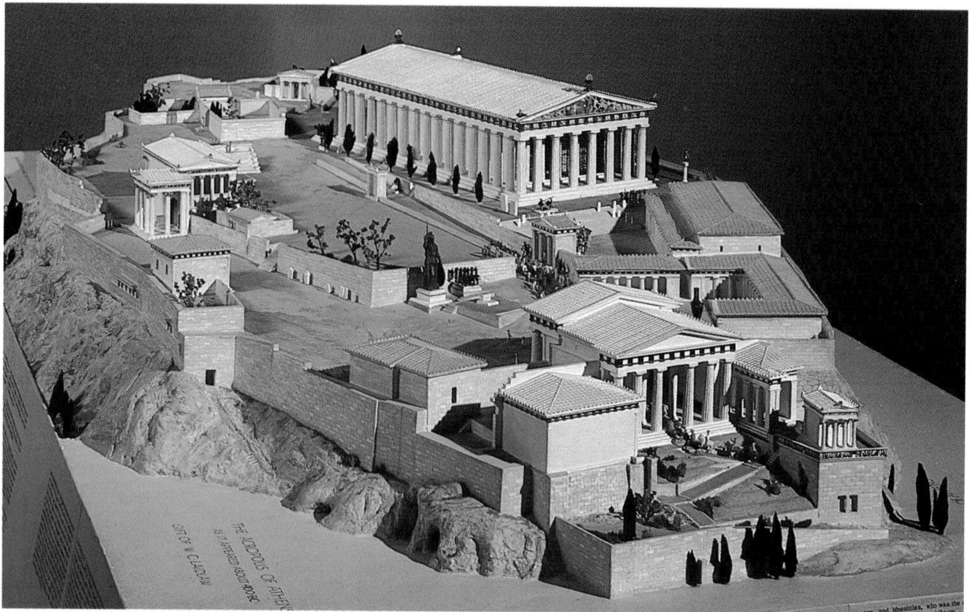

475 Ictinus and Callicrates. PARTHENON. Acropolis, Athens. 448-432 B.C.
a Copy of a model of the Acropolis by G. P. Stevens with artistic additions by Sylvia Hahn.
Courtesy of the Royal Ontario Museum, Toronto.

The city-state of Athens was the artistic and philosophical center of Classical Greek civilization. Above the city, on a large rock outcropping called the Acropolis, the Athenians built one of the world's most admired structures, the PARTHENON. Today, even in its ruined state, the PARTHENON continues to express the high ideals of the people who created it.

The largest of several sacred buildings on the Acropolis, the PARTHENON was designed and built as a gift to Athena Parthenos, goddess of wisdom, arts, industries, and prudent warfare, and protector of the Athenian navy.

When Ictinus and Callicrates designed the PARTHENON, they were following a well-established tradition in temple design based on the post-and-beam system of construction (see page 246). In the PARTHENON, the Greek temple concept reached its highest form of development. The structure was located so that it could be seen against the sky, the mountains, or the sea from vantage points around the city, and it was the focal point for processions and large outdoor religious ceremonies. Rites were performed on altars placed in front of the eastern entrance. The interior space was designed to house a 40-foot statue of Athena. The axis of the building was carefully calculated so that on Athena's birthday the rising sun coming through the huge east doorway would fully illuminate the towering gold-covered statue.

In its original form, the PARTHENON exhibited the refined clarity, harmony, and vigor that come from the heart of the Greek tradition. The proportions of the PARTHENON are based on harmonious ratios. The elevation of either end conforms to the Golden Ratio (see page 104). A different ratio is used elsewhere. The ratio of the height to the widths of the east and west ends is approximately 4 to 9. The ratio of the width to the length of the building is also 4 to 9. The diameter of the columns relates to the space between the columns at a ratio of 4 to 9, and so on.

None of the major lines of the building is perfectly straight. Experts believe that the subtle deviations were designed to correct optical illusions. The columns have an almost imperceptible bulge (called *entasis*) above the center, which causes them to appear straighter than if they were in fact straight-sided, and this gives the entire structure a tangible grace. Even the steps and tops of doorways rise slightly in perfect curves. Corner columns, seen against the light, are somewhat larger in diameter to counteract the diminishing effect of strong light in the background. The axis lines of the columns lean in a little at the top. If extended into space,

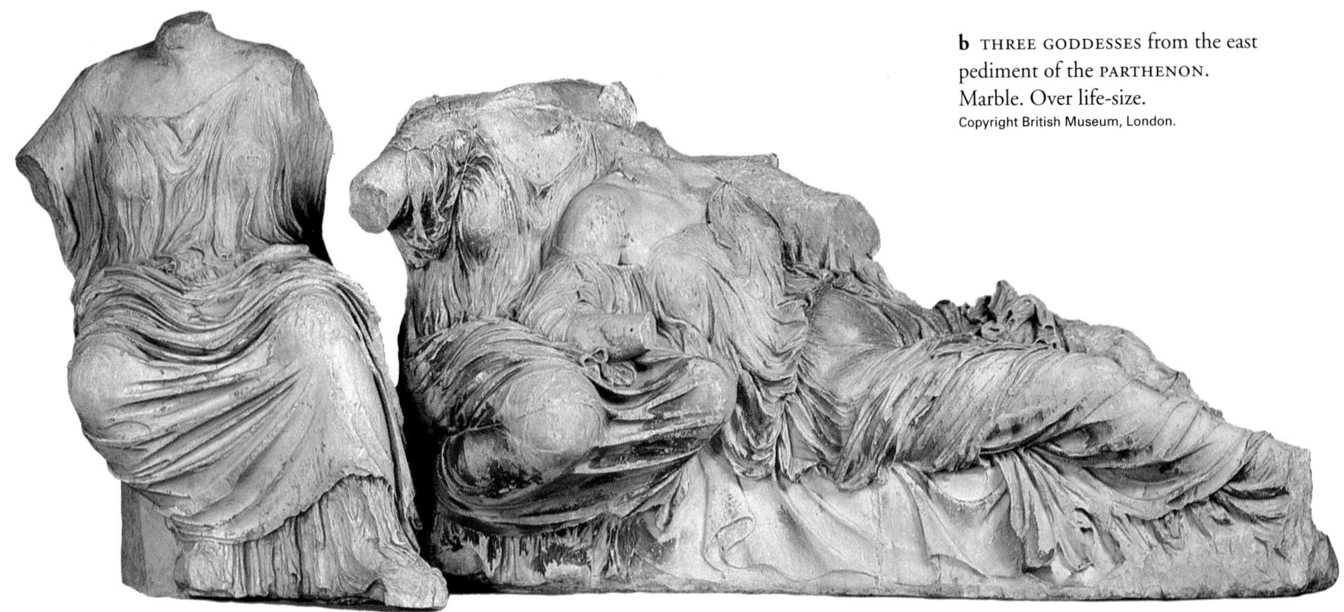

b THREE GODDESSES from the east pediment of the PARTHENON. Marble. Over life-size.

these lines would converge 5,856 feet above the building. These unexpected variations are not consciously seen, but they are felt.

The Greeks developed three COLUMN STYLES, or orders, of post-and-beam construction: Doric (used in the PARTHENON), Ionic, and Corinthian. Each order comprises a set of architectural elements and proportions. The most telling details for identification of the orders are the three types of capitals used at the tops of columns. Doric, which came first, is simple, geometric, and sturdy; Ionic is taller and more dynamic than Doric; Corinthian is complex and organic.

Although today we see Greek temples as white stone structures, some of the upper portions of exterior surfaces were once brightly painted. Parts of sculpture were also painted.

Some of the finest Greek sculpture was carved for the upper areas of the PARTHENON. Much of it, including the now headless GODDESSES, was removed by Lord Elgin in the early nineteenth century and is now in the British Museum. Most of the remaining sculpture has been badly damaged by war and air pollution.

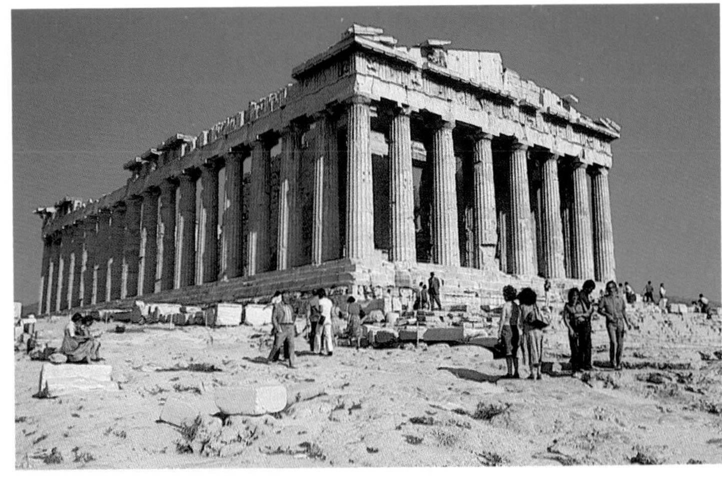

c View from the northwest.

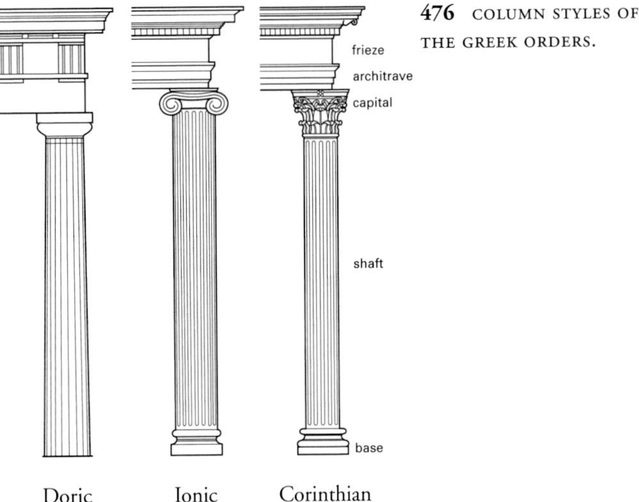

476 COLUMN STYLES OF THE GREEK ORDERS.

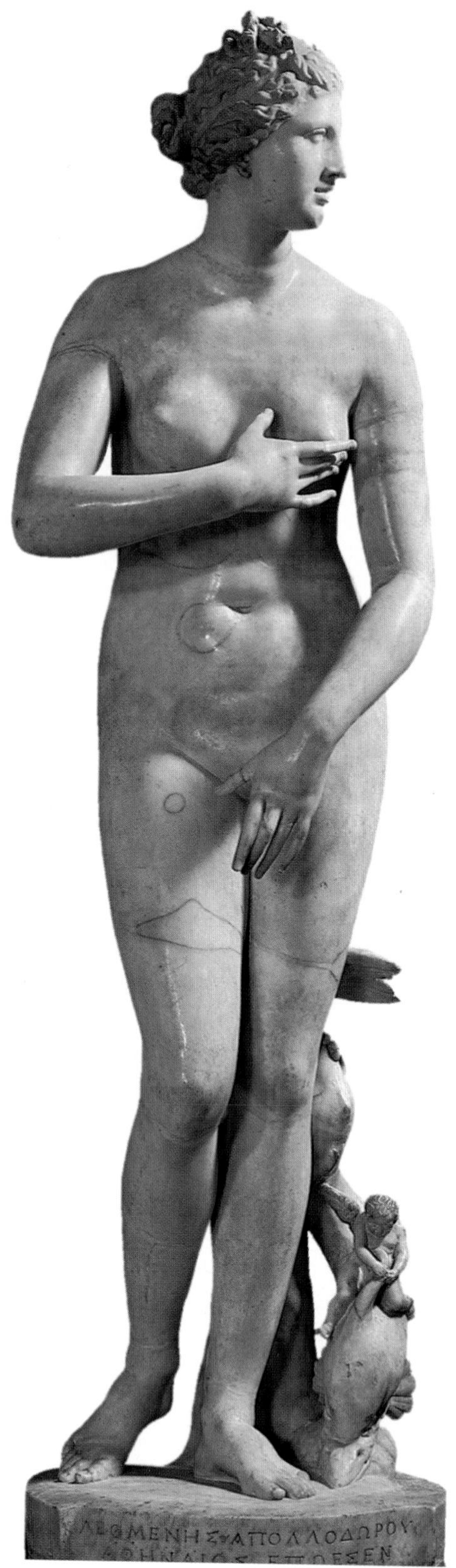

477 VENUS DE MEDICI. 3rd century B.C. Marble. Height 5'.
Uffizi Gallery, Florence.

Greek aesthetic principles from this period provide the basis for the concept of classicism, a recurrent sensibility in the history of art. *Classical* art emphasizes rational simplicity, order, and restrained emotion and is in contrast to the subjective, expressive, and exaggerated emotional qualities found in late (Hellenistic) Greek art and in the art of various subsequent periods.

VENUS DE MEDICI is a third-century B.C. Roman copy of a fourth-century B.C. Greek original. (Aphrodite, the Greek goddess of love and beauty, was known as Venus by the Romans.) The original sculpture was inspired by an Aphrodite by Praxitiles, one of the most famous sculptors of the Classical period. Because it was made to symbolize a goddess rather than to portray a real woman, the figure is more ideal than natural. Its refined profile is one of the most obvious features of the Greek idealization of human figures. But we can sense the emerging Hellenistic sensibility in the figure's sensuality—a mortal element foreign to Classical ideals.

After the decline of the Greek city-states at the end of the fourth century B.C., the art of the Mediterranean changed. Though it continued to be strongly influenced by earlier Greek art, and was often executed by Greek artists, it was produced for, and according to the preferences of, non-Greek patrons. Mediterranean art during this era is called *Hellenistic,* meaning Greek-like. The transition from Classical to Hellenistic coincided with the decline of Athens as a city-state and a loss of confidence due to a realization that the gods had failed to sustain the glory of Greece. People turned from the glorified idealizations of the Classical period to the subjective and imperfect aspects of life and humanity.

In the Hellenistic period, Greek art became more dynamic and less idealized. Everyday activities, historical subjects, myths, and portraiture were more common subjects for art than in the Classical period.

THE LAOCOÖN GROUP is a Roman copy of a late Hellenistic work. In Greek mythology, Laocoön was the Trojan priest who warned against bringing the wooden horse into Troy during the

Trojan War. Subsequently, he and his sons were attacked by serpents, an act the Trojans interpreted as a sign of the gods' disapproval of Laocoön's prophecy. Laocoön is shown in hierarchic proportion to his grown sons.

The rationalism, clarity, and restrained gestures of Classical sculpture have given way to writhing movement, tortured facial expressions, and strained muscles expressing emotional and physical anguish. When this sculpture was unearthed in Italy in 1506, it had an immediate influence on the young Michelangelo (see page 351).

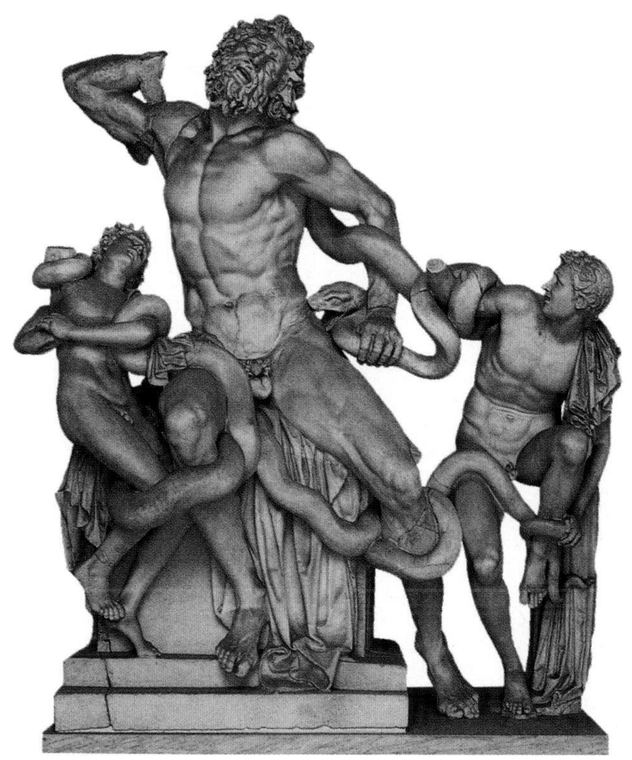

478 THE LAOCOÖN GROUP.
Roman copy of a 1st or 2nd century B.C. Greek original, perhaps after Agesander, Athenodorus, and Polydorus of Rhodes. c. 1st century A.D. Marble. Height 95¼".
Vatican Museum, Rome.

ROME

The Hellenistic era saw the rise of Rome, a formidable new force in the Mediterranean. By the second century B.C., Rome had become the major power in the Western world. At its height, the Roman Empire would include western Europe, North Africa, and the Near East as well as the shores of the Mediterranean (see map next page). The governance of a multitude of unique peoples and cultures was a prime example of the Roman genius for order and worldly action. Roman culture has affected our lives in many areas: our systems of law and government, our calendar, festivals, religions, and languages. We also inherited from the Romans the concept that art is worthy of historical study and critical appreciation.

The Romans were a practical, materialistic people, and their art reflects this. They made few changes in the general style of Greek art, which they admired, collected, and copied. But not all Roman art was imitative. Roman portraiture of the Republican period, such as the FEMALE PORTRAIT, achieved a high degree of individuality rarely found in Greek sculpture. The representationally accurate style probably grew out of the Roman custom of making wax death masks of ancestors for the family shrine or altar. Later, these images were recreated in marble to make them more durable. Roman sculp-

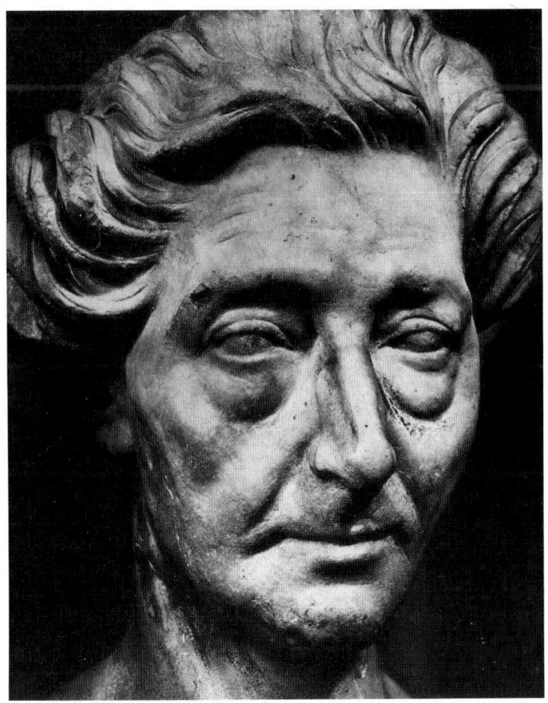

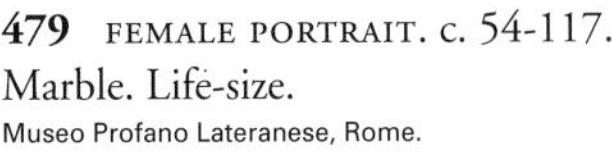

479 FEMALE PORTRAIT. c. 54-117.
Marble. Life-size.
Museo Profano Lateranese, Rome.

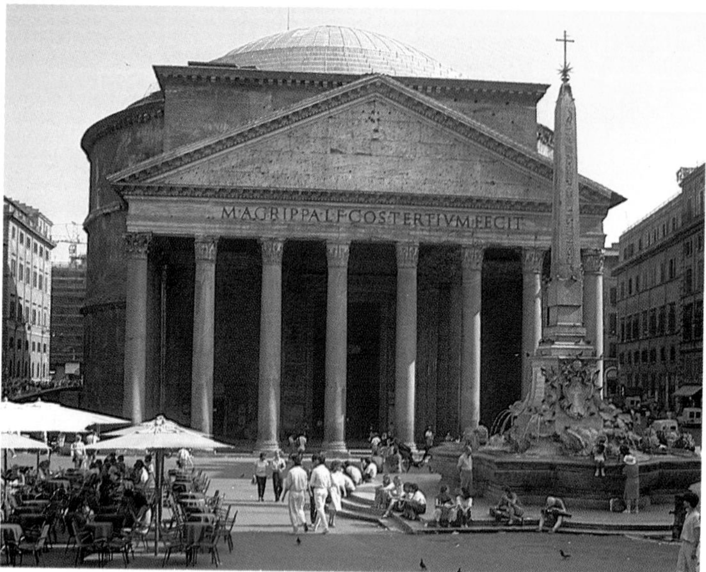

480 PANTHEON. Rome. 118-125.
a View of the entrance.

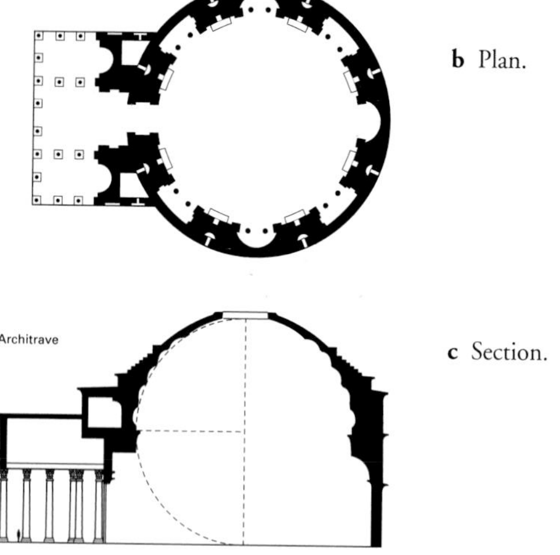

b Plan.

c Section.

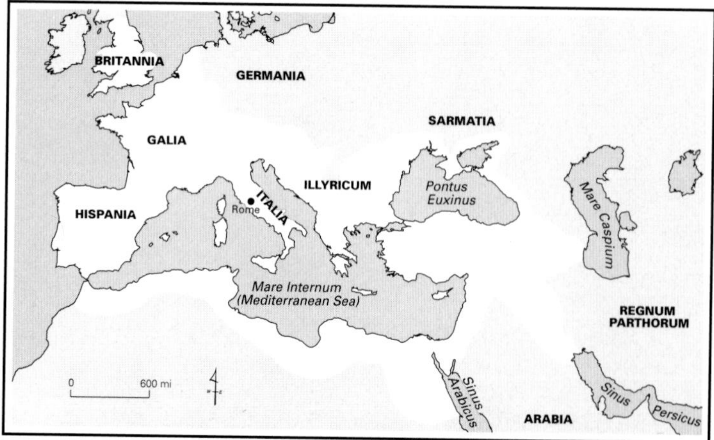

481 ROMAN EMPIRE, A.D. 117.

tors observed and carefully recorded those physical details and imperfections that give character to each person's face.

The Romans' greatest artistic achievements were in civil engineering, town planning, and architecture. They created utilitarian and religious structures of impressive beauty and grandeur that were to have a major influence on subsequent Western architecture. As we saw in Chapter 15, the outstanding feature of Roman architecture was the semicircular arch, which the Romans utilized and refined in the construction of arcades, barrel vaults, and domes (see the diagrams on pages 248 and 250).

By developing the structural use of concrete combined with semicircular arch and vault construction, the Romans were able to enclose large indoor spaces. Although a type of concrete was commonly used in Roman construction, the quality of cement (the chemically active ingredient in concrete) declined during the Middle Ages, and concrete was not widely used again until it was redeveloped in the nineteenth century.

In the PANTHEON, a major temple dedicated to all the gods, Roman builders created a domed interior space of immense scale. The building is essentially a cylinder, capped by a hemispherical dome, with a single entrance framed by a Greek porch, or *portico.*

Whereas Greek temples such as the PARTHENON were designed both as inner sanctuaries for priests and as focal points for outdoor religious ceremonies, later Roman temples, such as the PANTHEON, were focused inward: interior space became the place for public worship. Romans developed the ability to build large domed and vaulted interiors to accommodate their preference for gathering inside.

The PANTHEON's circular walls, which support the huge dome, are stone and concrete masonry, 20 feet thick and faced with brick. The dome diminishes in thickness toward the crown, and it is patterned on the interior surface with recessed squares called *coffers,* which both lighten and strengthen the structure. Originally covered with gold, the coffered ceiling symbolizes the dome of heaven. It was designed so that the distance from the summit to the floor is equal to the 143-foot diameter—making it a virtual globe of space. At the dome's crown, an opening called an *oculus,* or eye, 30 feet in diameter, provides daylight and ventilation to the interior. Neither verbal description nor views of the exterior and interior can evoke the awe one feels upon entering the PANTHEON.

Roman wall paintings are among the most interesting art produced during the period of the Roman Empire. The majority known to us come from Pompeii, Herculaneum, or other towns buried—and thus preserved—by the eruption of Mt. Vesuvius in A.D. 79. In the first century A.D., Roman artists continued the late Greek tradition of portraying depth in paintings of landscapes and urban views. The ROMAN PAINTING from a villa near Naples presents a complex urban scene painted with what may have been an intentionally unsystematic form of linear perspective. As is typical of Roman painting, the perspective lines are not systematically related to one another to create a sense of common space, nor is there controlled use of the effect of diminishing size relative to distance. Compare this painting with Raphael's SCHOOL OF ATHENS on page 63. Perhaps the artist intended viewers simply to enjoy the pleasing interwoven shapes, patterns, colors, and varied scale rather than to "enter" the illusory space he created. After the collapse of the Roman Empire, perspective was no longer applied, and the knowledge was forgotten until it was rediscovered and developed as a system during the Renaissance, more than one thousand years later.

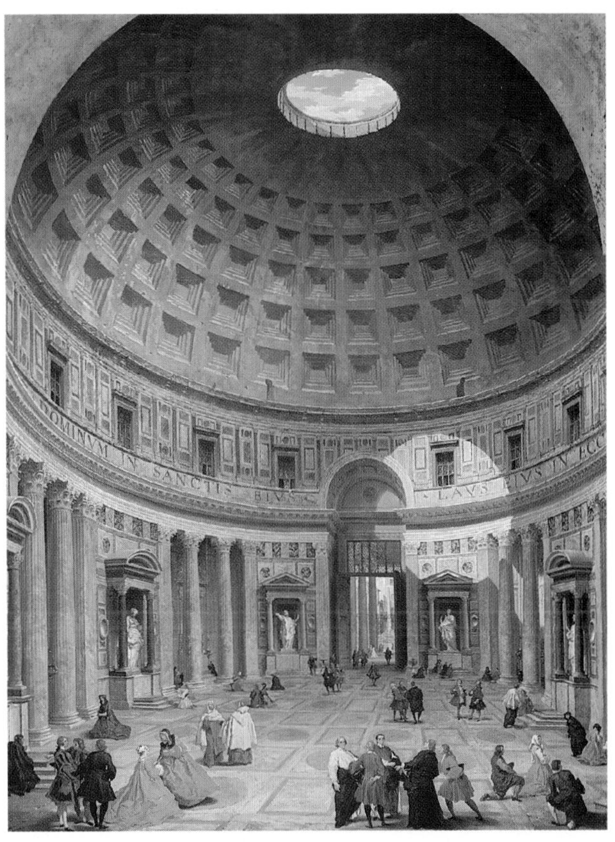

482 Giovanni Paolo Pannini.
THE INTERIOR OF THE PANTHEON. c. 1740.
Oil on canvas. 50½" × 39".

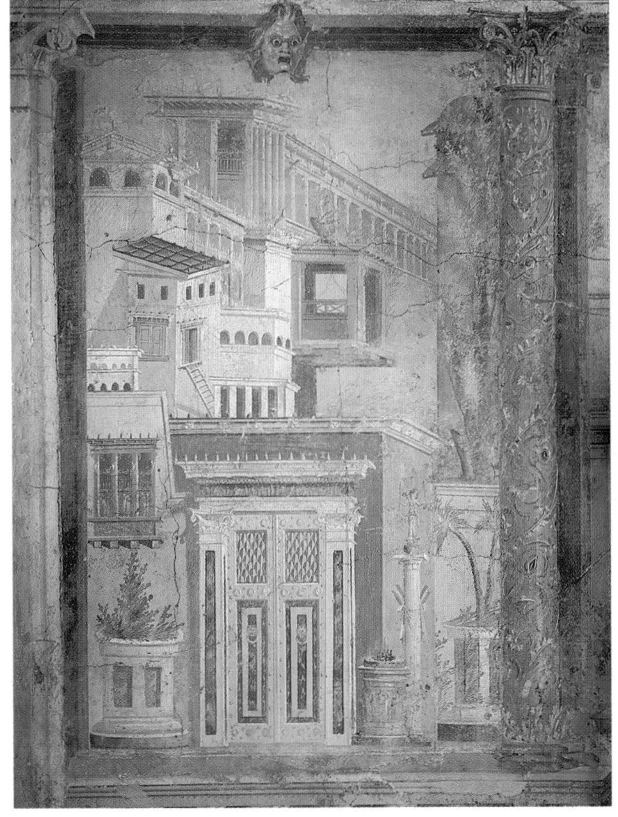

483 ROMAN PAINTING.
Detail of west wall in a villa at Boscoreale.
1st century B.C.
Fresco. Height: 8'.
The Metropolitan Museum of Art, New York. Rogers Fund, 1903. (03.14.13)

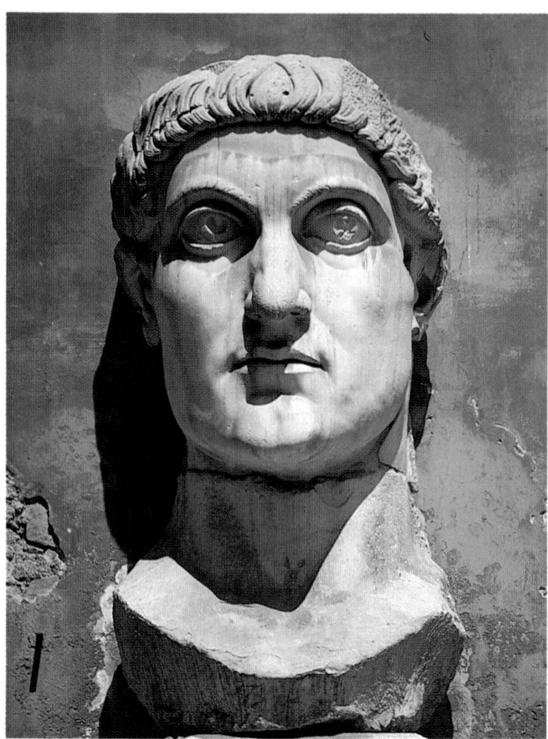

484 HEAD OF CONSTANTINE. c. 312.
Marble. Height 8'.
Museo dei Conservatori, Rome.

ROME, BYZANTIUM, AND EARLY CHRISTIAN ART

By the time Emperor Constantine converted to Christianity in 312, Roman attitudes had changed considerably. The grandeur of Rome was rapidly declining. As confidence in the material world fell, people turned inward to more spiritual values. The new orientation was reflected in art such as the colossal marble HEAD OF CONSTANTINE, once part of an immense figure. The superhuman head is an image of imperial majesty, yet the large eyes and immobile features express an inner spiritual life. The late Roman style of the facial features, particularly the eyes, is very different from the naturalism of earlier Roman portraits.

In 330, Constantine moved the capital of the Roman Empire east from Rome to the city of Byzantium, which he renamed Constantinople (present-day Istanbul). Although he could not have known it, the move would effectively split the empire in two. Under relentless attack from the Germanic tribes, the western portion of the empire soon collapsed, ushering in an era in Europe known as the Middle Ages.

The eastern portion of the empire, however, did not collapse. Indeed, the Byzantine Empire, as it came to be called, survived well into the fifteenth century. Founded as a Christian continuation of the Roman Empire, Byzantium developed a rich and distinctive artistic style that continues today in the mosaics, paintings, and architecture of the Orthodox church of Eastern Europe.

Not only did Constantine grant Christianity official recognition, he also sponsored an extensive building program. And so in the late Roman or early Byzantine empire we find the first great flowering of Christian art and architecture. (For a discussion of the Early Christian basilica, the model for the development of Western church architecture, see page 249.) Round or polygonal buildings crowned with domes had been used in earlier buildings such as Roman baths and later in the PANTHEON. Beginning in the fourth century, such buildings were built for Christian services and took on Christian meaning. Domed, central-plan

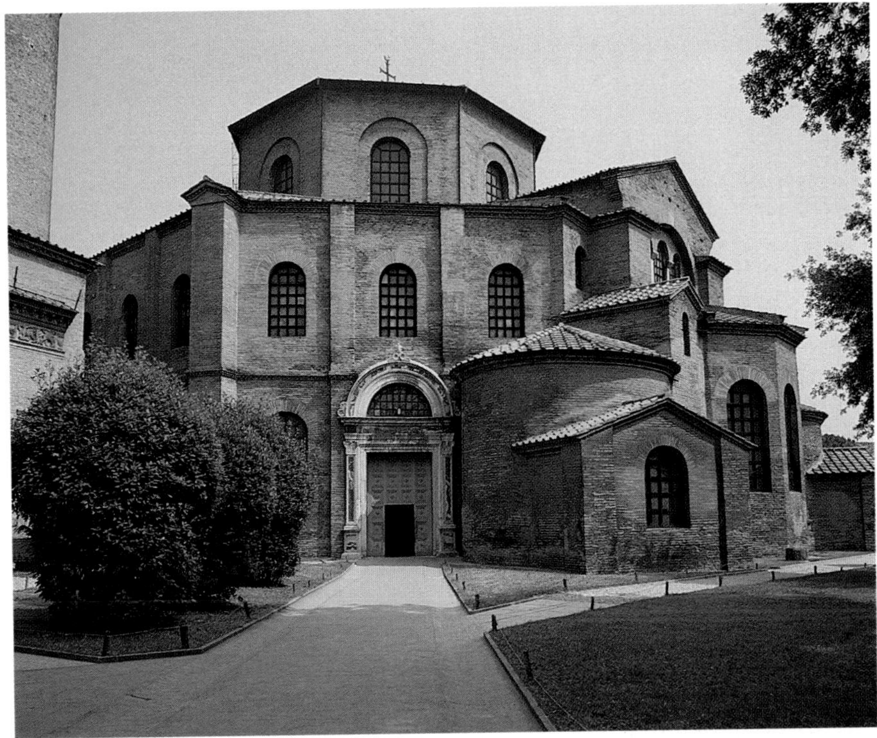

485 SAN VITALE. Ravenna, Italy. A.D. 526-547.
a Exterior.

churches have dominated the architecture of Eastern (Orthodox) Christianity ever since.

The inward focus of Roman temple architecture was adopted by the Early Christians for their churches, whose plain exteriors gave no hint of the light and beauty that lay inside.

The rapid construction of many large churches created a need for large paintings or other decorations to fill their walls. Mosaic technique (used by the Sumerians in the third millennium B.C. and later by the Greeks and Romans) was perfected and widely used in Early Christian churches. While earlier mosaics had been made of tiny pieces (tesserae) of colored marble, Early Christian wall mosaics were made of colored glass tesserae. Glass greatly expanded the range of colors and added a brilliance not found in earlier mosaics.

Ravenna, Italy, was briefly the capital of the Western Roman Empire (402–476), then recovered by Justinian for the Byzantine Empire (540–751). The many mosaics created in Ravenna in the fifth and sixth centuries show the transition from Early Christian to Byzantine style.

The most important sixth-century church is

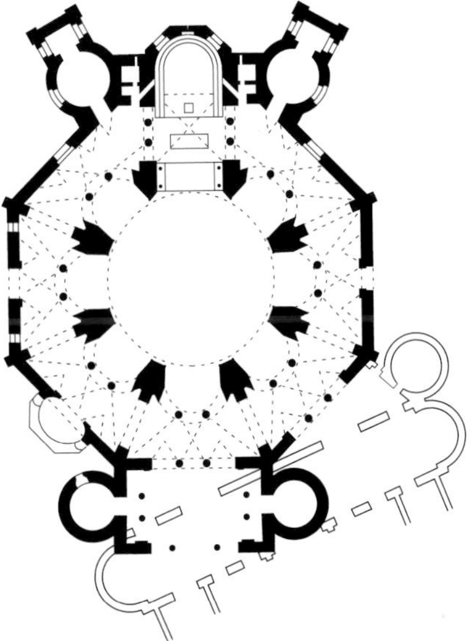

b Plan.

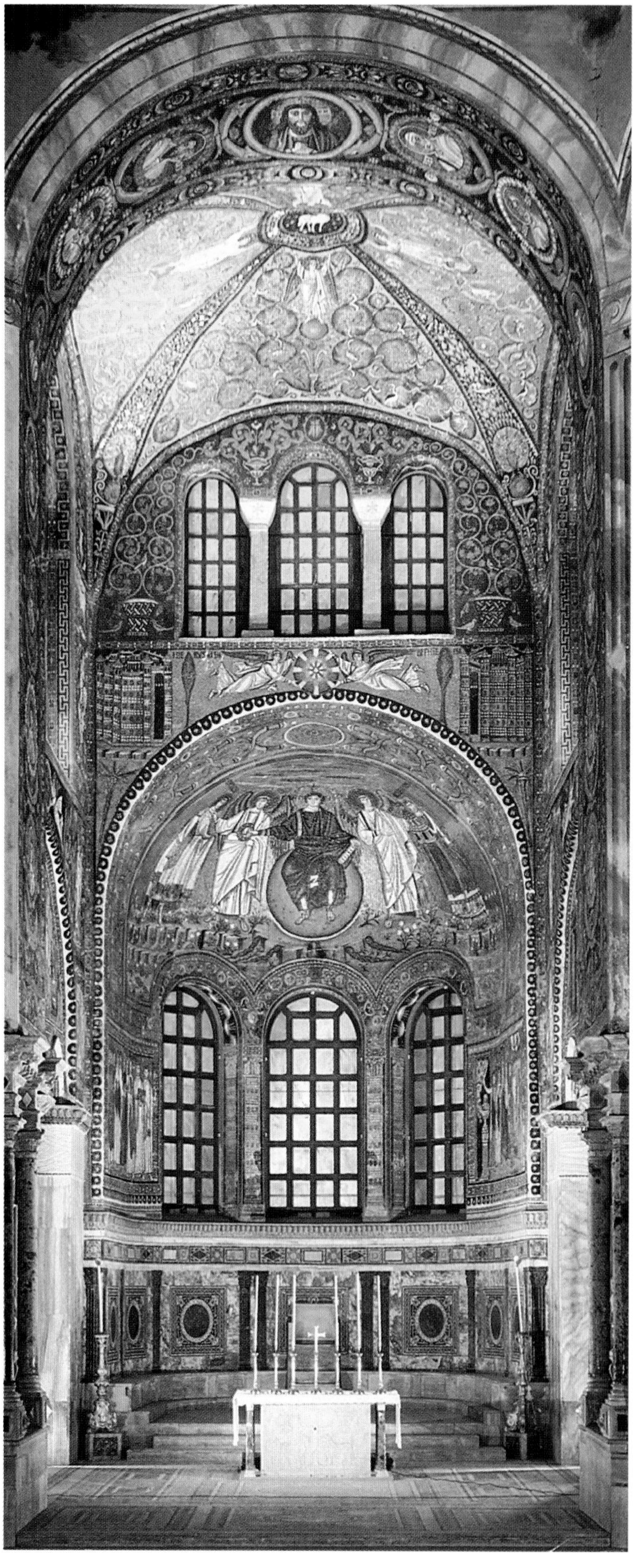

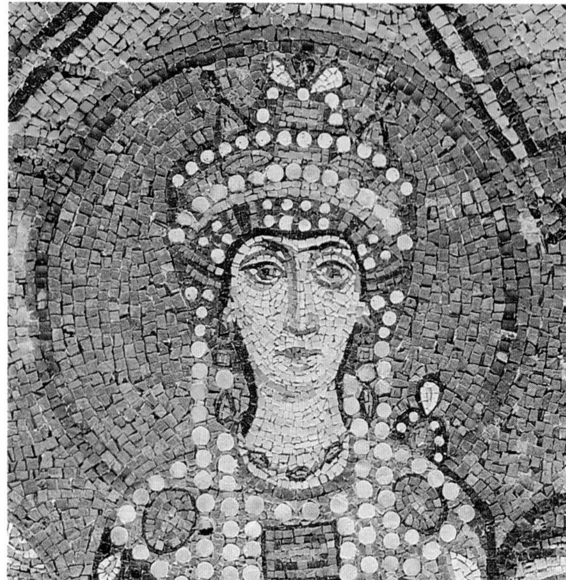

c Mosaic, detail of the Empress Theodora.

SAN VITALE in Ravenna. The glittering mosaic compositions that cover most of the interior surfaces depict the figures of Emperor Justinian and EMPRESS THEODORA in addition to religious figures and events. In a blending of religious and political authority, Justinian and Theodora are shown with halos, analogous to Christ and Mary, yet both are royally attired and bejeweled.

The elongated, abstracted figures provide symbolic rather than naturalistic depictions of the Christian and royal figures. Emphasis on the eyes is a Byzantine refinement of the stylized focus seen in the HEAD OF CONSTANTINE. Figures are depicted with heavy outline and stylized shading. The only suggestion of space is through overlap. Background and figures retain a flat, decorative richness typical of Byzantine art.

The arts of the Early Christian period were affected by an ongoing controversy between those who sought to follow the biblical prohibition against the making of images and those who wanted pictures to help tell the sacred stories. The Byzantine style developed as a way of inspiring the illiterate while keeping the biblical commandment that for-

d Interior.

bids the making of graven images. The Byzantine theory was that highly stylized (abstract) and decorative images could never be confused with a real person (as a naturalistic work might be). As a result, the naturalism and sense of depth found in Roman painting gradually gave way to abstraction.

By the tenth and eleventh centuries, Byzantine artists had created a distinct style that expressed Eastern Orthodox Christianity and also met the needs of a lavish court. The style had its roots in the Early Christian art of the late Roman Empire, as we have seen. But it also absorbed Eastern influences, particularly the flat patterns and nonrepresentational designs of Islam. Eastern influence continued with the hierarchical sizing and placement of subject matter in Byzantine church decoration.

High in the dome of the Church of the Dormition at Daphni, Greece, a Byzantine mosaic depicts CHRIST PANTOCRATOR, Lord of the Universe. This awesome religious image is one of the most powerful symbols of Christ. The scale of the figure emphasizes its spiritual importance to worshipers. The early Christian HEAD OF CONSTANTINE and the Byzantine CHRIST PANTOCRATOR exhibit similar intensity and emphasis on the eyes. The artist who created the Byzantine mosaic of Christ designed the features to indicate patriarchal authority.

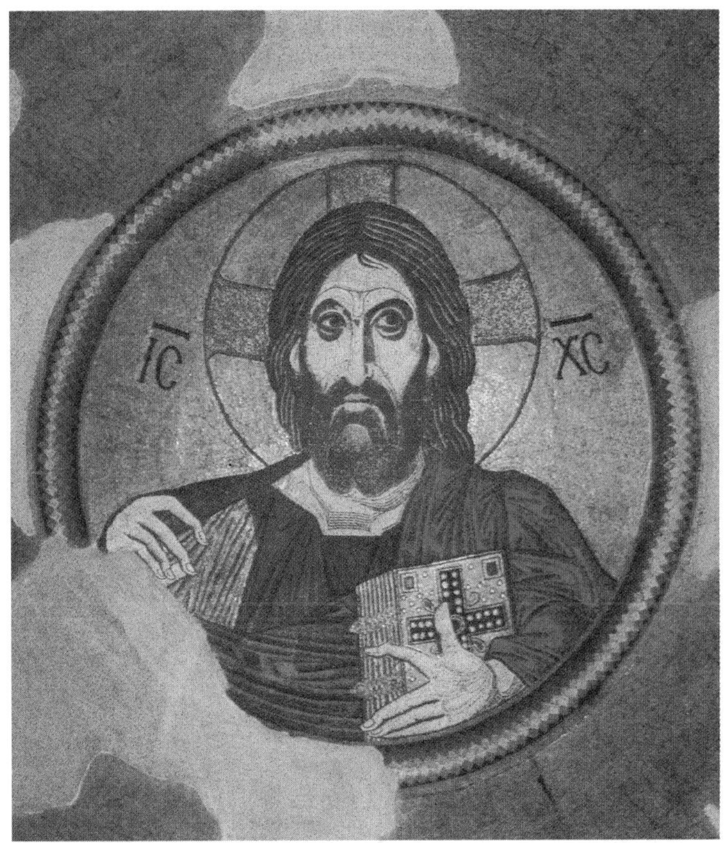

486 CHRIST PANTOCRATOR.
Dome of the Church of the Dormition, Daphni, Greece. c. 1080.
Mosaic.

A row of windows circles the base of the dome, bringing light to the church interior. The effect of the mosaic surfaces depends on the direction of light from the windows and from artificial sources such as candlelight; each small tessera was placed on the adhesive surface and tilted to catch the light, producing a shimmering effect.

The Byzantine style is still followed by painters and others working within the tradition of the Eastern Orthodox church. Clergy closely supervise the iconography and permit little room for individual interpretation. Artists of the Eastern Orthodox faith seek to portray the symbolic or mystical aspects of religious figures rather than their physical qualities. The figures are painted in conformity to a precise formula. Small paintings, referred to as *icons* (from the Greek *eikon,* meaning image), are holy images that inspire devotion but are not worshiped in them-

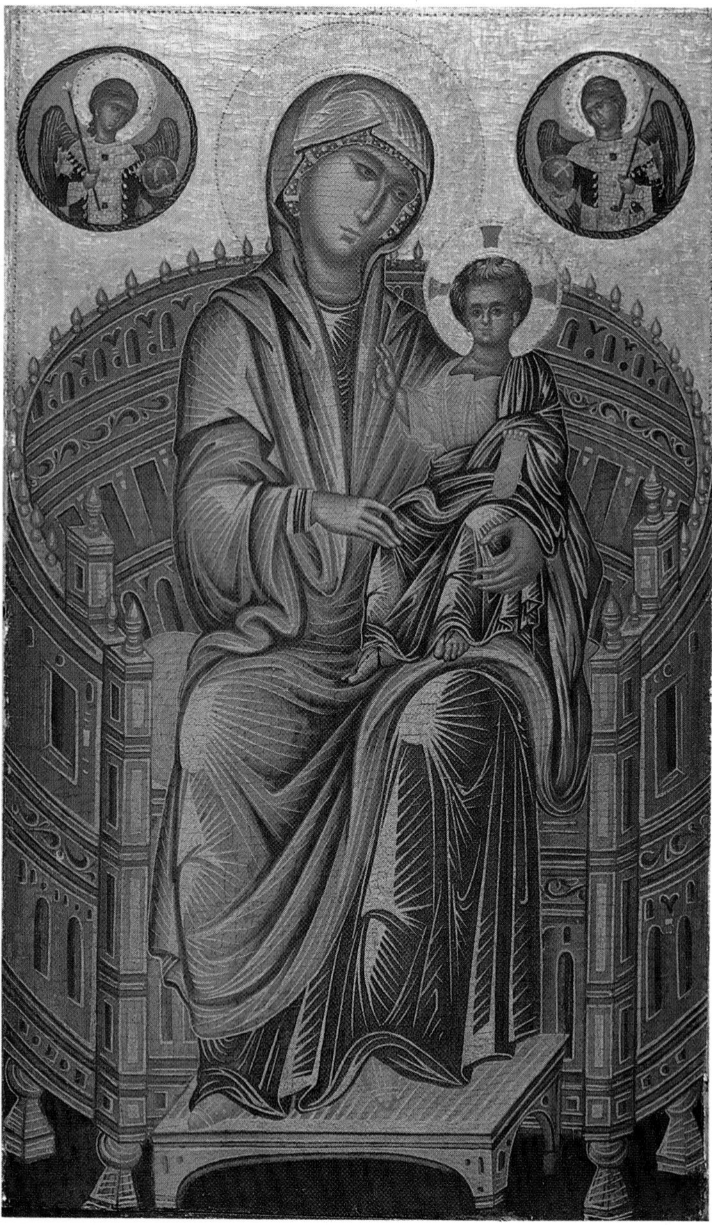

487 Byzantine School.
MADONNA AND CHILD ON A CURVED THRONE. 13th century.
Tempera on wood. 32⅛" × 19⅜".

selves. The making of portable icon paintings grew out of mosaic and fresco traditions.

The design of the icon painting MADONNA AND CHILD ON A CURVED THRONE is based on circular shapes and linear patterns. Mary's head repeats the circular shape of her halo; circles of similar size enclose angels, echoing the larger circle of the throne. The lines and shapes used in the draped robes that cover the figures give scarcely a hint of the bodies beneath. Divine light is symbolized by the gold background that surrounds the throne in which the Virgin Mary sits. The large architectural throne symbolizes Mary's position as Queen of the City of Heaven. Christ appears as a wise little man, supported on the lap of a heavenly, supernatural mother.

In order that they be worthy of dedication to God, icons are usually made of precious materials. Gold leaf was used here for the background and costly lapis lazuli for the Virgin's robe.

THE MIDDLE AGES IN EUROPE

In 395 the Roman Empire was officially divided in two, with one emperor in Rome and another in Constantinople—the center of what became known as Byzantium or the Byzantine Empire. Over the course of the next century the entire Empire, east and west, was repeatedly attacked by nomadic Germanic tribes—Visigoths, Astrogoths, Alans, Sneves, Bulgers, Vandals, and Huns (including Atilla). Byzantium successfully repelled its invaders; Rome was not so fortunate. Weakened from within by military rebellions and civil wars, the Western Roman Empire decayed and collapsed.

The one thousand years that followed the fall of the Western Roman Empire has been called the medieval period, or the Middle Ages, because it came between the time of ancient Greek and Roman civilizations and the rebirth, or renaissance, of Greco-Roman ideas in the fifteenth century.

Early Medieval Art

The art of the early Middle Ages took shape as Early Christian art absorbed a new influence: the art of the invaders. Many nomadic peoples traveled across the Eurasian grasslands called the Steppes, which extend from the Danube River in Europe to the borders of China. Their migrations occurred over a long period that began in the second millennium B.C. and lasted well into the Middle Ages. The Greeks called these uncivilized nomads (and other non-Greeks) "barbarians." What little we know about them is derived from artifacts and records of literate cultures of the Mediterranean, Near East, and China, to whom the nomads were a menace. The Great Wall of China and Hadrian's Wall in Britain were built to keep out such invaders.

A varied but interrelated art, known as the *animal style,* was developed by the Eurasian nomads. Because of their migrant way of life, their art consisted of small, easily portable objects such as items for personal adornment, weapons, and horse trappings. The style is characterized by active, intertwining shapes, often depicting wild animals in combat, as seen in the SCYTHIAN ANIMAL ornament. The vigor of the art reflects the mobile life of the people. The art of the animal style rarely depicts human beings; when it does, they play subordinate roles to animals.

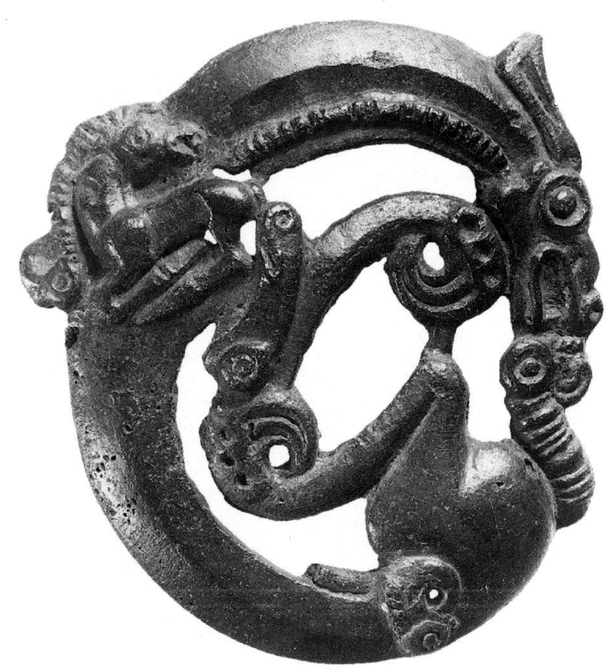

488 SCYTHIAN ANIMAL. 5th century B.C.
Bronze. Diameter 4".
Hermitage Museum, St. Petersburg.

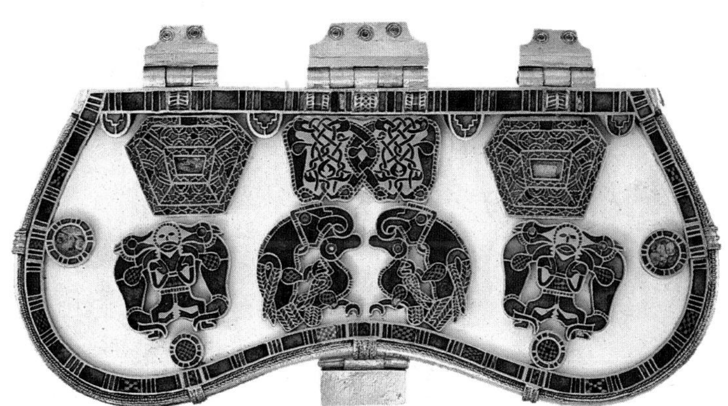

489 PURSE COVER.
From the Sutton Hoo Ship Burial, Suffolk, England. Before 655.
Gold and enamel. Length 7½".
Copyright British Museum, London.

Nomadic metalwork often exhibits exceptional craftsmanship. Because of frequent migrations and the durability and value of the art objects, the style was diffused over large geographic areas. Among the best known works of nomadic art are small gold and bronze ornaments produced by the Scythians, whose culture flourished between the eighth and fourth centuries B.C. Their abstracted animal forms appear to have been adopted by groups in the British Isles, Scandinavia, and China. In the art of medieval Europe, similar animal forms appear later in woodcarving, stonecarving, and manuscript illumination, as well as in metal.

The gold and enamel PURSE COVER found in a grave at Sutton Hoo belonged to a seventh-century East Anglian king. Its motifs are distinctly varied, indicating that they are derived from several sources.

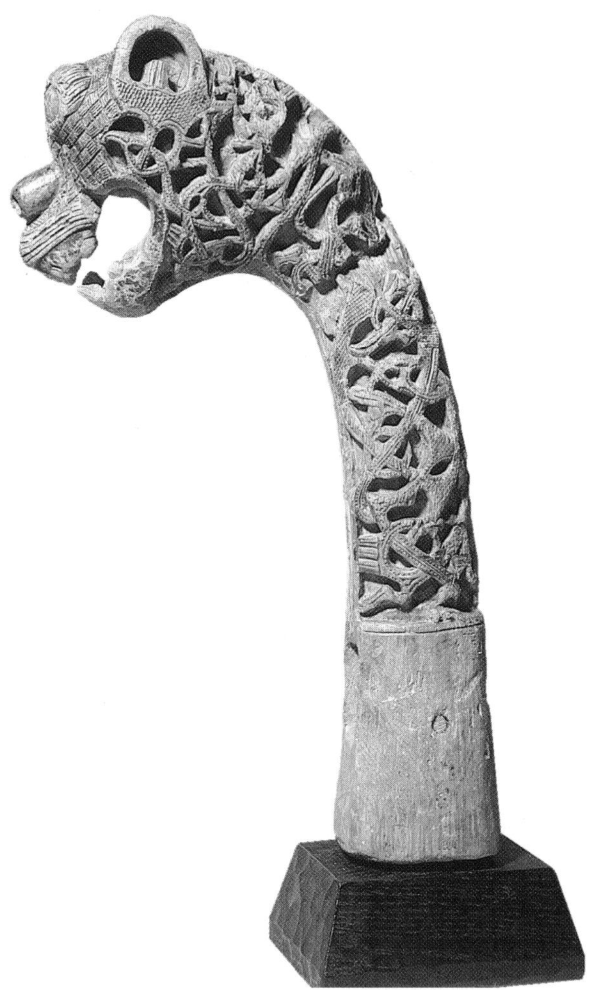

490 DRAGON'S HEAD.
Found at Oseberg, Norway. c. 820. Wood.
University Museum of
National Antiquities, Oslo, Norway.

The motif of a man standing between confronting animals appeared first in Sumerian art over three thousand years earlier (see page 318).

A great deal of woodcarving was done in Scandinavia, where the animal style flourished longer than anywhere else in the West. Protective animal spirits, like those in both the early Chinese RITUAL VESSEL (page 290) and the DRAGON'S HEAD from Norway, were felt to have power and symbolic significance beyond the decorative function we may associate with them. We know that Viking law required that figures such as the DRAGON'S HEAD be removed when a ship came into port so that the spirits of the land would not be frightened.

The meeting of decorative nomadic styles with Christianity can be seen most clearly in the illuminated holy books created in Ireland. The Irish had never been part of the Roman Empire, and in the fifth century they were Christianized without first becoming Romanized. During the chaotic centuries that followed the fall of Rome, Irish monasteries became the major centers of learning and the arts in Europe, and they produced hand-lettered copies of religious manuscripts in large numbers.

The initial letters in these manuscripts were embellished over time, moving first into the margin and then onto a separate page. This splendid initial page is the opening of St. Matthew's account of the Nativity in the BOOK OF KELLS, which contains the Latin Gospels. It is known as the CHI-RHO MONOGRAM because it is composed of the first two letters of Christ in Greek (XP, pronounced chi-rho) and is used to represent Christ or Christianity. Except for XP and two Latin words beginning the story of Christ's birth, most of the page is filled with a rich complexity of spirals and tiny interlacings. A close look at the knots and scrolls reveals angels to the left of the X, a man's head in the P, and cats and mice at the base.

491 CHI-RHO MONOGRAM (XP).
Page from the BOOK OF KELLS. Late 8th century.
Trinity College Library, Dublin, Ireland.

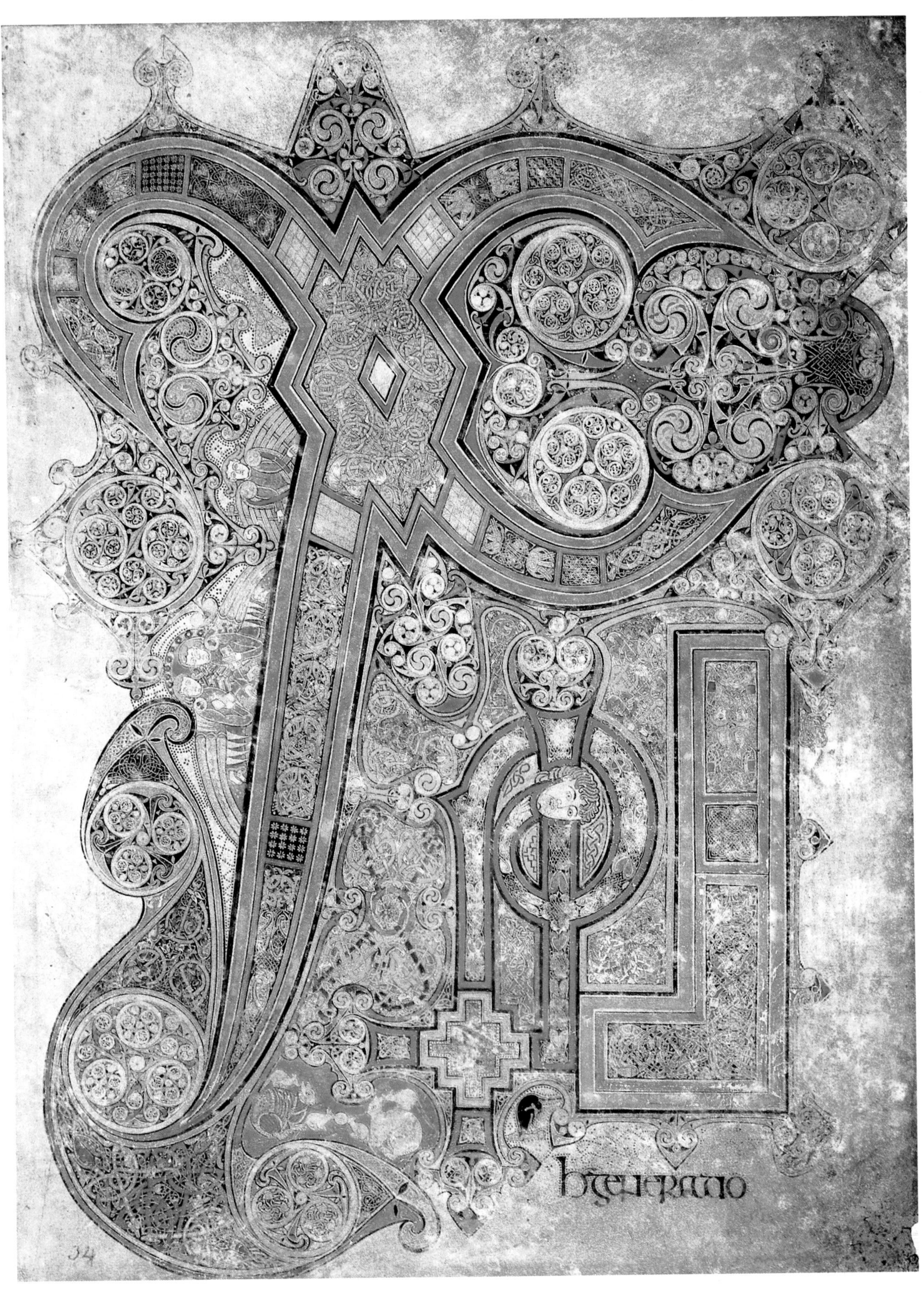
h generatio

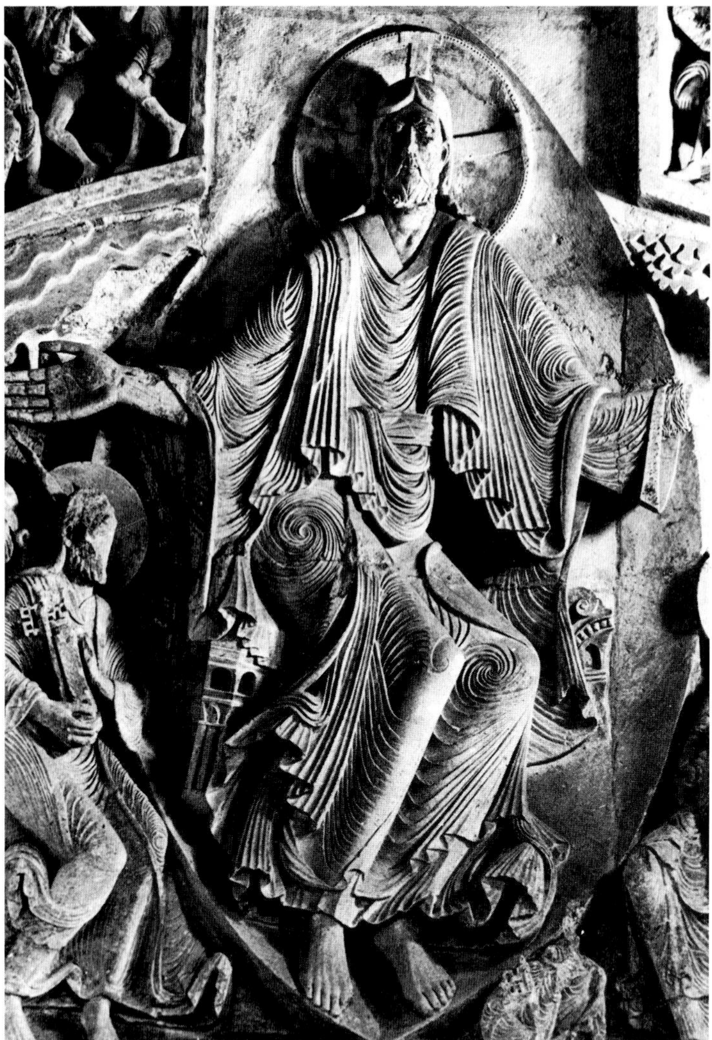

492 Detail of CHRIST OF THE PENTECOST.
Saint Madeleine Cathedral, Vézelay, France. 1125-1150.
Stone. Height of the tympanum 35½".

Romanesque

The stylistic term *Romanesque* was first used to designate European Christian architecture of the mid-eleventh to the mid-twelfth centuries, which revived Roman principles of stone construction, especially the round arch and the barrel vault (see the Romanesque vaulted interior on page 251). This term is now applied to all medieval art of western Europe during that period.

Byzantine art traditions continued in southeastern Europe, while Romanesque art developed in a western Europe dominated by feudalism and monasticism. Feudalism involved a complex system of local obligations and services based on economic, political, and property control, and wars to increase control. Monasteries provided shelter from a hostile world and served as the main sources of education.

Religious crusades and pilgrimages brought large groups of Christians even to remote places, necessitating larger churches. Romanesque builders increased the sizes of churches by doubling the length of the nave (the central space), doubling the side aisles, and building galleries above side aisles.

Churches continued to have wooden roofs, but stone vaults largely replaced fire-prone wooden ceilings, giving the new structures a close resemblance to Roman interiors. Consistent throughout the variety of regional styles was a common feeling of security provided by massive, fortresslike walls.

Romanesque sculpture is complex and highly imaginative, with the finest carvings an integral part of Romanesque architecture. Subjects and models came from miniature paintings in illuminated texts, but sculptors gradually added a degree of naturalism not found in earlier medieval work. In addition to stylized, and at times naive, figures from biblical stories, relief carvings include strange beasts and decorative plant forms. The largest and most elaborate figures were placed over the central doorways of churches. Such figures were the first large sculpture since Roman times.

Deviation from the standard human proportions enabled sculptors to give appropriately symbolic form to figures such as CHRIST OF THE PENTECOST. The mystical energy and compassion of

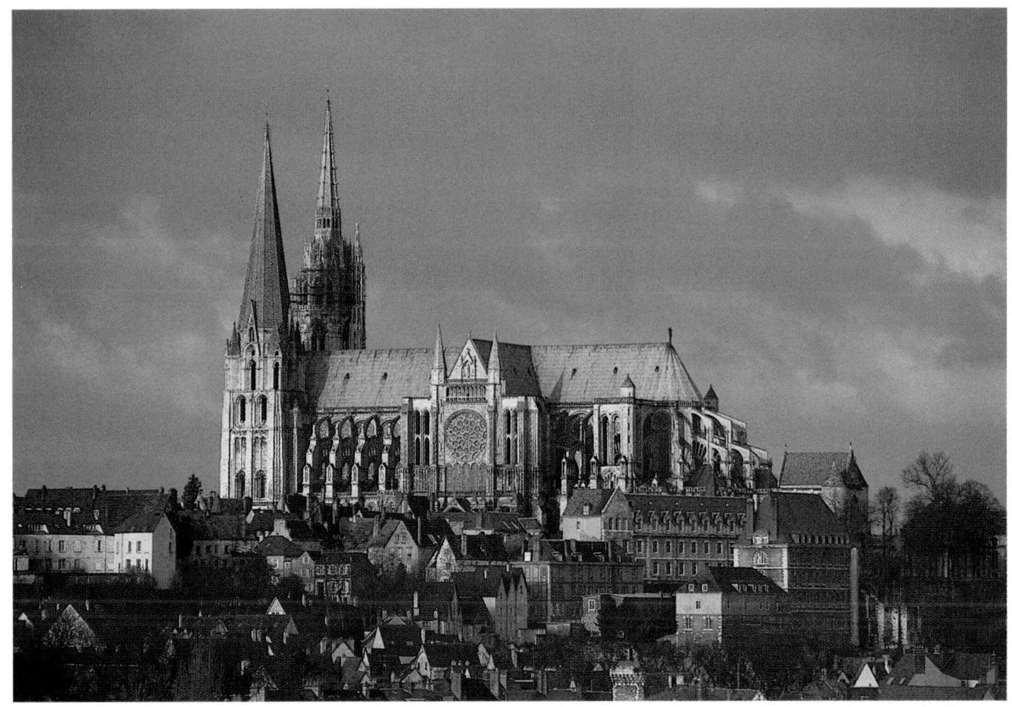

493 NOTRE DAME DE CHARTRES. Chartres, France. 1145-1513. Cathedral length 427'; facade height 157'; south tower height 344'; north tower height 377'.
a View from the southeast.
Photograph: © Adam Woolfitt.

Christ is depicted in this relief carving above the doorway of Saint Madeleine Cathedral at Vézelay, France. As worshipers enter the sanctuary, the image above them depicts Christ at the time he asked the Apostles and all Christians to take his message to the world. The image of Christ is larger in scale than the other figures, showing his relative importance. The sculptor achieved a monumental quality by making the head smaller than normal and by elongating the entire figure. Swirling folds of drapery are indicated with precise curves and spirals that show the continuing influence of the linear energy of the animal style and the CHI-RHO MONOGRAM. In abstract terms, the spiraling motion suggests Christ's cosmic power.

Gothic

One of the major differences between the cultures of the East and the West is the restless energy of Europeans. This restless energy caused frequent changes in attitude that resulted in the changing styles of Western art. The Romanesque style had lasted barely a hundred years when the Gothic style began to replace it in about 1145. The shift is seen most clearly in architecture, as the Romanesque round arch was superseded by the pointed Gothic arch, developed in the mid-twelfth century (discussed on page 252).

Gothic cathedrals were expressions of a new age of faith that grew out of medieval Christian theology and mysticism. The light-filled, upward-reaching structures symbolize the triumph of the spirit over the bonds of earthly life, evoking a sense of joyous spiritual elation. Inside, the faithful must have felt they had actually arrived at the visionary Heavenly City.

Gothic cathedrals such as NOTRE DAME DE CHARTRES (Our Lady of Chartres) were the center of community life. In many cases, they were the only indoor space that could hold all the townspeople at once; thus, they were used for meetings, concerts, and morality plays. But most of all, they were places of worship. Above the town of Chartres, the Cathedral rises, its spires visible for miles around.

The entire community cooperated in the building of NOTRE DAME DE CHARTRES, although those who began its construction never saw it in its final form. The cathedral continued to grow and change

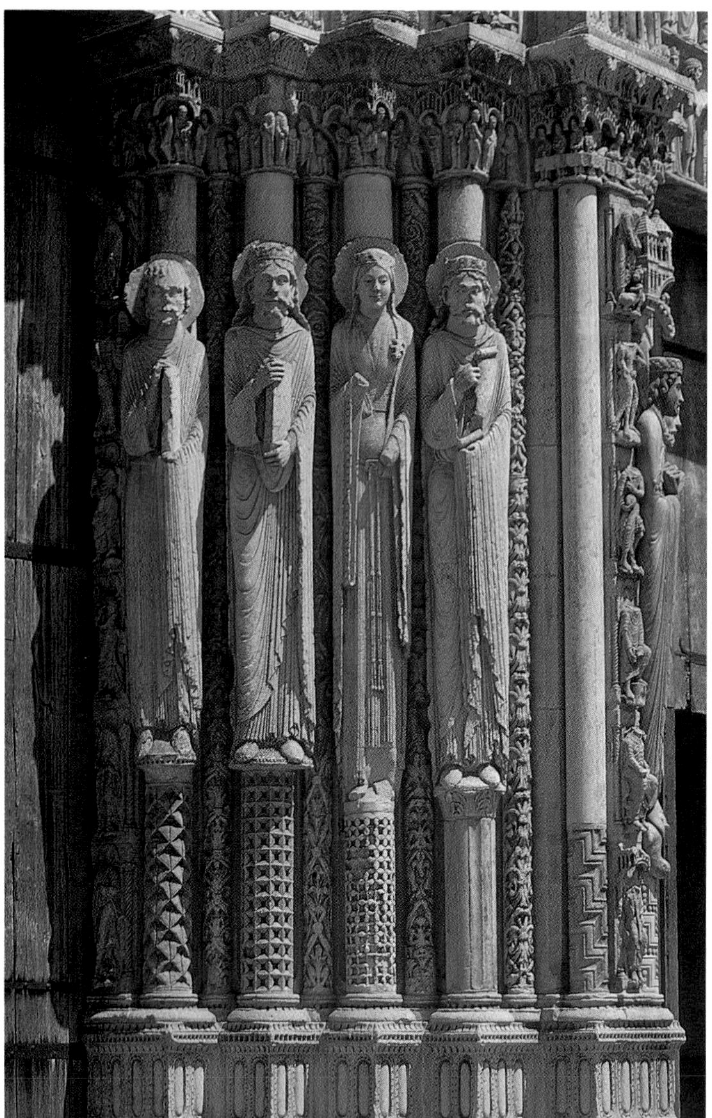

b OLD TESTAMENT PROPHET, KINGS, AND QUEEN. c. 1145-1170. Door-jamb statues from West (or Royal) Portal.

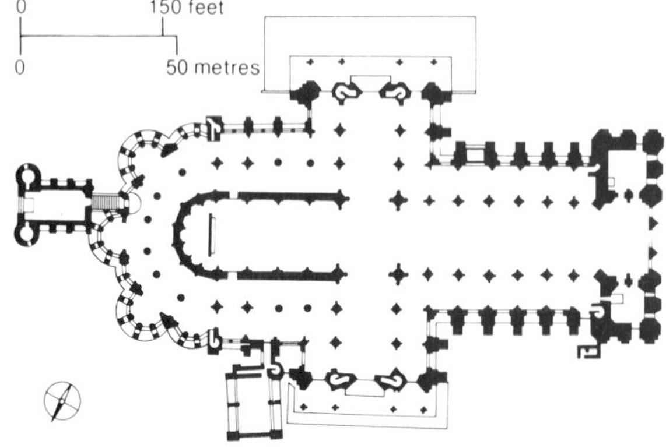

c Plan based on Latin cross.

in major ways for over three hundred years. Although the basic plan is symmetrical and logically organized, the architecture of CHARTRES has a rich, enigmatic complexity that is quite different from the easily grasped totality of the classical PARTHENON.

Chartres was partially destroyed by fire in 1194 and was rebuilt in the High Gothic style. One of the first cathedrals based on the full Gothic system, it helped set the standard for Gothic architecture in Europe. In its west facade, Chartres reveals the transition between the early and late phases of Gothic architecture. The massive lower walls and round arch portals were built in the mid-twelfth century. The north tower, on the left as one approaches the facade, was rebuilt with the intricate flamelike or flamboyant curves of the late Gothic style early in the sixteenth century, after the original tower collapsed in 1506.

Magnificent stained-glass windows of this period are so well integrated with the architecture that one is inconceivable without the other. The scriptures are told in imagery that transforms the sanctuary with showers of color, changing hour by hour. At Chartres, the brilliant north rose window, known as the ROSE DE FRANCE, is dedicated to the Virgin Mary, who sits in majesty, surrounded by doves, angels, and royal figures of the celestial hierarchy.

The statues of the OLD TESTAMENT PROPHET, KINGS, AND QUEEN to the right of the central doorway at the west entrance of CHARTRES are among the most impressive remaining examples of early Gothic sculpture. The kings and queen suggest Christ's royal heritage and also honor French monarchs of the time. The prophet on the left depicts Christ's mission as an apostle of God. In contrast to active, emotional Romanesque sculpture, the figures are passive and serene. Their typically Gothic, elongated forms allow them to blend readily with the vertical emphasis of the architecture.

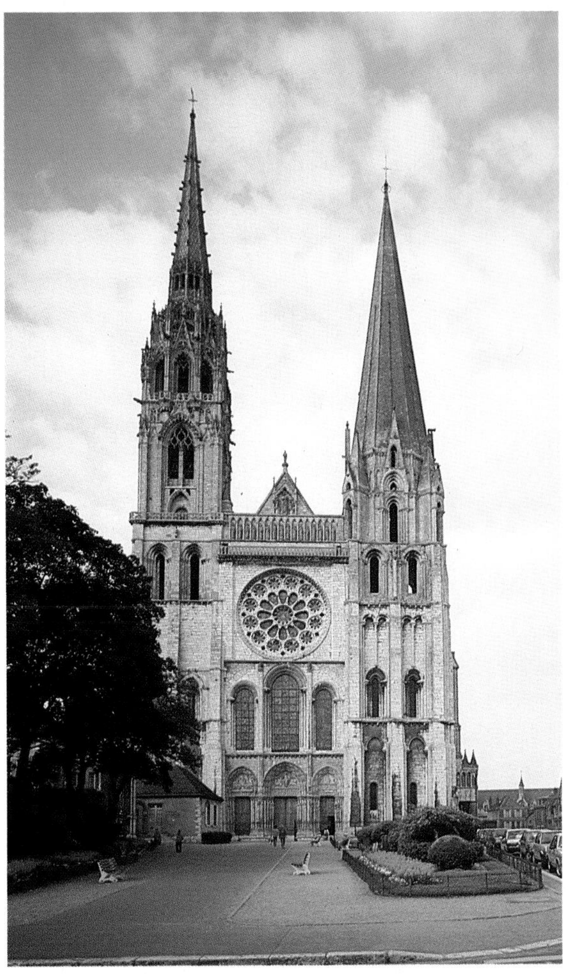

d West front.

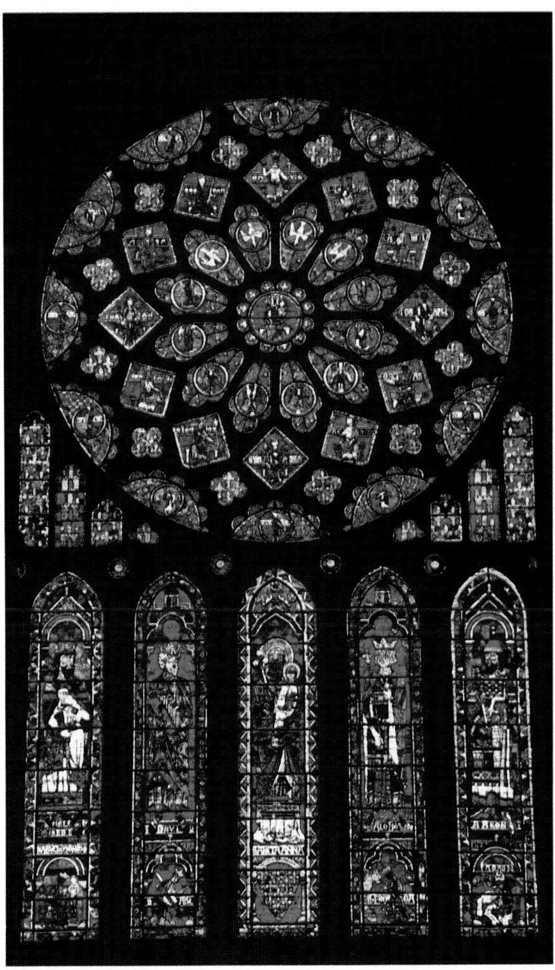

e "ROSE DE FRANCE" WINDOW. c. 1233.

Although they are part of the total scheme, the figures stand out from the columns behind them. Their draped bodies, and especially their heads, reveal a developing interest in portraying human features. Such interest eventually led again to full portraiture and freestanding figures.

In spite of the great differences in form and content between Hindu (see page 285) and Christian architecture and sculpture, their basic purposes are similar. Both the cathedral and the temple relate to an idea expressed by Abbot Suger, the man credited with starting the Gothic era. Art historian Erwin Panofsky has translated and paraphrased Suger's concept:

Every perceptible thing, manmade or natural, becomes a symbol of that which is not perceptible, a stepping stone on the road to Heaven; the human mind, abandoning itself to the "harmony and radiance"... which is the criterion of terrestrial beauty, finds itself "guided upward" to the transcendent cause of this "harmony and radiance" which is God.[1]

CHAPTER 19

Renaissance and Baroque

A shift in attitude occurred in Europe as the religious fervor of the Middle Ages was increasingly challenged by logical thought and the new philosophical, literary, and artistic movement called *humanism.* Leading humanist scholars did not discard theological concerns, but they reaffirmed the secular dimensions of life, pursued intellectual and scientific inquiry, and rediscovered the classical literature of Greece and Rome. The focus gradually shifted from God and the hereafter to mankind and the here and now.

For Europeans, the Renaissance was a period of achievement and worldwide exploration—a time of discovery and rediscovery of the world and of the seemingly limitless potential of individual human beings. The period began to take shape in the fourteenth century, reached its clear beginning in the early fifteenth century, and came to an end in the early seventeenth century. However, Renaissance thinking continues to influence our lives today, not only in Western countries but in all parts of the world where individualism, modern science, and technology impact on the way people live. In art, new and more scientific approaches were brought to the quest for representational accuracy. The resulting naturalism dominated Western art until the late nineteenth century.

The intellectuals of the time were the first in history to give their own era an identifying name. They named their period the *Renaissance*—literally, Rebirth—an apt description for the period of revived interest in the art and ideas of classical Greece and Rome. Fifteenth-century Italians believed they were responsible for the rebirth of "the glory of ancient Greece," which they considered the high point of Western civilization. Yet Greco-Roman culture was not really reborn, because this "classical" heritage had never disappeared from the medieval West. In essence, the Renaissance was a period of new and renewed understanding that transformed the medieval world and laid the foundation for modern society.

In art, we trace the beginnings of this new attitude to the twelfth century. While Gothic and Byzantine painters continued to employ relatively flat symbolic styles, Gothic sculptors were moving from stylized abstraction toward greater naturalism and individuality in their figures.

The humanist enthusiasm for classical antiquity and a growing secularism led to revolutionary thinking in many areas. The first writer to reveal evidence of Renaissance thinking was Italian poet Dante, who lived during the thirteenth and fourteenth centuries and belonged primarily to the Middle Ages. The last major writer of the Renaissance was Shakespeare, who lived three centuries later.

New values combined with technological advances brought forth an abundance of major artworks. Painting and sculpture were liberated from their medieval roles as supplements to architecture.

Artists, who had been viewed as anonymous craftsmen in the Middle Ages, came to be seen as individuals of creative genius.

The art of the Renaissance evolved in different ways in Northern and Southern Europe because the people of the two regions had different backgrounds, attitudes, and experiences. The Gothic style reached its high point in the north while Byzantine and Greco-Roman influences remained strong in the south. Italian Renaissance art grew from classical Mediterranean traditions that were human-centered and often emphasized monumentality and the ideal. In contrast, the art of the Northern Renaissance evolved out of pre-Christian, nature-centered religions that became God-centered through conversion to Christianity.

New directions in the course of human history are often begun by a small group or a single person of genius who seizes the opportunity that changing circumstances present. Such a person was proto-Renaissance Italian painter and architect Giotto di Bondone, known as Giotto. Giotto departed from the abstract Byzantine style by portraying the feelings and physical nature of human beings. His innovative depictions of light, space, and mass gave a renewed sense of realism to painting. In LAMENTATION, Giotto depicted physical as well as spiritual reality. His figures are shown as individuals within a shallow, stagelike space, and their expressions portray personal feelings of grief not often seen in medieval art.

In retrospect, we see Giotto not only as a precursor of the Renaissance but as the reinventor of naturalistic painting, which had not been seen in Europe since the decline of Rome a thousand years earlier. This "realism" is still an important current in Western painting.

The ancient Greeks had been concerned with idealized physical form; Roman artists had emphasized physical accuracy; and artists of the Middle Ages had focused on spiritual concerns rather than physical existence. With the Renaissance, as attention shifted from heaven to earth, artists portrayed Christian subjects in human terms. Italian leaders expressed a desire to equal or surpass the glory of ancient Greece and Rome and to imbue their achievements with the light of Christian understanding.

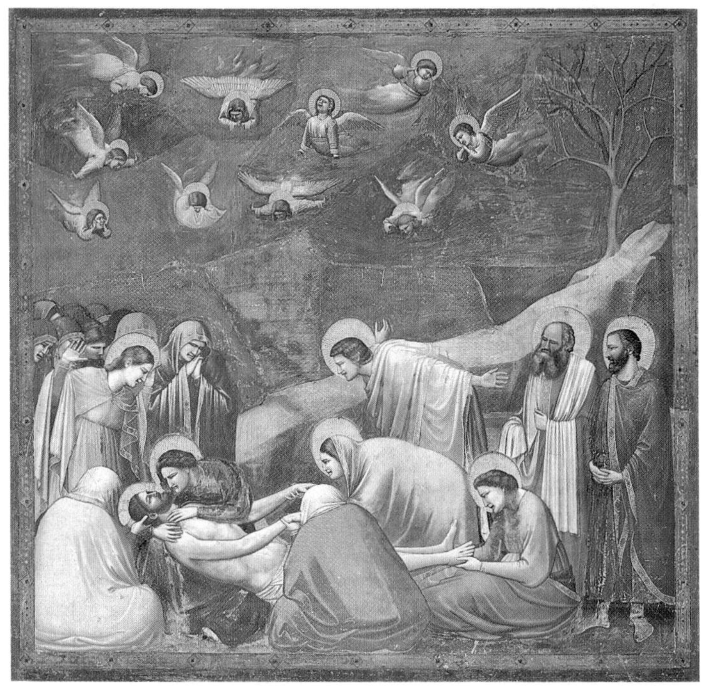

494 Giotto di Bondone.
LAMENTATION.
Arena Chapel, Padua, Italy. c. 1305.
Fresco. 185 cm × 200 cm.

Italy was the homeland of the Renaissance. In time the movement spread northward, but it did not flourish everywhere in the West; it came late to Spain and Portugal, and it barely touched Scandinavia.

THE RENAISSANCE IN ITALY

Artistic and intellectual developments in the Italian city-states were aided by a flourishing economic situation against a divided and chaotic political background. The great wealth of Italian merchants enabled them to compete with one another, and with the church officials and nobility, for the recognition and power that came with art patronage.

Italian architects, sculptors, and painters sought to integrate Christian spiritual traditions with the rational ordering of physical life in earthly space. Artists began an intense study of anatomy and light, and they applied geometry to the logical

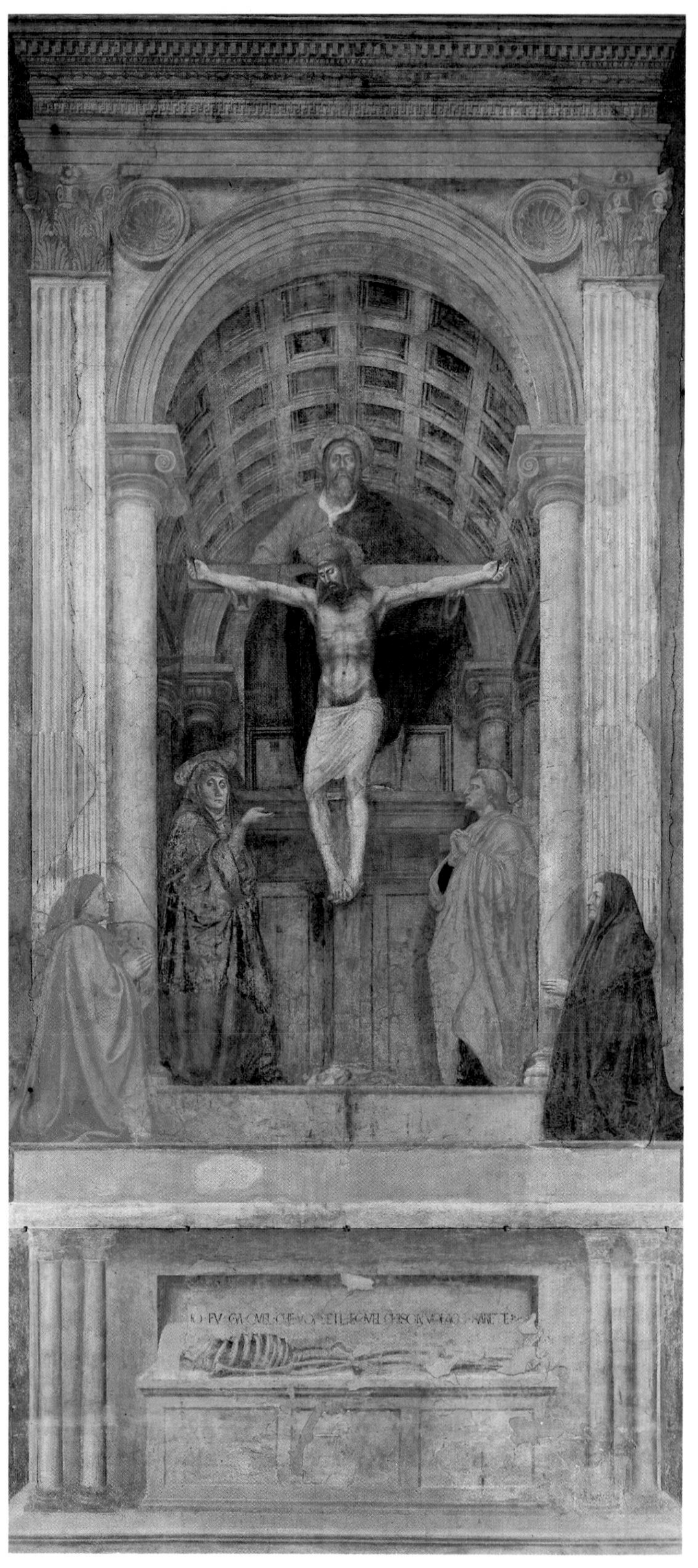

construction of implied space through the use of linear perspective (see page 61). In turn, the careful observation of nature initiated by Renaissance artists aided the growth of science.

About one hundred years after Giotto, Masaccio became the first major painter of the Italian Renaissance. In his fresco THE HOLY TRINITY, two donors (those who paid for the painting) kneel on either side of an open chapel in which the Trinity appears—God the Father, Christ the Son, and the Holy Spirit (represented by a white dove just above Christ's head). Below, a skeleton is shown lying on a sarcophagus beneath the inscription, "I was what you are, and what I am you shall become." If we view the painting from top to bottom, we move from spiritual reality to temporal reality.

THE HOLY TRINITY was the first painting based on the systematic use of linear perspective. Although perspective was known to the Romans in a limited way, it did not become a consistent science until architect Filippo Brunelleschi rediscovered and developed it in Florence early in the fifteenth century. Masaccio used perspective to construct an illusion of figures in three-dimensional space. The single vanishing point is below the base of the cross, about five feet above ground, at the viewer's eye level. Masaccio's perspective measurements were so precise that one can compute the dimensions of the interior of the illusionary chapel, which is seen as a believable extension of the space occupied by the viewer. The setting also reveals Masaccio's knowledge of the new Renaissance architecture developed by Brunelleschi, which was based on Roman prototypes.

The figures in THE HOLY TRINITY have a physical presence that shows what Masaccio learned from the work of Giotto. In Giotto's work, however, body and drapery still appear as one; Masaccio's figures are clothed nudes, with garments draped like real fabric.

495 Masaccio.
THE HOLY TRINITY. Santa Maria Novella, Florence. 1425.
Fresco. 21'10½" × 10'5".

During the Italian Renaissance, the nude became a major subject for art, as it had been in Greece and Rome. Unclothed subjects are rare in medieval art (Adam and Eve, sinners in Hell) and appear awkward, their bodies graceless. In contrast, sculpted and painted figures by Italian Renaissance artists appear as strong and natural as the Greek and Roman nudes that inspired them.

The great range and vitality of work by sculptor Donatello had a lasting influence on subsequent Renaissance sculpture and on European sculpture and painting for four centuries. Donatello brought the Greek ideal of what it means to be human into the Christian context. As a young adult, he made two trips to Rome where he studied medieval (Byzantine, Romanesque, and Gothic) as well as classical Greek and Roman art.

Donatello learned bronze casting technique at an early age by working in the studio of Ghiberti (see page 201). He achieved brilliant maturity even in his early work. His bronze figure of DAVID was the first life-size, freestanding nude statue since Roman times. In it Donatello went beyond the classical ideal by bringing in the dimension of personal expressiveness. Although he was greatly attracted to the classical ideal in art, Donatello's sculpture was less idealized and more naturalistic than that of ancient Greece. He chose to portray the biblical shepherd, David—slayer of the giant Goliath and later to be king of the Jews—as an adolescent youth rather than as a robust young man. The sculptor celebrated the sensuality of the boy's body by clothing him only in hat and boots. It is not so much the face, but every shift in the figure's weight and angle that is expressive. The figure's position is derived from classical contrapposto. The few nudes that appear in medieval art show no sensual appeal; to the medieval mind, nudity was associated with pagan idols. Because Greco-Roman "pagan idols" were used as artistic models during the humanist enlightenment, the unclothed figure reappeared as a major subject even for religious art.

During the Renaissance, artists received growing support from the new class of wealthy merchants and bankers, such as the Medici family of Florence. It is likely that Donatello created his bronze DAVID as a private commission for Cosimo de Medici, for the courtyard of the Medici palace.

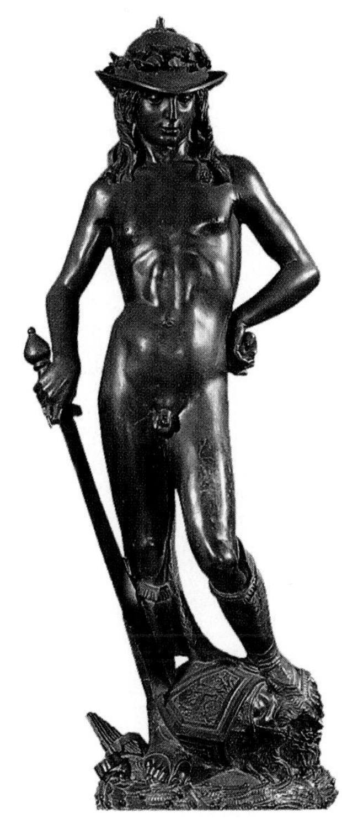

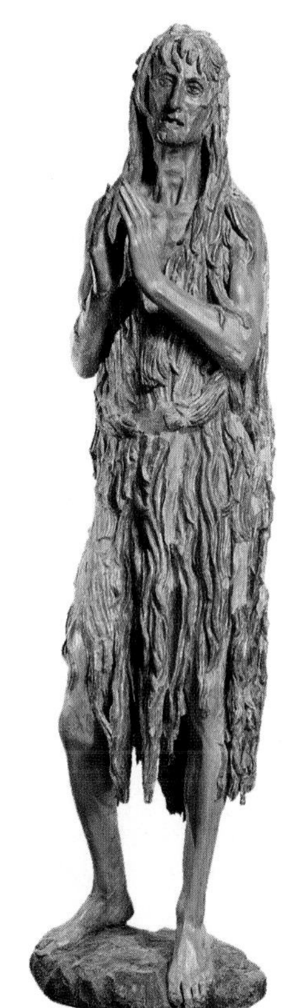

496 Donatello.
DAVID. c. 1425-1430.
Bronze. Height 62¼".
Museo Nazionale del Bargello, Florence.

497 Donatello.
MARY MAGDALEN. c. 1455.
Wood, partially gilded. Height 74".
Museo dell'Opera del Duomo, Florence.

A major influence on Donatello and other Renaissance artists was the renewal of Neoplatonist philosophy, embraced by the Medici family and their circle of philosophers, artists, historians, and humanists. These intellectuals believed that all sources of inspiration or revelation, whether from the Bible or classical mythology, are a means of ascending from earthly existence to mystical union with "the One." In this context, Donatello's DAVID was intended to be a symbol of divine beauty.

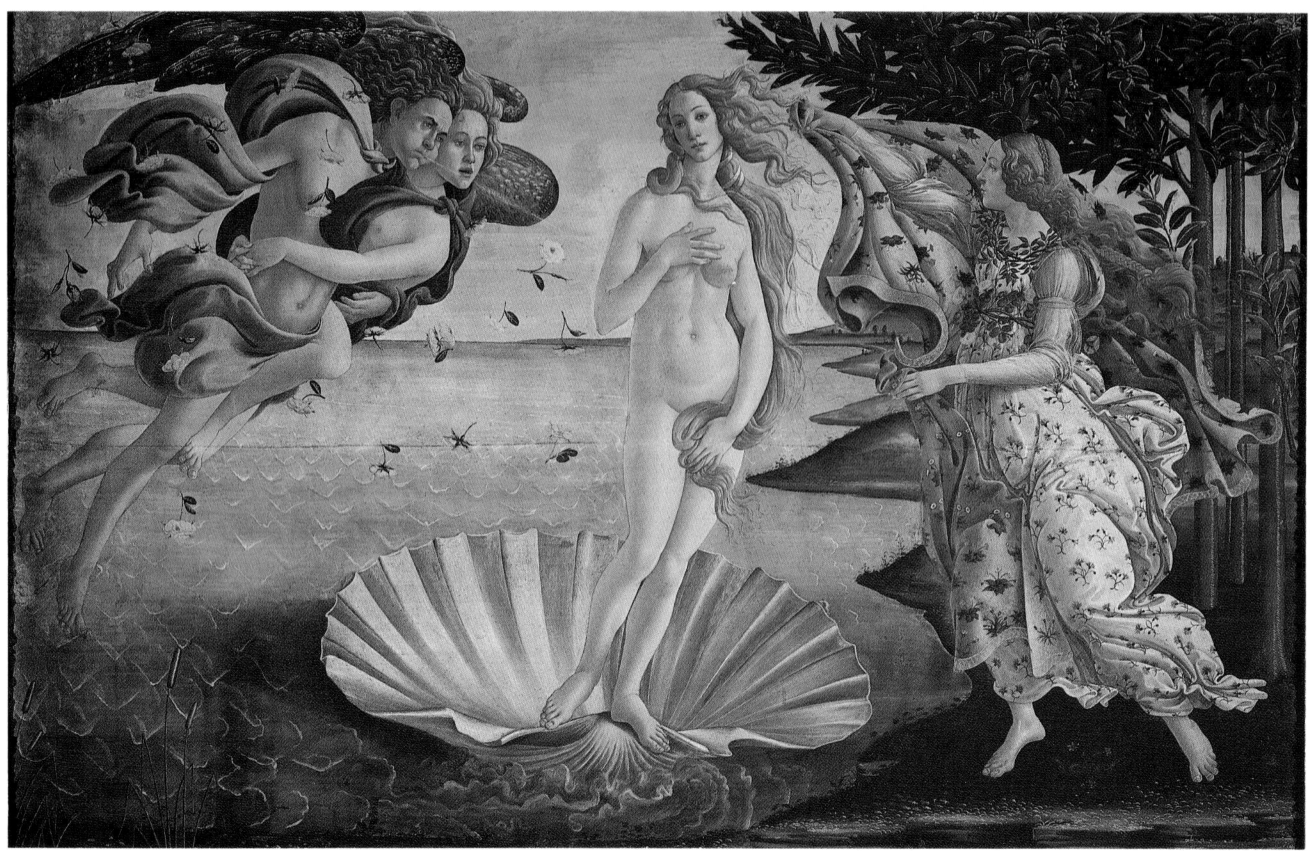

498 Sandro Botticelli.
BIRTH OF VENUS. c. 1480.
Tempera on canvas. 5'8⅞" × 9'1⅞".
Uffizi Gallery, Florence.

Donatello's work displayed a wide range of expression, from lyric joy to tragedy to extremes of religious passion. In contrast to the youthful and somewhat cocky DAVID, Donatello's MARY MAGDALEN is haggard and withdrawn—a forcefully expressive figure of old age and repentance. For this late work, Donatello chose painted wood, the favorite medium of northern Gothic sculptors.

Another Medici commission is Sandro Botticelli's BIRTH OF VENUS, one of the first paintings of an almost life-size nude since antiquity. The large painting, completed about 1480, depicts the Roman goddess of love just after she was born from the sea. She is being blown to shore by a handsome couple symbolizing the wind. As she arrives, Venus is greeted by a young woman who represents Spring. The lyric grace of Botticelli's lines shows Byzantine influence. The background is decorative and flat, giving no illusion of deep space. The figures appear to be in relief, not fully three-dimensional.

The posture and gestures of modesty were probably inspired by a third-century B.C. Greco-Roman sculpture of Venus that Botticelli would have seen in the Medici family collection (see page 326). In her posture of introspection and repose, Botticelli's Venus combines the classical Greek idealized human figure with a Renaissance concern for thought and feeling.

It was revolutionary for an artist working within the context of a Christian society to place a nude "pagan" goddess at the center of a large painting, in a position previously reserved for the Virgin Mary. Botticelli's apparent repudiation of Christian values was—like Donatello's—based on Neoplatonist philosophy. Botticelli's ethereal Venus was intended to portray divine love—a celestial Venus.

The High Renaissance

Between about 1490 and 1530—the period known as the High Renaissance—Italian art reached a peak of accomplishment in the cities of Florence, Rome, and Venice. The three artists who epitomized the period were Leonardo, Michelangelo, and Raphael (see page 63). They developed a style of art that was calm, balanced, and idealized, reconciling Christian theology with Greek philosophy and the science of the day.

Leonardo da Vinci was motivated by an insatiable curiosity and an optimistic belief in the human ability to understand the fascinating phenomena of the physical world. He believed that art and science are two means to the same end: knowledge.

Leonardo's investigative and creative mind is revealed in his journals, in which he documented his research in notes and drawings (see also page 133). His notebooks are filled with studies of anatomy and ideas for mechanical devices, explorations that put him in the forefront of the scientific development of his time. His study of an EMBRYO IN THE WOMB has a few errors, yet much of the drawing is so accurate that it could serve as an example in one of today's medical textbooks.

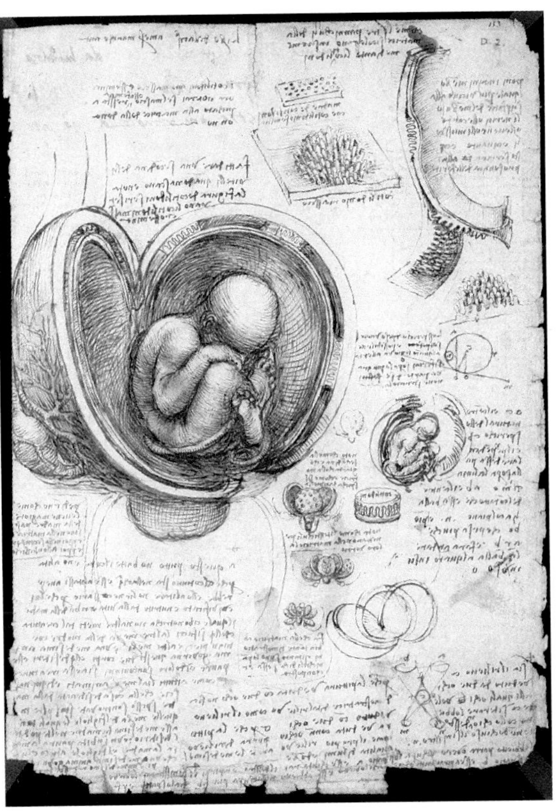

499 Leonardo da Vinci.
EMBRYO IN THE WOMB. c. 1510.
Pen and ink. 11⅞" × 8⅜".
Royal Library, Windsor Castle. © 1992 Her Majesty Queen Elizabeth II.

Leonardo was one of the first to give a clear description of the *camera obscura*, an optical device that captures light images in much the same way as the human eye (see page 172). The concept of photography began with the Renaissance desire to create an equivalent to our visual perception of reality.

In the famous ILLUSTRATION OF PROPORTIONS OF THE HUMAN FIGURE, Leonardo further developed a concept of Roman architect Vitruvius regarding the relationship between ideal human proportions, the circle, and the square. Ancient teaching, predating Roman times, held that the square symbolized the microcosm, or the finite world, and the circle symbolized the macrocosm, or the infinite cosmic sphere.

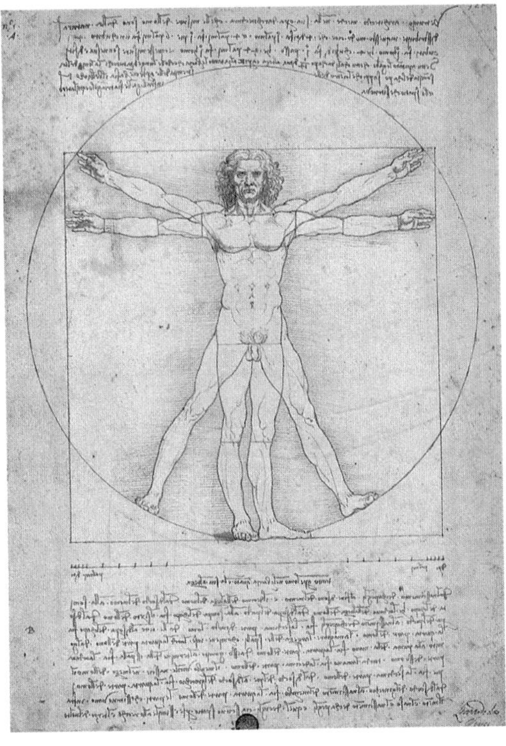

500 Leonardo da Vinci.
ILLUSTRATION OF PROPORTIONS OF THE HUMAN FIGURE.
c. 1485-1490.
Pen and ink. 13½" × 9¾".
Academy of Fine Arts, Venice.

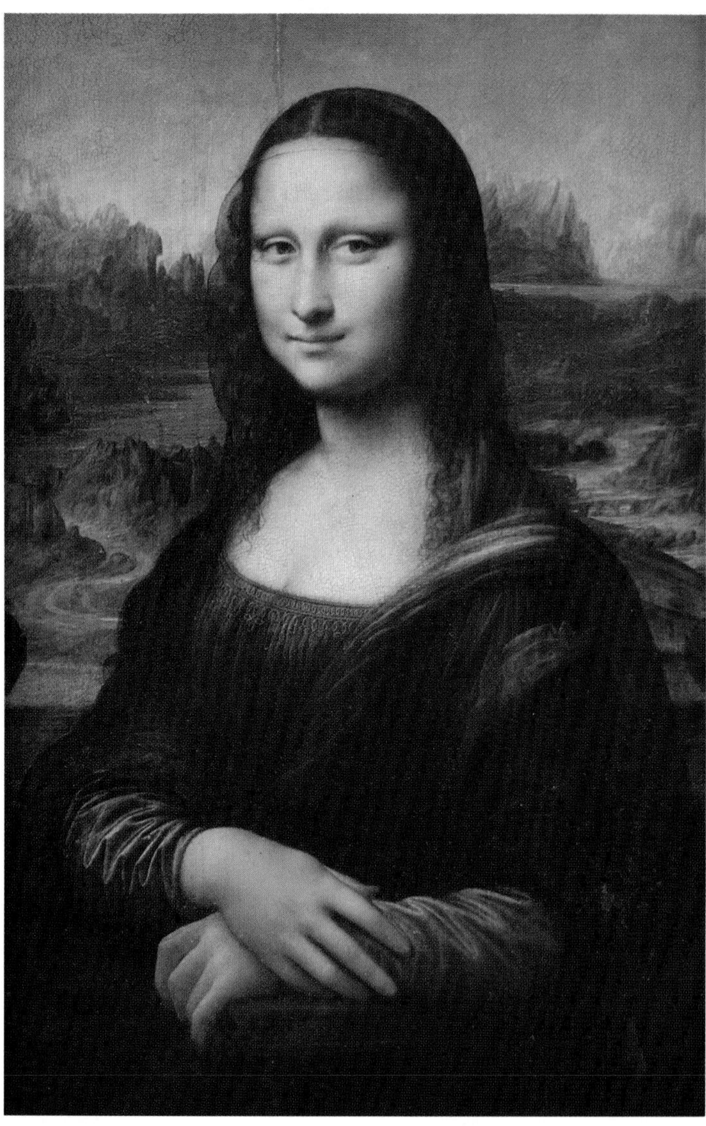

501 Leonardo da Vinci.
MONA LISA. c. 1503-1506.
Oil on wood. 30¼" × 21".
Musée du Louvre, Paris.

So frequently has Leonardo's world-famous portrait of MONA LISA been reproduced that it has become a cliché and the source of innumerable spoofs. Despite this overexposure, it is worthy of careful attention. It was one of Leonardo's favorite paintings. We can still be intrigued by the mysterious mood evoked by the faint smile and the strange, otherworldly landscape. The ambiguity is heightened by the hazy light quality that gives an amazing sense of atmosphere around the figure. This soft blurring of the edges—in Leonardo's words, "without lines or borders in the manner of smoke"—achieved through subtle value gradations, is called *sfumato* and was invented by Leonardo.[1] The effect, heightened by chiaroscuro (see page 74), amazed and impressed his contemporaries. MONA LISA's rich, luminous surface was achieved through the application of glazes (thin, translucent layers of paint).

The impact of Renaissance humanism becomes apparent when we compare THE LAST SUPPER by Leonardo da Vinci with the Byzantine mosaic CHRIST PANTOCRATOR on page 333. We must look up to the large Byzantine image of Christ, situated high in a dome; Leonardo's Christ sits across the table from us. The Byzantine mosaic is a stylized icon; Christ and his disciples are real people in an earthly setting. In his painting, Leonardo depicted the everyday world as one with the divine.

The naturalist style of the work contains a hidden geometry, which structures the design and strengthens the painting's symbolic content. The interior is based on a one-point linear perspective system (see page 61), with a single vanishing point in the middle of the composition, behind the head of Christ. Leonardo placed Christ in the center, at the point of greatest implied depth, associating him with infinity. Over Christ's head an architectural pediment suggests a halo, further setting him off from the irregular shapes and movements of the agitated disciples on either side. In contrast to the distraught figures surrounding him, Christ is shown with his arms outstretched in a gesture of acceptance, his image a stable triangle.

For a view and discussion of the current restoration of THE LAST SUPPER, see page 370.

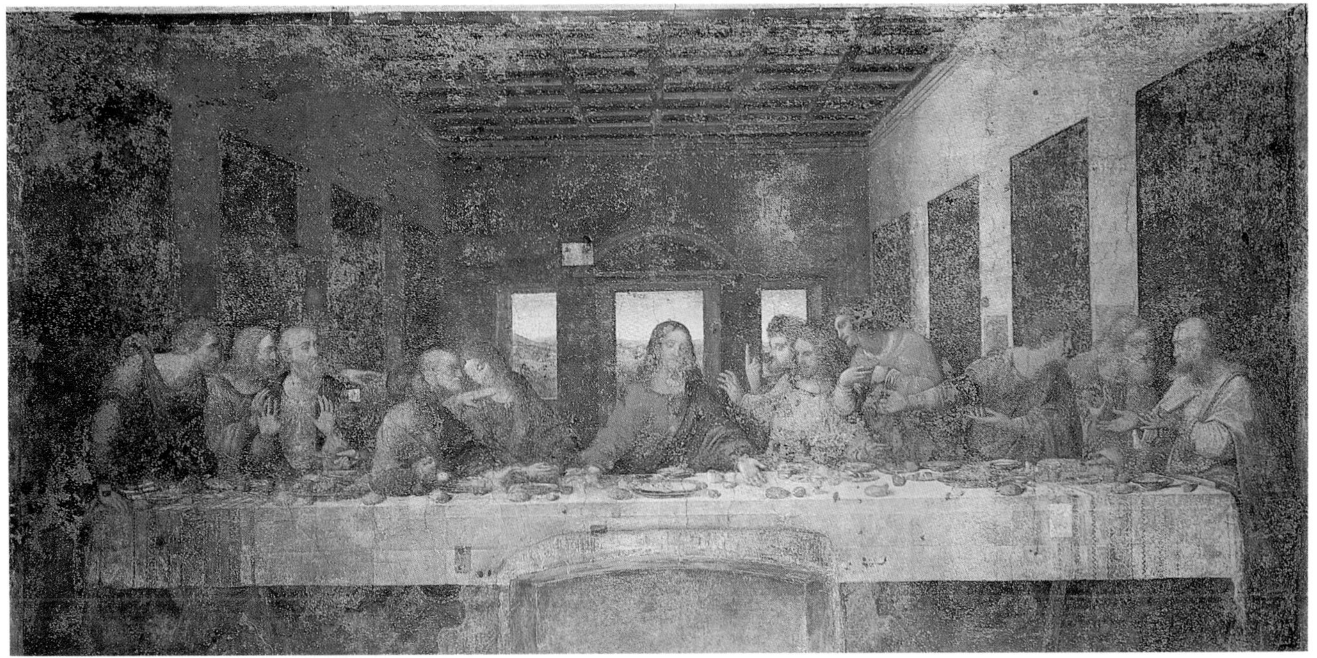

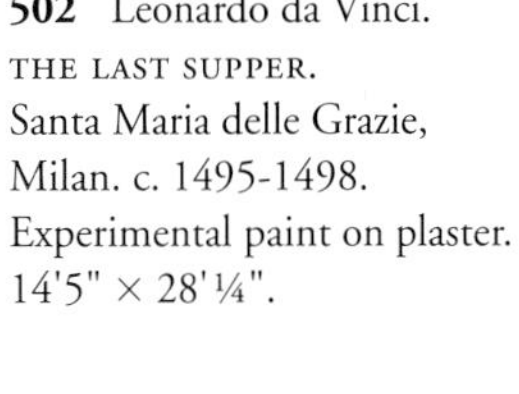

502 Leonardo da Vinci.
THE LAST SUPPER.
Santa Maria delle Grazie,
Milan. c. 1495-1498.
Experimental paint on plaster.
14'5" × 28'¼".

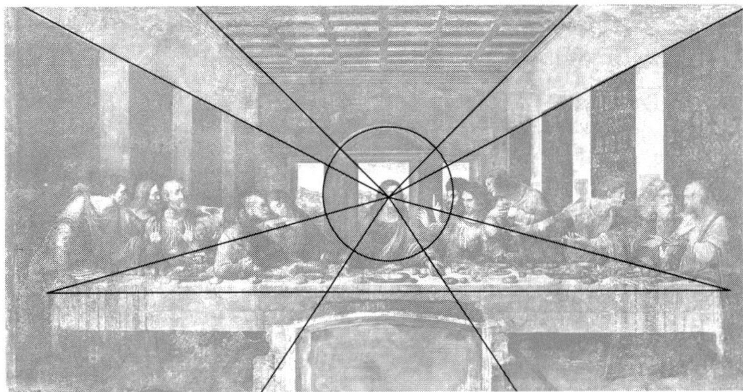

a Perspective lines as both organizing structure and symbol of content.

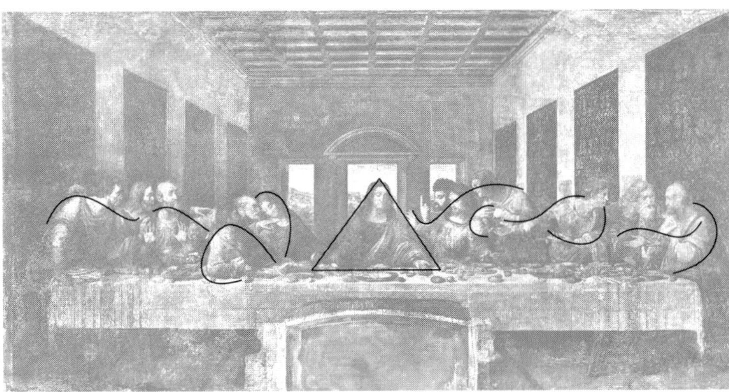

b Christ's figure as stable equilateral triangle, contrasting with active turmoil of the Disciples.

LEONARDO DA VINCI (1452–1519)

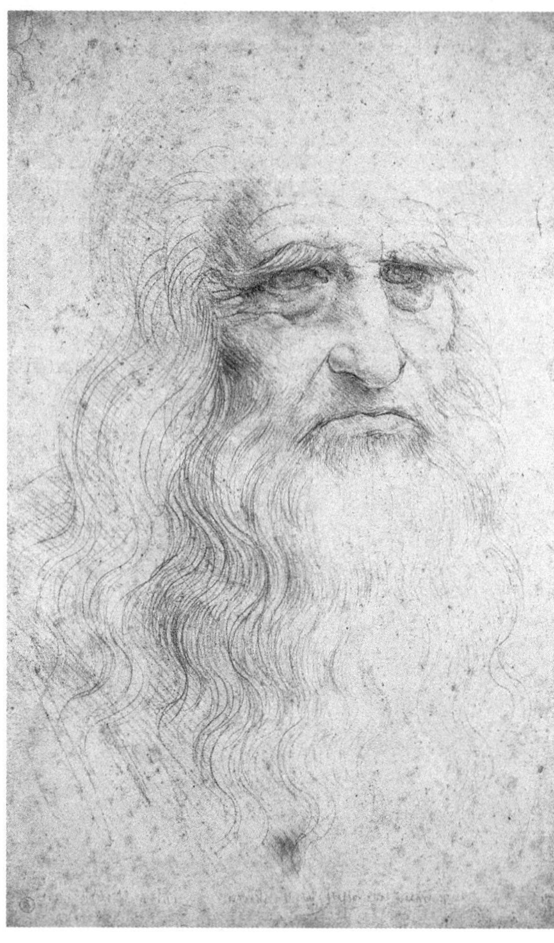

503 Leonardo da Vinci. SELF-PORTRAIT. c. 1512. Chalk on paper. 13" × 8¼". Biblioteca Reale, Turin, Italy.

Leonardo da Vinci—painter, sculptor, architect, town planner, writer, musician, scientist, engineer, and inventor—is the prototypical "Renaissance man," an extremely versatile individual with a record of high achievement in many fields.

Leonardo was the illegitimate son of a young notary, Piero da Vinci, and a peasant girl of whom we know nothing. He grew up an only child in his father's household, then in his mid-teens was apprenticed to Andrea del Verrochio, a leading artist in nearby Florence. Botticelli was one of his fellow apprentices.

Leonardo grew into a magnetic young man—tall, handsome, strong, graceful, charming, and endlessly talented. He played the lute, sang beautifully, and made fascinating conversation. People loved to be near him, yet he remained essentially solitary. He formed few friendships over the course of his life, and he never married.

At age thirty he began seventeen years in the service of the Duke of Milan, primarily as a military engineer and secondarily as a court painter, sculptor, and architect. He also entertained the court as a musician and satirist and designed scenery and costumes for pageants. During this period he painted several important works, including THE LAST SUPPER.

It was also in Milan that he started to keep his notebooks. After his few paintings, Leonardo's notebooks are his great legacy. They contain a lifetime of observations, inventions, and plans, all drawn in meticulous detail and annotated in secretive mirror writing. The range of subjects is enormous: mathematics, anatomy, architecture, optics, botany, geology, cartography, aeronautics, mechanics, civil engineering, urban planning, hydraulics, and weaponry all captured Leonardo's interest.

After Milan fell to French invaders in 1499, Leonardo fled to Venice where he was again employed as a military engineer. From there he went to Florence and worked on a portrait of an obscure merchant's third wife, the MONA LISA. The French called him back to Milan in 1506. He stayed until they were driven out six years later; then he journeyed to Rome, hoping the pope would have use for him.

Now in his sixties, Leonardo was increasingly haunted by a sense of futility. No building or invention of his had ever been built, no sculpture cast. Patrons had used his endless skills in frivolous or ignoble ways. Bored with what he could already do exquisitely well, he had left many paintings unfinished and ruined others with technical experiments.
"Tell me if anything at all was done," he wrote over and over in his last notebooks. "Tell me if anything at all . . ."[2]

Yet what little he had finished was so spectacular that his fame was well established. In 1516, the new King of France, Francis I, offered Leonardo a house, a stipend, and the title of First Painter and Engineer and Architect to the King. The title was a formality; Francis expected nothing in return but the honor of the great man's presence and the pleasure of his conversation. Leonardo died in Cloux, near Aboise, France, in 1519.

MICHELANGELO BUONARROTI (1475–1564)

Michelangelo Buonarroti was so greatly admired by his contemporaries that the poet Aristo referred to him as "Michael, more than human, Angel divine." Two biographies of Michelangelo were published in his lifetime. His noble, if irascible, character and his mistrust of human nature—including his own—make his life one of the most interesting known to us from the sixteenth century.

Michelangelo's father was a member of the minor nobility of Florence, a lazy, mean-spirited man who merely lived off the remains of the family fortune. Michelangelo's mother was unable to nurse him, so the infant was sent to stay with a wet nurse. The nurse's husband was a quarry worker in an area where stonecutting was a way of life. Michelangelo returned to his parents only for visits because his mother continued to suffer poor health. She died when Michelangelo was six years old. For four more years he continued to live as the son of the stonecutter and his wife, visiting his father only occasionally. He could neither read nor write, but he learned to use hammer and chisel.

When he was ten, his father remarried and Michelangelo returned home and was enrolled in school for the first time. In three years, he learned to read and write in Italian but absorbed little else. Michelangelo drew whenever he could and neglected his other studies. He decided to leave school to become an artist, starting as an apprentice to the painter Ghirlandaio. Pride in the family's social status was behind his father's opposition to his apprenticeship and to Michelangelo's later insistence that painting and sculpture required a high order of thinking (not just manual dexterity) and were therefore among the liberal arts. His father and uncles looked down on artists and thought it a disgrace to have one in the house. Michelangelo's father never realized the importance of the arts, even when Michelangelo gained fame and fortune.

After a year, Michelangelo transferred to the school in the Medici gardens, where he was inspired by the beauty of the Medici collection of contemporary Italian, ancient Greek, and Roman art. He studied there for several years, in the company of the leading artists and scholars of the time. During the turmoil following the death of his patron Lorenzo de Medici, Michelangelo left Florence for Rome. In Rome he completed the first of his major sculptures including the PIETÀ (see page 102) at age twenty-four. His handling of the difficult subject and the beautiful finish of the work established his reputation and led to important commissions, including the DAVID (see next page), when he returned to Florence. For the rest of his life, he went back and forth between Florence and Rome.

Although he considered himself primarily a sculptor, Michelangelo's painting on THE SISTINE CHAPEL ceiling is one of the world's most acclaimed works of art. The project was made Herculean by Michelangelo himself; although the original plan called for twelve figures, Michelangelo included over three hundred.

At the time Michelangelo was working on the Sistine ceiling, Raphael was commissioned to paint a series of frescoes including THE SCHOOL OF ATHENS (see page 63) in three rooms adjoining the chapel. Following the ceiling's unveiling, Raphael changed to a style clearly influenced by Michelangelo.

No other artist has left such masterful accomplishments in four major art forms: sculpture, painting, architecture—and poetry. If he had not been a supreme architect, sculptor, and painter, Michelangelo might have been known to us as a writer. Perhaps the most revealing writings are his poems, which express his innermost feelings about his mind and soul as well as his art.

In his later years, in addition to architectural commissions—including the rebuilding of St. Peter's in Rome—Michelangelo worked as a city planner, completed some of his most important sculpture, and wrote many of his finest sonnets.

Michelangelo was very different from Leonardo, who was twenty-three years older. Michelangelo saw human beings as unique, almost godlike, while Leonardo saw them as one part of nature, which he viewed as a scientist as well as an artist. Michelangelo believed that in an artist's hands, "life" could be created through inspiration from God. For Michelangelo, sculpture and the process of its creation reflected people's struggle with their imperfect selves—souls in struggle, bound in their bodies.

Michelangelo's life spanned nearly a century. From the time he was apprenticed at age thirteen until six days before his death at eighty-nine he worked continuously. His last words were "I regret that I have not done enough for the salvation of my soul and that I am dying just as I am beginning to learn the alphabet of my profession."[3]

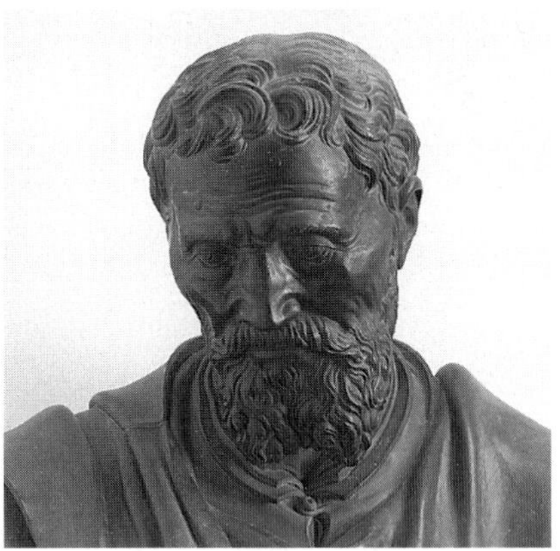

504 Daniele da Volterra. MICHELANGELO BUONARROTI. 1565. Detail of bronze bust. Height of entire work 32". Accademia, Florence.

In 1501, when he was twenty-six years old, Michelangelo obtained a commission from the city of Florence to carve a figure of David from an 18-foot block of marble that had been badly cut and then abandoned by another sculptor. The biblical hero David was an important symbol of freedom from tyranny for Florence, which had just become a republic. Other Renaissance artists had already given the city images of the young David (see page 345), but it was Michelangelo's figure that gave the most powerful expression to the idea of David as hero, the defender of a just cause.

Michelangelo took DAVID's stance, with the weight of the body on one foot, from Greek sculpture (see page 323). But the gestures, positions of the hands, and a tense frown indicate anxiety and readiness for conflict. Through changes in proportion and the depiction of inner feeling, Michelangelo humanized, then made monumental, the classical Greek athlete. Compare Michelangelo's DAVID with the earlier DAVID by Donatello and the later one by Bernini (page 361).

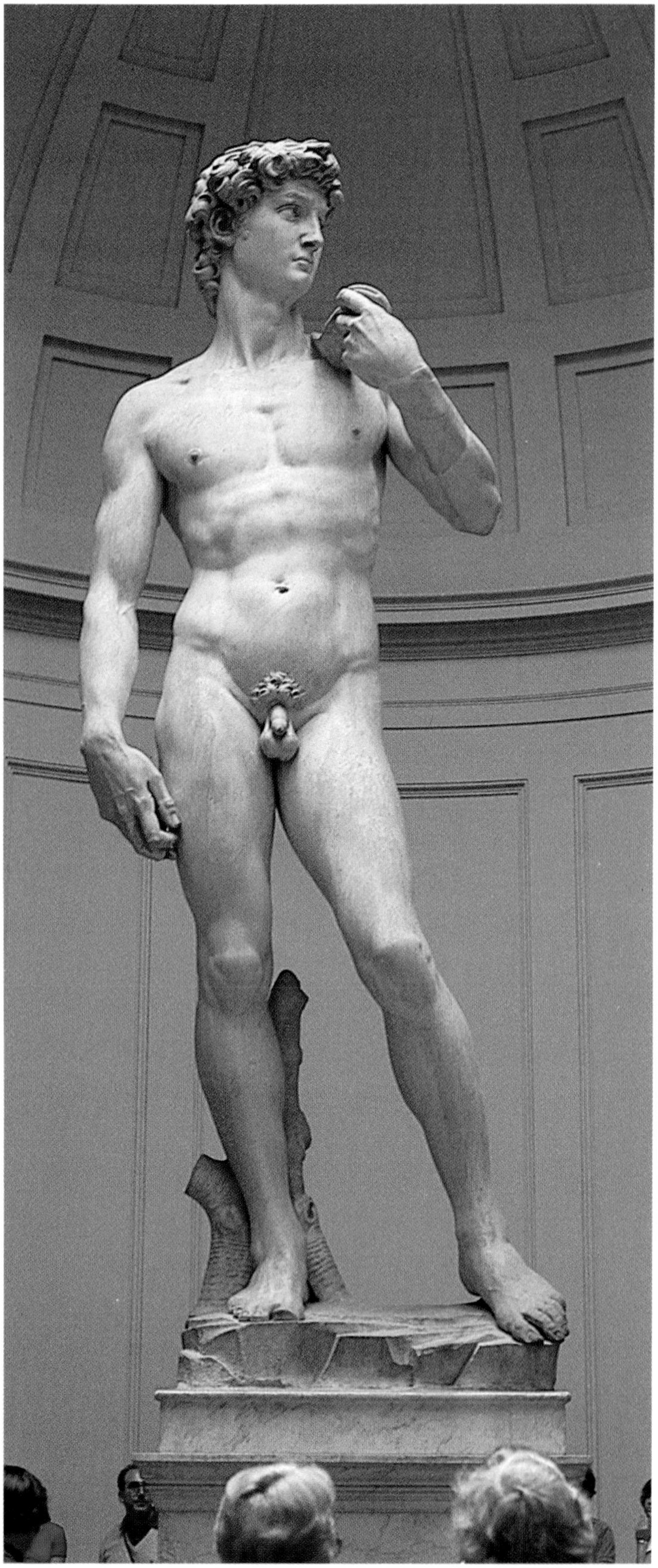

505 a Michelangelo Buonarroti.
DAVID. 1501-1504.
Marble. Height of figure 14'3".
Accademia, Florence.
b Detail of DAVID.

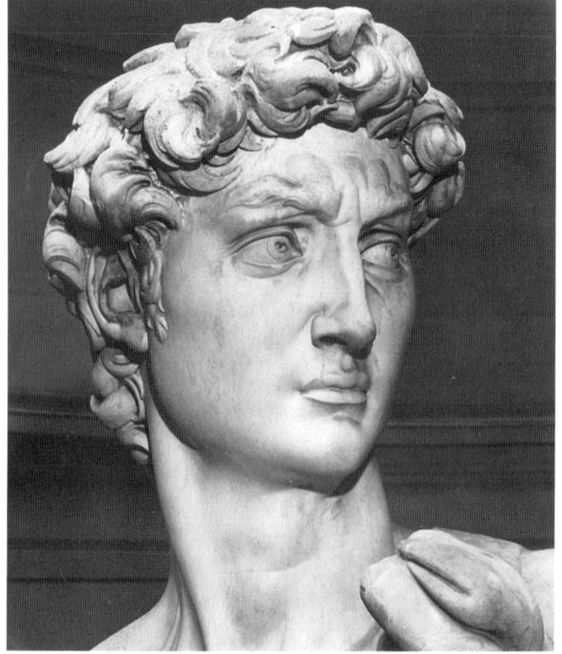

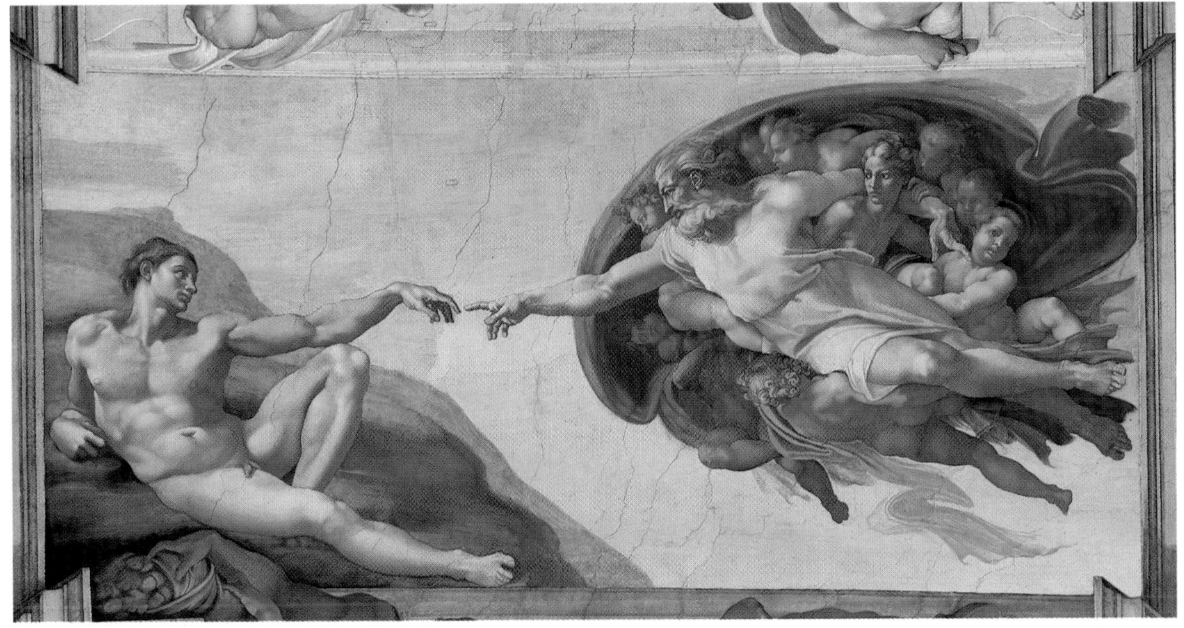

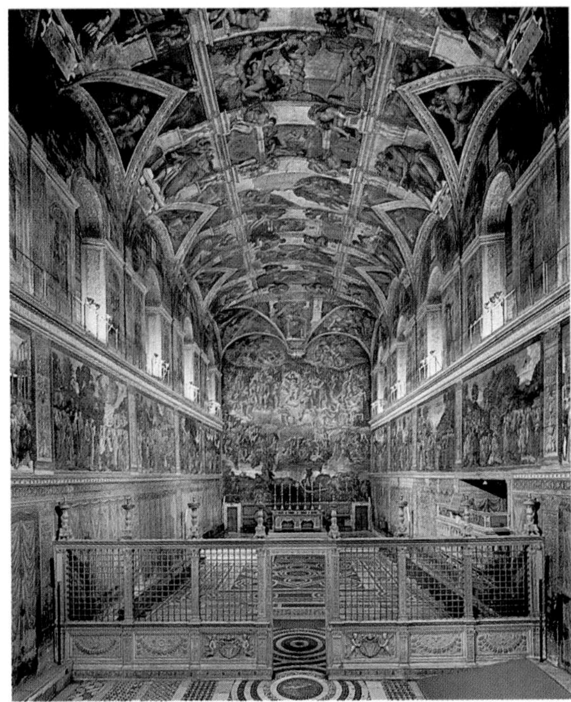

506 Michelangelo Buonarroti.
Frescoes on the ceiling and walls of THE SISTINE CHAPEL. Vatican, Rome. 1508-1512.
a THE CREATION OF ADAM, ceiling panel after restoration.
b THE SISTINE CHAPEL before restoration.

Michelangelo worked for three years on this sculpture. When it was finished and placed in the town square, the citizens of Florence were filled with admiration for the work and its creator. With this achievement, Michelangelo became known as the greatest sculptor since the Greeks.

Equally praised as a painter, Michelangelo had just begun work on what he thought would be his main sculptural commission, the tomb of Pope Julius II, when the pope all but forced him to accept a commission to paint THE SISTINE CHAPEL in the Vatican. Michelangelo began work on the ceiling in 1508 and finished it four years later. The surface is divided into three zones. In the highest are nine panels of scenes from Genesis, including THE CREATION OF ADAM. The next level contains prophets and sibyls (female prophets). The lowest level consists of groups of figures, some of which have been identified as Christ's biblical ancestors. *The Last Judgment,* painted later, fills the end wall above the altar.

The most-admired composition on the ceiling is the majestic portrayal of THE CREATION OF ADAM, in which God reaches out to give life to the first man. Eve, not yet mortal, stares at Adam from behind God's left arm.

It was long believed that Michelangelo intentionally used muted colors in the chapel frescoes, but a restoration and cleaning project begun in the 1970s revealed surprisingly brilliant colors. The discovery prompted a controversy over whether overcleaning had seriously distorted Michelangelo's painting (see page 370).

As the Early Renaissance was unfolding in Italy, there was a parallel new interest in realism in Northern Europe, where artists were even more concerned than the Italians with depicting life in the real world. Yet lingering medieval attitudes made the fifteenth-century art of the north as much a late phase of Gothic style as an early Renaissance style.

THE RENAISSANCE IN NORTHERN EUROPE

Jan van Eyck, the father of Flemish painting, was the leading artist in the low countries of Belgium, the Netherlands, and Luxembourg. He was one of the first to use linseed oil as a paint medium (see pages 151–152). The fine consistency and flexibility of the new oil medium made it possible to achieve a brilliance and transparency of color previously unattainable. His oil paintings remain in almost perfect condition, attesting to his skill and knowledge of materials. Italian artists admired and were influenced by the innovations of Van Eyck and other Flemish and Dutch artists.

On the same type of small wooden panels previously used for tempera painting, Van Eyck painted in minute detail, achieving an illusion of depth, directional light, mass, rich implied textures, and the physical likenesses of particular people. Human figures and their interior settings took on a new, believable presence. In spite of Van Eyck's realistic detail, GIOVANNI ARNOLFINI AND HIS BRIDE has a Gothic quality in its traditional symbolism, formality, and vertical emphasis of the figures.

At the time the portrait of the Arnolfini wedding was commissioned, the church did not always require the presence of clergy for a valid marriage contract, and thus it was easy to deny that a marriage had taken place. Van Eyck's painting is thought to be a testament to the oath of marriage between Giovanni Arnolfini and Giovanna Cenami. As witness to the event, Jan van Eyck placed his signature and the date, 1434, directly above the mirror—and he himself appears to be reflected in the mirror (see detail on page 86).

Today the painting's Christian iconography, well understood in the fifteenth century, needs explanation. Many of the ordinary objects portrayed with great care have sacred significance. The single lighted candle in the chandelier symbolizes the presence of Christ; the amber beads and the sunlight shining through them are symbols of purity; the dog indicates marital fidelity. The bride's holding up her skirt suggestively in front of her stomach may indicate her willingness to bear children. Green, a symbol of fertility, was often worn at weddings.

In the early sixteenth century in Germany, Northern Renaissance master Albrecht Dürer further developed the practice of presenting instructive symbolism through detailed realism. Minute details in THE GREAT PIECE OF TURF (page 21) reveal careful observation, while THE KNIGHT, DEATH AND THE DEVIL (page 43) combines Christian symbols with familiar subjects in the Flemish tradition of Van Eyck. Other Northern Renaissance masters include German painter Hans Holbein (page 92), and Flemish painters Pieter de Hooch (page 90) and Pieter Bruegel (page 356).

Bruegel was an independent thinker of far-reaching vision. As a young man he traveled extensively in France and Italy. Under the influence of Italian Renaissance painting, Bruegel developed a grand sense of composition and spatial depth. The focus of Bruegel's paintings was the lives and surroundings of common people, and toward the end of his life he did a series of paintings representing the activities of the twelve months of the year.

507 Jan van Eyck.
GIOVANNI ARNOLFINI AND HIS BRIDE. 1434.
Tempera and oil on panel. 33" × 22½".
Reproduced by courtesy of the Trustees, The National Gallery, London.

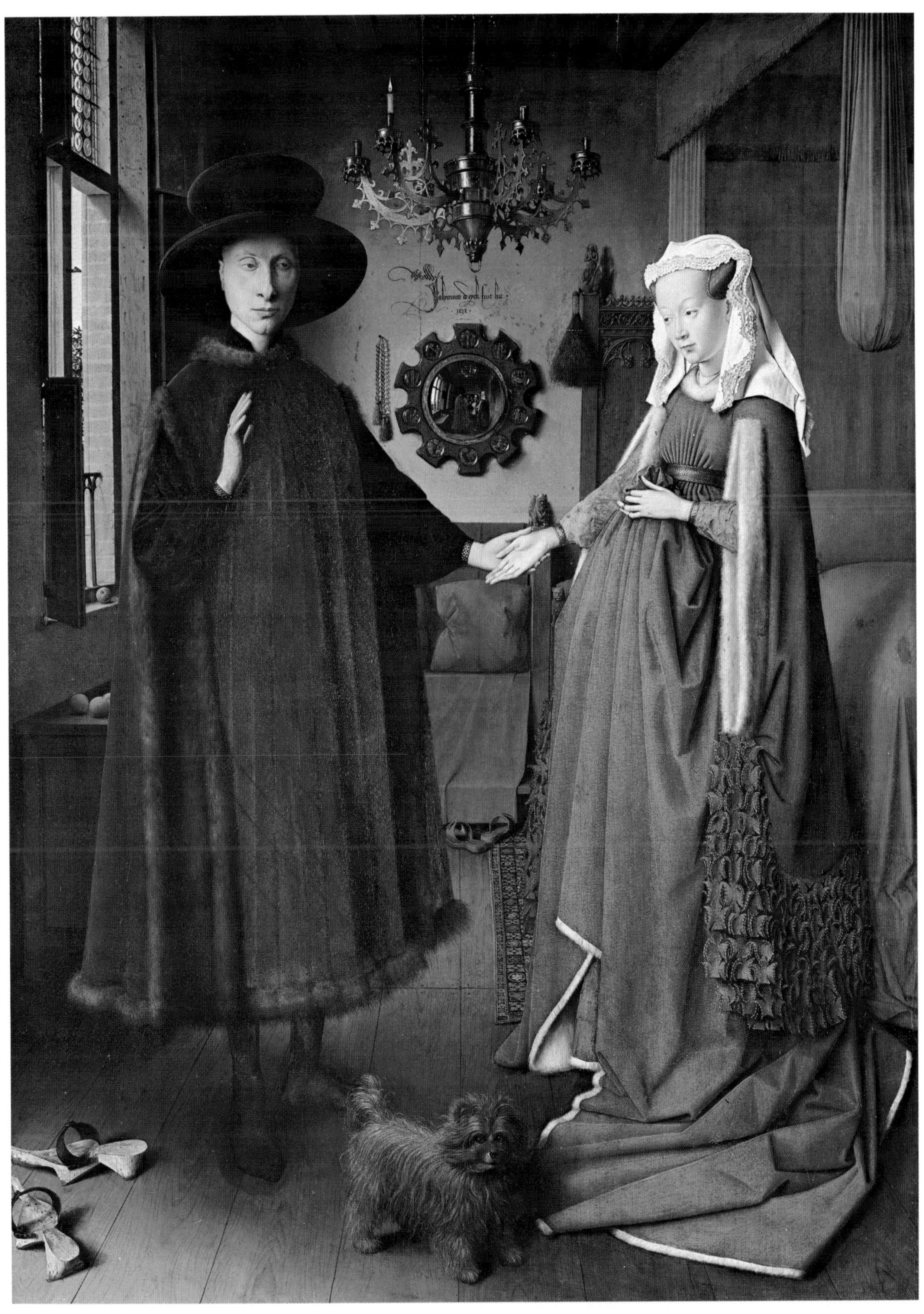

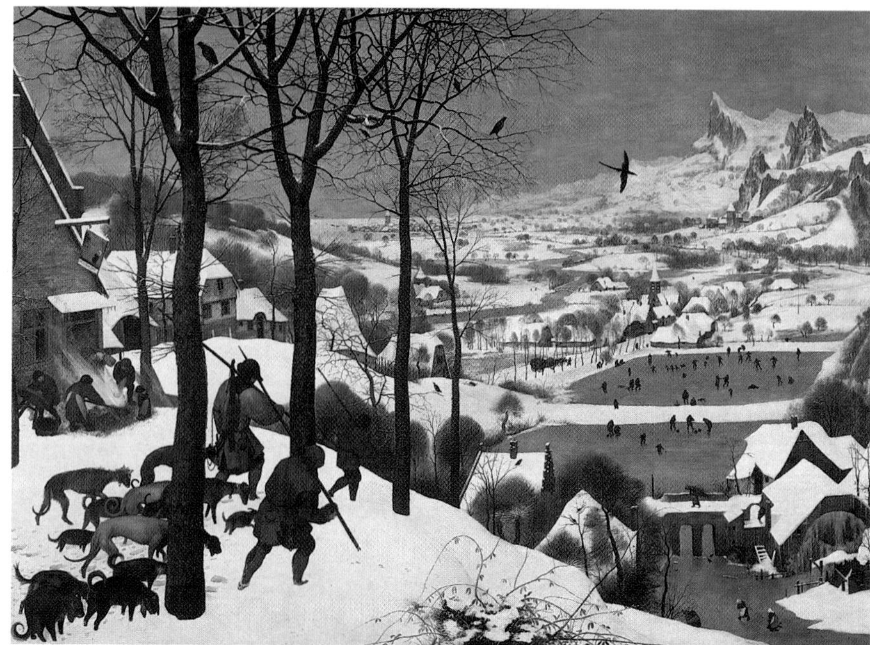

508 Pieter Bruegel.
THE RETURN OF THE HUNTERS. 1565.
Oil on panel. 46½" × 63¾".
Kunsthistorisches Museum, Vienna.

509 The Limbourg Brothers.
FEBRUARY, from LES TRÈS RICHES HEURES DU DUC DE BERRY. 1413-1416.
Musée Condé, Chantilly, France.

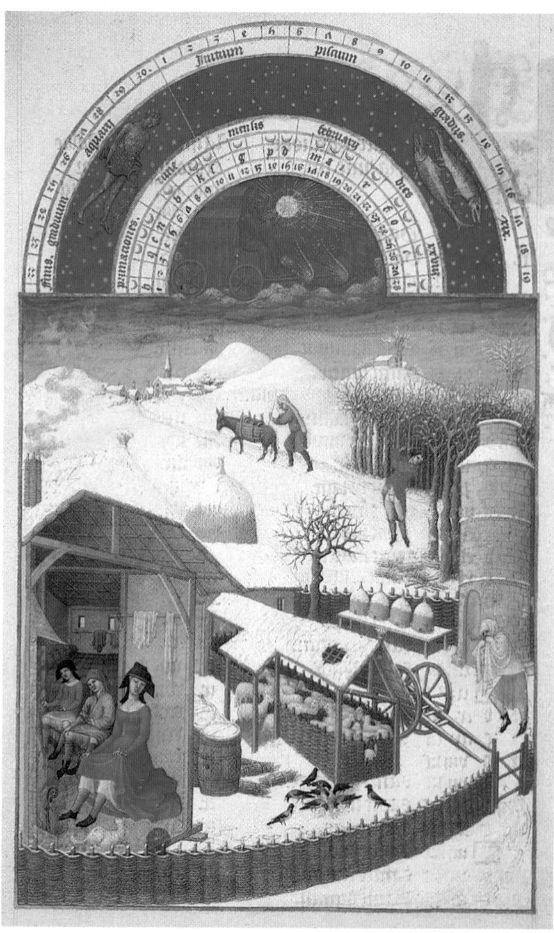

One of the most beloved of the series is his painting for January, RETURN OF THE HUNTERS. Following the precedent set by manuscript painters (illuminators) of medieval calendars, who depicted each month according to the agricultural labor appropriate to it, Bruegel shows peasants augmenting their winter diet by hunting. What is new here is the emphasis on nature's winter mood rather than on human activity. The illusion of deep space so important to this image came from the innovations of the Italians and was also inspired by Bruegel's journey over the Alps. Views from high vantage points are often seen in his work.

Compare Bruegel's painting with an illuminated page for FEBRUARY from a late Gothic book of hours painted by the Limbourg brothers in the early fifteenth century, before the Renaissance influence reached the north. Notice how far landscape painting evolved in just one hundred fifty years. Although there is a huge difference in the way space is depicted, in both paintings there is attention to nature and the details of everyday life. Bruegel achieved greater naturalism by portraying what could be seen from one vantage point at a particular time; the Limbourg brothers implied various moments in time by creating an imaginary composite view.

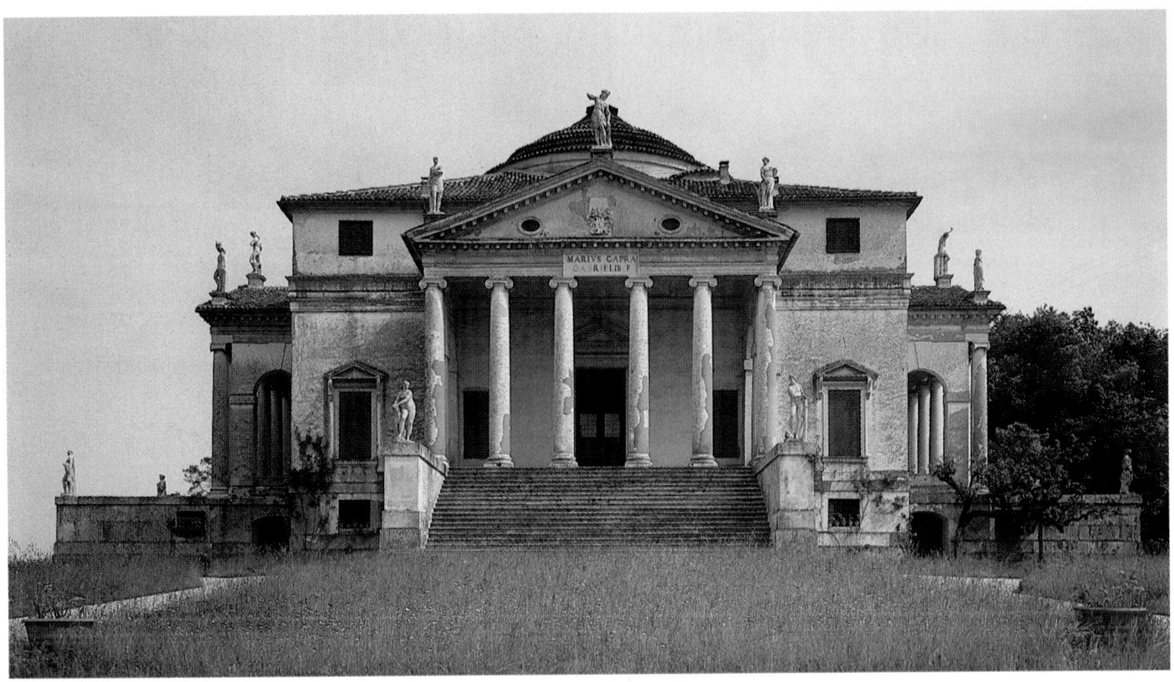

510 Andrea Palladio.
VILLA ROTONDA. Vicenza, Italy.
1567-1570.

LATE RENAISSANCE IN ITALY

The High Renaissance was followed by a period of turmoil, revolution, and new expectations. The early sixteenth century was a time of religious questioning and change that spawned the Protestant Reformation—the protest movement that sought to reform the western Christian Church and resulted in the division into Protestant and Catholic churches. The tensions and exaggerations brought on by social change were apparent in the major changes in art.

In the fifteenth century, Renaissance architects, sculptors, and painters had gone to great lengths to acquire knowledge of Greek and Roman ideas and to employ these ideas, along with contemporary concepts, in the creation of architecture they considered more beautiful than any done by their predecessors.

During the sixteenth century, architects made a deliberate effort to contradict classical rules. The most learned and influential architect was Andrea Palladio. His famous VILLA ROTONDA, or round villa, built near Vicenza, Italy, is intentionally unique, to the point of being capricious, yet reminiscent of the Roman Pantheon (see page 328). It has four identical sides, complete with porches resembling ancient temple facades, built around a central domed hall. The villa's design hardly satisfies the architectural goal of livability, but it was not intended for family living; it was designed for a retired monsignor as a kind of open summer house for social occasions. From its hilltop site, visitors standing in the central rotunda could enjoy four different views of the countryside.

Palladio's buildings had a major influence on English and American eighteenth-century architecture, one that can even be seen in some Post-Modern buildings of today. His villa, clearly separate from its natural surroundings, expresses a recurrent attitude in Western architecture: the separation of the humanmade from the natural.

By the sixteenth century, it had become increasingly difficult for artists to surpass such forebears as Raphael, Leonardo, and Michelangelo. While the ideas of the Renaissance spread north, Mediterranean artists also faced change. Mannerism,

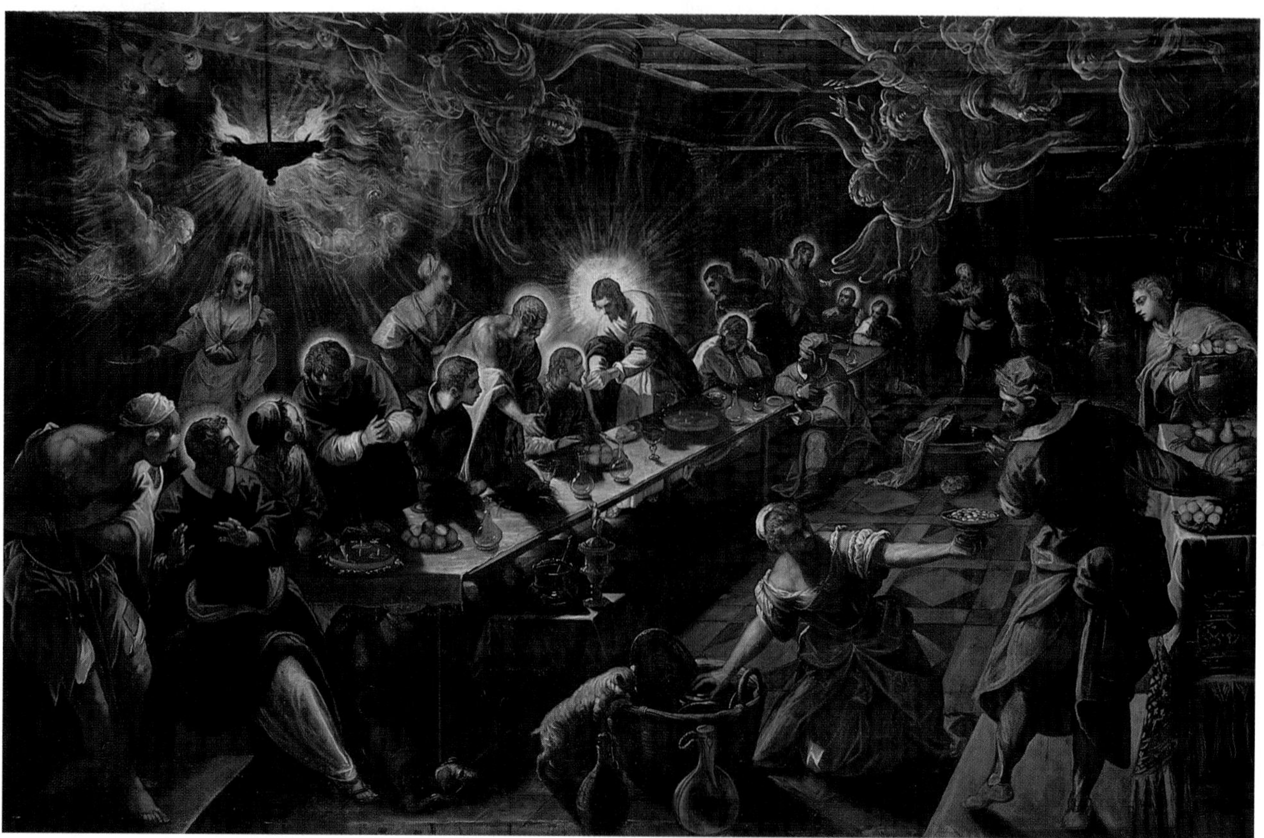

511 Jacopo Tintoretto.
THE LAST SUPPER. 1592-1594.
Oil on canvas. 12' × 18'8".
S. Giorgio Maggiore, Venice.

the key trend in southern Europe, dominated painting, sculpture, and architecture. Mannerist painters of the sixteenth century admired qualities of drama and emotion found in the late work of Michelangelo and Raphael. The younger generation exaggerated these qualities, sometimes in contrived or mannered ways, to achieve their own unique expression. Mannerism is characterized by distortions of perspective, scale, and proportion; exaggerated color; and increased value contrast—all aimed at provoking a sense of mystery and heightened emotion. The result was often ambiguous and disquieting, unlike the classical confidence inspired by High Renaissance art. Mannerism led from the High Renaissance of the early sixteenth century into Baroque art of the seventeenth century.

Paintings of Jacopo Tintoretto exhibit Mannerist qualities. His version of THE LAST SUPPER, completed when the artist was in his seventies, is a radical departure from Leonardo's calm, classical interpretation painted one hundred years earlier. After a lifetime working with the subject, Tintoretto transformed the earthly event into a supernatural vision. Christ seems farther away, distinguished only by a brilliant halo of light. The table, seen from a higher angle, is turned away from the picture plane in exaggerated perspective, creating a strong feeling of movement through diagonal forces. Angels appear overhead in the light and smoke of a blazing oil lamp. Disciples and attendants are caught in dramatic gestures at a moment of emotional intensity. Such vivid exaggerations of light, movement, spatial tension, and theatrical gesture became major storytelling devices for energetic seventeenth-century artists.

BAROQUE

The era known as the Baroque period includes the seventeenth and most of the eighteenth centuries in Europe. Although Baroque generally refers to a period, the term is also used to describe the art that arose in Italy around 1600 and spread through much of Europe during the next two hundred years.

The Baroque period had far more varied styles than the Renaissance, yet much of the art shows great energy and feeling, and a dramatic use of light, scale, and balance. The goal of balanced harmony achieved by Renaissance artists such as Raphael in his SCHOOL OF ATHENS (page 63) and Michelangelo in his DAVID was set aside first by Mannerists and later by Baroque artists as they explored more innovative uses of space and more intense ranges of light and shadow. Their art, with its frequent use of curves and countercurves, often appeals to the mind by way of the heart. Also, a new degree of vivid realism can be seen in compositions employing sharp diagonals and extreme foreshortening.

The Counter Reformation emerged in the late sixteenth and early seventeenth centuries as the Catholic Church's response to the Protestant Reformation and the growing impact of science. Many of the characteristics of the Baroque style were spawned and promoted by the Catholic Counter Reformation.

Michelangelo Merisi da Caravaggio's down-to-earth realism and dramatic use of light broke from Renaissance idealism and became the leading influences on other Baroque painters, north and south. Caravaggio created the most vivid and dramatic depictions of his time, using directed light and strong contrasts to guide the attention of the viewer and intensify the subject matter.

Emotional realism and a theatrical use of chiaroscuro, especially in Caravaggio's night effects (called *tenebrism*), influenced later Baroque painters such as Rubens, Rembrandt, and Zurbarán (see SAINT SERAPION, page 75). When displayed in a dark chapel, Caravaggio's paintings take on a lifelike quality intended to heighten the religious experience.

In THE CONVERSION OF SAINT PAUL, Caravaggio used light to create a blinding flash, symbolizing the evangelist's conversion: "And suddenly there shined around him a light from heaven: and he fell to the earth" (Acts 9:3). The figure of Paul, in Roman dress, is foreshortened and pushed into the foreground, presenting such a close view that we feel we are right there. In keeping with the supernatural character of the spiritual events he portrayed, Caravaggio evoked a feeling for the mystical dimension within the ordinary world. He wanted his paintings to be accessible and self-explanatory, and for this purpose he brought the emotional intensity of his own rowdy life to the stories of the Bible. Some of the clergy for whom he painted rejected his style; his emotional realism was too strong for people accustomed to idealized aristocratic images that demonstrated little more than gestures of piety.

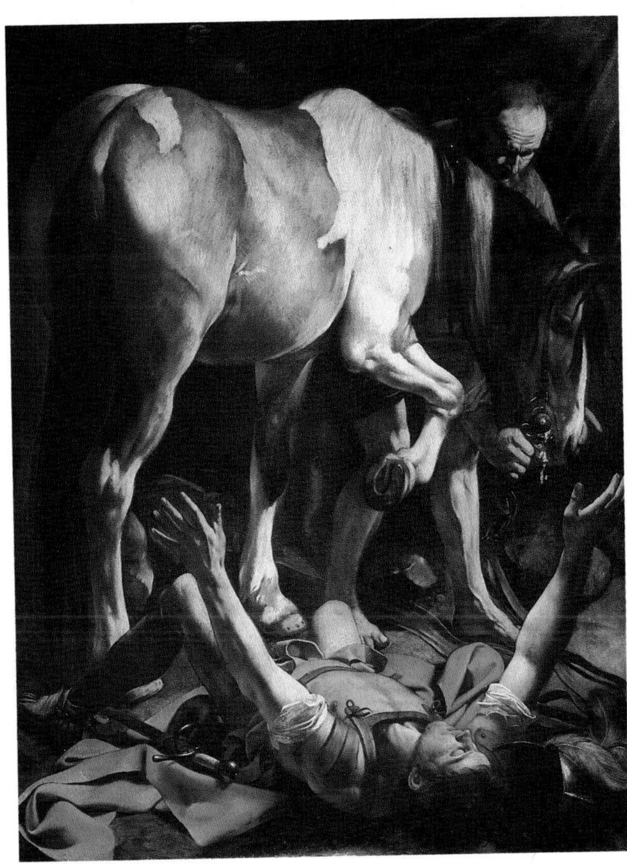

512 Michelangelo Merisi da Caravaggio.
THE CONVERSION OF SAINT PAUL. 1600-1601.
Oil on canvas. 100½" × 69".
Santa Maria del Popolo, Rome.

In post-Renaissance Rome, another artist who had as far-reaching an influence as Caravaggio was

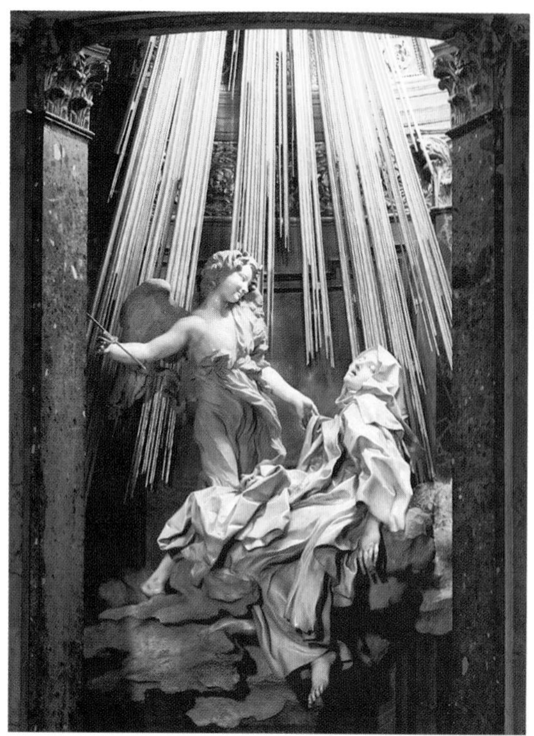

513 Gianlorenzo Bernini.
THE ECSTASY OF SAINT TERESA.
Detail of the altar, Cornaro Chapel,
Santa Maria della Vittoria, Rome. 1645-1652.
Marble. Life-size.

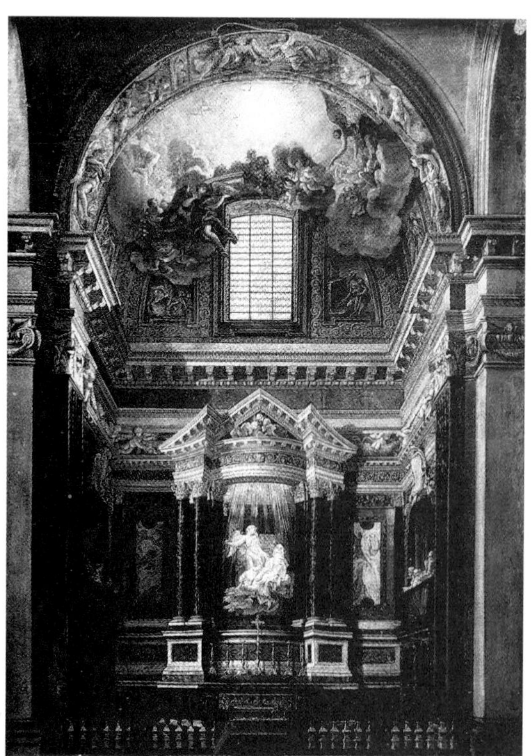

the sculptor and architect Gianlorenzo Bernini. Because Bernini's DAVID is life-size rather than monumental, viewers become engaged in the action. Rather than capture an introspective moment, as Michelangelo did (page 352), Bernini chose to depict David in a moment of tension, as he prepares to fling the stone at Goliath.

Bernini's elaborate orchestrations of the visual arts are the climax of Italian Baroque expression. The emotional intensity of his art is vividly apparent in his major work, THE ECSTASY OF SAINT TERESA. It features a life-size marble figure of the saint and depicts one of her visions as she recorded it in her diary. In this vision, she saw an angel who seemed to pierce her heart with a flaming arrow of gold, giving her great pain as well as pleasure and leaving her "all on fire with a great love of God."[4] Bernini made the visionary experience vivid by portraying the moment of greatest feeling, revealing spiritual passion through physical expression. Turbulent drapery heightens the emotional impact. His inventive departure from the naturalistic, classical norm soon influenced artists throughout Europe.

Bernini designed not only the figures of Saint Teresa and the angel but their altar setting and the entire CORNARO CHAPEL. Architecture, painting, and sculpture work together to enhance the drama of the central figures over the altar. Above the saint and her heavenly messenger, sunlight shines through a hidden window, illuminating the work in such a way that the figures appear to dematerialize. In box seats on either side of the altar, sculpted figures of the Cornaro family witness the event. Bernini intentionally crossed the lines usually drawn between architecture, painting, and sculpture, as well as those between illusion and reality. The complex scene is designed to be experienced as theater.

514 Gianlorenzo Bernini.
(18th-century painting by an unknown artist.)
CORNARO CHAPEL. 1645-1652.
Staatliches Museum, Schwerin, Germany.

Flemish painter Peter Paul Rubens, a renowned diplomat and humanist, was the most influential Baroque artist in Northern Europe. He studied painting in Antwerp, then traveled to Italy in 1600. During a stay of several years he was greatly influenced by the work of Michelangelo, and to a lesser degree by the work of Raphael, Leonardo, and Caravaggio. When Rubens returned north, he won increasing acclaim and patronage; being a sophisticated businessman, he enjoyed an aristocratic lifestyle. His work came to be in such demand by the nobility and royalty of Europe that he established a large studio with many assistants. The exuberant sensuality of his compositions took Baroque painting to new heights. Although Rubens was noted for the voluptuous quality of his nudes, there was a tendency for everything in his paintings to take on a similar sensuality. His free brushwork influenced many painters, including French and English masters, well into the nineteenth century.

THE RAPE OF THE DAUGHTERS OF LEUCIPPUS is based on a Greek legend. Rubens depicted the abduction of the daughters of the ancient Greek philosopher by the gods Castor and Pollux, who had fallen in love with them. The presence of two cupid figures and the expressions of both the men and the women suggest that this is a scene of passion—clearly not rape in the way we use the word today. The energy implied by the serpentine movement of the intertwined figures is typical of Baroque expression. An usually low eye level contributes to the monumental, superhuman quality of the figures and the event.

The natural human gestures and expressions in Bernini's and Caravaggio's work are also characteristic of the painting of Diego Rodríguez de Silva y Velázquez in Spain. Velázquez used grays to heighten the limited color in his painting of himself at work on the large canvas now known as LAS MENINAS (THE MAIDS OF HONOR). The Infanta Marguerita, the blonde daughter of the king, is

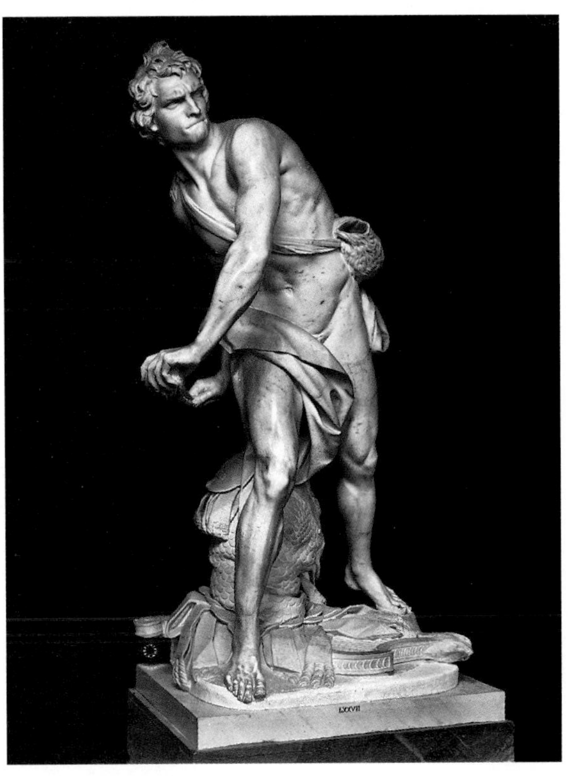

515 Gianlorenzo Bernini.
DAVID. 1623.
Marble. Life-size.

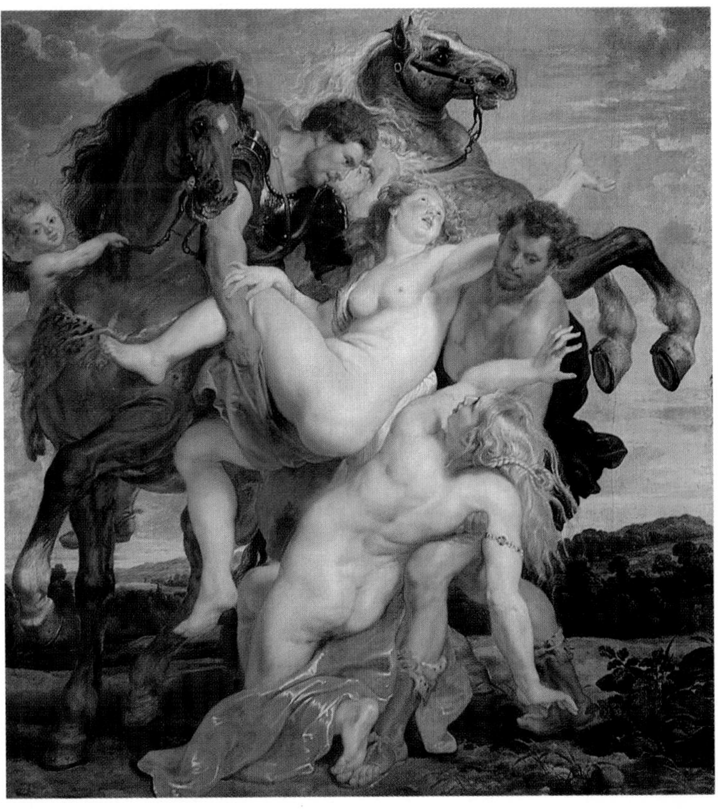

516 Peter Paul Rubens.
THE RAPE OF THE DAUGHTERS OF LEUCIPPUS. c. 1616-1617.
Oil on canvas. 7'3½" × 6'10¼".
Alte Pinakothek, Munich.

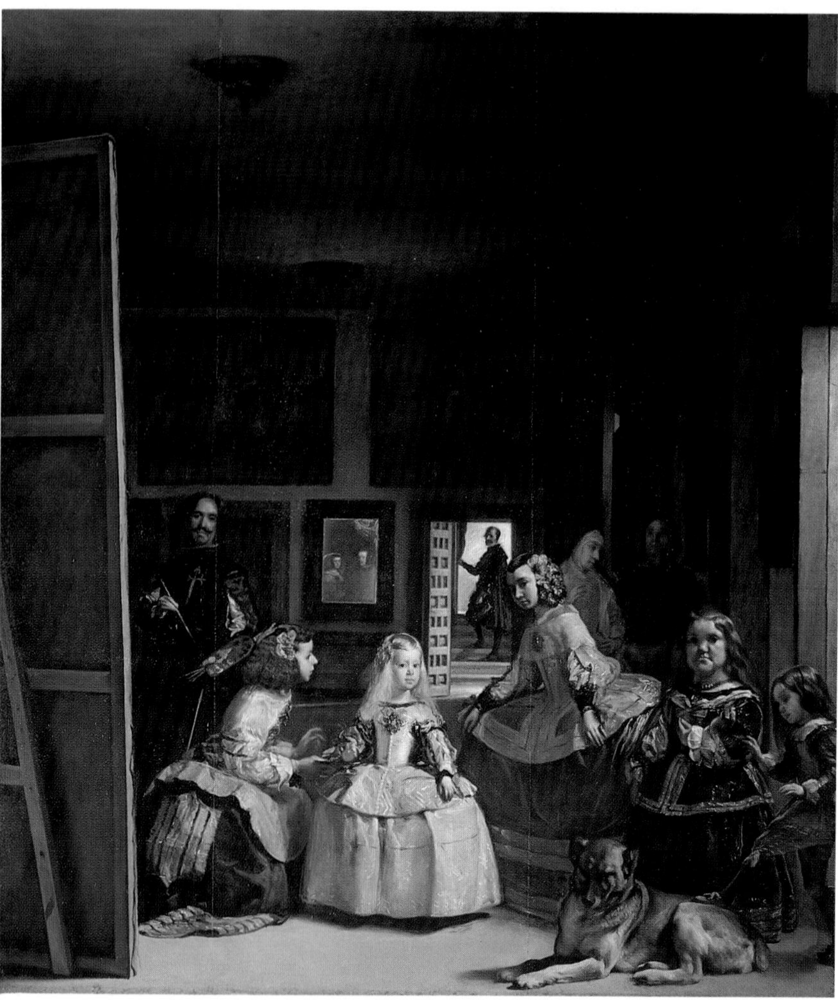

517 Diego Rodríguez de Silva y Velázquez.
LAS MENINAS (THE MAIDS OF HONOR). 1656.
Oil on canvas.
10'5" × 9'.
Museo del Prado, Madrid.

easily seen as the center of interest. Velázquez emphasized her by making her figure the clearest and lightest shape and by placing her near the center foreground. Around her, Velázquez created the appearance of his large studio, in which a complex group of life-size figures interact with the princess and the viewer. The viewer feels invited to join the participants in an ordinary moment in the studio. The king and queen also watched, and they saw themselves reflected in the mirror on the far wall. Although blurred, these two mirrored figures are a pivotal point for the entire composition. By controlling the light, color, and placement in space of everything in the room, Velázquez engages us in every aspect of the composition. LAS MENINAS gives us not only the artist's view of the court of Philip IV, but his view of the veils of illusion inherent in life itself. Velázquez placed himself in semi-shadow, brush in hand, his image acting as a kind of signature to the work.

We have seen that Baroque characteristics are found in art that depicts both religious and nonreligious subjects. This was primarily because artists no longer relied wholly on the church for their support; Velázquez was the court painter to the Spanish king. In fact, most art was commissioned not by the church but by middle-class merchants, bankers, and the aristocracy.

In Holland, Jan Vermeer, Rembrandt van Rijn, and their peers painted views of the rich interiors of merchant homes and portraits of the middle class and the wealthy. Along with the new emphasis on

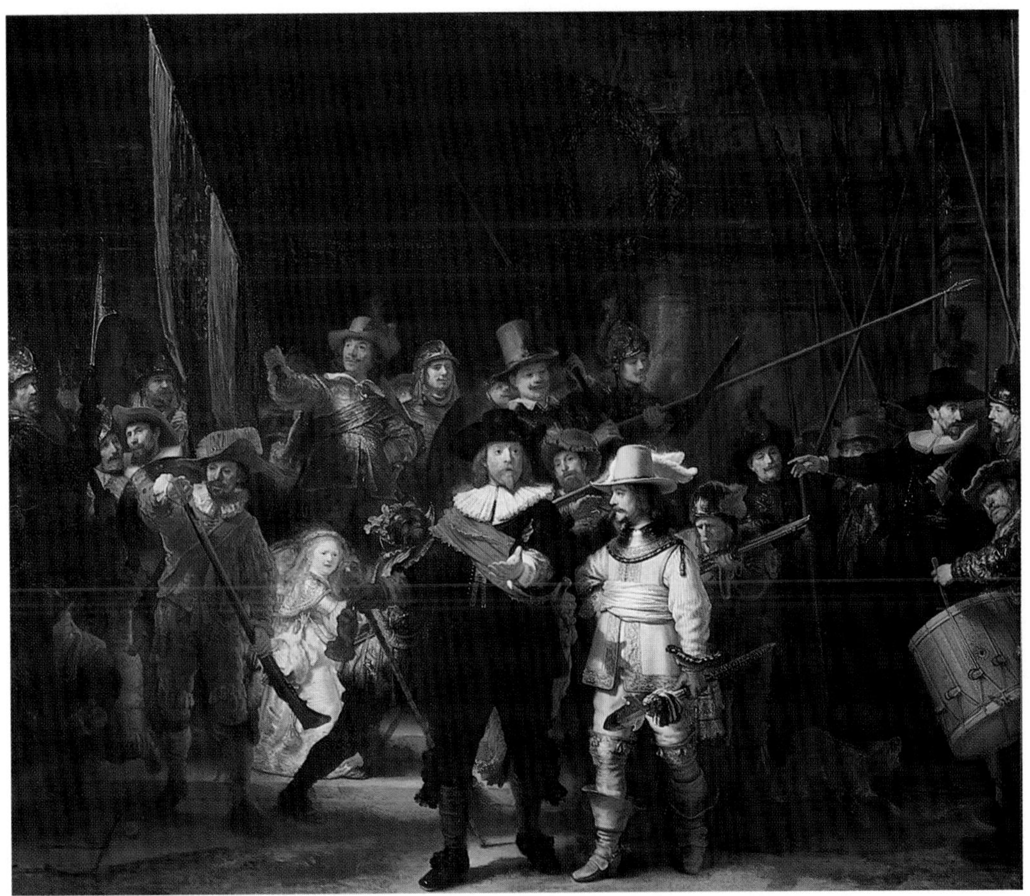

518 Rembrandt van Rijn.
THE NIGHT WATCH (THE COMPANY OF CAPTAIN FRANS BANNING COCQ). 1642.
Oil on canvas. 12'2" × 14'6".
Rijksmuseum, Amsterdam.

scenes of daily life, religious art continued as a strong current in the low countries; see, for example, Rembrandt's etching of the life of Christ (page 163).

As the result of recently won independence and booming international trade, Holland (the Netherlands) became a new type of society in the seventeenth century: predominantly middle class, wealthy, mercantile, materialistic, and Protestant. Among the middle and upper classes there was widespread enjoyment of and investment in contemporary art. Many people collected, traded, and resold paintings at a profit. Favored subjects were the same ones enjoyed to this day: landscape, still life, genre scenes (depictions of everyday life), and portraits. Through Dutch painters, art became accessible and understandable in everyday terms.

Rembrandt remains one of the world's most revered artists. At the peak of his career, he was commissioned to create a large group portrait of the militia (civic guard) company that was located near his home. The painting, THE COMPANY OF CAPTAIN FRANS BANNING COCQ, became known as THE NIGHT WATCH. The erroneous title was given to the work in the late eighteenth century—revarnishing and the accumulation of dirt caused the painting to darken and look like a night scene. (Painted in 1642, it was not restored to its present condition until the middle of the twentieth century.) Lasting damage had also been done to the painting in 1715 when it was cut down to fit it into a space in the Amsterdam Town Hall. Two figures were lost, as well as the bridge over which the men

REMBRANDT VAN RIJN (1606–1669)

Rembrandt Harmenszoon van Rijn was born in the elegant Dutch city of Leiden, the ninth of ten children of a prosperous miller. He began his art studies at fifteen, was apprenticed for three years to minor local artists, then traveled to Amsterdam to study briefly with a painter named Pieter Lastman, from whom he absorbed the influence of Caravaggio secondhand.

At nineteen, Rembrandt returned to Leiden and set up his own studio. Success came quickly, and in 1631 he moved to Amsterdam, a larger city offering more opportunities. There he married Saskia van Ulenborch, a beautiful, wealthy young woman from a good family. Judging from his paintings of her over the years, it was a happy marriage.

By the end of the decade Rembrandt was the most celebrated painter in the city. He bought a large house in a fine neighborhood, lived lavishly, and collected paintings, costumes, and precious objects on a grand scale. Among his portraits are many of himself in assorted costumes and guises (see page 9). He had so many pupils that he had to rent a warehouse for their work space.

Rembrandt's happiness was marred by the early deaths of their first three children. In 1641 his beloved son, Titus, was born. The next year, the same year he finished THE NIGHT WATCH, Saskia died, and everything began to change.

Rembrandt's art grew more introspective. He turned increasingly to biblical subjects and landscapes. Fashionable portraits, his bread and butter, interested him less and less. His style, no longer so popular, brought fewer commissions. When Geertge Dircx, a nurse he had hired to help with Titus, became his common-law wife, his personal life caused raised eyebrows. A few years later he fell in love with another household servant, Hendrickje Stoffels. Geertge's subsequent departure was an extended ordeal, involving lawsuits, countersuits, and criminal charges. Hendrickje bore Rembrandt two children and stayed with him until the end of her life. Because of a clause in Saskia's will, he was unable to marry Hendrickje, but his drawings and paintings of her are as affectionate as those of Saskia.

Rembrandt had always stretched his finances to the limit, and when the Dutch economy entered a shaky period in the 1650s he was forced into bankruptcy. His house and all his possessions were sold in a series of auctions. Ever loyal and supportive, Titus and Hendrickje formed a partnership to employ Rembrandt and to sell his work, thus shielding him legally from creditors. He moved with them to a smaller house in a far humbler part of town, where he lived in modest circumstances, continuing as a respected artist and receiving important commissions. Hendrickje died soon after in 1663; Titus died in 1668. The next year, Rembrandt followed them.

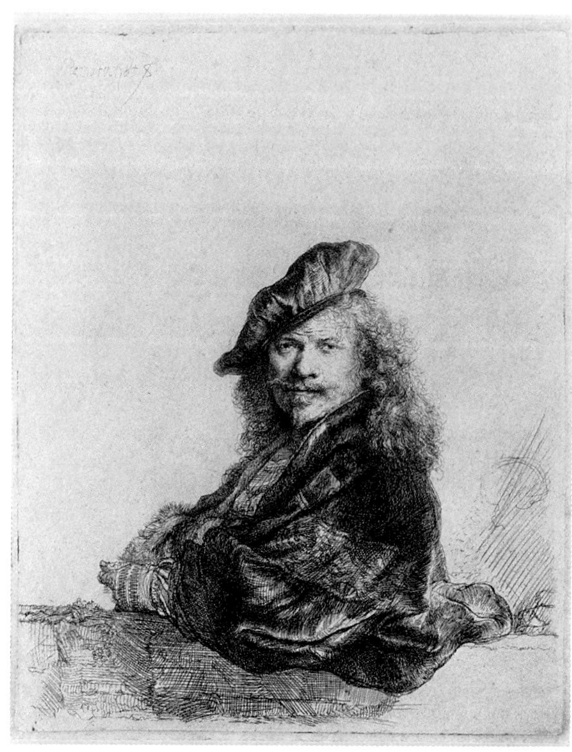

519 Rembrandt van Rijn. SELF-PORTRAIT AT AGE THIRTY-THREE. 1639. Etching, second state. 8 5/16" × 6 5/8". The Metropolitan Museum of Art. Bequest of Mrs. H. O. Havemeyer, 1929. The H. O. Havemeyer Collection (29.107.25).

Over two thousand drawings, etchings, and paintings survive, attesting to Rembrandt's vast output. To the very end Rembrandt's art grew deeper and more insightful. In his last self-portraits he had the look of a man whom nothing—no further drop of suffering could touch, and yet there is not the slightest hint of self-pity. The same understanding and compassion radiates from his biblical scenes and portraits, making Rembrandt the most warmly human of the artists we consider great masters.

were about to cross, and the balance of the composition was disrupted. Even in its altered state, however, THE NIGHT WATCH has long been admired.

Traditionally, group portraits depicted people lined up in rows. In contrast, Rembrandt chose to show the company as if on duty. Rembrandt subordinated individual portraits (paid for by each sitter) to the composition in order to turn an insignificant event into a pictorial drama. THE NIGHT WATCH has the dramatic action and theatrical light typical of Baroque painting. The dynamic group portrait typifies the Baroque spirit initiated by Caravaggio.

Upon inspection we realize that, for Rembrandt, meaning is conveyed through composition and paint application as well as subject matter. Rembrandt was among the first artists to demonstrate such delight in the visual eloquence that could be achieved with paint itself. The force of his brushwork is readily seen in his SELF-PORTRAITS on pages 9 and 153 and in his brush drawing on page 145.

Rembrandt's work has long influenced many painters—and, more recently, photographers—who have found his lighting technique useful in directing the attention of the viewer.

Jan Vermeer, another seventeenth-century Dutch painter, was also aware of the importance of light. His views of domestic life mark the high point of Dutch genre painting. Like Rembrandt, Vermeer was influenced by Caravaggio's use of light; unlike Caravaggio and Rembrandt, who used light for dramatic emphasis, Vermeer concentrated on the way light reveals each color, texture, and detail of the physical world. No one since Jan van Eyck (see page 355) had demonstrated such passion for seeing or such love for the visual qualities of the physical world.

To learn to see more accurately, Vermeer evidently used a table-model camera obscura (see page 172). His intimate portrait, THE GIRL WITH THE RED HAT, was painted on a small wooden panel similar in size to the frosted glass on which the image would have appeared using a camera obscura of the period. Thus Vermeer may have taught himself to see with photographic accuracy by copying images from the ground glass. In THE GIRL WITH THE RED HAT, the focus has a narrow range. Only part of the girl's collar and the left edge of her cheek are in sharp focus; everything in front of and behind that narrow band becomes increasingly blurred. The carved lion's head on the arm of the chair in the foreground looks like shimmering beads of light, just as it would appear in an out-of-focus photograph.

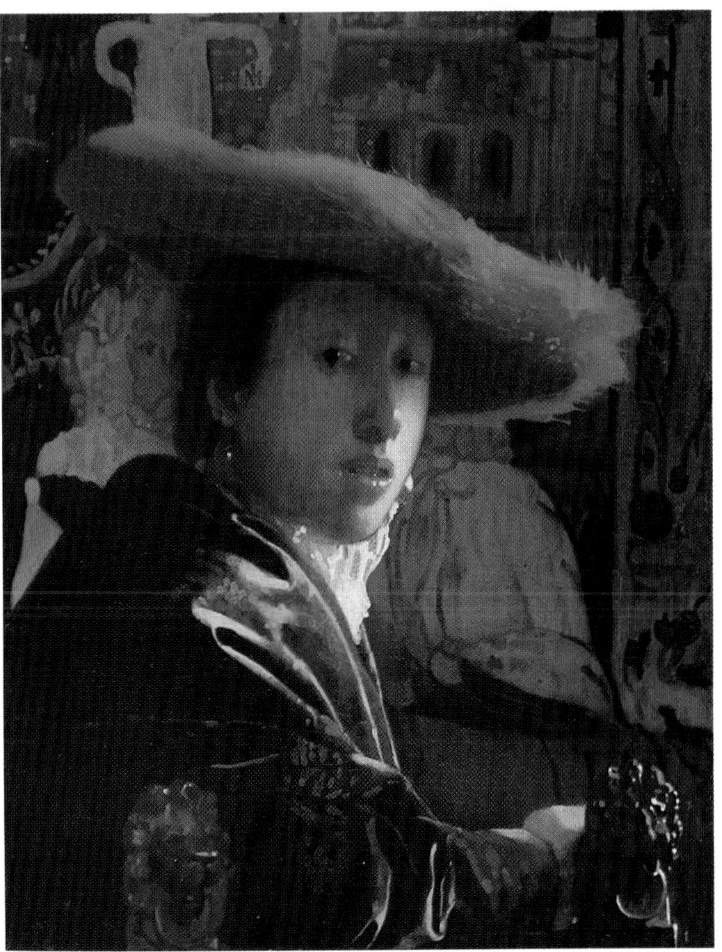

520 Jan Vermeer.
THE GIRL WITH THE RED HAT. c. 1665.
Oil on wood. 9⅛" × 7⅛".

Vermeer's understanding of the way light defines form enabled him to give his images a clear, luminous vitality. Much of the strength of THE KITCHEN MAID comes from a limited use of color: yellow and blue accented by red-orange surrounded by neutral tones. Vermeer gave equal attention to the details and the way each detail relates to the whole composition. Notice, for example, the immense care given to the rendering of the subtle surface qualities of the wall with its nail holes and stains.

Vermeer's painting THE ARTIST IN HIS STUDIO, known also as THE ART OF PAINTING, is evidently an allegorical statement of the position of the artist in seventeenth-century Holland. Through the use of symbols, Vermeer referred to the fame and fortune brought to Holland by her artists and merchant seamen. The woman, crowned with laurel (symbol of fame) and carrying a trumpet and book, represents Clio, the Greek muse of history. Behind her, a map of Holland carries the Dutch coat of arms and shows ships sailing. (Compare this work with another metaphorical painting by Vermeer's Spanish contemporary Velázquez on page 362.)

The heavy curtain in the left foreground gives a dynamic balance to the center of interest created by the black-and-white stripes on the artist's shirt. Looking over the artist's shoulder, we see that he is painting the laurel wreath on the model's head. The studio is illuminated by sunlight coming through an unseen window. The extraordinary appeal of this painting is in part the result of Vermeer's blending of Baroque drama and light with his precise down-to-earth Dutch realism.

During the Baroque period, French artists adopted Italian Renaissance ideas but made them their own; by the end of the seventeenth century, France had begun to take the lead in European art.

We can glimpse another view of seventeenth-century European life in the royal architecture and garden design of the French imperial villa of VERSAILLES built for King Louis XIV. The main palace and its gardens exemplify French Baroque architecture and landscape architecture. Throughout the palace and gardens, cool classical restraint and symmetry balance the romance of Baroque opulence and grand scale.

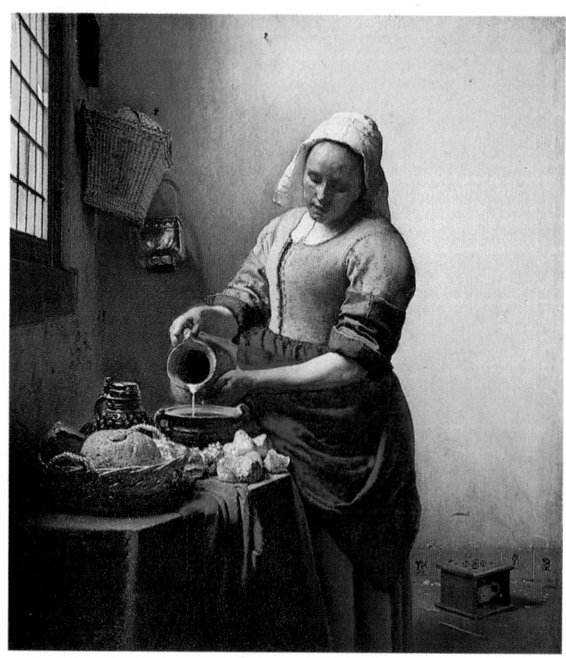

521 Jan Vermeer.
THE KITCHEN MAID. c. 1658.
Oil on canvas. 45.5 cm × 41 cm.
Rijksmuseum, Amsterdam.

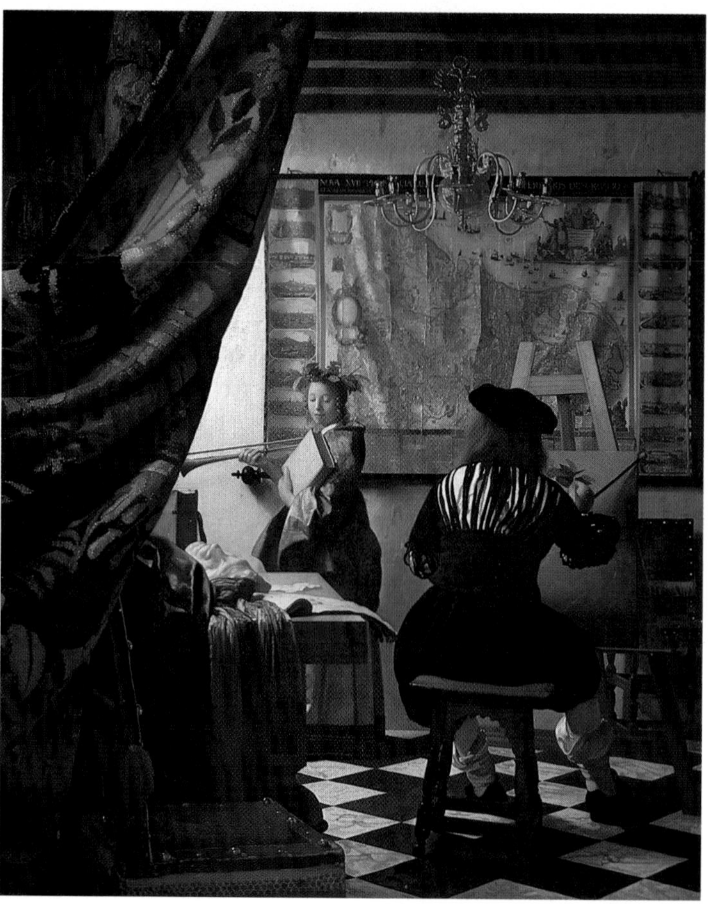

522 Jan Vermeer.
THE ARTIST IN HIS STUDIO (THE ART OF PAINTING). c. 1665.
Oil on canvas. 31⅜" × 26".
Kunsthistorisches Museum, Gemaeldegalerie, Vienna.

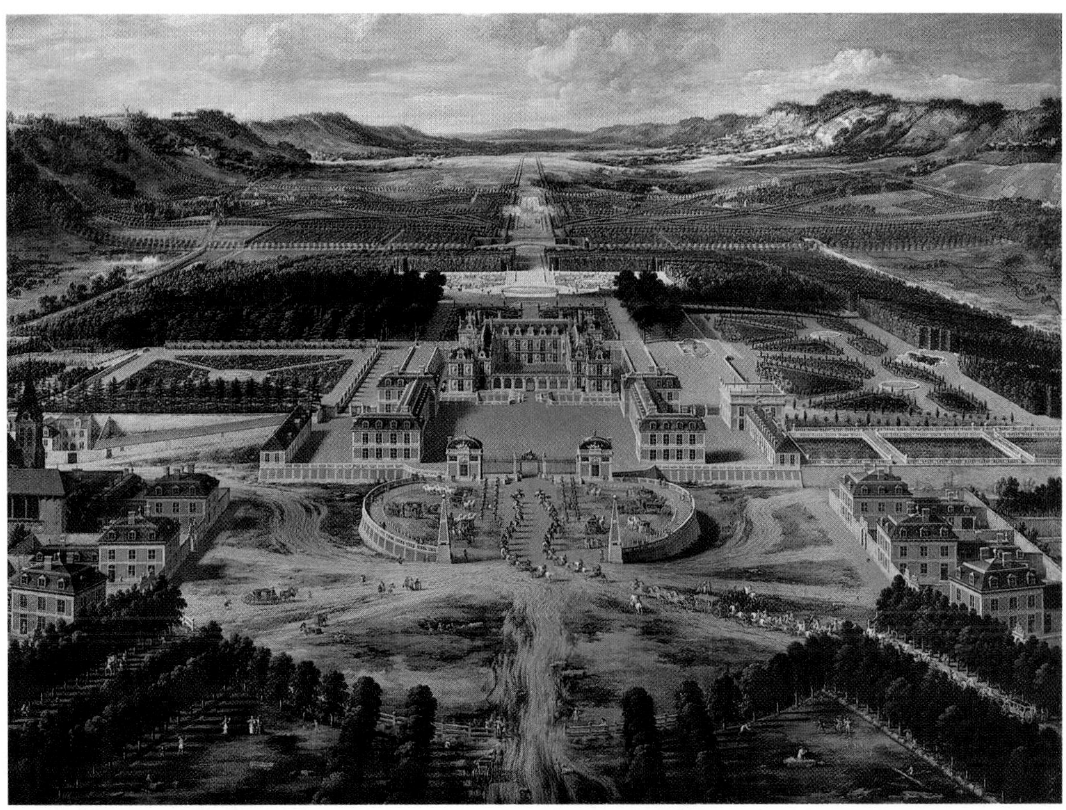

523 VERSAILLES. c. 1665.
Painting by Pierre Patel.
Musée du Louvre, Paris.

VERSAILLES expressed the king's desire to surpass all others in the splendor of his palace. It is an example of royal extravagance, originally set in fifteen thousand acres of manicured gardens, twelve miles south of Paris. The vast formal gardens, with their miles of clipped hedges, proclaimed the king's desire to rule even over nature. It is revealing to compare the contrasting attitudes behind VERSAILLES and KATSURA, the Japanese imperial villa built during the same century (see page 301).

Early in eighteenth-century France, the heavy, theatrical qualities of Italian Baroque art gradually gave way to the decorative Rococo style, a light, playful version of the Baroque. The curved shapes of shells were copied for elegantly paneled interiors and furniture, and they influenced the billowing shapes found in paintings. The arts moved out of the marble halls of palaces such as VERSAILLES and into fashionable town houses (called hotels) such as the HÔTEL DE SOUBISE.

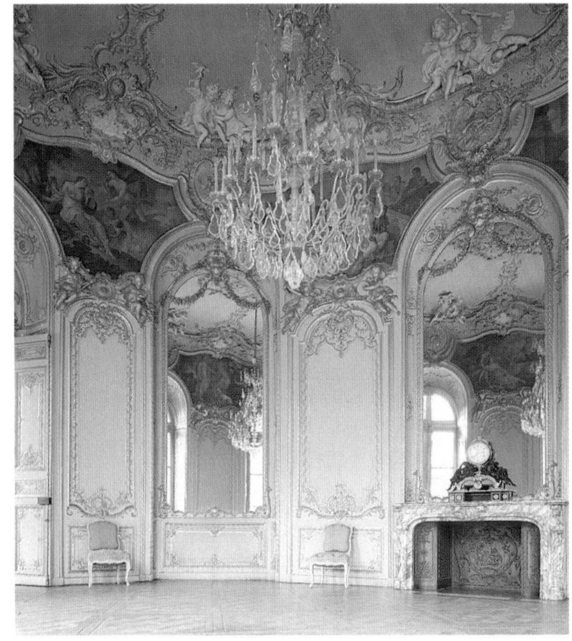

524 Germain Boffrand.
SALON DE LA PRINCESSE, HÔTEL DE SOUBISE.
Paris. Begun 1732.

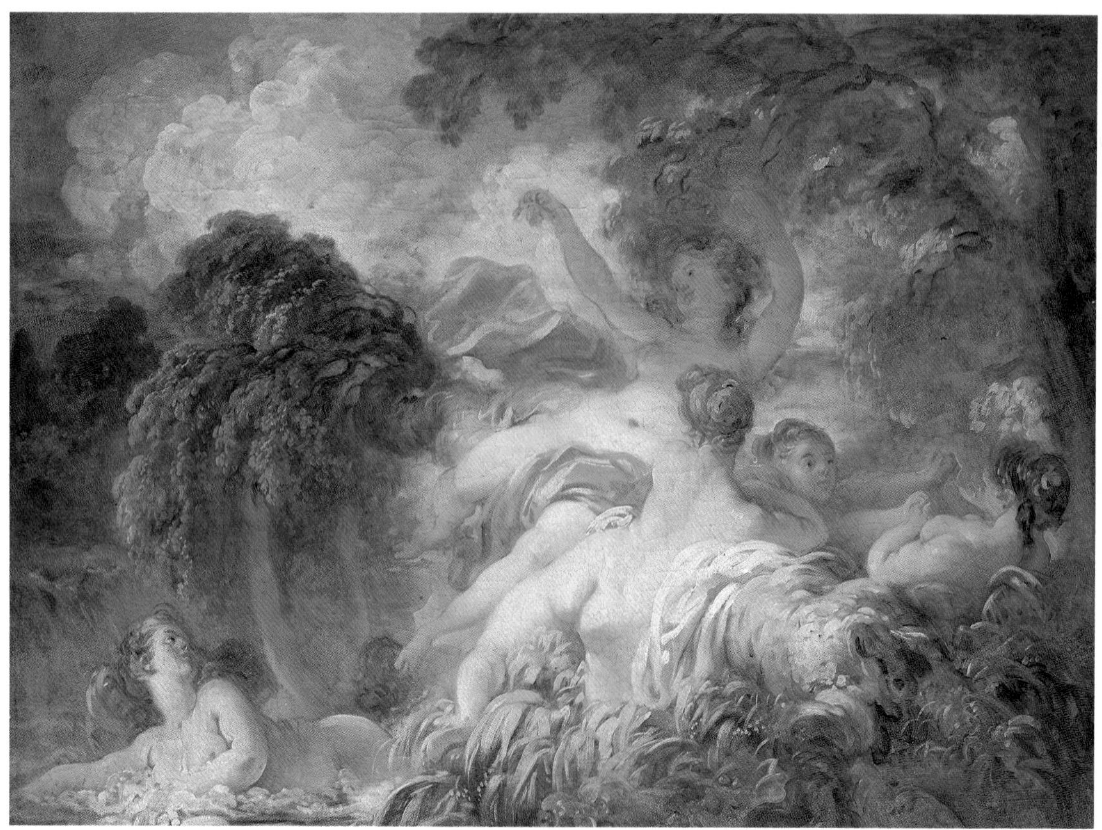

525 Jean-Honoré Fragonard.
THE BATHERS. c. 1765.
Oil on canvas. 25¼" × 31¼".
Musée du Louvre, Paris.

The enthusiastic sensuality of the Rococo style was particularly suited to the extravagant and often frivolous life led by the French court and aristocracy. Some of the movement, light, and gesture of the Baroque remained, but now the effect was one of lighthearted abandon rather than dramatic action or quiet repose. Rococo paintings provided romantic visions of life free from hardships, in which courtship and festive picnics filled the days.

Rococo painter Jean-Honoré Fragonard drew inspiration from French, Italian, and Flemish sources. The freedom of his brush technique and the vitality of his landscapes are seen in THE BATHERS. There is not a straight line in the entire composition—no hint of horizontal or vertical edges to stabilize the playful movement of the design.

As a period that lasted for almost two centuries and prevailed in Italy, France, Holland, and elsewhere, the Baroque was a complex and fruitful extension of Renaissance thinking. It is characterized by highly dramatic painters such as Caravaggio and serene and refined painters such as Vermeer, opulent painters such as Rubens and dignified and compassionate painters such as Velázquez. It produced equally varied and exuberant architecture and sculpture.

The Baroque era soon gave way to the Age of Reason. By the middle of the eighteenth century, political and economic strains had developed in France. The romance of Rococo no longer expressed the prevailing values of the time. A more conservative attitude led to the study and reinterpretation of the visual forms and symbolic content of classical Greek and Roman art. This movement, Neoclassicism, persisted in France until Napoleon was defeated in 1815.

PRESERVATION AND RESTORATION

Much of the art of the past that we enjoy today would have perished but for those people in each generation who cared for and restored selected works. Because art preserves tangible evidence of cultural history, it is essential to preserve major works for future generations.

Conservation may simply involve storing works where they cannot be damaged by heat, humidity, chemicals, and bacteria. For instance, works on paper usually need to be protected from contact with acid in other paper, from air that is too dry, too wet, or too hot, and from strong light.

Until recently, some of the best-preserved works of ancient art were Egyptian wall paintings long sealed in underground tombs.

For thousands of years, the tombs of Egyptian rulers and nobles were sealed against moisture, light, and bacteria. While nearly all had their contents stolen prior to their rediscovery in modern times, the painted walls were left intact because the tombs had been resealed. In recent decades, after the tombs were opened to tourists and scholars, the breath of large numbers of daily visitors has caused the humidity level to rise, leading to the growth of bacteria that is eating away ancient wall paintings.

While environmental effects and the normal course of deterioration lead to much of the damage, vandalism has been another source of destruction of art. Recent incidents involving major artworks have shocked the public. After Michelangelo's PIETÀ (page 102) was attacked with a hammer by a mentally unstable viewer, the piece was relocated behind a wall of bulletproof glass. Leonardo's MONA LISA (page 348) in the Louvre Museum in Paris is now also protected in a case behind bulletproof glass—where it is all but lost to viewers.

Vandalism of artworks is not just a recent phenomenon. In museums throughout the world, large numbers of sculptures of nudes, particularly Greek and Roman works, have had their noses and private parts broken off.

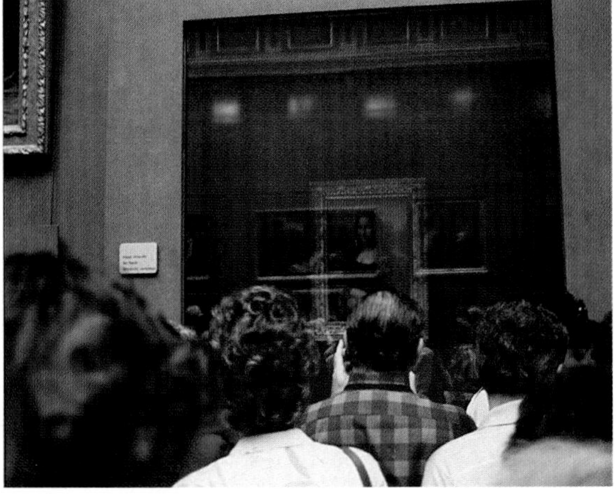

526 People viewing MONA LISA through bulletproof glass. (See also page 348.)

Outdoor art must face the additional challenges of dust, wind, rain, air pollution, and extremes of temperature. Within our lifetimes, floods and earthquakes have severely damaged or destroyed large quantities of works considered world art treasures.

Unfortunately, preservation, conservation, and restoration are issues that often arise late in the lives of art and architecture. The history of the PARTHENON (see page 324) illustrates some of the ways human values and actions have affected creative works of earlier peoples. Since its construction more than 2,400 years ago, the PARTHENON has been subjected to the ravages of human history. Conquering Romans used it as a brothel; Christians turned it into a church; the Turks refurbished it as a mosque, then stored explosives in it while they fought the Venetians. In 1687, a Venetian artillery shell exploded the Turks' store of gunpowder, causing major damage to the structure. From 1801 to 1803, while Greece remained under Turkish rule, Lord Elgin, the British ambassador to Turkey, was permitted to remove a large number of Greek sculptures, including many from the friezes of the PARTHENON.

Early in this century, would-be restorers inserted iron bars as reinforcements between the remaining stones of the PARTHENON's columns. The sea air soon corroded the iron, causing many stones to split. Nothing in its entire history, however, has been as hard on the PARTHENON as twentieth-century air pollution.

The marble of the PARTHENON and other buildings on the Acropolis is being eaten away by the sulphur dioxide produced when automobile and other fuel exhaust combines with moisture. Driving rain, windblown sand, and dirt now cause greater damage to the fragile surfaces of these structures in one year than weathering previously did in a century. Ironically, by being housed in the British Museum, the works removed (some would say stolen) by Lord Elgin have been protected not only from normal weathering, neglect, and the ravages of war, but also from air pollution.

It is ironic that the high-tech societies able to support specialized restoration technology are often the same societies in which air pollution from industrial production and traffic is rapidly destroying some of the world's finest art.

Restoration is a time-consuming and sometimes impossible task. Apart from the technical aspects, art restoration involves complex issues. Without knowledge of how a damaged work of art looked in its original condition, how do we know the artist's intent? And even

PRESERVATION AND RESTORATION

after we think we know how a piece of art should look, there are matters of time and money relative to the importance of the piece. Who decides which works are worth conserving? How far should restoration go before a piece ceases to be original? What should be done with previous restoration efforts that may have altered the original and even contributed to its deterioration? What responsibility for conservation rests on families, museums, communities, or nations that acquire works of art?

In the past, restoration was often so ill conceived that it did more harm than good, either by adding to and altering the original—as was done in previous centuries to Leonardo's THE LAST SUPPER—or by adding materials that caused new problems—as in the use of iron rods in the PARTHENON.

THE LAST SUPPER began to deteriorate soon after it was painted because Leonardo used an experimental mixture of oil and tempera that did not adhere permanently to the plaster wall (see also page 349). Numerous conservation and restoration attempts over the past 350 years further damaged the work, and only a fraction of Leonardo's painting remains today. The original portions have recently been uncovered and stabilized by the painstaking work of restorer Dr. Pinin Brambilla Barcilon. She also added watercolor (which can be easily removed) to bare spots to lessen contrast and maintain the visual continuity of the surface. Although we can only imagine the painting's original visual quality, much of its compelling strength survives even in its highly fragmented state.

The possibility of restoration doing permanent damage to an artist's work can cause public controversy, as was the case during the 1980s cleaning of THE SISTINE CHAPEL ceiling (page 353). The debate concerned whether Michelangelo painted simply in *buon fresco* (wet plaster) or used a *secco* (overpainting after the plaster had dried).

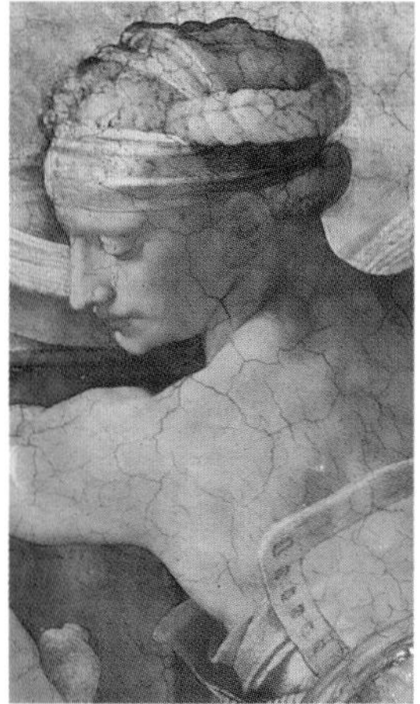

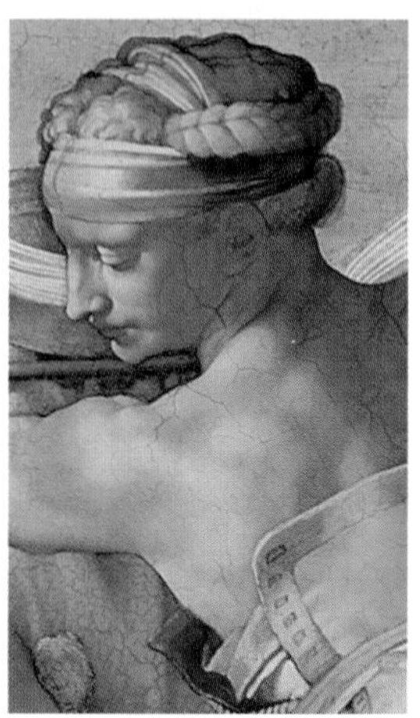

528 Michelangelo Buonarroti.
Detail of SISTINE CHAPEL ceiling frescoes, before and after 1980s restoration.
(See also page 353.)

Critics of the cleaning believe that Michelangelo painted a *secco,* and that the cleaning removed the brush strokes that he may have applied on top of the dried fresco to provide subtle shading. They claim that the cleaning went too far and removed the subtleties of Michelangelo's work.

Restoration director Fabrizio Mancinelli maintains that Michelangelo painted completely in *buon fresco,* and that layers of glue applied in the seventeenth and eighteenth centuries had dulled the bright colors. Ironically, the glue was applied as a varnish in attempts to brighten colors that had become darkened by layers of dirt. Prior to the twentieth century, the chapel was lit by candles and oil lamps and heated by charcoal braziers that generated greasy smoke and soot. The restorers say the cleaning reveals Michelangelo's revolutionary use of color. For those accustomed to the dark and muted colors of the unrestored frescoes, the change is extraordinary.

Today's well-trained, professional restorers are aware that they don't have all the answers, so they are careful to make as few additions as possible and use substances that can be easily removed if future technology provides better solutions.

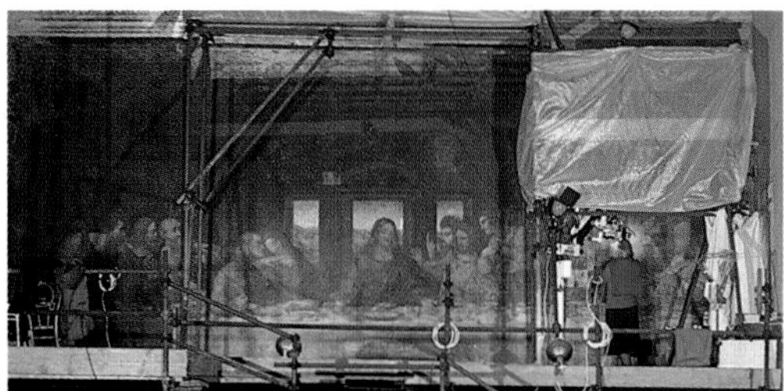

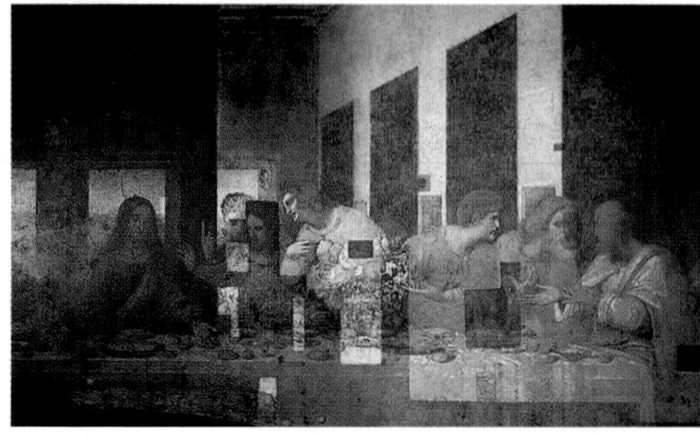

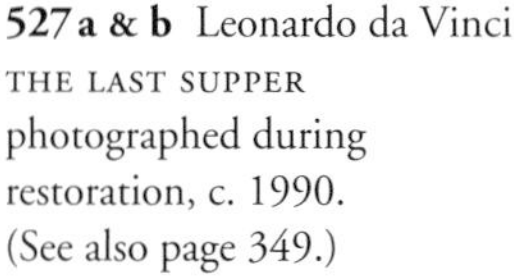

527 a & b Leonardo da Vinci.
THE LAST SUPPER
photographed during restoration, c. 1990.
(See also page 349.)

PART 7

THE MODERN WORLD

Consider . . .

What generalizations could you make about twentieth-century art after glancing at the photos in this book's last five chapters?

The invention of photography in the nineteenth century freed painting from the need to be realistic. Why do artists continue to paint portraits instead of simply using a camera to capture someone's likeness?

Since we usually group art movements by form rather than content, should feminist artists be placed in a separate category? Why?

Do the "stationary" visual arts such as painting and sculpture still have impact in a world dominated by film and television?

Is art today more or less difficult for the average person to understand than it was several hundred years ago? What changes might account for any difference?

Do artists build on the art of their predecessors in the way scientists build on the work of earlier scientists?

CHAPTER 20

Late Eighteenth and Nineteenth Centuries

Three revolutions—the Industrial Revolution, which began in Britain about 1760; the American Revolution in 1775; and the French Revolution in 1789—launched the period of great social and technological change we call the modern age. The Industrial Revolution brought about the most significant shift in the way people lived since the Neolithic agricultural revolution ten thousand years earlier. Since the start of the Industrial Revolution, technological change has occurred at an ever increasing rate.

The Enlightenment, or Age of Reason, as the eighteenth century has been called, was characterized by a shift to a more rational and scientific approach to religious, political, social, and economic issues. Belief in the importance of liberty, self-determination, and progress brought about an emphasis on democracy and secular concerns. Consistent belief systems that tended to unify the art of earlier societies became increasingly fragmented. Traditional values were challenged by the new atmosphere of independent investigation, by the radical changes brought about by technology, and by the increased mixing of peoples and cultures. Artists both expressed and abetted these changes.

In art, a new self-consciousness about styles led to increasing uncertainty about the place of art and artists in society. In earlier periods, within each society, artists had adhered to one dominant style. Following the French Revolution and the subsequent break with traditional art patronage in France, a variety of styles developed simultaneously. Artists were freed from the artistic constraints imposed by their traditional patrons (royalty, aristocracy, wealthy merchants and bankers, and the church), but they were left to struggle financially until a new system of patronage emerged. The support that developed came in the form of commercial galleries, private and corporate collectors, and museums.

NEOCLASSICISM

With the beginning of the French Revolution in 1789, the luxurious life that centered on the French court ended abruptly, and French society was disrupted and transformed. As the social structure and values changed, tastes changed.

One of the men who led the way to revolutions in both art and politics was painter Jacques-Louis David. Believing that the arts should serve a political purpose in a time of social and governmental reform, he rejected what he saw as the frivolous immorality associated with the aristocratic Rococo style. When he painted OATH OF THE HORATII, David used an austere style called Neoclassicism. Neoclassicism refers to the emulation of classical Greece and Rome; much of the subject matter in Neoclassical art was Roman because Rome represented a republican, or nonmonarchical, government.

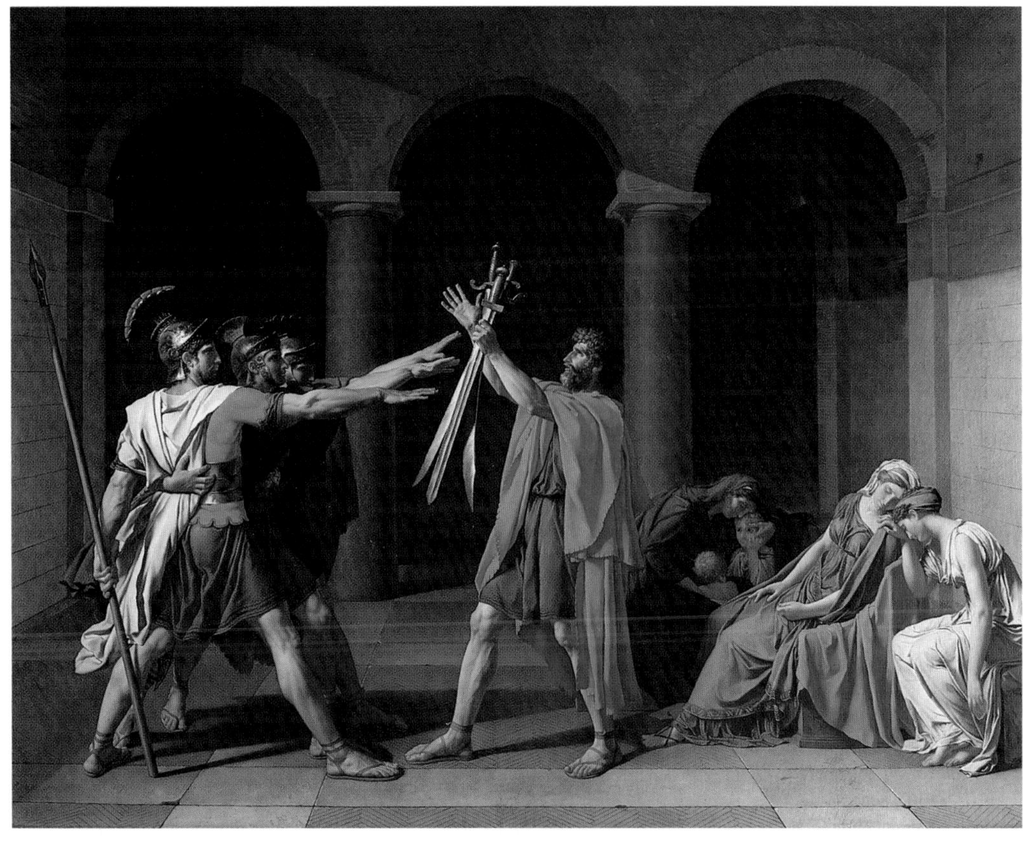

529 Jacques-Louis David.
OATH OF THE HORATII. 1784.
Oil on canvas.
10'10" × 14'.
Musée du Louvre, Paris.

The subject of OATH OF THE HORATII is a story of virtue and the readiness to die for liberty, in which three brothers pledge to take the sword offered by their father to defend Rome. With such paintings, David gave revolutionary leaders an inspiring image of themselves rooted in history. "Take courage," was the painting's message, "your cause is a noble one and has been fought before."

David's Neoclassicism, seen in the rational, geometric structure of his composition, provides strong contrast to the lyrical softness of Rococo designs. The painting has the quality of classical (Greco-Roman) relief sculpture, with strong side light emphasizing the figures in the foreground. Even the folds in the garments are more like carved marble than soft cloth. The three arches set on columns give strength to the design and provide an historically appropriate setting for the Roman figures. The two center columns separate the three major parts of the subject. Vertical and horizontal lines parallel the edges of the picture plane, forming a stable composition that resembles a stage set.

The new classical (that is, Neoclassical) spirit was also felt in architecture. American architecture achieved international stature for the first time with the work of American statesman and architect Thomas Jefferson. His original design for his home, MONTICELLO, was derived from Palladio's Renaissance reinterpretation of Roman country-style houses (see page 357). Then, during his years in Europe as Minister to France (1784–1789), Jefferson was strongly influenced by French, Italian, and Roman architecture. Thus, when he rebuilt his home between 1793 and 1806, he had the second story removed from the center of the building and replaced by a dome on an octagonal drum. He added a large Greco-Roman portico (a porchlike roof supported by columns), making the entire design reminiscent of the PANTHEON (see page 328) by way of contemporary French Neoclassical

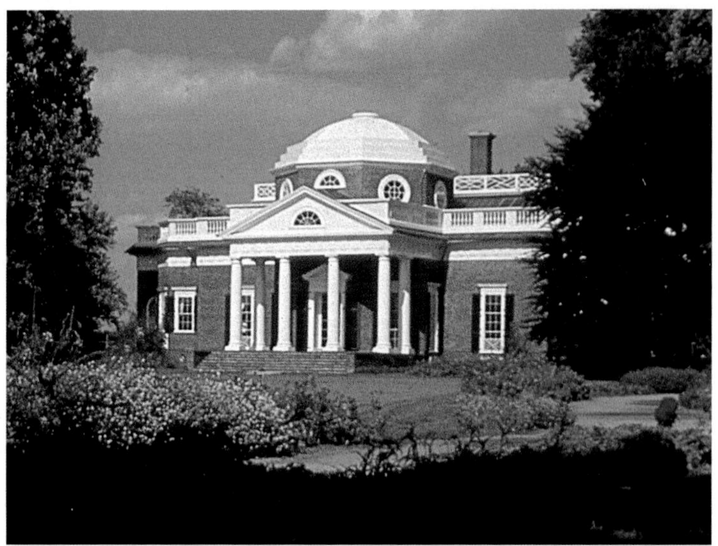

530 Thomas Jefferson.
MONTICELLO. Charlottesville, Virginia. 1793–1806.
Photograph: J. T. Tkatch.
Courtesy of the Thomas Jefferson Memorial Foundation.

architecture. In comparison with the first MONTICELLO, the second version has a monumental quality that reflects Jefferson's increasingly classical conception of architecture.

Both MONTICELLO and Jefferson's designs for the University of Virginia show the Roman phase of Neoclassical American architecture, often called the Federal or Jeffersonian Style. Jefferson aimed for an architecture capable of expressing the values of the new American republic. In its fusion of classical Greek, Roman, Renaissance (Palladian), and eighteenth-century forms, his architecture shows an originality that sets it apart. Jefferson's Neoclassical style is reflected in much of American architecture until the Civil War. Neoclassical architecture can be found in practically every city in the United States, and it continues to dominate Washington, D.C.

ROMANTICISM

The Enlightenment celebrated the power of human reason; however, an opposite reaction, called Romanticism, soon followed. This new wave of emotional expression dominated the arts in Europe from about 1825 to 1850. The word Romanticism comes from *romances,* popular medieval tales of adventure written in romance languages.

While Neoclassicism refers to a specific style, Romanticism refers to an attitude that inspired a number of styles. Romantic artists, musicians, and writers held the views that imagination and emotion are more valuable than reason, that nature is less corrupt than civilization, and that human beings are essentially good. Romantics championed the struggle for human liberty and celebrated the awe-inspiring qualities of nature, rural life, common people, and exotic subjects in art and literature. They wanted to assert the validity of subjective experience and to escape Neoclassicism's fixation on classical forms at the expense of feeling and spontaneity (see Blake's PITY, page 8).

Spanish artist Francisco Goya was a Romantic painter and printmaker. A contemporary of David, he was aware of the French Revolution and he personally experienced some of the worst aspects of the ensuing Napoleonic era, when French armies invaded Spain and much of the rest of Europe. Goya at first welcomed Napoleon's invading army because his sympathies were with the French Revolution and he had lost confidence in the king of Spain. But he soon discovered that the occupying army was destroying rather than defending the ideals he had associated with the Revolution. Madrid was occupied by Napoleon's troops in 1808. On May 2, a riot broke out against the French in the Puerto del Sol. Officers fired from a nearby hill, and the cavalry was ordered to cut down the crowds. The following night, a firing squad was set up to shoot anyone who appeared in the streets. Later, Goya vividly and bitterly depicted these brutalities in his powerful indictment of organized murder, THE THIRD OF MAY, 1808, painted in February 1814.

The painting is enormous yet so well conceived in every detail that it delivers its meaning in a visual flash. A clearly structured pattern of light and dark areas organizes the scene, giving it impact and underscoring its meaning. Goya focuses attention on the soldiers by means of value (light and dark) shifts that define a wedge shape formed by the edge of the hill and the edge of the brightly lighted area on the ground. Mechanical uniformity marks the faceless firing squad, in contrast with the ragged

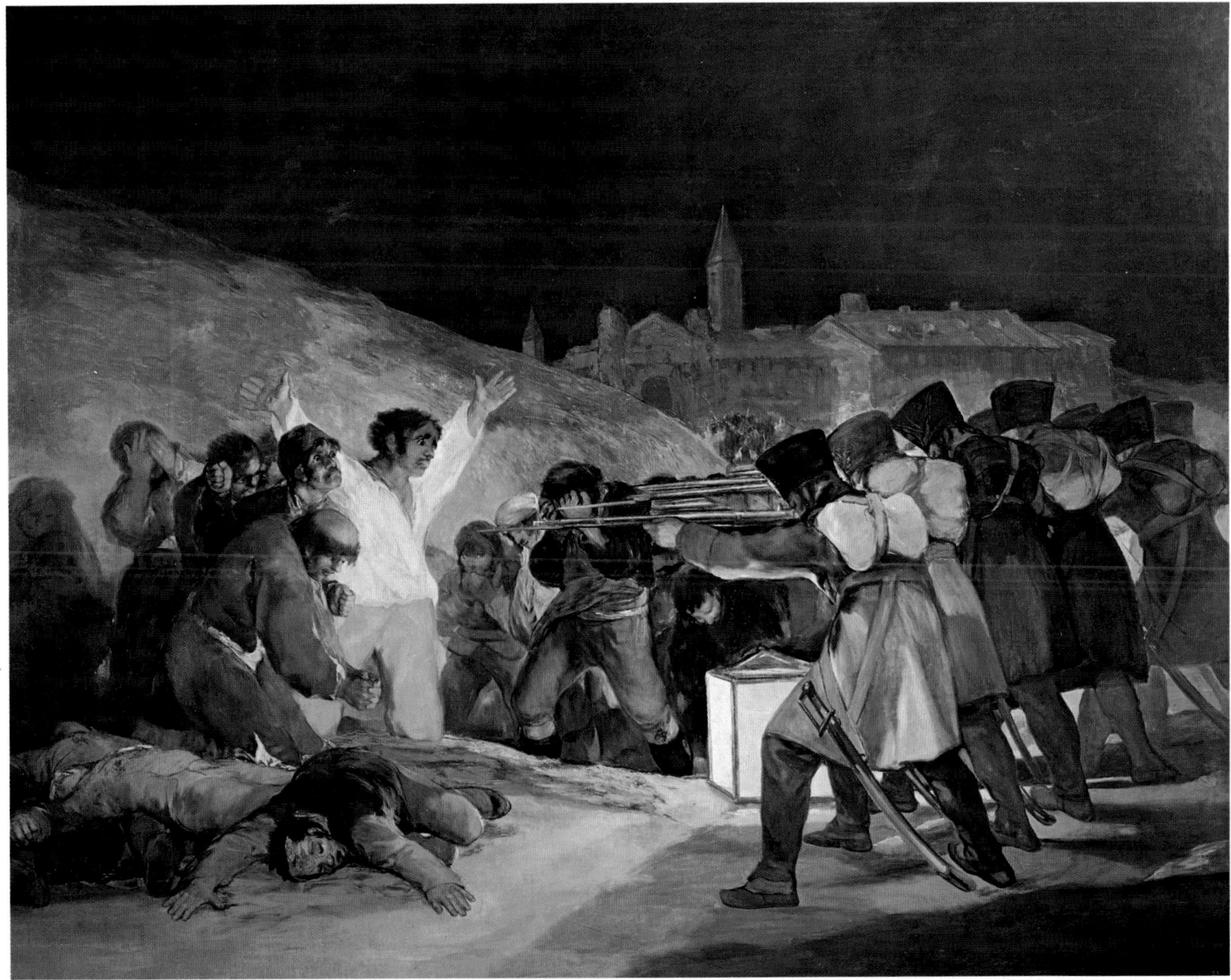

531 Francisco Goya.
THE THIRD OF MAY, 1808. 1814.
Oil on canvas. 8'9" × 13'4".
Museo del Prado, Madrid.

group that is the target. From the soldiers' dark shapes, we are led by the light and the lines of the rifles to the man in white. The dramatic painting spotlights this man, who raises his arms in a powerful gesture of defiance.

THE THIRD OF MAY, 1808 is not a mere reconstruction of history; it is a universal protest against the brutality of tyrannical governments. Its impact is similar to that of the photograph of a single man defying a row of oncoming tanks during the student demonstration in Tiananmen Square, Beijing, China, in 1989 (see page 16).

During the early nineteenth century, English painting was dominated by an interest in landscape—a response to the increasingly sooty air and sprawling factories of the Industrial Revolution.

The son of a wealthy miller, Romantic painter John Constable grew up in the English countryside and developed a love of nature that was to stay with him all his life. Although his detailed paintings were developed in his studio in the traditional way, they were preceded by numerous oil sketches completed outdoors. Constable was not the first to paint such studies on location, but he was unique in the

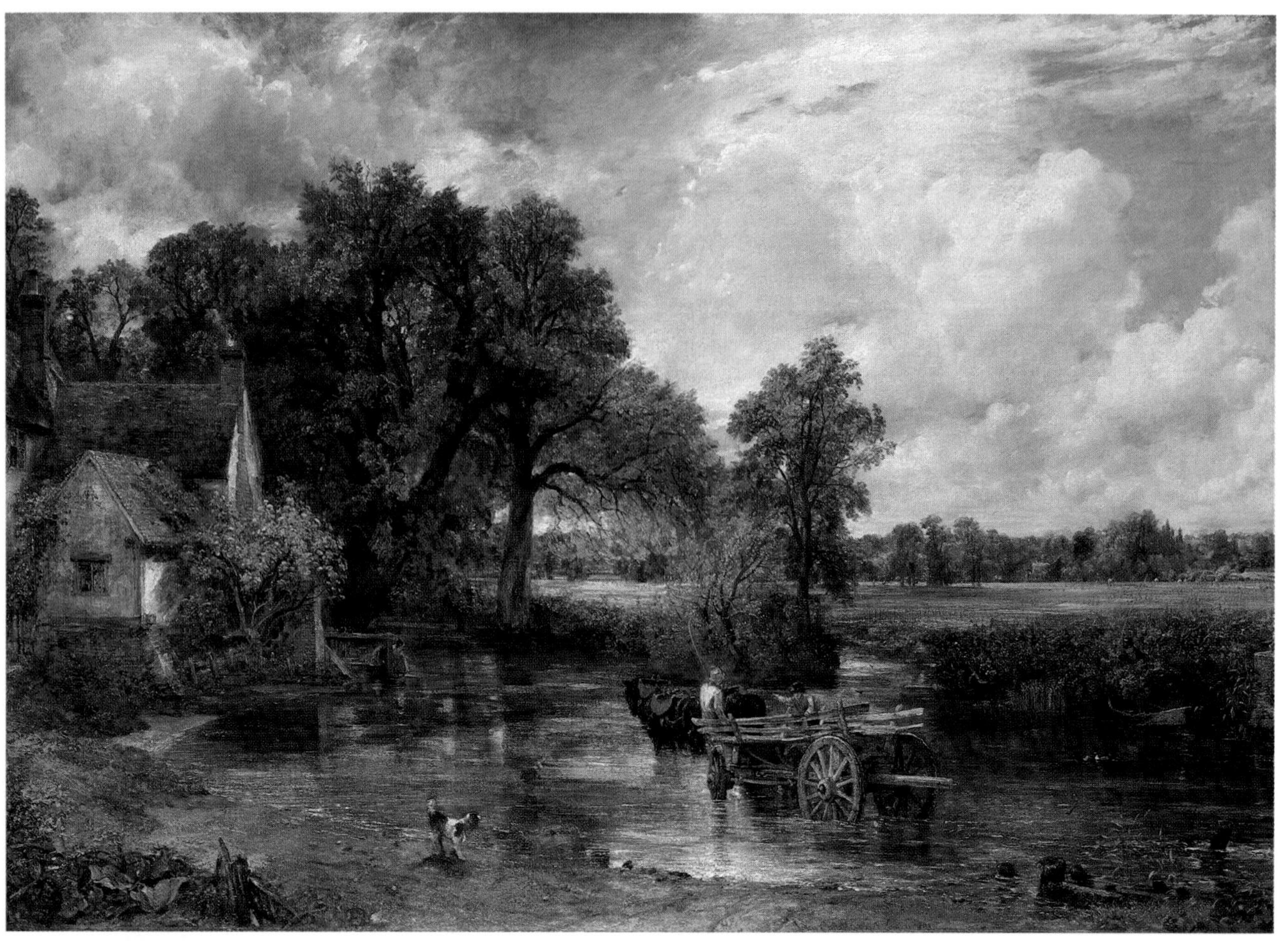

532 John Constable.
THE HAY WAIN. 1821.
Oil on canvas. 50½" × 73".

attention he gave to the intangible qualities of light and weather. He decried what he saw as the decline of art caused by "the imitation of preceding styles, with little reference to nature."[1]

When Constable's painting THE HAY WAIN was exhibited in the annual Paris exhibition of 1824, French artists were amazed by the English painter's vision of landscape. Eugène Delacroix (see page 378) is said to have been so inspired by the way the sky was painted in THE HAY WAIN that he repainted the sky in one of his own major works in a similar manner. Constable broke away from conventional formulas of color and technique. His innovative use of individual strokes of varied color and his use of flecks of white to suggest shimmering sunlight brought him ridicule from contemporary critics and, two generations later, praise from the French Impressionists (see pages 387–391).

In the United States, the work of Romantic painter Thomas Cole helped to stimulate enthusiasm for the grandeur and beauty of the vast American wilderness. Cole is recognized as the founder of the Hudson River School, an important group of American landscape painters. Like Constable, Cole began with on-site oil and pencil sketches, then made his large paintings in his studio. The broad, panoramic view, carefully rendered details, and light-filled atmosphere of paintings such as THE OXBOW became the inspiration for American landscape painting for several genera-

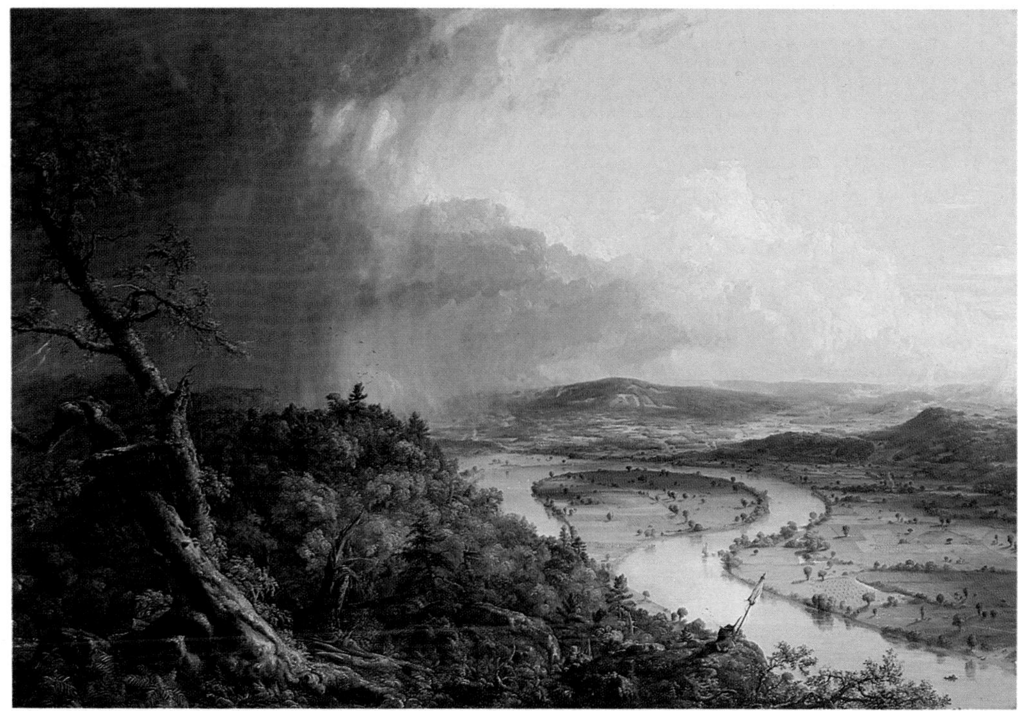

533 Thomas Cole.
THE OXBOW. 1836.
Oil on canvas. 51½" × 76".
The Metropolitan Museum of Art, New York. Gift of Mrs. Russell Sage, 1908 (08.228).

tions; see also Asher Durand's KINDRED SPIRITS on page 64.

In nineteenth-century America it was difficult for persons of European descent to receive the education they needed to become professional artists. For African Americans it was next to impossible. Nevertheless, with the help of antislavery sponsors, a few succeeded.

Robert S. Duncanson was one of the first African-American artists to earn an international reputation. As the son of a Scots-Canadian father and an African-American mother, he may have had an easier time gaining recognition as an artist than those who did not straddle the color line. Prior to settling in Cincinnati, he studied in Italy, France, and England, and he was heavily influenced by European Romanticism. With BLUE HOLE, LITTLE MIAMI RIVER, Duncanson reached artistic maturity. He modified the precise realism of the Hudson River School with an original, poetic softening. He orchestrated light, color, and detail to create an intimate and engaging reverie of man in nature.

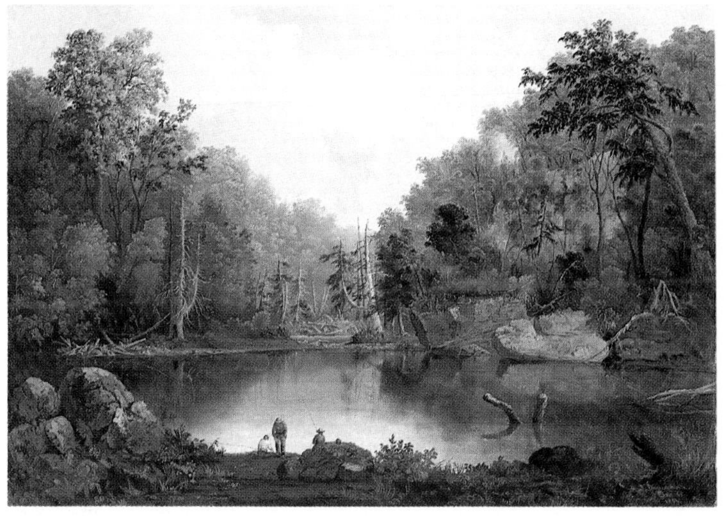

534 Robert S. Duncanson.
BLUE HOLE, LITTLE MIAMI RIVER. 1851.
Oil on canvas. 29¼" × 42¼".
Cincinnati Art Museum. Gift of Norbert Heerman and Arthur Helbig (1926.18).

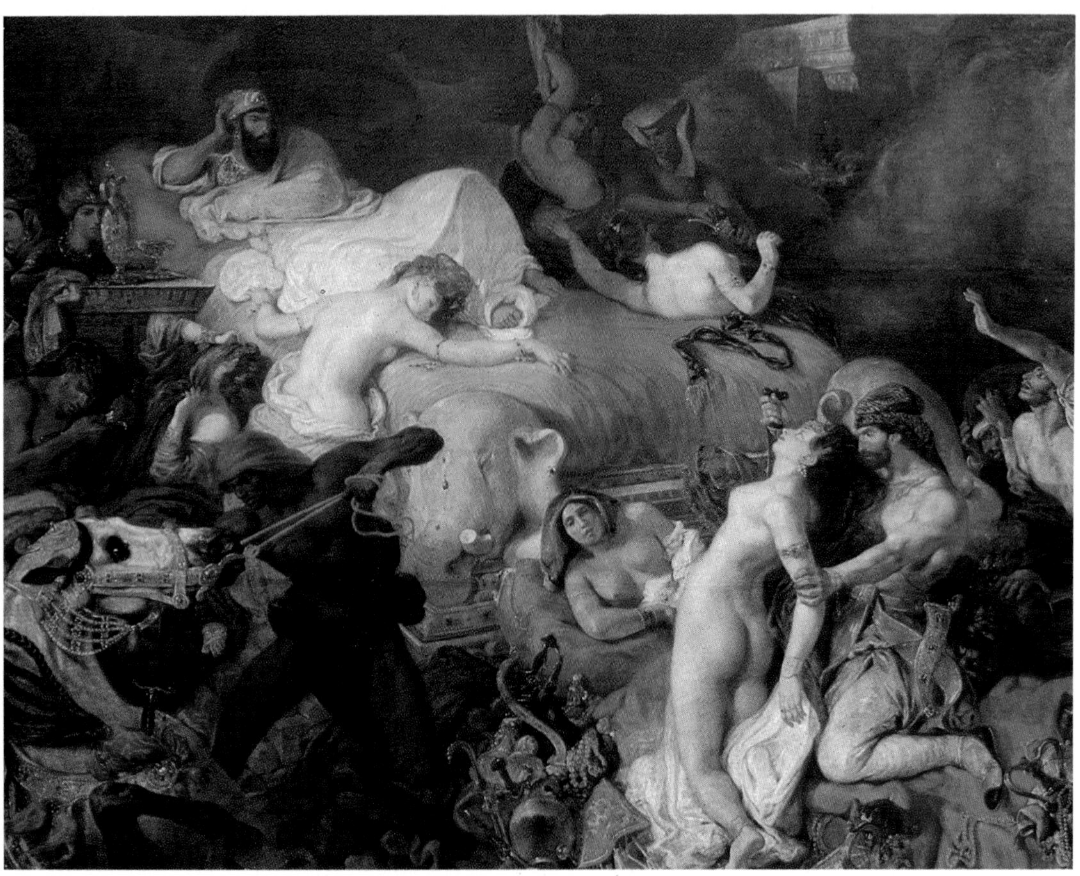

535 Eugène Delacroix.
THE DEATH OF SARDANAPALUS. 1827.
Oil on canvas. 12'1½" × 16'2⅞".
Musée du Louvre, Paris.

In France, the leading Romantic painter was Eugène Delacroix. Delacroix's painting THE DEATH OF SARDANAPALUS exhibits the many qualities that distinguish Romanticism from the Neoclassicism of David and his followers. The turbulent sensuality is based on Byron's poem, in which the legendary Assyrian ruler watches from his deathbed after ordering that his palace and all its contents be destroyed. The Romantic ideal stresses passionate involvement, color that is equal in importance to drawing, and dramatic movement—in contrast to the detached formal qualities of Neoclassicism. Delacroix's rich color and *painterly* execution (open form and sensual use of paint, with shapes defined by changes in color rather than line) was admired by later painters, particularly Van Gogh.

Both Neoclassicism and Romanticism had their beginnings in rebellion. But by mid-century each had become institutionalized, functioning instead as a conservative force in French artistic life. At the state-sponsored École des Beaux Arts, or School of Fine Arts, students were taught by members of the Academy of Fine Arts (an organization of government-approved artists) that "great painting" demanded "classical" technique and "elevated" subject matter found in history, mythology, literature, or exotic locations.

Delacroix accused Academy members of teaching beauty as though it were algebra. Today, we still use the term *academic art* for generally unimaginative works that follow generally stale formulas laid down by an academy or school, especially the

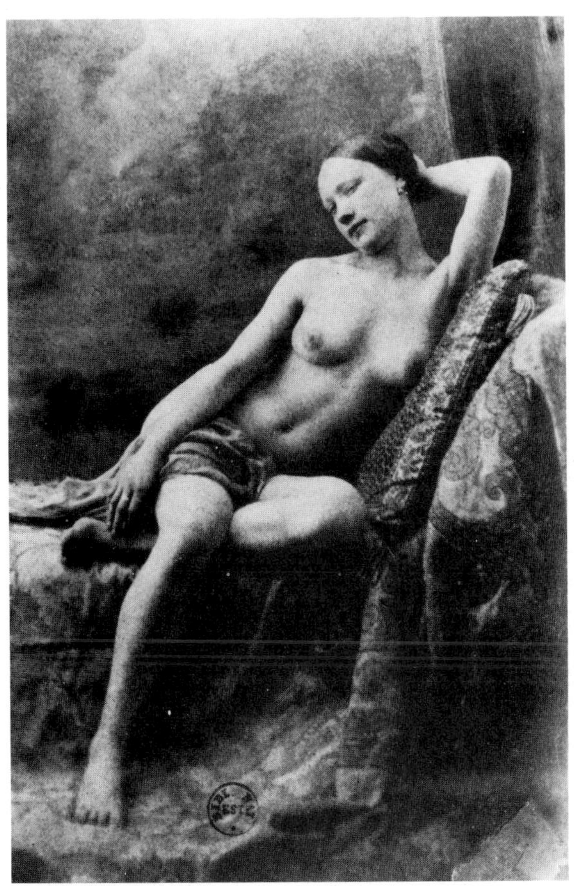

536 Eugène Durieu.
FIGURE STUDY. c. 1855.
Photograph.
Bibliothèque Nationale, Paris.

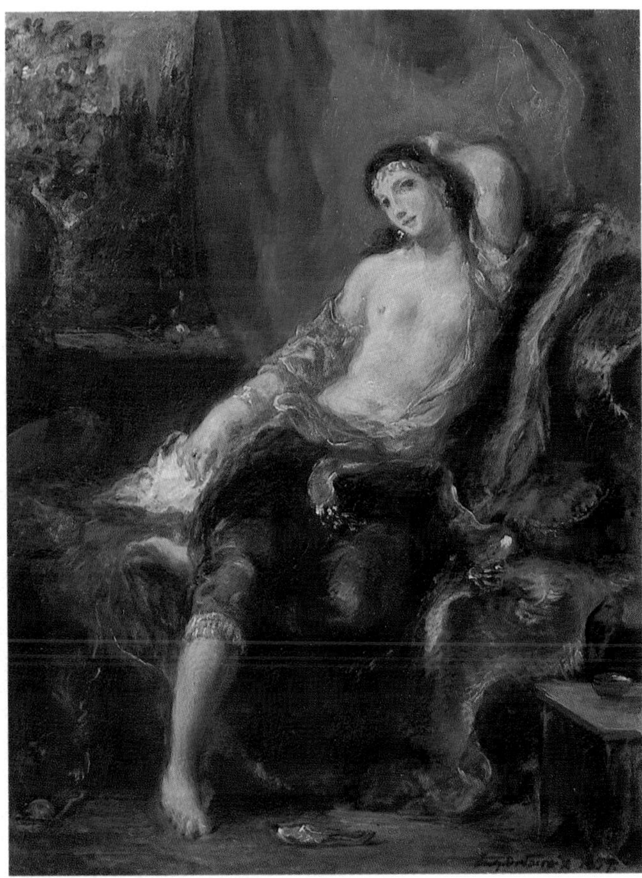

537 Eugène Delacroix.
ODALISQUE. 1857.
Oil on canvas. 35.5 cm × 30.5 cm.
Private collection.

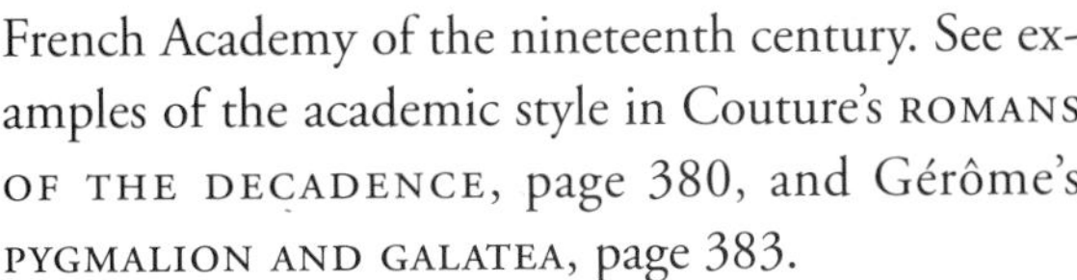

French Academy of the nineteenth century. See examples of the academic style in Couture's ROMANS OF THE DECADENCE, page 380, and Gérôme's PYGMALION AND GALATEA, page 383.

Academy members played a major role in selecting artists for a huge annual exhibition known as the Salon. Participating in the Salon was virtually the only way an artist might become known to the public and thus make a career. The art history of the rest of the nineteenth century is largely one of rebellion against such institutions and authority figures. Vast changes in art and the artist's role in society were about to topple the dominance of the French Academy.

PHOTOGRAPHY

The camera, perfected by the painter Daguerre (see page 173), was initially seen by landscape and portrait painters as a threat to their livelihood. In fact it freed painters from the roles of narrator and illustrator, allowing them to explore dimensions of inner experience that had been largely neglected in Western art since the Renaissance. Photography offered new opportunities to fuse images of objective reality with personal visions.

Delacroix occasionally drew and painted from early photographs. Two images reveal how he set up a painter's composition with a model, then with the help of his friend, photographer Eugène Durieu, made a photograph, FIGURE STUDY, that became the basis for the oil painting ODALISQUE.

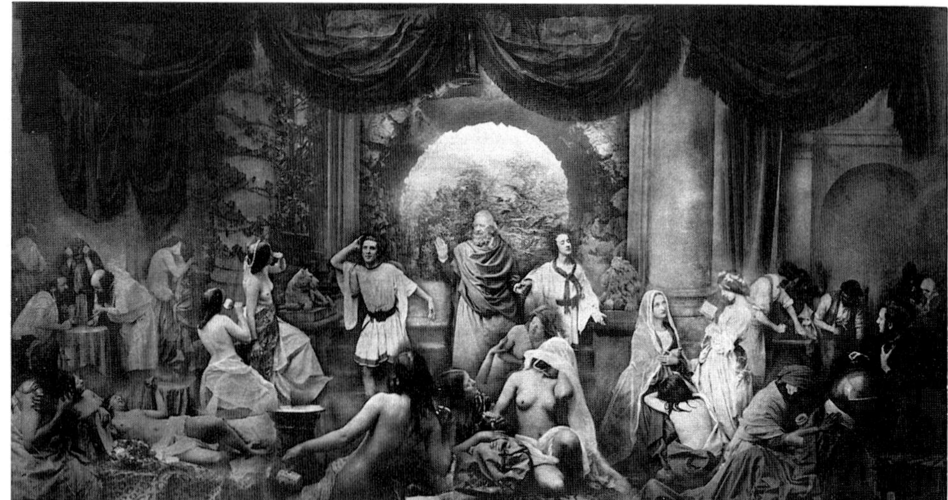

538 O. G. Rejlander.
THE TWO WAYS OF LIFE.
1857.
Photograph. 16" × 31".
Royal Photographic Society Collection, Bath, England.

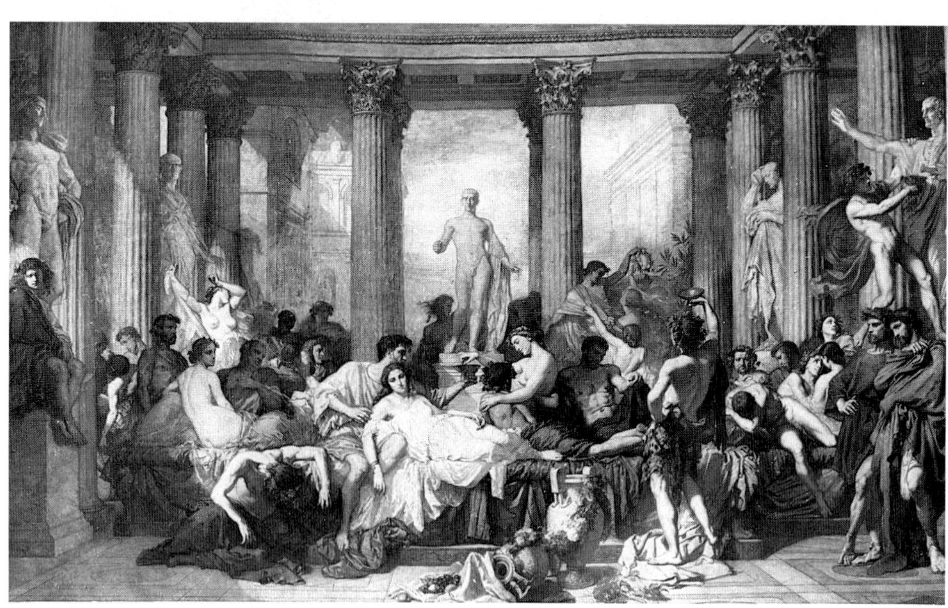

539 Thomas Couture.
ROMANS OF THE DECADENCE. 1847.
Oil on canvas.
15'1" × 25'4".
Musée du Louvre, Paris.

Delacroix was one of the first to recognize the difference between camera vision and human vision. He believed that photography was potentially of great benefit to art and artists. In an essay for students, Delacroix wrote:

A daguerreotype is a mirror of the object, certain details almost always overlooked in drawing from nature take on in it characteristic importance, and thus introduce the artist to complete knowledge of construction as light and shade are found in their true character.[2]

In an effort to convince doubting critics that photography could be art, many photographers imitated paintings and even copied the academic style. With great care, painter and photographer O. G. Rejlander combined over thirty negatives to achieve his technically ambitious and morally explicit photograph THE TWO WAYS OF LIFE.

Rejlander was determined to prove that it was possible to create photographs that were equal in importance to paintings. His opportunity came when he entered this photograph in the Manchester Art Treasures Exhibition of 1857. Queen Victoria of England, an amateur photographer herself, purchased the photograph.

Rejlander worked within the same academic style as Thomas Couture. But Rejlander's photograph measures 16 × 31 *inches,* while Couture's ROMANS OF THE DECADENCE is more than 15 × 25 *feet!* Couture's huge painting is a Romantic subject in a Neoclassical setting typical of nineteenth-century French academic art. It represents the dying gasp of pictorial themes that had been worked and reworked since the Renaissance. This painting nominally criticized Roman decadence, but it also presented an eroticism that was appealing and morally acceptable in an age of repressed sexuality.

Félix Tournachon, called Nadar, was—like many other photographers—an artist who came to prefer photography to drawing and printmaking. He gained fame as a balloonist, and from a hot air balloon he made the first aerial photographs. He even took the first underground photographs in the sewers and catacombs of Paris, using artificial lighting techniques and long exposures.

Nadar recognized that photography was merely a mechanical process and that the photographer had to be intelligent and creative in order to make significant works of art with a camera. The most notable artists, writers, and intellectuals of Paris went to him to have their portraits made. His photograph of French actress SARAH BERNHARDT is an evolutionary link between the Romantic painted portraits of nineteenth-century women and the glamour photography of today. Another pioneer portrait photographer was Julia Cameron, who began photographing at age forty-eight and created an impassioned body of work (see page 174).

As both a tool and a way of seeing, photography influenced the next major stylistic development: Realism.

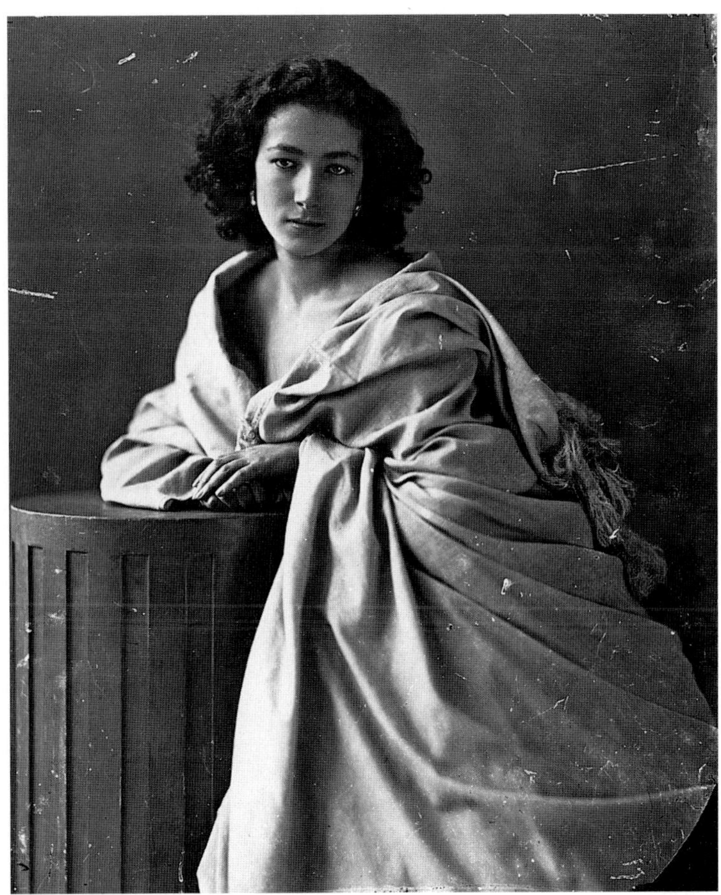

540 Nadar (Félix Tournachon).
SARAH BERNHARDT. 1855.
Photograph printed from a collodion negative.
International Museum of Photography at George Eastman House, Rochester, New York.

REALISM

Realism describes a style of art and literature that depicts ordinary existence without idealism, exoticism, or nostalgia. We have seen it before the nineteenth century, notably in Roman sculpture and Flemish and Dutch painting. By mid-century, a growing number of artists were dissatisfied with the Romantics' attachment to mythical, exotic, and historical subjects. They believed that art should deal with human experience and observation. They knew that people in the nineteenth century were living a new kind of life, and wanted art to show it.

In the 1850s, French painter Gustave Courbet revived Realism with new vigor by employing a direct, painterly technique and an objective vision to represent images of common life. In doing so, he laid the foundation for a rediscovery of the

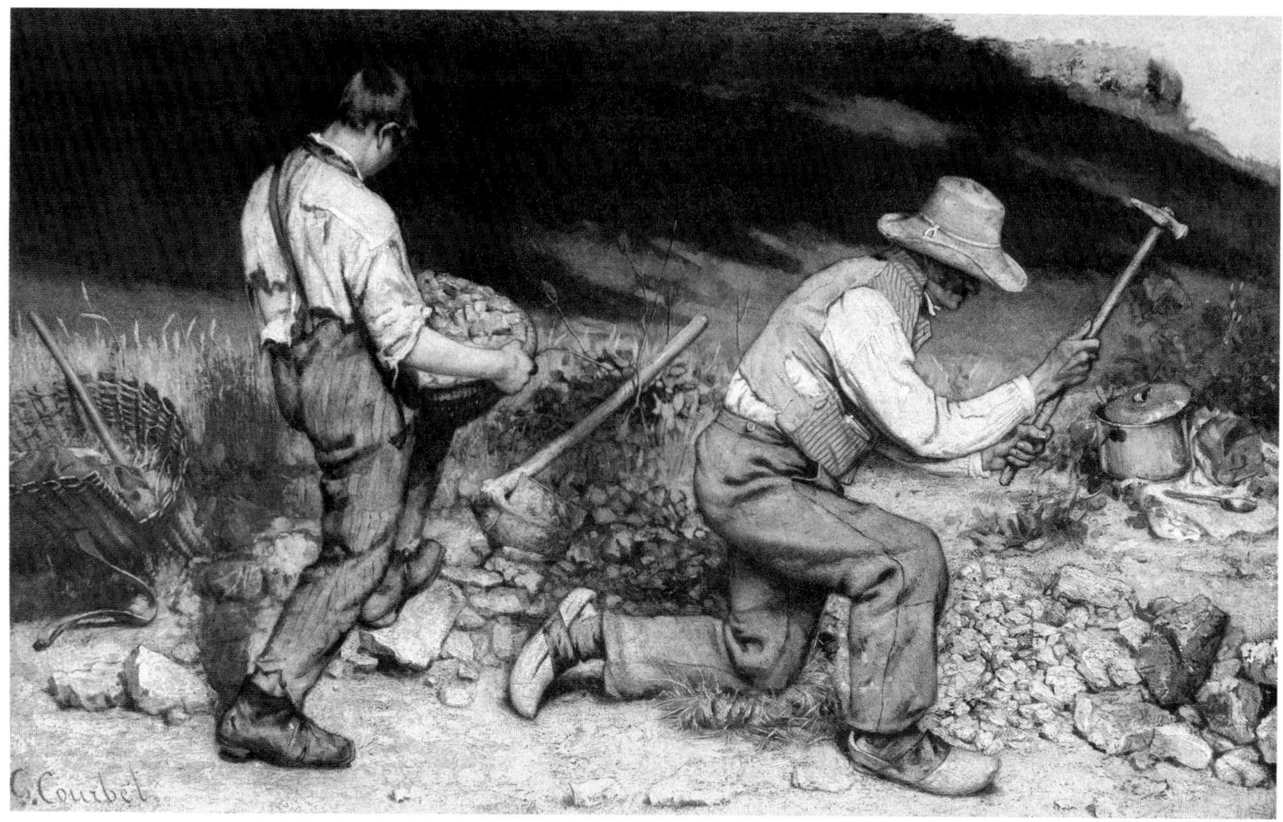

541 Gustave Courbet.
THE STONE BREAKERS. 1849
(destroyed during World War II).
Oil on canvas. 5'5" × 7'10".
Formerly in State Picture Gallery, Dresden, Germany.

extraordinary visual qualities of everyday experience.

THE STONE BREAKERS shows Courbet's rejection of Romantic and Neoclassical formulas. His subject is neither historical nor allegorical, religious nor heroic. The men breaking stones are ordinary road workers, presented almost life-size. Courbet did not idealize the work of breaking stones or dramatize the struggle for existence; he simply said, Look at this.

Courbet's detractors were sure that he was causing artistic and moral decline by painting what they considered unpleasant and trivial subjects on a grand scale. They accused him of raising "a cult of ugliness" against cherished concepts of Beauty and the Ideal. Realism was perceived as nothing less than the enemy of art, and many believed that photography was the source and the sponsor of this disaster. When THE STONE BREAKERS was exhibited in Paris in the Salon of 1850, it was attacked as unartistic, crude, and socialistic. From then on, Courbet set up his own exhibits—the beginning of the continuing practice of independent shows organized by artists themselves.

Courbet was one of the first to finish his paintings outdoors, working directly from nature. Previously, most landscape painting had been done in the artist's studio from memory, sketches, and reference materials such as rocks and plants brought in from outside. When portable tubes of oil paint became available in 1841, artists were able to paint outdoors without preliminary drawings or preconceived plans. By working directly from subjects outdoors, painters were able to capture first impressions. This shift in practice opened up whole new ways of seeing and painting.

Of his own work, Courbet said,

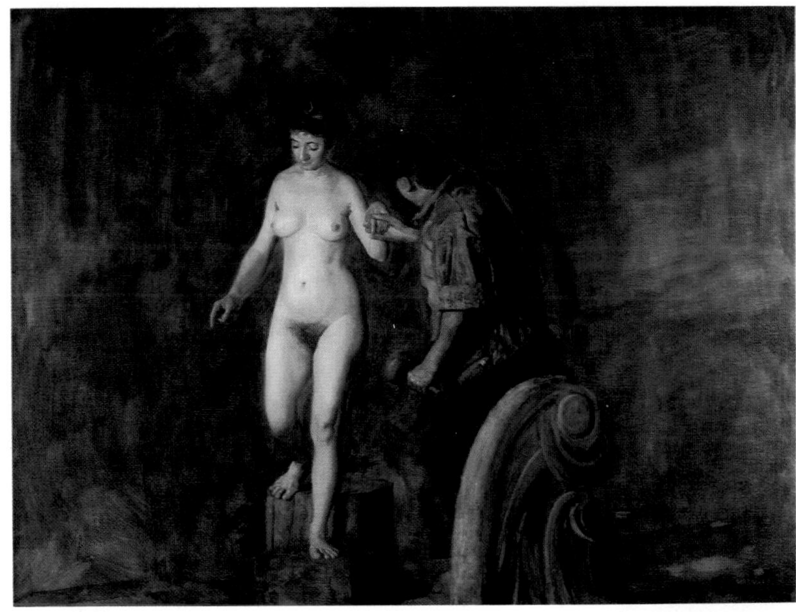

542 Thomas Eakins.
WILLIAM RUSH AND HIS MODEL. 1907-1908.
Oil on canvas. 35¼" × 47¼".
Honolulu Academy of Arts. Gift of Friends of the Academy.

543 Jean Léon Gérôme.
PYGMALION AND GALATEA.
c. 1860.
Oil on canvas. 35" × 27".
The Metropolitan Museum of Art, New York. Gift of Louis C. Raegner, 1927 (27.200).

To know in order to create, that was my idea. To be able to represent the customs, the ideas, the appearance of my own era ... to create living art; that is my aim.[3]

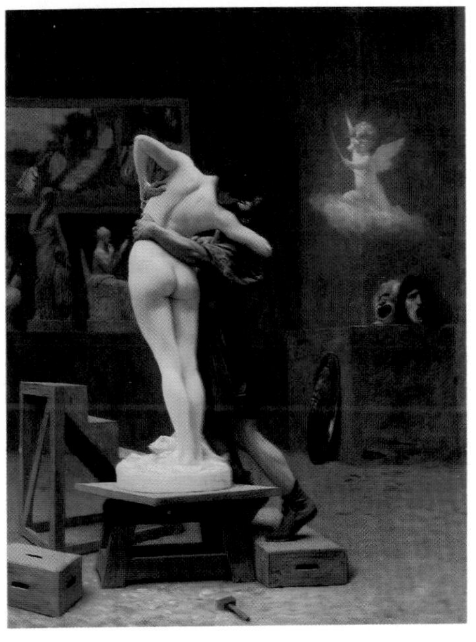

The Realist paintings of American artist Thomas Eakins are remarkable for their humanity and insight into the everyday world. A comparison of the paintings of Eakins and those of his teacher, Gérôme, shows the contrast between Realism and officially sanctioned academic art. The attitude Eakins presented is one of great respect for the beauty of the ordinary human being. Gérôme may have been equally interested in ordinary women, yet he created a painting based on classical and academic ideals. Eakins's insistence on painting people the way they actually look led him to escape the bondage of stylization imposed by the rules of the academy; it also led to shock and rejection by the public and much of the art world.

In the academic painting PYGMALION AND GALATEA, Gérôme placed the woman, Galatea, on a pedestal, both literally and figuratively. The Greek myth of Pygmalion tells of a sculptor who carved a statue of a woman so beautiful that he fell in love with his sculpture. Pygmalion prayed to Aphrodite, goddess of love, who responded by making the figure come to life. The sentimental approach (note the cupid), smooth finish, and mild eroticism are typical of academic art. In WILLIAM RUSH AND HIS MODEL, Eakins used his own likeness for Rush, an early nineteenth-century American sculptor whom Eakins greatly admired. The sculptor is depicted helping his model as she steps down from the stand, as if she were a queen being helped from a carriage, yet there is no hint of idealization or flattery.

THOMAS EAKINS (1844–1916)

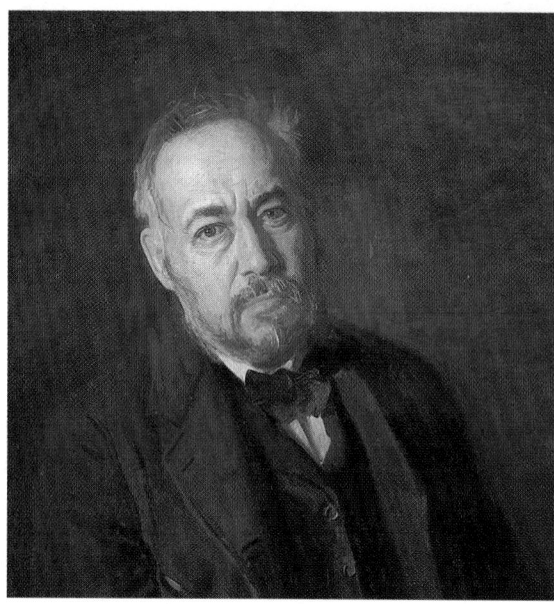

544 Thomas Eakins. Detail of SELF-PORTRAIT. 1902. Oil on canvas. Full painting 30" × 25". National Academy of Design, New York.

"I never knew but one artist, and that's Tom Eakins, who could resist the temptation to see what they think ought to be rather than what is."[4] Thus the great American poet Walt Whitman praised his friend and portraitist. Unfortunately, the quality Whitman most admired in Eakins was the quality the public and the critics liked least.

Thomas Eakins was an unlikely outcast. Growing up in a middle-class Philadelphia family, he expected nothing more than to fit in: to work hard, learn his trade, and take a useful place in society just like any other professional.

Work hard and learn his trade he did. A diligent student, he excelled in science, math, languages, and drawing. He went on to study art at the Pennsylvania Academy and anatomy at Jefferson Medical College.

In 1866 he traveled to Paris, where he studied for three years with the academic painter Léon Gérôme. Rembrandt became one of his artistic heroes. A year in Spain followed, where Eakins discovered his other artistic heroes in seventeenth-century painters such as Velásquez—"so good, so strong, so reasonable, so free of every affectation," he wrote home to his mother.[5] We use the same list of qualities to praise Eakins's work.

At twenty-seven, Eakins returned to Philadelphia and set to work painting the life and society he knew best. He painted portraits and family scenes. He painted Americans outdoors, in rowing races, baseball games, boxing, and skinny-dipping. He even painted a surgical operation, the new triumph of modern medicine. Critics respected Eakins's formidable technique, but they were variously offended, angered, depressed, or disappointed by his uncompromising realism. Few people saw that Eakins's greatness lay precisely in his capacity to accept contemporary life fully and without illusion.

Eakins had a disciplined, inquisitive mind, and he pursued complementary artistic and scientific interests. He loved anatomy, and his dissections were so expert that he read a paper before the Philadelphia Academy of Sciences on the action of certain muscles. He enjoyed mathematics and would relax after painting by reading logarithms or working out calculus problems. He invented and built the camera with which he took multiple-exposure action photographs such as the one on page 70.

As a teacher at the Pennsylvania Academy, he made waves by insisting that women receive the same rigorous training as men, including drawing from nude male as well as female models. Parents were shocked, and Eakins was forced to resign. As usual, what seemed common sense to Eakins seemed dangerously radical to his contemporaries.

As Eakins grew older, public and critical opinion passed from hostility to indifference. Young painters no longer flocked to study with him. Sustained by a modest family income, Eakins continued to paint, increasingly isolated and bitter. "My honors are misunderstanding, persecution, and neglect," he said, "enhanced because unsought."[6] His honors are such that today we realize he was one of the finest painters—and most original spirits—America ever produced.

Eakins's influence can be seen in the work of his student and friend Henry Ossawa Tanner, who was the best known African-American painter before the twentieth century. At the age of thirteen, Tanner watched a landscape painter at work and decided to become a painter. While studying with Eakins at the Academy of Fine Arts in Philadelphia, Tanner changed his subject matter from landscape to scenes of daily life. In 1891, after an exhibition of his work was largely ignored, Tanner moved to France, where he remained for most of the rest of his life. Tanner found less racial prejudice in Paris than in the United States. His paper "The American Negro in Art," presented at the 1893 World's Congress on Africa in Chicago, voiced the need for dignified portrayals of blacks, and he offered his painting THE BANJO LESSON as a model.

The lively realism of THE BANJO LESSON reveals Tanner's considerable insight into the feelings of his subjects, yet he avoids the sentimentality that was common in many late nineteenth-century American paintings. This painting shows the influence of Eakins in its detail and the influence of the Impressionists in Tanner's use of light and color.

The revolution that occurred in painting in the 1860s and 1870s has sometimes been referred to as the Manet revolution. Edouard Manet was a student of Couture who moved away from many of the artistic ideals of his teacher. Compare Couture's ROMANS OF THE DECADENCE (page 380) with Manet's LUNCHEON ON THE GRASS (see next page). Manet's study of the flat shapes of Japanese prints (see page 300) encouraged him to minimize illusionary space and to make powerful use of value, shape, and color. His painting style and choice of commonplace subjects reflect Courbet's influence. Manet fused Courbet's realism with his own concepts and sparked the enthusiasm for painterly brushwork and everyday visual experience that led to Impressionism.

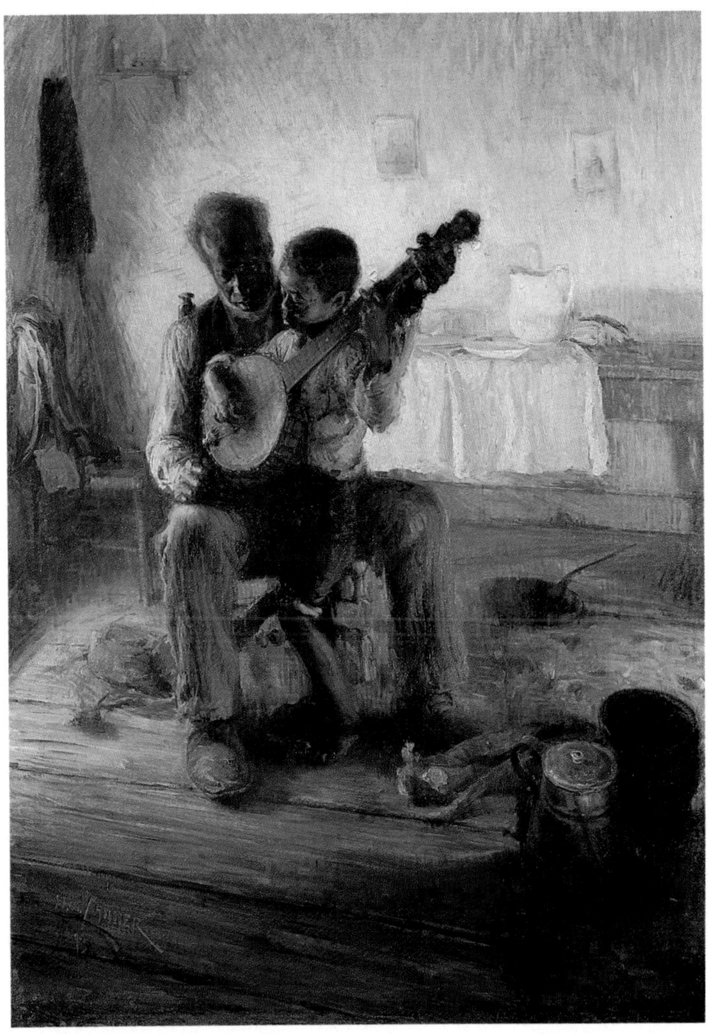

545 Henry Ossawa Tanner.
THE BANJO LESSON. 1893.
Oil on canvas. 4'1/2" × 3'11".
Hampton Institute, Hampton, Virginia.

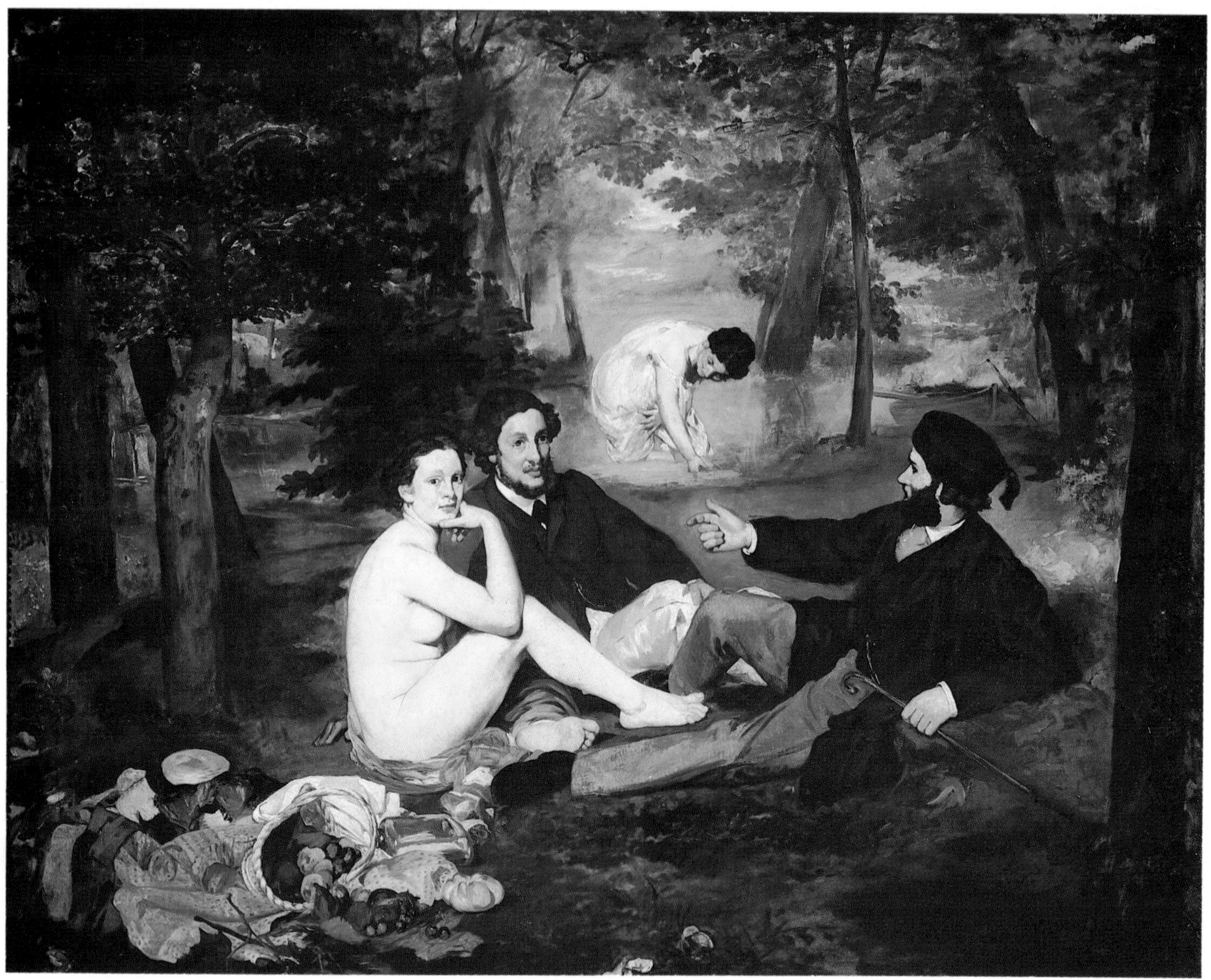

546 Edouard Manet.
LUNCHEON ON THE GRASS (LE DÉJEUNER SUR L'HERBE). 1863.
Oil on canvas. 84" × 106".
Musée du Louvre, Paris.

Manet's painting LUNCHEON ON THE GRASS scandalized French critics and the public—because of the way it was painted as well as the subject matter. Manet painted the female figure without shading, employed flat patches of color throughout the painting, and left bare canvas in some places. He concentrated on the interplay among the elements of form that make up the composition: light shapes against dark, cool colors accented by warm colors, directional forces, and active balance. What is revolutionary in Manet's work is his concern with visual issues over content or storytelling.

Renaissance illusion of depth is greatly diminished here. Manet's emphasis on the interaction of dark and light shapes and his de-emphasis of both chiaroscuro and perspective cause us to look at the surface of a painting rather than through an illusionary window onto nature.

The juxtaposition of a female nude with males dressed in clothing of the time shocked viewers, but such a combination was not new. Nude and clothed figures in landscape derives from a tradi-

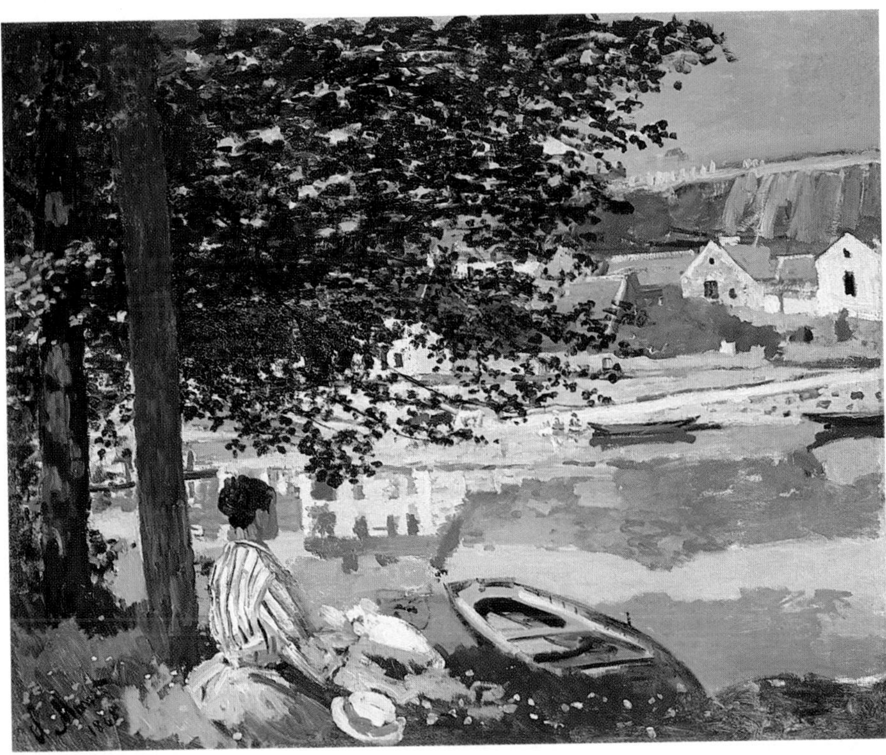

547 Claude Monet.
ON THE SEINE AT BENNECOURT (AU BORD DE L'EAU, BENNECOURT).
1868. Oil on canvas.
81.5 cm × 100.7 cm.
Potter Palmer Collection, 1922.427.

tion going back to Renaissance and even Roman compositions that depicted ancient myths or stories from the Bible. However, in Manet's painting, there is no allegory, no history, no mythology, and not even a significant title to suggest morally redeeming values. Manet based his composition (but not his content) on the figures in an engraving of a Renaissance drawing by Raphael, who in turn had been influenced by Roman relief sculpture.

It is ironic that Manet, who had such reverence for the art of the past, would be attacked by the public and the critics for his radical innovations. Simultaneously, he was championed by other artists as a leader of the avant-garde. Manet became the reluctant leader of an enthusiastic group of young painters who later formed the group known as the Impressionists.

Under Manet's influence, Claude Monet abandoned the use of heavy earth colors and broad-stroke painting techniques. Monet's paintings ON THE SEINE and BATHING AT LA GRENOUILLÈRE (see page 114) both pay homage to and progress from Manet's LUNCHEON ON THE GRASS. Monet had adopted Manet's color-patch technique and applied it to painting vivid colors generated by sunlight. Monet's idyllic glimpses of contemporary life, painted with an emphasis on qualities of light and color, are the beginnings of Impressionism.

IMPRESSIONISM

In 1874, a group of young painters who had been denied the right to show in the Salon of 1873 organized an independent exhibition of their work. These artists, opposing academic doctrines and Romantic ideals, turned instead to the portrayal of contemporary life. They sought to paint "impressions" of what the eye actually sees rather than what the mind knows. This is no simple goal; we usually generalize what we think we see from the most obvious fragments. The variety of colors in a river becomes a uniform blue-green in our minds, whereas direct, unconditioned seeing yields a rich diversity of colors.

Landscape and ordinary scenes painted outdoors in varied atmospheric conditions, seasons, and times of day were among their main subjects. They were dubbed Impressionists by a critic who

CLAUDE MONET (1840–1926)

Claude Monet grew up in Le Havre, a bustling port town on the north coast of France. In high school, he developed a reputation for drawing caricatures. A local picture framer took to exhibiting them in his shop, and there they caught the eye of a painter named Eugène Boudin.

Monet's senior by sixteen years, Boudin was a pioneer in the new practice of painting outdoors, working directly from nature. He encouraged Monet to pursue art seriously and invited him along on a painting excursion. The experience started Monet on the path he would follow all his life. "Boudin set up his easel and began to paint," Monet later recalled. "I looked on with some apprehension, then more attentively, and then suddenly it was as if a veil was torn from my eyes; I had understood. I had grasped what painting could be."[7]

Monet continued his studies in Paris, where he immersed himself in the lively artistic debates of the day. He met and admired the controversial painters Courbet and Manet. He met other art students, Renoir among them, who shared his passion for painting nature and modern life. In time, they would become famous as leading Impressionists.

Fame was long in coming, however; Monet was over forty before his paintings sold well enough to guarantee a living for himself and his family. In the meantime, life was difficult. From dawn to dusk he painted; in the evening, by lamplight, he wrote letters—letters asking for money, letters stalling creditors, letters trying to arrange for his work to be seen and sold.

As Monet's vision deepened, he realized that every shift in light and atmosphere created a new subject. He would arrive at a site with as many as a dozen canvases, working on each one in turn as the light changed. His painting grew increasingly subjective as he strove to express not only light but his feelings about the changing qualities of light. Relentlessly self-critical, he was often driven to despair by his work, and he destroyed hundreds of canvases he considered failures.

In back of his house at Giverny, the small town outside Paris where he finally settled, Monet created a water lily pond that became the favorite subject of his final years. In old age, he embarked on one of his most ambitious projects: a series of huge paintings of the water surface, its shimmering reflections of sky and clouds punctuated with floating flowers. Shown end to end, they form dazzling panoramas over six feet tall and twenty-eight feet long. Monet intended them as a gift to the French government, and one of his last acts before he died was to send a letter declaring them finished.

As you read in the next chapter about the radical movements that followed World War I, remember that the last and purest of the Impressionists was still painting from dawn to dusk every day, creating masterpieces of Impressionism long after the course of "art history" had moved on.

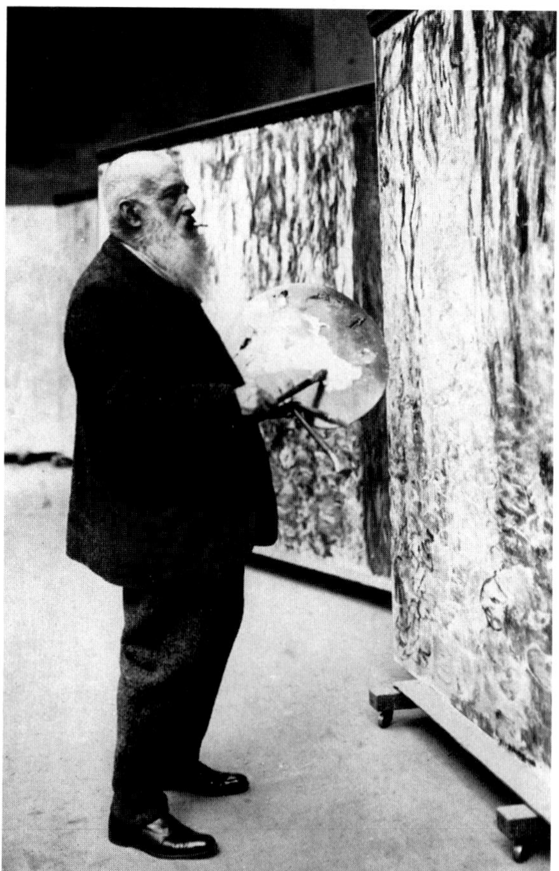

548 CLAUDE MONET
on his eightieth birthday. 1920.

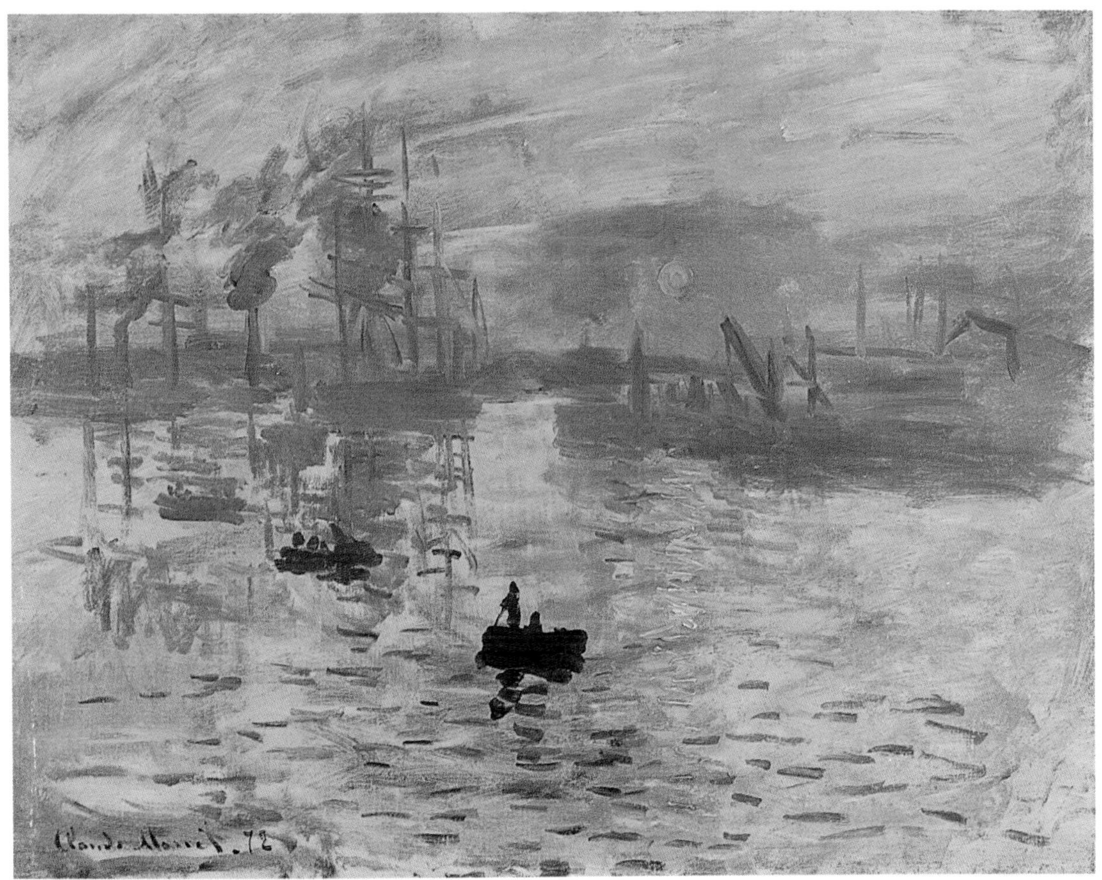

549 Claude Monet.
IMPRESSION: SUNRISE. 1872.
Oil on canvas. 19½" × 25½".
Musée Marmottan, Paris.

objected to the sketchy quality of their paintings. The term was suggested by one of Monet's versions of IMPRESSION: SUNRISE. Although the critic's label was intended to be derogatory, the artists adopted the term as a fitting description of their work.

From direct observation and from studies in physics, the Impressionists learned that light is seen as a complex of reflections received by the eye and reassembled by the mind during the process of perception. Therefore, they used small dabs of color that appear merely as separate strokes of paint when seen close up, yet become lively depictions of subjects when seen at a distance. Monet often applied strokes of color placed next to each other, rather than colors premixed or blended on the canvas. The viewer perceives a vibrancy that cannot be achieved with mixed color alone. The effect was startling to eyes accustomed to the muted, continuous tones of academic painting (see page 114).

The Impressionists enthusiastically affirmed modern life. They saw the beauty of the world as a gift and the forces of nature as aids to human progress. Although misunderstood by their public, the Impressionists made visible a widely held optimism about the promise of the new technology.

Impressionism was strongest between 1870 and 1880. After 1880, it was Claude Monet who continued for more than forty years to advance Impressionism's original premise. Instead of painting from sketches, he and most of the others in the group painted outdoors. Monet returned to the same subjects again and again in order to record the moods and qualities of light at different times of day and at different seasons.

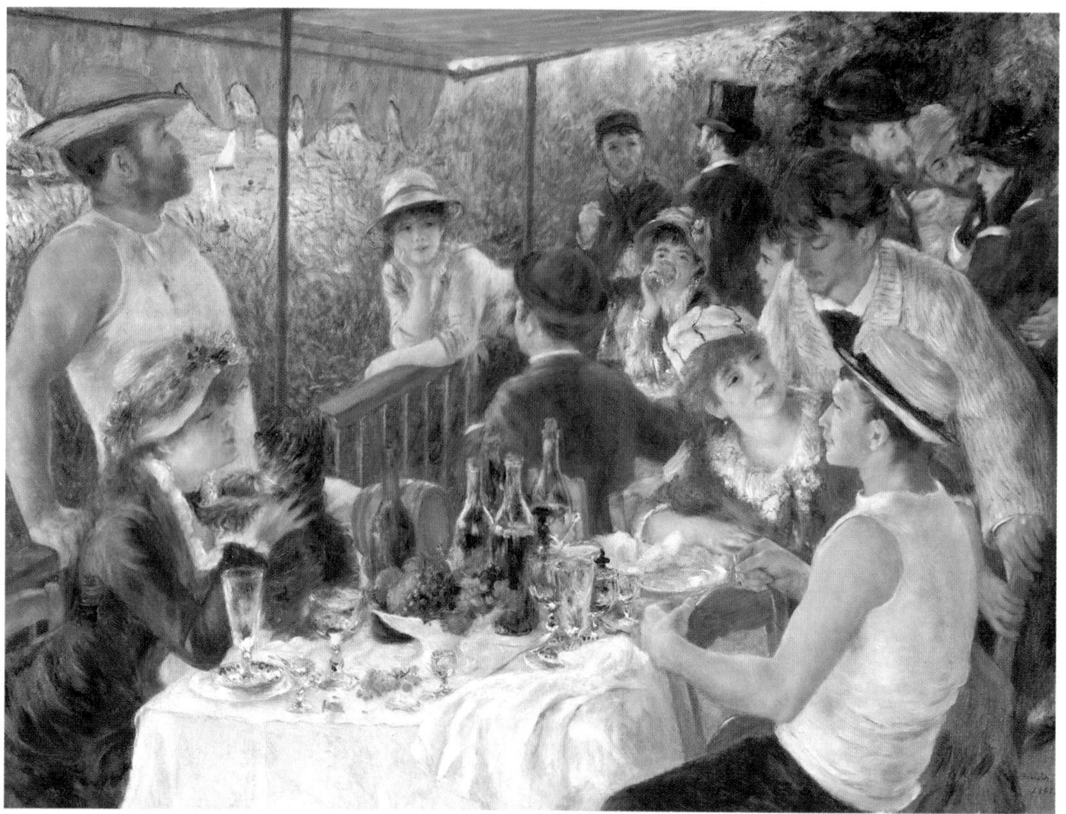

550 Pierre-Auguste Renoir.
THE LUNCHEON OF THE BOATING PARTY. 1881.
Oil on canvas. 51" × 68".
The Phillips Collection, Washington, D.C.

Monet's BATHING AT LA GRENOUILLÈRE (page 114) and Renoir's THE LUNCHEON OF THE BOATING PARTY both depict a popular Impressionist theme: people enjoying leisure activities along the Seine, the river that flows through Paris. These paintings also reveal similarities and differences between the styles of the two painters.

Monet's concern with the visual phenomena of light and color contrasts with the later work by Renoir, who by then was more concerned with composition. In THE LUNCHEON OF THE BOATING PARTY, as in Monet's paintings, rich colors, highlights, and shadows create a lively surface. But by 1881, Renoir had begun to move away from the lighter, more diffuse Impressionist imagery of the 1870s toward more solid forms and more structured design; compare this painting to his 1872 work on page 115. Renoir's disregard for true linear perspective, as seen in the lines of the railing and table top, reflects the declining interest in naturalistic illusions of depth. More obvious is his interest in portraying the solidity of the figures in a memorable composition.

The young men and women depicted are conversing, sipping wine, and generally enjoying the moment. The Industrial Revolution had created an urban middle class with leisure, a love of the new technology, and a taste for fashion.

French painter Camille Pissarro was hailed by fellow Impressionists as a leader and guide. As a student of a master landscape painter, he was advised to paint small sketches from nature and to study light and tonal values. Pissarro, in turn, was a highly influential teacher and friend to younger artists, including the seminal Post-Impressionist painters Cézanne and Gauguin; Cézanne was par-

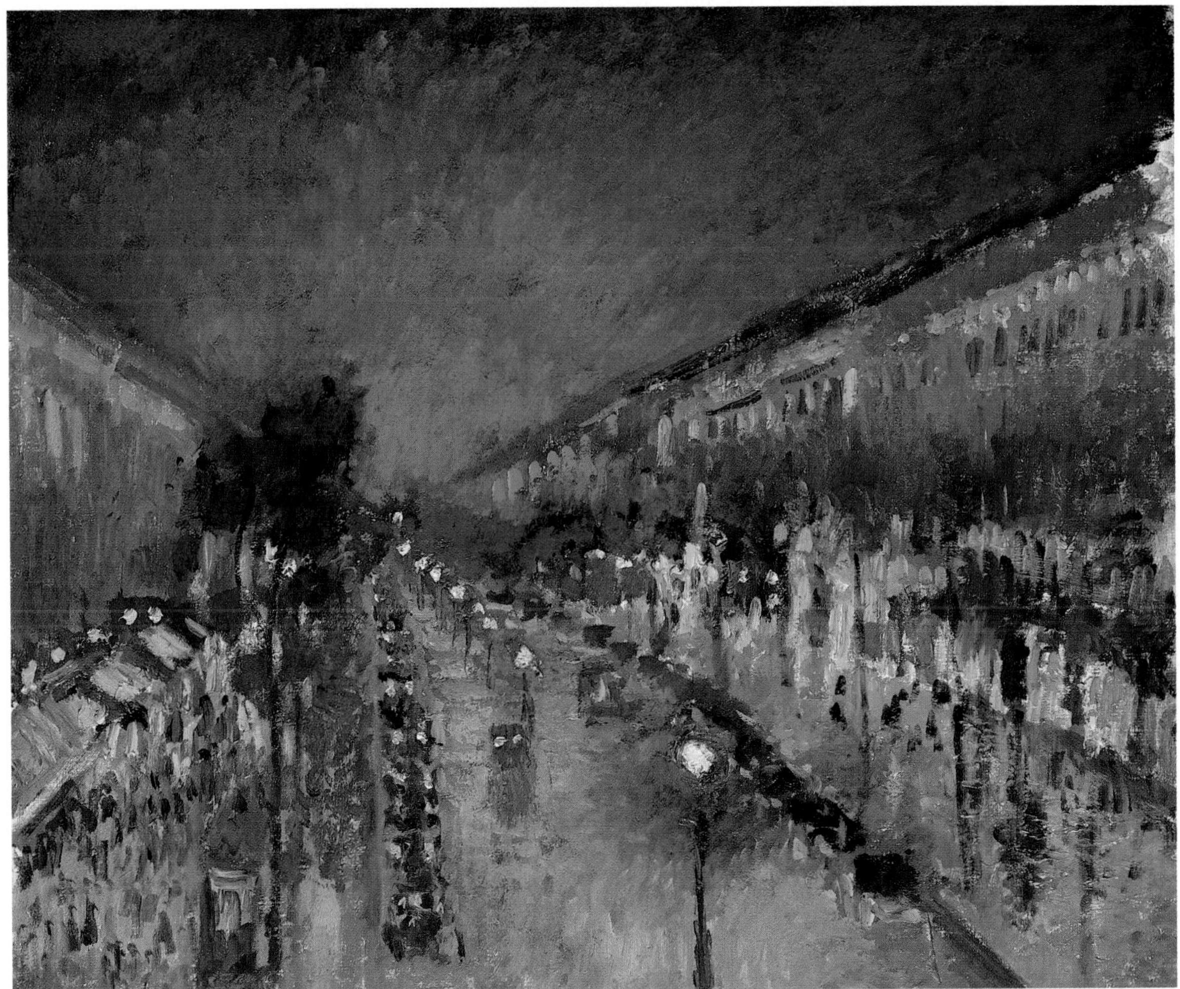

551 Camille Pissarro.
BOULEVARD MONTMARTRE, EFFET DE NUIT. 1887.
Oil on canvas. 21¼" × 25⅝".

ticularly impressed by Pissarro's use of a high vantage point and the structured composition of his paintings.

Although generally known for his landscapes, Pissarro painted a series of urban views, including BOULEVARD MONTMARTRE. In this quintessential Impressionist work, he captured the shimmering quality of reflected light on a rainy night. Loosely defined perspective lines give structure to this freely painted dance of color.

Edgar Degas exhibited with the Impressionists, although his approach differed from theirs. He shared with the Impressionists a directness of expression and an interest in portraying contemporary life, but he combined the immediacy of Impressionism with a highly inventive structured approach to design not found in the work of those painters. Degas, along with the Impressionists, was strongly influenced by the new ways of seeing and composing that were suggested in part by Japanese prints and by photography.

Conventional European compositions placed subjects within a central zone. Degas, however, used surprising, lifelike compositions and effects that often cut figures at the edge. The tipped-up ground planes and bold asymmetry found in Japanese prints inspired Degas to create paintings filled with intriguing visual tensions, such as those

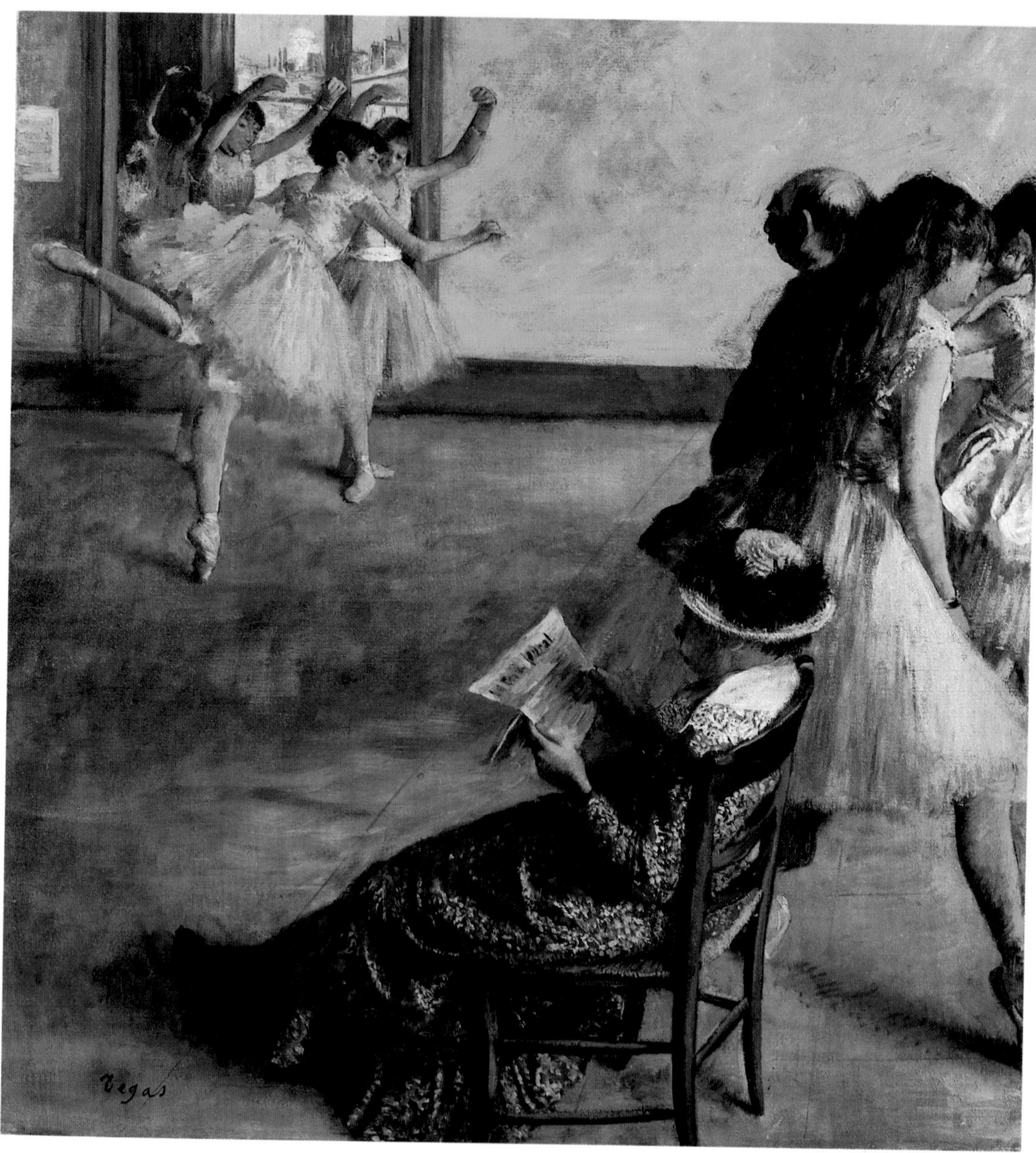

552 Edgar Degas.
THE BALLET CLASS. c. 1878-1880.
Oil on canvas. 32⅛" × 30⅛".
Philadelphia Museum of Art. W. P. Wilstach Collection.

seen in THE BALLET CLASS, in which two diagonal groups of figures appear on opposite sides of an empty center.

Degas depicted ballet classes in ways that showed their unglamorous character. Often, as here, he was able to turn his great ability to the task of defining human character and mood in a given situation. The painting builds from the quiet, uninterested woman in the foreground, up to the right, then across to the cluster of dancing girls, following the implied line of sight of the ballet master. The stability of the group on the right contrasts with the smaller, irregular shape of the girls before the mirror. Degas managed to balance spatial tensions between near and far and to create interesting contrasts between stable and unstable, large and

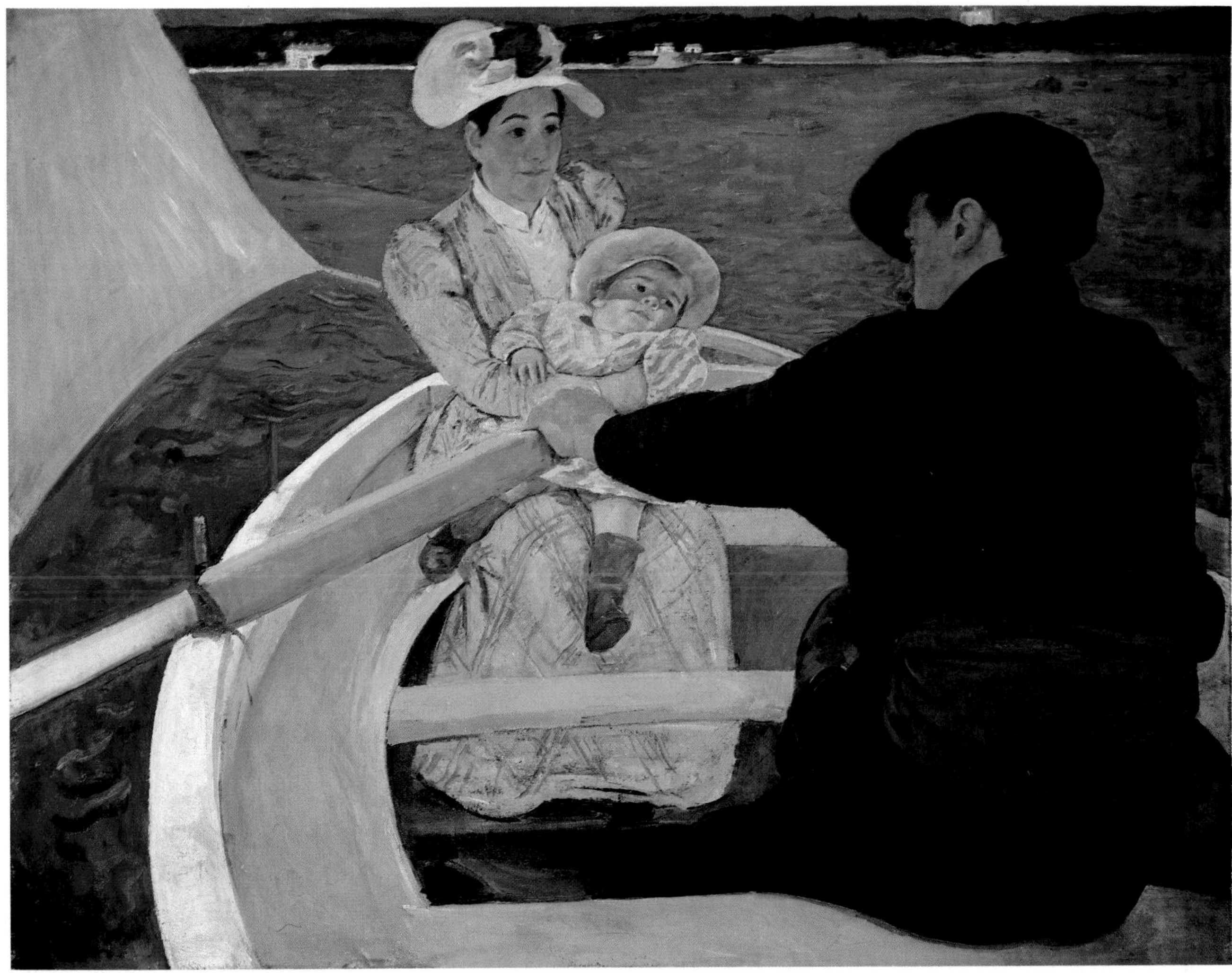

553 Mary Cassatt.
THE BOATING PARTY. 1893-1894.
Oil on canvas. 35½" × 46⅛".

small. He emphasized the line in the floor, which he brought together with the top of the woman's newspaper to guide the viewer's eye. The angle of the seated woman's foot brings us back around to begin again.

American painter Mary Cassatt went to Paris in the late 1860s to further her artistic development. She was strongly influenced by the work of Manet (page 386) and Degas. Following an invitation by Degas, she joined and exhibited with the Impressionists. Later, she was among the many European and American artists who were influenced by Japanese prints and "snapshot" compositions of late nineteenth-century do-it-yourself photography. A resemblance to Japanese prints is readily apparent in the simplicity and bold design of THE BOATING PARTY. Cassatt refined her subject in sweeping curves and almost flat shapes.

Painters such as Manet, Monet, Renoir, and Degas rejected the artificial poses and limited color prescribed by the Academy. Because they rebelled against accepted styles, they made few sales in their early years. Many who were considered outsiders, set apart from the conventional art of their time, we now consider masters of nineteenth-century art and precursors of twentieth-century art.

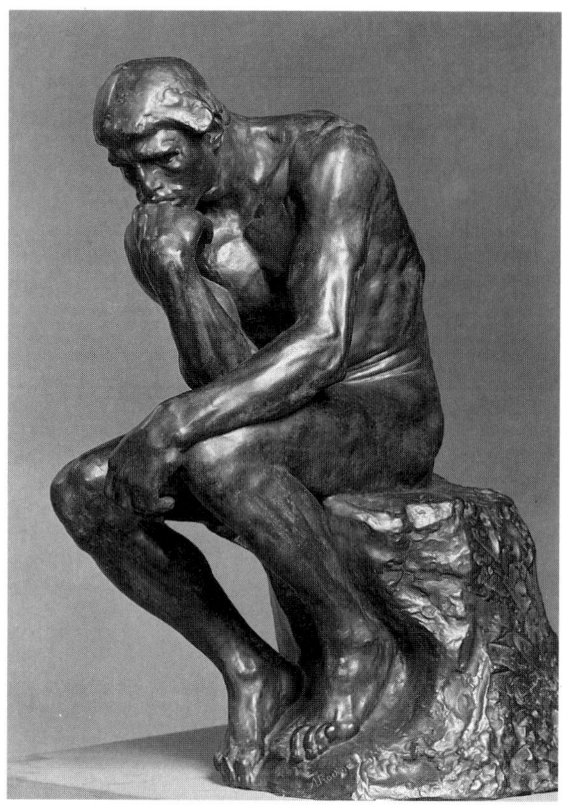

554 Auguste Rodin.
THE THINKER. 1879-1889.
Bronze. Life-size.
The Metropolitan Museum of Art. Gift of Thomas F. Ryan (1910).

The Impressionist group dissolved after its final exhibition in 1886, but its influence on art and public taste was immeasurable—in spite of the fact that Impressionist paintings were looked upon with indifference, even hostility, by most of the public and the critics until the 1920s. From the perspective of our time, Impressionism was the most important artistic movement of the nineteenth century.

French artist Auguste Rodin was at least as important to sculpture as his contemporaries, the Impressionist and Post-Impressionist painters, were to painting. Rodin became the first sculptor since Bernini (see page 360) to return sculpture to the status of a major art form, renewed with emotional and spiritual depth.

After training as a sculptor's helper, in 1875 Rodin traveled to Italy where he was impressed by the powerful work of the Renaissance masters Donatello and Michelangelo. Rodin was the first to use Michelangelo's unfinished pieces (see page 205) as an inspiration for making unfinishedness an expressive quality. In contrast to Michelangelo, however, Rodin was primarily a modeler rather than a carver.

In 1880 he was commissioned to make a bronze door, *The Gates of Hell,* for a proposed museum of decorative arts. The large project was unfinished at Rodin's death, but many of the figures that are part of the door, including THE THINKER, modeled in clay and cast in bronze, and THE KISS, carved in marble (page 38), were enlarged as independent pieces. Of THE THINKER, Rodin wrote that his first inspiration had been Dante, but he rejected the idea of a thin, ascetic figure.

Guided by my first inspiration I conceived another thinker, a naked man, seated upon a rock, his feet drawn under him, he dreams. The fertile thought slowly elaborates itself within his brain. He is no longer dreamer, he is creator.[8]

In the place of Christ in judgment, usually seen over the doorways of medieval churches (see page 338), Rodin projects the universal artist/poet as creator, judge, and witness, brooding over the human condition. Rodin's superb knowledge of anatomy and his modeling skill combine to create the fluid, tactile quality of hand-shaped clay. Rodin restored sculpture as a vehicle for personal expression after it had lapsed into mere decoration and heroic monuments.

THE POST-IMPRESSIONIST PERIOD

Post-Impressionism refers to trends in painting that followed Impressionism starting about 1885. The Post-Impressionist painters did not share a single style; rather, they built on or reacted to Impressionism in highly individual ways. Some felt that Impressionism had sacrificed solidity of form and composition for the sake of momentary impressions. Others felt that Impressionism's emphasis on the direct observation of nature and everyday life did not leave enough room for personal expression or spiritual content. Among those whose works best exemplify Post-Impressionist attitudes were Dutch

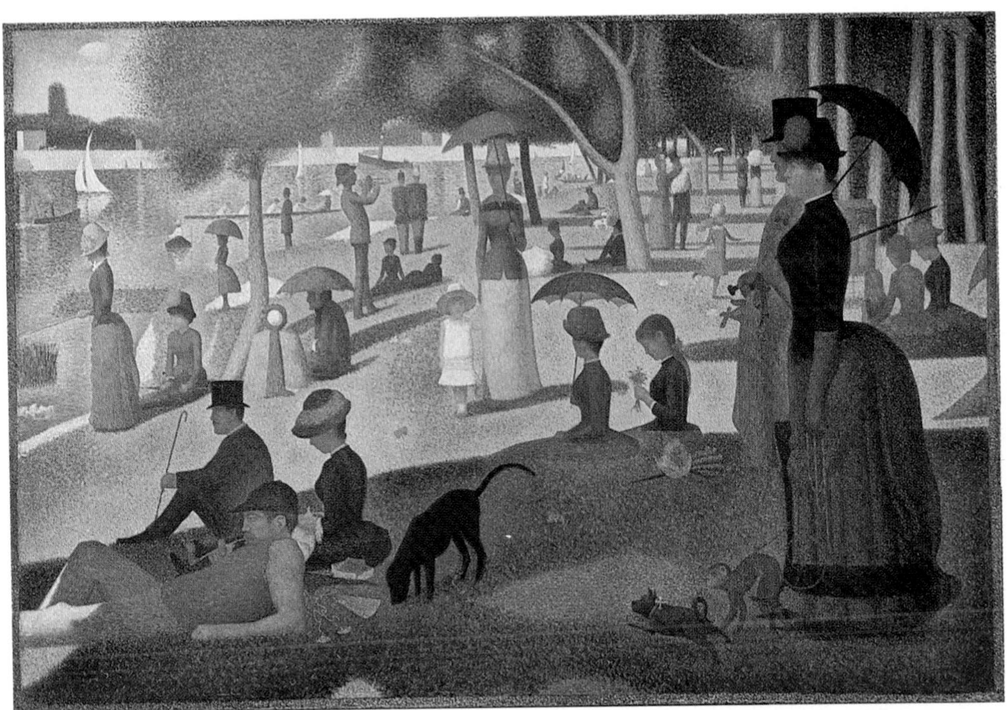

555 Georges Seurat.
A SUNDAY ON LA GRANDE JATTE. 1884-1886.
Oil on canvas. 81" × 120⅜".
Helen Birch Bartlett Memorial Collection, 1926.224.

artist Vincent van Gogh and French artists Paul Gauguin, Georges Seurat, and Paul Cézanne.

Gauguin and Van Gogh brought to their work expressive, emotional intensity and a desire to make their thoughts and feelings visible. They often used strong color contrasts, shapes with clear contours, bold brushwork, and, in Van Gogh's case, vigorous paint textures. Their art greatly influenced twentieth-century expressionist styles.

Seurat and Cézanne were interested in developing formal structure in their paintings. Each in his own way organized visual form to achieve structured clarity of design. Their paintings influenced twentieth-century formalist styles.

Cézanne and Seurat based their work on the observation of nature, and both used visibly separate strokes of color to build rich surfaces. Seurat's large painting A SUNDAY ON LA GRANDE JATTE has the subject matter, light, and color qualities of Impressionism, but this is not a painting of a fleeting moment. It is a carefully constructed composition of lasting impact. Seurat set out to systematize the optical color mixing of Impressionism and to create a more solid, formal organization with simplified shapes. He called his method *divisionism,* but it is more popularly known as *pointillism.* With it, Seurat tried to develop and apply a "scientific" technique. He arrived at his method by studying the principles of color optics that were being formulated at the time. Through the application of tiny dots of color, Seurat achieved a vibrant surface based on optical mixture (see page 81).

Seurat preceded LA GRANDE JATTE with more than fifty drawn and painted preliminary studies in which he explored the horizontal and vertical relationships, the character of each shape, and the patterns of light, shade, and color. The final painting shows the total control that Seurat sought through the application of his method. The frozen formality of the figures seems surprising, considering the casual nature of the subject matter; yet it is precisely this calm, formal grandeur that gives the painting its strength and enduring appeal.

Like Seurat, Cézanne sought to achieve strength in the formal structure of his paintings. "My aim," he said, "was to make Impressionism

PAUL CÉZANNE (1839–1906)

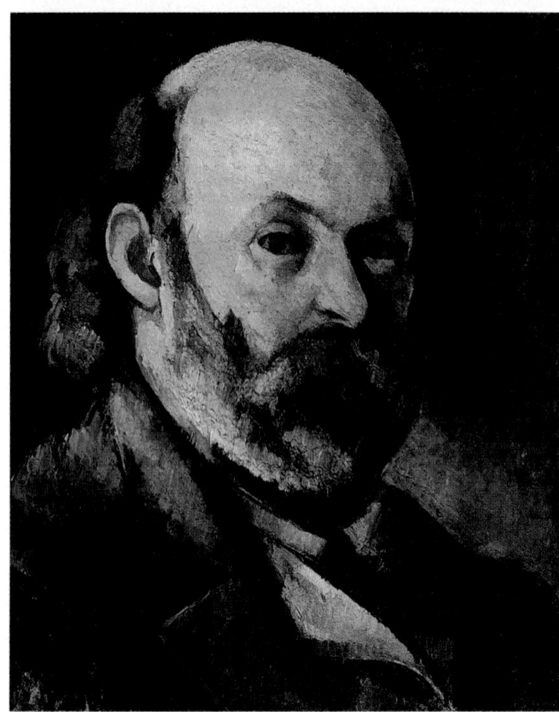

556 Paul Cézanne.
SELF-PORTRAIT.
Oil on canvas.
Hermitage Museum, St. Petersberg.

Paul Cézanne was born in Aix-en-Provence, a sleepy provincial town in the south of France. As a schoolboy his passion was poetry, and his friends, including the future novelist Emile Zola, thought of him as a budding literary genius. Bowing to the wishes of his father, a wealthy banker, Cézanne enrolled in a local college to study law. But Zola, who had gone to Paris to be in the thick of things, goaded Cézanne into declaring himself an artist and moving to the capital.

In Paris, Cézanne studied at the Académie Suisse, where his fellow students included many future Impressionists. In his early career, he painted from his imagination, not from nature; his subjects were often violent or erotic, the drawing seems barely competent, and the paint is laid on thickly, clumsily, passionately. The journey from these awkward beginnings to the mastery of his final years is one of the most impressive and moving self-transformations in the history of art.

Around 1870, Cézanne began to paint directly from nature and to discipline himself in this approach. For a time he worked side by side with the Impressionist painter Camille Pissarro, for whose patient guidance he remained grateful to the end of his life. Cézanne exhibited twice with the Impressionists, but the critics attacked him so viciously that he refused to show his work again. He returned to Aix, where for almost twenty years he worked in a self-imposed exile from the art world.

His personal life changed during those years as well: he married his mistress of seventeen years, when their son Paul was already twelve. Cézanne had kept their existence from his parents, afraid of angering his father and losing the meager allowance he provided. Later that year his father died, making Cézanne a wealthy man who was free to pursue his art without money worries.

In 1895, a young art dealer named Ambrose Vollard offered the reclusive painter a show in Paris. Cézanne sent one hundred fifty canvases, the cream of twenty years of work, wrapped in bundles of newsprint. The exhibit came as a revelation even to his old Impressionist friends. "It is great painting," wrote Pissarro. "My enthusiasm pales against Renoir's. Even Degas is seduced ... Monet, all of us."[9]

Cézanne was never popular with critics or the public during his lifetime, but he became a hero to the next generation of painters, many of whom made the pilgrimage to Aix to meet him. Still he worked all day every day, trying to realize more fully his sensations before nature.

In one of his last letters, he wrote his son, "Here on the bank of this river, the motifs multiply, the same subject seen from different angles gives a subject for study of the most powerful interest and so varied that I think I could occupy myself for months without changing position, simply bending a little more to the right or left."[10] This is as clear a description of a painter's state of grace as we are ever likely to have.

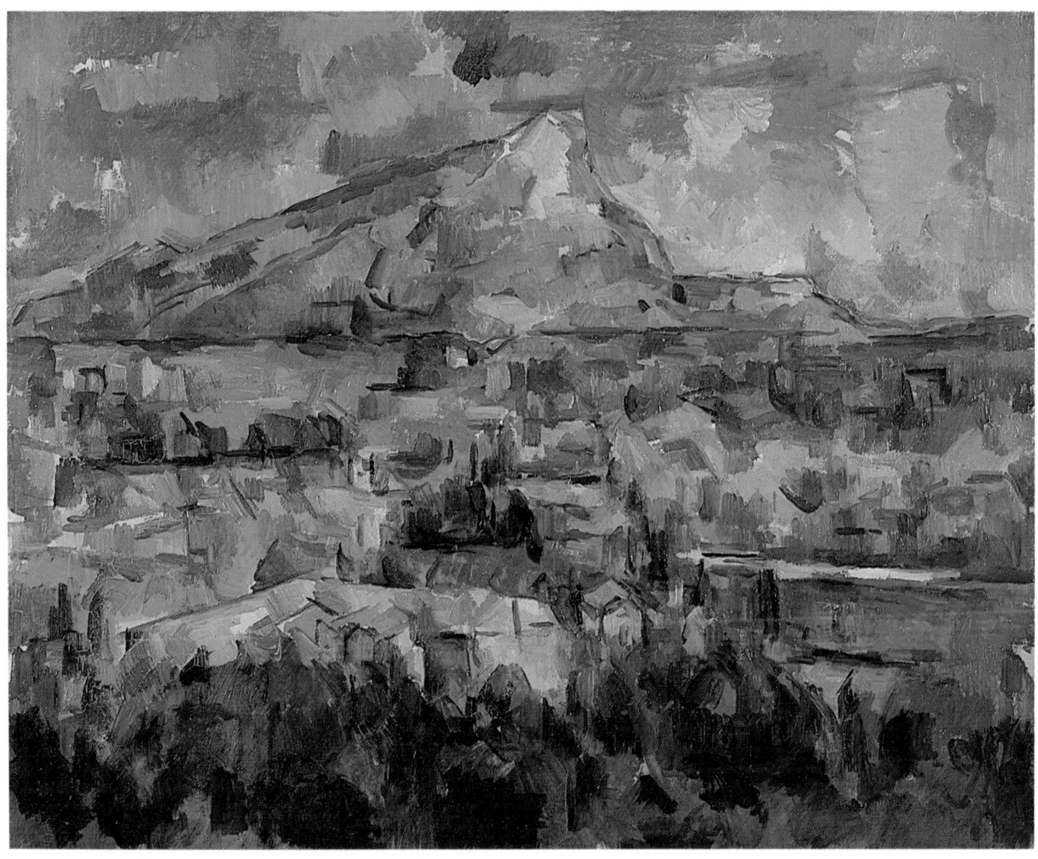

557 Paul Cézanne.
MONT SAINTE-VICTOIRE.
1902-1904.
Oil on canvas.
27½" × 35¼".
Philadelphia Museum of Art.
George W. Elkins Collection.

into something solid and enduring like the art of the museums."[11]

Cézanne saw the planar surfaces of his subjects in terms of color modulation. Instead of using light and shadow in a conventional way, he relied on carefully developed relationships between adjoining strokes of color to show solidity of form and receding space. He questioned, then abandoned, linear and atmospheric perspective and went beyond the appearance of nature, to reorganize it according to his own interpretation.

Landscape was one of Cézanne's main interests. In MONT SAINTE-VICTOIRE, we can see how he flattened space yet gave an impression of air and depth with some atmospheric perspective and the use of warm advancing and cool receding colors. The dark edge lines around the distant mountain help counter the illusion of depth. There is an important interplay between the illusion of depth and the fact of strokes of color on a flat surface. Cézanne simplified the houses and tree masses into patches of color that suggest almost geometric planes and masses. His open (not blended) brush strokes and his concept of a geometric substructure in nature and art offered a range of possibilities to those who studied his later paintings. Of the many great painters working in France around the turn of the century, Cézanne had the most lasting effect on the course of painting in the twentieth century. Compare this painting with Monet's LA GRENOUILLÈRE on page 114 to see how far Cézanne built on, yet departed from, Impressionism.

With Van Gogh, late nineteenth-century painting moved from an outer impression of what the eye sees to an inner expression of what the heart feels and the mind knows.

From Impressionism, Van Gogh learned the expressive potential of open brushwork and pure

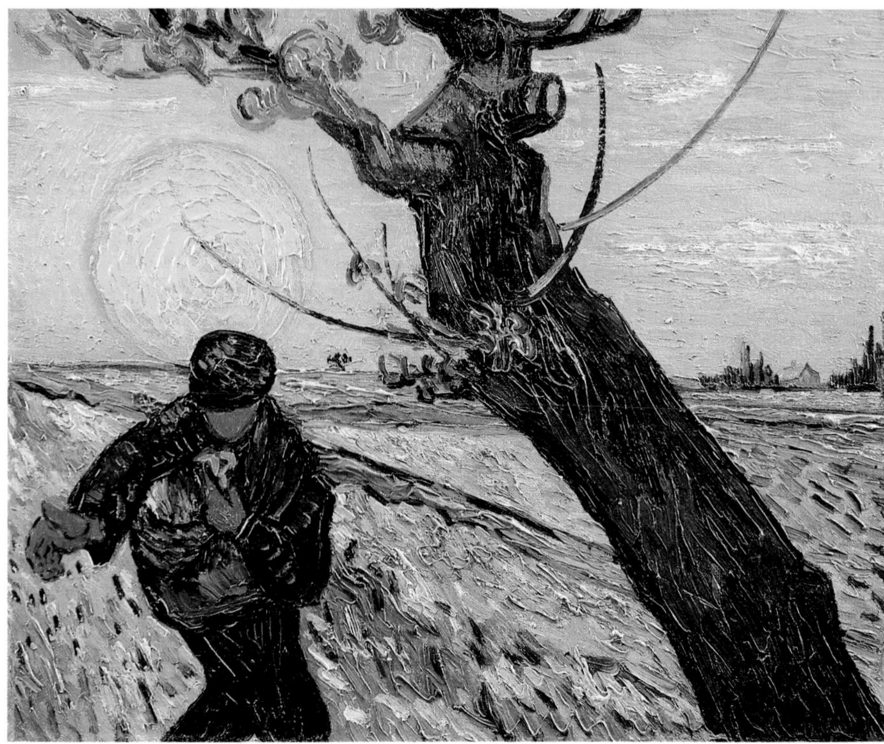

558 Vincent van Gogh.
THE SOWER. 1888.
Oil on canvas. 17⅜" × 22⅛".
Vincent van Gogh Foundation/Van Gogh Museum, Amsterdam.

559 Vincent van Gogh, after Hiroshige.
JAPONAISERIE: FLOWERING PLUM TREE. 1888.
Oil on canvas. 55 cm × 46 cm.
Vincent van Gogh Foundation/Van Gogh Museum, Amsterdam.

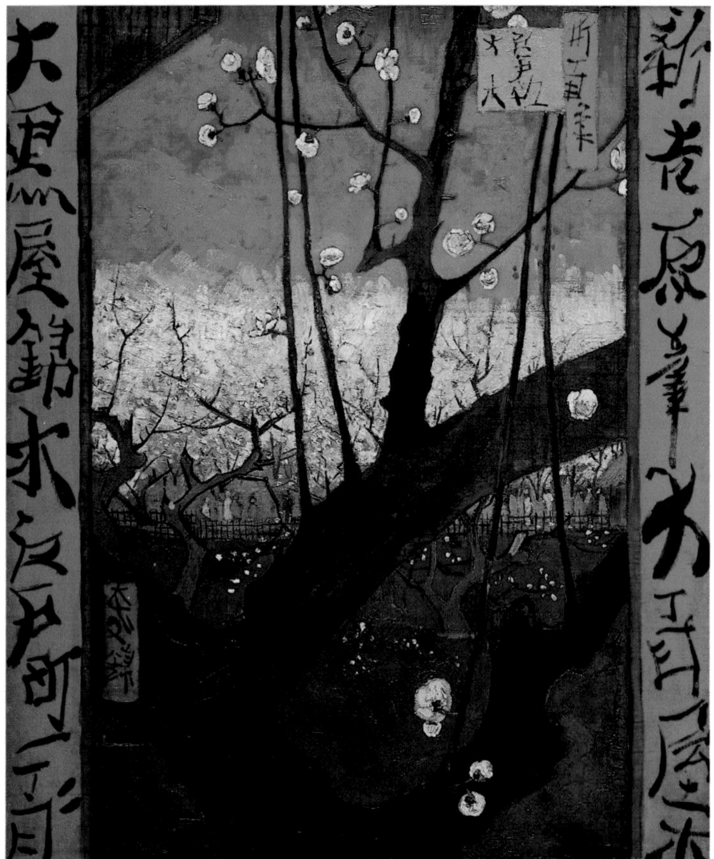

color; but the style did not provide enough freedom to satisfy his desire to express his feelings. Van Gogh intensified the surfaces of his paintings with textural brushwork that recorded each gesture of his hand and gave an overall rhythmic movement to his paintings. He began to use strong color in an effort to express his emotions more clearly. In letters to his brother Theo, he wrote,

... instead of trying to reproduce exactly what I have before my eyes, I use color more arbitrarily so as to express myself forcibly....

I am always in hope of making a discovery there to express the love of two lovers by a marriage of two complementary colors, their mingling and their opposition, the mysterious vibrations of kindred tones. To express the thought of a brow by the radiance of a light tone against somber background.[12]

As did other artists of the period, Van Gogh developed a new sense of design from studying—and even copying—Japanese prints, as in FLOWERING PLUM TREE. In THE SOWER, the Japanese influence

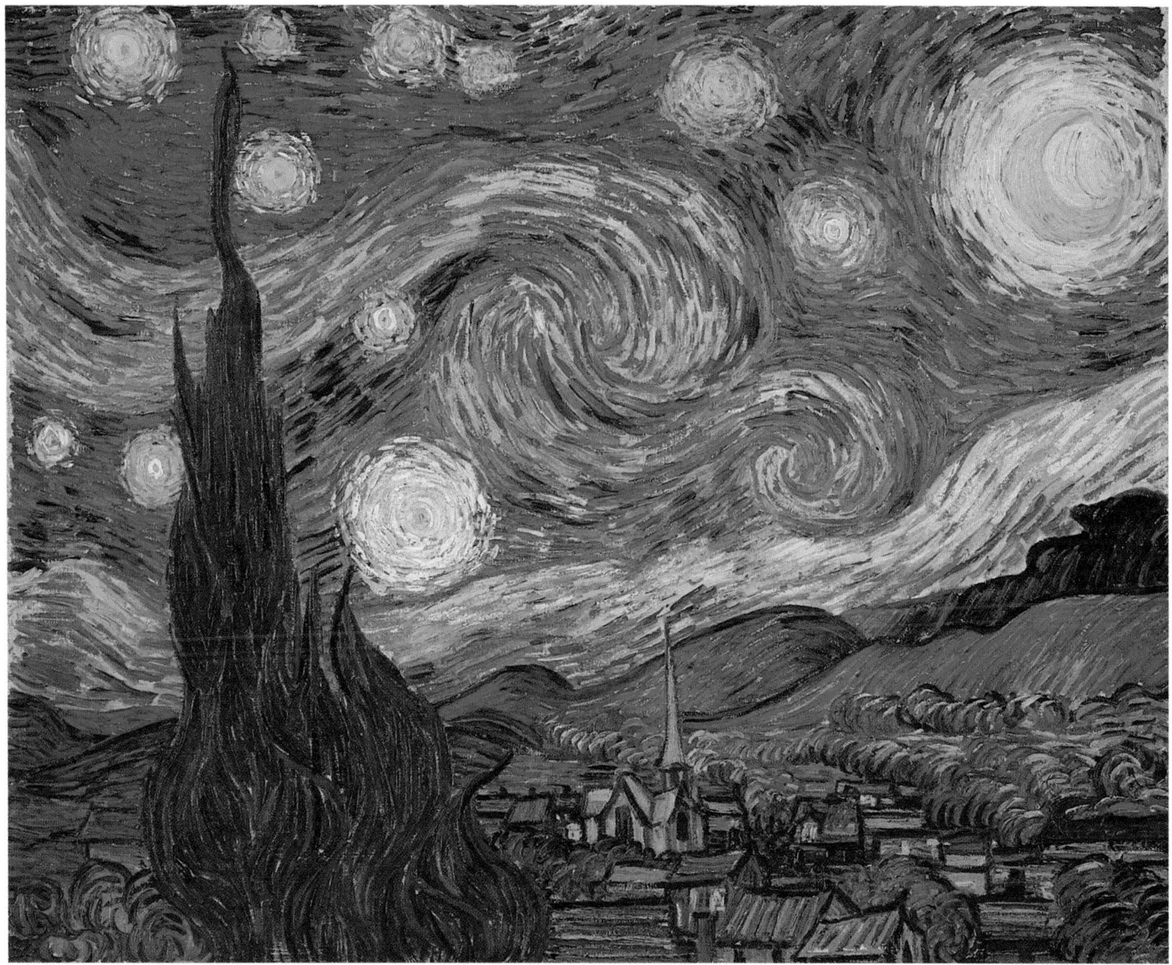

560 Vincent van Gogh.
THE STARRY NIGHT. 1889.
Oil on canvas. 29" × 36 1/4".
The Museum of Modern Art, New York. Acquired through the Lillie P. Bliss Bequest.

on Van Gogh's sense of design is clearly seen in the bold, simplified shapes and flat color areas. The wide band of a tree trunk cuts diagonally across the composition, its strength balancing the sun and its energy coming toward us with the movement of the sower.

A strong desire to share personal feelings and insights motivated Van Gogh. In THE STARRY NIGHT, his observation of a town at night became the point of departure for a powerful symbolic image. Hills seem to undulate, echoing tremendous cosmic forces in the sky. The small town nestled into the dark forms of the ground plane suggests the scale of human life. The church's spire reaches toward the heavens, echoed by the larger, more dynamic upward thrust of the cypress trees in the left foreground. (The evergreen cypress is traditionally planted beside graveyards in Europe as a symbol of eternal life.) All these elements are united by the surging rhythm of lines that express Van Gogh's passionate spirit and mystical vision. Many know of Van Gogh's bouts of mental illness, but few realize that his paintings were done between seizures, in moments of great clarity.

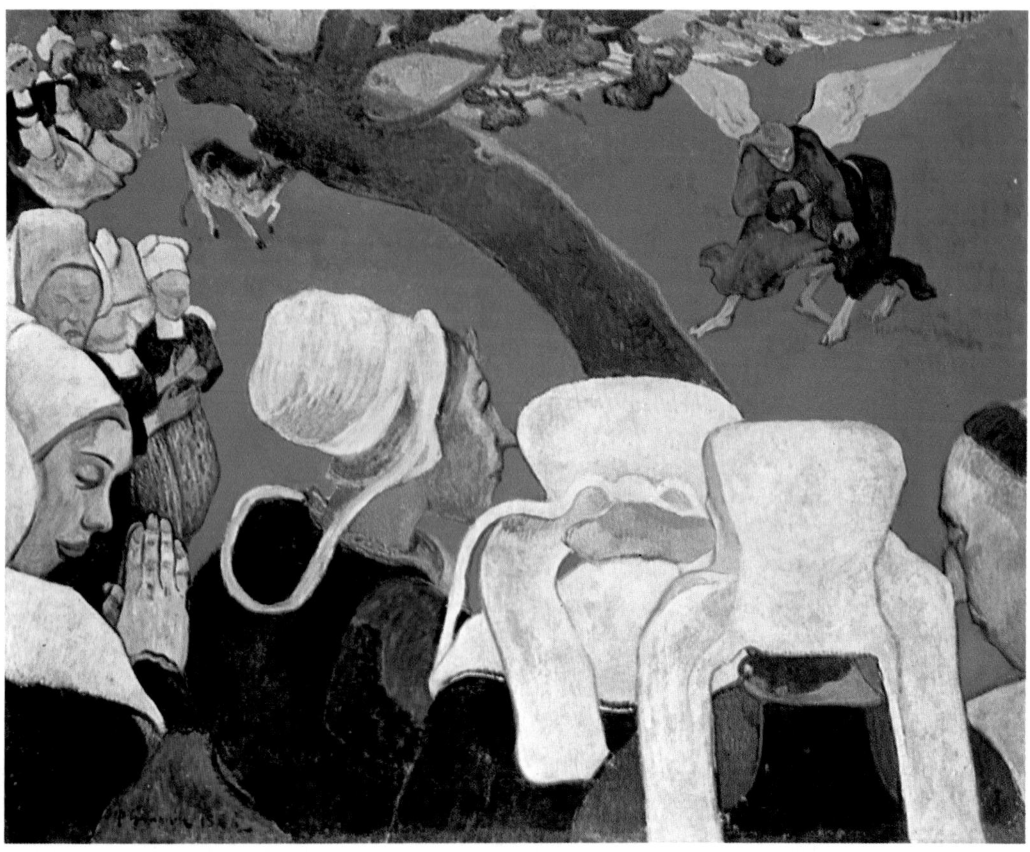

561 Paul Gauguin. THE VISION AFTER THE SERMON (JACOB WRESTLING WITH THE ANGEL). 1888. Oil on canvas. 28¾" × 36½". National Gallery of Scotland, Edinburgh.

French artist Paul Gauguin, like Van Gogh, was highly critical of the materialism of industrial society. This attitude led Gauguin to admire the honest life of the Brittany peasants of western France. In 1888, he completed THE VISION AFTER THE SERMON, the first major work in his revolutionary new style. The large, carefully designed painting shows Jacob and the angel as they appear to a group of Brittany peasants in a vision inspired by the sermon in their village church.

The symbolic representation of unquestioning faith is an image that originated in Gauguin's mind rather than in his eye. With it, Gauguin took a major step beyond Impressionism. In order to avoid what he considered the distraction of implied deep space, he tipped up the simplified background plane and painted it an intense, "unnatural" vermilion. The entire composition is divided diagonally by the trunk of the apple tree, in the manner of Japanese prints. Shapes have been reduced to flat curvilinear areas outlined in black, with shadows minimized or eliminated.

Both Van Gogh's and Gauguin's uses of color were important influences on twentieth-century painting. Their views on color were prophetic. The subject, Gauguin wrote, was only a pretext for symphonies of line and color.

In painting, one must search rather for suggestion than for description, as is done in music.... Think of the highly important musical role which colour will play henceforth in modern painting.[13]

Part Peruvian Indian, Gauguin retained memories of his childhood in Peru that persuaded him that the art of ancient and non-Western cultures had a spiritual strength that was lacking in the European art of his time. He wrote:

Keep the Persians, the Cambodians, and a bit of the Egyptians always in mind. The great error is the Greek, however beautiful it may be.[14]

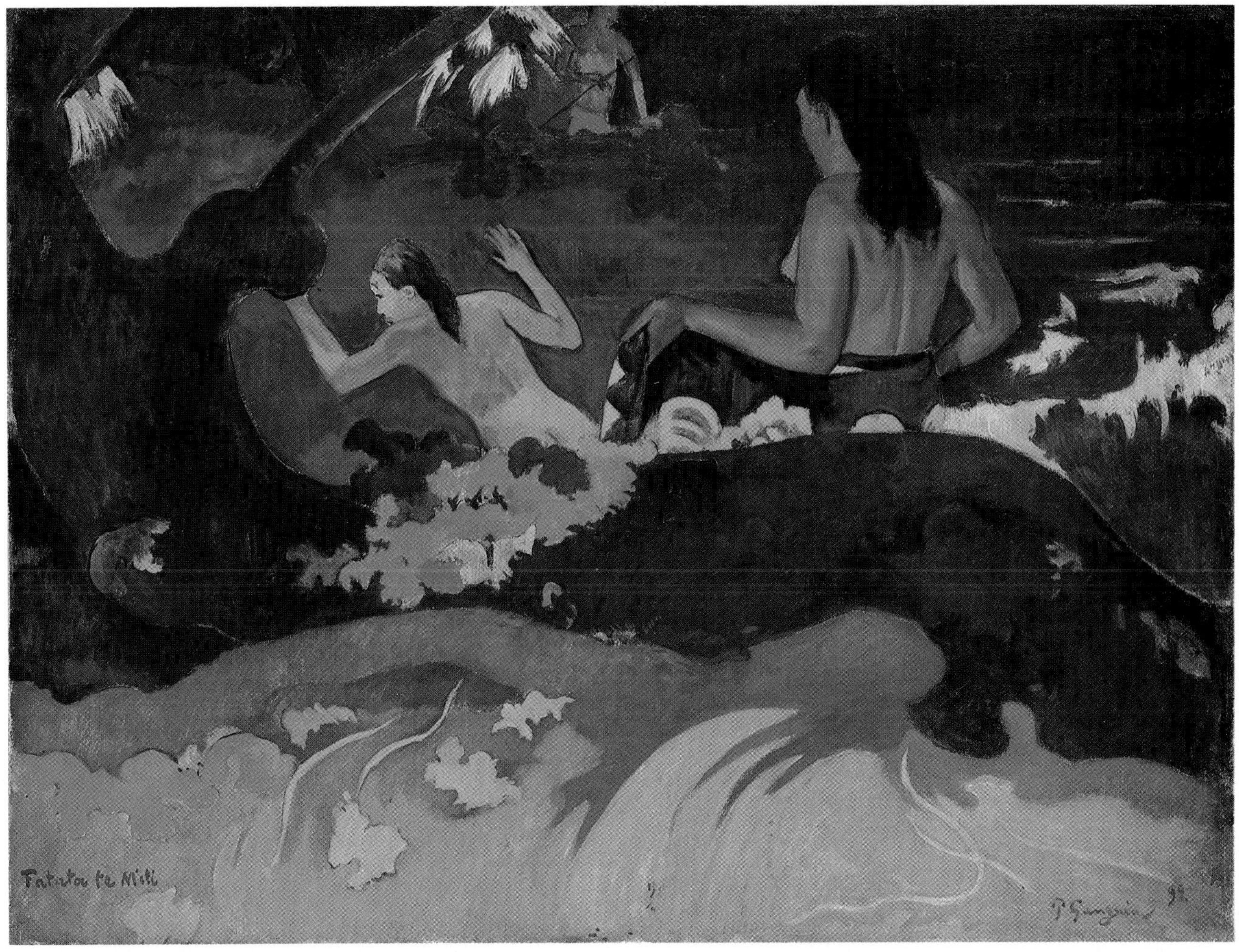

562 Paul Gauguin.
FATATA TE MITI (BY THE SEA). 1892.
Oil on canvas. 26¾" × 36".

A great thought system is written in gold in Far Eastern art.[15]

Gauguin's desire to rejuvenate European art and civilization with insights from non-Western traditions would be shared in the early twentieth century by Matisse, Picasso, and the German Expressionists. They adopted Gauguin's vision of the artist as a spiritual leader who could select from the past, and from various world cultures, anything capable of releasing the power of self-knowledge and inner life.

In the end, Gauguin tried to break completely with European civilization by going to Tahiti. In FATATA TE MITI, he combined flat, curvilinear shapes with tropical and fanciful colors.

For Gauguin, art had become above all a means of communicating through symbols, a "synthesis," he called it, of visual form carrying memory, feelings, and ideas. These beliefs link him to *Symbolism,* a movement in literature and the visual arts that developed around 1885.

Reacting against both Realism and Impressionism, Symbolist poets and painters sought to lift the mind from the mundane and the practical. They employed decorative forms and symbols that

PAUL GAUGUIN (1848–1903)

"I want to establish the right to dare everything," Gauguin wrote on the eve of his death.[16] Battered by bronchitis, neuralgia, syphilis, and a series of strokes, alone, impoverished, and halfway around the world from France, Gauguin had indeed dared everything, not only in his art but in his life.

Paul Gauguin was twenty-three when a family friend introduced him to the world of art and artists. Immersing himself in the new art of his day, he collected works by Cézanne, Degas, and others, and he began to paint in his spare time. By 1879 he was exhibiting with the Impressionist artists he so admired. His job as a stockbroker had become an unbearable distraction, and when he lost it in the aftermath of a financial crash a few years later, he decided not to look for another: he would be an artist. He was then thirty-five, with a pregnant wife and four children. It quickly became clear that he could not support his family as an artist, and after two years of arguments and compromises, his wife moved back to her family, taking the children with her.

Gauguin sought a place to paint that would nourish his vision of an art in touch with the primal mysteries of life. He moved first to Brittany, drawn to the primitive lives of the Breton peasants. In 1887 he painted on the Caribbean island of Martinique, but he fell ill, ran out of money, and had to return to France. The following year he joined Van Gogh in the south of France, but their idealistic plans for an artists' commune disintegrated into disastrous quarrels.

Convinced that he had to escape the "disease of civilization," Gauguin voyaged to Tahiti in 1891. He left its Westernized capital, Papeete, for a grass hut in a remote village, where he took a teenage bride, fathered a child, and steeped himself in the island's myths and legends. Despite the pressure of constant poverty, Gauguin transformed the raw material of Tahiti into a dream of earthly paradise, where a sensual people lived in harmony with their gods.

In 1893 Gauguin returned to France, confident that his Tahitian work would bring him success. Success did not come. Lonely and disillusioned, he returned to Tahiti in 1895 and found it more Westernized than before. Frustrated and angry, he fought with the colonial authorities and railed against the missionaries. His health was failing rapidly, he was desperate for money, and he grew so despondent he attempted suicide. Again he set off in search of a simpler life, sailing in 1901 to the Marquesas Islands, where he died two years later.

"It is true that I know very little," Gauguin wrote to a friend. "But who can say if even this little, worked on by others, will not become something great?"[17] In Paris, in 1906, a large retrospective of Gauguin's work made the extent of his achievement clear for the first time. His achievement was considerable, and, built on by Picasso and Matisse, and many others, his "little" did indeed become something great.

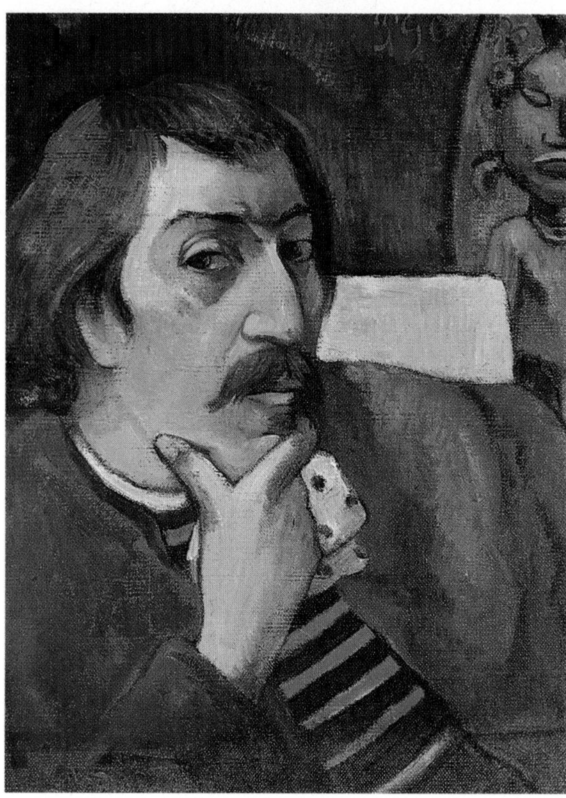

563 Paul Gauguin. PORTRAIT OF THE ARTIST WITH THE IDOL. c. 1893. Oil on canvas. 17¼" × 12⅞". McNay Art Museum, San Antonio, Texas. Bequest of Marion Koogler McNay.

were intentionally vague or open-ended in order to create imaginative suggestions. The poets held that the sounds and rhythms of words were part of their poems' deeper meaning; the painters recognized that line, color, and other visual elements were expressive in themselves. Symbolism, a trend rather than a specific style, provided the ideological background for twentieth-century abstraction; it has been seen as an outgrowth of Romanticism and a forerunner of Surrealism.

Henri de Toulouse-Lautrec, another Post-Impressionist, painted the gaslit interiors of Parisian nightclubs and brothels. His quick, long strokes of color define a world of sordid gaiety. Toulouse-Lautrec was influenced by Degas (see pages 143 and 392), whose work he greatly admired. In AT THE MOULIN ROUGE, Toulouse-Lautrec used unusual angles, cropped images, such as the face on the right, and expressive, unnatural color to heighten feelings about the people and the world he painted. His paintings, drawings, and prints of Parisian nightlife influenced the twentieth-century's expressionists and graphic designers (see page 167).

Norwegian painter Edvard Munch traveled to Paris to study the works of his contemporaries, especially Gauguin, Van Gogh, and Toulouse-Lautrec. What he learned from them, particularly from Gauguin's works, enabled him to carry Symbolism to a new level of expressive intensity. Munch's powerful paintings and prints explore depths of emotion—grief, loneliness, fear, love (see pages 106–109), sexual passion, jealousy, and death.

In THE SHRIEK, Munch takes the viewer far from the pleasures of Impressionism and extends considerably Van Gogh's expressive vision. In this powerful image of anxiety, the dominant figure is caught in isolation, fear, and loneliness. Despair reverberates in continuous linear rhythms. Munch's image has been called the soul-cry of our age.

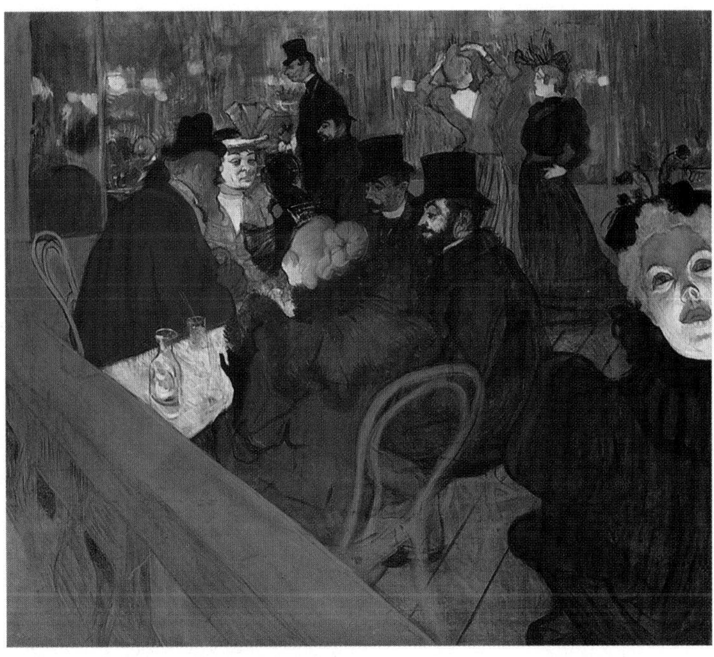

564 Henri de Toulouse-Lautrec.
AT THE MOULIN ROUGE. 1892-1895.
Oil on canvas. 48⅜" × 55¼".
Helen Birch Bartlett Memorial Collection 1928.610.

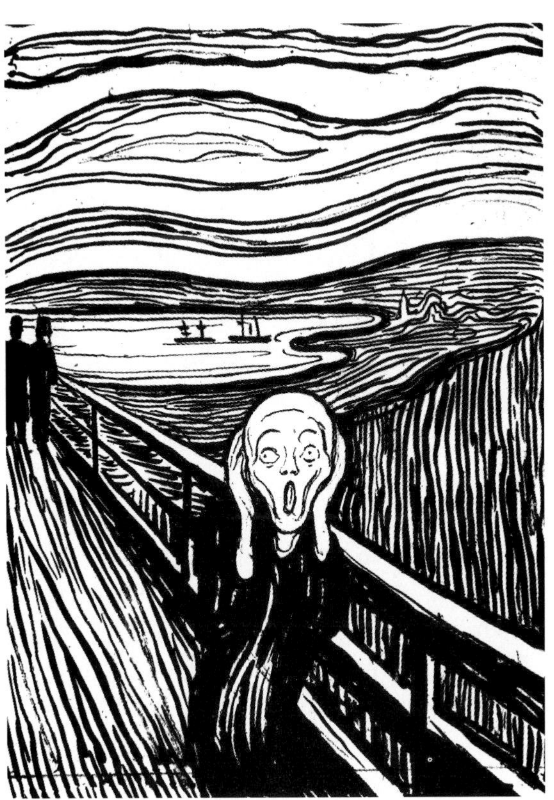

565 Edvard Munch.
THE SHRIEK (THE SCREAM). 1896.
Lithograph, printed in black. Sheet: 20⅝" × 15 13/16".
The Museum of Modern Art, New York. Matthew T. Mellon Fund.

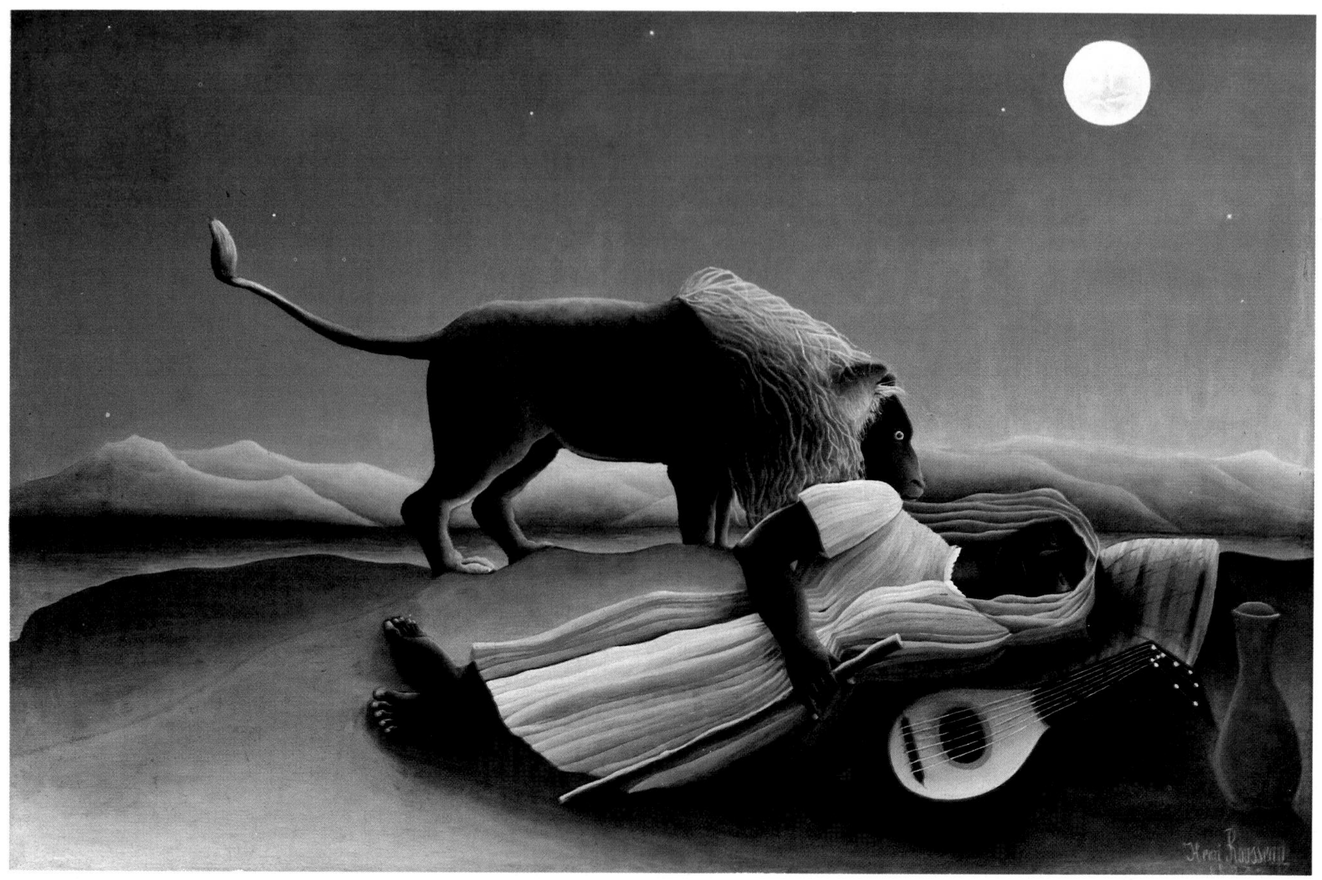

566 Henri Rousseau.
THE SLEEPING GYPSY. 1897.
Oil on canvas. 51" × 79".
The Museum of Modern Art, New York. Gift of Mrs. Simon Guggenheim.

The work of French painter Henri Rousseau reveals another aspect of the human psyche. Rousseau was an untrained amateur painter, not a member of the Paris art community. He did, however, catch the attention of many professional artists, including Picasso, who were looking for fresh approaches to visual form. Rousseau's naive purity, innate sense of design, imaginative use of color, and taste for exotic subjects gave his paintings a mysterious, magical quality. THE SLEEPING GYPSY appears to be the visualization of a dream.

The nineteenth-century invention of photography, along with the discovery of non-Western art and the rediscovery of pre-Renaissance art, strongly affected the direction of Western art. As the century progressed, artists sought a deeper reality by breaking away from the artificial idealism of officially recognized academic art.

This fresh beginning was full of self-assurance, as seen in the optimistic mood of Impressionism. Yet the process of seeing the visual world anew brought with it added levels of awareness, as the appearance of things came to be less important than the relationship between viewer and reality. It became, once again, the artist's task to probe and reveal hidden worlds, to make the invisible visible. Artists gave increasing importance to the elements of form and to the formal structure of seen and invented imagery. Nature was internalized and transformed in order to portray a greater reality as the stage was set for even bigger changes in the twentieth century.

WHERE WERE THE WOMEN?

Women artists have always existed, but they have often gone unrecognized or "underrecognized." Women have participated in every important art movement, yet they are rarely mentioned by historians. Until recently, two of the most widely used college textbooks on art history, covering prehistoric times to the present, showed no works by female artists.

The statement "Anonymous was a woman" reminds us that through the centuries, women's creative work was a part of the fabric of society but was rarely given credit. The academic emphasis on "fine art" over "craft" has helped to keep women's art invisible.

Art historian Linda Nochlin's essay "Why Have There Been No Great Women Artists?" was first published in the January 1971 issue of *Art News,* during the early period of the women's liberation movement. The same question can be asked of almost any professional field. Nochlin and other historians and writers continue to provoke soul-searching inquiry by both men and women. As Nochlin points out, to find answers, we need to ask more and perhaps different questions.

Have significant numbers of outstanding women artists existed but gone unrecognized? Have they been marginalized by male-dominated institutions and male critics and historians? Or have few great women artists existed because the conditions were not there to support their focused, creative development? The answers to such questions appear to be interconnected.

The conditions for producing great art—or for excelling in any discipline—include family support, educational opportunity, community support, and patronage, as well as aptitude. The situation has been and still is discouraging—even hostile at times—for anyone who is not born white, moderately affluent, and male. What is amazing, however, is that so many women and nonwhites have achieved so much against overwhelming odds. Obstacles begin with the attitudes and prejudgments of parents, teachers, and others in power—attitudes perpetuated by educational and other institutions.

We will never know whether stone age artists were men or women, but it is interesting to realize that a great deal of prehistoric art may have been made by women. We do know the names of distinguished women artists of ancient Greece and Rome. The numbers of women artists had increased greatly by the fifteenth century, but no woman had gained a reputation equal to that of her male counterparts.

During the Renaissance in Italy, it became socially and politically correct for aristocrats to educate daughters as well as sons in the social arts. While the idea was simply to produce women who could write poetry, dance, sing, paint, and be skilled in the art of conversation so that they would make good companions for aristocratic men, some women became highly accomplished artists. However, most were denied access to the academies and refused the training necessary for professional careers. Thus it is not surprising that, prior to the twentieth century, most of the women who achieved distinction in the visual arts had fathers or close male friends who were artists. A list of such women would include Rosa Bonheur and Marietta Tintoretto, both daughters of artists; Berthe Morisot (see page 162), who was closely associated with Manet; and Mary Cassatt (see page 393), who was a close friend of Degas.

Sofonisba Anguissola was the first woman of the Renaissance to gain an

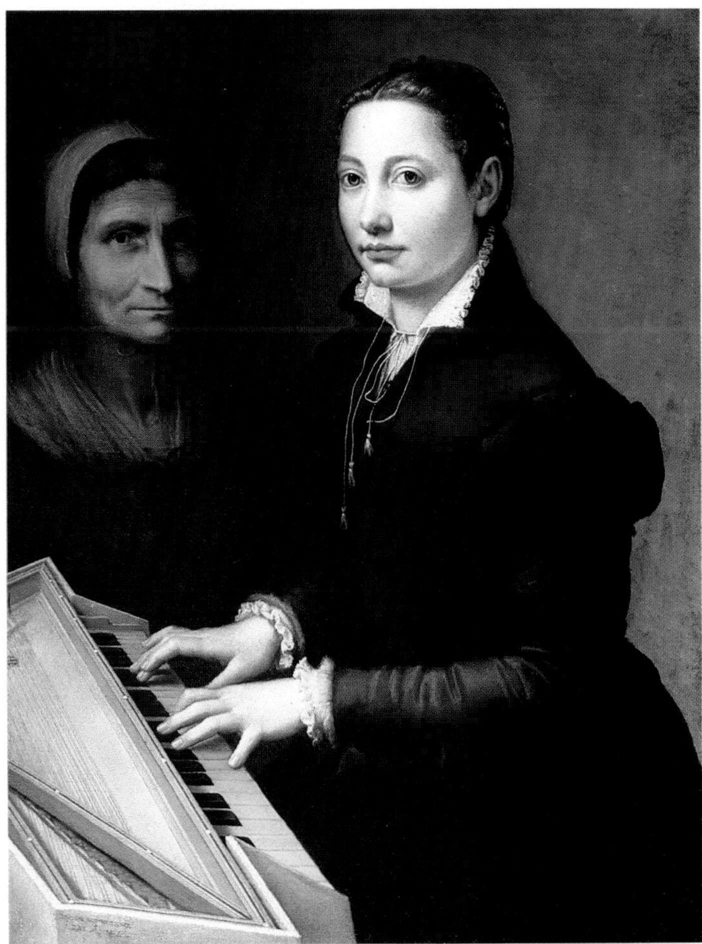

567 Sofonisba Anguissola. SELF-PORTRAIT. 1561. Oil on canvas. 35" × 32". Collection The Right Honorable Earl Spencer, Northampton, England.

WHERE WERE THE WOMEN?

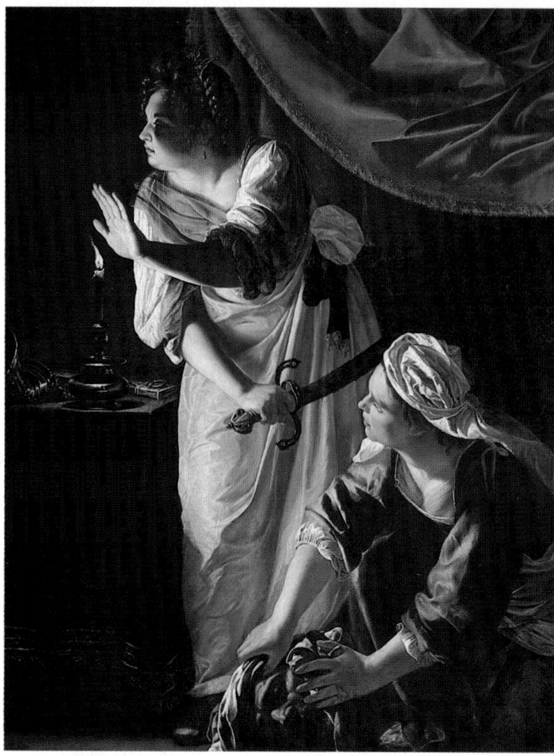

568 Artemisia Gentileschi. JUDITH AND MAIDSERVANT WITH THE HEAD OF HOLOFERNES. c. 1625. Oil on canvas, 6'½" × 4'7¾". The Detroit Institute of Arts. Gift of Mrs. Leslie H. Green.

international reputation. She is unusual in that her father was not an artist but a provincial nobleman. He educated all six of his daughters in Latin, music, and painting; only his son did not become a painter.

Anguissola studied with a portrait painter, and her well-publicized success led other male artists to accept female students. While still in her twenties, she became court painter to King Phillip II of Spain. Her SELF-PORTRAIT of 1561 employs subtle Mannerist qualities that evoke a mystical mood. The mysterious face of an older woman, barely visible in the upper left, provides an intriguing apparition.

Anguissola's first husband died after four years of marriage. She remarried and lived to about ninety.

European women artists were more numerous and better known during the Baroque period. Among the most remarkable was Artemisia Gentileschi, daughter of Orazio Gentileschi—long considered the best of Caravaggio's followers. Although some of today's art historians consider Gentileschi a better painter than her father, until recently, her work received limited recognition because she was a woman.

While in her late teens, Gentileschi was given drawing lessons by her father's friend and colleague Agostino Tassi. The lessons were to have been held in the company of a female chaperone, but evidently the student-teacher relationship broke down. In 1612 Orazio Gentileschi accused Tassi of raping his daughter. Tassi pleaded innocent, but Gentileschi did not waver in her testimony against him—despite being tortured with thumbscrews, ostensibly to illicit a confession of complicity or a denial of her claim. After a long trial, Tassi was acquitted of the charge.

Feminists and historians have made much of the relationship between Gentileschi's life—particularly the rape and its aftermath—and the violent subject matter of many of her paintings, including the series depicting the story of Judith from the Old Testament.

To save her town from the advancing Assyrian army, Judith crossed enemy lines, seduced Holofernes, the Assyrian general, then beheaded him with his own sword. Although JUDITH AND MAIDSERVANT WITH THE HEAD OF HOLOFERNES does not show the gory decapitation (featured in her other paintings of the subject), the intensity of the moment is communicated clearly. The drama is intensified by bold use of theatrical light, sweeping curves, dramatic gestures, and warm colors.

Rosa Bonheur was the most renowned animal painter of the nineteenth century. It seemed inevitable that she would become an artist; her father was a landscape painter, her mother had studied with him, and all three of her sisters became painters. She had the good fortune to reach artistic maturity during the middle

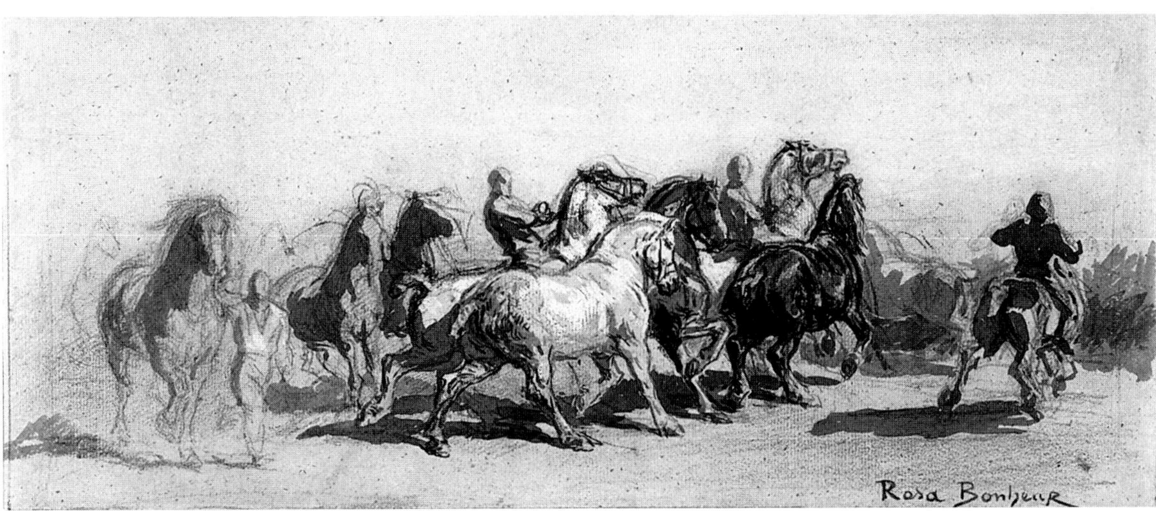

of the nineteenth century, at a time when small paintings of everyday subjects were favored over large history paintings. The rise of the middle class had created a population that wanted and could afford to buy such art. However, it was a huge painting, THE HORSE FAIR, exhibited at the Salon of 1853, that initially brought her critical acclaim and attracted public attention to her work. Concern with anatomical accuracy led Bonheur to visit slaughterhouses and horse fairs and to dissect animals—all highly unusual activities for a woman at that time. Her dynamic STUDY FOR "THE HORSE FAIR" appears to have been drawn quickly, using gestural lines to capture the feeling of motion.

Bonheur was ambitious and eccentric, choosing to wear trousers—for which she had to have a police permit—and keep her hair cropped short. She chose not to marry, believing that marriage meant an inevitable loss of self for women.

Among the constraints that kept women from becoming trained artists were the exclusion of women from art schools and a prohibition against women learning to draw the human figure. Art students traditionally studied classical Greek and Roman nude statues and drew from live nude models in order to learn human anatomy. When the influential French Academy was founded in 1648, female students were barred from its art classes, and they were generally not allowed to draw from the nude anywhere until the early twentieth century. Being barred from studying the human figure was a serious handicap in learning to draw people correctly, and it kept women from attempting large historical paintings that were the main avenue to success in Europe for many centuries.

Women themselves have contributed to the problem. The mother who wrote to the director of the Pennsylvania Academy of Art in the 1880s, complaining that her daughter, carefully raised, was being corrupted by exposure to nude models, represented widespread public opinion in the United States. This conservatism led to the firing of painter Thomas Eakins (see page 384) as head of the Pennsylvania Academy; Eakins strongly advocated the study of the human body.

569 Rosa Bonheur. STUDY FOR "THE HORSE FAIR". c. 1853. Black chalk, gray wash heightened with white on beige paper. 5⅜" × 13¼". The Metropolitan Museum of Art, New York. Bequest of Edith H. Proskauer (1975.319.2).

WHERE WERE THE WOMEN?

While women were discouraged from pursuing professions, including those in art, they were encouraged to make art a hobby by drawing flowers, painting miniatures, or doing household arts such as quilting. Today art historians are calling attention to women's accomplishments in these domains.

When women persisted in learning to draw or paint professionally, they faced additional difficulties in exhibiting their work; the large exhibitions were typically closed to women, although the French Salon was opened to women briefly after its founding in 1737 and then again after the French Revolution. The Royal Academy in London only periodically allowed women to exhibit in the main salons. The leading societies of artists were also closed to women. By and large, the official world of art was off-limits to women.

Women who wanted to study art—as did young Americans Mary Cassatt and Berthe Morisot, who went to Europe for training—were forced to study privately or to attend schools specifically set up for women. The attitude of the late nineteenth century was expressed by August Renoir, who is said to have called women painters "ridiculous."

Even generally supportive families had mixed feelings about women artists. At her death, Berthe Morisot's family left blank the space on her death certificate asking for her profession—as if her lifetime of painting was not worthy of being considered a profession.

History provides well-documented accounts of injustices and discrimination against women artists. Works by women have often been incorrectly attributed to male teachers or to male relatives—on the assumption that no really good art could have been done by a woman. In 1723, Dutch painter Margareta Haverman, the second woman of her century to be elected to the French Royal Academy of Fine Arts, was expelled from the institution when its members, without apparent reason, decided that the work she submitted had been painted by her teacher. In 1859, sculptor Harriet Hosmer threatened a libel suit to force magazines to retract claims that men had done the work that bore her name. In 1875, American sculptor Anne Whitney lost a major commission when the jurors discovered that the work they had selected was by a woman. Racism has compounded the problem for women who were not white.

A study released in 1992 indicated that in American schools, teachers were more likely to call on boys in class and to hold measurably higher expectations for boys than for girls. The educational community, including the teachers in the study group, were astonished by but did not contest the study's results. It appears that our individual and collective gender-related mind-sets are so much a part of our lives that most of us fail to recognize them, even in ourselves.

Not surprisingly, it is women who are researching and writing the emerging and expanding history of women's art. Few men write about women artists, while women art historians have until recently written primarily about men.

A group called the Guerilla Girls was organized in 1985 in New York to expose the inequalities still existing among critics, dealers, museums, and galleries. Their provocative performances and posters provide shocking statistics. The group has begun to achieve its goal: to be the "conscience of the art world" (see page 489).

The National Museum of Women in the Arts opened in Washington in 1987. We already have institutions classified by geography, ethnicity, and chronology; is it also appropriate to classify art history (or social history) by gender? Critics of the museum, both male and female, have suggested that the museum is ghettoizing women and that women artists have equal opportunity with men in museums and galleries. Supporters of the museum feel that statistics suggest otherwise. For instance, the modern wing of the Metropolitan Museum of Art opened in the 1980s with a display of 411 works by male artists and 28 by females.

At the end of the twentieth century, it is common for women artists to win major commissions, command high prices, and have exhibitions in major museums and galleries. However, their numbers are vastly fewer and their prices substantially lower than those of male artists. Women artists continue to face many of the same obstacles as their predecessors and women in other professions. Even today, young women believe they must choose between focusing on a career or profession or devoting their primary energy to being wives and mothers. Few men feel that they must choose one or the other.

In order to address inequities in the arts—or anywhere else—we need to look at and accept history for what it is, and then create a world in which equal opportunity is not only legislated but encouraged by families and community institutions.

CHAPTER 21

Early Twentieth Century

During the first decade of this century, Western views of reality underwent upheaval. In 1900, Sigmund Freud published *The Interpretation of Dreams,* a vast work that explored the structure and power of the subconscious mind. In 1903, the Wright brothers flew the first power-driven aircraft. In 1905, Albert Einstein changed our concepts of time, space, and substance with his theory of relativity. Matter could no longer be considered solid; it was recognized as a field of energy. Simultaneously, great changes occurred in art, and some of them were inspired by scientific discoveries. In 1913, Russian artist Wassily Kandinsky (see page 415) described how deeply he was affected by the discovery of subatomic particles:

A scientific event cleared my way of one of the greatest impediments. This was the further division of the atom. The crumbling of the atom was to my soul like the crumbling of the whole world.[1]

The art of the twentieth century is the result of a series of revolutions in thinking and seeing. Its characteristics are those of the century itself: rapid change, diversity, individualism, and exploration—followed by abundant discoveries. Twentieth-century artists, as well as scientists, have challenged preconceptions of the nature of reality, and they have made new levels of consciousness visible.

The explosion of new styles of art at the beginning of this century grew from Post-Impressionist trends. Yet in their search for forms to express the new age, European artists looked to ancient and non-Western cultures for inspiration and renewal. In so doing, they overturned the authority of the Renaissance, which had dominated Western artistic thought for five hundred years.

TOWARD ABSTRACTION

Early twentieth-century art continued the general shift from naturalistic to abstract art begun in the late nineteenth century. Our comparison in Chapter 3 of two works of sculpture, both titled THE KISS (pages 38 and 39), illustrates the transition from nineteenth- to twentieth-century thinking. Rodin, the leading sculptor of the nineteenth century, created a naturalistic work. Brancusi, the leading sculptor of the early twentieth century, produced an abstract interpretation.

Sculptor Constantin Brancusi changed the way we think about forms in space. Before Brancusi, sculptors in the Western world made statues. Since Brancusi, sculptors have made many other kinds of three-dimensional forms as well as statues—works collectively called sculpture. It was Brancusi's development of abstract and nonrepresentational sculpture that led to the shift.

A sequence of Brancusi's early work shows his radical break with the past. His SLEEP of 1908 has an appearance similar to Rodin's romantic natural-

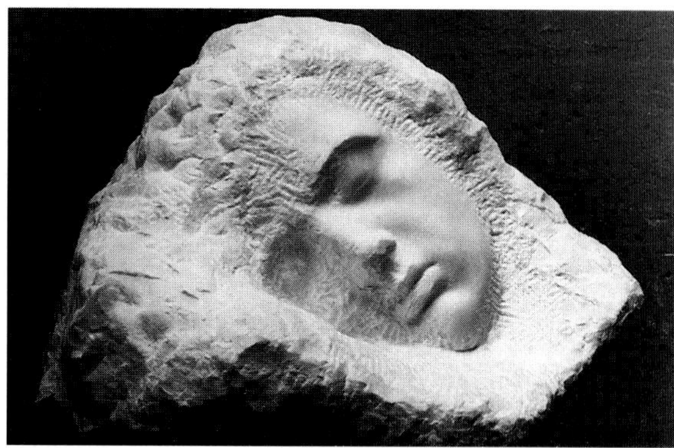

570 Constantin Brancusi.
SLEEP. 1908.
Marble. 6½" × 12".
National Museum, Bucharest, Romania. Photograph courtesy National Museum of Modern Art, Georges Pompidou Centre, Paris.

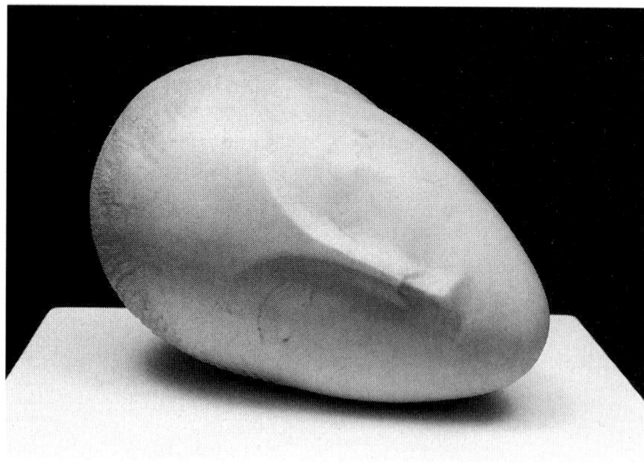

571 Constantin Brancusi.
SLEEPING MUSE. 1909-1911.
Marble. 7" × 10⅝" × 8".
Hirshhorn Museum and Sculpture Garden, Smithsonian Institution, Washington, D.C. Gift of Joseph H. Hirschhorn (1966).

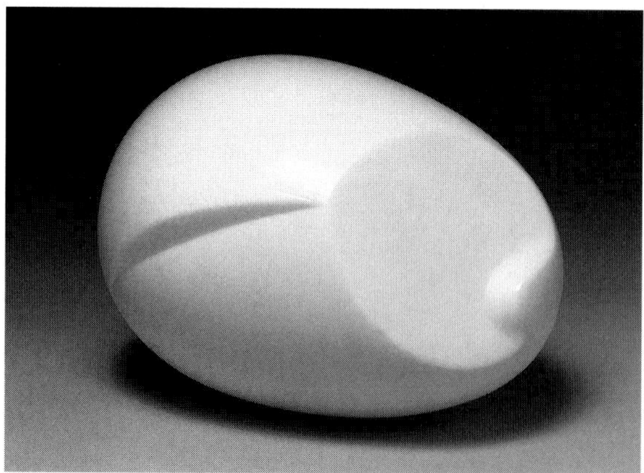

572 Constantin Brancusi.
THE NEWBORN. 1915.
Marble. 6" × 8½".
Philadelphia Museum of Art. The Louise and Walter Arensberg Collection.

ism. In his SLEEPING MUSE of 1911, Brancusi simplified the subject as he moved from naturalism to abstraction. THE NEWBORN of 1915 is stripped to essentials. Brancusi said, "Simplicity is not an end in art, but one arrives at simplicity in spite of oneself, in approaching the real sense of things."[2]

Comparisons can be made between Brancusi's work and Cycladic sculpture over four thousand years old, such as the CYCLADIC HEAD. Ancient sculpture from the Cyclades (islands of the Aegean Sea) has a distinctive, highly abstract elegance similar to Brancusi's. It is known that Brancusi spent time in the Louvre studying the collection of ancient sculpture.

Brancusi shared with other leading Parisian artists an interest in African and other non-Western arts, but the main influence on his sculpture was the folk art of his native Romania and his childhood in a peasant community, which had a strong woodcarving tradition.

In BIRD IN SPACE, Brancusi transformed inert mass into an elegant, uplifting form. The implied soaring motion embodies the idea of flight. The highly reflective polish adds to the form's weightless quality. Brancusi began work on this idea just after the Wright brothers initiated the age of flight, but long before streamlined aircraft, cars, pens, and telephones. Brancusi said, "All my life I have sought the essence of flight. Don't look for mysteries. I give you pure joy."[3]

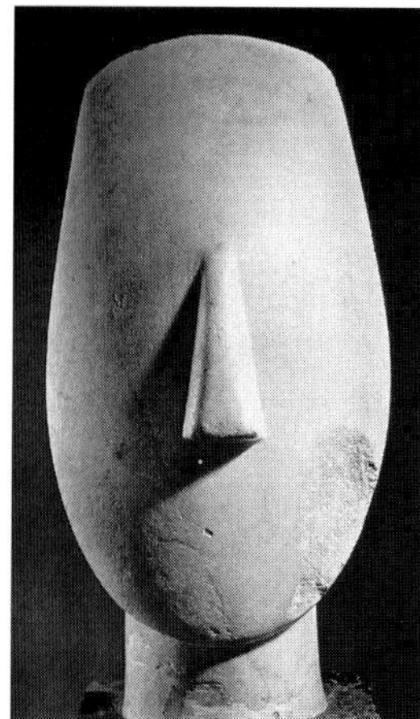

573 CYCLADIC HEAD.
2500-3000 B.C.
Marble. Height 10½".
Musée du Louvre, Paris.

574 Constantin Brancusi.
BIRD IN SPACE. (1928?).
Bronze (unique cast). Height 54".
The Museum of Modern Art, New York. Given anonymously.

CONSTANTIN BRANCUSI (1876–1957)

Constantin Brancusi was one of the most revered and influential artists of the early twentieth century. He was born in a village in Romania to a fairly prosperous peasant and his wife, a weaver. Like many peasant sons, he spent long hours tending sheep. As he grew older, he felt bullied by his father and older brothers and frequently ran away. He was brought back home, but his schooling was disrupted. When he was thirteen, Brancusi left his family for the last time.

He supported himself at menial jobs for several years before entering the Craiova School of Arts and Crafts. Graduating with honors, he immediately enrolled at the Bucharest School of Fine Arts and studied sculpture. The program, rigorous and traditional, was based on a close study of anatomy. After he graduated in 1902, he worked for a time as a carpenter.

In 1904 Brancusi made his way to Munich. Then, having exhausted his savings, he decided to walk to Paris—a distance of about 500 miles. Stopping at villages along the way, he walked a good part of the distance before collapsing. He then wrote to a Romanian friend in Paris who sent him the money to complete the trip by train.

He enrolled in the École des Beaux Arts (the French School of Fine Arts), where he demonstrated great skill.

He worked briefly in Rodin's studio in 1906–1907. When he was invited by Rodin to become his assistant,

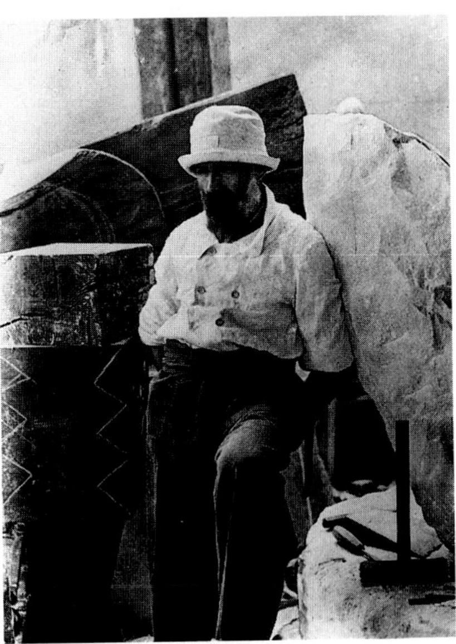

575 Constantin Brancusi.
SELF-PORTRAIT IN HIS STUDIO. c. 1921.
Photograph.
National Museum of Modern Art, Georges Pompidou Centre, Paris.

Brancusi is said to have turned him down with the reply, "Nothing can grow under big trees." His early work shows the influence of Rodin, but Brancusi went on to develop his own style. Brancusi's THE KISS was a determined rejection of the style of Rodin's famous piece of the same name.

Around 1910 he abandoned modeling in favor of direct carving. He was a superb craftsman who possessed great sensitivity to the character of his materials—primarily metal, stone, and wood. "We must try not to make materials speak our language. We must go with them to a point where others will understand their language."[4]

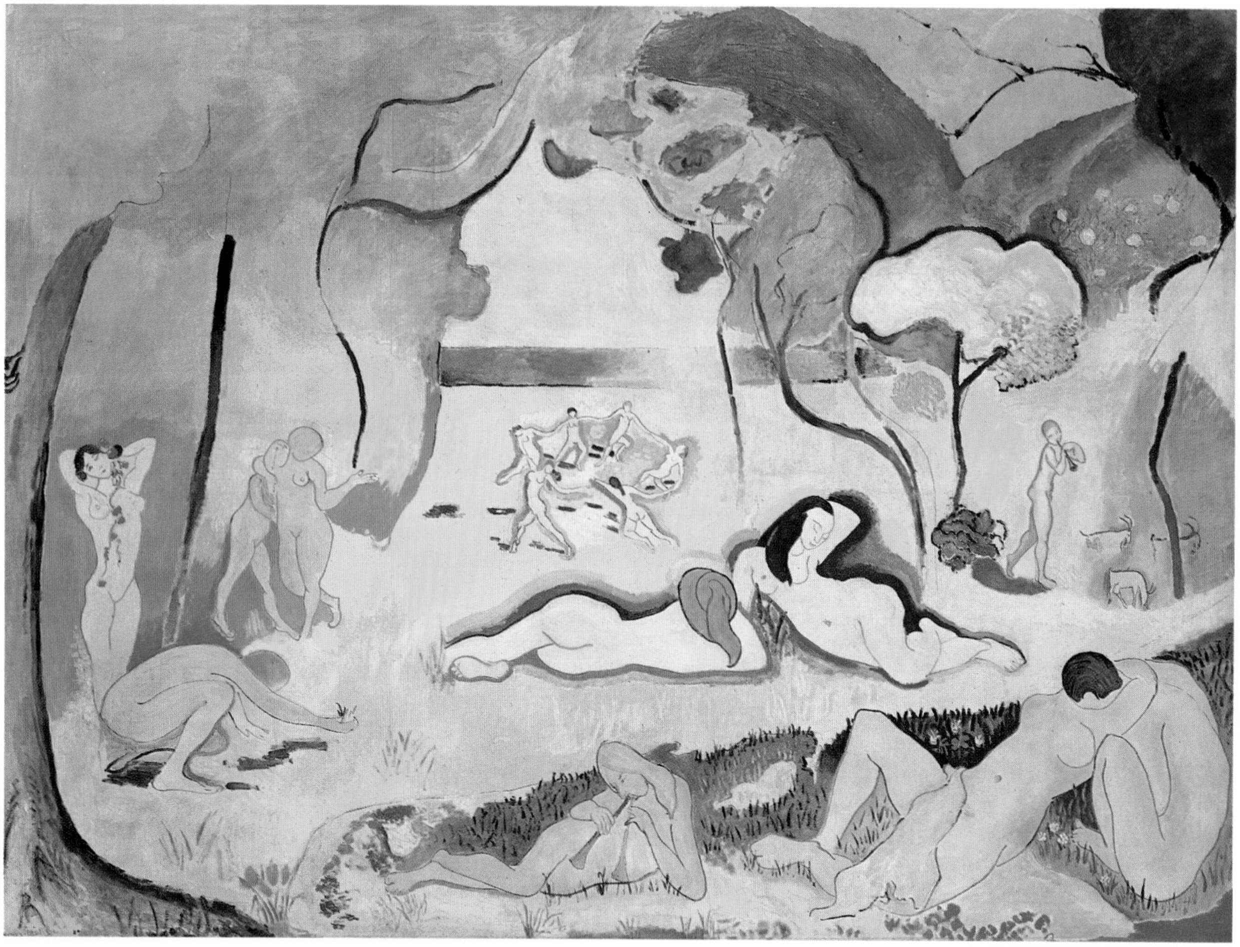

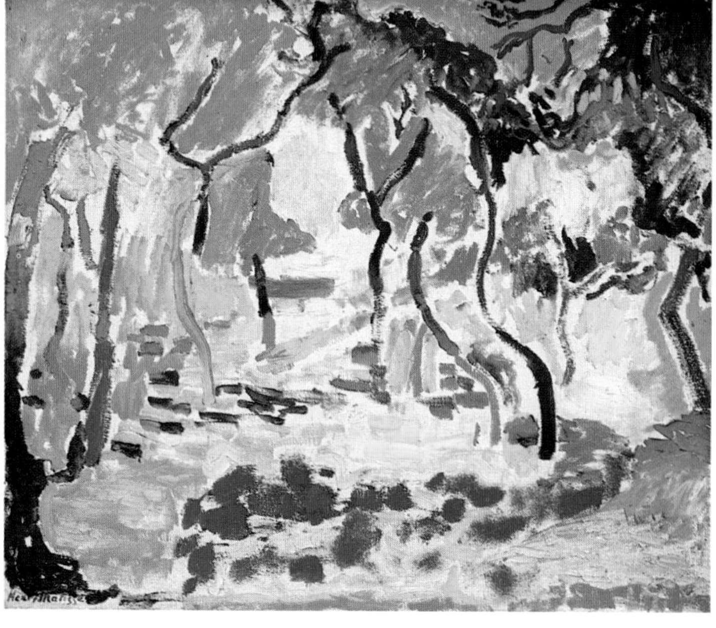

576 Henri Matisse.
JOY OF LIFE. 1905-1906.
Oil on canvas. 68½" × 93¾".
The Barnes Foundation, Merion Station, Pennsylvania.
Photograph © 1993 by The Barnes Foundation.

577 Henri Matisse.
LANDSCAPE. Study for JOY OF LIFE. 1905.
Oil on canvas. 46 cm × 44 cm.
Royal Museum of Fine Arts, Copenhagen. J. Rump Collection.

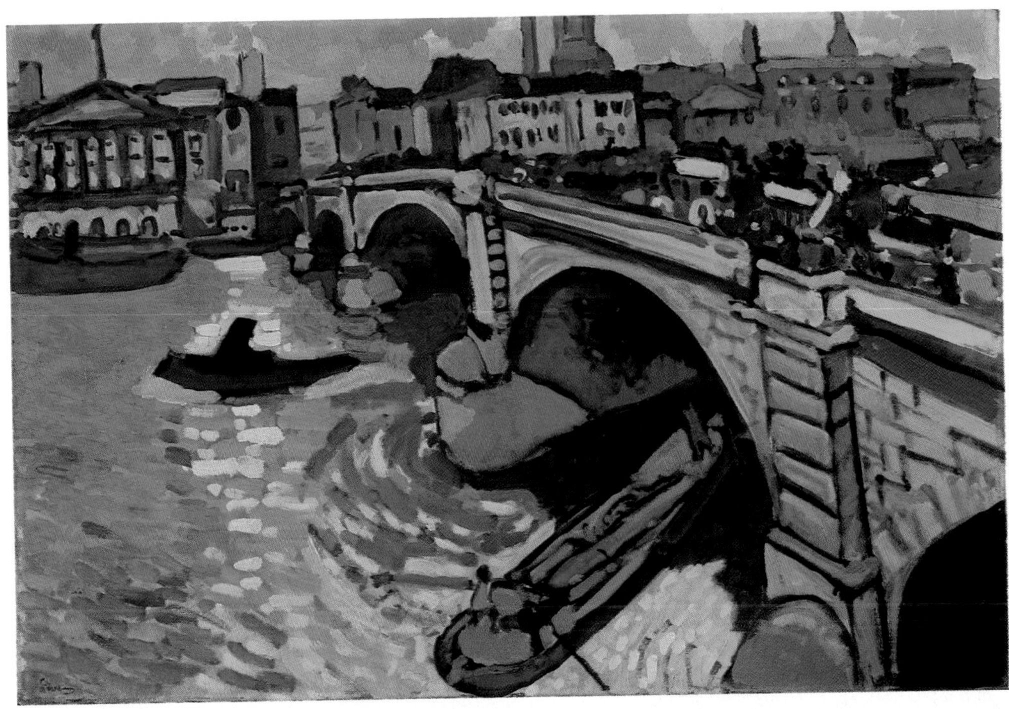

578 André Derain.
LONDON BRIDGE. 1906.
Oil on canvas. 26" × 39".
The Museum of Modern Art, New York. Gift of Mr. and Mrs. Charles Zadok.

THE FAUVES AND EXPRESSIONISM

By the turn of the century, many young painters in France had been attracted to Seurat's divisionist method. Its formalist, rational approach seemed perfectly suited to a progressive, scientific era. For some young painters just starting out, divisionism offered a systematic way to escape the weight of the past and to counter the oppressive influences of their academic teachers and the outdated Impressionists.

Soon, however, some of them felt imprisoned rather than liberated by divisionism. They wanted to express themselves more directly, more spontaneously. Led by Henri Matisse, a group of painters that included André Derain drew inspiration from the expressive color of Gauguin and Van Gogh. They studied Cézanne's pictorial constructions in colored planes. Their own use of color grew increasingly intense and subjective.

In 1905, their first group exhibit shocked the public. A critic of that show derisively called them *les fauves* (the wild beasts). According to Matisse, the epithet was never accepted by the group; it was merely a tag found useful by critics.

Matisse's painting JOY OF LIFE is a major early work in a long career and a masterpiece of what came to be known as Fauvism. Pure hues vibrate across the surface; lines, largely freed of their descriptive roles, align with simplified shapes to provide a lively rhythm in the composition. The seemingly careless depiction of the figures is based on Matisse's knowledge of human anatomy and drawing. The intentionally direct, childlike quality of the form serves to heighten the joyful content. LANDSCAPE was made as a study for JOY OF LIFE.

Until 1994 the Barnes Foundation, which owns JOY OF LIFE, did not allow color reproductions of works in its collection because Mr. Barnes felt color reproductions were too inaccurate. Color reproduction technology has greatly improved since Mr. Barnes took his stand.

In Derain's LONDON BRIDGE, brilliant, invented color is balanced by some use of traditional composition and perspective. Derain spoke of intentionally using discordant color. It is an indication of today's acceptance of strong color that Derain's painting does not appear disharmonious.

The Fauve movement lasted little more than two years, from 1905 to 1907, yet it was one of the most influential developments in early twentieth-century painting. The Fauves freed color from its

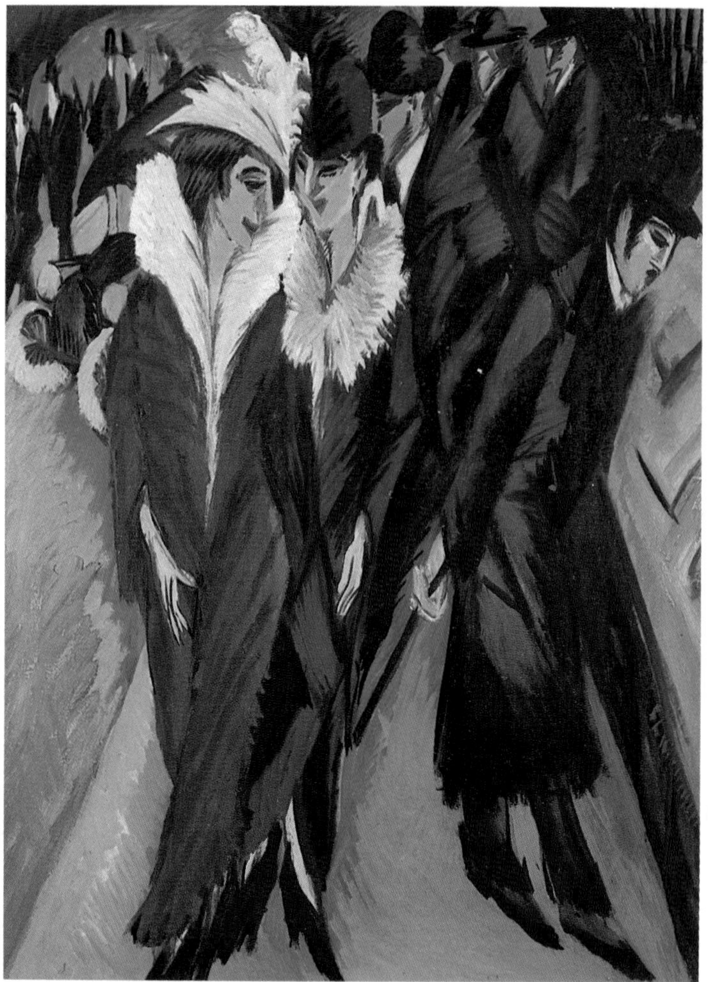

579 Ernst Ludwig Kirchner.
STREET, BERLIN. 1913.
Oil on canvas. 47½" × 35⅞".
The Museum of Modern Art, New York. Purchase.

traditional role of describing the natural appearance of an object. In this way, their work led to an increasing use of color as an independent expressive element.

We can categorize Fauvism as an expressive style. As we discussed in Chapter 6, expressionism is a general term for art that emphasizes inner feelings and emotions over objective depiction. In Europe, romantic or expressive tendencies can be traced from seventeenth-century Baroque art to the early nineteenth-century painting of Delacroix, who in turn influenced the expressive side of Post-Impressionism (particularly Van Gogh).

A few German artists at the beginning of the century shared the expressionist goals of the Fauves. Indeed, the German desire to express feelings and emotions was so pronounced and sustained that we call their art German Expressionism. Like their Fauve counterparts, the German Expressionists built on the achievements of Gauguin and Van Gogh. However, they were equally drawn to the bleak, soul-searching paintings of Edvard Munch. Like Munch, they felt compelled to use the power of expressionism to address the human condition, often exploring such themes as poverty, corruption, loneliness, sorrow, and passion. As their art developed, it absorbed formal influences from medieval German art, Fauvism, Slavic folk art, African and Oceanic art, and Cubism, but its subject matter remained urgently focused on social and moral issues.

The range of German Expressionist feeling is evident in the compassionate depictions of the poor and helpless by Käthe Kollwitz (pages 120–121), the earthy strength of images by Paula Modersohn-Becker (page 54), and the graphic clarity of prints by Emil Nolde (page 160).

Two groups typified the German Expressionist movement of the early twentieth century: the Bridge (*die Brücke*) and the Blue Rider (*der blaue Reiter*). Ernst Ludwig Kirchner, architecture student turned painter, was the founder of the Bridge. The group included several of his fellow architectural students, Emil Nolde, and others. They appealed to artists to revolt against academic painting and establish a new, vigorous aesthetic that would form a bridge between the Germanic past and modern experience. They first exhibited as a group in 1905, the year of the first Fauve exhibition.

Kirchner's concern for expressing human emotion gave his work a quality similar to that which he admired in Munch's work. Kirchner's early paintings employed the flat color areas of Fauvism; by 1913, he had developed a style that incorporated the angularities of Cubism, African sculpture, and German Gothic art. In STREET, BERLIN, elongated figures are crowded together with the use of repeated diagonal lines to create an urban atmosphere charged with energy. Dissonant colors, chopped out shapes, and rough, almost crude, brushwork heighten the emotional impact.

The Blue Rider group was led by Russian painter Wassily Kandinsky. Kandinsky lived in Munich between 1908 and 1914, and he shared with his German associates a concern for developing an art that would turn people away from false values, toward spiritual rejuvenation. He believed that a painting should be "an exact replica of some inner emotion"; in BLUE MOUNTAIN, painted in 1908, he created a "choir of colors" influenced by the vivid, freely expressive color of the Fauves.[5]

Kandinsky's paintings evolved toward an absence of representational subject matter. Already in BLUE MOUNTAIN, representational subject matter is secondary to the powerful effect of the visual elements released from descriptive roles.

By 1910, Kandinsky had made the shift to totally nonrepresentational imagery in order to concentrate on the expressive potential of pure form freed from associations with recognizable subjects. He sought a language of visual form comparable to the independent aural language we experience in music: the rhythms, melodies, and harmonies of music please or displease us because of the way the music affects us. By titling his painting WITH THE BLACK ARCH NO. 154, Kandinsky referred to the dominant visual element in the painting, which is similar to a composer's naming a composition "Symphony No. 2 in D Major." Weightless curves float across large free shapes in a painted world of interactive energies.

Kandinsky said that the content of his paintings was "what the spectator *lives* or *feels* while under the effect of the *form and color combinations* of the picture."[6] He was an outstanding innovator in the history of art, and his revolutionary nonfigurative works played a key role in the development of nonrepresentational styles. His purpose was not simply aesthetic: he saw his paintings as leading a way through an impending period of catastrophe to a great new era of spirituality.

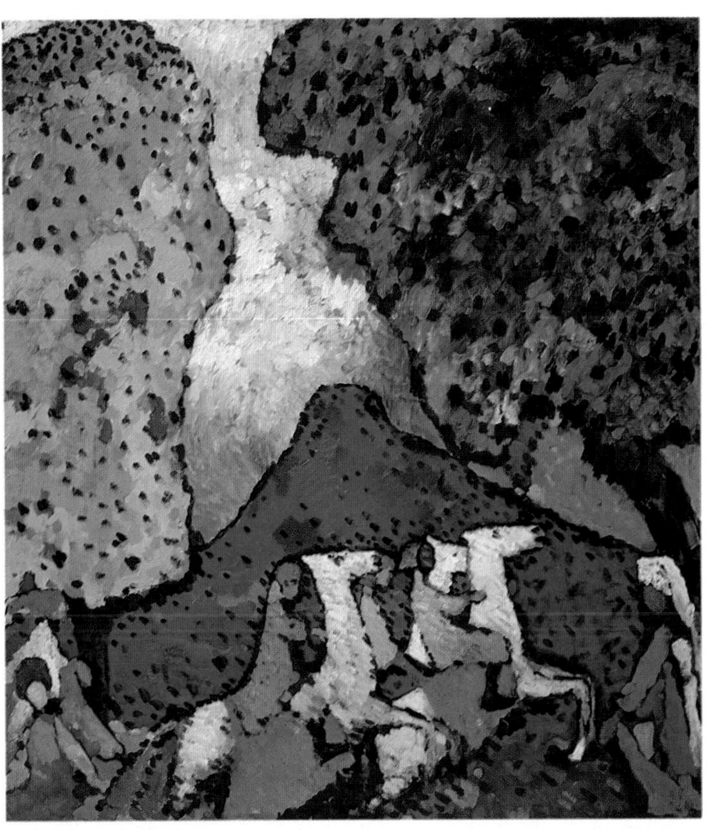

580 Wassily Kandinsky.
BLUE MOUNTAIN. 1908-1909.
Oil on canvas. 41¾" × 38".
© The Solomon R. Guggenheim Museum, New York. Gift of Solomon R. Guggenheim, 1941.

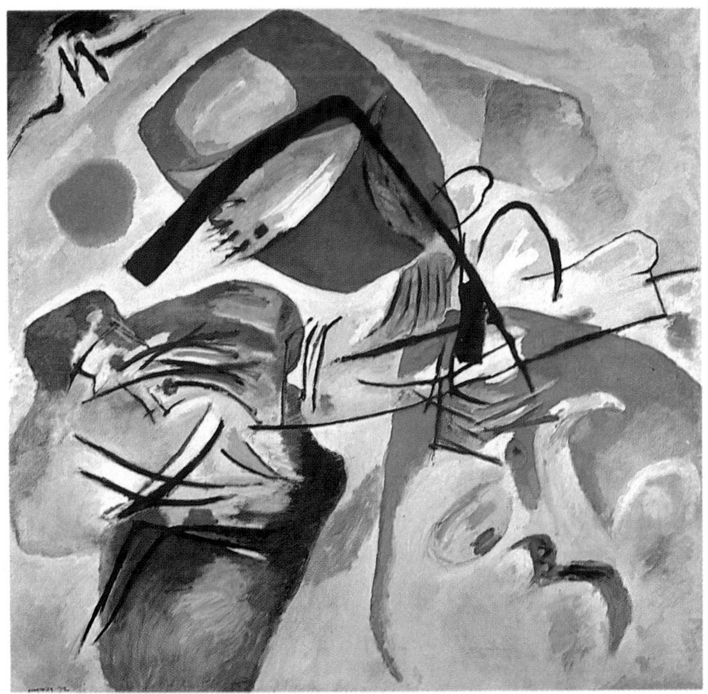

581 Wassily Kandinsky.
WITH THE BLACK ARCH NO. 154. 1912.
Oil on canvas. 74" × 77⅛".
National Museum of Modern Art, Georges Pompidou Centre, Paris. © ADAGP, Paris, 1993.

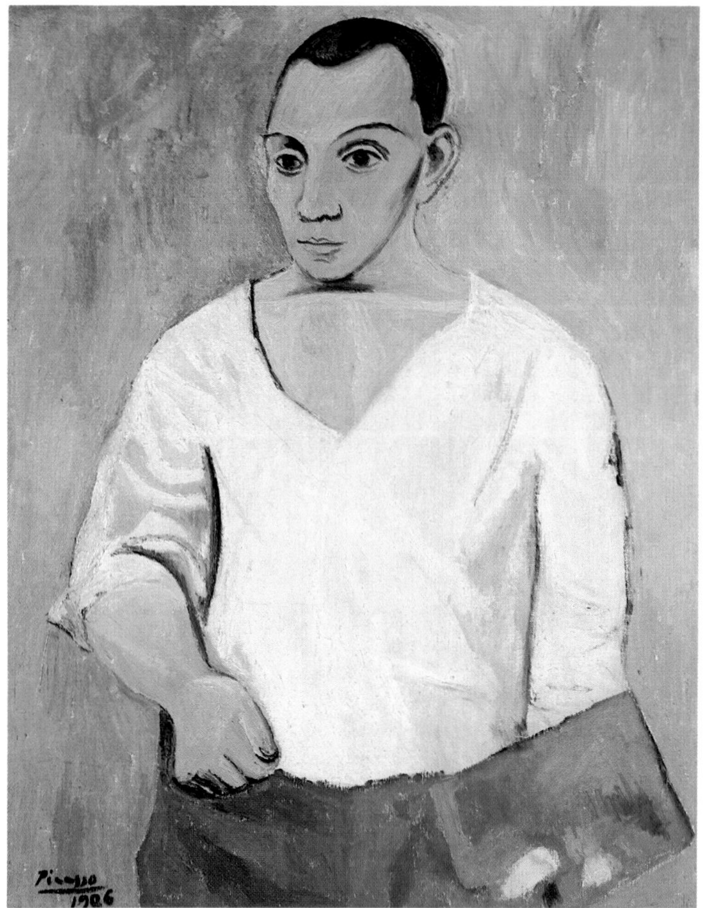

582 Pablo Picasso.
SELF-PORTRAIT WITH PALETTE. 1906.
Oil on canvas. 36¼" × 28¾".
Philadelphia Museum of Art. A. E. Gallatin Collection.

CUBISM

While living in Paris, Spanish artist Pablo Picasso shared ideas and influences with French artist Georges Braque. Together they pursued investigations that led to Cubism, the most influential movement of the early twentieth century. Cubism brought about the most radical and complete artistic revolution since the Renaissance. Through its indirect influence on architecture and the applied arts, it has become part of our daily lives. It is interesting to trace Picasso's artistic development in relation to the emergence of Cubism.

In 1906, the year Matisse completed JOY OF LIFE, Picasso painted SELF-PORTRAIT WITH PALETTE, which has a unique, abstract flatness not seen before in his work. The boldly simplified surfaces and shapes were influenced by the abstract, pre-Roman Iberian sculpture of Spain such as the IBERIAN STONE RELIEF.

Picasso absorbed influences quickly, keeping only what he needed to achieve his objectives. His breakthrough painting, LES DEMOISELLES D'AVIGNON, shows a radical departure from tradition. Rejecting the accepted European notion of Ideal Beauty, Picasso created an entirely personal vocabulary of form influenced by Cézanne's faceted reconstructions of nature and by the inventive abstraction, vitality, and power he admired in African sculpture such as the BAKOTA FUNERARY FIGURE and the ETOUMBI MASK.

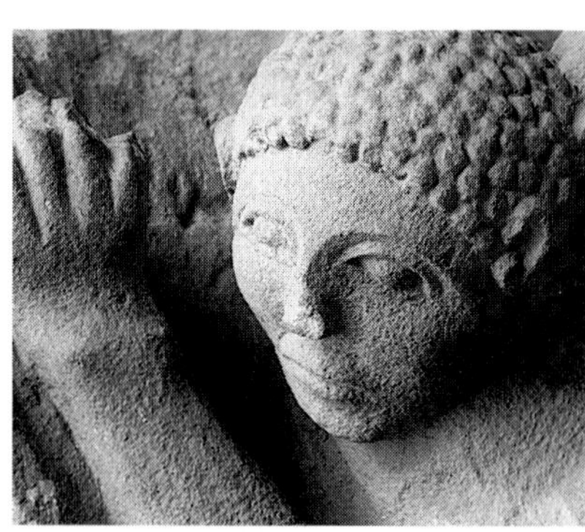

583 IBERIAN STONE RELIEF.
Museo Arqueológico Nacional, Madrid.

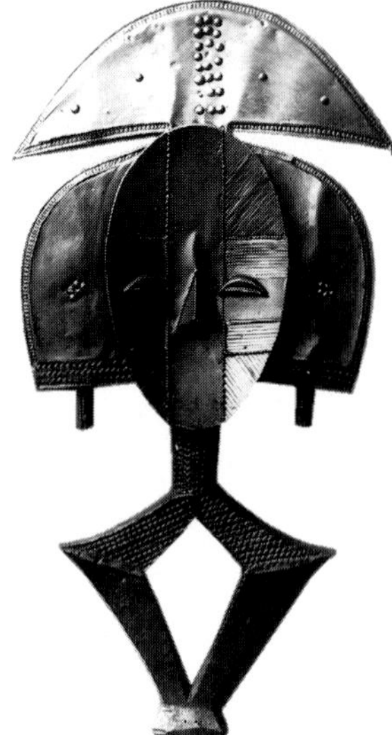

584 BAKOTA FUNERARY FIGURE.
French Equatorial Africa.
Probably 20th century.
Brass sheeting over wood.
Length 70.4 cm.
Department of Anthropology, Smithsonian Institution, Washington, D.C. Herbert Ward Collection (323683).

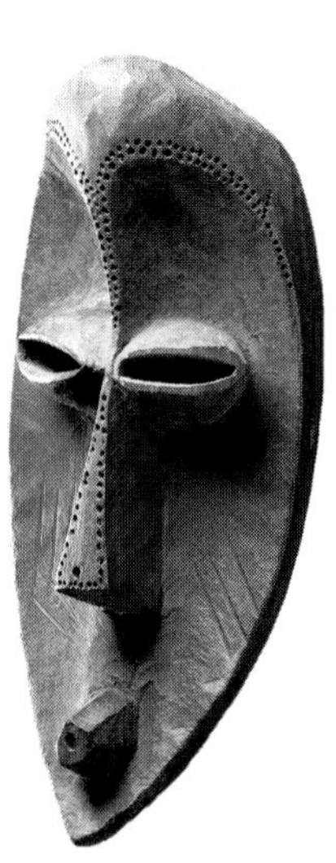

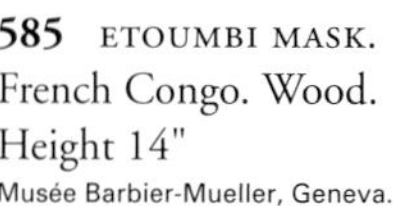

585 ETOUMBI MASK.
French Congo. Wood.
Height 14"
Musée Barbier-Mueller, Geneva.

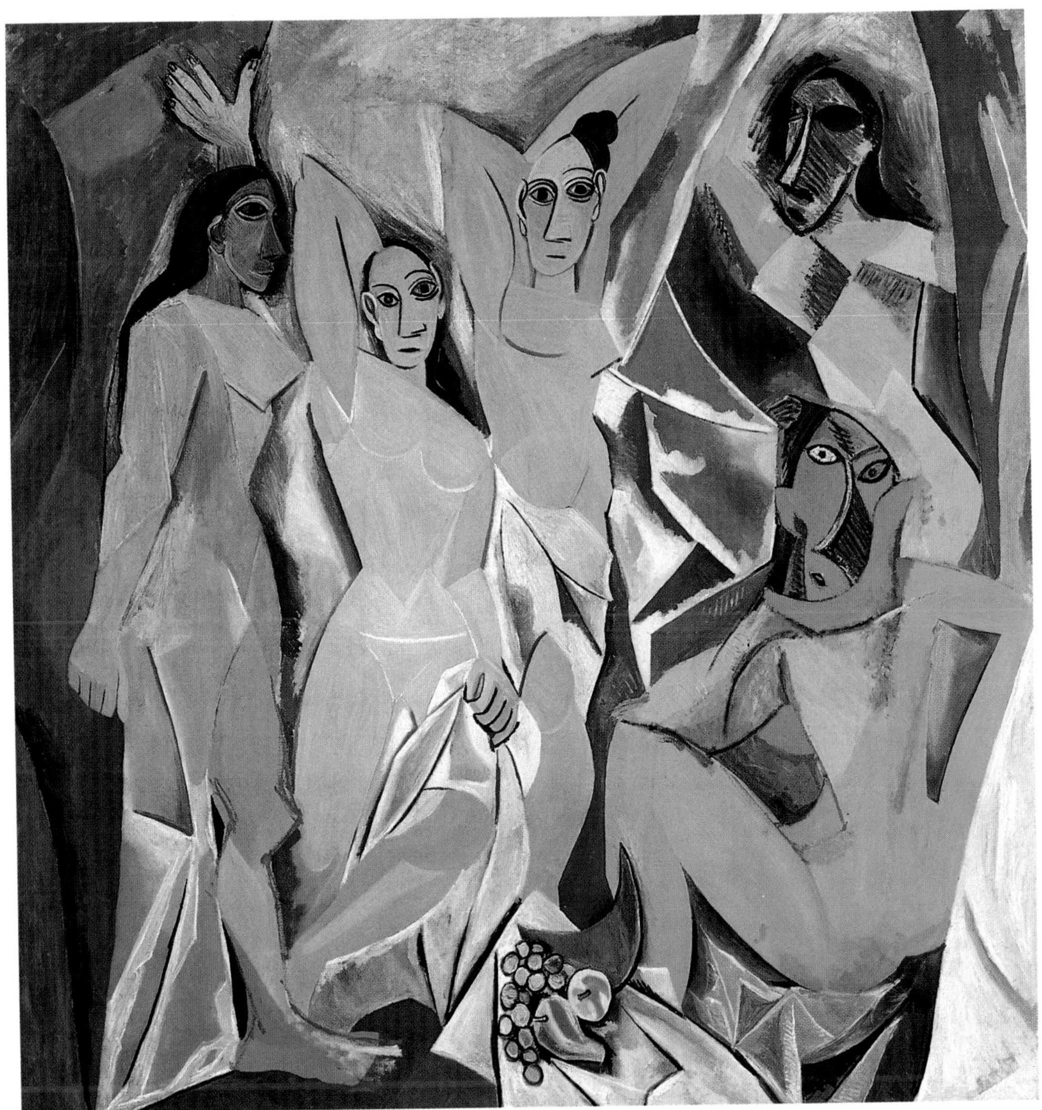

586 Pablo Picasso. LES DEMOISELLES D'AVIGNON. 1907.
Oil on canvas. 8' × 7'8".
The Museum of Modern Art, New York. Acquired through the Lillie P. Bliss Bequest.

Picasso's new approach astonished even his closest friends. Georges Braque, who did as much as Picasso to develop Cubism, was appalled when he first saw LES DEMOISELLES in 1907. "You may give all the explanations you like," he said, "but your painting makes one feel as if you were trying to make us eat cotton waste and wash it down with kerosene."[7] In LES DEMOISELLES D'AVIGNON, the fractured, angular figures intermingle with the sharp triangular shapes of the ground, activating the entire picture surface. This reconstruction of image and ground, suggesting shifting planes, was influenced by Cézanne's ideas about forms in space. In retrospect, we see that it was the fractured triangulation of forms and the merging of figure and ground in this large painting that was the turning point. With this painting, Picasso exploded the lingering Renaissance approach to the human figure in art and the legacy of Renaissance perspective. In short, he overturned the traditions of Western art. LES DEMOISELLES thus set the stage and provided the impetus for the development of Cubism. Even today, viewers are disturbed and challenged by the painting's hacked-out shapes and overall intensity.

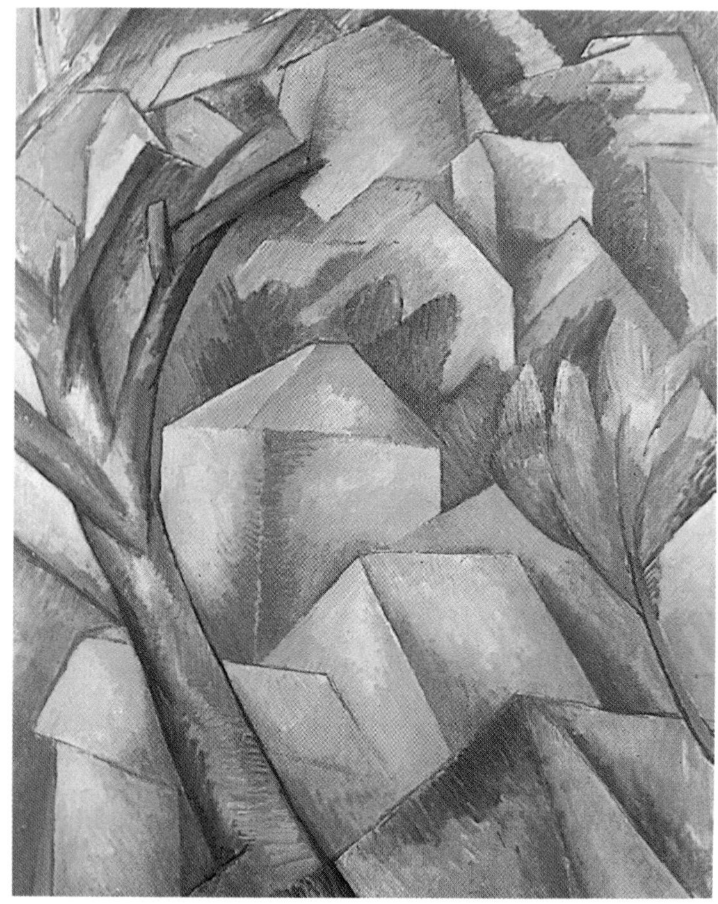

587 Georges Braque.
HOUSES AT L'ESTAQUE. 1908.
Oil on canvas. 73 cm × 59 cm.
Kunstmuseum, Bern, Switzerland.
Herman and Margit Rupf Foundation.

588 Paul Cézanne.
GARDANNE. 1885-1886.
Oil on canvas. 31½" × 25¼".
The Metropolitan Museum of Art, New York.
Gift of Dr. and Mrs. Franz H. Hirschland, 1957 (57.181).

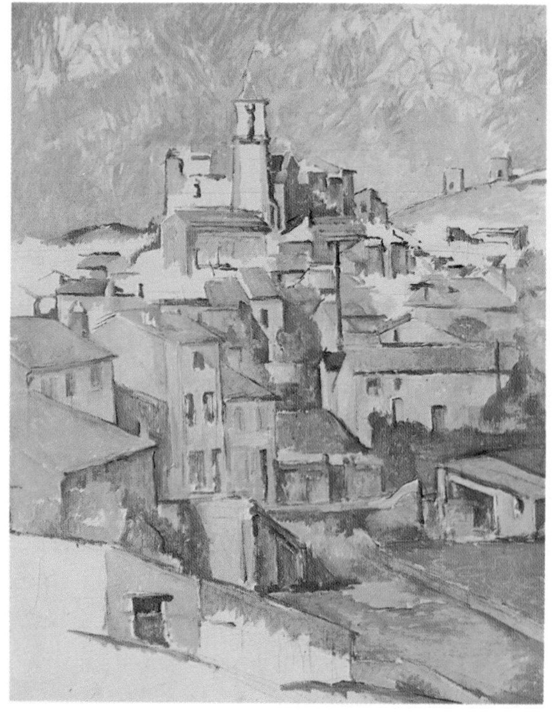

A comparison of three paintings—Cézanne's GARDANNE, Braque's HOUSES AT L'ESTAQUE, and Picasso's MAISONS SUR LA COLLINE—completed between 1886 and 1909, shows the beginning of the progression from Cézanne's Post-Impressionist style to the Cubist approach developed by Braque and Picasso.

Picasso made the first breakthrough, but Braque did the most to develop the refined vocabulary of Cubism. Braque admired Cézanne's continuous probing, his doubt, and his dogged determination to get at the truth of his subjects. In a series of landscapes painted in the south of France (where Cézanne had worked), Braque took Cézanne's faceted planar constructions a step further. Picasso's development of figure and ground interactions was also a springboard for paintings such as Braque's HOUSES AT L'ESTAQUE.

Instead of the sequential progression into depth

that had been common in European painting since the Renaissance, Braque's shapes define a rush of forms that pile up rhythmically in shallow, ambiguous space. Buildings and trees seem interlocked in an active spatial system that pushes and pulls across the picture surface.

HOUSES AT L'ESTAQUE, one of the first Cubist paintings, provided the impetus for the movement's name: when Matisse saw this painting, he declared it to be a bunch of little cubes. Although this observation does not accurately describe Cubist form, Cubism became the name by which the movement was identified.

From 1908 to 1914, Braque and Picasso were equally responsible for bringing Cubism to maturity. Picasso's MAISONS SUR LA COLLINE shows further development of Cubist ideas. While Cézanne structured his paintings with color, Braque and Picasso worked for a time in increasingly neutral tones, in an effort to achieve formal structure devoid of the emotional distractions of color.

By 1910, Cubism had become a fully developed style. During the *analytical* phase of Cubism (1910 to 1911), Picasso, Braque, and others analyzed their subjects from various angles, then painted abstract, geometric references to these views. Because mental concepts of familiar objects are based on experiences of seeing many sides, they aimed to show objects as the mind, rather than the eye, perceives them. In Picasso's PORTRAIT OF DANIEL HENRY KAHNWEILER, an art dealer, the analytical dissection and reintegration of the subject with its surrounding space reflect these multiple views. Figure and ground are one.

Cubism, although radical in appearance, can be seen as a new phase of the classical approach to visual form. It was a rational, formalist counterpart to the subjective emphasis of the Fauves and other expressionists. Above all, it was a reinvention of pictorial space. The Cubists realized that the two-dimensional space of the picture plane was unique—a form of space quite different from the three-dimensional space we occupy. Natural objects were points of departure for abstract images, demonstrating the essential unity of forms within the

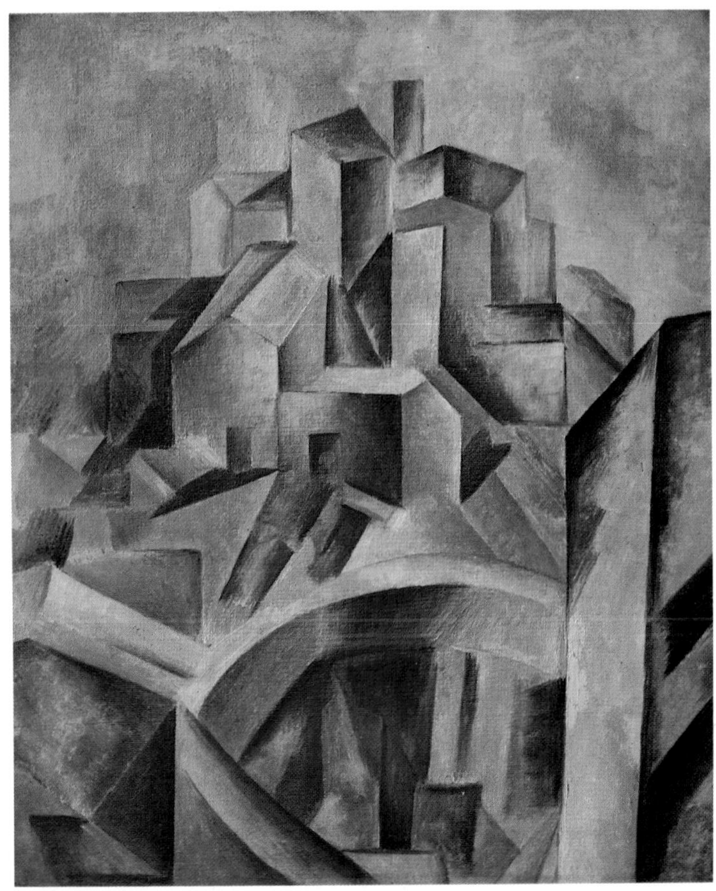

589 Pablo Picasso.
MAISONS SUR LA COLLINE (HOUSES ON THE HILL).
HORTA D'EBRO. 1909.
Oil on canvas. 31⅞" × 25¼".
Private collection.

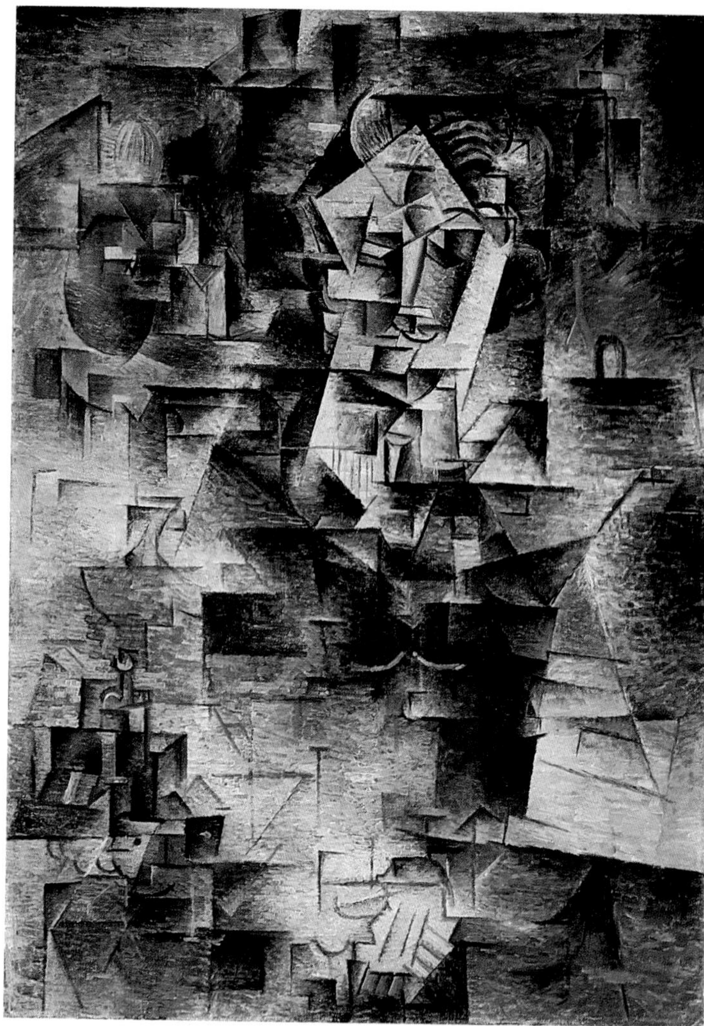

590 Pablo Picasso.
PORTRAIT OF DANIEL HENRY KAHNWEILER. 1910.
Oil on canvas. 39½" × 28⅝".
Gift of Mrs. Gilbert W. Chapman (1948.561). © 1994 The Art Institute of Chicago. All rights reserved.

spaces that surround and penetrate them. Cubism is a reconstruction of objects, based on geometric abstraction. By looking first at Cézanne's GARDANNE, then at Braque's HOUSES AT L'ESTAQUE and Picasso's MAISONS SUR LA COLLINE, and finally at PORTRAIT OF DANIEL HENRY KAHNWEILER, we see a progression in which forms seem to build, then spread across the surface in interwoven planes. Again, in Braque's VIOLIN AND PALETTE, objects and their background interpenetrate in shallow pictorial space.

A new kind of construction of planes in actual space came about when Picasso assembled his sheet-metal GUITAR and thereby extended the Cubist revolution to sculpture and collage as well as painting. Many consider GUITAR one of this century's most significant sculptures, since it began what has become a dominant trend toward sculptural construction. Before GUITAR, most sculpture was carved or modeled. Since GUITAR, much of contemporary sculpture has been constructed.

In 1912, Picasso and Braque modified Analytical Cubism with color, textured and patterned surfaces, and the use of cutout shapes. The resulting style came to be called Synthetic Cubism. Artists used actual two-dimensional objects as well as painted representational and invented surfaces. Pieces of newspaper, sheet music, wallpaper, and similar items were not re-presented but actually *presented* in a new context: the newspaper in THE VIOLIN is part of a real Paris newspaper. Shapes created by the exposed ground act simultaneously as major foreground elements; ground becomes figure, and figure becomes ground. Picasso chose traditional still-life objects; but rather than paint the fruit, he cut out and pasted printed images of fruit. Such compositions, called *papier colle* in French, or pasted paper, became known as *collage* in English. Analytical Cubism involved taking apart, or breaking down, the subject into its various aspects; Synthetic Cubism was a process of building up or combining bits and pieces of material.

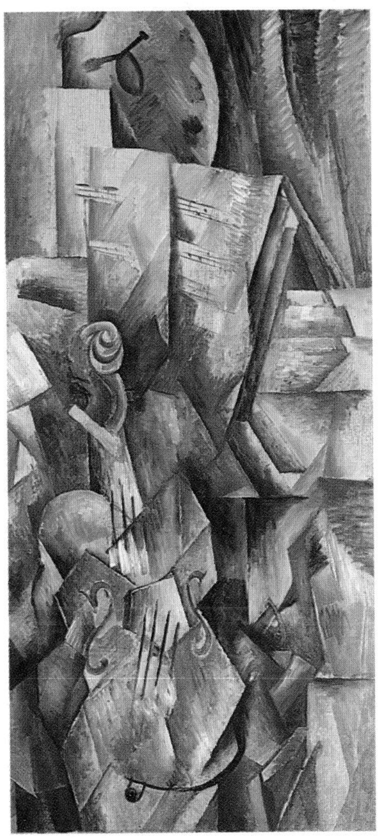

591 Georges Braque.
VIOLIN AND PALETTE. 1909-1910.
Oil on canvas. 36⅛" × 16⅞".
Solomon R. Guggenheim Museum, New York.

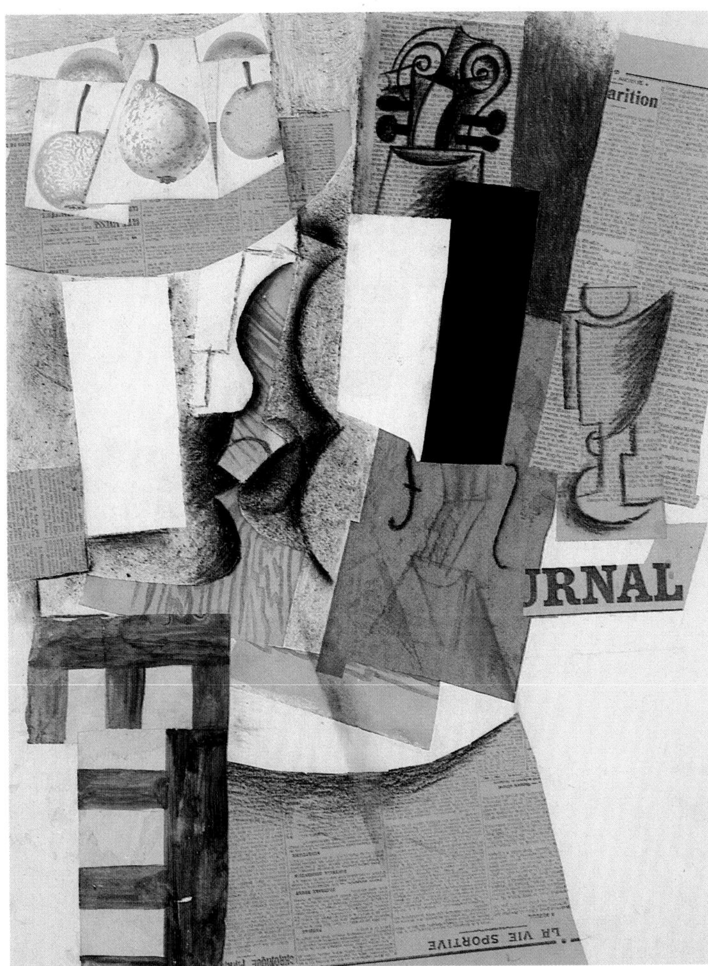

592 Pablo Picasso.
THE VIOLIN (VIOLIN AND FRUIT). 1913.
Paper, charcoal, gouache on paperboard. 25½" × 19½".
Philadelphia Museum of Art. A. E. Gallatin Collection.

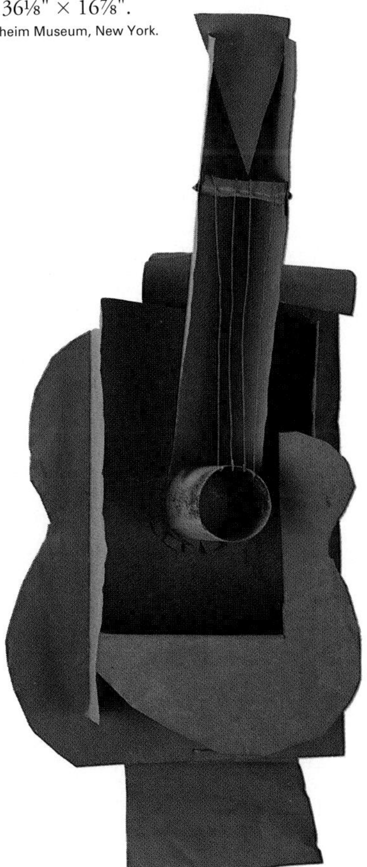

593 Pablo Picasso.
GUITAR. 1912-1913.
Sheet metal and wire.
30½" × 13⅛" × 7⅝".
The Museum of Modern Art, New York.
Gift of the artist.

PABLO PICASSO (1881–1973)

Even before he could talk, Picasso showed skill in drawing. Years later he could remember the colors of things he saw in early childhood.

Aided by the careful instruction of his artist father, Picasso mastered the basic techniques of representational drawing and painting by the time he was fourteen. By 1901, when he was twenty, he had assimilated the influences of several leading artists of his father's generation: Toulouse-Lautrec, Degas, Gauguin, and Van Gogh.

Between 1901 and 1904, Picasso depicted his poor, suffering neighbors in blue tones that deepened an impression of melancholy (see page 80). In the black-and-white drawing of a circus woman and her infant (page 49), sadness is replaced by gentleness. By 1905, sales of his work improved Picasso's economic situation and may have led to the more optimistic feeling in his work. He began painting circus people rather than the destitute; tints and shades of warm, delicate reds replaced somber blues.

At twenty-five, Picasso became fascinated with the expressive force of art from outside Western traditions. He became particularly interested in the African and Oceanic sculpture that Gauguin and later the Fauves had "discovered."

From 1904 to 1945 he lived in Paris. His early work shows his ability to assimilate varied influences and his interest in exploring new modes of expression.

There are conflicting accounts regarding when and where Picasso first saw African sculpture. He claimed that his first encounter with African sculpture and masks was in an exhibition late in 1907, after he had finished LES DEMOISELLES. Other artists and writers, including Matisse and Gertrude Stein, told of showing Picasso African sculpture in 1906. His paintings and sculpture of the period certainly show a familiarity with sculpture and masks of the Ivory Coast and the metal-covered figures of the Gabon. By 1909 Picasso had become a serious collector of African art.

In their development of Cubism, Picasso and Braque drew inspiration from the inventive abstractions of African sculpture and the structural translation of nature seen in paintings by Cézanne. The impact of Cubism on Western painting has been enormous.

Picasso exhibited in the first Surrealist exhibition in Paris in 1925, but he did not sign their manifesto. Like the Surrealists, he became increasingly involved with the political unrest in Europe during the 1930s. After a short period of rest and retreat, Picasso produced a long series of drawings and paintings that expressed his anguish over the growing political violence that led to World War II (see GUERNICA, page 443).

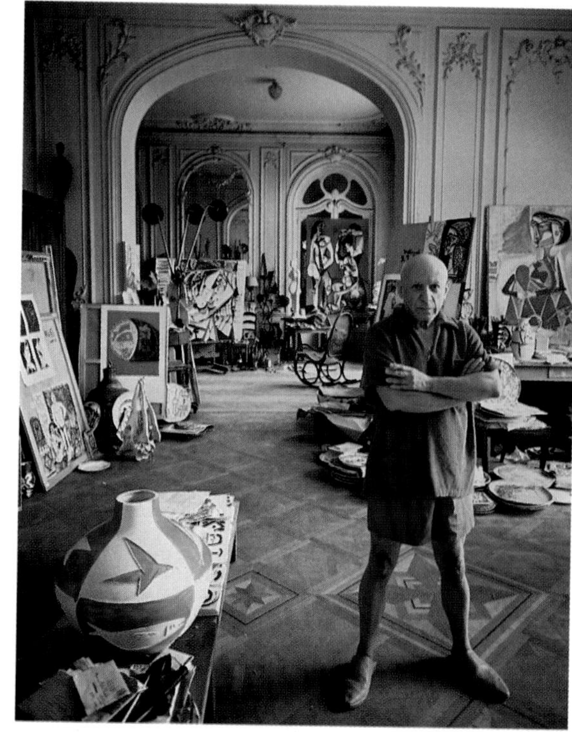

594 PICASSO IN HIS STUDIO AT CANNES. 1956.
Photograph: © Arnold Newman.

Any written biography of Picasso is only a footnote to the autobiographical content of much of his art. In his many variations on the themes of the artist at work and the artist with his model, we recognize that Picasso is commenting on his own experience. Within and beyond his images of the life of an artist there is the ebb and flow, the inspiration and the crisis of Picasso's turbulent love life. Five very different women, who (in succession) shared his life, appear again and again in his art.

His later work included ceramics and huge numbers of prints and drawings in addition to many paintings. Hardworking and prolific until the end of his life, he was a seminal figure who more than anyone else gave visual expression to the essential character of his time. In its diversity, Picasso's art relates to most of the twentieth century's art movements. With his prodigious imagination and many innovative changes in style and media, Picasso inspired generations of younger artists who often made whole careers sparked by just one phase of his creative evolution.

Picasso's stature in the twentieth century is comparable to that of Michelangelo's during the Renaissance: both artists lived nearly a century, both became famous early in life, both lived during periods of incredible change, and both were at the forefront of the artistic developments of their times. Picasso was the most representative artist of the twentieth century.

THE MODERN SPIRIT IN AMERICA

As Picasso and Braque took the steps that led to Cubism, American photographer Alfred Stieglitz was reconsidering the geometry of design on the picture plane. When Picasso saw Stieglitz's photograph THE STEERAGE, he said, "This photographer is working in the same spirit as I am."[8]

THE STEERAGE looked "chopped up" to many people. Some of the artist's friends felt that it should have been two photographs rather than one. Stieglitz, however, saw the complex scene as a pattern of interacting forces of light, shade, shape, and direction. Aboard a ship headed for Europe, he saw the composition of this photograph as "a round straw hat, the funnel leaning left, the stairway leaning right, the white drawbridge with its railings made of circular chains, white suspenders crossing on the back of a man on the steerage below, round shapes of iron machinery, a mast cutting into the sky, making a triangular shape.... I saw a picture of shapes and underlying that the feeling I had about life."[9] He rushed to his cabin to get his camera, hoping the relationships would not change. Nothing had shifted, and he made the photograph he considered his best.

Stieglitz made major contributions toward establishing photography as an art of comparable importance to traditional media. He also played a key role in introducing the new European painting and sculpture to Americans. In 1907, he opened a gallery in New York and began showing the work of the most progressive European artists, including photographers. He was the first in America to show works by Cézanne, Matisse, Brancusi, Picasso, and Braque. Following the exhibition of art by these pioneers, Stieglitz began to show work by those who would become leading American artists, including Georgia O'Keeffe (see pages 41–42 and 447).

Between 1905 and 1910, traditional concepts of form in space were being challenged in architecture as well as in sculpture, painting, and photography. While Cubism was developing in painting, leading American architect Frank Lloyd Wright was designing "prairie houses," in which he often omitted or minimized walls between living and

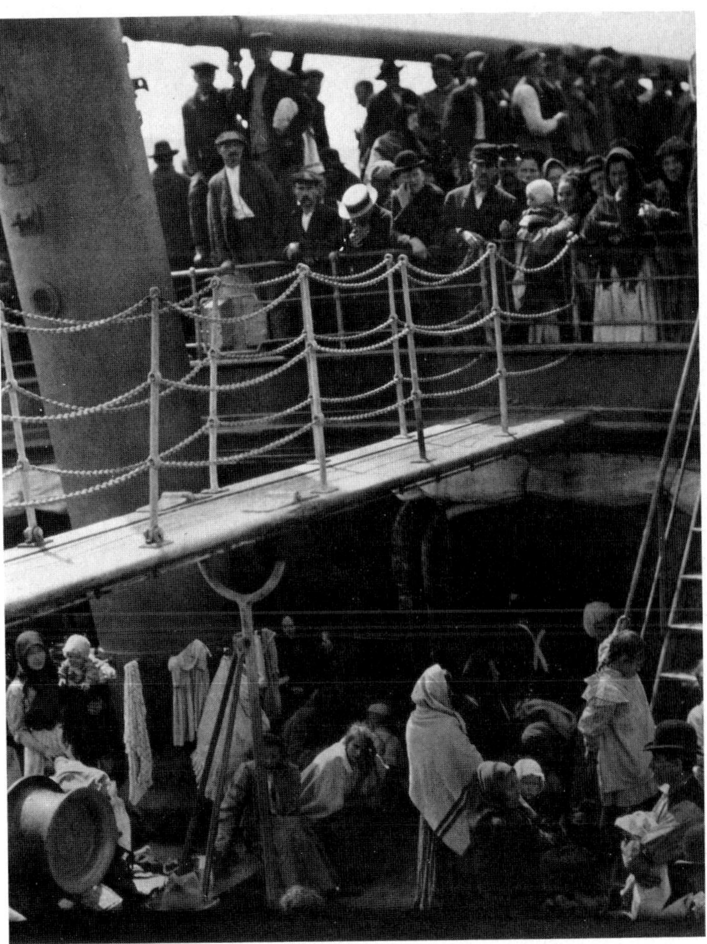

595 Alfred Stieglitz.
THE STEERAGE. 1907.
Photogravure (artist's proof) from *Camera Work*, No. 36 (1911).
Size of print: 7¾" × 6½".
The Museum of Modern Art, New York. Gift of the artist.

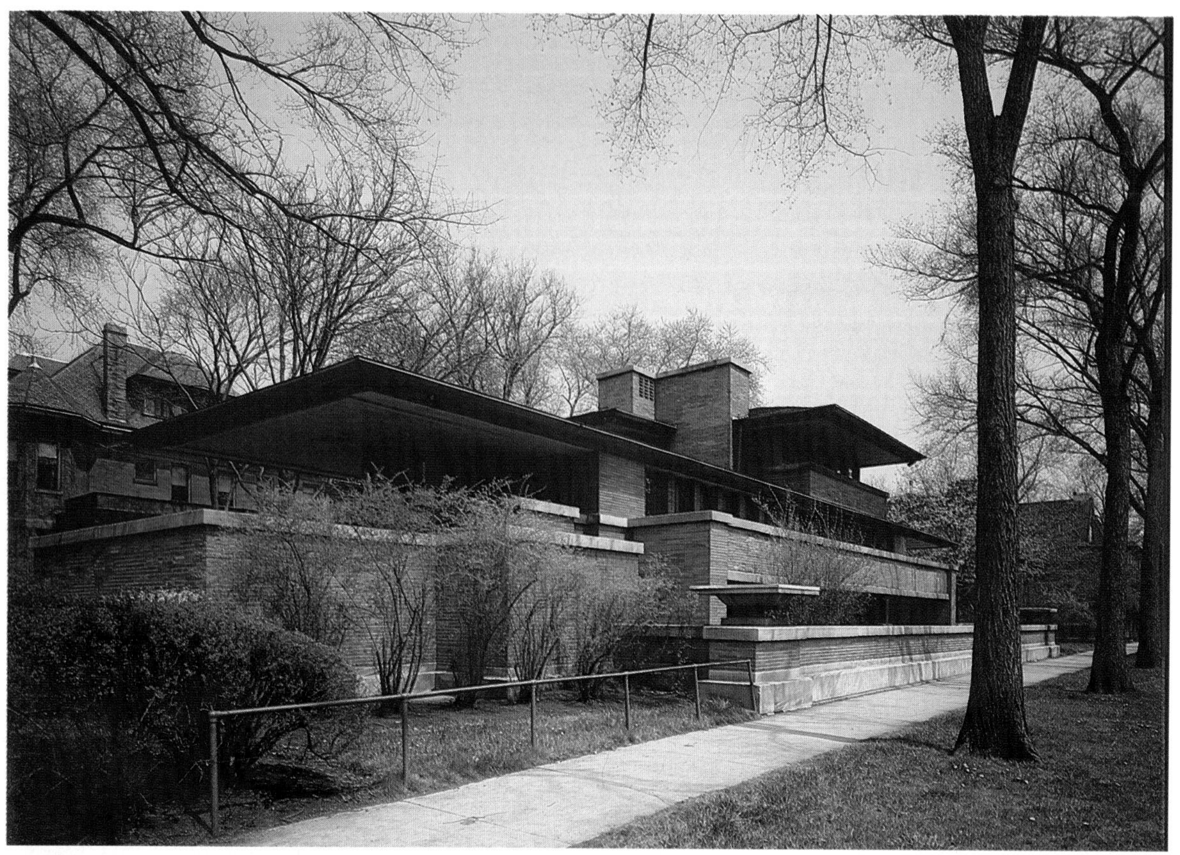

596 Frank Lloyd Wright. ROBIE HOUSE. Chicago, Illinois. 1909.

dining rooms and between interior and exterior spaces. Wright's concept of open plans has changed the way people design living spaces. In many contemporary homes, kitchen, dining room, and living room now join in one continuous space, and indoors often intermingles with outdoors.

In his ROBIE HOUSE of 1909, a striking cantilevered roof reaches out and unifies a fluid design of asymmetrically interconnected spaces. Through Wright's influence, the open flow of spaces became a major feature of contemporary architecture. To get a feeling of how far ahead of his time Wright was, imagine the incongruity of a new 1909 horseless carriage that could have been parked in front of the ROBIE HOUSE the year it was completed. (For more on Frank Lloyd Wright and his architecture, see pages 262–264.)

FUTURISM AND THE CELEBRATION OF MOTION

The Italian Futurists were among the many artists who gained their initial inspiration from Cubism. To the shifting planes and multiple vantage points of Cubism, Futurists such as Giacomo Balla (see page 71) and Umberto Boccioni added a sense of speed and motion and a celebration of the machine.

By multiplying the image of a moving object, Futurism expanded the Cubist concepts of simultaneity of vision and metamorphosis. In 1909, Marinetti, a poet, proclaimed in the *Initial Manifesto of Futurism:* "the world's splendor has been enriched by a new beauty; the beauty of speed ... a roaring motorcar ... is more beautiful than the Victory of Samothrace."[10] (NIKE OF SAMOTHRACE appears on page 70.)

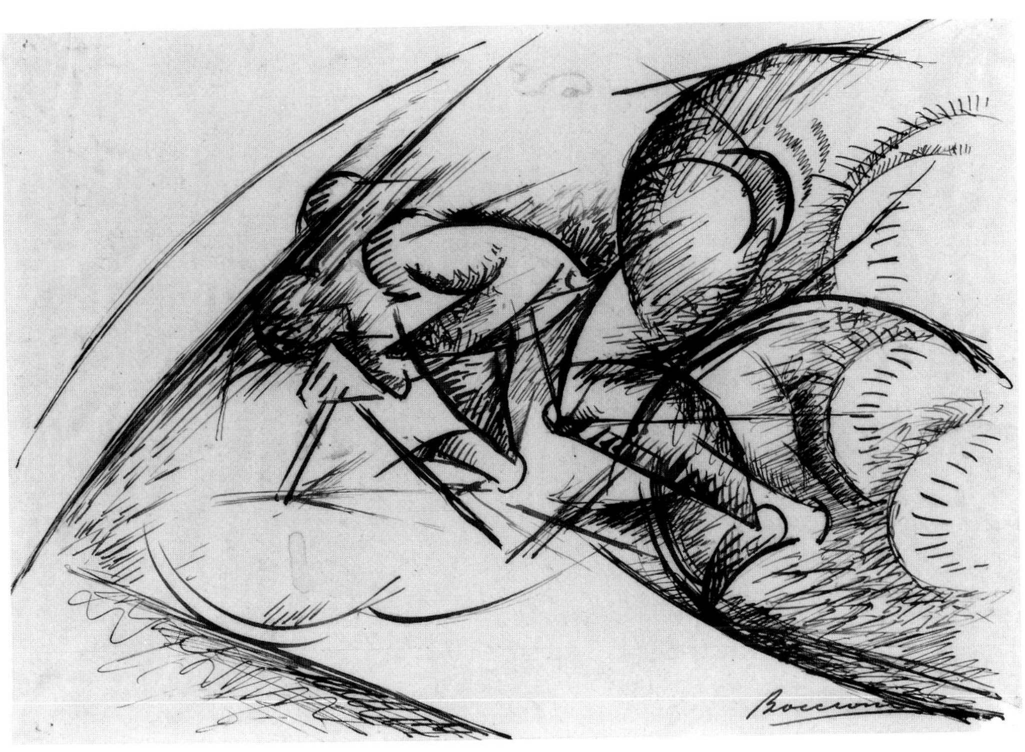

597 Umberto Boccioni.
STUDY FOR DYNAMIC FORCE OF A CYCLIST, I.
1913. Ink on paper.
8¼" × 12⅜".
Yale University Art Gallery, New Haven, Connecticut. Gift of Collection Société Anonyme.

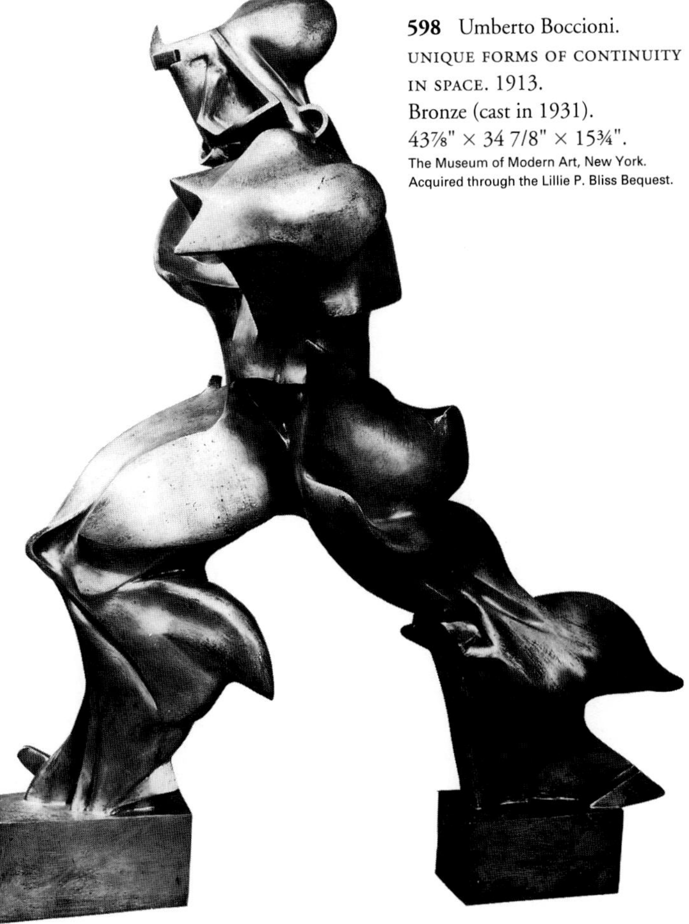

598 Umberto Boccioni.
UNIQUE FORMS OF CONTINUITY IN SPACE. 1913.
Bronze (cast in 1931).
43⅞" × 34 7/8" × 15¾".
The Museum of Modern Art, New York.
Acquired through the Lillie P. Bliss Bequest.

The Futurists translated the speed of modern life into works that captured the dynamic energy of the new century. In spite of their statements about the beauty of technology, even war machinery, much Futurist work is based on the dynamics of human figures and birds. Boccioni's drawing STUDY FOR DYNAMIC FORCE OF A CYCLIST, I is one of the most energized Futurist images.

An abstract sculpture of a striding figure climaxed a series of Boccioni's drawings, paintings, and sculpture. Boccioni insisted that sculpture should be released from its usual confining outer surfaces in order to open up and fuse the work with the space surrounding it. In UNIQUE FORMS OF CONTINUITY IN SPACE, muscular forms seem to leap outward in flamelike bursts of energy. During this period, the human experience of motion, time, and space was transformed by the development of the automobile, the airplane, and the movies. Futurist imagery reflects this exciting period of change.

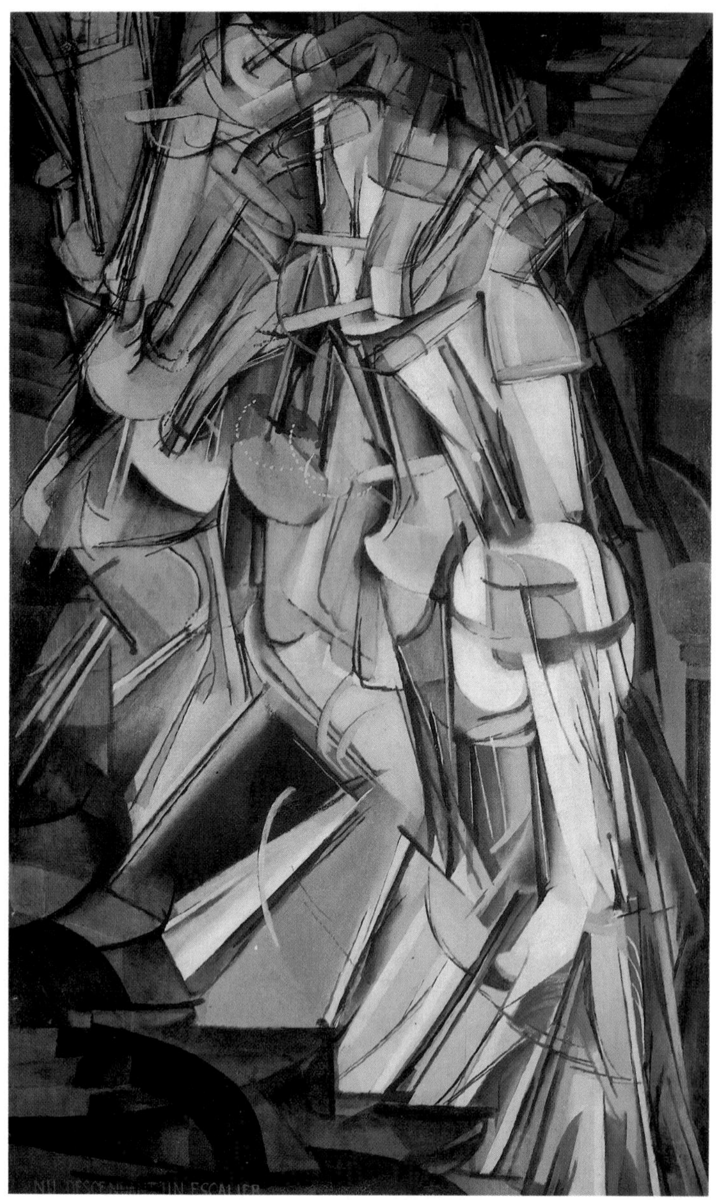

French artist Marcel Duchamp, working independently of the Futurists, brought the dimension of motion to Cubism. His NUDE DESCENDING A STAIRCASE, NO. 2 was in part inspired by the GEOMETRICAL CHRONOPHOTOGRAPH of nineteenth-century physiologist Etienne-Jules Marey, whose studies helped pave the way for the development of motion pictures. Superimposed sequential images photographed by Marey revealed patterns of movement in time and space.

In one of Marey's books, I saw an illustration of how he indicated people who fence, or horses galloping, with a system of dots delineating the different movements.... That's what gave me the idea for the execution of the "Nude Descending a Staircase." I used this method a little in the sketch, but especially in the final form of the picture.... At the same time, I retained a lot of Cubism, at least in the color harmony. From things I had seen at Braque's or Picasso's. But I was trying to apply a slightly different formula.... Also there was no Futurism, since I didn't know the Futurists.[11]

Duchamp's NUDE DESCENDING A STAIRCASE works in a way that film cannot. Through sequential, diagonally placed, abstract references to the figure, the painting presents the movement of a body through space, seen all at once, in a single rhythmic progression. Our sense of gravity intensifies the overall feeling of motion. When the painting was displayed at the Armory Show in New York in 1913, it caused cries of dismay and was seen as the ultimate Cubist madness. The painting, once described as "an explosion in a shingle factory," has remained an inspiration to painters who use repetition and rhythm to express motion.

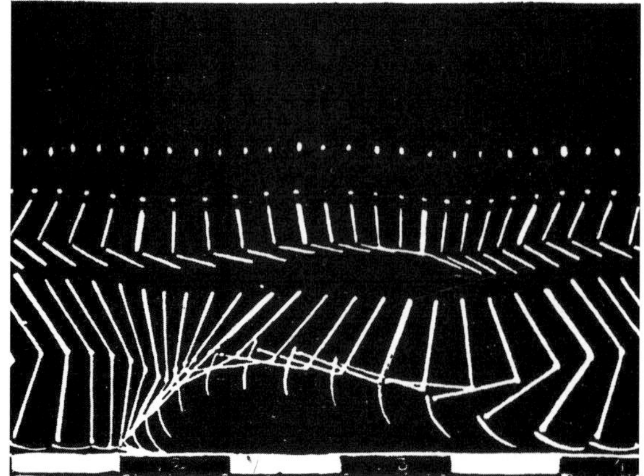

599 Marcel Duchamp.
NUDE DESCENDING A STAIRCASE, NO. 2. 1912.
Oil on canvas. 58" × 35".
Philadelphia Museum of Art. Louise and Walter Arensberg Collection.

600 Etienne-Jules Marey.
GEOMETRICAL CHRONOPHOTOGRAPH. c. 1883.
Image of runner dressed in black with white lines and points attached.
International Museum of Photography at George Eastman House, Rochester, New York.

CHAPTER 22

Between World Wars

In 1914, enthusiasm for grand patriotic solutions to international tensions led citizens of many countries into World War I, a murderous and protracted conflict involving many European countries and eventually the United States. History has revealed that the war was far more devastating than the people of the time were led to believe. Over ten million were killed and twice that number wounded by machinery devised, but no longer controlled, by human reason. Many of the best-educated youth of Europe were lost in the world's first experience with mechanized mass killing.

As a result of the war, the political and cultural landscape was changed forever. The war set the stage for the Russian Revolution and paved the way for the Nazis of Germany and the Fascists of Italy. Governments assumed new powers to mobilize people and material, to dictate economic life, to censor public expression, and to manipulate the way people thought by controlling information. Dissent was denounced as unpatriotic.

Writers, photographers, and artists were prevented by governments and the self-censoring press from communicating the horror of the war. Many writers and artists produced propaganda, remained silent, or fought in the war. A great many were killed.

It was not until after the war had ended that those artists and writers who survived were able to express their perceptions of the catastrophe that shaped the world. Many sensitive people either were stifled by cynicism or sought relief in idealistic schemes for reform.

During the postwar era there was a gap between the older generation who had "bought" the propaganda and the young who had been in the trenches, between the official party line and the reality understood by the informed public. In the arts, movements emerged to protest the insanity and to mend the gulf between idealism and actuality.

DADA

Dada began in protest against the horrors of World War I. It became an aggressive assault on corrupt values by an international group of young writers and artists. Those who began the movement in Zurich chose the intentionally ambiguous word *Dada* as their rallying cry. One member of the group assumed that it referred to *da, da,* Slavic for "yes, yes." The two-syllable word was well-suited for expressing the essence of what was an attitude, not a style. In the eyes of the Dadaists, the destructive absurdity of war was caused by traditional, narrow-minded values, which they set out to overturn. According to artist Marcel Janco,

Dada was not a school of artists, but an alarm signal against declining values, routine and speculation, a desperate appeal on behalf of all forms of art, for a creative basis on which to build a new and universal consciousness of art.[1]

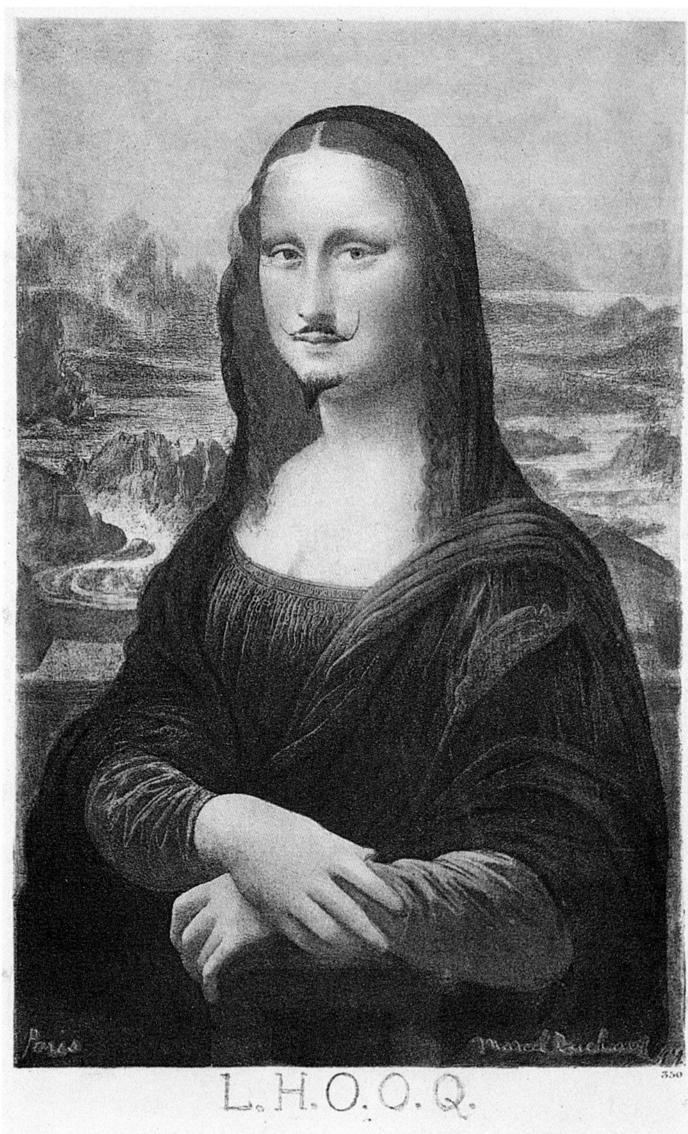

601 Marcel Duchamp.
L.H.O.O.Q. 1919.
"Corrected ready-made."
Private collection. On loan to the Philadelphia Museum of Art.

French artist and poet Jean Arp said,

While the thunder of guns rolled in the distance, we sang, painted, glued, and composed for all our worth. We are seeking an art that would heal mankind from the madness of the age.[2]

Dadaists maintained that humankind had demonstrated that it was without reason. In order to make a new beginning, the Dadaists rejected all accepted moral, social, political, and aesthetic values. They felt it was pointless to try to find order and meaning in a world in which so-called rational behavior had produced only chaos and destruction. They sought to shock the middle class into seeing the absurdity of the Western world's social and political situation.

The Dadaists celebrated play and spontaneity. Their literature, art, and staged events were often based on chance rather than premeditation. Poets selected words at random; artists joined elements in startling, irrational combinations.

For Duchamp, mechanically produced things were a reservoir of un-self-conscious art objects. In his view, a reproduction of the MONA LISA was a ready-made object, in the same class as bicycle wheels, kitchen stools (see page 458), and snow shovels. L.H.O.O.Q. is a "corrected" ready-made by Duchamp, expressing his view that art had become simply a precious commodity. He poked fun with his "corrections," a penciled moustache and goatee and a new title. The unusual title is a pun in French, comprehensible to those who can hear the sentence in the sound of the letters pronounced in French. Translated into English, it reads, "She has a hot tail." Duchamp's outrageous irreverence toward one of the world's most revered paintings was an attempt to shake people out of a pattern of automatic acceptance of cultural values.

Man Ray, an American, was a friend of Duchamp. His Dada works include paintings, photographs, and assembled objects. In 1921, in Paris, Man Ray saw an iron displayed in front of a shop selling housewares. He purchased the iron, a box of tacks, and a tube of glue. After gluing a row of tacks

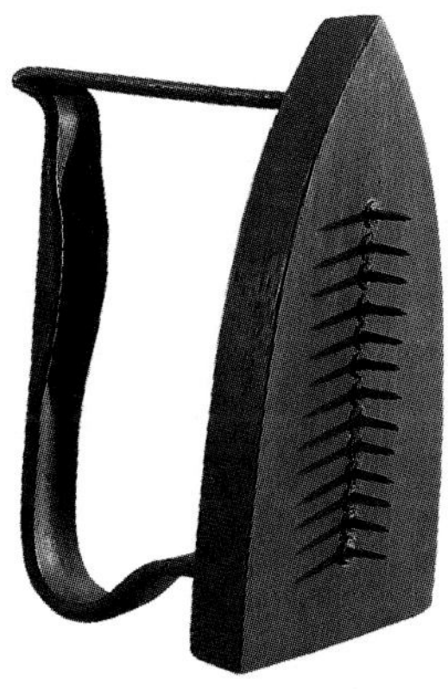

602 Man Ray.
CADEAU (THE GIFT). c. 1958 (replica of 1921 original). Flatiron with metal tacks. 16⅛" × 3⅝" × 4½".
The Museum of Modern Art, New York. James Thrall Soby Fund.

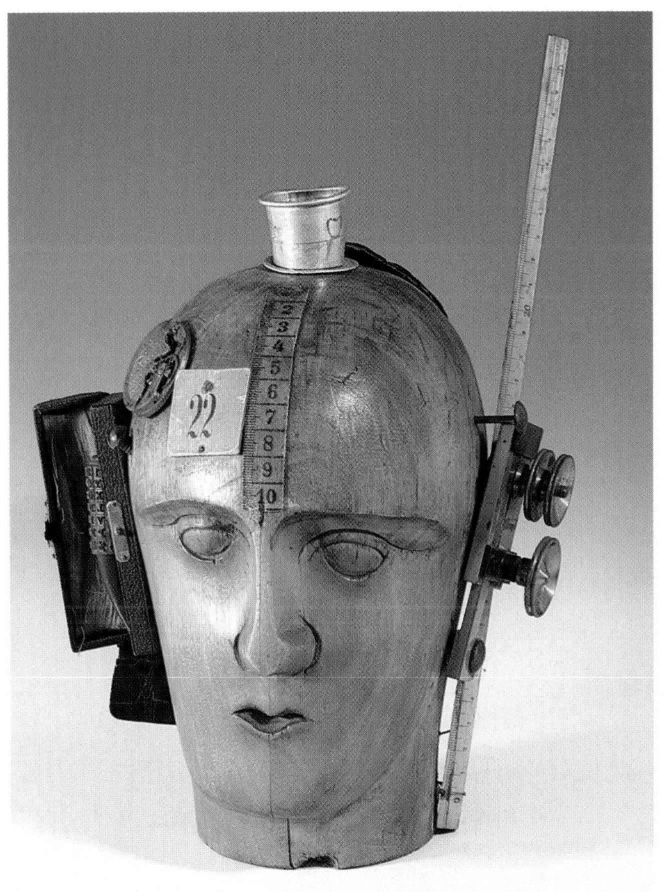

to the smooth surface of the iron, he titled his assemblage THE GIFT—thus creating an ironic contradiction.

One memorable Dada sculpture, Raoul Hausmann's THE SPIRIT OF OUR TIME, continues to express a truth about the twentieth century. We would like to know ourselves, yet we succumb to the playthings of our technology and ignore the sound of silence. Have the artifacts of our mass production turned us into hollow-headed robots who simply receive and transmit information and are unable to think for ourselves? Hausmann seems to have anticipated the world of artificial intelligence and the ubiquitous Walkman.

Dadaists expanded on the Cubist idea of collage with *photomontage,* in which parts of photographs are combined in new ways. In THE MULTI-MILLIONAIRE, by Dadaist Hannah Höch, man, the artifact-making industrialist, stands as a fractured giant among the things he has produced.

Some Dadaists maintained that "Art is dead." They often intended to be antiaesthetic. Ironically, they created a new aesthetic that has had lasting influence on the twentieth century.

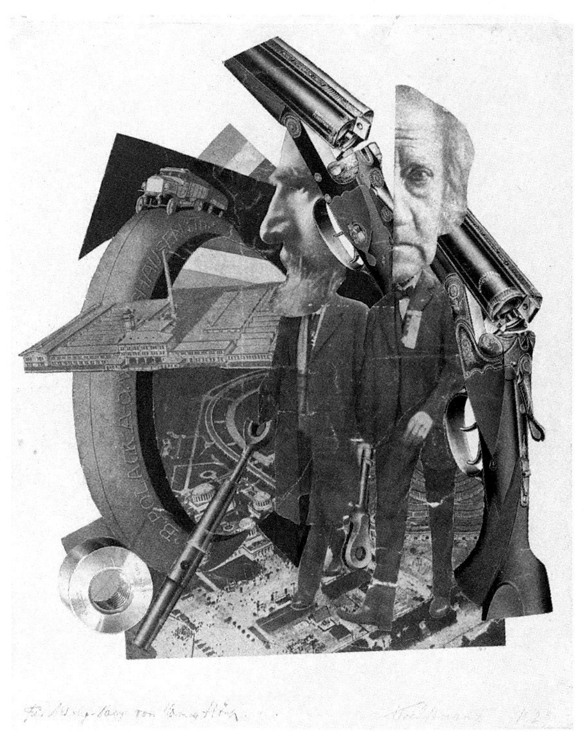

603 Raoul Hausmann.
THE SPIRIT OF OUR TIME. 1919.
Combine. Height 12¾".
National Museum of Modern Art, Georges Pompidou Centre, Paris. © ADAGP, Paris, 1993.

604 Hannah Höch.
THE MULTI-MILLIONAIRE. 1923.
Photomontage. 36 cm × 31 cm.
Galerie Berinson, Berlin.

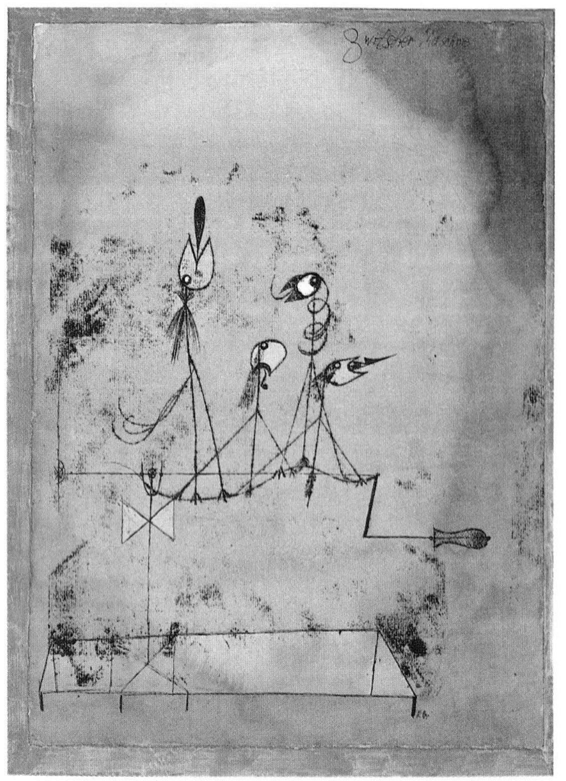

605 Paul Klee.
TWITTERING MACHINE. 1922.
Oil on transfer drawing on paper, mounted on cardboard.
16¼" × 12".
The Museum of Modern Art, New York. Purchase.

FANTASY AND METAPHYSICS

The highly personal and inventive art of Paul Klee provided inspiration for both Dadaists and their heirs, the Surrealists (see page 432). Although Klee belonged to neither group, his work paralleled these movements and he exhibited with both groups.

As Klee worked to develop his art, he tried to free himself from the accumulation of history in an effort to begin all over again. He discovered ways to tap the resources of his own unconscious, enabling him to create fantastic images. Klee spoke of his receptivity to such inspiration:

> *. . . everything vanishes around me and good works rise from me of their own accord. My hand is entirely the implement of a distant sphere. It is not my head that functions but something else, something higher, something more remote. I must have great friends there, dark as well as bright. . . . They are all very kind to me.*[3]

Both whimsy and mystery pervade Klee's fantastic TWITTERING MACHINE. A major part of the intrigue comes from the title and its relationship to the "machine." We participate in the fun as we imagine the twittering sounds that will come forth when the crank is turned. As a machine it is absurd—a kind of useless Dada object.

Earlier in the century, when Cubism was maturing, Marc Chagall assimilated the influence of the Cubists by blending their use of geometric abstraction with his own imaginative use of subject matter. His fantasy-filled paintings such as THE BIRTHDAY and I AND THE VILLAGE (page 50) incorporate symbolism drawn from eastern Jewish Hasidism, folklore, and childhood memories of Russian life.

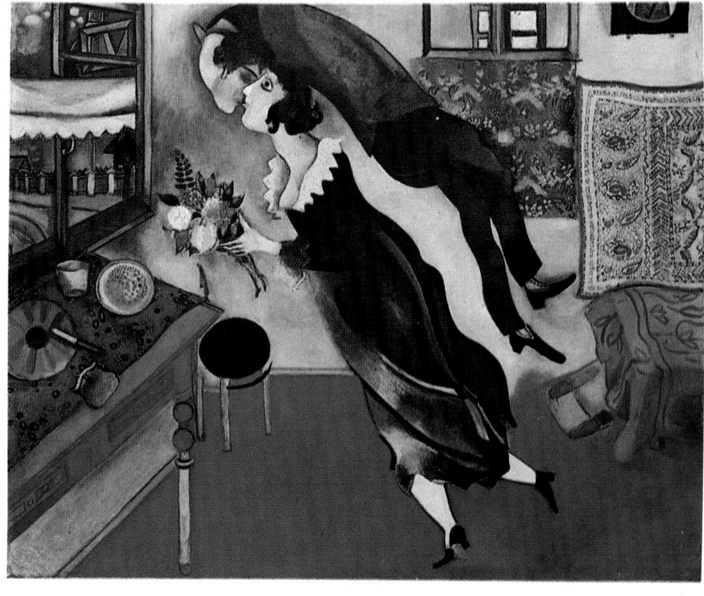

606 Marc Chagall.
THE BIRTHDAY. 1915.
Oil on canvas. 31¾" × 39¼".
The Museum of Modern Art, New York.
Acquired through the Lillie P. Bliss Bequest.

Shortly before Chagall's marriage, his bride-to-be, Bella, brought him flowers on his birthday. In Bella's autobiography, she wrote of their rapture:

Soon I forget the flowers. You work with your brushes ... You pour on color ... Suddenly you jump in the air ... You float among the rafters. You turn your head and you twist mine too ... and both together we rise over the clean little room.

"How do you like my picture?" you ask ... You wait and are afraid of what I may tell you. "It's very good ... you float away so beautifully. We'll call it the Birthday."[4]

Many of Chagall's paintings show people "flying" or with their feet off the ground, as a metaphor for love. Chagall's immense outpouring of work included prints and stained glass as well as paintings. His images are filled with delightful combinations of gestures, objects, environments, and figures from his life and imagination.

Italian metaphysical painter Giorgio De Chirico had a more direct role as a precursor of Surrealism than Klee or Chagall. In THE MYSTERY AND MELANCHOLY OF A STREET, De Chirico used distorted linear perspective, with conflicting vanishing points, to create an eerie space peopled by faceless shadows. The painting speaks the symbolic language of dreams and mystery. According to the artist,

everything has two aspects: the current aspect, which we see nearly always and which ordinary men see, and the ghostly and metaphysical aspect, which only rare individuals may see in moments of clairvoyance and metaphysical abstraction.[5]

Painters of the metaphysical sought to create an alternative reality that could communicate with the unconscious by removing objects from the real world and presenting them in incongruous relationships.

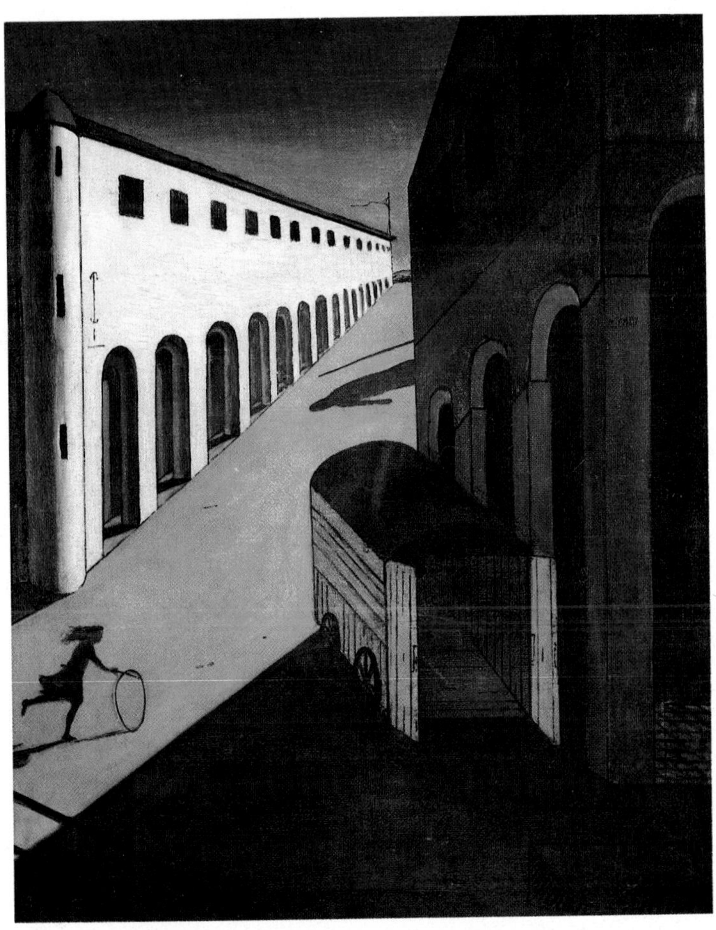

607 Giorgio De Chirico.
THE MYSTERY AND MELANCHOLY OF A STREET. 1914.
Oil on canvas. 34¼" × 28⅛".
Private collection.

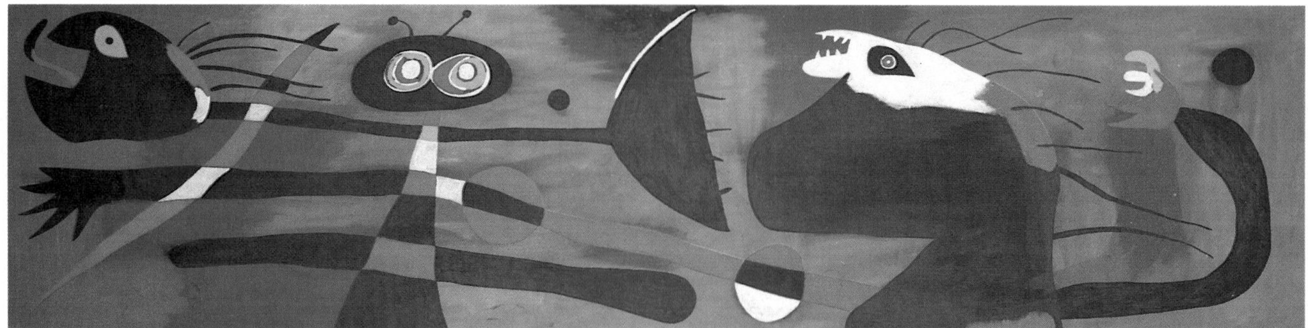

608 Joan Miró.
WOMAN HAUNTED BY THE PASSAGE OF THE DRAGON-FLY, BIRD OF BAD OMEN (also called NURSERY DECORATION). 1938.
Oil on canvas. 31½" × 124".
The Toledo Museum of Art, Toledo, Ohio. Purchased with funds from the Libbey Endowment. Gift of Edward Drummond Libbey.

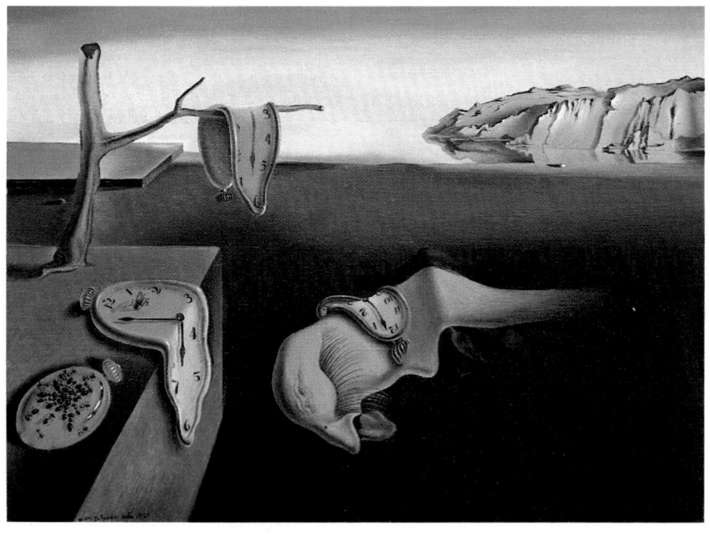

609 Salvador Dali.
THE PERSISTENCE OF MEMORY. 1931.
Oil on canvas. 9½" × 13".
The Museum of Modern Art, New York. Anonymous gift.

SURREALISM

In the 1920s, a group of writers and painters gathered to proclaim the omnipotence of the unconscious mind, thought to be a higher reality than the conscious mind. Their goal was to make visible the imagery of the unconscious. They were indebted to the shocking irrationality of Dadaism, the fantastic creations of Chagall and Klee, and especially the dream images of De Chirico. They also drew heavily on the new psychology of Sigmund Freud.

Surrealism was officially launched in Paris in 1924 with the publication of its first manifesto, written by poet-painter André Breton. In it he defined the movement's purpose as

the future resolution of these two states, dream and reality, which are seemingly so contradictory, into a kind of absolute reality, a surreality, if one may so speak.[6]

Among the members of the Surrealist group were Spanish painters Salvador Dali and Joan Miró.

Dali's THE PERSISTENCE OF MEMORY evokes the eerie quality of some dreams. Mechanical time wilts in a deserted landscape of infinite space. The warped, headlike image in the foreground may be the last remnant of a vanished humanity. It may also be a self-portrait, complete with protruding tongue.

Dali and Miró represent two opposite tendencies operating in Surrealism. Dali's illusionary deep space and representational techniques create near-photographic dream images that make the impossible seem believable. The startling juxtaposition of unrelated objects creates a nightmarish sense of a superreality beyond the everyday world. This approach has been called representational Surrealism. In contrast, Miró's abstract Surrealism provides suggestive elements that give the widest possible play to the viewer's imagination and emphasize color and design rather than storytelling content.

To probe deep into the unconscious, Miró and others used automatic processes, sometimes called *automatism,* in which chance was a key factor. With the adoption of spontaneous and "automatic" methods, the Surrealists sought to expand consciousness by transcending limits of rational thought.

Miró's evocative paintings often depict imaginary creatures. The bold, organic shapes in WOMAN HAUNTED BY THE PASSAGE OF THE DRAGON-FLY, BIRD OF BAD OMEN are typical of his mature work. The wild, tormented quality, however, is unusual for Miró and reflects his reaction to the times. Miró pointed out that this painting was done at the time of the Munich crisis that helped precipitate World War II. Even though there's a sense of terror here, Miró's underlying playful optimism is apparent.

Almost all forms of contemporary art have prototypes in the past. Surrealism has been compared to the fantastic art of Flemish painter Hieronymus Bosch, active between 1488 and 1516. In the center panel of his three-part altarpiece, THE GARDEN OF EARTHLY DELIGHTS, Bosch depicted indulgence in delights of the flesh.

Belgian Surrealist René Magritte used an illogical form of realism, similar to Dali's in surface appearance but quite different in content. In Magritte's paintings, witty humor replaces the macabre quality often found in Dali's work. Everything depicted in PORTRAIT is ordinary; the impact of the painting comes from the bizarre combination of everyday objects. The disturbing effect of many Surrealist paintings and sculptures (see page 85) results

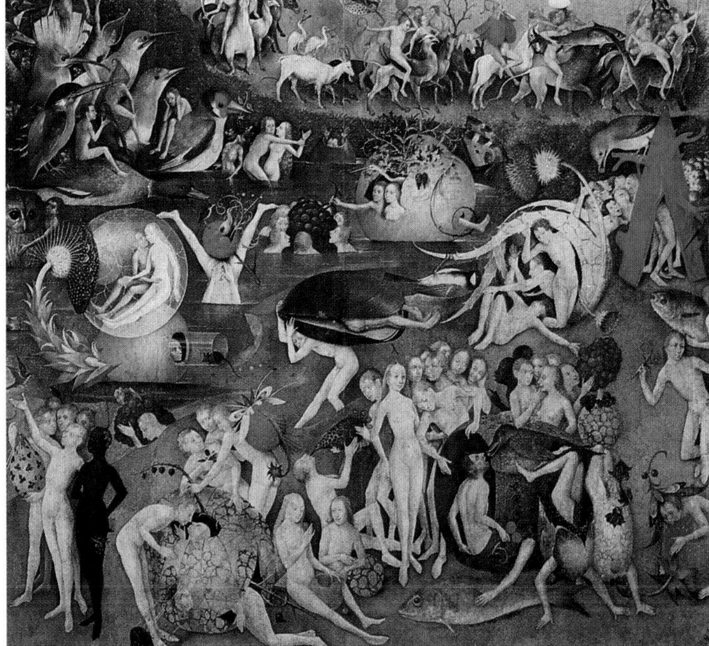

610 Hieronymus Bosch.
Detail of center panel, THE GARDEN OF EARTHLY DELIGHTS.
c. 1505-1510.
Oil on canvas.
Museo del Prado, Madrid.

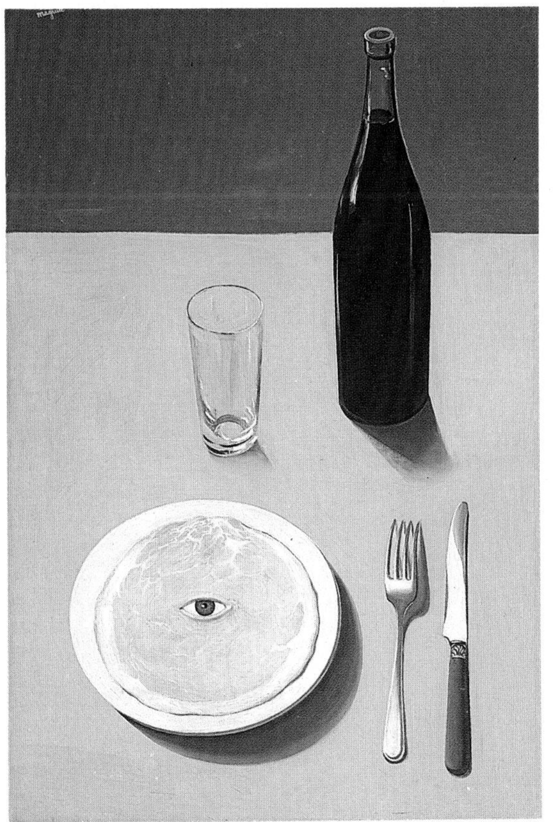

611 René Magritte.
PORTRAIT. 1935.
Oil on canvas. 28⅞" × 19⅞".
The Museum of Modern Art, New York.
Gift of Mrs. Kay Sage Tanguy.

from the transformation of familiar objects through absurd juxtapositions and dreamlike settings.

Mexican painter Frida Kahlo was one of many artists who, though not a part of the Surrealist movement in Europe, worked in a similar vein. Her first large painting, THE TWO FRIDAS, was painted during the period between her two marriages to Diego Rivera. The self-portrait on the right, the Frida whom Rivera had loved, derives her life's blood from the miniature portrait of Rivera that she holds in her hand. The blood runs in an exposed artery to her heart, which is laid out on her breast, then, after winding around her neck, proceeds to the second Frida, the one Rivera no longer loves. The rejected Frida tries to stop the flow of blood with a forceps.

Surrealist influence continues to be seen in record album covers, advertising, magazine illustrations, science fiction movies, television, and music videos. Like other revolutionary art movements, Dada and Surrealism did not greatly alter the world; but these movements did call attention to the fact that the world was undergoing radical change.

FRIDA KAHLO (1907–1954)

Frida Kahlo was a strong-willed, determined woman in a society that taught women to be passive.

Born in a suburb of Mexico City, she was the child of a photographer of German descent and a part Spanish, part Indian mother. When she was six years old she was stricken with polio. The painful disease caused her to be isolated for nine months and left her with one leg shorter and thinner than the other. At age eighteen she was in a trolley car accident that was followed by ineffective orthopedic treatments and thirty-two operations over the course of her life.

Chronic physical suffering caused by her illness and the accident led to a preoccupation with her ruined body—often the central subject in her paintings. In spite of her pain, her art reveals her feelings of connection with nature and with the creative energy that flows through all life. In her paintings, lovingly rendered details of nature are integrated with elements of dreams and fantasies.

When her work was shown in Paris in 1938, it received favorable attention from leading Surrealists. However, Kahlo's unique style is probably more indebted to Mexican narrative folk painting than to European Surrealism. Her paintings contain a mixture of folk art motifs, Surrealist elements, and autobiographical variations on the theme of mythical woman.

Her life was as unconventional as her art: she had two stormy marriages to Diego Rivera, numerous affairs, and friendships with leading international leftist and Surrealist leaders.

Kahlo's dramatic, bohemian personality enriched her distinctive painting style. Since her death in 1954, her international reputation has greatly increased. In the 1980s her psychologically loaded self-portraits found an appreciative new audience. Kahlo has become the heroine of the Mexican avant-garde and the subject of several books and a feature-length movie.

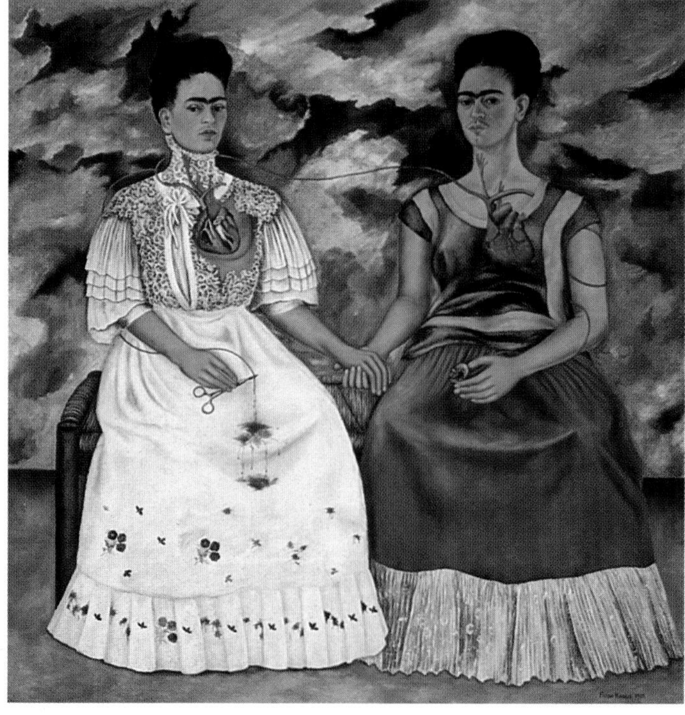

612 Frida Kahlo.
THE TWO FRIDAS. 1939.
Oil on canvas. 5'8" × 5'8".
Museo de Arte Moderno, Mexico City.

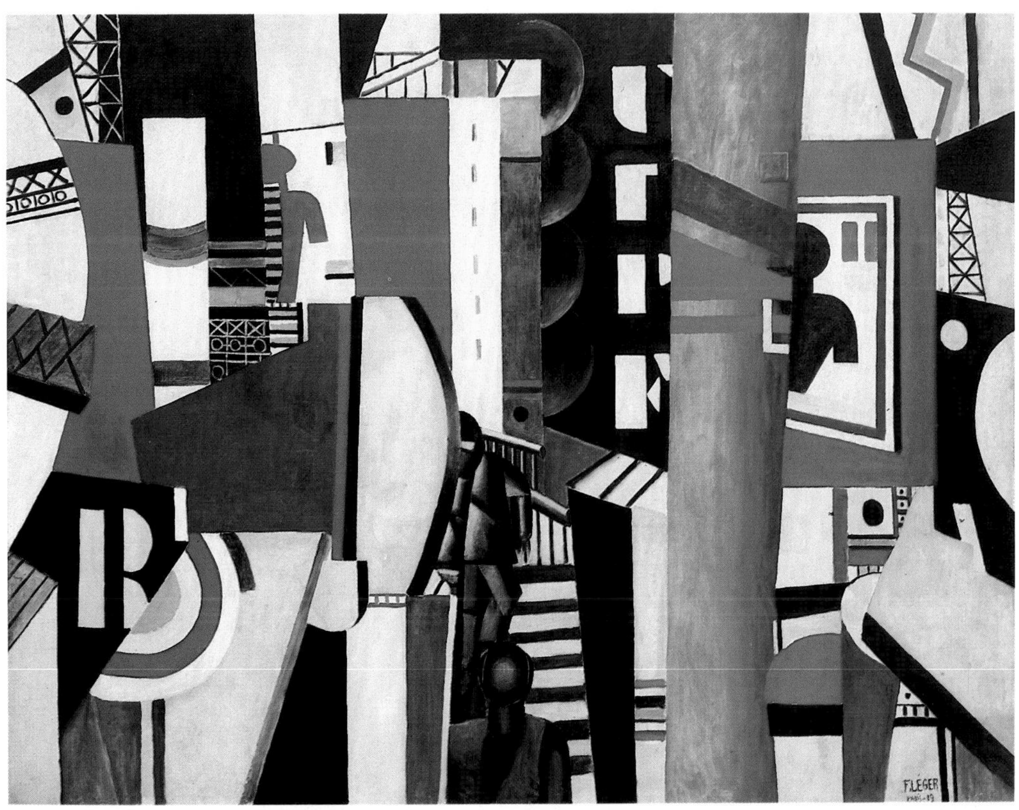

THE INFLUENCE OF CUBISM

After the original phase of Analytical Cubism, many painters adopted its basic spatial concept. One was Fernand Léger. In his painting THE CITY, he used Cubist overlapping planes in compact, shallow space to depict the rhythms and complexity of modern city life.

In twentieth-century cities, the buildings, signs, people, and traffic crowd together between reflective surfaces in a giant assemblage of overlapping, disjointed forms. To the photographer's eye, as seen in REFLECTIONS, these phenomena join in a collage experience similar to the spatial phenomena explored by Cubism.

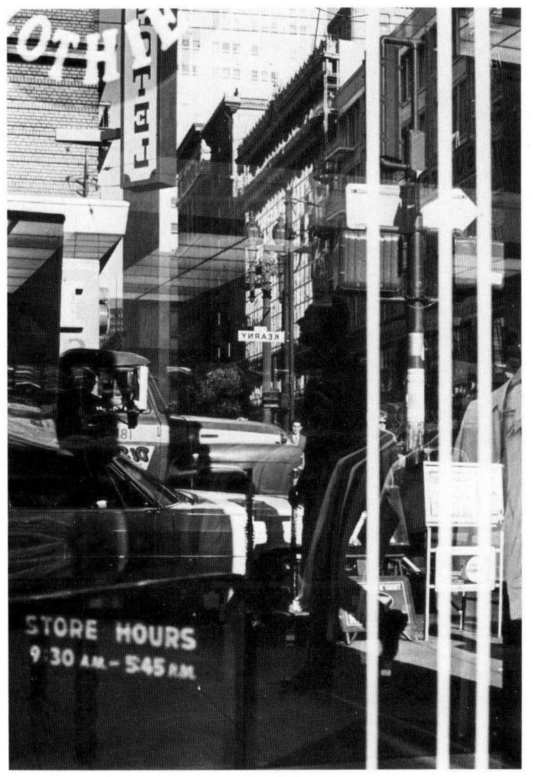

613 Fernand Léger.
THE CITY. 1919.
Oil on canvas.
90¾" × 117¼".
Philadelphia Museum of Art. A. E. Gallatin Collection.

614 REFLECTIONS. 1972.
Photograph.

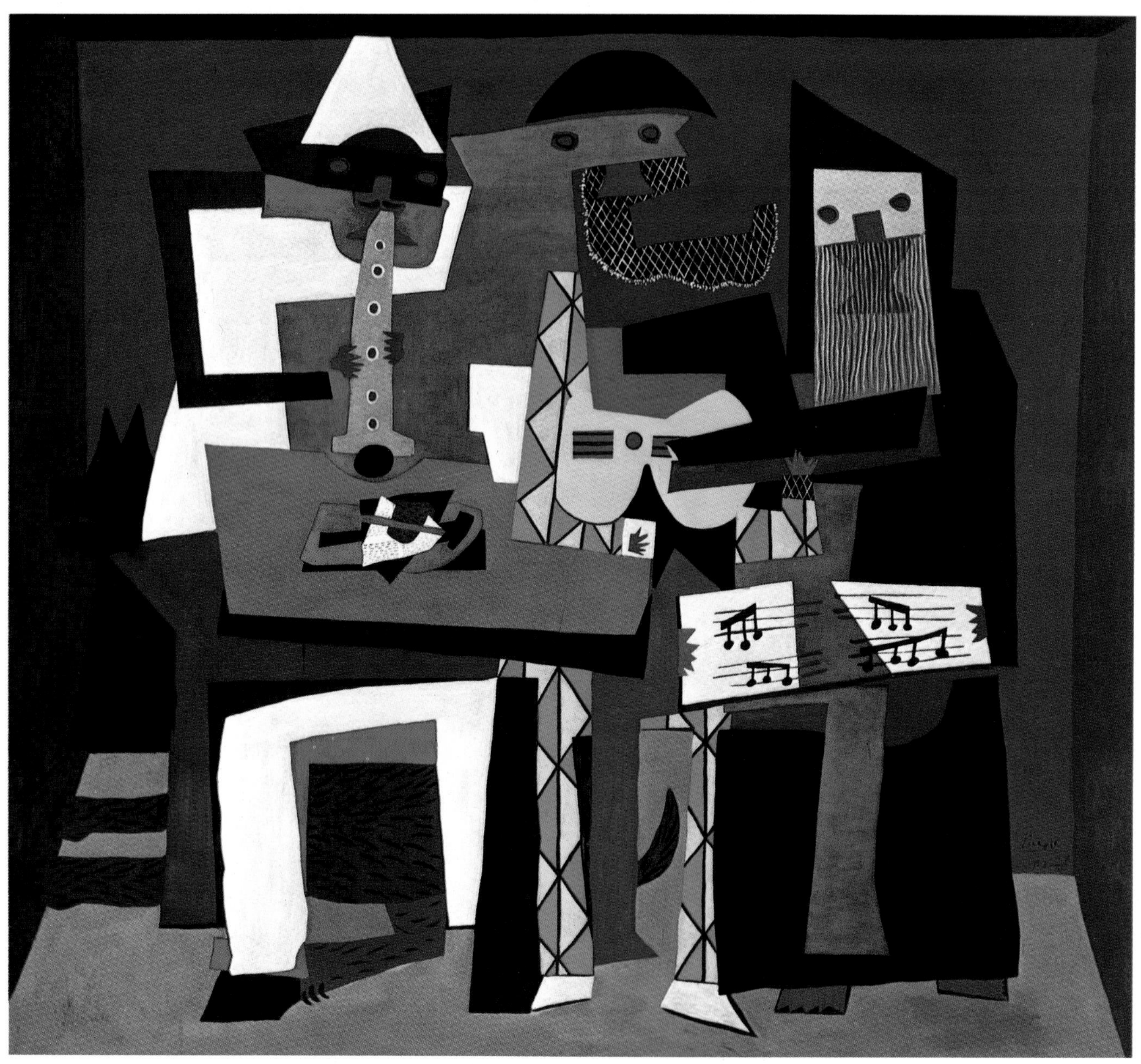

615 Pablo Picasso. THREE MUSICIANS. 1921.
Oil on canvas. 6'7" × 7'3¾".
The Museum of Modern Art, New York. Mrs. Simon Guggenheim Fund.

Picasso painted THREE MUSICIANS in the flat, decorative style of Synthetic Cubism. Although it is a painting, its form is heavily influenced by the cutout shapes of Cubist collages. Two of the life-size figures are the traditional characters of French comedy—Pierrot, in white, playing a recorder, and a brightly costumed Harlequin in the center, playing a guitar. The third figure wears a black monk's habit and a veiled mask, and he sings from the sheet of music he holds. Behind the trio, a black dog lies with tail raised. Although abstract, the figures have a real presence. The work is solemn and whimsical at the same time.

Throughout his life Picasso shifted his approach, going from one style to another. He painted THREE MUSICIANS at the same time he was reexamining and working with the style and subject matter of ancient Greece, creating figures that had the solid appearance of classical sculpture (see HEAD OF A YOUNG MAN, page 55). As a teenager, Picasso had made detailed drawings of plaster casts of Greek sculpture, as did all art students of the nineteenth and early twentieth centuries. Some were surprised to see the adult artist return to a source rejected by his colleagues. As we look back over his career, we see that the dramatic shifts in style are indicative of Picasso's extraordinary inventive ability.

Cubism brought about the most radical and complete artistic revolution since the Renaissance. Through its indirect influence on architecture and the applied arts, it has become part of our daily lives.

BUILDING A NEW SOCIETY

Several art movements emerged in the years after World War I. Pioneer abstractionists felt that the nonrepresentational language of form they were creating would provide an ideal basis for the utopian society they sought. Constructivism, in Russia, focused on nonrepresentational forms for a new industrial age. De Stijl, in Holland, advocated the use of basic forms, particularly rectangles, horizontals, and verticals. Both movements spread throughout Europe and were picked up by the Bauhaus in Germany.

Constructivism

Constructivism was a revolutionary sculptural movement that began in Russia, inspired in part by Cubist abstraction. Seeking to create art that was relevant to modern life in form and content, Constructivists began making the first nonrepresentational constructions out of such modern materials as plastic and electroplated metal.

The Constructivists were in concert with the Cubists in rejecting the traditional view of sculpture as a static volume defined by mass and created by modeling and carving. The name of the movement came from their preference for constructing planar and linear forms that suggested a dynamic quality and, whenever possible, contained moving elements.

Mass had previously been the main element in sculpture; with the Constructivists, space became primary. Naum Gabo concentrated on space by minimizing mass and employing lines and planes. He made variations of LINEAR CONSTRUCTION over several decades.

In the early 1920s, the Russian government decided to tolerate only art that could be easily understood by the public. Gabo and other leading artists realized that they must work elsewhere in order to develop and promote their ideas. By leaving Russia, he and other Constructivists were able to make a contribution to international sculpture, architecture, and applied design, and to a lesser degree, painting.

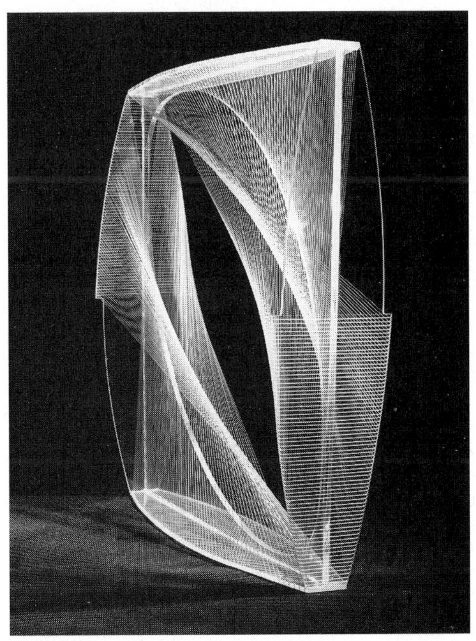

616 Naum Gabo.
LINEAR CONSTRUCTION NO. I.
1942-1943 (variation of 1921 original).
Plastic and nylon thread. 24½" × 24½".
Tate Gallery, London.

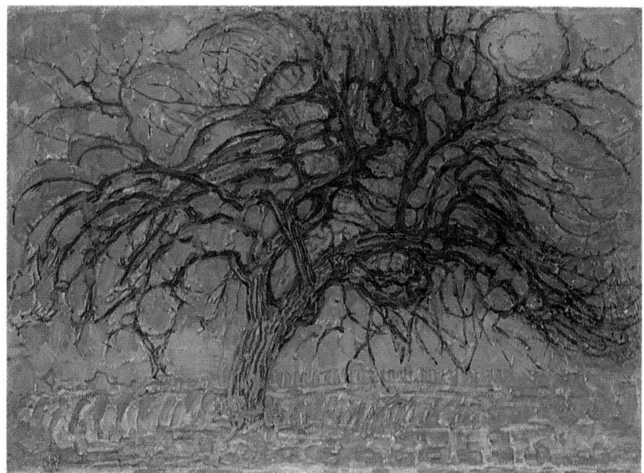

617 Piet Mondrian.
RED TREE. 1908.
Oil on canvas. 27½" × 39".
Haags Gemeentemuseum, The Hague.

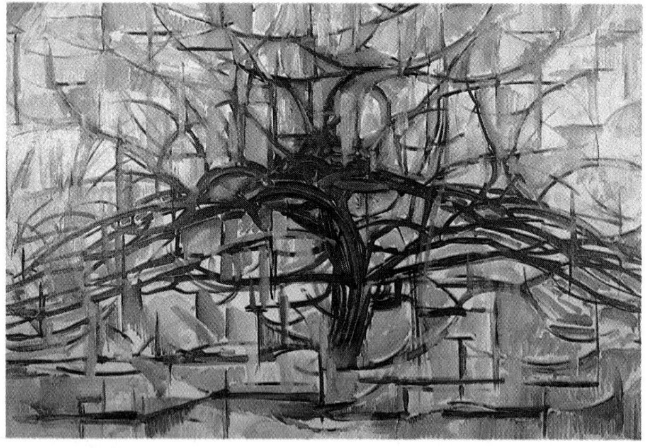

618 Piet Mondrian.
HORIZONTAL TREE. 1911.
Oil on canvas. 29⅝" × 43⅞".
Munson-Williams-Proctor Institute, Utica, New York.

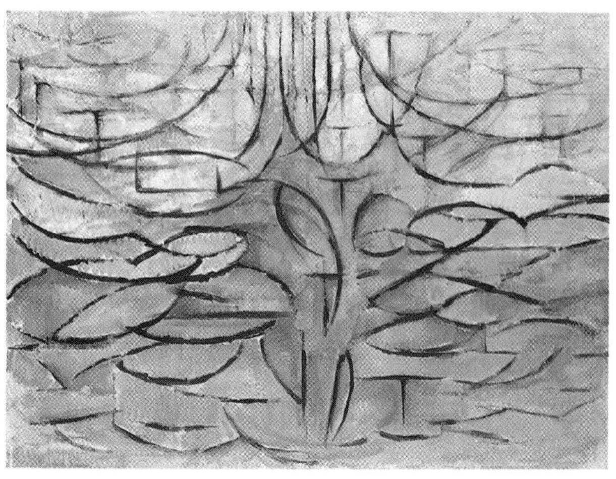

619 Piet Mondrian.
FLOWERING APPLE TREES. 1912.
Oil on canvas. 30¾" × 41¾".
Haags Gemeentemuseum, The Hague.

De Stijl

Another of the many movements inspired by the formal qualities of Cubism was *De Stijl* (The Style). In 1917, a small group of Dutch artists, led by painter Piet Mondrian, began to employ nonrepresentational geometric elements in a group style that involved both two- and three-dimensional art forms. Their goal was the creation of a world of universal harmony. Armed with the newly independent vocabulary of "pure" visual form, they created an inventive body of work in painting, architecture, furniture, and graphic design.

Mondrian's evolution as an artist reflects the origin and essence of De Stijl. Working to free painting completely from both the depiction of nameable objects and the expression of personal feelings, he developed an austere style based on the expressive potential of fundamental visual elements and their relationships. He sought to create a new aesthetic that would provide a poetic vitality capable of setting standards of harmony for the new technological age.

In three paintings of trees completed between 1908 and 1912, we see Mondrian's progression toward increasingly abstract imagery. Between 1910 and 1916, Mondrian did his paintings in sequence. He started with naturalistic sketches of trees and landscapes and gradually transformed them into abstract visual relationships. His personal philosophy led him to search for an art that was objective (impersonal) and universal. His formalist, classical approach to absolute form was the opposite of Kandinsky's personal, romantic expressionism (see page 415).

Mondrian's 1908 painting RED TREE shows the artist's early concern with the visual pattern or structure created by the tree branches and the spaces between them. Mondrian was beginning his lifelong quest for the purest means by which art can express fundamental truth. Through what he saw as the "essential plastic means of art"—line and color freed from any particular subject—he emphasized the expressive qualities of primary form:

Non-figurative art . . . shows that "art" is not the expression of the appearance of reality such as we see it, nor of the life which we live, but that it is the expression of true reality and true life.[7]

When he painted HORIZONTAL TREE in 1911, Mondrian concentrated on the rhythmic curves of the branches and on the patterns of the spaces between the branches. He became increasingly aware of the strong expressive character of simple horizontal and vertical lines defining rectilinear shapes. FLOWERING APPLE TREES of 1912 shows a further shift toward nonrepresentational imagery.

From 1917 until his death in 1944, Mondrian was the leading spokesman for an art reflecting universal order.

The new art has continued and culminated the art of the past in such a way that the new painting, by employing "neutral," or universal forms, expresses itself only through the relationships of line and color.[8]

For Mondrian, these universal elements were straight lines and primary colors. He reduced painting to four elements: line, shape, color, and space. COMPOSITION WITH RED, YELLOW, AND BLUE, completed in 1930, exemplifies his totally nonrepresentational later work.

In 1940, Mondrian left Europe for New York, where he spent the last four years of his life. New York was a joy to him because it seemed to be a celebration of human achievement. He was fascinated by the geometric, technological world, its neon lights, and especially the staccato rhythms of American jazz. His enthusiasm for music, dancing, and his new environment gave his final paintings, such as BROADWAY BOOGIE-WOOGIE, a pulsing, rhythmic energy.

620 Piet Mondrian.
COMPOSITION WITH RED, YELLOW, AND BLUE. 1930.
Oil on canvas. 19" × 19".
Private collection.

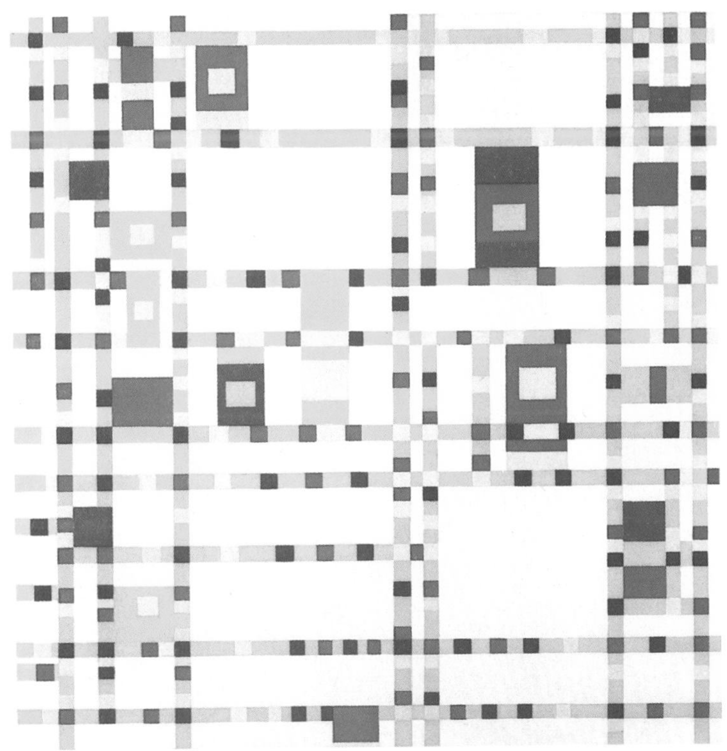

621 Piet Mondrian.
BROADWAY BOOGIE-WOOGIE. 1942-1943.
Oil on canvas. 50" × 50".
The Museum of Modern Art, New York. Given anonymously.

As he moved from representation to nonrepresentation, Mondrian placed greater and greater emphasis on the fundamental qualities of proportion, balance, and rhythm. Within the strict limitations he set for himself, he was able to express his sense of fundamental harmony in a rich variety of compositions.

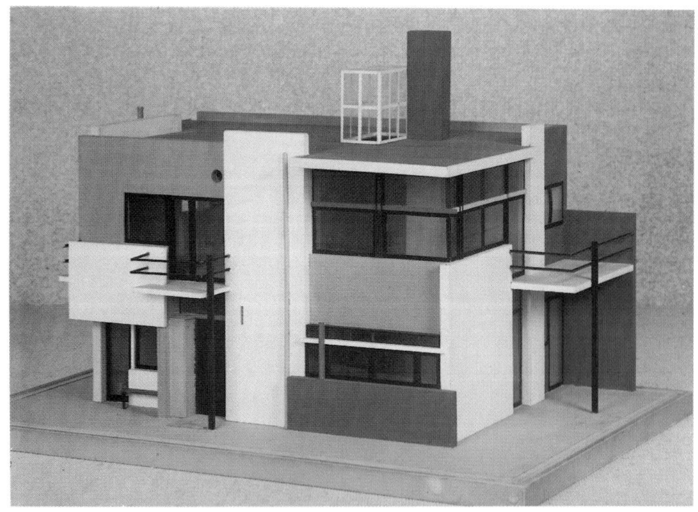

622 Gerrit Rietveld.
MODEL OF THE SCHRODER HOUSE. 1923-1934.
Glass and wood. 17⅜" × 28⅜" × 19⅓".
Stedelijk Museum, Amsterdam, Netherlands.

International Style

The search for a new language of form was carried on by architects as well as painters. Ideas about form developed by Frank Lloyd Wright, the Cubist painters, and the De Stijl artists were carried further by architects stimulated by the structural possibilities of modern materials including steel, plate glass, and reinforced concrete.

About 1918, a new style of architecture emerged simultaneously in Germany, France, and the Netherlands and came to be called the International Style. Steel-frame curtain-wall construction methods made it possible to build structures characterized by undecorated rectilinear planes. Extensive use of glass in non-load-bearing exterior walls brings abundant light and flexible space to interiors. In many International Style buildings, asymmetrical designs create dynamic balances of voids and solids. Unlike Frank Lloyd Wright, who blended houses with their natural surroundings (see page 262), architects working in the International Style deliberately created a visual contrast between natural and manufactured forms.

Dutch architect Gerrit Rietveld was associated with Mondrian and De Stijl. His SCHRODER HOUSE in Utrecht was an early classic of the International Style, its design of interacting planes, spaces, and primary colors closely related to Mondrian's work.

In France, the principles of the International Style of architecture were basic to the early work of

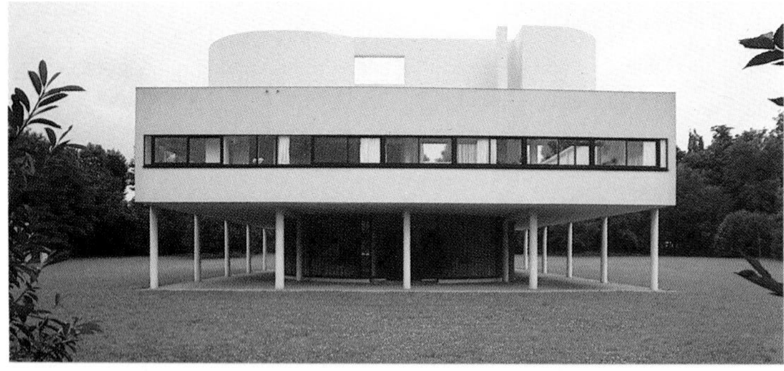

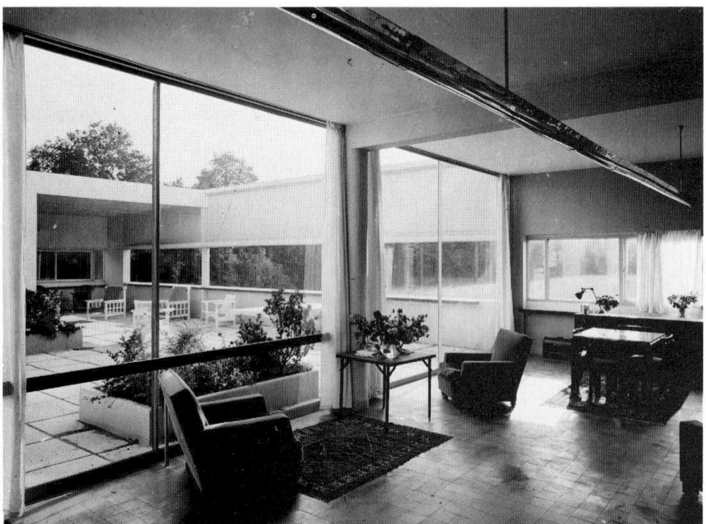

623 Le Corbusier.
VILLA SAVOYE. Poissy, France. 1928-1930.
a Exterior.
b Interior.

leading architect, city planner, and painter Charles-Édouard Jeanneret, known by the pseudonym Le Corbusier. His drawing on page 257 represents his philosophy that a basic structural frame allows complete freedom in terms of the placement of interior and exterior walls. His most significant early work is the VILLA SAVOYE at Poissy, France, built between 1928 and 1930. The second-floor living area seems to float on slender reinforced-concrete columns above a smaller, deeply recessed entrance and service area on the ground. A private interior terrace opens to the sky on the upper level, joined to the living room by floor-to-ceiling panels of plate glass. Le Corbusier called his houses "machines for living."

The International Style buildings designed by Walter Gropius for the Bauhaus (see page 257) clearly reflect the the concepts of both De Stijl and Constructivism. Today, the spare style that Mondrian and the Bauhaus helped to initiate can be seen in the design not only of buildings but of books, interiors, clothing, furnishings, and many other articles of daily life.

Architect and designer Ludwig Mies van der Rohe was one of the most influential figures associated with the Bauhaus and the International Style. His imaginative and highly refined GERMAN PAVILION, built for the International Exposition at Barcelona in 1929, served as a model of excellence for other architects. In its refinement, simplification, and elegance of materials and proportions, the design exemplifies his maxim, "Less is more." The pavilion was dismantled following the exposition, but it was considered so important to the history of architecture that it was carefully rebuilt in exactly the same location in 1986. (Mies van der Rohe designed the BARCELONA CHAIR, page 240, for this building.)

In 1938, Mies van der Rohe emigrated to the United States. There, his ideas and works such as the SEAGRAM BUILDING (page 258) strongly influenced the post–World War II development of the rectilinear, metal-and-glass-sheathed, steel-frame skyscraper.

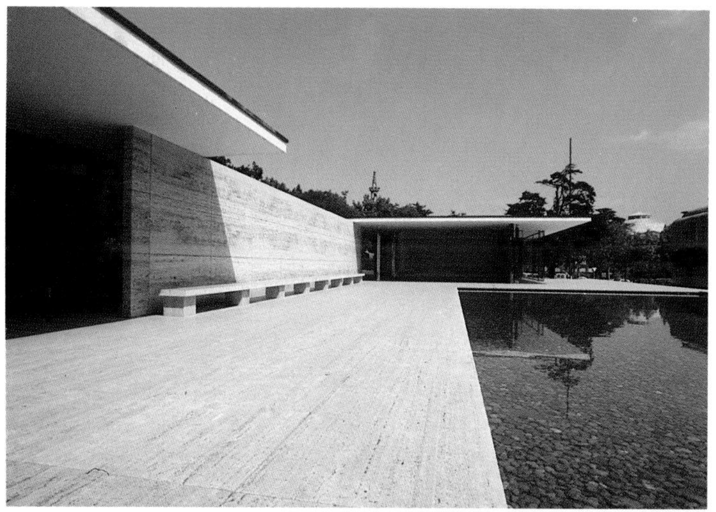

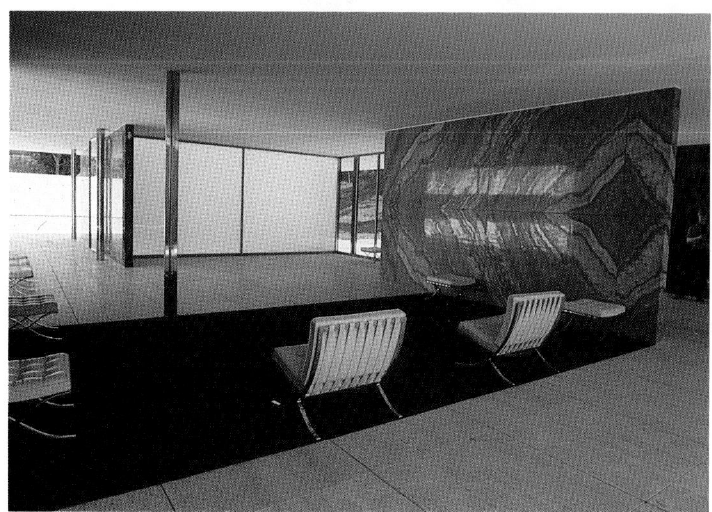

624 Ludwig Mies van der Rohe.
GERMAN PAVILION, International Exposition. Barcelona. 1929 (dismantled in 1930, and rebuilt in 1986).
Photographs: Prithwish Neogy.

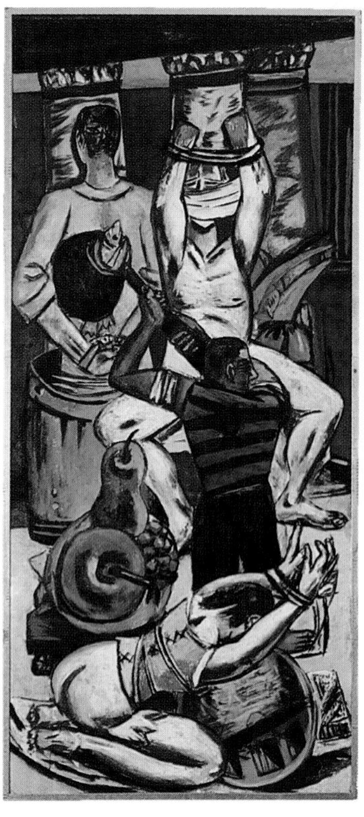
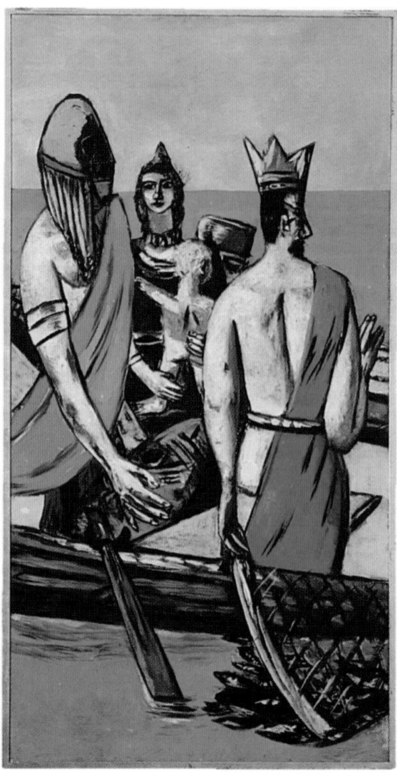
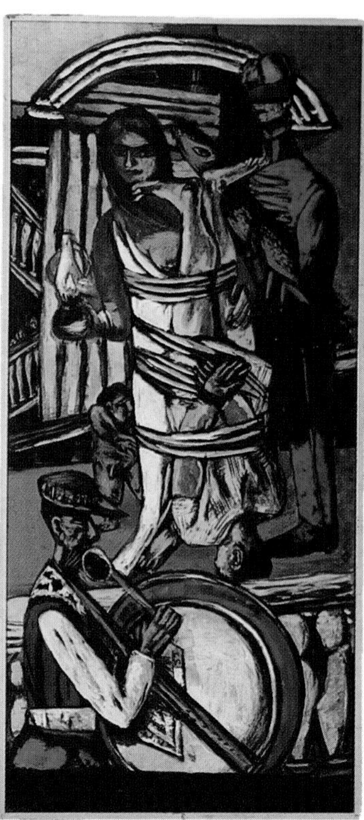

625 Max Beckmann.
DEPARTURE. 1932-1933.
Oil on canvas; triptych, center panel 7'¾" × 45⅜"; side panels each 7'¾" × 39¼".
The Museum of Modern Art, New York. Given anonymously (by exchange).

POLITICAL PROTEST

Expressionism continued as the dominant trend in German art despite the fact that the Bridge and Blue Rider groups were largely dispersed by the devastation of World War I. Reactions to the war and the social and political situation of the 1920s and 1930s led to some of Expressionism's major works. Two exponents of German Expressionism and its values were Käthe Kollwitz (see pages 120–121) and Max Beckmann.

Beckmann's experience working in a field hospital during World War I led him to shift from his early Impressionist-influenced mode to an expressive style in which he could speak forcefully of the misery he saw. As he built his own visual vocabulary, he was influenced by Gothic abstraction, naive art, and Cubism.

After years of public acceptance and professional success, Beckmann was classified as a degenerate artist by the Nazis. Fifteen German museums were forced to remove his paintings. He painted his great triptych (three-panel painting) DEPARTURE in secret during the early years of Nazi tyranny. Suggestions of Christian symbolism include the altarpiece-related triptych format and a Christlike fisherman-king. Beckmann's moral content and symbolism are presented with the direct vigor of a circus sideshow. When the triptych was shipped out of Germany in 1937, Beckmann fooled Hitler's inspectors by labeling it "Scenes from Shakespeare's *Tempest.*" Beckmann, forced to go into hiding, fled first to Holland, then to the United States. In retrospect, we see DEPARTURE as an allegory of good and evil as well as a portrayal of Beckmann's personal

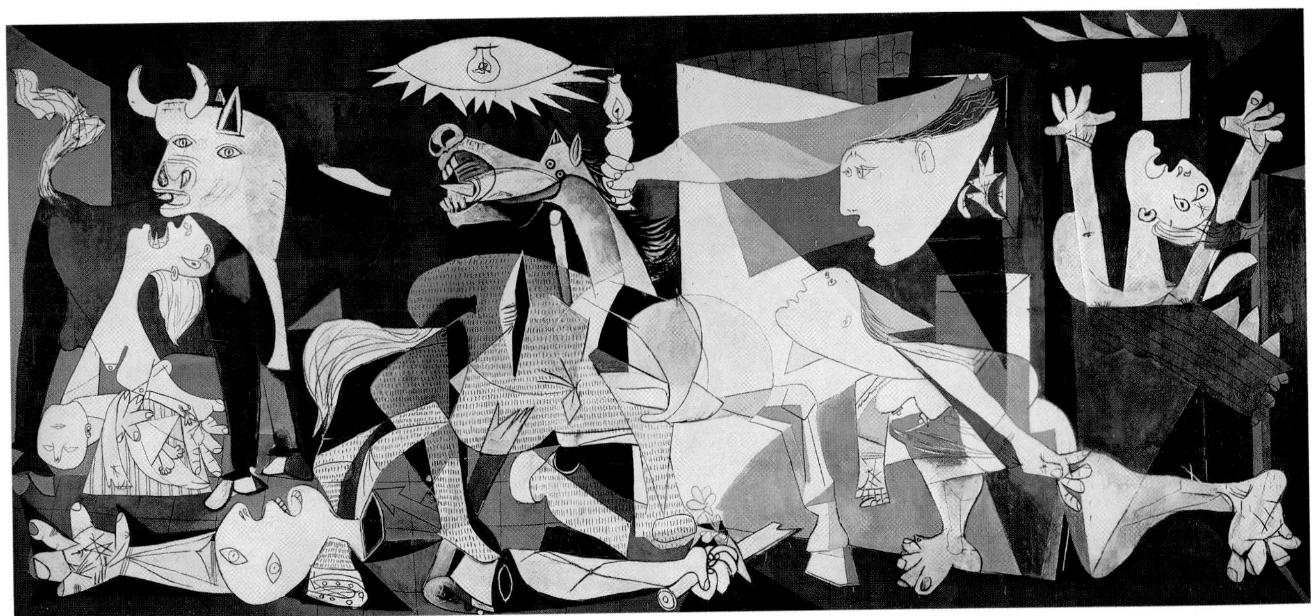

626 Pablo Picasso.
GUERNICA. 1937.
Oil on canvas. 11'5½" × 25'5¼".
Museo del Prado, Madrid.

experience and desire to escape a society gone mad.

Hitler's rise to power in the 1920s and 1930s all but destroyed the German Expressionist movement, although many of its leading artists had already left Germany by then. The Bauhaus, the most influential art school of the twentieth century, was closed by the Nazis in 1933. In 1938, about five thousand paintings and sculptures and twelve thousand prints and drawings by German Expressionist artists were confiscated.

Between 1936 and 1939, while Hitler held power in Germany, Spain underwent a bloody civil war. With military support from Germany and Italy, General Francisco Franco emerged as dictator.

Throughout the 1920s and into the 1930s, Spanish-born Pablo Picasso continued to produce innovative drawings, paintings, prints, posters, and sculptures. Many of these works were filled with strange distortions and dislocations related to Surrealism. In 1937, while the Spanish Civil War was in progress, Picasso was commissioned by the doomed Spanish democratic government to paint a mural for the Paris Exposition. For several months he was unable to begin work. Suddenly, on April 26, 1937, he was shocked into action by the "experimental" mass bombing of the defenseless Basque town of Guernica. To aid his bid for power, General Franco had allowed Hitler to use his war machinery on the town as a demonstration of military power. The bombing, which occurred at night, was the first incidence of saturation bombing in the history of warfare; according to witnesses, one of every seven people in the town was killed.

Picasso, appalled by this brutality against the people of his native country, called upon all his powers to create the mural-size painting GUERNICA. Although Picasso's GUERNICA stems from a specific incident, it has universal significance as a statement of protest against the senseless brutality of war. More than one hundred years earlier, another Spaniard, Goya, painted a large canvas that also depicts the inhumanity of war (see page 375).

GUERNICA covers a huge canvas more than 25 feet long. It is painted in somber black, blue-blacks, whites, and grays. A large triangle embedded under the smaller shapes holds the whole scene of chaotic

DIEGO RIVERA (1886–1957)

"The earliest memory I have," Diego Rivera wrote, "is that I was drawing."[9] He drew all the time and on anything he could find.

Rivera grew up in Mexico City. From age twelve he attended a prestigious art school. At twenty he won a scholarship to Europe. He settled in Paris, where he quickly caught up with the latest developments in art and became known as a leading Cubist painter.

In 1918, Rivera abandoned Cubism and looked increasingly back at art history. In medieval cathedrals and Renaissance frescoes art had a task, an important story to tell to an entire society. Was this no longer possible? Did art now have to appeal only to the few? Did modern society have no great tasks for its artists?

An answer came in 1920 from Mexico. The revolution begun in 1911 had triumphed at last, and the new government planned an ambitious public works program. It called on its artists to beautify public buildings with murals that would celebrate the country's rich cultural heritage and teach a largely illiterate people the history of their own political struggle. Rivera returned to Mexico the next year. "My homecoming produced an aesthetic exhilaration which it is impossible to describe," he later recalled. "In everything I saw a potential masterpiece—the crowds, the markets, the festivals, the marching battalions, the working men in the shops and in the fields."[10]

Rivera believed that the New World should declare its artistic independence from Europe. He looked to the living tradition of folk art and to the ancient works of the Aztec, Inca, and other American civilizations to provide healthy roots for new artistic growth.

Rivera had three wives in the course of his life, including the painter Frida Kahlo (see page 434), whom he married in 1929. They made a striking couple—he was enormous, she was slight. Her parents said it was "like a marriage between an elephant and a dove."[11] Yet in temperament she was every inch his equal.

As champion of the overworked and underpaid, Rivera provided lasting statements on the social issues of his day. He was the most celebrated muralist of the twentieth century.

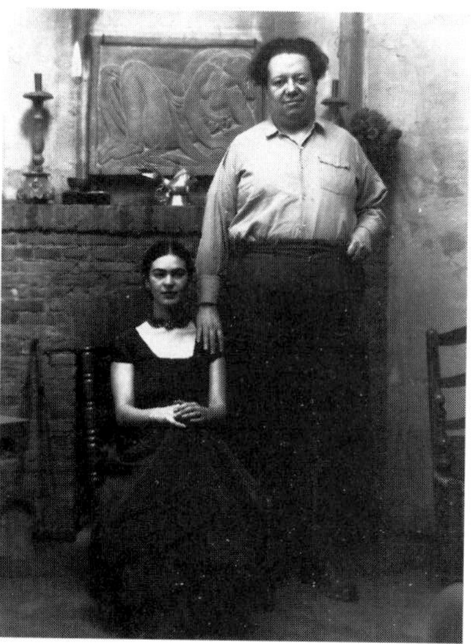

627 DIEGO RIVERA AND FRIDA KAHLO AT COYOACÁN. c. 1930.
Photograph: Peter Juley.
Peter A. Juley & Son Collection. National Museum of American Art, Smithsonian Institution.

destruction together as a unified composition. GUERNICA combines Cubism's intellectual structuring of form with the emotional intensity of earlier forms of expressionism and Abstract Surrealism. Details show some of the personal symbolism Picasso used to portray ideas and feelings beyond the protest of a single incident. In dream symbolism, a horse often represents a dreamer's creativity. Here the horse is speared and is dying in anguish. Beneath the horse's feet a soldier lies in pieces; near his broken sword a faint flower suggests hope. Above, a woman reaches out from an open window, an oil lamp in hand. Near the old-fashioned lamp and above the horse's head is an eyelike shape with an electric light bulb at the center. Jagged rays of light radiate out from the bottom edge. The sun? An eye? Sometimes an eye representing the eye of God was painted on the ceiling of medieval churches. The juxtaposition between old and new sources of illumination could be a metaphor relating to enlightenment. God's eye, in this context, may symbolize the creative energy of God subverted by human beings for destructive rather than creative ends.

During the 1940s, while German forces occupied France, Picasso was allowed to paint in his studio in Paris even though his art was considered degenerate by the Nazis. One day German soldiers came to his door with a small reproduction of GUERNICA. They asked, "Did you do this?" Picasso replied, "No, you did."[12] On another occasion during the war, Picasso remarked that "painting is not done to decorate apartments. It is an instrument of war for attack and defense against the enemy."[13]

While various schools of abstract art were emerging in Europe, some repressive governments restricted artists to an illustrative, realistic style that they considered politically advantageous. As its name implies, *social realism* is a style of painting with social or political content. Social realism was used as a propaganda tool by political leaders in Nazi Germany, Communist Russia, and Communist China. For many decades, prior to recent trends toward modernization and reconciliation, neither Russia nor China would permit any other mode. Forms of social realism, influenced but not dictated

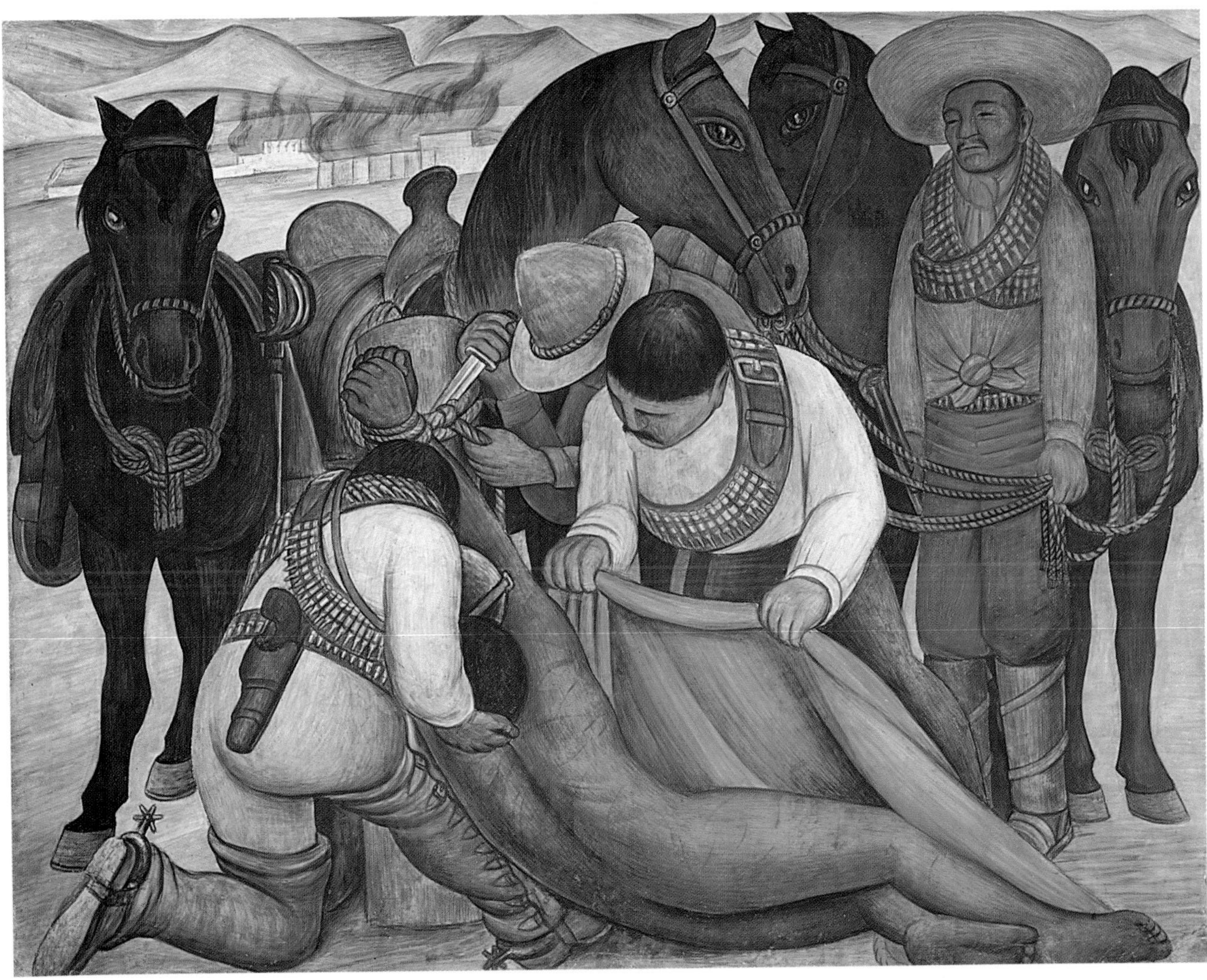

628 Diego Rivera.
THE LIBERATION OF THE PEON. 1931.
Fresco. 74" × 95".
Philadelphia Museum of Art. Given by Mr. and Mrs. Herbert C. Morris.

by government, came to prominence in Mexico and the United States in the 1920s and 1930s.

The Mexican mural renaissance, led by Diego Rivera with help from José Clemente Orozco (see page 100) and others, influenced artists in both Mexico and the United States. Inspired by the Italian murals he had seen in Europe, Rivera envisioned a national art that would glorify the traditional Mexican heritage and promote the aims and accomplishments of the new, revolutionary government. Rivera consciously integrated what he learned as a student in Paris with influences from Renaissance frescoes and the indigenous arts of his native Mexico.

During the 1920s and 1930s, large frescoes painted on public buildings throughout Mexico and in a few places in the United States emphasized revolutionary themes. Rivera's THE LIBERATION OF THE PEON summarizes agrarian reform. The landlord's house burns in the distance, while revolutionary soldiers free the peon from servitude and cover his naked body, scarred from repeated lashings.

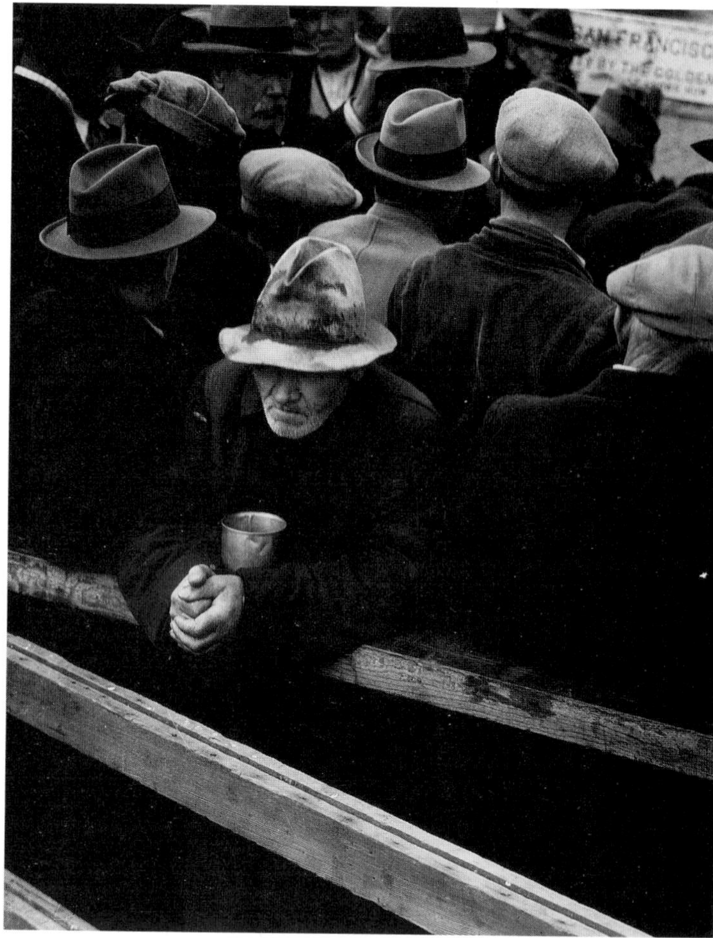

629 Dorothea Lange.
A DEPRESSION BREADLINE, SAN FRANCISCO. 1933.
Photograph.
The Oakland Museum. Dorothea Lange Collection.

This painting is a variation of a large fresco on a wall of the Ministry of Education in Mexico City.

During the Depression years of the 1930s, the United States government maintained an active program of subsidy for the arts. The Works Progress Administration (WPA) commissioned painters to paint murals in public buildings, and the Farm Security Administration (FSA) hired photographers and filmmakers to record the eroding dustbowl and its workworn inhabitants. With government support, the art of documentary filmmaking reached a peak of achievement.

One photographer, Dorothea Lange, documented the helplessness and hopelessness of the urban unemployed. Her sensitive study, A DEPRESSION BREADLINE, SAN FRANCISCO, is a powerful icon of a difficult period.

AMERICAN PAINTING

The American public had its first extensive look at leading developments in European art during the Armory Show held in New York in 1913. This show of over sixteen hundred works became the best known and the most influential art exhibition ever held in the United States. Americans, especially young American artists, were able to see key works by Impressionists, Post-Impressionists, and Fauves—particularly Matisse, who was much maligned by the critics. Also shown were paintings by Picasso, Braque, Léger, and Duchamp, and sculpture by Brancusi. As a result, Cubism and other forms of abstract art spread to America. Among the Americans who exhibited in the Armory show were Charles Sheeler (see page 142) and Edward Hopper.

Americans saw Europe as the center of traditional culture as well as the source of the modern movement. In the early twentieth century, it was common for American artists to go to Europe to study. Georgia O'Keeffe was an exception. She stayed in New York, yet she was influenced by the revolutionary changes in European art. O'Keeffe's personal style is apparent in her majestic paintings of flowers and her interpretations of the American Southwest (see pages 41–42). In BLACK CROSS,

NEW MEXICO, the single dominant shape of the cross pushes forward from the infinite vista of the subtle glowing landscape behind it. Here, as in much of O'Keeffe's work, she achieved a powerful simplicity through subtle shading and careful design.

Edward Hopper made several trips to Europe between 1906 and 1910, but he remained apart from European avant-garde movements as he portrayed the loneliness that permeated much of American life. NIGHTHAWKS shows Hopper's fascination with the visual mood of people in a particular place and time. The haunting effect of his paintings comes largely from his carefully organized compositions and his emphasis on controlled use of light and shadow areas. Hopper and the Impressionists were both interested in light, but for different purposes: Hopper employed it to clarify and organize structure, while the Impressionists used light in ways that seemed to dissolve structure.

In the 1930s, the spread of the Depression, along with political upheaval, helped motivate artists in America to search for both national and personal identity. American artists were caught between a largely indifferent public at home and a feeling, both at home and abroad, that American art was merely provincial. In this atmosphere of cultural inferiority, an American regionalism developed, based on the idea that artists in the United

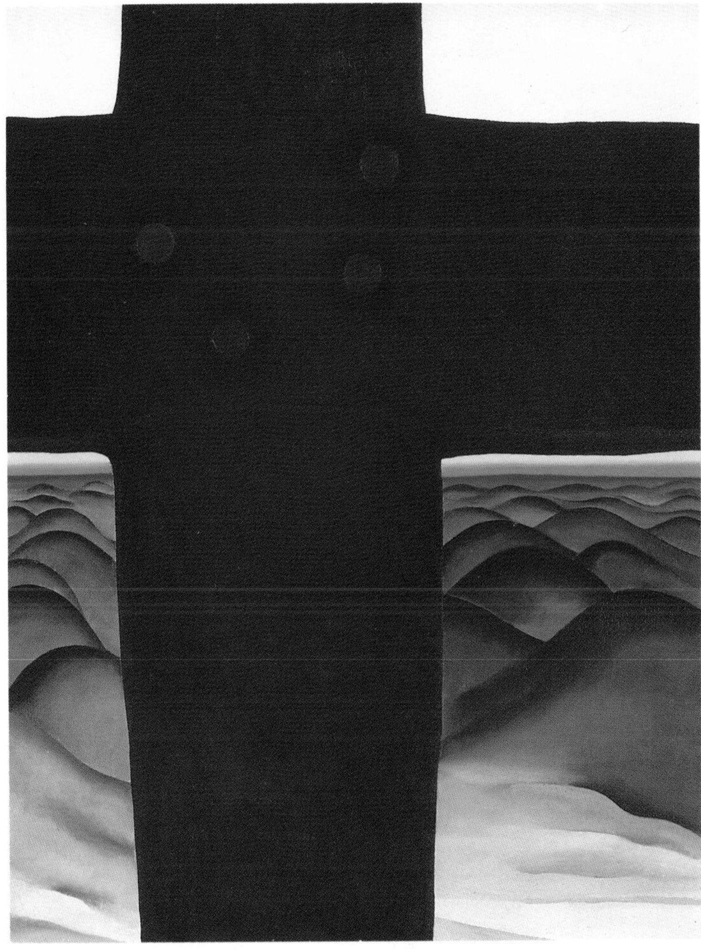

630 Georgia O'Keeffe.
BLACK CROSS, NEW MEXICO. 1929.
Oil on canvas. 39" × 30".
The Art Institute Fund (1943.95).

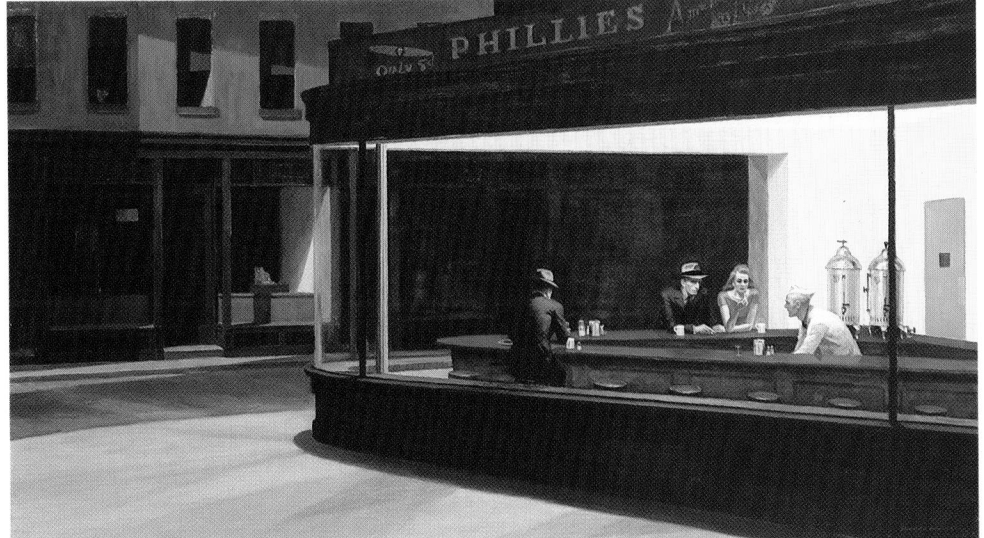

631 Edward Hopper.
NIGHTHAWKS. 1942.
Oil on canvas. 30" × 60".
Friends of American Art Collection (1942.51).

States could find their identity by focusing attention on the subject matter that was uniquely American.

Regional painter Grant Wood studied art in Paris in the early 1920s. Although he never worked with Cubist or expressionist ideas, he did identify with the modern trends, and he began making freely brushed paintings derived from Impressionism. After years with little success, Wood returned to his birthplace in rural midwestern America and dedicated himself to memorializing the unique character of the land, the people, and their way of life. Childhood experience as an Iowa farm boy and the perception of his artistic maturity combined to make Grant Wood an astute observer of rural America.

Wood's personal style of crisp realism was inspired by the paintings of the Northern Renaissance masters such as Van Eyck, Dürer, and Holbein. He also drew on American folk painting and the characteristically stiff, long-exposure portraits taken by late nineteenth-century photographers. Wood, like Van Eyck, calculated every aspect of design and all details of the subject matter to enhance the content of his paintings.

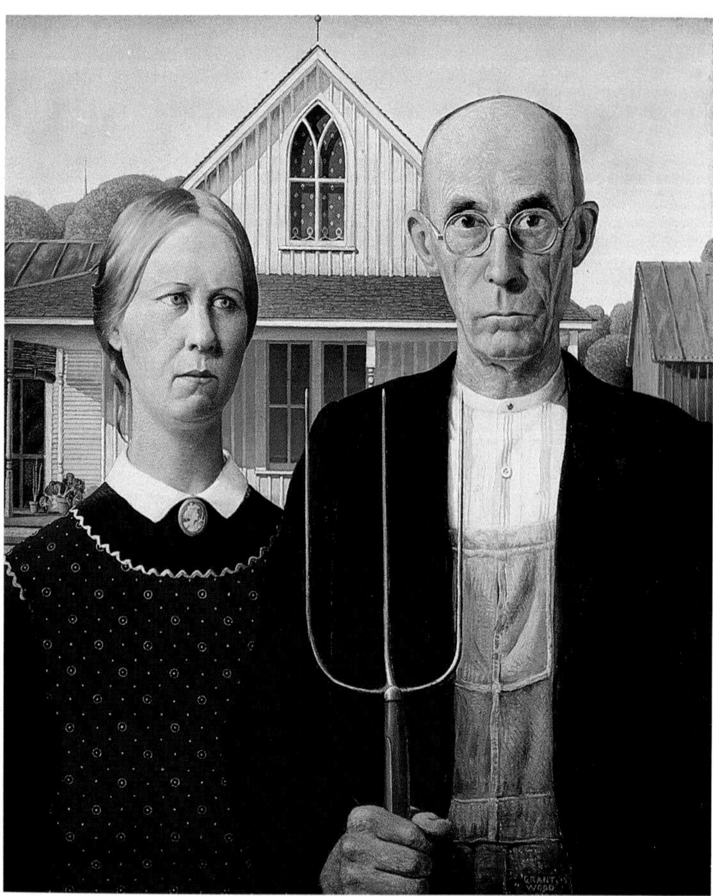

632 Grant Wood.
AMERICAN GOTHIC. 1930.
Oil on beaver board. 29⅞" × 24⅞".
Friends of American Art Collection (1930.934).

The idea for the famous painting AMERICAN GOTHIC came to Wood when he saw a modest farmhouse built in Carpenter Gothic style. The restrained color, simplification of round masses such as trees and people, and use of detail are typical of Wood's paintings. The two figures are echoed in the pointed-arch window shapes. Vertical lines and paired elements dominate. For example, the lines of the pitchfork are repeated in the man's overalls and shirt front. The upright tines of the fork seem to symbolize the pair's firm, traditional stance and hard-won virtue. Wood's AMERICAN GOTHIC, has become a national icon that speaks clearly to many. It continues to spark a wealth of responses.

By far the most forceful spokesman for the idea of an independent American art was Thomas Hart Benton. In 1908, Benton went to Paris to study European art. He and Rivera both studied there during the development of Cubism. In contrast to Rivera, Benton decried the influence of Cubism. His conservative midwestern background and traditional art training led him to be more impressed with the work of Italian Renaissance masters than with the French moderns.

After 1918, Benton worked to create an art that was American in both form and content—a realistic style that would be easily understood by all, based on the clear depiction of American themes. Some of the strength for both figures and composition came from the influence of Michelangelo. Benton transformed Renaissance and modern influences in a highly personal style in which all forms are conditioned by strong curvilinear rhythms. The push and pull of shapes in shallow space, emphasized by contrasting light and dark edges, shows what Benton learned from Cubism.

PALISADES was part of a series of paintings, titled AMERICAN HISTORICAL EPIC, which Benton never completed. In contrast to conventional histories that feature great men, Benton wanted to create a people's history, one that depicted the actions of ordinary people on the land. Here, the European colonizers are staking out and dividing up the land, while the Indians, in contrast, are sharing their knowledge of growing corn, which the newcomers will need for survival.

Benton's passionate love of grass-roots American life is expressed as much in his dynamic compositions as in his choice of subjects. In his print HUCK FINN, Benton translated Mark Twain's classic story of the adventures of Huckleberry Finn and his friend Jim into visual form. Benton's own experiences on the Mississippi River contributed to the vitality of the image. This lithograph is part of a series in which Benton captured the essence of three murals he had painted earlier for the Missouri State Capitol.

The emigration of large numbers of people to the United States just before and after World War II brought about a reexamination of the role of art in modern life. Expatriated European artists brought new ideas and purposes to America. As a result, the regional, narrative styles of painters such as Thomas Hart Benton lost favor, and New York became the new center for the exchange of creative energies among artists from many nations.

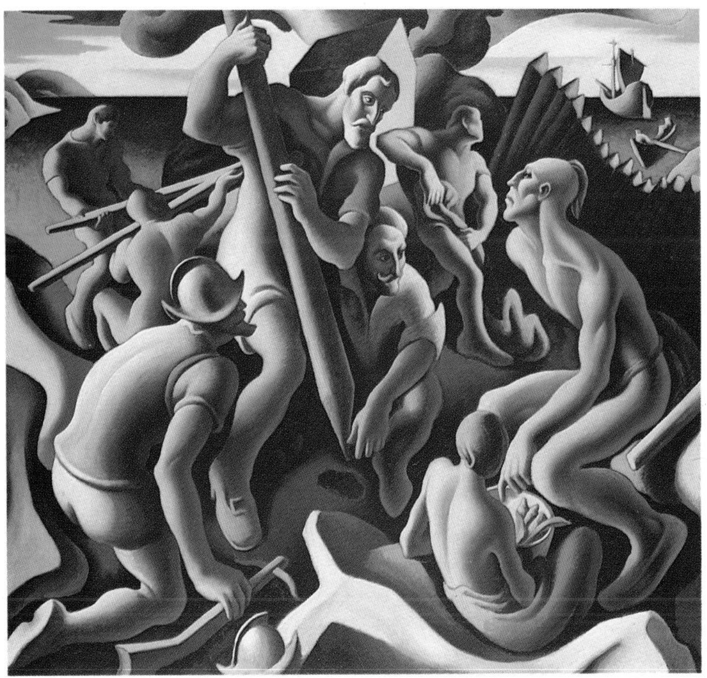

633 Thomas Hart Benton.
PALISADES, from the series AMERICAN HISTORICAL EPIC. 1919–1924.
Oil on cotton duck on aluminum honeycomb panel. 66⅛" × 72".
The Nelson-Atkins Museum of Art, Kansas City, Missouri. Bequest of Thomas Hart Benton.

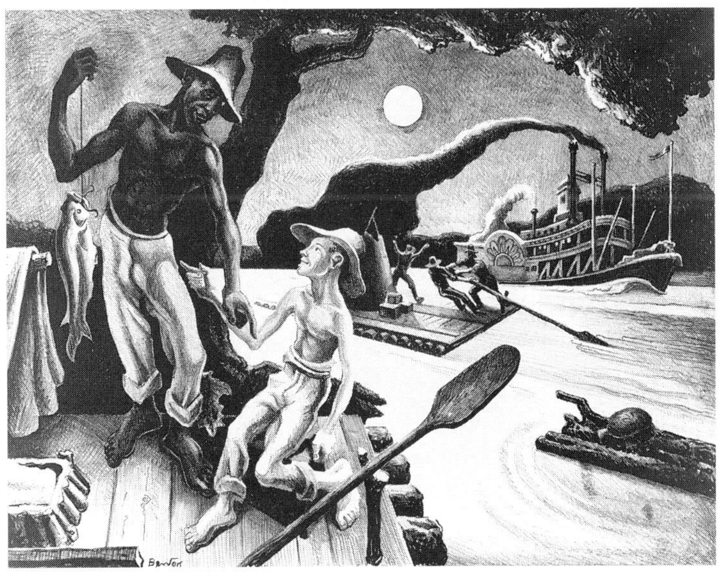

634 Thomas Hart Benton.
HUCK FINN. 1936.
Lithograph. 16⅝" × 21¹¹⁄₁₆".
Honolulu Academy of Arts.

CHAPTER 23

Accelerated Change: Art after 1945

At the end of World War II, Europe lay in ruins—financially, emotionally, and physically. Many prominent European artists had fled from Nazi oppression to the United States, which emerged from the war economically strong and optimistic. This influx from Europe coincided with America's newfound confidence: as artists flocked to New York in the way they once had to Paris, the center of contemporary Western art shifted from Europe to America.

Three artists who settled in New York were Mondrian, Léger, and Hofmann. They worked, taught, exhibited, and generally stirred things up, opening new possibilities for American artists. Modernism was no longer a distant, European phenomena; its leading practitioners were here in the United States.

War had altered the consciousness of the developed world in subtle but profound ways. The Nazi genocide machine had taken human cruelty to a new low, and the atom bomb gave humankind terrifying new powers: we were now living in a world we had the technology to destroy. These conditions have formed the background for art and life to the present day.

ABSTRACT EXPRESSIONISM AND RELATED ART

The horrors of World War II, in which millions of people lost their lives in battle or in concentration camps, led artists to rethink the relationship between art and life. Again, dislocations caused by war inspired artists to explore visual realms other than the representational and narrative. The result was Abstract Expressionism, a culmination of the expressive tendencies in painting from Van Gogh and Gauguin through Fauvism and German Expressionism. Immediate inspiration came from the motives and spontaneous methods of Surrealism—in particular, the abstract Surrealism of Miró—and the stimulating ideas and methods of Hofmann.

German artist Hans Hofmann was one of the most influential of the European immigrants. Both a painter and a well-loved teacher, he made a major contribution to new American art during the 1930s and 1940s. Hofmann stressed a balance between spontaneity and formal structure, and this approach became a model for generations of American painters. By 1940, he had begun using poured paint and bold color. THE GOLDEN WALL (see page 154), painted in 1961 when Hofmann was eighty-one, shows the strength of his later work. The canvas glows with warm color set off by cool accents. Hofmann's emphasis on color as form influenced abstract painters and even realist painters of the 1960s and 1970s.

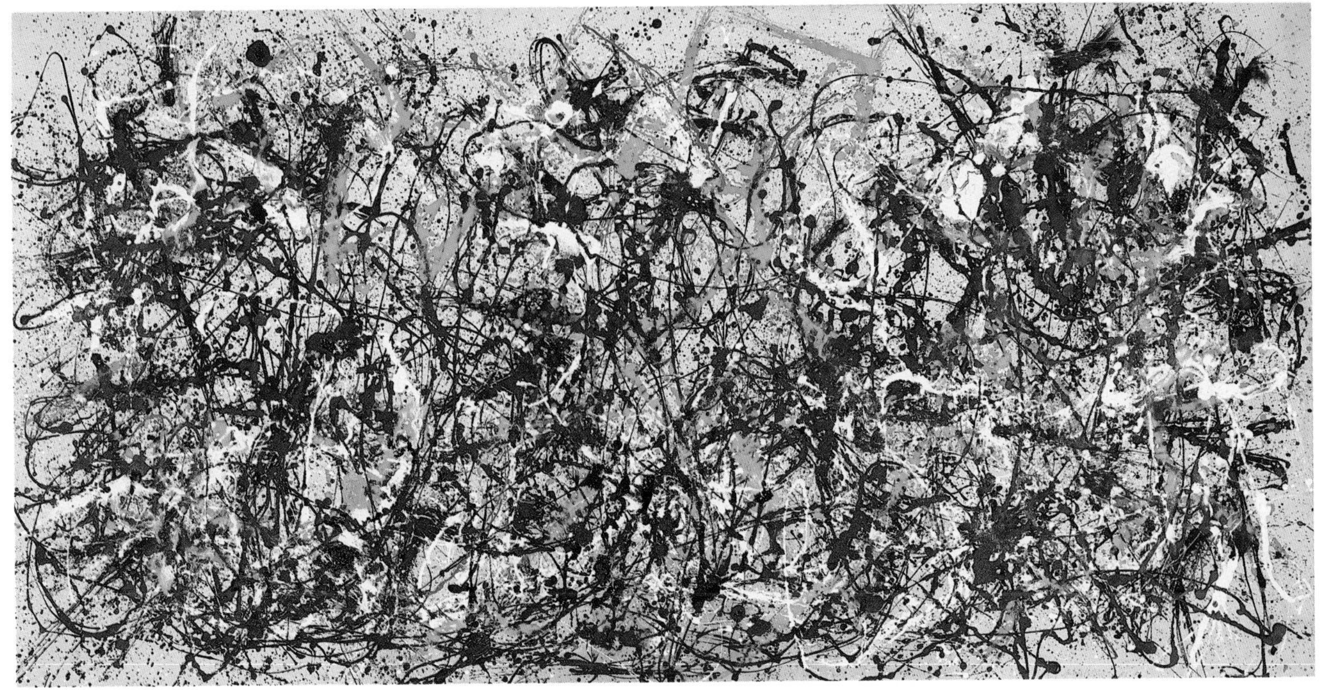

Jackson Pollock, the leading innovator of Abstract Expressionism, studied with Thomas Hart Benton in the 1930s. The rhythmic structure of Benton's style (see page 449) and Hofmann's early drip-and-pour techniques were influences on Pollock's poured paintings of the late 1940s and early 1950s. Searching for ways to express primal human nature, Pollock also studied Navajo sand painting (see page 4) and psychologist Carl Jung's theories of the unconscious.

The act of painting itself became a major part of the content of Pollock's paintings. Pollock created AUTUMN RHYTHM by dripping thin paint onto the canvas rather than brushing it on. By working on huge canvases placed on the floor, Pollock was able to enter the space of the painting physically and psychologically. The huge format allowed ample room for his sweeping gestural lines. Pollock dripped, poured, and flung his paint, yet he exercised control and selection by the rhythmical, dancing movements of his body. A similar approach in the work of many of his colleagues led to the term *action painting*.

A different, but related, painting style that evolved at about the same time was *color field*, a

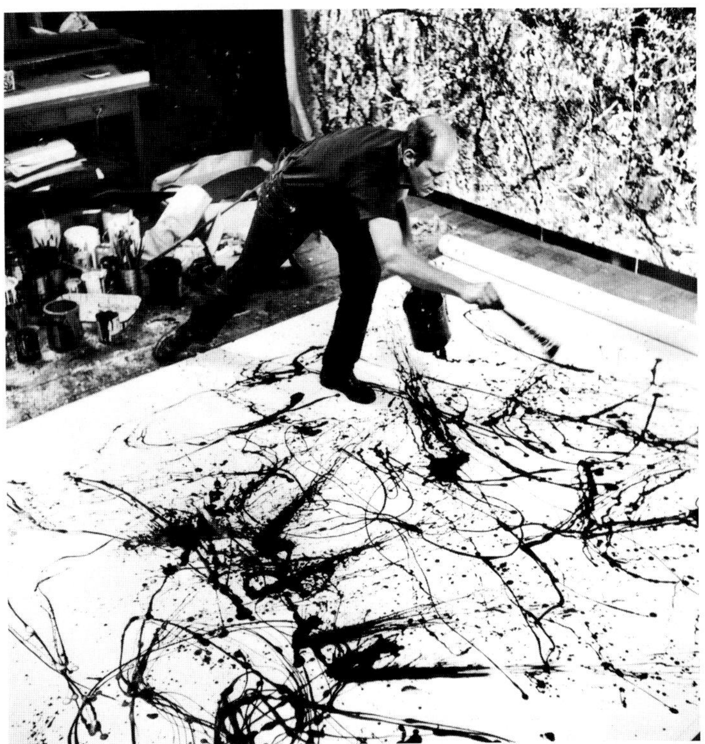

635 Jackson Pollock.
AUTUMN RHYTHM. 1950.
Oil on canvas. 8'9" × 17'3".
The Metropolitan Museum of Art. George A. Hearn Fund, 1957 (57.92).

636 JACKSON POLLOCK AT WORK.
Photograph: Hans Namuth.

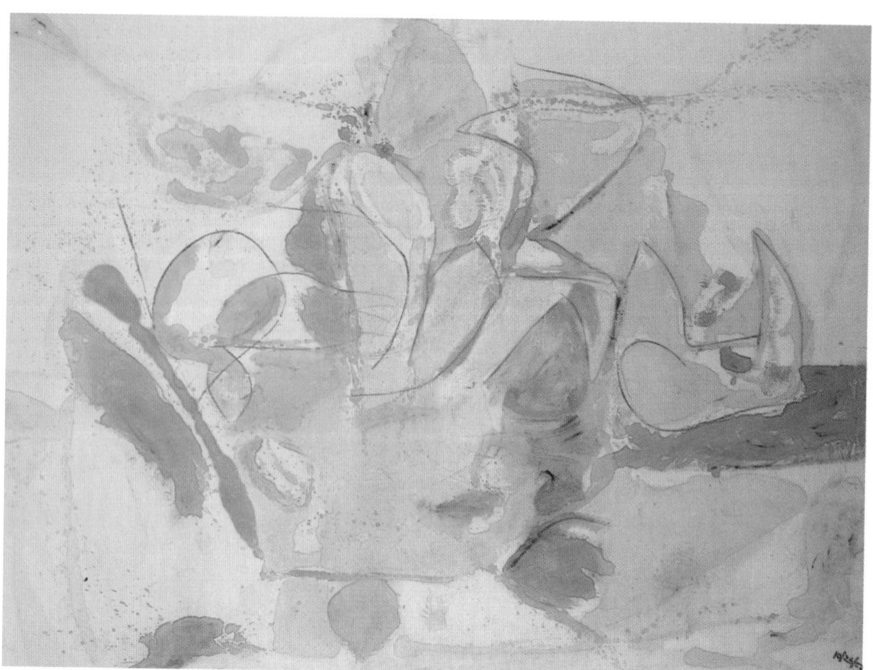

637 Helen Frankenthaler.
MOUNTAINS AND SEA. 1952.
Oil on canvas. 7'2⅝" × 9'9¼".
Collection of the artist, on loan to The National Gallery of Art, Washington, D.C.
© Helen Frankenthaler 1992.

638 Mark Rothko.
BLUE, ORANGE, RED. 1961.
Oil on canvas. 90¼" × 81¼".
Hirshhorn Museum and Sculpture Garden, Smithsonian Institution, Washington, D.C.
Gift of Joseph H. Hirshhorn Foundation (1966).

term for painting that consists of large areas of color, with no obvious structure, central focus, or dynamic balance. The canvases of color field painters are dominated by unified images, images so huge that they engulf the viewer. They are not about environments; they are environments in themselves.

Mark Rothko is now best known as a pioneer of color field painting, although his early works of the 1930s were urban scenes. By the 1940s, influenced by Surrealism, he began producing paintings inspired by myths and rituals. In the late 1940s, he gave up the figure and began to work primarily through color in works such as BLUE, ORANGE, RED. Rothko was able to use color to evoke moods ranging from joy and serenity to melancholy and death. By superimposing thin layers of paint, he achieved a variety of qualities from dense or heavy to atmospheric and luminous. While Rothko drew upon the intellect, his paintings have a highly sensuous appeal. Their size and image quality gives them a monumental presence.

Helen Frankenthaler's work also evolved during the height of Abstract Expressionism. In 1952, she pioneered staining techniques as an extension of Jackson Pollock's poured paint and Mark Rothko's

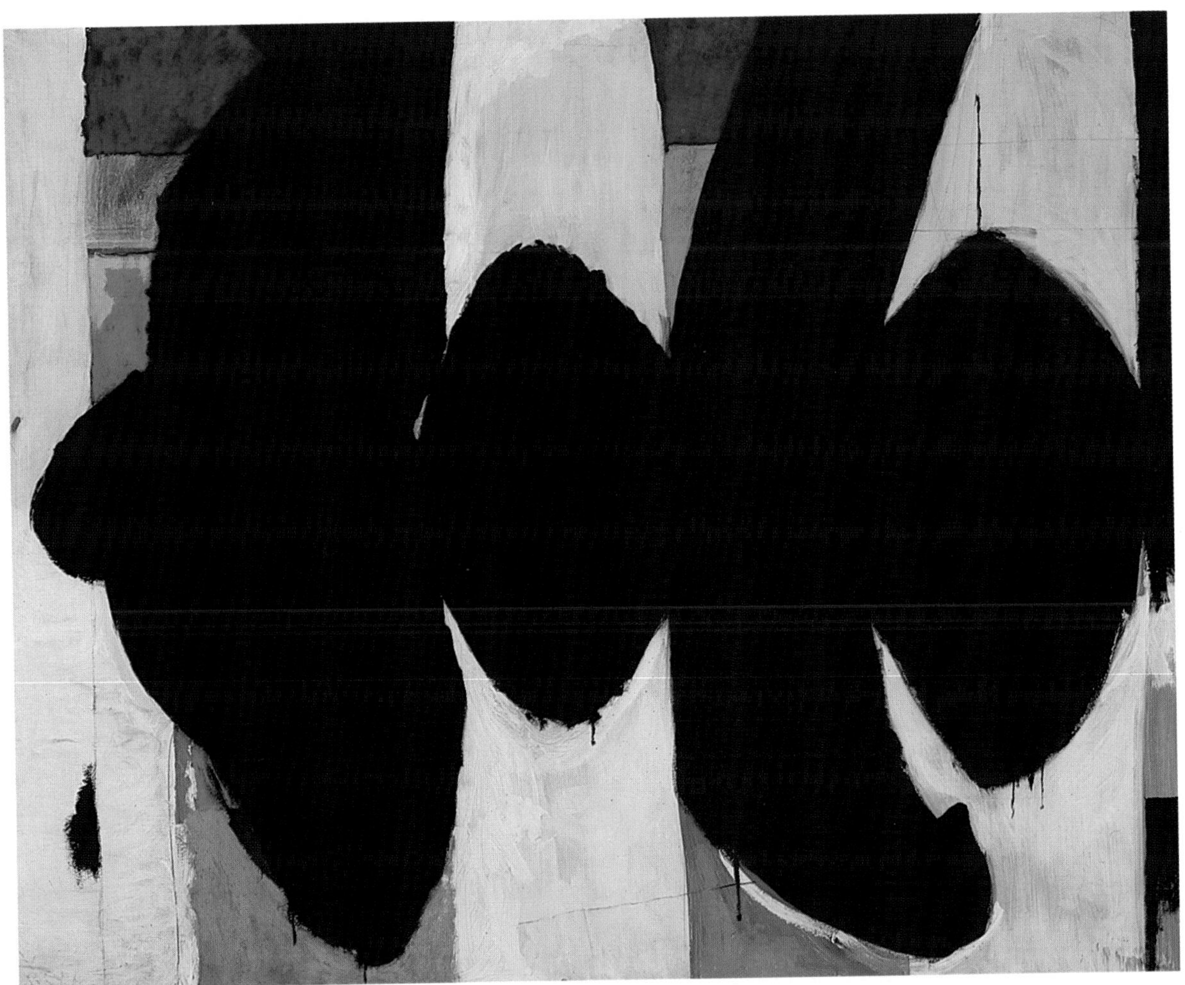

639 Robert Motherwell.
ELEGY TO THE SPANISH REPUBLIC NO. 34. 1953-1954.
Oil on canvas. 80" × 100".
Albright-Knox Art Gallery, Buffalo, N. Y. Gift of Seymour H. Knox (1957).

fields of color. Brush strokes and paint texture were eliminated as she spread liquid colors across horizontal, unprimed canvas. The thin pigment soaked into the raw fabric, producing fluid, lyrical shapes. Pale, subtle, and spontaneous, MOUNTAINS AND SEA marked the beginning of a series of paintings that emphasize softness and openness and the expressive power of color. The twenty-four-year-old Frankenthaler painted it in one day, after a trip to Nova Scotia. This large, influential painting is a pivotal work in the history of twentieth-century art. Among the artists who were influenced by Frankenthaler was Morris Louis, who adopted her staining technique and made it his own (see page 155).

Robert Motherwell's series of paintings titled ELEGY TO THE SPANISH REPUBLIC is permeated with a tragic sense of history. Unlike many Abstract Expressionists, Motherwell began with a specific subject as his starting point. His elegies brood over the destruction of the young Spanish democracy by General Franco in the bloody Spanish Civil War of the 1930s. Heavy black shapes crush and obliterate the lighter passages behind them. In these large paintings, Motherwell expresses outrage at the crushing of human rights in Spain.

The influence of Expressionist and Surrealist attitudes on Willem de Kooning's work is evident in his crashing brushwork and provocative distor-

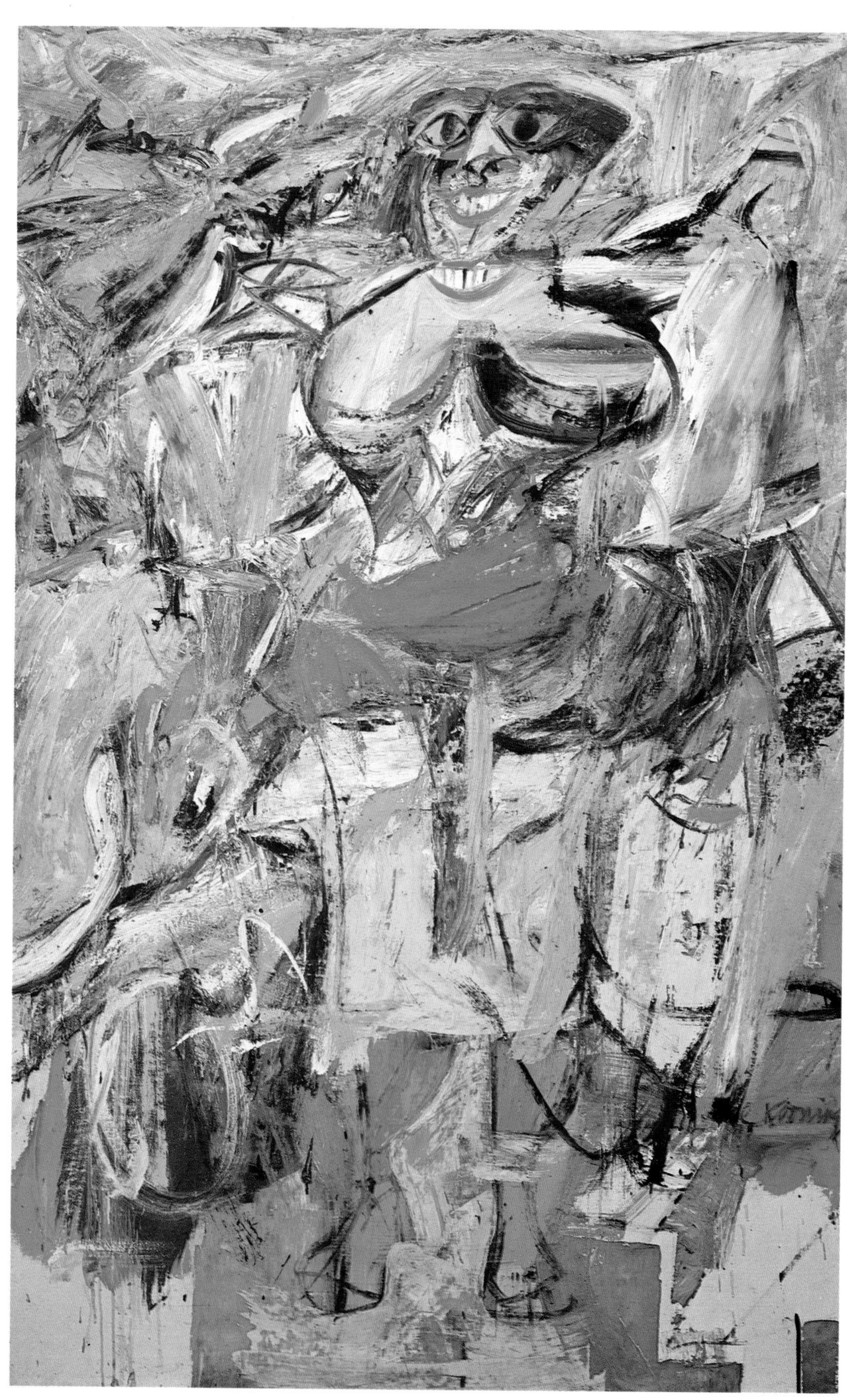

640 Willem de Kooning.
WOMAN AND BICYCLE.
1952-1953.
Oil on canvas. 76½" × 49".
Collection of Whitney Museum of American Art, New York. Purchase (55.35).

tions of human form. Throughout his career, De Kooning emphasized abstract imagery, yet he felt no compulsion to ban recognizable subject matter. After several years of working without subjects, he began a series of large paintings in which ferocious female figures appear. These canvases, painted with slashing attacks of the brush, have a violent, overwhelming power. In WOMAN AND BICYCLE, the toothy smile is repeated in a savage necklace that caps tremendous breasts.

Although Abstract Expressionism had its roots and parallels in Europe, critics see it as America's most significant contribution in visual art. An outstanding regional variation on Abstract Expressionism was initiated in the mid-1950s by several California painters who returned to the figure after years as nonrepresentational abstractionists. They employed Abstract Expressionist brushwork to depict people, light, color, and space. The group included Richard Diebenkorn, whose JULY evokes a feeling of the bright light of midsummer.

641 Richard Diebenkorn. JULY. 1957.
Oil on canvas. 59" × 54".
Courtesy of the artist's estate. Photograph: © 1988 Sotheby's, Inc.

In the 1960s, Diebenkorn's paintings again moved toward abstraction as he became intrigued with the formal possibilities of the windows in his Ocean Park, California, studio. The figure disappeared, and window frame, ocean, horizon, and sky became the dominant elements in a series of geometric abstractions. He developed his new style from a synthesis of the formalist qualities of Mondrian and Hopper and the expressionist tendencies of Matisse. OCEAN PARK #29 is from his series based on the light and color of the California land and seascape. Compare JULY and OCEAN PARK #29, and you will see the origins of the later painting.

David Smith, for many critics the most important American sculptor of the postwar period, took the formal ideas of Cubism and gave them an American vigor. His assembled metal sculpture balanced formal qualities with the heroic energy of Abstract Expressionist painting. His use of factory

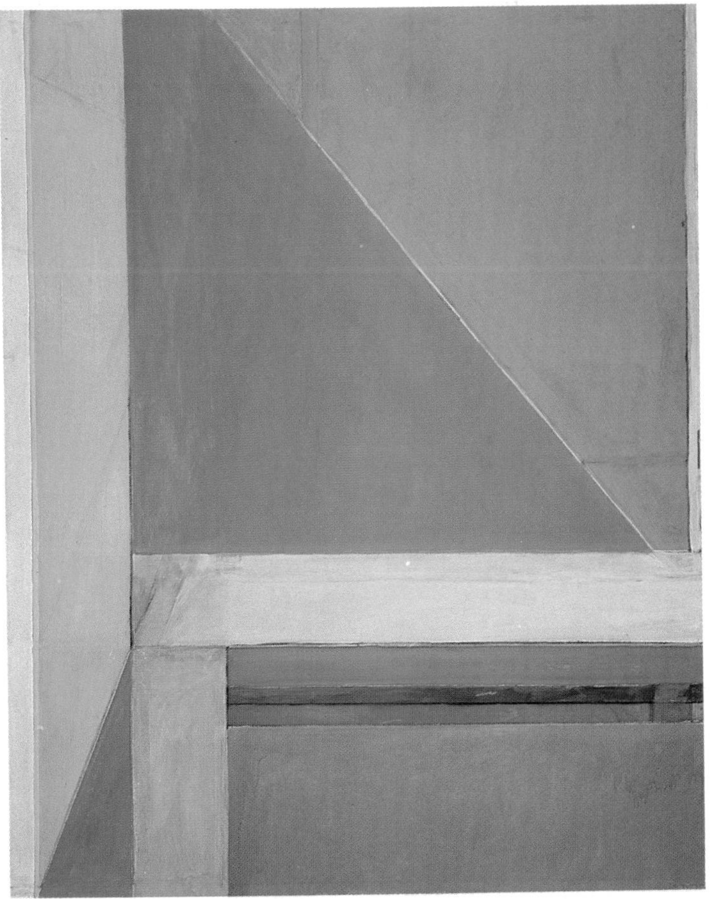

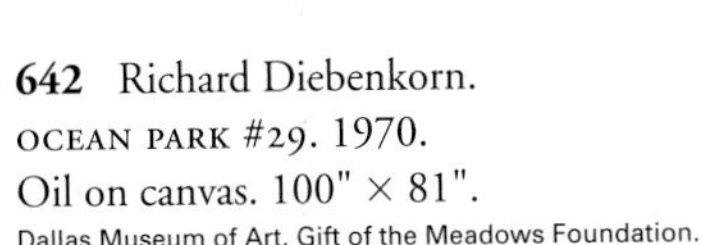

642 Richard Diebenkorn.
OCEAN PARK #29. 1970.
Oil on canvas. 100" × 81".
Dallas Museum of Art. Gift of the Meadows Foundation.

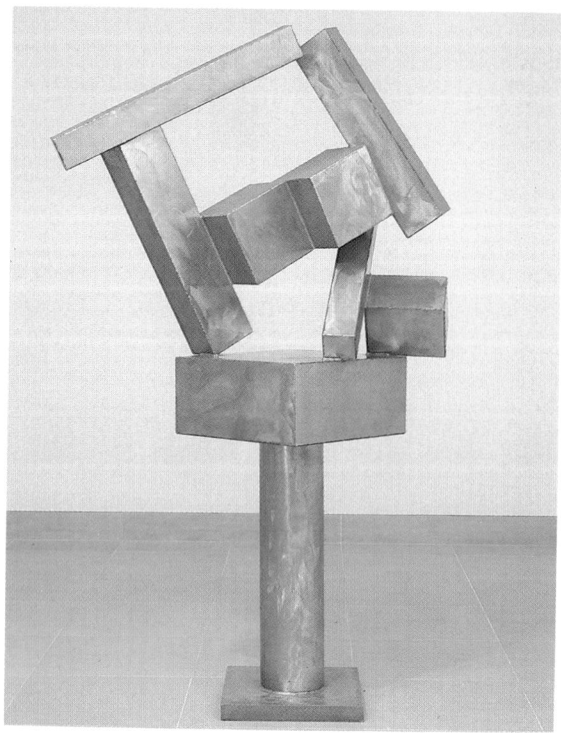

643 David Smith.
CUBI XVII. 1963.
Polished stainless steel. 107¾" × 64⅜" × 38⅛".
Dallas Museum of Art.
The Eugene and Margaret McDermott Fund.

methods and materials provided new options for the next generation of sculptors. Smith's late work included the stainless steel CUBI series, based on cubic masses and planes balanced dynamically above the viewer's eye level. The scoured surfaces of the steel reflect light in ways that seem to dissolve their solidity. Smith intended the sculpture to be viewed outdoors in strong light, set off by green landscape.

NEO-DADA

Most leading artists of the 1940s and 1950s chose not to deal with recognizable subject matter. They avoided any reference to the appearance of the environment in which they lived. In the mid-1950s, a few young artists began to acknowledge, confront, and even celebrate the visual diversity of the urban scene; they wanted to move beyond the exclusive, personal nature of Abstract Expressionism.

Under the influence of composer John Cage, who urged artists to pay attention to the lives they were living, Robert Rauschenberg began combining ordinary objects and collage materials with abstract expressionistic brushwork in what he called "combine-paintings." Rauschenberg's CANYON recalls the work of Dada artists (see pages 427–429); the strange assemblage offers glimpses of seemingly unrelated objects and events and acts as a symbol for the wild juxtapositions of modern life. Instead of blocking out the chaotic messages of city streets, TV, and magazines, Rauschenberg incorporates the trash of urban civilization in his art, renewing our sense of mystery.

In the early 1960s, with the aid of the new technique of photographic screen printing, Rauschenberg brought together images from art history and documentary photographs. In TRACER he combined expressionist painting with modified parts of art reproductions and news photographs so that art history, the Vietnam War, and street life interact with one another. Just as we may move

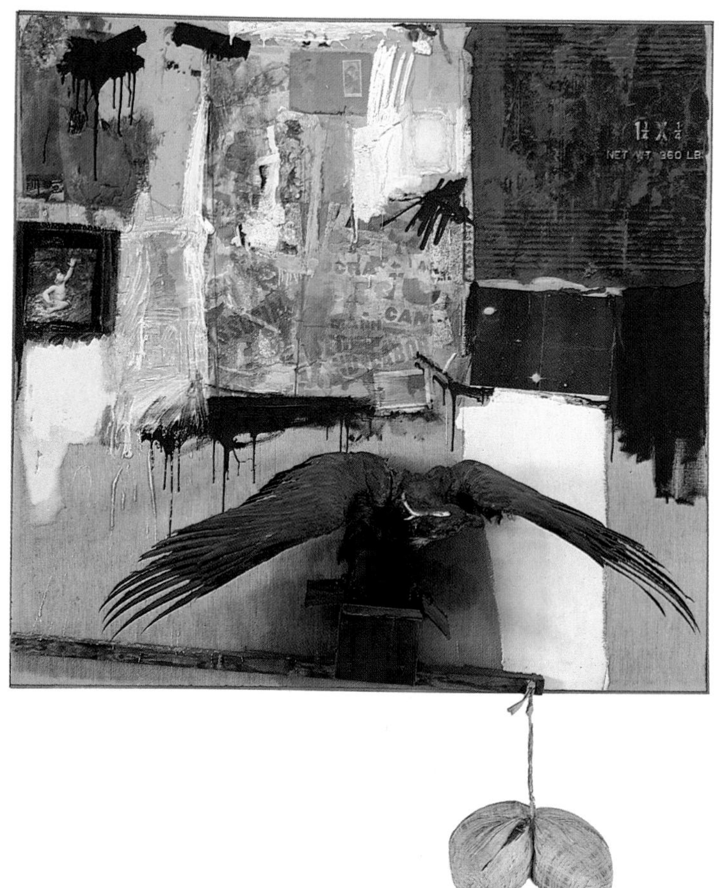

644 Robert Rauschenberg.
CANYON. 1959.
"Combine-painting" of oil on canvas, wood, printed matter, stuffed eagle, pillow tied with cord, etc. 6'1" × 5'6" × 24¾".
Private collection. Photograph courtesy of Leo Castelli Gallery, New York.

ROBERT RAUSCHENBERG (BORN 1925)

If it weren't for the navy, Robert Rauschenberg might never have discovered art at all.

One-quarter Cherokee, Rauschenberg was born in Port Arthur, Texas. He had little exposure to art before he was seventeen, and originally he intended to become a pharmacist. Growing up, he enjoyed drawing, but "art" was something for other people.

He spent three years in the navy during World War II, working in a naval hospital. One day, while on leave in California, he wandered into his first museum. Among the paintings he saw were two he recognized from reproductions on playing cards. "That was the first time I realized you could actually *be* an artist," he recalled.[1]

But how to become one? Again chance stepped in: a girlfriend in Los Angeles was returning home to Kansas City; if she could get him into the Kansas City Art Institute, would he come with her? Rauschenberg studied at the Institute for about a year. Next he went briefly to Paris (he thought all artists were supposed to). Then he spent time at the experimental Black Mountain College in North Carolina, where he met and began working with avant-garde composer John Cage. Eventually, he settled in New York, where he supplemented his income by designing window displays for fashionable Fifth Avenue stores. He continued to work with Cage, and he met Jasper Johns. Rauschenberg and Johns became the inspiration for a new avant-garde, a new synthesis of art and ordinary life.

New York now has hundreds of galleries for new art, but in the 1950s there were only five. The community of artists was small, intense, and poor, yet there was high energy and optimism. Rauschenberg experimented endlessly. When he ran out of canvas, he painted on whatever came to hand—most notoriously, his old bed quilt. Soon he was using ordinary objects almost exclusively, connecting art to daily life in a direct, exhilarating way. Anything that looked interesting could find itself in a Rauschenberg.

In 1964, he received international acclaim when he won the grand prize for painting at the Venice Biennale.

Today Rauschenberg lives on a Florida island where he works with a crew of artist assistants and devotes most of his energy (and income) to a project called ROCI (pronounced "rocky"), the Rauschenberg Overseas Cultural Interchange. ROCI grew out of the artist's experiences collaborating with traditional craftsworkers and artists in China, India, and Tibet in the 1970s. He was struck by how little the peoples of the world know about each other and how effectively making art together improved communication.

ROCI is a constantly evolving collaborative enterprise that includes rooms full of images and objects from many cultures and eras. In each country ROCI visits, local artists work with Rauschenberg to modify the ongoing work. The ultimate purpose of the project is to promote peace and understanding by celebrating diversity.

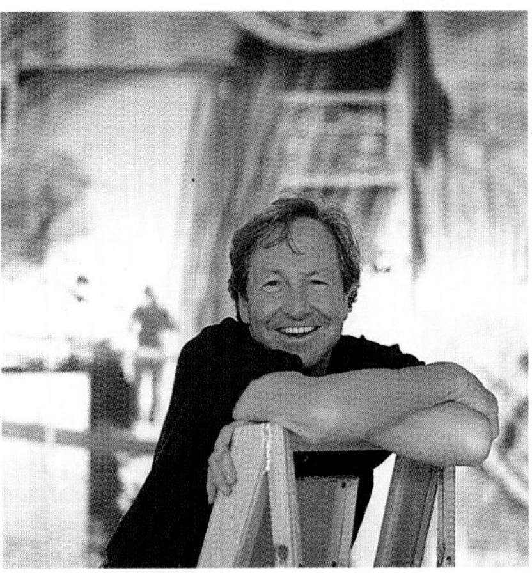

645 ROBERT RAUSCHENBERG.
Photograph: © Ed Chappell.

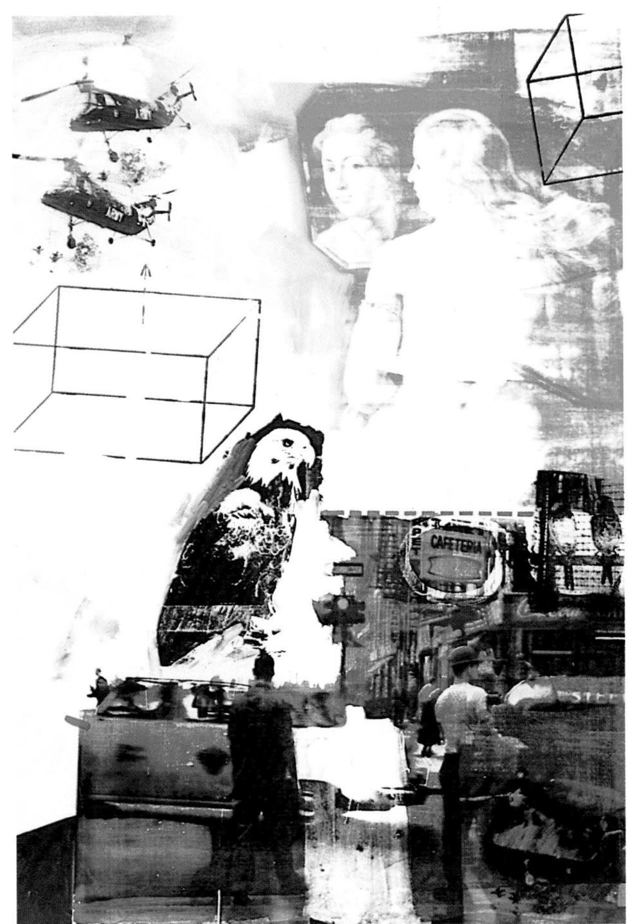

646 Robert Rauschenberg.
TRACER. 1964.
Mixed media. 84" × 60".
Nelson-Atkins Museum of Art, Kansas City, Missouri.
Photograph courtesy of Leo Castelli Gallery, New York.

from sports to dinner to televised wars and sitcoms, Rauschenberg's work assembles the unrelated bits and pieces of everyday experience.

Rauschenberg often discussed art-making with Jasper Johns during their formative years in the 1950s. Whereas Rauschenberg's work is filled with visual complexity, Johns's work is deceptively simple. Johns's large early paintings were based on common graphic forms such as targets, maps, flags, and numbers. He was interested in the difference between signs (emblems that carry meaning) and art. In Johns's work, common signs play a dual role: they have the power of Abstract Expressionist forms in their size and painterly surface qualities, yet they represent familiar, everyday objects and thus bring art back to everyday life. In his TARGET WITH FOUR FACES, a sign (target) becomes a painting, while the faces (sculpture) become a sign.

As with Duchamp's BICYCLE WHEEL and Man Ray's THE GIFT (page 429), Johns's common subjects are now objects of contemplation. His irony relates back to Dada and forward to Conceptual Art. The Neo-Dada works of Johns and Rauschenberg provided a bridge between Abstract Expressionism and Pop Art. Properly speaking, Johns and Rauschenberg are not Pop artists but champions of art in an environment saturated with popular culture.

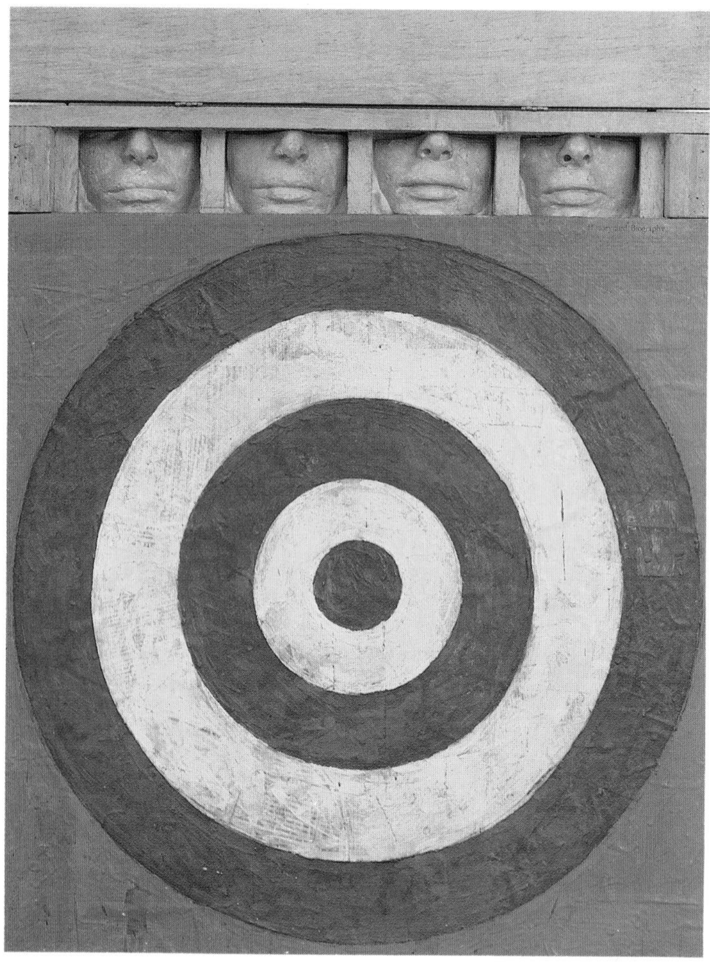

647 Jasper Johns.
TARGET WITH FOUR FACES. 1955.
Assemblage: encaustic and collage on canvas with objects, 26" × 26", surmounted by four tinted plaster faces in wood box with hinged front. Box, closed, 3¾" × 26" × 3½". Overall dimensions with box open, 33⅝" × 26" × 3".
The Museum of Modern Art, New York. Gift of Mr. and Mrs. Robert C. Scull.

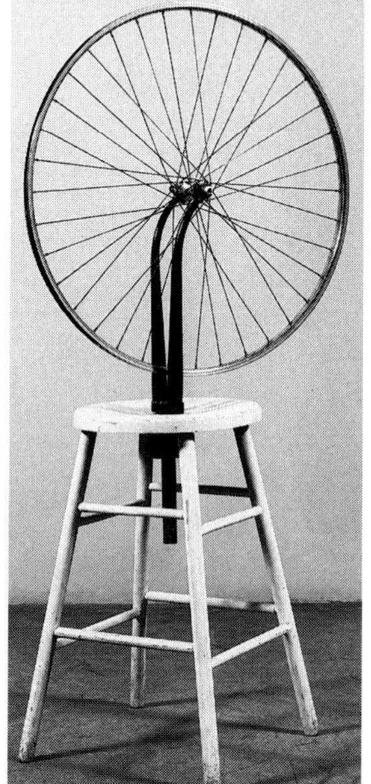

648 Marcel Duchamp.
BICYCLE WHEEL. 1951 (third version after lost original of 1913).
Assemblage: metal wheel, diameter 25½"; mounted on painted wooden stool, 23¾" high; overall height 50½".
The Sidney and Harriet Janis Collection. Gift to the Museum of Modern Art, New York.

POP AND POP-RELATED ART

Inspired by Neo-Dada, Pop Art emerged as human contact with the natural world was rapidly being cut off by a flood of manufactured objects, advertising signs, and urban sprawl. Poet Ogden Nash summed up the situation: "I think that I shall never see / A billboard lovely as a tree. / Perhaps unless the billboards fall, / I'll never see a tree at all."[2]

Although the term Pop is short for "popular," it does not refer to art popular with the public, but to art that deals with the images of popular culture. Pop artists, like the Dadaists and Neo-Dadaists before them, wanted to challenge cultural assumptions.

While Abstract Expressionism had celebrated each artist's individual feelings and personal touch, Pop artists created cool, mechanical images that hid all evidence of their hands at work. Commercial art, which had long been looked down on by fine artists, became a source of inspiration. Pop painters used photographic screenprinting and airbrush techniques to achieve the surface characteristics of mass-produced imagery such as advertising, food labels, and comic books.

Pop Art appeared almost simultaneously in London and the United States. In London, a group of young artists made collages with images cut from popular, mostly American, magazines. Decades earlier, Dada artists such as Hannah Höch (see page 429) had produced photomontages with similar raw material. But for the Londoners, the purposes were different. In 1957, English artist Richard Hamilton published a somewhat tongue-in-cheek list of characteristics of Pop Art for the London artists who were beginning to work in this vein. The list includes qualities of contemporary mass culture these artists chose to address. Hamilton wrote that Pop Art should be:

Popular (designed for a mass audience)
Transient (short-term solution)
Expendable (easily forgotten)
Low-cost
Mass-produced
Young (aimed at youth)
Witty
Sexy
Gimmicky
Glamorous
Big business[3]

Pop Art's media sources include the comic strip, the advertising blowup, the famous-name-brand package, and the visual clichés of billboard, newspaper, movie theater, and television. Elements from all these mass media are included in Hamilton's collage JUST WHAT IS IT THAT MAKES TODAY'S HOME SO DIFFERENT, SO APPEALING? Hamilton's work is a hilarious parody of the superficiality and materialism of modern popular culture. In it, we see the word Pop along with the origins and images of the Pop style.

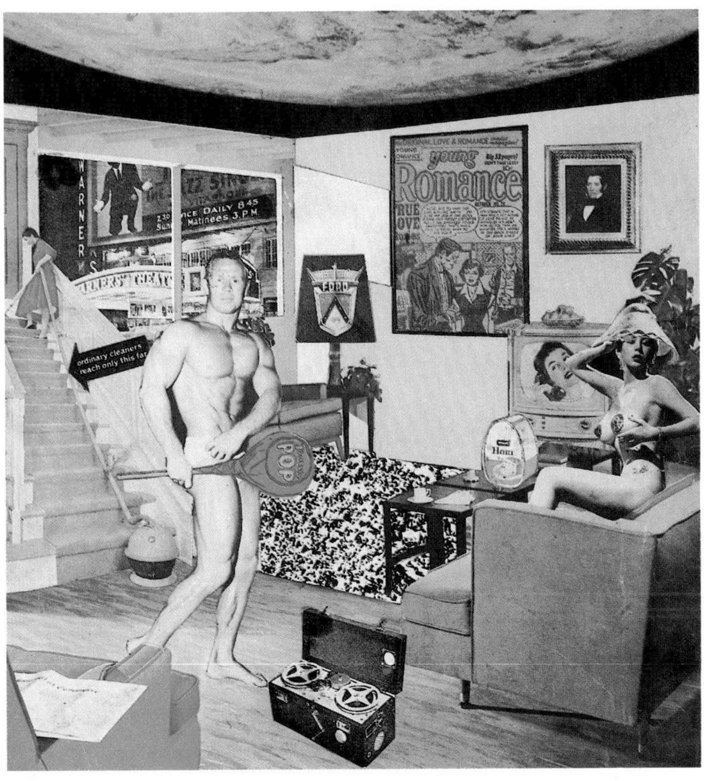

649 Richard Hamilton.
JUST WHAT IS IT THAT MAKES TODAY'S HOME SO DIFFERENT, SO APPEALING? 1956.
Collage. 10¼" × 9¾".
Kunsthalle Museum, Tubingen, Germany.

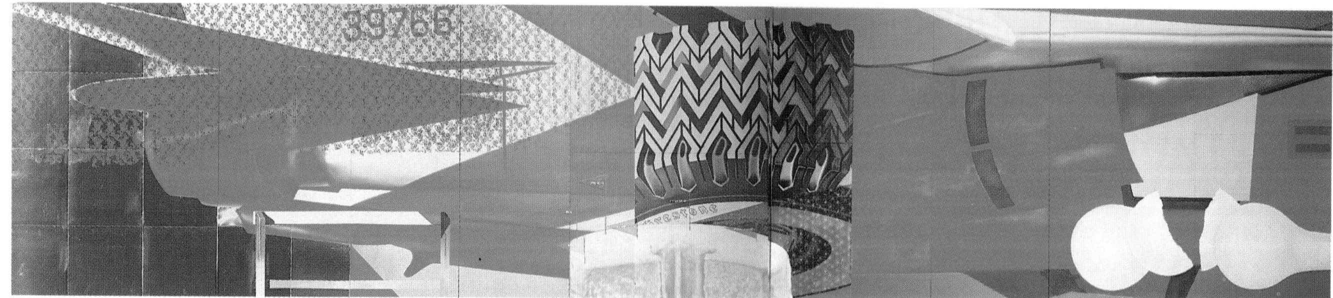

James Rosenquist worked as a billboard painter after attending art school and college. Later, he incorporated his experiences in a mature style that presents impersonally rendered montages of contemporary American popular culture. He drew upon the techniques and imagery of his sign painting experience, painting huge close-up details of faces, natural forms, and industrial objects with a mechanical airbrush.

Rosenquist's enormous mural F-111 filled all four walls of the Leo Castelli Gallery in New York City when it was first presented in 1965. The image of an F-111 jet—an enormously expensive experimental bomber—sweeps across his wall-to-wall environment of sixties Americana. Rosenquist mixed symbols of affluence and destruction in his billboard-sized painting, which includes—in addition to jet parts—a hair dryer, a child of ambitious parents, a tire, light bulbs, a beach umbrella, and a mushroom cloud from an atomic bomb.

No American artist in the 1960s sparked more public indignation than Andy Warhol. He didn't invent Pop Art, but he was its most visible and controversial exponent. Like Rosenquist, Warhol began his career as a commercial artist. When he moved into the fine-art sphere in the early 1960s, Warhol came as an inventive subversive. 200 CAMPBELL'S SOUP CANS is characteristic of his paintings, in which common, mass-produced objects are mechanically repeated, as if seen on supermarket shelves. Warhol's work called attention to the pervasive and uniformly insistent character of our commercial environment. The repetition of mass imagery has become our cultural landscape and our mythology; the "canned" popular image is a giant filter and equalizer of everything from processed foods to presidential candidates. Slight variations exist within bland uniformity: tomato, pepperpot, bean with bacon.

In DROWNING GIRL (page 12) and other paintings, Roy Lichtenstein uses comic book images with their bright primary colors, impersonal surfaces, and characteristic printing dots. His work is a commentary on a world obsessed with consumer goods, sex, and violence. He sees Pop Art as "involvement with what I think to be the most brazen and threatening characteristics of our culture, things we hate, but which are also powerful in their impingement on us."[4]

For several decades, Claes Oldenburg has been finding inspiration in the common, mass-produced artifacts of American society. His lumpy, gloopy TWO CHEESEBURGERS WITH EVERYTHING (known as DUAL HAMBURGERS) needs no explanation. There it is! Oldenburg enjoys taking mundane objects and remaking them into icons; see also his giant clothespin on page 101. Rather than turn away from the funk of neo-America, Oldenburg embraces it:

I am for Kool-Art, 7-UP art, Pepsi-art, Sunshine art, 39 cents art . . . Menthol art . . . Rx art . . . Now art . . . I am for U. S. Government Inspected Art, Grade A art, Regular Price art, Yellow Ripe art, Extra Fancy art, Ready-to-eat art.[5]

Since prehistoric times, art has helped people to describe, to understand, and to gain a sense of positive interaction with their surroundings. Cave

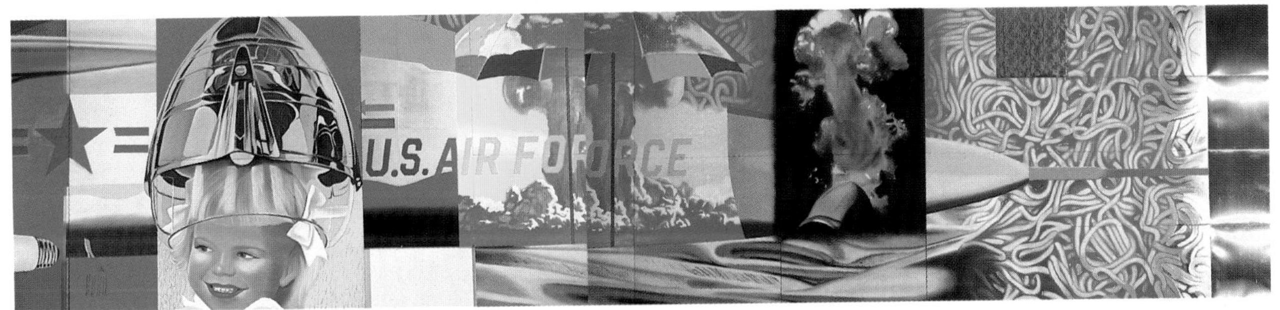

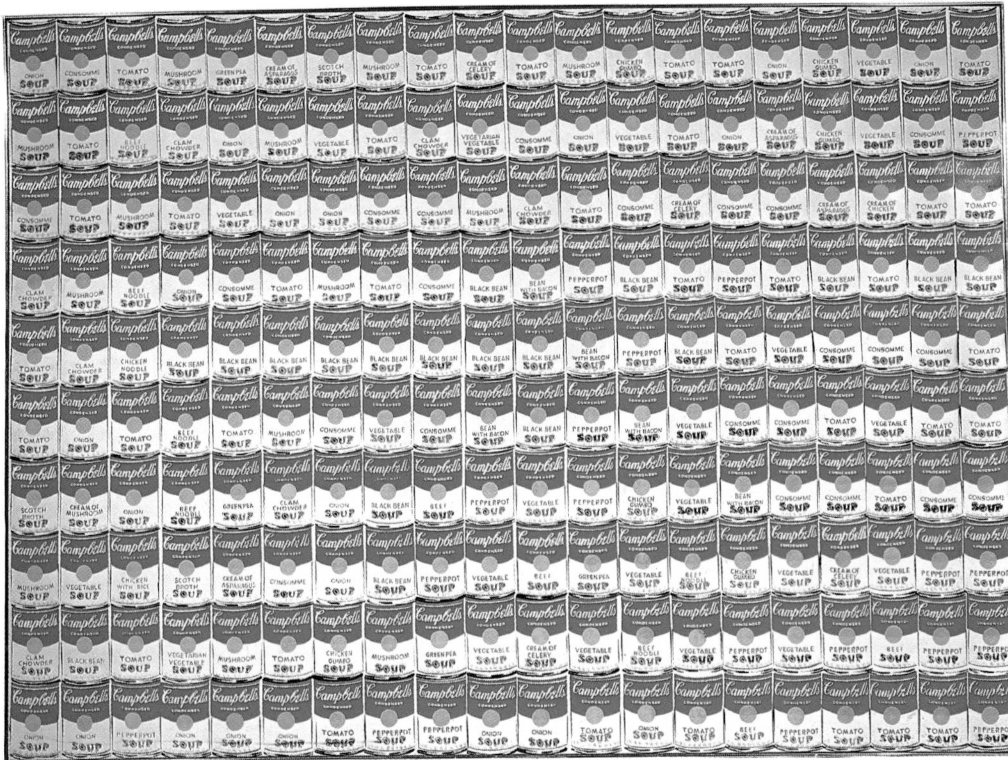

650 James Rosenquist.
F-III. 1965.
Oil on canvas with aluminum, four parts. 10' × 86'.
Private collection.
Photographs courtesy of Leo Castelli Gallery, New York.

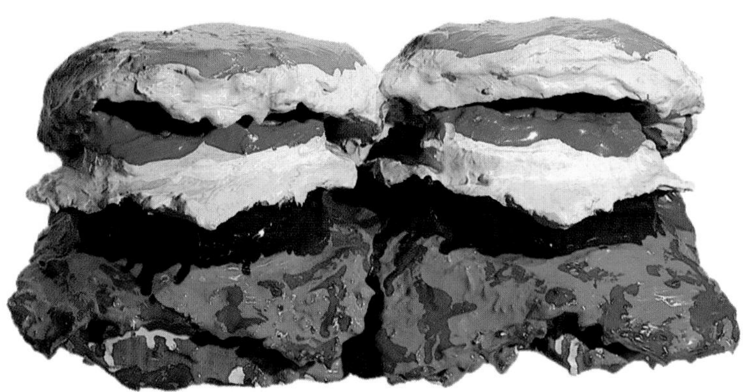

651 Andy Warhol.
200 CAMPBELL'S SOUP CANS. 1962.
Oil on canvas. 72" × 100".
Private collection.
Photograph courtesy of Leo Castelli Gallery, New York.

652 Claes Oldenburg
TWO CHEESEBURGERS WITH EVERYTHING (DUAL HAMBURGERS). 1962.
Burlap soaked in plaster, painted with enamel.
7" × 14¾" x 8⅝".
The Museum of Modern Art, New York. Philip Johnson Fund.

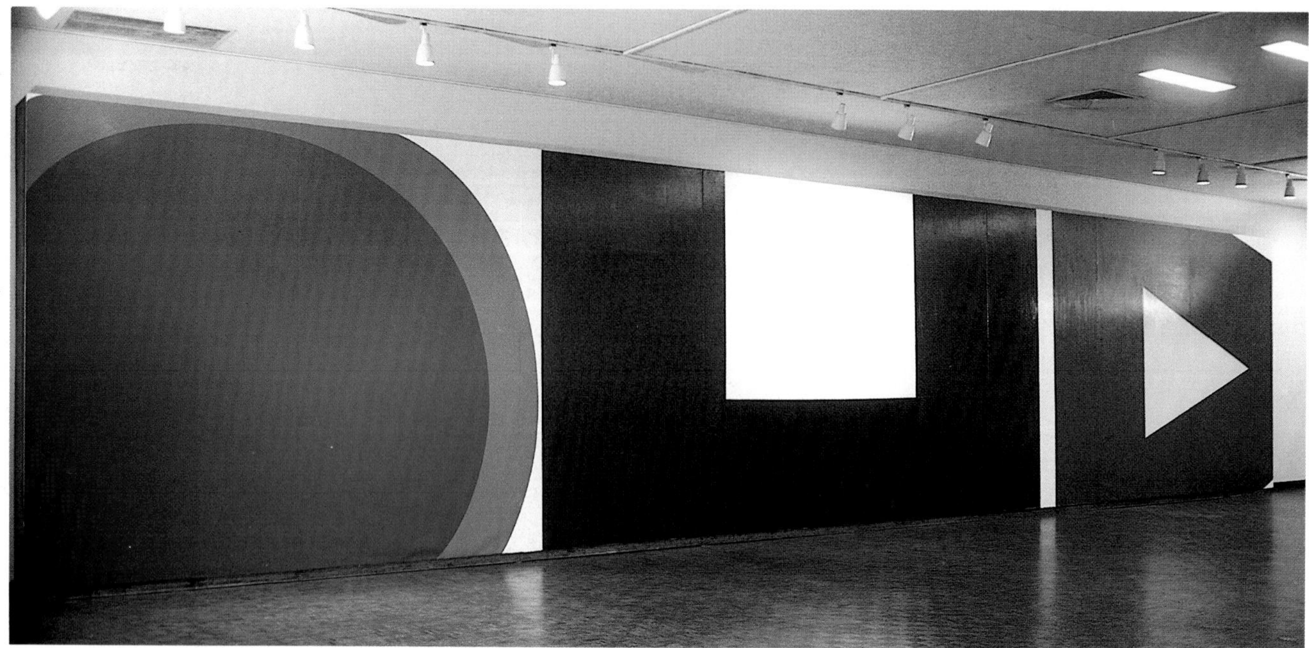

653 Al Held.
GREEK GARDEN. 1966.
Acrylic on canvas. 12' × 56'.
Collection of the artist. Photograph courtesy of Andre Emmerich Gallery, New York.

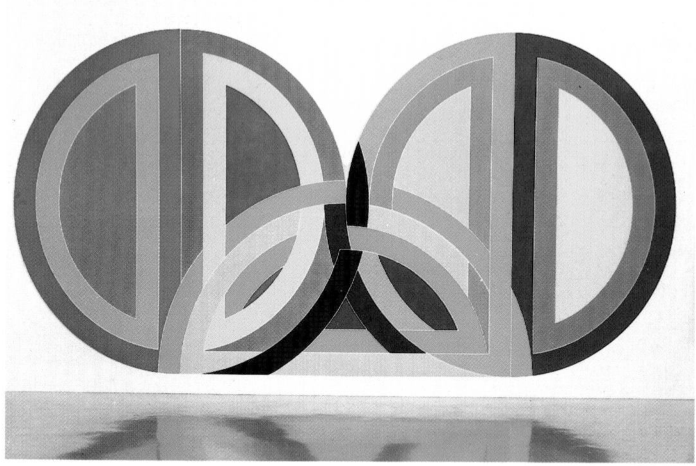

654 Frank Stella.
HIRAQLA I. 1968.
Acrylic polymer and fluorescent polymer paint on canvas.
10' × 20'.
Private collection.

dwellers at Lascaux painted the animals that were a major feature of their environment; modern city dwellers draw inspiration from an urban environment, making art of the signs and symbols of popular culture.

HARD-EDGE AND MINIMAL

Pop Art was just one reaction against the self-absorbed quality of Abstract Expressionism. Other painters and sculptors took different approaches. Some painters shared an interest in what they saw as the essence of painting: a flat, colored surface. Quick-drying acrylic paints, which were developed at this time, lend themselves to uniform application and to the use of tape to obtain shapes with precise edges—a style called *hard-edge.* This somewhat misleading term refers to works concerned not only with linear definition but with the relationship of color to form. It is a cooler, more geometrical approach to color than that seen in color field painting.

Frank Stella's rigorous hard-edge paintings of the 1960s emphasize the flatness of the picture plane and its boundaries. He treated his paintings like constructed objects rather than pictures. In HIRAQLA, Stella replaced the traditional rectangular format with a distinctive outer profile to further extend the concept of the surface as an object in its own right rather than as a field for illusions. External boundaries of the overall shape are arrived at internally. There is no figure-ground relationship; within the painting, everything is figure. Interwoven bands of both muted and intense Day-Glo acrylic colors pull together in a tight spatial weave.

Stella's intellectual conception of the painting-as-object brought him close to the realm of sculpture and aligned him with Minimalism. Minimalists admired the unified, all-at-once, nonrelational character of works by such artists as Pollock and Rothko. Minimalism depends on a total impression—an instant gestalt. To achieve this, it reduces its properties to the most essential. The idea of reducing art to a minimal image was first explored by the Russian Kasimir Malevich in the early twentieth century (see page 75). American Minimalists developed their own spare style.

The most complete application of Minimalism occurs in sculpture, yet painters were also involved. As paintings became objects rather than reflections of objects, they began to function as environments in themselves instead of as representations of environments. Both Color Field and Minimalist painters employ scale to help create environments rather than "pictures." Al Held cut off his shapes at the edge of the picture plane in such a way that they seem even more gigantic than they are. The Minimalist forms of Held's GREEK GARDEN fill an entire gallery wall and appear to exude a massive inner force.

In the late 1950s and early 1960s, a number of artists who began as painters rejected painting altogether because they felt it lacked the concreteness and presence of three-dimensional forms. Minimalist sculpture frequently has more in common with architecture and painting than with traditional sculpture. Instead of being emotionally charged, the works are nonsensual, impersonal, geometric structures—presented without interpretation.

Among those who went from painting to sculpture was Donald Judd. He works with industrial materials such as sheet metal, aluminum, and molded plastics, which had not previously been used for art; his UNTITLED combines stainless steel and plexiglass. Judd has been a leading artist and the major spokesman for the Minimalist movement. In his essay "Specific Objects," he wrote about the aims of his art:

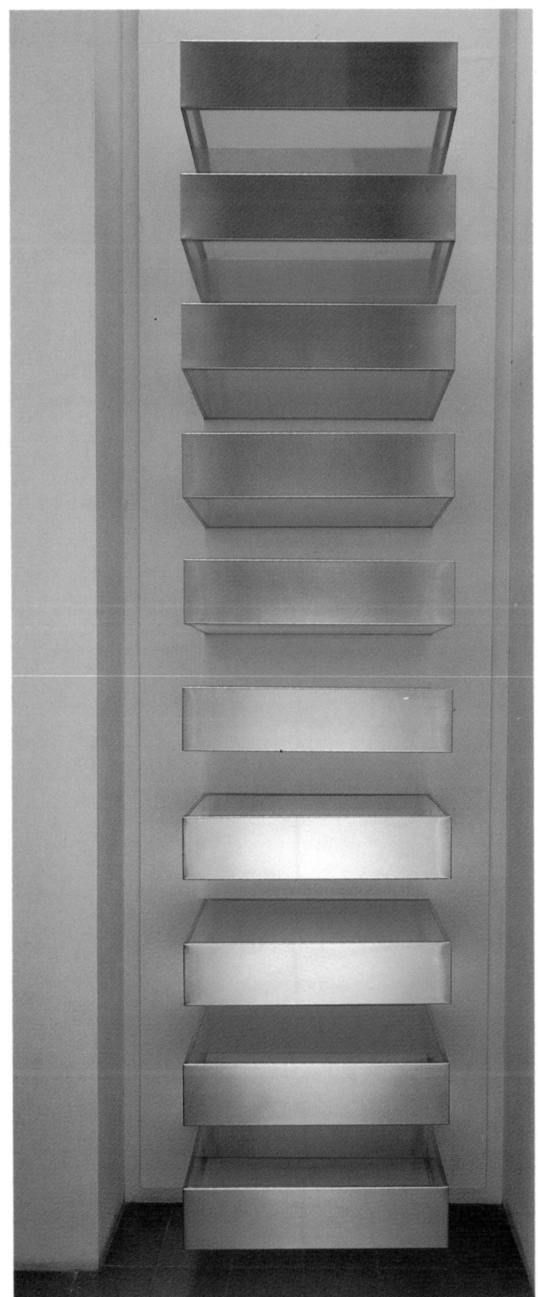

655 Donald Judd.
UNTITLED. 1967.
Stainless steel and plexiglass. Height 14'3".
Collection, Modern Art Museum of Fort Worth. The Benjamin J. Tillar Memorial Trust.

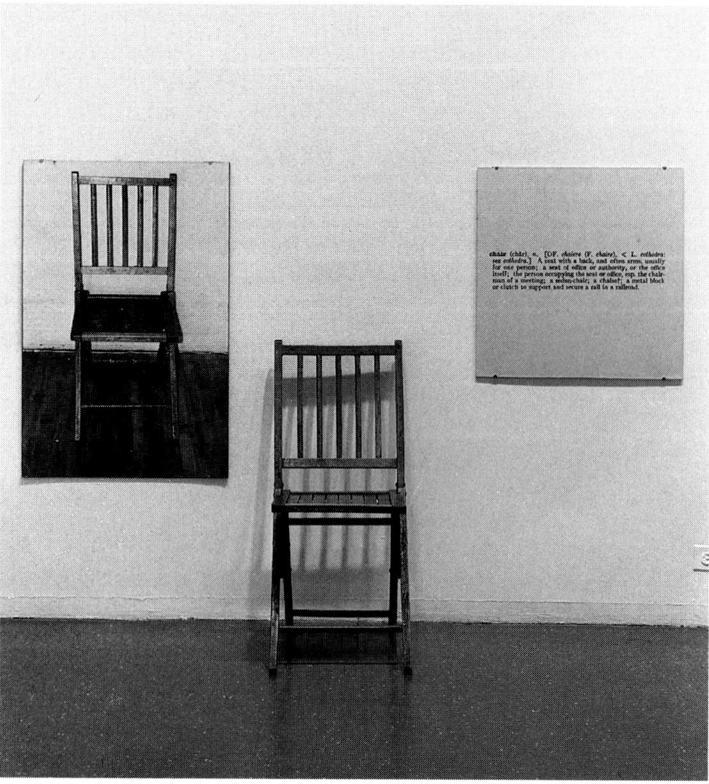

656 Joseph Kosuth.
ONE AND THREE CHAIRS. 1965.
Wooden folding chair, photographic copy of a chair, and photographic enlargement of dictionary definition of chair.
Chair, 32⅜" × 14⅞" × 20⅞"; photo panel, 36" × 24⅛"; text panel, 24" × 24⅛".
The Museum of Modern Art, New York. Larry Aldrich Foundation Fund.

It isn't necessary for a work to have a lot of things to look at, to compare, to analyze one by one, to contemplate. The thing as a whole, its quality as a whole, is what is interesting.... In the new work the shape, image, color, and surface are single, and not partial and scattered.[6]

CONCEPTUAL ART

During the last decades of the twentieth century, artists have reacted ever more quickly to each successive aesthetic movement. Pushing back the limits, the next reductive step after Minimalist art became no art at all—that is, an art of ideas rather than objects. Conceptual art, in which an idea takes the place of the art object, was an outgrowth of Minimalism and a reaction to Pop. The Conceptual movement was heavily indebted to Marcel Duchamp, the first champion of an art of ideas.

Joseph Kosuth, the most rigorous early Conceptualist, was angered at the materialism of the art market and Pop Art's embrace of commercialism. In 1965, he produced ONE AND THREE CHAIRS, which consisted of a wooden chair, a photograph of the same chair, and a photographic enlargement of a dictionary definition of the word "chair."

Another notable Conceptual work was *Ice,* by Rafael Ferrer. In 1969, Ferrer put together an assemblage of ice blocks and autumn leaves on the Whitney Museum's entry ramp. When collectors complained about the ephemeral nature of his creation, Ferrer suggested that the iceman's bill might be collected as a kind of "drawing." In the true spirit of Conceptualism, this work is not illustrated here.

SITE WORKS AND EARTHWORKS

In the late 1960s, a number of artists working under the influence of Minimalism and Conceptual Art went beyond the prevailing idea of sculpture as a portable precious object. They began creating works that are inseparable from the sites for which they were designed. In *site-specific* works, the artist's sensitivity to the location determines the composition, scale, medium, and even the content of each piece.

Walter De Maria's THE LIGHTNING FIELD is a site sculpture designed to be viewed over a period of time. The work consists of four hundred stainless steel poles arranged in a rectangular grid over an area measuring one mile by one kilometer in west central New Mexico. The sharpened tips of the poles form a level plane, a kind of monumental bed of nails. Each of the poles can act as a lightning conductor during the electrical storms that occur frequently over the desert. Actual strikes are rare, however. Early and late in the day the poles reflect the sun, creating accents of technological precision in sharp contrast to the otherwise natural landscape. Purposely isolated from the art-viewing public, THE LIGHTNING FIELD combines aspects of both Conceptual and Minimalist art. Viewers must arrange their visits through the Dia Foundation, which commissioned the piece. Once

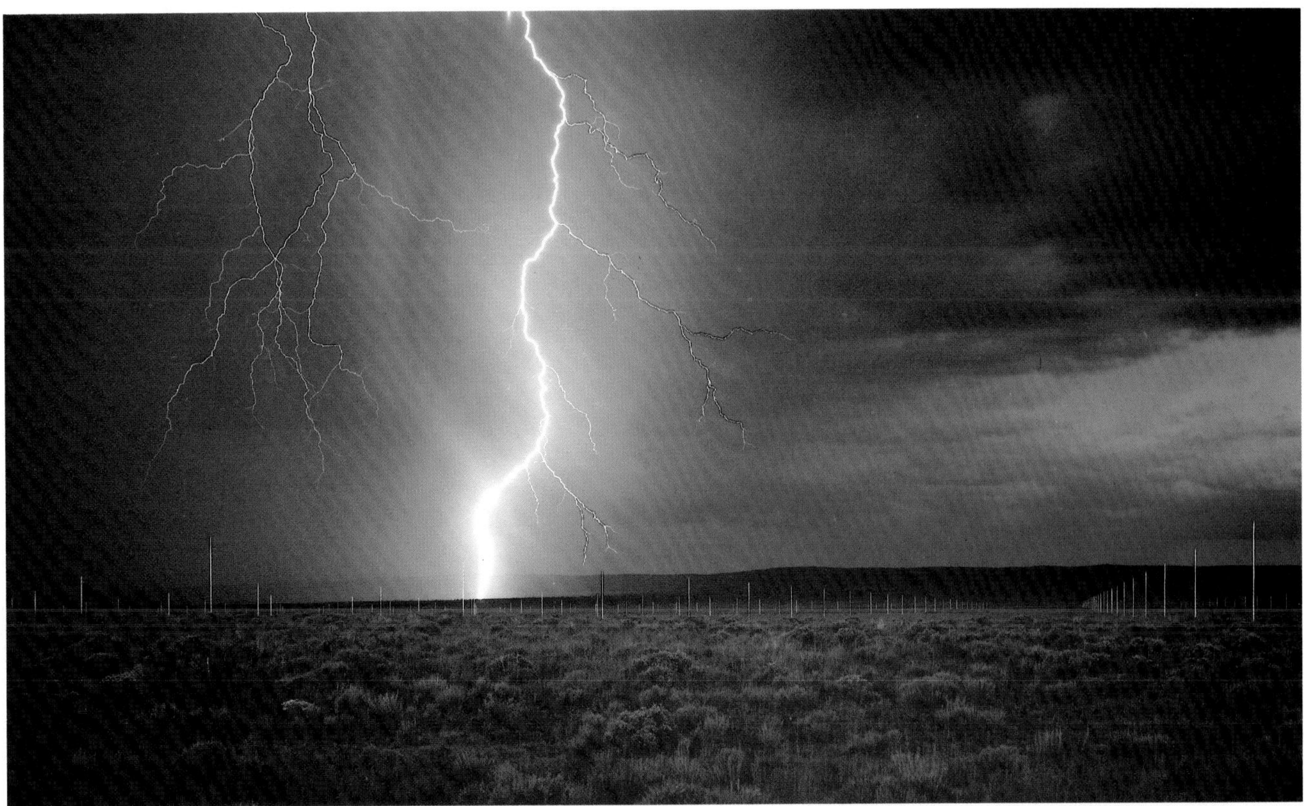

657 Walter De Maria.
THE LIGHTNING FIELD. New Mexico. 1971-1977.
400 stainless-steel poles, average height 20'7";
land area 1 mile × 1 kilometer.
Photograph: John Cliett. © Dia Art Foundation 1980.

there, they are left to study the work and make their own interpretations.

When Bulgarian artist Christo was a student, he was alienated by the narrowness of his country's officially prescribed social realist art. His enthusiasm was aroused, however, by government-sponsored trips to the countryside, during which he and other art students covered hay and old farm equipment with tarpaulins in order to improve the appearance of the landscape for foreigners traveling on the *Orient Express.*

Christo was first known in Europe as a gifted portrait painter. Later, he joined a group of artists in Paris who were presenting objects as art rather than painting or sculpting representations of objects. In the late 1950s, he gained notoriety when he closed off a Paris alley with a wall of 50-gallon

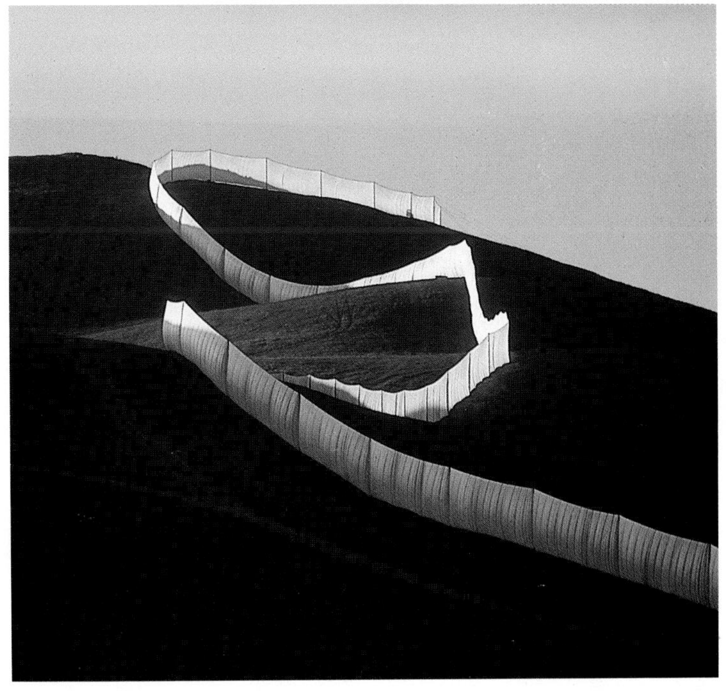

658 Christo.
RUNNING FENCE. Sonoma and Marin counties, California.
1972-1976.
Nylon fabric and steel poles. 18' × 24½ miles.
Photograph: © Wolfgang Volz.

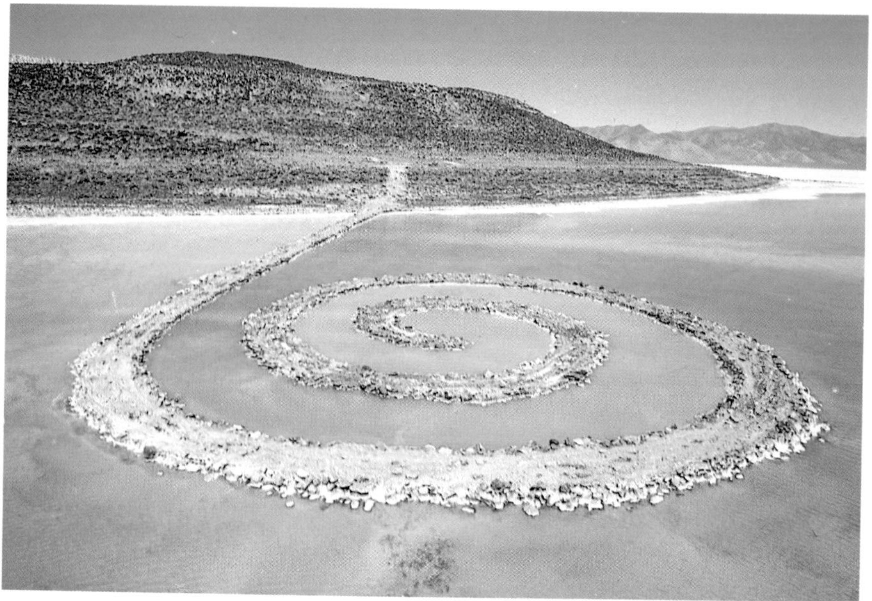

659 Robert Smithson.
SPIRAL JETTY.
Great Salt Lake, Utah. 1970.
Earthwork. Length 1500', width 15'.
Photograph: © 1989 Gianfranco Gorgoni/Contact Press Images, Inc.

oil drums. Then he began wrapping in fabric objects ranging in size and complexity from a motorcycle to a mile of sea cliffs in Australia. This was just the beginning for an artist who makes art by interacting with sites throughout the world.

One of Christo's most ambitious projects was RUNNING FENCE, a temporary environmental artwork that was as much a process and an event as it was sculpture. The 18-foot-high white nylon fence ran from the ocean at Bodega Bay in Sonoma County, California, through 24½ miles of agricultural and dairy land. RUNNING FENCE was a unique event, ultimately involving thousands of people. The project required political action, the agreement of landowners, and the help of hundreds of volunteers. Christo raised the necessary funds by selling preliminary drawings and collages of the work.

RUNNING FENCE celebrated landscape, light, and vision. The seemingly endless ribbon of white cloth made the wind visible and caught the changing light as it stretched across the gently rolling hills, appearing and disappearing on the horizon. The simplicity of RUNNING FENCE relates it to Minimalist art, but the fence itself was not presented as an art object. It was the focal point for a work that included the interweaving of people, process, object, and place. Christo's works are conceptual in the way they alert viewers to the fact that art is an experience before and after it is anything else.

As an idea and a process, RUNNING FENCE may have helped protect not only the land it temporarily graced but other landscapes as well. Christo's ideas may enable people to become more perceptive, particularly of the beauty and character of open countryside. The 280-page Environmental Impact Statement required by the Sonoma County Superior Court concluded that "the only large scale irreversible change may very well be in the ideas and attitudes of the people."[7]

Earthworks are sculptural forms made of materials such as earth, rocks, and sometimes plants. They are often very large, and they may be executed in remote locations. Earthworks are usually designed to merge with or complement the landscape. *Site works* are environmental constructions, frequently made of sculptural materials, designed to interact with, but not permanently alter, the environment. These art forms often indicate a positive interest in ecology and in the earthworks of ancient America.

Robert Smithson was one of the founders of the earthworks movement. His SPIRAL JETTY, completed at Great Salt Lake, Utah, in 1970, has since been lost to view because of the rising water level.

Its natural surroundings emphasized its form as willful human design. Although our society has no supportive, agreed-upon symbolism or iconography, we instinctively respond to universal signs like the spiral, which are found in nature and in ancient art.

The earthworks and site works movements have helped redirect relationships among architecture, sculpture, and the environment.

While site-specific works can be commissioned, they are almost never resold unless someone buys the land of which they are a part. Project drawings and photographs, however, can be collected. Conceptual art, earthworks, site works, and performance art share a common desire to subvert the gallery-museum-collector syndrome, to present art as an experience rather than as a commodity.

INSTALLATIONS AND ENVIRONMENTS

While some artists were creating outdoor earthworks and site works, others were moving beyond the traditional concepts of painting and sculpture indoors. Since the mid-1960s, artists from diverse backgrounds and points of view have fabricated interior installations and environments rather than portable works of art. Some installations alter the entire spaces they occupy; others are experienced as large sculpture; most of them assume the viewer to be a part of the piece.

James Turrell's installations challenge assumptions about the truth of what we see. With light and space defining walls, Turrell designs environments that create shifts in perception. His work goes beyond the lean physical structures of Minimalism, and beyond Conceptualism's reliance on words and ideas, to dwell on the mysterious and at times awe-inspiring interaction of light, space, and time. Light becomes a tangible physical presence in works such as AMBA, where viewers are coaxed into paying attention to their own perceptions.

The work is about your seeing. It is responsive to the viewer. As you move within the space or as you decide to see it, one way or another, its reality can change.[8]

What really interests me is having the viewer make discoveries the same way the artist does ... instead of having the viewer participate vicariously, through someone else.... You determine the reality of what you see. The work is the product of my vision, but it's about your seeing. The poles of the realm in which I operate are the physical limitations of human vision and the learned limits of perception, or what I call "prejudiced perception." Encountering these prejudices

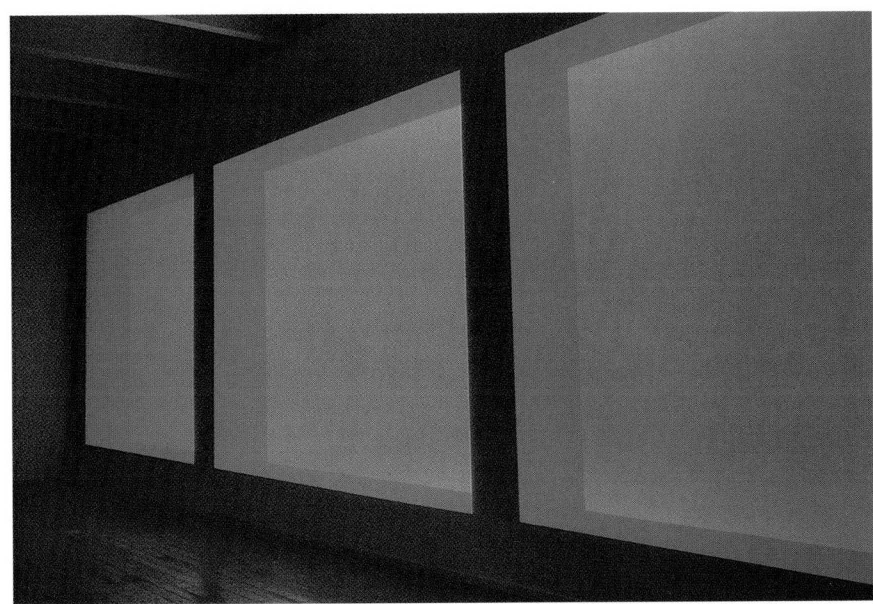

660 James Turrell.
AMBA. 1982.
Light installation.
Photograph courtesy of the artist.

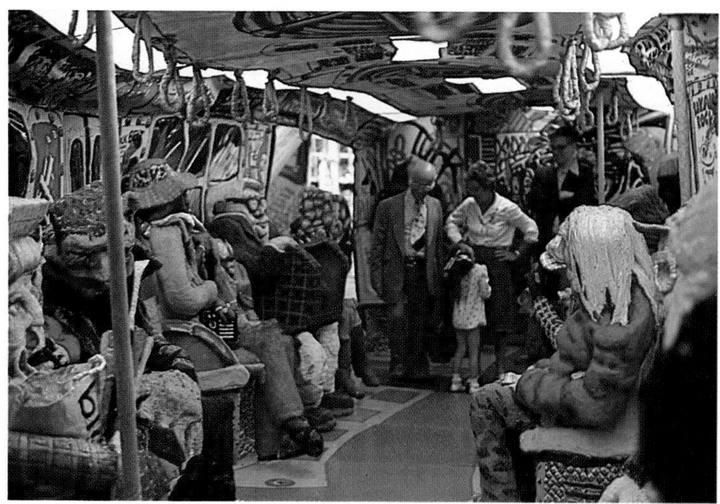

661 Red Grooms and the Ruckus Construction Company. RUCKUS MANHATTAN. 1976.
Mixed media installation.
Photographed at Marlborough Gallery, New York.

can be an amazing experience, and if someone can come to these discoveries directly, the way the artist does, the impact is greater and so is the joy.[9]

Turrell also creates what he calls Skyspaces by removing sections of ceilings to expose the sky. From within such installations, the sky appears to be on the same plane as the opening, and therefore it seems to be not sky but ceiling. Seen from within, from sunset through twilight, the sky-ceiling undergoes an amazing transformation as it changes in color and intensity in relation to the room.

A far cry from Turrell's cool perceptual magic are the narrative, whimsical installations of Red Grooms. RUCKUS MANHATTAN, a refreshing, wildly humorous installation, was created by Grooms and a group called the Ruckus Construction Company. Grooms defines *ruckus* as "a beautiful southern word meaning a disorderly commotion."[10] The elaborate sculptural extravaganza featured caricatures of many famous New York City landmarks, including a 30-foot-tall World Trade Center, a subway train, the Woolworth Building, a Times Square porno shop, a Staten Island ferry one could "ride" on, and the Statue of Liberty in red platform shoes, holding a cigar in her raised right hand. The installation was a marvelous cartoon mix of theater, circus, carnival, parade, and amusement park. Realistic details were everywhere, including steam puffing out of manholes.

Viewers became a part of the work as they mingled with papier-mâché and cutout figures in a complex of walk-in buildings, shops, subway cars and bridges that was installed first in Manhattan's Marlborough Gallery in the summer of 1976. As living people and papier-mâché people blended in the chaos of the minicity, it seemed as though all Manhattan and all the world were a giant cartoon.

EVENTS, HAPPENINGS, AND PERFORMANCE ART

Artists have continued to extend the boundaries of the visual arts until they can no longer be simply defined as aesthetic objects. In addition to easel paintings, there are now room-size installation pieces; in addition to traditional sculpture, there are earthworks. And, in addition to stationary art objects, there are living, moving art events.

For Swiss sculptor Jean Tinguely, life was play, movement, perpetual change. Tinguely made machines that do just about everything except work in the manner expected of machines. Although much kinetic art has celebrated science and technology, Tinguely enjoyed a mocking yet sympathetic relationship to machines and machine fallibility. "I try to distill the frenzy I see in the world, the mechanical frenzy of our joyful, industrial confusion."[11] Clearly, Tinguely was the artistic grandson of both Duchamp (see BICYCLE WHEEL, page 458) and Klee (see TWITTERING MACHINE, page 430).

In 1960, Tinguely built a large piece of mechanized sculpture that he put together from materials gathered from junkyards and stores in and around New York City. The result was a giant assemblage designed to destroy itself at the turn of a switch—which it did in the courtyard of the Museum of Modern Art in New York City on March 17, 1960. The environmental sculpture was appropriately called HOMAGE TO NEW YORK: A SELF-CONSTRUCTING, SELF-DESTRUCTING WORK OF ART. Tinguely's HOMAGE TO NEW YORK was an event, similar in its effect to a Happening.

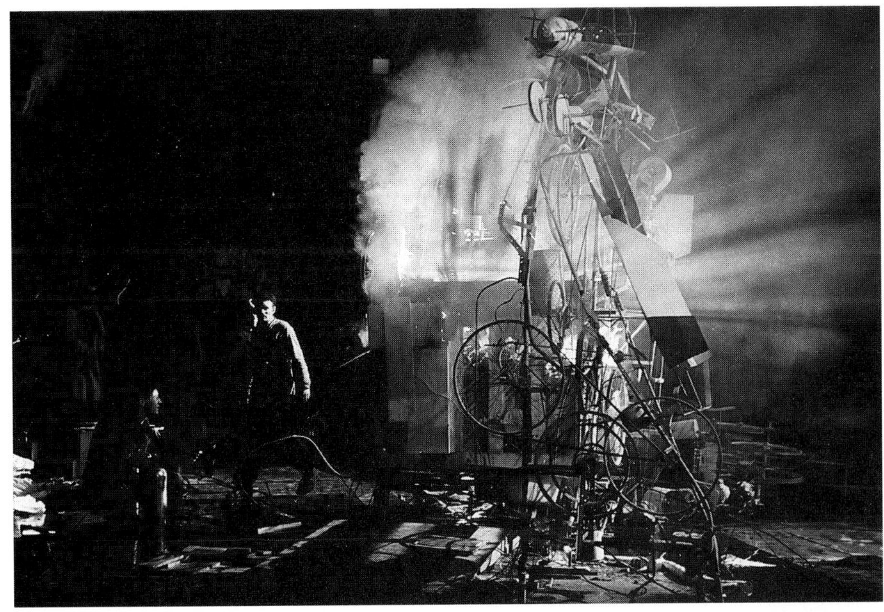

662 Jean Tinguely. HOMAGE TO NEW YORK: A SELF-CONSTRUCTING, SELF-DESTRUCTING WORK OF ART. 1960. Photograph: David Gahr.

Happenings were cooperative events in which viewers became active participants in partly planned, partly spontaneous performances that combined loose scenarios and considerable improvisation. Strictly speaking, Happenings were drama with "structure but no plot, words but no dialogue, actors but no characters, and above all, nothing logical or continuous."[12] Unlike Dada and Surrealist events, the first Happenings were frequently nihilistic, without a relieving sense of humor. No help was given the viewer, who was expected to find his or her own answers. Happenings led to more controlled, more focused types of art events.

The term Happening was first used by Allan Kaprow in the late 1950s. There were no spectators at Kaprow's Happening, HOUSEHOLD. At a preliminary meeting, participants were given parts. The action took place at an isolated rural dump, amid smoldering piles of refuse. The men built a wooden tower on a trash pile while the women constructed a nest on another mound. During the course of a series of interrelated events, the men destroyed the nest and the women retaliated by pulling down the men's tower. In the process, participants gained a new perspective on the theater of life in our time.

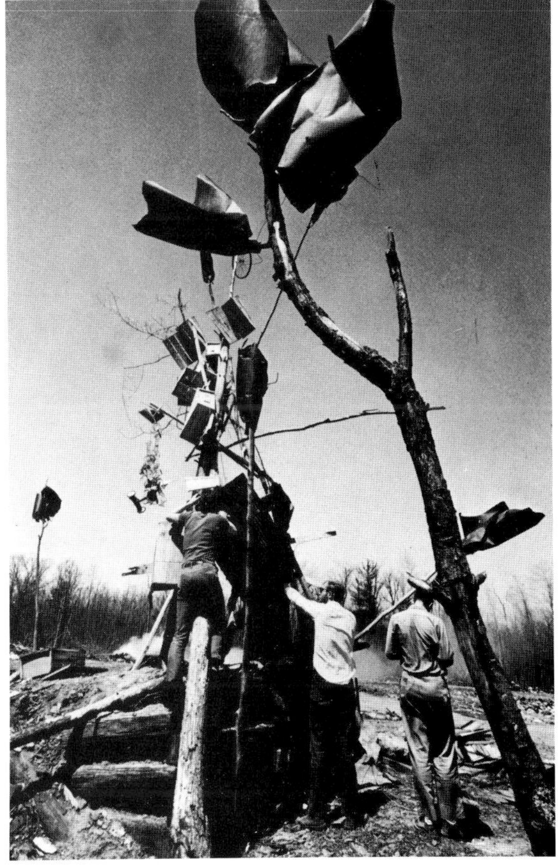

663 Allan Kaprow. HOUSEHOLD. Happening commissioned by Cornell University, performed May 1964. Photograph: Solomon A. Goldberg.

Performance art—which falls somewhere between visual art and drama—can be traced to Futur-

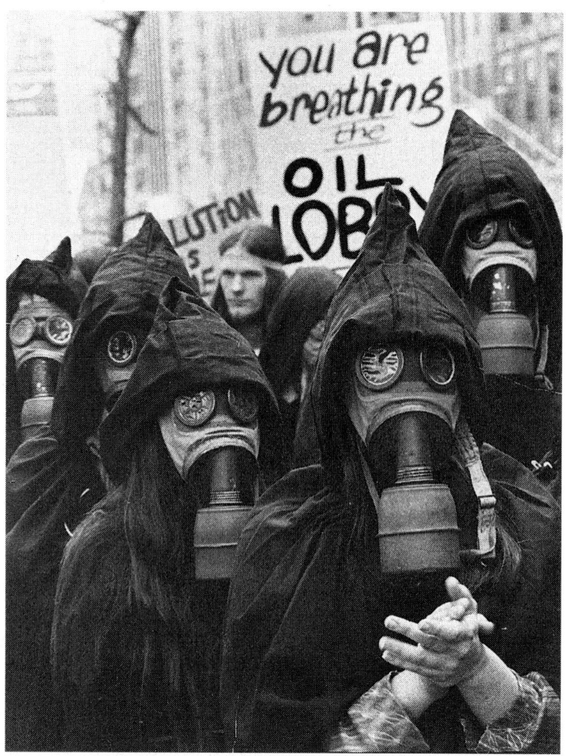

664 ANTI-AUTO POLLUTION DEMONSTRATION.
New York. 1971.
Photograph: Horst Schafer.

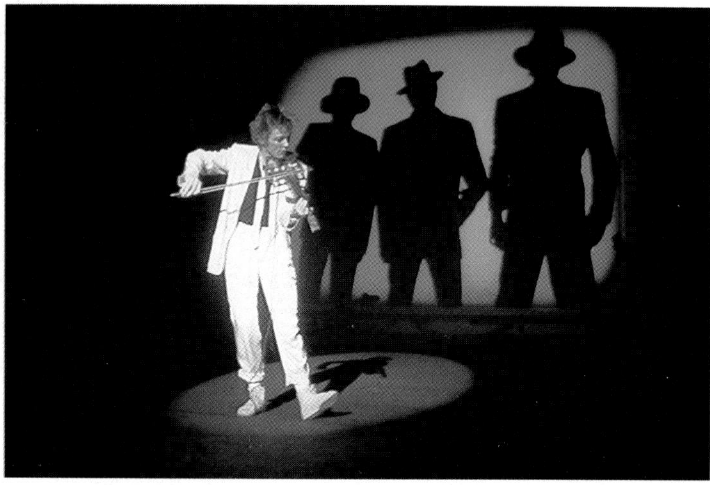

665 Laurie Anderson.
From HOME OF THE BRAVE. 1986.
Film.
Photograph courtesy of Original Artists, New York, and Les Fincher.

ist and Dada performances of the early twentieth century as well as to expressionist painting. An Abstract Expressionist painting is the frozen record of an event (the act of making a painting). The next step was easy: eliminate the record and concentrate on the event itself. In Happenings, the process was everything. The record was in the remembered experience of the participants and in a few photographs. Forms of art such as Conceptual art (page 464), which emphasize idea and process over art-as-object, are related to current modes of performance art.

Street protests can also work as performance art, as frequently was the case in the late 1960s and early 1970s. When the participants in the event have a sense of symbolic drama, the result can be highly effective, media-attracting communication, as the photograph of the ANTI-AUTO POLLUTION DEMONSTRATION suggests.

Laurie Anderson is a multitalented performance artist whose social commentary makes the familiar seem unfamiliar. Her mastery of electronic equipment has helped her to move from solo street performances to audio recordings to videos to films. HOME OF THE BRAVE, Anderson's first film, employs the performance/rock video format.

Anderson's performances are filled with stories and anecdotes that seem unrelated but add up to a strong comment on the love-hate relationship Americans have with technology. As a performance artist and musician, she depends on both body language and spoken language; her trademark is a talking violin. Anderson is a storyteller with a social conscience, a zany sense of humor, and incredible energy and imagination.

Performance art can be thought-provoking and technically innovative. In many instances, it combines the gestures of Abstract Expressionism, the ideas of Conceptualism, the images of Pop Art, and the expansiveness of installations.

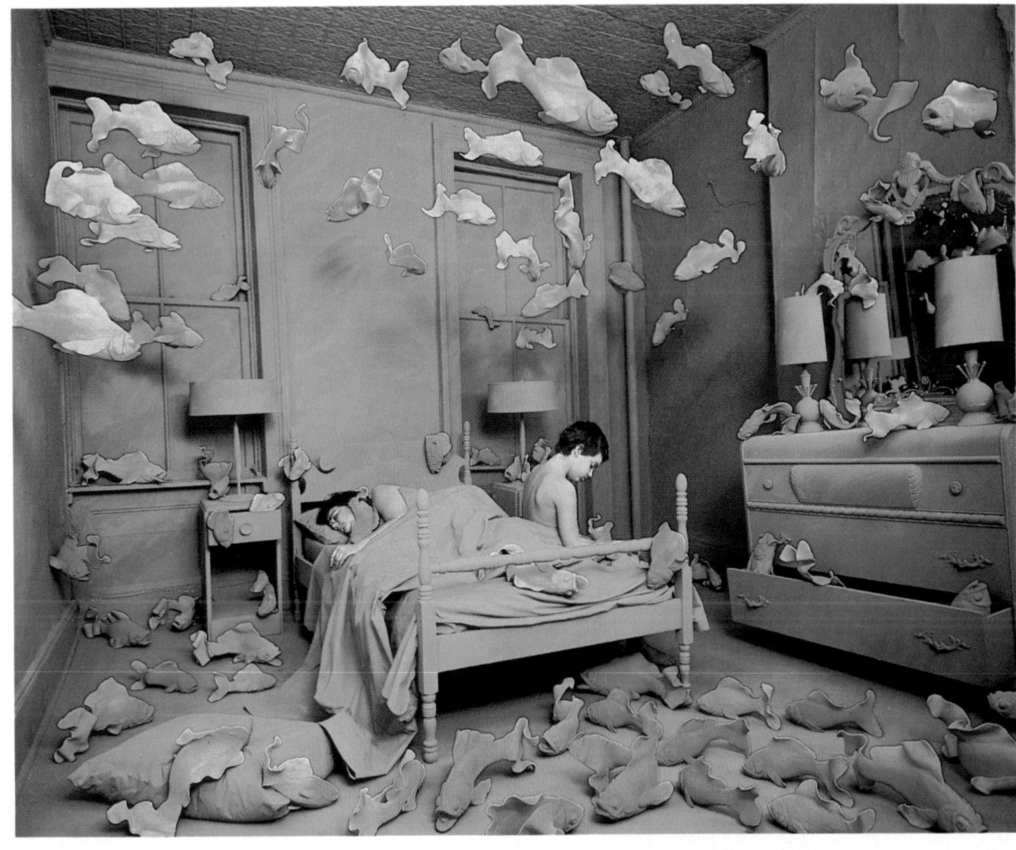

666 Sandy Skoglund.
REVENGE OF THE GOLDFISH.
1981.
Cibachrome print.
30" × 40".
Courtesy of the artist.

PHOTOGRAPHY

Photography, like performance art, crosses boundaries. Best known as a method for capturing the qualities of a moment—whether for journalism or for the family photo album—photography has not won easy recognition and support as a fine art medium. Until recently, photography has been left out of art history because of a bias in favor of more traditional, less technological media. Many critics, historians, and museums now acknowledge the importance of photography as an art form.

John Pfahl both challenges and affirms the flat character of the picture plane by carefully placing additions to his chosen subjects. In AUSTRALIAN PINES, the band of blue water between the white sand and the distant horizon appears to be on the same plane as the tree trunks in the foreground as a consequence of Pfahl's strategically placed foil wrappings. The formal composition teases eye and mind.

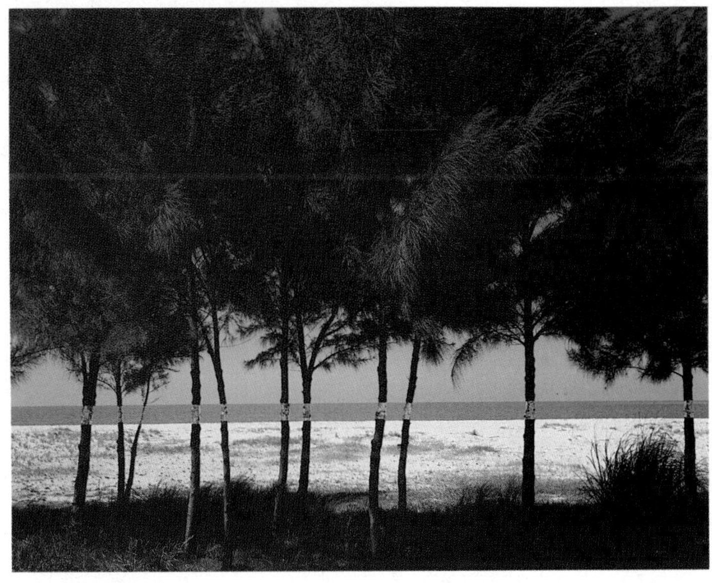

667 John Pfahl.
AUSTRALIAN PINES (FORT DESOTO, FLORIDA). 1977.
Ektacolor c-print. 8" × 10".
Courtesy of the artist.

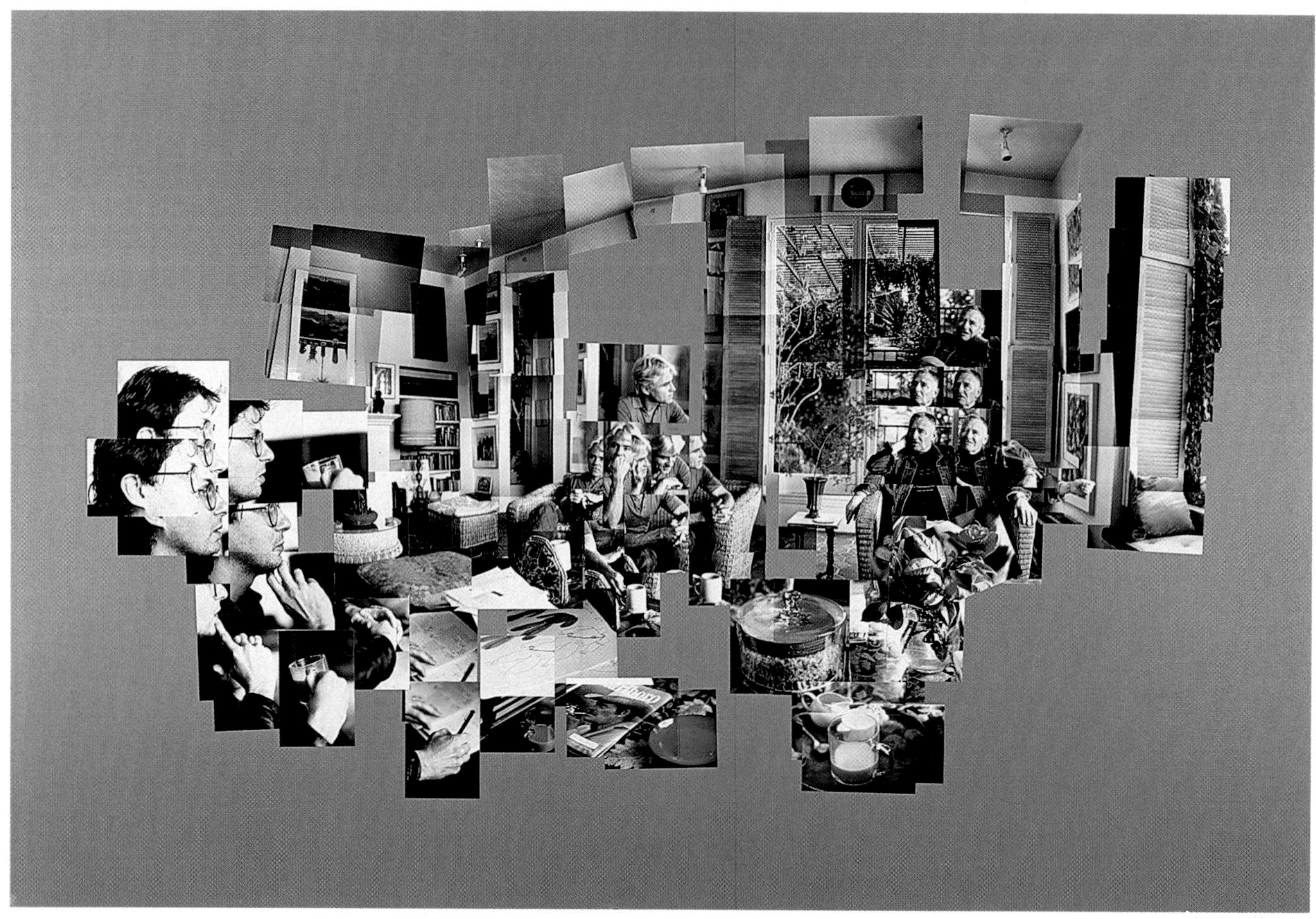

668 David Hockney.
CHRISTOPHER ISHERWOOD TALKING TO BOB HOLMAN, SANTA MONICA, MARCH 14, 1983 #3. 1983.
Photographic collage. 43½" × 64½".
The Contemporary Museum, Honolulu.

The present generation of photographers has challenged the conventions of photography in many ways; making studio setups and directing live models are among the current approaches. In her humorous REVENGE OF THE GOLDFISH (page 471), Sandy Skoglund took advantage of the inherent believability of photography to convince the viewer of the truth of her brilliantly created surreal world. The realization of her concept entailed sculpting dozens of goldfish, transforming her studio with furnishings and color, and directing models.

Qualities of light, color, and lifestyle have been central to English artist David Hockney's paintings (see page 155) and photographs. For images such as CHRISTOPHER ISHERWOOD TALKING TO BOB HOLMAN, Hockney used a Polaroid camera to construct a montage of impressions of a particular occasion. Here, as silent participants, we observe the interrelationships among people and a particular setting.

Hockney's photographs are about both the subject and the process of seeing. Our perception of this work is very different from that of a single photograph in which everything is seen at once. This montage realizes the idea often suggested as central to Cubism: the simultaneous presentation of multiple views. It recalls Cubist portraits and the multiple views of Eakins's photographs (see page 70).

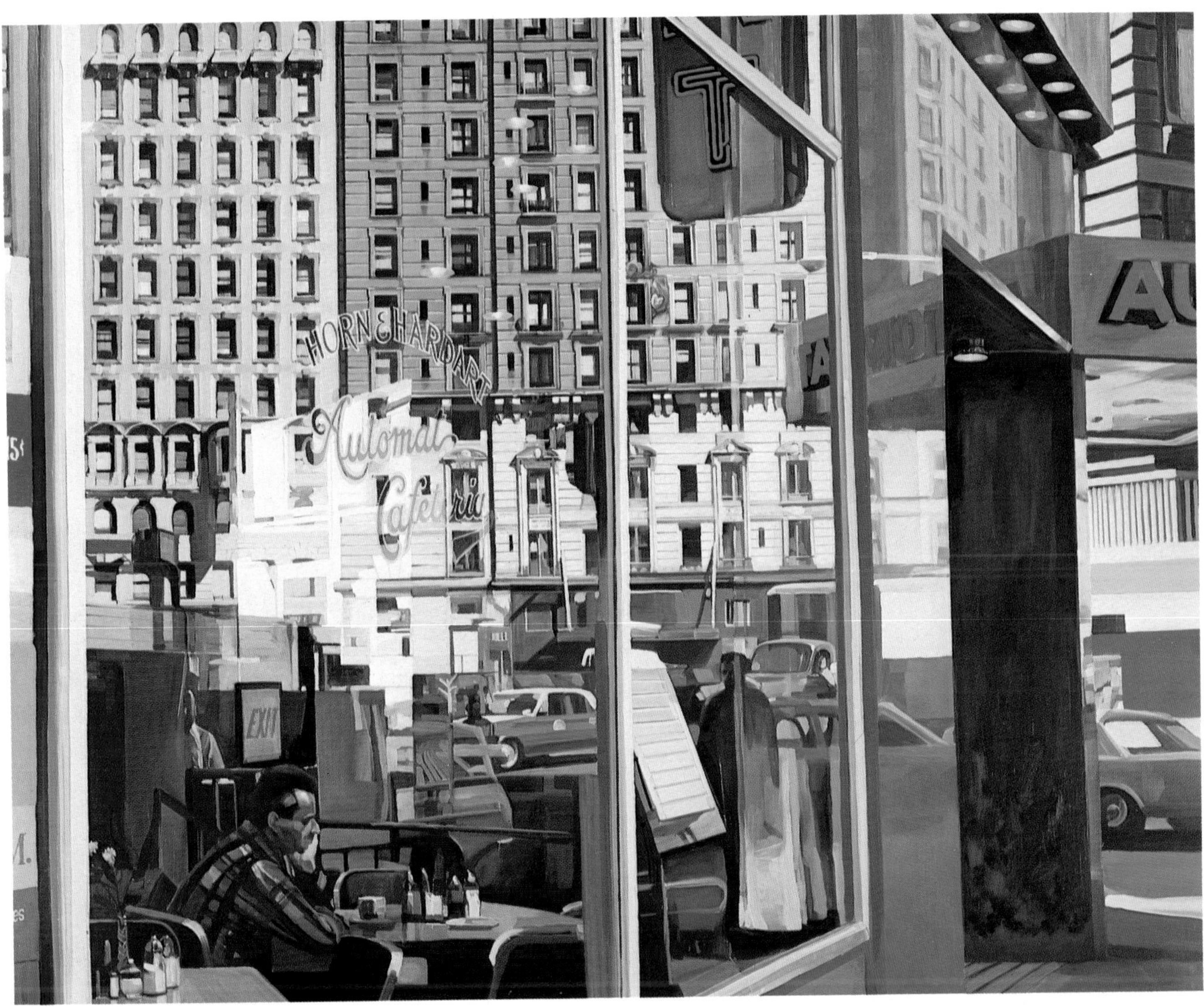

669 Richard Estes.
HORN AND HARDART AUTOMAT. 1967.
Oil on masonite. 48" × 60".
Collection of Mr. and Mrs. Stephen D. Paine, Boston.

PHOTOREALIST PAINTING AND SUPERREALIST SCULPTURE

Just as painting has influenced photography, so photography has had its influences on painting. A major example is the impersonal, highly realistic quality that is central to the late-sixties, post-Pop style of painting called Photorealism.

Despite the movements that rejected realism in favor of nonrepresentational form, it was inevitable that some artists would continue to paint realistically while others would return to some aspect of art's role as a recorder of appearances. The principal difference between the paintings of Photorealists and most earlier realist painting is that the Photorealists are not telling stories; most of them, including Richard Estes, choose subjects with no narrative significance. A notable exception is Audrey Flack (see page 45), whose Photorealist paintings contain objects loaded with psychological symbolism. The cool objectivity of Photorealism shows the influence of Pop Art, but Photorealism does not use Pop's mass-media subjects.

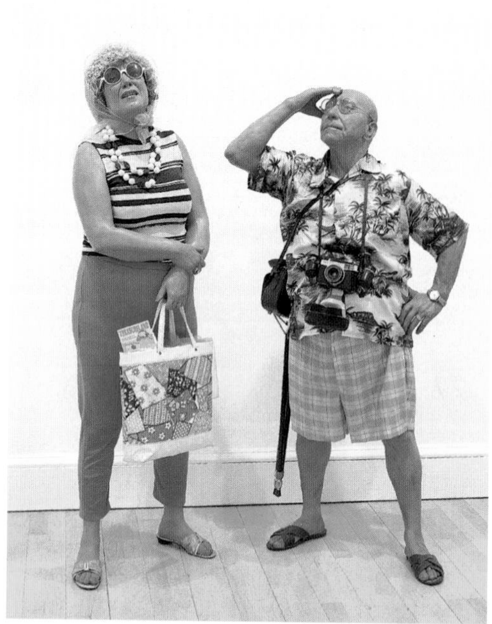

670 Duane Hanson.
TOURISTS. 1970.
Fiberglass and polychromed polyester. 64" × 65" × 67".
Scottish National Gallery of Modern Art.

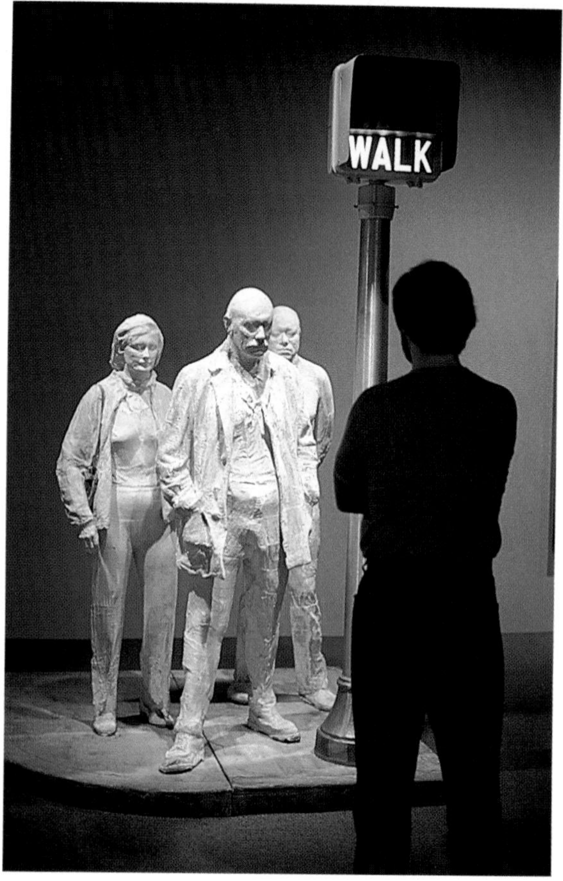

671 George Segal.
WALK, DON'T WALK. 1976.
Museum installation, with viewer. Plaster, cement, metal, painted wood, and electric light. 104" × 72" × 72".
Collection of Whitney Museum of American Art, New York. Purchase, with funds from the Louis and Bessie Adler Foundation, Inc., Seymour M. Klein, President, the Gilman Foundation, Inc., and the National Endowment for the Arts (79.4).

In preparation for each of his paintings, Estes takes many photographs. He then paints complex composite images of common cityscapes, often devoid of people but full of the character of urban life. Estes painted HORN AND HARDART AUTOMAT with a traditional brush, giving the surface an active and personal paint quality when viewed at close range. His sensitive application of abstract values in each composition makes Estes one of the most consistently rewarding of the artists who work with photographically inspired realism.

A sculptural counterpart to Photorealism can be seen in the work of Duane Hanson. His super-realist figures, cast in polyester and fiberglass and then painted in minute detail, are unsettling when experienced face-to-face. Viewers marvel at the incredible technique, but for Hanson, technique is a means, not an end. Hanson not only imitates reality, he sometimes presents ideas about reality that are unpleasant. He takes a documentary approach to realist sculpture. His figures are ordinary people, with no trace of idealism. Carefully selected clothing and other props are important parts of each of Hanson's pieces, and he gives considerable thought to relationships among figure, clothing, and articles.

Hanson's figures are so intensely realistic, having lifelike hair, clothing, and skin, that people who come upon them often begin to interact with them before realizing that they are not alive.

TOURISTS is a pointed social comment on Americans in general and American tourists in particular. The overweight figures, encumbered with possessions, look like people we know or have seen many times. The content of this piece suggests a love-hate relationship with middle-class America.

Similar to Hanson's figures are those by John DeAndrea (see page 204), who uses the same materials and a similar technique to achieve a different goal. DeAndrea's figures are usually beautiful young adults without clothing or other evidence of their life experience, while Hanson's are very much a part of the everyday world.

Both Hanson and DeAndrea followed the lead of George Segal, a sculptor with a more symbolic approach. Segal makes "sculptural situations" by combining life-size plaster casts of people with props that designate particular environments. Because he doesn't paint the detailed features of his people, Segal's expressionless white figures become types rather than individuals. Segal's figures are a part of the viewers' space, rather than separated by a pedestal or frame. With works such as WALK, DON'T WALK he entices us into contemplating the character of life today.

POST-MODERN ARCHITECTURE

The history of architecture has been yet another series of refinements followed by overturnings, with the young and the imaginative always finding some degree of inadequacy in the work of their immediate predecessors. A growing discontent with the sterile anonymity of the mid-century International style led many architects to rebel and to look once again at meaning, history, tradition, and context. Their departure from architectural modernism was dubbed Post-Modern in the late 1970s.

Post-Modernists feel that the unadorned functional purity of the International Style makes all buildings look the same, offers no identity relative to purpose, no symbolism, no meaning, no mystery, no excitement. Post-Modern architects enjoy the very qualities of modern life that the proponents of machine aesthetics sought to escape: complexity, ambiguity, contradiction, nostalgia, and the rich vulgarity of popular taste.

Post-Modern would become the catchall label of the 1980s, applied in retrospect to much of the art of the 1960s and 1970s. It is a term for an art based on freedom of choice and tolerance. Post-Modernists embrace an eclectic mix of historical influences, decorative tendencies, expressionism, symbolism, and the popular styles of architecture and applied arts enjoyed by the general public. They divorce themselves and their work from the accepted meanings of "traditional" and "modern" and do not value one more than the other. The attitudes associated with Post-Modernism are a part of all the arts, and they are particularly recognized in literature. In the visual arts, Post-Modern is best known and most easily seen in architecture.

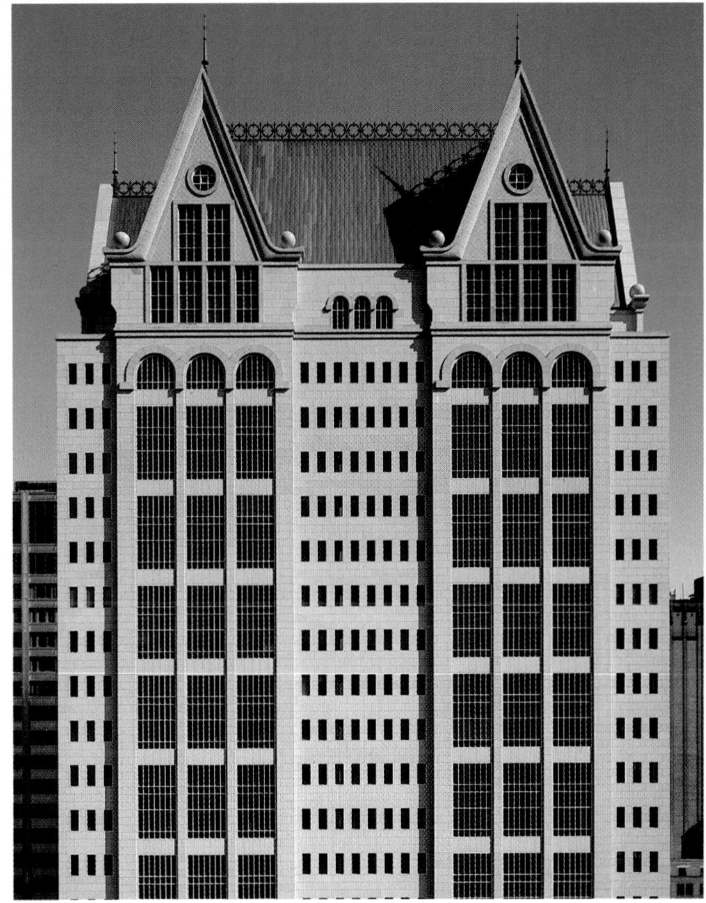

672 John Burgee Architects with Philip Johnson. 190 SOUTH LASALLE STREET. Chicago. 1987.
Photograph: Hedrich-Blessing

Architect Philip Johnson's career has spanned both the modern and Post-Modern movements. He has been known since mid-century as an advocate of modernism and, with Mies van der Rohe, designed the SEAGRAM BUILDING (page 258), a landmark of International Style. But the pure glass-enclosed box, repeated a thousand times in cities throughout the world, became too severe, too limited for Johnson and his younger colleagues. In high-rise buildings like 190 SOUTH LASALLE

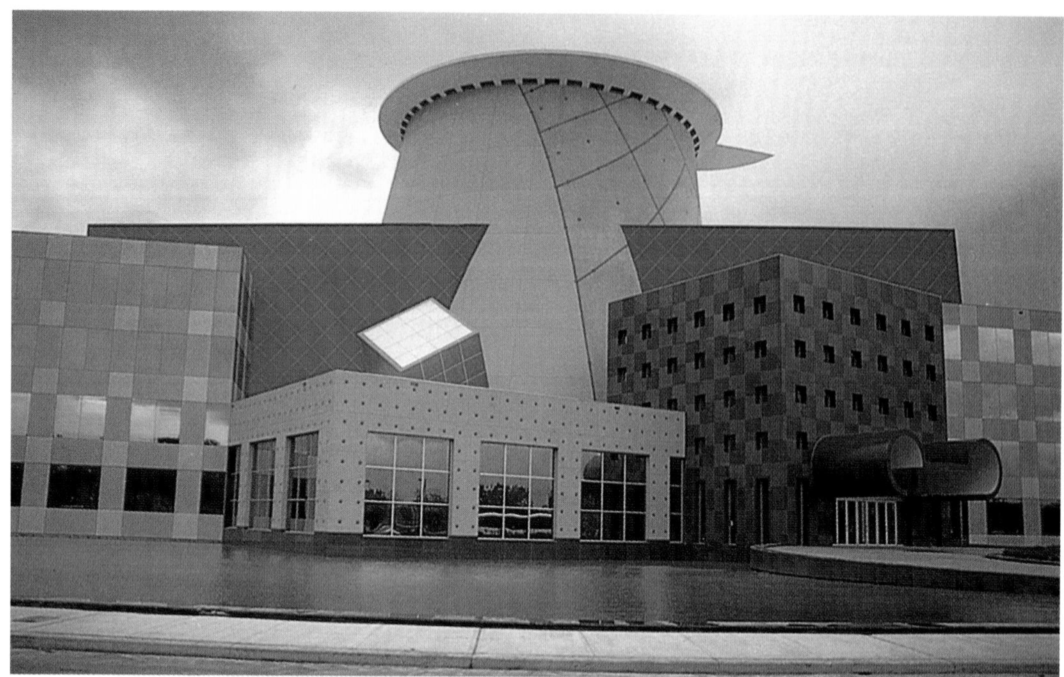

673 Arata Isozaki.
TEAM DISNEY BUILDING.
Florida. 1990.
Photograph: © Charles Jencks.

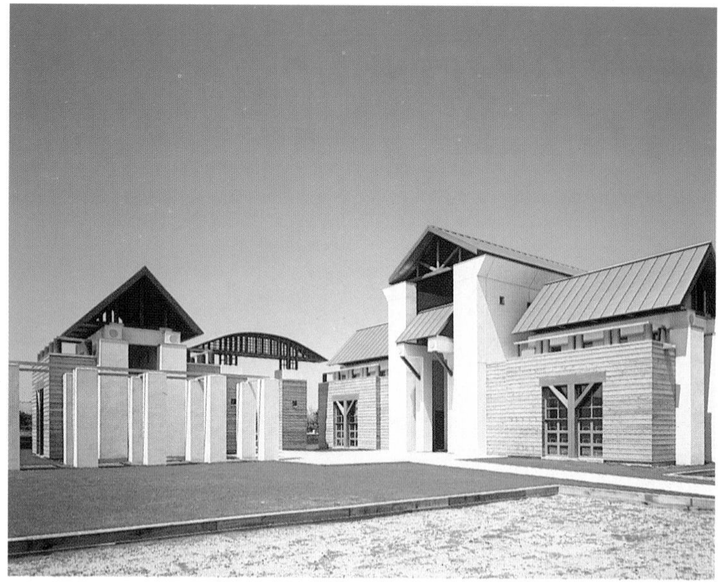

674 Michael Graves.
ENVIRONMENTAL
EDUCATION CENTER.
Liberty State Park, Jersey City, New Jersey. 1980.

STREET in Chicago, he reversed himself. Here Johnson and John Burgee brought back warmth and delight with a decorative upper story that brings together elements from several historical styles.

The architecture of Michael Graves reflects a personal blend of traditional classicism and inventive irony. His ENVIRONMENTAL EDUCATION CENTER is both formal and playful. The Center consists of a series of wood-frame pavilions that contain exhibitions. The combined colors and textures of simple, traditional materials—gray cedar siding, yellow stucco, red-brown timbers, and copper roofs—create articulated sculptural form.

When Japanese architect Arata Isozaki made his first trip to Europe in 1960, he expected to admire the great modern architecture of such pioneers as Le Corbusier (page 440). Instead, he became fascinated by the classical architectural spaces of ancient Rome, by medieval towns, and by the villas of Andrea Palladio (see page 357).

Isozaki, who calls himself a "guerilla architect," seeks to create buildings with mystery, excitement, and surprise rather than quiet beauty. His TEAM DISNEY BUILDING shows a playful departure from the cool rationality of modernism.

CENSORSHIP

Congress shall make no law ... abridging the freedom of speech, or of the press.

From the first amendment to the *Constitution*

In the United States, the word *speech* has been broadly interpreted to include all forms of expression. The first amendment guarantee of freedom of expression is part of the foundation of our democracy.

Censorship and *freedom* are words that raise issues about which people feel strongly and hold widely differing opinions. Freedom without responsibility leads to wanton disregard for the welfare of others, and irresponsible censorship kills creative freedom, the wellspring of art.

Censoring is the prohibiting of what is considered morally, politically, or otherwise objectionable. In the United States, artists and writers have the freedom to paint, photograph, and write what they please. The issue of censorship does not usually arise until works that offend some portion of the population are displayed or distributed in public places.

Censorship has most often been an issue when publicly supported institutions or public funds are involved. It is one thing to be broad-minded and opposed to censorship in theory and quite another to confront something one finds morally offensive.

The National Endowment for the Arts (NEA) was established by Congress in 1965 "to help create and sustain not only a climate encouraging freedom of thought, imagination, and inquiry, but also the material conditions facilitating the release of this creative talent." In the following twenty-five years, over 85,000 individual and group projects were partially or fully funded by the NEA. Of these grants, only about twenty were controversial.

In the late 1980s and early 1990s, the NEA received publicity that stirred considerable debate about how to protect artistic freedom while preserving public values. Many political leaders felt that public money should not be spent to support any art that offended the majority of taxpayers.

Potentially offensive subjects include racism, police brutality, unpopular political views, feminism, sex, homosexuality, and AIDS. Where should the line be drawn? What exactly does freedom of expression mean, and how far does it go?

The United States Supreme Court has upheld the right to ban obscenity in speech, writing, and art; the problem lies in determining what is obscene. The 1973 California case *Miller v. California* held that a work is obscene if the "average person applying contemporary community standards" would find it obscene and if "the work taken as a whole lacks serious literary, artistic, political or scientific value." While this landmark case provided a legal precedent, it raised as many questions as it answered. Who decides what is obscene and what is art? Should public funds be used only for art that is acceptable to *all* taxpayers? Or *most* taxpayers? Would that leave us an enlightening variety of art?

As a form of government, democracy is often less orderly than a dictatorship. Democracy encourages free exchange of ideas and freedom of expression—and disagreement is common. Dictatorship depends on controlling or censoring ideas and expressions. In Hitler's Germany, there was no tolerance of art or ideas that differed from the official position. Many major artists had their work scorned, banned, and even destroyed by the Nazi regime.

Censorship can be a problem for publishers and writers who seek to bring this issue to public attention. The printers of *Artforms* refused to print a 1990 issue of an art magazine as it was first submitted because it contained a photograph by Robert Mapplethorpe that press executives deemed pornographic. The photograph showed a girl, about four years old, sitting in a way that revealed she wasn't wearing anything under her dress. Is such an image a depiction of the innocence of a child, or is it child pornography? If the photograph had been taken by almost anyone other than Mapplethorpe it might have drawn little or no attention. Mapplethorpe, known for his technically superb, sensuous photographs of flowers and people, evoked an enormous public outcry with his 1989 exhibition that contained a number of photographs with homoerotic content.

Recently, an illustrator of elementary school textbooks was told to remove udders from pictures of cows because udders are sexually explicit.

When a museum curator or gallery director chooses to show works by some artists and not others, are those who are not selected victims of censorship? Most people would say no, the experts are simply doing their job.

All art involves selection—the process of retaining the significant and discarding the irrelevant. If artists tell the truth as they see it, they may inevitably offend some people. But this may be a small price to pay to protect the foundation of liberty—the tolerance and protection of all points of view.

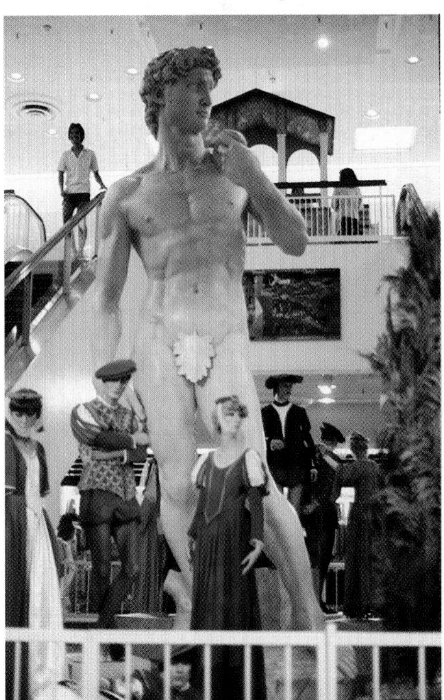

675 Department store DAVID—censored.

CHAPTER 24

Recent Diversity

In the late twentieth century, people of the world have witnessed widespread disintegration of centralized authority, the collapse of political empires, and challenges to long-standing social, religious, and scientific dogma. Art reflects this breakdown of authority in the questioning of the notion that the history of art flows as a single current. A more fitting metaphor than "mainstream" for present-day art might be "delta," the network of branching streams where a river meets the ocean.

In the 1980s, four decades after the center of the gallery and museum art world shifted from Paris to New York, there was a new, less complete shift, a move away from New York to regional art centers in the United States and around the world.

Since the late eighties, what had been an emphasis on form has for many become an emphasis on content. Among the streams visible in contemporary art, we find renewed political and environmental consciousness, multiculturalism, feminism, and the reinterpretation of earlier forms of art. It is not surprising that the often abrasive and confusing qualities of modern life have found full force in contemporary art. Some people find recent art hard to deal with partly for this reason; others find the most avant-garde work exciting and challenging.

Each generation of artists addresses what it perceives as the inadequacies of the previous generation. Since any solution can only be partial, each generation's shortcomings provide opportunities for the succeeding generation. For some, the issues are primarily questions of form; for others, they are questions of content.

The controlled, formal work of the 1960s and 1970s created an emotional vacuum that erupted in the next generation. The 1980s produced a strong reaction. Shock value was often emphasized over visual form, personality over lasting value.

However, a number of contemporary artists are thoughtful creators of works with potential staying power. Recent developments in art, like those in science and other fields, are often too close to us in time to be perceived clearly, but by learning to "read" the art of our time, we can become more fully aware of what is happening in the world of today.

Each person's creative output is more important than any category or label we apply to it. You will notice that many of the artists discussed in this chapter could be placed in more than one category, and most would prefer not to be categorized at all.

ISSUE-RELATED ART

A good place to begin looking at contemporary art is with the work of Neo-Expressionist Anselm Kiefer. The West German artist combines the aggressive paint application of Abstract Expressionism with nineteenth-century feelings for history and mythology. In contrast to Abstract Expressionists who emphasize aesthetic issues and downplay content, Kiefer gives equal attention to moral and aes-

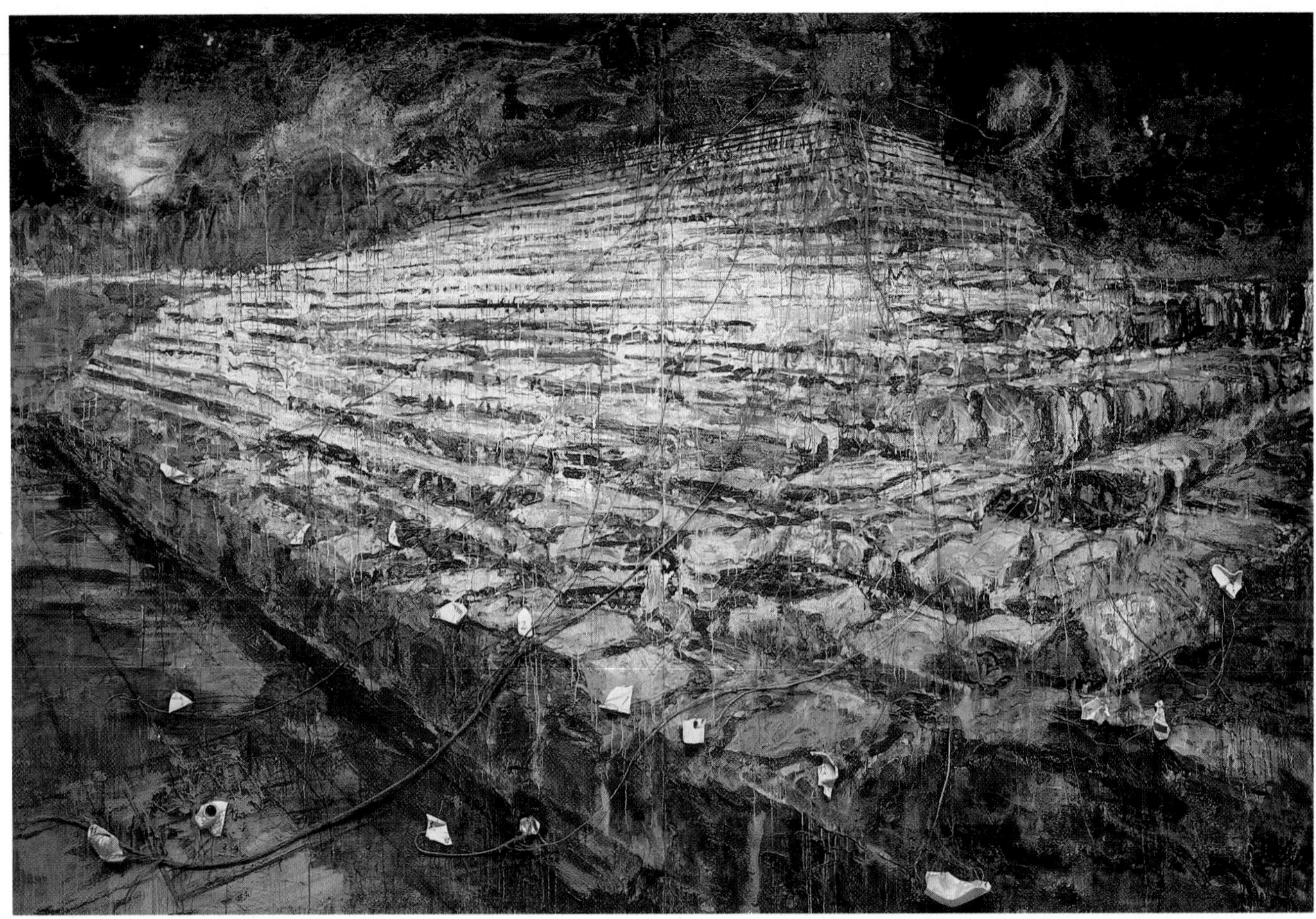

676 Anselm Kiefer.
OSIRIS AND ISIS. 1985-1987.
Mixed media on canvas. 150" × 220½" × 6½".
San Francisco Museum of Modern Art.
Purchased through a gift of Jean Stein, by exchange,
the Mrs. Paul L. Wattis Fund, and the Doris and Donald Fisher Fund.

thetic issues. His paintings, loaded with symbolism, mythology, and religion, probe the German national conscience and reveal the grim confusion felt by many postwar Germans. Kiefer sees art as having the power to provide a spiritual catharsis; yet his disturbing work presents more questions than answers.

OSIRIS AND ISIS joins an ancient Egyptian myth with the reality of nuclear energy and the potential of nuclear destruction. Osiris symbolized the indestructible creative forces of nature; according to legend, the god was slain and cut into pieces by his evil brother. Isis, sister and wife of Osiris, found and buried the pieces, making each burial place sacred. In another version of the story, Isis collected the pieces and brought Osiris back to life. In Kiefer's huge painting, the goddess Isis (in the form of a TV circuit board) sits on top of a pyramid, sending out a network of wires attached to fragments of the dismembered Osiris. The heavily textured surface, consisting of paint, mud, earth, rock, tar, and bits of ceramic and metal, intensifies the image's disturbing power. Some see Kiefer's angst-filled, end-of-the-world paintings as dreary and depressing; others feel Kiefer is awakening his fellow Germans to their tragic heritage and helping them to move beyond guilt to an era of renewed hope.

American painter Neil Jenney also exhibits a

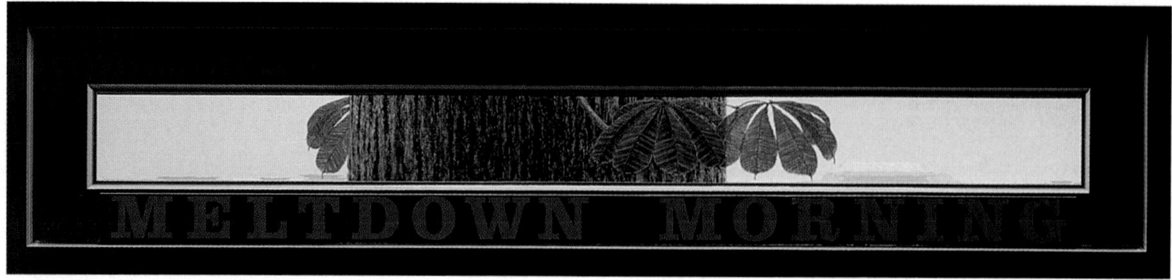

677 Neil Jenney.
MELTDOWN MORNING. 1975.
Oil on panel. 25⅜" × 112½".
Philadelphia Museum of Art. Purchased: Samuel S. White III and Vera White Collection (by exchange) and funds contributed by the Daniel W. Dietrich Foundation in honor of Mrs. H. Gates Lloyd.

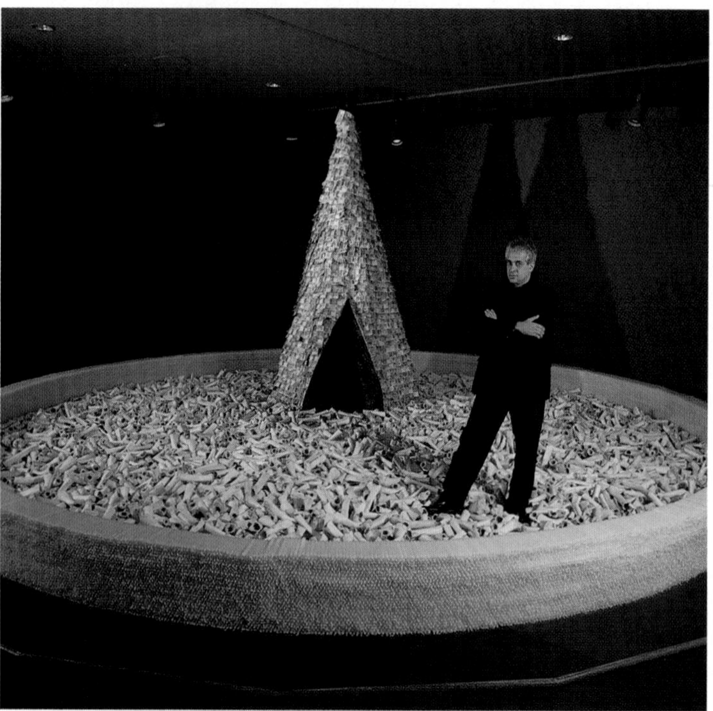

678 Cildo Meireles.
OLVIDO (OBLIVION). 1990.
Mixed media.
Photograph: © 1993 by Claudio Edinger.

social conscience in his concern for the environmental destruction facing the planet. Jenney's best-known works of the 1970s and 1980s are a series of very narrow, horizontal paintings, heavily framed in black wood, with the titles often painted right on the frames. One of his favorites is MELTDOWN MORNING, a centered section of tree trunk with a few leaves against a background of poisonous-looking haze. Jenney's stark juxtaposition of nature with a subtle reminder of impending destruction makes a forceful statement. At first we see natural beauty, then comes the startling realization of the ominous threat.

Brazilian artist Cildo Meireles communicates his concerns about social destruction through the heightened impact of large-scale installations such as OLVIDO (OBLIVION). A tepeelike form shingled with paper money stands on a deep layer of bones—symbols of death. Candles, important to Catholic religious practice, form an encircling wall. The leaflike money on the tepee is currency from all the nations of North, Central, and South America in which members of the once predominant native cultures are being wiped out; the money represents the greed and exploitation that have doomed generations of Native Americans. The installation includes a subtle sound track that evokes sounds of chanting priests or perhaps distant traffic—but is actually the sound of chain saws rapidly destroying rain forests.

From the other side of the world, a humorous piece suggests the widespread influence of installation art. The communal apartment, a familiar environment in the former Soviet Union, is a place where families live crowded together in small, dimly lit units, sharing a kitchen and standing in line to get into the bathroom. Imagine yourself living in a cramped communal apartment and becoming so depressed, frustrated, and claustrophobic that you build a catapult to propel yourself through the roof, leaving your shoes behind in the escape!

Such a visualization is the essence of Russian artist Ilya Kabakov's installation THE MAN WHO FLEW INTO SPACE FROM HIS APARTMENT. This piece is a metaphor for the life he and millions of other Russians have lived, and for the recent moves by the peoples of the Iron Curtain countries to break out of a life-denying political and social system. Russian artists determined to make critical social comments have long worked in secrecy because Communist controls outlawed any style except social realism. With the breakup of the Communist Party stranglehold, Kabakov has been able to move from working in secrecy to receiving international recognition.

Billy Curmano is a performance artist whose concern over the pollution of the Mississippi River led to an ongoing piece called SWIMMIN' THE RIVER. Between July 1987 and August 1992, he swam 1183 miles of the river in what is projected to be a six-year performance piece. He began at the headwaters at Lake Itaska in Minnesota and, amid fanfare and publicity, made daily rest stops along the way. In August 1992 he reached St. Louis, where the Mayor proclaimed August 18 as Billy X. Curmano Day. Curmano's witty bravado and the accompanying publicity bring his political-ecological message to the attention of the novelty-hungry media, who become unwitting partners in the process of raising public awareness. This piece is as much conceptual art as it is a performance.

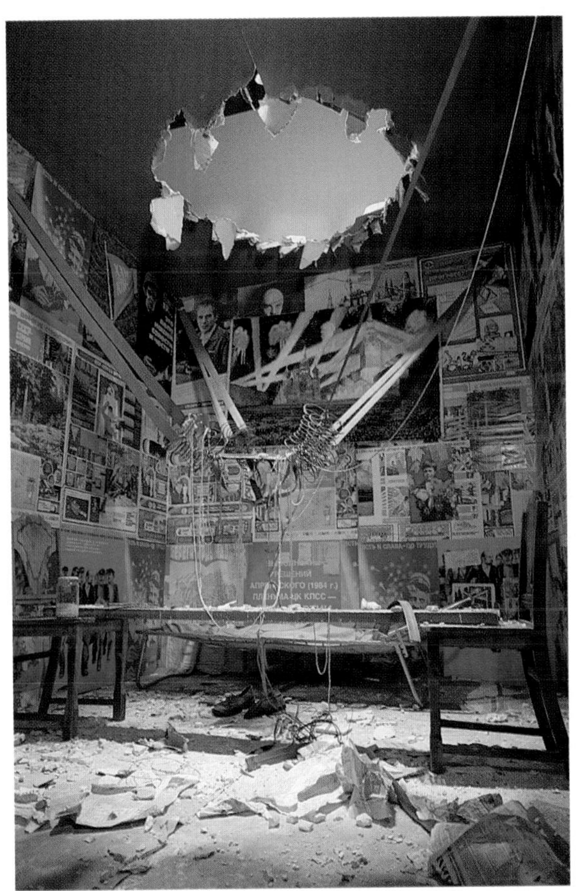

680 Ilya Kabakov.
THE MAN WHO FLEW INTO SPACE FROM HIS APARTMENT.
A room from "TEN CHARACTERS." 1981-1988.
Photograph: © Katherine Lambert. All rights reserved.

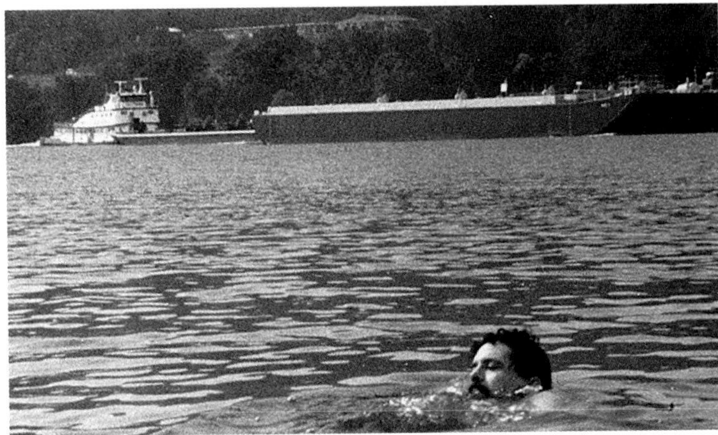

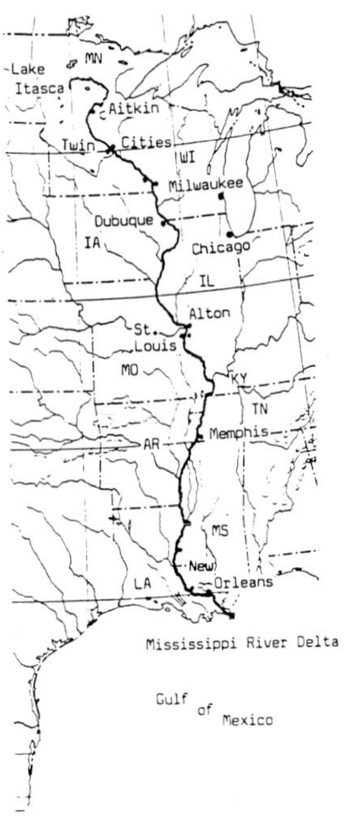

679 Billy Curmano.
SWIMMIN' THE RIVER. Mississippi River. Begun 1987.
Performance.
Map: 2,552-mile performance channel.
Photograph: Mary Coughlan.
© 1989 Billy Curmano.

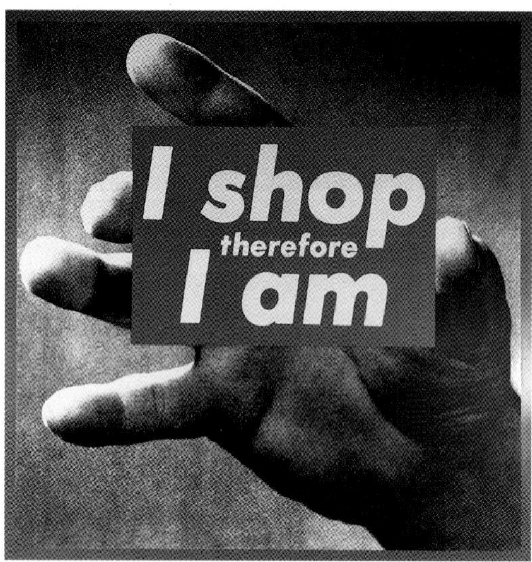

681 Barbara Kruger.
UNTITLED (I SHOP THEREFORE I AM). 1987.
Photographic silkscreen/vinyl. 111" × 113".
Private collection. Courtesy of Mary Boone Gallery, New York.

Barbara Kruger combines black-and-white photographs with texts that appear to consist of words cut from magazines or newspapers. While her words and images each have meanings of their own, taken together they have further implications, as in UNTITLED. Kruger uses elements from mass media to create images that call attention to major social and psychological concerns.

California artist Rupert Garcia opposes political repression from the perspective of experience. Garcia studied art at San Francisco State College during the turbulent late sixties, when a student strike almost closed the campus. It was then that he realized the important role artists can play in bringing about political reform. Garcia adopts and alters photographs from magazines and newspapers, emphasizing and simplifying shapes to create bold, graphic images, many of which are printed as posters. His process of simplifying and abstracting creates memorable interacting shapes of vibrant contrasting colors. For his pastel MEXICO, CHILE, SOWETO, Garcia was inspired by two separate news photographs. He combined the shape of the slain figure from one and the soldier's feet from the other to create an image of a victim of officially sanctioned brutality.

My art is committed to the paradox that in using mass-media I am using a source which I despise and with which I am at war. In using the images of mass-media I am taking an art form whose motives are debased, exploitive, and indifferent to human welfare, and setting it into a totally new moral context. I am, so to speak, reversing the process by which mass-media betray the masses, and betraying the images of mass-media to moral purposes for which they were not designed: the art of social protest.[1]

Among the century's most powerful antiwar statements are Picasso's GUERNICA (page 443) and Arneson's NUCLEAR WAR HEAD (page 16).

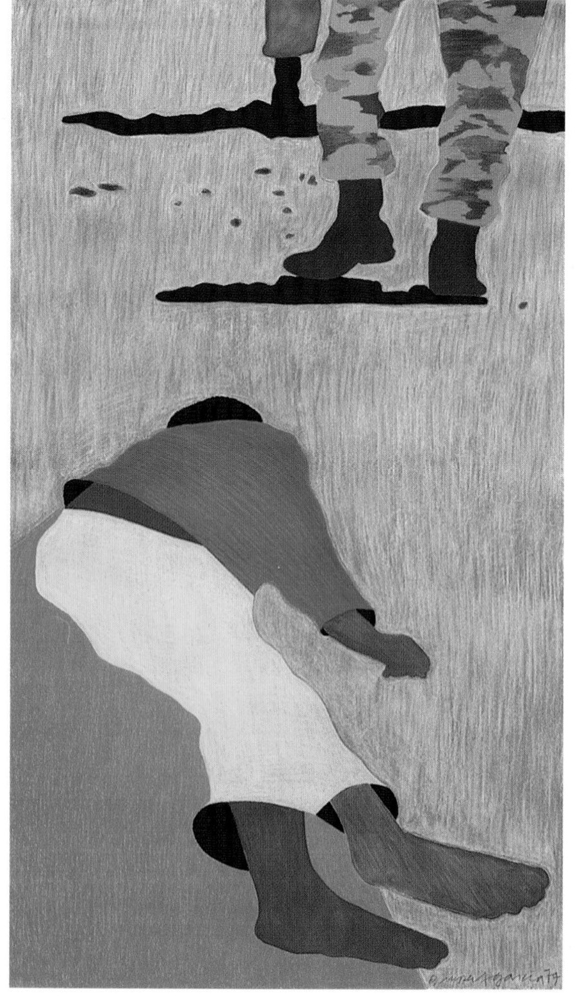

682 Rupert Garcia.
MEXICO, CHILE, SOWETO. 1977.
Pastel on paper. 51" × 36".
Courtesy of the artist and Rena Bransten Gallery, Daniel Saxon Gallery, and Galerie Claude Samuel.

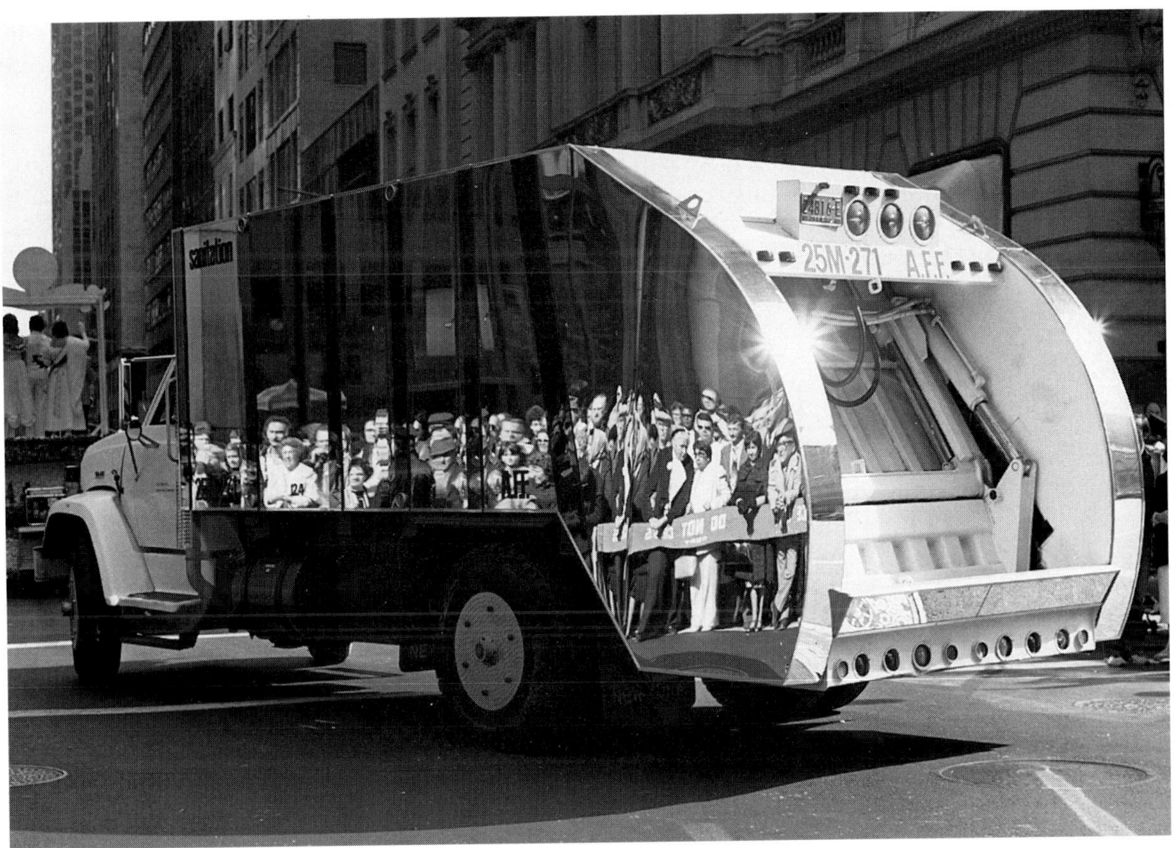

683 Mierle Laderman Ukeles.
THE SOCIAL MIRROR. New York. 1983.
20-cubic-yard garbage collection truck fitted with hand-tempered glass mirror with additional strips of mirrored acrylic.
Photograph: The New York City Department of Sanitation.

COMMUNITY ARTISTS

Some artists who address social issues in their work prefer to operate in a context of direct community involvement. *Community artists* are innovators and problem solvers who forgo the process of making precious art objects in order to use artistic and organizational skills to empower the people of their communities to interact productively in creative processes. The interaction between artists and others becomes an important dimension of the work.

New York's garbage crisis in the seventies and her own experiences as a mother led Mierle Laderman Ukeles to consider the importance of maintenance work. Since 1978, Ukeles has been an unsalaried artist-in-residence for the New York City Department of Sanitation. Her self-effacing, conceptual approach to art permeates everything she does. In 1979 and 1980 she joined the daily rounds of sanitation workers and their supervisors; then for eleven months she completed an eight-hour-a-day performance piece in which she shook the hands of the more than 8,500 workers taking care of New York's mountains of garbage. With each handshake she said, "Thank you for keeping New York City alive."

For a parade, Ukeles covered the sides of a garbage truck with mirrors, creating THE SOCIAL MIRROR. The piece enabled people to see themselves as the starting point of the process, the source of the garbage. More recently she has been involved with the design of a "maintenance installation" intended to provide new insight into the drama of waste disposal.

When photographer and photojournalist Jim

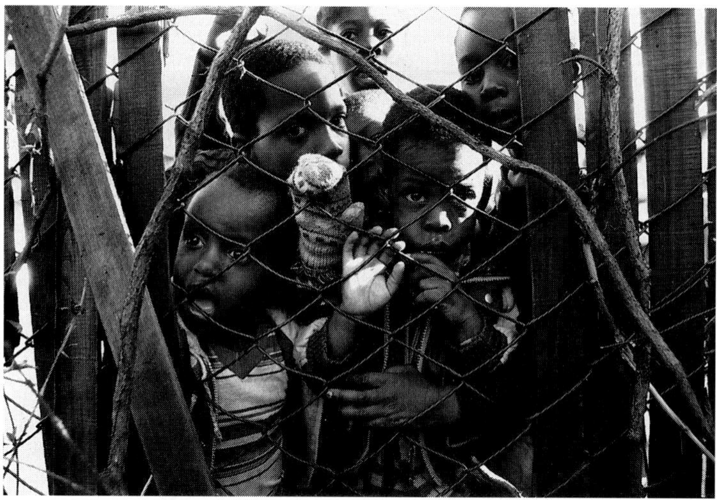

684 Jim Hubbard.
SHUT IN AND SHUT OUT. 1987.
Photograph.
Number 33 from *American Refugees.*

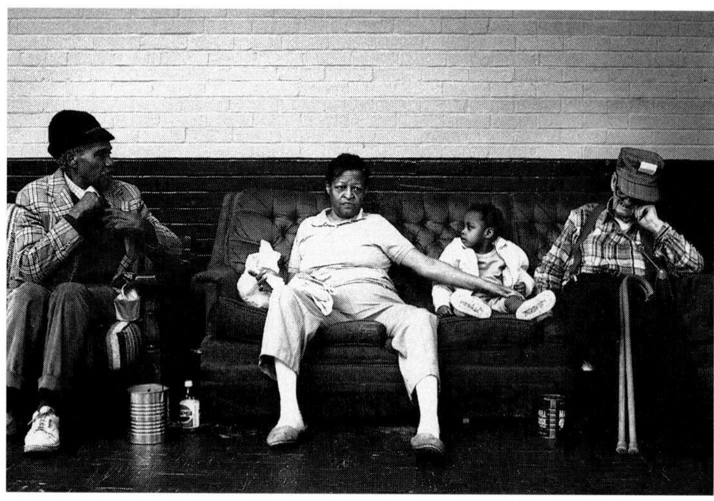

685 Norman Heflin, age 8.
COMMON LIVING AREA. 1990.
Photograph, silver print. 11" × 14".
Courtesy of Shooting Back, Inc., Washington, D.C.

Hubbard began to document the lives of the homeless in Washington, D.C., he was increasingly drawn to the children and became obsessed with finding a way to end their plight. Whenever he photographed them, as in SHUT IN AND SHUT OUT, he saw that children were fascinated with his camera and wanted to hold it and look through it. Their curiosity and enthusiasm inspired Hubbard to develop a program that would enable them to document their own lives.

He realized that teaching children creative thinking skills could give them a much-needed chance to succeed in the world. He called his new education and media center Shooting Back, Inc. (Asked why he was photographing his surroundings, a child had replied, "I'm shooting back.")

Hubbard notes that while professionals who document the poor and homeless generally emphasize pathos and tragedy, children's views are far more balanced. Consider COMMON LIVING AREA and BOXCAR POSE; children tend to photograph what they see, without distortion, often showing the beauty and good times along with the despair and violence.

In many cities, the American mural movement of the 1960s developed into a community-based means of expressing cultural heritage, unity, desires, and needs. In California, murals have been influenced by the student movement and counterculture. The American mural movement brought about renewed interest in its predecessors: the Mexican mural movement of the 1920s and 1930s (see page 445) and the wall paintings created in the United States under the WPA.

Los Angeles has become the new mural center of the world. Many of the murals are painted by teams of people that include both community artists and nonartists from schools, community centers, or organizations. These murals communicate key experiences and concerns of the individuals and groups who participate. The murals are the most democratic works of art this country has produced.

Since the early seventies, Judy Baca, founder of Citywide Murals of Los Angeles, has coordinated the design and painting of murals. In 1976, the

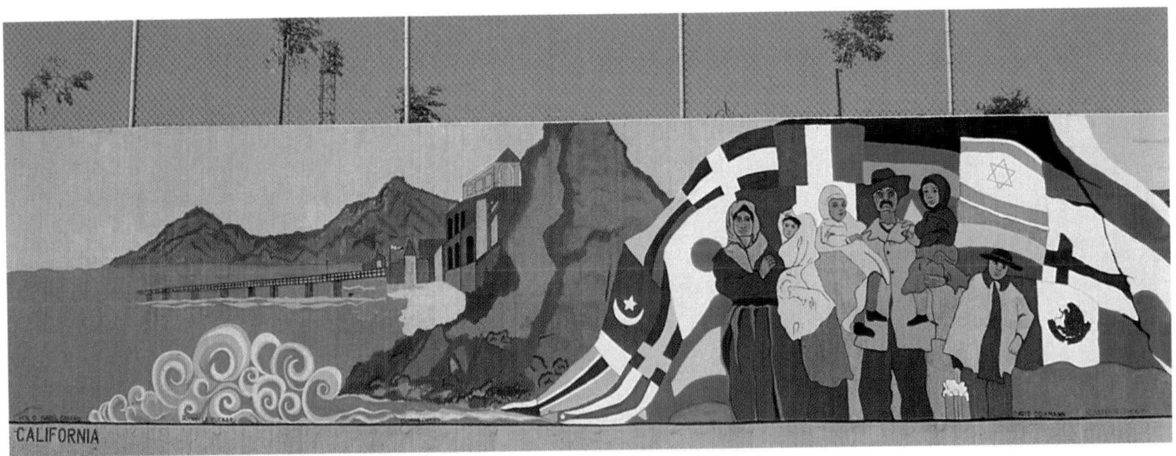

686 Judy Baca, director; Isabel Castro, designer.
"1900 IMIGRANT CALIFORNIA,"
GREAT WALL OF LOS ANGELES.
Photograph: Social and Public Resource Center. San Fernando Valley, California. 1976.

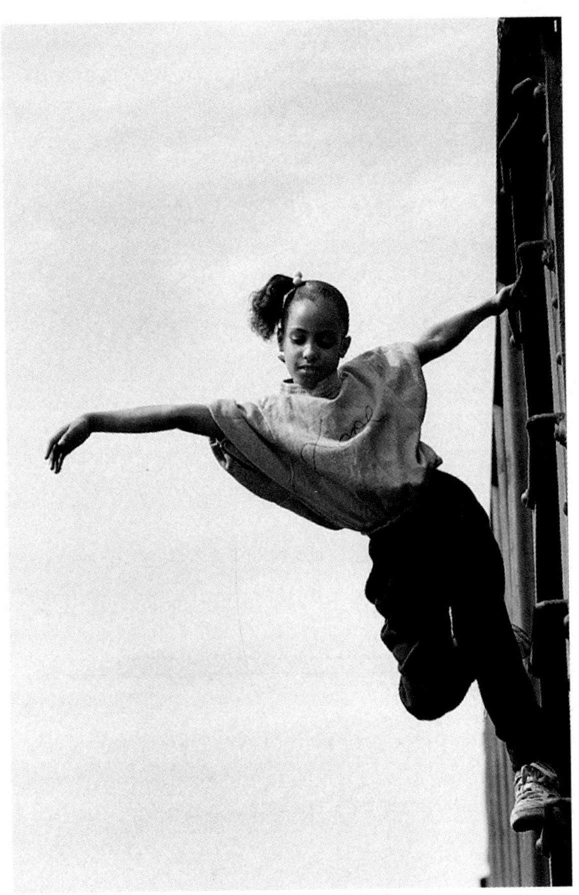

687 Shawn Nixon, age 18.
BOXCAR POSE. 1990.
Photograph, silver print. 20" × 16".
Courtesy of Shooting Back, Inc., Washington, D.C.

U.S. Army Corps of Engineers asked Baca to paint one or two murals on the concrete wall of a flood-control channel in the San Fernando Valley. The concept has grown into an annual summer project involving over fifty artists and hundreds of volunteers, mostly teenagers, from widely varied backgrounds. Each section of the mural, which depicts the ethnic history of Los Angeles, is conceived and completed by a team under the direction of a supervising artist. Volunteers learn, play, and cooperate with one another as they work on each 350-foot section of the longest mural in the world, now known as the GREAT WALL.

Baca and other community artists are consciously integrating art with the realities of their communities. Private initiative, combined with financial support from foundations, companies, and government agencies at all levels, has played a major role in sustaining the mural movement.

Some observers categorize the 1990s as a period of "politically correct" art. Works that reflect political, environmental, sexual, economic, ethnic, and other concerns may indeed be great art, but the mere presence of such subject matter does not guarantee excellence in a visual statement.

CULTURAL PLURALISM

America is seen as a melting pot in which people of many ethnic backgrounds become part of a flavorful national blend. It is encouraging when art celebrates rather than erases racial and cultural differences.

Well into the twentieth century, many artists avoided subjects and styles that might cause their work to be labeled and dismissed as ethnic art. Most artists of all ethnic backgrounds sought to be a part of the mainstream, Eurocentric styles. At the end of the twentieth century in the United States, a shift is taking place toward the acknowledgement and appreciation of the nation's distinctive ethnic identities. This movement is related to legal and social shifts in civil rights and equal opportunity.

The Harlem Renaissance, which began in the twenties, sought to address these issues. A group of prominent African-American artists, musicians, and writers encouraged one another and younger generations to create from their own experience. Romare Bearden (see page 11) was one of these leaders.

In art, the maker's cultural or ethnic identity or gender may or may not be evident in style or subject matter. Martin Puryear's powerful sculpture does not reveal that he is black or male (see page 495). On the other hand, works by Romare Bearden and Faith Ringgold (page 223) celebrate their African-American heritage while projecting a universal message. Culturally or ethnically based subject matter is often used in humorous or poignant ways.

Multicultural complexity is communicated by the meticulous paintings of Masami Teraoka, in a style based on the traditional Ukiyo-e woodblock prints popular in Japan from the seventeenth through the nineteenth centuries (see page 300). Both Ukiyo-e prints and Teraoka's paintings refer to worldly pleasures, but Teraoka's works, with references to hamburgers, ice cream cones, cameras, and condoms, are clearly late twentieth-century.

With great wit and skillful design, Teraoka combines clichés of Eastern tradition and Western subject matter in highly inventive images that play on some of the ironies of contemporary East-West relations or focus on social and environmental hazards. In his GEISHA AND AIDS NIGHTMARE the despairing courtesan realizes that it is already too late for the protection she clutches.

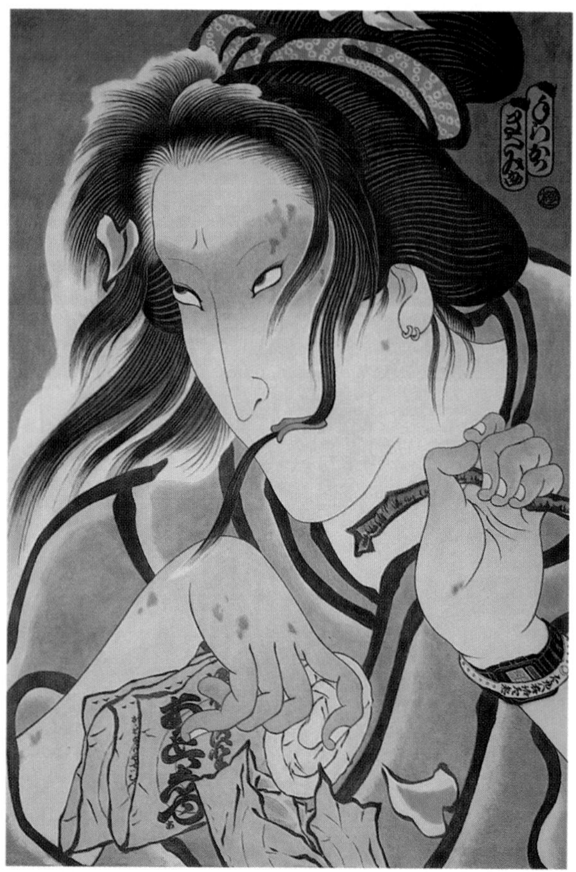

688 Masami Teraoka.
GEISHA AND AIDS NIGHTMARE from the AIDS SERIES.
1989-1990.
Watercolor on canvas. 106¼" × 72".
Courtesy of the artist and Pamela Auchincloss Gallery.

Native Americans share the extra perspective of being both traditionally linked "natives" and contemporary Americans. Painter Fritz Scholder, who is one-quarter Indian, gained recognition and provoked controversy by dealing with the tragic—yet at times comic—situation of the Native American.

Scholder's painting style has the fluid paint application of Abstract Expressionism and some of the irony of Pop. His series on Indians has been denounced by some Native American artists—those who see his paintings as an insult to Indian customs and dignity rather than as ironic symbols. Scholder, who considers himself a non-Indian Indian, has enjoyed the process of painting while overturning romantic clichés associated with Native Americans. Scholder wrote a narrative to accompany SUPER INDIAN NO. 2:

He tried to ignore the hoard of ugly tourists as he left the others. In the old days there were few white watchers along with the professional Indian lovers. Now it had turned into a carnival. He stepped up to the red, white, and blue concession stand and ordered an ice cream cone—a double-dip strawberry.[2]

Jaune Quick-to-See Smith uses a linear Abstract Expressionist style that links the symbols and markings of her French Cree, Shoshone, and Flathead Native American heritage with the influences

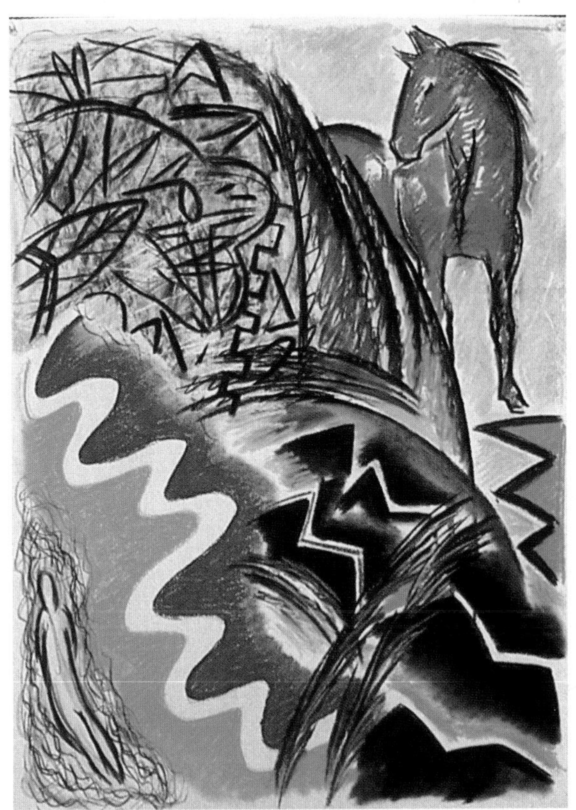

690 Jaune Quick-to-See Smith.
PETROGLYPH PARK. 1986.
Pastel on paper. 30" × 22".
Private collection. Courtesy Steinbaum Krauss Gallery, New York.

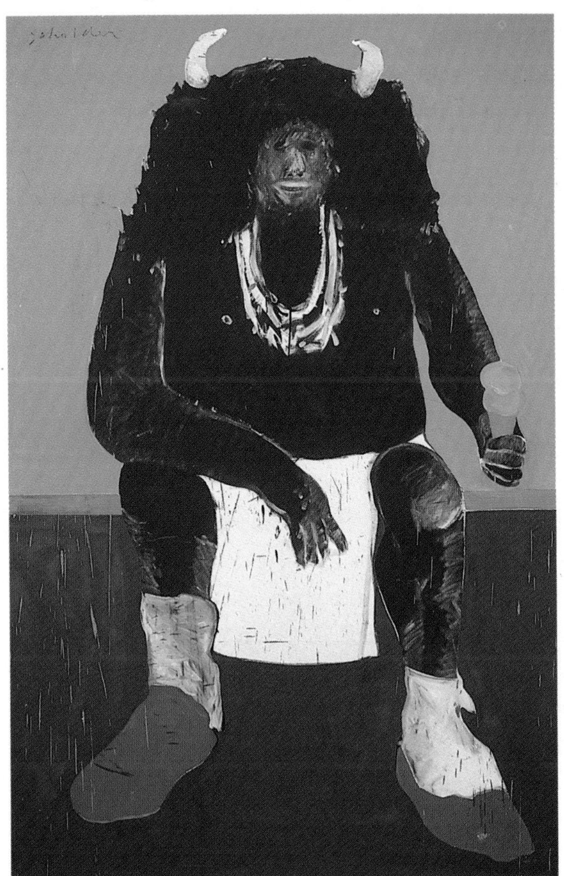

689 Fritz Scholder.
SUPER INDIAN NO. 2. 1971.
Oil on canvas. 90" × 60".
Photograph courtesy of Aberbach Fine Art, New York.

of modern Expressionist painters. In PETROGLYPH PARK, Smith used colors and motifs of the Southwest landscape and the horse, a symbolically important animal to many Native American cultures.

Within recent decades the richness of Hispanic art in the United States has emerged from the barrios and moved into the wider community. Hispanic art is often expressive and vibrantly colorful. Some works are created by naive or folk artists; others are highly sophisticated and may have been inspired by Hispanic traditions and experiences. One's outlook may be primarily cultural or racial, or it may be formed by shared experience that has nothing to do with race or ethnicity. Frida Kahlo (page 434), Judy Baca (page 485), Marisol (page 208), Rupert Garcia (page 482), and Cildo Miereles (page 480) reflect the diversity of work by Hispanic artists.

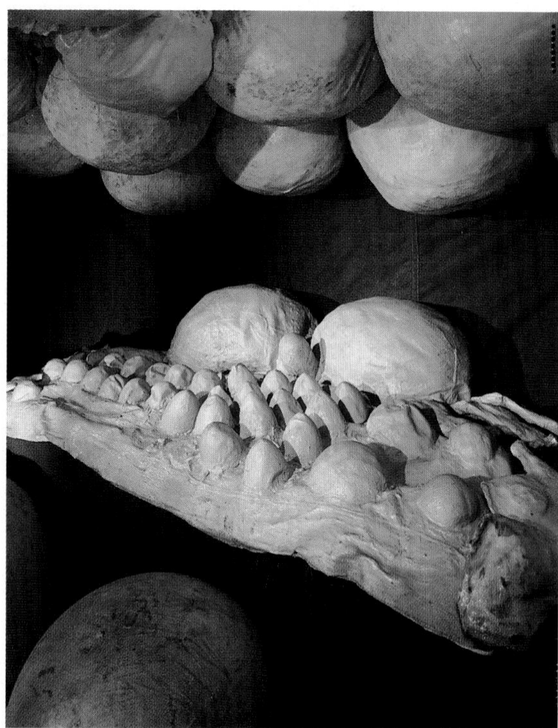

691 Louise Bourgeois.
Detail of THE DESTRUCTION OF THE FATHER. 1974.
Latex, plaster, and mixed media. 93⅝" × 142⅝" × 97⅞".
Courtesy Robert Miller Gallery, New York. Photograph: Peter Moore.

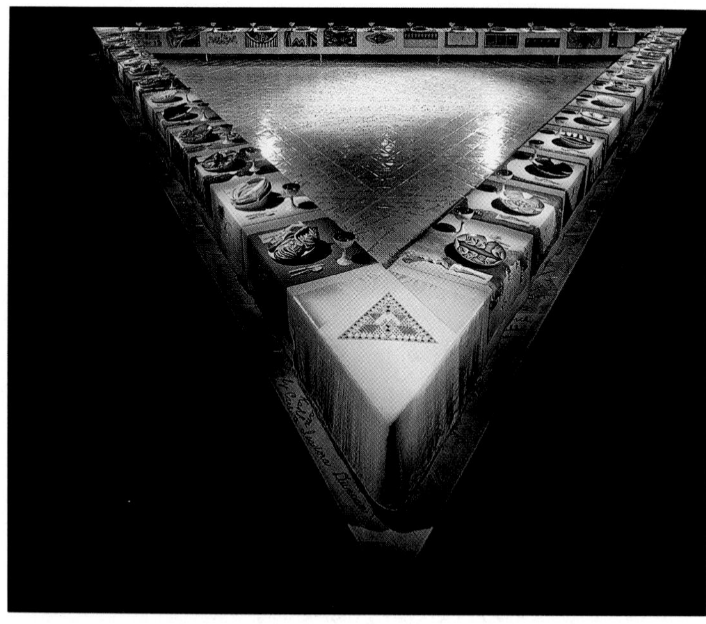

692 Judy Chicago, in cooperation with a working community of 300 women and men.
THE DINNER PARTY. 1979. (Dismantled.)
Mixed media. Triangle, 48' each side.
Photograph courtesy ACA Gallery, New York.

FEMINISM

Setting aside questions of recognition and status (often the result of political, social, and economic forces rather than artistic merit—see pages 405–408), is the work of female artists inherently distinguishable from that of male artists?

Lucy Lippard, an influential art critic and a strong supporter of women artists, argues, "The overwhelming fact remains that a woman's experience in this society—social and biological—is simply not like that of a man. If art comes from the inside, as it must, then the art of men and women must be different, too."[3] Not everyone would agree with Lippard's assessment. Yet the work of some women artists definitely is influenced by their gender and their interest in feminist issues.

Sculptor Louise Bourgeois, born in France, became an American citizen and went on to create an acclaimed body of work. While not considered a "feminist artist"—her intentions are more aesthetic and psychological than political—Bourgeois creates works about clearly feminine concerns.

Bourgeois depicts femaleness from within instead of looking at it from the outside, as male artists have done for centuries. Her sculpture describes the experience of being female in terms of organic shapes placed in tenuous relationships. It explores helplessness, fear, nurturing, and sexuality—as well as aggression, rage, and protest.

According to Bourgeois, the underlying motivations for her art stem from unresolved psychological conflicts of her childhood. In one of her most powerful works, THE DESTRUCTION OF THE FATHER, she alludes to the Greek myth of Cronos devouring his children. In this sculpture, Bourgeois turned to an ancient myth to exorcise her fear of her domineering father. "It is a very murderous piece," Bourgeois pointed out in her retrospective catalogue. Its inspiration lay in the "impulse that comes when one is under too much stress and one turns against those one loves the most."[4] Bourgeois's monumental rubber and mixed-media sculpture is profoundly threatening; it describes a deep division between genders and generations.

The feminist movement became visible in art

in the 1970s, in part through the work of Judy Chicago. This feminist artist confronted those who sought to maintain a distinction between "high" art and decorative arts. Feminist art focuses on content and the use of materials and media long associated with women, and it often gives as much importance to political as to aesthetic concerns.

THE DINNER PARTY was a collaboration of many women (and a few men), both fine artists and craftspeople, organized and directed by Judy Chicago over a period of five years. This cooperative venture was in itself a political statement about the supportive nature of female experience, as opposed to the frequently competitive nature of the male.

A large triangular table contains place settings for thirty-nine women who made important contributions to world history. The names of 999 other notable women of achievement are inscribed on ceramic tiles below the table. Each place setting includes a hand-embroidered fabric runner and a porcelain plate designed in honor of that woman. Some of the plates are painted with flat designs; others have modeled and painted relief motifs; many are explicitly sexual, embellished with flower-like unfoldings of female genitalia. The project proved to be as controversial as it was erotic.

Some female artists are less interested in working with specific female imagery than in equalizing the age-old male-female imbalance in the art world. In 1985, provocative GUERILLA GIRLS posters featuring women wearing gorilla masks appeared in SoHo, an area of New York City where many contemporary art galleries are located. One poster listed twenty major galleries beneath an announcement: "These Galleries Show No More Than 10% Women Artists or None at All." It was signed: "A Public Service Message from Guerrilla Girls—Conscience of the Art World." Another poster asked: "Do Women Have To Be Naked To Get Into The Met. Museum?" The answer: "Less than 5% of the artists in the Modern Art Sections are women, but 85% of the nudes are female."

No one is sure how many women artists are members of the Guerrilla Girls—some say as many

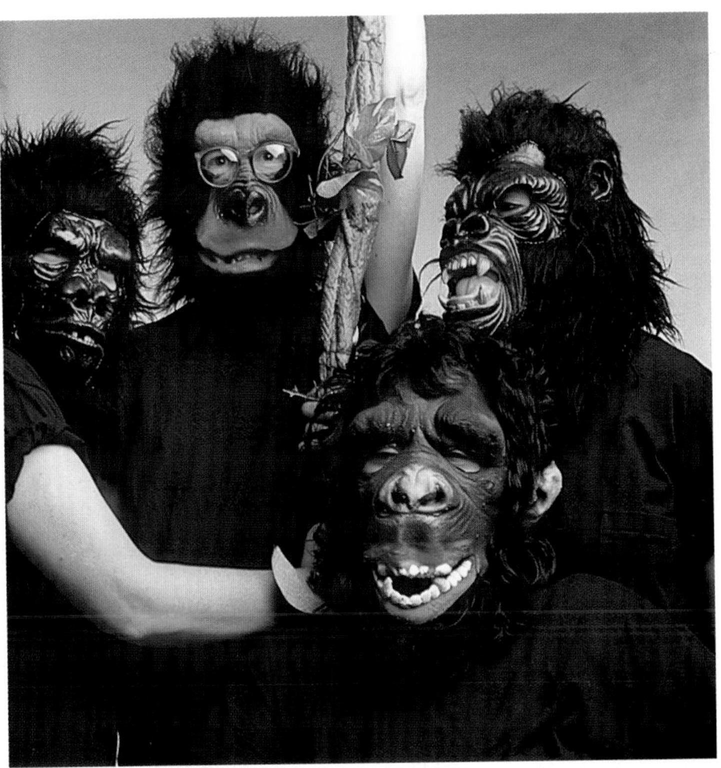

693 GUERILLA GIRLS. 1992.
Photograph: Mark Seliger / Outline.

as one hundred. They have remained anonymous so that they can speak out without jeopardizing their careers. The Guerrilla Girls shine a needed spotlight on sexism in museums and galleries.

Cindy Sherman's photographs of herself are not self-portraits. Her real subjects are the stereotypes that belittle females. Sherman arranges narrative settings, casting herself as the only character. She stands in for America's sweetheart, the girl next door, the young housewife, Daddy's little girl, the girl detective, the girl left behind. In her Untitled Film Stills series, each character is a cliché out of a "B" movie, with the entire drama condensed to a single shot.

Sherman's UNTITLED FILM STILL #48 shows a young blonde woman hitchhiking on a deserted road at dusk. She stands with her back to us, looking up the highway, her suitcase at her side. The disturbing photo evokes feelings of dread and danger; like the lurid jacket of a cheap novel, it teases us with the premise of a story about to unfold. Sherman works at the edge of two visual art forms, photography and film, and at the edge of two artistic styles, Realism and Surrealism.

When the National Museum of Women in the Arts opened in Washington D.C. in 1987, many people expressed concern that the creation of such a museum would further marginalize, rather than truly recognize, women's art. They believed it would be better to work for more balanced representation in "mainstream" museums.

694 Cindy Sherman.
UNTITLED FILM STILL # 48. 1979.
Photograph.
Courtesy Metro Pictures.

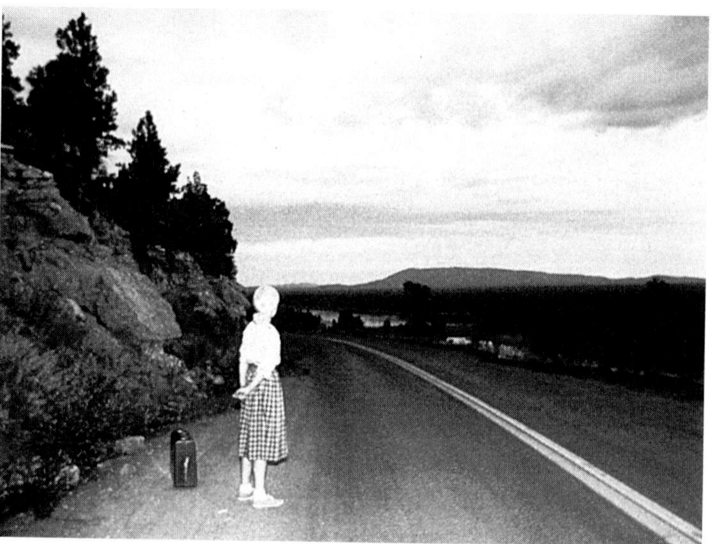

PUBLIC ART

We have seen that cultural diversity and rapid change have led to variety in styles of art and personal responses to works of art. Because there is no longer general agreement on what constitutes "good" art, selection of a work of art for a public place can be an emotional and often a political issue. While most people will readily accept the decisions of experts in other areas, many believe they have the right to view or not view art and to decide for themselves what art they want to see. The placement of an artwork in a public space makes it accessible, but this may lead to a feeling that some so-called art experts have decided what the public should learn to like. In the case of government art commissions, people who dislike the "art" may be further distressed when they realize that their tax dollars helped pay for it.

The idea of public art goes back to ancient times. Government and religious leaders have commissioned many of history's best-known artists to execute works for the public. In the United States, however, public art (other than architecture) was largely confined to commemorative statues and monuments in parks until almost the middle of this century. The short-lived WPA (see page 446) federal art program of the late 1930s and early 1940s provided modest support for the participating artists, who created a great number of public murals, easel paintings, prints, photographs, and sculpture. However, it is only in recent decades that we have seen a steady stream of commissions given to large numbers of American artists for public art.

During the 1960s, when the American economy was strong, government leaders began to spend money in new areas. Since the arts are considered beneficial for individuals and communities, it seemed appropriate that city, state, and national governments become involved in bringing the arts to the public. A high percentage of today's public art is now commissioned by government agencies.

Among the largest sponsors of public art is the federal government's General Services Administration (GSA) Art-in-Architecture program, begun in 1962 during John F. Kennedy's presidency. The program requires that 0.05 percent of the cost of each new government building be spent for art to be located in or around the new building. States, cities, and counties subsequently implemented similar programs, with varying percentages designated for the purchase or commissioning of works of art.

The federal government's National Endowment for the Arts (NEA) was created in 1965. Among the NEA's many programs is the Art in Public Places Program, from which communities can request matching funds for commissions of large outdoor artworks.

Corporations have also become involved in supporting the arts. Many have found that by providing more rewarding environments for their own employees and by making cultural contributions to the larger community, they generate goodwill both within their own companies and with the general public. Corporate support for the arts ranges from buying or commissioning artworks to sponsoring public television programs and traveling art exhibitions.

Public art programs have had problems and failures as well as successes. In some instances, the results have been cosmetic attempts to hide inferior architecture, or simply "decoration" inappropriately applied as an afterthought. To insure effective, integrated results, architects, landscape architects, interior designers, and artists need to work with each other and with clients, starting at the conceptual and planning stages of projects.

Most art in outdoor public places takes the form of large sculpture or murals; problems of theft and vandalism are minimized when the works are durable and immovable. Occasionally, existing art is purchased for outdoor locations, but more often artists are commissioned to design site-specific pieces.

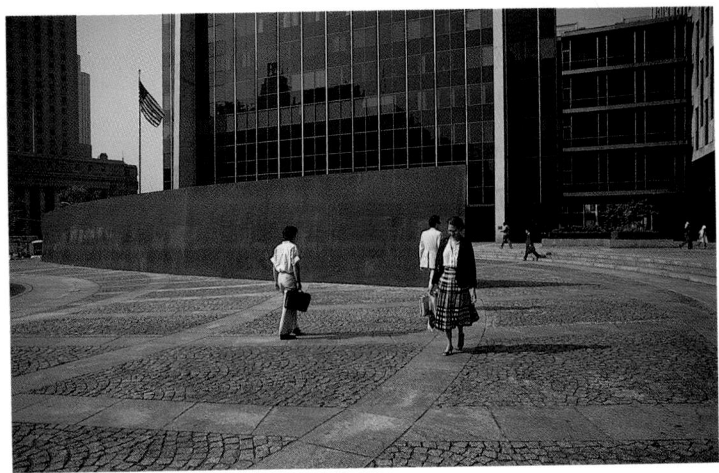

695 Richard Serra.
TILTED ARC. New York City. 1981.
Cor-ten steel. 12' × 120'.

Disputes may arise when the tastes and views of those who select the art are at odds with the preferences of the public. Two of the most highly publicized public art controversies in recent years concerned minimal sculptures, each in the form of a wall—one by sculptor Richard Serra, the other by then architecture student Maya Lin.

In 1979, Richard Serra was selected by a panel of art professionals working with the GSA to submit a proposal for a sculpture to be located in the plaza at the corner of Broadway and Lafayette Street in New York City. The panel subsequently approved the design, and in 1981 TILTED ARC was fabricated and installed. The sculpture was made of Cor-ten steel, which is supposed to develop a thin layer of rust. In time, the surface of TILTED ARC acquired its patina of rust—and also graffiti. The site-specific work was a slightly curved wall weighing 73 tons and measuring 120 feet long by 12 feet high. It was positioned so that it seemed to turn its back on the large fountain that had been the focal point of the plaza. It blocked the view of a tree-filled park from the entrance of the Jacob K. Javits Federal Building and the view up Broadway from the entrance to the Courthouse.

TILTED ARC was greeted with enormous hostility from people who worked in the buildings facing the plaza. In protest, thirteen hundred government

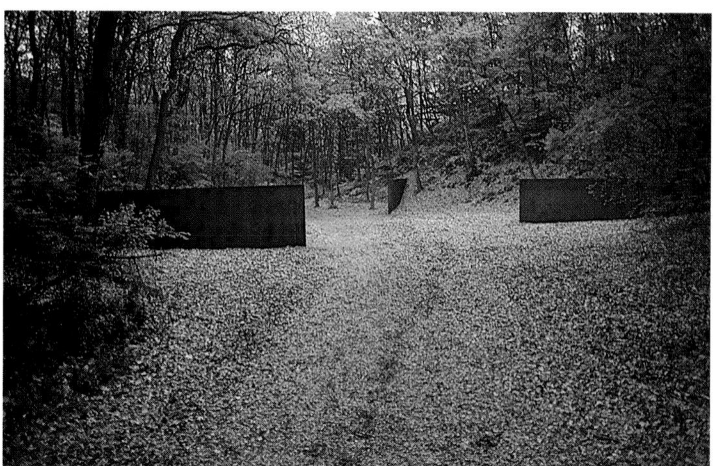

696 Richard Serra.
SPIN OUT. 1973.
Hot-rolled steel. Three plates, each 10' × 40' × 1½".
Kröller-Müller Rijksmuseum, Otterlo, Netherlands.

employees signed petitions demanding the removal of the sculpture. The work became the subject of a lengthy, heated battle involving artists, art critics, the press, public hearings, administrative panels, and a United States District Court. Following a GSA panel's recommendation that the work be relocated at an estimated cost of $50,000, Serra filed a lawsuit against the GSA, seeking $30 million in damages. Serra maintained that relocation of the site-specific work would destroy its integrity and therefore destroy the piece itself. The dispute caused a split in the art community, and it further divided art professionals from a public wary of much contemporary art. TILTED ARC was dismantled in 1989 after Serra's appeals had been exhausted.

Serra saw the intent of TILTED ARC as "a way to dislocate or alter the decorative function of the plaza, and actively bring people into the sculpture's context."[5] The employees and many others didn't like either the "dislocation" or the "sculpture's context." In retrospect, given the confrontational nature of much of Serra's previous work, the GSA took a risk in selecting Serra in the first place.

For an earlier commission for the Kröller-Müller Museum's sculpture park, Serra designed a related minimal sculpture. SPIN OUT consists of hot-rolled steel walls which emerge from wooded slopes around a clearing. The implied convergence of the walls punctuates rather than disrupts the continuity of the forest clearing.

The highly publicized VIETNAM VETERANS MEMORIAL, located on the Mall in Washington, D.C., sparked a different kind of controversy. The 250-foot-long, V-shaped black granite wall bears the names of the nearly sixty thousand American servicemen and women who died or are missing in Southeast Asia. The nonprofit Vietnam Veterans Memorial Fund, Inc. (VVMF) was formed in 1979 by a group of Vietnam veterans who believed that a symbol of recognition of the human cost of the war would help speed the process of national reconciliation. Controversy over American involvement in the war had caused returning veterans to receive less than a hero's welcome.

In 1980, Congress authorized the site, and the VVMF announced a national design competition. The VVMF set design criteria specifying that the memorial be reflective and contemplative in character, harmonize with its surroundings, contain the names of all those who died or remain missing, and make no political statement about the war. After examining 1,421 anonymously submitted entries, the jury of internationally recognized artists and designers unanimously selected the design of twenty-one-year-old Maya Ying Lin of Athens, Ohio, then a student at Yale University. Lin had visited the site and created a design that would work with the land rather than dominate it. "I had an impulse to cut open the earth ... an initial violence that in time would heal. The grass would grow back, but the cut would remain, a pure, flat surface, like a geode when you cut it open and polish the edge.... I chose black granite to make the surface reflective and peaceful."[6]

Initial reaction by the press was favorable, and in spring 1981 the Commission of Fine Arts and other government agencies approved the design. But several months later, a Vietnam veteran appeared before the commission and called the proposed design a "black gash of shame." He hit a nerve, and subsequent accusations in the press called the design "unheroic," "defeatist," and "death-oriented."

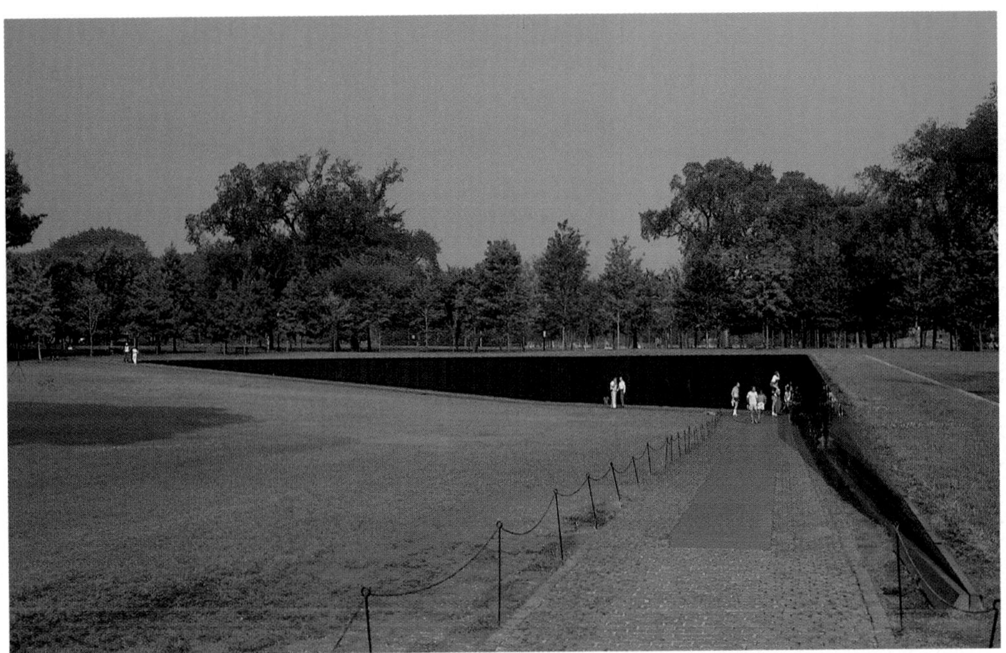

697 Maya Lin.
VIETNAM VETERANS MEMORIAL. The Mall, Washington, D.C. 1980-1982.
Black granite. Each wall 10'1" × 246'9".

Veterans were divided on the issue. It was, indeed, a hard design to explain. In January 1982, Secretary of the Interior James Watt put the project on hold.

A compromise was reached several months later when it was decided that a figurative sculpture and a flag would be added to the site. Frederick Hart was chosen to create a naturalistic bronze statue to be located in a cluster of small trees near the wall. In time, the compromise seemed to please all sides. The wall was dedicated on Veterans Day 1982, and the Hart statue in 1984. Most of the modernists who were dismayed at the idea of cluttering up the site with yet another bronze commemorative statue were pleasantly surprised by the quality of the figurative VIETNAM MEMORIAL SCULPTURE and the fact that it complements the wall from a distance rather than competes with it. Yet, despite public clamor for a traditional monument, a majority of the thousands of tourists who flock to the memorial each day never see the Hart sculpture; they are drawn to the wall.

Lin's bold, eloquently simple design creates a memorial park within a larger park. The polished black surface reflects the surrounding trees and lawn, and the tapering segments point to the Washington Monument in one direction and the Lincoln

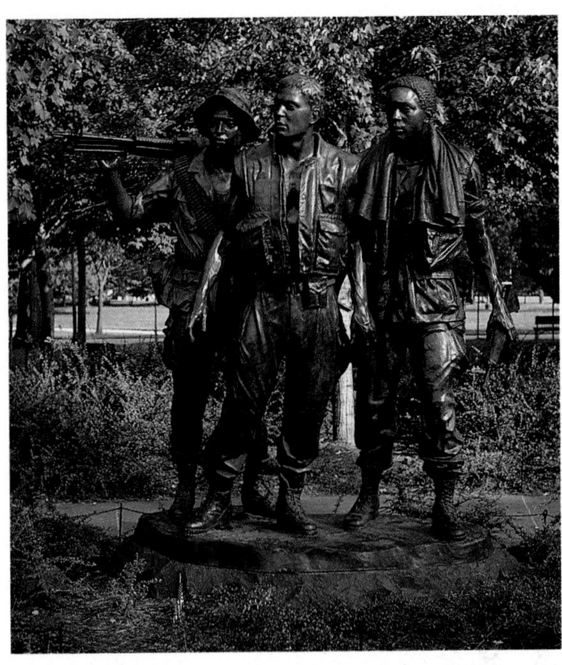

698 Frederick Hart.
VIETNAM MEMORIAL SCULPTURE.
The Mall, Washington, D.C. 1984.
Bronze. Life-size.

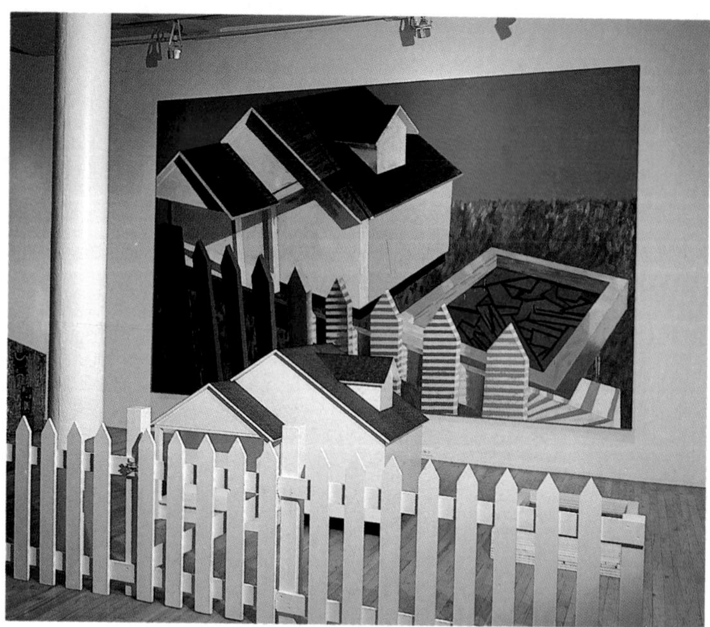

699 Jennifer Bartlett.
WHITE HOUSE. 1985.
Installation view. Oil on canvas, wood, enamel paint, metal, tar paper.
Painting, 10' × 16'; fence, 3' × 12' and 10¼" × 5';
house, 45" × 60" × 58¼"; swimming pool, 7" × 43¾" × 31½".
Photograph: Geoffrey Clements. Courtesy of Paula Cooper Gallery, New York.

Memorial in the other. Names are inscribed in chronological order by date of death, each name given a place in history. As visitors walk toward the center, the wall becomes higher and the names pile up inexorably. The monument, visited by more than ten thousand people a day, has the power to console and heal.

The fragmented nature of contemporary American culture presents a dilemma for both artists and those who sponsor public art. Should the freedom of the creative individual be unquestioned, with the hope that the public will follow, or at least accept, the art that results? Or should the public, or some part of the public, have a voice in setting guidelines for selection or actually select the art that becomes part of the public environment—particularly when the art is paid for by tax dollars? Just how democratic should the process be? On the one hand, we could rely entirely on "art experts," whose tastes are often different from those of the public; at the other extreme, with a lot of public input, we might yield to the lowest common denominator of popular taste. Recent controversies have caused everyone involved in public art commissions, as well as other concerned citizens, to give serious thought to the procedures involved.

RECENT SCULPTURE

The question of how to integrate and support the art of women and ethnic minorities is just one aspect of the increasingly complex nature of the art world. It is no longer even clear how to draw distinctions among art forms themselves. More and more artists use elements of both painting and sculpture.

Jennifer Bartlett's mixed-media works reflect the tendency of many contemporary artists to blur the distinction between painting and sculpture. In WHITE HOUSE, as in other installations of the mid-eighties, Bartlett combined landscape paintings with objects—small boats, fences, houses. With the actual object and the illusion of the object presented simultaneously, the viewer is brought into the art process in a surprising way.

Since many contemporary artists combine media and approaches, it is difficult to label them. Martin Puryear compounds the difficulty of categorizing art. Like craft artists, Puryear makes beautifully constructed, handmade objects; yet he is one of today's best sculptors. He deals not only with techniques and materials but with ideas and dreams. Is Puryear's work craft or sculpture? And since Puryear is an African-American, should he be seen as a minority artist even when his work is more universal than specifically ethnic in its concerns? Old categories are quickly breaking down and often seem irrelevant.

Combining elegant craftsmanship, organic creativity, and humor, Puryear's deceptively simple sculptures include references to shelters, canoes, trestle bridges, coffins, and basketry. Puryear's work has a distinctly American eloquence that arises from a pioneering tradition of self-reliance and disciplined craftsmanship. His OLD MOLE recalls the delicate skeleton of a natural creature, the whimsical humor of a folk tale, and the austere sophistication of Minimalist sculpture.

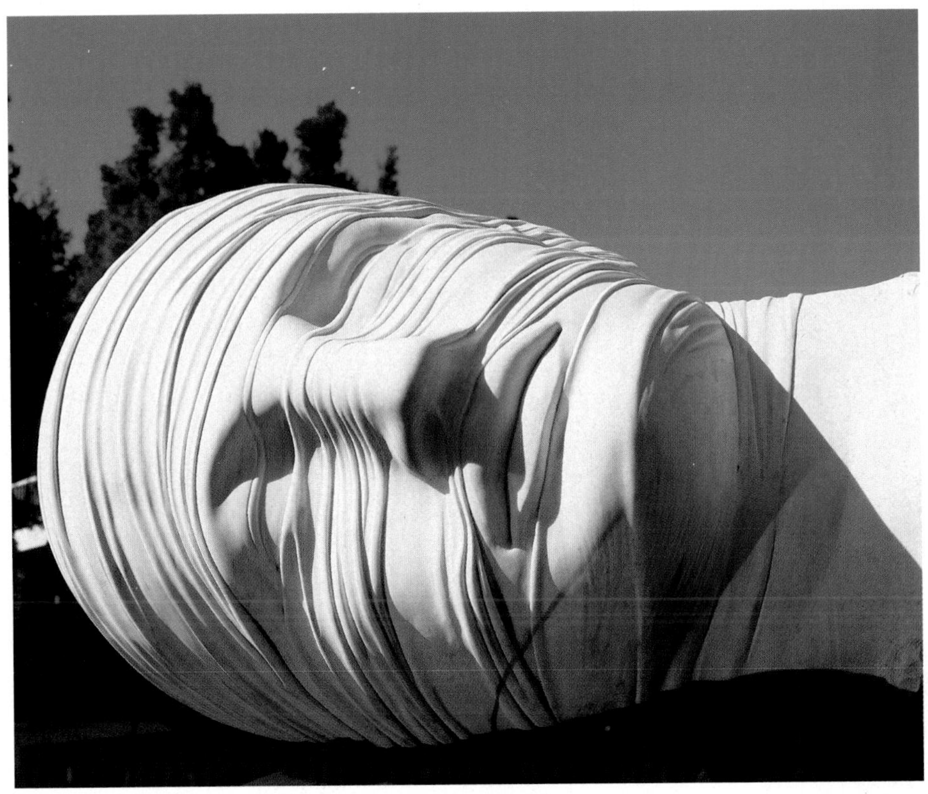

700 Igor Mitoraj.
SLEEPING HEAD. 1983.
Marble. 105" × 172" × 133".
Hakone Open Air Museum, Japan.
Courtesy of the artist.

Austere sophistication in a representational mode is seen in the sculpture of German-born Igor Mitoraj. In works such as SLEEPING HEAD, Mitoraj evokes a sense of timeless mystery by bringing qualities of ancient Greek art to contemporary sculpture. In his return to the figure and to classical, pre-Cubist attitudes, Mitoraj takes a Post-Modern approach. The monumental size of his figure fragments contributes to their impact. Whether his sculptures exist outdoors or indoors, their large scale intensifies their heroic mood.

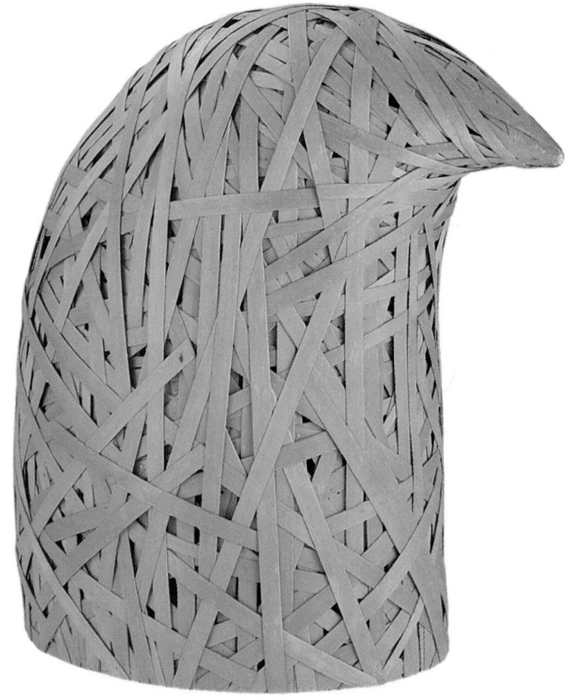

701 Martin Puryear.
OLD MOLE. 1985.
Red cedar. 61" × 61" × 32".
Philadelphia Museum of Art. Purchased: Samuel S. White III and Vera White Collection (by exchange) and gift of Mr. and Mrs. C.G. Chaplin (by exchange), funds contributed by Marion Stroud Swingle, and funds contributed by friends and family in memory of Mrs. H. Gates Lloyd.

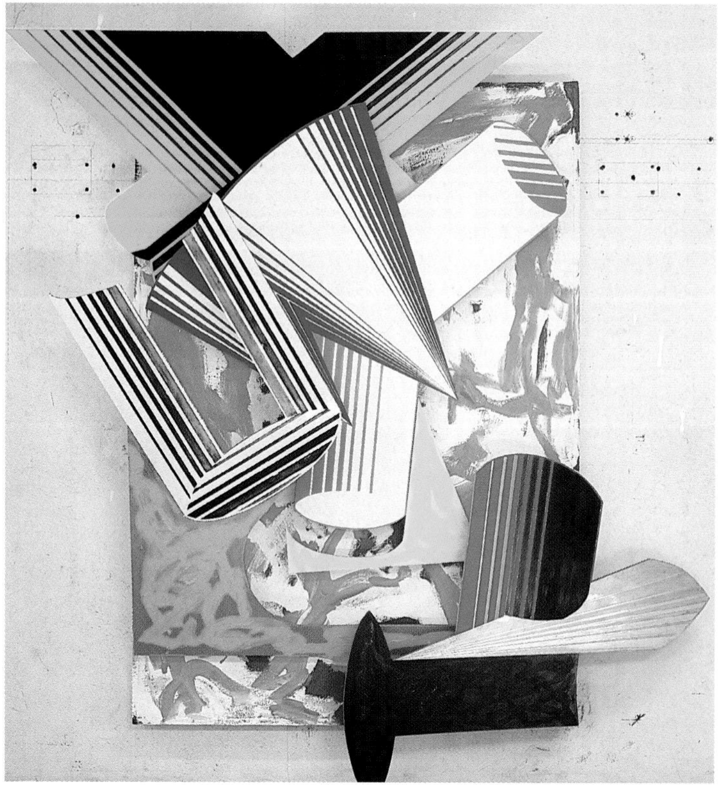

702 Frank Stella.
LO SCIOCCO SENZO PAURA (#1, 4X). 1984.
Oil, urethane enamel, fluorescent alkyd, acrylic, and printing ink on canvas, etched magnesium, aluminum, and fiberglass.
130" × 127" × 23".
Collection of Ann and Robert L. Freedman, New York.
Photograph courtesy of M. Knoedler & Company, New York.

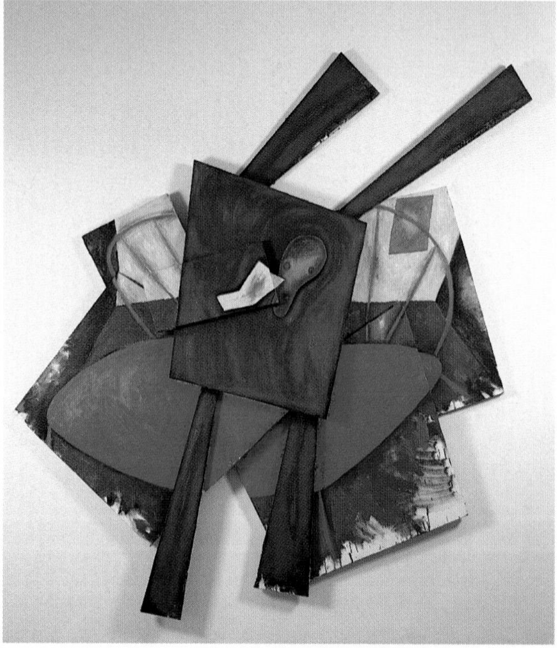

703 Elizabeth Murray.
MORE THAN YOU KNOW. 1983.
Oil on nine canvases. 108" × 111" × 8".
Collection of The Edward R. Broida Trust, Florida.

RECENT PAINTING

Just as some artists are rediscovering representation, others are reinventing abstraction. During a career spanning more than three decades, Frank Stella has moved from Minimalism to hard-edge abstraction to constructions that might be called painted wall sculpture. To see a part of this evolution, compare Stella's HIRAQLA I of 1968 (page 462) with his LO SCIOCCO SENZO PAURA of 1984. He uses some of the same geometric shapes and bright colors in each case, but in the later work the flat application of color has yielded to a more painterly approach. Further, he has broken apart the symmetry of the earlier painting, leaving fragments of unmatched shapes clinging to one another.

Each of Stella's progressive phases, logical in its own way, is a clear, if surprising, outgrowth of the preceding work. He has taken his painting from cool, formal, shaped flatness to hot, highly expressive, three-dimensional projections—pure visual razzle-dazzle. His large painted constructions of the 1980s reach out aggressively toward the viewer. LO SCIOCCO SENZO PAURA may be a caricature of the idea of modernism as well as a comment on the manufactured madness of our times.

Just a glance will confirm that Elizabeth Murray's work is related to that of Frank Stella. In MORE THAN YOU KNOW, Murray uses colorful, assembled shapes similar to Stella's, but she infuses them with an emotional energy all her own. While both artists manage a high-intensity balancing act, Murray explores narrative situations that Stella intentionally keeps out of his work. She responds to domestic scenes and human emotions while remaining true to rigorous formal issues.

Modernism—including Abstract Expressionism and hard-edge abstraction—stressed the flatness of the picture plane and rejected narration. In time, some artists found this approach inadequate for communicating their feelings and concerns. In the late 1960s, a few daring artists found a way out of this aesthetic corner.

Susan Rothenberg began a career as a nonrepresentational painter in the formalist sixties. In the seventies, she brought into her work references to the physical world. Thanks to the cleansing blankness of Minimalism, a leading explorer such as Rothenberg could return to figurative images with original vision. What emerges is almost ethereal.

Rothenberg is a tonal painter who here uses a muted palette of white, beige, silvery or dark gray, with a bit of blue. Her UNTITLED (BLUE), which outlines a horse's head in front of a human hand, is a haunting image that remains outside persistent attempts at explanation. It is a primal sign operating in the interval between the known material world and the mystery beyond.

At times during the twentieth century, the human image has all but disappeared from the mainstream of art. Since the 1970s, however, an increasing number of artists have returned to the human figure as a major subject.

Eric Fischl is another master of painterly brushwork. Like Rothenberg, he moved from nonrepresentation to representation. His UNTITLED view of children washing sand from their bathing suits shows a love of gesture and color. Fischl paints with direct fluidity, drawing the viewer into the magical process of creating pictures out of paint. His seductive paint application is often overshadowed by subject matter that shocks viewers with its psychological and sexual implications.

Consciously or unconsciously, artists speak for their eras as well as for themselves. It is difficult to look the present in the eye. It is natural to feel more comfortable with the art of the past, which has been around long enough to be sorted out and understood through the perspective of time. It is too soon to know which contemporary works will prove to be of lasting artistic value. But it is worthwhile to experience the currents of thought and feeling that recent art communicates. In making this effort, we come into closer touch with our time and with ourselves.

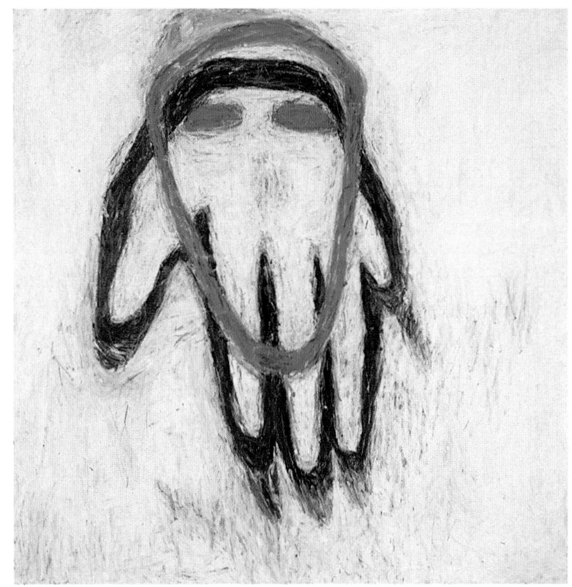

704 Susan Rothenberg.
UNTITLED (BLUE). 1980-1981.
Acrylic and flashe on canvas. 114" × 114".
Virginia Museum of Fine Arts, Richmond. Gift of the Sydney & Frances Lewis Foundation.

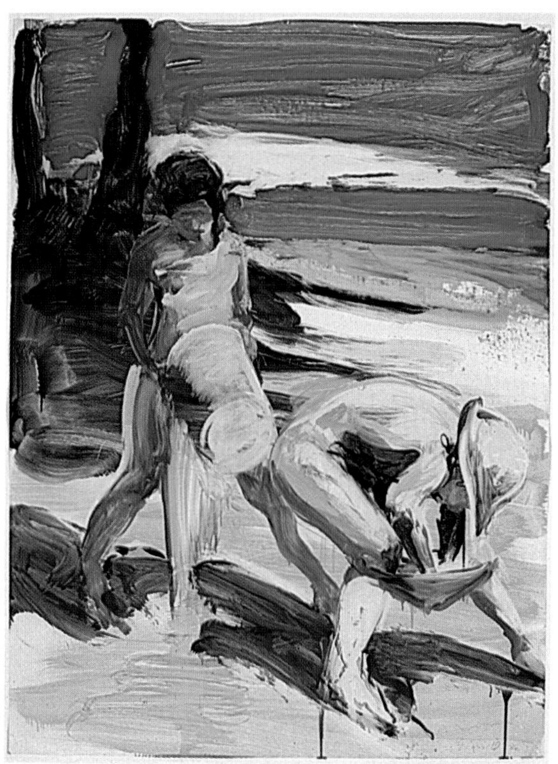

705 Eric Fischl.
UNTITLED. 1986.
Oil on paper. 46" × 35".
Private collection. Courtesy Mary Boone Gallery, New York.

THE ROLE OF THE ARTIST TODAY

If they blow [the world] up, that's not my business. My business is to work.

Louise Nevelson[7]

I'm questioning the cultural and societal changes in the role of the artist.... I'm afraid that if we don't address broader issues in art-making, we'll be left with an empty bag.

Keith Sonnier[8]

Through most of history, artists have been primarily occupied with serving the needs of their communities. Whether a society's needs were part of a tribal tradition or dictated by priests or rulers, the expressive individuality of artists was of secondary importance. In the West, the Renaissance emphasis on the individual brought about significant changes in both artists' and society's views of the role of artists.

As we approach the end of the twentieth century, art-making is undergoing a quiet revolution. From prehistoric times through the Renaissance, art functioned as a keeper of mythological and sacred traditions. Western art grew increasingly secular by the seventeenth century, as artists became involved in social record-keeping. After the development of photography in the mid-nineteenth century, art began to center on the expression of individual and formal issues. By the middle of the twentieth century, art entered mass culture and became commodified. Artists and their patrons had succeeded in pulling art out of the caves and cathedrals and into the shops and galleries and museums.

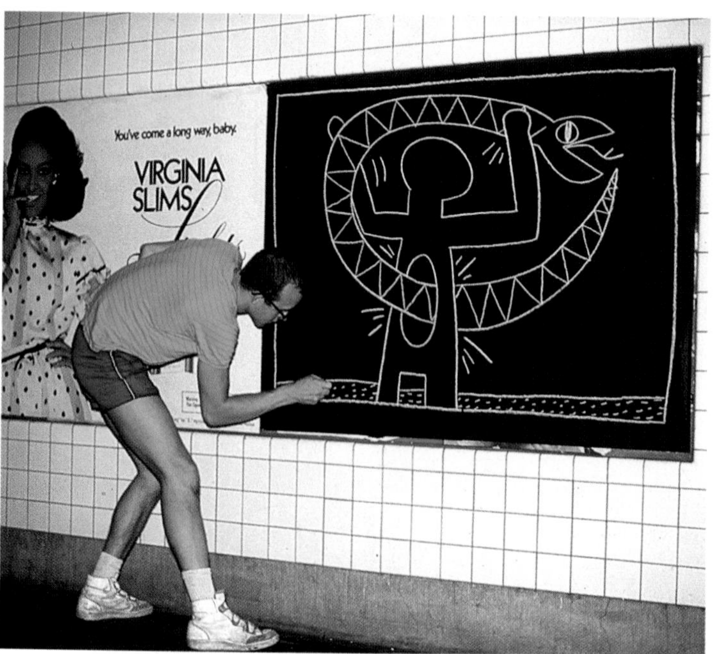

706 KEITH HARING AT WORK.
Photograph: Tseng Kwong Chi, New York.

Some artists have worked to bring art out of the galleries and museums and into the street. Vigilante artist Keith Haring created and presented his art, not on the street, but in the New York subway stations. Solid black paper on empty advertising signboards provided surfaces for Haring to make line drawings in white chalk. His drawings became so popular that in the mid-1980s, he became commercially successful as an artist.

Occasionally, advertisements on adjacent panels provided inspiration or created humorous associations. Even when Haring's drawings remained only a short time before they were covered by new advertisements, they were seen and enjoyed by thousands of people—many more than would have seen them in a gallery or a museum. The influence of Haring's popular style on graphic and textile designers has further extended the impact of his work.

What is the role of the artist today? This question returns us to the question with which this book began: What is the purpose of art?

After sorting through many possible answers, Ellen Dissanayake (in her book *What is Art For?*) concludes that art is a biological necessity, as important to long-term human survival as food and safety. She believes that educated people in a post-Darwinian, post-Freudian, post-Einsteinian world can no longer believe that their particular world view is the only one possible. Yet neither can human beings live without a sense of meaning and purpose. Within a multitude of cultures, beliefs, values, and customs, we need to embrace multiplicity and rediscover the importance of individual insights and expressions.

Art is the widest path to both goals. It allows us to experience the full range of otherness while deep-

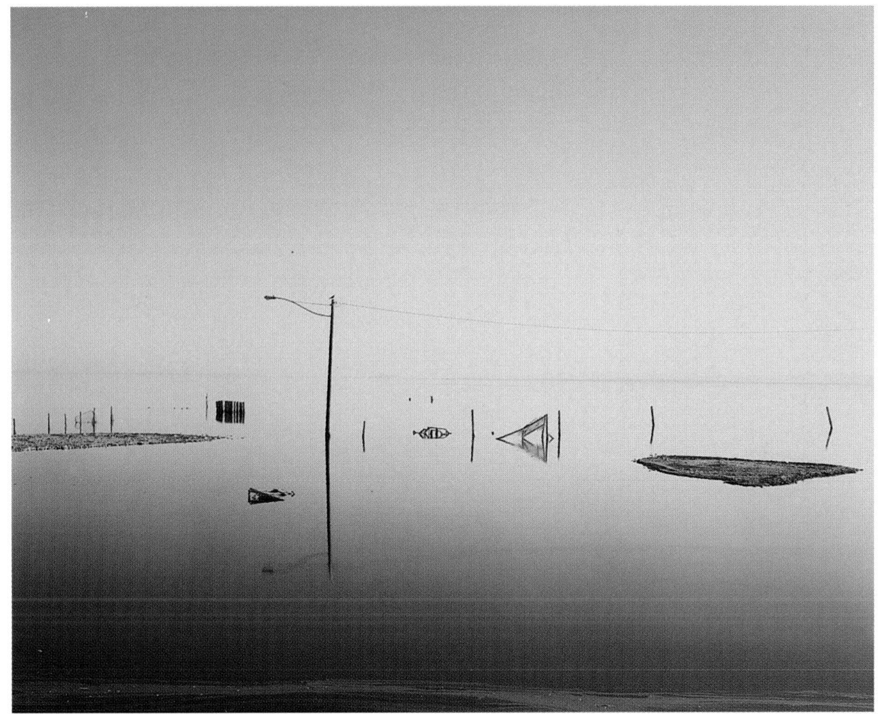

707 Richard Misrach. SUBMERGED LAMPOST, SALTON SEA. 1985. Photograph (chromogenic color print).
Courtesy Robert Mann Gallery.

ening our inwardness—our own dreams, memories, myths, and rituals. The more satisfying the art, the more likely it is to reach outward to the universal and inward to the particular.

What is the function of art today? Is its function to provide visual pleasure? To act as society's mirror? To challenge prevailing prejudices and misguided values? To uplift, inform, and enlighten? All of the above, and more, according to artists.

Each artist has his or her own intentions. Some simply create pretty images; some draw on their own experiences to create images with universal significance; some create memorable images that help bring about positive social change.

Often it seems that artists are ahead of their time. In fact, they are among the few who are truly with their time. Marshall McLuhan referred to art as an early warning system that helps us see who we have become and where we are headed.

Richard Misrach is one of a growing number of artists who use the power of aesthetic appeal to give clarity and weight to their messages of concern for what human beings are doing to each other and to their environment. His photograph SUBMERGED LAMPPOST, SALTON SEA captures the silent beauty of a small town in California that was flooded by a misguided irrigation system. Artists' commitment to social values and reform is certainly not new—Goya (page 375) and Daumier (page 165) worked for social change, and many more recent examples are included throughout *Artforms.*

In her book *The Reenchantment of Art,* Suzi Gablik promotes the concept of a value-based art, an art that increases awareness of the interconnectedness of the individual and the world and actively promotes social change. Gablik advocates an evolution in human consciousness in which each individual is engaged in the world as an active participant rather than a passive observer.

Each day massive quantities of pollutants are emitted into the air and large areas of forest lands are dying from the effects of acid rain. Our lakes, rivers, and oceans are being contaminated by toxic waste. Worldwide, slash-and-burn forest clearing is depleting the forests and affecting the climate. Can artists afford to continue to make art that is without moral conscience, art that places form above content, art that ignores a world in crisis?

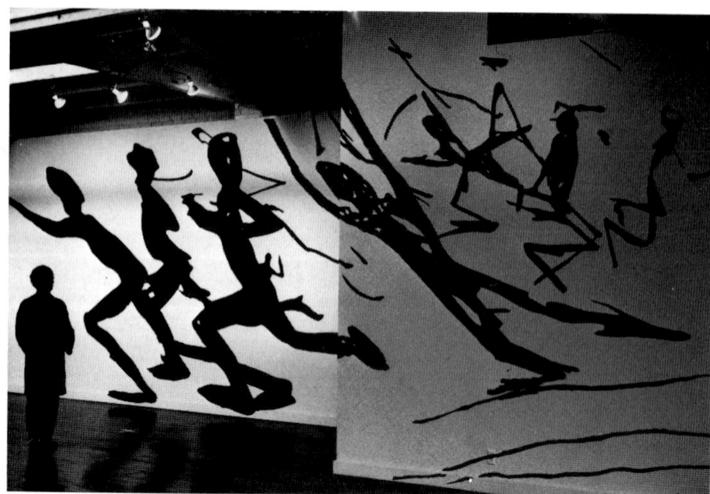

708 Jonathan Borofsky.
RUNNING PEOPLE AT 2,661,216. 1979.
Latex paint on two walls and ceiling beams. 14' × 18'.
Installation, Portland Center for Visual Arts, Portland, Oregon.

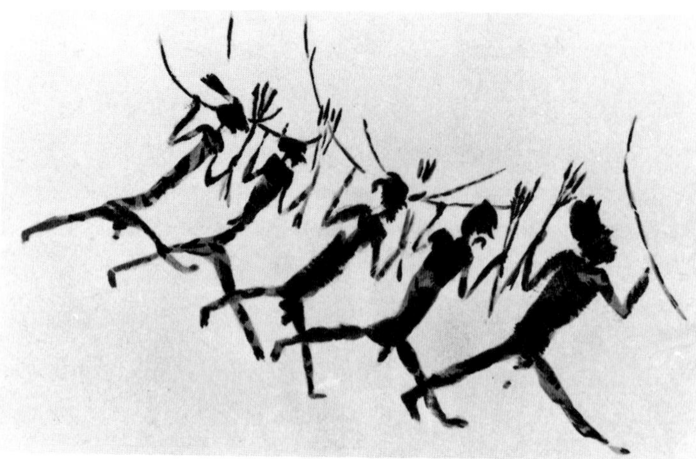

709 WARRIORS. Gasulla Gorge, Castellon, Spain.
c. 8000-3000 B.C.
Approx. 9" wide.

Art is in a transitional period as the twentieth century draws to a close. It is not clear whether signs of a return to content over form will persist, or whether emphasis on content, in turn, will be superseded by the needs of the next generation.

The best art responds to its time while maintaining its connection to the past. The two images on this page were created at least five thousand years apart. The size and energy of Jonathan Borofsky's RUNNING PEOPLE sweeps the viewer into the painting. These running figures are among the many images that result from the artist's practice of drawing quickly after dreaming, then enlarging the drawings on wall surfaces.

Compare Borofsky's painting with WARRIORS, a prehistoric painting of marching figures, painted five to ten thousand years ago. While the sizes of the two images are vastly different (the recent painting is 28 feet long; the prehistoric one is 9 inches across), each is a response to human experience. These artists were attempting to understand and interact with life, to find purpose and meaning.

Art and human life have changed considerably since prehistoric times, but art's primary purpose endures. Creative expression is a function of being human, a response to being alive.

Appreciation for the artistic dimension within each of us is as important as the recognition of the roles of art and artists in society at large. If, in the process of strengthening our understanding and appreciation for the art produced by recognized masters, we neglect the art within ourselves, we will be worse off than when we started. To prevent such a dead end, it is necessary to give equal care and attention to the development of the artist within.

Art offers us a way to go beyond mere physical existence. We, the creatures with the most advanced consciousness, have been described as nature becoming aware of itself.

We form art. Art forms us.

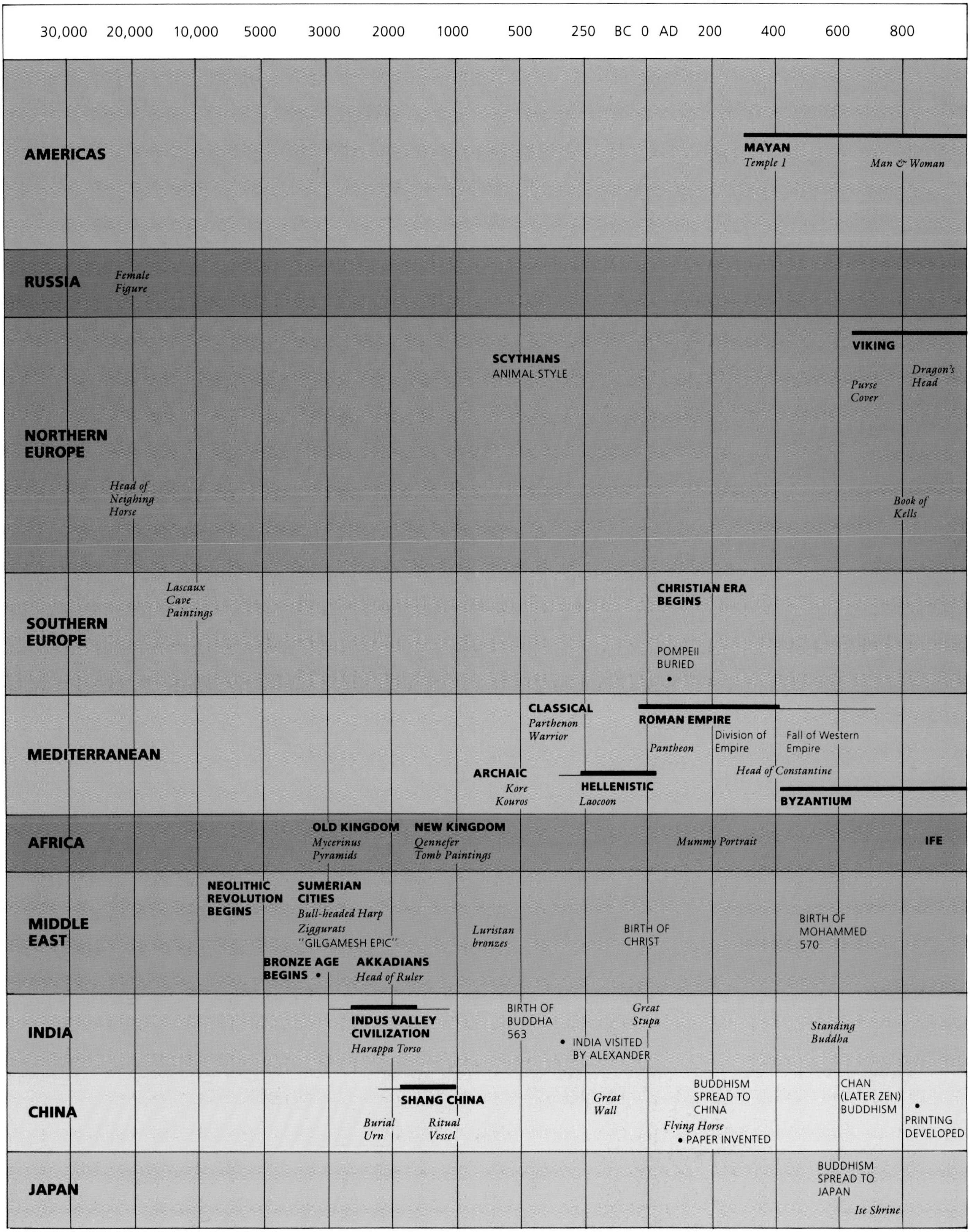

30,000	20,000	10,000	5000	3000	2000	1000	500	250	BC 0 AD	200	400	600	800

Region	Entries (left to right along the timeline)
AMERICAS	**MAYAN** *Temple 1*; *Man & Woman*
RUSSIA	*Female Figure*
NORTHERN EUROPE	*Head of Neighing Horse*; **SCYTHIANS** ANIMAL STYLE; **VIKING** *Purse Cover*; *Dragon's Head*; *Book of Kells*
SOUTHERN EUROPE	*Lascaux Cave Paintings*; **CHRISTIAN ERA BEGINS**; POMPEII BURIED •
MEDITERRANEAN	**ARCHAIC** *Kore Kouros*; **CLASSICAL** *Parthenon Warrior*; **HELLENISTIC** *Laocoon*; **ROMAN EMPIRE** *Pantheon*; Division of Empire; Fall of Western Empire; *Head of Constantine*; **BYZANTIUM**
AFRICA	**OLD KINGDOM** *Mycerinus Pyramids*; **NEW KINGDOM** *Qennefer Tomb Paintings*; *Mummy Portrait*; **IFE**
MIDDLE EAST	**NEOLITHIC REVOLUTION BEGINS**; **BRONZE AGE BEGINS** •; **SUMERIAN CITIES** *Bull-headed Harp* *Ziggurats* "GILGAMESH EPIC"; **AKKADIANS** *Head of Ruler*; *Luristan bronzes*; BIRTH OF CHRIST; BIRTH OF MOHAMMED 570
INDIA	**INDUS VALLEY CIVILIZATION** *Harappa Torso*; BIRTH OF BUDDHA 563; • INDIA VISITED BY ALEXANDER; *Great Stupa*; *Standing Buddha*
CHINA	*Burial Urn*; **SHANG CHINA**; *Ritual Vessel*; *Great Wall*; BUDDHISM SPREAD TO CHINA; *Flying Horse*; • PAPER INVENTED; CHAN (LATER ZEN) BUDDHISM; • PRINTING DEVELOPED
JAPAN	BUDDHISM SPREAD TO JAPAN; *Ise Shrine*

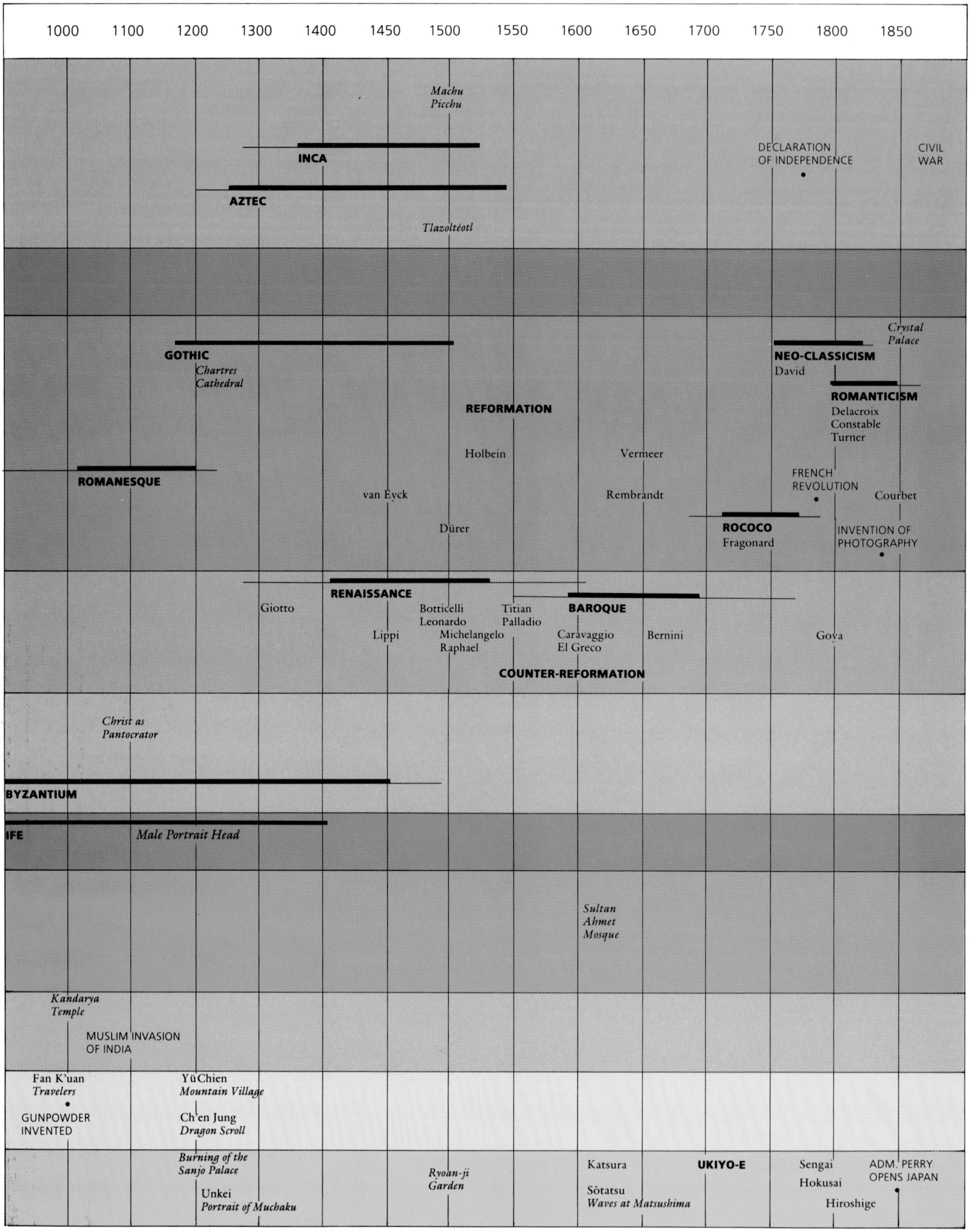

1000 | 1100 | 1200 | 1300 | 1400 | 1450 | 1500 | 1550 | 1600 | 1650 | 1700 | 1750 | 1800 | 1850

Machu Picchu

INCA

AZTEC

Tlazoltéotl

DECLARATION OF INDEPENDENCE

CIVIL WAR

GOTHIC

Chartres Cathedral

ROMANESQUE

van Eyck

REFORMATION

Holbein

Dürer

Vermeer

Rembrandt

Crystal Palace

NEO-CLASSICISM

David

ROMANTICISM

Delacroix

Constable

Turner

FRENCH REVOLUTION

Courbet

ROCOCO

Fragonard

INVENTION OF PHOTOGRAPHY

Giotto

RENAISSANCE

Lippi

Botticelli

Leonardo

Michelangelo

Raphael

Titian

Palladio

BAROQUE

Caravaggio

El Greco

Bernini

COUNTER-REFORMATION

Goya

Christ as Pantocrator

BYZANTIUM

IFE

Male Portrait Head

Sultan Ahmet Mosque

Kandarya Temple

MUSLIM INVASION OF INDIA

Fan K'uan
Travelers

GUNPOWDER INVENTED

Yü Chien
Mountain Village

Ch'en Jung
Dragon Scroll

Burning of the Sanjo Palace

Unkei
Portrait of Muchaku

Ryoan-ji Garden

Katsura

Sôtatsu
Waves at Matsushima

UKIYO-E

Sengai

Hokusai

Hiroshige

ADM. PERRY OPENS JAPAN

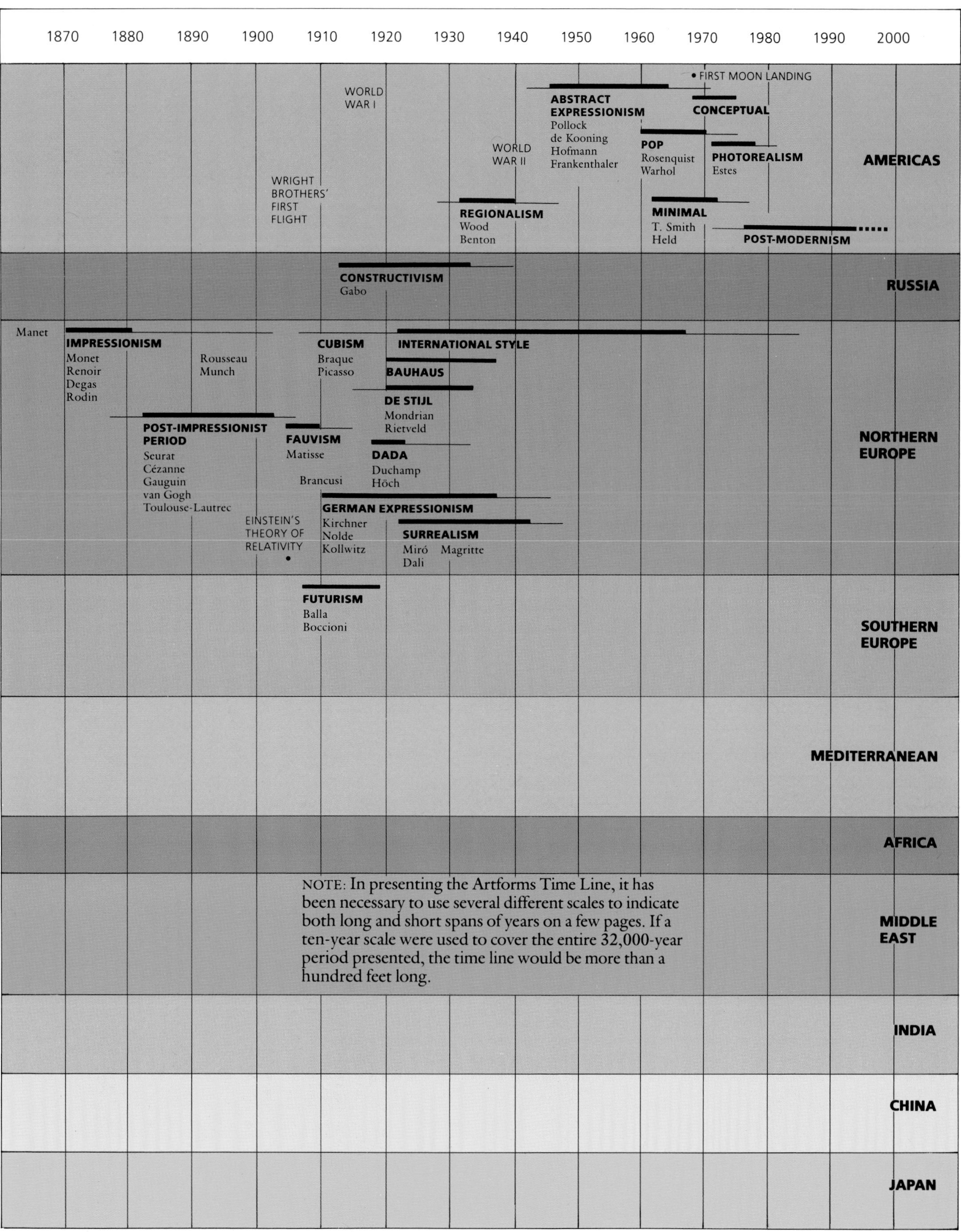

NOTE: In presenting the Artforms Time Line, it has been necessary to use several different scales to indicate both long and short spans of years on a few pages. If a ten-year scale were used to cover the entire 32,000-year period presented, the time line would be more than a hundred feet long.

GLOSSARY

The following terms are defined according to their usage in the visual arts. A term in *italics* has its own listing in the glossary.

abstract art Art that departs significantly from natural appearances. Forms are modified or changed to varying degrees in order to emphasize certain qualities or content. Recognizable references to original appearances may be slight. The term is also used to describe art that is *nonrepresentational.*

Abstract Expressionism An art movement, primarily in painting, that originated in the United States in the 1940s and remained strong through the 1950s. Artists working in many different styles emphasized spontaneous personal expression in large paintings that are *abstract* or *nonrepresentational.* One type of Abstract Expressionism is called *action painting.* See also *expressionism.*

Abstract Surrealism See *Surrealism.*

academic art Art governed by rules, especially art sanctioned by an official institution, academy, or school. Originally applied to art that conformed to standards established by the French Academy regarding composition, drawing, and color usage. The term has come to mean conservative and lacking in originality.

academy An institution of artists and scholars, originally formed during the Renaissance to free artists from control by guilds and to elevate them from artisan to professional status. In an academy, art is taught as a *humanist* discipline along with other disciplines of the liberal arts.

achromatic Having no color or *hue*; without identifiable hue. Most blacks, whites, grays, and browns are achromatic.

acrylic (acrylic resin) A clear plastic used as a *binder* in paint and as a casting material in sculpture.

action painting A style of *nonrepresentational* painting that relies on the physical movement of the artist in using such gestural techniques as vigorous brushwork, dripping, and pouring. Dynamism is often created through the interlaced directions of the paint. A subcategory of *Abstract Expressionism.*

additive color mixture When light colors are combined (as with overlapping spotlights), the result becomes successively lighter. Light primaries, when combined, create white light. See also *subtractive color mixture.*

additive sculpture Sculptural form produced by combining or building up material from a core or *armature.* Modeling in clay and welding steel are additive processes.

aerial perspective See *perspective.*

aesthetic Relating to the sense of the beautiful and to heightened sensory perception in general.

aesthetics The study and philosophy of the quality and nature of sensory responses related to, but not limited by, the concept of beauty.

afterimage The visual impression that remains after the initial stimulus is removed. Staring at a single intense *hue* may cause the cones, or color receptors, of the eye to become so fatigued that they perceive only the complement of the original hue when it has been removed.

airbrush A small-scale paint sprayer that allows the artist to control a fine mist of paint.

analogous colors or **analogous hues** Closely related *hues*, especially those in which we can see a common hue; hues that are neighbors on the color wheel, such as blue, blue-green, and green.

Analytical Cubism See *Cubism.*

aperture In photography, the *camera* lens opening and its relative diameter. Measured in f-stops, such as f/8, f/11, etc. As the number increases, the size of the aperture decreases, thereby reducing the amount of light passing through the *lens* and striking the film.

applied art Art in which aesthetic values are used in the design or decoration of utilitarian objects.

aquatint An *intaglio* printmaking process in which value areas rather than lines are etched on the printing plate. Powdered resin is sprinkled on the plate and heated until it adheres. The plate is then immersed in an acid bath. The acid bites around the resin particles, creating a rough surface that holds ink. Also, a *print* made using this process.

arabesque Ornament or surface decoration with intricate curves and flowing lines based on plant forms.

arcade A series of *arches* supported by columns or piers. Also, a covered passageway between two series of arches or between a series of arches and a wall.

arch A curved structure designed to span an opening, usually made of stone or other masonry. Roman arches are semicircular; Islamic and Gothic arches come to a point at the top.

armature A rigid framework serving as a supporting inner core for clay or other soft sculpting material.

Art Nouveau A style that originated in the late 1880s, based on the sinuous curves of plant forms, used primarily in architectural detailing and the applied arts.

assemblage Sculpture using preexisting, sometimes "found" objects that may or may not contribute their original identities to the total content of the work.

asymmetrical Without *symmetry.*

atmospheric perspective See *perspective.*

automatism Automatic or unconscious action. Employed by *Surrealist* writers and artists to allow unconscious ideas and feelings to be expressed.

avant-garde French for "'advance guard" or "vanguard." Those considered the leaders (and often regarded as radicals) in the invention and application of new concepts in a given field.

axis An implied straight line in the center of a form along its dominant direction.

balance An arrangement of parts achieving a state of equilibrium between opposing forces or influences. Major types are symmetrical and *asymmetrical.* See *symmetry.*

Baroque The seventeenth-century period in Europe characterized in the visual arts by dramatic light and shade, turbulent composition, and exaggerated emotional expression.

barrel vault See *vault.*

bas-relief See *relief sculpture.*

Bauhaus German art school in existence from 1919 to 1933, best known for its influence on design, leadership in art education, and a radically innovative philosophy of applying design principles to machine technology and mass production.

beam The horizontal stone or timber placed across an architectural space to take the weight of the roof or wall above; also called a lintel.

binder The material used in paint that causes *pigment* particles to adhere to one another and to the *support*; for example, linseed oil or acrylic polymer.

buttress A *support,* usually exterior, for a wall, *arch,* or *vault,* that opposes the lateral forces of these structures. A flying buttress consists of a strut or segment of an arch carrying the thrust of a vault to a vertical pier positioned away from the main portion of the building. An important element in *Gothic* cathedrals.

Byzantine art Styles of painting, design, and architecture developed from the fifth century A.D. in the Byzantine Empire of eastern Europe. Characterized in architecture by round *arches,* large *domes,* and extensive use of *mosaic;* characterized in painting by formal design, *frontal* and *stylized* figures, and a rich use of color, especially gold, in generally religious subject matter.

calligraphy The art of beautiful writing. Broadly, a flowing use of line, often varying from thick to thin.

camera obscura A dark room (or box) with a small hole in one side, through which an inverted image of the view outside is projected onto the opposite wall, screen, or mirror. The image is then traced. This forerunner of the modern camera was a tool for recording an optically accurate image.

cantilever A beam or slab projecting a substantial distance beyond its supporting post or wall; a projection supported at only one end.

capital In architecture, the top part, capstone, or head of a column or pillar.

caricature A representation in which the subject's distinctive features are exaggerated.

cartoon 1. A humorous or satirical drawing. 2. A drawing completed as a full-scale working drawing, usually for a *fresco* painting, *mural,* or tapestry.

carving A *subtractive* process in which a sculpture is formed by removing material from a block or mass of wood, stone, or other material, using sharpened tools.

casein A white, tasteless, odorless milk protein used in making paint as well as plastics, adhesives, and foods.

casting A process that involves pouring liquid material such as molten metal, clay, wax, or plaster into a mold. When the liquid hardens, the mold is removed, leaving a form in the shape of the mold.

ceramic Objects made of clay hardened into a relatively permanent material by firing. Also, the process of making such objects.

chiaroscuro Italian for "light-dark." The gradations of light and dark *values* in *two-dimensional* imagery; especially the illusion of rounded, three-dimensional form created through gradations of light and shade rather than line. Highly developed by *Renaissance* painters.

chroma See *intensity.*

cinematography The art and technique of making motion pictures, especially the work done by motion picture camera operators.

classical 1. The art of ancient Greece and Rome. More specifically, Classical refers to the style of Greek art that flourished during the fifth century B.C. 2. Any art based on a clear, rational, and regular structure, emphasizing horizontal and vertical directions, and organizing its parts with special emphasis on balance and proportion. The term classic is also used to indicate recognized excellence.

closed form A self-contained or explicitly limited form; having a resolved balance of tensions, a sense of calm completeness implying a totality within itself.

cluster houses Residential units placed close together in order to maximize the usable exterior space of the surrounding area, within the concept of single-family dwellings.

coffer In architecture, a decorative sunken panel on the underside of a ceiling.

collage From the French *coller,* to glue. A work made by gluing materials such as paper scraps, photographs, and cloth on to a flat surface.

colonnade A row of columns usually spanned or connected by *beams* (lintels).

color field painting A movement that grew out of *Abstract Expressionism,* in which large stained or painted areas or "fields" of color evoke aesthetic and emotional responses.

color wheel A circular arrangement of contiguous spectral *hues* used in some color systems. Also called a color circle.

complementary colors Two *hues* directly opposite one another on a *color wheel* which, when mixed together in proper proportions, produce a neutral gray. The true complement of a color can be seen in its *afterimage.*

composition The bringing together of parts or elements to form a whole; the structure, organization, or total form of a work of art. See also *design.*

Conceptual art An art form in which the originating idea and the process by which it is presented take precedence over a tangible product. Conceptual works are sometimes produced in visible form, but they often exist only as descriptions of mental concepts or ideas. This trend developed in the late 1960s, in part as a way to avoid the commercialization of art.

content Meaning or message contained and communicated by a work of art, including its emotional, intellectual, symbolic, thematic, and narrative connotations.

contour The edge or apparent line that separates one area or mass from another; a line following a surface drawn to suggest volume.

contrapposto Italian for "counterpoise." The counterpositioning of parts of the human figure about a central vertical axis, as when the weight is placed on one foot, causing the hip and shoulder lines to counterbalance each other, often in a graceful S-curve.

cool colors Colors whose relative visual temperatures make them seem cool. Cool colors generally include green, blue-green, blue, blue-violet, and violet. The quality of warmness or coolness is relative to adjacent hues. See also *warm colors.*

cross-hatching See *hatching.*

Cubism The most influential style of the twentieth century, developed in Paris by Picasso and Braque, beginning in 1907. The early mature phase of the style, called Analytical Cubism, lasted from 1909 through 1911. Cubism is based on the simultaneous presentation of multiple views, disintegration, and the geometric reconstruction of subjects in flattened, ambiguous pictorial space; figure and ground merge into one interwoven surface of shifting planes. Color is limited to *neutrals.* By 1912 the more decorative phase called Synthetic (or Collage) Cubism, began to appear; it was characterized by fewer, more solid forms, conceptual rather than observed subject matter, and richer color and texture.

curtain wall A non-load-bearing wall.

curvilinear Formed or characterized by curving lines or edges.

Dada A movement in art and literature, founded in Switzerland in the early twentieth century, which ridiculed contemporary culture and conventional art. The Dadaists shared an antimilitaristic and antiaesthetic attitude, generated in part by the horrors of World War I and in part by a rejection of accepted canons of morality and taste. The anarchic spirit of Dada can be seen in the works of Duchamp, Man Ray, Hoch, Miró, and Picasso. Many Dadaists later explored *Surrealism.*

depth of field The area of sharp focus in a photograph. Depth of field becomes greater as the f-stop number is increased.

design Both the process and the result of structuring the elements of visual form; composition.

De Stijl Dutch for "the style,"a purist art movement begun in the Netherlands during World War I by Mondrian and others. It involved painters, sculptors, designers, and architects whose works and ideas were expressed in *De Stijl* magazine. De Stijl was aimed at creating a universal language of *form* that would be independent of individual emotion. Visual form was pared down to primary colors, plus black and white, and rectangular shapes. The movement was influential primarily in architecture.

divisionism See *pointillism.*

dome A generally hemispherical roof or *vault.* Theoretically, an *arch* rotated 360 degrees on its vertical *axis.*

drypoint An *intaglio* printmaking process in which lines are scratched directly into a metal plate with a steel needle. Also, the resulting *print.*

earth art; earthworks Sculptural forms of earth, rocks, or sometimes plants, often on a vast scale and in remote locations. Some are deliberately impermanent.

eclecticism The practice of selecting or borrowing from earlier styles and combining the borrowed elements.

edition In printmaking, the total number of *prints* made and approved by an artist, usually numbered consecutively. Also, a limited number of multiple originals of a single design in any medium.

elevation In architecture, a scale drawing of any vertical side of a given structure.

encaustic A painting medium in which *pigment* is suspended in a *binder* of hot wax.

engraving An *intaglio* printmaking process in which grooves are cut into a metal or wood surface with a sharp cutting tool called a burin or graver. Also, the resulting *print.*

entasis In *classical* architecture, the slight swelling or bulge in the center of a column, which corrects the illusion of concave tapering produced by parallel straight lines.

etching An *intaglio* printmaking process in which a metal plate is first coated with acid-resistant wax, then scratched to expose the metal to the bite of nitric acid where lines are desired. Also, the resulting *print.*

expressionism The broad term that describes emotional art, most often boldly executed and making free use of distortion and symbolic or invented color. More specifically, Expressionism refers to individual and group styles originating in Europe in the late nineteenth and early twentieth centuries. See also *Abstract Expressionism.*

eye level The height of the viewer's eyes above the ground plane.

facade In architecture, a term used to refer to the front exterior of a building. Also, other exterior sides when they are emphasized.

Fauvism A style of painting introduced in Paris in the early twentieth century, characterized by areas of bright, contrasting color and simplified shapes. The name *les fauves* is French for "the wild beasts."

figure Separate shape(s) distinguishable from a background or *ground.*

fine art Art created for purely aesthetic expression, communication, or contemplation. Painting and sculpture are the best known of the fine arts.

flamboyant Any design dominated by flamelike, curvilinear rhythms. In architecture, having complex, flamelike forms characteristic of fifteenth- and sixteenth-century *Gothic* style.

flying buttress See *buttress.*

folk art Art of people who have had no formal, academic training, but whose works are part of an established tradition of style and craftsmanship.

foreshortening The representation of *forms* on a *two-dimensional* surface by presenting the length in such a way that the long *axis* appears to project toward or recede away from the viewer.

form In the broadest sense, the total physical characteristics of an object, event, or situation.

formalist Having an emphasis on highly structured visual relationships rather than on subject matter or nonvisual content.

format The shape or proportions of a *picture plane.*

fresco A painting technique in which *pigments* suspended in water are applied to a damp lime-plaster surface. The pigments dry to become part of the plaster wall or surface.

frontal An adjective describing an object that faces the viewer directly, rather than being set at an angle or *foreshortened.*

Futurism A group movement that originated in Italy in 1909. One of several movements to grow out of *Cubism.* Futurists added implied motion to the shifting planes and multiple observation points of the Cubists; they celebrated natural as well as mechanical motion and speed. Their glorification of danger, war, and the machine age was in keeping with the martial spirit developing in Italy at the time.

geodesic A geometric form basic to structures using short sections of lightweight material joined into interlocking polygons. Also a structural system developed by R. Buckminster Fuller to create *domes* using the above principle.

gesso A mixture of glue and either chalk or plaster of paris applied as a *ground* or coating to surfaces in order to give them the correct properties to receive paint. Gesso can also be built up or molded into *relief* designs, or carved.

glaze In *ceramics,* a vitreous or glassy coating applied to seal and decorate surfaces. Glaze may be colored, transparent, or opaque. In oil painting, a thin transparent or translucent layer brushed over another layer of paint, allowing the first layer to show through but altering its color slightly.

Gothic Primarily an architectural style that prevailed in western Europe from the twelfth through the fifteenth centuries, characterized by pointed *arches,* ribbed *vaults,* and flying *buttresses,* that made it possible to create stone buildings that reached great heights.

gouache An opaque, water-soluble paint. *Watercolor* to which opaque white has been added.

green belt A strip of planned or protected open space, consisting of recreational parks, farm land, or uncultivated land, often used to define and limit the boundaries of a community and prevent urban sprawl.

ground The background in two-dimensional works—the area around and between *figures.* Also, the surface onto which paint is applied.

Happening An event conceived by artists and performed by artists and others, usually unrehearsed and without a specific script or stage.

hard-edge A term first used in the 1950s to distinguish styles of painting in which shapes are precisely defined by sharp edges, in contrast to the usually blurred or soft edges in *Abstract Expressionist* paintings.

hatching A technique used in drawing and linear forms of printmaking, in which lines are placed in parallel series to darken the value of an area. Cross-hatching is drawing one set of hatchings over another in a different direction so that the lines cross.

Hellenistic Style of the last of three phases of ancient Greek art (300-100 B.C.), characterized by emotion, drama, and the interaction of sculptural forms with the surrounding space.

hierarchic proportion Use of unnatural *proportion* to show the relative importance of figures.

high key Exclusive use of pale or light *values* within a given area or surface.

horizon line In linear *perspective,* the implied or actual line or edge placed on a *two-dimensional* surface to represent the place in nature where the sky meets the horizontal land or water plane. The horizon line matches the *eye level* on a two-dimensional surface. Lines or edges parallel to the ground plane and moving away from the viewer appear to converge at *vanishing points* on the horizon line.

hue That property of a color identifying a specific, named wavelength of light such as green, red, violet, and so on.

humanism A cultural and intellectual movement during the *Renaissance,* following the rediscovery of the art and literature of ancient Greece and Rome. A philosophy or attitude concerned with the interests, achievements, and capabilities of human beings rather than with the abstract concepts and problems of theology or science.

icon An image or symbolic representation often with sacred significance.

iconography The symbolic meanings of subjects and signs used to convey ideas important to particular cultures or religions, and the conventions governing the use of such forms.

impasto In painting, thick paint applied to a surface in a heavy manner, having the appearance and consistency of buttery paste.

Impressionism A style of painting that originated in France about 1870. Paintings of casual subjects, executed outdoors, using divided brush strokes to capture the mood of a particular moment as defined by the transitory effects of light and color. The first Impressionist exhibit was held in 1874.

intaglio Any printmaking technique in which lines and areas to be inked and transferred to paper are recessed below the surface of the printing plate. *Etching, engraving, drypoint,* and *aquatint* are all intaglio processes. See also *print.*

intensity The relative purity or saturation of a *hue* (color), on a scale from bright (pure) to dull (mixed with another hue or a *neutral*). Also called chroma.

intermediate color A *hue* between a primary and a secondary on the color wheel, such as yellow-green, a mixture of yellow and green.

International Style An architectural style that emerged in several European countries between 1910 and 1920. Related to purism and *De Stijl* in painting, it joined structure and exterior design into a noneclectic form based on rectangular geometry and growing out of the basic function and structure of the building.

kiln An oven in which pottery or *ceramic* ware is fired.

kinetic art Art that incorporates actual movement as part of the design.

kore Greek for "maiden." An Archaic Greek statue of a standing clothed young woman.

kouros Greek for "youth." An Archaic Greek statue of a standing nude young male.

lens The part of a camera that concentrates light and focuses the image.

linear perspective See *perspective.*

lintel See *beam.*

lithography A planographic printmaking technique based on the antipathy of oil and water. The image is drawn with a grease crayon or painted with *tusche* on a stone or grained aluminum plate. The surface is then chemically treated and dampened so that it will accept ink only where the crayon or tusche has been used.

local color The actual color as distinguished from the apparent color of objects and surfaces; true color, without shadows or reflections.

logo Short for "logotype." Sign, name, or trademark of an institution, firm, or publication, consisting of letter forms borne on one printing plate or piece of type.

loom A device for producing cloth by interweaving fibers at right angles.

low key Consistent use of dark *values* within a given area or surface.

lumina The use of actual light as an art *medium.*

Mannerism A style that developed in the sixteenth century as a reaction to the classical rationality and balanced harmony of the High *Renaissance;* characterized by the dramatic use of space and light, exaggerated color, elongation of figures, and distortions of *perspective, scale,* and *proportion.*

mass Three-dimensional form having physical bulk. Also, the illusion of such a form on a *two-dimensional* surface.

mat Border of cardboard or similar material placed around a picture as a neutral area between the frame and the picture.

matte A dull finish or surface, especially in painting, photography, and *ceramics.*

medium (pl. media or mediums) 1. A particular material along with its accompanying technique; a specific type of artistic technique or means of expression determined by the use of particular materials. 2. In paint, the fluid in which *pigment* is suspended, allowing it to spread and adhere to the surface.

Minimalism A *nonrepresentational* style of sculpture and painting, usually severely restricted in the use of visual elements and often consisting of simple geometric shapes or masses. The style came to prominence in the late 1960s.

mixed media Works of art made with more than one *medium.*

mobile A type of sculpture in which parts move, often activated by air currents. See also *kinetic art.*

modeling 1. Working pliable material such as clay or wax into *three-dimensional* forms. 2. In drawing or painting, the effect of light falling on a three-dimensional object so that the illusion of its *mass* is created and defined by *value* gradations.

modernism Theory and practice in late nineteenth- and twentieth-century art, which holds that each new generation must build on past styles in new ways or break with the past in order to make the next major historical contribution. Characterized by idealism;

seen as "high art," as differentiated from popular art. In painting, most clearly seen in the work of the *Post-Impressionists,* beginning in 1885; in architecture, most evident in the work of *Bauhaus* and *International Style* architects, beginning about 1920.

module A standard unit of measure in architecture. The part of a structure used as a standard by which the rest is proportioned.

monochromatic A color scheme limited to variations of one *hue;* a hue with its *tints* and/or *shades.*

montage 1. A composition made up of pictures or parts of pictures previously drawn, painted, or photographed. 2. In motion pictures, the combining of separate bits of film to portray the character of a single event through multiple views.

mosaic An art medium in which small pieces of colored glass, stone, or ceramic tile called tessera are embedded in a background material such as plaster or mortar. Also, works made using this technique.

mural A large wall painting, often executed in fresco.

naturalism Representational art in which the artist presents a subjective interpretation of visual reality while retaining something of the natural appearance or look of the objects depicted. Naturalism varies greatly from artist to artist, depending on the degree and kind of subjective interpretation.

naive art Art made by people with no formal art training.

nave The tall central space of a church or cathedral, usually flanked by side aisles.

negative shape A background or *ground* shape seen in relation to foreground or *figure* shapes.

Neoclassicism New classicism. A revival of classical Greek and Roman forms in art, music, and literature, particularly during the eighteenth and nineteenth centuries in Europe and America. It was part of a reaction to the excesses of *Baroque* and *Rococo* art.

neutrals Not associated with any single *hue.* Blacks, whites, grays, and dull gray-browns. A neutral can be made by mixing complementary hues.

nonobjective See *nonrepresentational* and *abstract art.*

nonrepresentational Art without reference to anything outside itself—without representation. Also called nonobjective—without recognizable objects.

offset printing Planographic printing by indirect image-transfer from photomechanical plates. The plate transfers ink to a rubber-covered cylinder, which "offsets" the ink to the paper. Also called photo-offset and offset lithography.

oil paint Paint in which the *pigment* is held together with a *binder* of oil, usually linseed oil.

opaque Impenetrable by light; not transparent or translucent.

open form A form whose contour is irregular or broken, having a sense of growth, change, or unresolved tension; form in a state of becoming.

optical color mixture Apparent rather than actual color mixture, produced by interspersing brush strokes or dots of color instead of physically mixing them. The implied mixing occurs in the eye of the viewer and produces a lively color sensation.

painterly Painting characterized by openness of form, in which shapes are defined by loose brushwork in light and dark color areas rather than by outline or contour.

pastels 1. Sticks of powdered pigment held together with a gum binding agent. 2. Pale colors or *tints.*

performance art Dramatic presentation by visual artists (as distinguished from theater artists such as actors and dancers) before an audience, usually apart from a formal theatrical setting.

perspective A system for creating an illusion of depth or *three-dimensional* space on a *two-dimensional* surface. Usually refers to linear perspective, which is based on the fact that parallel lines or edges appear to converge and objects appear smaller as the distance between them and the viewer increases. Atmospheric perspective (aerial perspective) creates the illusion of distance by reducing color saturation, value contrast, and detail in order to imply the hazy effect of atmosphere between the viewer and distant objects. *Isometric perspective* is not a visual or optical interpretation, but a mechanical means to show space and volume in rectangular forms. Parallel lines remain parallel; there is no convergence.

perspective rendering A view of an architectural structure drawn in linear *perspective,* usually from a three-quarter view or similar vantage point that shows two sides of the proposed building.

photorealism A style of painting that became prominent in the 1970s, based on the cool objectivity of photographs as records of subjects.

pictorial space In a painting or other *two-dimensional* art, illusionary space which appears to recede backward into depth from the *picture plane.*

picture plane The *two-dimensional* picture surface.

pigment Any coloring agent, made from natural or synthetic substances, used in paints or drawing materials.

plan In architecture, a *scale* drawing in diagrammatic form showing the basic layout of the interior and exterior spaces of a structure, as if seen in a cutaway view from above.

plastic 1. Pliable; capable of being shaped. Pertaining to the process of shaping or modeling (i.e., the plastic arts). 2. Synthetic polymer substances, such as *acrylic.*

pointillism A system of painting using tiny dots or "points" of color, developed by French artist Georges Seurat in the 1880s. Seurat systematized the divided brushwork and *optical color mixture* of the *Impressionists* and called this technique divisionism.

polychromatic Having many colors; random or intuitive use of color combinations as opposed to color selection based on a specific color scheme.

Pop Art A style of painting and sculpture that developed in the late 1950s and early 1960s, in Britain and the United States; based on the visual clichés, subject matter, and impersonal style of popular mass-media imagery.

positive shape A *figure* or foreground shape, as opposed to a *negative* ground or background shape.

post-and-beam system (post and lintel) In architecture, a structural system that uses two or more uprights or posts to support a horizontal beam (or lintel) which spans the space between them.

Post-Impressionism A general term applied to various personal styles of painting by French artists (or artists living in France) that developed from about 1885 to 1900 in reaction to what these artists saw as the somewhat formless and aloof quality of *Impressionist* painting. Post-Impressionist painters were concerned with the significance of form, symbols, expressiveness, and psychological intensity. They can be broadly separated into two groups, *expressionists,* such as Gauguin and Van Gogh, and *formalists,* such as Cézanne and Seurat.

Post-Modern An attitude or trend of the 1970s, 1980s, and 1990s, in which artists and architects accept all that *modernism* rejects. In architecture, the movement away from or beyond what had become boring adaptations of the *International Style,* in favor of an imaginative, eclectic approach. In the other visual arts, Post-Modern is characterized by an acceptance of all periods and styles, including modernism, and a willingness to combine elements of all styles and periods. Although modernism makes distinctions between high art and popular taste, Post-Modernism makes no such value judgments.

prehistoric art Art created before written history. Often the only record of early cultures.

primary colors Those *hues* that cannot be produced by mixing other hues. *Pigment* primaries are red, yellow, and blue; light primaries are red, green, and blue. Theoretically, pigment primaries can be mixed together to form all the other hues in the spectrum.

prime In painting, a first layer of paint or sizing applied to a surface that is to be painted.

print (artist's print) A multiple-original impression made from a plate, stone, wood block, or screen by an artist or made under the artist's supervision. Prints are usually made in *editions,* with each print numbered and signed by the artist.

proportion The size relationship of parts to a whole and to one another.

realism 1. A type of *representational art* in which the artist depicts as closely as possible what the eye sees. 2. Realism. The mid-nineteenth-century style of Courbet and others, based on the idea that ordinary people and everyday activities are worthy subjects for art.

registration In color printmaking or machine printing, the process of aligning the impressions of blocks or plates on the same sheet of paper.

reinforced concrete (ferroconcrete) Concrete with steel mesh or bars embedded in it to increase its tensile strength.

relief printing A printing technique in which the parts of the printing surface that carry ink are left raised, while the remaining areas are cut away. Woodcuts and linoleum prints (linocuts) are relief prints.

relief sculpture Sculpture in which *three-dimensional* forms project from a flat background of which they are a part. The degree of projection can vary and is described by the terms high relief and low relief (bas-relief).

Renaissance Period in Europe from the late fourteenth through the sixteenth centuries, characterized by a renewed interest in human-centered *classical* art, literature, and learning. See also *humanism.*

representational art Art in which it is the artist's intention to present again or represent a particular subject; especially pertaining to realistic portrayal of subject matter.

reproduction A mechanically produced copy of an original work of art; not to be confused with an original *print* or fine print.

rhythm The regular or ordered repetition of dominant and subordinate elements or units within a design.

ribbed vault See *vault.*

Rococo From the French *rocaille* meaning "rock work." This late *Baroque* (c. 1715-1775) style used in interior decoration and painting was characteristically playful, pretty, romantic, and visually loose or soft; it used small *scale* and ornate decoration, *pastel* colors, and asymmetrical arrangement of curves. Rococo was popular in France and southern Germany in the 18th century.

Romanesque A style of European architecture prevalent from the ninth to the twelfth centuries, with round *arches* and barrel *vaults* influenced by Roman architecture and characterized by heavy stone construction.

Romanticism 1. A literary and artistic movement of late eighteenth- and nineteenth-century Europe, aimed at asserting the validity of subjective experience as a countermovement to the often cold formulas of *Neoclassicism;* characterized by intense emotional excitement and depictions of powerful forces in nature, exotic lifestyles, danger, suffering, and nostalgia. 2. Art of any period based on spontaneity, intuition, and emotion rather than carefully organized rational approaches to form.

salon A general term for a group art exhibition in France.

saturation See *intensity.*

scale The size or apparent size of an object seen in relation to other objects, people, or its environment or *format.* Also used to refer to the quality or monumentality found in some objects regardless of their size. In architectural drawings, the ratio of the measurements in the drawing to the measurements in the building.

school of art A group of artists whose work demonstrates a common influence or unifying belief. Schools of art are often defined by geographic origin. When the term is applied to a particular artist, it may refer to work done by the artist's pupils or assistants or to work that imitates the artist's style.

screenprinting (serigraphy) A printmaking technique in which stencils are applied to fabric stretched across a frame. Paint or ink is forced with a squeegee through the unblocked portions of the screen onto paper or other surface beneath.

secondary colors Pigment secondaries are the *hues* orange, violet, and green, which may be produced in slightly dulled form by mixing two *primaries.*

section In architecture, a *scale* drawing of part of a building as seen along an imaginary *plane* that passes through a building vertically.

serigraphy See *screenprinting.*

setback The legal distance that a building must be from property lines. Early setback requirements often increased with the height of a building, resulting in steplike recessions in the rise of tall buildings.

shade A *hue* with black added.

shape A *two-dimensional* or implied two-dimensional area defined by line or changes in value and/or color.

shutter In photography, the part of the camera that controls the length of time the light is allowed to strike the photosensitive film.

silk screen See *screenprinting.*

simultaneous contrast An optical effect caused by the tendency of contrasting forms and colors to emphasize their difference when they are placed together.

site-specific art Any work made for a certain place, which cannot be separated or exhibited apart from its intended environment.

size Any of several substances made from glue, wax, or clay, used as a filler for porous material such as paper, canvas or other cloth, or wall surfaces. Used to protect the surface from the deteriorating effects of paint, particularly oil paint.

still life A painting or other *two-dimensional* work of art representing inanimate objects such as bottles, fruit, and flowers. Also, the arrangement of these objects from which a drawing, painting, or other work is made.

stupa The earliest form of Buddhist architecture, probably derived from Indian funeral mounds.

style A characteristic handling of *media* and elements of form that gives a work its identity as the product of a particular person, group, art movement, period, or culture.

stylized Simplified or exaggerated visual *form* which emphasizes particular or contrived design qualities.

subtractive color mixture Combining of colored *pigments* in the form of paints, inks, pastels, and so on. Called subtractive because reflected light is reduced as pigment colors are combined. See *additive color mixture.*

subtractive sculpture Sculpture made by removing material from a larger block or form.

support The physical material that provides the base for and sustains a *two-dimensional* work of art. Paper is the usual support for drawings and prints; canvas and panels are supports in painting.

Surrealism A movement in literature and the visual arts that developed in the mid-1920s and remained strong until the mid-1940s, growing out of *Dada* and *automatism.* Based upon revealing the unconscious mind in dream images, the irrational, and the fantastic, Surrealism took two directions: *representational* and *abstract.* Dali's and Magritte's paintings, with their uses of impossible combinations of objects depicted in realistic detail, typify representational Surrealism. Miró's paintings, with their use of abstract and fantastic shapes and vaguely defined creatures, are typical of abstract Surrealism.

symbol A form or image implying or representing something beyond its obvious and immediate meaning.

symmetry A design (or composition) with identical or nearly identical form on opposite sides of a dividing line or central *axis;* formal *balance.*

Synthetic Cubism See *Cubism.*

tempera A water-based paint that uses egg, egg yolk, glue, or *casein* as a *binder.* Many commercially made paints identified as tempera are actually *gouache.*

tessera Bit of colored glass, ceramic tile, or stone used in a *mosaic.*

texture The tactile quality of a surface or the representation or invention of the appearance of such a surface quality.

three-dimensional Having height, width, and depth.

throwing The process of forming clay objects on a potter's wheel.

tint A *hue* with white added.

townhouse One of a row of houses connected by common side walls.

trompe l'oeil French for "fool the eye." A *two-dimensional* representation that is so naturalistic that it looks actual or real (*three-dimensional*).

truss In architecture, a structural framework of wood or metal based on a triangular system, used to span, reinforce, or support walls, ceilings, piers, or beams.

tunnel vault (barrel vault) See *vault.*

tusche In *lithography,* a waxy liquid used to draw or paint images on a lithographic stone or plate.

two-dimensional Having the dimensions of height and width only.

typography The art and technique of composing printed materials from type.

unity The appearance of similarity, consistency, or oneness. Interrelational factors that cause various elements to appear as part of a single complete form.

value The lightness or darkness of tones or colors. White is the lightest value; black is the darkest. The value halfway between these extremes is called middle gray.

vanishing point In linear *perspective,* the point on the *horizon line* at which lines or edges that are parallel appear to converge.

vantage point The position from which the viewer looks at an object or visual field; also called observation point or viewpoint.

vault A masonry roof or ceiling constructed on the principle of the *arch.* A tunnel or barrel vault is a semicircular arch extended in depth: a continuous series of arches, one behind the other. A groin vault is formed when two barrel vaults intersect. A ribbed vault is a vault reinforced by masonry ribs.

vehicle Liquid emulsion used as a carrier or spreading agent in paints.

video Television. "Video" emphasizes the visual rather than the audio aspects of the television *medium.* The term is also used to distinguish television used as an art medium from general broadcast television.

visualize To form a mental image or vision; to imagine.

volume 1. Space enclosed or filled by a three-dimensional object or figure. 2. The implied space filled by a painted or drawn object or figure. Synonym: *mass.*

warm colors Colors whose relative visual temperature makes them seem warm. Warm colors or *hues* include red-violet, red, red-orange, orange, yellow-orange, and yellow. See also *cool colors.*

warp In weaving, the threads that run lengthwise in a fabric, crossed at right angles by the *weft.* Also, the process of arranging yarn or thread on a *loom* so as to form a warp.

wash A thin, transparent layer of paint or ink.

watercolor Paint that uses water-soluble gum as the *binder* and water as the *vehicle.* Characterized by transparency. Also, the resulting painting.

weft In weaving, the horizontal threads interlaced through the *warp.* Also called woof.

woodcut A type of *relief print* made from an image that is left raised on a block of wood.

PRONUNCIATION GUIDE

Magdalena Abakanowicz (mahg-dah-*lay*-nuh ah-bah-kah-*no*-vich)
Fra Angelico (frah ahn-*jay*-lee-coe)
Sofonisba Anguissola (so-fah-*niss*-bah ahn-*gwees*-so-la)
Richard Anuszkiewicz (ah-*nuhs*-ke-vich)
Giacomo Balla (*jah*-koh-moh *bahl*-la)
Ernst Barlach (airnst *bahr*-lahk)
Benin (ben-in)
Gianlorenzo Bernini (jahn-low-*ren*-tsoh ber-*nee*-nee)
Umberto Boccioni (oom-*bair*-toh boh-*choh*-nee)
Pierre Bonnard (pee-*air* baw-*nar*)
Hieronymous Bosch (heer-*ahn*-ni-mus *bosh*)
Sandro Botticelli (bought-tee-*chel*-lee)
Louise Bourgeois (boorzh-*wah*)
Constantin Brancusi (*kahn*-stuhn-teen brahn-*koo*-see)
Georges Braque (zhorzh brahk)
Pieter Bruegel (*pee*-ter *broy*-guhl)
Michelangelo Buonarroti, see *Michelangelo*
Callicrates (kah-*lik*-rah-teez)
Michelangelo da Caravaggio (my-kel-*an*-jay-loe da car-ah-*vah*-jyoh)
Henri Cartier-Bresson (on-*ree* car-tee-*ay* bruh-*sohn*)
Mary Cassatt (cah-*sat*)
Paul Cézanne (say-*zahn*)
Marc Chagall (shah-gahl)
Chartres (*shahr*-truh)
Maria Chino (*chee*-noh)
Giorgio de Chirico (*johr*-jyo de *key*-ree-co)
Christo (*kree*-stoh)
Constantine (*kahn*-stuhn-teen)
Billy Curmano (kuhr-*mah*-no)
Gustave Courbet (*goos*-tahv koor-*bay*)
Thomas Couture (toh-*mah* koo-*tyoor*)
Cycladic (sik-*lad*-ik)
Louis Jacques Mandé Daguerre (loo-*ee* zhahk mon-*day* dah-*gair*)
Salvador Dali (*sahl*-vah-dore *dah*-lee)
Honoré Daumier (awn-ohr-*ay doh*-mee-ay)
Jacques Louis David (*zhahk* loo-*ee* dah-*veed*)
John DeAndrea (dee-*ann*-dray-ah)
Edgar Degas (ed-gahr duh-*gah*)
Willem de Kooning (*vill*-em duh *koe*-ning)
Eugène Delacroix (oo-*zhen* duh-lah-*kwah*)
Charles Demuth (day-mooth)
André Derain (on-*dray* duh-*ran*)
Richard Diebenkorn (*dee*-ben-korn)
Henry Dreyfuss (*dray*-fuhs)
Marcel Duchamp (mahr-*sell* doo-*shahm*)
Albrecht Dürer (*ahl*-brekht *duh*-ruhr)
Eugène Durieu (oo-*zhen* doo-ree-*yuh*)
Thomas Eakins (*ay*-kins)
Charles and Ray Eames (eems)
Sergei Eisenstein (sair-gay *eye*-zen-styn)
M. C. Escher (*esh*-uhr)
Fan Kuan (fahn kwahn)
Jean-Honoré Fragonard (zhon oh-no-*ray* fra-go-*nahr*)
Helen Frankenthaler (frank-en-*thahl*-er)
Naum Gabo (nawm *gah*-boh)
Ganges (*gan*-jeez)
Paul Gauguin (go-*gan*)
Jean Léon Gérôme (zhon *lay*-on zhay-*roam*)
Lorenzo Ghiberti (low-*rent*-soh ghee-*bair*-tee)
Alberto Giacometti (ahl-*bair*-toh jah-ko-*met*-tee)
Giotto di Bondone (*joht*-toe dee bone-*doe*-nay)
Giza (*ghee*-zuh)
Francisco Goya (fran-*sis*-coe *go*-yah)
Walter Gropius (*val*-tuhr *grow*-pee-us)
Guan Yin (Kwan Yin) (*gwan* yeen)
Guernica (*gwar*-nih-kah)
Heiji Monogatari (hay-jee mo-no-gah-*tah*-ree)
Hannah Höch (*hahn*-nuh *hohk*)
Hans Hofmann (*hahns hohf*-mahn)
Hokusai (hohk-*sy*)
Hans Holbein (*hahns hohl*-byn)
Pieter de Hooch (*pee*-tuhr duh *hohk*)
Huangshan (hwanhng-shahn)
Ictinus (ick-*tee*-nuhs)
Inca (*eenk*-ah)
Ise (*ee*-say)
Arata Isozaki (ahr-ah-tah ee-so-*zah*-kee)
Ilya Kabakov (*ill*-ya *kob*-ah-kohv)
Kandarya Mahadeva (gan-dahr-reeah mah-hah-*day*-vuh)
Vasily Kandinsky (vass-see-lee can-*din*-skee)
Katsura (kah-*tsoo*-rah)
Anselm Kiefer (*ahn*-sehlm *kee*-fuhr)
Ernst Ludwig Kirchner (*airnst loot*-vik *keerkh*-ner)
Paul Klee (clay)
Gustav Klimt (*goos*-tahv *kleemt*)
Käthe Kollwitz (*kay*-teh *kahl*-wits)
Torii Kiyonobu (tor-ee-ee kee-oh-*noh*-boo)
Torii Kiyotada (tor-ee-ee kee-oh-*tah*-dah)
Konarak (*kohn*-ahr-ok) or (kohn-ehr-rek)
Krishna (*krish*-nuh)
Laocoön (lay-*ah*-koh-ahn)
Lascaux (lass-coe)
Le Corbusier (luh core-boo-zee-ay)
Fernand Léger (fair-*non* lay-*zhay*)
Pierre Charles L'Enfant (pee-*air* sharl lon-*fon*)
Roy Lichtenstein (*lick*-ten-steen)
Maya Lin (*my*-uh *lin*)
Fra Filippo Lippi (frah fill-*leep*-poh *leep*-pee)
Marshall Lomokema (loh-moh-kem-ah)
Machu Picchu (*mah*-choo *peek*-choo)
René Magritte (ruh-*nay* muh-*greet*)
Kasimir Malevich (*kah*-sim-eer mahl-*yay*-vitch)
Edouard Manet (ay-*dwahr* mah-*nay*)
Giacomo Manzu (jah-koh-moh mahn-*dzoo*)
Etienne-Jules Marey (ay-tee-*en* zhyool mah-*ray*)
Marisol (mah-ree-*sohl*)
Masaccio (mah-*sach*-chyo)
Henri Matisse (on-*ree* mah-*tees*)
Maya (*my*-uh)
Michelangelo Buonarroti (my-kel-*an*-jay-loe bwoh-nah-*roe*-tee)
Ludwig Mies van der Rohe (*loot-vik mees* vahn dair *roh*-eh)
Mi Fei (mee fay)
Joan Miró (*zhoh*-ahn mee-*roh*)
Richard Misrach (*miz*-rahk)
Paula Modersohn-Becker (*moh*-dur-zohn *bek*-ur)
Piet Mondrian (*peet mohn*-dree-ahn)
Claude Monet (*klohd* muh-*nay*)
Berthe Morisot (*bairt* moh-ree-*zoh*)
mosque (mahsk)
Edvard Munch (*ed*-vard *moonk*)
Mu Qi (Mu Ch'i) (moo-kee) or (moo-chee)
Eadweard Muybridge (*ed*-wurd *my*-brij)
Mycerinus (miss-uh-*ree*-nuhs)
Emil Nolde (*ay*-muhl *nohl*-duh)
Notre Dame de Chartres (*noh*-truh dahm duh *shahr*-truh)
Claes Oldenburg (klahs ol-den-burg)
José Clemente Orozco (hō-*say* cleh-*men*-tay oh-*rohs*-coh)
Padmapani (*padh*-muh-*pah*-nee)
Nam June Paik (nahm joon pahk)
Andrea Palladio (ahn-*dray*-uh pahl-*lah*-dyo)
Giovanni Paolo Pannini (jyo-*vahn*-nee *pah-oh*-lo pah-*nee*-nee)
John Pfahl (fall)
Pablo Picasso (pab-lo pee-*cah*-so)
Marianna Pineda (pin-*ay*-duh)
Michelangelo Pistoletto (my-kel-*an*-jay-loh pee-stoh-*let*-toh)
Jackson Pollock (*pah*-lock)

Polyclitus (pol-ee-*cly*-tus)
Pompeii (pahm-*pay*)
Pierre-Paul Prud'hon (proo-*dohn*)
Angelo Puccinelli (poo-chee-*nell*-lee)
Radha (*rad*-duh)
Robert Rauschenberg (*roh*-shen-buhrg)
Ad Reinhardt (add *ryn*-hahrt)
Gerrit Reitveld (*gair*-it *ryt*-velt)
O. G. Rejlander (*ray*-lahn-der)
Rembrandt van Rijn (*rem*-brant van *ryne*)
Pierre August Renoir (pee-*err* oh-*goost* ren-*wahr*)
Leni Riefenstahl (len-ee *ree*-fen-stahl)
Diego Rivera (dee-*ay*-goh ree-*vay*-rah)
Sabatino Rodia (roh-*dee*-uh)
Francois August Rodin (frahn-*swah* oh-*goost* roh-*dan*)
Henri Rousseau (on-*ree* roo-*soh*)
Ryoan-ji (ryoh-ahn-jee)
Eero Saarinen (*eer*-oh *sahr*-uh-nen)
Moshe Safdie (*mosh*-uh *sahf*-dee)
Sāñchī (*sahn*-chee)
Raphael Sanzio (ra-fay-el *sahn*-zee-oh)
Hideo Sasaki (hid-ay-oh sah-sah-kee)
Sassetta (suh-*set*-tuh)
Fritz Scholder (*showl*-duhr)
George Segal (*see*-guhl)
Sengai (sen-guy)
Sesshū (seh-shoo)
Georges Seurat (zhorzh sir-*ah*)
Shiva Nātarāja (*shih*-vuh nah-tah-*rah*-jah)
Tawaraya Sōtatsu (tah-wa-*rah*-ya *soh*-taht-soo)
Alfred Stieglitz (*steeg*-lits)
St. Savin-sur-Gartempe (san sah-*vanh* suhr gahr-*tom*)
stupa (*stoo*-pah)
Tagasode (ta-ga-so-day)
Toshiko Takaezu (tosh-ko tah-kah-*ay*-zoo)
Kenzo Tange (ken-zo tahn-gay)
Masami Teraoka (ma-sah-mee tair-ah-oh-ka)
Wayne Thiebaud (*tee*-boh)
Jean Tinguely (zhon tan-*glee*)
Tlingit (*tling*-git)
Henri de Toulouse-Lautrec (on-*ree* duh too-*looz* low-*trek*)
James Turrell (tuh-*rell*)
Tutankhamen (too-tahn-*kahm*-uhn)
Jerry Uelsmann (*uhlz*-man)
Unkei (ung-kay)
Mierle Laderman Ukeles (murl *lad*-er-man oo-*kel*-leez)
Ur (er)
Kitagawa Utamaro (kit-ah-*gah*-wah ut-ah-*mah*-roh)
Theo van Doesburg (*tay*-oh van dohz-*buhrg*)
Jan van Eyck (*yahn* van *ike*)
Vincent van Gogh (*vin*-sent van goe; also, van *gawk*)
Diego Velázquez (dee-*aye*-goh bay-*lahth*-kehth; also, vay-las-kes)
Robert Venturi (ven-*tuhr*-ee)
Jan Vermeer (*yahn* ver-*mair*)
Versailles (vair-*sy*)
Leonardo da Vinci (lay-oh-*nahr*-doh dah *veen*-chi)
Peter Voulkos (*vool*-kohs)
Andy Warhol (*wohr*-hohl)
Yu-Jian (Yü-Chien) (yu-jee-en)
Shibata Zeshin (she-bah-tah zeh-sheen)
ziggurat (*zig*-uh-raht)
Francisco de Zurbaran (frahn-*thee*-skoh de thoor-bah-*rahn;* also, frahn-see-skoh de soor-bar-rahn)

NOTES

Chapter 1

1. C. L. Barnhart and Jess Stein, eds., *The American College Dictionary* (New York: Random House, 1963), 70.

2. Georgia O'Keeffe, *Georgia O'Keeffe* (New York: Viking, 1976), opposite plate 13.

3. Charles Glueck, "A Brueghel from Harlem," *New York Times,* February 22, 1970: sec. 2, 29. Copyright © by The New York Times Company. Reprinted by permission.

4. Julia Marcus, "Romare Bearden," *Smithsonian,* March 1981: 74.

5. Ibid., 72.

Chapter 2

1. Leo Tolstoy, *What Is Art?* (London: Walter Scott, 1899), 50.

2. Don Fabun, *The Dynamics of Change* (Englewood Cliffs, NJ: Prentice Hall, 1968), 9.

3. Lawrence Weschler, *Seeing Is Forgetting the Name of the Thing One Sees: A Life of Contemporary Artist Robert Irwin* (Berkeley: University of California Press, 1982).

4. Edward Weston, *The Daybooks of Edward Weston,* edited by Nancy Newhall (Millerton, NY: Aperture, 1973), vol. 2, 181.

5. Ibid., 154.

6. Henri Matisse, "The Nature of Creative Activity," *Education and Art,* edited by Edwin Ziegfeld (New York: UNESCO, 1953), 21.

7. Rev. Paul S. Osumi, "Today's Thought," *Honolulu Advertiser,* November 26, 1976, F-11.

8. Douglas Davis, "New Architecture: Building for Man," *Newsweek,* April 19, 1971: 80.

9. Betty Burroughs, ed., *Vasari's Lives of the Artists* (New York: Simon & Schuster, 1946), 191.

10. Bergen Evans, *Dictionary of Quotations* (New York: Delacorte Press, 1968), 340.

11. Erich Fromm, "The Creative Attitude," *Creativity and Its Cultivation,* edited by Harold H. Anderson (New York: HarperCollins, 1959), 44.

12. John Holt, *How Children Fail* (New York: Pitman, 1964), 167.

Chapter 3

1. Gyorgy Kepes, *The Language of Vision* (Chicago: Paul Theobald, 1944), 9.

2. "Notes d'un peintre sur son dessin," *Le Point IV,* 1939: 14.

3. Jean Schuster, "Marcel Duchamp, vite," *le surréalisme,* Spring 1957: 143.

4. "Interview with Roger Reynolds," *John Cage* (New York: Henmar Press, 1962), 47.

5. Georgia O'Keeffe, *Georgia O'Keeffe* (New York: Viking, 1976), opposite plate 23.

6. Audrey Flack, *Audrey Flack on Painting* (New York: Abrams, 1980), 90.

Chapter 4

1. Maurice Denis, *Theories 1870–1910* (Paris: Hermann, 1964), 13.

2. Henry Moore, *Henry Moore* (London: Edbury Press, 1986), 125.

3. Ray Bethers, *Composition in Pictures* (New York: Pitman, 1949), 163; originally in *Manifesto of the Futurist Painters* (Italy, 1910).

4. Faber Birren, *Color Psychology and Color Theory* (New Hyde Park, NY: University Books, 1961), 20.

Chapter 5

1. R. G. Swenson, "What is Pop Art," *Art News,* November 1963: 62.

2. Elizabeth McCausland, "Jacob Lawrence," *Magazine of Art,* November 1945: 254.

3. Jack D. Flam, *Matisse on Art* (New York: Dutton, 1978), 36; originally in "Notes d'un peintre," *La Grande Revue* (Paris, 1908).

4. Ibid.

5. Frederick B. Deknatel, *Edvard Munch* (New York: Museum of Modern Art, 1950), 10.

6. Ragna Thiis Stang, *Edvard Munch* (New York: Abbeville, 1979), 74.

Chapter 6

1. Jack D. Flam, *Matisse on Art* (New York: Dutton, 1978), 35.

2. Henri Matisse, "Notes of a Painter," translated by Alfred H. Barr, Jr., *Problems of Aesthetics,* edited by Eliseo Vivas and Murray Krieger (New York: Holt, 1953), 256; originally in "Notes d'un peintre," *La Grande Revue* (Paris, 1908).

3. Ibid., 259-260.

4. Ibid., 260.

5. Ibid.

6. *The Diaries and Letters of Kaethe Kollwitz,* translated by Richard and Clara Winston (Chicago: Henry Regnery, 1955), 52.

7. *Louise Nevelson: Atmospheres and Environments* (New York: Whitney Museum, 1980), 55.

8. Diana MacKown, *Dawns and Dusk* (New York: Scribner, 1976), 14

9. "Louise Nevelson: a Conversation with Barbara Diamonstein," *Nevelson: Maquettes for Monumental Sculpture* (New York: Pace Gallery, 1980), 2.

10. Ibid., 7.

Chapter 7

1. Lucy Lippard, *From the Center: Feminist Essays on Women's Art* (New York: Dutton, 1976), 22.

2. Martin Filler, "The Shock of the Hughes," *Vanity Fair,* November 1990: 226.

3. *Time,* April 29, 1991: 29.

4. *Time,* September 23, 1991: 75.

5. "Robert Hughes," *Esquire,* June 1988: 223.

6. Filler, p. 226.

7. Rick Steves, *Mona Winks: Self-guided Tours of Europe's Top Museums* (London: John Muir; New York: Norton, 1988).

Chapter 8

1. Frederick Franck, *The Zen of Seeing: Seeing/Drawing as Meditation* (New York: Vintage, 1973), 6.

2. Betty Edwards, *Drawing on the Right Side of the Brain* (Los Angeles: Tarcher, 1979).

3. David Hockney, *David Hockney* (New York: Abrams, 1977), 271.

4. Anthony Blunt, *Picasso's Guernica* (New York: Oxford University Press, 1969), 28.

5. Ichitaro Kondo and Elsie Grilli, *Katsushika Hokusai* (Rutland, VT: Tuttle, 1955), 13.

Chapter 10

1. Joan Hall, Artist's statement to accompany *New Faculty Exhibition,* Department of Art, University of Hawaii, 1992.

Chapter 11

1. *The Art of Photography* (New York: Time-Life, 1981), 12.

2. "Edwin Land," *Time,* June 26, 1972: 84.

3. Henri Cartier-Bresson, *The Decisive Moment* (New York: Simon & Schuster, 1952), 14.

4. Richard Stengel, "The Old Master of Majesty," *Time,* May 7, 1984: 124.

5. Ibid.

6. Minor White, Foreword to *Ansel Adams,* edited by Liliane De Cock (New York Graphic Society, 1972).

7. James L. Enyeart, *Jerry N. Uelsmann, Twenty-Five Years: A Retrospective* (Boston: Little, Brown, 1982), 37.

Chapter 12

1. Betty Burroughs, ed., *Vasari's Lives of the Artists* (New York: Simon & Schuster, 1946), 62.

2. Ruth Butler, *Western Sculpture: Definitions of Man* (New York: HarperCollins, 1975), 249; from an unpublished manuscript in the possession of Roberta Gonzales, translated and included in the appendices of a Ph.D dissertation by Josephine Whithers, *The Sculpture of Julio Gonzales: 1926–1942* (New York: Columbia University, 1971).

3. Brassai, *Conversations with Picasso* (Paris: Gallimard, 1964), 67.

4. Ibid.

5. *Alexander Calder* (New York: Abrams, 1979), 13.

6. Ibid., 15.

Chapter 13

1. John Coyne, "Handcrafts," *Today's Education,* November-December 1976: 75.

2. Henry Hopkins, *Fifty West Coast Artists* (San Francisco: Chronicle Books, 1981), 25.

3. Kathleen McCann, "Diane Itter: Paying Tribute to the Artist," *Fiberarts,* September-October 1992: 46. Reprinted by permission of the Publisher, Altamont Press, Inc., Asheville NC.

4. *Abakanowicz* (New York: Abbeville, 1982), 127.

5. Ibid., 18.

6. Ibid., 27.

Chapter 14

1. Henry Dreyfuss, *Designing for People* (New York: Paragraphic Books, 1967), iii.

Chapter 15

1. Louis Sullivan, "The Tall Office Building Artistically Considered," *Lippincott Monthly Magazine,* March 1896: 408.

2. Frank Lloyd Wright, *The Future of Architecture* (New York: Horizon Press, 1953), 227.

3. Michael Demarest, "He Digs Downtown," *Time,* August 24, 1981: 46.

4. Peter Blake, "The Ugly American," *Horizon,* May 1961: 6.

5. Mac Margolis, "A Third World City that Works," *World Monitor,* March, 1992: 42.

Chapter 16

1. "Picasso Speaks," *The Arts,* May 1923: 319.

2. Jacob Bronowski, *The Ascent of Man* (Boston: Little, Brown, 1973), 42.

Chapter 17

1. James Cooke, *A Voyage to the Pacific Ocean* (Dublin, 1784), vol. 2, 206.

Chapter 18

1. Erwin Panofsky, *Meaning in the Visual Arts* (Garden City, NY: Doubleday, 1955), 128.

Chapter 19

1. David Piper, *The Illustrated History of Art* (New York, Crescent Books, 1991), 130.

2. Jacob Bronowski, "Leonardo da Vinci," *Renaissance Profiles,* edited by J. H. Plumb (New York: HarperCollins, 1976), 84.

3. *The World of Michelangelo* (New York: Time-Life, 1966), 192.

4. Saint Teresa of Jesus, *The Life of Saint Teresa of Jesus,* translated by David Lewis, edited by Benedict Zimmerman (Westminster, MD: Newman, 1947), 266.

Chapter 20

1. C. R. Leslie, *Memoirs of the Life of John Constable* (London: J. M. Dent, 1913), 274.

2. Beaumont Newhall, "Delacroix and Photography," *Magazine of Art,* November 1952: 300.

3. Margaretta Salinger, *Gustave Courbet, 1819–1877, Miniature Album XH* (New York: Metropolitan Museum of Art, 1955), 24.

4. Lloyd Goodrich, *Thomas Eakins* (Cambridge: Harvard University Press, 1982), vol. 2, 34.

5. James Flexner, *19th Century American Painting* (New York: Putnam, 1970), 229.

6. Goodrich, *Thomas Eakins,* vol. 2, 160.

7. William Seitz, *Claude Monet* (New York: Abrams, 1982), 13.

8. Albert E. Elsen, *Rodin* (New York: Museum of Modern Art, 1963), 53; from a letter to critic Marcel Adam, published in an article in *Gil Blas* (Paris), July 7, 1904.

9. John Rewald, *Cézanne: A Biography* (New York: Abrams, 1986), 208.

10. Michael Howard, *Cézanne* (London: Bison Group, 1990), 6.

11. *Cézanne and the Post-Impressionists,* McCall's Collection of Modern Art (New York: McCall Books, 1970), 5.

12. Vincent van Gogh, *Further Letters of Vincent van Gogh to His Brother, 1886–1889* (London: Constable, 1929), 139, 166.

13. Ronald Alley, *Gauguin* (Middlesex, England: Hamlyn, 1968), 8.

14. Paul Gauguin, *Lettres de Paul Gauguin à Georges-Daniel de Monfried* (Paris: Georges Cres, 1918), 89.

15. John Russell, *The Meanings of Modern Art* (New York: HarperCollins, 1974), 35.

16. Jean Leymerie, "Paul Gauguin," *Encyclopedia of World Art* (London: McGraw-Hill, 1971), vol. 6, 42.

17. Yann Le Pichon, *Gauguin: Life, Art, Inspiration* (New York: Abrams, 1987), 240.

Chapter 21

1. Wassily Kandinsky, "Reminiscences," *Modern Artists on Art,* edited by Robert L. Herbert (Englewood Cliffs, NJ: Prentice-Hall, 1964), 27.

2. Alfred H. Barr, Jr., ed., *Masters of Modern Art* (New York: Museum of Modern Art, 1955), 124.

3. H. H. Arnason, *History of Modern Art,* rev. ed. (New York: Abrams, 1977), 146.

4. Dorothy Dudley, "Brancusi," *Dial,* February 1927: 124.

5. William Fleming, *Art, Music and Ideas* (New York: Holt, 1970), 342.

6. Ibid.

7. Roland Penrose, *Picasso: His Life and Work* (New York: Schocken, 1966), 125.

8. Nathan Lyons, ed., *Photographers on Photography* (Englewood Cliffs, NJ: Prentice-Hall, 1966), 133.

9. Beaumont Newhall, *The History of Photography* (New York: Museum of Modern Art, 1964), 111.

10. Joshua C. Taylor, *Futurism* (New York: Museum of Modern Art, 1961), 124.

11. Jasper Johns, "Marcel Duchamp (1887–1968)," *Artforum,* November 1968: 6. Reprinted by permission of *Artforum,* NY.

12. Barr, *Masters of Modern Art,* 137.

Chapter 22

1. Hans Richter, *Dada 1916–1966* (Munich: Goethe Institut, 1966), 22.

2. Paride Accetti, Raffaele De Grada, and Arturo Schwarz, *Cinquant'annia Dada—Dada in Italia 1916–1966* (Milan: Galleria Schwarz, 1966), 39.

3. Alfred H. Barr, Jr., ed., *Masters of Modern Art* (New York: Museum of Modern Art, 1955), 131.

4. Ibid., 133.

5. William Fleming, *Art, Music and Ideas* (New York: Holt, 1970), 346.

6. André Breton, *Manifestos of Surrealism,* translated by Richard Seaver and Helen R. Lane (Ann Arbor: University of Michigan Press, 1972), 14.

7. Piet Mondrian, "Plastic Art and Pure Plastic Art," *Circle,* edited by J. L. Martin, Ben Nicholson, and N. Gabo (New York: Praeger, 1971), 53.

8. Piet Mondrian, "Neo-Plasticism," *Abstraction-creation,* 1932: 25.

9. David Wolfe, *The Fabulous Life of Diego Rivera* (New York: Stein and Day, 1963), 18.

10. *Diego Rivera: A Retrospective* (New York: Norton, 1986), 19.

11. *The Concise Oxford Dictionary of Art and Artists* (Oxford: Oxford University Press, 1990), 398.

12. Lael Wertenbaker, *The World of Picasso* (New York: Time-Life, 1967), 130.

13. Herbert Read, *A Concise History of Modern Painting* (New York: Praeger, 1959), 160.

Chapter 23

1. Barbara Rose, *An Interview with Robert Rauschenberg* (New York: Vintage, 1987), 9.

2. Ogden Nash, "Song of the Open Road" (after "Trees" by Joyce Kilmer), © 1932. Originally published in the *New Yorker.* Reprinted by permission.

3. *Richard Hamilton: Catalogue of an exhibition at the Tate Gallery,* March 12–April 19, 1970 (London: Tate Gallery, 1970), 31.

4. R. G. Swenson, "What Is Pop Art?" *Art News,* November 1963: 25.

5. Claes Oldenburg, "I am for an art ...," from *Store Days, Documents from the Store (1961) and Ray Gun Theater (1962),* selected by Claes Oldenburg and Emmett Williams, (New York: Copyright Claes Oldenburg, 1967).

6. Donald Judd, "Specific Objects," *Arts Yearbook 8,* 1965: 78. Reprinted by permission of *Arts Yearbook.*

7. Werner Spies, *The Running Fence Project, Christo,* (New York: Abrams, 1977), unpaged.

8. Julia Brown, *Occluded Front: James Turrell* (Los Angeles: Fellows of Contemporary Art, Lapis Press, 1985), 15.

9. Patricia Failing, "James Turrell's New Light on the Universe," *Art News,* April 1985: 71. Copyright 1985 Patricia Failing. Reprinted by permission of *Artnews,* New York.

10. Grace Glueck, "Odd Man Out: Red Grooms, the Ruckus Kid," *Art News,* December 1973: 27.

11. Edward Lucie-Smith, *Sculpture Since 1945* (London: Phaidon, 1987), 77.

12. Calvin Tomkins, *The World of Marcel Duchamp* (New York: Time-Life, 1966), 162.

Chapter 24

1. Ramon Favela, *The Art of Rupert Garcia: A Survey Exhibition* (San Francisco: Chronicle, 1986), 19.

2. Fritz Scholder, *Scholder/Indians* (Flagstaff, AZ: Northland Press, 1972), 14.

3. Lucy R. Lippard, *From the Center: Feminist Essays on Women's Art.* (New York: Dutton, 1976), 48.

4. *Louise Bourgeois* (New York: Museum of Modern Art, 1982), 95.

5. Clara Weyergraf, ed., *Richard Serra: Interviews, Etc.* (Yonkers: Hudson River Museum, 1980), 168.

6. Joel L. Swerdlow, "To Heal a Nation," *National Geographic,* May 1985: 557.

7. Suzy Gablik, *The Reenchantment of Art,* (New York: Thames and Hudson, 1991), 115.

8. Ibid., 132.

SUGGESTED READING

General Reference

Barnet, Sylvan. *A Short Guide to Writing About Art*, 4th ed. New York: HarperCollins, 1993.

Dissanayake, Ellen. *Homo Aestheticus: Where Art Comes From and Why*. New York: Free Press, 1992.

Dissanayake, Ellen. *What Is Art For?* Seattle: University of Washington Press, 1988.

Gablik, Suzi. *The Reenchantment of Art*. New York: Thames and Hudson, 1991.

Goldwater, Robert, and Marco Treves, eds. *Artists on Art*. New York: Pantheon, 1958.

Gowing, Sir Lawrence, ed. *Encyclopedia of Visual Art*. Englewood Cliffs, N.J.: Prentice-Hall, 1983.

Lucie-Smith, Edward, ed. *The Thames and Hudson Dictionary of Art Terms*. New York: Thames and Hudson, 1984.

Read, Herbert, and Nikos Stangos, eds. *The Thames and Hudson Dictionary of Art and Artists*. London: Thames and Hudson, 1985.

PART 1 What Is Art For?

Canaday, John. *What is Art? An Introduction to Painting, Sculpture & Architecture*. New York: Knopf, 1980.

Edwards, Betty. *Drawing on the Artist Within: A Guide to Innovation, Invention and Creativity*. New York: Simon and Schuster, 1986.

Johnson, Jay. *American Folk Art of the Twentieth Century*. New York: Rizzoli, 1983.

London, Peter. *No More Secondhand Art: Awakening the Artist Within*. Boston: Shambhala, 1989.

Lowenfeld, Viktor. *Creative and Mental Growth*, 8th ed. New York: Macmillan, 1987.

May, Rollo. *The Courage to Create*. New York: W. W. Norton, 1975.

McKim, Robert. *Experiences in Visual Thinking*, 2nd ed. Monterey, California: Brooks/Cole, 1980.

Samuels, Mike, M.D., and Nancy Samuels. *Seeing with the Mind's Eye: The History, Techniques and Uses of Visualization*. New York: Random House, 1975.

PART 2 The Language of Visual Experience

Anderson, Donald M. *The Art of Written Forms*. New York: Holt, Rinehart & Winston, 1969.

Arnheim, Rudolf. *Art and Visual Perception*, rev. ed. Berkeley: University of California Press, 1974.

Dosczi, Gyorgy. *The Power of Limits: Proportional Harmonies in Nature, Art and Architecture*. Boulder: Shambhala, 1981.

Kepes, Gyorgy. *Language of Vision*. Chicago: Paul Theobald, 1949.

Nelson, George. *How to See*. Boston: Little, Brown, 1977.

Shahn, Ben. *The Shape of Content*. New York: Random House, 1957.

Varley, Helen, ed. *Colour*. London: Mitchell Beazley, 1980.

PART 3 Two-Dimensional Media

Cartier-Bresson, Henri. *The Decisive Moment*. New York: Simon & Schuster, 1952.

Castleman, Riva. *Prints of the Twentieth Century*, rev. ed. New York: Thames and Hudson, 1988.

Edwards, Betty. *Drawing on the Right Side of the Brain*, rev. ed. Los Angeles: Tarcher, 1989.

Franck, Frederick. *The Zen of Seeing: Drawing as Meditation*. New York: Random House, 1973.

Goldstein, Nathan. *The Art of Responsive Drawing*, 4th ed. Englewood Cliffs, N.J.: Prentice-Hall, 1992.

Goodman, Cynthia. *Digital Visions: Computers and Art*. New York: Abrams, 1987.

Ivins, William M. *Prints and Visual Communication*. New York: Plenum, 1969.

Loveless, Richard L. *The Computer Revolution and the Arts*. Tampa: University of South Florida Press, 1989.

Mast, Gerald. *A Short History of the Movies*. New York: Macmillan, 1986.

Mayer, A. Hyatt. *Prints and People: A Social History of Printed Pictures*. Princeton: Princeton University Press, 1980.

Mayer, Ralph. *Artists Handbook of Materials and Techniques*, 5th ed. New York: Viking, 1991.

Newhall, Beaumont. *The History of Photography*, rev. ed. New York, Museum of Modern Art, 1982.

Nicolaides, Kimon. *The Natural Way to Draw*. Boston: Houghton Mifflin, 1975.

Piper, David. *Looking at Art: An Introduction to Enjoying Great Paintings of the World*. New York: Random House, 1984.

Sachs, Paul J. *Modern Prints and Drawings: A Guide to a Better Understanding of Modern Draughtsmanship*. New York: Knopf, 1954.

Smith, Stan, and Friso Ten Holt, eds. *The Artist's Manual: Equipment, Materials, Techniques*. New York: Mayflower Books, 1980.

London, Barbara with John Upton. *Photography*, 5th ed. New York: HarperCollins, 1994.

Wilson, Marjorie. *Teaching Children to Draw: a Guide for Teachers & Parents*. Englewood Cliffs, N.J.: Prentice-Hall, 1982.

PART 4 Three-Dimensional Media

Le Normand-Romain, Antoinette, et al. *Sculpture: The Adventure of Modern Sculpture in the Nineteenth and Twentieth Centuries*. New York: Rizzoli, 1986.

Lucie-Smith, Edward. *The Story of Craft: The Craftsman's Role in Society*. Ithaca, New York: Cornell University Press, 1981.

Smith, Paul J., and Edward Lucie-Smith. *Craft Today: Poetry of the Physical*. New York: American Craft Council, 1986.

Mayer, Barbara. *Contemporary American Craft Art*. Salt Lake City: Gibbs M. Smith, 1988.

Rubinstein, Charlotte Streifer. *American Women Sculptors: A History of Women Working in Three Dimensions*. Boston: G. K. Hall, 1990.

Speight, Charlotte. *Hands in Clay: An Introduction to Ceramics*. Mountain View, Calif.: Mayfield, 1989.

Zelanski, Paul, and Mary Pat Fisher. *Shaping Space: The Dynamics of Three-Dimensional Design*. New York: Holt, Rinehart & Winston, 1987.

PART 5 Design Disciplines

Bacon, Edmund N. *The Design of Cities,* rev. ed. New York: Penguin, 1976.

Gardiner, Stephen. *Introduction to Architecture.* Oxford: Equinox, 1983.

Heller, Steven, ed. *Innovators of American Illustration.* New York: Van Nostrand Reinhold, 1986.

Macaulay, David. *Cathedral: The Story of Its Construction.* Boston: Houghton Mifflin, 1973.

Meggs, Philip B. *A History of Graphic Design.* New York: Van Nostrand Reinhold, 1992.

Rudofsky, Bernard. *Architecture without Architects: A Short Introduction to Non-pedigreed Architecture.* New York: Doubleday, 1964.

Salvadori, Mario. *Why Buildings Stand Up.* New York: W. W. Norton, 1980.

Scully, Vincent, Jr. *Modern Architecture: The Architecture of Democracy.* New York: Braziller, 1977.

Thomas, Michel, Cristine Mainguy, and Sophie Pommier. *Textile Art.* New York: Rizzoli, 1985.

Watkin, David A. *A History of Western Architecture.* London: Barrie & Jenkins, 1986.

Wines, James. *De-Architecture.* New York: Rizzoli, 1987.

PART 6 Art as Cultural Heritage

Chadwick, Whitney. *Women, Art, and Society.* London: Thames and Hudson, 1990.

Coe, Ralph T. *Lost and Found Traditions: Native American Art 1965-1985.* New York: American Federation of the Arts. 1986.

Cole, Herbert M. *Icons: Ideals and Power in the Art of Africa.* Washington: Smithsonian, 1989.

Dreamings: The Art of Aboriginal Australia. New York: Braziller and the Asia Society Galleries, 1988.

Dwyer, Jane P., and Edward B. Dwyer. *Traditional Arts of Africa, Oceania and the Americas.* San Francisco: The Fine Arts Museums of San Francisco, 1973.

Fine, Elsa H. *Women and Art: A History of Women Painters and Sculptors from the Renaissance to the 20th Century.* Montclair, N.J.: Allanheld & Schram, 1978.

Fleming, William. *Art, Music, and Ideas,* 8th ed. New York: Holt, Rinehart & Winston, 1991.

Gardner, Helen. *Art Through the Ages,* 9th ed. San Diego: Harcourt, Brace, Jovanovich, 1991.

Gillon, Werner. *A Short History of African Art.* New York: Facts on File, 1984.

Gombrich, E.H. *The Story of Art,* 15th ed. Englewood Cliffs, N.J.: Prentice-Hall, 1989.

Heller, Nancy G. *Women Artists: An Illustrated History.* New York: Abbeville, 1987.

Herbert, Robert L., ed. *Modern Artists on Art.* Englewood Cliffs, N.J.: Prentice-Hall, 1964.

Janson, H. W. *History of Art,* 4th ed., revised by Anthony Janson. New York: Abrams, 1991.

Kennedy, Jean. *New Currents, Ancient Rivers: Contemporary African Artists in a Generation of Change.* Washington, D. C.: Smithsonian, 1992.

Lee, Sherman. *A History of Far Eastern Art,* 4th ed. Englewood Cliffs, New Jersey: Prentice-Hall, 1982; New York: Abrams, 1982.

Malraux, Andre, trans. Stuart Gilbert and Francis Price. *Museums without Walls.* Garden City, N.Y.: Doubleday, 1967.

Mead, S. M. *Exploring the Visual Arts of Oceania.* Honolulu: University Press of Hawaii, 1979.

Newhall, Beaumont. *The History of Photography.* rev. ed. New York: The Museum of Modern Art, 1982.

Nochlin, Linda. *Women, Art, and Power: and Other Essays.* New York: Harper & Row, 1988.

Peterson, Karen, and J. J. Wilson. *Women Artists: Recognition and Reappraisal from the Early Middle Ages to the Twentieth Century.* New York: New York University Press, 1976.

Pfeiffer, John E. *The Creative Explosion: An Inquiry into the Origins of Art and Religion.* New York: Harper & Row, 1982.

Piper, David. *The Illustrated History of Art.* New York: Crescent, 1991.

Reti, Ladislao, ed. *The Unknown Leonardo.* New York: McGraw-Hill, 1974.

Ruspoli, Mario. *The Cave of Lascaux: The Final Photographic Record.* London: Thames & Hudson, 1987.

Stanley-Baker, Joan. *Japanese Art.* New York: Thames & Hudson, 1984.

Sullivan, Michael. *The Arts of China,* 3d ed. Berkeley: University of California, 1984.

Wood, Michael. *Art of the Western World.* New York: Simon and Schuster, 1989.

PART 7 The Modern World

Arnason, H. H. *History of Modern Art: Painting, Sculpture, Architecture, Photography.* New York: Abrams, 4th ed. 1986.

Ashton, Dore. *Twentieth-Century Artists on Art.* New York: Pantheon, 1985.

Banfield, Edward C. *The Democratic Muse: Visual Arts and the Public Interest.* New York: Basic Books, 1984.

Beardsley, John. *Earthworks and Beyond.* New York: Abbeville, 1984.

Beckett, Wendy. *Contemporary Women Artists.* New York: Universe, 1988.

Brown, Milton Wolf. *The Story of the Armory Show,* 2d ed. New York: Abbeville, 1988.

Bruckner, D.J.R., Seymour Chwast, and Steven Heller. *Art Against War.* New York: Abbeville, 1984.

Canaday, John. *Mainstreams of Modern Art,* 2nd ed. New York: Henry Holt, 1981.

Cockcroft, Eva, John Weber, and James C. Cockcroft. *Toward a People's Art: A Contemporary Mural Movement.* New York: Dutton, 1977.

Encyclopedia of American Art. New York: Dutton, 1981.

Felshin, Nina. *Disarming Images: Art for Nuclear Disarmament.* New York: Adama Books, 1984.

Ferrier, Jean-Louis and Yann Le Pichon. *Art of Our Century.* New York: Prentice-Hall, 1989.

Fleming, Ronald Lee, and Renata von Tscharner. *Place Makers: Creating Public Art That Tells You Where You Are.* New York: Harcourt, Brace, Jovanovich, 1986.

Friedman, Mildred. *De Stijl: 1917-1931.* New York: Abbeville, 1992.

Goldberg, Vicki. *The Power of Photography: How Photographs Changed Our Lives.* New York: Abbeville, 1991.

Harris, Ann Sutherland, and Linda Nochlin. *Women Artists: 1550-1950.* New York: Knopf, 1977.

Henri, Adrian. *Total Art: Environment, Happenings, and Performance.* New York: Praeger, 1974.

Hughes, Robert. *The Shock of the New,* 2nd ed. New York: McGraw-Hill, 1991.

Hunter, Sam, and John Jacobus. *Modern Art.* New York: Abrams, 1985.

Jencks, Cahrles. *The Language of Post-Modern.* New York: Rizzoli, 1991.

Jencks, Charles. *Post-Modernism: The New Classicism in Art and Architecture.* London: Academy Editions, 1987.

Johnson, Ellen H. *American Artists on Art from 1940 to 1980.* New York: Harper & Row, 1982.

Klotz, Heinrich. *The History of Postmodern Architecture.* Cambridge: MIT Press, 1988.

Lancaster, Clay. *The Japanese Influence in America.* New York: Abbeville, 1985.

Lippard, Lucy. *From the Center: Feminist Essays on Women's Art.* New York: Dutton, 1976.

_____. *Mixed Blessings: New Art in a Multicultural America.* New York: Pantheon 1990.

_____. *Pop Art.* New York: Praeger, 1966

Lovejoy, Margot. *Postmodern Currents: Art and Artists in the Age of Electronic Media.* Englewood Cliffs, N.J.: Prentice-Hall, 1992.

Neff, Terry Ann R. *In the Mind's Eye: Dada and Surrealism.* New York: Abbeville, 1985.

Pelfrey, Robert H. with Mary Hall-Pelfrey. *Art and Mass Media.* New York: Harper & Row, 1985.

Quirarte, Jacinto. *Mexican American Artists.* Austin: University of Texas Press, 1973.

Richter, Hans. *Dada: Art and Anti-Art.* New York: Abrams, 1970.

Rickey, George. *Constructivism: Origins and Evolution.* New York: Braziller, 1967.

Robbins, Corrine. *The Pluralist Era: American Art, 1968-1981.* New York: Harper & Row, 1984.

Rose, Barbara. *American Art Since 1900,* rev. ed. New York: Praeger, 1975.

Rubin, William, and Kirk Varnadoe, eds. *Primitivism in 20th Century Art: Affinity of the Tribal and the Modern,* 2 vols. New York: The Museum of Modern Art, 1984.

Sandler, Irving. *American Art of the 1960s.* New York: Harper & Row, 1988.

Seitz, William. *Abstract Expressionist Painting in America.* Cambridge: Harvard University Press, 1983.

Selz, Peter. *Art in Our Times: A Pictorial History, 1890-1980.* New York: Abrams, 1981.

Smagula, Howard. *Currents: Contemporary Directions in the Visual Arts,* 2nd ed. Englewood Cliffs, N.J.: Prentice-Hall, 1989.

Sonfist, Alan, ed. *Art in the Land: A Critical Anthology of Environmental Art.* New York: Dutton, 1983.

Stern, Robert A. M. *American Architecture: Innovation and Tradition.* New York: Rizzoli, 1985.

Tuchman, Maurice, *The Spiritual in Art: Abstract Painting 1890-1985.* New York: Abbeville, 1986.

Wheeler, Daniel. *Art Since Mid-Century.* New York: Vendome, 1991.

PHOTOGRAPHIC CREDITS

The authors and publisher wish to thank artists, owners, museums, galleries, and others for supplying photographs and permission to reproduce them. The following credits are in addition to those provided in captions. Copyright for each photograph is in the name of the photographer unless otherwise specified. Artists' copyrights have been cleared through the appropriate rights-clearance organizations unless otherwise specified. All references are to figure numbers.

Abbreviations
AR: Art Resource, New York
A/AR: Alinari/Art Resource, New York
G/AR: Giraudon/Art Resource, New York
S/AR: Scala/Art Resource, New York

Chapter 1
2: Jack Parsons. 4: Erich Lessing/AR. 5: D. Preble. 8: AR. 11: Lee Stalsworth. 13: Bernard Brown, Bourne, MA. 16: D. Preble. 19: G/AR. 21: Reproduced courtesy of The American Cancer Society. 22: Permission granted by Liggett Group Inc. to use the EVE advertisement. All rights reserved. 24: Stuart Franklin/Magnum.

Chapter 2
32, 33: D. Preble. 34: Reproduced with permission of the Macmillan Company. From *Creative and Mental Growth* by Viktor Lowenfeld and W. Lambert Brittain. 1970 by the Macmillan Company. 35, 40 a, b: D. Preble.

Chapter 3
42: Collection Frederick R. Weisman. 43: (c) 1992 National Gallery of Art, Washington, D.C. 45: Ferdinand Boesch/The Pace Gallery. 49: Elliot Erwitt/Magnum. 52: (c) 1987 Malcolm Varon, NYC. 53: Yousuf Karsh/Woodfin Camp & Associates. 58: Gift of the Amanson Foundation.

Chapter 4
59: Hans Hinz, Basel, Switzerland. 62: © 1960 by Saul Steinberg. Reprinted by permission of Wendy Weil Agency. 65: Graphische Sammlung. 73: D. Preble. 74: G/AR. 75: Reproduced courtesy of the Trustees of the British Museum. 79: Lars Lohrisch Photograf, Bremen, West Germany. 89: Reprinted by permission of Mitchell Beazley International, LTD. 90: Photograph courtesy of the Vatican Museums. 101: Marburg/AR. 106a, b: Chesterwood Museum Archives, Chesterwood, Stockbridge, Massachusetts, a Property for the National Trust for Historic Preservation. Photograph by DeWitt Ward. 119: (c) 1993, The Art Institute of Chicago. All rights reserved. 120: S/AR. 124: Leo Castelli Gallery, New York City. 128: Verlag Galerie Welz, Salzburg, Austria.

Chapter 5
131: © 1993 The Museum of Modern Art, New York. 133: © Reunion des Musees Nationaux. 140: S/AR. 143: D. Preble. 146: A/AR. 147: Ryzard Petrajtis, Gdansk, Poland. 151: Munch Museum, Oslo, 1992.

Chapter 6
158: Poster Photo Archives, Posters Please, Inc., New York City. 157: Bastin & Evrard, Brussels. 161: © Reunion des Musees Nationaux. 162: (c) Succession Henri Matisse, Bridgeman/AR. 163: S/AR. 164a: © Succession Henri Matisse/AR. © SPADEM. 164b: © Succession Henri Matisse, 1988. 173: © 1993 Hans Namuth.

Chapter 7
174: From *Men, Women and Dogs* (Harcourt Brace Jovanovich, Inc.) © 1943 James Thurber, © 1971 Helen Thurber and Rosemary A. Thurber. 176: © 1945 by Saul Steinberg. Reprinted by permission of Wendy Weil Agency. 178: Drawing by Modell; © 1983 The New Yorker Magazine, Inc.

Chapter 8
180: From *The Zen of Seeing* by Frederick Franck. New York: Random House, 1973, p. 6. Reproduced by permission of the author. 183: From *Drawing on the Right Side of the Brain* by Betty Edwards. Los Angeles, California: J. P. Tarcher, 1979. Reproduced by permission of the author. 184: Gift of Wallace and Wilhelmina Holladay. 196: D. Preble. 203: Reproduced courtesy of the Trustees of the British Museum.

Chapter 9
208: S/AR. 212: AR.

Chapter 10
227: Edita S.A., Lausanne, Switzerland. 230: AR. Copyright 1991 the Estate and Foundation of Andy Warhol/ARS, New York.

Chapter 11
239, 241a, b: D. Preble. 245: Magnum Photos, Inc., New York City. 246: Collection of Walter and Naomi Rosenblum. 257: Library of Congress.

Chapter 12
277: Hirmer Photoarchiv, Munich. 278: D. Preble. 279: S/AR. 283: D. Preble. 285: A/AR. 286: Heinz-Peter Cordes, Hamburg West Germany. 289: AR. 297: S. Preble.

Chapter 13
300: Frank Wing Photography. 302: D. Preble. 309: AR. 312: Photo courtesy American Craft Museum, from the exhibition "Craft Today: Poetry of the Physical", 1986. 314: Karen Bell. 316: Jan Michlewski, courtesy of Magdalena Abakanowicz.

Chapter 14
319: From *Symbol Sourcebook* (McGraw-Hill, Inc.), (c) 1972 by Henry Dreyfuss. All rights reserved. 322: CBS, Inc. 333: © 1960 the Norman Rockwell Family Trust.

Chapter 15
348, 349, 350: D. Preble. 355a: Hirmer Fotoarchiv, Munich. 355b: S/AR. 358a: S/AR. 359: AR. 366: Hedrich Blessing, Ltd. 368: Lucia Moholy, Zurich, Switzerland. 371b: Stubbins Associates, Inc., Boston. 373: Osamu Murai, Tokyo. 386a, b: D. Preble. 388: © David Bradford/Envision. 389, 390 D. Preble. 393: Reprinted by permission of Doubleday & Company, Inc. From *Who Designs America* by Laurence B. Holland. Copyright 1966 by the Trustees of Princeton University for the Program in American Civilization at Princeton University. 394: D. Preble. 398: © 1992 Carlos Humberto TDC/Contact Press Images.

Chapter 16

399: Reproduced by permission of Alpine Book Company. From *Scythian Art* by Georges Charriere. New York: Alpine Fine Arts Collections, 1979, p. 33. 400: Colorphoto Hans Hinz. 401, 402: © Reunion des Musees Nationaux.

Chapter 17

412: Prithwish Neogy. 413b Colorphoto Hans Hinz. 415: Luc Joubert. 416: Photographic Collection, Boltin, negative no. 323051, Department of Library Services, American Museum of Natural History, New York. 417: Robert Harding Picture Library, Ltd., London. 422: From *China: Land of Charm and Beauty*. Shanghai: The Shanghai People's Fine Arts Publishing House, 1964. 423: Kyodo News International. 432: Hans Namuth/Photo Researchers. 433: AR. 434: Werner Forman/AR. 440: Alaska Pictorial Service, Anchorage, Alaska. 441: Photograph by Axel Poignant. From *Oceanic Mythology* by Roslyn Poignant, published 1971 by the Hamlyn Publishing Group, London. Reproduced with permission of the author and photographer. 444: Jan Newhouse, Molokai, Hawaii. 445: Reproduced courtesy of the Trustees of the British Museum. 447: Photograph by Axel Poignant. From *Oceanic Mythology* by Roslyn Poignant, published 1971 by the Hamlyn Publishing Group, London. Reproduced with permission of the author. 449: Pascal James Imperato, M. D. 450: The estate of Eliott Elisofon. 453: Wettsin and Kaaf. 455: Franko Khoury, National Museum of African Art, Eliot Elisofon Archives, Smithsonian Institution. 456: D. Preble. 462: Superstock.

Chapter 18

466: Hirmer Photo Archive. 467: D. Preble. 470: Superstock. 471: Reproduced courtesy of the Trustees of the British Museum. 474: S/AR. 475 b: Reproduced courtesy of the Trustees of the British Museum. 475c: D. Preble. 477: S/AR. 478: D. Preble. 479: Phaidon Press, London. 480, 484: D. Preble. 485a: Guglielmo Mairani/Grazia Neri. 485c, d: S/AR. 486: Ancient Art & Architecture Collection. 489: Reproduced courtesy of the Trustees of the British Museum. 491: Reproduced courtesy of the Board of Trinity College Library, Dublin, Ireland. 492: Reproduced by permission of Harvard University Press. From *Art East and West* by Benjamin Rowland. Cambridge, MA: Harvard University Press, 1954. 493a: © Adam Woolfitt/Woodfin Camp. 493b, d, e: Duane Preble.

Chapter 19

494, 495, 496, 497, 498: S/AR. 500: Camerafoto, Venice. 501, 502, 503: S/AR. 504: A/AR. 505a: D. Preble. 505b: A/AR. 506a, b: Vatican Museums. 510, 511, 512, 513: S/AR. 515: A/AR. 516: ARTOTHEK, Peissenberg, Germany. 522: Erich Lessing/AR. 523: G/AR. 524: Hirmer Fotoarchiv, Munich. 525: © Reunion des Musees Nationaux. 527a: © Enrico Ferorelli, New York. 527b: Olivetti, by permission of the Superintendency for Fine Arts of Milan. Photo: Quattrone. 528a: S/AR. 528b: Vatican Museums.

Chapter 20

529: S/AR. 535: Kavalar/AR. 537: A. C. Cooper Ltd., London. 539: © Reunion des Musees Nationaux. 541: Gerhard Reinhold, Leipzig-Molkau, East Germany. 546: © Reunion des Musees Nationaux. 548: Roger-Viollet, Paris. 556: S/AR. 567: Beedle & Cooper, Northampton, England.

Chapter 21

570: ADAGP, Paris, 1933. 571: Lee Stalsworth. 573: © Reunion des Musees Nationaux. 580: David Heald. (c) The Solomon R. Guggenheim Foundation, New York. 583: Ampliaciones y Reproducciones MAS, Barcelona. 585: P.A. Ferrazzini. 587: AR. 589: G/AR. 591: David Heald. (c) Solomon R. Guggenheim Foundation, New York. 596: Hedrich Blessing.

Chapter 22

601: Philadelphia Museum of Art. Reproduced by permission of the owners. 607: Allen Mitchell, New Canaan, Connecticut. 612: Reproduction authorized by the Instituto Nacional de Bellas Artes y Literatura, Mexico. 614: D. Preble. 620: Alfred Roth, Zurich, Switzerland. 614: D. Preble. 623a: Prithwish Neogy. 623b: Lucien Herve, Paris. 624a, b: Prithwish Neogy.

Chapter 23

638: Lee Stalsworth. 654: Graham Gund, Boston. 661, 671: D. Preble. 674: Paschall/Taylor. 675: D. Preble.

Chapter 24

682: Ben Blackwell. 688: Lynda Hess. 695, 696, 697, 698: D. Preble. 708: Reproduced courtesy of Paula Cooper Gallery. Photograph by Jon Borofsky. 709: Ampliaciones y Reproducciones MAS, Barcelona, Spain.

INDEX

ABOUT THE AUTHORS

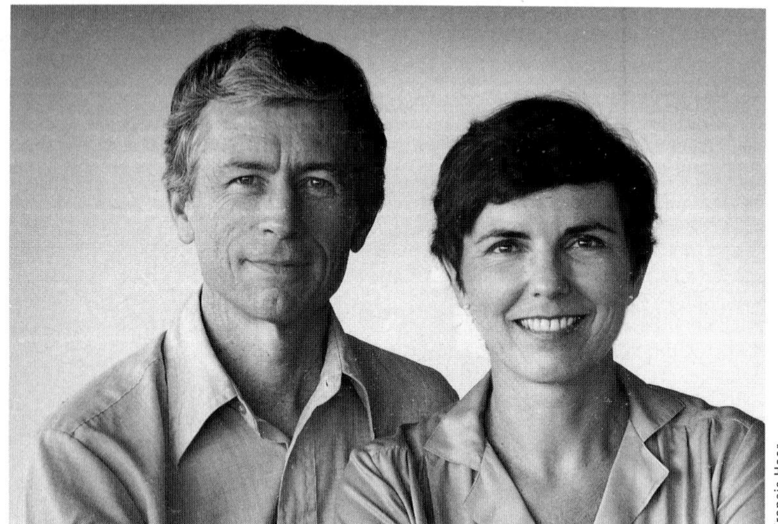

Francis Haar

Extensive travel has given Duane and Sarah Preble a global perspective. Duane taught on two round-the-world Semester at Sea voyages with the Institute for Shipboard Education, University of Pittsburgh, and he has led study tours in the United States, Europe, and Japan for the University of Hawaii. Research for ARTFORMS has taken the Prebles to Europe and to towns and cities throughout the United States.

After completing his BA in painting, graphics, and sculpture at UCLA, Duane received his Master of Fine Arts degree from the University of Hawaii. From 1961 to 1991 he was a member of the art faculty at the University of Hawaii as well as an exhibiting artist. He has taught a wide variety of courses, including introduction to the visual arts, art history, photography, drawing, and design. In 1975, Duane was selected for listing in *Outstanding Educators of America.*

Sarah studied art and psychology at St. Lawrence University and the University of Hawaii. After receiving her BA and Master of Library Science degrees from the University of Hawaii, she worked at the University of Hawaii libraries for several years before becoming an art librarian at the Hawaii State Library.

The Prebles live at the edge of a tropical forest overlooking Honolulu and the Pacific Ocean. They are active in their community and have served on boards of governmental, environmental, and arts organizations. Duane is on the Board of Trustees of Hawaii's major art museum, the Honolulu Academy of Arts, and is a frequent consultant to art and educational organizations.